Index to Irish Statutory Instruments

Richard F. Humphreys

Volume 2
Enabling Acts

Dublin · Butterworths · 1988

Republic of Ireland	Butterworths (Ireland) Ltd, DUBLIN and ABINGDON (U.K.)
United Kingdom	Butterworth & Co (Publishers) Ltd, 88 Kingsway, LONDON WC2B 6AB and 61A North Castle Street, EDINBURGH EH2 3LJ
Australia	Butterworths Pty Ltd, SYDNEY, MELBOURNE, BRISBANE, ADELAIDE, PERTH, CANBERRA and HOBART
Canada	Butterworths, A division of Reed Inc, TORONTO and VANCOUVER
Ireland	Butterworth (Ireland) Limited, DUBLIN
Malaysia	Malayan Law Journal PTE Limited, KUALA LUMPUR
New Zealand	Butterworths of New Zealand Ltd, WELLINGTON and AUCKLAND
Singapore	Butterworth & Co (Asia) Pte Ltd, Singapore
USA	Butterworths Legal Publishers, ST PAUL, Minnesota, SEATTLE, Washington, BOSTON, Massachusetts, AUSTIN, Texas and D & S Publishers, CLEARWATER, Florida

© Butterworths (Ireland) Ltd 1988

ISBN for the complete set 0 86205 232 7

Phototypesetting from discs supplied by OPUS, Oxford
Printed in Great Britain by Hartnolls Ltd., Bodmin, Cornwall

Preface

In the course of preparing this Index, I contacted the Oireachtas Library to ask whether there was any record of a Statutory Instrument having been annulled by resolution of either House of the Oireachtas. The reply came back in the negative. From this it is tempting to conclude that Parliamentary review of subordinate legislation has become a moribund exercise.

Many of the Regulations featured in this work are breathtaking in their scope. This is particularly true in areas where the Executive has traditionally enjoyed a special position, such as security, international affairs, and finance. Organisations can be suppressed, special courts established, internment introduced, broadcasts censored and extradition arrangements introduced by Executive order. Taxes and Duties can be imposed by Dail Resolution or Governmental decision. Imports and Exports can be halted. And European Community law can be implemented, including if required the repeal of entire Acts of the Oireachtas, simply by a flourish of the Ministerial pen. The statute roll is liberally daubed with other examples of powers to carve out exceptions to general statutory norms, and to otherwise modify or amend statutory provisions. The suspicion lingers that some of this delegatory largesse has, like other notions, floated to our shores from across the Irish Sea, like a sort of intellectual radiation.

The Seanad Select Committees on Statutory Instruments succeeded in achieving some improvement in the drafting of Instruments, but did little to address the growth of the delegatee's empire. Even despite their efforts, severe drafting difficulties remain, of which the worst is the epidemic of regulation by reference. To take the most extreme example, the amendments to the Defence Forces (Pensions) Scheme, 1937, listed in the Subject Index span to over 27 pages. Other drafting aberrations include titles of unwieldy length (such as the record 25-word, 184-character title to S.I. No.46 of 1971) or the citation of enabling powers which have already been repealed (S.I. No.427 of 1986). Neither the Seanad Committees nor the Joint Committee on Secondary Legislation of the European Communities seems to have been sufficiently galvanised into action to cause the introduction of a motion to annul any Instrument.

The Constitution provides by Article 25.4.5 for the enrolment of Acts with the Supreme Court Registrar as a matter of record. There is no corresponding provision concerning Statutory Instruments (section 3 of the Statutory Instruments Act, 1947 does contain a limited publication requirement, but even this is avoidable). By Article 25.4.4, Irish translations of English-language Acts must be issued, and vice versa. Again, there is no such requirement in the case of Statutory Instruments. This is not simply an issue of sterile legalism. It was not until January 1988 that I was able to obtain a copy of the last instrument of 1986. During the period of compilation of this Book, the last bound version of Statutory Instruments to hand dated from 1982. The last bi-lingual bound version dated from 1980. 1980 was eight years ago.

The Rules Publication Act, the precursor of our own 1947 legislation, was enacted in 1893. It provided that 40 days' notice be given of a proposal to make Statutory Rules. It allowed for copies of the Rules to be made available in advance to public bodies, and for representations to be taken into account. These essentially democratic safeguards were not continued by the Act of 1947. Today, by the time you get a bound volume into your hand, there is a serious risk that the relevant Instrument has long since ceased to be.

The task of this Book, however, is not to evangelise for a total reform of the administrative system, desirable though that may be. Its purpose is simply to forge a trail through the labyrinth, and hopefully to assist those who travel its passageways. I would be very grateful for any comments or criticisms, as it is planned to update this work in due course.

Ní amháin gur téacs-leabhar dlí é an leabhar seo; ríomhann sé stair sóisialta na hÉireann le trí scór blian anuas. Tá súil agam mar sin go mbeidh sé ina dhídl spéise do lucht léitheoireachta níos forleithne ná dlíodóirí amháin. Is é mo ghuí go mbeidh muintir na hÉireann amach anseo ábalta ceachtanna a fhoghlaim as na fadhbanna dlí a cíoradh insan leabhar seo.

Richard F. Humphreys.
23 March, 1988.

Acknowledgments

My heartfelt thanks are due to all of the many people who helped me in completing this Book. In particular I offer thanks:

Firstly, to Mr. Stephen M. Brien, Mr. Douglas A. Reynolds and Mr. Eoin Flood, who jointly devised and wrote all the software for the Book. Their skill and ingenuity in overcoming all technical hurdles, their dexterity in handling the immense and complex software problems presented by this Book, their capacity to work day and night to see the project to completion, and their heroic patience in the face of ever-changing design specifications has been unsurpassable. Without their help, this Book would never have come to life. Indeed for Mr. Brien, his help with this book is but the latest of many kindnesses over the years. To them all, my first and special thanks.

For early encouragement, to Mr. Peter Prendergast, Mr. Iarflaith O'Neill B.L., Mr. D. Finbarr Murphy B.L. and Mr. Owen Drumm. For carefully compiling the Table of Cases incorporated in Volume I, to Mr. T. John O'Dowd. For their meticulous work in assisting the proof-reading, Ms. Deborah Rennick, Mr. Stephen J. Costello, Ms. Barbara Jordan, Mr. Declan Ryan, Mr. Robert Cremins, Ms. Grainne McArdle and Mr. Ronan M. Murphy B.L. For the thankless task of typing the data, to Mr. Tony Doherty, Ms. Persis Quinn, Ms. Karen King and Mr. Ciaran McGoldrick.

To all the staff of the following institutions: U.C.D. Computer Centre, especially Helen Brangan, Sinead Guilfoyle, Miriam Allen, Bonnie McGregor and Dr. Michael Norris; U.C.D. Law Library, especially Ms. Esther Semple and Mr. Tony Eklof; T.C.D. Library; The National Library of Ireland, especially Mr. Jim O'Neill; The Government Publications Sale Office, especially Frank; R.D.S. Library; The Oireachtas Library, especially Ms. Maura Corcoran.

To Mr. Justice Walsh for his kind introduction, and to all who kindly offered comments on parts of my original draft, especially Dr. Robert Clark B.L., Mr. Justice Costello, Mr. Nial Fennelly S.C., Dr. Michael Forde B.L., Mr. Justice Johnson, Mr. Justice Keane, Dr. Andrew B. Lyall B.L., Mr. Justice McCarthy, Mr. Paul O'Higgins B.L. and Mr. John D. Rogers S.C.

Finally, to those who have had to endure this project with me; Mark, Frank and Joe; and my parents Richard and Deirdre, to whom I owe the greatest debt of thanks. Without their support, in every way, this Book could not have been begun, let alone finished. My deepest thanks are due to them.

Contents

List of Subject Headings

Agriculture
Allotments and Smallholdings
Animals
Arbitration
Armed Forces
Aviation
Banking
Betting, Gaming and Lotteries
Building
Building Societies
Burial and Cremation
Charities
Children
Civil defence
Companies
Compulsory Acquisition
Constitutional Law
Copyright
Coroners
Courts
Criminal Law
Customs and Excise
Education
Elections
Electricity
Employment
European Communities
Evidence
Explosives and Firearms
Extradition
Fire Services
Fisheries
Food
Forestry
Friendly Societies and Industrial
    Assurance
Gaeilge
Gas
Health and safety at Work
Housing
Insurance
International Affairs
Juries

Landlord and Tenant
Legal Aid
Licensing and Liquor Duties
Local Government
Matrimonial Law
Medicine and Health
Mental Health
Mines, Minerals and Quarries
Money
Nationality and Immigration
Open Spaces and Historic Buildings
Parliament
Patents and Designs
Pensions and Superannuation
Petroleum
Planning Law
Police
Post Office
Prisons
Rating
Real Property
Road Traffic
Sale of Goods
Savings Banks
Sheriffs and Bailiffs
Shipping and Navigation
Social Welfare
Solicitors
Taxation
Telecommunications and Broadcasting
Theatres and Other Places of
    Entertainment
Time
Trade and Industry
Trade Marks and Trade Names
Transport
Trusts
Value Added Tax
War and Emergency
Water Supply
Weights and Measures
Wills

Guide to the Use of this Book

1. Scope

This Book Indexes all Statutory Instruments, Rules and Orders made in the period 6 December, 1922 to 31 December, 1986, which were numbered by the Stationery Office and published in the Annual Volumes of Statutory Instruments or in the pre-1948 set of Bound Volumes of the Statutory Rules and Orders. Approximately 20,000 Instruments are covered.

2. Notation

Bold Type indicates an Instrument is in force. Italic Type indicates that the Instrument is not in force. Each Instrument is deemed to be in force for the purposes of this Index unless expressly revoked or terminated, disallowed through exercise of a relevant statutory power, expired whether expressly or by reason of reference to temporary circumstances appearing upon the face of the Instrument, disenabled through the repeal or termination of all of its enabling authority, or declaration of invalidity of the Instrument or its entire enabling power by a Court. Instruments merely revoking other Instruments, or fixing a now past date for the commencement of statutory or other provisions, are deemed to have expired for this purpose.

Hence it will appear that although some Instruments are Indexed in bold type in accordance with this convention, they have in fact ceased to have force due to implicit revocation, oblique expiry not appearing on the face of the Instrument, or the creation of new and superseding factual or legal circumstances.

References to Volume and page numbers after Instrument titles are to the 40-Volume set of Statutory Rules and Orders, published by the Stationery Office to cover the period 1922–1947. During this period, Instruments were not issued in Annual Volumes.

3. Arrangement

Volume I is an alphabetical Index of all Instruments. It lays out the title, enabling authority and any subsequent enactments which may have affected the Instrument. The possible effects are listed in para.4 below. Where the Instrument is still in force, a section-by-section account is given of changes to it.

Volume II is an alphabetical Index of all Enabling Enactments. It lists the enabling sections of each Act in numerical order, and, in a separate column, the Instruments made thereunder.

Volume III is a Subject Index covering Instruments still in force. It is closely based on the headings used in Halsbury's Statutory Instruments. To use the Subject Index, first consult the list of subject headings contained at the start of Volume III. Every Instrument is included under one or more of the headings in this list. Reference to the list should immediately point up the most likely heading to search in the Subject Index itself. The Index is thoroughly cross-referenced.

4. Operations

The possible effects of a subsequent enactment upon a previous one, which occur in Volume I of the Index, are as follows:

- Invalid
- Enabled
- Enablement
- Continued   (Normally where the enabling power is repealed and the Instruments are expressly continued)
- Referred to
- Disallowed
- Revoked
- Cesser   (Terminated otherwise than by express Revocation)
- Disenabled   (Entire enabling authority has been terminated)
- Continued
- Revived
- Added   (A new paragraph or other numbered subdivision is inserted)
- Substituted   (A paragraph or other numbered subdivision is revoked and an identically numbered paragraph replaces it)
- Renumbered
- Amended   (Other forms of amendment, including partial addition, substitution or revocation; i.e. where the words added or deleted are part only of a paragraph, and do not constitute in themselves a numbered subdivision of the Instrument)
- Applied   (Where the application of the Instrument is in some way extended)
- Restricted   (Where the application of the Instrument is reduced in scope although no words are deleted)
- Entitled   (A title is provided by a subsequent enactment)

5. Alphabetical Order

The alphabetical order used in Volumes I and II is standard lexicographical order with the following adjustments:

(a) The Principal Instrument is sorted before amending Instruments; hence Tea Order, simpliciter, would sort before any other Instruments beginning with the word 'Tea', such as Tea (Amendment) Order.

(b) Numbers, and words representing numbers, sort consecutively.

(c) Characters such as brackets are disregarded for sorting purposes.

(d) Sorting is not sensitive as to case.

Otherwise lexicographical order is followed: hence numbers sort before letters, for example. For technical reasons, the alphabetical order used in Volume III is standard lexicographical order, without the modifications set out at (a)-(d) above.

6. Note on Customs

Since the Customs Tariff was totally revised in 1987 just outside the period of this Index, the Subject Index treatment of this heading is somewhat less detailed than would otherwise have been the case.

Introduction

Since the setting up of the State the field of subordinate legislation has achieved such great dimensions that it is now impossible for any person, lawyer or layman, to claim to be familiar with all of it. The excellent index now presented to us by Mr. Humphreys will be an indispensable guide to tracking down not only the birth of the vast number of our pieces of subordinate legislation, but, even more importantly, this work indicates the demise of many hundreds of such pieces of legislation. To know that certain statutory instruments are no longer in force, or have been superseded by others, can be knowledge of the greatest value and importance. Unfortunately it has not always been easy to acquire it. The format of this work makes that task simple.

The Statutory Instruments Act, 1947, defines the expression "statutory instrument" as an order, regulation, rule, scheme or by-law made in exercise of a power conferred by statute. That is a most important definition because it brings to mind immediately that all such forms of subordinate legislation are but the creatures of statute. I prefer to use the term subordinate legislation rather than delegated legislation as the Oireachtas has no power to delegate the legislative function conferred upon it by the Constitution. Article 15, s. 2, subs. 1 of the Constitution vests in the Oireachtas the sole and exclusive power of making laws for the State. Save to the extent that that has now been modified by the amendments to Article 29 of the Constitution consequent upon our membership of the European Communities that provision still stands not only as a declaration of the sovereignty of the Oireachtas in law making, but also as a constitutional curb upon the powers of the executive. Unlike the position in the United Kingdom where by means of Orders in Council the sovereign can in effect make laws, or the position in France where the Government is in many particular circumstances entitled to legislate by decree. The Constitution of Ireland does not permit of any law-making by those who exercise the executive power save in such as may be enjoyed during a period of emergency as defined by the Constitution.

Even Plato, who was not at all committed to open government, acknowledged that the law-giver of necessity must in all matters involving matters of detail leave gaps and that from time to time rules must be made to regulate the satisfactory working of such laws. As the state becomes more and more involved, both directly and indirectly, in almost every aspect of our social and economic life it was inevitable that a great deal of regulation would be required. This is particularly so in a state which is as centralised as Ireland.

The function of this subordinate legislation is to provide the administration with the means of bringing the laws into operation, not in any attempt to alter their provisions, but simply to act as the machinery necessary to give effect to the statutes. The Oireachtas can, and sometimes does, regulate highly technical questions by direct legislation, but this is not always feasible. Yet in the absence of any general ordaining power in the executive it is obvious that all such administrative machinery must be founded upon statute. It goes without saying that any such subordinate legislation can never purport to exercise power beyond limits set by the statute. Superior to all statutes and therefore superior to all subordinate legislation the Constitution stands as the basic law of the State and must not in any way be infringed by either statute law or subordinate legislation. That is the ultimate protection against the excesses of subordinate legislation.

There is a presumption that all enactments of the Oireachtas established by the Constitution are not repugnant to the Constitution. It therefore follows that any subordinate legislation, purporting to be based upon statute, which infringes the Constitution would be deemed to be *ultra vires* the statute unless it was clear that the statute itself purported to authorise such an instrument. In that case the statute must fall and with it will fall all the subordinate legislation authorised by it.

Our case law has clearly established that even in the area of subordinate legislation there is no such thing as an unfettered discretion in the widest sense. A discretion where conferred must be exercised in accordance with the objectives of the statute conferring the rule making power. No statute or subordinate legislation can validly authorise any judging procedure which does not comply with requirements of constitutional justice. In addition account must be taken of the rapidly growing jurisprudence of the European Court of Human Rights in its development of Article 6 of the European Convention on Human Rights. This jurisprudence is having a profound effect on the administrative adjudicating procedures in all of the member states of the Council of Europe by ensuring that these procedures must be fair and that those exercising the power of adjudicating must be independent and impartial.

While many pieces of legislation may require very elaborate procedures for their implementation none the less the constitutional requirements must be observed in all cases.

Our own constitutional jurisprudence has shown that the Courts are ready to strike down any unauthorised delegation of legislative power while at the same time recognising that in the complex and frequently changing situations which confront the modern state there is a necessity for subordinate legislation. In his book *Constitutional Law in Ireland* Professor Casey has correctly summed up the position by saying that "the Oireachtas, it seems, may delegate a power to put flesh on the bones of an Act; but anything going beyond this would be constitutionally suspect."

While statutory instruments or statutory orders may for all general purposes be regarded as part of the law none the less they are not "laws" in the strict meaning of the Constitution because such expression must be construed in accordance with Article 15 and be confined to an Act of the Oireachtas. There has been one apparent exception to this but it is really more apparent than real and it arose out of the decision by the Supreme Court in *The State (Gilliland)* v. *The Governor of Mountjoy Prison*. That was a case concerning an extradition treaty made by the Government (which by virtue of the provisions of Part II of the Extradition Act, 1965, could be made without the necessity of a statutory ratification) and empowering the Government to apply the Act by statutory instrument. Thus the statutory instrument became the only ordinance in existence to give effect to the Treaty. It fell for straying outside the constraints of the Constitution.

Because of the necessity for a statutory basis for all subordinate legislation and because of the dominant position of the Constitution the ordinary Courts frequently find themselves dealing with the type of case which in civil law countries would almost invariably go to the administrative Courts. The French concept of the constitutional separation of powers does not permit of the ordinary Courts intervening in administrative matters. Our conception of the constitutional separation of powers envisages judicial review of all legislative and administrative acts. While it cannot be denied that the Conseil d'Etat can usually provide speedier and certainly cheaper remedies than our Courts nevertheless our system has a much wider scope and, therefore, a greater capacity for righting a wrong. Professor Stout in his book *Administrative Law in Ireland* draws attention to the fact that administrative law has not been recognised as a category of law in the Irish Digests. However, today, the expression "administrative law", like the expression "public law", is now used in this country. It is to be hoped that this category of law will find a place in future Digests.

An interesting analysis of the nature and development of administrative law in Ireland was made by a committee under the chairmanship of Chief Justice Cearbhall O Dalaigh and published as a note on "Administrative Law and Procedure" in an appendix to the first "Devlin Report". Perhaps it should be looked at again.

Mr. Humphreys is to be warmly congratulated upon his industry in producing this invaluable work. All of those on the Bench and at the Bar who toil in the fields of administrative law will find in this work an invaluable aid. It will greatly lighten their burden and for this he deserves our deepest gratitude.

BRIAN WALSH
The Supreme Court
March 1988

Statutory Authority	Section	Statutory Instrument
Abandonment of Railways Act, No. 83 of 1850		**Dundalk Newry and Greenore Railway (Abandonment) Warrant, S.I. No. 397 of 1953**
Acquisition of Derelict Sites Act, No. 29 of 1940	1	**Acquisition of Derelict Sites Regulations [Vol. XXV p. 1] S.R.& O. No. 268 of 1940**
	6(1)	**Acquisition of Derelict Sites Regulations [Vol. XXV p. 1] S.R.& O. No. 268 of 1940**
	12	**Acquisition of Derelict Sites Regulations [Vol. XXV p. 1] S.R.& O. No. 268 of 1940**
Acquisition of Land (Allotments) Act, No. 8 of 1926	4	**Acquisition of Land (Allotments) (Forms) Order [Vol. II p. 1] S.R.& O. No. 39 of 1936**
Acquisition of Land (Allotments) (Amendment) Act, No. 7 of 1934	2	**Allotments (Unemployed Persons) Regulations [Vol. XXV p. 7] S.R.& O. No. 99 of 1945**
	2(2)	**Allotments (Unemployed Persons) Regulations, 1945 (Amendment) Regulations, S.I. No. 74 of 1960**
Adaptation of Charters Act, No. 6 of 1926	1	**Saint Patrick's Hospital, Dublin (Adaptation of Charters) Order [Vol. II p. 15] S.R.& O. No. 29 of 1926**
		Royal College of Physicians (Ireland) (Adaptation of Charters) Order [Vol. II p. 19] S.R.& O. No. 38 of 1926
		Ballaghadereen Markets and Fairs (Adaptation of Charter) Order [Vol. II p. 25] S.R.& O. No. 2 of 1927
		City of Dublin Skin and Cancer Hospital (Adaptation of Charter) Order [Vol. II p. 29] S.R.& O. No. 3 of 1927
		Royal Hospital for Incurables, Donnybrook (Adaptation of Charter) Order [Vol. II p. 33] S.R.& O. No. 44 of 1929
	1(1)	**National University of Ireland (Adaptation of Charter) Order [Vol. II p. 37] S.R.& O. No. 33 of 1935**
		Royal Hibernian Academy (Adaptation of Charter) Order [Vol. XXV p. 19] S.R.& O. No. 331 of 1940
		Institute of Chartered Accountants in Ireland (Adaptation of Charter) Order [Vol. XXV p. 13] S.R.& O. No. 479 of 1941
Adaptation of Enactments Act, No. 2 of 1922		**Revenue Commissioners Order (Executive Council Order No.2), 1923**
		Postal Order (Inland) Amendment (No.4) Regulations, S.I. No. 294 of 1951
	5	**Solicitors' Remuneration General Order, 1957 (Disallowance) Order, S.I. No. 232 of 1957**
		Solicitors' Remuneration General Order, 1971 (Disallowance) Order, S.I. No. 61 of 1972

Statutory Authority	Section	Statutory Instrument
Adaptation of Enactments Act, No. 2 of 1922 (*Cont.*)	7	**Rates Advisory Committee Order [Vol. II p. 193] S.R.& O. No. 11 of 1925**
		Saorstat Eireann Forestry Commissioners Order [Vol. II p. 275] S.R.& O. No. 68 of 1927
	9	**Estate Duty Grant (No.1) Order [Vol. II p. 163] S.R.& O. No. 16 of 1924**
		Irish Church Temporalities Fund (Apportionment of Grant) Order [Vol. II p. 173] S.R.& O. No. 22 of 1924
		Judicial Savings (Apportionment of Grant) Order [Vol. II p. 177] S.R.& O. No. 23 of 1924
		Agricultural Education (Apportionment of Grant) Order [Vol. II p. 181] S.R.& O. No. 24 of 1924
		Teachers' Salaries Grant (Apportionment) Order [Vol. II p. 185] S.R.& O. No. 25 of 1924
		Local Taxation (Customs and Excise) Duties Grant Order [Vol. II p. 189] S.R.& O. No. 26 of 1924
		Judicial Savings (Apportionment of Grant) Order [Vol. II p. 265] S.R.& O. No. 38 of 1927
		Local Taxation Account (Licence Duty Grant) Order [Vol. II p. 285] S.R.& O. No. 83 of 1927
		Exchequer Contribution Order [Vol. II p. 291] S.R.& O. No. 84 of 1927
		General Cattle Diseases Fund (Cattle Pleuropneumonia Account) Apportionment Order [Vol. II p. 305] S.R.& O. No. 97 of 1927
	10	**National Health Insurance (Arrears) Amendment Regulations [Vol. XVII p. 25] S.R.& O. No. 1 of 1924**
		Revenue and Post Office (Powers and Duties) Order [Vol. XII p. 97] S.R.& O. No. 30 of 1925
		Weights and Measures (Alteration of Fees) Order [Vol. XXII p. 345] S.R.& O. No. 19 of 1926
		Weights and Measures (Verification and Stamping Fees) Order [Vol. XXII p. 357] S.R.& O. No. 23 of 1929
		Merchant Shipping (Pilot Signals) Order [Vol. XVIII p. 135] S.R.& O. No. 115 of 1934
		Solicitors' Remuneration General Order, 1957 (Disallowance) Order, S.I. No. 232 of 1957
		Solicitors' Remuneration General Order, 1971 (Disallowance) Order, S.I. No. 61 of 1972
	11	**Pier at Clogherhead in the County of Louth Bye-Laws, S.I. No. 125 of 1960**
		Bantry Pier Bye-Laws, S.I. No. 183 of 1968
		Harbour at Burtonport, County Donegal (Bye-Laws for the Regulation of the) S.I. No. 427 of 1986
		Harbour at Rathmullan, County Donegal (Bye-Laws for the Regulation of the) S.I. No. 428 of 1986
		Harbour at Greencastle, County Donegal (Bye-Laws for the Regulation of the) S.I. No. 429 of 1986

Adaptation of Enactments Act, No. 2 of 1922 (*Cont.*)	12	**Fairs (Ireland) Act, 1868 – Adaptation Order [Vol. II p. 199] S.R.& O. No. 60 of 1925**
		Sheriffs (Ireland) Act, 1920, Adaptation Order [Vol. II p. 203] S.R.& O. No. 65 of 1925
		Pharmacy Act (Ireland) 1875, Adaptation Order [Vol. II p. 207] S.R.& O. No. 1 of 1926
		Dangerous Drugs Act, 1920, Adaptation Order [Vol. II p. 211] S.R.& O. No. 10 of 1926
		Dublin Traffic Act, 1875, Adaptation Order [Vol. II p. 215] S.R.& O. No. 16 of 1926
		Explosives Act, 1875, Adaptation Order [Vol. II p. 219] S.R.& O. No. 22 of 1926
		Harbours Act, 1814, Adaptation Order [Vol. II p. 223] S.R.& O. No. 34 of 1926
		Registrar of Friendly Societies (Adaptation) Order [Vol. II p. 227] S.R.& O. No. 43 of 1926
		Charles Shiels' Almshouses Charity Act, 1864, Adaptation Order [Vol. II p. 233] S.R.& O. No. 7 of 1927
		Public Offices Fees Act, 1879, Adaptation Order [Vol. II p. 237] S.R.& O. No. 8 of 1927
		Dublin Port and Docks Act, 1898, Adaptation Order [Vol. II p. 241] S.R.& O. No. 12 of 1927
		Assay (Gold and Silver Plate and Watch Cases) Adaptation Order [Vol. II p. 245] S.R.& O. No. 18 of 1927
		Waterford Infirmary Act, 1896, Adaptation Order [Vol. II p. 253] S.R.& O. No. 19 of 1927
		Shops Act, 1912, Adaptation Order [Vol. II p. 257] S.R.& O. No. 26 of 1927
		Public Offices Fees Act, 1879, Adaptation (No.2) Order [Vol. II p. 261] S.R.& O. No. 28 of 1927
		Municipal Corporations (Ireland) Act, 1840, Adaptation Order [Vol. II p. 271] S.R.& O. No. 47 of 1927
		Merchant Shipping Act, 1894, Adaptation Order [Vol. II p. 281] S.R.& O. No. 80 of 1927
		Estate Duty Grant Order [Vol. II p. 299] S.R.& O. No. 94 of 1927
		Merchant Shipping Act, 1894, Adaptation (No.2) Order [Vol. II p. 311] S.R.& O. No. 106 of 1927
		Air Navigation Act, 1920, Adaptation Order [Vol. II p. 315] S.R.& O. No. 5 of 1928
		Assurance Companies Act, 1909, Adaptation Order [Vol. II p. 321] S.R.& O. No. 7 of 1928
		Children Act, 1908, Adaptation Order [Vol. II p. 327] S.R.& O. No. 8 of 1928
		Sale of Food and Drugs Acts Adaptation Order [Vol. II p. 337] S.R.& O. No. 16 of 1928
		Official Secrets Acts, 1911 and 1920, Adaptation Order [Vol. II p. 341] S.R.& O. No. 36 of 1928

Statutory Authority	Section	Statutory Instrument

Adaptation of Enactments Act,
No. 2 of 1922 (*Cont.*)

Prevention of Corruption Acts, 1889 to 1916, Adaptation Order [Vol. II p. 353] S.R.& O. No. 37 of 1928

Advertisements Regulation Act, 1907, Adaptation Order [Vol. II p. 361] S.R.& O. No. 55 of 1928

Lunacy Acts (Adaptation) Order [Vol. II p. 365] S.R.& O. No. 26 of 1929

Forfeiture Act, 1870 (Adaptation) Order [Vol. II p. 369] S.R.& O. No. 29 of 1929

Public Health Acts Amendment Act, 1890, Adaptation Order [Vol. II p. 381] S.R.& O. No. 28 of 1930

Marine Works (Ireland) Act, 1902, Adaptation Order [Vol. II p. 385] S.R.& O. No. 38 of 1930

Ministry of Munitions (Cessation) Order, 1921 Adaptation Order [Vol. II p. 389] S.R.& O. No. 45 of 1930

Tribunals of Inquiry (Evidence) Act, 1921, Adaptation Order [Vol. II p. 393] S.R.& O. No. 48 of 1930

Public Health Acts Amendment Act, 1907, Adaptation Order [Vol. II p. 397] S.R.& O. No. 41 of 1931

Motor Car (International Circulation) Act, 1909, Adaptation Order [Vol. II p. 401] S.R.& O. No. 62 of 1931

Post Office Act, 1908, Adaptation Order [Vol. II p. 405] S.R.& O. No. 15 of 1932

Superannuation (Prison Officers) Act, 1919, Adaptation Order [Vol. II p. 409] S.R.& O. No. 71 of 1933

Poisons (Ireland) Act, 1870, Adaptation Order [Vol. II p. 413] S.R.& O. No. 79 of 1933

Explosives Act, 1875, Adaptation Order [Vol. II p. 417] S.R.& O. No. 79 of 1935

Gold and Silver Wares Act, 1854, Adaptation Order [Vol. II p. 421] S.R.& O. No. 249 of 1935

Tribunals of Inquiry (Evidence) Act, 1921, Adaptation Order [Vol. II p. 425] S.R.& O. No. 25 of 1936

Marriages (Ireland) Act, 1844, Adaptation Order [Vol. II p. 429] S.R.& O. No. 42 of 1936

Local Government (Application of Enactments) Order, 1898, Adaptation Order [Vol. II p. 133] S.R.& O. No. 122 of 1936

Petty Sessions (Ireland) Act, 1851, Adaptation Order [Vol. II p. 463] S.R.& O. No. 300 of 1938

Alkali etc., Works Regulation Act, 1906, Adaptation Order [Vol. XXV p. 25] S.R.& O. No. 221 of 1939

Irish Church Act, 1869 Adaptation Order [Vol. XXV p. 61] S.R.& O. No. 34 of 1940

Pilotage Act, 1913, Adaptation Order [Vol. XXV p. 77] S.R.& O. No. 311 of 1940

Statutory Authority	Section	Statutory Instrument
Adaptation of Enactments Act, No. 2 of 1922 (*Cont.*)		**Irish Universities Act, 1908, Adaptation Order [Vol. XXV p. 67] S.R.& O. No. 476 of 1942**
		Merchant Shipping Act, 1906, Adaptation Order [Vol. XXV p. 71] S.R.& O. No. 484 of 1942
		Merchant Shipping Acts, 1894 to 1921, Adaptation Order [Vol. XXXI p. 5] S.R.& O. No. 273 of 1945
		Dublin Carriage Act, 1853, Adaptation Order [Vol. XXXVI p. 1] S.R.& O. No. 137 of 1946
		Solicitors' Remuneration Act, 1881, Adaptation Order [Vol. XXXVI p. 9] S.R.& O. No. 208 of 1946
		Solicitors (Ireland) Act, 1898, Adaptation Order [Vol. XXXVI p. 5] S.R.& O. No. 235 of 1946
		Towns Improvement (Ireland) Act, 1854, Adaptation Order [Vol. XXXVI p. 13] S.R.& O. No. 410 of 1947
		Merchant Shipping Act, 1894 (Adaptation) Order, S.I. No. 398 of 1953
		Land Transfer (Ireland) Act, 1848 (Adaptation) Order, S.I. No. 280 of 1956
		Registry of Deeds (Ireland) Act, 1832 (Adaptation) Order, S.I. No. 281 of 1956
		Saint Stephen's Green (Dublin) Act, 1877 (Adaptation) Order, S.I. No. 153 of 1962
		Offences Against the Person Act, 1861 (Section 9) Adaptation Order, S.I. No. 356 of 1973
		Merchant Shipping Act, 1894 (Adaptation) Order, S.I. No. 223 of 1983
	13	*Customs (Land Frontier) Regulations [Vol. II p. 129] S.R.& O. No. 11 of 1923*
		Customs (Land Frontier) Regulations [Vol. II p. 167] S.R.& O. No. 20 of 1924
		Customs (Land Frontier) Regulations [Vol. II p. 373] S.R.& O. No. 52 of 1929
		Customs (Land Frontier) Regulations [Vol. II p. 439] S.R.& O. No. 226 of 1937
		Customs (Land Frontier) Regulations [Vol. II p. 449] S.R.& O. No. 129 of 1938
		Customs (Land Frontier) Regulations [Vol. XXV p. 31] S.R.& O. No. 105 of 1939
		Customs (Land Frontier) Regulations [Vol. XXV p. 47] S.R.& O. No. 304 of 1943
		Customs (Land Frontier) Regulations, S.I. No. 258 of 1951
		Customs (Land Frontier) Regulations, S.I. No. 258 of 1952
		Customs (Land Frontier) Regulations, S.I. No. 226 of 1962
		Customs (Land Frontier) Regulations, S.I. No. 84 of 1965
		Customs (Land Frontier) Regulations, S.I. No. 117 of 1968

Statutory Authority	Section	Statutory Instrument
Adaptation of Enactments Act, No. 2 of 1922 (*Cont.*)		**Customs (Land Frontier) Regulations, S.I. No. 324 of 1978**
	16	**Ministry of Munitions (Cessation) Order, 1921 Adaptation Order [Vol. II p. 389] S.R.& O. No. 45 of 1930**
	16(2)	**Assay (Gold and Silver Plate and Watch Cases) Adaptation Order [Vol. II p. 245] S.R.& O. No. 18 of 1927**
		Local Government (Application of Enactments) Order, 1898, Adaptation Order [Vol. II p. 133] S.R.& O. No. 122 of 1936
Adaptation of Enactments Act, No. 34 of 1931	2	**26 Geo. III, C.57 (Irish) Adaptation Order [Vol. II p. 469] S.R.& O. No. 69 of 1931**
		Irish Lights Commissioners (Adaptation) Order [Vol. II p. 473] S.R.& O. No. 661 of 1935
		Marsh's Library (Adaptation) Order, S.I. No. 8 of 1970
Adoption Act, No. 25 of 1952		*Adoption Act, 1952 Rules, S.I. No. 104 of 1953*
	2	*Adoption Act, 1952 (Commencement) Order, S.I. No. 380 of 1952*
	5	*Adoption Rules, S.I. No. 19 of 1965*
		Adoption Rules, S.I. No. 216 of 1976
		Adoption Rules, S.I. No. 134 of 1984
	22	**Short Birth Certificate Regulations, S.I. No. 215 of 1953**
Agricultural and Fishery Products (Regulation of Export) Act, No. 18 of 1947		*Agricultural and Fishery Products (Regulation of Export) Act, 1947 (Export of Poultry and Rabbits) Order, 1950 (Temporary Amendment) Order, S.I. No. 112 of 1951*
		Prohibition of Storage of Rabbits Order, S.I. No. 113 of 1951
		Prohibition of Storage of Rabbits Order, S.I. No. 60 of 1952
		Agricultural and Fishery Products (Regulation of Export) Act, 1947 (Export of Poultry and Rabbits) Order, 1950 (Temporary Amendment) Order, S.I. No. 61 of 1952
		Prohibition of Storage of Rabbits Order, S.I. No. 110 of 1953
		Agricultural and Fishery Products (Regulation of Export) Act, 1947 (Export of Poultry and Rabbits) Order, 1950 (Temporary Amendment) Order, S.I. No. 111 of 1953
		Agricultural and Fishery Products (Regulation of Export) Act, 1947 (Export of Poultry and Rabbits) Order, 1950 (Temporary Amendment) Order, S.I. No. 49 of 1954
		Prohibition of Storage of Rabbits Order, S.I. No. 50 of 1954

Agricultural and Fishery Products
(Regulation of Export) Act, No. 18
of 1947 (*Cont.*)

Prohibition of Storage of Rabbits Order, 1954 (Revocation) Order, S.I. No. 188 of 1954

Agricultural and Fishery Products (Regulation of Export) Act, 1947 (Export of Poultry and Rabbits) Order, 1950 (Temporary Amendment) (Revocation) Order, S.I. No. 189 of 1954

Agricultural and Fishery Products (Regulation of Export) Act, 1947 (Export of Poultry and Rabbits) Order, 1950 (Partial Revocation) Order, S.I. No. 194 of 1954

2 *Agricultural and Fishery Products (Regulation of Export) Act, 1947 (Export of Salmon) Order [Vol. XXXVI p. 283] S.R.& O. No. 408 of 1947*

Agricultural and Fishery Products (Regulation of Export) Act, 1947 (Export of Venison) Order, S.I. No. 62 of 1949

Agriculture and Fishery Products (Regulation of Export) Act, 1947 (Export of Salmon) Order, S.I. No. 90 of 1950

Agricultural and Fishery Products (Regulations of Export) Act, 1947 (Export of Fish Pastes and Fish Jellies) Order, S.I. No. 266 of 1950

Agricultural and Fishery Products (Regulation of Export) Act, 1947 (Export of Poultry and Rabbits) Order, S.I. No. 302 of 1950

Agricultural and Fishery Products (Regulation of Exports) Act, 1947 (Export of Eggs) Order, S.I. No. 202 of 1952

Regulation of Export (Christmas Season Exemption) Order, S.I. No. 323 of 1952

Shellfish (Regulation of Export) Order, S.I. No. 159 of 1953

Agricultural Products (Restriction of Export) Order, S.I. No. 234 of 1953

Regulation of Export (Christmas Season Exemption) Order, S.I. No. 349 of 1953

Grass Seed (Regulation of Export) Order, S.I. No. 195 of 1954

Agricultural and Fishery Products (Regulation of Export) Act, 1947 (Export of Eggs) Order, 1952 (Amendment) S.I. No. 242 of 1954

Agricultural and Fishery Products (Regulation of Export) Act, 1947 (Export of Poultry and Rabbits) Order, 1950 (Amendment) Order, S.I. No. 244 of 1954

Agricultural and Fishery Products (Regulation of Export) Act, 1947 (Export of Poultry and Rabbits) Order, 1950 (Temporary Amendment) Order, S.I. No. 247 of 1954

Agricultural Products (Restriction of Export) Order, S.I. No. 262 of 1954

Regulation of Export (Orders relating to Venison, Fish Pastes and Fish Jellies) (Revocation) Order, S.I. No. 263 of 1954

Agricultural and Fishery Products (Regulation of Export) Act, No. 18 of 1947 (*Cont.*)		*Agricultural and Fishery Products (Regulation of Export) Act, 1947 (Export of Salmon) Order, S.I. No. 275 of 1954*
		Agricultural and Fishery Products (Regulation of Export) Act, 1947 (Export of Poultry and Rabbits) Order, 1950 (Amendment) Order, S.I. No. 200 of 1955
		Agricultural and Fishery Products (Regulation of Export) Act, 1947 (Export of Poultry and Rabbits) Order, 1950 (Temporary Amendment) Order, S.I. No. 201 of 1955
		Agricultural Products (Restriction of Export) Order, S.I. No. 56 of 1956
		Agricultural Products (Restriction of Export) (No.2) Order, S.I. No. 94 of 1956
		Agricultural and Fishery Products (Regulation of Export) Act, 1947 (Export of Poultry and Rabbits) Order, 1950 (Temporary Amendment) Order, S.I. No. 272 of 1956
		Agricultural Products (Restriction of Export) Order, 1956 (Amendment) Order, S.I. No. 2 of 1957
		Hares (Regulation of Export) Order, S.I. No. 6 of 1957
		Agricultural Products (Restriction of Export) Order, 1956 (Amendment) (No.2) Order, S.I. No. 7 of 1957
		Agricultural Products (Restriction of Export) Order, 1956 (Amendment) (No.3) Order, S.I. No. 153 of 1957
		Agricultural and Fishery Products (Regulation of Export) Act, 1947 (Export of Poultry and Rabbits) Order, 1950 (Temporary Amendment) O, S.I. No. 210 of 1957
		Agricultural Products (Restriction of Export) Order, 1956 (Amendment) Order, S.I. No. 80 of 1958
		Agricultural and Fishery Products (Regulation of Export) Act, 1947 (Export of Poultry and Rabbits) Order, 1950 (Temporary Amendment) Order, S.I. No. 217 of 1958
		Shellfish (Regulation of Export) Order, S.I. No. 223 of 1958
		Agricultural Products (Restriction of Export) Order, 1956 (Amendment) Order, S.I. No. 53 of 1959
		Agricultural and Fishery Products (Regulation of Export) Act, 1947 (Export of Poultry and Rabbits) Order, 1950 (Amendment) Order, S.I. No. 171 of 1959
		Agricultural and Fishery Products (Export of Poultry and Rabbits) (Temporary Amendment) Order, S.I. No. 188 of 1959
		Horses (Regulation of Export) Order, S.I. No. 226 of 1960

Statutory Authority	Section	Statutory Instrument

Agricultural and Fishery Products (Regulation of Export) Act, No. 18 of 1947 (*Cont.*)

Agricultural and Fishery Products (Export of Poultry and Rabbits) (Temporary Amendment) Order, S.I. No. 231 of 1960

Agricultural and Fishery Products (Export of Poultry and Rabbits) (Temporary Amendment) Order, S.I. No. 263 of 1961

Partridge, Pheasant and Grouse (Regulation of Export) Order, S.I. No. 151 of 1962

Agricultural Products (Restriction of Export of Sugar Syrups) Order, S.I. No. 59 of 1963

Agricultural Products (Restriction of Export of Sugar Commodities) Order, S.I. No. 60 of 1963

Agricultural Products (Restriction of Export of Sugar Commodities) (No.2) Order, S.I. No. 170 of 1963

Agricultural Products (Restriction of Export of Sugar Syrups and Inert Sugar) Order, S.I. No. 171 of 1963

Agricultural Products (Restriction of Export) Order, S.I. No. 26 of 1964

Live Pigs (Regulation of Export) Order, S.I. No. 104 of 1964

Agricultural Products (Restriction of Export of Commodities) (No.2) Order, 1963 (Revocation) Order, S.I. No. 249 of 1964

Agricultural Products (Restriction of Export of Sugar Syrups and Invert Sugar) Order, 1963 (Revocation) Order, S.I. No. 250 of 1964

Warble Fly Order, S.I. No. 246 of 1965

Agricultural and Fishery Products (Regulation of Export) Act, 1947 (Export of Salmon and Trout) Order, S.I. No. 86 of 1966

Agricultural Products (Restriction of Export) Order, 1953 (Amendment) Order, S.I. No. 140 of 1966

Agricultural and Fishery Products (Regulation of Export to Southern Rhodesia) Order, S.I. No. 105 of 1969

Control of Exports (Southern Rhodesia) (No.2) Order, S.I. No. 106 of 1969

Tomatoes (Regulation of Export) Order, S.I. No. 127 of 1970

Control of Exports (Southern Rhodesia) Order, S.I. No. 140 of 1970

Agricultural Products (Restriction of Export) Order, S.I. No. 153 of 1970

Control of Exports (Southern Rhodesia) Order, S.I. No. 192 of 1971

Fishery Products (Regulation of Export) Order, S.I. No. 314 of 1971

Agricultural Products (Restriction of Export of Sugar Commodities and Sweetened Milk Powder Commodities) Order, S.I. No. 69 of 1972

Statutory Authority	Section	Statutory Instrument
Agricultural and Fishery Products (Regulation of Export) Act, No. 18 of 1947 (*Cont.*)		**Agricultural Products (Restriction of Export of Unsweetened Milk Powder Commodities) Order, S.I. No. 70 of 1972**
		Agricultural Products (Restriction of Export of Sugar Syrups Invert Sugar and Liquid Sugar) Order, S.I. No. 71 of 1972
		Control of Exports (Southern Rhodesia) Order, S.I. No. 153 of 1972
		Agricultural Products (Restriction of Export) Order, S.I. No. 254 of 1972
		Agricultural Products (Restriction of Export) (No.2) Order, S.I. No. 307 of 1972
		Fishery Products (Regulation of Export) Order, S.I. No. 10 of 1973
		Shellfish (Regulation of Export) (Revocation) Order, S.I. No. 25 of 1973
		Control of Exports (Southern Rhodesia) Order, S.I. No. 162 of 1973
		Fishery Products (Regulation of Export) (No.2) Order, S.I. No. 218 of 1973
		Control of Exports (Southern Rhodesia) Order, S.I. No. 181 of 1974
		Control of Exports (Southern Rhodesia) Order, S.I. No. 122 of 1975
		Agricultural Products (Restriction of Export) Order, S.I. No. 126 of 1975
		Control of Exports (Southern Rhodesia) Order, S.I. No. 123 of 1976
		Control of Exports (Southern Rhodesia) Order, S.I. No. 170 of 1977
		Control of Exports (Southern Rhodesia) Order, S.I. No. 164 of 1978
		Control of Exports (Southern Rhodesia) Order, S.I. No. 213 of 1979
		Partridge, Pheasant and Grouse (Regulation of Export) (Amendment) Order, S.I. No. 238 of 1979
		Control of Exports (Southern Rhodesia) (Revocation) Order, S.I. No. 24 of 1980
		Agriculture and Fishery Products (Regulation of Export to Southern Rhodesia) (Revocation) (No.2) Order, S.I. No. 69 of 1980
		Agriculture and Fishery Products (Regulation of Export to Southern Rhodesia) (Revocation) Order, S.I. No. 70 of 1980
		Agricultural Products (Regulation of Export to Iran) Order, S.I. No. 145 of 1980
		Control of Exports (Iran) Order, S.I. No. 146 of 1980
		Control of Exports (Iran) (Revocation) Order, S.I. No. 27 of 1981
		Agricultural Products (Regulation of Export to Iran) (Revocation) Order, S.I. No. 40 of 1981

Statutory Authority	Section	Statutory Instrument
Agricultural and Fishery Products (Regulation of Export) Act, No. 18 of 1947 (*Cont.*)		**Agricultural and Fishery Products (Regulation of Export) Act, 1947 (Export of Salmon and Trout) (Amendment) Order, S.I. No. 372 of 1984**
	2(2)	**Agricultural Products (Restriction of Export) Order, 1953 (Amendment) Order, S.I. No. 11 of 1978**
	5	**Agricultural and Fishery Products (Regulation of Export) Act, 1947 (Transfer of Powers) Order, S.I. No. 52 of 1956**
		Agricultural and Fishery Products (Regulation of Export) Act, 1947 (Transfer of Powers) Order, 1956 (Amendment) Order, S.I. No. 209 of 1972
	5(2)	**Agricultural and Fishery Products (Regulation of Export) Act, 1947 (Transfer of Powers) Order, 1956 (Amendment) Order, S.I. No. 21 of 1963**
	5(3)	**Agricultural and Fishery Products (Regulation of Export) Act, 1947 (Transfer of Powers) Order, 1956 (Amendment) Order, S.I. No. 21 of 1963**
Agricultural Co-operative Societies (Debentures) Act, No. 39 of 1934		**Agricultural Co-operative Societies (Debentures) Regulations, S.I. No. 141 of 1949**
	12	*Agricultural Co-operative Societies (Debentures) Regulations [Vol. III p. 45] S.R.& O. No. 325 of 1934*
Agricultural Credit Act, No. 24 of 1927	25(8)	**Chattel Mortgages (Registration) Order [Vol. III p. 63] S.R.& O. No. 40 of 1928**
Agricultural Credit Act, No. 14 of 1947	6	*Agricultural Credit Act, 1947 (Part II) Appointed Day Order, S.R.& O. No. 337 of 1947*
	26	*Agricultural Credit Act, 1947 (Section 26 (1) – Forms) Regulations, S.I. No. 269 of 1954*
		Agricultural Credit Act, 1947 (Sections 26 and 29 – Forms) Regulations, S.I. No. 42 of 1956
	29	*Agricultural Credit Act, 1947 (Sections 26 and 29 – Forms) Regulations, S.I. No. 42 of 1956*
Agricultural Credit Act, No. 2 of 1978	2	*Agricultural Credit Act, 1978 (Commencement) Order, S.I. No. 49 of 1978*
	28	**Agricultural Credit Act, 1978 (Sections 28 and 31 – Forms) Regulations, S.I. No. 170 of 1978**
	31	**Agricultural Credit Act, 1978 (Sections 28 and 31 – Forms) Regulations, S.I. No. 170 of 1978**
Agricultural Produce (Cereals) Act, No. 7 of 1933		**Agricultural Produce (Cereals) (Wheat Growing and Feeding Stuffs) Regulations [Vol. III p. 93] S.R.& O. No. 57 of 1933**
		Agricultural Produce (Maize Meal Mixture) Regulations [Vol. III p. 171] S.R.& O. No. 89 of 1933
		Agricultural Produce (Maize Meal Mixture) No.2 Regulations [Vol. III p. 177] S.R.& O. No. 113 of 1933

Statutory Authority	Section	Statutory Instrument
Agricultural Produce (Cereals) Act, No. 7 of 1933 (*Cont.*)		*Agricultural Produce (Maize Meal Mixture) Regulations [Vol. III p. 185] S.R.& O. No. 145 of 1934*
		Agricultural Produce (Maize Meal Mixture) No.2 Regulations [Vol. III p. 193] S.R.& O. No. 241 of 1934
		Agricultural Produce (Maize Meal Mixture) Regulations [Vol. III p. 201] S.R.& O. No. 157 of 1935
		Agricultural Produce (Maize Meal Mixture) No.2 Regulations [Vol. III p. 209] S.R.& O. No. 536 of 1935
		Agricultural Produce (Maize Meal Mixture) No.3 Regulations [Vol. III p. 215] S.R.& O. No. 657 of 1935
	2	*Agricultural Produce (Cereals) Act, 1933 (Parts I to VII) (Commencement) Order [Vol. III p. 69] S.R.& O. No. 65 of 1933*
	6	*Millable Wheat Regulations [Vol. III p. 221] S.R.& O. No. 100 of 1933*
		Millable Wheat Regulations, S.I. No. 210 of 1958
		Millable Wheat Regulations, S.I. No. 114 of 1959
		Millable Wheat Regulations, S.I. No. 140 of 1961
		Millable Wheat Regulations, S.I. No. 213 of 1965
	7(2)	*Home-Grown Wheat (Standard Prices) Order [Vol. III p. 295] S.R.& O. No. 174 of 1934*
	12(3)	**Agricultural Produce (Cereals) Act (Part I) Regulations [Vol. III p. 73] S.R.& O. No. 64 of 1933**
	16	**Agricultural Produce (Cereals) Act (Part II) Regulations [Vol. III p. 77] S.R.& O. No. 66 of 1933**
	29	*Home-Grown Wheat (National Percentage for Cereal Year 1933–34) Order [Vol. III p. 225] S.R.& O. No. 105 of 1933*
		Home-Grown Wheat (National Percentage for Cereal Year 1933–34) (Varying) Order [Vol. III p. 231] S.R.& O. No. 182 of 1934
		Home-Grown Wheat (National Percentage for Cereal Year 1934–35) Order [Vol. III p. 235] S.R.& O. No. 258 of 1934
		Home-Grown Wheat (National Percentage for Cereal Year 1934–35) (Varying) Order [Vol. III p. 241] S.R.& O. No. 350 of 1934
		Home-Grown Wheat (National Percentage for Cereal Year 1934–35) (Varying) (No.2) Order [Vol. III p. 247] S.R.& O. No. 134 of 1935
	31	**Milling Licences (Times for Making Returns) Regulations, S.I. No. 282 of 1953**
	31(1)	**Milling Licences (Returns) Regulations [Vol. III p. 155] S.R.& O. No. 81 of 1933**

Statutory Authority	Section	Statutory Instrument
Agricultural Produce (Cereals) Act, No. 7 of 1933 (*Cont.*)	32	**Agricultural Produce (Cereals) Acts (Records No.1) Regulations [Vol. III p. 317] S.R.& O. No. 185 of 1936**
		Agricultural Produce (Cereals) Acts (Records No.2) Regulations [Vol. III p. 331] S.R.& O. No. 186 of 1936
	44(1)	**Agricultural Produce (Cereals) Act (Part IV) Regulations [Vol. III p. 87] S.R.& O. No. 63 of 1933**
	55(1)	**Registered Flour Importers and Registered Distillers (Returns) Regulations [Vol. III p. 159] S.R.& O. No. 82 of 1933**
	67(2)	*Home-Grown Wheat (Standard Prices) Order [Vol. III p. 165] S.R.& O. No. 86 of 1933*
	67(4)	*Home-Grown Wheat (Increase of Standard Prices) Order [Vol. III p. 301] S.R.& O. No. 175 of 1934*
	78	*Agricultural Produce (Sale of Maize Meal) Regulations [Vol. III p. 253] S.R.& O. No. 168 of 1933*
		Agricultural Produce (Sale of Maize Meal) Regulations [Vol. III p. 257] S.R.& O. No. 55 of 1936
	90(2)	*Agricultural Produce (Cereals) (Scheduled Feeding Stuffs) Order [Vol. III p. 263] S.R.& O. No. 19 of 1934*
		Agricultural Produce (Cereals) (Scheduled Feeding Stuffs) No.3 Order [Vol. III p. 271] S.R.& O. No. 82 of 1934
		Agricultural Produce (Cereals) (Scheduled Feeding Stuffs) No.2 Order [Vol. III p. 267] S.R.& O. No. 136 of 1934
		Agricultural Produce (Cereals) (Scheduled Feeding Stuffs) No.1 Order [Vol. III p. 275] S.R.& O. No. 96 of 1935
		Agricultural Produce (Cereals) (Scheduled Feeding Stuffs) No.2 Order [Vol. III p. 279] S.R.& O. No. 468 of 1935
		Agricultural Produce (Cereals) (Scheduled Feeding Stuffs) No.1 Order [Vol. III p. 283] S.R.& O. No. 257 of 1936
		Agricultural Produce (Cereals) (Scheduled Feeding Stuffs) No.2 Order [Vol. III p. 287] S.R.& O. No. 385 of 1936
	94	*Wheat Offals (Restriction on Exportation) Order [Vol. III p. 291] S.R.& O. No. 148 of 1934*
		Beet Pulp (Restriction on Exportation) Order [Vol. III p. 307] S.R.& O. No. 261 of 1934
	Part IV	**Agricultural Produce (Cereals) (Wheat Growing and Feeding Stuffs) Amendment Regulations [Vol. III p. 113] S.R.& O. No. 605 of 1935**
Agricultural Produce (Cereals) Act, No. 41 of 1934	11	**Agricultural Produce (Cereals) Acts (Records No.1) Regulations [Vol. III p. 317] S.R.& O. No. 185 of 1936**

Statutory Authority	Section	Statutory Instrument
Agricultural Produce (Cereals) Act, No. 41 of 1934 (*Cont.*)		**Agricultural Produce (Cereals) Acts (Records No.2) Regulations [Vol. III p. 331] S.R.& O. No. 186 of 1936**
	30	*Compound Feeding Stuffs (Indication of Place of Manufacture) Regulations [Vol. III p. 371] S.R.& O. No. 317 of 1934*
	36	*Agricultural Produce (Cereals) Act, 1934 (Operation of Part IV) Order [Vol. III p. 349] S.R.& O. No. 273 of 1934*
	37(1)	**Agricultural Produce (Cereals) Act, 1934 (Cesser of operation of Part IV) Order [Vol. XXV p. 113] S.R.& O. No. 195 of 1939**
	56(1)	*Home-Grown Barley (Minimum Prices) Order [Vol. III p. 377] S.R.& O. No. 322 of 1934*
	56(2)	*Home-Grown Barley (Minimum Prices) (Revocation) Order [Vol. III p. 383] S.R.& O. No. 631 of 1935*
	Part IV	*Agricultural Produce (Cereals) Act, 1934 (Part IV) Regulations [Vol. III p. 353] S.R.& O. No. 323 of 1934*
Agricultural Produce (Cereals) Act, No. 26 of 1935	6(1)	*Home-Grown Wheat (National Percentage for Cereal Year 1935–36) Order [Vol. III p. 387] S.R.& O. No. 314 of 1935*
		Home-Grown Wheat (National Percentage for Cereal Year 1936–37) Order [Vol. III p. 397] S.R.& O. No. 19 of 1936
		Home-Grown Wheat (National Percentage for Cereal Year 1935–36) (Variation) Order [Vol. III p. 391] S.R.& O. No. 131 of 1936
		Home-Grown Wheat (National Percentage for Cereal Year 1937–38) Order [Vol. III p. 415] S.R.& O. No. 390 of 1936
		Home-Grown Wheat (National Percentage for Cereal Year 1936–37) (Variation) Order [Vol. III p. 403] S.R.& O. No. 18 of 1937
		Home-Grown Wheat (National Percentage for Cereal Year 1936–37) (Variation) (No.2) Order [Vol. III p. 409] S.R.& O. No. 149 of 1937
		Home-Grown Wheat (National Percentage for Cereal Year 1937–38) (Variation) Order [Vol. III p. 419] S.R.& O. No. 262 of 1937
		Home-Grown Wheat (National Percentage for Cereal Year 1938–39) Order [Vol. III p. 425] S.R.& O. No. 325 of 1937
		Home-Grown Wheat (National Percentage for Cereal Year 1938–39) (Variation) Order [Vol. III p. 429] S.R.& O. No. 276 of 1938
		Home-Grown Wheat (National Percentage for Cereal Year 1939–40) Order [Vol. III p. 435] S.R.& O. No. 341 of 1938
		Home-Grown Wheat (National Percentage for Cereal Year 1938–39) (Variation No.2) Order [Vol. XXV p. 151] S.R.& O. No. 95 of 1939

Statutory Authority	Section	Statutory Instrument
Agricultural Produce (Cereals) Act, No. 26 of 1935 (*Cont.*)		*Home-Grown Wheat (National Percentage for Cereal Year 1939–40) (Variation) Order [Vol. XXV p. 145] S.R.& O. No. 310 of 1939*
		Home-Grown Wheat (National Percentage for Cereal Year 1940–41) Order, (1939) [Vol. XXV p. 117] S.R.& O. No. 12 of 1940
		Home-Grown Wheat (National Percentage for Cereal Year 1940–41) (Variation) Order [Vol. XXV p. 157] S.R.& O. No. 277 of 1940
		Home-Grown Wheat (National Percentage for Cereal Year 1941–42) Order [Vol. XXV p. 121] S.R.& O. No. 393 of 1940
		Home-Grown Wheat (National Percentage for Cereal Year 1940–41) (Variation No.2) Order [Vol. XXV p. 163] S.R.& O. No. 61 of 1941
		Home-Grown Wheat (National Percentage for Cereal Year 1940–41) (Variation No.3) Order [Vol. XXV p. 169] S.R.& O. No. 207 of 1941
		Home-Grown Wheat (National Percentage for Cereal Year 1942–43) Order [Vol. XXV p. 125] S.R.& O. No. 580 of 1941
		Home-Grown Wheat (National Percentage for Cereal Year 1943–44) Order [Vol. XXV p. 129] S.R.& O. No. 541 of 1942
		Home-Grown Wheat (National Percentage for Cereal Year 1942–43) (Variation) Order [Vol. XXV p. 175] S.R.& O. No. 223 of 1943
		Home-Grown Wheat (National Percentage for Cereal Year 1943–44) (Variation) Order [Vol. XXV p. 181] S.R.& O. No. 336 of 1943
		Home-Grown Wheat (National Percentage for Cereal Year 1944–45) Order [Vol. XXV p. 133] S.R.& O. No. 431 of 1943
		Home-Grown Wheat (National Percentage for Cereal Year 1944–45) (Variation No.2) Order [Vol. XXV p. 187] S.R.& O. No. 226 of 1944
		Home-Grown Wheat (National Percentage for Cereal Year 1945–46) Order [Vol. XXV p. 137] S.R.& O. No. 342 of 1944
		Home-Grown Wheat (National Percentage for Cereal Year 1944–45) (Variation) Order [Vol. XXV p. 191] S.R.& O. No. 33 of 1945
		Home-Grown Wheat (National Percentage for Cereal Year 1946–47) Order [Vol. XXV p. 141] S.R.& O. No. 327 of 1945
		Home-Grown Wheat (National Percentage for Cereal Year 1945–46) (Variation) Order [Vol. XXXVI p. 51] S.R.& O. No. 211 of 1946
		Home-Grown Wheat (National Percentage for Cereal Year 1947–48) Order [Vol. XXXVI p. 63] S.R.& O. No. 379 of 1946
		Home-Grown Wheat (National Percentage for Cereal Year 1946–47) (Variation) Order [Vol. XXXVI p. 57] S.R.& O. No. 251 of 1947

Statutory Authority	Section	Statutory Instrument
Agricultural Produce (Cereals) Act, No. 26 of 1935 (*Cont.*)		*Home-Grown Wheat (National Percentage for Cereal Year 1948–49) Order [Vol. XXXVI p. 67] S.R.& O. No. 435 of 1947*
		Home-Grown Wheat (National Percentage for Cereal Year 1947–48) (Variation) Order, S.I. No. 262 of 1948
		Home-Grown Wheat (National Percentage for Cereal Year 1949–50) Order, S.I. No. 436 of 1948
		Home-Grown Wheat (National Percentage for Cereal Year 1948–49) (Variation) Order, S.I. No. 239 of 1949
		Home-Grown Wheat (National Percentage for Cereal Year 1950–51) Order, S.I. No. 342 of 1949
		Home-Grown Wheat (National Percentage for Cereal Year 1949–50) (Variation) Order, S.I. No. 210 of 1950
		Home-Grown Wheat (National Percentage for Cereal Year 1951–52) Order, S.I. No. 307 of 1950
		Home-Grown Wheat (National Percentage for Cereal Year 1950–51) (Variation) Order, S.I. No. 236 of 1951
		Home-Grown Wheat (National Percentage for Cereal Year 1952–53) Order, S.I. No. 322 of 1951
		Home-Grown Wheat (National Percentage for Cereal Year 1951–52) (Variation) Order, S.I. No. 246 of 1952
		Home-Grown Wheat (National Percentage for Cereal Year 1953–54) Order, S.I. No. 345 of 1952
		Home-Grown Wheat (National Percentage for Cereal Year 1952–53) (Variation) Order, S.I. No. 138 of 1953
		Home-Grown Wheat (National Percentage for Cereal Year 1954–55) Order, S.I. No. 374 of 1953
		Home-Grown Wheat (National Percentage for Cereal Year 1953–54) (Variation) Order, S.I. No. 127 of 1954
		Home-Grown Wheat (National Percentage for Cereal Year 1955–56) Order, S.I. No. 282 of 1954
		Home-Grown Wheat (National Percentage for Cereal Year 1954–55) (Variation) Order, S.I. No. 138 of 1955
		Home-Grown Wheat (National Percentage for Cereal Year 1956–57) Order, S.I. No. 247 of 1955
		Home-Grown Wheat (National Percentage for Cereal Year 1955–56) (Variation) Order, S.I. No. 190 of 1956
		Home-Grown Wheat (National Percentage for Cereal Year 1957–58) Order, S.I. No. 309 of 1956
		Home-Grown Wheat (National Percentage for Cereal Year 1956–57) (Variation) Order, S.I. No. 145 of 1957
		Home-Grown Wheat (National Percentage for Cereal Year 1957–58) (Variation) Order, S.I. No. 213 of 1957

Statutory Authority	Section	Statutory Instrument
Agricultural Produce (Cereals) Act, No. 26 of 1935 (*Cont.*)		*Home-Grown Wheat (National Percentage for Cereal Year 1958–59) Order, S.I. No. 266 of 1957*
		Home-Grown Wheat (National Percentage for Cereal Year 1957–58) (Variation No.2) Order, S.I. No. 174 of 1958
		Home-Grown Wheat (National Percentage for Cereal Year 1959–60) Order, S.I. No. 263 of 1958
		Home-Grown Wheat (National Percentage for Cereal Year 1958–59) (Variation) Order, S.I. No. 84 of 1959
		Home-Grown Wheat (National Percentage for Cereal Year 1960–61) Order, S.I. No. 222 of 1959
		Home-Grown Wheat (National Percentage for Cereal Year 1959–60) (Variation) Order, S.I. No. 130 of 1960
		Home-Grown Wheat (National Percentage for Cereal Year 1961–62) Order, S.I. No. 262 of 1960
		Home-Grown Wheat (National Percentage for Cereal Year 1960–61) (Variation) Order, S.I. No. 114 of 1961
		Home-Grown Wheat (National Percentage for Cereal Year 1960–61) (Variation No.2) Order, S.I. No. 185 of 1961
		Home-Grown Wheat (National Percentage for Cereal Year 1962–63) Order, S.I. No. 301 of 1961
		Home-Grown Wheat (National Percentage for Cereal Year 1961–62) (Variation) Order, S.I. No. 141 of 1962
		Home-Grown Wheat (National Percentage for Cereal Year 1963–64) Order, S.I. No. 229 of 1962
		Home-Grown Wheat (National Percentage for Cereal Year 1962–63) (Variation) Order, S.I. No. 138 of 1963
		Home-Grown Wheat (National Percentage for Cereal Year 1964–65) Order, S.I. No. 256 of 1963
		Home-Grown Wheat (National Percentage for Cereal Year 1963–64) (Variation) Order, S.I. No. 195 of 1964
		Home-Grown Wheat (National Percentage for Cereal Year 1965–66) Order, S.I. No. 285 of 1964
		Home-Grown Wheat (National Percentage for Cereal Year 1964–65) (Variation) Order, S.I. No. 167 of 1965
		Home-Grown Wheat (National Percentage for Cereal Year 1966–67) Order, S.I. No. 250 of 1965
		Home-Grown Wheat (National Percentage for Cereal Year 1965–66) (Variation) Order, S.I. No. 191 of 1966
		Home-Grown Wheat (National Percentage for Cereal Year 1967–68) Order, S.I. No. 272 of 1966
		Home-Grown Wheat (National Percentage for Cereal Year 1966–67) (Variation) Order, S.I. No. 191 of 1967

Statutory Authority	Section	Statutory Instrument
Agricultural Produce (Cereals) Act, No. 26 of 1935 (*Cont.*)		*Home-Grown Wheat (National Percentage for Cereal Year 1968–69) Order, S.I. No. 280 of 1967*
		Home-Grown Wheat (National Percentage for Cereal Year 1967–68) (Variation) Order, S.I. No. 159 of 1968
		Home-Grown Wheat (National Percentage for Cereal Year 1969–70) Order, S.I. No. 259 of 1968
		Home-Grown Wheat (National Percentage for Cereal Year 1968–69) (Variation) Order, S.I. No. 159 of 1969
		Home-Grown Wheat (National Percentage for Cereal Year 1970–71) Order, S.I. No. 243 of 1969
		Home-Grown Wheat (National Percentage for Cereal Year 1969–70) (Variation) Order, S.I. No. 150 of 1970
		Home-Grown Wheat (National Percentage for Cereal Year 1971–72) Order, S.I. No. 293 of 1970
		Home-Grown Wheat (National Percentage for Cereal Year 1970–71) (Variation) Order, S.I. No. 202 of 1971
		Home-Grown Wheat (National Percentage for Cereal Year 1972–73) Order, S.I. No. 325 of 1971
		Home-Grown Wheat (National Percentage for Cereal Year 1971–72) (Variation) Order, S.I. No. 148 of 1972
	7(1)	*Home-Grown Wheat (Storage and Drying Plant for Cereal Year 1935–36) Order [Vol. III p. 439] S.R.& O. No. 315 of 1935*
		Home-Grown Wheat (Storage and Drying Plant for Cereal Year 1936–37) Order [Vol. III p. 445] S.R.& O. No. 263 of 1936
		Home-Grown Wheat (Storage and Drying Plant for Cereal Year 1937–38) Order [Vol. III p. 451] S.R.& O. No. 170 of 1937
		Home-Grown Wheat (Storage and Drying Plant for Cereal Year 1938–39) Order [Vol. III p. 457] S.R.& O. No. 60 of 1938
		Home-Grown Wheat (Storage and Drying Plant for Cereal Year 1939–40) Order [Vol. XXV p. 239] S.R.& O. No. 59 of 1939
		Home-Grown Wheat (Storage and Drying Plant for Cereal Year 1940–41) Order [Vol. XXV p. 245] S.R.& O. No. 212 of 1940
		Home-Grown Wheat (Storage and Drying Plant for Cereal Year 1941–42) Order [Vol. XXV p. 251] S.R.& O. No. 81 of 1941
		Home-Grown Wheat (Storage and Drying Plant for Cereal Year 1942–43) Order [Vol. XXV p. 257] S.R.& O. No. 196 of 1942
		Home-Grown Wheat (Storage and Drying Plant for Cereal Year 1943–44) Order [Vol. XXV p. 263] S.R.& O. No. 105 of 1943

Statutory Authority	Section	Statutory Instrument
Agricultural Produce (Cereals) Act, No. 26 of 1935 (*Cont.*)		*Home-Grown Wheat (Storage and Drying Plant for Cereal Year 1944–45) Order [Vol. XXV p. 269]* S.R.& O. No. 79 of 1944
		Home-Grown Wheat (Storage and Drying Plant for Cereal Year 1945–46) Order [Vol. XXV p. 275] S.R.& O. No. 50 of 1945
		Home-Grown Wheat (Storage and Drying Plant for Cereal Year 1946–47) Order [Vol. XXXVI p. 83] S.R.& O. No. 132 of 1946
		Home-Grown Wheat (Storage and Drying Plant for Cereal Year 1947–48) Order [Vol. XXXVI p. 89] S.R.& O. No. 261 of 1947
		Home-Grown Wheat (Storage and Drying Plant for Cereal Year 1948–49) Order, S.I. No. 205 of 1948
		Home-Grown Wheat (Storage and Drying Plant for Cereal Year 1949–50) Order, S.I. No. 89 of 1949
		Home-Grown Wheat (Storage and Drying Plant for Cereal Year 1950–51) Order, S.I. No. 38 of 1950
		Home-Grown Wheat (Storage and Drying Plant for Cereal Year 1951–52) Order, S.I. No. 159 of 1951
		Home-Grown Wheat (Storage and Drying Plant for Cereal Year 1952–53) Order, S.I. No. 148 of 1952
		Home-Grown Wheat (Storage and Drying Plant for Cereal Year 1953–54) Order, S.I. No. 238 of 1953
		Home-Grown Wheat (Storage and Drying Plant for Cereal Year 1954–55) Order, S.I. No. 109 of 1954
		Home-Grown Wheat (Storage and Drying Plant for Cereal Year 1955–56) Order, S.I. No. 71 of 1955
		Home-Grown Wheat (Storage and Drying Plant for Cereal Year 1956–57) Order, S.I. No. 143 of 1956
		Home-Grown Wheat (Storage and Drying Plant for Cereal Year 1957–58) Order, S.I. No. 126 of 1957
		Home-Grown Wheat (Storage and Drying Plant for Cereal Year 1958–59) Order, S.I. No. 130 of 1958
	10(1)	*Home-Grown Wheat (Purchase Percentage for Cereal Year 1935–36) Order [Vol. III p. 463]* S.R.& O. No. 316 of 1935
		Home-Grown Wheat (Purchase Percentage for Cereal Year 1936–37) Order [Vol. III p. 475] S.R.& O. No. 262 of 1936
		Home-Grown Wheat (Purchase Percentage for Cereal Year 1937–38) Order [Vol. III p. 481] S.R.& O. No. 150 of 1937
		Home-Grown Wheat (Purchase Percentage for Cereal Year 1938–39) Order [Vol. III p. 487] S.R.& O. No. 179 of 1938
		Home-Grown Wheat (Purchase Percentage for Cereal Year 1939–40) Order [Vol. XXV p. 197] S.R.& O. No. 145 of 1939
		Home-Grown Wheat (Purchase Percentage for Cereal Year 1940–41) Order [Vol. XXV p. 203] S.R.& O. No. 158 of 1940

Statutory Authority	Section	Statutory Instrument
Agricultural Produce (Cereals) Act, No. 26 of 1935 *(Cont.)*		*Home-Grown Wheat (Purchase Percentage for Cereal Year 1941–42) Order [Vol. XXV p. 209] S.R.& O. No. 289 of 1941*
		Home-Grown Wheat (Purchase Percentage for Cereal Year 1941–42) (Amendment) Order [Vol. XXV p. 233] S.R.& O. No. 25 of 1942
		Home-Grown Wheat (Purchase Percentage for Cereal Year 1942–43) Order [Vol. XXV p. 215] S.R.& O. No. 209 of 1942
		Home-Grown Wheat (Purchase Percentage for Cereal Year 1943–44) Order [Vol. XXV p. 221] S.R.& O. No. 266 of 1943
		Home-Grown Wheat (Purchase Percentage for Cereal Year 1944–45) Order [Vol. XXV p. 227] S.R.& O. No. 211 of 1944
		Home-Grown Wheat (Purchase Percentage for Cereal Year 1945–46) Order [Vol. XXV p. 281] S.R.& O. No. 104 of 1945
		Home-Grown Wheat (Purchase Percentage for Cereal Year 1946–47) Order [Vol. XXXVI p. 71] S.R.& O. No. 133 of 1946
		Home-Grown Wheat (Purchase Percentage for Cereal Year 1947–48) Order [Vol. XXXVI p. 77] S.R.& O. No. 208 of 1947
		Home-Grown Wheat (Purchase Percentage for Cereal Year 1948–49) Order, S.I. No. 187 of 1948
		Home-Grown Wheat (Purchase Percentage for Cereal Year 1949–50) Order, S.I. No. 147 of 1949
		Home-Grown Wheat (Purchase Percentage for Cereal Year 1950–51) Order, S.I. No. 118 of 1950
		Home-Grown Wheat (Purchase Percentage for Cereal Year 1951–52) Order, S.I. No. 158 of 1951
		Home-Grown Wheat (Purchase Percentage for Cereal Year 1952–53) Order, S.I. No. 139 of 1952
		Home-Grown Wheat (Purchase Percentage for Cereal Year 1953–54) Order, S.I. No. 204 of 1953
		Home-Grown Wheat (Purchase Percentage for Cereal Year 1954–55) S.I. No. 96 of 1954
		Home-Grown Wheat (Purchase Percentage for Cereal Year 1955–56) Order, S.I. No. 117 of 1955
		Home-Grown Wheat (Purchase Percentage for Cereal Year 1956–57) Order, S.I. No. 139 of 1956
		Home-Grown Wheat (Purchase Percentage for Cereal Year 1957–58) Order, S.I. No. 90 of 1957
		Home-Grown Wheat (Purchase Percentage for Cereal Year 1958–59) Order, S.I. No. 185 of 1958
		Home-Grown Wheat (Purchase Percentage for Cereal Year 1959–60) Order, S.I. No. 111 of 1959
		Home-Grown Wheat (Purchase Percentage for Cereal Year 1960–61) Order, S.I. No. 121 of 1960
		Home-Grown Wheat (Purchase Percentage for Cereal Year 1962–63) Order, S.I. No. 78 of 1962
		Home-Grown Wheat (Purchase Percentage for Cereal Year 1963–64) Order, S.I. No. 106 of 1963

Statutory Authority	Section	Statutory Instrument
Agricultural Produce (Cereals) Act, No. 26 of 1935 (*Cont.*)		*Home-Grown Wheat (Purchase Percentage for Cereal Year 1964–1965) Order, S.I. No. 133 of 1964*
	10(2)	*Home-Grown Wheat (Purchase Percentage for Cereal Year 1935–36) (Amendment) Order [Vol. III p. 469] S.R.& O. No. 656 of 1935*
		Home-Grown Wheat (Purchase Percentage for Cereal Year 1952–53) (Amendment) Order, S.I. No. 80 of 1953
	12(2)	*Home-Grown Millable Wheat (Minimum Prices for Sale (Wheat) Year 1937–38) Order [Vol. III p. 493] S.R.& O. No. 402 of 1935*
		Home-Grown Millable Wheat (Minimum Prices for Sale (Wheat) Year 1938–39) Order [Vol. III p. 503] S.R.& O. No. 241 of 1936
		Home-Grown Millable Wheat (Minimum Prices for Sale (Wheat) Year 1939–40) Order [Vol. III p. 513] S.R.& O. No. 195 of 1937
		Home-Grown Millable Wheat (Minimum Prices for Sale (Wheat) Year 1940–41) Order [Vol. III p. 521] S.R.& O. No. 211 of 1938
		Home-Grown Millable Wheat (Minimum Prices for Sale (Wheat) Year 1941–42) Order [Vol. XXV p. 287] S.R.& O. No. 204 of 1939
	12(3)	*Home-Grown Millable Wheat (Minimum Prices for Sale (Wheat) Year 1937–38) Order [Vol. III p. 493] S.R.& O. No. 402 of 1935*
		Home-Grown Millable Wheat (Minimum Prices for Sale (Wheat) Year 1938–39) Order [Vol. III p. 503] S.R.& O. No. 241 of 1936
		Home-Grown Millable Wheat (Minimum Prices for Sale (Wheat) Year 1939–40) Order [Vol. III p. 513] S.R.& O. No. 195 of 1937
		Home-Grown Millable Wheat (Minimum Prices for Sale (Wheat) Year 1940–41) Order [Vol. III p. 521] S.R.& O. No. 211 of 1938
	14(1)	**Home-Grown Wheat (Determination of Class) Order [Vol. III p. 529] S.R.& O. No. 266 of 1936**
Agricultural Produce (Cereals) Act, No. 30 of 1936		*Agricultural Produce (Maize Meal Mixture) Regulations [Vol. III p. 539] S.R.& O. No. 243 of 1936*
		Agricultural Produce (Maize Meal Mixture) No.2 Regulations [Vol. III p. 547] S.R.& O. No. 289 of 1936
		Maize Meal Mixture (Indication of Weight of Component Parts) Regulations [Vol. III p. 567] S.R.& O. No. 383 of 1936
		Agricultural Produce (Maize Meal Mixture) Regulations [Vol. III p. 555] S.R.& O. No. 100 of 1937
		Agricultural Produce (Maize Meal Mixture) Regulations [Vol. III p. 561] S.R.& O. No. 216 of 1938
	5	*Agricultural Produce (Maize Meal Mixture) Regulations [Vol. XXV p. 295] S.R.& O. No. 135 of 1939*

Statutory Authority	Section	Statutory Instrument
Agricultural Produce (Cereals) Act, No. 30 of 1936 (*Cont.*)		**Agricultural Produce (Maize Meal Mixture) No.2 Regulations [Vol. XXV p. 301] S.R.& O. No. 187 of 1939**
	14(4)	*Home-Grown Wheat (Purchase Percentage for Cereal Year 1961–62) Order, S.I. No. 147 of 1961*
	22(1)	*Agricultural Produce (Cereals) Act, 1936 (Part IV) (Appointed Day) Order [Vol. III p. 535] S.R.& O. No. 244 of 1936*
Agricultural Produce (Cereals) Act, No. 16 of 1938	10(2)	*Agricultural Produce (Cereals) Act, 1938 (Section 10) (Exemption) Order [Vol. III p. 603] S.R.& O. No. 165 of 1938*
		Agricultural Produce (Cereals) Act, 1938 (Section 10) (Exemption) Order, S.I. No. 29 of 1957
		Agricultural Produce (Cereals) Act, 1938 (Section 10) (Exemption) Order, S.I. No. 141 of 1966
	18(2)	**Agricultural Produce (Cereals) Act, 1938 (Section 18 (2)) Order [Vol. XXV p. 329] S.R.& O. No. 365 of 1939**
		Agricultural Produce (Cereals) Act, 1938 (Section 18 (2)) (No.2) Order, (1939) [Vol. XXV p. 333] S.R.& O. No. 24 of 1940
	18(3)	*Agricultural Produce (Cereals) (Exempted Feeding Stuffs) Order [Vol. XXV p. 345] S.R.& O. No. 146 of 1939*
	18(4)	*Agricultural Produce (Cereals) (Exempted Feeding Stuffs) Order, 1939 (Revocation) Order [Vol. XXV p. 349] S.R.& O. No. 364 of 1939*
	19(2)	**Agricultural Produce (Cereals) Act, 1938 (Section 19 (2)) Order, S.I. No. 124 of 1957**
		Agricultural Produce (Cereals) Act, 1938 (Section 19 (2)) Order, S.I. No. 197 of 1957
	19(3)	**Agricultural Produce (Cereals) (Scheduled Feeding Stuff) Order, (1939) [Vol. XXV p. 341] S.R.& O. No. 25 of 1940**
	20(2)	*Agricultural Produce (Cereals) Act, 1938 (Section 20 (2)) (Exemption) Order [Vol. III p. 593] S.R.& O. No. 127 of 1938*
		Agricultural Produce (Cereals) Act, 1938 (Section 20 (2)) (Exemption) Order, S.I. No. 171 of 1955
		Agricultural Produce (Cereals) Act, 1938 (Section 20 (2)) Exemption Order, S.I. No. 123 of 1957
	20(3)	**Agricultural Produce (Cereals) Act, 1938 (Section 20 (3)) (Exemption) Order [Vol. III p. 597] S.R.& O. No. 128 of 1938**
	20(4)	*Agricultural Produce (Cereals) Act, 1938 (Section 20 (2)) (Exemption) Order, 1938 (Revocation) Order S.R.&O. No. 363 of 1939*

Statutory Authority	Section	Statutory Instrument
Agricultural Produce (Cereals) Act, No. 16 of 1938 (*Cont.*)	24	**Feeding Stuffs (Restriction of Export) Order, S.I. No. 233 of 1953** **Feeding Stuffs (Restriction of Export) Order, S.I. No. 93 of 1956** **Feeding Stuffs (Restriction of Export) Order, S.I. No. 178 of 1957** **Feeding Stuffs (Restriction of Export) Order, S.I. No. 138 of 1966**
Agricultural Produce (Cereals) Act, No. 22 of 1939	3(1)	**Agricultural Produce (Cereals) Act, 1939 (Suspendable Provisions under Section 3) (Suspending) Order [Vol. XXV p. 353] S.R.& O. No. 280 of 1939**
	4(1)	**Agricultural Produce (Cereals) Act, 1939 (Suspendable Provisions under Section 4) (Suspending) Order [Vol. XXV p. 357] S.R.& O. No. 239 of 1939**
Agricultural Produce (Cereals) Act, No. 47 of 1961	2	*Agricultural Produce (Cereals) Act, 1961 (Commencement) Order, S.I. No. 2 of 1962*
Agricultural Produce (Cereals) Acts, 1933 and 1934,		*Wheat Bounty (Cereal Year 1934–35) Regulations [Vol. III p. 311] S.R.& O. No. 321 of 1934*
Agricultural Produce (Cereals) Acts, 1933 to 1936,		**Agricultural Produce (Cereals) (Wheat Growing and Feeding Stuffs) Amendment Regulations [Vol. III p. 125] S.R.& O. No. 384 of 1936** **Agricultural Produce (Cereals) (Wheat Growing and Feeding Stuffs) Amendment Regulations [Vol. III p. 141] S.R.& O. No. 263 of 1937**
Agricultural Produce (Cereals) (Amendment) Act, No. 49 of 1933	4	**Sale of Wheat Seed (Purchaser's Undertaking) Regulations [Vol. III p. 343] S.R.& O. No. 106 of 1934**
Agricultural Produce (Cereals) (Amendment) Act, No. 56 of 1936	2(1)	*Home-Grown Millable Wheat (Minimum Prices for Sale (Wheat) Year 1937–38) (Substitutive) Order [Vol. III p. 573] S.R.& O. No. 32 of 1937* *Home-Grown Millable Wheat (Minimum Prices for Sale (Wheat) Year 1938–39) (Substitutive) Order [Vol. III p. 583] S.R.& O. No. 33 of 1937* *Home-Grown Millable Wheat (Minimum Prices for Sale (Wheat) Year 1940–41) Substitutive Order [Vol. XXV p. 309] S.R.& O. No. 88 of 1940* *Home-Grown Millable Wheat (Minimum Prices for Sale (Wheat) Year 1941–42) Substitutive Order [Vol. XXV p. 319] S.R.& O. No. 27 of 1941*
Agricultural Produce (Cereals) (Amendment) Act, No. 5 of 1956	2	*Wheat Order, S.I. No. 196 of 1956* *Wheat Order, S.I. No. 133 of 1957* *Wheat Order, 1957 (Amendment) Order, S.I. No. 218 of 1957* *Wheat Order, S.I. No. 162 of 1958* *Wheat Regulations, S.I. No. 123 of 1959* *Wheat Order, S.I. No. 148 of 1960* *Wheat (Amendment) Order, S.I. No. 195 of 1960* *Wheat Order, S.I. No. 141 of 1961*

Statutory Authority	Section	Statutory Instrument
Agricultural Produce (Cereals) (Amendment) Act, No. 5 of 1956 (*Cont.*)		*Wheat (Amendment) Order, S.I. No. 155 of 1961*
		Wheat Order, S.I. No. 119 of 1962
		Wheat Order, S.I. No. 149 of 1963
		Wheat Order, S.I. No. 194 of 1964
		Wheat Order, S.I. No. 159 of 1965
		Wheat Order, S.I. No. 182 of 1966
		Wheat Order, S.I. No. 177 of 1967
		Wheat Order, S.I. No. 166 of 1968
		Wheat Order, S.I. No. 162 of 1969
		Wheat Order, S.I. No. 176 of 1970
		Wheat Order, S.I. No. 211 of 1971
		Wheat Order, S.I. No. 190 of 1972
	3	**Wheat Milling (General Quota Variation) Order, S.I. No. 6 of 1958**
	16	*Agricultural Produce (Cereals) (Amendment) Act, 1956 (Commencement) Order, S.I. No. 90 of 1956*
Agricultural Produce (Cereals) (Amendment) Act, No. 24 of 1958	2	*Agricultural Produce (Cereals) (Amendment) Act, 1958 (Appointed Day) Order, S.I. No. 169 of 1958*
	3	*Wheat Levy Order, S.I. No. 171 of 1958*
		Wheat Levy Order, S.I. No. 159 of 1960
		Wheat Levy Order, S.I. No. 157 of 1961
		Wheat Levy Order, S.I. No. 124 of 1962
		Wheat Levy (Amendment) Order, S.I. No. 167 of 1962
		Wheat Levy Order, S.I. No. 226 of 1969
		Wheat Levy Order, S.I. No. 251 of 1970
		Wheat Levy Order, S.I. No. 302 of 1971
		Wheat Levy Order, S.I. No. 270 of 1972
	7	*An Bord Grain (Additional Function) Order, S.I. No. 273 of 1961*
		An Bord Grain (Assignment of Additional Function) (No.2) Order, S.I. No. 168 of 1962
		An Bord Grain (Assignment of Additional Function) (No.3) Order, S.I. No. 176 of 1962
		An Bord Grain (Assignment of Additional Function) (No.4) Order, S.I. No. 194 of 1962
		An Bord Grain (Assignment of Additional Function) (No.5) Order, S.I. No. 230 of 1962
		An Bord Grain (Assignment of Additional Functions) Order, S.I. No. 160 of 1963
		An Bord Grain (Assignment of Additional Functions) (Amendment) Order, S.I. No. 108 of 1964
		An Bord Grain (Assignment of Additional Functions) Order, S.I. No. 196 of 1964
		An Bord Grain (Assignment of Additional Function) Order, S.I. No. 65 of 1965

Statutory Authority	Section	Statutory Instrument
Agricultural Produce (Cereals) (Amendment) Act, No. 24 of 1958 (*Cont.*)		*An Bord Grain (Assignment of Additional Functions) Order, S.I. No. 180 of 1968*
		An Bord Grain (Assignment of Additional Function) Order, S.I. No. 262 of 1973
	7(1)	*An Bord Grain (Assignment of Additional Function) Order, S.I. No. 128 of 1962*
Agricultural Produce (Eggs) Act, No. 35 of 1924		*Agricultural Produce (Eggs) Regulations, 1925 Amendment Regulations (No.2) [Vol. III p. 639] S.R.& O. No. 30 of 1929*
	20	*Agricultural Produce (Eggs) Regulations [Vol. III p. 607] S.R.& O. No. 26 of 1925*
		Agricultural Produce (Eggs) Regulations, 1925 Amendment Regulations [Vol. III p. 631] S.R.& O. No. 11 of 1929
Agricultural Produce (Eggs) Act, No. 2 of 1939		*Agricultural Produce (Eggs) Regulations [Vol. XXV p. 495] S.R.& O. No. 169 of 1939*
		Agricultural Produce (Eggs) (Amendment) Regulations [Vol. XXV p. 545] S.R.& O. No. 342 of 1939
		Agricultural Produce (Eggs) (Amendment) Regulations [Vol. XXV p. 553] S.R.& O. No. 101 of 1940
		Agricultural Produce (Eggs) (Amendment) Regulations (No.2) [Vol. XXV p. 563] S.R.& O. No. 204 of 1940
		Agricultural Produce (Eggs) (Amendment) Regulations (No.3) [Vol. XXV p. 567] S.R.& O. No. 322 of 1940
		Agricultural Produce (Eggs) (Amendment) Regulations [Vol. XXV p. 569] S.R.& O. No. 45 of 1941
		Agricultural Produce (Eggs) (Amendment) Regulations (No.2) [Vol. XXV p. 583] S.R.& O. No. 56 of 1941
		Agricultural Produce (Eggs) (Amendment) Regulations (No.3) [Vol. XXV p. 587] S.R.& O. No. 502 of 1941
		Agricultural Produce (Eggs) (Amendment) Regulations [Vol. XXV p. 591] S.R.& O. No. 279 of 1942
		Agricultural Produce (Eggs) (Amendment) Regulations (No.2) [Vol. XXV p. 595] S.R.& O. No. 406 of 1942
		Agricultural Produce (Eggs) (Amendment) Regulations [Vol. XXV p. 599] S.R.& O. No. 225 of 1945
		Agricultural Produce (Eggs) (Amendment) Regulations, 1945 (Revocation) Regulations, S.I. No. 292 of 1948
		Agricultural Produce (Eggs) (Amendment) Regulations, S.I. No. 19 of 1949

Statutory Authority	Section	Statutory Instrument
Agricultural Produce (Eggs) Act, No. 2 of 1939 *(Cont.)*		*Agricultural Produce (Eggs) (Amendment) Regulations, S.I. No. 127 of 1950*
		Agricultural Produce (Eggs) (Amendment) Regulations, S.I. No. 114 of 1951
		Agricultural Produce (Eggs) (Amendment) (No.2) Regulations, S.I. No. 235 of 1951
		Agricultural Produce (Eggs) (Amendment) Regulations, S.I. No. 86 of 1952
		Agricultural Produce (Eggs) (Temporary Amendment) Regulations, S.I. No. 131 of 1953
		Agricultural Produce (Eggs) (Amendment) Regulations, S.I. No. 64 of 1954
		Agricultural Produce (Eggs) (Amendment) (No.2) Regulations, S.I. No. 197 of 1954
	1(2)	*Agricultural Produce (Eggs) Act, 1939 (Commencement) Order [Vol. XXV p. 491] S.R.&O. No. 215 of 1939*
	4	*Agricultural Produce (Eggs) (Amendment) Regulations, S.I. No. 206 of 1961*
	35	*Agricultural Produce (Eggs) (Amendment) Regulations, S.I. No. 206 of 1961*
	38	*Agricultural Produce (Eggs) (Amendment) Regulations, S.I. No. 40 of 1955*
		Agricultural Produce (Eggs) (Amendment) Regulations, S.I. No. 206 of 1961
	42	*Agricultural Produce (Eggs) (Amendment) Regulations, S.I. No. 206 of 1961*
	52	*Agricultural Produce (Eggs) (Amendment) Regulations, S.I. No. 116 of 1960*
	59	*Agricultural Produce (Eggs) (Amendment) Regulations, S.I. No. 206 of 1961*
Agricultural Produce (Eggs) Act, No. 15 of 1961	5	*Agricultural Produce (Eggs) Act, 1961 (Commencement) Order, S.I. No. 205 of 1961*
Agricultural Produce (Eggs) Acts, 1924 and 1930,		*Agricultural Produce (Eggs) Regulations [Vol. III p. 643] S.R.& O. No. 23 of 1931*
		Agricultural Produce (Eggs) (Amending) Regulations [Vol. III p. 671] S.R.& O. No. 66 of 1932
		Agricultural Produce (Eggs) (Amending) Regulations (No.2) [Vol. III p. 675] S.R.& O. No. 122 of 1933
		Agricultural Produce (Eggs) (Amendment) Regulations [Vol. III p. 679] S.R.& O. No. 50 of 1936
		Agricultural Produce (Eggs) (Amendment) (No.2) Regulations [Vol. III p. 687] S.R.& O. No. 205 of 1936
		Agricultural Produce (Eggs) (Amendment) Regulations [Vol. III p. 691] S.R.& O. No. 180 of 1937
		Agricultural Produce (Eggs) (Amendment) Regulations [Vol. III p. 697] S.R.& O. No. 282 of 1938

Statutory Authority	Section	Statutory Instrument
Agricultural Produce (Eggs) Acts, 1924 and 1930 (*Cont.*)		*Agricultural Produce (Eggs) (Amendment) Regulations (No.1) [Vol. XXV p. 361] S.R.& O. No. 27 of 1939*
		Agricultural Produce (Eggs) (Amendment) Regulations (No.2) [Vol. XXV p. 367] S.R.& O. No. 48 of 1939
		Agricultural Produce (Eggs) (Code-marking) (No.1) Regulations [Vol. XXV p. 391] S.R.& O. No. 56 of 1939
		Agricultural Produce (Eggs) (Code-marking) (No.2) Regulations [Vol. XXV p. 395] S.R.& O. No. 68 of 1939
		Agricultural Produce (Eggs) (Code-marking) (No.3) Regulations [Vol. XXV p. 399] S.R.& O. No. 70 of 1939
		Agricultural Produce (Eggs) (Code-marking) (No.4) Regulations [Vol. XXV p. 403] S.R.& O. No. 78 of 1939
		Agricultural Produce (Eggs) (Code-marking) (No.5) Regulations [Vol. XXV p. 407] S.R.& O. No. 79 of 1939
		Agricultural Produce (Eggs) (Code-marking) (No.6) Regulations [Vol. XXV p. 411] S.R.& O. No. 90 of 1939
		Agricultural Produce (Eggs) (Code-marking) (No.7) Regulations [Vol. XXV p. 415] S.R.& O. No. 96 of 1939
		Agricultural Produce (Eggs) (Code-marking) (No.8) Regulations [Vol. XXV p. 419] S.R.& O. No. 106 of 1939
		Agricultural Produce (Eggs) (Code-marking) (No.9) Regulations [Vol. XXV p. 423] S.R.& O. No. 116 of 1939
		Agricultural Produce (Eggs) (Code-marking) (No.10) Regulations [Vol. XXV p. 427] S.R.& O. No. 124 of 1939
		Agricultural Produce (Eggs) (Code-marking) (No.12) Regulations [Vol. XXV p. 435] S.R.& O. No. 133 of 1939
		Agricultural Produce (Eggs) (Code-marking) (No.13) Regulations [Vol. XXV p. 439] S.R.& O. No. 144 of 1939
		Agricultural Produce (Eggs) (Code-marking) (No.11) Regulations [Vol. XXV p. 431] S.R.& O. No. 150 of 1939
		Agricultural Produce (Eggs) (Code-marking) (No.14) Regulations [Vol. XXV p. 443] S.R.& O. No. 151 of 1939
		Agricultural Produce (Eggs) (Code-marking) (No.15) Regulations [Vol. XXV p. 447] S.R.& O. No. 157 of 1939
		Agricultural Produce (Eggs) (Code-marking) (No.16) Regulations [Vol. XXV p. 451] S.R.& O. No. 160 of 1939

Statutory Authority	Section	Statutory Instrument
Agricultural Produce (Eggs) Acts, 1924 and 1930 (*Cont.*)		*Agricultural Produce (Eggs) (Code-marking) (No.17) Regulations [Vol. XXV p. 455] S.R.& O. No. 172 of 1939*
		Agricultural Produce (Eggs) (Code-marking) (No.18) Regulations [Vol. XXV p. 459] S.R.& O. No. 179 of 1939
		Agricultural Produce (Eggs) (Code-marking) (No.19) Regulations [Vol. XXV p. 463] S.R.& O. No. 186 of 1939
		Agricultural Produce (Eggs) (Code-marking) (No.20) Regulations [Vol. XXV p. 467] S.R.& O. No. 191 of 1939
		Agricultural Produce (Eggs) (Code-marking) (No.21) Regulations [Vol. XXV p. 471] S.R.& O. No. 193 of 1939
		Agricultural Produce (Eggs) (Code-marking) (No.22) Regulations [Vol. XXV p. 475] S.R.& O. No. 196 of 1939
		Agricultural Produce (Eggs) (Code-marking) (No.23) Regulations [Vol. XXV p. 479] S.R.& O. No. 216 of 1939
		Agricultural Produce (Eggs) (Code-marking) (No.24) Regulations [Vol. XXV p. 487] S.R.& O. No. 218 of 1939
		Agricultural Produce (Eggs) (Code-marking) (No.25) Regulations [Vol. XXV p. 487] S.R.& O. No. 227 of 1939
Agricultural Produce (Fresh Meat) Act, No. 10 of 1930		*Agricultural Produce (Fresh Meat) Act, 1930 (Beef, Pork and Mutton) (Commencement) Order [Vol. III p. 705] S.R.& O. No. 59 of 1930*
		Agricultural Produce (Fresh Meat) (Beef, Pork and Mutton) Regulations [Vol. III p. 709] S.R.& O. No. 62 of 1930
		Agricultural Produce (Fresh Meat) (Beef, Pork and Mutton) Regulations [Vol. III p. 743] S.R.& O. No. 357 of 1934
		Agricultural Produce (Fresh Meat) (Beef, Pork and Mutton) (Amendment) Regulations [Vol. XXV p. 607] S.R.& O. No. 268 of 1942
	2(4)	*Agricultural Produce (Fresh Meat) Act, 1930 (Horse-flesh) (Commencement) Order, S.I. No. 83 of 1958*
	2(7)	*Agricultural Produce (Fresh Meat) Act, 1930 (Application to Dead Poultry) (Commencement) Order [Vol. III p. 761] S.R.& O. No. 320 of 1938*
	18	**Agricultural Produce (Fresh Meat) (Horse-Flesh) Regulations, S.I. No. 84 of 1958**
	26	**Agricultural Produce (Fresh Meat) (Horse-Flesh) Regulations, S.I. No. 84 of 1958**
	26A	*Fresh Meat (Beef Carcase Classifications) Regulations, S.I. No. 274 of 1979*
		Fresh Meat (Beef Carcase Classification) (Amendment) Regulations, S.I. No. 385 of 1979

Statutory Authority	Section	Statutory Instrument
Agricultural Produce (Fresh Meat) Act, No. 10 of 1930 (*Cont.*)	27	**Agricultural Produce (Fresh Meat) (Beef, Pork and Mutton) (Amendment) Regulations [Vol. XXV p. 603] S.R.& O. No. 83 of 1939**
		Agricultural Produce (Fresh Meat) (Beef, Pork and Mutton) (Amendment) Regulations, S.I. No. 145 of 1954
		Agricultural Produce (Fresh Meat) (Horse-Flesh) Regulations, S.I. No. 84 of 1958
		Agricultural Produce (Fresh Meat) (Horse-Flesh) (Amendment) Regulations, S.I. No. 17 of 1967
	28	**Agricultural Produce (Fresh Meat) (Horse-Flesh) Regulations, S.I. No. 84 of 1958**
	29	**Agricultural Produce (Fresh Meat) (Horse-Flesh) Regulations, S.I. No. 84 of 1958**
	30	**Agricultural Produce (Fresh Meat) (Horse-Flesh) Regulations, S.I. No. 84 of 1958**
	34	**Agricultural Produce (Fresh Meat) (Horse-Flesh) Regulations, S.I. No. 84 of 1958**
		Agricultural Produce (Fresh Meat) (Beef, Pork and Mutton) (Amendment) Regulations, S.I. No. 260 of 1985
	42(1)	*Export of Fresh Meat (Prohibition) Order [Vol. III p. 749] S.R.& O. No. 63 of 1930*
		Export of Fresh Meat (Prohibition) Order [Vol. III p. 755] S.R.& O. No. 96 of 1933
	44(1)	*Dead Turkeys (Packing for Export) Regulations [Vol. III p. 765] S.R.& O. No. 321 of 1938*
		Dead Turkeys (Packing for Export) Regulations, 1938 (Revocation) Regulations [Vol. XXV p. 613] S.R.& O. No. 517 of 1941
	51	**Agricultural Produce (Fresh Meat) (Horse-Flesh) Regulations, S.I. No. 84 of 1958**
		Agricultural Produce (Fresh Meat) Act, 1930 (Exporters' Licences) (Fees) Regulations, S.I. No. 36 of 1964
		Agricultural Produce (Fresh Meat) Act, 1930 (Exporters' Licences) (Fees) Regulations, S.I. No. 216 of 1973
		Agricultural Produce (Fresh Meat) Act, 1930 (Exporters' Licences) (Fees) Regulations, S.I. No. 106 of 1976
		Agricultural Produce (Fresh Meat) Act, 1930 (Exporters' Licences) (Fees) Regulations, S.I. No. 53 of 1978
		Fresh Meat (Beef Carcase Classifications) Regulations, S.I. No. 274 of 1979
		Fresh Meat (Beef Carcase Classification) (Amendment) Regulations, S.I. No. 385 of 1979
		Agricultural Produce (Fresh Meat) Act, 1930 (Exporters' Licences) (Fees) Regulations, S.I. No. 393 of 1980

Statutory Authority	Section	Statutory Instrument
Agricultural Produce (Fresh Meat) Act, No. 10 of 1930 (*Cont.*)		*Agricultural Produce (Fresh Meat) Act, 1930 (Exporters' Licences) (Fees) Regulations, S.I. No. 154 of 1982*
		Agricultural Produce (Fresh Meat) Act, 1930 (Exporters' Licences) (Fees) (No.2) Regulations, S.I. No. 383 of 1982
		Agricultural Produce (Fresh Meat) Act, 1930 (Exporters' Licences) (Fees) Regulations, S.I. No. 412 of 1983
		Agricultural Produce (Fresh Meat) Act, 1930 (Exporters' Licences) (Fees) Regulations, S.I. No. 246 of 1985
	Sch.	*Agricultural Produce (Fresh Meat) Act, 1930 (Exporters' Licences) (Fees) (No.2) Regulations, S.I. No. 383 of 1982*
		Agricultural Produce (Fresh Meat) Act, 1930 (Exporters' Licences) (Fees) Regulations, S.I. No. 412 of 1983
		Agricultural Produce (Fresh Meat) Act, 1930 (Exporters' Licences) (Fees) Regulations, S.I. No. 246 of 1985
	Sch. par. 2	*Agricultural Produce (Fresh Meat) Act, 1930 (Exporters' Licences) (Fees) Regulations, S.I. No. 36 of 1964*
		Agricultural Produce (Fresh Meat) Act, 1930 (Exporters' Licences) (Fees) Regulations, S.I. No. 216 of 1973
		Agricultural Produce (Fresh Meat) Act, 1930 (Exporters' Licences) (Fees) Regulations, S.I. No. 106 of 1976
		Agricultural Produce (Fresh Meat) Act, 1930 (Exporters' Licences) (Fees) Regulations, S.I. No. 53 of 1978
		Agricultural Produce (Fresh Meat) Act, 1930 (Exporters' Licences) (Fees) Regulations, S.I. No. 393 of 1980
		Agricultural Produce (Fresh Meat) Act, 1930 (Exporters' Licences) (Fees) Regulations, S.I. No. 154 of 1982
Agricultural Produce (Potatoes) Act, No. 26 of 1931		**Agricultural Produce (Potatoes) Regulations [Vol. III p. 779] S.R.& O. No. 87 of 1931**
		Agricultural Produce (Potatoes) Regulations [Vol. III p. 799] S.R.& O. No. 60 of 1935
		Agricultural Produce (Potatoes) Regulations [Vol. XXV p. 617] S.R.& O. No. 185 of 1944
		Agricultural Produce (Potatoes) Regulations [Vol. XXV p. 623] S.R.& O. No. 48 of 1945
	1(2)	*Agricultural Produce (Potatoes) Act, 1931 (Commencement) Order [Vol. III p. 775] S.R.&O. No. 82 of 1931*
	26(1)	*Agricultural Produce (Potatoes) (Time of Exemption) Order [Vol. III p. 805] S.R.& O. No. 52 of 1932*

Statutory Authority	Section	Statutory Instrument
Agricultural Produce (Potatoes) Act, No. 26 of 1931 (*Cont.*)		*Agricultural Produce (Potatoes) (Time of Exemption) Order [Vol. III p. 809] S.R.& O. No. 74 of 1933*
		Agricultural Produce (Potatoes) (Time of Exemption) Order [Vol. III p. 813] S.R.& O. No. 144 of 1934
		Agricultural Produce (Potatoes) (Time of Exemption) Order [Vol. III p. 817] S.R.& O. No. 155 of 1935
		Agricultural Produce (Potatoes) (Time of Exemption) Order [Vol. III p. 821] S.R.& O. No. 124 of 1936
		Agricultural Produce (Potatoes) (Time of Exemption) Order [Vol. III p. 825] S.R.& O. No. 93 of 1937
		Agricultural Produce (Potatoes) (Time of Exemption) Order [Vol. III p. 829] S.R.& O. No. 119 of 1938
		Agricultural Produce (Potatoes) (Time of Exemption) Order [Vol. XXV p. 627] S.R.& O. No. 97 of 1939
		Agricultural Produce (Potatoes) (Time of Exemption) Order [Vol. XXV p. 631] S.R.& O. No. 131 of 1940
Agricultural Products (Regulation of Export) Act, No. 26 of 1933		*Pig Carcases (Regulation of Export) Order [Vol. III p. 1169] S.R.& O. No. 141 of 1933*
		Cattle (Regulation of Export) Order [Vol. III p. 1135] S.R.& O. No. 188 of 1933
		Pigs (Regulation of Export) Order [Vol. III p. 1165] S.R.& O. No. 180 of 1934
		Wool (Regulation of Export to Germany) Order [Vol. III p. 1173] S.R.& O. No. 57 of 1935
		Feathers (Regulation of Export to Germany) Order [Vol. III p. 1147] S.R.& O. No. 355 of 1935
	2	*Bacon and Pigs (Quota) (No.1) Order [Vol. III p. 833] S.R.& O. No. 169 of 1933*
		Bacon and Pigs (Quota) (No.2) Order [Vol. III p. 837] S.R.& O. No. 7 of 1934
		Bacon and Pigs (Quota) (Amendment) Order [Vol. III p. 835] S.R.& O. No. 8 of 1934
		Bacon and Pigs (Quota) (No.3) Order [Vol. III p. 939] S.R.& O. No. 21 of 1934
		Bacon and Pigs (Quota) (No.4) Order [Vol. III p. 841] S.R.& O. No. 58 of 1934
		Bacon and Pigs (Quota) (No.4) (Amendment) Order [Vol. III p. 843] S.R.& O. No. 120 of 1934
		Bacon and Pigs (Quota) (No.5) Order [Vol. III p. 845] S.R.& O. No. 121 of 1934
		Bacon and Pigs (Quota) (No.6) Order [Vol. III p. 847] S.R.& O. No. 142 of 1934
		Bacon and Pigs (Quota) (No.7) Order [Vol. III p. 849] S.R.& O. No. 165 of 1934

Statutory Authority	Section	Statutory Instrument
Agricultural Products (Regulation of Export) Act, No. 26 of 1933 (*Cont.*)		*Bacon and Pigs (Quota) (No.8) Order [Vol. III p. 851] S.R.& O. No. 199 of 1934*
		Bacon and Pigs (Quota) (No.9) Order [Vol. III p. 853] S.R.& O. No. 233 of 1934
		Bacon and Pigs (Quota) (No.9) (Amendment) Order [Vol. III p. 855] S.R.& O. No. 247 of 1934
		Bacon and Pigs (Quota) (No.10) Order [Vol. III p. 859] S.R.& O. No. 268 of 1934
		Bacon and Pigs (Quota) (No.11) Order [Vol. III p. 863] S.R.& O. No. 336 of 1934
		Bacon and Pigs (Quota) (No.11) (Amendment) Order [Vol. III p. 867] S.R.& O. No. 337 of 1934
		Bacon and Pigs (Quota) (No.12) Order [Vol. III p. 871] S.R.& O. No. 363 of 1934
		Bacon and Pigs (Quota) (No.1) Order [Vol. III p. 875] S.R.& O. No. 12 of 1935
		Bacon and Pigs (Quota) (No.2) Order [Vol. III p. 879] S.R.& O. No. 29 of 1935
		Bacon and Pigs (Quota) (No.3) Order [Vol. III p. 883] S.R.& O. No. 56 of 1935
		Bacon and Pigs (Quota) (No.4) Order [Vol. III p. 887] S.R.& O. No. 77 of 1935
		Bacon and Pigs (Quota) (No.5) Order [Vol. III p. 891] S.R.& O. No. 117 of 1935
		Bacon and Pigs (Quota) (No.6) Order [Vol. III p. 895] S.R.& O. No. 146 of 1935
		Bacon and Pigs (Quota) (No.7) Order [Vol. III p. 899] S.R.& O. No. 178 of 1935
		Bacon and Pigs (Quota) (No.8) Order [Vol. III p. 903] S.R.& O. No. 258 of 1935
		Bacon and Pigs (Quota) (No.9) Order [Vol. III p. 907] S.R.& O. No. 403 of 1935
		Bacon and Pigs (Quota) (No.10) Order [Vol. III p. 911] S.R.& O. No. 565 of 1935
		Bacon and Pigs (Quota) (No.10) (Amendment) Order [Vol. III p. 915] S.R.& O. No. 620 of 1935
		Bacon and Pigs (Quota) (No.11) Order [Vol. III p. 919] S.R.& O. No. 621 of 1935
		Bacon and Pigs (Quota) (No.12) Order [Vol. III p. 923] S.R.& O. No. 654 of 1935
		Bacon and Pigs (Quota) (No.1) Order [Vol. III p. 927] S.R.& O. No. 2 of 1936
		Bacon and Pigs (Quota) (No.2) Order [Vol. III p. 931] S.R.& O. No. 29 of 1936
		Bacon and Pigs (Quota) (No.3) Order [Vol. III p. 935] S.R.& O. No. 63 of 1936
		Bacon and Pigs (Quota) (No.4) Order [Vol. III p. 939] S.R.& O. No. 85 of 1936
		Butter (Regulation of Export to Germany) Order [Vol. III p. 1109] S.R.& O. No. 87 of 1936
		Butter (Regulation of Export to Belgium) Order [Vol. III p. 1119] S.R.& O. No. 88 of 1936

Statutory Authority	Section	Statutory Instrument
Agricultural Products (Regulation of Export) Act, No. 26 of 1933 (*Cont.*)		*Eggs (Regulation of Export to Germany) Order [Vol. III p. 1125] S.R.& O. No. 89 of 1936*
		Bacon and Pigs (Quota) (No.5) Order [Vol. III p. 943] S.R.& O. No. 126 of 1936
		Bacon and Pigs (Quota) (No.6) Order [Vol. III p. 947] S.R.& O. No. 156 of 1936
		Bacon and Pigs (Quota) (No.7) Order [Vol. III p. 951] S.R.& O. No. 195 of 1936
		Bacon and Pigs (Quota) (No.8) Order [Vol. III p. 955] S.R.& O. No. 213 of 1936
		Bacon and Pigs (Quota) (No.9) Order [Vol. III p. 959] S.R.& O. No. 255 of 1936
		Bacon and Pigs (Quota) (No.10) Order [Vol. III p. 963] S.R.& O. No. 274 of 1936
		Bacon and Pigs (Quota) (No.11) Order [Vol. III p. 967] S.R.& O. No. 318 of 1936
		Bacon and Pigs (Quota) (No.12) Order [Vol. III p. 971] S.R.& O. No. 359 of 1936
		Bacon and Pigs (Quota) (No.1) Order [Vol. III p. 975] S.R.& O. No. 1 of 1937
		Bacon and Pigs (Quota) (No.2) Order [Vol. III p. 979] S.R.& O. No. 19 of 1937
		Bacon and Pigs (Quota) (No.3) Order [Vol. III p. 983] S.R.& O. No. 41 of 1937
		Bacon and Pigs (Quota) (No.4) Order [Vol. III p. 987] S.R.& O. No. 63 of 1937
		Bacon and Pigs (Quota) (No.5) Order [Vol. III p. 991] S.R.& O. No. 90 of 1937
		Bacon and Pigs (Quota) (No.6) Order [Vol. III p. 995] S.R.& O. No. 130 of 1937
		Bacon and Pigs (Quota) (No.7) Order [Vol. III p. 999] S.R.& O. No. 156 of 1937
		Bacon and Pigs (Quota) (No.8) Order [Vol. III p. 1003] S.R.& O. No. 188 of 1937
		Bacon and Pigs (Quota) (No.9) Order [Vol. III p. 1007] S.R.& O. No. 239 of 1937
		Bacon and Pigs (Quota) (No.10) Order [Vol. III p. 1011] S.R.& O. No. 256 of 1937
		Bacon and Pigs (Quota) (No.11) Order [Vol. III p. 1015] S.R.& O. No. 283 of 1937
		Bacon and Pigs (Quota) (No.12) Order [Vol. III p. 1019] S.R.& O. No. 308 of 1937
		Bacon and Pigs (Quota) (No.1) Order [Vol. III p. 1023] S.R.& O. No. 9 of 1938
		Bacon and Pigs (Quota) (No.2) Order [Vol. III p. 1027] S.R.& O. No. 14 of 1938
		Bacon and Pigs (Quota) (No.3) Order [Vol. III p. 1031] S.R.& O. No. 35 of 1938
		Wool (Regulation of Export to Germany) (Revocation) Order [Vol. III p. 1179] S.R.& O. No. 68 of 1938

Statutory Authority	Section	Statutory Instrument
Agricultural Products (Regulation of Export) Act, No. 26 of 1933 (*Cont.*)		*Feathers (Regulation of Export to Germany) (Revocation) Order [Vol. III p. 1155] S.R.& O. No. 69 of 1938*
		Bacon and Pigs (Quota) (No.4) Order [Vol. III p. 1035] S.R.& O. No. 76 of 1938
		Bacon and Pigs (Quota) (No.4) (Amendment) Order [Vol. III p. 1039] S.R.& O. No. 106 of 1938
		Bacon and Pigs (Quota) (No.5) Order [Vol. III p. 1043] S.R.& O. No. 107 of 1938
		Bacon and Pigs (Quota) (No.6) Order [Vol. III p. 1047] S.R.& O. No. 171 of 1938
		Bacon and Pigs (Quota) (No.6) (Amendment) Order [Vol. III p. 1051] S.R.& O. No. 172 of 1938
		Bacon and Pigs (Quota) (No.7) Order [Vol. III p. 1055] S.R.& O. No. 191 of 1938
		Bacon and Pigs (Quota) (No.8) Order [Vol. III p. 1059] S.R.& O. No. 208 of 1938
		Bacon and Pigs (Quota) (No.9) Order [Vol. III p. 1063] S.R.& O. No. 243 of 1938
		Bacon and Pigs (Quota) (No.10) Order [Vol. III p. 1067] S.R.& O. No. 275 of 1938
		Bacon and Pigs (Quota) (No.11) Order [Vol. III p. 1071] S.R.& O. No. 301 of 1938
		Bacon and Pigs (Quota) (No.11) (Amendment) Order [Vol. III p. 1075] S.R.& O. No. 302 of 1938
		Bacon and Pigs (Quota) (No.12) Order [Vol. III p. 1079] S.R.& O. No. 322 of 1938
		Bacon and Pigs (Quota) (No.1) Order [Vol. XXVI p. 1] S.R.& O. No. 25 of 1939
		Bacon and Pigs (Quota) (No.2) Order [Vol. XXVI p. 9] S.R.& O. No. 64 of 1939
		Bacon and Pigs (Quota) (No.3) Order [Vol. XXVI p. 13] S.R.& O. No. 88 of 1939
		Bacon and Pigs (Quota) (No.4) Order [Vol. XXVI p. 17] S.R.& O. No. 125 of 1939
		Bacon and Pigs (Quota) (No.5) Order [Vol. XXVI p. 21] S.R.& O. No. 136 of 1939
		Bacon and Pigs (Quota) (No.6) Order [Vol. XXVI p. 25] S.R.& O. No. 158 of 1939
		Bacon and Pigs (Quota) (No.7) Order [Vol. XXVI p. 29] S.R.& O. No. 182 of 1939
		Bacon and Pigs (Quota) (No.8) Order [Vol. XXVI p. 33] S.R.& O. No. 217 of 1939
		Bacon and Pigs (Quota) (No.9) Order [Vol. XXVI p. 37] S.R.& O. No. 304 of 1939
		Bacon and Pigs (Quota) (No.10) Order [Vol. XXVI p. 41] S.R.& O. No. 305 of 1939
	2(1)	*Bacon and Pigs (Regulation of Export) Order [Vol. III p. 1083] S.R.& O. No. 167 of 1933*

Statutory Authority	Section	Statutory Instrument
Agricultural Products (Regulation of Export) Act, No. 26 of 1933 (*Cont.*)	2(2)	*Cattle (Regulation of Export) (Revocation) Order [Vol. III p. 1139] S.R.& O. No. 1 of 1934*
		Bacon and Pigs (Regulation of Export) (Amendment) Order [Vol. III p. 1107] S.R.& O. No. 194 of 1934
		Eggs (Regulation of Export to Germany) (Revocation) Order [Vol. III p. 1131] S.R.& O. No. 342 of 1938
		Butter (Regulation of Export to Germany) (Revocation) Order [Vol. III p. 1115] S.R.& O. No. 343 of 1938
		Bacon and Pigs (Quota) (No.1) (Amendment) Order [Vol. XXVI p. 5] S.R.& O. No. 26 of 1939
		Bacon and Pigs (Regulation of Export) Order (Revocation) Order [Vol. XXVI p. 45] S.R.& O. No. 297 of 1939
		Sheep (Regulation of Export) Order (Revocation) Order [Vol. XXVI p. 79] S.R.& O. No. 355 of 1940
Agricultural Products (Regulation of Export) Acts, 1933 and 1935,		*Grass Seed (Regulation of Export) Order [Vol. III p. 1161] S.R.& O. No. 139 of 1938*
		Cattle (Regulation of Export from Greenore) Order [Vol. III p. 1141] S.R.& O. No. 140 of 1938
		Sheep (Regulation of Export) Order [Vol. XXVI p. 73] S.R.& O. No. 285 of 1940
		Cattle (Regulation of Export) Order [Vol. XXVI p. 49] S.R.& O. No. 516 of 1941
		Cattle (Regulation of Export) Order [Vol. XXVI p. 53] S.R.& O. No. 9 of 1942
		Cattle (Regulation of Export) Order, 1942 (Revocation) Order [Vol. XXVI p. 59] S.R.& O. No. 17 of 1942
		Live Goats (Regulation of Export) Order [Vol. XXVI p. 63] S.R.& O. No. 123 of 1942
		Live Goats (Regulation of Export) Order, 1942 (Revocation) Order [Vol. XXVI p. 69] S.R.& O. No. 233 of 1944
Agricultural Products (Regulation of Export) (Amendment) Act, No. 15 of 1935	3(1)	*Agricultural Products (Feathers) (Transfer of Functions) Order [Vol. III p. 1185] S.R.& O. No. 184 of 1935*
		Agricultural Products (Hides and Skins of Animals) (Transfer of Functions) Order [Vol. III p. 1189] S.R.& O. No. 185 of 1935
		Agricultural Products (Wool) (Transfer of Functions) Order [Vol. III p. 1193] S.R.& O. No. 615 of 1935
Agricultural Products (Regulation of Import) Act, No. 14 of 1938	2	*Bacon (Regulation of Import) Order [Vol. III p. 1197] S.R.& O. No. 135 of 1938*
		Pigs (Regulation of Import) Order [Vol. III p. 1239] S.R.& O. No. 136 of 1938
		Fruit (Regulation of Import) Order [Vol. III p. 1215] S.R.& O. No. 137 of 1938

Agricultural Products (Regulation of Import) Act, No. 14 of 1938 (*Cont.*)		*Grass Seed (Regulation of Import) Order [Vol. III p. 1221] S.R.& O. No. 138 of 1938*
		Fish (Regulation of Import) Order [Vol. III p. 1203] S.R.& O. No. 204 of 1938
		Fish (Regulation of Import) (No.2) Order [Vol. III p. 1209] S.R.& O. No. 266 of 1938
		Onions (Regulation of Import) Order [Vol. III p. 1233] S.R.& O. No. 283 of 1938
		Meat (Regulation of Import) Order [Vol. III p. 1227] S.R.& O. No. 336 of 1938
		Onions (Regulation of Import) (Revocation) Order [Vol. XXVI p. 101] S.R.& O. No. 17 of 1939
		Pigs (Regulation of Import) Order [Vol. XXVI p. 123] S.R.& O. No. 148 of 1939
		Tomatoes (Regulation of Import) Order [Vol. XXVI p. 143] S.R.& O. No. 240 of 1939
		Apples (Regulation of Import) Order [Vol. XXVI p. 83] S.R.& O. No. 329 of 1939
		Apples (Regulation of Import) (Revocation) Order [Vol. XXVI p. 105] S.R.& O. No. 43 of 1940
		Tomatoes (Regulation of Import) Order [Vol. XXVI p. 149] S.R.& O. No. 150 of 1940
		Apples (Regulation of Import) Order [Vol. XXVI p. 89] S.R.& O. No. 222 of 1940
		Onions (Regulation of Import) (Revocation) Order [Vol. XXVI p. 119] S.R.& O. No. 26 of 1941
		Apples (Regulation of Import) (Revocation) Order [Vol. XXVI p. 193] S.R.& O. No. 32 of 1941
		Tomatoes (Regulation of Import) Order [Vol. XXVI p. 155] S.R.& O. No. 288 of 1941
		Apples (Regulation of Import) Order [Vol. XXVI p. 95] S.R.& O. No. 362 of 1941
		Onions (Regulation of Import) Order [Vol. XXVI p. 113] S.R.& O. No. 374 of 1941
		Tomatoes (Regulation of Import) Order [Vol. XXVI p. 161] S.R.& O. No. 186 of 1942
		Seeds (Regulation of Import) Order [Vol. XXVI p. 129] S.R.& O. No. 347 of 1942
		Seeds (Regulation of Import) (Amendment) Order [Vol. XXVI p. 135] S.R.& O. No. 176 of 1943
		Tomatoes (Regulation of Import) Order [Vol. XXVI p. 167] S.R.& O. No. 225 of 1943
		Tomatoes (Regulation of Import) Order [Vol. XXVI p. 173] S.R.& O. No. 177 of 1944
		Seeds (Regulation of Import) (Amendment) Order [Vol. XXVI p. 139] S.R.& O. No. 11 of 1945
		Tomatoes (Regulation of Import) Order [Vol. XXVI p. 179] S.R.& O. No. 135 of 1945
		Apples (Regulation of Import) (Revocation) Order [Vol. XXVI p. 109] S.R.& O. No. 217 of 1945
		Dried Peas (Regulation of Import) Order [Vol. XXXVI p. 101] S.R.& O. No. 86 of 1946

Statutory Authority	Section	Statutory Instrument
Agricultural Products (Regulation of Import) Act, No. 14 of 1938 (*Cont.*)		*Tomatoes (Regulation of Import) Order [Vol. XXXVI p. 123] S.R.& O. No. 165 of 1946*
		Apples (Regulation of Import) Order [Vol. XXXVI p. 95] S.R.& O. No. 272 of 1946
		Onions (Regulation of Import) Order, 1941 (Revocation) Order [Vol. XXXVI p. 109] S.R.&O. No. 383 of 1946
		Tomatoes (Regulation of Import) Order [Vol. XXXVI p. 129] S.R.& O. No. 230 of 1947
		Onions (Regulation of Import) Order [Vol. XXXVI p. 113] S.R.& O. No. 296 of 1947
		Onions (Regulation of Import) Order, 1947 (Revocation) Order [Vol. XXXVI p. 119] S.R.&O. No. 383 of 1947
		Tomatoes (Regulation of Import) Order, S.I. No. 225 of 1948
		Grass Seed (Regulation of Import) Order, 1938 (Revocation) Order, S.I. No. 245 of 1948
		Dried Peas (Regulation of Import) Order, 1946 (Revocation) Order, S.I. No. 193 of 1950
		Apples (Regulation of Import) Order, S.I. No. 88 of 1951
		Grass Seed (Regulation of Import) Order, S.I. No. 277 of 1952
		Seeds (Regulation of Import) Order, S.I. No. 177 of 1955
		Sugar (Regulation of Import) Order, S.I. No. 215 of 1962
		Fruit (Regulation of Import) Order, S.I. No. 143 of 1966
		Seeds (Regulation of Import) Order, S.I. No. 144 of 1966
		Meat (Regulation of Import) (Amendment) Order, S.I. No. 146 of 1966
		Fish (Regulation of Import) Order, S.I. No. 148 of 1966
		Broiler Chickens, Turkeys and Eggs (Regulation of Import) Order, S.I. No. 154 of 1966
		Meat (Regulation of Import) Order, S.I. No. 108 of 1969
		Fish Diseases (Control of Imports) Order, S.I. No. 18 of 1973
		Fish (Regulation of Import) Order, S.I. No. 26 of 1973
		Bees (Regulation of Import) Order, S.I. No. 161 of 1980
		Potatoes (Regulation of Import) Order, S.I. No. 78 of 1981
	2(2)	*Tomatoes (Regulation of Import) (Revocation) Order [Vol. XXVI p. 185] S.R.& O. No. 330 of 1939*

Statutory Authority	Section	Statutory Instrument
Agricultural Products (Regulation of Import) Act, No. 14 of 1938 (*Cont.*)		*Tomatoes (Regulation of Import) (Revocation) Order [Vol. XXVI p. 189] S.R.& O. No. 319 of 1940*
Agricultural Seeds Act, No. 14 of 1936		**Agricultural Seeds (Seeds of Injurious Weeds) Regulations [Vol. III p. 1249] S.R.& O. No. 161 of 1937**
	2(1)	**Agricultural Seeds (Specification) Order [Vol. III p. 1245] S.R.& O. No. 121 of 1936**
	6(2)	**Agricultural Seeds (Restriction on Cleaning of Grass Seeds) Order, S.I. No. 211 of 1956**
	12	*Agricultural Seeds (Protection of Sugar Beet Seeds) Order [Vol. XXVI p. 197] S.R.& O. No. 42 of 1942*
Agricultural Wages Act, No. 53 of 1936		**Committees for Agricultural Wages Areas (Procedure) Regulations [Vol. III p. 1267] S.R.& O. No. 200 of 1937**
	3(1)	*Agricultural Wages Districts and Areas Order [Vol. III p. 1257] S.R.& O. No. 75 of 1937*
	4(1)	*Agricultural Wages Districts and Areas Order [Vol. III p. 1257] S.R.& O. No. 75 of 1937*
	17	*Agricultural Wages (Minimum Rates) Order [Vol. III p. 1275] S.R.& O. No. 228 of 1937*
		Agricultural Wages (Minimum Rates) Order [Vol. III p. 1291] S.R.& O. No. 150 of 1938
		Agricultural Wages (Minimum Rates) Order [Vol. XXVI p. 233] S.R.& O. No. 6 of 1939
		Agricultural Wages (Minimum Rates) Order [Vol. XXVI p. 259] S.R.& O. No. 45 of 1940
		Agricultural Wages (Minimum Rates) Order [Vol. XXVI p. 303] S.R.& O. No. 89 of 1942
		Agricultural Wages (Minimum Rates) Order [Vol. XXVI p. 347] S.R.& O. No. 30 of 1943
		Agricultural Wages (Minimum Rates) Order [Vol. XXVI p. 391] S.R.& O. No. 42 of 1944
		Agricultural Wages (Minimum Rates) Order, 1944 (Revocation) Order [Vol. XXXVI p. 135] S.R.& O. No. 45 of 1946
		Agricultural Wages (Minimum Rates) Order [Vol. XXXVI p. 139] S.R.& O. No. 46 of 1946
		Agricultural Wages (Minimum Rates) Order, 1946 (Revocation) Order [Vol. XXXVI p. 227] S.R.& O. No. 196 of 1946
		Agricultural Wages (Minimum Rates) (No.2) Order [Vol. XXXVI p. 231] S.R.& O. No. 197 of 1946
		Agricultural Wages (Minimum Rates) (No.2) Order, 1946 (Revocation) Order [Vol. XXXVI p. 279] S.R.& O. No. 192 of 1947

Statutory Authority	Section	Statutory Instrument
Agricultural Wages Act, No. 53 of 1936 (*Cont.*)		*Agricultural Wages (Minimum Rates) Order [Vol. XXXVI p. 179] S.R.& O. No. 193 of 1947*
		Agricultural Wages (Minimum Rates) Order, 1947 (Revocation) Order, S.I. No. 58 of 1948
		Agricultural Wages (Minimum Rates) Order, S.I. No. 59 of 1948
		Agricultural Wages (Minimum Rates) Order, 1948 (Revocation) Order, S.I. No. 401 of 1948
		Agricultural Wages (Minimum Rates) (No.2) Order, S.I. No. 402 of 1948
		Agricultural Wages (Minimum Rates) (No.2) Order, 1948 (Amendment) Order, S.I. No. 63 of 1949
		Agricultural Workers (Holiday Remuneration) Order, S.I. No. 229 of 1950
		Agricultural Wages (Minimum Rates) (No.2) Order, 1948 (Amendment) Order, S.I. No. 232 of 1950
		Agricultural Wages (Minimum Rates) Orders (Revocation) Order, S.I. No. 187 of 1951
		Agricultural Wages (Minimum Rates) Order, S.I. No. 188 of 1951
		Agricultural Wages (Minimum Rates) (Female Workers) Order, S.I. No. 1 of 1952
		Agricultural Wages (Minimum Rates) Order, 1951 (Revocation) Order, S.I. No. 91 of 1952
		Agricultural Wages (Minimum Rates) Order, S.I. No. 92 of 1952
		Agricultural Wages (Minimum Rates) (Female Workers) Order, 1952 (Amendment) Order, S.I. No. 197 of 1952
		Agricultural Wages (Minimum Rates) Order, 1952 (Revocation) Order, S.I. No. 26 of 1953
		Agricultural Wages (Minimum Rates) Order, S.I. No. 27 of 1953
		Agricultural Wages (Minimum Rates) (Weekly Half-Holidays) Order, S.I. No. 42 of 1953
		Agricultural Wages (Minimum Rates) Order, 1953 (Revocation) Order, S.I. No. 9 of 1954
		Agricultural Wages (Minimum Rates) Order, S.I. No. 10 of 1954
		Agricultural Wages (Minimum Rates) Order, 1954 (Revocation) Order, S.I. No. 161 of 1955
		Agricultural Wages (Minimum Rates) Order, S.I. No. 162 of 1955
		Agricultural Wages (Minimum Rates) Order, 1955 (Revocation) Order, S.I. No. 102 of 1956
		Agricultural Wages (Minimum Rates) Order, S.I. No. 103 of 1956
		Agricultural Wages (Minimum Rates) Order, S.I. No. 18 of 1959

Statutory Authority	Section	Statutory Instrument
Agricultural Wages Act, No. 53 of 1936 (*Cont.*)		*Agricultural Wages (Minimum Rates) Order, 1956 (Revocation) Order, S.I. No. 19 of 1959*
		Agricultural Wages (Minimum Rates) Order, 1959 (Revocation) Order, S.I. No. 32 of 1960
		Agricultural Wages (Minimum Rates) Order, S.I. No. 33 of 1960
		Agricultural Wages (Minimum Rates) Order, 1960 (Revocation) Order, S.I. No. 188 of 1960
		Agricultural Wages (Minimum Rates) (No.2) Order, S.I. No. 189 of 1960
		Agricultural Wages (Minimum Rates) (No.2) Order, 1960 (Revocation) Order, S.I. No. 221 of 1961
		Agricultural Wages (Minimum Rates) Order, S.I. No. 222 of 1961
		Agricultural Wages (Minimum Rates) Order, 1961 (Revocation) Order, S.I. No. 81 of 1962
		Agricultural Wages (Minimum Rates) Order, S.I. No. 82 of 1962
		Agricultural Wages (Minimum Rates) Order, 1962 (Revocation) Order, S.I. No. 248 of 1963
		Agricultural Wages (Minimum Rates) Order, S.I. No. 249 of 1963
		Agricultural Wages (Minimum Rates) Order, 1963 (Amendment) Order, S.I. No. 89 of 1964
		Agricultural Wages (Minimum Rates) Orders (Revocation) Order, S.I. No. 74 of 1965
		Agricultural Wages (Minimum Rates) Order, S.I. No. 75 of 1965
		Agricultural Wages (Minimum Rates) Order, 1965 (Revocation) Order, S.I. No. 102 of 1966
		Agricultural Wages (Minimum Rates) Order, S.I. No. 103 of 1966
		Agricultural Wages (Minimum Rates) Order, 1966 (Revocation) Order, S.I. No. 162 of 1967
		Agricultural Wages (Minimum Rates) Order, S.I. No. 163 of 1967
		Agricultural Wages (Minimum Rates) Order, 1967 (Revocation) Order, S.I. No. 39 of 1968
		Agricultural Wages (Minimum Rates) Order, S.I. No. 40 of 1968
		Agricultural Wages (Minimum Rates) Order, 1968 (Revocation) Order, S.I. No. 41 of 1969
		Agricultural Wages (Minimum Rates) Order, S.I. No. 42 of 1969
		Agricultural Wages (Minimum Rates) Order, 1969 (Revocation) Order, S.I. No. 36 of 1970
		Agricultural Wages (Minimum Rates) Order, S.I. No. 37 of 1970
		Agricultural Workers (Holiday Remuneration) Order, 1950 (Amendment) Order, S.I. No. 38 of 1970

Agricultural Wages Act, No. 53 of
1936 (*Cont.*)

*Agricultural Wages (Minimum Rates) Order, 1970
(Revocation) Order, S.I. No. 177 of 1970*

*Agricultural Wages (Minimum Rates) (No.2) Order,
S.I. No. 178 of 1970*

*Agricultural Wages (Minimum Rates) (No.2) Order,
1970 (Revocation) Order, S.I. No. 148 of 1971*

*Agricultural Wages (Minimum Rates) Order, S.I.
No. 149 of 1971*

*Agricultural Wages (Minimum Rates) Order, 1971
(Revocation) Order, S.I. No. 84 of 1972*

*Agricultural Wages (Minimum Rates) Order, S.I.
No. 85 of 1972*

*Agricultural Wages (Minimum Rates) Order, 1972
(Revocation) Order, S.I. No. 87 of 1973*

*Agricultural Wages (Minimum Rates) Order, S.I.
No. 88 of 1973*

*Agricultural Wages (Minimum Rates) Order, 1973
(Revocation) (No.2) Order, S.I. No. 275 of 1973*

*Agricultural Wages (Minimum Rates) (No.2) Order,
S.I. No. 276 of 1973*

*Agricultural Wages (Minimum Rates) (No.2) Order,
1973 (Revocation) Order, S.I. No. 106 of 1974*

*Agricultural Wages (Minimum Rates) Order, S.I.
No. 107 of 1974*

*Agricultural Wages (Minimum Rates) Order, 1974
(Revocation) (No.2) Order, S.I. No. 367 of 1974*

*Agricultural Wages (Minimum Rates) (No.2) Order,
S.I. No. 368 of 1974*

*Agricultural Wages (Minimum Rates) (No.2) Order,
1974 (Revocation) Order, S.I. No. 97 of 1975*

*Agricultural Wages (Minimum Rates) Order, S.I.
No. 98 of 1975*

*Agricultural Wages (Minimum Rates) Order, 1975
(Revocation) (No.2) Order, S.I. No. 256 of 1975*

*Agricultural Wages (Minimum Rates) (No.2) Order,
S.I. No. 257 of 1975*

*Agricultural Wages (Minimum Rates) (No.2) Order,
1975 (Revocation) Order, S.I. No. 242 of 1976*

*Agricultural Wages (Minimum Rates) Order, S.I.
No. 243 of 1976*

17(4) *Agricultural Wages (Minimum Rates) (Revocation)
Order [Vol. III p. 1287] S.R.& O. No. 103 of
1938*

*Agricultural Wages (Minimum Rates) (Revocation)
Order [Vol. XXVI p. 431] S.R.& O. No. 5 of
1939*

*Agricultural Wages (Minimum Rates) (Revocation)
Order [Vol. XXVI p. 437] S.R.& O. No. 46 of
1940*

*Agricultural Wages (Minimum Rates) (Revocation)
Order [Vol. XXVI p. 441] S.R.& O. No. 88 of
1942*

Statutory Authority	Section	Statutory Instrument
Agricultural Wages Act, No. 53 of 1936 (*Cont.*)		*Agricultural Wages (Minimum Rates) (Revocation) Order [Vol. XXVI p. 445] S.R.& O. No. 29 of 1943*
		Agricultural Wages (Minimum Rates) (Revocation) Order [Vol. XXVI p. 449] S.R.& O. No. 41 of 1944
	24(2)	*Agricultural Wages Act, 1936 (Commencement) Order [Vol. III p. 1253] S.R.& O. No. 82 of 1937*
Agricultural Workers (Holidays) Act, No. 21 of 1950	1	*Agricultural Workers (Holidays) Act, 1950 (Commencement) Order, S.I. No. 230 of 1950*
Agricultural Workers (Holidays) (Amendment) Act, No. 36 of 1961	1	*Agricultural Workers (Holidays) (Amendment) Act, 1961 (Commencement) Order, S.I. No. 181 of 1961*
Agricultural Workers (Holidays) (Amendment) Act, No. 7 of 1975	3(3)	*Agricultural Workers (Holidays) (Amendment) Act, 1975 (Commencement) Order, S.I. No. 110 of 1975*
Agricultural Workers (Holidays and Wages) Act, No. 17 of 1969	1(4)	*Agricultural Workers (Holidays and Wages) Act, 1969 (Commencement) Order, S.I. No. 150 of 1969*
Agricultural Workers (Weekly Half-Holidays) Act, No. 26 of 1952	1	*Agricultural Workers (Weekly Half-Holidays) Act, 1952 (Commencement) Order, S.I. No. 54 of 1953*
	6	*Agricultural Workers (Weekly Half-Holidays in Winter Periods) (Qualifying Period of Work) Regulations, S.I. No. 207 of 1969*
Agriculture Act, No. 8 of 1931		**Foreign Animals Order, 1931, Amendment Order [Vol. X p. 513] S.R.& O. No. 38 of 1931**
		Foot and Mouth Disease (Imported Packing) Order, 1923 Amendment Order [Vol. X p. 223] S.R.& O. No. 39 of 1931
		Foreign Hay and Straw (Ireland) Order of 1912 Amendment Order [Vol. X p. 135] S.R.& O. No. 40 of 1931
		Diseases of Animals (Disinfection) Order [Vol. X p. 587] S.R.& O. No. 59 of 1931
		Exportation of Animals (Irish Free State) Order [Vol. X p. 181] S.R.& O. No. 63 of 1931
		Foreign Animals Order [Vol. X p. 517] S.R.& O. No. 17 of 1932
		Foot and Mouth Disease (Imported Packing) Order [Vol. X p. 227] S.R.& O. No. 18 of 1932
		Foreign Hay and Straw Order [Vol. X p. 593] S.R.& O. No. 19 of 1932
		Foreign Animals Order of 1932 No.2 [Vol. X p. 521] S.R.& O. No. 48 of 1932
		Foreign Animals Order of 1932 No.2 Revocation Order [Vol. X p. 597] S.R.& O. No. 85 of 1932
		Foot and Mouth Disease (Importation of Rodents and Insectivora) Order [Vol. X p. 601] S.R.& O. No. 10 of 1933

Statutory Authority	Section	Statutory Instrument

Agriculture Act, No. 8 of 1931
(*Cont.*)

Diseases of Animals Act, 1894 (Extension to Rodents and Insectivora) Order [Vol. X p. 607] S.R.& O. No. 11 of 1933

Foreign Animals Order, 1931, Amendment Order [Vol. X p. 611] S.R.& O. No. 12 of 1933

Foot and Mouth Disease (Imported Packing) Order, 1923 Amendment Order [Vol. X p. 615] S.R.& O. No. 13 of 1933

Foreign Hay and Straw (Ireland) Order of 1912 Amendment Order [Vol. X p. 619] S.R.& O. No. 14 of 1933

Rabies Order [Vol. X p. 623] S.R.& O. No. 16 of 1933

Diseases of Animals Act, 1894 (Extension to Horses, Asses, Mules, Dogs and Cats) Order [Vol. X p. 645] S.R.& O. No. 17 of 1933

Diseases of Animals Act, 1894 (Extension to Rabies) Order [Vol. X p. 649] S.R.& O. No. 18 of 1933

Foot and Mouth Disease and Swine Fever (Boiling of Animal Foodstuffs) Order [Vol. X p. 653] S.R.& O. No. 39 of 1933

Transit of Animals Order [Vol. X p. 659] S.R.& O. No. 42 of 1933

County Dublin (Special Dipping Area) Sheep Dipping Order [Vol. X p. 667] S.R.& O. No. 68 of 1933

Portal Inspection Order, 1924 (Revocation) Order [Vol. X p. 681] S.R.& O. No. 88 of 1933

County Dublin (Special Dipping Area) Sheep Dipping Order, 1933 Revocation Order [Vol. X p. 677] S.R.& O. No. 121 of 1933

Portal Inspection Order [Vol. X p. 685] S.R.& O. No. 175 of 1935

Portal Inspection Order of 1935, Amendment Order [Vol. X p. 689] S.R.& O. No. 651 of 1935

Warble Fly (Treatment of Cattle) Order [Vol. X p. 695] S.R.& O. No. 20 of 1936

Diseases of Animals Act, 1894 (Extension to Warble Fly Infestation) Order [Vol. X p. 717] S.R.& O. No. 43 of 1936

Sale of Milk (Ireland) Regulations, 1901 (Revocation) Regulations [Vol. XX p. 1] S.R.&O. No. 79 of 1936

Warble Fly (Treatment of Cattle) (Amendment) Order [Vol. X p. 711] S.R.& O. No. 371 of 1936

Sheep Dipping Order [Vol. X p. 721] S.R.& O. No. 169 of 1937

Foot and Mouth Disease (Disposal of Swill) Order [Vol. X p. 741] S.R.& O. No. 337 of 1937

Diseases of Animals Act, 1894 (Extension to Poultry and Poultry Diseases) Order [Vol. X p. 745] S.R.& O. No. 23 of 1938

Agriculture Act, No. 8 of 1931
(*Cont.*)

Importation of Carcases (Prohibition) (Amendment) Order [Vol. X p. 751] S.R.& O. No. 65 of 1938

Foreign Animals Order, 1931, Amendment Order [Vol. X p. 755] S.R.& O. No. 66 of 1938

Sheep Scab (Leitrim and Cavan) Order [Vol. X p. 759] S.R.& O. No. 99 of 1938

Dublin Swine Fever Orders, 1903 to 1928 (Revocation) Order [Vol. X p. 769] S.R.& O. No. 104 of 1938

Exportation of Animals (Irish Free State) Order [Vol. X p. 773] S.R.& O. No. 110 of 1938

Diseases of Animals Act, 1894 (Extension to Poultry and Poultry Diseases) (No.2) Order [Vol. X p. 779] S.R.& O. No. 125 of 1938

Poultry and Poultry Eggs (Importation) Order [Vol. X p. 785] S.R.& O. No. 126 of 1938

Hay, Straw and Peat Moss Litter Order [Vol. X p. 793] S.R.& O. No. 230 of 1938

Sheep Scab (Leitrim and Cavan) (Amendment) Order [Vol. X p. 801] S.R.& O. No. 231 of 1938

Sheep Dipping (Amendment) Order [Vol. X p. 805] S.R.& O. No. 232 of 1938

Foot and Mouth Disease (Imported Carcases and Packing Materials) Order [Vol. X p. 811] S.R.& O. No. 273 of 1938

Foot and Mouth Disease (Imported Carcases and Packing Materials) (Amendment) Order [Vol. X p. 821] S.R.& O. No. 287 of 1938

Black Scab in Potatoes (Special Area) Order [Vol. XXVIII p. 979] S.R.& O. No. 36 of 1945

Colorado Beetle Order [Vol. XXV p. 83] S.R.& O. No. 228 of 1945

Importation of Strawberry Plants and Blackcurrant and Gooseberry Bushes Order [Vol. XXXVII p. 133] S.R.& O. No. 358 of 1946

Sale of Diseased Plants (Ireland) Order, 1922 (Second Amendment) Order [Vol. XXXVII p. 141] S.R.& O. No. 359 of 1946

Black Scab in Potatoes (Special Area) Order, 1933 (Amendment) Order, S.I. No. 375 of 1948

Importation of Forest Trees (Prohibition) Order, S.I. No. 292 of 1949

Foot and Mouth Disease Order, S.I. No. 79 of 1950

Potato Root Eelworm Order, S.I. No. 372 of 1951

Foot and Mouth Disease Order, 1950 (Amendment) Order, S.I. No. 147 of 1952

Importation of Forest Trees (Prohibition) Order, 1949 (Amendment) Order, S.I. No. 371 of 1952

4   **Beet Eelworm Order, S.I. No. 313 of 1956**

Shipment of Livestock (Port of Dublin) Order, S.I. No. 221 of 1959

Agriculture Act, No. 8 of 1931
(*Cont.*)

Importation of Wool Order, 1946 (Amendment) Order, S.I. No. 8 of 1960

Horses (Carriage by Sea) Order, S.I. No. 227 of 1960

Shipment of Livestock (Port of Dublin) Order, 1959 (Revocation) Order, S.I. No. 123 of 1961

Foot and Mouth Disease (Importation of Plants) Order, S.I. No. 4 of 1962

Diseases of Animals (Licensing of Pig Dealers) Order, 1957 (Revocation) Order, S.I. No. 85 of 1962

Importation of Meat and Animal Products Order, S.I. No. 186 of 1963

Importation of Meat and Animal Products (Amendment) Order, S.I. No. 197 of 1964

Sheep Dipping Order, S.I. No. 105 of 1965

Importation of Meat and Animal Products (Amendment) Order, S.I. No. 148 of 1965

Importation of Meat and Animal Products (Amendment) Order, S.I. No. 27 of 1966

Sheep Dipping Order, 1965 (Amendment) Order, S.I. No. 98 of 1966

Bee Pest Prevention (Amendment) Regulations, S.I. No. 151 of 1978

8   **Bee Pest Prevention (Ireland) (Amendment) Regulations, S.I. No. 82 of 1971**

11(1)   **Agricultural Production Council Order, S.I. No. 261 of 1956**

Western Agriculture Consultative Council Order, S.I. No. 174 of 1965

25(1)   **Agricultural Committees (Local Inquiries) Regulations [Vol. III p. 1] S.R.& O. No. 47 of 1932**

27(1)   *Committees of Agriculture (Salaries of Officers) Regulations [Vol. III p. 7] S.R.& O. No. 41 of 1933*

Committees of Agriculture (Salaries of Officers) Regulations [Vol. III p. 23] S.R.& O. No. 51 of 1936

Committees of Agriculture (Salaries of Officers) (Amendment) Regulations [Vol. XXV p. 101] S.R.& O. No. 69 of 1944

Committees of Agriculture (Salaries of Officers) (Amendment) Regulations [Vol. XXV p. 107] S.R.& O. No. 2 of 1945

Committees of Agriculture (Salaries of Officers) (Amendment) Regulations [Vol. XXXVI p. 27] S.R.& O. No. 13 of 1946

Committees of Agriculture (Salaries of Officers) Regulations [Vol. XXXVI p. 33] S.R.& O. No. 218 of 1947

Committees of Agriculture (Salaries of Officers) Regulations, S.I. No. 232 of 1949

Agriculture Act, No. 8 of 1931
(*Cont.*)

Committees of Agriculture (Salaries of Officers) Regulations, 1949 (Amendment) Regulations, S.I. No. 207 of 1951

Committees of Agriculture (Salaries of Officers) Regulations, S.I. No. 317 of 1952

Committees of Agriculture (Salaries of Officers) Regulations, 1952 (Amendment) Regulations, S.I. No. 303 of 1953

Committees of Agriculture (Salaries of Officers) Regulations, 1952 (Amendment) Regulations, S.I. No. 69 of 1956

Committees of Agriculture (Salaries of Officers) Regulations, 1952 (Amendment) Regulations, S.I. No. 140 of 1958

Committees of Agriculture (Salaries of Officers) Regulations, 1952 (Amendment) (No.2) Regulations, S.I. No. 208 of 1958

Committees of Agriculture (Salaries of Officers) Regulations, 1952 (Amendment) Regulations, S.I. No. 225 of 1959

Committees of Agriculture (Salaries of Officers) Regulations, 1952 (Amendment) Regulations, S.I. No. 45 of 1960

Committees of Agriculture (Salaries of Officers) Regulations, 1952 (Amendment) (No.2) Regulations, S.I. No. 213 of 1960

Committees of Agriculture (Salaries of Officers) Regulations, 1952 (Amendment) Regulations, S.I. No. 12 of 1961

Committees of Agriculture (Salaries of Officers) Regulations, S.I. No. 95 of 1961

Committees of Agriculture (Salaries of Officers) Regulations, S.I. No. 185 of 1962

Committees of Agriculture (Salaries of Officers) (Amendment) Regulations, S.I. No. 270 of 1963

Committees of Agriculture (Salaries of Officers) Regulations, S.I. No. 239 of 1964

Committees of Agriculture (Salaries of Officers) Regulations, S.I. No. 67 of 1965

Committees of Agriculture (Salaries of Officers) Regulations, S.I. No. 187 of 1966

Committees of Agriculture (Salaries of Officers) Regulations, S.I. No. 65 of 1968

Committees of Agriculture (Salaries of Officers) Regulations, S.I. No. 333 of 1975

28   *Committees of Agriculture (Officers' Travelling Expenses and Maintenance Allowance and Expenses) Regulations [Vol. III p. 35] S.R.& O. No. 97 of 1936*

Committees of Agriculture (Officers' Travelling Expenses and Maintenance Allowance and Expenses) (Amendment) Regulations [Vol. XXV p. 93] S.R.& O. No. 95 of 1945

Agriculture Act, No. 8 of 1931
(*Cont.*)

Committees of Agriculture (Officers' Travelling Expenses and Maintenance Allowance and Expenses) Regulations [Vol. XXXVI p. 17] S.R. & O. No. 349 of 1947

Committees of Agriculture (Officers' Travelling Expenses and Maintenance Allowance and Expenses) Regulations, S.I. No. 318 of 1952

Committees of Agriculture (Officers' Travelling Expenses and Maintenance Allowance and Expenses) Regulations, S.I. No. 70 of 1956

Committees of Agriculture (Officers' Travelling Expenses and Maintenance Allowance and Expenses) Regulations, 1956 (Amendment) Regulations, S.I. No. 92 of 1957

Committees of Agriculture (Officers' Travelling Expenses and Maintenance Allowance and Expenses) Regulations, 1956 (Amendment) Regulations, S.I. No. 221 of 1958

Committees of Agriculture (Officers' Travelling Expenses and Maintenance Allowance and Expenses) Regulations, 1956 (Amendment) Regulations, S.I. No. 226 of 1959

Committees of Agriculture (Officers' Travelling Expenses and Maintenance Allowance and Expenses) Regulations, 1956 (Amendment) Regulations, S.I. No. 149 of 1960

Committees of Agriculture (Officers' Travelling Expenses and Maintenance Allowance and Expenses) Regulations, 1956 (Amendment) Regulations, S.I. No. 244 of 1961

Committees of Agriculture (Officers' Travelling Expenses and Maintenance Allowance and Expenses) Regulations, 1956 (Amendment) Regulations, S.I. No. 226 of 1963

Committees of Agriculture (Officers' Travelling Expenses and Maintenance Allowance and Expenses) Regulations, S.I. No. 22 of 1965

Committees of Agriculture (Officers' Travelling Expenses and Maintenance Allowance and Expenses) (Amendment) Regulations, S.I. No. 183 of 1965

Committees of Agriculture (Officers' Travelling Expenses and Maintenance Allowance and Expenses) (Amendment) Regulations, S.I. No. 126 of 1966

Committees of Agriculture (Officers' Travelling Expenses and Maintenance Allowance and Expenses) (Amendment) Regulations, S.I. No. 60 of 1967

Committees of Agriculture (Officers' Travelling Expenses and Maintenance Allowance and Expenses) (Amendment) Regulations, S.I. No. 18 of 1969

Committees of Agriculture (Officers' Travelling Expenses and Maintenance Allowance and Expenses) (Amendment) (No.2) Regulations, S.I. No. 203 of 1969

Statutory Authority	Section	Statutory Instrument
Agriculture Act, No. 8 of 1931 (*Cont.*)		**Committees of Agriculture (Officers' Travelling Expenses and Maintenance Allowance and Expenses) (Amendment) Regulations, S.I. No. 311 of 1970**
		Committees of Agriculture (Officers' Travelling Expenses and Maintenance Allowance and Expenses) (Amendment) Regulations, S.I. No. 68 of 1971
		Committees of Agriculture (Officers' Travelling Expenses and Maintenance Allowance and Expenses) (Amendment) Regulations, S.I. No. 64 of 1972
		Committees of Agriculture (Officers' Travelling Expenses and Maintenance Allowance and Expenses) (Amendment) (No.2) Regulations, S.I. No. 139 of 1972
		Committees of Agriculture (Officers' Travelling Expenses and Maintenance Allowance and Expenses) (Amendment) Regulations, S.I. No. 251 of 1973
		Committees of Agriculture (Officers' Travelling Expenses and Maintenance Allowance and Expenses) (Amendment) Regulations, S.I. No. 303 of 1974
		Committees of Agriculture (Officers' Travelling Expenses and Maintenance Allowance and Expenses) (Amendment) (No.2) Regulations, S.I. No. 354 of 1974
		Committees of Agriculture (Officers' Travelling Expenses and Maintenance Allowance and Expenses) (Amendment) Regulations, S.I. No. 186 of 1975
		Committees of Agriculture (Officers' Travelling Expenses and Maintenance Allowance and Expenses) (Amendment) Regulations, S.I. No. 58 of 1976
	Sch. II par. 2(2)	**Committees of Agriculture (Nominations by Voluntary Rural Organisations) Order, S.I. No. 240 of 1980**
		Committees of Agriculture (Nominations by Voluntary Rural Organisations) (Amendment) Order, S.I. No. 267 of 1980
		Committees of Agriculture (Nominations by Voluntary Rural Organisations) (Amendment) Order, S.I. No. 167 of 1985
Agriculture Acts, 1931 to 1944,		*Diseases of Animals Act, 1894 (Extension to Certain Fur-Bearing Animals) Order, S.I. No. 57 of 1949*
		Foot and Mouth Disease (Importation of Rodents and Insectivora Order, 1933 (Amendment) Order, S.I. No. 58 of 1949
Agriculture Acts, 1931 to 1948		*Sheep Dipping Order, S.I. No. 157 of 1948*

Statutory Authority	Section	Statutory Instrument

Agriculture Acts, 1931 to 1948 (*Cont.*)

Poultry, Poultry Carcases and Poultry Eggs (Restriction on Importation) Order, S.I. No. 293 of 1949

Fowl Pest Order, S.I. No. 15 of 1950

Diseases of Animals Act, 1894 (Extension to Poultry and Poultry Diseases) Order, S.I. No. 16 of 1950

Diseases of Animals Act, 1894 (Extension to Poultry and Poultry Diseases) (Amendment) Order, S.I. No. 17 of 1950

Fowl Pest (Amendment) Order, S.I. No. 18 of 1950

Foot and Mouth Disease (Importation of Animals) Order, S.I. No. 356 of 1951

Foot and Mouth Disease (Importation of Plants) Order, S.I. No. 134 of 1952

Importation of Wool Order, 1946 (Amendment) Order, S.I. No. 135 of 1952

Foreign Animals Order, 1931 (Amendment) Order, S.I. No. 136 of 1952

Foot and Mouth Disease (Importation of Animals) Order, 1951 (Revocation) Order, S.I. No. 268 of 1953

Foreign Animals Order of 1931 (Amendment) Order, S.I. No. 39 of 1954

Importation of Wool Order, 1946 (Amendment) Order, S.I. No. 113 of 1954

Rodents and Insectivora (Restriction on Importation) Order, S.I. No. 114 of 1954

Diseases of Animals Act, 1894 (Extension to Rodents, Insectivora and Myxomatosis) Order, S.I. No. 115 of 1954

Transit of Greyhounds Order, S.I. No. 121 of 1954

Agriculture Acts, 1931 to 1955,

Johne's Disease Order, S.I. No. 86 of 1955

Live Pigeons (Prohibition of Export) Order, S.I. No. 222 of 1956

Swine Fever Infected Area Order, S.I. No. 223 of 1956

Swine Fever (Dublin) Order, S.I. No. 242 of 1956

Swine Fever Infected Area Order, 1956 (Amendment) Order, S.I. No. 276 of 1956

Foot and Mouth Disease Order, S.I. No. 324 of 1956

Swine Fever Infected Area Order, 1956 (Amendment) Order, S.I. No. 107 of 1957

Swine Fever (Restriction of Movement of Pigs) Order, S.I. No. 128 of 1957

Swine Fever (Restriction of Movement of Pigs) Order, 1957 (Amendment) Order, S.I. No. 166 of 1957

Swine Fever (Restriction of Movement of Pigs) Order, 1957 (Amendment) (No.2) Order, S.I. No. 189 of 1957

Statutory Authority	Section	Statutory Instrument
Agriculture Acts, 1931 to 1955 (*Cont.*)		*Diseases of Animals (Licensing of Pig Dealers) Order, S.I. No. 202 of 1957*
		Swine Fever (Controlled Area) Order, S.I. No. 255 of 1957
		Transit of Animals Order, 1927 (Swine Fever) (Amendment) Order, S.I. No. 65 of 1958
Agriculture Acts, 1931 to 1958,		**Swine Fever (Controlled Area) Order, 1957 (Amendment) Order, S.I. No. 234 of 1958**
		Swine Fever (Controlled Area) Order, 1957 (Revocation) Order, S.I. No. 45 of 1959
		Foot and Mouth Disease (Importation of Animals) Order, S.I. No. 225 of 1960
		Foot and Mouth Disease (Importation of Animals) Order, 1960 (Revocation) Order, S.I. No. 20 of 1961
		Foot and Mouth Disease (Importation of Animals) Order, S.I. No. 50 of 1961
		Foot and Mouth Disease (Importation of Animals) Order, 1961 (Revocation) Order, S.I. No. 100 of 1961
Agriculture Acts, 1931 to 1964,		*Live Pigeons (Prohibition of Export) Order, 1956 (Revocation) Order, S.I. No. 232 of 1964*
Agriculture (Amendment) Act, No. 24 of 1948	3	**Committees of Agriculture (Allowances to Members) Rules, S.I. No. 100 of 1959**
		Committees of Agriculture (Allowances to Members) (Amendment) Rules, S.I. No. 139 of 1964
		Committees of Agriculture (Allowances to Members) (Amendment) Rules, S.I. No. 70 of 1969
		Committees of Agriculture (Allowances to Members) (Amendment) Rules, S.I. No. 295 of 1972
		Committees of Agriculture (Allowances to Members) (Amendment) Rules, S.I. No. 36 of 1975
	3(3)	*Committees of Agriculture (Allowances to Members) Rules, S.I. No. 13 of 1949*
Agriculture (Amendment) Act, No. 17 of 1958	6	*Committees of Agriculture (Officers' Travelling Expenses and Maintenance Allowance and Expenses) Regulations, 1956 (Amendment) Regulations, S.I. No. 149 of 1960*
		Committees of Agriculture (Salaries of Officers) Regulations, 1952 (Amendment) Regulations, S.I. No. 12 of 1961
		Committees of Agriculture (Salaries of Officers) Regulations, S.I. No. 95 of 1961
		Committees of Agriculture (Officers' Travelling Expenses and Maintenance Allowance and Expenses) Regulations, 1956 (Amendment) Regulations, S.I. No. 226 of 1963
		Committees of Agriculture (Salaries of Officers) (Amendment) Regulations, S.I. No. 270 of 1963
		Committees of Agriculture (Salaries of Officers) Regulations, S.I. No. 239 of 1964

Agriculture (Amendment) Act,
No. 17 of 1958 (*Cont.*)

Committees of Agriculture (Officers' Travelling Expenses and Maintenance Allowance and Expenses) Regulations, S.I. No. 22 of 1965

Committees of Agriculture (Salaries of Officers) Regulations, S.I. No. 67 of 1965

Committees of Agriculture (Officers' Travelling Expenses and Maintenance Allowance and Expenses) (Amendment) Regulations, S.I. No. 183 of 1965

Committees of Agriculture (Officers' Travelling Expenses and Maintenance Allowance and Expenses) (Amendment) Regulations, S.I. No. 126 of 1966

Committees of Agriculture (Salaries of Officers) Regulations, S.I. No. 187 of 1966

Committees of Agriculture (Officers' Travelling Expenses and Maintenance Allowance and Expenses) (Amendment) Regulations, S.I. No. 60 of 1967

Committees of Agriculture (Salaries of Officers) Regulations, S.I. No. 65 of 1968

Committees of Agriculture (Officers' Travelling Expenses and Maintenance Allowance and Expenses) (Amendment) Regulations, S.I. No. 18 of 1969

Committees of Agriculture (Officers' Travelling Expenses and Maintenance Allowance and Expenses) (Amendment) (No.2) Regulations, S.I. No. 203 of 1969

Committees of Agriculture (Officers' Travelling Expenses and Maintenance Allowance and Expenses) (Amendment) Regulations, S.I. No. 68 of 1971

Committees of Agriculture (Officers' Travelling Expenses and Maintenance Allowance and Expenses) (Amendment) Regulations, S.I. No. 64 of 1972

Committees of Agriculture (Officers' Travelling Expenses and Maintenance Allowance and Expenses) (Amendment) (No.2) Regulations, S.I. No. 139 of 1972

Committees of Agriculture (Officers' Travelling Expenses and Maintenance Allowance and Expenses) (Amendment) Regulations, S.I. No. 251 of 1973

Committees of Agriculture (Officers' Travelling Expenses and Maintenance Allowance and Expenses) (Amendment) Regulations, S.I. No. 303 of 1974

Committees of Agriculture (Officers' Travelling Expenses and Maintenance Allowance and Expenses) (Amendment) (No.2) Regulations, S.I. No. 354 of 1974

Statutory Authority	Section	Statutory Instrument
Agriculture (Amendment) Act, No. 17 of 1958 *(Cont.)*		**Committees of Agriculture (Officers' Travelling Expenses and Maintenance Allowance and Expenses) (Amendment) Regulations, S.I. No. 186 of 1975**
		Committees of Agriculture (Salaries of Officers) Regulations, S.I. No. 333 of 1975
		Committees of Agriculture (Officers' Travelling Expenses and Maintenance Allowance and Expenses) (Amendment) Regulations, S.I. No. 58 of 1976
Agriculture (An Chomhairle Oiliuna Talmhaiochta) Act, No. 9 of 1979	1(2)	*Agriculture (An Chomhairle Oiliuna Talmhaiochta) Act, 1979 (Commencement) Order, S.I. No. 248 of 1979*
		Agriculture (An Chomhairle Oiliuna Talmhaiochta) Act, 1979 (Commencement) Order, S.I. No. 53 of 1980
		Agriculture (An Chomhairle Oiliuna Talmhaiochta) Act, 1979 (Commencement) (No.2) Order, S.I. No. 81 of 1980
Agriculture (An Foras Taluntais) Act, No. 1 of 1958	1	*Agriculture (An Foras Taluntais) Act, 1958 (Commencement) Order, S.I. No. 123 of 1958*
	5(8)	*An Foras Taluntais (Nomination of Members of the Council by Agricultural and Rural Organisations) Order, S.I. No. 102 of 1958*
		An Foras Taluntais (Nomination of Members of the Council by Agricultural and Rural Organisations) Order, S.I. No. 197 of 1973
	5(11)	*An Foras Taluntais (Nomination of Members of the Council by Agricultural and Rural Organisations) (Amendment) Order, S.I. No. 98 of 1961*
		An Foras Taluntais (Nomination of Members of the Council by Agricultural and Rural Organisations) (Amendment) Order, S.I. No. 82 of 1964
		An Foras Taluntais (Nomination of Members of the Council by Agricultural and Rural Organisations) (Amendment) Order, S.I. No. 119 of 1967
		An Foras Taluntais (Nomination of Members of the Council by Agricultural and Rural Organisations) (Amendment) Order, S.I. No. 121 of 1970
		An Foras Taluntais (Nomination of Members of the Council by Agricultural and Rural Organisations) (Amendment) Order, S.I. No. 289 of 1979
Agriculture and Technical Instruction (Ireland) Act, No. 50 of 1899		*Bovine Tuberculosis Order [Vol. X p. 351] S.R.& O. No. 18 of 1926*
		Landing of Carcases Order [Vol. X p. 379] S.R.& O. No. 32 of 1926
		Landing of Carcases Order, 1926, Amendment Order [Vol. X p. 385] S.R.& O. No. 33 of 1926
		Peat Moss Litter (Prohibition) Order [Vol. X p. 389] S.R.& O. No. 36 of 1926

Statutory Authority	Section	Statutory Instrument

Agriculture and Technical Instruction (Ireland) Act, No. 50 of 1899 (*Cont.*)

Importation of Carcases (Prohibition) Order [Vol. X p. 393] S.R.& O. No. 66 of 1926

Transit of Animals Order [Vol. X p. 409] S.R.& O. No. 39 of 1927

Parasitic Mange (Cattle) Order [Vol. X p. 469] S.R.& O. No. 48 of 1927

Importation of Carcases (Prohibition) (Amendment) Order [Vol. X p. 403] S.R.& O. No. 49 of 1927

Foot and Mouth Disease (Boiling of Animal Foodstuffs) Order [Vol. X p. 475] S.R.& O. No. 50 of 1927

Foreign Animals Order [Vol. X p. 495] S.R.& O. No. 62 of 1928

Importation of Dogs and Cats Order [Vol. X p. 525] S.R.& O. No. 4 of 1929

Hay and Straw Orders (Amendment) Order [Vol. X p. 541] S.R.& O. No. 6 of 1929

Anthrax Order [Vol. X p. 545] S.R.& O. No. 57 of 1930

Transit of Animals Order of 1927 Amendment Order [Vol. X p. 459] S.R.& O. No. 61 of 1930

Sheep Dipping (Local Regulations) Order [Vol. X p. 579] S.R.& O. No. 8 of 1931

Foreign Animals Order [Vol. X p. 503] S.R.& O. No. 9 of 1931

Air Companies Act, No. 4 of 1966 — 23(2) — *Air Companies Act, 1966 (Commencement) Order, S.I. No. 61 of 1966*

Air Navigation Act, No. 80 of 1920

Air Navigation (International Lines) Order [Vol. IV p. 145] S.R.& O. No. 560 of 1935

1 — *Air Navigation (No.1) Regulations [Vol. IV p. 9] S.R.& O. No. 68 of 1928*

Air Navigation (No.1) Regulations [Vol. IV p. 19] S.R.& O. No. 24 of 1929

Air Navigation (No.2) Regulations [Vol. IV p. 25] S.R.& O. No. 34 of 1929

Air Navigation (General) Regulations [Vol. IV p. 31] S.R.& O. No. 26 of 1930

Air Navigation (Eucharistic Congress) Regulations [Vol. IV p. 131] S.R.& O. No. 53 of 1932

12 — *Air Navigation (Investigation of Accidents) Regulations [Vol. IV p. 1] S.R.& O. No. 21 of 1928*

17(2) — **Air Navigation (Amendment) Regulations [Vol. IV p. 139] S.R.& O. No. 245 of 1934**

Air Navigation and Transport Act, No. 40 of 1936

Air Navigation and Transport Act, 1936 (Aviation Business) Regulations [Vol. XXXVI p. 287] S.R.& O. No. 1 of 1947

Air Navigation and Transport (Compulsory Acquisition of Land) (No.1) Order [Vol. XXXVI p. 341] S.R.& O. No. 433 of 1947

Statutory Authority	Section	Statutory Instrument
Air Navigation and Transport Act, No. 40 of 1936 (*Cont.*)		**Air Navigation and Transport Act, 1936 (Aviation Business) Regulations, S.I. No. 228 of 1953**
	5	**Air Navigation and Transport Act, 1936 (Non-International Carriage) Order, S.I. No. 264 of 1964**
	15	**Air Navigation (Amendment) Regulations [Vol. IV p. 155] S.R.& O. No. 108 of 1938**
		Air Navigation (Amendment) Regulations [Vol. XXVI p. 453] S.R.& O. No. 53 of 1939
		Air Navigation (Amendment) Regulations [Vol. XXVI p. 459] S.R.& O. No. 47 of 1940
		Air Navigation (Amendment) Regulations [Vol. XXVI p. 465] S.R.& O. No. 347 of 1943
	17(2)	**Warsaw Convention (High Contracting Parties) Order, S.I. No. 18 of 1964**
	20	*Air Navigation and Transport Act, 1936 (Non-International Carriage) Order, S.I. No. 110 of 1956*
		Air Navigation and Transport Act, 1936 (Non-International Carriage) Order, S.I. No. 264 of 1964
	41	**Air Navigation and Transport (Compulsory Acquisition of Land) Order, S.I. No. 403 of 1951**
	58	*Signals of Distress (Ships and Seaplanes on the Water) Order, S.I. No. 186 of 1965*
		Collision Regulations (Ships and Water Craft on the Water) Order, S.I. No. 229 of 1977
	60	*Air Navigation (Investigation of Accidents) Regulations, 1928 (Amendment) Regulations [Vol. XXVI p. 471] S.R.& O. No. 288 of 1943*
		Air Navigation (Investigation of Accidents) Regulations, S.I. No. 19 of 1957
	79(1)	*Subsidy (Aer-Rianta, Teoranta) Order [Vol. XXVI p. 475] S.R.& O. No. 31 of 1939*
		Subsidy (Aer-Rianta, Teoranta) (No.2) Order [Vol. XXVI p. 481] S.R.& O. No. 156 of 1939
	81	*Aer-Rianta, Teoranta (Accounts) Regulations [Vol. IV p. 161] S.R.& O. No. 177 of 1938*
		Aer Lingus, Teoranta (Accounts) Regulations [Vol. IV p. 171] S.R.& O. No. 178 of 1938
	86	*Air Navigation and Transport Act, 1936 (Part X) (Appointed Day) Order [Vol. XXXVI p. 327] S.R.& O. No. 376 of 1946*
Air Navigation and Transport Act, No. 23 of 1946		*Air Navigation (Rules of the Air) Order, S.I. No. 96 of 1949*
		Air Navigation (Foreign Military Aircraft) Order, S.I. No. 74 of 1952
	5	*Air Navigation (General) Regulations, 1930 (Amendment) Order, S.I. No. 187 of 1962*

Air Navigation and Transport Act,
No. 23 of 1946 (*Cont.*)

Air Navigation (Rules of the Air) Order, S.I. No. 7 of 1963

Air Navigation (Fees) Order, S.I. No. 65 of 1963

Air Navigation and Transport (Fares and Rates) Order, S.I. No. 87 of 1963

Air Navigation (Nationality and Registration of Aircraft) Order, S.I. No. 88 of 1963

Air Navigation (Operations) Order, S.I. No. 140 of 1964

Air Navigation (Airworthiness of Aircraft) Order, S.I. No. 141 of 1964

Air Navigation (Personnel Licensing) Order, S.I. No. 165 of 1966

Air Navigation (Rules of the Air) (Amendment) Order, S.I. No. 273 of 1966

Air Navigation (Rules of the Air) (Amendment) (No.2) Order, S.I. No. 272 of 1967

Air Navigation (Rules of the Air) (Amendment) Order, S.I. No. 26 of 1968

Air Navigation (Definition of Aircraft) Order, S.I. No. 134 of 1968

Air Navigation (Rules of the Air) (Amendment) Order, S.I. No. 147 of 1969

Air Navigation (Aerodromes and Visual Ground Aids) Order, S.I. No. 291 of 1970

Air Navigation (Noise Certification and Limitation) Order, S.I. No. 280 of 1972

Air Navigation (Rules of the Air) Order, S.I. No. 22 of 1973

Air Navigation (Airworthiness of Aircraft) (Amendment) Order, S.I. No. 102 of 1973

Air Navigation (Noise Certification and Limitation) (Amendment) Order, S.I. No. 187 of 1973

Air Navigation (Carriage of Munitions of War, Weapons and Dangerous Goods) Order, S.I. No. 224 of 1973

Air Navigation (Rules of the Air) (Amendment) Order, S.I. No. 18 of 1974

Air Navigation (Rules of the Air) (Amendment) Regulations, S.I. No. 7 of 1975

Air Navigation (Fees) Order, S.I. No. 60 of 1976

Air Navigation (Noise Certification and Limitation) Order, S.I. No. 250 of 1976

Air Navigation (Nationality and Registration of Aircraft) (Amendment) Order, S.I. No. 194 of 1979

Air Navigation (Fees) Order, S.I. No. 335 of 1979

Air Navigation (Fees) Order, S.I. No. 307 of 1980

Air Navigation (Fees) Order, S.I. No. 349 of 1981

Air Navigation (Fees) Order, S.I. No. 47 of 1983

Air Navigation (Noise Certification and Limitation) Order, S.I. No. 13 of 1984

Statutory Authority	Section	Statutory Instrument
Air Navigation and Transport Act, No. 23 of 1946 (*Cont.*)		**Air Navigation (Nationality and Registration of Aircraft) (Amendment) Order, S.I. No. 15 of 1984**
		Air Navigation (Fees) Order, S.I. No. 261 of 1985
		Air Navigation (Operations) Order, S.I. No. 62 of 1986
	5(5)	**Air Navigation (Amendment) Order, S.I. No. 31 of 1951**
		Air Navigation and Transport (Fares and Rates) Order, 1963 (Revocation) Order, S.I. No. 120 of 1963
	8	*Chicago Convention (Commencement) Order [Vol. XXXVI p. 337] S.R.& O. No. 109 of 1947*
	9	**Air Navigation (General Regulations) Order [Vol. XXXVI p. 305] S.R.& O. No. 113 of 1947**
		Air Navigation (Personnel Licensing) (Fees) Order, S.I. No. 65 of 1951
		Air Navigation (General) Regulations, 1930 (Amendment) Order, S.I. No. 187 of 1962
		Air Navigation (Rules of the Air) Order, S.I. No. 7 of 1963
		Air Navigation (Fees) Order, S.I. No. 65 of 1963
		Air Navigation and Transport (Fares and Rates) Order, S.I. No. 87 of 1963
		Air Navigation (Nationality and Registration of Aircraft) Order, S.I. No. 88 of 1963
		Air Navigation (Operations) Order, S.I. No. 140 of 1964
		Air Navigation (Airworthiness of Aircraft) Order, S.I. No. 141 of 1964
		Air Navigation (Personnel Licensing) Order, S.I. No. 165 of 1966
		Air Navigation (Aerodromes and Visual Ground Aids) Order, S.I. No. 291 of 1970
		Air Navigation (Noise Certification and Limitation) Order, S.I. No. 280 of 1972
		Air Navigation (Rules of the Air) Order, S.I. No. 22 of 1973
		Air Navigation (Airworthiness of Aircraft) (Amendment) Order, S.I. No. 102 of 1973
		Air Navigation (Noise Certification and Limitation) (Amendment) Order, S.I. No. 187 of 1973
		Air Navigation (Carriage of Munitions of War, Weapons and Dangerous Goods) Order, S.I. No. 224 of 1973
		Air Navigation (Rules of the Air) (Amendment) Order, S.I. No. 18 of 1974
		Air Navigation (Rules of the Air) (Amendment) Regulations, S.I. No. 7 of 1975
		Air Navigation (Fees) Order, S.I. No. 60 of 1976
		Air Navigation (Noise Certification and Limitation) Order, S.I. No. 250 of 1976

Air Navigation and Transport Act,
No. 23 of 1946 (*Cont.*)

Air Navigation (Nationality and Registration of Aircraft) (Amendment) Order, S.I. No. 194 of 1979

Air Navigation (Fees) Order, S.I. No. 335 of 1979

Air Navigation (Fees) Order, S.I. No. 307 of 1980

Air Navigation (Fees) Order, S.I. No. 349 of 1981

Air Navigation (Fees) Order, S.I. No. 47 of 1983

Air Navigation (Noise Certification and Limitation) Order, S.I. No. 13 of 1984

Air Navigation (Nationality and Registration of Aircraft) (Amendment) Order, S.I. No. 15 of 1984

Air Navigation (Fees) Order, S.I. No. 261 of 1985

Air Navigation (Operations) Order, S.I. No. 62 of 1986

11 *Air Navigation (General) Regulations, 1930 (Amendment) Order, S.I. No. 187 of 1962*

Air Navigation (Rules of the Air) Order, S.I. No. 7 of 1963

Air Navigation (Fees) Order, S.I. No. 65 of 1963

Air Navigation (Nationality and Registration of Aircraft) Order, S.I. No. 88 of 1963

Air Navigation (Operations) Order, S.I. No. 140 of 1964

Air Navigation (Airworthiness of Aircraft) Order, S.I. No. 141 of 1964

Air Navigation (Personnel Licensing) Order, S.I. No. 165 of 1966

Air Navigation (Aerodromes and Visual Ground Aids) Order, S.I. No. 291 of 1970

Air Navigation (Noise Certification and Limitation) Order, S.I. No. 280 of 1972

Air Navigation (Rules of the Air) Order, S.I. No. 22 of 1973

Air Navigation (Airworthiness of Aircraft) (Amendment) Order, S.I. No. 102 of 1973

Air Navigation (Noise Certification and Limitation) (Amendment) Order, S.I. No. 187 of 1973

Air Navigation (Carriage of Munitions of War, Weapons and Dangerous Goods) Order, S.I. No. 224 of 1973

Air Navigation (Rules of the Air) (Amendment) Order, S.I. No. 18 of 1974

Air Navigation (Fees) Order, S.I. No. 60 of 1976

Air Navigation (Noise Certification and Limitation) Order, S.I. No. 250 of 1976

Air Navigation (Nationality and Registration of Aircraft) (Amendment) Order, S.I. No. 194 of 1979

Air Navigation (Fees) Order, S.I. No. 335 of 1979

Air Navigation (Fees) Order, S.I. No. 307 of 1980

Air Navigation (Fees) Order, S.I. No. 349 of 1981

Statutory Authority	Section	Statutory Instrument
Air Navigation and Transport Act, No. 23 of 1946 *(Cont.)*		*Air Navigation (Fees) Order, S.I. No. 47 of 1983*
		Air Navigation (Noise Certification and Limitation) Order, S.I. No. 13 of 1984
		Air Navigation (Nationality and Registration of Aircraft) (Amendment) Order, S.I. No. 15 of 1984
		Air Navigation (Fees) Order, S.I. No. 261 of 1985
		Air Navigation (Operations) Order, S.I. No. 62 of 1986
	11(j)	*Air Navigation (Personnel Licensing) (Fees) Order, S.I. No. 65 of 1951*
	16	*Air Navigation (Rules of the Air) Order, S.I. No. 7 of 1963*
		Air Navigation (Nationality and Registration of Aircraft) Order, S.I. No. 88 of 1963
		Air Navigation (Operations) Order, S.I. No. 140 of 1964
		Air Navigation (Airworthiness of Aircraft) Order, S.I. No. 141 of 1964
		Air Navigation (Personnel Licensing) Order, S.I. No. 165 of 1966
		Air Navigation (Noise Certification and Limitation) Order, S.I. No. 280 of 1972
		Air Navigation (Rules of the Air) Order, S.I. No. 22 of 1973
		Air Navigation (Airworthiness of Aircraft) (Amendment) Order, S.I. No. 102 of 1973
		Air Navigation (Noise Certification and Limitation) (Amendment) Order, S.I. No. 187 of 1973
		Air Navigation (Carriage of Munitions of War, Weapons and Dangerous Goods) Order, S.I. No. 224 of 1973
		Air Navigation (Rules of the Air) (Amendment) Order, S.I. No. 18 of 1974
		Air Navigation (Noise Certification and Limitation) Order, S.I. No. 250 of 1976
		Air Navigation (Noise Certification and Limitation) Order, S.I. No. 13 of 1984
		Air Navigation (Operations) Order, S.I. No. 62 of 1986
Air Navigation and Transport Act, No. 4 of 1950		*Shannon Airport Bye-Laws, S.I. No. 150 of 1953*
		Dublin Airport Bye-Laws, S.I. No. 151 of 1953
		Shannon Airport (Amendment) Bye-Laws, S.I. No. 60 of 1954
		Dublin Airport (Amendment) Bye-Laws, S.I. No. 61 of 1954
		Cork Airport Bye-Laws, S.I. No. 229 of 1961
		Cork Airport (Amendment) Bye-Laws, S.I. No. 59 of 1962
		Shannon Airport (Amendment) Bye-Laws, S.I. No. 81 of 1969
		Airport Bye-Laws, S.I. No. 225 of 1978

Statutory Authority	Section	Statutory Instrument
Air Navigation and Transport Act, No. 4 of 1950 (*Cont.*)	16	**Shannon Airport (Small Public Service Vehicles) Bye-Laws, S.I. No. 89 of 1980**
	16(1)	*Dublin Airport (Admission Charges) Bye-Laws, S.I. No. 292 of 1953*
		Shannon Airport (Admission Charges) Bye-Laws, S.I. No. 293 of 1953
		Dublin Airport (Admission Charges) Bye-Laws, 1953 (Revocation) Bye-Laws, S.I. No. 134 of 1956
		Shannon Airport (Admission Charges) (Revocation) Bye-Laws, S.I. No. 168 of 1960
	16(1)(l)	**Airport Bye-Laws, S.I. No. 361 of 1980**
	16(3)	*Dublin Airport (Parking Fees) Bye-Laws, S.I. No. 133 of 1956*
		Dublin Airport (Parking Fees) Bye-Laws, S.I. No. 161 of 1960
		Shannon Airport (Parking Fees) Bye-Laws, S.I. No. 169 of 1960
		Cork Airport (Parking Fees) Bye-Laws, S.I. No. 123 of 1962
		Dublin Airport (Parking Fees) (Amendment) Bye-Laws, S.I. No. 68 of 1963
		Cork Airport (Parking Fees) Bye-Laws, S.I. No. 241 of 1964
		Dublin Airport (Parking Fees) (Amendment) Bye-Laws, S.I. No. 14 of 1968
		Dublin Airport (Parking Fees) (Amendment) Bye-Laws, S.I. No. 191 of 1970
		Shannon Airport (Parking Fees) Bye-Laws, S.I. No. 19 of 1971
		Cork Airport (Parking Fees) Bye-Laws, S.I. No. 20 of 1971
		Dublin Airport (Parking Fees) Bye-Laws, S.I. No. 21 of 1971
		Dublin Airport (Parking Fees) Bye-Laws, S.I. No. 48 of 1975
		Shannon Airport (Parking Fee) Bye-Laws, S.I. No. 205 of 1975
		Cork Airport (Parking-Fees) Bye-Laws, S.I. No. 70 of 1976
		Dublin Airport (Parking Fees) Bye-Laws, S.I. No. 92 of 1977
Air Navigation and Transport Act, No. 1 of 1959	2(2)	*Air Navigation and Transport Act, 1959 (Parts III and IV and Schedule) (Commencement) Order, S.I. No. 148 of 1963*
	7(2)	**Hague Protocol to the Warsaw Convention (High Contracting Parties) Order, S.I. No. 184 of 1965**
Air Navigation and Transport Act, No. 6 of 1965	6(2)	*Air Navigation and Transport Act, 1965 (Commencement of Sections 6 and 19) Order, S.I. No. 94 of 1966*
	7	**Air Services Authorisation Order, S.I. No. 95 of 1966**

Statutory Authority	Section	Statutory Instrument
Air Navigation and Transport Act, No. 6 of 1965 (*Cont.*)		*Air Services Authorisation (Amendment) Order, S.I. No. 177 of 1975*
		Air Services Authorisation (Amendment) Order, S.I. No. 201 of 1976
	8	**Air Navigation and Transport Act, 1965 (Section 8) Regulations, S.I. No. 96 of 1966**
Air Navigation and Transport Act, No. 29 of 1973	19(3)	*Air Navigation and Transport Act, 1973 (Commencement) Order, S.I. No. 343 of 1973*
Air Navigation and Transport Acts, 1936 to 1942,		*Subsidy (Aer-Rianta, Teoranta) Order [Vol. XXXVI p. 347] S.R.& O. No. 146 of 1946*
		Subsidy (Aer-Rianta, Teoranta) (No.1) Order [Vol. XXXVI p. 353] S.R.& O. No. 101 of 1947
Air Navigation and Transport Acts, 1936 to 1946,		*Subsidy (Aer-Rianta, Teoranta) (No.2) Order [Vol. XXXVI p. 331] S.R.& O. No. 145 of 1947*
		Subsidy (Aer-Rianta, Teoranta) (No.1) Order, S.I. No. 86 of 1948
Air Navigation and Transport Acts, 1936 to 1950,		*Subsidy (Aer-Rianta, Teoranta) Order, S.I. No. 86 of 1950*
		Subsidy (Aer-Rianta, Teoranta) (No.2) Order, S.I. No. 159 of 1950
		Air Navigation (Personnel Licensing) Order, S.I. No. 33 of 1951
		Air Navigation (Operations) Order, S.I. No. 96 of 1953
		Air Navigation (Personnel Licensing) Order, S.I. No. 353 of 1953
		Air Navigation (Operations) Order, 1953 (Amendment) Order, S.I. No. 118 of 1954
Air Navigation and Transport (Preinspection) Act, No. 18 of 1986	2	*Air Navigation and Transport (Preinspection) Act, 1986 (Competent Authority) Order, S.I. No. 229 of 1986*
Air Navigation (Eurocontrol) Act, No. 15 of 1963	1	*Air Navigation (Eurocontrol) Act, 1963 (Commencement) Order, S.I. No. 291 of 1964*
	4(1)	**Air Navigation (Eurocontrol) Order, S.I. No. 243 of 1985**
		Air Navigation (Eurocontrol) (No.2) Order, S.I. No. 434 of 1985
	12	*Air Navigation (Eurocontrol) (Route Charges) Regulations, S.I. No. 290 of 1971*
		Air Navigation (Eurocontrol) (Route Charges) (Amendment) Regulations, S.I. No. 59 of 1972
		Air Navigation (Eurocontrol) (Route Charges) (Amendment) (No.2) Regulations, S.I. No. 160 of 1972
		Air Navigation (Eurocontrol) (Route Charges) (Amendment) Regulations, S.I. No. 214 of 1973

Statutory Authority	Section	Statutory Instrument
Air Navigation (Eurocontrol) Act, No. 15 of 1963 (*Cont.*)		*Air Navigation (Eurocontrol) (Route Charges) (Amendment) (No.2) Regulations, S.I. No. 290 of 1973*
		Air Navigation (Eurocontrol) (Route Charges) (Amendment) (No.3) Regulations, S.I. No. 327 of 1973
		Air Navigation (Eurocontrol) (Route Charges) (Amendment) Regulations, S.I. No. 249 of 1975
		Air Navigation (Eurocontrol) (Route Charges) (Amendment) Regulations, S.I. No. 83 of 1977
		Air Navigation (Eurocontrol) (Route Charges) (Amendment) Regulations, S.I. No. 35 of 1978
		Air Navigation (Eurocontrol) (Route Charges) (Amendment) Regulations, S.I. No. 76 of 1979
		Air Navigation (Eurocontrol) (Route Charges) Regulations, S.I. No. 78 of 1980
		Air Navigation (Eurocontrol) (Route Charges) (Amendment) Regulations, S.I. No. 104 of 1981
		Air Navigation (Eurocontrol) (Route Charges) (Amendment) (No.2) Regulations, S.I. No. 343 of 1981
		Air Navigation (Eurocontrol) (Route Charges) (Amendment) Regulations, S.I. No. 70 of 1982
		Air Navigation (Eurocontrol) (Route Charges) (Amendment) (No.2) Regulations, S.I. No. 307 of 1982
		Air Navigation (Eurocontrol) (Route Charges) (Amendment) Regulations, S.I. No. 82 of 1983
		Air Navigation (Eurocontrol) (Route Charges) (Amendment) (No.2) Regulations, S.I. No. 418 of 1983
		Air Navigation (Eurocontrol) (Route Charges) (Amendment) Regulations, S.I. No. 435 of 1985
Air Navigation (Eurocontrol) Act, No. 38 of 1983	16(3)	*Air Navigation (Eurocontrol) Act, 1983 (Commencement) Order, S.I. No. 436 of 1985*
Air Navigation (General) Regulations [Vol. IV p. 31] S.R.& O. No. 26 of 1930	88	*Air Navigation (Aircraft Equipment) Directions [Vol. IV p. 151] S.R.& O. No. 263 of 1938*
		Air Navigation (Navigators' Licences) Directions [Vol. XXXVI p. 259] S.R.& O. No. 132 of 1947
Air-Raid Precautions Act, No. 21 of 1939		**Air-Raid Precautions (Register of Designated Premises) Regulations [Vol. XXVI p. 541] S.R.& O. No. 59 of 1940**
	10(2)	**Air-Raid Precautions (Cesser of Certain Scheduled Urban Areas) Order, S.I. No. 63 of 1960**
	26(1)	**Air-Raid Precautions Act, 1939 (Appeals under Sections 22 and 25) Rules [Vol. XXVI p. 487] S.R.& O. No. 89 of 1940**
	36	**Air-Raid Precautions Schemes (Prescribed Provisions) Regulations [Vol. XXVI p. 543] S.R.& O. No. 238 of 1939**

Statutory Authority	Section	Statutory Instrument
Air-Raid Precautions Act, No. 21 of 1939 (*Cont.*)		**Air-Raid Precautions (Approval of Expenditure by Local Authorities) Regulations [Vol. XXVI p. 513] S.R.& O. No. 401 of 1939**
		Air-Raid Precautions Schemes (Prescribed Provisions) (Amendment) Regulations [Vol. XXVI p. 553] S.R.& O. No. 264 of 1941
		Air-Raid Precautions (Approval of Expenditure by Local Authorities) (Amendment) Regulations [Vol. XXVI p. 523] S.R.& O. No. 345 of 1941
		Air-Raid Precautions Schemes (Prescribed Provisions) (Amendment) (No.2) Regulations [Vol. XXVI p. 555] S.R.& O. No. 58 of 1942
		Air-Raid Precautions Schemes (Prescribed Provisions) (Amendment) (No.3) Regulations [Vol. XXVI p. 559] S.R.& O. No. 326 of 1943
		Air-Raid Precautions (Approval of Expenditure by Local Authorities) (Amendment) (No.2) Regulations [Vol. XXVI p. 525] S.R.& O. No. 327 of 1943
		Air-Raid Precautions (Approval of Expenditure by Local Authorities) (Amendment) Regulations, S.I. No. 126 of 1959
	48	**Air-Raid Precautions (Essential Undertakers) Schemes (Prescribed Provisions) Regulations [Vol. XXVI p. 537] S.R.& O. No. 179 of 1940**
		Air-Raid Precautions (Approval of Expenditure by Essential Undertakers) Regulations [Vol. XXVI p. 499] S.R.& O. No. 180 of 1940
		Air-Raid Precautions (Approval of Expenditure by Essential Undertakers) (Amendment) Regulations [Vol. XXVI p. 505] S.R.& O. No. 72 of 1942
		Air-Raid Precautions (Approval of Expenditure by Essential Undertakers) (No.2) Regulations [Vol. XXVI p. 507] S.R.& O. No. 157 of 1944
	58	**Air-Raid Precautions Act, 1939 (Grants under Section 58) Regulations [Vol. XXVI p. 491] S.R.& O. No. 83 of 1940**
		Air-Raid Precautions Act, 1939 (Grants under Section 58) (Amendment) Regulations [Vol. XXVI p. 497] S.R.& O. No. 300 of 1940
	61	**Air-Raid Precautions Equipment (Storage and Loan) Regulations [Vol. XXVI p. 531] S.R.& O. No. 184 of 1940**
	63	*Air-Raid Precautions Equipment (Importation and Sale) Order [Vol. XXVI p. 527] S.R.& O. No. 54 of 1940*
		Air-Raid Shelters (Sale) Order [Vol. XXVI p. 617] S.R.& O. No. 215 of 1940
		Air-Raid Precautions Equipment (Importation and Sale) Order, 1940 (Revocation) Order, S.I. No. 219 of 1960
	64	*Air-Raid Precautions Services (Compensation for Personal Injuries) Scheme [Vol. XXVI p. 563] S.R.& O. No. 319 of 1942*

Air-Raid Precautions Act, No. 21 of 1939 *(Cont.)*

Air-Raid Precautions Services (Compensation for Personal Injuries) Scheme, 1942 (First Amendment) Scheme [Vol. XXVI p. 607] S.R.& O. No. 415 of 1943

Air-Raid Precautions Services (Compensation for Personal Injuries) Scheme, 1942 (Second Amendment) Scheme, S.I. No. 43 of 1949

Air-Raid Precautions Services (Compensation for Personal Injuries) Scheme, 1942 (Third Amendment) Scheme, S.I. No. 50 of 1957

Air-Raid Precautions Services (Compensation for Personal Injuries) Scheme, S.I. No. 104 of 1973

Air-Raid Precautions Services (Compensation for Personal Injuries) Scheme, 1973 (First Amendment) Scheme, S.I. No. 268 of 1973

Air-Raid Precautions Services (Compensation for Personal Injuries) (Second Amendment) Scheme, S.I. No. 179 of 1975

Air-Raid Precautions Services (Compensation for Personal Injuries) (Third Amendment) Scheme, S.I. No. 27 of 1976

Air-Raid Precautions Services (Compensation for Personal Injuries) (Fourth Amendment) Scheme, S.I. No. 183 of 1976

Aliens Act, No. 14 of 1935   5

Aliens Order [Vol. IV p. 187] S.R.& O. No. 108 of 1935

Aliens Order [Vol. XXVI p. 619] S.R.& O. No. 291 of 1939

Aliens Order [Vol. XXVI p. 635] S.R.& O. No. 290 of 1941

Aliens Order [Vol. XXVI p. 639] S.R.& O. No. 169 of 1943

Aliens Order [Vol. XXXVI p. 363] S.R.& O. No. 395 of 1946

Aliens Order, S.I. No. 276 of 1949

Aliens (Amendment) Order, S.I. No. 112 of 1962

Aliens (Amendment) Order, S.I. No. 12 of 1966

Aliens (Amendment) Order, S.I. No. 182 of 1972

Aliens (Amendment) (No.2) Order, S.I. No. 232 of 1972

Aliens Order, S.I. No. 233 of 1974

Aliens (No.2) Order, S.I. No. 234 of 1974

Aliens (No.3) Order, S.I. No. 235 of 1974

Aliens (No.4) Order, S.I. No. 237 of 1974

Aliens (No.5) Order, S.I. No. 239 of 1974

Aliens (No.6) Order, S.I. No. 240 of 1974

Aliens (Amendment) Order, S.I. No. 128 of 1975

Aliens Order, S.I. No. 161 of 1976

Aliens (Amendment) Order, S.I. No. 351 of 1978

Aliens Order, S.I. No. 77 of 1985

Aliens (Amendment) Order, S.I. No. 154 of 1985

Aliens (Amendment) Order, S.I. No. 31 of 1986

Statutory Authority	Section	Statutory Instrument
Aliens Act, No. 14 of 1935 (*Cont.*)	5(7)	*Aliens (Amendment) Order [Vol. IV p. 225] S.R.& O. No. 75 of 1936*
		Aliens Order [Vol. IV p. 229] S.R.& O. No. 141 of 1938
		Aliens Order, 1949 (Revocation) Order, S.I. No. 38 of 1952
		Aliens Orders, 1974 (Revocation) Order, S.I. No. 248 of 1974
	8(6)	*Aliens Act, 1935 (Sections 8 and 9, Appointed Day) Order [Vol. IV p. 213] S.R.& O. No. 604 of 1935*
	10	*Aliens (Exemption) Order, 1935 (Revocation) Order, S.I. No. 113 of 1962*
	10(1)	*Aliens (Exemption) Order [Vol. IV p. 181] S.R.& O. No. 80 of 1935*
	11(1)	**Aliens (Name Licence) Regulations [Vol. IV p. 217] S.R.& O. No. 65 of 1936**
Aliens Restriction Act, No. 12 of 1914		*Aliens Order [Vol. IV p. 233] S.R.& O. No. 2 of 1925*
Anchors and Chain Cables Act, No. 23 of 1899	8	**Chain Cables Order [Vol. IV p. 271] S.R.& O. No. 83 of 1930**
Animal Remedies Act, No. 41 of 1956	5	**Animal Remedies (Control of Sale) Regulations, S.I. No. 258 of 1985**
	7	**Animal Remedies (Control of Oestrogenic Substances) Regulations, S.I. No. 96 of 1962**
		Animal Remedies (Control of Certain Anti-Abortion Vaccines) Regulations, S.I. No. 112 of 1965
		Animal Remedies (Control of Chloramphenicol) Regulations, S.I. No. 10 of 1974
		Animal Remedies (Registration of Manufacturers, Importers and Wholesalers) Regulations, S.I. No. 115 of 1980
		Animal Remedies (Control of Sale) Regulations, S.I. No. 258 of 1985
		Animal Remedies (Control of Sale) (Amendment) Regulations, S.I. No. 235 of 1986
Animals Act, No. 11 of 1985	9	*Animals Act, 1985 (Commencement) Order, S.I. No. 305 of 1985*
Apprenticeship Act, No. 56 of 1931		*Hairdressing Trade (Constitution of Apprenticeship Committee) Regulations [Vol. XXVI p. 743] S.R.& O. No. 338 of 1945*
	2(1)	*Apprenticeship Act (Hairdressing Trade) Special Order [Vol. IV p. 317] S.R.& O. No. 195 of 1934*
		Apprenticeship Act (Furniture Trade) Special Order [Vol. IV p. 305] S.R.& O. No. 271 of 1934
		Apprenticeship Act (Brush and Broom Trade) Special Order [Vol. IV p. 299] S.R.& O. No. 36 of 1935
		Apprenticeship Act (House Painting and Decorating Trade) Special Order [Vol. IV p. 323] S.R.& O. No. 566 of 1935

Statutory Authority	Section	Statutory Instrument
Apprenticeship Act, No. 56 of 1931 *(Cont.)*		*Apprenticeship Act (Furniture Trade) Special Order [Vol. IV p. 311] S.R.& O. No. 292 of 1936*
		Apprenticeship Act (Boot and Shoe Repairing Trade) Special Order [Vol. XXVI p. 657] S.R.& O. No. 153 of 1939
		Apprenticeship Act (Hairdressing Trade) Special Order [Vol. XXVI p. 661] S.R.& O. No. 249 of 1945
	3	*Apprenticeship Act (Hairdressing Trade) Apprenticeship District Order, S.R.& O. No. 196 of 1934*
		Apprenticeship Act (Furniture Trade) Apprenticeship District Order [Vol. IV p. 335] S.R.& O. No. 272 of 1934
		Apprenticeship Act (Brush and Broom Trade) Apprenticeship District Order [Vol. IV p. 329] S.R.& O. No. 37 of 1935
		Apprenticeship Act (House Painting and Decorating Trade) Apprenticeship District Order [Vol. IV p. 351] S.R.& O. No. 567 of 1935
		Apprenticeship Act (Furniture Trade) Apprenticeship District Order [Vol. IV p. 341] S.R.& O. No. 293 of 1936
		Apprenticeship District (Boot and Shoe Repairing Trade) Order [Vol. XXVI p. 729] S.R.& O. No. 154 of 1939
		Apprenticeship District (Hairdressing Trade) Order [Vol. XXVI p. 735] S.R.& O. No. 248 of 1945
	3(1)	*Apprenticeship Act (Hairdressing Trade) Apprenticeship District Order, S.R.& O. No. 196 of 1934*
		Apprenticeship Act (Furniture Trade) Apprenticeship District Order [Vol. IV p. 335] S.R.& O. No. 272 of 1934
		Apprenticeship Act (Brush and Broom Trade) Apprenticeship District Order [Vol. IV p. 329] S.R.& O. No. 37 of 1935
		Apprenticeship Act (House Painting and Decorating Trade) Apprenticeship District Order [Vol. IV p. 351] S.R.& O. No. 567 of 1935
		Apprenticeship Act (Furniture Trade) Apprenticeship District Order [Vol. IV p. 341] S.R.& O. No. 293 of 1936
	4(4)	*Furniture Trade (Constitution of Apprenticeship Committee) Regulations [Vol. IV p. 423] S.R.& O. No. 342 of 1934*
		Hairdressing Trade (Constitution of Apprenticeship Committee) Regulations [Vol. IV p. 443] S.R.& O. No. 353 of 1934
		Brush and Broom Trade (Constitution of Apprenticeship Committee) Regulations [Vol. IV p. 415] S.R.& O. No. 67 of 1935
		House Painting and Decorating Trade (Constitution of Apprenticeship Committee) Regulations [Vol. IV p. 455] S.R.& O. No. 616 of 1935

Statutory Authority	Section	Statutory Instrument
Apprenticeship Act, No. 56 of 1931 *(Cont.)*		*Furniture Trade (Constitution of Apprenticeship Committee) Regulations [Vol. IV p. 433] S.R.& O. No. 320 of 1937*
		Furniture Trade (Constitution of Apprenticeship Committee) (Amendment) Regulations [Vol. XXVI p. 737] S.R.& O. No. 29 of 1939
	6(4)	*Furniture Trade (Constitution of Apprenticeship Committee) Regulations [Vol. IV p. 423] S.R.& O. No. 342 of 1934*
		Hairdressing Trade (Constitution of Apprenticeship Committee) Regulations [Vol. IV p. 443] S.R.& O. No. 353 of 1934
		Brush and Broom Trade (Constitution of Apprenticeship Committee) Regulations [Vol. IV p. 415] S.R.& O. No. 67 of 1935
		House Painting and Decorating Trade (Constitution of Apprenticeship Committee) Regulations [Vol. IV p. 455] S.R.& O. No. 616 of 1935
		Furniture Trade (Constitution of Apprenticeship Committee) Regulations [Vol. IV p. 433] S.R.& O. No. 320 of 1937
	8(4)	*Apprenticeship (Notice of Intention to Make Rules) Regulations [Vol. IV p. 293] S.R.& O. No. 116 of 1935*
	9	*Apprenticeship Committee for the Hairdressing Trade (Dublin) (Confirmation of Rules) Order, S.I. No. 359 of 1952*
		Apprenticeship Committee for the Brush and Broom Trade (Confirmation of Rules) Order, S.I. No. 266 of 1953
		Apprenticeship Committee for the Hairdressing Trade (Dublin) (Confirmation of Rules) Order, S.I. No. 238 of 1956
		Apprenticeship Committee for the Hairdressing Trade (Dublin) (Confirmation of Rules) Order, S.I. No. 114 of 1958
	9(1)	*Apprenticeship Committee for the Hairdressing Trade (Dublin) Confirmation of Rules Order [Vol. IV p. 383] S.R.& O. No. 91 of 1936*
		Apprenticeship Committee for the Brush and Broom Trade Confirmation of Rules Order [Vol. IV p. 355] S.R.& O. No. 39 of 1937
		Apprenticeship Committee for the Furniture Trade (Dublin) Confirmation of Rules Order [Vol. IV p. 3] S.R.& O. No. 168 of 1938
		Apprenticeship Committee for the Hairdressing Trade (Dublin) Confirmation of Rules Order [Vol. IV p. 391] S.R.& O. No. 196 of 1938
		Apprenticeship Committee for the House Painting and Decorating Trade Confirmation of Rules Order [Vol. IV p. 403] S.R.& O. No. 219 of 1938
		Apprenticeship Committee for the House Painting and Decorating Trade (Confirmation of Rules) Order [Vol. XXVI p. 699] S.R.& O. No. 152 of 1939

Apprenticeship Act, No. 56 of 1931
(*Cont.*)

Apprenticeship Act, 1931 Apprenticeship Committee for the Furniture Trade (Dublin) Confirmation of Rules Order [Vol. XXVI p. 645] S.R.& O. No. 278 of 1941

Apprenticeship Committee for the Hairdressing Trade (Dublin) (Confirmation of Rules) Order, (1941) [Vol. XXVI p. 675] S.R.& O. No. 118 of 1942

Apprenticeship Act, 1931 Apprenticeship Committee for the Furniture Trade (Dublin) Confirmation of Rules Order [Vol. XXVI p. 651] S.R.& O. No. 22 of 1943

Apprenticeship Committee for the Hairdressing Trade (Dublin) (Confirmation of Rules) Order [Vol. XXVI p. 685] S.R.& O. No. 118 of 1944

Apprenticeship Act, 1931 Apprenticeship Committee for the Furniture Trade (Dublin) Confirmation of Rules Order [Vol. XXVI p. 669] S.R.& O. No. 344 of 1944

Apprenticeship Committee for the Hairdressing Trade (Dublin) (Confirmation of Rules) Order [Vol. XXVI p. 691] S.R.& O. No. 15 of 1945

Apprenticeship Committee for the House Painting and Decorating Trade (Confirmation of Rules) Order [Vol. XXVI p. 709] S.R.& O. No. 42 of 1945

Apprenticeship Committee for the Hairdressing Trade (Cork) (Confirmation of Rules) Order [Vol. XXXVI p. 409] S.R.& O. No. 313 of 1946

Apprenticeship Committee for the Hairdressing Trade (Dublin) (Confirmation of Rules) Order [Vol. XXXVI p. 427] S.R.& O. No. 374 of 1946

Apprenticeship Committee for the Furniture Trade (Dublin) (Confirmation of Rules) Order [Vol. XXXVI p. 393] S.R.& O. No. 375 of 1946

Apprenticeship Committee for the Furniture Trade (Dublin) (Confirmation of Rules) Order [Vol. XXXVI p. 401] S.R.& O. No. 392 of 1947

Apprenticeship Committee for the Hairdressing Trade (Dublin) (Confirmation of Rules) Order, S.I. No. 66 of 1948

Apprenticeship Committee for the Furniture Trade (Dublin) (Confirmation of Rules) Order, S.I. No. 237 of 1949

Apprenticeship Committee (No.2) for the Furniture Trade (Confirmation of Rules) Order, S.I. No. 219 of 1950

Apprenticeship Committee for the Furniture Trade (Confirmation of Rules) Order, S.I. No. 265 of 1953

Apprenticeship Committee (No.2) for the Furniture Trade (Confirmation of Rules) Order, S.I. No. 267 of 1953

Apprenticeship Committee for the Hairdressing Trade (Cork) (Confirmation of Rules) Order, S.I. No. 270 of 1955

Statutory Authority	Section	Statutory Instrument
Apprenticeship Act, No. 56 of 1931 (*Cont.*)		*Apprenticeship Committee for the Furniture Trade (Dublin) (Confirmation of Rules) Order, S.I. No. 50 of 1956*
		Apprenticeship Committee (No.2) for the Furniture Trade (Confirmation of Rules) Order, S.I. No. 68 of 1956
		Apprenticeship Committee for the House Painting and Decorating Trade (Confirmation of Rules) Order, S.I. No. 127 of 1956
		Apprenticeship Committee for the House Painting and Decorating Trade (Confirmation of Rules) Order, S.I. No. 74 of 1957
		Apprenticeship Committee for the House Painting and Decorating Trade (Confirmation of Rules) (No.2) Order, S.I. No. 120 of 1957
		Apprenticeship Committee for the Furniture Trade (Dublin) (Confirmation of Rules) Order, S.I. No. 254 of 1957
		Apprenticeship Committee (No.2) for the Furniture Trade (Confirmation of Rules) Order, S.I. No. 22 of 1958
		Apprenticeship Committee for the Furniture Trade (Dublin) (Confirmation of Rules) Order, S.I. No. 101 of 1958
		Apprenticeship Committee for the Furniture Trade (Dublin) (Confirmation of Rules) (No.2) Order, S.I. No. 196 of 1958
		Apprenticeship Committee for the Furniture Trade (Dublin) (Confirmation of Rules) (No.3) Order, S.I. No. 209 of 1958
		Apprenticeship Committee (No.2) for the Furniture Trade (Confirmation of Rules) (No.2) Order, S.I. No. 220 of 1958
		Apprenticeship Committee (No.2) for the Furniture Trade (Confirmation of Rules) Order, S.I. No. 36 of 1960
		Apprenticeship Committee for the Furniture Trade (Dublin) (Confirmation of Rules) Order, S.I. No. 41 of 1960
		Apprenticeship Committee for the Hairdressing Trade (Dublin) (Confirmation of Rules) Order, S.I. No. 53 of 1960
		Apprenticeship Committee for the Furniture Trade (Dublin) (Confirmation of Rules) Order, S.I. No. 230 of 1961
		Apprenticeship Committee (No.2) for the Furniture Trade (Confirmation of Rules) Order, S.I. No. 253 of 1961
		Apprenticeship Committee for the Hairdressing Trade (Dublin) (Confirmation of Rules) Order, S.I. No. 68 of 1962
	36	*Apprenticeship (Notice of Intention to Make Rules) Regulations [Vol. IV p. 293] S.R.& O. No. 116 of 1935*

Statutory Authority	Section	Statutory Instrument
Apprenticeship Act, No. 56 of 1931 (*Cont.*)	38(1)	*Apprenticeship Act, 1931 (General) Regulations [Vol. IV p. 277] S.R.& O. No. 341 of 1934*
		Furniture Trade (Constitution of Apprenticeship Committee) Regulations [Vol. IV p. 423] S.R.& O. No. 342 of 1934
		Hairdressing Trade (Constitution of Apprenticeship Committee) Regulations [Vol. IV p. 443] S.R.& O. No. 353 of 1934
		Brush and Broom Trade (Constitution of Apprenticeship Committee) Regulations [Vol. IV p. 415] S.R.& O. No. 67 of 1935
		House Painting and Decorating Trade (Constitution of Apprenticeship Committee) Regulations [Vol. IV p. 455] S.R.& O. No. 616 of 1935
		Furniture Trade (Constitution of Apprenticeship Committee) Regulations [Vol. IV p. 433] S.R.& O. No. 320 of 1937
Apprenticeship Act, No. 39 of 1959	3	*Apprenticeship Act, 1959 (Establishment Day) Order, S.I. No. 75 of 1960*
	7(4)	*Apprenticeship Act, 1959 (Appointed Day) Order, S.I. No. 172 of 1963*
	21(1)	**Apprenticeship Act (Designated Trade) (Motor Mechanic) Order, S.I. No. 28 of 1962**
		Apprenticeship Act (Designated Trade) (Electrician) Order, S.I. No. 29 of 1962
		Apprenticeship Act (Designated Trade) (Furniture Trade) Order, S.I. No. 30 of 1962
		Apprenticeship Act (Designated Trade) (Engineering and Metal Trade) Order, S.I. No. 154 of 1964
		Apprenticeship Act (Designated Trade) (Trade of Building and Construction) Order, S.I. No. 117 of 1965
		Apprenticeship Act (Designated Trade) (Dental Craftsmen) Order, S.I. No. 194 of 1965
		Apprenticeship Act (Designated Trade) (Printing Trade) Order, S.I. No. 24 of 1966
		Apprenticeship Act (Designated Trade) (Printing Trade) (No.2) Order, S.I. No. 207 of 1966
	21(3)	*Apprenticeship Act (Designated Trade) (Printing Trade) Order, 1966 (Revocation) Order, S.I. No. 206 of 1966*
	22(1)	**Apprenticeship Act (Trade of Motor Mechanic) (Apprenticeship District and Apprenticeship Committee) Order, S.I. No. 31 of 1962**
		Apprenticeship Act (Trade of Electrician) (Apprenticeship District and Apprenticeship Committee) Order, S.I. No. 32 of 1962
		Apprenticeship Act (Furniture Trade) (Apprenticeship District and Apprenticeship Committee) Order, S.I. No. 33 of 1962

Statutory Authority	Section	Statutory Instrument
Apprenticeship Act, No. 39 of 1959 (*Cont.*)		**Apprenticeship Act (Engineering and Metal Trade) (Apprenticeship District and Apprenticeship Committee) Order, S.I. No. 155 of 1964**
		Apprenticeship Act (Trade of Building and Construction) (Apprenticeship District and Apprenticeship Committee) Order, S.I. No. 118 of 1965
		Apprenticeship Act (Trade of Dental Craftsman) (Apprenticeship District and Apprenticeship Committee) Order, S.I. No. 224 of 1965
		Apprenticeship Act (Printing Trade) (Apprenticeship District and Apprenticeship Committee) Order, S.I. No. 25 of 1966
		Apprenticeship Act (Printing Trade) (Apprenticeship District and Apprenticeship Committee) (No.2) Order, S.I. No. 208 of 1966
	55	*Apprenticeship Act (Initial Registration Fee) Rules, S.I. No. 53 of 1963*
Appropriation Act, No. 34 of 1924	4	**Pensions – Declarations by Pensioners [Vol. IV p. 489] S.R.& O. No. 3 of 1925**
Appropriation Act, No. 19 of 1962	5	**Pensions Declaration Rules, S.I. No. 134 of 1966**
		Appropriation Act, 1962 (Commencement of Section 5) Order, S.I. No. 135 of 1966
Appropriation Acts		**Pensions – Declarations by Pensioners [Vol. IV p. 489] S.R.& O. No. 3 of 1925**
Approved Investments Act, No. 34 of 1933	15	*Approved Investments (Application for Approval of Securities) Regulations [Vol. IV p. 493] S.R.& O. No. 259 of 1934*
Acquisition of Land (Assessment of Compensation) Act, No. 57 of 1919		**Shannon Electricity (Assessment of Compensation) Rules [Vol. XX p. 397] S.R.& O. No. 83 of 1926**
		Property Values (Arbitrations and Appeals) Rules, S.I. No. 91 of 1961
	3(6)	**Acquisition of Land (Assessment of Compensation) Fees Rules, S.I. No. 49 of 1962**
Arbitration Act, No. 26 of 1954	1(3)	*Arbitration Act, 1954 (Section 12(2) and Part V) (Commencement) Order, S.I. No. 14 of 1960*
	54(1)(a)	**Arbitration (Foreign Awards) Order, S.I. No. 15 of 1960**
	54(1)(b)	**Arbitration (Foreign Awards) (Amendment) Order, S.I. No. 148 of 1964**
Arbitration Act, No. 7 of 1980	3	*Arbitration Act, 1980 (Part IV) (Commencement) Order, S.I. No. 356 of 1980*
		Arbitration Act, 1980 (Part III) (Commencement) Order, S.I. No. 195 of 1981

Statutory Authority	Section	Statutory Instrument
Arbitration Act, No. 7 of 1980 (*Cont.*)	6(2)	*Arbitration Act, 1980 (New York Convention) Order, S.I. No. 175 of 1981*
		Arbitration Act, 1980 (New York Convention) Order, S.I. No. 350 of 1983
	6(3)	**Arbitration Act, 1980 (New York Convention) Order, S.I. No. 350 of 1983**
Army Pensions Act, No. 26 of 1923	6	**Army Pensions (Medical Examination and Re-examination) Regulations [Vol. IV p. 507] S.R.& O. No. 187 of 1933**
	6(1)	**Army Pensions (Medical Examination and Re-examination) Regulations [Vol. IV p. 503] S.R.& O. No. 65 of 1928**
Army Pensions Act, No. 12 of 1927		**Army Pensions (Expenses and Allowances) Regulations, (1927) [Vol. IV p. 549] S.R.& O. No. 3 of 1928**
	5(6)	**Army Pensions Board (Functions and Procedure) Rules [Vol. IV p. 565] S.R.& O. No. 64 of 1928**
		Army Pensions Board (Functions and Procedure) Rules [Vol. IV p. 571] S.R.& O. No. 185 of 1933
	27(1)	**Army Pensions (Forms of Application) Regulations [Vol. IV p. 513] S.R.& O. No. 74 of 1927**
		Army Pensions (Expenses and Allowances) Regulations, (1927) [Vol. IV p. 549] S.R.& O. No. 3 of 1928
		Army Pensions (Investigation of Applications) Regulations [Vol. IV p. 555] S.R.& O. No. 6 of 1928
Army Pensions Act, No. 24 of 1932		*Army Pensions (Form of Service Certificate) Regulations [Vol. IV p. 643] S.R.& O. No. 183 of 1933*
		Army Pensions (Form of Service Certificate) Regulations [Vol. IV p. 707] S.R.& O. No. 278 of 1937
	6(6)	*Military Service Registration Board (Procedure) Rules [Vol. IV p. 627] S.R.& O. No. 182 of 1933*
		Military Service Registration Board (Procedure) Rules [Vol. IV p. 691] S.R.& O. No. 277 of 1937
		Military Service Registration Board (Procedure) Rules, 1937 (Amendment) Rules, S.I. No. 111 of 1954
	9	*Army Pensions Board (Investigation of Applications under Part II of the Army Pensions Act, 1932) Regulations [Vol. IV p. 669] S.R.& O. No. 186 of 1933*
		Army Pensions Board (Investigation of Applications under Part II of the Army Pensions Act, 1932) Regulations [Vol. IV p. 725] S.R.& O. No. 279 of 1937

Statutory Authority	Section	Statutory Instrument
Army Pensions Act, No. 24 of 1932 (*Cont.*)	20	**Army Pensions (Forms of Application) Regulations [Vol. IV p. 583] S.R.& O. No. 181 of 1933**
		Army Pensions (Expenses and Allowances) Regulations [Vol. IV p. 659] S.R.& O. No. 184 of 1933
		Army Pensions (Medical Examination and Re-examination) Regulations [Vol. IV p. 507] S.R.& O. No. 187 of 1933
		Army Pensions (Expenses and Allowances) Regulations, S.I. No. 110 of 1954
	20(4)	*Army Pensions (Form of Service Certificate) Regulations [Vol. IV p. 643] S.R.& O. No. 183 of 1933*
		Army Pensions (Form of Service Certificate) Regulations [Vol. IV p. 707] S.R.& O. No. 278 of 1937
Army Pensions Act, No. 15 of 1937	33	**Army Pensions (Expenses and Allowances) Regulations, S.I. No. 110 of 1954**
	45	**Army Pensions (Expenses and Allowances) Regulations, S.I. No. 110 of 1954**
Army Pensions Act, No. 23 of 1953	9(2)	**Army Pensions (Form of Service Certificate) Regulations, S.I. No. 112 of 1954**
	11	**Army Pensions (Expenses and Allowances) Regulations, S.I. No. 110 of 1954**
Army Pensions Act, No. 12 of 1968	7	**Army Pensions (Increase) Regulations, S.I. No. 191 of 1969**
		Army Pensions (Increase) (No.2) Regulations, S.I. No. 236 of 1969
		Army Pensions (Increase) Regulations, S.I. No. 51 of 1971
		Army Pensions (Increase) Regulations, S.I. No. 101 of 1972
		Army Pensions (Increase) Regulations, S.I. No. 141 of 1973
		Army Pensions (Increase) Regulations, S.I. No. 222 of 1974
		Army Pensions (Increase) Regulations, S.I. No. 8 of 1975
		Army Pensions (Increase) Regulations, S.I. No. 119 of 1976
		Army Pensions (Increase) Regulations, S.I. No. 369 of 1977
		Army Pensions (Increase) Regulations, S.I. No. 143 of 1978
		Army Pensions (Increase) (No.2) Regulations, S.I. No. 378 of 1978
		Army Pensions (Increase) Regulations, S.I. No. 310 of 1980
		Army Pensions (Increase) Regulations, S.I. No. 136 of 1982

Statutory Authority	Section	Statutory Instrument
Army Pensions Act, No. 12 of 1968 (*Cont.*)		**Army Pensions (Increase) (No.2) Regulations, S.I. No. 226 of 1982**
		Army Pensions (Increase) Regulations, S.I. No. 59 of 1984
		Army Pensions (Increase) (No.2) Regulations, S.I. No. 98 of 1984
		Army Pensions (Increase) (No.3) Regulations, S.I. No. 157 of 1984
		Army Pensions (Increase) (No.4) Regulations, S.I. No. 236 of 1984
		Army Pensions (Increase) (No.5) Regulations, S.I. No. 357 of 1984
		Army Pensions (Increase) Regulations, S.I. No. 292 of 1985
		Army Pensions (Increase) (No.2) Regulations, S.I. No. 417 of 1985
Army Pensions Act, No. 21 of 1980	7	**Army Pensions Regulations, S.I. No. 50 of 1981**
		Army Pensions Regulations, S.I. No. 359 of 1985
Arterial Drainage Act, No. 33 of 1925	23(3)	**Arterial Drainage (Membership and Procedure of Joint Committees) (Regulations) Order [Vol. XXVI p. 753] S.R.& O. No. 257 of 1945**
Arterial Drainage Act, No. 3 of 1945	21	*Arterial Drainage Act, 1945, Section 21 Appointed Day [Vol. XXVI p. 763] S.R.& O. No. 49 of 1945*
	23(4)	**Arterial Drainage (Membership and Procedure of Joint Committees) (Regulations) Order [Vol. XXVI p. 753] S.R.& O. No. 257 of 1945**
Arts Act, No. 9 of 1951	3(4)	**Arts Act, 1951 (Additional Function) Order, S.I. No. 8 of 1953**
		Arts Act, 1951 (Additional Function) Order, S.I. No. 155 of 1966
		Arts Act, 1951 (Additional Function) (Amendment) Order, S.I. No. 276 of 1980
Assurance Companies Act, No. 49 of 1909	2	**Insurance (Deposits) Rules [Vol. XXVI p. 767] S.R.& O. No. 78 of 1940**
	2(6)	*Assurance Companies (Deposit of Securities) Rules [Vol. IV p. 805] S.R.& O. No. 63 of 1928*
		Assurance Companies (Deposits in Respect of Mechanically Propelled Vehicle Insurance Business) Rules [Vol. IV p. 809] S.R.& O. No. 140 of 1933
Auctioneers and House Agents Act, No. 10 of 1947	12	**Auctioneers and House Agents Act, 1947 (Accounts Examination and Certificate) Regulations, S.I. No. 10 of 1968**
Bee Pest Prevention (Ireland) Act, No. 34 of 1908		**Bee Pest Prevention (Ireland) (Amendment) Regulations, S.I. No. 254 of 1950**
	6	**Bee Pest Prevention (Ireland) (Amendment) Regulations, S.I. No. 82 of 1971**

Statutory Authority	Section	Statutory Instrument
Bee Pest Prevention (Ireland) Act, No. 34 of 1908 (*Cont.*)	8	**Bee Pest Prevention (Ireland) (Amendment) Regulations, S.I. No. 82 of 1971**
Beet Sugar (Subsidy) Act, No. 37 of 1925	5	**Beet Sugar (Subsidy) Regulations [Vol. V p. 1] S.R.& O. No. 67 of 1926**
Betting Act, No. 38 of 1926	28(1)	*Betting Act, 1926 (Revenue Forms) Regulations [Vol. V p. 29] S.R.& O. No. 60 of 1926*
	28(2)	*Betting Act (District Court and Garda Siochana) Regulations [Vol. V p. 12] S.R.& O. No. 49 of 1926*
Betting Act, No. 27 of 1931	35(1)	**Betting Act (District Court and Garda Siochana) Regulations [Vol. V p. 67] S.R.& O. No. 81 of 1931**
	35(2)	**Betting Act (Revenue Forms) Regulations [Vol. V p. 49] S.R.& O. No. 80 of 1931**
		Betting Act (Revenue Forms) Regulations, S.I. No. 246 of 1954
	38(2)	*Betting Act, 1931 (Commencement) Order [Vol. V p. 45] S.R.& O. No. 79 of 1931*
Blessington and Poula-Phouca Steam Tramway Company Order, 1889	37	**Blessington and Poula-Phouca Steam Tramway Company (Cesser of Powers) Order [Vol. V p. 87] S.R.& O. No. 43 of 1928**
Bord na Gaeilge (Acht um) No. 14 of 1978	21(2)	*Bord na Gaeilge, 1978 (Tosach Feidhme) (An tOrdu fan Acht um) S.I. No. 293 of 1978*
Boundary Survey Act, No. 17 of 1854	11	**Boundaries (Townlands of Ballymartin and Castletown, County Limerick) Order, S.I. No. 238 of 1966**
		Maritime Boundaries (County Borough of Dublin) Order, S.I. No. 122 of 1985
	12	**Boundaries (Townlands of Ballymartin and Castletown, County Limerick) Order, S.I. No. 238 of 1966**
		Maritime Boundaries (County Borough of Dublin) Order, S.I. No. 122 of 1985
Boundary Survey (Ireland) Act, No. 8 of 1859	4	**Boundaries (Townlands of Ballymartin and Castletown, County Limerick) Order, S.I. No. 238 of 1966**
		Maritime Boundaries (County Borough of Dublin) Order, S.I. No. 122 of 1985
Bourn Vincent Memorial Park Act, No. 31 of 1932		**Bourn Vincent Memorial Park Bye-Laws, S.I. No. 234 of 1971**
Bovine Diseases (Levies) Act, No. 26 of 1979	2(2)	*Bovine Diseases (Levies) Regulations, S.I. No. 101 of 1981*
		Bovine Diseases (Levies) Regulations, S.I. No. 400 of 1983
		Bovine Diseases (Levies) Regulations, S.I. No. 272 of 1984

Statutory Authority	Section	Statutory Instrument
Bovine Diseases (Levies) Act, No. 26 of 1979 (*Cont.*)		*Bovine Diseases (Levies) Regulations, S.I. No. 428 of 1985*
	4(2)	**Bovine Diseases (Levies) Act, 1979 (Commencement and Returns) Order, S.I. No. 272 of 1979**
	19	**Bovine Diseases (Levies) Act, 1979 (Commencement and Returns) Order, S.I. No. 272 of 1979**
	19(1)	*Bovine Diseases (Levies) Regulations, S.I. No. 101 of 1981*
		Bovine Diseases (Levies) Regulations, S.I. No. 400 of 1983
		Bovine Diseases (Levies) Regulations, S.I. No. 272 of 1984
		Bovine Diseases (Levies) Regulations, S.I. No. 428 of 1985
	26(2)	**Bovine Diseases (Levies) Act, 1979 (Commencement and Returns) Order, S.I. No. 272 of 1979**
Bread (Regulation of Prices) Act, No. 29 of 1936		*Fancy Bread (Prices) Order [Vol. XXXVI p. 441] S.R.& O. No. 120 of 1946*
		Bread (Prices) Order [Vol. XXXVI p. 433] S.R.& O. No. 350 of 1947
		Bread (Dublin City and County, Bray and Greystones) (Prices) Order, S.I. No. 265 of 1948
		Bread (Prices) Order, S.I. No. 123 of 1951
		Bread (Prices) Order, S.I. No. 183 of 1952
		Bread (Prices) Order, 1952 (Amendment) Order, S.I. No. 268 of 1952
		Bread (Prices) Order, 1952 (Amendment) Order, S.I. No. 83 of 1954
		Bread (Prices) Order, S.I. No. 164 of 1955
		Bread (Prices) Order, 1955 (Revocation) Order, S.I. No. 93 of 1957
	2(1)	*Bread (Standard Price of Flour) (No.1) Order [Vol. V p. 113] S.R.& O. No. 319 of 1936*
		Bread (Standard Price of Flour) (No.9) Order [Vol. V p. 151] S.R.& O. No. 133 of 1938
		Bread (Standard Price of Flour) (No.10) Order [Vol. V p. 157] S.R.& O. No. 221 of 1938
		Bread (Standard Price of Flour) (No.11) Order [Vol. V p. 163] S.R.& O. No. 279 of 1938
		Bread (Standard Price of Flour) (No.12) Order [Vol. XXVIII p. 1] S.R.& O. No. 263 of 1939
		Bread (Standard Price of Flour) (No.13) Order [Vol. XXVIII p. 7] S.R.& O. No. 30 of 1940
		Bread (Standard Price of Flour) (No.14) Order [Vol. XXVIII p. 13] S.R.& O. No. 121 of 1940
		Bread (Standard Price of Flour) (No.16) Order [Vol. XXVIII p. 19] S.R.& O. No. 405 of 1943
	2(3)	*Bread (Standard Price of Flour) (No.2) Order [Vol. V p. 119] S.R.& O. No. 362 of 1936*

Statutory Authority	Section	Statutory Instrument
Bread (Regulation of Prices) Act, No. 29 of 1936 (*Cont.*)		*Bread (Standard Price of Flour) (No.3) Order [Vol. V p. 123] S.R.& O. No. 58 of 1937*
		Bread (Standard Price of Flour) (No.4) Order [Vol. V p. 127] S.R.& O. No. 79 of 1937
		Bread (Standard Price of Flour) (No.5) Order [Vol. V p. 131] S.R.& O. No. 131 of 1937
		Bread (Standard Price of Flour) (No.6) Order [Vol. V p. 137] S.R.& O. No. 151 of 1937
		Bread (Standard Price of Flour) (No.7) Order [Vol. V p. 141] S.R.& O. No. 201 of 1937
		Bread (Standard Price of Flour) (No.8) Order [Vol. V p. 145] S.R.& O. No. 253 of 1937
		Bread (Standard Price of Flour) (No.9) Order [Vol. V p. 151] S.R.& O. No. 133 of 1938
		Bread (Standard Price of Flour) (No.10) Order [Vol. V p. 157] S.R.& O. No. 221 of 1938
		Bread (Standard Price of Flour) (No.11) Order [Vol. V p. 163] S.R.& O. No. 279 of 1938
		Bread (Standard Price of Flour) (No.12) Order [Vol. XXVIII p. 1] S.R.& O. No. 263 of 1939
		Bread (Standard Price of Flour) (No.13) Order [Vol. XXVIII p. 7] S.R.& O. No. 30 of 1940
		Bread (Standard Price of Flour) (No.14) Order [Vol. XXVIII p. 13] S.R.& O. No. 121 of 1940
		Bread (Standard Price of Flour) (No.16) Order [Vol. XXVIII p. 19] S.R.& O. No. 405 of 1943
	3	*Fancy Bread (Prices) Order [Vol. XXVIII p. 23] S.R.& O. No. 265 of 1942*
		Fancy Bread (Prices) (No.2) Order [Vol. XXVIII p. 29] S.R.& O. No. 386 of 1942
		Fancy Bread (Prices) Order [Vol. XXVIII p. 37] S.R.& O. No. 388 of 1943
		Fancy Bread (Prices) Order, 1943 (Amendment) Order [Vol. XXVIII p. 45] S.R.& O. No. 151 of 1944
		Bread (Prices) Order, 1955 (Amendment) Order, S.I. No. 215 of 1956
	3(1)	*Bread (Price) (No.1) Order [Vol. V p. 89] S.R.& O. No. 320 of 1936*
		Bread (Price) (No.2) Order [Vol. V p. 103] S.R.& O. No. 202 of 1937
	3(2)(f)	*Bread (Price) (No.1) (Amendment) Order [Vol. V p. 99] S.R.& O. No. 343 of 1936*
		Bread (Revocation of Prices Orders) Order, S.I. No. 9 of 1949
	4	*Fancy Bread (Prices) Order [Vol. XXVIII p. 23] S.R.& O. No. 265 of 1942*
Bretton Woods Agreements (Amendment) Act, No. 10 of 1969	8	*Bretton Woods Agreements (Amendment) Act, 1969 (Commencement of Sections 4 (1), 5 and 6) Order, S.I. No. 122 of 1969*

Statutory Authority	Section	Statutory Instrument
Broadcasting Authority Act, No. 10 of 1960	2	*Broadcasting Authority Act, 1960 (Establishment Day) Order, S.I. No. 107 of 1960*
	31(1)	*Broadcasting Authority Act, 1960 (Section 31) Order, S.I. No. 7 of 1977*
		Broadcasting Authority Act, 1960 (Section 31) Order, S.I. No. 10 of 1978
		Broadcasting Authority Act, 1960 (Section 31) Order, S.I. No. 16 of 1980
		Broadcasting Authority Act, 1960 (Section 31) Order, S.I. No. 21 of 1981
		Broadcasting Authority Act, 1960 (Section 31) (No.2) Order, S.I. No. 51 of 1981
		Broadcasting Authority Act, 1960 (Section 31) (No.2) Order, S.I. No. 21 of 1982
		Broadcasting Authority Act, 1960 (Section 31) Order, S.I. No. 17 of 1983
	31(1A)	*Broadcasting Authority Act, 1960 (Section 31) Order, S.I. No. 9 of 1979*
		Broadcasting Authority Act, 1960 (Section 31) Order, S.I. No. 9 of 1982
		Broadcasting Authority Act, 1960 (Section 31) Order, S.I. No. 12 of 1984
		Broadcasting Authority Act, 1960 (Section 31) Order, S.I. No. 10 of 1985
		Broadcasting Authority Act, 1960 (Section 31) Order, S.I. No. 10 of 1986
Broadcasting (Offences) Act, No. 35 of 1968	10(2)	*Broadcasting (Offences) Act, 1968 (Commencement) Order, S.I. No. 209 of 1968*
Building Societies Act, No. 38 of 1976	3	*Building Societies Act, 1976 (Commencement) Order, S.I. No. 118 of 1977*
	5	**Building Societies Regulations, S.I. No. 119 of 1977**
	18	**Building Societies Regulations, S.I. No. 119 of 1977**
	20	**Building Societies Regulations, S.I. No. 119 of 1977**
	38(1)	**Building Societies (Prescribed Investments) Regulations, S.I. No. 186 of 1984**
Butter and Margarine Act, No. 21 of 1907		*Public Health (Saorstat Eireann) (Preservatives, etc., in Food) Regulations [Vol. XVIII p. 867] S.R.& O. No. 54 of 1928*
	7	**Public Health (Preservatives, etc., in Food) Regulations 1928 and 1943 (Amendment) Regulations, S.I. No. 46 of 1972**
Canals Act, No. 3 of 1986	20	**Canals Act, 1986 (Vesting Day) Order, S.I. No. 207 of 1986**
Capital Acquisitions Tax Act, No. 8 of 1976	66	**Double Taxation Relief (Taxes on Estates of Deceased Persons and Inheritances and on Gifts) (United Kingdom) Order, S.I. No. 279 of 1978**

Statutory Authority	Section	Statutory Instrument
Capital Gains Tax (Amendment) Act, No. 33 of 1978	3(5)	**Capital Gains Tax (Multipliers) (1979–80) Regulations, S.I. No. 197 of 1979**
		Capital Gains Tax (Multipliers) (1980–81) Regulations, S.I. No. 148 of 1980
		Capital Gains Tax (Multipliers) (1981–82) Regulations, S.I. No. 209 of 1981
		Capital Gains Tax (Multipliers) (1982–83) Regulations, S.I. No. 173 of 1982
		Capital Gains Tax (Multipliers) (1983–84) Regulations, S.I. No. 160 of 1983
		Capital Gains Tax (Multipliers) (1984–85) Regulations, S.I. No. 166 of 1984
		Capital Gains Tax (Multipliers) (1985–86) Regulations, S.I. No. 181 of 1985
		Capital Gains Tax (Multipliers) (1986–87) Regulations, S.I. No. 272 of 1986
Casual Trading Act, No. 43 of 1980	4(10)	**Casual Trading Act, 1980 (Licence Fees) Regulations, S.I. No. 328 of 1984**
	21	*Casual Trading Act, 1980 (Commencement) Order, S.I. No. 43 of 1981*
Cement Act, No. 17 of 1933	2	*Cement Act, 1933 (Date of Commencement) Order [Vol. V p. 169] S.R.& O. No. 121 of 1935*
	6	*Cement Act (Collection of Fees on Import Licences) Regulations [Vol. V p. 173] S.R.& O. No. 122 of 1935*
		Cement (Manufacture and Import) Regulations [Vol. V p. 179] S.R.& O. No. 123 of 1935
		Cement Act, 1933 (Part IV) Regulations Order [Vol. V p. 189] S.R.& O. No. 268 of 1936
	9	*Portland Cement (Standard of Quality) Order, S.I. No. 165 of 1953*
		Portland Cement (Standard of Quality) Order, S.I. No. 264 of 1971
	9(1)	*Portland Cement (Standard of Quality) Order [Vol. V p. 235] S.R.& O. No. 144 of 1938*
	28	*Cement Act (Transport Works) (Aerial Ropeway) Order [Vol. V p. 191] S.R.& O. No. 89 of 1937*
		Cement Act, 1933 (Transport Works) (Railway) Order [Vol. V p. 203] S.R.& O. No. 22 of 1938
	29	*Cement Act, 1933 (Transport Works) (Railway) Order [Vol. V p. 203] S.R.& O. No. 22 of 1938*
	30	**Cement Act, 1933 (Transport Works) (Railway) Order, 1938 (Amendment) Order, S.I. No. 242 of 1963**
		Cement Acts, 1933 and 1938 (Transport Works) (Railway Sidings) Order, 1939 (Amendment) Order, S.I. No. 243 of 1963
Cement Acts, 1933 to 1938		**Cement Acts, 1933 and 1938 (Transport Works) (Railway Sidings) Order [Vol. XXVIII p. 51] S.R.& O. No. 396 of 1939**

Statutory Authority	Section	Statutory Instrument
Cement (Amendment) Act, No. 4 of 1962	2	*Cement (Amendment) Act, 1962 (Commencement) Order, S.I. No. 70 of 1962*
Censorship of Films Act, No. 23 of 1923	11	*Censorship of Films Act, 1923 (Fees) Order [Vol. XXVIII p. 71] S.R.& O. No. 143 of 1944*
		Censorship of Films Act, 1923 (Fees) Order, 1944 (Amendment) Order [Vol. XXXVI p. 449] S.R.& O. No. 319 of 1946
		Censorship of Films Act, 1923 (Fees) Order, 1944 (Amendment) Order, S.I. No. 340 of 1949
		Censorship of Films Act, 1923 (Fees) Order, S.I. No. 4 of 1955
		Censorship of Films Act, 1923 (Amendment of Fees) Order, S.I. No. 115 of 1959
		Censorship of Films Act, 1923 (Amendment of Fees) Order, S.I. No. 218 of 1961
		Censorship of Films (Fees) Order, S.I. No. 72 of 1969
		Censorship of Films (Fees) Order, S.I. No. 253 of 1976
		Censorship of Films (Fees) Order, S.I. No. 120 of 1980
		Censorship of Films (Fees) Order, S.I. No. 113 of 1983
	12	**Censorship of Films (Exhibition of Censor's Certificate) Regulations [Vol. V p. 273] S.R.& O. No. 13 of 1926**
		Censorship of Films (Exhibition of Censor's Certificate) (Amendment) Regulations, S.I. No. 55 of 1961
		Censorship of Films (Exhibition of Censor's Certificate) (Amendment) Regulations, S.I. No. 46 of 1962
		Censorship of Films (Fees) Order, S.I. No. 72 of 1969
		Censorship of Films (Fees) Order, S.I. No. 253 of 1976
		Censorship of Films (Fees) Order, S.I. No. 120 of 1980
		Censorship of Films (Exhibition of Censor's Certificate) (Amendment) Regulations, S.I. No. 68 of 1983
		Censorship of Films (Fees) Order, S.I. No. 113 of 1983
	12(1)	**Censorship of Films (No.1) Order [Vol. V p. 259] S.R.& O. No. 40 of 1925**
		Censorship of Films (No.2) Order [Vol. V p. 263] S.R.& O. No. 41 of 1925
Censorship of Films (Amendment) Act, No. 21 of 1925	7	**Censorship of Films (Exhibition of Censor's Certificate) Regulations [Vol. V p. 273] S.R.& O. No. 13 of 1926**
		Censorship of Films (Exhibition of Censor's Certificate) (Amendment) Regulations, S.I. No. 68 of 1983

Statutory Authority	Section	Statutory Instrument
Censorship of Publications Act, No. 21 of 1929	20(1)	Censorship of Publications Regulations [Vol. V p. 277] S.R.& O. No. 32 of 1930
		Censorship of Publications Regulations, 1930 (Amendment) Order [Vol. V p. 285] S.R.& O. No. 58 of 1930
Censorship of Publications Act, No. 1 of 1946	20	Censorship of Publications Act, 1946, Regulations [Vol. XXXVI p. 453] S.R.& O. No. 254 of 1946
		Censorship of Publications Act, 1946, Regulations [Vol. XXXVI p. 475] S.R.& O. No. 42 of 1947
		Censorship of Publications (Amendment) Regulations, S.I. No. 212 of 1960
		Censorship of Publications Regulations, S.I. No. 292 of 1980
Central Bank Act, No. 22 of 1942	3	Central Bank Act, 1942 (Appointed Day) Order [Vol. XXVIII p. 85] S.R.& O. No. 505 of 1942
	11	**Central Bank of Ireland (Form of Statement of Accounts) (Amendment) Regulations, S.I. No. 148 of 1970**
	42(3)	Banker's Deposit (Permission for Reduced Deposit) Order [Vol. XXVIII p. 77] S.R.& O. No. 542 of 1942
	47	Banker's Licences Regulations [Vol. XXVIII p. 1] S.R.& O. No. 481 of 1942
Central Bank Act, No. 24 of 1971	1	Central Bank Act, 1971 (Commencement) Order, S.I. No. 228 of 1971
	10(4)	**Central Bank Act, 1971 (Condition of Licences) Order, S.I. No. 283 of 1971**
	33	**Central Bank Act (Approval of Scheme of the National Bank of Ireland Limited and The Governor and Company of the Bank of Ireland) Order, S.I. No. 20 of 1972**
		Central Bank Act (Approval of Scheme of the Hibernian Bank of Ireland Limited and The Governor and Company of the Bank of Ireland) Order, S.I. No. 21 of 1972
		Central Bank Act (Approval of Scheme of the Munster and Leinster Bank Limited and Allied Irish Banks Limited) Order, S.I. No. 22 of 1972
		Central Bank Act (Approval of Scheme of the Royal Bank of Ireland Limited and Allied Irish Banks Limited) Order, S.I. No. 24 of 1972
		Central Bank Act (Approval of Scheme of Lombard and Ulster Banking (Ireland) Limited and Lombard and Ulster Banking Ireland Limited) Order, S.I. No. 25 of 1972
		Conditions of Employment (Precision Engineering and Toolmaking Industry) (Exclusion) Regulations, S.I. No. 23 of 1977
		Central Bank Act (Approval of Scheme of Forward Trust (Ireland) Limited and Northern Bank Finance Corporation Limited) Order, S.I. No. 98 of 1986

Statutory Authority	Section	Statutory Instrument
Central Bank Act, No. 24 of 1971 (*Cont.*)		**Central Bank Act (Approval of Scheme of Northern Bank Limited and Northern Bank (Ireland) Limited) Order, S.I. No. 99 of 1986**
		Central Bank Act (Approval of Scheme of Anglo-Irish Bank Limited and City of Dublin plc) Order, S.I. No. 385 of 1986
	49	*Central Bank Act, 1971 (Section 49) (Commencement) Order, S.I. No. 345 of 1971*
	50	*Central Bank Act, 1971 (Section 50) (Commencement) Order, S.I. No. 170 of 1972*
Central Criminal Lunatic Asylum (Ireland) Act, No. 107 of 1845	9	*Dundrum Central Lunatic Asylum (Visiting Committee) Regulations, S.I. No. 425 of 1948*
		Central Mental Hospital (Visiting Committee) Regulations, S.I. No. 231 of 1963
Central Fund Act, No. 4 of 1965	4	**National Bonds Regulations, S.I. No. 55 of 1966**
		National Bonds 1966–67 (Draws for Redemption) Regulations, S.I. No. 56 of 1966
		National Bonds 1966–67 (Draws for Redemption) (Amendment) Regulations, S.I. No. 282 of 1966
Children Act, No. 67 of 1908	75(1)	**Reformatory and Industrial Schools (Average Cost of Maintenance of Youthful Offenders and Children) Order, S.I. No. 231 of 1958**
	130	**Reformatory and Industrial Schools (Average Cost of Maintenance of Youthful Offenders and Children) Order, S.I. No. 231 of 1958**
Children Act, No. 12 of 1941	21	*Children Act, 1941 (Section 21) Regulations [Vol. XXVIII p. 107] S.R.& O. No. 428 of 1942*
		Children Act, 1941 (Section 21) Regulations [Vol. XXVIII p. 111] S.R.& O. No. 260 of 1944
		Children Act, 1941 (Section 21) Regulations [Vol. XXXVI p. 479] S.R.& O. No. 287 of 1946
		Children Act, 1941 (Section 21) Regulations [Vol. XXXVI p. 483] S.R.& O. No. 453 of 1947
		Children Act, 1941 (Section 21) Regulations, S.I. No. 61 of 1951
		Children Act, 1941 (Section 21) Regulations, S.I. No. 80 of 1952
		Children Act, 1941 (Section 21) Regulations, S.I. No. 12 of 1958
		Children Act, 1941 (Section 21) Regulations, S.I. No. 162 of 1964
		Children Act, 1941 (Section 21) Regulations, S.I. No. 58 of 1965

Statutory Authority	Section	Statutory Instrument
Children Act, No. 12 of 1941 (*Cont.*)		*Children Act, 1941 (Section 21) Regulations, S.I. No. 148 of 1968*
		Children Act, 1941 (Section 21) Regulations, S.I. No. 216 of 1969
		Children Act, 1941 (Section 21) Regulations, S.I. No. 125 of 1972
		Children Act, 1941 (Section 21) Regulations, S.I. No. 326 of 1973
		Children Act, 1941 (Section 41) Regulations, S.I. No. 144 of 1974
		Children Act, 1941 (Section 21) Regulations, S.I. No. 378 of 1974
		Children Act, 1941 (Section 21) Regulations, S.I. No. 195 of 1976
		Children Act, 1941 (Section 21) Regulations, S.I. No. 82 of 1977
		Children Act, 1941 (Section 21) Regulations, 1977 (No.2 of 1977) S.I. No. 151 of 1977
		Children Act, 1941 (Section 21) Regulations, S.I. No. 210 of 1978
		Children Act, 1941 (Section 21) Regulations, S.I. No. 190 of 1979
		Children Act, 1941 (Section 21) Regulations, 1979 (No.2 of 1979) S.I. No. 397 of 1979
		Children Act, 1941 (Section 21) Regulations, S.I. No. 212 of 1980
		Children Act, 1941 (Section 21) Regulations, S.I. No. 96 of 1981
		Children Act, 1941 (Section 21) Regulations, S.I. No. 83 of 1982
		Children Act, 1941 (Section 21) Regulations, S.I. No. 44 of 1983
		Children Act, 1941 (Section 21) Regulations, S.I. No. 182 of 1984
	31	*Children Act, 1941 (Commencement of Sections 1, 6, 7, 9 to 11, 13, 16 to 20 and 23 to 31) Order [Vol. XXVIII p. 99] S.R.& O. No. 271 of 1942*
		Children Act, 1941 (Commencement of Sections 2 to 5, 8, 12, 14, 15, 21 and 22) Order [Vol. XXVIII p. 103] S.R.& O. No. 427 of 1942
Children (Amendment) Act, No. 6 of 1949	3(2)	*Children (Amendment) Act, 1949 (Commencement of Part II) Order, S.I. No. 231 of 1949*
Children's Allowance Act, No. 2 of 1944		*Children's Allowances Act, 1944 (General) Regulations [Vol. XXVIII p. 115] S.R.& O. No. 137 of 1944*
	2(1)	**Children's Allowances Act, 1944 (Section 2) Order [Vol. XXVIII p. 159] S.R.& O. No. 80 of 1944**
	20	**Social Welfare (Children's Allowances) (General) (Amendment) Regulations, S.I. No. 197 of 1974**
		Social Welfare (Children's Allowances) (General) (Amendment) Regulations, S.I. No. 325 of 1978

Statutory Authority	Section	Statutory Instrument
Children's Allowance Act, No. 2 of 1944 (*Cont.*)	20(1)	*Children's Allowances Act, 1944 (Qualifying Dates) Regulations [Vol. XXVIII p. 165] S.R.& O. No. 81 of 1944*
	20(1)(k)	**Social Welfare (Payments to Appointed Persons) Regulations, S.I. No. 143 of 1973**
Children's Allowances Acts, 1944 and 1946,		*Children's Allowances (General) Regulations [Vol. XXXVI p. 487] S.R.& O. No. 116 of 1946*
		Children's Allowances (Qualifying Dates) (No.1) Regulations [Vol. XXXVI p. 521] S.R.& O. No. 140 of 1946
		Children's Allowances (Qualifying Dates) (No.2) Regulations [Vol. XXXVI p. 527] S.R.& O. No. 285 of 1946
Children's Allowances Acts, 1944 to 1952		**Children's Allowances (Qualifying Dates) (No.2) Regulations, 1946 (Amendment) Regulations, S.I. No. 204 of 1952**
		Social Welfare (Children's Allowances) (General) Regulations, S.I. No. 222 of 1952
		Social Welfare (Children's Allowances) (Normal Residence) Rules, S.I. No. 224 of 1952
Children's Allowances (Amendment) Act, No. 8 of 1946	2	*Children's Allowances (Amendment) Act, 1946 (Commencement) Order [Vol. XXXVI p. 533] S.R.& O. No. 153 of 1946*
	5(2)	*Children's Allowances (Normal Residence) Rules [Vol. XXXVI p. 537] S.R.& O. No. 152 of 1946*
		Children's Allowances (Normal Residence) Rules [Vol. XXXVI p. 543] S.R.& O. No. 168 of 1947
		Social Welfare (Children's Allowances) (Normal Residence) Rules, S.I. No. 120 of 1967
		Social Welfare (Children's Allowances) (Normal Residence) Rules, S.I. No. 198 of 1974
City and County Management (Amendment) Act, No. 12 of 1955	9	**Public Bodies (Temporary Provisions) Order, S.I. No. 155 of 1955**
		Public Bodies (Temporary Provisions) Order, S.I. No. 174 of 1960
		Public Bodies (Amendment) Order, S.I. No. 167 of 1975
		Public Bodies (Amendment) Order, S.I. No. 173 of 1977
		Public Bodies (Amendment) (No.2) Order, S.I. No. 353 of 1977
		Public Bodies (Amendment) (No.2) Order, S.I. No. 271 of 1979
		Public Bodies (Amendment) Order, S.I. No. 17 of 1982
		Public Bodies (Amendment) Order, S.I. No. 66 of 1983
		Public Bodies (Amendment) (No.2) Order, S.I. No. 415 of 1983

Statutory Authority	Section	Statutory Instrument
City and County Management (Amendment) Act, No. 12 of 1955 (*Cont.*)		**Public Bodies (Amendment) Order, S.I. No. 342 of 1984**
		Public Bodies (Amendment) Order, S.I. No. 340 of 1985
	10	**Public Bodies (Temporary Provisions) Order, S.I. No. 155 of 1955**
		Public Bodies (Temporary Provisions) Order, S.I. No. 174 of 1960
		Public Bodies (Amendment) Order, S.I. No. 167 of 1975
		Public Bodies (Amendment) (No.2) Order, S.I. No. 353 of 1977
		Public Bodies (Amendment) (No.2) Order, S.I. No. 271 of 1979
		Public Bodies (Amendment) Order, S.I. No. 17 of 1982
		Public Bodies (Amendment) Order, S.I. No. 66 of 1983
		Public Bodies (Amendment) (No.2) Order, S.I. No. 415 of 1983
		Public Bodies (Amendment) Order, S.I. No. 342 of 1984
	13	**County Management (Kilkenny and Waterford) Order, S.I. No. 3 of 1965**
		County Management (Tipperary North Riding and Tipperary South Riding) Order, S.I. No. 8 of 1969
		County Management (Carlow and Kildare) Order, S.I. No. 305 of 1974
		County Management (Sligo and Leitrim) Order, S.I. No. 220 of 1976
		County Management (Longford and Westmeath) Order, S.I. No. 296 of 1976
		County Management (Laoighis and Offaly) Order, S.I. No. 391 of 1981
	21	**Public Bodies (Temporary Provisions) Order, S.I. No. 174 of 1960**
		Public Bodies (Amendment) Order, S.I. No. 167 of 1975
		Public Bodies (Amendment) Order, S.I. No. 173 of 1977
		Public Bodies (Amendment) (No.2) Order, S.I. No. 353 of 1977
		Public Bodies (Amendment) (No.2) Order, S.I. No. 271 of 1979
		Public Bodies (Amendment) Order, S.I. No. 17 of 1982
		Public Bodies (Amendment) Order, S.I. No. 66 of 1983
		Public Bodies (Amendment) (No.2) Order, S.I. No. 415 of 1983

Statutory Authority	Section	Statutory Instrument
City and County Management (Amendment) Act, No. 12 of 1955 *(Cont.)*		**Public Bodies (Amendment) Order, S.I. No. 342 of 1984**
		Public Bodies (Amendment) Order, S.I. No. 340 of 1985
	24	*City and County Management (Amendment) Act, 1955 (Date of Commencement) Order, S.I. No. 130 of 1955*
		City and County Management (Amendment) Act, 1955 (Commencement) Order, S.I. No. 303 of 1956
		City and County Management (Amendment) Act, 1955 (Commencement) Order, S.I. No. 134 of 1957
Civil Service Commissioners Act, No. 45 of 1956	1(2)	*Civil Service Commissioners Act, 1956 (Commencement) Order, S.I. No. 17 of 1957*
Civil Service Regulation Act, No. 5 of 1924	9(1)	*Civil Service (Stabilisation of Bonus) Regulations [Vol. XXVIII p. 203] S.R.& O. No. 177 of 1940*
		Civil Service (Stabilisation of Bonus) (Amendment) Regulations [Vol. XXVIII p. 211] S.R.& O. No. 258 of 1942
		Civil Service (Emergency Bonus) Regulations [Vol. XXVIII p. 175] S.R.& O. No. 1 of 1943
		Civil Service (Emergency Bonus) Regulations [Vol. XXVIII p. 185] S.R.& O. No. 43 of 1944
		Civil Service (Bonus) Regulations [Vol. XXVIII p. 169] S.R.& O. No. 364 of 1944
		Civil Service (Emergency Bonus) Regulations [Vol. XXVIII p. 195] S.R.& O. No. 345 of 1945
		Civil Service (Remuneration) Regulations [Vol. XXXVI p. 547] S.R.& O. No. 182 of 1947
		Civil Service (Remuneration) Regulations, S.I. No. 6 of 1951
		Civil Service (Remuneration) (No.2) Regulations, S.I. No. 288 of 1951
		Civil Service (Remuneration) Regulations, S.I. No. 250 of 1953
		Civil Service (Remuneration) Regulations, S.I. No. 24 of 1955
		Civil Service (Remuneration) Regulations, S.I. No. 95 of 1956
Civil Service Regulation Act, No. 46 of 1956	22(2)	*Civil Service Regulations 1924 (Revocation) Regulations, S.I. No. 27 of 1957*
	23(2)	*Civil Service Regulation Act, 1956 (Commencement) Order, S.I. No. 18 of 1957*
Clean Wool Act, No. 27 of 1947	6	**Clean Wool Act, 1947 (Section 6) (No.1) Order [Vol. XXXVI p. 587] S.R.& O. No. 273 of 1947**
	14	*Clean Wool Act, 1947 (Commencement) Order [Vol. XXXVI p. 583] S.R.& O. No. 272 of 1947*

Statutory Authority	Section	Statutory Instrument
Coal Mines Act, No. 50 of 1911	61	*Coal Mines (Storage and Use of Explosives) Order, S.I. No. 288 of 1952*
	86	*Coal Mines (Diesel Locomotive) General Regulations, S.I. No. 3 of 1952*
		Metalliferous Mines (General) Regulations, S.I. No. 273 of 1956
		Quarries (General) Regulations, S.I. No. 274 of 1956
Coinage Act, No. 14 of 1926	2(4)	*Coinage (Dimensions and Designs) Order [Vol. V p. 315] S.R.& O. No. 76 of 1928*
		Coinage (Dimensions and Designs) Order [Vol. V p. 321] S.R.& O. No. 78 of 1938
Coinage Act, No. 32 of 1950	2	*Coinage Act, 1950 (Commencement) Order, S.I. No. 111 of 1951*
	5(6)	**Coinage (Dimensions and Designs) Regulations, S.I. No. 137 of 1951**
		Coinage (Dimensions and Designs) (Silver Coin in Respect of the Year 1966) Regulations, S.I. No. 71 of 1966
	11	**Coinage (Calling In) Order, S.I. No. 12 of 1969**
		Coinage (Calling In) (No.2) Order, S.I. No. 113 of 1969
Combat Poverty Agency Act, No. 14 of 1986	2	*Combat Poverty Agency Act, 1986 (Establishment Day) Order, S.I. No. 308 of 1986*
Commissioners for Oaths (Diplomatic and Consular) Act, No. 9 of 1931		*Diplomatic and Consular Fees (Amendment) Regulations, S.I. No. 365 of 1948*
		Diplomatic and Consular Fees Regulations, S.I. No. 263 of 1956
	3	*Diplomatic and Consular Fees (Amendment) Regulations, S.I. No. 334 of 1974*
		Diplomatic and Consular Fees (Amendment) Regulations, S.I. No. 268 of 1975
		Diplomatic and Consular Fees (Amendment) Regulations, S.I. No. 272 of 1976
		Diplomatic and Consular Fees (Amendment) Regulations, S.I. No. 95 of 1980
		Diplomatic and Consular Fees (Amendment) Regulations, S.I. No. 260 of 1981
		Diplomatic and Consular Fees (Amendment) Regulations, S.I. No. 6 of 1982
		Diplomatic and Consular Fees Regulations, S.I. No. 344 of 1982
	3(1)	*Commissioners for Oaths (Diplomatic and Consular) Fees Regulations [Vol. V p. 325] S.R.& O. No. 234 of 1934*
Companies Act, No. 33 of 1963	1(2)	*Companies Act, 1963 (Commencement) Order, S.I. No. 41 of 1964*
	44	*Companies (Stock Exchange) Order, S.I. No. 43 of 1964*

Statutory Authority	Section	Statutory Instrument
Companies Act, No. 33 of 1963 (*Cont.*)		**Companies (Stock Exchange) Order, S.I. No. 198 of 1975**
	45	*Companies (Stock Exchange) Order, S.I. No. 43 of 1964*
		Companies (Stock Exchange) Order, S.I. No. 198 of 1975
	47	**Companies (Forms) Order, S.I. No. 45 of 1964**
	99	**Companies (Forms) Order, S.I. No. 45 of 1964**
	101	**Companies (Forms) Order, S.I. No. 45 of 1964**
	103	**Companies (Fees) Order, S.I. No. 44 of 1964**
		Companies (Fees) Order, S.I. No. 64 of 1976
		Companies (Fees) Order, S.I. No. 400 of 1980
		Companies (Fees) Order, S.I. No. 259 of 1983
	111	**Companies (Forms) Order, S.I. No. 45 of 1964**
	112	**Companies (Fees) Order, S.I. No. 44 of 1964**
		Companies (Fees) Order, S.I. No. 64 of 1976
		Companies (Fees) Order, S.I. No. 400 of 1980
		Companies (Fees) Order, S.I. No. 259 of 1983
	128	**Companies (Forms) Order, S.I. No. 45 of 1964**
	169	**Companies (Fees) Order, S.I. No. 44 of 1964**
	204	**Companies (Forms) Order, S.I. No. 45 of 1964**
	250	**Companies (Recognition of Countries) Order, S.I. No. 42 of 1964**
	352	**Companies (Forms) Order, S.I. No. 45 of 1964**
	353	**Companies (Forms) Order, S.I. No. 45 of 1964**
	354	**Companies (Forms) Order, S.I. No. 45 of 1964**
	361	*Companies (Stock Exchange) Order, S.I. No. 43 of 1964*
		Companies (Forms) Order, S.I. No. 45 of 1964
		Companies (Stock Exchange) Order, S.I. No. 198 of 1975
	362	*Companies (Stock Exchange) Order, S.I. No. 43 of 1964*
		Companies (Stock Exchange) Order, S.I. No. 198 of 1975
	364	**Companies (Forms) Order, S.I. No. 45 of 1964**
	367	**Companies (Recognition of Countries) Order, S.I. No. 42 of 1964**
	388	**Companies (Recognition of Countries) Order, S.I. No. 42 of 1964**
	389	**Companies (Recognition of Countries) Order, S.I. No. 42 of 1964**
	395	*Companies (Fees) Order, S.I. No. 64 of 1976*
		Companies (Fees) Order, S.I. No. 400 of 1980
		Companies (Fees) Order, S.I. No. 259 of 1983

Statutory Authority	Section	Statutory Instrument
Companies Act, No. 33 of 1963 (*Cont.*)	396	**Companies (Forms) Order, S.I. No. 45 of 1964** **Companies (Forms) Order, S.I. No. 256 of 1982** **Companies (Forms) Order, S.I. No. 289 of 1983**
	Sch. VI par. 28	*Companies (Stock Exchange) Order, S.I. No. 43 of 1964* **Companies (Stock Exchange) Order, S.I. No. 198 of 1975**
Companies (Amendment) Act, No. 31 of 1977	1(1)	**Companies (Amendment) Act, 1977 (Designation of Stock Exchange Nominee) Regulations, S.I. No. 122 of 1979**
	11(3)	*Companies (Amendment) Act, 1977 (Commencement) Order, S.I. No. 95 of 1978*
Companies (Amendment) Act, No. 10 of 1982	3	**Companies (Forms) Order, S.I. No. 256 of 1982**
	24(3)	*Companies (Amendment) Act, 1982 (Commencement) Order, S.I. No. 255 of 1982*
Companies (Amendment) Act, No. 13 of 1983	1(3)	*Companies (Amendment) Act, 1983 (Commencement) Order, S.I. No. 288 of 1983*
	59	**Companies (Forms) Order, S.I. No. 289 of 1983**
Companies (Amendment) Act, No. 25 of 1986	25(4)	*Companies (Amendment) Act, 1986 (Commencement) Order, S.I. No. 257 of 1986*
	25(5)	*Companies (Amendment) Act, 1986 (Commencement) Order, S.I. No. 257 of 1986*
Companies (Consolidation) Act, No. 69 of 1908	118	*Companies Acts Forms Order [Vol. V p. 339] S.R.& O. No. 12 of 1923* *Companies Acts Forms No.1 Order [Vol. V p. 347] S.R.& O. No. 19 of 1924* *Companies Acts Forms No.1 Order [Vol. V p. 351] S.R.& O. No. 9 of 1925*
	118(2)	*Companies Acts, 1908 to 1959 (Forms) Order, S.I. No. 16 of 1960*
Companies (Particulars as Directors) Act, No. 28 of 1917	2(1)	*Companies Acts Forms No.1 Order [Vol. V p. 347] S.R.& O. No. 19 of 1924*
Conditions of Employment Act, No. 2 of 1936	1(2)	*Conditions of Employment Act, 1936 (Date of Commencement) Order [Vol. V p. 359] S.R.& O. No. 139 of 1936*
	11	**Conditions of Employment (No.1) Order [Vol. V p. 417] S.R.& O. No. 167 of 1936** *Conditions of Employment (Prescribed Abstract) Order [Vol. V p. 555] S.R.& O. No. 164 of 1937* *Conditions of Employment (Prescribed Abstract) Regulations [Vol. XXXVI p. 591] S.R.& O. No. 300 of 1946* **Conditions of Employment (Prescribed Abstract) Regulations, S.I. No. 6 of 1964**

Statutory Authority	Section	Statutory Instrument
Conditions of Employment Act, No. 2 of 1936 (*Cont.*)	15(1)	**Conditions of Employment (Manufacture of Paper) (Proportion of Young Persons to other Workers) Regulations [Vol. V p. 615] S.R.& O. No. 228 of 1938**
	17(1)	**Conditions of Employment (Men's and Boys' Tailoring) (Prohibition of Employment of Outworkers) Order [Vol. V p. 589] S.R.& O. No. 270 of 1937**
	17(2)	**Conditions of Employment (Men's and Boys' Tailoring) (Prohibition of Employment of Outworkers) Order [Vol. V p. 589] S.R.& O. No. 270 of 1937**
	29	**Conditions of Employment (Telegraphic Construction etc.) (Exclusion) Regulations [Vol. XXVIII p. 243] S.R.& O. No. 71 of 1940**
		Conditions of Employment (Malting) (Exclusion) Regulations [Vol. XXVIII p. 235] S.R.& O. No. 152 of 1940
		Conditions of Employment (Boilermen and Enginemen) (Exclusion and Period of Rest) Regulations [Vol. XXVIII p. 221] S.R.& O. No. 240 of 1942
		Conditions of Employment (Turf Industry) (Exclusion) Order [Vol. XXXVI p. 617] S.R.& O. No. 97 of 1947
		Conditions of Employment (Ship Repairing Industry, Dublin) (Exclusion) Order [Vol. XXXVI p. 613] S.R.& O. No. 175 of 1947
		Conditions of Employment (Match Manufacturing Industry) (Exclusion) Regulations, S.I. No. 90 of 1951
		Conditions of Employment (Turf Industry) (Exclusion) Order, S.I. No. 154 of 1951
		Conditions of Employment (Woollen and Worsted Industry) (Exclusion) Regulations, S.I. No. 371 of 1953
		Conditions of Employment (Linen and Cotton Textile Industry) (Exclusion and Young Persons deemed to be Adult Workers) Regulations, S.I. No. 272 of 1954
		Conditions of Employment (Rayon Industry) (Exclusion and Young Persons deemed to be Adult Workers) Regulations, S.I. No. 156 of 1955
		Conditions of Employment (Rubber Footwear Industry) (Exclusion) Regulations, S.I. No. 36 of 1959
		Conditions of Employment (Nylon, Rayon and Terylene Yarn Winding Industry) (Exclusion) Regulations, S.I. No. 120 of 1959
		Conditions of Employment (Peat Moss Flower Pots Industry) (Exclusion) Regulations, S.I. No. 245 of 1960
		Conditions of Employment (Biscuit and Chocolate Confectionery Industry) (Exclusion) Regulations, S.I. No. 252 of 1960

Statutory Authority	Section	Statutory Instrument

Conditions of Employment Act,
No. 2 of 1936 (*Cont.*)

Conditions of Employment (Glass Cloth Industry) (Exclusion) Regulations, S.I. No. 68 of 1961

Conditions of Employment (Chewing Gum Industry) (Exclusion) Regulations, S.I. No. 69 of 1961

Conditions of Employment (Frozen Sugar Confectionery) (Exclusion) Regulations, S.I. No. 82 of 1961

Conditions of Employment (Rope Industry) (Exclusion) Regulations, S.I. No. 119 of 1961

Conditions of Employment (Woollen and Cotton Garments Industry) (Exclusion) Regulations, S.I. No. 176 of 1961

Conditions of Employment (Terylene Yarns Industry) (Exclusion) Regulations, S.I. No. 184 of 1961

Conditions of Employment (Crown Cork Industry) (Exclusion) Regulations, S.I. No. 190 of 1961

Conditions of Employment (Cigarette Industry) (Exclusion) Regulations, S.I. No. 192 of 1961

Conditions of Employment (Plastic Packaging Industry) (Exclusion) Regulations, S.I. No. 271 of 1961

Conditions of Employment (Carpet Weaving Industry) (Exclusion) Regulations, S.I. No. 282 of 1961

Conditions of Employment (Glass-fibre Cloth Industry) (Exclusion) Regulations, S.I. No. 292 of 1961

Conditions of Employment (Worsted Spinning Industry) (Exclusion) Regulations, S.I. No. 1 of 1962

Conditions of Employment (Instant Potato Flake Industry) (Exclusion) Regulations, S.I. No. 63 of 1962

Conditions of Employment (Electric Lamp Industry) (Exclusion) Regulations, S.I. No. 65 of 1962

Conditions of Employment (Paper Sacks Industry) (Exclusion) Regulations, S.I. No. 125 of 1962

Conditions of Employment (Laundry Industry at Whitegate) (Exclusion) Regulations, S.I. No. 127 of 1962

Conditions of Employment (Accelerated Freeze Drying Industry) (Exclusion) Regulations, S.I. No. 129 of 1962

Conditions of Employment (Woollen Industry at Foxford) (Exclusion) Regulations, S.I. No. 149 of 1962

Conditions of Employment (Hairdressing Products Industry) (Exclusion) Regulations, S.I. No. 174 of 1962

Conditions of Employment (Food Processing Industry) (Exclusion) Regulations, S.I. No. 181 of 1962

Conditions of Employment Act,
No. 2 of 1936 (*Cont.*)

Conditions of Employment (Accelerated Freeze Drying and Air-Drying Industry) (Exclusion) Regulations, S.I. No. 196 of 1962

Conditions of Employment (Celluloid Spectacle Frames) (Exclusion) Regulations, S.I. No. 234 of 1962

Conditions of Employment (Sugar Packaging Industry) (Exclusion) Regulations, S.I. No. 46 of 1963

Conditions of Employment (Braids Industry) (Exclusion) Regulations, S.I. No. 85 of 1963

Conditions of Employment (Veneer Industry) (Exclusion) Regulations, S.I. No. 86 of 1963

Conditions of Employment (Fruit and Vegetable Canning and Freezing Industry) (Exclusion) Regulations, S.I. No. 130 of 1963

Conditions of Employment (Iron Castings Industry) (Exclusion) Regulations, S.I. No. 133 of 1963

Conditions of Employment (Men's Clothing and Shirt Making Industry) (Exclusion) Regulations, S.I. No. 140 of 1963

Conditions of Employment (Knitted Rayon Lining) (Exclusion) Regulations, S.I. No. 195 of 1963

Conditions of Employment (Carpet Weaving Industry) (Exclusion) Regulations, S.I. No. 197 of 1963

Conditions of Employment (Woollen Industry at Tralee) (Exclusion) Regulations, S.I. No. 198 of 1963

Conditions of Employment (Moquette Weaving Industry) (Exclusion) Order, S.I. No. 251 of 1963

Conditions of Employment (Sugar Confectionery Industry) (Exclusion) Regulations, S.I. No. 2 of 1964

Conditions of Employment (Jute Industry) (Exclusion) Regulations, S.I. No. 92 of 1964

Conditions of Employment (Surgical Instruments Industry) (Exclusion) Regulations, S.I. No. 205 of 1964

Conditions of Employment (Beer Bottling Industry) (Exclusion) Regulations, S.I. No. 207 of 1964

Conditions of Employment (Raschel Knitting Machines Industry) (Exclusion) Regulations, S.I. No. 208 of 1964

Conditions of Employment (Packing of Flower Pots) (Exclusion) Regulations, S.I. No. 233 of 1964

Conditions of Employment (Plastic Moulding) (Exclusion) Regulations, S.I. No. 254 of 1964

Conditions of Employment (Ladies Clothes and Household Piece Goods) (Exclusion) Regulations, S.I. No. 261 of 1964

Conditions of Employment (Pharmaceutical and Allied Products Industry) (Exclusion) Regulations, S.I. No. 262 of 1964

Statutory Authority	Section	Statutory Instrument

Conditions of Employment Act,
No. 2 of 1936 (*Cont.*)

Conditions of Employment (Chocolate and Sweets Industry) (Exclusion) Regulations, S.I. No. 263 of 1964

Conditions of Employment (Calendaring of Printed Sheets) (Exclusion) Regulations, S.I. No. 283 of 1964

Conditions of Employment (Ship Building and Repairing Industry) (Exclusion) Regulations, S.I. No. 295 of 1964

Conditions of Employment (Tufted Carpeting) (Exclusion) Regulations, S.I. No. 25 of 1965

Conditions of Employment (Knitted Garments Industry) (Exclusion) Regulations, S.I. No. 45 of 1965

Conditions of Employment (Certain Electric Fittings) (Exclusion) Regulations, S.I. No. 46 of 1965

Conditions of Employment (Plastic Moulding) (Exclusion) Regulations, S.I. No. 53 of 1965

Conditions of Employment (Flax Spinning Industry) (Exclusion) Regulations, S.I. No. 151 of 1965

Conditions of Employment (Polythene Film Bags) (Exclusion) Regulations, S.I. No. 152 of 1965

Conditions of Employment (Ice Cones and Wafers) (Exclusion) Regulations, S.I. No. 160 of 1965

Conditions of Employment (Electric Motors) (Exclusion) Regulations, S.I. No. 181 of 1965

Conditions of Employment (Electronic Components Industry at Shannon Industrial Estate) (Exclusion) Regulations, S.I. No. 204 of 1965

Conditions of Employment (Curtain Materials and Bedspreads) (Exclusion) Regulations, S.I. No. 215 of 1965

Conditions of Employment (Printing and Box-Making Industry) (Exclusion) Regulations, S.I. No. 222 of 1965

Conditions of Employment (Paper Bags Industry) (Exclusion) Regulations, S.I. No. 247 of 1965

Conditions of Employment (Rubber Soles) (Exclusion) Regulations, S.I. No. 259 of 1965

Conditions of Employment (Toilet Rolls) (Exclusion) Regulations, S.I. No. 260 of 1965

Conditions of Employment (Plastic Moulding) (Exclusion) (No.2) Regulations, S.I. No. 20 of 1966

Conditions of Employment (Electronic Components Industry) (Exclusion) Regulations, S.I. No. 29 of 1966

Conditions of Employment (Electronic Components Industry) (Exclusion) Regulations, S.I. No. 81 of 1966

Conditions of Employment (Golf Balls) (Exclusion) Regulations, S.I. No. 56 of 1967

Conditions of Employment Act, No. 2 of 1936 (*Cont.*)		Conditions of Employment (Nylon Stockings Industry) (Exclusion) Regulations, S.I. No. 66 of 1967
		Conditions of Employment (Electronic Components Industry) (Exclusion) Regulations, S.I. No. 136 of 1967
		Conditions of Employment (Tobacco Pouches) (Exclusion) Regulations, S.I. No. 137 of 1967
		Conditions of Employment (Processing and Packaging of Tobacco) (Exclusion) Regulations, S.I. No. 138 of 1967
		Conditions of Employment (Yarn-dyeing Industry) (Exclusion) Regulations, S.I. No. 178 of 1967
		Conditions of Employment (Wool Top Industry) (Exclusion) Regulations, S.I. No. 179 of 1967
		Conditions of Employment (Jersey Fabrics Industry) (Exclusion) Regulations, S.I. No. 180 of 1967
		Conditions of Employment (Jetty Construction) (Exclusion) Regulations, S.I. No. 195 of 1967
		Conditions of Employment (Carding and Spinning of Cotton and Synthetic Fibres) (Exclusion) Regulations, S.I. No. 201 of 1967
		Conditions of Employment (Drying and Conditioning of Native Grain) (Exclusion) Regulations, S.I. No. 210 of 1967
		Conditions of Employment (Towel Weaving Industry) (Exclusion) (No.2) Regulations, S.I. No. 270 of 1967
		Conditions of Employment (Continuous Filament Bulked Synthetic Yarns) (Exclusion) (No.2) Regulations, S.I. No. 292 of 1967
		Conditions of Employment (Continuous Filament Bulked Synthetic Yarns) (Exclusion) Regulations, S.I. No. 293 of 1967
		Conditions of Employment (Towel Weaving Industry) (Exclusion) Regulations, S.I. No. 294 of 1967
		Conditions of Employment (Yarn Processing) (Exclusion) Regulations, S.I. No. 19 of 1968
		Conditions of Employment (Chewing Gum and Confectionery Industry) (Exclusion) Regulations, S.I. No. 23 of 1968
		Conditions of Employment (Nylon Stockings Industry) (Exclusion) Regulations, S.I. No. 33 of 1968
		Conditions of Employment (Polypropylene Industry) (Exclusion) Regulations, S.I. No. 41 of 1968
		Conditions of Employment (Welding Electrodes) (Exclusion) Regulations, S.I. No. 84 of 1968
		Conditions of Employment (Polypropylene Industry) (Exclusion) Regulations (No.2) S.I. No. 115 of 1968
		Conditions of Employment (Cosmetics Industry) (Exclusion) Regulations, S.I. No. 151 of 1968

Conditions of Employment Act,
No. 2 of 1936 (*Cont.*)

Conditions of Employment (Sugar and Chocolate Confectionery Industry) (Exclusion) Regulations, S.I. No. 175 of 1968

Conditions of Employment (Mechanical Handling Equipment) (Exclusion) Regulations, S.I. No. 192 of 1968

Conditions of Employment (Pharmaceutical Preparations Industry) (Exclusion) Regulations, S.I. No. 197 of 1968

Conditions of Employment (Weft Winding) (Exclusion) Regulations, S.I. No. 216 of 1968

Conditions of Employment (Automobile Rear-View Mirrors Industry) (Exclusion) Regulations, S.I. No. 221 of 1968

Conditions of Employment (Chemical Processing Industry) (Exclusion) Regulations, S.I. No. 232 of 1968

Conditions of Employment (Woollen Fabrics Industry) (Exclusion) Regulations, S.I. No. 258 of 1968

Conditions of Employment (Paper Cream Containers) (Exclusion) Regulations, S.I. No. 280 of 1968

Conditions of Employment (Plastic Extrusion) (Exclusion) Regulations, S.I. No. 66 of 1969

Conditions of Employment (Knitted Elasticated Fabrics) (Exclusion) Regulations, S.I. No. 96 of 1969

Conditions of Employment (Rayon Industry) (Exclusion) Regulations, S.I. No. 189 of 1969

Conditions of Employment (Potato Processing) (Exclusion) Regulations, S.I. No. 202 of 1969

Conditions of Employment (Woollen and Worsted Industry) (Exclusion) Regulations, S.I. No. 165 of 1970

Conditions of Employment (Towel Weaving) (Exclusion) Regulations, S.I. No. 278 of 1970

Conditions of Employment (Pen Assembly Industry) (Exclusion) Regulations, S.I. No. 45 of 1971

Conditions of Employment (Radiator Valve Industry) (Exclusion) Order, S.I. No. 53 of 1971

Conditions of Employment (Textile Industry) (Exclusion) Regulations, S.I. No. 75 of 1971

Conditions of Employment (Baked Products) (Exclusion) Regulations, S.I. No. 210 of 1971

Conditions of Employment (Carpet Weaving) (Exclusion) Regulations, S.I. No. 227 of 1971

Conditions of Employment (Rubber Tape and Thread) (Exclusion) Regulations, S.I. No. 253 of 1971

Conditions of Employment (Industrial Fasteners) (Exclusion) Regulations, S.I. No. 254 of 1971

Conditions of Employment (Twine and Rope Industry) (Exclusion) Regulations, S.I. No. 329 of 1971

Conditions of Employment Act,
No. 2 of 1936 (*Cont.*)

Conditions of Employment (Textile Machinery Components) (Exclusion) Regulations, S.I. No. 342 of 1971

Conditions of Employment (Aluminium Foundry Work) (Exclusion) Regulations, S.I. No. 10 of 1972

Conditions of Employment (Chipboard Manufacture) (Exclusion) Regulations, S.I. No. 57 of 1972

Conditions of Employment (Polypropylene Tape Industry) (Exclusion) Regulations, S.I. No. 63 of 1972

Conditions of Employment (Cotton and Yarn Spinning) (Exclusion) Regulations, S.I. No. 66 of 1972

Conditions of Employment (Gum Base Production) (Exclusion) Regulations, S.I. No. 214 of 1972

Conditions of Employment (Surgical Castings Inspection) (Exclusion) Regulations, S.I. No. 215 of 1972

Conditions of Employment (Nylon Yarn Industry) (Exclusion) Regulations, S.I. No. 250 of 1972

Conditions of Employment (Automatic Turned Parts Industry) (Exclusion) Regulations, S.I. No. 278 of 1972

Conditions of Employment (Medical Products Assembly) (Exclusion) Regulations, S.I. No. 244 of 1973

Conditions of Employment (Tobacco Packaging Industry) (Exclusion) Regulations, S.I. No. 245 of 1973

Conditions of Employment (Cheese Manufacturing Industry) (Exclusion) Regulations, S.I. No. 310 of 1973

Conditions of Employment (Switch Gear Component Assembly) (Exclusion) Regulations, S.I. No. 312 of 1973

Conditions of Employment (Colour Film Processing) (Exclusion) Order, S.I. No. 96 of 1974

Conditions of Employment (Biscuit Packaging) (Exclusion) Regulations, S.I. No. 218 of 1974

Conditions of Employment (Kitchen Furniture Industry) (Exclusion) Regulations, S.I. No. 228 of 1974

Conditions of Employment (Food Processing Industry) (Exclusion) Regulations, S.I. No. 229 of 1974

Conditions of Employment (Marine Oil Terminal Industry) (Exclusion) Regulations, S.I. No. 238 of 1974

Conditions of Employment (Cutlery and Steelware Components Industry) (Exclusion) Regulations, S.I. No. 327 of 1974

Statutory Authority	Section	Statutory Instrument
Conditions of Employment Act, No. 2 of 1936 (*Cont.*)		Conditions of Employment (Tennis Balls Industry) (Exclusion) Regulations, S.I. No. 361 of 1974
		Conditions of Employment (Fertiliser Industry) (Exclusion) Regulations, S.I. No. 379 of 1974
		Conditions of Employment (Printing Industry) (Exclusion) Regulations, S.I. No. 81 of 1975
		Conditions of Employment (Carpet Tufting Industry) (Exclusion) Regulations, S.I. No. 95 of 1975
		Conditions of Employment (Boiler Tube Industry) (Exclusion) Regulations, S.I. No. 96 of 1975
		Conditions of Employment (Synthetic Screen Seaming Industry) (Exclusion) Regulations, S.I. No. 149 of 1975
		Conditions of Employment (Wallpaper Industry) (Exclusion) Regulations, S.I. No. 150 of 1975
		Conditions of Employment (Metal Working Industry) (Exclusion) Regulations, S.I. No. 152 of 1975
		Conditions of Employment (Plaster and Plasterboard Manufacturing Industry) (Exclusion) Regulations, S.I. No. 161 of 1975
		Conditions of Employment (Whey Processing Industry) (Exclusion) Regulations, S.I. No. 244 of 1975
		Conditions of Employment (Greeting Card Industry) (Exclusion) Regulations, S.I. No. 278 of 1975
		Conditions of Employment (Car Component Manufacturing Industry) (Exclusion) Regulations, S.I. No. 14 of 1976
		Conditions of Employment (China Sanitary Ware Manufacturing Industry) (Exclusion) Regulations, S.I. No. 15 of 1976
		Conditions of Employment (Sweet Packaging Industry) (Exclusion) Regulations, S.I. No. 23 of 1976
		Conditions of Employment (Domestic Electrical Appliances Industry) (Exclusion) Regulations, S.I. No. 31 of 1976
		Conditions of Employment (Pharmaceutical Products Industry) (Exclusions) Regulations, S.I. No. 47 of 1976
		Conditions of Employment (Fish Processing Industry) (Exclusion) Regulations, S.I. No. 73 of 1976
		Conditions of Employment (Home Care Products Industry) (Exclusion) Regulations, S.I. No. 152 of 1976
		Conditions of Employment (Electro-Mechanical Assemblies Industry) (Exclusion) Regulations, S.I. No. 158 of 1976
		Conditions of Employment (Pasta Products Industry) (Exclusion) Regulations, S.I. No. 190 of 1976

Conditions of Employment Act,
No. 2 of 1936 (*Cont.*)

Conditions of Employment (Textile Shipping Industry) (Exclusion) Regulations, S.I. No. 215 of 1976

Conditions of Employment (Cassette Manufacturing Industry) (Exclusion) Regulations, S.I. No. 233 of 1976

Conditions of Employment (Canning and Bottling of Soft Drinks Industry) (Exclusion) Regulations, S.I. No. 270 of 1976

Conditions of Employment (Medical Equipment Manufacturing Industry) (Exclusion) Regulations, S.I. No. 271 of 1976

Conditions of Employment (Industrial Components Manufacturing Industry) (Exclusion) Regulations, S.I. No. 290 of 1976

Conditions of Employment (Nylon Yarn Spinning Industry) (Exclusion) Regulations 1076, S.I. No. 321 of 1976

Conditions of Employment (Photographic Equipment Manufacturing Industry) (Exclusion) Regulations, S.I. No. 15 of 1977

Conditions of Employment (Precision Engineering and Toolmaking Industry) (Exclusion) Regulations, S.I. No. 23 of 1977

Conditions of Employment (Carpet Manufacturing Industry) Exclusion, Regulations, S.I. No. 24 of 1977

Conditions of Employment (Telecommunications Equipment Industry) (Exclusion) Regulations, S.I. No. 25 of 1977

Conditions of Employment (Chocolate Confectionery and Biscuits Industry) (Exclusion) Regulations, S.I. No. 93 of 1977

Conditions of Employment (Aluminium Products Industry) (Exclusion) Regulations, S.I. No. 147 of 1977

Conditions of Employment (Assembly of Telephone Equipment Industry) (Exclusion) Regulations, S.I. No. 188 of 1977

Conditions of Employment (Milk Powder Packaging Industry) (Exclusion) Regulations, S.I. No. 189 of 1977

Conditions of Employment (Textile Manufacturing, Wool and Fibre Yarn Spinning) (Exclusion) Regulations, S.I. No. 190 of 1977

Conditions of Employment (Paper Converting and Packaging Industry) (Exclusion) Regulations, S.I. No. 191 of 1977

Conditions of Employment (Quarried Limestone Products Industry) (Exclusion) Regulations, S.I. No. 192 of 1977

Conditions of Employment (Acrylic Fibre Manufacturing Industry) (Exclusion) Regulations, S.I. No. 223 of 1977

Conditions of Employment Act,
No. 2 of 1936 (*Cont.*)

Conditions of Employment (Whey Processing Industry) (Exclusion) Regulations, S.I. No. 244 of 1977

Conditions of Employment (Acrylic Yarn Spinning Industry) (Exclusion) Regulations, S.I. No. 245 of 1977

Conditions of Employment (Manufacture of Games and Puzzles Industry) (Exclusion) Regulations, S.I. No. 263 of 1977

Conditions of Employment (Manufacture of Knitted Vegetable Bags) (Exclusion) Regulations, S.I. No. 264 of 1977

Conditions of Employment (Paper-Making Industry) (Exclusion) Regulations, S.I. No. 276 of 1977

Conditions of Employment (Manufacture of Polyester-type Fabric Industry) (Exclusion) Regulations, S.I. No. 277 of 1977

Conditions of Employment (Manufacture of Stainless Steel Products Industry) (Exclusion) Regulations, S.I. No. 280 of 1977

Conditions of Employment (Manufacture of Surgical Instruments Industry) (Exclusion) Regulations, S.I. No. 304 of 1977

Conditions of Employment (Manufacture of Sports, Surgical and Music Strings Industry) (Exclusion) Regulations, S.I. No. 323 of 1977

Conditions of Employment (Manufacture of Canned Dog and Cat Food Industry) (Exclusion) Regulations, S.I. No. 343 of 1977

Conditions of Employment (Manufacture of Industrial Safety Equipment Industry) (Exclusion) Regulations, S.I. No. 357 of 1977

Conditions of Employment (Manufacture of Pharmaceutical Products Industry) (Exclusion) Regulations, S.I. No. 360 of 1977

Conditions of Employment (Precision Sheet Metal Work Industry) (Exclusion) Regulations, S.I. No. 7 of 1978

Conditions of Employment (Manufacture of Corrugated Container Industry) (Exclusion) Regulations, S.I. No. 8 of 1978

Conditions of Employment (Manufacture of Medical Health Care Products Industry) (Exclusion) Regulations, S.I. No. 24 of 1978

Conditions of Employment (Manufacture of Laminate and Pre-Impregnated Cloths Industry) (Exclusion) Regulations, S.I. No. 131 of 1978

Conditions of Employment (Manufacture of Jewellery Industry) (Exclusion) Regulations, S.I. No. 141 of 1978

Conditions of Employment (Manufacture of Records and Tape Duplication Industry) (Exclusion) Regulations, S.I. No. 142 of 1978

Conditions of Employment Act, No. 2 of 1936 (*Cont.*)		**Conditions of Employment (Distribution of Gas) (Exclusion) Regulations, S.I. No. 90 of 1979**
		Conditions of Employment (Whey Processing Industry) (Exclusion) Regulations, S.I. No. 91 of 1979
		Conditions of Employment (Rolling of Dental Root Canal Points) (Exclusion) Regulations, S.I. No. 92 of 1979
		Conditions of Employment (Manufacture and Assembly of Tools) (Exclusion) Regulations, S.I. No. 150 of 1979
		Conditions of Employment (Manufacture of Ladies Nylon Hosiery Industry) (Exclusion) Regulations, S.I. No. 154 of 1979
		Conditions of Employment (Manufacture of Castors and Wheels) (Exclusion) Regulations, S.I. No. 155 of 1979
		Conditions of Employment (Manufacture of Analytical Instruments) (Exclusion) Regulations, S.I. No. 169 of 1979
		Conditions of Employment (Manufacture of Pharmaceutical Products) (Exclusion) Regulations, S.I. No. 223 of 1979
		Conditions of Employment (Manufacture of Central Heating Radiators Industry) (Exclusion) Regulations, S.I. No. 365 of 1979
		Conditions of Employment (Manufacture of Wire Nails Industry) (Exclusion) Regulations, S.I. No. 366 of 1979
		Conditions of Employment (Manufacture of Removable Magnetic Storage Media for Computers) (Exclusion) Regulations, S.I. No. 367 of 1979
		Conditions of Employment (Manufacture of Steel Reinforcement) (Exclusion) Regulations, S.I. No. 368 of 1979
		Conditions of Employment (Manufacture of Corrugated Containers Industry) (Exclusion) Regulations, S.I. No. 371 of 1979
		Conditions of Employment (Manufacture of Windscreens Industry) (Exclusion) Regulations, S.I. No. 381 of 1979
		Conditions of Employment (Manufacture of Nylon Yarn Industry) (Exclusion) Regulations, S.I. No. 394 of 1979
		Conditions of Employment (Manufacture and Packaging of Confectionery Products Industry) (Exclusion) Regulations, S.I. No. 396 of 1979
		Conditions of Employment (Manufacture of Textiles) (Exclusion) Regulations, S.I. No. 40 of 1980
		Conditions of Employment (Manufacture of Components for the Motor Industry) (Exclusion) Regulations, S.I. No. 63 of 1980

Conditions of Employment Act,
No. 2 of 1936 (*Cont.*)

Conditions of Employment (Manufacture of Mechanical Packings Industry) (Exclusion) Regulations, S.I. No. 124 of 1980

Conditions of Employment (Manufacture of Audio Cassette Tapes Industry) (Exclusion) Regulations, S.I. No. 131 of 1980

Conditions of Employment (Manufacture of Workmates, Jobbers and Drill Attachments) (Exclusion) Regulations, S.I. No. 138 of 1980

Conditions of Employment (Assembly of Lighters and Small Domestic Appliances Industry) (Exclusion) Regulations, S.I. No. 164 of 1980

Conditions of Employment (Manufacture of Cut Rug Yarn Industry) (Exclusion) Regulations, S.I. No. 174 of 1980

Conditions of Employment (Manufacture of Typewriter Ribbons Industry) (Exclusion) Regulations, S.I. No. 191 of 1980

Conditions of Employment (Polypropylene Foam Injection Moulding Industry) (Exclusion) Regulations, S.I. No. 217 of 1980

Conditions of Employment (Manufacture of Tapes and Laces Industry) (Exclusion) Regulations, S.I. No. 269 of 1980

Conditions of Employment (Aluminium Tubes Industry) (Exclusion) Regulations, S.I. No. 275 of 1980

Conditions of Employment (Weaving of Synthetic Fibres) (Exclusion) Regulations, S.I. No. 280 of 1980

Conditions of Employment (Manufacture of Plastic Moulded Parts and Tubing) (Exclusion) Regulations, S.I. No. 303 of 1980

Conditions of Employment (Manufacture of Cosmetic Cases Industry) (Exclusion) Regulations, S.I. No. 304 of 1980

Conditions of Employment (Assembly of Industrial Control Equipment) (Exclusion) Regulations, S.I. No. 305 of 1980

Conditions of Employment (Beverage Can Tops Industry) (Exclusion) Regulations, S.I. No. 308 of 1980

Conditions of Employment (Manufacture of Felt Insulation Industry) (Exclusion) Regulations, S.I. No. 312 of 1980

Conditions of Employment (Bubble Gum and Confectionery Industry) (Exclusion) Regulations, S.I. No. 313 of 1980

Conditions of Employment (Manufacture of Wheels) (Exclusion) Regulations, S.I. No. 314 of 1980

Conditions of Employment (Collapsible Aluminium Tubes) (Exclusion) Regulations, S.I. No. 348 of 1980

Conditions of Employment (Wire Weaving Industry) (Exclusion) Regulations, S.I. No. 375 of 1980

Conditions of Employment Act, No. 2 of 1936 (*Cont.*)	29(1)	Conditions of Employment (Jute Manufacture) (Exclusion) Order [Vol. V p. 363] S.R.& O. No. 158 of 1936
		Conditions of Employment (Gas Undertakings) (Exclusion) Order [Vol. V p. 371] S.R.& O. No. 159 of 1936
		Conditions of Employment (Women Cleaners) (Exclusion) Order [Vol. V p. 379] S.R.& O. No. 160 of 1936
		Conditions of Employment (Railways: Public Service Vehicles) (Exclusion) Order [Vol. V p. 385] S.R.& O. No. 161 of 1936
		Conditions of Employment (Electricity Undertakings) (Exclusion) Order [Vol. V p. 393] S.R.& O. No. 162 of 1936
		Conditions of Employment (Maintenance of Machinery and Plant) (Exclusion) Order [Vol. V p. 401] S.R.& O. No. 163 of 1936
		Conditions of Employment (Boilermen and Enginemen) (Exclusion) Order [Vol. V p. 409] S.R.& O. No. 164 of 1936
		Conditions of Employment (Bakeries) (Exclusion) Order [Vol. V p. 433] S.R.& O. No. 168 of 1936
		Conditions of Employment (Cotton and Linen Industry) (Exclusion) Order [Vol. V p. 441] S.R.& O. No. 175 of 1936
		Conditions of Employment (Tramways) (Exclusion) Order [Vol. V p. 449] S.R.& O. No. 191 of 1936
		Conditions of Employment (Turf Industry) (Exclusion) Order [Vol. V p. 455] S.R.& O. No. 288 of 1936
		Conditions of Employment (Boot and Shoe Industry) (Exclusion) Order [Vol. V p. 467] S.R.& O. No. 315 of 1936
		Conditions of Employment (Bacon Curing Industry) (Exclusion) Order [Vol. V p. 475] S.R.& O. No. 349 of 1936
		Conditions of Employment (Sausage Making) (Exclusion) Order [Vol. V p. 481] S.R.& O. No. 350 of 1936
		Conditions of Employment (Sugar Industry) (Shift Workers) (Exclusion) Order [Vol. V p. 487] S.R.& O. No. 351 of 1936
		Conditions of Employment (Sugar Industry) (Sugar Cooking) (Exclusion) Order [Vol. V p. 491] S.R.& O. No. 352 of 1936
		Conditions of Employment (Creameries) (Exclusion) Order [Vol. V p. 495] S.R.& O. No. 353 of 1936
		Conditions of Employment (Condensed Milk) (Exclusion) Order [Vol. V p. 501] S.R.& O. No. 354 of 1936
		Conditions of Employment (Maintenance and Repair of Mail Vans) (Exclusion) Order [Vol. V p. 519] S.R.& O. No. 367 of 1936

Conditions of Employment Act, No. 2 of 1936 (*Cont.*)

Conditions of Employment (Malting) (Exclusion) Order [Vol. V p. 531] S.R.& O. No. 387 of 1936

Conditions of Employment (Glass Bottle Works) (Exclusion) Order [Vol. V p. 543] S.R.& O. No. 391 of 1936

Conditions of Employment (Pottery) (Exclusion) Order [Vol. V p. 549] S.R.& O. No. 127 of 1937

Conditions of Employment (Peat Bog Development) (Exclusion) Order [Vol. V p. 583] S.R.& O. No. 184 of 1937

Conditions of Employment (Sheet Glass Works) (Exclusion) Order [Vol. V p. 601] S.R.& O. No. 193 of 1938

Conditions of Employment (Sewer Cleaning) (Exclusion) Order [Vol. V p. 619] S.R.& O. No. 338 of 1938

34   **Conditions of Employment (Boiler Tube Industry) (Exclusion) Regulations, S.I. No. 96 of 1975**

Conditions of Employment (Plaster and Plasterboard Manufacturing Industry) (Exclusion) Regulations, S.I. No. 161 of 1975

40   *Conditions of Employment (Spinning and Weaving of Jute) (Young Persons deemed to be Adult Workers) Regulations, S.I. No. 93 of 1950*

Conditions of Employment (Gas Installation Dublin) (Young Persons deemed to be Adult Workers) Regulations, S.I. No. 266 of 1951

Conditions of Employment (Linen and Cotton Textile Industry) (Exclusion and Young Persons deemed to be Adult Workers) Regulations, S.I. No. 272 of 1954

Conditions of Employment (Rayon Industry) (Exclusion and Young Persons deemed to be Adult Workers) Regulations, S.I. No. 156 of 1955

Conditions of Employment (Glass Cutting, Waterford Glass Ltd.) (Young Persons deemed to be Adult Workers) Regulations, S.I. No. 72 of 1960

Conditions of Employment (Manufacture of Jute Goods, J. & L. F. Goodbody, Limited) (Young Persons Deemed to be Adult Workers) Regulations, S.I. No. 175 of 1961

Conditions of Employment (Manufacture of Jute Goods) (Young Persons deemed to be Adult Workers) Regulations, S.I. No. 71 of 1962

Conditions of Employment (Manufacture of Fully-Fashioned Woollen and Cotton Garments) (Young Persons deemed to be Adult Workers) Regulations, S.I. No. 74 of 1962

40(1)   *Conditions of Employment (Boot and Shoe Industry: Young Persons deemed to be Adult Workers) Order [Vol. V p. 461] S.R.& O. No. 314 of 1936*

Statutory Authority	Section	Statutory Instrument
Conditions of Employment Act, No. 2 of 1936 *(Cont.)*	40(1)	*Conditions of Employment (Woollen and Worsted Industry: Young Persons deemed to be Adult Workers) Order [Vol. V p. 507] S.R.& O. No. 355 of 1936*
		Conditions of Employment (Enamelware Industry: Young Persons deemed to be Adult Workers) Order [Vol. V p. 525] S.R.& O. No. 369 of 1936
		Conditions of Employment (Wallpaper Industry: Young Persons deemed to be Adult Workers) Order [Vol. V p. 595] S.R.& O. No. 37 of 1938
		Conditions of Employment (Worsted Spinning: Young Persons deemed to be Adult Workers) Order [Vol. V p. 625] S.R.& O. No. 339 of 1938
	47(2)	*Conditions of Employment (Sugar Beet Factories) (Employment of Young Persons at Night) Order [Vol. V p. 513] S.R.& O. No. 364 of 1936*
		Conditions of Employment (Glass Bottle Works) (Employment of Young Persons at Night) Order [Vol. V p. 537] S.R.& O. No. 388 of 1936
		Conditions of Employment (Manufacture of Paper) (Employment of Young Persons at Night) Order [Vol. V p. 607] S.R.& O. No. 213 of 1938
		Conditions of Employment (Glass Manufacture) (Employment of Young Persons at Night) Regulations, S.I. No. 31 of 1952
	49	**Conditions of Employment (Boilermen and Enginemen) (Exclusion and Period of Rest) Regulations [Vol. XXVIII p. 221] S.R.& O. No. 240 of 1942**
	49(1)(e)	**Conditions of Employment (Maintenance and Repair of Mail Vans) (Exclusion) Order [Vol. V p. 519] S.R.& O. No. 367 of 1936**
	49(4)	**Conditions of Employment (Maintenance of Machinery and Plant) (Repair of Moulds for Glass Bottles) (Period of Rest) Regulations [Vol. XXVIII p. 229] S.R.& O. No. 50 of 1940**
		Conditions of Employment (Electricity Undertakings) Period of Rest) Regulations, S.I. No. 108 of 1954
	52	**Conditions of Employment (Malting) (Exclusion) Regulations [Vol. XXVIII p. 235] S.R.& O. No. 152 of 1940**
		Conditions of Employment (Boilermen and Enginemen) (Exclusion and Period of Rest) Regulations [Vol. XXVIII p. 221] S.R.& O. No. 240 of 1942
		Conditions of Employment (Turf Industry) (Exclusion) Order [Vol. XXXVI p. 617] S.R.& O. No. 97 of 1947
		Conditions of Employment (Match Manufacturing Industry) (Exclusion) Regulations, S.I. No. 90 of 1951
		Conditions of Employment (Turf Industry) (Exclusion) Order, S.I. No. 154 of 1951

Conditions of Employment Act, No. 2 of 1936 (*Cont.*)		**Conditions of Employment (Woollen and Worsted Industry) (Exclusion) Regulations, S.I. No. 371 of 1953**
		Conditions of Employment (Linen and Cotton Textile Industry) (Exclusion and Young Persons deemed to be Adult Workers) Regulations, S.I. No. 272 of 1954
		Conditions of Employment (Rayon Industry) (Exclusion and Young Persons deemed to be Adult Workers) Regulations, S.I. No. 156 of 1955
		Conditions of Employment (Rubber Footwear Industry) (Exclusion) Regulations, S.I. No. 36 of 1959
		Conditions of Employment (Nylon, Rayon and Terylene Yarn Winding Industry) (Exclusion) Regulations, S.I. No. 120 of 1959
		Conditions of Employment (Peat Moss Flower Pots Industry) (Exclusion) Regulations, S.I. No. 245 of 1960
		Conditions of Employment (Biscuit and Chocolate Confectionery Industry) (Exclusion) Regulations, S.I. No. 252 of 1960
		Conditions of Employment (Glass Cloth Industry) (Exclusion) Regulations, S.I. No. 68 of 1961
		Conditions of Employment (Chewing Gum Industry) (Exclusion) Regulations, S.I. No. 69 of 1961
		Conditions of Employment (Frozen Sugar Confectionery) (Exclusion) Regulations, S.I. No. 82 of 1961
		Conditions of Employment (Rope Industry) (Exclusion) Regulations, S.I. No. 119 of 1961
		Conditions of Employment (Woollen and Cotton Garments Industry) (Exclusion) Regulations, S.I. No. 176 of 1961
		Conditions of Employment (Terylene Yarns Industry) (Exclusion) Regulations, S.I. No. 184 of 1961
		Conditions of Employment (Crown Cork Industry) (Exclusion) Regulations, S.I. No. 190 of 1961
		Conditions of Employment (Cigarette Industry) (Exclusion) Regulations, S.I. No. 192 of 1961
		Conditions of Employment (Plastic Packaging Industry) (Exclusion) Regulations, S.I. No. 271 of 1961
		Conditions of Employment (Carpet Weaving Industry) (Exclusion) Regulations, S.I. No. 282 of 1961
		Conditions of Employment (Glass-fibre Cloth Industry) (Exclusion) Regulations, S.I. No. 292 of 1961
		Conditions of Employment (Worsted Spinning Industry) (Exclusion) Regulations, S.I. No. 1 of 1962

Conditions of Employment Act,
No. 2 of 1936 (*Cont.*)

Conditions of Employment (Sugar Confectionery Industry) (Exclusion) Regulations, S.I. No. 2 of 1964

Conditions of Employment (Jute Industry) (Exclusion) Regulations, S.I. No. 92 of 1964

Conditions of Employment (Surgical Instruments Industry) (Exclusion) Regulations, S.I. No. 205 of 1964

Conditions of Employment (Beer Bottling Industry) (Exclusion) Regulations, S.I. No. 207 of 1964

Conditions of Employment (Raschel Knitting Machines Industry) (Exclusion) Regulations, S.I. No. 208 of 1964

Conditions of Employment (Packing of Flower Pots) (Exclusion) Regulations, S.I. No. 233 of 1964

Conditions of Employment (Plastic Moulding) (Exclusion) Regulations, S.I. No. 254 of 1964

Conditions of Employment (Ladies Clothes and Household Piece Goods) (Exclusion) Regulations, S.I. No. 261 of 1964

Conditions of Employment (Pharmaceutical and Allied Products Industry) (Exclusion) Regulations, S.I. No. 262 of 1964

Conditions of Employment (Chocolate and Sweets Industry) (Exclusion) Regulations, S.I. No. 263 of 1964

Conditions of Employment (Calendaring of Printed Sheets) (Exclusion) Regulations, S.I. No. 283 of 1964

Conditions of Employment (Tufted Carpeting) (Exclusion) Regulations, S.I. No. 25 of 1965

Conditions of Employment (Knitted Garments Industry) (Exclusion) Regulations, S.I. No. 45 of 1965

Conditions of Employment (Certain Electric Fittings) (Exclusion) Regulations, S.I. No. 46 of 1965

Conditions of Employment (Plastic Moulding) (Exclusion) Regulations, S.I. No. 53 of 1965

Conditions of Employment (Flax Spinning Industry) (Exclusion) Regulations, S.I. No. 151 of 1965

Conditions of Employment (Polythene Film Bags) (Exclusion) Regulations, S.I. No. 152 of 1965

Conditions of Employment (Ice Cones and Wafers) (Exclusion) Regulations, S.I. No. 160 of 1965

Conditions of Employment (Electric Motors) (Exclusion) Regulations, S.I. No. 181 of 1965

Conditions of Employment (Electronic Components Industry at Shannon Industrial Estate) (Exclusion) Regulations, S.I. No. 204 of 1965

Conditions of Employment (Curtain Materials and Bedspreads) (Exclusion) Regulations, S.I. No. 215 of 1965

Conditions of Employment Act,
No. 2 of 1936 (*Cont.*)

Conditions of Employment (Printing and Box-Making Industry) (Exclusion) Regulations, S.I. No. 222 of 1965

Conditions of Employment (Paper Bags Industry) (Exclusion) Regulations, S.I. No. 247 of 1965

Conditions of Employment (Rubber Soles) (Exclusion) Regulations, S.I. No. 259 of 1965

Conditions of Employment (Toilet Rolls) (Exclusion) Regulations, S.I. No. 260 of 1965

Conditions of Employment (Plastic Moulding) (Exclusion) (No.2) Regulations, S.I. No. 20 of 1966

Conditions of Employment (Electronic Components Industry) (Exclusion) Regulations, S.I. No. 29 of 1966

Conditions of Employment (Electronic Components Industry) (Exclusion) Regulations, S.I. No. 81 of 1966

Conditions of Employment (Golf Balls) (Exclusion) Regulations, S.I. No. 56 of 1967

Conditions of Employment (Nylon Stockings Industry) (Exclusion) Regulations, S.I. No. 66 of 1967

Conditions of Employment (Electronic Components Industry) (Exclusion) Regulations, S.I. No. 136 of 1967

Conditions of Employment (Tobacco Pouches) (Exclusion) Regulations, S.I. No. 137 of 1967

Conditions of Employment (Processing and Packaging of Tobacco) (Exclusion) Regulations, S.I. No. 138 of 1967

Conditions of Employment (Yarn-dyeing Industry) (Exclusion) Regulations, S.I. No. 178 of 1967

Conditions of Employment (Wool Top Industry) (Exclusion) Regulations, S.I. No. 179 of 1967

Conditions of Employment (Jersey Fabrics Industry) (Exclusion) Regulations, S.I. No. 180 of 1967

Conditions of Employment (Jetty Construction) (Exclusion) Regulations, S.I. No. 195 of 1967

Conditions of Employment (Carding and Spinning of Cotton and Synthetic Fibres) (Exclusion) Regulations, S.I. No. 201 of 1967

Conditions of Employment (Drying and Conditioning of Native Grain) (Exclusion) Regulations, S.I. No. 210 of 1967

Conditions of Employment (Towel Weaving Industry) (Exclusion) (No.2) Regulations, S.I. No. 270 of 1967

Conditions of Employment (Continuous Filament Bulked Synthetic Yarns) (Exclusion) (No.2) Regulations, S.I. No. 292 of 1967

Conditions of Employment (Continuous Filament Bulked Synthetic Yarns) (Exclusion) Regulations, S.I. No. 293 of 1967

Conditions of Employment Act, No. 2 of 1936 (*Cont.*)

Conditions of Employment (Towel Weaving Industry) (Exclusion) Regulations, S.I. No. 294 of 1967

Conditions of Employment (Yarn Processing) (Exclusion) Regulations, S.I. No. 19 of 1968

Conditions of Employment (Chewing Gum and Confectionery Industry) (Exclusion) Regulations, S.I. No. 23 of 1968

Conditions of Employment (Nylon Stockings Industry) (Exclusion) Regulations, S.I. No. 33 of 1968

Conditions of Employment (Polypropylene Industry) (Exclusion) Regulations, S.I. No. 41 of 1968

Conditions of Employment (Welding Electrodes) (Exclusion) Regulations, S.I. No. 84 of 1968

Conditions of Employment (Polypropylene Industry) (Exclusion) Regulations (No.2) S.I. No. 115 of 1968

Conditions of Employment (Cosmetics Industry) (Exclusion) Regulations, S.I. No. 151 of 1968

Conditions of Employment (Sugar and Chocolate Confectionery Industry) (Exclusion) Regulations, S.I. No. 175 of 1968

Conditions of Employment (Mechanical Handling Equipment) (Exclusion) Regulations, S.I. No. 192 of 1968

Conditions of Employment (Pharmaceutical Preparations Industry) (Exclusion) Regulations, S.I. No. 197 of 1968

Conditions of Employment (Weft Winding) (Exclusion) Regulations, S.I. No. 216 of 1968

Conditions of Employment (Automobile Rear-View Mirrors Industry) (Exclusion) Regulations, S.I. No. 221 of 1968

Conditions of Employment (Chemical Processing Industry) (Exclusion) Regulations, S.I. No. 232 of 1968

Conditions of Employment (Woollen Fabrics Industry) (Exclusion) Regulations, S.I. No. 258 of 1968

Conditions of Employment (Paper Cream Containers) (Exclusion) Regulations, S.I. No. 280 of 1968

Conditions of Employment (Plastic Extrusion) (Exclusion) Regulations, S.I. No. 66 of 1969

Conditions of Employment (Knitted Elasticated Fabrics) (Exclusion) Regulations, S.I. No. 96 of 1969

Conditions of Employment (Rayon Industry) (Exclusion) Regulations, S.I. No. 189 of 1969

Conditions of Employment (Potato Processing) (Exclusion) Regulations, S.I. No. 202 of 1969

Statutory Authority	Section	Statutory Instrument

Conditions of Employment Act,
No. 2 of 1936 (*Cont.*)

Conditions of Employment (Woollen and Worsted Industry) (Exclusion) Regulations, S.I. No. 165 of 1970

Conditions of Employment (Towel Weaving) (Exclusion) Regulations, S.I. No. 278 of 1970

Conditions of Employment (Pen Assembly Industry) (Exclusion) Regulations, S.I. No. 45 of 1971

Conditions of Employment (Radiator Valve Industry) (Exclusion) Order, S.I. No. 53 of 1971

Conditions of Employment (Textile Industry) (Exclusion) Regulations, S.I. No. 75 of 1971

Conditions of Employment (Baked Products) (Exclusion) Regulations, S.I. No. 210 of 1971

Conditions of Employment (Carpet Weaving) (Exclusion) Regulations, S.I. No. 227 of 1971

Conditions of Employment (Rubber Tape and Thread) (Exclusion) Regulations, S.I. No. 253 of 1971

Conditions of Employment (Industrial Fasteners) (Exclusion) Regulations, S.I. No. 254 of 1971

Conditions of Employment (Twine and Rope Industry) (Exclusion) Regulations, S.I. No. 329 of 1971

Conditions of Employment (Textile Machinery Components) (Exclusion) Regulations, S.I. No. 342 of 1971

Conditions of Employment (Aluminium Foundry Work) (Exclusion) Regulations, S.I. No. 10 of 1972

Conditions of Employment (Chipboard Manufacture) (Exclusion) Regulations, S.I. No. 57 of 1972

Conditions of Employment (Polypropylene Tape Industry) (Exclusion) Regulations, S.I. No. 63 of 1972

Conditions of Employment (Cotton and Yarn Spinning) (Exclusion) Regulations, S.I. No. 66 of 1972

Conditions of Employment (Gum Base Production) (Exclusion) Regulations, S.I. No. 214 of 1972

Conditions of Employment (Surgical Castings Inspection) (Exclusion) Regulations, S.I. No. 215 of 1972

Conditions of Employment (Nylon Yarn Industry) (Exclusion) Regulations, S.I. No. 250 of 1972

Conditions of Employment (Automatic Turned Parts Industry) (Exclusion) Regulations, S.I. No. 278 of 1972

Conditions of Employment (Medical Products Assembly) (Exclusion) Regulations, S.I. No. 244 of 1973

Conditions of Employment (Tobacco Packaging Industry) (Exclusion) Regulations, S.I. No. 245 of 1973

Statutory Authority	Section	Statutory Instrument
Conditions of Employment Act, No. 2 of 1936 (*Cont.*)		**Conditions of Employment (Cheese Manufacturing Industry) (Exclusion) Regulations, S.I. No. 310 of 1973**
		Conditions of Employment (Switch Gear Component Assembly) (Exclusion) Regulations, S.I. No. 312 of 1973
		Conditions of Employment (Colour Film Processing) (Exclusion) Order, S.I. No. 96 of 1974
		Conditions of Employment (Biscuit Packaging) (Exclusion) Regulations, S.I. No. 218 of 1974
		Conditions of Employment (Kitchen Furniture Industry) (Exclusion) Regulations, S.I. No. 228 of 1974
		Conditions of Employment (Food Processing Industry) (Exclusion) Regulations, S.I. No. 229 of 1974
		Conditions of Employment (Marine Oil Terminal Industry) (Exclusion) Regulations, S.I. No. 238 of 1974
		Conditions of Employment (Cutlery and Steelware Components Industry) (Exclusion) Regulations, S.I. No. 327 of 1974
		Conditions of Employment (Tennis Balls Industry) (Exclusion) Regulations, S.I. No. 361 of 1974
		Conditions of Employment (Fertiliser Industry) (Exclusion) Regulations, S.I. No. 379 of 1974
		Conditions of Employment (Printing Industry) (Exclusion) Regulations, S.I. No. 81 of 1975
		Conditions of Employment (Carpet Tufting Industry) (Exclusion) Regulations, S.I. No. 95 of 1975
		Conditions of Employment (Synthetic Screen Seaming Industry) (Exclusion) Regulations, S.I. No. 149 of 1975
		Conditions of Employment (Wallpaper Industry) (Exclusion) Regulations, S.I. No. 150 of 1975
		Conditions of Employment (Metal Working Industry) (Exclusion) Regulations, S.I. No. 152 of 1975
		Conditions of Employment (Whey Processing Industry) (Exclusion) Regulations, S.I. No. 244 of 1975
		Conditions of Employment (Greeting Card Industry) (Exclusion) Regulations, S.I. No. 278 of 1975
		Conditions of Employment (Car Component Manufacturing Industry) (Exclusion) Regulations, S.I. No. 14 of 1976
		Conditions of Employment (China Sanitary Ware Manufacturing Industry) (Exclusion) Regulations, S.I. No. 15 of 1976
		Conditions of Employment (Sweet Packaging Industry) (Exclusion) Regulations, S.I. No. 23 of 1976

Conditions of Employment Act, No. 2 of 1936 (*Cont.*)

Conditions of Employment (Domestic Electrical Appliances Industry) (Exclusion) Regulations, S.I. No. 31 of 1976

Conditions of Employment (Pharmaceutical Products Industry) (Exclusions) Regulations, S.I. No. 47 of 1976

Conditions of Employment (Fish Processing Industry) (Exclusion) Regulations, S.I. No. 73 of 1976

Conditions of Employment (Home Care Products Industry) (Exclusion) Regulations, S.I. No. 152 of 1976

Conditions of Employment (Electro-Mechanical Assemblies Industry) (Exclusion) Regulations, S.I. No. 158 of 1976

Conditions of Employment (Pasta Products Industry) (Exclusion) Regulations, S.I. No. 190 of 1976

Conditions of Employment (Textile Shipping Industry) (Exclusion) Regulations, S.I. No. 215 of 1976

Conditions of Employment (Cassette Manufacturing Industry) (Exclusion) Regulations, S.I. No. 233 of 1976

Conditions of Employment (Canning and Bottling of Soft Drinks Industry) (Exclusion) Regulations, S.I. No. 270 of 1976

Conditions of Employment (Medical Equipment Manufacturing Industry) (Exclusion) Regulations, S.I. No. 271 of 1976

Conditions of Employment (Industrial Components Manufacturing Industry) (Exclusion) Regulations, S.I. No. 290 of 1976

Conditions of Employment (Nylon Yarn Spinning Industry) (Exclusion) Regulations 1076, S.I. No. 321 of 1976

Conditions of Employment (Photographic Equipment Manufacturing Industry) (Exclusion) Regulations, S.I. No. 15 of 1977

Conditions of Employment (Precision Engineering and Toolmaking Industry) (Exclusion) Regulations, S.I. No. 23 of 1977

Conditions of Employment (Carpet Manufacturing Industry) Exclusion, Regulations, S.I. No. 24 of 1977

Conditions of Employment (Telecommunications Equipment Industry) (Exclusion) Regulations, S.I. No. 25 of 1977

Conditions of Employment (Chocolate Confectionery and Biscuits Industry) (Exclusion) Regulations, S.I. No. 93 of 1977

Conditions of Employment (Aluminium Products Industry) (Exclusion) Regulations, S.I. No. 147 of 1977

Conditions of Employment Act,
No. 2 of 1926 (*Cont.*)

Conditions of Employment (Assembly of Telephone Equipment Industry) (Exclusion) Regulations, S.I. No. 188 of 1977

Conditions of Employment (Milk Powder Packaging Industry) (Exclusion) Regulations, S.I. No. 189 of 1977

Conditions of Employment (Textile Manufacturing, Wool and Fibre Yarn Spinning) (Exclusion) Regulations, S.I. No. 190 of 1977

Conditions of Employment (Paper Converting and Packaging Industry) (Exclusion) Regulations, S.I. No. 191 of 1977

Conditions of Employment (Quarried Limestone Products Industry) (Exclusion) Regulations, S.I. No. 192 of 1977

Conditions of Employment (Acrylic Fibre Manufacturing Industry) (Exclusion) Regulations, S.I. No. 223 of 1977

Conditions of Employment (Whey Processing Industry) (Exclusion) Regulations, S.I. No. 244 of 1977

Conditions of Employment (Acrylic Yarn Spinning Industry) (Exclusion) Regulations, S.I. No. 245 of 1977

Conditions of Employment (Manufacture of Games and Puzzles Industry) (Exclusion) Regulations, S.I. No. 263 of 1977

Conditions of Employment (Manufacture of Knitted Vegetable Bags) (Exclusion) Regulations, S.I. No. 264 of 1977

Conditions of Employment (Paper-Making Industry) (Exclusion) Regulations, S.I. No. 276 of 1977

Conditions of Employment (Manufacture of Polyester-type Fabric Industry) (Exclusion) Regulations, S.I. No. 277 of 1977

Conditions of Employment (Manufacture of Stainless Steel Products Industry) (Exclusion) Regulations, S.I. No. 280 of 1977

Conditions of Employment (Manufacture of Surgical Instruments Industry) (Exclusion) Regulations, S.I. No. 304 of 1977

Conditions of Employment (Manufacture of Sports, Surgical and Music Strings Industry) (Exclusion) Regulations, S.I. No. 323 of 1977

Conditions of Employment (Manufacture of Canned Dog and Cat Food Industry) (Exclusion) Regulations, S.I. No. 343 of 1977

Conditions of Employment (Manufacture of Industrial Safety Equipment Industry) (Exclusion) Regulations, S.I. No. 357 of 1977

Conditions of Employment (Manufacture of Pharmaceutical Products Industry) (Exclusion) Regulations, S.I. No. 360 of 1977

Statutory Authority	Section	Statutory Instrument

Conditions of Employment Act,
No. 2 of 1936 (*Cont.*)

Conditions of Employment (Precision Sheet Metal Work Industry) (Exclusion) Regulations, S.I. No. 7 of 1978

Conditions of Employment (Manufacture of Corrugated Container Industry) (Exclusion) Regulations, S.I. No. 8 of 1978

Conditions of Employment (Manufacture of Medical Health Care Products Industry) (Exclusion) Regulations, S.I. No. 24 of 1978

Conditions of Employment (Manufacture of Laminate and Pre-Impregnated Cloths Industry) (Exclusion) Regulations, S.I. No. 131 of 1978

Conditions of Employment (Manufacture of Jewellery Industry) (Exclusion) Regulations, S.I. No. 141 of 1978

Conditions of Employment (Manufacture of Records and Tape Duplication Industry) (Exclusion) Regulations, S.I. No. 142 of 1978

Conditions of Employment (Gramophone Record Industry) (Exclusion) Regulations, S.I. No. 165 of 1978

Conditions of Employment (Polyester Yarn Processing) (Exclusion) Regulations, S.I. No. 188 of 1978

Conditions of Employment (Manufacture of Plastic Strapping and Yarn Industry) (Exclusion) Regulations, S.I. No. 189 of 1978

Conditions of Employment (Structural Steel Work Industry) (Exclusion) Regulations, S.I. No. 268 of 1978

Conditions of Employment (Manufacture of Ceramics) (Exclusion) Regulations, S.I. No. 285 of 1978

Conditions of Employment (Textile Bleaching, Dyeing and Printing) (Exclusion) Regulations, S.I. No. 294 of 1978

Conditions of Employment (Spinning and Dyeing of Carpet Yarns Industry) (Exclusion) Regulations, S.I. No. 296 of 1978

Conditions of Employment (Manufacture of Bulk Fine Chemicals) (Exclusion) Regulations, S.I. No. 300 of 1978

Conditions of Employment (Manufacture of Steel Stoves) (Exclusion) Regulations, S.I. No. 333 of 1978

Conditions of Employment (Manufacture of Toys Industry) (Exclusion) Regulations, S.I. No. 355 of 1978

Conditions of Employment (Manufacture of Turned Metal Components) (Exclusion) Regulations, S.I. No. 367 of 1978

Conditions of Employment (Manufacture and Assembly of Car Mirrors) (Exclusion) Regulations, S.I. No. 368 of 1978

Conditions of Employment Act,
No. 2 of 1936 (*Cont.*)

Conditions of Employment (Brewing Industry) (Exclusion) Regulations, S.I. No. 25 of 1979

Conditions of Employment (Printing, Packaging and Manufacture of Bags Industry) (Exclusion) Regulations, S.I. No. 34 of 1979

Conditions of Employment (Manufacture of Gases) (Exclusion) Regulations, S.I. No. 35 of 1979

Conditions of Employment (Operation and Maintenance of an Onshore Gas Metering Terminal) (Exclusion) Regulations, S.I. No. 36 of 1979

Conditions of Employment (Injection Moulding and Vacuum Metalizing Industry) (Exclusion) Regulations, S.I. No. 39 of 1979

Conditions of Employment (Manufacture of Toiletry Products and Adhesives) (Exclusion) Regulations, S.I. No. 69 of 1979

Conditions of Employment (Manufacture of Transformers) (Exclusion) Regulations, S.I. No. 81 of 1979

Conditions of Employment (Distribution of Gas) (Exclusion) Regulations, S.I. No. 90 of 1979

Conditions of Employment (Whey Processing Industry) (Exclusion) Regulations, S.I. No. 91 of 1979

Conditions of Employment (Rolling of Dental Root Canal Points) (Exclusion) Regulations, S.I. No. 92 of 1979

Conditions of Employment (Manufacture and Assembly of Tools) (Exclusion) Regulations, S.I. No. 150 of 1979

Conditions of Employment (Manufacture of Ladies Nylon Hosiery Industry) (Exclusion) Regulations, S.I. No. 154 of 1979

Conditions of Employment (Manufacture of Castors and Wheels) (Exclusion) Regulations, S.I. No. 155 of 1979

Conditions of Employment (Manufacture of Analytical Instruments) (Exclusion) Regulations, S.I. No. 169 of 1979

Conditions of Employment (Manufacture of Pharmaceutical Products) (Exclusion) Regulations, S.I. No. 223 of 1979

Conditions of Employment (Manufacture of Central Heating Radiators Industry) (Exclusion) Regulations, S.I. No. 365 of 1979

Conditions of Employment (Manufacture of Wire Nails Industry) (Exclusion) Regulations, S.I. No. 366 of 1979

Conditions of Employment (Manufacture of Removable Magnetic Storage Media for Computers) (Exclusion) Regulations, S.I. No. 367 of 1979

Conditions of Employment (Manufacture of Steel Reinforcement) (Exclusion) Regulations, S.I. No. 368 of 1979

Statutory Authority	Section	Statutory Instrument
Conditions of Employment Act, No. 2 of 1936 (*Cont.*)		**Conditions of Employment (Manufacture of Corrugated Containers Industry) (Exclusion) Regulations, S.I. No. 371 of 1979**
		Conditions of Employment (Manufacture of Windscreens Industry) (Exclusion) Regulations, S.I. No. 381 of 1979
		Conditions of Employment (Manufacture of Nylon Yarn Industry) (Exclusion) Regulations, S.I. No. 394 of 1979
		Conditions of Employment (Manufacture and Packaging of Confectionery Products Industry) (Exclusion) Regulations, S.I. No. 396 of 1979
		Conditions of Employment (Manufacture of Textiles) (Exclusion) Regulations, S.I. No. 40 of 1980
		Conditions of Employment (Manufacture of Components for the Motor Industry) (Exclusion) Regulations, S.I. No. 63 of 1980
		Conditions of Employment (Manufacture of Mechanical Packings Industry) (Exclusion) Regulations, S.I. No. 124 of 1980
		Conditions of Employment (Manufacture of Audio Cassette Tapes Industry) (Exclusion) Regulations, S.I. No. 131 of 1980
		Conditions of Employment (Manufacture of Workmates, Jobbers and Drill Attachments) (Exclusion) Regulations, S.I. No. 138 of 1980
		Conditions of Employment (Assembly of Lighters and Small Domestic Appliances Industry) (Exclusion) Regulations, S.I. No. 164 of 1980
		Conditions of Employment (Manufacture of Cut Rug Yarn Industry) (Exclusion) Regulations, S.I. No. 174 of 1980
		Conditions of Employment (Manufacture of Typewriter Ribbons Industry) (Exclusion) Regulations, S.I. No. 191 of 1980
		Conditions of Employment (Polypropylene Foam Injection Moulding Industry) (Exclusion) Regulations, S.I. No. 217 of 1980
		Conditions of Employment (Manufacture of Tapes and Laces Industry) (Exclusion) Regulations, S.I. No. 269 of 1980
		Conditions of Employment (Aluminium Tubes Industry) (Exclusion) Regulations, S.I. No. 275 of 1980
		Conditions of Employment (Weaving of Synthetic Fibres) (Exclusion) Regulations, S.I. No. 280 of 1980
		Conditions of Employment (Manufacture of Plastic Moulded Parts and Tubing) (Exclusion) Regulations, S.I. No. 303 of 1980
		Conditions of Employment (Manufacture of Cosmetic Cases Industry) (Exclusion) Regulations, S.I. No. 304 of 1980

Conditions of Employment Act, No. 2 of 1936 (*Cont.*)

Conditions of Employment (Assembly of Industrial Control Equipment) (Exclusion) Regulations, S.I. No. 305 of 1980

Conditions of Employment (Beverage Can Tops Industry) (Exclusion) Regulations, S.I. No. 308 of 1980

Conditions of Employment (Manufacture of Felt Insulation Industry) (Exclusion) Regulations, S.I. No. 312 of 1980

Conditions of Employment (Bubble Gum and Confectionery Industry) (Exclusion) Regulations, S.I. No. 313 of 1980

Conditions of Employment (Manufacture of Wheels) (Exclusion) Regulations, S.I. No. 314 of 1980

Conditions of Employment (Collapsible Aluminium Tubes) (Exclusion) Regulations, S.I. No. 348 of 1980

Conditions of Employment (Wire Weaving Industry) (Exclusion) Regulations, S.I. No. 375 of 1980

Conditions of Employment (Manufacture of Cassette Deck Cleaners) (Exclusion) Regulations, S.I. No. 379 of 1980

Conditions of Employment (Distribution of Gas) (Exclusion) Regulations, S.I. No. 30 of 1981

Conditions of Employment (Laboratory Technicians) (Exclusion) Regulations, S.I. No. 65 of 1981

Conditions of Employment (Magic Mop) Exclusion, Regulations, S.I. No. 84 of 1981

Conditions of Employment (Laboratory Technicians) (Exclusion) Regulations, S.I. No. 85 of 1981

Conditions of Employment (Plastic Injection Moulding) (Exclusion) Regulations, S.I. No. 105 of 1981

Conditions of Employment (Manufacture of Textiles) (Exclusion) Regulations, S.I. No. 125 of 1981

Conditions of Employment (Adhesives and Solvents) (Exclusion) Regulations, S.I. No. 129 of 1981

Conditions of Employment (Boilerhouse) (Exclusion) Regulations, S.I. No. 166 of 1981

Conditions of Employment (Manufacture of Worsted Yarns) (Comer Yarns (Donegal) Limited) (Exclusion) Regulations, S.I. No. 167 of 1981

Conditions of Employment (Manufacture of Worsted Yarns) (Comer International Limited) (Exclusion) Regulations, S.I. No. 168 of 1981

Conditions of Employment (Laboratory Analysis) (Exclusion) Regulations, S.I. No. 171 of 1981

Conditions of Employment (Cardboard Jewellery Boxes) (Exclusion) Regulations, S.I. No. 177 of 1981

Conditions of Employment Act, No. 2 of 1936 (*Cont.*)		**Conditions of Employment (Plastics Manufacture) Exclusion Regulations, S.I. No. 178 of 1981**
		Conditions of Employment (Manufacture of Bulk Pharmaceuticals) (Exclusion) Regulations, S.I. No. 228 of 1981
		Conditions of Employment (Artificial Kidney Supplies) (Exclusion) Regulations, S.I. No. 229 of 1981
		Conditions of Employment (Laboratory Disposals) (Exclusion) Regulations, S.I. No. 230 of 1981
		Conditions of Employment (Manufacture of Electronic Components) (Exclusion) Regulations, S.I. No. 234 of 1981
		Conditions of Employment (Manufacture of Slates) (Exclusion) Regulations, S.I. No. 235 of 1981
		Conditions of Employment (Manufacture of Artificial Kidney Supplies) (Exclusion) Regulations, S.I. No. 252 of 1981
		Conditions of Employment (Manufacture of Seals and Liquid Products) (Exclusion) Regulations, S.I. No. 253 of 1981
		Conditions of Employment (Manufacture of Cheese) (Exclusion) Regulations, S.I. No. 254 of 1981
		Conditions of Employment (Manufacture of Contact Lenses) (Exclusion) Regulations, S.I. No. 261 of 1981
		Conditions of Employment (Ribbon Re-Reeling) (Exclusion) Regulations, S.I. No. 273 of 1981
		Conditions of Employment (Manufacture of Liqueur) (Exclusion) Regulations, S.I. No. 274 of 1981
		Conditions of Employment (Assembly of Computer Modules) (Exclusion) Regulations, S.I. No. 292 of 1981
		Conditions of Employment (Regeneration of Nylon) (Exclusion) Regulations, S.I. No. 293 of 1981
		Conditions of Employment (Plastic Injection Moulding and Grinding) (Exclusion) Regulations, S.I. No. 334 of 1981
		Conditions of Employment (Mirrors and Windows) (Exclusion) Regulations, S.I. No. 335 of 1981
		Conditions of Employment (Manufacture of Laboratory Products) (Exclusion) Regulations, S.I. No. 344 of 1981
		Conditions of Employment (Manufacture of Nylon Hosiery) (Exclusion) Regulations, S.I. No. 78 of 1985
		Conditions of Employment (Manufacture of Nylon Hosiery) (Exclusion) (No.2) Regulations, S.I. No. 338 of 1985
		Conditions of Employment (Manufacture of Disposable Health Products) (Exclusion) Regulations, S.I. No. 213 of 1986

Statutory Authority	Section	Statutory Instrument
Conditions of Employment Act, No. 2 of 1936 (*Cont.*)		Conditions of Employment (Creameries) (Exclusion) Order [Vol. V p. 495] S.R.& O. No. 353 of 1936
		Conditions of Employment (Condensed Milk) (Exclusion) Order [Vol. V p. 501] S.R.& O. No. 354 of 1936
		Conditions of Employment (Maintenance and Repair of Mail Vans) (Exclusion) Order [Vol. V p. 519] S.R.& O. No. 367 of 1936
		Conditions of Employment (Malting) (Exclusion) Order [Vol. V p. 531] S.R.& O. No. 387 of 1936
		Conditions of Employment (Glass Bottle Works) (Exclusion) Order [Vol. V p. 543] S.R.& O. No. 391 of 1936
		Conditions of Employment (Pottery) (Exclusion) Order [Vol. V p. 549] S.R.& O. No. 127 of 1937
		Conditions of Employment (Peat Bog Development) (Exclusion) Order [Vol. V p. 583] S.R.& O. No. 184 of 1937
		Conditions of Employment (Sheet Glass Works) (Exclusion) Order [Vol. V p. 601] S.R.& O. No. 193 of 1938
		Conditions of Employment (Sewer Cleaning) (Exclusion) Order [Vol. V p. 619] S.R.& O. No. 338 of 1938
	57	Conditions of Employment (Jute Manufacture) (Exclusion) Order [Vol. V p. 363] S.R.& O. No. 158 of 1936
		Conditions of Employment (Gas Undertakings) (Exclusion) Order [Vol. V p. 371] S.R.& O. No. 159 of 1936
		Conditions of Employment (Women Cleaners) (Exclusion) Order [Vol. V p. 379] S.R.& O. No. 160 of 1936
		Conditions of Employment (Railways: Public Service Vehicles) (Exclusion) Order [Vol. V p. 385] S.R.& O. No. 161 of 1936
		Conditions of Employment (Electricity Undertakings) (Exclusion) Order [Vol. V p. 393] S.R. & O. No. 162 of 1936
		Conditions of Employment (Maintenance of Machinery and Plant) (Exclusion) Order [Vol. V p. 401] S.R.& O. No. 163 of 1936
		Conditions of Employment (Boilermen and Enginemen) (Exclusion) Order [Vol. V p. 409] S.R. & O. No. 164 of 1936
		Conditions of Employment (Bakeries) (Exclusion) Order [Vol. V p. 433] S.R.& O. No. 168 of 1936
		Conditions of Employment (Cotton and Linen Industry) (Exclusion) Order [Vol. V p. 441] S.R. & O. No. 175 of 1936
		Conditions of Employment (Tramways) (Exclusion) Order [Vol. V p. 449] S.R.& O. No. 191 of 1936

Statutory Authority	Section	Statutory Instrument
Conditions of Employment Act, No. 2 of 1936 (*Cont.*)		*Conditions of Employment (Turf Industry) (Exclusion) Order [Vol. V p. 455] S.R.& O. No. 288 of 1936*
		Conditions of Employment (Malting) (Exclusion) Regulations [Vol. XXVIII p. 235] S.R.& O. No. 152 of 1940
		Conditions of Employment (Boilermen and Enginemen) (Exclusion and Period of Rest) Regulations [Vol. XXVIII p. 221] S.R.& O. No. 240 of 1942
		Conditions of Employment (Match Manufacturing Industry) (Exclusion) Regulations, S.I. No. 90 of 1951
		Conditions of Employment (Manufacture of Jute Goods) (Young Persons deemed to be Adult Workers) Regulations, S.I. No. 71 of 1962
		Conditions of Employment (Carpet Weaving Industry) (Exclusion) Regulations, S.I. No. 197 of 1963
		Conditions of Employment (Moquette Weaving Industry) (Exclusion) Order, S.I. No. 251 of 1963
	58(1)	**Conditions of Employment (Division of Industrial Undertaking) (Cork County Council) Order [Vol. V p. 611] S.R.& O. No. 220 of 1938**
	64	**Conditions of Employment (Records) Regulations [Vol. XXXVI p. 607] S.R.& O. No. 200 of 1947**
Connaught Rangers (Pensions) Act, No. 37 of 1936	20(2)	**Connaught Rangers Pensions (Expenses and Allowances) Regulations [Vol. V p. 631] S.R.& O. No. 342 of 1936**
Constabulary and Police (Ireland) Act, No. 68 of 1919	4	**Dublin Metropolitan Police Pay Order [Vol. V p. 635] S.R.& O. No. 3 of 1924**
		Dublin Metropolitan Police Pensions Order [Vol. V p. 639] S.R.& O. No. 4 of 1924
Constitution (Consequential Provisions) Act, No. 40 of 1937	4	**Solicitors' Remuneration General Order, 1957 (Disallowance) Order, S.I. No. 232 of 1957**
		Solicitors' Remuneration General Order, 1971 (Disallowance) Order, S.I. No. 61 of 1972
	5	**Petty Sessions (Ireland) Act, 1851, Adaptation Order [Vol. II p. 463] S.R.& O. No. 300 of 1938**
		Alkali etc., Works Regulation Act, 1906, Adaptation Order [Vol. XXV p. 25] S.R.& O. No. 221 of 1939
		Irish Church Act, 1869 Adaptation Order [Vol. XXV p. 61] S.R.& O. No. 34 of 1940
		Pilotage Act, 1913, Adaptation Order [Vol. XXV p. 77] S.R.& O. No. 311 of 1940
		Saorstat Eireann Enactments (Adaptation) Order [Vol. XXVIII p. 267] S.R.& O. No. 204 of 1944

Statutory Authority	Section	Statutory Instrument
Constitution (Consequential Provisions) Act, No. 40 of 1937 (*Cont.*)		**Electoral Act, 1923, Adaptation Order [Vol. XXVIII p. 251] S.R.& O. No. 331 of 1945**
		Offences Against the Person Act, 1861 (Section 9) Adaptation Order, S.I. No. 356 of 1973
		Merchant Shipping Act, 1894 (Adaptation) Order, S.I. No. 223 of 1983
	5(1)	**Currency Act, 1927, Adaptation Order [Vol. V p. 693] S.R.& O. No. 102 of 1938**
		Oireachtas (Payment of Members) Act, 1933, Adaptation Order [Vol. V p. 697] S.R.& O. No. 192 of 1938
		Electoral Act, 1923, Adaptation Order [Vol. V p. 701] S.R.& O. No. 209 of 1938
		Police Forces Amalgamation Act, 1925, Adaptation Order [Vol. V p. 715] S.R.& O. No. 244 of 1938
		Dentists Act, 1928, Adaptation Order [Vol. XXVIII p. 247] S.R.& O. No. 1 of 1941
		Medical Practitioners Act, 1927, Adaptation Order [Vol. XXVIII p. 263] S.R.& O. No. 2 of 1941
		Veterinary Surgeons Act, 1931, Adaptation Order [Vol. XXVIII p. 271] S.R.& O. No. 4 of 1941
Consular Conventions Act, No. 10 of 1954	2(2)	**Consular Conventions Act, 1954 (United States of America) Order, S.I. No. 133 of 1954**
Consumer Information Act, No. 1 of 1978	10	*Consumer Information (Miscellaneous Goods) (Marking) Order, S.I. No. 178 of 1984*
	11	**Consumer Information (Advertisements) (Disclosure of Business Interest) Order, S.I. No. 168 of 1984**
Continental Shelf Act, No. 14 of 1968	2(3)	**Continental Shelf (Designated Areas) Order, S.I. No. 182 of 1968**
		Continental Shelf (Designated Areas) Order, S.I. No. 96 of 1970
		Continental Shelf (Designated Areas) Order, S.I. No. 36 of 1974
		Continental Shelf (Designated Areas) (No.2) Order, S.I. No. 371 of 1974
		Continental Shelf (Designated Areas) Order, S.I. No. 164 of 1976
		Continental Shelf (Designated Areas) Order, S.I. No. 21 of 1977
		Continental Shelf (Designated Areas) (No.2) Order, S.I. No. 22 of 1977
	6(1)	**Continental Shelf (Protection of Installations) (Kinsale Head Field) Order, S.I. No. 285 of 1977**
	10	**Social Welfare (Continental Shelf) Regulations, S.I. No. 19 of 1978**

Statutory Authority	Section	Statutory Instrument
Continuation of Compensation Schemes Act, No. 19 of 1946	1	Emergency Powers (Compensation for Personal Injuries) (Civilians) Scheme, 1942 (Third Amendment) Scheme, S.I. No. 222 of 1949
		Emergency Powers (Compensation for Personal Injuries) (Civilians) Scheme, 1942 (Fourth Amendment) Scheme, S.I. No. 162 of 1960
		Emergency Powers (Compensation for Personal Injuries) (Civilians) Scheme, 1942 (Fifth Amendment) Scheme, S.I. No. 185 of 1972
		Emergency Powers (Compensation for Personal Injuries) (Civilians) Scheme, 1942 (Sixth Amendment) Scheme, S.I. No. 75 of 1974
		Emergency Powers (Compensation for Personal Injuries) (Civilians) Scheme, 1942 (Seventh Amendment) Scheme, S.I. No. 313 of 1974
		Emergency Powers (Compensation for Personal Injuries) (Civilians) Scheme, 1942 (Eighth Amendment) Scheme, S.I. No. 142 of 1975
		Emergency Powers (Compensation for Personal Injuries) (Civilians) Scheme, 1942 (Ninth Amendment) Scheme, S.I. No. 159 of 1976
		Emergency Powers (Compensation for Personal Injuries) (Civilians) Scheme, 1942 (Tenth Amendment) Scheme, S.I. No. 397 of 1977
		Emergency Powers (Compensation for Personal Injuries) (Civilians) Scheme, 1942 (Eleventh Amendment) Scheme, S.I. No. 262 of 1978
	2	Emergency Powers (Compensation for Personal Injuries) (Local Defence Force) Scheme, 1942 (Second Amendment) Scheme, S.I. No. 272 of 1949
		Emergency Powers (Compensation for Personal Injuries) (Local Defence Force) Scheme, 1942 (Third Amendment) Scheme, S.I. No. 178 of 1961
	3	Local Security Force (Compensation for Personal Injuries) Scheme, 1943 (Second Amendment) Scheme, S.I. No. 270 of 1949
		Local Security Force (Compensation for Personal Injuries) Scheme, 1943 (Third Amendment) Scheme, S.I. No. 158 of 1960
		Local Security Force (Compensation for Personal Injuries) Scheme, 1943 (Fourth Amendment) Scheme, S.I. No. 327 of 1975
		Local Security Force (Compensation for Personal Injuries) Scheme, 1943 (Fifth Amendment) Scheme, S.I. No. 386 of 1979
Control of Bulls for Breeding Act, No. 13 of 1985	3	Control of Bulls for Breeding (Permits) Regulations, S.I. No. 333 of 1986
	11	Control of Bulls for Breeding (Permits) Regulations, S.I. No. 333 of 1986
	14(2)	*Control of Bulls for Breeding Act, 1985 (Commencement) Order, S.I. No. 334 of 1986*

Statutory Authority	Section	Statutory Instrument
Control of Exports Act, No. 35 of 1983	2	**Control of Exports Order, S.I. No. 405 of 1983** **Control of Exports Order, 1983 (Amendment) Order, S.I. No. 286 of 1984**
Control of Exports (Temporary Provisions) Act, No. 1 of 1956	2	*Control of Exports Order, S.I. No. 57 of 1956* *Control of Exports (Amendment) Order, S.I. No. 207 of 1956* *Control of Exports Order, S.I. No. 64 of 1957* *Control of Exports Order (Amendment) Order, S.I. No. 139 of 1957* *Control of Exports Order, S.I. No. 79 of 1958* *Control of Exports (No.2) Order, S.I. No. 52 of 1959* *Control of Exports (No.2) Order, S.I. No. 61 of 1960* *Control of Exports (No.3) Order, S.I. No. 59 of 1961* *Control of Exports Order, S.I. No. 27 of 1962* *Control of Exports Order, S.I. No. 28 of 1963* *Control of Exports Order, S.I. No. 33 of 1964* *Control of Exports (No.2) Order, S.I. No. 80 of 1964* *Control of Exports Order, S.I. No. 35 of 1965* *Control of Exports Order, S.I. No. 33 of 1966* *Control of Exports (Amendment) Order, S.I. No. 281 of 1966* *Control of Imports Order, S.I. No. 36 of 1967* *Control of Exports (Southern Rhodesia) Order, S.I. No. 40 of 1967* *Control of Exports (Amendment) Order, S.I. No. 165 of 1967* *Control of Exports Order, S.I. No. 36 of 1968* *Control of Exports (Southern Rhodesia) Order, S.I. No. 48 of 1968* *Control of Exports Order, S.I. No. 32 of 1969* *Control of Exports (Southern Rhodesia) Order, S.I. No. 35 of 1969* *Control of Exports (Southern Rhodesia) (No.2) Order, S.I. No. 106 of 1969* *Control of Exports Order, S.I. No. 32 of 1970* *Control of Exports (Southern Rhodesia) Order, S.I. No. 140 of 1970* *Control of Exports Order, S.I. No. 73 of 1971* *Control of Exports (Southern Rhodesia) Order, S.I. No. 192 of 1971* *Control of Exports Order, S.I. No. 38 of 1972* *Control of Exports (Southern Rhodesia) Order, S.I. No. 153 of 1972* *Control of Exports (Amendment) Order, S.I. No. 308 of 1972* *Control of Exports Order, S.I. No. 51 of 1973* *Control of Exports (Southern Rhodesia) Order, S.I. No. 162 of 1973*

Statutory Authority	Section	Statutory Instrument
Control of Exports (Temporary Provisions) Act, No. 1 of 1956 (*Cont.*)		*Control of Exports (No.2) Order, S.I. No. 344 of 1973*
		Control of Exports Order, S.I. No. 179 of 1974
		Control of Exports (Southern Rhodesia) Order, S.I. No. 181 of 1974
		Control of Exports Order, 1974 (Revocation) Order, S.I. No. 264 of 1974
		Control of Exports (No.2) Order, S.I. No. 369 of 1974
		Control of Exports (Southern Rhodesia) Order, S.I. No. 122 of 1975
		Control of Exports Order, S.I. No. 125 of 1975
		Control of Exports (Southern Rhodesia) Order, S.I. No. 123 of 1976
		Control of Exports Order, S.I. No. 132 of 1976
		Control of Exports (Amendment) Order, S.I. No. 301 of 1976
		Control of Exports (Southern Rhodesia) Order, S.I. No. 170 of 1977
		Control of Exports Order, S.I. No. 195 of 1977
		Control of Exports (No.2) Order, S.I. No. 373 of 1977
		Control of Exports (Southern Rhodesia) Order, S.I. No. 164 of 1978
		Control of Exports Order, S.I. No. 369 of 1978
		Control of Exports (Southern Rhodesia) Order, S.I. No. 213 of 1979
		Control of Exports Order, S.I. No. 403 of 1979
		Conditions of Employment (Southern Rhodesia) (Revocation) Order, S.I. No. 24 of 1980
		Control of Exports (Iran) Order, S.I. No. 146 of 1980
		Control of Exports Order, S.I. No. 385 of 1980
		Control of Exports (Iran) (Revocation) Order, S.I. No. 27 of 1981
		Control of Exports Order, S.I. No. 415 of 1981
		Control of Exports Order, S.I. No. 387 of 1982
	2(2)	*Control of Exports Order, S.I. No. 28 of 1959*
		Control of Exports Order, S.I. No. 35 of 1960
		Control of Exports Order, S.I. No. 33 of 1961
		Control of Exports (No.2) Order, S.I. No. 54 of 1961
Control of Imports Act, No. 12 of 1934		*Control of Imports (Quota No.11, First Period, Additional Quota) Order [Vol. VI p. 719] S.R.& O. No. 161 of 1935*
		Control of Imports (Quota No.17, First Period, Additional Quota) Order [Vol. VII p. 45] S.R.& O. No. 237 of 1935
		Control of Imports (Quota No.17, Third Period, Additional Quota) Order [Vol. VII p. 63] S.R.& O. No. 64 of 1936
		Control of Imports (Quota No.30, First Period, Additional Quota) Order [Vol. VII p. 651] S.R.& O. No. 173 of 1936

Statutory Authority	Section	Statutory Instrument
Control of Imports Act, No. 12 of 1934 (*Cont.*)		*Control of Imports (Quota No.23, Fourth Period, Additional Quota) Order [Vol. VII p. 365] S.R.& O. No. 121 of 1937*
		Control of Imports (Quota No.13, Sixth Period, Additional Quota) Order [Vol. VI p. 857] S.R.& O. No. 126 of 1937
		Control of Imports (Quota No.34, Second Period, Additional Quota) Order [Vol. VII p. 837] S.R.& O. No. 326 of 1937
	3	*Control of Imports (Quota No.1) Order [Vol. VI p. 41] S.R.& O. No. 230 of 1934*
		Control of Imports (Quota No.2) Order [Vol. VI p. 135] S.R.& O. No. 231 of 1934
		Control of Imports (Quota No.3) Order [Vol. VI p. 231] S.R.& O. No. 242 of 1934
		Control of Imports (Quota No.4) Order [Vol. VI p. 305] S.R.& O. No. 243 of 1934
		Control of Imports (Quota No.5) Order [Vol. VI p. 403] S.R.& O. No. 255 of 1934
		Control of Imports (Quota No.6) Order [Vol. VI p. 455] S.R.& O. No. 264 of 1934
		Control of Imports (Quota No.7) Order [Vol. VI p. 501] S.R.& O. No. 265 of 1934
		Control of Imports (Quota No.8) Order [Vol. VI p. 577] S.R.& O. No. 287 of 1934
		Control of Imports (Quota No.9) Order [Vol. VI p. 625] S.R.& O. No. 288 of 1934
		Control of Imports (Quota No.10) Order [Vol. VI p. 663] S.R.& O. No. 289 of 1934
		Control of Imports (Quota No.11) Order [Vol. VI p. 707] S.R.& O. No. 379 of 1934
		Control of Imports (Quota No.12) Order [Vol. VI p. 753] S.R.& O. No. 16 of 1935
		Control of Imports (Quota No.13) Order [Vol. VI p. 815] S.R.& O. No. 59 of 1935
		Control of Imports (Quota No.14) Order [Vol. VI p. 893] S.R.& O. No. 64 of 1935
		Control of Imports (Quota No.15) Order [Vol. VI p. 947] S.R.& O. No. 65 of 1935
		Control of Imports (Quota No.16) Order [Vol. VII p. 1] S.R.& O. No. 66 of 1935
		Control of Imports (Quota No.17) Order [Vol. VII p. 35] S.R.& O. No. 97 of 1935
		Control of Imports (Quota No.18) Order [Vol. VII p. 101] S.R.& O. No. 115 of 1935
		Control of Imports (Quota No.19) Order [Vol. VII p. 137] S.R.& O. No. 158 of 1935
		Control of Imports (Quota No.20) Order [Vol. VII p. 175] S.R.& O. No. 159 of 1935
		Control of Imports (Quota No.21) Order [Vol. VII p. 253] S.R.& O. No. 182 of 1935
		Control of Imports (Quota No.22) Order [Vol. VII p. 295] S.R.& O. No. 183 of 1935

Statutory Authority	Section	Statutory Instrument

Control of Imports Act, No. 12 of 1934 (*Cont.*)

Control of Imports (Quota No.23) Order [Vol. VII p. 337] S.R.& O. No. 261 of 1935

Control of Imports (Quota No.24) Order [Vol. VII p. 389] S.R.& O. No. 469 of 1935

Control of Imports (Quota No.25) Order [Vol. VII p. 429] S.R.& O. No. 569 of 1935

Control of Imports (Quota No.26) Order [Vol. VII p. 461] S.R.& O. No. 14 of 1936

Control of Imports (Quota No.27) Order [Vol. VII p. 505] S.R.& O. No. 15 of 1936

Control of Imports (Quota No.28) Order [Vol. VII p. 549] S.R.& O. No. 16 of 1936

Control of Imports (Quota No.29) Order [Vol. VII p. 593] S.R.& O. No. 17 of 1936

Control of Imports (Quota No.30) Order [Vol. VII p. 639] S.R.& O. No. 58 of 1936

Control of Imports (Quota No.31) Order [Vol. VII p. 667] S.R.& O. No. 238 of 1936

Control of Imports (Quota No.32) Order [Vol. VII p. 727] S.R.& O. No. 239 of 1936

Control of Imports (Quota No.33) Order [Vol. VII p. 771] S.R.& O. No. 56 of 1937

Control of Imports (Quota No.34) Order [Vol. VII p. 813] S.R.& O. No. 146 of 1937

Control of Imports (Quota No.35) Order [Vol. VII p. 865] S.R.& O. No. 217 of 1937

Control of Imports (Quota No.37) Order [Vol. VII p. 927] S.R.& O. No. 288 of 1937

Control of Imports (Quota No.36) Order [Vol. VII p. 893] S.R.& O. No. 314 of 1937

Control of Imports (Quota No.38) Order [Vol. XXVII p. 1005] S.R.& O. No. 139 of 1939

Control of Imports (Quota No.39) Order [Vol. XXVII p. 1091] S.R.& O. No. 200 of 1940

Control of Imports (Quota No.40) Order [Vol. XXVII p. 1139] S.R.& O. No. 201 of 1940

Control of Imports (Quota No.41) Order [Vol. XXVII p. 1181] S.R.& O. No. 202 of 1940

Control of Imports (Quota No.42) Order [Vol. XXVII p. 1221] S.R.& O. No. 203 of 1940

Control of Imports (Quota No.53) (Miscellaneous Brushes) Order, S.I. No. 116 of 1966

6   *Control of Imports (Quota No.2, Sixty-First Period) (Cycle Tyres) Order, S.I. No. 374 of 1985*

Control of Imports (Quota No.51, Twenty-Second Period) (Miscellaneous Textiles) Order, S.I. No. 375 of 1985

Control of Imports (Quota No.52, Twenty-Second Period) (Miscellaneous Textile Piece Goods) Order, S.I. No. 376 of 1985

Control of Imports (Quota No.2, Sixty-Second Period) (Cycle Tyres) Order, S.I. No. 382 of 1986

Control of Imports (Quota No.51, Twenty-Third Period) (Miscellaneous Textiles) Order, S.I. No. 383 of 1986

Statutory Authority	Section	Statutory Instrument
Control of Imports Act, No. 12 of 1934 (*Cont.*)		*Control of Imports (Quota No.52, Twenty-Third Period) (Miscellaneous Textile Piece Goods) Order, S.I. No. 384 of 1986*
	6(1)	*Control of Imports (Quota No.1, First Period) Order [Vol. VI p. 71] S.R.& O. No. 239 of 1934*
		Control of Imports (Quota No.2, First Period) Order [Vol. VI p. 151] S.R.& O. No. 240 of 1934
		Control of Imports (Quota No.3, First Period) Order [Vol. VI p. 241] S.R.& O. No. 256 of 1934
		Control of Imports (Quota No.4, First Period) Order [Vol. VI p. 321] S.R.& O. No. 257 of 1934
		Control of Imports (Quota No.5, First Period) Order [Vol. VI p. 409] S.R.& O. No. 260 of 1934
		Control of Imports (Quota No.6, First Period) Order [Vol. VI p. 463] S.R.& O. No. 314 of 1934
		Control of Imports (Quota No.7, First Period) Order [Vol. VI p. 507] S.R.& O. No. 315 of 1934
		Control of Imports (Quota No.8, First Period) Order [Vol. VI p. 580] S.R.& O. No. 327 of 1934
		Control of Imports (Quota No.9, First Period) Order [Vol. VI p. 631] S.R.& O. No. 328 of 1934
		Control of Imports (Quota No.10, First Period) Order [Vol. VI p. 669] S.R.& O. No. 329 of 1934
		Control of Imports (Quota No.11, First Period) Order [Vol. VI p. 713] S.R.& O. No. 11 of 1935
		Control of Imports (Quota No.12, First Period) Order [Vol. VI p. 763] S.R.& O. No. 26 of 1935
		Control of Imports (Quota No.13, First Period) Order [Vol. VI p. 825] S.R.& O. No. 69 of 1935
		Control of Imports (Quota No.14, First Period) Order [Vol. VI p. 905] S.R.& O. No. 74 of 1935
		Control of Imports (Quota No.15, First Period) Order [Vol. VI p. 959] S.R.& O. No. 75 of 1935
		Control of Imports (Quota No.16, First Period) Order [Vol. VII p. 9] S.R.& O. No. 76 of 1935
		Control of Imports (Quota No.17, First Period) Order [Vol. VII p. 39] S.R.& O. No. 120 of 1935
		Control of Imports (Quota No.18, First Period) Order [Vol. VII p. 107] S.R.& O. No. 127 of 1935
		Control of Imports (Quota No.20, First Period) Order [Vol. VII p. 179] S.R.& O. No. 170 of 1935
		Control of Imports (Quota No.19, First Period) Order [Vol. VII p. 149] S.R.& O. No. 179 of 1935
		Control of Imports (Quota No.21, First Period) Order [Vol. VII p. 259] S.R.& O. No. 239 of 1935
		Control of Imports (Quota No.22, First Period) Order [Vol. VII p. 301] S.R.& O. No. 240 of 1935

Statutory Authority	Section	Statutory Instrument
Control of Imports Act, No. 12 of 1934 (*Cont.*)		*Control of Imports (Quota No.23, First Period) Order [Vol. VII p. 343] S.R.& O. No. 263 of 1935*
		Control of Imports (Quota No.24, First Period) Order [Vol. VII p. 395] S.R.& O. No. 558 of 1935
		Control of Imports (Quota No.25, First Period) Order [Vol. VII p. 435] S.R.& O. No. 591 of 1935
		Control of Imports (Quota No.29, First Period) Order [Vol. VII p. 599] S.R.& O. No. 31 of 1936
		Control of Imports (Quota No.26, First Period) Order [Vol. VII p. 471] S.R.& O. No. 34 of 1936
		Control of Imports (Quota No.27, First Period) Order [Vol. VII p. 515] S.R.& O. No. 35 of 1936
		Control of Imports (Quota No.28, First Period) Order [Vol. VII p. 559] S.R.& O. No. 36 of 1936
		Control of Imports (Quota No.30, First Period) Order [Vol. VII p. 645] S.R.& O. No. 62 of 1936
		Control of Imports (Quota No.31, First Period) Order [Vol. VII p. 679] S.R.& O. No. 250 of 1936
		Control of Imports (Quota No.32, First Period) Order [Vol. VII p. 731] S.R.& O. No. 251 of 1936
		Control of Imports (Quota No.33, First Period) Order [Vol. VII p. 777] S.R.& O. No. 57 of 1937
		Control of Imports (Quota No.34, First Period) Order [Vol. VII p. 825] S.R.& O. No. 152 of 1937
		Control of Imports (Quota No.35, First Period) Order [Vol. VII p. 871] S.R.& O. No. 225 of 1937
		Control of Imports (Quota No.37, First Period) Order [Vol. VII p. 935] S.R.& O. No. 307 of 1937
		Control of Imports (Quota No.36, First Period) Order [Vol. VII p. 899] S.R.& O. No. 311 of 1937
		Control of Imports (Quota No.38, First Period) Order [Vol. XXVII p. 1013] S.R.& O. No. 155 of 1939
		Control of Imports (Quota No.39, First Period) Order [Vol. XXVII p. 1099] S.R.& O. No. 223 of 1940
		Control of Imports (Quota No.40, First Period) Order [Vol. XXVII p. 1147] S.R.& O. No. 224 of 1940
		Control of Imports (Quota No.41, First Period) Order [Vol. XXVII p. 1189] S.R.& O. No. 225 of 1940
		Control of Imports (Quota No.42, First Period) Order [Vol. XXVII p. 1229] S.R.& O. No. 226 of 1940

Statutory Authority	Section	Statutory Instrument
Control of Imports Act, No. 12 of 1934 (*Cont.*)	6(2)	*Control of Imports (Quota No.1, Second Period) Order [Vol. VI p. 77] S.R.& O. No. 343 of 1934*
		Control of Imports (Quota No.2, Second Period) Order [Vol. VI p. 163] S.R.& O. No. 344 of 1934
		Control of Imports (Quota No.3, Second Period) Order [Vol. VI p. 247] S.R.& O. No. 345 of 1934
		Control of Imports (Quota No.4, Second Period) Order [Vol. VI p. 327] S.R.& O. No. 346 of 1934
		Control of Imports (Quota No.5, Second Period) Order [Vol. VI p. 419] S.R.& O. No. 347 of 1934
		Control of Imports (Quota No.2, First Period, Additional Quota) Order [Vol. VI p. 157] S.R.& O. No. 348 of 1934
		Control of Imports (Quota No.6, Second Period) Order [Vol. VI p. 467] S.R.& O. No. 377 of 1934
		Control of Imports (Quota No.7, Second Period) Order [Vol. VI p. 519] S.R.& O. No. 378 of 1934
		Control of Imports (Quota No.1, Third Period) Order [Vol. VI p. 87] S.R.& O. No. 44 of 1935
		Control of Imports (Quota No.2, Third Period) Order [Vol. VI p. 171] S.R.& O. No. 45 of 1935
		Control of Imports (Quota No.5, Third Period) Order [Vol. VI p. 423] S.R.& O. No. 47 of 1935
		Control of Imports (Quota No.3, Third Period) Order [Vol. VI p. 257] S.R.& O. No. 54 of 1935
		Control of Imports (Quota No.6, Third Period) Order [Vol. VI p. 473] S.R.& O. No. 61 of 1935
		Control of Imports (Quota No.7, Third Period) Order [Vol. VI p. 525] S.R.& O. No. 62 of 1935
		Control of Imports (Quota No.12, Second Period) Order [Vol. VI p. 767] S.R.& O. No. 90 of 1935
		Control of Imports (Quota No.14, Second Period) Order [Vol. VI p. 909] S.R.& O. No. 129 of 1935
		Control of Imports (Quota No.2, Fourth Period) Order [Vol. VI p. 183] S.R.& O. No. 131 of 1935
		Control of Imports (Quota No.5, Fourth Period) Order [Vol. VI p. 429] S.R.& O. No. 132 of 1935
		Control of Imports (Quota No.15, Second Period) Order [Vol. VI p. 967] S.R.& O. No. 133 of 1935
		Control of Imports (Quota No.4, Third Period) Order [Vol. VI p. 337] S.R.& O. No. 140 of 1935
		Control of Imports (Quota No.1, Fourth Period) Order [Vol. VI p. 93] S.R.& O. No. 142 of 1935
		Control of Imports (Quota No.8, Second Period) Order [Vol. VI p. 595] S.R.& O. No. 143 of 1935
		Control of Imports (Quota No.9, Second Period) Order [Vol. VI p. 637] S.R.& O. No. 144 of 1935
		Control of Imports (Quota No.10, Second Period) Order [Vol. VI p. 675] S.R.& O. No. 145 of 1935
		Control of Imports (Quota No.6, Fourth Period) Order [Vol. VI p. 477] S.R.& O. No. 168 of 1935
		Control of Imports (Quota No.7, Fourth Period) Order [Vol. VI p. 529] S.R.& O. No. 169 of 1935

Statutory Authority	Section	Statutory Instrument
Control of Imports Act, No. 12 of 1934 (*Cont.*)		*Control of Imports (Quota No.11, Second Period) Order [Vol. VI p. 725] S.R.& O. No. 171 of 1935*
		Control of Imports (Quota No.13, Second Period) Order [Vol. VI p. 829] S.R.& O. No. 173 of 1935
		Control of Imports (Quota No.20, Second Period) Order [Vol. VII p. 183] S.R.& O. No. 238 of 1935
		Control of Imports (Quota No.17, Second Period) Order [Vol. VII p. 51] S.R.& O. No. 250 of 1935
		Control of Imports (Quota No.4, Fourth Period) Order [Vol. VI p. 349] S.R.& O. No. 311 of 1935
		Control of Imports (Quota No.5, Fifth Period) Order [Vol. VI p. 439] S.R.& O. No. 312 of 1935
		Control of Imports (Quota No.1, Fifth Period) Order [Vol. VI p. 99] S.R.& O. No. 320 of 1935
		Control of Imports (Quota No.2, Fifth Period) Order [Vol. VI p. 189] S.R.& O. No. 321 of 1935
		Control of Imports (Quota No.3, Fourth Period) Order [Vol. VI p. 263] S.R.& O. No. 322 of 1935
		Control of Imports (Quota No.14, Third Period) Order [Vol. VI p. 913] S.R.& O. No. 323 of 1935
		Control of Imports (Quota No.15, Third Period) Order [Vol. VI p. 971] S.R.& O. No. 324 of 1935
		Control of Imports (Quota No.6, Fifth Period) Order [Vol. VI p. 481] S.R.& O. No. 539 of 1935
		Control of Imports (Quota No.7, Fifth Period) Order [Vol. VI p. 533] S.R.& O. No. 540 of 1935
		Control of Imports (Quota No.20, Third Period) Order [Vol. VII p. 193] S.R.& O. No. 542 of 1935
		Control of Imports (Quota No.16, Second Period) Order [Vol. VII p. 13] S.R.& O. No. 556 of 1935
		Control of Imports (Quota No.23, Second Period) Order [Vol. VII p. 349] S.R.& O. No. 557 of 1935
		Control of Imports (Quota No.13, Third Period) Order [Vol. VI p. 835] S.R.& O. No. 559 of 1935
		Control of Imports (Quota No.22, Second Period) Order [Vol. VII p. 307] S.R.& O. No. 607 of 1935
		Control of Imports (Quota No.12, Third Period) Order [Vol. VI p. 773] S.R.& O. No. 610 of 1935
		Control of Imports (Quota No.17, Third Period) Order [Vol. VII p. 57] S.R.& O. No. 611 of 1935
		Control of Imports (Quota No.21, Second Period Order [Vol. VII p. 265] S.R.& O. No. 612 of 1935
		Control of Imports (Quota No.4, Fifth Period) Order [Vol. VI p. 355] S.R.& O. No. 632 of 1935
		Control of Imports (Quota No.5, Sixth Period) Order [Vol. VI p. 445] S.R.& O. No. 636 of 1935
		Control of Imports (Quota No.19, Second Period) Order [Vol. VII p. 155] S.R.& O. No. 637 of 1935

Control of Imports Act, No. 12 of
1934 (*Cont.*)

*Control of Imports (Quota No.8, Third Period)
Order [Vol. VI p. 601] S.R.& O. No. 639 of 1935*

*Control of Imports (Quota No.9, Third Period)
Order [Vol. VI p. 643] S.R.& O. No. 640 of 1935*

*Control of Imports (Quota No.18, Second Period)
Order [Vol. VII p. 113] S.R.& O. No. 641 of
1935*

*Control of Imports (Quota No.10, Third Period)
Order [Vol. VI p. 681] S.R.& O. No. 645 of 1935*

*Control of Imports (Quota No.1, Sixth Period)
Order [Vol. VI p. 105] S.R.& O. No. 649 of 1935*

*Control of Imports (Quota No.14, Fourth Period)
Order [Vol. VI p. 919] S.R.& O. No. 650 of 1935*

*Control of Imports (Quota No.7, Sixth Period)
Order [Vol. VI p. 539] S.R.& O. No. 667 of 1935*

*Control of Imports (Quota No.24, Second Period)
Order [Vol. VII p. 401] S.R.& O. No. 669 of
1935*

*Control of Imports (Quota No.11, Third Period)
Order [Vol. VI p. 731] S.R.& O. No. 674 of 1935*

*Control of Imports (Quota No.4, Sixth Period)
Order [Vol. VI p. 361] S.R.& O. No. 30 of 1936*

*Control of Imports (Quota No.2, Sixth Period)
Order [Vol. VI p. 195] S.R.& O. No. 53 of 1936*

*Control of Imports (Quota No.15, Fourth Period)
Order [Vol. VI p. 977] S.R.& O. No. 54 of 1936*

*Control of Imports (Quota No.3, Fifth Period)
Order [Vol. VI p. 269] S.R.& O. No. 56 of 1936*

*Control of Imports (Quota No.5, Seventh Period)
Order [Vol. VI p. 449] S.R.& O. No. 57 of 1936*

*Control of Imports (Quota No.7, Seventh Period)
Order [Vol. VI p. 543] S.R.& O. No. 81 of 1936*

*Control of Imports (Quota No.13, Fourth Period)
Order [Vol. VI p. 839] S.R.& O. No. 82 of 1936*

*Control of Imports (Quota No.24, Third Period)
Order [Vol. VII p. 405] S.R.& O. No. 83 of 1936*

*Control of Imports (Quota No.21, Third Period)
Order [Vol. VII p. 269] S.R.& O. No. 93 of 1936*

*Control of Imports (Quota No.22, Third Period)
Order [Vol. VII p. 313] S.R.& O. No. 94 of 1936*

*Control of Imports (Quota No.12, Fourth Period)
Order [Vol. VI p. 777] S.R.& O. No. 103 of 1936*

*Control of Imports (Quota No.17, Fourth Period)
Order [Vol. VII p. 69] S.R.& O. No. 104 of 1936*

*Control of Imports (Quota No.4, Seventh Period)
Order [Vol. VI p. 367] S.R.& O. No. 143 of 1936*

*Control of Imports (Quota No.8, Fourth Period)
Order [Vol. VI p. 605] S.R.& O. No. 144 of 1936*

*Control of Imports (Quota No.25, Second Period)
Order [Vol. VII p. 441] S.R.& O. No. 146 of
1936*

*Control of Imports (Quota No.29, Second Period)
Order [Vol. VII p. 605] S.R.& O. No. 147 of
1936*

Statutory Authority	Section	Statutory Instrument

Control of Imports Act, No. 12 of
1934 (*Cont.*)

*Control of Imports (Quota No.20, Fourth Period)
Order [Vol. VII p. 201] S.R.& O. No. 151 of
1936*

*Control of Imports (Quota No.26, Second Period)
Order [Vol. VII p. 477] S.R.& O. No. 152 of
1936*

*Control of Imports (Quota No.27, Second Period)
Order [Vol. VII p. 521] S.R.& O. No. 153 of
1936*

*Control of Imports (Quota No.28, Second Period)
Order [Vol. VII p. 565] S.R.& O. No. 154 of
1936*

*Control of Imports (Quota No.30, Second Period)
Order [Vol. VII p. 657] S.R.& O. No. 155 of
1936*

*Control of Imports (Quota No.20, Fifth Period)
Order [Vol. VII p. 205] S.R.& O. No. 170 of
1936*

*Control of Imports (Quota No.23, Third Period)
Order [Vol. VII p. 353] S.R.& O. No. 174 of
1936*

*Control of Imports (Quota No.7, Eighth Period)
Order [Vol. VI p. 549] S.R.& O. No. 177 of 1936*

*Control of Imports (Quota No.20, Sixth Period)
Order [Vol. VII p. 211] S.R.& O. No. 212 of
1936*

*Control of Imports (Quota No.3, Sixth Period)
Order [Vol. VI p. 275] S.R.& O. No. 231 of 1936*

*Control of Imports (Quota No.2, Seventh Period)
Order [Vol. VI p. 207] S.R.& O. No. 233 of 1936*

*Control of Imports (Quota No.15, Fifth Period)
Order [Vol. VI p. 987] S.R.& O. No. 234 of 1936*

*Control of Imports (Quota No.26, Third Period)
Order [Vol. VII p. 481] S.R.& O. No. 235 of
1936*

*Control of Imports (Quota No.27, Third Period)
Order [Vol. VII p. 525] S.R.& O. No. 236 of
1936*

*Control of Imports (Quota No.28, Third Period)
Order [Vol. VII p. 569] S.R.& O. No. 237 of
1936*

*Control of Imports (Quota No.20, Seventh Period)
Order [Vol. VII p. 217] S.R.& O. No. 252 of
1936*

*Control of Imports (Quota No.13, Fifth Period)
Order [Vol. VI p. 845] S.R.& O. No. 253 of 1936*

*Control of Imports (Quota No.6, Sixth Period)
Order [Vol. VI p. 485] S.R.& O. No. 259 of 1936*

*Control of Imports (Quota No.16, Third Period)
Order [Vol. VII p. 17] S.R.& O. No. 260 of 1936*

*Control of Imports (Quota No.24, Fourth Period)
Order [Vol. VII p. 411] S.R.& O. No. 261 of
1936*

Control of Imports Act, No. 12 of
1934 (*Cont.*)

Control of Imports (Quota No.12, Fifth Period)
Order [Vol. VI p. 781] S.R.& O. No. 285 of 1936

Control of Imports (Quota No.21, Fourth Period)
Order [Vol. VII p. 275] S.R.& O. No. 286 of
1936

Control of Imports (Quota No.22, Fourth Period)
Order [Vol. VII p. 319] S.R.& O. No. 287 of
1936

Control of Imports (Quota No.17, Sixth Period)
Order [Vol. VII p. 81] S.R.& O. No. 297 of 1936

Control of Imports (Quota No.8, Fifth Period)
Order [Vol. VI p. 609] S.R.& O. No. 324 of 1936

Control of Imports (Quota No.9, Fourth Period)
Order [Vol. VI p. 647] S.R.& O. No. 325 of 1936

Control of Imports (Quota No.10, Fifth Period)
Order [Vol. VI p. 689] S.R.& O. No. 326 of 1936

Control of Imports (Quota No.18, Third Period)
Order [Vol. VII p. 119] S.R.& O. No. 327 of
1936

Control of Imports (Quota No.25, Third Period)
Order [Vol. VII p. 445] S.R.& O. No. 328 of
1936

Control of Imports (Quota No.1, Seventh Period)
Order [Vol. VI p. 111] S.R.& O. No. 332 of 1936

Control of Imports (Quota No.4, Eighth Period)
Order [Vol. VI p. 373] S.R.& O. No. 333 of 1936

Control of Imports (Quota No.14, Fifth Period)
Order [Vol. VI p. 923] S.R.& O. No. 334 of 1936

Control of Imports (Quota No.19, Third Period)
Order [Vol. VII p. 165] S.R.& O. No. 335 of
1936

Control of Imports (Quota No.23, Fourth Period)
Order [Vol. VII p. 359] S.R.& O. No. 336 of
1936

Control of Imports (Quota No.29, Third Period)
Order [Vol. VII p. 609] S.R.& O. No. 337 of
1936

Control of Imports (Quota No.31, Second Period)
Order [Vol. VII p. 685] S.R.& O. No. 338 of
1936

Control of Imports (Quota No.32, Second Period)
Order [Vol. VII p. 735] S.R.& O. No. 339 of
1936

Control of Imports (Quota No.7, Ninth Period)
Order [Vol. VI p. 553] S.R.& O. No. 365 of 1936

Control of Imports (Quota No.11, Fourth Period)
Order [Vol. VI p. 737] S.R.& O. No. 379 of 1936

Control of Imports (Quota No.3, Seventh Period)
Order [Vol. VI p. 281] S.R.& O. No. 20 of 1937

Control of Imports (Quota No.4, Ninth Period)
Order [Vol. VI p. 379] S.R.& O. No. 23 of 1937

Control of Imports (Quota No.29, Fourth Period)
Order [Vol. VII p. 615] S.R.& O. No. 24 of 1937

Control of Imports Act, No. 12 of 1934 (*Cont.*)

Control of Imports (Quota No.17, Seventh Period) Order [Vol. VII p. 85] S.R.& O. No. 25 of 1937

Control of Imports (Quota No.26, Fourth Period) Order [Vol. VII p. 487] S.R.& O. No. 26 of 1937

Control of Imports (Quota No.27, Fourth Period) Order [Vol. VII p. 531] S.R.& O. No. 27 of 1937

Control of Imports (Quota No.28, Fourth Period) Order [Vol. VII p. 575] S.R.& O. No. 28 of 1937

Control of Imports (Quota No.32, Third Period) Order [Vol. VII p. 741] S.R.& O. No. 29 of 1937

Control of Imports (Quota No.13, Sixth Period) Order [Vol. VI p. 851] S.R.& O. No. 54 of 1937

Control of Imports (Quota No.31, Third Period) Order [Vol. VII p. 691] S.R.& O. No. 55 of 1937

Control of Imports (Quota No.21, Fifth Period) Order [Vol. VII p. 281] S.R.& O. No. 80 of 1937

Control of Imports (Quota No.22, Fifth Period) Order [Vol. VII p. 325] S.R.& O. No. 81 of 1937

Control of Imports (Quota No.12, Sixth Period) Order [Vol. VI p. 787] S.R.& O. No. 83 of 1937

Control of Imports (Quota No.20, Eighth Period) Order [Vol. VII p. 223] S.R.& O. No. 97 of 1937

Control of Imports (Quota No.32, Fourth Period) Order [Vol. VII p. 747] S.R.& O. No. 120 of 1937

Control of Imports (Quota No.7, Tenth Period) Order [Vol. VI p. 557] S.R.& O. No. 129 of 1937

Control of Imports (Quota No.17, Eighth Period) Order [Vol. VII p. 91] S.R.& O. No. 137 of 1937

Control of Imports (Quota No.20, Ninth Period) Order [Vol. VII p. 227] S.R.& O. No. 138 of 1937

Control of Imports (Quota No.23, Fifth Period) Order [Vol. VII p. 371] S.R.& O. No. 139 of 1937

Control of Imports (Quota No.31, Fourth Period) Order [Vol. VII p. 697] S.R.& O. No. 159 of 1937

Control of Imports (Quota No.13, Seventh Period) Order [Vol. VI p. 863] S.R.& O. No. 173 of 1937

Control of Imports (Quota No.33, Second Period) Order [Vol. VII p. 783] S.R.& O. No. 174 of 1937

Control of Imports (Quota No.3, Eighth Period) Order [Vol. VI p. 287] S.R.& O. No. 189 of 1937

Control of Imports (Quota No.4, Tenth Period) Order [Vol. VI p. 385] S.R.& O. No. 190 of 1937

Control of Imports (Quota No.29, Fifth Period) Order [Vol. VII p. 621] S.R.& O. No. 191 of 1937

Control of Imports (Quota No.1, Eighth Period) Order [Vol. VI p. 117] S.R.& O. No. 208 of 1937

Control of Imports (Quota No.2, Eighth Period) Order [Vol. VI p. 213] S.R.& O. No. 210 of 1937

Statutory Authority	Section	Statutory Instrument
Control of Imports Act, No. 12 of 1934 (*Cont.*)		*Control of Imports (Quota No.12, Seventh Period) Order [Vol. VI p. 791] S.R.& O. No. 212 of 1937*
		Control of Imports (Quota No.14, Sixth Period) Order [Vol. VI p. 929] S.R.& O. No. 214 of 1937
		Control of Imports (Quota No.15, Sixth Period) Order [Vol. VI p. 993] S.R.& O. No. 216 of 1937
		Control of Imports (Quota No.6, Seventh Period) Order [Vol. VI p. 489] S.R.& O. No. 244 of 1937
		Control of Imports (Quota No.20, Tenth Period) Order [Vol. VII p. 233] S.R.& O. No. 247 of 1937
		Control of Imports (Quota No.24, Fifth Period) Order [Vol. VII p. 417] S.R.& O. No. 248 of 1937
		Control of Imports (Quota No.34, Second Period) Order [Vol. VII p. 831] S.R.& O. No. 251 of 1937
		Control of Imports (Quota No.16, Fourth Period) Order [Vol. VII p. 23] S.R.& O. No. 252 of 1937
		Control of Imports (Quota No.21, Sixth Period) Order [Vol. VII p. 285] S.R.& O. No. 274 of 1937
		Control of Imports (Quota No.13, Eighth Period) Order [Vol. VI p. 869] S.R.& O. No. 280 of 1937
		Control of Imports (Quota No.33, Third Period) Order [Vol. VII p. 789] S.R.& O. No. 281 of 1937
		Control of Imports (Quota No.23, Sixth Period) Order [Vol. VII p. 375] S.R.& O. No. 287 of 1937
		Control of Imports (Quota No.32, Fifth Period) Order [Vol. VII p. 753] S.R.& O. No. 293 of 1937
		Control of Imports (Quota No.9, Fifth Period) Order [Vol. VI p. 651] S.R.& O. No. 299 of 1937
		Control of Imports (Quota No.18, Fourth Period) Order [Vol. VII p. 125] S.R.& O. No. 300 of 1937
		Control of Imports (Quota No.25, Fourth Period) Order [Vol. VII p. 451] S.R.& O. No. 301 of 1937
		Control of Imports (Quota No.35, Second Period) Order [Vol. VII p. 877] S.R.& O. No. 302 of 1937
		Control of Imports (Quota No.10, Sixth Period) Order [Vol. VI p. 695] S.R.& O. No. 303 of 1937
		Control of Imports (Quota No.26, Fifth Period) Order [Vol. VII p. 493] S.R.& O. No. 304 of 1937
		Control of Imports (Quota No.27, Fifth Period) Order [Vol. VII p. 537] S.R.& O. No. 305 of 1937
		Control of Imports (Quota No.28, Fifth Period) Order [Vol. VII p. 581] S.R.& O. No. 306 of 1937

Statutory Authority	Section	Statutory Instrument
Control of Imports Act, No. 12 of 1934 (*Cont.*)		*Control of Imports (Quota No.8, Sixth Period) Order [Vol. VI p. 615] S.R.& O. No. 312 of 1937*
		Control of Imports (Quota No.31, Fifth Period) Order [Vol. VII p. 703] S.R.& O. No. 313 of 1937
		Control of Imports (Quota No.11, Fifth Period) Order [Vol. VI p. 743] S.R.& O. No. 332 of 1937
		Control of Imports (Quota No.12, Eighth Period) Order [Vol. VI p. 797] S.R.& O. No. 333 of 1937
		Control of Imports (Quota No.7, Eleventh Period) Order [Vol. VI p. 563] S.R.& O. No. 334 of 1937
		Control of Imports (Quota No.34, Third Period) Order [Vol. VII p. 843] S.R.& O. No. 335 of 1937
		Control of Imports (Quota No.36, Second Period) Order [Vol. VII p. 905] S.R.& O. No. 17 of 1938
		Control of Imports (Quota No.15, Seventh Period) Order [Vol. VI p. 999] S.R.& O. No. 39 of 1938
		Control of Imports (Quota No.35, Third Period) Order [Vol. VII p. 881] S.R.& O. No. 40 of 1938
		Control of Imports (Quota No.14, Seventh Period) Order [Vol. VI p. 935] S.R.& O. No. 41 of 1938
		Control of Imports (Quota No.29, Sixth Period) Order [Vol. VII p. 627] S.R.& O. No. 42 of 1938
		Control of Imports (Quota No.3, Ninth Period) Order [Vol. VI p. 293] S.R.& O. No. 43 of 1938
		Control of Imports (Quota No.1, Ninth Period) Order [Vol. VI p. 123] S.R.& O. No. 45 of 1938
		Control of Imports (Quota No.4, Eleventh Period) Order [Vol. VI p. 391] S.R.& O. No. 52 of 1938
		Control of Imports (Quota No.37, Second Period) Order [Vol. VII p. 941] S.R.& O. No. 53 of 1938
		Control of Imports (Quota No.33, Fourth Period) Order [Vol. VII p. 795] S.R.& O. No. 71 of 1938
		Control of Imports (Quota No.31, Sixth Period) Order [Vol. VII p. 709] S.R.& O. No. 72 of 1938
		Control of Imports (Quota No.13, Ninth Period) Order [Vol. VI p. 875] S.R.& O. No. 73 of 1938
		Control of Imports (Quota No.34, Fourth Period) Order [Vol. VII p. 849] S.R.& O. No. 74 of 1938
		Control of Imports (Quota No.12, Ninth Period) Order [Vol. VI p. 803] S.R.& O. No. 92 of 1938
		Control of Imports (Quota No.21, Seventh Period) Order [Vol. VII p. 289] S.R.& O. No. 93 of 1938
		Control of Imports (Quota No.22, Sixth Period) Order [Vol. VII p. 331] S.R.& O. No. 94 of 1938
		Control of Imports (Quota No.36, Third Period) Order [Vol. VII p. 909] S.R.& O. No. 143 of 1938
		Control of Imports (Quota No.37, Third Period) Order [Vol. VII p. 947] S.R.& O. No. 161 of 1938

Statutory Authority	Section	Statutory Instrument

Control of Imports Act, No. 12 of
1934 (*Cont.*)

*Control of Imports (Quota No.20, Eleventh Period)
Order [Vol. VII p. 237] S.R.& O. No. 162 of
1938*

*Control of Imports (Quota No.32, Sixth Period)
Order [Vol. VII p. 759] S.R.& O. No. 164 of
1938*

*Control of Imports (Quota No.7, Twelfth Period)
Order [Vol. VI p. 567] S.R.& O. No. 180 of 1938*

*Control of Imports (Quota No.31, Seventh Period)
Order [Vol. VII p. 715] S.R.& O. No. 181 of
1938*

*Control of Imports (Quota No.20, Twelfth Period)
Order [Vol. VII p. 243] S.R.& O. No. 182 of
1938*

*Control of Imports (Quota No.23, Seventh Period)
Order [Vol. VII p. 381] S.R.& O. No. 183 of
1938*

*Control of Imports (Quota No.34, Fifth Period)
Order [Vol. VII p. 855] S.R.& O. No. 184 of
1938*

*Control of Imports (Quota No.35, Fourth Period)
Order [Vol. VII p. 887] S.R.& O. No. 206 of
1938*

*Control of Imports (Quota No.36, Fourth Period)
Order [Vol. VII p. 915] S.R.& O. No. 212 of
1938*

*Control of Imports (Quota No.3, Tenth Period)
Order [Vol. VI p. 299] S.R.& O. No. 237 of 1938*

*Control of Imports (Quota No.4, Twelfth Period)
Order [Vol. VI p. 397] S.R.& O. No. 238 of 1938*

*Control of Imports (Quota No.29, Seventh Period)
Order [Vol. VII p. 633] S.R.& O. No. 239 of
1938*

*Control of Imports (Quota No.14, Eighth Period)
Order [Vol. VI p. 941] S.R.& O. No. 245 of 1938*

*Control of Imports (Quota No.15, Eighth Period)
Order [Vol. VI p. 1005] S.R.& O. No. 246 of
1938*

*Control of Imports (Quota No.1, Tenth Period)
Order [Vol. VI p. 129] S.R.& O. No. 247 of 1938*

*Control of Imports (Quota No.2, Tenth Period)
Order [Vol. VI p. 225] S.R.& O. No. 248 of 1938*

*Control of Imports (Quota No.24, Sixth Period)
Order [Vol. VII p. 423] S.R.& O. No. 256 of
1938*

*Control of Imports (Quota No.33, Fifth Period)
Order [Vol. VII p. 807] S.R.& O. No. 258 of
1938*

*Control of Imports (Quota No.13, Tenth Period)
Order [Vol. VI p. 887] S.R.& O. No. 260 of 1938*

*Control of Imports (Quota No.16, Fifth Period)
Order [Vol. VII p. 29] S.R.& O. No. 261 of 1938*

*Control of Imports (Quota No.6, Eighth Period)
Order [Vol. VI p. 495] S.R.& O. No. 269 of 1938*

Control of Imports Act, No. 12 of 1934 (*Cont.*)		*Control of Imports (Quota No.36, Fifth Period) Order [Vol. VII p. 921] S.R.& O. No. 294 of 1938*
		Control of Imports (Quota No.12, Tenth Period) Order [Vol. VI p. 809] S.R.& O. No. 295 of 1938
		Control of Imports (Quota No.8, Seventh Period) Order [Vol. VI p. 619] S.R.& O. No. 304 of 1938
		Control of Imports (Quota No.9, Sixth Period) Order [Vol. VI p. 657] S.R.& O. No. 305 of 1938
		Control of Imports (Quota No.10, Seventh Period) Order [Vol. VI p. 701] S.R.& O. No. 306 of 1938
		Control of Imports (Quota No.18, Fifth Period) Order [Vol. VII p. 131] S.R.& O. No. 307 of 1938
		Control of Imports (Quota No.25, Fifth Period) Order [Vol. VII p. 455] S.R.& O. No. 308 of 1938
		Control of Imports (Quota No.26, Sixth Period) Order [Vol. VII p. 499] S.R.& O. No. 314 of 1938
		Control of Imports (Quota No.27, Sixth Period) Order [Vol. VII p. 543] S.R.& O. No. 315 of 1938
		Control of Imports (Quota No.28, Sixth Period) Order [Vol. VII p. 587] S.R.& O. No. 316 of 1938
		Control of Imports (Quota No.32, Seventh Period) Order [Vol. VII p. 765] S.R.& O. No. 317 of 1938
		Control of Imports (Quota No.37, Fourth Period) Order [Vol. VII p. 951] S.R.& O. No. 318 of 1938
		Control of Imports (Quota No.31, Eighth Period) Order [Vol. VII p. 721] S.R.& O. No. 328 of 1938
		Control of Imports (Quota No.34, Sixth Period) Order [Vol. VII p. 859] S.R.& O. No. 333 of 1938
		Control of Imports (Quota No.7, Thirteenth Period) Order [Vol. VI p. 571] S.R.& O. No. 334 of 1938
		Control of Imports (Quota No.35, Fifth Period) Order [Vol. XXVII p. 835] S.R.& O. No. 18 of 1939
		Control of Imports (Quota No.1, Eleventh Period) Order [Vol. XXVII p. 7] S.R.& O. No. 33 of 1939
		Control of Imports (Quota No.2, Eleventh Period) Order [Vol. XXVII p. 41] S.R.& O. No. 34 of 1939
		Control of Imports (Quota No.3, Eleventh Period) Order [Vol. XXVII p. 87] S.R.& O. No. 35 of 1939
		Control of Imports (Quota No.14, Ninth Period) Order [Vol. XXVII p. 441] S.R.& O. No. 36 of 1939

Statutory Authority	Section	Statutory Instrument
Control of Imports Act, No. 12 of 1934 (*Cont.*)		*Control of Imports (Quota No.15, Ninth Period) Order [Vol. XXVII p. 475] S.R.& O. No. 37 of 1939*
		Control of Imports (Quota No.4, Thirteenth Period) Order [Vol. XXVII p. 157] S.R.& O. No. 41 of 1939
		Control of Imports (Quota No.29, Eighth Period) Order [Vol. XXVII p. 675] S.R.& O. No. 42 of 1939
		Control of Imports (Quota No.33, Sixth Period) Order [Vol. XXVII p. 793] S.R.& O. No. 71 of 1939
		Control of Imports (Quota No.13, Eleventh Period) Order [Vol. XXVII p. 363] S.R.& O. No. 72 of 1939
		Control of Imports (Quota No.36, Sixth Period) Order [Vol. XXVII p. 873] S.R.& O. No. 75 of 1939
		Control of Imports (Quota No.12, Eleventh Period) Order [Vol. XXVII p. 307] S.R.& O. No. 92 of 1939
		Control of Imports (Quota No.21, Eighth Period) Order [Vol. XXVII p. 555] S.R.& O. No. 93 of 1939
		Control of Imports (Quota No.22, Seventh Period) Order [Vol. XXVII p. 565] S.R.& O. No. 94 of 1939
		Control of Imports (Quota No.32, Eighth Period) Order [Vol. XXVII p. 729] S.R.& O. No. 137 of 1939
		Control of Imports (Quota No.34, Seventh Period) Order [Vol. XXVII p. 819] S.R.& O. No. 174 of 1939
		Control of Imports (Quota No.31, Ninth Period) Order [Vol. XXVII p. 699] S.R.& O. No. 175 of 1939
		Control of Imports (Quota No.1, Twelfth Period) Order [Vol. XXVII p. 13] S.R.& O. No. 197 of 1939
		Control of Imports (Quota No.2, Twelfth Period) Order [Vol. XXVII p. 47] S.R.& O. No. 198 of 1939
		Control of Imports (Quota No.14, Tenth Period) Order [Vol. XXVII p. 447] S.R.& O. No. 199 of 1939
		Control of Imports (Quota No.15, Tenth Period) Order [Vol. XXVII p. 481] S.R.& O. No. 200 of 1939
		Control of Imports (Quota No.35, Sixth Period) Order [Vol. XXVII p. 841] S.R.& O. No. 201 of 1939
		Control of Imports (Quota No.3, Twelfth Period) Order [Vol. XXVII p. 93] S.R.& O. No. 219 of 1939

Statutory Authority	Section	Statutory Instrument
Control of Imports Act, No. 12 of 1934 (*Cont.*)		*Control of Imports (Quota No.4, Fourteenth Period) Order [Vol. XXVII p. 163] S.R.& O. No. 233 of 1939*
		Control of Imports (Quota No.29, Ninth Period) Order [Vol. XXVII p. 681] S.R.& O. No. 234 of 1939
		Control of Imports (Quota No.38, Second Period) Order [Vol. XXVII p. 1019] S.R.& O. No. 251 of 1939
		Control of Imports (Quota No.6, Ninth Period) Order [Vol. XXVII p. 191] S.R.& O. No. 290 of 1939
		Control of Imports (Quota No.16, Sixth Period) Order [Vol. XXVII p. 521] S.R.& O. No. 294 of 1939
		Control of Imports (Quota No.33, Seventh Period) Order [Vol. XXVII p. 805] S.R.& O. No. 308 of 1939
		Control of Imports (Quota No.13, Twelfth Period) Order [Vol. XXVII p. 375] S.R.& O. No. 309 of 1939
		Control of Imports (Quota No.24, Seventh Period) Order [Vol. XXVII p. 581] S.R.& O. No. 314 of 1939
		Control of Imports (Quota No.36, Seventh Period) Order [Vol. XXVII p. 879] S.R.& O. No. 320 of 1939
		Control of Imports (Quota No.12, Twelfth Period) Order [Vol. XXVII p. 319] S.R.& O. No. 321 of 1939
		Control of Imports (Quota No.32, Ninth Period) Order [Vol. XXVII p. 735] S.R.& O. No. 355 of 1939
		Control of Imports (Quota No.37, Sixth Period) Order [Vol. XXVII p. 933] S.R.& O. No. 356 of 1939
		Control of Imports (Quota No.38, Third Period) Order [Vol. XXVII p. 1025] S.R.& O. No. 357 of 1939
		Control of Imports (Quota No.10, Eighth Period) Order [Vol. XXVII p. 277] S.R.& O. No. 358 of 1939
		Control of Imports (Quota No.18, Sixth Period) Order [Vol. XXVII p. 537] S.R.& O. No. 359 of 1939
		Control of Imports (Quota No.25, Sixth Period) Order [Vol. XXVII p. 597] S.R.& O. No. 360 of 1939
		Control of Imports (Quota No.9, Seventh Period) Order [Vol. XXVII p. 247] S.R.& O. No. 361 of 1939
		Control of Imports (Quota No.8, Eighth Period) Order [Vol. XXVII p. 211] S.R.& O. No. 362 of 1939

Statutory Authority	Section	Statutory Instrument
Control of Imports Act, No. 12 of 1934 (*Cont.*)		*Control of Imports (Quota No.26, Seventh Period) Order [Vol. XXVII p. 627] S.R.& O. No. 368 of 1939*
		Control of Imports (Quota No.27, Seventh Period) Order [Vol. XXVII p. 643] S.R.& O. No. 369 of 1939
		Control of Imports (Quota No.28, Seventh Period) Order [Vol. XXVII p. 659] S.R.& O. No. 370 of 1939
		Control of Imports (Quota No.13, Thirteenth Period) Order [Vol. XXVII p. 385] S.R.& O. No. 399 of 1939
		Control of Imports (Quota No.36, Eighth Period) Order [Vol. XXVII p. 883] S.R.& O. No. 13 of 1940
		Control of Imports (Quota No.35, Seventh Period) Order [Vol. XXVII p. 847] S.R.& O. No. 40 of 1940
		Control of Imports (Quota No.1, Thirteenth Period) Order [Vol. XXVII p. 19] S.R.& O. No. 62 of 1940
		Control of Imports (Quota No.3, Thirteenth Period) Order [Vol. XXVII p. 99] S.R.& O. No. 63 of 1940
		Control of Imports (Quota No.2, Thirteenth Period) Order [Vol. XXVII p. 59] S.R.& O. No. 64 of 1940
		Control of Imports (Quota No.14, Eleventh Period) Order [Vol. XXVII p. 453] S.R.& O. No. 65 of 1940
		Control of Imports (Quota No.15, Eleventh Period) Order [Vol. XXVII p. 493] S.R.& O. No. 66 of 1940
		Control of Imports (Quota No.4, Fifteenth Period) Order [Vol. XXVII p. 169] S.R.& O. No. 67 of 1940
		Control of Imports (Quota No.29, Tenth Period) Order [Vol. XXVII p. 685] S.R.& O. No. 68 of 1940
		Control of Imports (Quota No.37, Seventh Period) Order [Vol. XXVII p. 939] S.R.& O. No. 69 of 1940
		Control of Imports (Quota No.38, Fourth Period) Order [Vol. XXVII p. 1031] S.R.& O. No. 70 of 1940
		Control of Imports (Quota No.12, Thirteenth Period) Order [Vol. XXVII p. 325] S.R.& O. No. 110 of 1940
		Control of Imports (Quota No.13, Fourteenth Period) Order [Vol. XXVII p. 397] S.R.& O. No. 115 of 1940
		Control of Imports (Quota No.36, Ninth Period) Order [Vol. XXVII p. 887] S.R.& O. No. 116 of 1940
		Control of Imports (Quota No.22, Eighth Period) Order [Vol. XXVII p. 571] S.R.& O. No. 118 of 1940

Statutory Authority	Section	Statutory Instrument
Control of Imports Act, No. 12 of 1934 (*Cont.*)		*Control of Imports (Quota No.32, Tenth Period) Order [Vol. XXVII p. 773] S.R.& O. No. 159 of 1940*
		Control of Imports (Quota No.37, Eighth Period) Order [Vol. XXVII p. 945] S.R.& O. No. 160 of 1940
		Control of Imports (Quota No.38, Fifth Period) Order [Vol. XXVII p. 1037] S.R.& O. No. 161 of 1940
		Control of Imports (Quota No.31, Tenth Period) Order [Vol. XXVII p. 705] S.R.& O. No. 185 of 1940
		Control of Imports (Quota No.34, Eighth Period) Order [Vol. XXVII p. 825] S.R.& O. No. 186 of 1940
		Control of Imports (Quota No.35, Eighth Period) Order [Vol. XXVII p. 853] S.R.& O. No. 244 of 1940
		Control of Imports (Quota No.4, Sixteenth Period) Order [Vol. XXVII p. 175] S.R.& O. No. 254 of 1940
		Control of Imports (Quota No.29, Eleventh Period) Order [Vol. XXVII p. 71] S.R.& O. No. 255 of 1940
		Control of Imports (Quota No.1, Fourteenth Period) Order [Vol. XXVII p. 25] S.R.& O. No. 257 of 1940
		Control of Imports (Quota No.2, Fourteenth Period) Order [Vol. XXVII p. 65] S.R.& O. No. 258 of 1940
		Control of Imports (Quota No.3, Fourteenth Period) Order [Vol. XXVII p. 105] S.R.& O. No. 259 of 1940
		Control of Imports (Quota No.14, Twelfth Period) Order [Vol. XXVII p. 459] S.R.& O. No. 260 of 1940
		Control of Imports (Quota No.15, Twelfth Period) Order [Vol. XXVII p. 499] S.R.& O. No. 261 of 1940
		Control of Imports (Quota No.24, Eighth Period) Order [Vol. XXVII p. 587] S.R.& O. No. 288 of 1940
		Control of Imports (Quota No.16, Seventh Period) Order [Vol. XXVII p. 527] S.R.& O. No. 289 of 1940
		Control of Imports (Quota No.13, Fifteenth Period) Order [Vol. XXVII p. 403] S.R.& O. No. 290 of 1940
		Control of Imports (Quota No.6, Tenth Period) Order [Vol. XXVII p. 197] S.R.& O. No. 291 of 1940
		Control of Imports (Quota No.39, Second Period) Order [Vol. XXVII p. 1105] S.R.& O. No. 293 of 1940

Statutory Authority	Section	Statutory Instrument
Control of Imports Act, No. 12 of 1934 (*Cont.*)		*Control of Imports (Quota No.40, Second Period) Order [Vol. XXVII p. 1153] S.R.& O. No. 294 of 1940*
		Control of Imports (Quota No.41, Second Period) Order [Vol. XXVII p. 1195] S.R.& O. No. 295 of 1940
		Control of Imports (Quota No.42, Second Period) Order [Vol. XXVII p. 1235] S.R.& O. No. 296 of 1940
		Control of Imports (Quota No.36, Tenth Period) Order [Vol. XXVII p. 893] S.R.& O. No. 320 of 1940
		Control of Imports (Quota No.12, Fourteenth Period) Order [Vol. XXVII p. 331] S.R.& O. No. 321 of 1940
		Control of Imports (Quota No.26, Eighth Period) Order [Vol. XXVII p. 633] S.R.& O. No. 343 of 1940
		Control of Imports (Quota No.27, Eighth Period) Order [Vol. XXVII p. 649] S.R.& O. No. 344 of 1940
		Control of Imports (Quota No.28, Eighth Period) Order [Vol. XXVII p. 665] S.R.& O. No. 345 of 1940
		Control of Imports (Quota No.32, Eleventh Period) Order [Vol. XXVII p. 779] S.R.& O. No. 346 of 1940
		Control of Imports (Quota No.37, Ninth Period) Order [Vol. XXVII p. 957] S.R.& O. No. 347 of 1940
		Control of Imports (Quota No.38, Sixth Period) Order [Vol. XXVII p. 1043] S.R.& O. No. 348 of 1940
		Control of Imports (Quota No.8, Ninth Period) Order [Vol. XXVII p. 217] S.R.& O. No. 349 of 1940
		Control of Imports (Quota No.9, Eighth Period) Order [Vol. XXVII p. 253] S.R.& O. No. 350 of 1940
		Control of Imports (Quota No.10, Ninth Period) Order [Vol. XXVII p. 283] S.R.& O. No. 351 of 1940
		Control of Imports (Quota No.18, Seventh Period) Order [Vol. XXVII p. 543] S.R.& O. No. 352 of 1940
		Control of Imports (Quota No.25, Seventh Period) Order [Vol. XXVII p. 603] S.R.& O. No. 353 of 1940
		Control of Imports (Quota No.39, Third Period) Order [Vol. XXVII p. 1119] S.R.& O. No. 385 of 1940
		Control of Imports (Quota No.40, Third Period) Order [Vol. XXVII p. 1163] S.R.& O. No. 386 of 1940

Statutory Authority	Section	Statutory Instrument
Control of Imports Act, No. 12 of 1934 (*Cont.*)		*Control of Imports (Quota No.41, Third Period) Order [Vol. XXVII p. 1201] S.R.& O. No. 387 of 1940*
		Control of Imports (Quota No.42, Third Period) Order [Vol. XXVII p. 1241] S.R.& O. No. 388 of 1940
		Control of Imports (Quota No.35, Ninth Period) Order [Vol. XXVII p. 857] S.R.& O. No. 24 of 1941
		Control of Imports (Quota No.2, Fifteenth Period) Order [Vol. XXVII p. 77] S.R.& O. No. 50 of 1941
		Control of Imports (Quota No.14, Thirteenth Period) Order [Vol. XXVII p. 461] S.R.& O. No. 51 of 1941
		Control of Imports (Quota No.15, Thirteenth Period) Order [Vol. XXVII p. 505] S.R.& O. No. 52 of 1941
		Control of Imports (Quota No.29, Twelfth Period) Order [Vol. XXVII p. 691] S.R.& O. No. 53 of 1941
		Control of Imports (Quota No.4, Seventeenth Period) Order [Vol. XXVII p. 181] S.R.& O. No. 54 of 1941
		Control of Imports (Quota No.1, Fifteenth Period) Order [Vol. XXVII p. 31] S.R.& O. No. 65 of 1941
		Control of Imports (Quota No.3, Fifteenth Period) Order [Vol. XXVII p. 111] S.R.& O. No. 66 of 1941
		Control of Imports (Quota No.13, Sixteenth Period) Order [Vol. XXVII p. 421] S.R.& O. No. 125 of 1941
		Control of Imports (Quota No.40, Fourth Period) Order [Vol. XXVII p. 1169] S.R.& O. No. 126 of 1941
		Control of Imports (Quota No.36, Eleventh Period) Order [Vol. XXVII p. 899] S.R.& O. No. 192 of 1941
		Control of Imports (Quota No.12, Fifteenth Period) Order [Vol. XXVII p. 337] S.R.& O. No. 199 of 1941
		Control of Imports (Quota No.37, Tenth Period) Order [Vol. XXVII p. 963] S.R.& O. No. 262 of 1941
		Control of Imports (Quota No.38, Seventh Period) Order [Vol. XXVII p. 1049] S.R.& O. No. 269 of 1941
		Control of Imports (Quota No.31, Eleventh Period) Order [Vol. XXVII p. 711] S.R.& O. No. 314 of 1941
		Control of Imports (Quota No.39, Fourth Period) Order [Vol. XXVII p. 1133] S.R.& O. No. 333 of 1941

Statutory Authority	Section	Statutory Instrument
Control of Imports Act, No. 12 of 1934 (*Cont.*)		*Control of Imports (Quota No.40, Fifth Period) Order [Vol. XXVII p. 1175] S.R.& O. No. 334 of 1941*
		Control of Imports (Quota No.41, Fourth Period) Order [Vol. XXVII p. 1215] S.R.& O. No. 335 of 1941
		Control of Imports (Quota No.42, Fourth Period) Order [Vol. XXVII p. 1247] S.R.& O. No. 336 of 1941
		Control of Imports (Quota No.35, Tenth Period) Order [Vol. XXVII p. 863] S.R.& O. No. 370 of 1941
	6(3)	*Control of Imports (Quota No.11, First Period) Order [Vol. VI p. 713] S.R.& O. No. 11 of 1935*
		Control of Imports (Quota No.17, First Period) Order [Vol. VII p. 39] S.R.& O. No. 120 of 1935
		Control of Imports (Quota No.11, Second Period) Order [Vol. VI p. 725] S.R.& O. No. 171 of 1935
		Control of Imports (Quota No.17, Second Period) Order [Vol. VII p. 51] S.R.& O. No. 250 of 1935
		Control of Imports (Quota No.17, Third Period) Order [Vol. VII p. 57] S.R.& O. No. 611 of 1935
		Control of Imports (Quota No.11, Third Period) Order [Vol. VI p. 731] S.R.& O. No. 674 of 1935
		Control of Imports (Quota No.30, First Period) Order [Vol. VII p. 645] S.R.& O. No. 62 of 1936
		Control of Imports (Quota No.17, Fourth Period) Order [Vol. VII p. 69] S.R.& O. No. 104 of 1936
		Control of Imports (Quota No.17, Fifth Period) Order [Vol. VII p. 75] S.R.& O. No. 210 of 1936
		Control of Imports (Quota No.11, Fourth Period) Order [Vol. VI p. 737] S.R.& O. No. 379 of 1936
		Control of Imports (Quota No.11, Fifth Period) Order [Vol. VI p. 743] S.R.& O. No. 332 of 1937
		Control of Imports (Quota No.20, Eleventh Period) Order [Vol. VII p. 237] S.R.& O. No. 162 of 1938
		Control of Imports (Quota No.20, Twelfth Period) Order [Vol. VII p. 243] S.R.& O. No. 182 of 1938
		Control of Imports (Quota No.37, Fifth Period) Order [Vol. XXVII p. 921] S.R.& O. No. 138 of 1939
		Control of Imports (Quota No.38, First Period) Order [Vol. XXVII p. 1013] S.R.& O. No. 155 of 1939
		Control of Imports (Quota No.38, Second Period) Order [Vol. XXVII p. 1019] S.R.& O. No. 251 of 1939
		Control of Imports (Quota No.33, Seventh Period) Order [Vol. XXVII p. 805] S.R.& O. No. 308 of 1939

Control of Imports Act, No. 12 of 1934 (*Cont.*)

Control of Imports (Quota No.13, Twelfth Period) Order [Vol. XXVII p. 375] S.R.& O. No. 309 of 1939

Control of Imports (Quota No.38, Third Period) Order [Vol. XXVII p. 1025] S.R.& O. No. 357 of 1939

Control of Imports (Quota No.13, Thirteenth Period) Order [Vol. XXVII p. 385] S.R.& O. No. 399 of 1939

Control of Imports (Quota No.38, Fourth Period) Order [Vol. XXVII p. 1031] S.R.& O. No. 70 of 1940

Control of Imports (Quota No.13, Fourteenth Period) Order [Vol. XXVII p. 397] S.R.& O. No. 115 of 1940

Control of Imports (Quota No.38, Fifth Period) Order [Vol. XXVII p. 1037] S.R.& O. No. 161 of 1940

Control of Imports (Quota No.39, First Period) Order [Vol. XXVII p. 1099] S.R.& O. No. 223 of 1940

Control of Imports (Quota No.40, First Period) Order [Vol. XXVII p. 1147] S.R.& O. No. 224 of 1940

Control of Imports (Quota No.41, First Period) Order [Vol. XXVII p. 1189] S.R.& O. No. 225 of 1940

Control of Imports (Quota No.42, First Period) Order [Vol. XXVII p. 1229] S.R.& O. No. 226 of 1940

Control of Imports (Quota No.13, Fifteenth Period) Order [Vol. XXVII p. 403] S.R.& O. No. 290 of 1940

Control of Imports (Quota No.39, Second Period) Order [Vol. XXVII p. 1105] S.R.& O. No. 293 of 1940

Control of Imports (Quota No.40, Second Period) Order [Vol. XXVII p. 1153] S.R.& O. No. 294 of 1940

Control of Imports (Quota No.41, Second Period) Order [Vol. XXVII p. 1195] S.R.& O. No. 295 of 1940

Control of Imports (Quota No.42, Second Period) Order [Vol. XXVII p. 1235] S.R.& O. No. 296 of 1940

Control of Imports (Quota No.38, Sixth Period) Order [Vol. XXVII p. 1043] S.R.& O. No. 348 of 1940

Control of Imports (Quota No.39, Third Period) Order [Vol. XXVII p. 1119] S.R.& O. No. 385 of 1940

Control of Imports (Quota No.40, Third Period) Order [Vol. XXVII p. 1163] S.R.& O. No. 386 of 1940

Control of Imports (Quota No.41, Third Period) Order [Vol. XXVII p. 1201] S.R.& O. No. 387 of 1940

Statutory Authority	Section	Statutory Instrument
Control of Imports Act, No. 12 of 1934 (*Cont.*)		*Control of Imports (Quota No.42, Third Period) Order [Vol. XXVII p. 1241] S.R.& O. No. 388 of 1940*
		Control of Imports (Quota No.40, Fourth Period) Order [Vol. XXVII p. 1169] S.R.& O. No. 126 of 1941
		Control of Imports (Quota No.38, Seventh Period) Order [Vol. XXVII p. 1049] S.R.& O. No. 269 of 1941
		Control of Imports (Quota No.39, Fourth Period) Order [Vol. XXVII p. 1133] S.R.& O. No. 333 of 1941
		Control of Imports (Quota No.40, Fifth Period) Order [Vol. XXVII p. 1175] S.R.& O. No. 334 of 1941
		Control of Imports (Quota No.41, Fourth Period) Order [Vol. XXVII p. 1215] S.R.& O. No. 335 of 1941
		Control of Imports (Quota No.42, Fourth Period) Order [Vol. XXVII p. 1247] S.R.& O. No. 336 of 1941
	6(4)	*Control of Imports (Quota No.5, First Period, Additional Quota) Order [Vol. VI p. 415] S.R.& O. No. 339 of 1934*
		Control of Imports (Quota No.7, First Period, Additional Quota) Order [Vol. VI p. 513] S.R.& O. No. 376 of 1934
		Control of Imports (Quota No.3, Second Period, Additional Quota) Order [Vol. VI p. 251] S.R.& O. No. 20 of 1935
		Control of Imports (Quota No.4, Second Period, Additional Quota) Order [Vol. VI p. 331] S.R.& O. No. 21 of 1935
		Control of Imports (Quota No.1, Second Period, Additional Quota) Order [Vol. VI p. 81] S.R.& O. No. 24 of 1935
		Control of Imports (Quota No.2, Second Period, Additional Quota) Order [Vol. VI p. 167] S.R.& O. No. 25 of 1935
		Control of Imports (Quota No.15, First Period, Additional Quota) Order [Vol. VI p. 963] S.R.& O. No. 128 of 1935
		Control of Imports (Quota No.2, Third Period, Additional Quota) Order [Vol. VI p. 177] S.R.& O. No. 130 of 1935
		Control of Imports (Quota No.5, Fourth Period, Additional Quota) Order [Vol. VI p. 435] S.R.& O. No. 180 of 1935
		Control of Imports (Quota No.20, Second Period, Additional Quota) Order [Vol. VII p. 187] S.R.& O. No. 541 of 1935
		Control of Imports (Quota No.20, Third Period, Additional Quota) Order [Vol. VII p. 197] S.R.& O. No. 134 of 1936

Statutory Authority	Section	Statutory Instrument

Control of Imports Act, No. 12 of 1934 (*Cont.*)

Control of Imports (Quota No.2, Sixth Period, Additional Quota) Order [Vol. VI p. 201] S.R.& O. No. 207 of 1936

Control of Imports (Quota No.15, Fourth Period, Additional Quota) Order [Vol. VI p. 983] S.R.& O. No. 208 of 1936

Control of Imports (Quota No.19, Second Period, Additional Quota) Order [Vol. VII p. 159] S.R.& O. No. 209 of 1936

11

Control of Imports (Quota No.3) (Amendment) Order [Vol. VI p. 237] S.R.& O. No. 18 of 1935

Control of Imports (Quota No.4) (Amendment) Order [Vol. VI p. 311] S.R.& O. No. 19 of 1935

Control of Imports (Quota No.1) (Amendment) Order [Vol. VI p. 49] S.R.& O. No. 34 of 1935

Control of Imports (Quota No.2) (Amendment) Order [Vol. VI p. 141] S.R.& O. No. 46 of 1935

Control of Imports (Quota No.1) (Amendment No.2) Order [Vol. VI p. 53] S.R.& O. No. 160 of 1935

Control of Imports (Quota No.4, Third Period) (Amendment) Order [Vol. VI p. 343] S.R.& O. No. 174 of 1935

Control of Imports (Quota No.16) (Amendment) Order [Vol. VII p. 5] S.R.& O. No. 606 of 1935

Control of Imports (Quota No.1) (Amendment No.3) Order [Vol. VI p. 59] S.R.& O. No. 666 of 1935

Control of Imports (Quota No.19) (Amendment) Order [Vol. VII p. 143] S.R.& O. No. 668 of 1935

Control of Imports (Quota No.4) (Amendment No.2) Order [Vol. VI p. 315] S.R.& O. No. 13 of 1936

Control of Imports (Quota No.26) (Amendment) Order [Vol. VII p. 467] S.R.& O. No. 178 of 1936

Control of Imports (Quota No.27) (Amendment) Order [Vol. VII p. 511] S.R.& O. No. 179 of 1936

Control of Imports (Quota No.28) (Amendment) Order [Vol. VII p. 555] S.R.& O. No. 180 of 1936

Control of Imports (Quota No.30) (Revocation) Order [Vol. VII p. 663] S.R.& O. No. 182 of 1936

Control of Imports (Quota No.13) (Amendment) Order [Vol. VI p. 821] S.R.& O. No. 53 of 1937

Control of Imports (Quota No.31) (Amendment) Order [Vol. VII p. 673] S.R.& O. No. 147 of 1937

Control of Imports (Quota No.19) (Revocation) Order [Vol. VII p. 171] S.R.& O. No. 206 of 1937

Control of Imports (Quota No.1) (Amendment No.4) Order [Vol. VI p. 65] S.R.& O. No. 207 of 1937

Control of Imports (Quota No.2) (Amendment No.2) Order [Vol. VI p. 145] S.R.& O. No. 209 of 1937

Control of Imports (Quota No.12) (Amendment) Order [Vol. VI p. 757] S.R.& O. No. 211 of 1937

Statutory Authority	Section	Statutory Instrument

Control of Imports Act, No. 12 of
1934 (*Cont.*)

Control of Imports (Quota No.14) (Amendment) Order [Vol. VI p. 899] S.R.& O. No. 213 of 1937

Control of Imports (Quota No.15) (Amendment) Order [Vol. VI p. 953] S.R.& O. No. 215 of 1937

Control of Imports (Quota No.17) (Revocation) Order [Vol. VII p. 97] S.R.& O. No. 310 of 1937

Control of Imports (Quota No.11) (Revocation) Order [Vol. VI p. 749] S.R.& O. No. 163 of 1938

Control of Imports (Quota No.8) (Amendment) Order [Vol. VI p. 583] S.R.& O. No. 175 of 1938

Control of Imports (Quota No.34) (Amendment) Order [Vol. VII p. 821] S.R.& O. No. 176 of 1938

Control of Imports (Quota No.23) (Revocation) Order [Vol. VII p. 385] S.R.& O. No. 280 of 1938

Control of Imports (Quota No.20) (Revocation) Order [Vol. VII p. 249] S.R.& O. No. 281 of 1938

Control of Imports (Quota No.7) (Revocation) Order [Vol. XXVII p. 207] S.R.& O. No. 164 of 1939

Control of Imports (Quota No.34) (Amendment) Order [Vol. XXVII p. 815] S.R.& O. No. 173 of 1939

Control of Imports (Quota No.21) (Revocation) Order [Vol. XXVII p. 561] S.R.& O. No. 188 of 1939

Control of Imports (Quota No.37) (Amendment) Order [Vol. XXVII p. 927] S.R.& O. No. 295 of 1939

Control of Imports (Quota No.13, Twelfth Period) (Amendment) Order [Vol. XXVII p. 381] S.R.& O. No. 353 of 1939

Control of Imports (Quota No.33) (Revocation) Order [Vol. XXVII p. 811] S.R.& O. No. 354 of 1939

Control of Imports (Quotas No.1 to 32) (Amendment) Order [Vol. XXVII p. 741] S.R.& O. No. 402 of 1939

Control of Imports (Quota No.13, Thirteenth Period) (Amendment) Order [Vol. XXVII p. 391] S.R.& O. No. 41 of 1940

Control of Imports (Quota No.37, Eighth Period) (Amendment) Order [Vol. XXVII p. 951] S.R.& O. No. 199 of 1940

Control of Imports (Quota No.13, Fifteenth Period) (Amendment) (No.2) Order [Vol. XXVII p. 409] S.R.& O. No. 317 of 1940

Control of Imports (Quota No.22) (Revocation) Order [Vol. XXVII p. 577] S.R.& O. No. 342 of 1940

Control of Imports (Quota No.40) (Amendment) Order [Vol. XXVII p. 1159] S.R.& O. No. 383 of 1940

Control of Imports Act, No. 12 of
1934 (*Cont.*)

Control of Imports (Quota No.34) (Revocation)
Order [Vol. XXVII p. 831] S.R.& O. No. 209 of
1941

Control of Imports (Quotas No.35 and 36)
(Amendment) Order [Vol. XXVII p. 905] S.R.&
O. No. 351 of 1941

Control of Imports (Quota No.10) Order, 1934
(Road Vehicle Bodies) (Amendment) Order, S.I.
No. 138 of 1952

Control of Imports (Quota No.6) (Revocation)
Order, S.I. No. 92 of 1963

Control of Imports (Quota No.2) (Amendment)
Order, S.I. No. 118 of 1963

Control of Imports (Amendment of Quota No.3 and
Revocation of Quota No.4) Order, S.I. No. 261 of
1965

Control of Imports (Miscellaneous Quotas) (Revo-
cation) Order, S.I. No. 106 of 1966

Control of Imports (Quota No.50) (Super-
phosphates) (Amendment) Order, S.I. No. 107 of
1966

Control of Imports (Quota No.12) (Silk or Artificial
Silk Hose) (Amendment) Order, S.I. No. 109 of
1966

Control of Imports (Quota No.28) (Miscellaneous
Brushes) (Amendment) Order, S.I. No. 114 of
1966

Control of Imports (Quota No.54) (Revocation)
Order, S.I. No. 251 of 1969

Control of Imports (Quota No.3) (Revocation)
Order, S.I. No. 139 of 1970

Control of Imports (Quota No.31) (Revocation)
Order, S.I. No. 315 of 1972

Control of Imports (Miscellaneous Quotas)
(Revocation) Order, S.I. No. 135 of 1975

Control of Imports (Quota No.51) (Miscellaneous
Textiles) (Amendment) Order, S.I. No. 283 of
1975

Control of Imports (Quota No.52) (Miscellaneous
Textile Piece Goods) (Amendment) Order, S.I.
No. 284 of 1975

Control of Imports (Quota No.2) (Cycle Tyres)
(Amendment) Order, S.I. No. 319 of 1975

Control of Imports (Quota No.51) (Miscellaneous
Textiles) (Amendment) Order, S.I. No. 107 of
1977

Control of Imports (Quota No.52) (Miscellaneous
Textile Piece Goods) (Amendment) Order, S.I.
No. 108 of 1977

Control of Imports (Quota No.52) (Miscellaneous
Textile Piece Goods) (Amendment) (No.2) Order,
S.I. No. 257 of 1977

Control of Imports (Quota No.51) (Miscellaneous
Textiles) (Amendment) (No.2) Order, S.I. No. 266
of 1977

Statutory Authority	Section	Statutory Instrument
Control of Imports Act, No. 12 of 1934 (*Cont.*)	13	*Control of Imports (Regulations) Order [Vol. VI p. 1] S.R.& O. No. 223 of 1934*
		Control of Imports (Regulations) Order [Vol. VI p. 11] S.R.& O. No. 197 of 1937
		Control of Imports (Regulations) (Amendment) Order [Vol. XXVII p. 1] S.R.& O. No. 214 of 1940
		Control of Imports (Regulations) (Amendment) Order, S.I. No. 357 of 1949
Control of Imports Acts,		*Control of Imports (Quota No.33, Fourth Period, Additional Quota) Order [Vol. VII p. 801] S.R.& O. No. 257 of 1938*
		Control of Imports (Quota No.13, Ninth Period, Additional Quota) Order [Vol. VI p. 881] S.R.& O. No. 259 of 1938
		Control of Imports (Quota No.33, Fifth Period, Additional Quota) Order [Vol. XXVII p. 787] S.R.& O. No. 30 of 1939
		Control of Imports (Quota No.16, Fifth Period, Additional Quota) Order [Vol. XXVII p. 515] S.R.& O. No. 39 of 1939
		Control of Imports (Quota No.13, Tenth Period, Additional Quota) Order [Vol. XXVII p. 357] S.R.& O. No. 113 of 1939
		Control of Imports (Quota No.12, Eleventh Period, Additional Quota) Order [Vol. XXVII p. 313] S.R.& O. No. 252 of 1939
		Control of Imports (Quota No.33, Sixth Period, Additional Quota) Order [Vol. XXVII p. 799] S.R.& O. No. 292 of 1939
		Control of Imports (Quota No.13, Eleventh Period, Additional Quota) Order [Vol. XXVII p. 369] S.R.& O. No. 293 of 1939
		Control of Imports (Quota No.2, Twelfth Period, Additional Quota) Order [Vol. XXVII p. 53] S.R.& O. No. 37 of 1940
		Control of Imports (Quota No.15, Tenth Period, Additional Quota) Order [Vol. XXVII p. 487] S.R.& O. No. 38 of 1940
		Control of Imports (Quota No.39, Second Period, Additional Quota) Order [Vol. XXVII p. 1111] S.R.& O. No. 382 of 1940
		Control of Imports (Quota No.42) (Amendment) Order [Vol. XXVII p. 1253] S.R.& O. No. 384 of 1940
		Control of Imports (Quota No.13, Fifteenth Period, Additional Quota) Order [Vol. XXVII p. 413] S.R.& O. No. 67 of 1941
		Control of Imports (Quota No.39, Third Period, Additional Quota) Order [Vol. XXVII p. 1125] S.R.& O. No. 250 of 1941
		Control of Imports (Quota No.41, Third Period, Additional Quota) Order [Vol. XXVII p. 1207] S.R.& O. No. 251 of 1941

Statutory Authority	Section	Statutory Instrument
Control of Imports Acts (*Cont.*)		*Control of Imports (Quota No.13, Sixteenth Period, Additional Quota) Order [Vol. XXVII p. 427] S.R.& O. No. 344 of 1941*
		Control of Imports (Quota No.12, Fifteenth Period, Additional Quota) Order [Vol. XXVII p. 343] S.R.& O. No. 365 of 1941
		Control of Imports (Quota No.13, Sixteenth Period, Amendment and Second Additional Quota) Order [Vol. XXVII p. 435] S.R.& O. No. 382 of 1941
		Control of Imports (Quota No.29, Thirteenth Period) Order [Vol. XXVII p. 695] S.R.& O. No. 388 of 1941
		Control of Imports (Quota No.4, Eighteenth Period) Order [Vol. XXVII p. 187] S.R.& O. No. 389 of 1941
		Control of Imports (Quota No.14, Fourteenth Period) Order [Vol. XXVII p. 475] S.R.& O. No. 392 of 1941
		Control of Imports (Quota No.15, Fourteenth Period) Order [Vol. XXVII p. 511] S.R.& O. No. 393 of 1941
		Control of Imports (Quota No.1, Sixteenth Period) Order [Vol. XXVII p. 37] S.R.& O. No. 394 of 1941
		Control of Imports (Quota No.2, Sixteenth Period) Order [Vol. XXVII p. 83] S.R.& O. No. 395 of 1941
		Control of Imports (Quota No.3, Sixteenth Period) Order [Vol. XXVII p. 117] S.R.& O. No. 396 of 1941
		Control of Imports (Quota No.12, Fifteenth Period, Amendment and Second Additional Quota) Order [Vol. XXVII p. 349] S.R.& O. No. 422 of 1941
		Control of Imports (Quota No.24, Ninth Period) Order [Vol. XXVII p. 593] S.R.& O. No. 423 of 1941
		Control of Imports (Quota No.6, Eleventh Period) Order [Vol. XXVII p. 203] S.R.& O. No. 426 of 1941
		Control of Imports (Quota No.16, Eighth Period) Order [Vol. XXVII p. 533] S.R.& O. No. 452 of 1941
		Control of Imports (Quota No.32, Twelfth Period) Order [Vol. XXVII p. 783] S.R.& O. No. 467 of 1941
		Control of Imports (Quota No.36, Twelfth Period) Order [Vol. XXVII p. 917] S.R.& O. No. 469 of 1941
		Control of Imports (Quota No.26, Ninth Period) Order [Vol. XXVII p. 639] S.R.& O. No. 521 of 1941
		Control of Imports (Quota No.27, Ninth Period) Order [Vol. XXVII p. 655] S.R.& O. No. 522 of 1941

Statutory Authority	Section	Statutory Instrument
Control of Imports Acts (*Cont.*)		*Control of Imports (Quota No.28, Ninth Period) Order [Vol. XXVII p. 671] S.R.& O. No. 523 of 1941*
		Control of Imports (Quota No.38, Eighth Period) Order [Vol. XXVII p. 1055] S.R.& O. No. 524 of 1941
		Control of Imports (Quota No.37, Eleventh Period) Order [Vol. XXVII p. 969] S.R.& O. No. 525 of 1941
		Control of Imports (Quota No.3, Seventeenth Period) Order [Vol. XXVII p. 121] S.R.& O. No. 537 of 1941
		Control of Imports (Quota No.18, Eighth Period) Order [Vol. XXVII p. 547] S.R.& O. No. 538 of 1941
		Control of Imports (Quota No.25, Eighth Period) Order [Vol. XXVII p. 607] S.R.& O. No. 539 of 1941
		Control of Imports (Quota No.8, Tenth Period) Order [Vol. XXVII p. 223] S.R.& O. No. 540 of 1941
		Control of Imports (Quota No.10, Tenth Period) Order [Vol. XXVII p. 287] S.R.& O. No. 541 of 1941
		Control of Imports (Quota No.9, Ninth Period) Order [Vol. XXVII p. 257] S.R.& O. No. 542 of 1941
		Control of Imports (Quota No.35, Eleventh Period) Order [Vol. XXVII p. 869] S.R.& O. No. 16 of 1942
		Control of Imports (Quota No.38, Ninth Period) Order [Vol. XXVII p. 1059] S.R.& O. No. 197 of 1942
		Control of Imports (Quota No.37, Twelfth Period) Order [Vol. XXVII p. 973] S.R.& O. No. 198 of 1942
		Control of Imports (Quota No.3, Eighteenth Period) Order [Vol. XXVII p. 125] S.R.& O. No. 224 of 1942
		Control of Imports (Quota No.31, Twelfth Period) Order [Vol. XXVII p. 717] S.R.& O. No. 260 of 1942
		Control of Imports (Quota No.3, Nineteenth Period) Order [Vol. XXVII p. 129] S.R.& O. No. 485 of 1942
		Control of Imports (Quota No.8, Eleventh Period) Order [Vol. XXVII p. 227] S.R.& O. No. 486 of 1942
		Control of Imports (Quota No.9, Tenth Period) Order [Vol. XXVII p. 261] S.R.& O. No. 487 of 1942
		Control of Imports (Quota No.10, Eleventh Period) Order [Vol. XXVII p. 291] S.R.& O. No. 488 of 1942

Statutory Authority	Section	Statutory Instrument

Control of Imports Acts (*Cont.*)

Control of Imports (Quota No.18, Ninth Period) Order [Vol. XXVII p. 551] S.R.& O. No. 489 of 1942

Control of Imports (Quota No.25, Ninth Period) Order [Vol. XXVII p. 611] S.R.& O. No. 490 of 1942

Control of Imports (Quota No.37, Thirteenth Period) Order [Vol. XXVII p. 977] S.R.& O. No. 491 of 1942

Control of Imports (Quota No.38, Tenth Period) Order [Vol. XXVII p. 1063] S.R.& O. No. 492 of 1942

Control of Imports (Quota No.31, Thirteenth Period) Order [Vol. XXVII p. 721] S.R.& O. No. 528 of 1942

Control of Imports (Quota No.3, Twentieth Period) Order [Vol. XXVII p. 133] S.R.& O. No. 205 of 1943

Control of Imports (Quota No.37, Fourteenth Period) Order [Vol. XXVII p. 981] S.R.& O. No. 206 of 1943

Control of Imports (Quota No.38, Eleventh Period) Order [Vol. XXVII p. 1067] S.R.& O. No. 207 of 1943

Control of Imports (Quota No.3, Twenty-First Period) Order [Vol. XXVII p. 137] S.R.& O. No. 374 of 1943

Control of Imports (Quota No.8, Twelfth Period) Order [Vol. XXVII p. 231] S.R.& O. No. 375 of 1943

Control of Imports (Quota No.9, Eleventh Period) Order [Vol. XXVII p. 265] S.R.& O. No. 376 of 1943

Control of Imports (Quota No.10, Twelfth Period) Order [Vol. XXVII p. 295] S.R.& O. No. 377 of 1943

Control of Imports (Quota No.25, Tenth Period) Order [Vol. XXVII p. 615] S.R.& O. No. 378 of 1943

Control of Imports (Quota No.37, Fifteenth Period) Order [Vol. XXVII p. 985] S.R.& O. No. 379 of 1943

Control of Imports (Quota No.38, Twelfth Period) Order [Vol. XXVII p. 1071] S.R.& O. No. 380 of 1943

Control of Imports (Quota No.3, Twenty-Second Period) Order [Vol. XXVII p. 141] S.R.& O. No. 164 of 1944

Control of Imports (Quota No.37, Sixteenth Period) Order [Vol. XXVII p. 989] S.R.& O. No. 165 of 1944

Control of Imports (Quota No.38, Thirteenth Period) Order [Vol. XXVII p. 1075] S.R.& O. No. 166 of 1944

Statutory Authority	Section	Statutory Instrument
Control of Imports Acts (*Cont.*)		*Control of Imports (Quota No.3, Twenty-Third Period) Order [Vol. XXVII p. 145] S.R.& O. No. 329 of 1944*
		Control of Imports (Quota No.8, Thirteenth Period) Order [Vol. XXVII p. 235] S.R.& O. No. 330 of 1944
		Control of Imports (Quota No.9, Twelfth Period) Order [Vol. XXVII p. 269] S.R.& O. No. 331 of 1944
		Control of Imports (Quota No.10, Thirteenth Period) Order [Vol. XXVII p. 299] S.R.& O. No. 332 of 1944
		Control of Imports (Quota No.25, Eleventh Period) Order [Vol. XXVII p. 619] S.R.& O. No. 333 of 1944
		Control of Imports (Quota No.37, Seventeenth Period) Order [Vol. XXVII p. 993] S.R.& O. No. 334 of 1944
		Control of Imports (Quota No.38, Fourteenth Period) Order [Vol. XXVII p. 1079] S.R.& O. No. 335 of 1944
		Control of Imports (Quota No.3, Twenty-Fourth Period) Order [Vol. XXVII p. 149] S.R.& O. No. 130 of 1945
		Control of Imports (Quota No.37, Eighteenth Period) Order [Vol. XXVII p. 997] S.R.& O. No. 131 of 1945
		Control of Imports (Quota No.38, Fifteenth Period) Order [Vol. XXVII p. 1083] S.R.& O. No. 132 of 1945
		Control of Imports (Quota No.8, Thirteenth Period, Additional Quota) Order [Vol. XXVII p. 239] S.R.& O. No. 244 of 1945
		Control of Imports (Quota No.31, Fourteenth Period) Order [Vol. XXVII p. 725] S.R.& O. No. 305 of 1945
		Control of Imports (Quota No.8, Fourteenth Period) Order [Vol. p. 243] S.R.& O. No. 316 of 1945
		Control of Imports (Quota No.9, Thirteenth Period) Order [Vol. XXVII p. 273] S.R.& O. No. 317 of 1945
		Control of Imports (Quota No.10, Fourteenth Period) Order [Vol. XXVII p. 303] S.R.& O. No. 318 of 1945
		Control of Imports (Quota No.25, Twelfth Period) Order [Vol. XXVII p. 623] S.R.& O. No. 319 of 1945
		Control of Imports (Quota No.3, Twenty-Fifth Period) Order [Vol. XXVII p. 153] S.R.& O. No. 339 of 1945
		Control of Imports (Quota No.38, Sixteenth Period) Order [Vol. XXVII p. 1087] S.R.& O. No. 340 of 1945

Control of Imports Acts (*Cont.*)

Control of Imports (Quota No.37, Nineteenth Period) Order [Vol. XXVII p. 1001] S.R.& O. No. 341 of 1945

Control of Imports (Quota No.35, Twelfth Period) Order [Vol. XXXVI p. 727] S.R.& O. No. 25 of 1946

Control of Imports (Quota No.31, Fifteenth Period) Order [Vol. XXXVI p. 705] S.R.& O. No. 32 of 1946

Control of Imports (Quota No.36, Thirteenth Period) Order [Vol. XXXVI p. 747] S.R.& O. No. 49 of 1946

Control of Imports (Quota No.35, Thirteenth Period) Order [Vol. XXXVI p. 731] S.R.& O. No. 71 of 1946

Control of Imports (Quota No.38, Seventeenth Period) Order [Vol. XXXVI p. 783] S.R.& O. No. 184 of 1946

Control of Imports (Quota No.3, Twenty-Sixth Period) Order [Vol. XXXVI p. 629] S.R.& O. No. 185 of 1946

Control of Imports (Quota No.31, Sixteenth Period) Order [Vol. XXXVI p. 709] S.R.& O. No. 247 of 1946

Control of Imports (Quota No.36, Fourteenth Period) Order [Vol. XXXVI p. 751] S.R.& O. No. 299 of 1946

Control of Imports (Quota No.35, Fourteenth Period) Order [Vol. XXXVI p. 735] S.R.& O. No. 321 of 1946

Control of Imports (Quotas No.1 to 32) (Amendment) Order, 1939 (Amendment) Order [Vol. XXXVI p. 623] S.R.& O. No. 345 of 1946

Control of Imports (Quotas No.35 and 36) (Amendment) Order, 1941 (Amendment) Order [Vol. XXXVI p. 721] S.R.& O. No. 346 of 1946

Control of Imports (Quotas No.37 to 42) (Amendment) Order [Vol. XXXVI p. 763] S.R.& O. No. 347 of 1946

Control of Imports (Quota No.37, Twentieth Period) Order [Vol. XXXVI p. 771] S.R.& O. No. 404 of 1946

Control of Imports (Quota No.3, Twenty-Seventh Period) Order [Vol. XXXVI p. 633] S.R.& O. No. 405 of 1946

Control of Imports (Quota No.10, Fifteenth Period) Order [Vol. XXXVI p. 669] S.R.& O. No. 406 of 1946

Control of Imports (Quota No.9, Fourteenth Period) Order [Vol. XXXVI p. 661] S.R.& O. No. 407 of 1946

Control of Imports (Quota No.38, Eighteenth Period) Order [Vol. XXXVI p. 787] S.R.& O. No. 408 of 1946

Statutory Authority	Section	Statutory Instrument
Control of Imports Acts (*Cont.*)		*Control of Imports (Quota No.8, Fifteenth Period) Order [Vol. XXXVI p. 653] S.R.& O. No. 409 of 1946*
		Control of Imports (Quota No.25, Thirteenth Period) Order [Vol. XXXVI p. 685] S.R.& O. No. 410 of 1946
		Control of Imports (Quota No.36, Fifteenth Period) Order [Vol. XXXVI p. 755] S.R.& O. No. 84 of 1947
		Control of Imports (Quota No.35, Fifteenth Period) Order [Vol. XXXVI p. 739] S.R.& O. No. 125 of 1947
		Control of Imports (Quota No.3, Twenty-Eighth Period) Order [Vol. XXXVI p. 637] S.R.& O. No. 214 of 1947
		Control of Imports (Quota No.31, Seventeenth Period) Order [Vol. XXXVI p. 713] S.R.& O. No. 215 of 1947
		Control of Imports (Quota No.38, Nineteenth Period) Order [Vol. XXXVI p. 791] S.R.& O. No. 216 of 1947
		Control of Imports (Quota No.12, Sixteenth Period) Order [Vol. XXXVI p. 677] S.R.& O. No. 239 of 1947
		Control of Imports (Quota No.37, Twenty-First Period) Order [Vol. XXXVI p. 775] S.R.& O. No. 240 of 1947
		Control of Imports (Quota No.6, Twelfth Period) Order [Vol. XXXVI p. 645] S.R.& O. No. 246 of 1947
		Control of Imports (Quota No.31, Eighteenth Period) Order [Vol. XXXVI p. 717] S.R.& O. No. 268 of 1947
		Control of Imports (Quota No.36, Sixteenth Period) Order [Vol. XXXVI p. 759] S.R.& O. No. 324 of 1947
		Control of Imports (Quota No.12, Seventeenth Period) Order [Vol. XXXVI p. 681] S.R.& O. No. 369 of 1947
		Control of Imports (Quota No.35, Sixteenth Period) Order [Vol. XXXVI p. 743] S.R.& O. No. 376 of 1947
		Control of Imports (Quota No.6, Thirteenth Period) Order [Vol. XXXVI p. 649] S.R.& O. No. 442 of 1947
		Control of Imports (Quota No.28, Tenth Period) Order [Vol. XXXVI p. 801] S.R.& O. No. 443 of 1947
		Control of Imports (Quota No.37, Twenty-Second Period) Order [Vol. XXXVI p. 779] S.R.& O. No. 444 of 1947
		Control of Imports (Quota No.3, Twenty-Ninth Period) Order [Vol. XXXVI p. 641] S.R.& O. No. 445 of 1947

Statutory Authority	Section	Statutory Instrument

Control of Imports Acts (*Cont.*)

Control of Imports (Quota No.27, Tenth Period) Order [Vol. XXXVI p. 697] S.R.& O. No. 446 of 1947

Control of Imports (Quota No.26, Tenth Period) Order [Vol. XXXVI p. 693] S.R.& O. No. 447 of 1947

Control of Imports (Quota No.25, Fourteenth Period) Order [Vol. XXXVI p. 689] S.R.& O. No. 448 of 1947

Control of Imports (Quota No.10, Sixteenth Period) Order [Vol. XXXVI p. 673] S.R.& O. No. 449 of 1947

Control of Imports (Quota No.8, Sixteenth Period) Order [Vol. XXXVI p. 657] S.R.& O. No. 450 of 1947

Control of Imports (Quota No.9, Fifteenth Period) Order [Vol. XXXVI p. 665] S.R.& O. No. 451 of 1947

Control of Imports (Quota No.38, Twentieth Period) Order [Vol. XXXVI p. 795] S.R.& O. No. 452 of 1947

Control of Imports (Quota No.13, Seventeenth Period) Order, S.I. No. 17 of 1948

Control of Imports (Quota No.31, Nineteenth Period) Order, S.I. No. 31 of 1948

Control of Imports (Quota No.12, Eighteenth Period) Order, S.I. No. 32 of 1948

Control of Imports (Quota No.8) (Amendment) Order, 1938 (Amendment) Order, S.I. No. 50 of 1948

Control of Imports (Quota No.36, Seventeenth Period) Order, S.I. No. 54 of 1948

Control of Imports (Quota No.35, Seventeenth Period) Order, S.I. No. 95 of 1948

Control of Imports (Quota No.13) (Amendment) Order, S.I. No. 97 of 1948

Control of Imports (Quota No.6, Fourteenth Period) Order, S.I. No. 195 of 1948

Control of Imports (Quota No.26, Eleventh Period) Order, S.I. No. 196 of 1948

Control of Imports (Quota No.27, Eleventh Period) Order, S.I. No. 197 of 1948

Control of Imports (Quota No.28, Eleventh Period) Order, S.I. No. 198 of 1948

Control of Imports (Quota No.38, Twenty-First Period) Order, S.I. No. 199 of 1948

Control of Imports (Quota No.37, Twenty-Third Period) Order, S.I. No. 200 of 1948

Control of Imports (Quota No.3, Thirteenth Period) Order, S.I. No. 201 of 1948

Control of Imports (Quota No.1, Seventeenth Period) Order, S.I. No. 233 of 1948

Control of Imports (Quota No.2, Seventeenth Period) Order, S.I. No. 234 of 1948

Statutory Authority	Section	Statutory Instrument
Control of Imports Acts (*Cont.*)		*Control of Imports (Quota No.4, Nineteenth Period) Order, S.I. No. 235 of 1948*
		Control of Imports (Quota No.14, Fifteenth Period) Order, S.I. No. 236 of 1948
		Control of Imports (Quota No.15, Fifteenth Period) Order, S.I. No. 237 of 1948
		Control of Imports (Quota No.29, Fourteenth Period) Order, S.I. No. 238 of 1948
		Control of Imports (Quota No.13, Eighteenth period) Order, S.I. No. 254 of 1948
		Control of Imports (Quota No.12, Nineteenth period) Order, S.I. No. 255 of 1948
		Control of Imports (Quota No.31, Twentieth period) Order, S.I. No. 256 of 1948
		Control of Imports (Quota No.36, Eighteenth Period) Order, S.I. No. 288 of 1948
		Control of Imports (Quota No.35, Eighteenth Period) Order, S.I. No. 316 of 1948
		Control of Imports (Quota No.6, Fifteenth Period) Order, S.I. No. 393 of 1948
		Control of Imports (Quota No.8, Seventh Period) Order, S.I. No. 394 of 1948
		Control of Imports (Quota No.9, Sixteenth Period) Order, S.I. No. 395 of 1948
		Control of Imports (Quota No.10, Seventeenth Period) Order, S.I. No. 396 of 1948
		Control of Imports (Quota No.25, Fifteenth Period) Order, S.I. No. 397 of 1948
		Control of Imports (Quota No.37, Twenty-Fourth Period) Order, S.I. No. 398 of 1948
		Control of Imports (Quota No.26, Twelfth Period) Order, S.I. No. 406 of 1948
		Control of Imports (Quota No.27, Twelfth Period) Order, S.I. No. 407 of 1948
		Control of Imports (Quota No.28, Twelfth Period) Order, S.I. No. 408 of 1948
		Control of Imports (Quota No.38, Thirty-Second Period) Order, S.I. No. 409 of 1948
		Control of Imports (Quota No.3, Thirty-First Period) Order, S.I. No. 415 of 1948
		Control of Imports (Quota No.29, Fifteenth Period) Order, S.I. No. 424 of 1948
		Control of Imports (Quota No.12, Twentieth Period) Order, S.I. No. 24 of 1949
		Control of Imports (Quota No.13, Nineteenth Period) Order, S.I. No. 25 of 1949
		Control of Imports (Quota No.31, Twenty-First Period) Order, S.I. No. 26 of 1949
		Control of Imports (Quota No.36, Nineteenth Period) Order, S.I. No. 41 of 1949
		Control of Imports (Quota No.35, Nineteenth Period) Order, S.I. No. 72 of 1949

Control of Imports Acts (*Cont.*)

Control of Imports (Quota No.31, Twenty-Second Period) Order, S.I. No. 124 of 1949

Control of Imports (Quota No.37, Twenty-Fifth Period) Order, S.I. No. 163 of 1949

Control of Imports (Quota No.6, Sixteenth Period) Order, S.I. No. 164 of 1949

Control of Imports (Quota No.26, Thirteenth Period) Order, S.I. No. 165 of 1949

Control of Imports (Quota No.27, Thirteenth Period) Order, S.I. No. 166 of 1949

Control of Imports (Quota No.28, Thirteenth Period) Order, S.I. No. 167 of 1949

Control of Imports (Quota No.38, Twenty-Third Period) Order, S.I. No. 168 of 1949

Control of Imports (Quota No.3, Thirty-Second Period) Order, S.I. No. 181 of 1949

Control of Imports (Quota No.13) (Amendment) Order, S.I. No. 195 of 1949

Control of Imports (Quota No.1, Eighteenth Period) Order, S.I. No. 199 of 1949

Control of Imports (Quota No.14, Sixteenth Period) Order, S.I. No. 200 of 1949

Control of Imports (Quota No.2, Eighteenth Period) Order, S.I. No. 201 of 1949

Control of Imports (Quota No.15, Sixteenth Period) Order, S.I. No. 202 of 1949

Control of Imports (Quota No.4, Twentieth Period) Order, S.I. No. 206 of 1949

Control of Imports (Quota No.29, Sixteenth Period) Order, S.I. No. 207 of 1949

Control of Imports (Quota No.13, Twentieth Period) Order, S.I. No. 212 of 1949

Control of Imports (Quota No.31, Twenty-Third Period) Order, S.I. No. 225 of 1949

Control of Imports (Quota No.12, Twenty-First Period) Order, S.I. No. 226 of 1949

Control of Imports (Quota No.36, Twentieth Period) Order, S.I. No. 242 of 1949

Control of Imports (Quota No.35, Twentieth Period) Order, S.I. No. 255 of 1949

Control of Imports (Quota No.31, Twenty-Fourth Period) Order, S.I. No. 279 of 1949

Control of Imports (Quota No.3, Thirty-Third Period) Order, S.I. No. 308 of 1949

Control of Imports (Quota No.6, Seventeenth Period) Order, S.I. No. 309 of 1949

Control of Imports (Quota No.8, Eighteenth Period) Order, S.I. No. 310 of 1949

Control of Imports (Quota No.9, Seventeenth Period) Order, S.I. No. 311 of 1949

Control of Imports (Quota No.10, Eighteenth Period) Order, S.I. No. 312 of 1949

Statutory Authority	Section	Statutory Instrument
Control of Imports Acts (*Cont.*)		*Control of Imports (Quota No.25, Sixteenth Period) Order, S.I. No. 313 of 1949*
		Control of Imports (Quota No.26, Fourteenth Period) Order, S.I. No. 314 of 1949
		Control of Imports (Quota No.27, Fourteenth Period) Order, S.I. No. 315 of 1949
		Control of Imports (Quota No.28, Fourteenth Period) Order, S.I. No. 316 of 1949
		Control of Imports (Quota No.37, Twenty-Sixth Period) Order, S.I. No. 317 of 1949
		Control of Imports (Quota No.38, Twenty-Fourth Period) Order, S.I. No. 318 of 1949
		Control of Imports (Quota No.43) Order, S.I. No. 328 of 1949
		Control of Imports (Quota No.44) Order, S.I. No. 329 of 1949
		Control of Imports (Quota No.45) Order, S.I. No. 330 of 1949
		Control of Imports (Quota No.46) Order, S.I. No. 331 of 1949
		Control of Imports (Quota No.1, Nineteenth Period) Order, S.I. No. 345 of 1949
		Control of Imports (Quota No.2, Nineteenth Period) Order, S.I. No. 346 of 1949
		Control of Imports (Quota No.4, Twenty-First Period) Order, S.I. No. 347 of 1949
		Control of Imports (Quota No.14, Seventeenth Period) Order, S.I. No. 348 of 1949
		Control of Imports (Quota No.15, Seventeenth Period) Order, S.I. No. 349 of 1949
		Control of Imports (Quota No.29, Seventeenth Period) Order, S.I. No. 350 of 1949
		Control of Imports (Quota No.12, Twenty-Second Period) Order, S.I. No. 26 of 1950
		Control of Imports (Quota No.13, Twenty-First Period) Order, S.I. No. 27 of 1950
		Control of Imports (Quota No.43, First Period) Order, S.I. No. 34 of 1950
		Control of Imports (Quota No.44, First Period) Order, S.I. No. 35 of 1950
		Control of Imports (Quota No.45, First Period) Order, S.I. No. 36 of 1950
		Control of Imports (Quota No.46, First Period) Order, S.I. No. 37 of 1950
		Control of Imports (Quota No.36, Twenty-First Period) Order, S.I. No. 50 of 1950
		Control of Imports (Quota No.35 Twenty-First Period) Order, S.I. No. 80 of 1950
		Control of Imports (Quota No.43, Second Period) Order, S.I. No. 110 of 1950
		Control of Imports (Quota No.44, Second Period) Order, S.I. No. 111 of 1950

Statutory Authority	Section	Statutory Instrument
Control of Imports Acts (*Cont.*)		*Control of Imports (Quota No.45, Second Period) Order, S.I. No. 112 of 1950*
		Control of Imports (Quota No.46, Second Period) Order, S.I. No. 113 of 1950
		Control of Imports (Quota No.31, Twenty-Fifth Period) Order, S.I. No. 115 of 1950
		Control of Imports (Quota No.3, Thirty-Fourth Period) Order, S.I. No. 139 of 1950
		Control of Imports (Quota No.6, Eighteenth Period) Order, S.I. No. 140 of 1950
		Control of Imports (Quota No.26, Fifteenth Period) Order, S.I. No. 141 of 1950
		Control of Imports (Quota No.27, Fifteenth Period) Order, S.I. No. 142 of 1950
		Control of Imports (Quota No.28, Fifteenth Period) Order, S.I. No. 143 of 1950
		Control of Imports (Quota No.37, Twenty-Seventh Period) Order, S.I. No. 144 of 1950
		Control of Imports (Quota No.38, Twenty-Fifth Period) Order, S.I. No. 145 of 1950
		Control of Imports (Quota No.1, Twentieth Period) Order, S.I. No. 164 of 1950
		Control of Imports (Quota No.2, Twentieth Period) Order, S.I. No. 165 of 1950
		Control of Imports (Quota No.14, Eighteenth Period) Order, S.I. No. 166 of 1950
		Control of Imports (Quota No.15, Eighteenth Period) Order, S.I. No. 167 of 1950
		Control of Imports (Quota No.37) (Amendment) Order, S.I. No. 173 of 1950
		Control of Imports (Quota No.13, Twenty-Second Period) Order, S.I. No. 199 of 1950
		Control of Imports (Quota No.12, Twenty-Third Period) Order, S.I. No. 200 of 1950
		Control of Imports (Quota No.36, Twenty-Second Period) Order, S.I. No. 226 of 1950
		Control of Imports (Quota No.35, Twenty-Second Period) Order, S.I. No. 244 of 1950
		Control of Imports (Quota No.43, Third Period) Order, S.I. No. 274 of 1950
		Control of Imports (Quota No.44, Third Period) Order, S.I. No. 275 of 1950
		Control of Imports (Quota No.45, Third Period) Order, S.I. No. 276 of 1950
		Control of Imports (Quota No.46, Third Period) Order, S.I. No. 277 of 1950
		Control of Imports (Quota No.31, Twenty-Sixth Period) Order, S.I. No. 278 of 1950
		Control of Imports (Quota No.3, Thirty-Fifth Period) Order, S.I. No. 294 of 1950
		Control of Imports (Quota No.6, Nineteenth Period) Order, S.I. No. 295 of 1950

Statutory Authority	Section	Statutory Instrument
Control of Imports Acts (*Cont.*)		*Control of Imports (Quota No.8, Nineteenth Period) Order, S.I. No. 296 of 1950*
		Control of Imports (Quota No.9, Eighteenth Period) Order, S.I. No. 297 of 1950
		Control of Imports (Quota No.10, Nineteenth Period) Order, S.I. No. 298 of 1950
		Control of Imports (Quota No.25, Seventeenth Period) Order, S.I. No. 299 of 1950
		Control of Imports (Quota No.37, Twenty-Eighth Period) Order, S.I. No. 300 of 1950
		Control of Imports (Quota No.38, Twenty-Sixth Period) Order, S.I. No. 301 of 1950
		Control of Imports (Quota No.1, Twenty-First Period) Order, S.I. No. 318 of 1950
		Control of Imports (Quota No.2, Twenty-First Period) Order, S.I. No. 319 of 1950
		Control of Imports (Quota No.14, Nineteenth Period) Order, S.I. No. 320 of 1950
		Control of Imports (Quota No.15, Nineteenth Period) Order, S.I. No. 321 of 1950
		Control of Imports (Quota No.4, Twenty-Second Period) Order, S.I. No. 322 of 1950
		Control of Imports (Quota No.29, Eighteenth Period) Order, S.I. No. 323 of 1950
		Control of Imports (Quota No.12, Twenty-Fourth Period) Order, S.I. No. 25 of 1951
		Control of Imports (Quota No.13, Twenty-Third Period) Order, S.I. No. 26 of 1951
		Control of Imports (Quota No.36, Twenty-Third Period) Order, S.I. No. 54 of 1951
		Control of Imports (Quota No.35, Twenty-Third Period) Order, S.I. No. 84 of 1951
		Control of Imports (Quota No.31, Twenty-Seventh Period) Order, S.I. No. 121 of 1951
		Control of Imports (Quota No.26, Sixteenth Period) Order, S.I. No. 146 of 1951
		Control of Imports (Quota No.27, Sixteenth Period) Order, S.I. No. 147 of 1951
		Control of Imports (Quota No.28, Sixteenth Period) Order, S.I. No. 148 of 1951
		Control of Imports (Quota No.37, Twenty-Ninth Period) Order, S.I. No. 149 of 1951
		Control of Imports (Quota No.38, Twenty-Seventh Period) Order, S.I. No. 150 of 1951
		Control of Imports (Quota No.1, Twenty-Second Period) Order, S.I. No. 180 of 1951
		Control of Imports (Quota No.2, Twenty-Second Period) Order, S.I. No. 181 of 1951
		Control of Imports (Quota No.14, Twentieth Period) Order, S.I. No. 182 of 1951
		Control of Imports (Quota No.15, Twentieth Period) Order, S.I. No. 183 of 1951

Statutory Authority	Section	Statutory Instrument
Control of Imports Acts (*Cont.*)		*Control of Imports (Quota No.12, Twenty-Fifth Period) Order, S.I. No. 219 of 1951*
		Control of Imports (Quota No.13, Twenty-Fourth Period) Order, S.I. No. 220 of 1951
		Control of Imports (Quota No.37) (Amendment) Order, S.I. No. 237 of 1951
		Control of Imports (Quota No.36, Twenty-Fourth Period) Order, S.I. No. 248 of 1951
		Control of Imports (Quota No.35) (Sparking Plugs) (Twenty-Fourth Period) Order, S.I. No. 274 of 1951
		Control of Imports (Quota No.43, Fourth Period) (Cotton Piece Goods) Order, S.I. No. 296 of 1951
		Control of Imports (Quota No.44, Fourth Period) (Cotton Piece Goods) Order, S.I. No. 297 of 1951
		Control of Imports (Quota No.45, Fourth Period) (Cotton Piece Goods) Order, S.I. No. 298 of 1951
		Control of Imports (Quota No.46, Fourth Period) (Cotton Piece Goods) Order, S.I. No. 299 of 1951
		Control of Imports (Quota No.31, Twenty-Eighth Period) Order, S.I. No. 301 of 1951
		Control of Imports (Quota No.3, Thirty-Sixth Period) (Leather Footwear) Order, S.I. No. 342 of 1951
		Control of Imports (Quota No.6, Twentieth Period) (Rubber Proofed Clothing) Order, S.I. No. 343 of 1951
		Control of Imports (Quota No.8, Twentieth Period) (Motor Cars) Order, S.I. No. 344 of 1951
		Control of Imports (Quota No.9, Nineteenth Period) (Motor Car Chassis) Order, S.I. No. 345 of 1951
		Control of Imports (Quota No.10, Twentieth Period) (Motor Car Bodies) Order, S.I. No. 346 of 1951
		Control of Imports (Quota No.25, Eighteenth Period) (Motor Car Body Balloons) Order, S.I. No. 347 of 1951
		Control of Imports (Quota No.26, Eighteenth Period) (Domestic Brushes) Order, S.I. No. 348 of 1951
		Control of Imports (Quota No.27, Eighteenth Period) (Toilet Brushes) Order, S.I. No. 349 of 1951
		Control of Imports (Quota No.28, Eighteenth Period) (Miscellaneous Brushes) Order, S.I. No. 350 of 1951
		Control of Imports (Quota No.37, Thirtieth Period) (Women's Felt Hats) Order, S.I. No. 351 of 1951
		Control of Imports (Quota No.38, Twenty-Eighth Period) (Wood Screws) Order, S.I. No. 352 of 1951
		Control of Imports (Quota No.1, Twenty-Third Period) (Motor Tyres) Order, S.I. No. 375 of 1951

Statutory Authority	Section	Statutory Instrument
Control of Imports Acts (*Cont.*)		*Control of Imports (Quota No.2, Twenty-Third Period) (Cycle Tyres) Order, S.I. No. 376 of 1951*
		Control of Imports (Quota No.14, Twenty-First Period) (Motor Tubes) Order, S.I. No. 377 of 1951
		Control of Imports (Quota No.15, Twenty-First Period) (Cycle Tubes) Order, S.I. No. 378 of 1951
		Control of Imports (Quota No.4, Twenty-Third Period) (Rubber Footwear) Order, S.I. No. 379 of 1951
		Control of Imports (Quota No.29, Nineteenth Period) (Heeled Rubber Shoes) Order, S.I. No. 380 of 1951
		Control of Imports (Quota No.13, Twenty-Fifth Period) (Woven Woollen Tissues) Order, S.I. No. 9 of 1952
		Control of Imports (Quota No.12, Twenty-Sixth Period) (Silk or Artificial Silk Hose) Order, S.I. No. 24 of 1952
		Control of Imports (Quota No.36, Twenty-Fifth Period) (Laminated Springs) Order, S.I. No. 45 of 1952
		Control of Imports (Quota No.35) (Sparking Plugs) (Twenty-Fifth Period) Order, S.I. No. 79 of 1952
		Control of Imports (Quota No.43, Fifth Period) (Cotton Piece Goods) Order, S.I. No. 102 of 1952
		Control of Imports (Quota No.44, Fifth Period) (Cotton Piece Goods) Order, S.I. No. 103 of 1952
		Control of Imports (Quota No.45, Fifth Period) (Cotton Piece Goods) Order, S.I. No. 104 of 1952
		Control of Imports (Quota No.46, Fifth Period) (Cotton Piece Goods) Order, S.I. No. 105 of 1952
		Control of Imports (Quota No.31, Twenty-Ninth Period) (Electric Filament Lamps) Order, S.I. No. 113 of 1952
		Control of Imports (Quota No.26, Eighteenth Period) (Domestic Brushes) Order, S.I. No. 128 of 1952
		Control of Imports (Quota No.27, Eighteenth Period) (Toilet Brushes) Order, S.I. No. 129 of 1952
		Control of Imports (Quota No.28, Eighteenth Period) (Miscellaneous Brushes) Order, S.I. No. 130 of 1952
		Control of Imports (Quota No.37, Thirty-First Period) (Women's Felt Hats) Order, S.I. No. 131 of 1952
		Control of Imports (Quota No.38, Twenty-Ninth Period) (Wood Screws) Order, S.I. No. 132 of 1952
		Control of Imports (Quota No.47) (Road Vehicles) Order, S.I. No. 137 of 1952

Statutory Authority	Section	Statutory Instrument
Control of Imports Act, No. 12 of 1934 (*Cont.*)		**Control of Imports (Quota No.13) (Artificial Silk Piece Goods Amendment) Order, S.I. No. 145 of 1952**
		Control of Imports (Quota No.48) (Woollen and Worsted Yarns) Order, S.I. No. 189 of 1952
		Control of Imports (Quota No.1, Twenty-Fourth Period) (Motor Tyres) Order, S.I. No. 190 of 1952
		Control of Imports (Quota No.2, Twenty-Fourth Period) (Cycle Tyres) Order, S.I. No. 191 of 1952
		Control of Imports (Quota No.14, Twenty-Second Period) (Motor Tubes) Order, S.I. No. 192 of 1952
		Control of Imports (Quota No.15, Twenty-Second Period) (Cycle Tubes) Order, S.I. No. 193 of 1952
		Control of Imports (Quota No.47, First Period) (Road Vehicles) Order, S.I. No. 215 of 1952
		Control of Imports (Quota No.49) (Single Cotton Yarns) Order, S.I. No. 221 of 1952
		Control of Imports (Quota No.13, Twenty-Sixth Period) (Woven Woollen Tissues and Artificial Silk Piece Goods) Order, S.I. No. 235 of 1952
		Control of Imports (Quota No.12, Twenty-Seventh Period) (Silk or Artificial Silk Hose) Order, S.I. No. 237 of 1952
		Control of Imports (Quota No.48, First Period) (Woollen and Worsted Yarns) Order, S.I. No. 239 of 1952
		Control of Imports (Quota No.49, First Period) (Single Cotton Yarns) Order, S.I. No. 244 of 1952
		Control of Imports (Quota No.36, Twenty-Sixth Period) (Laminated Springs) Order, S.I. No. 256 of 1952
		Control of Imports (Quota No.35) (Sparking Plugs) (Twenty-Sixth Period) Order, S.I. No. 284 of 1952
		Control of Imports (Quota No.31, Thirtieth Period) (Electric Filament Lamps) Order, S.I. No. 303 of 1952
		Control of Imports (Quota No.43, Sixth Period) (Cotton Piece Goods) Order, S.I. No. 304 of 1952
		Control of Imports (Quota No.44, Sixth Period) (Cotton Piece Goods) Order, S.I. No. 305 of 1952
		Control of Imports (Quota No.45, Sixth Period) (Cotton Piece Goods) Order, S.I. No. 306 of 1952
		Control of Imports (Quota No.49, Second Period) (Single Cotton Yarns) Order, S.I. No. 307 of 1952
		Control of Imports (Amendment of Quota No.45 and Revocation of Quota No.46) Order, S.I. No. 308 of 1952

Control of Imports Acts (*Cont.*)

Control of Imports (Quota No.8, Twenty-First Period) (Motor Cars) Order, S.I. No. 330 of 1952

Control of Imports (Quota No.9, Twentieth Period) (Motor Vehicles Chassis) Order, S.I. No. 331 of 1952

Control of Imports (Quota No.10, Twenty-First Period) (Road Vehicle Bodies) Order, S.I. No. 332 of 1952

Control of Imports (Quota No.25, Nineteenth Period) (Motor Car Body Balloons) Order, S.I. No. 333 of 1952

Control of Imports (Quota No.47, Second Period) (Road Vehicles) Order, S.I. No. 334 of 1952

Control of Imports (Quota No.38, Thirtieth Period) (Wood Screws) Order, S.I. No. 335 of 1952

Control of Imports (Quota No.6, Twenty-First Period) (Rubber-Proofed Clothing) Order, S.I. No. 336 of 1952

Control of Imports (Quota No.26, Nineteenth Period) (Domestic Brushes) Order, S.I. No. 337 of 1952

Control of Imports (Quota No.27, Nineteenth Period) (Toilet Brushes) Order, S.I. No. 338 of 1952

Control of Imports (Quota No.28, Nineteenth Period) (Miscellaneous Brushes) Order, S.I. No. 339 of 1952

Control of Imports (Quota No.3, Thirty-Seventh Period) (Leather Footwear) Order, S.I. No. 340 of 1952

Control of Imports (Quota No.37, Thirty-Second Period) (Womens' Felt Hats) Order, S.I. No. 341 of 1952

Control of Imports (Quota No.1, Twenty-Fifth Period) (Motor Tyres) Order, S.I. No. 362 of 1952

Control of Imports (Quota No.2, Twenty-Fifth Period) (Cycle Tyres) Order, S.I. No. 363 of 1952

Control of Imports (Quota No.14, Twenty-Third Period) (Motor Tubes) Order, S.I. No. 364 of 1952

Control of Imports (Quota No.15, Twenty-Third Period) (Cycle Tubes) Order, S.I. No. 365 of 1952

Control of Imports (Quota No.4, Twenty-Fourth Period) (Rubber Footwear) Order, S.I. No. 366 of 1952

Control of Imports (Quota No.29, Twentieth Period) (Heeled Rubber Shoes) Order, S.I. No. 367 of 1952

Control of Imports (Quota No.48, Second Period) (Woollen and Worsted Yarns) Order, S.I. No. 368 of 1952

Control of Imports (Quota No.13) (Artificial Silk Piece Goods Amendment) Order, S.I. No. 39 of 1953

Control of Imports Acts (*Cont.*)

Control of Imports (Quota No.12, Twenty-Eighth Period) (Silk or Artificial Silk Hose) Order, S.I. No. 47 of 1953

Control of Imports (Quota No.49, Third Period) (Single Cotton Yarns) Order, S.I. No. 48 of 1953

Control of Imports (Quota No.13, Twenty-Seventh Period) (Woven Woollen Tissues and Artificial Silk Piece Goods) Order, S.I. No. 49 of 1953

Control of Imports (Quota No.36, Twenty-Seventh Period) (Laminated Springs) Order, S.I. No. 74 of 1953

Control of Imports (Quota No.35, Twenty-Seventh Period) (Sparking Plugs) Order, S.I. No. 101 of 1953

Control of Imports (Quota No.31, Thirty-First Period) (Electric Filament Lamps) Order, S.I. No. 145 of 1953

Control of Imports (Quota No.43, Seventh Period) (Cotton Piece Goods) Order, S.I. No. 146 of 1953

Control of Imports (Quota No.44, Seventh Period) (Cotton Piece Goods) Order, S.I. No. 147 of 1953

Control of Imports (Quota No.45, Seventh Period) (Cotton Piece Goods) Order, S.I. No. 148 of 1953

Control of Imports (Quota No.26, Twentieth Period) (Domestic Brushes) Order, S.I. No. 172 of 1953

Control of Imports (Quota No.27, Twentieth Period) (Toilet Brushes) Order, S.I. No. 173 of 1953

Control of Imports (Quota No.28, Twentieth Period) (Miscellaneous Brushes) Order, S.I. No. 174 of 1953

Control of Imports (Quota No.37, Thirty-Third Period) (Women's Felt Hats) Order, S.I. No. 175 of 1953

Control of Imports (Quota No.38, Thirty-First Period) (Wood Screws) Order, S.I. No. 176 of 1953

Control of Imports (Quota No.1, Twenty-Sixth Period) (Motor Tyres) Order, S.I. No. 210 of 1953

Control of Imports (Quota No.2, Twenty-Sixth Period) (Cycle Tyres) Order, S.I. No. 211 of 1953

Control of Imports (Quota No.14, Twenty-Fourth Period) (Motor Tubes) Order, S.I. No. 212 of 1953

Control of Imports (Quota No.15, Twenty-Fourth Period) (Cycle Tubes) Order, S.I. No. 213 of 1953

Control of Imports (Quota No.49) (Single Cotton Yarns) (Revocation) Order, S.I. No. 216 of 1953

Control of Imports (Quotas No.13 and 45) (Amendment) (Moquette and Plush) Order, S.I. No. 220 of 1953

Control of Imports Acts (*Cont.*)

Control of Imports (Quota No.48) (Woollen and Worsted Yarns) (Revocation) Order, S.I. No. 221 of 1953

Control of Imports (Quota No.18) (Mechanically Propelled Bicycles) (Revocation) Order, S.I. No. 222 of 1953

Control of Imports (Quota No.24) (Perambulators) (Revocation) Order, S.I. No. 223 of 1953

Control of Imports (Quota No.32) (Marble Chippings) (Revocation) Order, S.I. No. 224 of 1953

Control of Imports (Quota No.13, Twenty-Eighth Period) (Woven Woollen Tissues and Artificial Silk Piece Goods) Order, S.I. No. 262 of 1953

Control of Imports (Quota No.12, Twenty-Ninth Period) (Silk or Artificial Silk Hose) Order, S.I. No. 264 of 1953

Control of Imports (Quota No.10) Order, 1934 (Road Vehicle Bodies) (Amendment) Order, S.I. No. 273 of 1953

Control of Imports (Quota No.36, Twenty-Eighth Period) (Laminated Springs) Order, S.I. No. 283 of 1953

Control of Imports (Quota No.13) (Artificial Silk Piece Goods Amendment) (No.2) Order, S.I. No. 300 of 1953

Control of Imports (Quota No.35, Twenty-Eighth Period) (Sparking Plugs) Order, S.I. No. 304 of 1953

Control of Imports (Quota No.31, Thirty-Second Period) (Electric Filament Lamps) Order, S.I. No. 329 of 1953

Control of Imports (Quota No.43, Eighth Period) (Cotton Piece Goods) Order, S.I. No. 330 of 1953

Control of Imports (Quota No.44, Eighth Period) (Cotton Piece Goods) Order, S.I. No. 331 of 1953

Control of Imports (Quota No.45, Eighth Period) (Cotton Piece Goods) Order, S.I. No. 332 of 1953

Control of Imports (Quota No.3, Thirty-Eighth Period) (Leather Footwear) Order, S.I. No. 357 of 1953

Control of Imports (Quota No.6, Twenty-Second Period) (Rubber-Proofed Clothing) Order, S.I. No. 358 of 1953

Control of Imports (Quota No.8, Twenty-Second Period) (Motor Cars) Order, S.I. No. 359 of 1953

Control of Imports (Quota No.9, Twenty-First Period) (Motor Vehicle Chassis) Order, S.I. No. 360 of 1953

Control of Imports (Quota No.10, Twenty-Second Period) (Road Vehicle Bodies) Order, S.I. No. 361 of 1953

Control of Imports (Quota No.25, Twentieth Period) (Motor Car Body Balloons) Order, S.I. No. 362 of 1953

Statutory Authority	Section	Statutory Instrument
Control of Imports Acts (*Cont.*)		*Control of Imports (Quota No.37, Thirty-Fourth Period) (Women's Felt Hats) Order, S.I. No. 363 of 1953*
		Control of Imports (Quota No.38, Thirty-Second Period) (Wood Screws) Order, S.I. No. 364 of 1953
		Control of Imports (Quota No.47, Third Period) (Road Vehicles) Order, S.I. No. 365 of 1953
		Control of Imports (Quota No.1, Twenty-Seventh Period) (Motor Tyres) Order, S.I. No. 400 of 1953
		Control of Imports (Quota No.2, Twenty-Seventh Period) (Cycle Tyres) Order, S.I. No. 401 of 1953
		Control of Imports (Quota No.14, Twenty-Fifth Period) (Motor Tubes) Order, S.I. No. 402 of 1953
		Control of Imports (Quota No.15, Twenty-Fifth Period) (Cycle Tubes) Order, S.I. No. 403 of 1953
		Control of Imports (Quota No.4, Twenty-Fifth Period) (Rubber Footwear) Order, S.I. No. 404 of 1953
		Control of Imports (Quota No.29, Twenty-First Period) (Heeled Rubber Shoes) Order, S.I. No. 405 of 1953
		Control of Imports (Quota No.13, Twenty-Ninth Period) (Woven Woollen Tissues and Artificial Silk Piece Goods) Order, S.I. No. 406 of 1953
		Control of Imports (Quota No.12, Thirtieth Period) (Silk or Artificial Silk Hose) Order, S.I. No. 13 of 1954
		Control of Imports (Quota No.36, Twenty-Ninth Period) (Laminated Springs) Order, S.I. No. 33 of 1954
		Control of Imports (Quota No.26, Twenty-First Period) (Domestic Brushes) Order, S.I. No. 35 of 1954
		Control of Imports (Quota No.27, Twenty-First Period) (Toilet Brushes) Order, S.I. No. 36 of 1954
		Control of Imports (Quota No.28, Twenty-First Period) (Miscellaneous Brushes) Order, S.I. No. 37 of 1954
		Control of Imports (Quota No.31, Thirty-Third Period) (Electric Filament Lamps) Order, S.I. No. 86 of 1954
		Control of Imports (Quota No.43, Ninth Period) (Cotton Piece Goods) Order, S.I. No. 87 of 1954
		Control of Imports (Quota No.44, Ninth Period) (Cotton Piece Goods) Order, S.I. No. 88 of 1954
		Control of Imports (Quota No.45, Ninth Period) (Cotton Piece Goods) Order, S.I. No. 89 of 1954
		Control of Imports (Quota No.38, Thirty-Third Period) (Wood Screws) Order, S.I. No. 105 of 1954

Control of Imports Acts (*Cont.*)		*Control of Imports (Quota No.1, Twenty-Eighth Period) (Motor Tyres) Order, S.I. No. 135 of 1954*
		Control of Imports (Quota No.2, Twenty-Eighth Period) (Cycle Tyres) Order, S.I. No. 136 of 1954
		Control of Imports (Quota No.14, Twenty-Sixth Period) (Motor Tubes) Order, S.I. No. 137 of 1954
		Control of Imports (Quota No.15, Twenty-Sixth Period) (Cycle Tubes) Order, S.I. No. 138 of 1954
		Control of Imports (Quota No.12, Thirty-First Period) (Silk or Artificial Silk Hose) Order, S.I. No. 152 of 1954
		Control of Imports (Quota No.13, Thirtieth Period) (Woven Woollen Tissues and Artificial Silk Piece Goods) Order, S.I. No. 153 of 1954
		Control of Imports (Quota No.35, Twenty-Ninth Period) (Sparking Plugs) Order, S.I. No. 204 of 1954
		Control of Imports (Quota No.13) (Woven Woollen and Synthetic and Artificial Fabrics) (Amendment) Order, S.I. No. 227 of 1954
		Control of Imports (Quota No.31, Thirty-Fourth Period) (Electric Filament Lamps) Order, S.I. No. 229 of 1954
		Control of Imports (Quota No.43, Tenth Period) (Cotton Piece Goods) Order, S.I. No. 230 of 1954
		Control of Imports (Quota No.45, Tenth Period) (Cotton Piece Goods) Order, S.I. No. 231 of 1954
		Control of Imports (Quota No.3, Thirty-Ninth Period) (Leather Footwear) Order, S.I. No. 251 of 1954
		Control of Imports (Quota No.6, Twenty-Third Period) (Rubber-Proofed Clothing) Order, S.I. No. 252 of 1954
		Control of Imports (Quota No.8, Twenty-Third Period) (Motor Cars) Order, S.I. No. 253 of 1954
		Control of Imports (Quota No.9, Twenty-Second Period) (Motor Vehicle Chassis) Order, S.I. No. 254 of 1954
		Control of Imports (Quota No.25, Twenty-Third Period) (Road Vehicle Bodies) Order, S.I. No. 255 of 1954
		Control of Imports (Quota No.25, Twenty-First Period) (Motor Car Body Balloons) Order, S.I. No. 256 of 1954
		Control of Imports (Quota No.37, Thirty-Fifth Period) (Women's Felt Hats) Order, S.I. No. 257 of 1954
		Control of Imports (Quota No.38, Thirty-Fourth Period) (Wood Screws) Order, S.I. No. 258 of 1954
		Control of Imports (Quota No.47, Fourth Period) (Road Vehicles) Order, S.I. No. 259 of 1954

Statutory Authority	Section	Statutory Instrument
Control of Imports Acts (*Cont.*)		*Control of Imports (Quota No.1, Twenty-Ninth Period) (Motor Tyres) Order, S.I. No. 283 of 1954*
		Control of Imports (Quota No.2, Twenty-Ninth Period) (Cycle Tyres) Order, S.I. No. 284 of 1954
		Control of Imports (Quota No.14, Twenty-Seventh Period) (Motor Tubes) Order, S.I. No. 285 of 1954
		Control of Imports (Quota No.15, Twenty-Seventh Period) (Cycle Tubes) Order, S.I. No. 286 of 1954
		Control of Imports (Quota No.4, Twenty-Sixth Period) (Rubber Footwear) Order, S.I. No. 287 of 1954
		Control of Imports (Quota No.29, Twenty-Second Period) (Heeled Rubber Shoes) Order, S.I. No. 288 of 1954
		Control of Imports (Quota No.12, Thirty-Second Period) (Silk or Artificial Silk Hose) Order, S.I. No. 12 of 1955
		Control of Imports (Quota No.13, Thirty-First Period) (Woven Woollen and Synthetic and Artificial Fabrics) Order, S.I. No. 13 of 1955
		Control of Imports (Quota No.13) (Woven Woollen and Synthetic and Artificial Fabrics) (Amendment) Order, S.I. No. 14 of 1955
		Control of Imports (Quota No.26, Twenty-Second Period) (Domestic Brushes) Order, S.I. No. 26 of 1955
		Control of Imports (Quota No.27, Twenty-Second Period) (Toilet Brushes) Order, S.I. No. 27 of 1955
		Control of Imports (Quota No.28, Twenty-Second Period) (Miscellaneous Brushes) Order, S.I. No. 28 of 1955
		Control of Imports (Quota No.36, Thirtieth Period) (Laminated Springs) Order, S.I. No. 29 of 1955
		Control of Imports (Quota No.43, Eleventh Period) (Cotton Piece Goods) Order, S.I. No. 76 of 1955
		Control of Imports (Quota No.44, Tenth Period) (Cotton Piece Goods) Order, S.I. No. 77 of 1955
		Control of Imports (Quota No.45, Eleventh Period) (Cotton Piece Goods) Order, S.I. No. 78 of 1955
		Control of Imports (Quota No.38, Thirty-Fifth Period) (Wood Screws) Order, S.I. No. 89 of 1955
		Control of Imports (Quota No.13) (Woven Woollen and Synthetic and Artificial Fabrics) (Amendment) (No.2) Order, S.I. No. 108 of 1955
		Control of Imports (Quota No.1, Thirtieth Period) (Motor Tyres) Order, S.I. No. 123 of 1955
		Control of Imports (Quota No.2, Thirtieth Period) (Cycle Tyres) Order, S.I. No. 124 of 1955

Statutory Authority	Section	Statutory Instrument

Control of Imports Acts (*Cont.*)

Control of Imports (Quota No.14, Twenty-Eighth Period) (Motor Tubes) Order, S.I. No. 125 of 1955

Control of Imports (Quota No.15, Twenty-Eighth Period) (Cycle Tubes) Order, S.I. No. 126 of 1955

Control of Imports (Quota No.12, Thirty-Third Period) (Silk or Artificial Silk Hose) Order, S.I. No. 140 of 1955

Control of Imports (Quota No.13, Thirty-Second Period) (Woven Woollen and Synthetic and Artificial Fabrics) Order, S.I. No. 147 of 1955

Control of Imports (Quota No.3, Thirty-Ninth Period, Additional Quota) (Leather Footwear) Order, S.I. No. 175 of 1955

Control of Imports (Quota No.35, Thirtieth Period) (Sparking Plugs) Order, S.I. No. 178 of 1955

Control of Imports (Quota No.31, Thirty-Fifth Period) (Electric Filament Lamps) Order, S.I. No. 204 of 1955

Control of Imports (Amendment of Quota No.45 and Revocation of Quotas Nos.43 and 44) Order, S.I. No. 205 of 1955

Control of Imports (Quota No.45, Twelfth Period) (Cotton Piece Goods) Order, S.I. No. 206 of 1955

Control of Imports (Quota No.8, Twenty-Fourth Period) (Motor Cars) Order, S.I. No. 224 of 1955

Control of Imports (Quota No.9, Twenty-Third Period) (Motor Vehicle Chassis) Order, S.I. No. 225 of 1955

Control of Imports (Quota No.10, Twenty-Fourth Period) (Road Vehicle Bodies) Order, S.I. No. 226 of 1955

Control of Imports (Quota No.25, Twenty-Second Period) (Motor Car Body Balloons) Order, S.I. No. 227 of 1955

Control of Imports (Quota No.47, Fifth Period) (Road Vehicles) Order, S.I. No. 228 of 1955

Control of Imports (Quota No.3, Fortieth Period) (Leather Footwear) Order, S.I. No. 235 of 1955

Control of Imports (Quota No.37, Thirty-Sixth Period) (Women's Felt Hats) Order, S.I. No. 236 of 1955

Control of Imports (Quota No.6, Twenty-Fourth Period) (Rubber-Proofed Clothing) Order, S.I. No. 237 of 1955

Control of Imports (Quota No.6) (Personal Clothing) (Amendment) Order, S.I. No. 248 of 1955

Control of Imports (Quota No.1, Thirty-First Period) (Motor Tyres) Order, S.I. No. 254 of 1955

Control of Imports (Quota No.2, Thirty-First Period) (Cycle Tyres) Order, S.I. No. 255 of 1955

Statutory Authority	Section	Statutory Instrument

Control of Imports Acts (*Cont.*)

Control of Imports (Amendment of Quota No.1 and Revocation of Quota No.14) Order, S.I. No. 256 of 1955

Control of Imports (Amendment of Quota No.2 and Revocation of Quota No.15) Order, S.I. No. 257 of 1955

Control of Imports (Amendment of Quota No.4 and Revocation of Quota No.29) Order, S.I. No. 258 of 1955

Control of Imports (Quota No.4, Twenty-Seventh Period) (Rubber Footwear) Order, S.I. No. 259 of 1955

Control of Imports (Quota No.13, Thirty-Third Period) (Woven Woollen and Synthetic and Artificial Fabrics) O, S.I. No. 4 of 1956

Control of Imports (Quota No.12, Thirty-Fourth Period) (Silk or Artificial Silk Hose) Order, S.I. No. 5 of 1956

Control of Imports (Quota No.36, Thirty-First Period) (Laminated Springs) Order, S.I. No. 23 of 1956

Control of Imports (Quota No.28, Twenty-Third Period) (Miscellaneous Brushes) Order, S.I. No. 24 of 1956

Control of Imports (Revocation of Quotas Nos 26 and 27 and Amendment of Quota No.28) Order, S.I. No. 25 of 1956

Control of Imports (Quota No.38, Thirty-Sixth Period) (Wood Screws) Order, S.I. No. 131 of 1956

Control of Imports (Quota No.13) (Woven Woollen and Synthetic and Artificial Fabrics) (Amendment) Order, S.I. No. 206 of 1956

Control of Imports (Quota No.13, Thirty-Fourth Period) (Woven Woollen and Synthetic and Artificial Fabrics) Order, S.I. No. 217 of 1956

Control of Imports (Quota No.35, Thirty-First Period) (Sparking Plugs) Order, S.I. No. 247 of 1956

Control of Imports (Quota No.45, Thirteenth Period) (Cotton Piece Goods) Order, S.I. No. 268 of 1956

Control of Imports (Quota No.31, Thirty-Sixth Period) (Electric Filament Lamps) Order, S.I. No. 269 of 1956

Control of Imports (Quota No.8, Twenty-Fifth Period) (Motor Cars) Order, S.I. No. 294 of 1956

Control of Imports (Quota No.9, Twenty-Fourth Period) (Motor Vehicle Chassis) Order, S.I. No. 295 of 1956

Control of Imports (Quota No.10, Twenty-Fifth Period) (Road Vehicle Bodies) Order, S.I. No. 296 of 1956

Control of Imports (Quota No.25, Twenty-Third Period) (Motor Car Body Balloons) Order, S.I. No. 297 of 1956

Control of Imports Acts (*Cont.*)

Control of Imports (Quota No.47, Sixth Period) (Road Vehicles) Order, S.I. No. 298 of 1956

Control of Imports (Quota No.3, Forty-First Period) (Leather Footwear) Order, S.I. No. 299 of 1956

Control of Imports (Quota No.37, Thirty-Seventh Period) (Women's Felt Hats) Order, S.I. No. 300 of 1956

Control of Imports (Quota No.6, Twenty-Fifth Period) (Rubber-Proofed Clothing) Order, S.I. No. 301 of 1956

Control of Imports (Quota No.1, Thirty-Second Period) (Motor Tyres) Order, S.I. No. 325 of 1956

Control of Imports (Quota No.2, Thirty-Second Period) (Cycle Tyres) Order, S.I. No. 326 of 1956

Control of Imports (Quota No.4, Twenty-Eighth Period) (Rubber Footwear) Order, S.I. No. 327 of 1956

Control of Imports (Quota No.12, Thirty-Fifth Period) (Silk or Artificial Silk Hose) Order, S.I. No. 9 of 1957

Control of Imports (Quota No.13, Thirty-Fifth Period) (Woven Woollen and Synthetic and Artificial Fabrics) Order, S.I. No. 10 of 1957

Control of Imports (Quota No.36, Thirty-Second Period) (Laminated Springs) Order, S.I. No. 33 of 1957

Control of Imports (Quota No.28, Twenty-Fourth Period) (Miscellaneous Brushes) Order, S.I. No. 34 of 1957

Control of Imports (Quota No.16) (Fertilisers) (Revocation) Order, S.I. No. 44 of 1957

Control of Imports (Quota No.38, Thirty-Seventh Period) (Wood Screws) Order, S.I. No. 113 of 1957

Control of Imports (Quota No.45) (Amendment) Order, S.I. No. 147 of 1957

Control of Imports (Quota No.13, Thirty-Sixth Period) (Woven Woollen and Synthetic and Artificial Fabrics) Order, S.I. No. 164 of 1957

Control of Imports (Quota No.35, Thirty-Second Period) (Sparking Plugs) Order, S.I. No. 190 of 1957

Control of Imports (Quota No.31, Thirty-Seventh Period) (Electric Filament Lamps) Order, S.I. No. 222 of 1957

Control of Imports (Quota No.45, Fourteenth Period) (Cotton Piece Goods) Order, S.I. No. 224 of 1957

Control of Imports (Quota No.8, Twenty-Sixth Period) (Motor Cars) Order, S.I. No. 242 of 1957

Control of Imports (Quota No.9, Twenty-Fifth Period) (Motor Vehicle Chassis) Order, S.I. No. 243 of 1957

Control of Imports Acts (*Cont.*)

Control of Imports (Quota No.10, Twenty-Sixth Period) (Road Vehicle Bodies) Order, S.I. No. 244 of 1957

Control of Imports (Quota No.25, Twenty-Fourth Period) (Motor Car Body Balloons) Order, S.I. No. 245 of 1957

Control of Imports (Quota No.47, Seventh Period) (Road Vehicles) Order, S.I. No. 246 of 1957

Control of Imports (Quota No.3, Forty-Second Period) (Leather Footwear) Order, S.I. No. 247 of 1957

Control of Imports (Quota No.37, Thirty-Eighth Period) (Women's Felt Hats) Order, S.I. No. 248 of 1957

Control of Imports (Quota No.6, Twenty-Sixth Period) (Rubber-Proofed Clothing) Order, S.I. No. 249 of 1957

Control of Imports (Quota No.1, Thirty-Third Period) (Motor Tyres) Order, S.I. No. 272 of 1957

Control of Imports (Quota No.2, Thirty-Third Period) (Cycle Tyres) Order, S.I. No. 273 of 1957

Control of Imports (Quota No.4, Twenty-Ninth Period) (Rubber Footwear) Order, S.I. No. 274 of 1957

Control of Imports (Quota No.12, Thirty-Sixth Period) (Silk or Artificial Hose) Order, S.I. No. 20 of 1958

Control of Imports (Quota No.13, Thirty-Seventh Period) (Woven Woollen and Synthetic and Artificial Fabrics) Order, S.I. No. 21 of 1958

Control of Imports (Quota No.13) (Woven Woollen and Synthetic and Artificial Fabrics) (Amendment) Order, S.I. No. 29 of 1958

Control of Imports (Quota No.36, Thirty-Third Period) (Laminated Springs) Order, S.I. No. 53 of 1958

Control of Imports (Quota No.28, Twenty-Fifth Period) (Miscellaneous Brushes) Order, S.I. No. 54 of 1958

Control of Imports (Quota No.38, Thirty-Eighth Period) (Wood Screws) Order, S.I. No. 124 of 1958

Control of Imports (Quota No.45) (Cotton Piece Goods) (Amendment) Order, S.I. No. 134 of 1958

Control of Imports (Quota No.45) (Cotton Piece Goods) (Amendment) (No.2) Order, S.I. No. 154 of 1958

Control of Imports (Quota No.13) (Woven Woollen and Synthetic and Artificial Fabrics) (Amendment) (No.2) Order, S.I. No. 167 of 1958

Control of Imports (Quotas Nos.1 to 32) (Amendment) Order, 1939 (Amendment) Order, S.I. No. 168 of 1958

Statutory Authority	Section	Statutory Instrument
Control of Imports Acts (*Cont.*)		*Control of Imports (Quota No.35, Thirty-Third Period) (Sparking Plugs) Order, S.I. No. 197 of 1958*
		Control of Imports (Quota No.45, Fifteenth Period) (Cotton Piece Goods) Order, S.I. No. 215 of 1958
		Control of Imports (Quota No.31, Thirty-Eighth Period) (Electric Filament Lamps) Order, S.I. No. 216 of 1958
		Control of Imports (Quota No.8, Twenty-Seventh Period) (Motor Cars) Order, S.I. No. 236 of 1958
		Control of Imports (Quota No.9, Twenty-Sixth Period) (Motor Vehicle Chassis) Order, S.I. No. 237 of 1958
		Control of Imports (Quota No.10, Twenty-Seventh Period) (Road Vehicle Bodies) Order, S.I. No. 238 of 1958
		Control of Imports (Quota No.25, Twenty-Fifth Period) (Motor Car Body Balloons) Order, S.I. No. 239 of 1958
		Control of Imports (Quota No.47, Eighth Period) (Road Vehicles) Order, S.I. No. 240 of 1958
		Control of Imports (Quota No.3, Forty-Third Period) (Leather Footwear) Order, S.I. No. 241 of 1958
		Control of Imports (Quota No.37, Thirty-Ninth Period) (Women's Felt Hats) Order, S.I. No. 242 of 1958
		Control of Imports (Quota No.6, Twenty-Seventh Period) (Rubber-Proofed Clothing) Order, S.I. No. 243 of 1958
		Control of Imports (Quota No.1, Thirty-Fourth Period) (Motor Tyres) Order, S.I. No. 272 of 1958
		Control of Imports (Quota No.2, Thirty-Fourth Period) (Cycle Tyres) Order, S.I. No. 273 of 1958
		Control of Imports (Quota No.4, Thirtieth Period) (Rubber Footwear) Order, S.I. No. 274 of 1958
		Control of Imports (Quota No.12, Thirty-Seventh Period) (Silk or Artificial Silk Hose) Order, S.I. No. 12 of 1959
		Control of Imports (Quota No.13, Thirty-Eighth Period) (Woven Woollen and Synthetic and Artificial Fabrics) Order, S.I. No. 13 of 1959
		Control of Imports (Quota No.36, Thirty-Fourth Period) (Laminated Springs) Order, S.I. No. 26 of 1959
		Control of Imports (Quota No.28, Twenty-Sixth Period) (Miscellaneous Brushes) Order, S.I. No. 27 of 1959
		Control of Imports (Quota No.38, Thirty-Ninth Period) (Wood Screws) Order, S.I. No. 95 of 1959
		Control of Imports (Quota No.13, Thirty-Ninth Period) (Woven Woollen and Synthetic and Artificial Fabrics) Order, S.I. No. 128 of 1959

Statutory Authority	Section	Statutory Instrument

Control of Imports Acts (*Cont.*)

Control of Imports (Quota No.50) (Super-phosphates) Order, S.I. No. 129 of 1959

Control of Imports (Quota No.50, First Period) (Superphosphates) Order, S.I. No. 130 of 1959

Control of Imports (Quota No.35, Thirty-Fourth Period) (Sparking Plugs) Order, S.I. No. 160 of 1959

Control of Imports (Quota No.31, Thirty-Ninth Period) (Electric Filament Lamps) Order, S.I. No. 176 of 1959

Control of Imports (Quota No.45, Sixteenth Period) (Cotton Piece Goods) Order, S.I. No. 177 of 1959

Control of Imports (Quota No.3, Forty-Fourth Period) (Leather Footwear) Order, S.I. No. 201 of 1959

Control of Imports (Quota No.6, Twenty-Eighth Period) (Rubber Proofed Clothing) Order, S.I. No. 202 of 1959

Control of Imports (Quota No.37, Fortieth Period) (Women's Felt Hats) Order, S.I. No. 203 of 1959

Control of Imports (Quota No.50, Second Period) (Superphosphates) Order, S.I. No. 204 of 1959

Control of Imports (Quota No.9, Twenty-Seventh Period) (Motor Vehicle Chassis) Order, S.I. No. 205 of 1959

Control of Imports (Quota No.8, Twenty-Eighth Period) (Motor Cars) Order, S.I. No. 206 of 1959

Control of Imports (Quota No.10, Twenty-Eighth Period) (Road Vehicle Bodies) Order, S.I. No. 207 of 1959

Control of Imports (Quota No.25, Twenty-Sixth Period) (Motor Car Body Balloons) Order, S.I. No. 208 of 1959

Control of Imports (Quota No.47, Ninth Period) (Road Vehicles) Order, S.I. No. 209 of 1959

Control of Imports (Quota No.1, Thirty-Fifth Period) (Motor Tyres) Order, S.I. No. 237 of 1959

Control of Imports (Quota No.2, Thirty-Fifth Period) (Cycle Tyres) Order, S.I. No. 238 of 1959

Control of Imports (Quota No.4, Thirty-First Period) (Rubber Footwear) Order, S.I. No. 239 of 1959

Control of Imports (Quota No.13, Fortieth Period) (Woven Woollen and Synthetic and Artificial Fabrics) Order, S.I. No. 18 of 1960

Control of Imports (Quota No.12, Thirty-Eighth Period) (Silk or Artificial Silk Hose) Order, S.I. No. 19 of 1960

Control of Imports (Quota No.36, Thirty-Fifth Period) (Laminated Springs) Order, S.I. No. 39 of 1960

Control of Imports (Quota No.28, Twenty-Seventh Period) (Miscellaneous Brushes) Order, S.I. No. 40 of 1960

Statutory Authority	Section	Statutory Instrument
Control of Imports Acts (*Cont.*)		**Control of Imports (Quota No.45) (Cotton Piece Goods) (Amendment) Order, S.I. No. 98 of 1960**
		Control of Imports (Quota No.50, Third Period) (Superphosphates) Order, S.I. No. 111 of 1960
		Control of Imports (Quota No.38, Fortieth Period) (Wood Screws) Order, S.I. No. 112 of 1960
		Control of Imports (Quota No.13, Forty-First Period) (Woven Woollen and Synthetic and Artificial Fabrics) Order, S.I. No. 160 of 1960
		Control of Imports (Quota No.35, Thirty-Fifth Period) (Sparking Plugs) Order, S.I. No. 207 of 1960
		Control of Imports (Quota No.31, Fortieth Period) (Electric Filament Lamps) Order, S.I. No. 210 of 1960
		Control of Imports (Quota No.45, Seventeenth Period) (Cotton Piece Goods) Order, S.I. No. 217 of 1960
		Control of Imports (Quota No.3, Forty-Fifth Period) (Leather Footwear) Order, S.I. No. 234 of 1960
		Control of Imports (Quota No.6, Twenty-Ninth Period) (Rubber Proofed Clothing) Order, S.I. No. 237 of 1960
		Control of Imports (Quota No.37, Forty-First Period) (Women's Felt Hats) Order, S.I. No. 238 of 1960
		Control of Imports (Quota No.8, Twenty-Ninth Period) (Motor Cars) Order, S.I. No. 239 of 1960
		Control of Imports (Quota No.9, Twenty-Eighth Period) (Motor Vehicle Chassis) Order, S.I. No. 240 of 1960
		Control of Imports (Quota No.10, Twenty-Ninth Period) (Road Vehicle Bodies) Order, S.I. No. 241 of 1960
		Control of Imports (Quota No.25, Twenty-Seventh Period) (Motor Car Body Balloons) Order, S.I. No. 242 of 1960
		Control of Imports (Quota No.47, Tenth Period) (Road Vehicles) Order, S.I. No. 243 of 1960
		Control of Imports (Quota No.1, Thirty-Sixth Period) (Motor Tyres) Order, S.I. No. 266 of 1960
		Control of Imports (Quota No.2, Thirty-Sixth Period) (Cycle Tyres) Order, S.I. No. 267 of 1960
		Control of Imports (Quota No.4, Thirty-Second Period) (Rubber Footwear) Order, S.I. No. 268 of 1960
		Control of Imports (Quota No.12, Thirty-Ninth Period) (Silk or Artificial Silk Hose) Order, S.I. No. 13 of 1961
		Control of Imports (Quota No.13, Forty-Second Period) (Woven Woollen and Synthetic and Artificial Fabrics) Order, S.I. No. 14 of 1961

Control of Imports Acts (*Cont.*)

Control of Imports (Quota No.28, Twenty-Eighth Period) (Miscellaneous Brushes) Order, S.I. No. 43 of 1961

Control of Imports (Quota No.36, Thirty-Sixth Period) (Laminated Springs) Order, S.I. No. 44 of 1961

Control of Imports (Quota No.50, Fourth Period) (Superphosphates) Order, S.I. No. 109 of 1961

Control of Imports (Quota No.38, Forty-First Period) (Wood Screws) Order, S.I. No. 110 of 1961

Control of Imports (Quota No.13, Forty-Third Period) (Woven Woollen and Synthetic and Artificial Fabrics) Order, S.I. No. 163 of 1961

Control of Imports (Quota No.35, Thirty-Sixth Period) (Sparking Plugs) Order, S.I. No. 220 of 1961

Control of Imports (Quota No.31, Forty-First Period) (Electric Filament Lamps) Order, S.I. No. 242 of 1961

Control of Imports (Quota No.45, Eighteenth Period) (Cotton Piece Goods) Order, S.I. No. 243 of 1961

Control of Imports (Quota No.47, Eleventh Period) (Road Vehicles) Order, S.I. No. 284 of 1961

Control of Imports (Quota No.25, Twenty-Eighth Period) (Motor Car Body Balloons) Order, S.I. No. 285 of 1961

Control of Imports (Quota No.9, Twenty-Ninth Period) (Motor Vehicle Chassis) Order, S.I. No. 286 of 1961

Control of Imports (Quota No.6, Thirtieth Period) (Rubber-Proofed Clothing) Order, S.I. No. 287 of 1961

Control of Imports (Quota No.8, Thirtieth Period) (Motor Cars) Order, S.I. No. 288 of 1961

Control of Imports (Quota No.10, Thirtieth Period) (Road Vehicle Bodies) Order, S.I. No. 289 of 1961

Control of Imports (Quota No.37, Forty-Second Period) (Womens' Felt Hats) Order, S.I. No. 290 of 1961

Control of Imports (Quota No.3, Forty-Sixth Period) (Leather Footwear) Order, S.I. No. 291 of 1961

Control of Imports (Quota No.1, Thirty-Seventh Period) (Motor Tyres) Order, S.I. No. 303 of 1961

Control of Imports (Quota No.4, Thirty-Third Period) (Rubber Footwear) Order, S.I. No. 304 of 1961

Control of Imports (Quota No.2, Thirty-Seventh Period) (Cycle Tyres) Order, S.I. No. 305 of 1961

Control of Imports Acts (*Cont.*)

Control of Imports (Quota No.13) (Woven Woollen and Synthetic and Artificial Fabrics) (Amendment) Order, S.I. No. 10 of 1962

Control of Imports (Quota No.12, Fortieth Period) (Silk or Artificial Silk Hose) Order, S.I. No. 22 of 1962

Control of Imports (Quota No.13, Forty-Fourth Period) (Woven Woollen and Synthetic and Artificial Fabrics) Order, S.I. No. 23 of 1962

Control of Imports (Quota No.28, Twenty-Ninth Period) (Miscellaneous Brushes) Order, S.I. No. 36 of 1962

Control of Imports (Quota No.36, Thirty-Seventh Period) (Laminated Springs) Order, S.I. No. 37 of 1962

Control of Imports (Quota No.3, Forty-Seventh Period) (Leather Footwear) Order, S.I. No. 98 of 1962

Control of Imports (Quota No.38, Forty-Second Period) (Wood Screws) Order, S.I. No. 99 of 1962

Control of Imports (Quota No.50, Fifth Period) (Superphosphates) Order, S.I. No. 100 of 1962

Control of Imports (Quota No.13, Forty-Fifth Period) (Woven Woollen and Synthetic and Artificial Fabrics) Order, S.I. No. 139 of 1962

Control of Imports (Quota No.35, Thirty-Seventh Period) (Sparking Plugs) Order, S.I. No. 162 of 1962

Control of Imports (Quota No.45, Nineteenth Period) (Cotton Piece Goods) Order, S.I. No. 189 of 1962

Control of Imports (Quota No.31, Forty-Second Period) (Electric Filament Lamps) Order, S.I. No. 190 of 1962

Control of Imports (Quota No.3, Forty-Eighth Period) (Leather Footwear) Order, S.I. No. 218 of 1962

Control of Imports (Quota No.6, Thirty-First Period) (Rubber-Proofed Clothing) Order, S.I. No. 219 of 1962

Control of Imports (Quota No.8, Thirty-First Period) (Motor Cars) Order, S.I. No. 220 of 1962

Control of Imports (Quota No.9, Thirtieth Period) (Motor Vehicle Chassis) Order, S.I. No. 221 of 1962

Control of Imports (Quota No.10, Thirty-First Period) (Road Vehicle Bodies) Order, S.I. No. 222 of 1962

Control of Imports (Quota No.25, Twenty-Ninth Period) (Motor Car Body Balloons) Order, S.I. No. 223 of 1962

Control of Imports (Quota No.37, Forty-Third Period) (Women's Felt Hats) Order, S.I. No. 224 of 1962

Control of Imports Acts (*Cont.*)

Control of Imports (Quota No.47, Twelfth Period) (Road Vehicles) Order, S.I. No. 225 of 1962

Control of Imports (Quota No.1, Thirty-Eighth Period) (Motor Tyres) Order, S.I. No. 237 of 1962

Control of Imports (Quota No.2, Thirty-Eighth Period) (Cycle Tyres) Order, S.I. No. 238 of 1962

Control of Imports (Quota No.4, Thirty-Fourth Period) (Rubber Footwear) Order, S.I. No. 239 of 1962

Control of Imports (Quota No.12, Forty-First Period) (Silk or Artificial Silk Hose) Order, S.I. No. 37 of 1963

Control of Imports (Quota No.13, Forty-Sixth Period) (Woven Woollen and Synthetic and Artificial Fabrics) Order, S.I. No. 38 of 1963

Control of Imports (Quota No.28, Thirtieth Period) (Miscellaneous Brushes) Order, S.I. No. 41 of 1963

Control of Imports (Quota No.36, Thirty-Eighth Period) (Laminated Springs) Order, S.I. No. 42 of 1963

Control of Imports (Quota No.1, Thirty-Ninth Period) (Motor Tyres) Order, S.I. No. 93 of 1963

Control of Imports (Quota No.3, Forty-Ninth Period) (Leather Footwear) Order, S.I. No. 94 of 1963

Control of Imports (Quota No.12, Forty-Second Period) (Silk or Artificial Silk Hose) Order, S.I. No. 95 of 1963

Control of Imports (Quota No.13, Forty-Seventh Period) (Woven Woollen and Synthetic and Artificial Fabrics) Order, S.I. No. 96 of 1963

Control of Imports (Quota No.28, Thirty-First Period) (Miscellaneous Brushes) Order, S.I. No. 97 of 1963

Control of Imports (Quota No.36, Thirty-Ninth Period) (Laminated Springs) Order, S.I. No. 98 of 1963

Control of Imports (Quota No.38, Forty-Third Period) (Wood Screws) Order, S.I. No. 99 of 1963

Control of Imports (Quota No.50, Sixth Period) (Superphosphates) Order, S.I. No. 100 of 1963

Control of Imports (Quota No.2, Thirty-Ninth Period) (Cycle Tyres) Order, S.I. No. 101 of 1963

Control of Imports (Quota No.4, Thirty-Fifth Period) (Rubber Footwear) Order, S.I. No. 102 of 1963

Control of Imports (Quota No.35, Thirty-Eighth Period) (Sparking Plugs) Order, S.I. No. 185 of 1963

Control of Imports (Quota No.45, Twentieth Period) (Cotton Piece Goods) Order, S.I. No. 212 of 1963

Control of Imports Acts (*Cont.*)

Control of Imports (Quota No.31, Forty-Third Period) (Electric Filament Lamps) Order, S.I. No. 225 of 1963

Control of Imports (Quota No.8, Thirty-Second Period) (Motor Cars) Order, S.I. No. 232 of 1963

Control of Imports (Quota No.9, Thirty-First Period) (Motor Vehicle Chassis) Order, S.I. No. 233 of 1963

Control of Imports (Quota No.10, Thirty-Second Period) (Road Vehicle Bodies) Order, S.I. No. 234 of 1963

Control of Imports (Quota No.25, Thirtieth Period) (Motor Car Body Balloons) Order, S.I. No. 235 of 1963

Control of Imports (Quota No.47, Thirteenth Period) (Road Vehicles) Order, S.I. No. 236 of 1963

Control of Imports (Quota No.3, Fiftieth Period) (Leather Footwear) Order, S.I. No. 252 of 1963

Control of Imports (Quota No.4, Thirty-Sixth Period) (Rubber Footwear) Order, S.I. No. 253 of 1963

Control of Imports (Quota No.13, Forty-Eighth Period) (Woven Woollen and Synthetic and Artificial Fabrics) Order, S.I. No. 254 of 1963

Control of Imports (Quota No.37, Forty-Fourth Period) (Women's Felt Hats) Order, S.I. No. 255 of 1963

Control of Imports (Quota No.1, Fortieth Period) (Motor Tyres) Order, S.I. No. 277 of 1963

Control of Imports (Quota No.2, Fortieth Period) (Cycle Tyres) Order, S.I. No. 278 of 1963

Control of Imports (Quota No.12, Forty-Third Period) (Silk or Artificial Silk Hose) Order, S.I. No. 14 of 1964

Control of Imports (Quota No.28, Thirty-Second Period) (Miscellaneous Brushes) Order, S.I. No. 31 of 1964

Control of Imports (Quota No.36, Fortieth Period) (Laminated Springs) Order, S.I. No. 32 of 1964

Control of Imports (Quota No.38, Forty-Fourth Period) (Wood Screws) Order, S.I. No. 135 of 1964

Control of Imports (Quota No.3, Fifty-First Period) (Leather Footwear) Order, S.I. No. 136 of 1964

Control of Imports (Quota No.4, Thirty-Seventh Period) (Rubber Footwear) Order, S.I. No. 137 of 1964

Control of Imports (Quota No.50, Seventh Period) (Superphosphates) Order, S.I. No. 138 of 1964

Control of Imports (Quota No.13, Forty-Ninth Period) (Woven Woollen and Synthetic and Artificial Fabrics) Order, S.I. No. 184 of 1964

Statutory Authority	Section	Statutory Instrument
Control of Imports Acts (*Cont.*)		*Control of Imports (Quota No.35, Thirty-Ninth Period) (Sparking Plugs) Order, S.I. No. 225 of 1964*
		Control of Imports (Quota No.31, Forty-Fourth Period) (Electric Filament Lamps) Order, S.I. No. 251 of 1964
		Control of Imports (Quota No.45, Twenty-First Period) (Cotton Piece Goods) Order, S.I. No. 258 of 1964
		Control of Imports (Quota No.8, Thirty-Third Period) (Motor Cars) Order, S.I. No. 268 of 1964
		Control of Imports (Quota No.9, Thirty-Second Period) (Motor Vehicle Chassis) Order, S.I. No. 269 of 1964
		Control of Imports (Quota No.10, Thirty-Third Period) (Road Vehicle Bodies) Order, S.I. No. 270 of 1964
		Control of Imports (Quota No.25, Thirty-First Period) (Motor Car Body Balloons) Order, S.I. No. 271 of 1964
		Control of Imports (Quota No.47, Fourteenth Period) (Road Vehicles) Order, S.I. No. 272 of 1964
		Control of Imports (Quota No.3, Fifty-Second Period) (Leather Footwear) Order, S.I. No. 287 of 1964
		Control of Imports (Quota No.37, Forty-Fifth Period) (Women's Felt Hats) Order, S.I. No. 288 of 1964
		Control of Imports (Quota No.4, Thirty-Eighth Period) (Rubber Footwear) Order, S.I. No. 289 of 1964
		Control of Imports (Quota No.51) (Miscellaneous Textiles) Order, S.I. No. 297 of 1964
		Control of Imports (Quota No.52) (Miscellaneous Textile Piece Goods) Order, S.I. No. 298 of 1964
		Control of Imports (Quota No.51, First Period) (Miscellaneous Textiles) Order, S.I. No. 299 of 1964
		Control of Imports (Quota No.52, First Period) (Miscellaneous Textile Piece Goods) Order, S.I. No. 300 of 1964
		Control of Imports (Quota No.1, Forty-First Period) (Motor Tyres) Order, S.I. No. 301 of 1964
		Control of Imports (Quota No.2, Forty-First Period) (Cycle Tyres) Order, S.I. No. 302 of 1964
		Control of Imports (Quota No.12, Forty-Fourth Period) (Silk or Artificial Silk Hose) Order, S.I. No. 14 of 1965
		Control of Imports (Quota No.13, Fiftieth Period) (Woven Woollen and Synthetic and Artificial Fabrics) Order, S.I. No. 15 of 1965
		Control of Imports (Quota No.28, Thirty-Third Period) (Miscellaneous Brushes) Order, S.I. No. 37 of 1965

Statutory Authority	Section	Statutory Instrument
Control of Imports Acts (*Cont.*)		*Control of Imports (Quota No.36, Forty-First Period) (Laminated Springs) Order, S.I. No. 38 of 1965*
		Control of Imports (Quota No.50, Eighth Period) (Superphosphates) Order, S.I. No. 115 of 1965
		Control of Imports (Quota No.38, Forty-Fifth Period) (Wood Screws) Order, S.I. No. 119 of 1965
		Control of Imports (Quota No.4, Thirty-Ninth Period) (Rubber Footwear) Order, S.I. No. 120 of 1965
		Control of Imports (Quota No.3, Fifty-Third Period) (Leather Footwear) Order, S.I. No. 121 of 1965
		Control of Imports (Quota No.13, Fifty-First Period) (Woven Woollen and Synthetic and Artificial Fabrics) Order, S.I. No. 187 of 1965
		Control of Imports (Quota No.35, Fortieth Period) (Sparking Plugs) Order, S.I. No. 207 of 1965
		Control of Imports (Quota No.31, Forty-Fifth Period) (Electric Filament Lamps) Order, S.I. No. 214 of 1965
		Control of Imports (Quota No.45, Twenty-Second Period) (Cotton Piece Goods) Order, S.I. No. 217 of 1965
		Control of Imports (Quota No.37, Forty-Sixth Period) (Women's Felt Hats) Order, S.I. No. 234 of 1965
		Control of Imports (Quota No.3, Fifty-Fourth Period) (Leather Footwear) Order, S.I. No. 235 of 1965
		Control of Imports (Quota No.51, Second Period) (Miscellaneous Textiles) Order, S.I. No. 237 of 1965
		Control of Imports (Quota No.52, Second Period) (Miscellaneous Textile Piece Goods) Order, S.I. No. 238 of 1965
		Control of Imports (Quota No.4, Fortieth Period) (Rubber Footwear) Order, S.I. No. 239 of 1965
		Control of Imports (Quota No.8, Thirty-Fourth Period) (Motor Cars) Order, S.I. No. 240 of 1965
		Control of Imports (Quota No.9, Thirty-Third Period) (Motor Vehicle Chassis) Order, S.I. No. 241 of 1965
		Control of Imports (Quota No.10, Thirty-Fourth Period) (Road Vehicle Bodies) Order, S.I. No. 242 of 1965
		Control of Imports (Quota No.25, Thirty-Second Period) (Motor Car Body Balloons) Order, S.I. No. 243 of 1965
		Control of Imports (Quota No.47, Fifteenth Period) (Road Vehicles) Order, S.I. No. 244 of 1965
		Control of Imports (Quota No.1, Forty-Second Period) (Motor Tyres) Order, S.I. No. 263 of 1965

Statutory Authority	Section	Statutory Instrument

Control of Imports Acts (*Cont.*)

Control of Imports (Quota No.2, Forty-Second Period) (Cycle Tyres) Order, S.I. No. 264 of 1965

Control of Imports (Quota No.13, Fifty-Second Period) (Woven Woollen and Synthetic and Artificial Fabrics) Order, S.I. No. 14 of 1966

Control of Imports (Quota No.12, Forty-Fifth Period) (Silk or Artificial Silk Hose) Order, S.I. No. 16 of 1966

Control of Imports (Quota No.28, Thirty-Fourth Period) (Miscellaneous Brushes) Order, S.I. No. 45 of 1966

Control of Imports (Quota No.36, Forty-Second Period) (Laminated Springs) Order, S.I. No. 46 of 1966

Control of Imports (Quota No.50, Ninth Period) (Superphosphates) Order, S.I. No. 108 of 1966

Control of Imports (Quota No.12, Forty-Sixth Period) (Silk or Artificial Silk Hose) (Amendment) Order, S.I. No. 110 of 1966

Control of Imports (Quota No.3, Fifty-Fifth Period) (Leather Footwear) Order, S.I. No. 111 of 1966

Control of Imports (Quota No.36, Forty-Third Period) (Laminated Springs) Order, S.I. No. 112 of 1966

Control of Imports (Quota No.35, Forty-First Period) (Sparking Plugs) Order, S.I. No. 113 of 1966

Control of Imports (Quota No.28, Thirty-Fifth Period) (Miscellaneous Brushes) Order, S.I. No. 115 of 1966

Control of Imports (Quota No.53, First Period) (Miscellaneous Brushes) Order, S.I. No. 117 of 1966

Control of Imports (Quota No.31, Forty-Sixth Period) (Electric Filament Lamps) Order, S.I. No. 245 of 1966

Control of Imports (Quota No.51, Third Period) (Miscellaneous Textiles) Order, S.I. No. 259 of 1966

Control of Imports (Quota No.52, Third Period) (Miscellaneous Textile Piece Goods) Order, S.I. No. 260 of 1966

Control of Imports (Quota No.3, Fifty-Sixth Period) (Leather Footwear) Order, S.I. No. 263 of 1966

Control of Imports (Quota No.2, Forty-Third Period) (Cycle Tyres) Order, S.I. No. 290 of 1966

Control of Imports (Quota No.54) (Pneumatic Tyres) Order, S.I. No. 134 of 1967

Control of Imports (Quota No.3, Fifty-Seventh Period) (Leather Footwear) Order, S.I. No. 140 of 1967

Control of Imports (Quota No.12, Forty-Seventh Period) (Silk or Artificial Silk Hose) Order, S.I. No. 141 of 1967

Statutory Authority	Section	Statutory Instrument
Control of Imports Acts (*Cont.*)		*Control of Imports (Quota No.28, Thirty-Sixth Period) (Miscellaneous Brushes) Order, S.I. No. 142 of 1967*
		Control of Imports (Quota No.53, Second Period) (Miscellaneous Brushes) Order, S.I. No. 143 of 1967
		Control of Imports (Quota No.35, Forty-Second Period) (Sparking Plugs) Order, S.I. No. 144 of 1967
		Control of Imports (Quota No.36, Forty-Fourth Period) (Laminated Springs) Order, S.I. No. 145 of 1967
		Control of Imports (Quota No.50, Tenth Period) (Superphosphates) Order, S.I. No. 146 of 1967
		Control of Imports (Quota No.54, First Period) (Pneumatic Tyres) Order, S.I. No. 159 of 1967
		Control of Imports (Quota No.31, Forty-Seventh Period) (Electric Filament Lamps) Order, S.I. No. 228 of 1967
		Control of Imports (Quota No.3, Fifty-Eighth Period) Leather Footwear Order, S.I. No. 251 of 1967
		Control of Imports (Quota No.51, Fourth Period) (Miscellaneous Textiles) Order, S.I. No. 260 of 1967
		Control of Imports (Quota No.52, Fourth Period) (Miscellaneous Textile Piece Goods) Order, S.I. No. 261 of 1967
		Control of Imports (Quota No.54, Second Period) (Pneumatic Tyres) Order, S.I. No. 262 of 1967
		Control of Imports (Quota No.2, Forty-Fourth Period) (Cycle Tyres) Order, S.I. No. 308 of 1967
		Control of Imports (Quota No.12, Forty-Eighth Period) (Silk or Artificial Silk Hose) Order, S.I. No. 125 of 1968
		Control of Imports (Quota No.28, Thirty-Seventh Period) (Miscellaneous Brushes) Order, S.I. No. 126 of 1968
		Control of Imports (Quota No.35, Forty-Third Period) (Sparking Plugs) Order, S.I. No. 127 of 1968
		Control of Imports (Quota No.36, Forty-Fifth Period) (Laminated Springs) Order, S.I. No. 128 of 1968
		Control of Imports (Quota No.50, Eleventh Period) (Superphosphates) Order, S.I. No. 129 of 1968
		Control of Imports (Quota No.53, Third Period) (Miscellaneous Brushes) Order, S.I. No. 130 of 1968
		Control of Imports (Quota No.3, Fifty-Ninth Period) (Leather Footwear) Order, S.I. No. 131 of 1968
		Control of Imports (Quota No.54, Third Period) (Pneumatic Tyres) Order, S.I. No. 133 of 1968

Statutory Authority	Section	Statutory Instrument

Control of Imports Acts (*Cont.*)

Control of Imports (Quota No.3, Sixtieth Period) (Leather Footwear) Order, S.I. No. 186 of 1968

Control of Imports (Quota No.31, Forty-Eighth Period) (Electric Filament Lamps) Order, S.I. No. 223 of 1968

Control of Imports (Quota No.51, Fifth Period) (Miscellaneous Textiles) Order, S.I. No. 243 of 1968

Control of Imports (Quota No.52, Fifth Period) (Miscellaneous Textile Piece Goods) Order, S.I. No. 244 of 1968

Control of Imports (Quota No.54, Fourth Period) (Pneumatic Tyres) Order, S.I. No. 245 of 1968

Control of Imports (Quota No.2, Forty-Fifth Period) (Cycle Tyres) Order, S.I. No. 288 of 1968

Control of Imports (Quota No.54, Fifth Period) (Pneumatic Tyres) Order, S.I. No. 84 of 1969

Control of Imports (Quota No.3, Sixty-First Period) (Leather Footwear) Order, S.I. No. 86 of 1969

Control of Imports (Quota No.12, Forty-Ninth Period) (Silk or Artificial Silk Hose) Order, S.I. No. 88 of 1969

Control of Imports (Quota No.28, Thirty-Eighth Period) (Miscellaneous Brushes) Order, S.I. No. 89 of 1969

Control of Imports (Quota No.53, Fourth Period) (Miscellaneous Brushes) Order, S.I. No. 90 of 1969

Control of Imports (Quota No.35, Forty-Fourth Period) (Sparking Plugs) Order, S.I. No. 91 of 1969

Control of Imports (Quota No.36, Forty-Sixth Period) (Laminated Springs) Order, S.I. No. 92 of 1969

Control of Imports (Quota No.50, Twelfth Period) (Superphosphates) Order, S.I. No. 93 of 1969

Control of Imports (Quota No.31, Forty-Ninth Period) (Electric Filament Lamps) Order, S.I. No. 197 of 1969

Control of Imports (Quota No.51, Sixth Period) (Miscellaneous Textiles) Order, S.I. No. 233 of 1969

Control of Imports (Quota No.52, Sixth Period) (Miscellaneous Textile Piece Goods) Order, S.I. No. 234 of 1969

Control of Imports (Quota No.3, Sixty-Second Period) (Leather Footwear) Order, S.I. No. 235 of 1969

Control of Imports (Quota No.2, Forty-Sixth Period) (Cycle Tyres) Order, S.I. No. 255 of 1969

Control of Imports (Quota No.12, Fiftieth Period) (Silk or Artificial Silk Hose) Order, S.I. No. 111 of 1970

Statutory Authority	Section	Statutory Instrument
Control of Imports Acts (*Cont.*)		*Control of Imports (Quota No.28, Thirty-Ninth Period) (Miscellaneous Brushes) Order, S.I. No. 112 of 1970*
		Control of Imports (Quota No.53, Fifth Period) (Miscellaneous Brushes) Order, S.I. No. 113 of 1970
		Control of Imports (Quota No.35, Forty-Fifth Period) (Sparking Plugs) Order, S.I. No. 114 of 1970
		Control of Imports (Quota No.36, Forty-Seventh Period) (Laminated Springs) Order, S.I. No. 115 of 1970
		Control of Imports (Quota No.50, Thirteenth Period) (Superphosphates) Order, S.I. No. 116 of 1970
		Control of Imports (Quota No.31, Fiftieth Period) (Electric Filament Lamps) Order, S.I. No. 253 of 1970
		Control of Imports (Quota No.51, Seventh Period) (Miscellaneous Textiles) Order, S.I. No. 273 of 1970
		Control of Imports (Quota No.52, Seventh Period) (Miscellaneous Textile Piece Goods) Order, S.I. No. 274 of 1970
		Control of Imports (Quota No.2, Forty-Seventh Period) (Cycle Tyres) Order, S.I. No. 295 of 1970
		Control of Imports (Quota No.12, Fifty-First Period) (Silk or Artificial Silk Hose) Order, S.I. No. 169 of 1971
		Control of Imports (Quota No.28, Fortieth Period) (Miscellaneous Brushes) Order, S.I. No. 170 of 1971
		Control of Imports (Quota No.53, Sixth Period) (Miscellaneous Brushes) Order, S.I. No. 171 of 1971
		Control of Imports (Quota No.31, Fifty-First Period) (Electric Filament Lamps) Order, S.I. No. 172 of 1971
		Control of Imports (Quota No.35, Forty-Sixth Period) (Sparking Plugs) Order, S.I. No. 173 of 1971
		Control of Imports (Quota No.36, Forty-Eighth Period) (Laminated Springs) Order, S.I. No. 174 of 1971
		Control of Imports (Quota No.50, Fourteenth Period) (Superphosphates) Order, S.I. No. 175 of 1971
		Control of Imports (Quota No.51, Eighth Period) (Miscellaneous Textiles) Order, S.I. No. 311 of 1971
		Control of Imports (Quota No.52, Eighth Period) (Miscellaneous Textile Piece Goods) Order, S.I. No. 312 of 1971
		Control of Imports (Quota No.31, Fifty-Second Period) (Electric Filament Lamps) (No.2) Order, S.I. No. 317 of 1971

Control of Imports Acts (*Cont.*)

Control of Imports (Quota No.2, Forty-Eight Period) (Cycle Tyres) Order, S.I. No. 350 of 1971

Control of Imports (Quota No.31, Fifty-Third Period) (Electric Filament Lamps) Order, S.I. No. 122 of 1972

Control of Imports (Quota No.12, Fifty-Second Period) (Silk or Artificial Silk Hose) Order, S.I. No. 131 of 1972

Control of Imports (Quota No.28, Forty-First Period) (Miscellaneous Brushes) Order, S.I. No. 132 of 1972

Control of Imports (Quota No.53, Seventh Period) (Miscellaneous Brushes) Order, S.I. No. 133 of 1972

Control of Imports (Quota No.35, Forty-Seventh Period) (Sparking Plugs) Order, S.I. No. 134 of 1972

Control of Imports (Quota No.36, Forty-Ninth Period) (Laminated Springs) Order, S.I. No. 135 of 1972

Control of Imports (Quota No.50, Fifteenth Period) (Superphosphates) Order, S.I. No. 136 of 1972

Control of Imports (Quota No.51, Ninth Period) (Miscellaneous Textiles) Order, S.I. No. 285 of 1972

Control of Imports (Quota No.52, Ninth Period) (Miscellaneous Textile Piece Goods) Order, S.I. No. 286 of 1972

Control of Imports (Quota No.12, Fifty-Third Period) (Silk or Artificial Silk Hose) (No.2) Order, S.I. No. 287 of 1972

Control of Imports (Quota No.28, Forty-Second Period) (Miscellaneous Brushes) (No.2) Order, S.I. No. 288 of 1972

Control of Imports (Quota No.53, Eighth Period) (Miscellaneous Brushes) (No.2) Order, S.I. No. 289 of 1972

Control of Imports (Quota No.35, Forty-Eighth Period) (Sparking Plugs) (No.2) Order, S.I. No. 290 of 1972

Control of Imports (Quota No.36, Fiftieth Period) (Laminated Springs) (No.2) Order, S.I. No. 291 of 1972

Control of Imports (Quota No.50, Sixteenth Period) (Superphosphates) (No.2) Order, S.I. No. 292 of 1972

Control of Imports (Quota No.2, Forty-Ninth Period) (Cycle Tyres) Order, S.I. No. 330 of 1972

Control of Imports (Quota No.12, Fifty-Fourth Period) (Silk or Artificial Silk Hose) Order, S.I. No. 122 of 1973

Control of Imports (Quota No.28, Forty-Third Period) (Miscellaneous Brushes) Order, S.I. No. 123 of 1973

Statutory Authority	Section	Statutory Instrument
Control of Imports Acts (*Cont.*)		*Control of Imports (Quota No.53, Ninth Period) (Miscellaneous Brushes) Order, S.I. No. 124 of 1973*
		Control of Imports (Quota No.35, Forty-Ninth Period) (Sparking Plugs) Order, S.I. No. 125 of 1973
		Control of Imports (Quota No.36, Fifty-First Period) (Laminated Springs) Order, S.I. No. 126 of 1973
		Control of Imports (Quota No.50, Seventeenth Period) (Superphosphates) Order, S.I. No. 316 of 1973
		Control of Imports (Quota No.51, Tenth Period) (Miscellaneous Textiles) Order, S.I. No. 317 of 1973
		Control of Imports (Quota No.52, Tenth Period) (Miscellaneous Textile Piece Goods) Order, S.I. No. 318 of 1973
		Control of Imports (Quota No.2, Fiftieth Period) (Cycle Tyres) Order, S.I. No. 332 of 1973
		Control of Imports (Quota No.12, Fifty-Fifth Period) (Silk or Artificial Silk Hose) Order, S.I. No. 155 of 1974
		Control of Imports (Quota No.28, Forty-Fourth Period) (Miscellaneous Brushes) Order, S.I. No. 156 of 1974
		Control of Imports (Quota No.53, Tenth Period) (Miscellaneous Brushes) Order, S.I. No. 157 of 1974
		Control of Imports (Quota No.35, Fiftieth Period) (Sparking Plugs) Order, S.I. No. 158 of 1974
		Control of Imports (Quota No.36, Fifty-Second Period) (Laminated Springs) Order, S.I. No. 159 of 1974
		Control of Imports (Quota No.50, Eighteenth Period) (Superphosphates) Order, S.I. No. 346 of 1974
		Control of Imports (Quota No.51, Eleventh Period) (Miscellaneous Textiles) Order, S.I. No. 347 of 1974
		Control of Imports (Quota No.52, Eleventh Period) (Miscellaneous Textile Piece Goods) Order, S.I. No. 348 of 1974
		Control of Imports (Quota No.2, Fifty-First Period) (Cycle Tyres) Order, S.I. No. 372 of 1974
		Control of Imports (Quota No.51, Twelfth Period) (Miscellaneous Textiles) Order, S.I. No. 285 of 1975
		Control of Imports (Quota No.52, Twelfth Period) (Miscellaneous Textile Piece Goods) Order, S.I. No. 286 of 1975
		Control of Imports (Quota No.2, Fifty-Second Period) (Cycle Tyres) Order, S.I. No. 289 of 1976
		Control of Imports (Quota No.51, Thirteenth Period) (Miscellaneous Textiles) Order, S.I. No. 291 of 1976

Control of Imports Acts (*Cont.*)

Control of Imports (Quota No.52, Thirteenth Period) (Miscellaneous Textile Piece Goods) Order, S.I. No. 292 of 1976

Control of Imports (Quota No.2, Fifty-Third Period) (Cycle Tyres) Order, S.I. No. 354 of 1977

Control of Imports (Quota No.52, Fourteenth Period) (Miscellaneous Textile Piece Goods) Order, S.I. No. 355 of 1977

Control of Imports (Quota No.51, Fourteenth Period) (Miscellaneous Textiles) Order, S.I. No. 356 of 1977

Control of Imports (Quota No.2, Fifty-Fourth Period) (Cycle Tyres) Order, S.I. No. 313 of 1978

Control of Imports (Quota No.51, Fifteenth Period) (Miscellaneous Textiles) Order, S.I. No. 316 of 1978

Control of Imports (Quota No.52, Fifteenth Period) (Miscellaneous Textile Piece Goods) Order, S.I. No. 317 of 1978

Control of Imports (Quota No.2, Fifty-Fifth Period) (Cycle Tyres) Order, S.I. No. 358 of 1979

Control of Imports (Quota No.51, Sixteenth Period) (Miscellaneous Textiles) Order, S.I. No. 372 of 1979

Control of Imports (Quota No.52, Sixteenth Period) (Miscellaneous Textile Piece Goods) Order, S.I. No. 373 of 1979

Control of Imports (Quota No.2, Fifty-Sixth Period) (Cycle Tyres) Order, S.I. No. 330 of 1980

Control of Imports (Quota No.51, Seventeenth Period) (Miscellaneous Textiles) Order, S.I. No. 349 of 1980

Control of Imports (Quota No.52, Seventeenth Period) (Miscellaneous Textile Piece Goods) Order, S.I. No. 350 of 1980

Control of Imports (Quota No.2, Fifty-Seventh Period) (Cycle Tyres) Order, S.I. No. 385 of 1981

Control of Imports (Quota No.51, Eighteenth Period) (Miscellaneous Textiles) Order, S.I. No. 405 of 1981

Control of Imports (Quota No.52, Eighteenth Period) (Miscellaneous Textile Piece Goods) Order, S.I. No. 406 of 1981

Control of Imports (Quota No.2, Fifty-Eighth Period) (Cycle Tyres) Order, S.I. No. 332 of 1982

Control of Imports (Quota No.51, Nineteenth Period) (Miscellaneous Textiles) Order, S.I. No. 333 of 1982

Control of Imports (Quota No.52, Nineteenth Period) (Miscellaneous Textile Piece Goods) Order, S.I. No. 334 of 1982

Control of Imports (Quota No.2, Fifty-Ninth Period) (Cycle Tyres) Order, S.I. No. 346 of 1983

Statutory Authority	Section	Statutory Instrument
Control of Imports Act, No. 12 of 1934 (*Cont.*)		*Control of Imports (Quota No.51, Twentieth Period) (Miscellaneous Textiles) Order, S.I. No. 347 of 1983*
		Control of Imports (Quota No.52, Twentieth Period) (Miscellaneous Textiles Piece Goods) Order, S.I. No. 348 of 1983
		Control of Imports (Quota No.2, Sixtieth Period) (Cycle Tyres) Order, S.I. No. 322 of 1984
		Control of Imports (Quota No.51, Twenty-First Period) (Miscellaneous Textiles) Order, S.I. No. 323 of 1984
		Control of Imports (Quota No.52, Twenty-First Period) (Miscellaneous Textile Piece Goods) Order, S.I. No. 324 of 1984
Control of Imports (Amendment) Act, No. 8 of 1937	2	**Control of Imports (Quota No.34) (Amendment) Order [Vol. XXVII p. 815] S.R.& O. No. 173 of 1939**
		Control of Imports (Quota No.37) (Amendment) Order [Vol. XXVII p. 927] S.R.& O. No. 295 of 1939
		Control of Imports (Quota No.33) (Revocation) Order [Vol. XXVII p. 811] S.R.& O. No. 354 of 1939
		Control of Imports (Quotas No.1 to 32) (Amendment) Order [Vol. XXVII p. 741] S.R.& O. No. 402 of 1939
		Control of Imports (Quota No.37, Eighth Period) (Amendment) Order [Vol. XXVII p. 951] S.R.& O. No. 199 of 1940
		Control of Imports (Quota No.34) (Revocation) Order [Vol. XXVII p. 831] S.R.& O. No. 209 of 1941
		Control of Imports (Quotas No.35 and 36) (Amendment) Order [Vol. XXVII p. 905] S.R.& O. No. 351 of 1941
	3	**Control of Imports (Quota No.34) (Amendment) Order [Vol. XXVII p. 815] S.R.& O. No. 173 of 1939**
		Control of Imports (Quota No.37) (Amendment) Order [Vol. XXVII p. 927] S.R.& O. No. 295 of 1939
		Control of Imports (Quota No.33) (Revocation) Order [Vol. XXVII p. 811] S.R.& O. No. 354 of 1939
		Control of Imports (Quotas No.1 to 32) (Amendment) Order [Vol. XXVII p. 741] S.R.& O. No. 402 of 1939
		Control of Imports (Quota No.37, Eighth Period) (Amendment) Order [Vol. XXVII p. 951] S.R.& O. No. 199 of 1940

Statutory Authority	Section	Statutory Instrument
Control of Imports (Amendment) Act, No. 8 of 1937 (*Cont.*)		**Control of Imports (Quota No.34) (Revocation) Order** *[Vol. XXVII p. 831]* **S.R.& O. No. 209 of 1941**
		Control of Imports (Quotas No.35 and 36) (Amendment) Order [Vol. XXVII p. 905] S.R.& O. No. 351 of 1941
Control of Imports (Amendment) Act, No. 13 of 1963	3	**Control of Imports (Quota No.2) (Amendment) Order, S.I. No. 118 of 1963**
		Control of Imports (Quota No.50) (Superphosphates) (Amendment) Order, S.I. No. 107 of 1966
	3	**Road Vehicles (Registration and Licensing) Regulations, S.I. No. 13 of 1958**
Control of Manufactures Act, No. 21 of 1932	12	*Control of Manufactures Regulations, 1932 (Amendment) Regulations, S.I. No. 77 of 1953*
		Control of Manufactures, 1932 (Amendment) Regulations, S.I. No. 98 of 1964
	12(1)	*Control of Manufactures Regulations [Vol. VIII p. 5] S.R.& O. No. 108 of 1932*
	16(2)	*Control of Manufactures Act, 1932 (Date of Commencement) Order [Vol. VIII p. 1] S.R.& O. No. 9 of 1933*
Control of Manufactures Act, No. 36 of 1934	6	*Control of Manufactures Regulations [Vol. VIII p. 7] S.R.& O. No. 362 of 1934*
		Control of Manufactures Regulations [Vol. VIII p. 25] S.R.& O. No. 156 of 1935
	17(1)	*Reserved Commodity (Sewing Cotton) Order [Vol. VIII p. 31] S.R.& O. No. 176 of 1935*
	18	*Control of Manufactures Act, 1934 (Sewing Cotton) (Appointed Day) Order [Vol. VIII p. 37] S.R.& O. No. 309 of 1935*
Control of Prices Act, No. 33 of 1932	3(2)	*Control of Prices (Scheduled Commodity) (Furniture) Order [Vol. VIII p. 57] S.R.& O. No. 660 of 1935*
	6	*Control of Prices Regulations [Vol. VIII p. 47] S.R.& O. No. 83 of 1933*
	17(1)	*Prices Commission (Proceedings) Regulations [Vol. VIII p. 41] S.R.& O. No. 69 of 1933*
Control of Prices Act, No. 26 of 1937	1(2)	*Control of Prices Act, 1937 (Commencement) Order [Vol. VIII p. 61] S.R.& O. No. 27 of 1938*
	5	*Price Certificate (Form) Regulations [Vol. VIII p. 65] S.R.& O. No. 55 of 1938*
	16(1)	*Prices Commission (Proceedings) Regulations [Vol. VIII p. 71] S.R.& O. No. 63 of 1938*

Statutory Authority	Section	Statutory Instrument
Control of Prices Act, No. 26 of 1937 (*Cont.*)	42	*Retail Prices (Display) (No.1) Order, 1938 (Revocation) Order, S.I. No. 182 of 1955*
	42(1)	*Retail Prices (Display) (No.1) Order [Vol. VIII p. 77] S.R.& O. No. 83 of 1938*
	42(3)	*Retail Prices (Display) (No.1) (Amendment) Order [Vol. VIII p. 87] S.R.& O. No. 122 of 1938*
		Retail Prices (Display) (No.1) Order, 1938 (Amendment) Order [Vol. XXVIII p. 275] S.R.& O. No. 192 of 1939
Copyright Act, No. 10 of 1963	1(2)	*Copyright Act, 1963 (Commencement) Order, S.I. No. 177 of 1964*
	12(6)	**Copyright (Publication of Certain Works) Regulations, S.I. No. 180 of 1964**
	13	**Copyright (Royalties on Records) Regulations, S.I. No. 179 of 1964**
	28	**Copyright (Customs) Regulations, S.I. No. 231 of 1964**
	35	**Copyright (Proceedings Before the Controller) Rules, S.I. No. 204 of 1964**
	36	**Copyright (Proceedings Before the Controller) Rules, S.I. No. 204 of 1964**
	43	**Copyright (Foreign Countries) Order, S.I. No. 132 of 1978**
		Copyright (Foreign Countries) (No.2) Order, S.I. No. 133 of 1978
	55(3)	**Copyright (Register of Dramatic Works) Rules, S.I. No. 178 of 1964**
	56(1)	**Copyright (Exemption from Delivery of Books to certain Libraries) Regulations, S.I. No. 181 of 1964**
Coras Beostoic agus Feola Act, No. 25 of 1979	2	*Coras Beostoic agus Feola Act, 1979 (Establishment Day) Order, S.I. No. 325 of 1979*
	28(3)	*Coras Beostoic agus Feola Act, 1979 (Levy on Slaughtered or Exported Livestock) Order, S.I. No. 231 of 1982*
		Coras Beostoic agus Feola Act, 1979 (Levy on Slaughtered or Exported Livestock) Order, S.I. No. 427 of 1985
	29(6)	**Coras Beostoic agus Feola (Levy on Exported Livestock) Regulations, S.I. No. 324 of 1979**
		Coras Beostoic agus Feola (Levy on Exported Livestock) (Amendment) Regulations, S.I. No. 230 of 1982
Coras Iompair Eireann (Additional Powers) Order, S.I. No. 366 of 1977	4	**Coras Iompair Eireann Salaried Officers' and Clerks' (G. N. R., C. D. R. and I. R. C. H.) Superannuation Scheme, 1977 (Confirmation) Order, S.I. No. 339 of 1978**

Statutory Authority	Section	Statutory Instrument
Coras Iompair Eireann (Additional Powers) Order, S.I. No. 366 of 1977 (*Cont.*)		**Coras Iompair Eireann Salaried Officers' and Clerks' (G. N. R., C. D. R., I. R. C. H.) Superannuation (Amendment) (Confirmation) Order, S.I. No. 184 of 1982**
Cork City Management Act, No. 1 of 1929	8(2)	**Cork and Limerick City Management (Reserved Functions) Order, S.I. No. 43 of 1986**
Cork City Management (Amendment) Act, No. 5 of 1941	4	*Cork County Borough (Electoral Areas) Order, S.I. No. 249 of 1965*
		Cork County Borough (Electoral Areas) Order, S.I. No. 27 of 1974
		Cork County Borough (Electoral Areas) Order, S.I. No. 111 of 1985
Cork Fever Hospital (Amendment) Act, No. 24 of 1954	3	*Cork Fever Hospital (Amendment) Act, 1954 (Appointed Day) Order, S.I. No. 79 of 1955*
Cork Milling Company Railway Act, No. 3 of 1935(Private)	10	**Cork Milling Company Railway Act, 1935, Regulations [Vol. VIII p. 93] S.R.& O. No. 168 of 1937**
Cork Tramways (Employees' Compensation) Act, No. 27 of 1933	3	**Cork Tramways (Employees' Compensation) Act, 1933 (Regulations) Order [Vol. VIII p. 97] S.R.& O. No. 101 of 1933**
Coroners Act, No. 9 of 1962	1(2)	*Coroners Act, 1962 (Commencement) Regulations, S.I. No. 93 of 1962*
	3(1)	*Coroners Act, 1962 (Fees and Expenses) Regulations, S.I. No. 92 of 1962*
		Coroners Act, 1962 (Forms) Regulations, S.I. No. 94 of 1962
		Coroners Act, 1962 (Particulars for Registration of Death) Regulations, S.I. No. 95 of 1962
		Coroners Act, 1962 (Fees and Expenses) Regulations, S.I. No. 145 of 1963
		Coroners Act, 1962 (Fees and Expenses) Regulations, S.I. No. 32 of 1965
		Coroners Act, 1962 (Fees and Expenses) Regulations, S.I. No. 196 of 1970
		Coroners Act, 1962 (Fees and Expenses) Regulations, S.I. No. 256 of 1973
		Coroners Act, 1962 (Fees and Expenses) Regulations, S.I. No. 88 of 1976
		Coroners Act, 1962 (Fees and Expenses) (No.2) Regulations, S.I. No. 199 of 1976
		Coroners Act, 1962 (Fees and Expenses) Regulations, S.I. No. 337 of 1977
		Coroners Act, 1962 (Fees and Expenses) Regulations, S.I. No. 11 of 1979
		Coroners Act, 1962 (Fees and Expenses) (No.2) Regulations, S.I. No. 72 of 1979
		Coroners Act, 1962 (Fees and Expenses) Regulations, S.I. No. 167 of 1980
		Coroners Act, 1962 (Fees and Expenses) (No.2) Regulations, S.I. No. 381 of 1980

Statutory Authority	Section	Statutory Instrument
Coroners Act, No. 9 of 1962 (*Cont.*)		*Coroners Act, 1962 (Fees and Expenses) Regulations, S.I. No. 201 of 1981*
		Coroners Act, 1962 (Fees and Expenses) (No.2) Regulations, S.I. No. 416 of 1981
		Coroners Act, 1962 (Fees and Expenses) Regulations, S.I. No. 196 of 1984
	29	**Coroners Act, 1962 (Fees and Expenses) Regulations, S.I. No. 196 of 1984**
	57	*Coroners Act, 1962 (Fees and Expenses) Regulations, S.I. No. 201 of 1981*
		Coroners Act, 1962 (Fees and Expenses) (No.2) Regulations, S.I. No. 416 of 1981
		Coroners Act, 1962 (Fees and Expenses) Regulations, S.I. No. 196 of 1984
County Borough of Cork (Extension of Boundary) Provisional Order, 1965		*County Borough of Cork (Extension of Boundary) Provisional Order, 1965 (Commencement) Order, S.I. No. 141 of 1965*
County Management Act, No. 12 of 1940	2	*County Management Act, 1940 (Date of Commencement) Order [Vol. XXVIII p. 279] S.R. & O. No. 365 of 1942*
	5(3)	**County Management (Joint Bodies) Order, S.I. No. 214 of 1952**
	8	**County Management (Joint Bodies) Order, S.I. No. 214 of 1952**
		County Management (Joint Bodies) Order, S.I. No. 122 of 1960
		County Management (Joint Bodies) (No.2) Order, S.I. No. 142 of 1960
	16(3)	**County Management (Reserved Functions) Order, S.I. No. 45 of 1948**
		County Management (Reserved Functions) Order, S.I. No. 341 of 1985
	22	**Public Bodies (Temporary Provisions) Order, S.I. No. 232 of 1954**
	23	**Public Bodies (Temporary Provisions) Order, S.I. No. 232 of 1954**
Court Officers Act, No. 27 of 1926	47(1)	*District Court (Areas) Order [Vol. VIII p. 141] S.R.& O. No. 52 of 1926*
	47(2)	*District Court (Areas) Order [Vol. VIII p. 141] S.R.& O. No. 52 of 1926*
	47(3)	*District Court (New Districts) Order [Vol. VIII p. 245] S.R.& O. No. 102 of 1927*
		District Court (New Areas) Order [Vol. VIII p. 295] S.R.& O. No. 103 of 1927

Statutory Authority	Section	Statutory Instrument

Court Officers Act, No. 27 of 1926
(*Cont.*)

District Court (New Areas) Order, 1927 (Variation Order, No.1) [Vol. VIII p. 477] S.R.& O. No. 51 of 1929

District Court (New Areas) Order, 1927 (Variation Order, No.2) [Vol. VIII p. 481] S.R.& O. No. 59 of 1929

District Court (New Areas) Order, 1927 (Variation Order, No.3) [Vol. VIII p. 485] S.R.& O. No. 60 of 1929

District Court (New Areas) Order, 1927 (Variation Order, No.4) [Vol. VIII p. 489] S.R.& O. No. 61 of 1929

District Court (New Areas) Order, 1927 (Variation Order, No.5) [Vol. VIII p. 493] S.R.& O. No. 62 of 1929

District Court (New Areas) Order, 1927 (Variation Order, No.6) [Vol. VIII p. 497] S.R.& O. No. 63 of 1929

District Court (New Areas) Order, 1927 (Variation Order, No.7) [Vol. VIII p. 501] S.R.& O. No. 64 of 1929

District Court (New Areas) Order, 1927 (Variation Order, No.8) [Vol. VIII p. 505] S.R.& O. No. 65 of 1929

District Court (New Areas) Order, 1927 (Variation Order, No.9) [Vol. VIII p. 509] S.R.& O. No. 66 of 1929

District Court (New Areas) Order, 1927 (Variation Order, No.10) [Vol. VIII p. 513] S.R.& O. No. 67 of 1929

District Court (New Areas) Order, 1927 (Variation Order, No.11) [Vol. VIII p. 517] S.R.& O. No. 68 of 1929

District Court (New Areas) Order, 1927 (Variation Order, No.12) [Vol. VIII p. 521] S.R.& O. No. 69 of 1929

District Court (New Areas) Order, 1927 (Variation Order, No.13) [Vol. VIII p. 525] S.R.& O. No. 6 of 1930

District Court (New Areas) Order, 1927 (Variation Order, No.14) [Vol. VIII p. 529] S.R.& O. No. 7 of 1930

District Court (New Areas) Order, 1927 (Variation Order, No.15) [Vol. VIII p. 533] S.R.& O. No. 8 of 1930

District Court (New Areas) Order, 1927 (Variation Order, No.16) [Vol. VIII p. 539] S.R.& O. No. 9 of 1930

District Court (New Areas) Order, 1927 (Variation Order, No.17) [Vol. VIII p. 545] S.R.& O. No. 10 of 1930

District Court (New Areas) Order, 1927 (Variation Order, No.18) [Vol. VIII p. 551] S.R.& O. No. 11 of 1930

Statutory Authority	Section	Statutory Instrument
Court Officers Act, No. 27 of 1926 (*Cont.*)		*District Court (New Areas) Order, 1927 (Variation Order, No.19) [Vol. VIII p. 557] S.R.& O. No. 12 of 1930*
		District Court (New Areas) Order, 1927 (Variation Order, No.20) [Vol. VIII p. 561] S.R.& O. No. 16 of 1930
		District Court (New Areas) Order, 1927 (Variation Order, No.21) [Vol. VIII p. 565] S.R.& O. No. 24 of 1930
		District Court (New Areas) Order, 1927 (Variation Order, No.22) [Vol. VIII p. 569] S.R.& O. No. 39 of 1930
		District Court (New Areas) Order, 1927 (Variation Order, No.23) [Vol. VIII p. 577] S.R.& O. No. 91 of 1930
		District Court (New Areas) Order, 1927 (Variation Order, No.24) [Vol. VIII p. 581] S.R.& O. No. 6 of 1931
		District Court (New Areas) Order, 1927 (Variation Order, No.25) [Vol. VIII p. 585] S.R.& O. No. 7 of 1931
		District Court (New Areas) Order, 1927 (Variation Order, No.26) [Vol. VIII p. 589] S.R.& O. No. 15 of 1931
		District Court (New Areas) Order, 1927 (Variation Order, No.27) [Vol. VIII p. 593] S.R.& O. No. 16 of 1931
		District Court (New Areas) Order, 1927 (Variation Order, No.28) [Vol. VIII p. 599] S.R.& O. No. 17 of 1931
		District Court (New Areas) Order, 1927 (Variation Order, No.29) [Vol. VIII p. 603] S.R.& O. No. 18 of 1931
		District Court (New Areas) Order, 1927 (Variation Order, No.30) [Vol. VIII p. 607] S.R.& O. No. 32 of 1931
		District Court (New Areas) Order, 1927 (Variation Order, No.31) [Vol. VIII p. 613] S.R.& O. No. 64 of 1931
		District Court (New Areas) Order, 1927 (Variation Order, No.32) [Vol. VIII p. 617] S.R.& O. No. 65 of 1931
		District Court (New Areas) Order, 1927 (Variation Order, No.33) [Vol. VIII p. 621] S.R.& O. No. 74 of 1931
		Game Birds Protection (No.1) Order, 1930 (Continuing) Order [Vol. XII p. 689] S.R.& O. No. 99 of 1932
		District Court (New Areas) Order, 1927 (Variation Order, No.35) [Vol. VIII p. 629] S.R.& O. No. 109 of 1932
		District Court (New Areas) Order, 1927 (Variation Order, No.36) [Vol. VIII p. 635] S.R.& O. No. 6 of 1933

Statutory Authority	Section	Statutory Instrument
Court Officers Act, No. 27 of 1926 (*Cont.*)		*District Court (New Areas) Order, 1927 (Variation Order, No.37) [Vol. VIII p. 639] S.R.& O. No. 27 of 1933*
		District Court (New Areas) Order, 1927 (Variation Order, No.38) [Vol. VIII p. 645] S.R.& O. No. 59 of 1933
		District Court (New Areas) Order, 1927 (Variation Order, No.39) [Vol. VIII p. 649] S.R.& O. No. 60 of 1933
		District Court (New Areas) Order, 1927 (Variation Order, No.40) [Vol. VIII p. 653] S.R.& O. No. 78 of 1933
		District Court (New Areas) Order, 1927 (Variation Order, No.41) [Vol. VIII p. 657] S.R.& O. No. 114 of 1933
		District Court (New Areas) Order, 1927 (Variation Order, No.42) [Vol. VIII p. 663] S.R.& O. No. 134 of 1933
		District Court (New Areas) Order, 1927 (Variation Order, No.43) [Vol. VIII p. 667] S.R.& O. No. 165 of 1933
		District Court (New Areas) Order, 1927 (Variation Order, No.44) [Vol. VIII p. 671] S.R.& O. No. 132 of 1934
		District Court (New Areas) Order, 1927 (Variation Order, No.45) [Vol. VIII p. 675] S.R.& O. No. 133 of 1934
		District Court (New Areas) Order, 1927 (Variation Order, No.46) [Vol. VIII p. 679] S.R.& O. No. 152 of 1934
		District Court (New Areas) Order, 1927 (Variation Order, No.47) [Vol. VIII p. 683] S.R.& O. No. 192 of 1934
		District Court (New Areas) Order, 1927 (Variation Order, No.48) [Vol. VIII p. 687] S.R.& O. No. 286 of 1934
		District Court (New Areas) Order, 1927 (Variation Order, No.49) [Vol. VIII p. 691] S.R.& O. No. 638 of 1935
		District Court (New Areas) Order, 1927 (Variation Order, No.50) [Vol. VIII p. 695] S.R.& O. No. 296 of 1936
		District Court (New Areas) Order, 1927 (Variation Order, No.51) [Vol. VIII p. 699] S.R.& O. No. 313 of 1936
		District Court (New Areas) Order, 1927 (Variation Order, No.52) [Vol. VIII p. 703] S.R.& O. No. 67 of 1937
		District Court (New Areas) Order, 1927 (Variation Order, No.53) [Vol. VIII p. 707] S.R.& O. No. 68 of 1937
		District Court (New Areas) Order, 1927 (Variation Order, No.54) [Vol. VIII p. 711] S.R.& O. No. 267 of 1937

Statutory Authority	Section	Statutory Instrument
Court Officers Act, No. 27 of 1926 *(Cont.)*		*District Court (New Areas) Order, 1927 (Variation Order, No.55) [Vol. VIII p. 717] S.R.& O. No. 282 of 1937*
		District Court (New Areas) Order, 1927 (Variation Order, No.56) [Vol. VIII p. 721] S.R.& O. No. 336 of 1937
		District Court (New Areas) Order, 1927 (Variation Order, No.57) [Vol. VIII p. 725] S.R.& O. No. 7 of 1938
		District Court (New Areas) Order, 1927 (Variation Order, No.58) [Vol. VIII p. 729] S.R.& O. No. 8 of 1938
		District Court (New Areas) Order, 1927 (Variation Order, No.59) [Vol. VIII p. 733] S.R.& O. No. 100 of 1938
		District Court (New Areas) Order, 1927 (Variation Order, No.60) [Vol. VIII p. 737] S.R.& O. No. 101 of 1938
		District Court (New Areas) Order, 1927 (Variation Order, No.61) [Vol. VIII p. 741] S.R.& O. No. 174 of 1938
		District Court (New Areas) Order, 1927 (Variation Order, No.62) [Vol. VIII p. 745] S.R.& O. No. 277 of 1938
		District Court (New Areas) Order, 1927 (Variation Order, No.63) [Vol. VIII p. 749] S.R.& O. No. 297 of 1938
		District Court (New Areas) Order, 1927 (Variation Order, No.64) [Vol. VIII p. 753] S.R.& O. No. 299 of 1938
		District Court (New Areas) Order, 1927 (Variation Order, No.65) [Vol. XXVIII p. 291] S.R.& O. No. 55 of 1939
		District Court (New Areas) Order, 1927 (Variation Order, No.66) [Vol. XXVIII p. 295] S.R.& O. No. 131 of 1939
		District Court (New Areas) Order, 1927 (Variation Order, No.67) [Vol. XXVIII p. 299] S.R.& O. No. 203 of 1939
		District Court (New Areas) Order, 1927 (Variation Order, No.68) [Vol. XXVIII p. 303] S.R.& O. No. 331 of 1939
		District Court (New Areas) Order, 1927 (Variation Order, No.69) [Vol. XXVIII p. 307] S.R.& O. No. 198 of 1940
		District Court (New Areas) Order, 1927 (Variation Order, No.70) [Vol. XXVIII p. 311] S.R.& O. No. 366 of 1940
		District Court (New Areas) Order, 1927 (Variation Order, No.71) [Vol. XXVIII p. 315] S.R.& O. No. 299 of 1941
		District Court (New Areas) (Variation No.93) Order [Vol. XXVIII p. 321] S.R.& O. No. 215 of 1943
		District Court (Areas) Order [Vol. XXVIII p. 283] S.R.& O. No. 301 of 1943

Court Officers Act, No. 27 of 1926
(Cont.)

District Court Districts (Donegal and Leitrim) Order [Vol. XXVIII p. 329] S.R.& O. No. 302 of 1943

District Court Districts (Dublin) Order [Vol. XXVIII p. 335] S.R.& O. No. 279 of 1945

District Court (New Areas) Order, 1927 (Variation No.94) Order [Vol. XXXVI p. 799] S.R.& O. No. 40 of 1946

District Court (New Areas) Order, 1927 (Variation No.95) Order [Vol. XXXVI p. 803] S.R.& O. No. 335 of 1946

District Court (New Areas) Order, 1927 (Variation No.97) Order [Vol. XXXVI p. 821] S.R.& O. No. 380 of 1946

District Court (New Areas) Order, 1927 (Variation No.98) Order [Vol. XXXVI p. 827] S.R.& O. No. 384 of 1946

District Court (New Areas) Order, 1927 (Variation No.100) Order [Vol. XXXVI p. 835] S.R.& O. No. 402 of 1946

District Court (New Areas) Order, 1927 (Variation No.101) Order [Vol. XXXVI p. 841] S.R.& O. No. 403 of 1946

District Court (New Areas) Order, 1927 (Variation No.102) Order [Vol. XXXVI p. 849] S.R.& O. No. 63 of 1947

District Court (New Districts) Order, 1927 (Variation, No.2) Order [Vol. XXXVI p. 905] S.R.& O. No. 86 of 1947

District Court (New Areas) Order, 1927 (Variation No.103) Order [Vol. XXXVI p. 855] S.R.& O. No. 87 of 1947

District Court (New Areas) Order, 1927 (Variation No.104) Order [Vol. XXXVI p. 859] S.R.& O. No. 88 of 1947

District Court (New Areas) Order, 1927 (Variation No.105) Order [Vol. XXXVI p. 867] S.R.& O. No. 146 of 1947

District Court (New Areas) Order, 1927 (Variation No.107) Order [Vol. XXXVI p. 873] S.R.& O. No. 263 of 1947

District Court (New Areas) Order, 1927 (Variation No.108) Order [Vol. XXXVI p. 879] S.R.& O. No. 264 of 1947

District Court (New Areas) Order, 1927 (Variation No.96) Order [Vol. XXXVI p. 813] S.R.& O. No. 302 of 1947

District Court (New Areas) Order, 1927 (Variation No.109) Order [Vol. XXXVI p. 889] S.R.& O. No. 371 of 1947

District Court (New Areas) Order, 1927 (Variation No.110) Order [Vol. XXXVI p. 895] S.R.& O. No. 386 of 1947

District Court (New Areas) Order, 1927 (Variation No.111) Order [Vol. XXXVI p. 901] S.R.& O. No. 411 of 1947

Statutory Authority	Section	Statutory Instrument
Court Officers Act, No. 27 of 1926 *(Cont.)*		*District Court (New Areas) Order, 1927 (Variation No.113) Order, S.I. No. 220 of 1948*
		District Court (New Areas) Order, 1927 (Variation No.114) Order, S.I. No. 221 of 1948
		District Court (New Areas) Order, 1927 (Variation No.115) Order, S.I. No. 222 of 1948
		District Court (New Areas) Order, 1927 (Variation No.116) Order, S.I. No. 223 of 1948
		District Court (New Areas) Order, 1927 (Variation No.117) Order, S.I. No. 271 of 1948
		District Court (New Areas) Order, 1927 (Variation No.118) Order, S.I. No. 381 of 1948
		District Court (New Areas) Order, 1927 (Variation No.119) Order, S.I. No. 413 of 1948
		District Court (New Areas) Order, 1927 (Variation No.120) Order, S.I. No. 414 of 1948
		District Court (New Areas) Order, 1927 (Variation No.122) Order, S.I. No. 20 of 1949
		District Court (New Areas) Order, 1927 (Variation No.123) Order, S.I. No. 40 of 1949
		District Court (New Areas) Order, 1927 (Variation No.121) Order, S.I. No. 93 of 1949
		District Court (New Areas) Order, 1927 (Variation No.124) Order, S.I. No. 98 of 1949
		District Court (New Areas) Order, 1927 (Variation No.125) Order, S.I. No. 139 of 1949
		District Court (New Areas) Order, 1927 (Variation No.126) Order, S.I. No. 193 of 1949
		District Court (New Areas) Order, 1927 (Variation No.127) Order, S.I. No. 229 of 1949
		District Court (New Areas) Order, 1927 (Variation No.128) Order, S.I. No. 306 of 1949
		District Court (New Areas) Order, 1927 (Variation No.129) Order, S.I. No. 323 of 1949
		District Court (New Areas) Order, 1927 (Variation No.130) Order, S.I. No. 11 of 1950
		District Court (New Areas) Order, 1927 (Variation No.131) Order, S.I. No. 20 of 1950
		District Court (New Areas) Order, 1927 (Variation No.134) Order, S.I. No. 68 of 1950
		District Court (New Areas) Order, 1927 (Variation No.132) Order, S.I. No. 81 of 1950
		District Court (New Areas) Order, 1927 (Variation No.133) Order, S.I. No. 82 of 1950
		District Court Districts (Limerick) Order, S.I. No. 83 of 1950
		District Court (New Areas) Order, 1927 (Variation No.135) Order, S.I. No. 207 of 1950
		District Court (New Areas) Order, 1927 (Variation No.136) Order, S.I. No. 231 of 1950
		District Court (New Areas) Order, 1927 (Variation No.137) Order, S.I. No. 268 of 1950

Statutory Authority	Section	Statutory Instrument
Court Officers Act, No. 27 of 1926 (*Cont.*)		*District Court (New Areas) Order, 1927 (Variation No.139) Order, S.I. No. 287 of 1950*
		District Court (New Areas) Order, 1927 (Variation No.140) Order, S.I. No. 315 of 1950
		District Court (New Areas) Order, 1927 (Variation No.141) Order, S.I. No. 64 of 1951
		District Court (New Areas) Order, 1927 (Variation No.142) Order, S.I. No. 70 of 1951
		District Court (New Areas) Order, 1927 (Variation No.143) Order, S.I. No. 156 of 1951
		District Court (New Areas) Order, 1927 (Variation No.144) Order, S.I. No. 169 of 1951
		District Court (New Areas) Order, 1927 (Variation No.145) Order, S.I. No. 260 of 1951
		District Court (New Areas) Order, 1927 (Variation No.146) Order, S.I. No. 262 of 1951
		District Court (New Areas) Order, 1927 (Variation No.138) Order, S.I. No. 311 of 1951
		District Court (New Areas) Order, 1927 (Variation No.147) Order, S.I. No. 336 of 1951
		District Court (New Areas) Order, 1927 (Variation No.148) Order, S.I. No. 374 of 1951
		District Court (New Areas) Order, 1927 (Variation No.149) Order, S.I. No. 411 of 1951
		District Court (New Areas) Order, 1927 (Variation No.150) Order, S.I. No. 47 of 1952
		District Court (New Areas) Order, 1927 (Variation No.151) Order, S.I. No. 320 of 1952
		District Court (New Areas) Order, 1927 (Variation No.153) Order, S.I. No. 167 of 1953
		District Court (New Areas) Order, 1927 (Variation No.152) Order, S.I. No. 169 of 1953
		District Court (New Areas) Order, 1927 (Variation No.154) Order, S.I. No. 237 of 1953
		District Court (New Areas) Order, 1927 (Variation No.155) Order, S.I. No. 370 of 1953
		District Court (New Areas) Order, 1927 (Variation No.156) Order, S.I. No. 42 of 1954
		District Court (New Areas) Order, 1927 (Variation No.157) Order, S.I. No. 59 of 1954
		District Court (New Areas) Order, 1927 (Variation No.158) Order, S.I. No. 154 of 1954
		District Court (New Areas) Order, 1927 (Variation No.159) Order, S.I. No. 191 of 1954
		District Court (New Areas) Order, 1927 (Variation No.160) Order, S.I. No. 221 of 1954
		District Court (New Areas) Order, 1927 (Variation No.161) Order, S.I. No. 10 of 1955
		District Court (New Areas) Order, 1927 (Variation No.162) Order, S.I. No. 45 of 1955
		District Court (New Areas) Order, 1927 (Variation No.163) Order, S.I. No. 62 of 1955

Statutory Authority	Section	Statutory Instrument
Court Officers Act, No. 27 of 1926 (*Cont.*)		*District Court (New Areas) Order, 1927 (Variation No.164) Order, S.I. No. 65 of 1955*
		District Court (New Areas) Order, 1927 (Variation No.166) Order, S.I. No. 150 of 1955
		District Court (New Areas) Order, 1927 (Variation No.167) Order, S.I. No. 195 of 1955
		District Court (New Districts) Order, 1927 (Variation No.3) Order, S.I. No. 196 of 1955
		District Court (New Areas) Order, 1927 (Variation No.168) Order, S.I. No. 201 of 1956
		District Court (New Areas) Order, 1927 (Variation No.171) Order, S.I. No. 292 of 1956
		District Court (New Areas) Order, 1927 (Variation No.169) Order, S.I. No. 310 of 1956
		District Court (New Areas) Order, 1927 (Variation No.170) Order, S.I. No. 328 of 1956
		District Court (New Areas) Order, 1927 (Variation No.172) Order, S.I. No. 8 of 1957
		District Court (New Areas) Order, 1927 (Variation No.173) Order, S.I. No. 110 of 1957
		District Court (New Areas) Order, 1927 (Variation No.174) Order, S.I. No. 67 of 1958
		District Court (New Areas) Order, 1927 (Variation No.175) Order, S.I. No. 175 of 1958
		District Court (New Areas) Order, 1927 (Variation No.176) Order, S.I. No. 25 of 1959
		District Court (New Areas) Order, 1927 (Variation No.177) Order, S.I. No. 75 of 1959
		District Court (New Areas) Order, 1927 (Variation No.178) Order, S.I. No. 52 of 1960
		District Court (New Areas) Order, 1927 (Variation No.179) Order, S.I. No. 114 of 1960
		District Court (New Areas) Order, 1927 (Variation No.180) Order, S.I. No. 144 of 1960
	49(2)	*Court Officers Act, 1926 (Appointed Day) Order [Vol. VIII p. 757] S.R.& O. No. 10 of 1928*
	51	**Fines and Penalties (Disposal) Order, S.I. No. 241 of 1954**
		Fines and Penalties (Disposal) Order, S.I. No. 188 of 1961
		Fines and Penalties (Disposal) Order, S.I. No. 6 of 1966
		Fines and Penalties (Disposal) Order, S.I. No. 165 of 1969
	51(4)	**Fines and Penalties (Disposal) Order [Vol. VIII p. 761] S.R.& O. No. 12 of 1928**
		Fines and Penalties (Disposal) Order [Vol. VIII p. 775] S.R.& O. No. 10 of 1937
		Fines and Penalties (Disposal) (No.2) Order [Vol. VIII p. 781] S.R.& O. No. 122 of 1937
		Fines and Penalties (Disposal) Order [Vol. XXVIII p. 347] S.R.& O. No. 267 of 1942

Statutory Authority	Section	Statutory Instrument
Court Officers Act, No. 27 of 1926 (*Cont.*)		**Fines and Penalties (Disposal) Order [Vol. XXVIII p. 353] S.R.& O. No. 115 of 1943**
		Fines and Penalties (Disposal) Order [Vol. XXVIII p. 359] S.R.& O. No. 264 of 1945
		Fines and Penalties (Disposal) Order [Vol. XXXVI p. 911] S.R.& O. No. 141 of 1946
	54	**Sheriffs' Fees Order, S.I. No. 1 of 1958**
	56	*District Probate Registry, Tuam (Closing) Order [Vol. VIII p. 787] S.R.& O. No. 44 of 1930*
		District Probate Registry, Mullingar (Closing) Order, S.I. No. 245 of 1953
	57(1)	*Court Fees (Supreme Court and High Court) Order [Vol. VIII p. 221] S.R.& O. No. 53 of 1926*
		District Court (Fees) Order [Vol. VIII p. 229] S.R.& O. No. 54 of 1926
		District Court (Fees) Order [Vol. VIII p. 237] S.R.& O. No. 76 of 1927
		Circuit Court (Fees) Order [Vol. VIII p. 789] S.R.& O. No. 84 of 1931
Court Officers Act, No. 25 of 1945	11	*District Court (New Areas) Order, 1927 (Variation No.94) Order [Vol. XXXVI p. 799] S.R.& O. No. 40 of 1946*
		District Court (New Areas) Order, 1927 (Variation No.113) Order, S.I. No. 220 of 1948
		District Court (New Areas) Order, 1927 (Variation No.114) Order, S.I. No. 221 of 1948
		District Court (New Areas) Order, 1927 (Variation No.115) Order, S.I. No. 222 of 1948
		District Court (New Areas) Order, 1927 (Variation No.116) Order, S.I. No. 223 of 1948
		District Court (New Areas) Order, 1927 (Variation No.117) Order, S.I. No. 271 of 1948
		District Court (New Areas) Order, 1927 (Variation No.118) Order, S.I. No. 381 of 1948
		District Court (New Areas) Order, 1927 (Variation No.119) Order, S.I. No. 413 of 1948
		District Court (New Areas) Order, 1927 (Variation No.120) Order, S.I. No. 414 of 1948
		District Court (New Areas) Order, 1927 (Variation No.122) Order, S.I. No. 20 of 1949
		District Court (New Areas) Order, 1927 (Variation No.123) Order, S.I. No. 40 of 1949
		District Court (New Areas) Order, 1927 (Variation No.121) Order, S.I. No. 93 of 1949
		District Court (New Areas) Order, 1927 (Variation No.124) Order, S.I. No. 98 of 1949
		District Court (New Areas) Order, 1927 (Variation No.125) Order, S.I. No. 139 of 1949
		District Court (New Areas) Order, 1927 (Variation No.126) Order, S.I. No. 193 of 1949

Statutory Authority	Section	Statutory Instrument
Court Officers Act, No. 25 of 1945 (*Cont.*)		*District Court (New Areas) Order, 1927 (Variation No.127) Order, S.I. No. 229 of 1949*
		District Court (New Areas) Order, 1927 (Variation No.128) Order, S.I. No. 306 of 1949
		District Court (New Areas) Order, 1927 (Variation No.129) Order, S.I. No. 323 of 1949
		District Court (New Areas) Order, 1927 (Variation No.130) Order, S.I. No. 11 of 1950
		District Court (New Areas) Order, 1927 (Variation No.131) Order, S.I. No. 20 of 1950
		District Court (New Areas) Order, 1927 (Variation No.134) Order, S.I. No. 68 of 1950
		District Court (New Areas) Order, 1927 (Variation No.132) Order, S.I. No. 81 of 1950
		District Court (New Areas) Order, 1927 (Variation No.135) Order, S.I. No. 207 of 1950
		District Court (New Areas) Order, 1927 (Variation No.136) Order, S.I. No. 231 of 1950
		District Court (New Areas) Order, 1927 (Variation No.137) Order, S.I. No. 268 of 1950
		District Court (New Areas) Order, 1927 (Variation No.139) Order, S.I. No. 287 of 1950
		District Court (New Areas) Order, 1927 (Variation No.140) Order, S.I. No. 315 of 1950
		District Court (New Areas) Order, 1927 (Variation No.141) Order, S.I. No. 64 of 1951
		District Court (New Areas) Order, 1927 (Variation No.142) Order, S.I. No. 70 of 1951
		District Court (New Areas) Order, 1927 (Variation No.143) Order, S.I. No. 156 of 1951
		District Court (New Areas) Order, 1927 (Variation No.144) Order, S.I. No. 169 of 1951
		District Court (New Areas) Order, 1927 (Variation No.145) Order, S.I. No. 260 of 1951
		District Court (New Areas) Order, 1927 (Variation No.146) Order, S.I. No. 262 of 1951
		District Court (New Areas) Order, 1927 (Variation No.138) Order, S.I. No. 311 of 1951
		District Court (New Areas) Order, 1927 (Variation No.147) Order, S.I. No. 336 of 1951
		District Court (New Areas) Order, 1927 (Variation No.148) Order, S.I. No. 374 of 1951
		District Court (New Areas) Order, 1927 (Variation No.149) Order, S.I. No. 411 of 1951
		District Court (New Areas) Order, 1927 (Variation No.150) Order, S.I. No. 47 of 1952
		District Court (New Areas) Order, 1927 (Variation No.151) Order, S.I. No. 320 of 1952
		District Court (New Areas) Order, 1927 (Variation No.153) Order, S.I. No. 167 of 1953
		District Court (New Areas) Order, 1927 (Variation No.152) Order, S.I. No. 169 of 1953

Statutory Authority	Section	Statutory Instrument
Court Officers Act, No. 25 of 1945 (*Cont.*)		*District Court (New Areas) Order, 1927 (Variation No.154) Order, S.I. No. 237 of 1953*
		District Court (New Areas) Order, 1927 (Variation No.155) Order, S.I. No. 370 of 1953
		District Court (New Areas) Order, 1927 (Variation No.156) Order, S.I. No. 42 of 1954
		District Court (New Areas) Order, 1927 (Variation No.157) Order, S.I. No. 59 of 1954
		District Court (New Areas) Order, 1927 (Variation No.158) Order, S.I. No. 154 of 1954
		District Court (New Areas) Order, 1927 (Variation No.159) Order, S.I. No. 191 of 1954
		District Court (New Areas) Order, 1927 (Variation No.160) Order, S.I. No. 221 of 1954
		District Court (New Areas) Order, 1927 (Variation No.161) Order, S.I. No. 10 of 1955
		District Court (New Areas) Order, 1927 (Variation No.162) Order, S.I. No. 45 of 1955
		District Court (New Areas) Order, 1927 (Variation No.163) Order, S.I. No. 62 of 1955
		District Court (New Areas) Order, 1927 (Variation No.164) Order, S.I. No. 65 of 1955
		District Court (New Areas) Order, 1927 (Variation No.166) Order, S.I. No. 150 of 1955
		District Court (New Areas) Order, 1927 (Variation No.167) Order, S.I. No. 195 of 1955
		District Court (New Areas) Order, 1927 (Variation No.168) Order, S.I. No. 201 of 1956
		District Court (New Areas) Order, 1927 (Variation No.171) Order, S.I. No. 292 of 1956
		District Court (New Areas) Order, 1927 (Variation No.169) Order, S.I. No. 310 of 1956
		District Court (New Areas) Order, 1927 (Variation No.170) Order, S.I. No. 328 of 1956
		District Court (New Areas) Order, 1927 (Variation No.172) Order, S.I. No. 8 of 1957
		District Court (New Areas) Order, 1927 (Variation No.173) Order, S.I. No. 110 of 1957
		District Court (New Areas) Order, 1927 (Variation No.174) Order, S.I. No. 67 of 1958
		District Court (New Areas) Order, 1927 (Variation No.175) Order, S.I. No. 175 of 1958
		District Court (New Areas) Order, 1927 (Variation No.176) Order, S.I. No. 25 of 1959
		District Court (New Areas) Order, 1927 (Variation No.177) Order, S.I. No. 75 of 1959
		District Court (New Areas) Order, 1927 (Variation No.178) Order, S.I. No. 52 of 1960
		District Court (New Areas) Order, 1927 (Variation No.179) Order, S.I. No. 114 of 1960
		District Court (New Areas) Order, 1927 (Variation No.180) Order, S.I. No. 144 of 1960

Statutory Authority	Section	Statutory Instrument
Court Officers Act, No. 25 of 1945 *(Cont.)*	12	**Sheriffs' Fees Order, S.I. No. 1 of 1958**
	12(3)(c)	**Court Officers Act, 1945 (Section 12) (County Borough of Dublin) Order, S.I. No. 303 of 1964**
		Court Officers Act, 1945 (Section 12) (County of Dublin) Order, S.I. No. 304 of 1964
		Court Officers Act, 1945 (Section 12) (County Borough of Cork) Order, S.I. No. 305 of 1964
		Court Officers Act, 1945 (Section 12) (County of Cork) Order, S.I. No. 306 of 1964
Courts Act, No. 11 of 1964	3	**Circuit Court (Alteration of Circuit) Order, S.I. No. 9 of 1986**
	3(1)	**Circuit Court (Alteration of Circuits) Order, S.I. No. 206 of 1964**
		Circuit Court (Alteration of Circuits) Order, S.I. No. 201 of 1969
		Circuit Court (Alteration of Circuits) Order, S.I. No. 327 of 1978
Courts of Justice Act, No. 10 of 1924	36	*Criminal Appeal Rules (1924) July 24*
		Auctioneers and House Agents Act, Rules [Vol. XXXVI p. 1073] S.R.& O. No. 319 of 1947
		High Court Rules, S.I. No. 224 of 1951
		High Court Rules (No.1) Order, S.I. No. 97 of 1952
		High Court Rules (No.2) Order, S.I. No. 98 of 1952
		High Court Rules, S.I. No. 200 of 1953
		High Court Rules (No.2) S.I. No. 254 of 1953
		High Court (Social Welfare Act, 1952) Rules, S.I. No. 25 of 1954
		Central Criminal Court Rules, S.I. No. 129 of 1954
		Rules of the High Court and Supreme Court, 1954 (Additional Rule in Order XVI of 1926 Rules) S.I. No. 131 of 1954
		High Court (Funds in Court) Rules, (1954) S.I. No. 2 of 1955
		High Court (Appeals from Circuit Court) Rules, (1954) S.I. No. 3 of 1955
		Solicitors Act Rules, S.I. No. 81 of 1955
		High Court Rules, S.I. No. 82 of 1956
		Criminal Appeal Rules, S.I. No. 252 of 1956
		High Court Rules (No.2) S.I. No. 282 of 1956
		High Court Rules, S.I. No. 12 of 1957
		High Court Rules, S.I. No. 159 of 1958
		High Court Rules, S.I. No. 139 of 1959
		High Court Rules (No.2) S.I. No. 189 of 1959
		High Court Rules, S.I. No. 92 of 1961
		Rules of the High Court and Supreme Court Mode of Address, S.I. No. 130 of 1961
		Rules of the Superior Courts, S.I. No. 72 of 1962
		Rules of the Superior Courts (No.1) S.I. No. 105 of 1963

Statutory Authority	Section	Statutory Instrument
Court of Justice Act, No. 10 of 1924 (*Cont.*)		*Rules of the Superior Courts (No.2) S.I. No. 224 of 1963*
		Rules of the Superior Courts (No.1) S.I. No. 38 of 1964
		Rules of the Superior Courts (No.2) S.I. No. 96 of 1964
		Rules of the Superior Courts (No.3) S.I. No. 166 of 1964
		Rules of the Superior Courts (No.4) S.I. No. 168 of 1964
		Rules of the Superior Courts (No.5) (1964) S.I. No. 29 of 1965
		Rules of the Superior Courts (No.1) S.I. No. 28 of 1966
		Rules of the Superior Courts (No.2) S.I. No. 169 of 1966
		Rules of the Superior Courts (No.3) S.I. No. 185 of 1966
		Rules of the Superior Courts (No.1) S.I. No. 63 of 1967
		Rules of the Superior Courts (No.2) S.I. No. 219 of 1967
		Rules of the Superior Courts (No.1) S.I. No. 66 of 1968
		Rules of the Superior Courts (No.3) (1970) S.I. No. 27 of 1971
		Rules of the Superior Courts (No.1) (1970) S.I. No. 37 of 1971
		Rules of the Superior Courts (No.2) (1970) S.I. No. 38 of 1971
		Rules of the Superior Courts (No.1) S.I. No. 129 of 1971
		Rules of the Superior Courts (No.2) S.I. No. 226 of 1971
		Rules of the Superior Courts (No.3) S.I. No. 284 of 1971
		Rules of the Superior Courts (No.1) S.I. No. 300 of 1972
		Rules of the Superior Courts (No.1) S.I. No. 220 of 1973
		Rules of the Superior Courts (No.1) S.I. No. 256 of 1974
		Rules of the Superior Courts (No.2) S.I. No. 261 of 1974
		Rules of the Superior Courts (No.1) S.I. No. 15 of 1975
		Rules of the Superior Courts (No.1) S.I. No. 286 of 1976
		Rules of the Superior Courts (No.1) S.I. No. 194 of 1977
		Rules of the Superior Courts (No.1) S.I. No. 295 of 1978

Statutory Authority	Section	Statutory Instrument
Courts of Justice Act, No. 10 of 1924 (*Cont.*)		*Rules of the Superior Courts (No.1) S.I. No. 48 of 1980*
		Rules of the Superior Courts (No.2) S.I. No. 127 of 1980
		Rules of the Superior Courts (No.3) S.I. No. 319 of 1980
		Rules of the Superior Courts (No.4) S.I. No. 384 of 1980
		Rules of the Superior Courts (No.1) S.I. No. 32 of 1981
		Rules of the Superior Courts (No.3) S.I. No. 124 of 1981
		Rules of the Superior Courts (No.2) S.I. No. 130 of 1981
		Rules of the Superior Courts (No.4) S.I. No. 237 of 1981
		Rules of the Superior Courts (No.5) S.I. No. 245 of 1981
		Rules of the Superior Courts (No.1) S.I. No. 125 of 1983
		Rules of the Superior Courts (No.2) S.I. No. 283 of 1983
		Rules of the Superior Courts (No.3) S.I. No. 370 of 1983
		Rules of the Superior Courts, S.I. No. 15 of 1986
	66	*Circuit Court Rules, S.I. No. 261 of 1948*
		Rules of the Circuit Court, S.I. No. 179 of 1950
		Circuit Court Rules, S.I. No. 212 of 1954
		Circuit Court Rules, S.I. No. 1 of 1955
		Circuit Court Rules, S.I. No. 270 of 1956
		Circuit Court Rules, S.I. No. 148 of 1961
		Circuit Court Rules, S.I. No. 84 of 1962
		Circuit Court Rules (No.2) S.I. No. 164 of 1962
		Circuit Court Rules, S.I. No. 3 of 1963
		Circuit Court Rules (No.1) S.I. No. 167 of 1964
		Circuit Court Rules (No.1) S.I. No. 202 of 1965
		Circuit Court Rules, S.I. No. 128 of 1966
		Circuit Court Rules, S.I. No. 37 of 1967
		Circuit Court Rules (No.2) S.I. No. 118 of 1967
		Circuit Court Rules (No.3) S.I. No. 215 of 1967
		Circuit Court Rules (No.1) S.I. No. 149 of 1970
		Circuit Court Rules (No.2) S.I. No. 308 of 1970
		Circuit Court Rules, S.I. No. 41 of 1971
		Circuit Court Rules (No.1) S.I. No. 129 of 1972
		Circuit Court Rules (No.2) S.I. No. 189 of 1972
		Circuit Court Rules (No.3), S.I. No. 322 of 1972
		Circuit Court Rules (No.1) S.I. No. 120 of 1975
		Circuit Court Rules (No.1) S.I. No. 266 of 1976
		Circuit Court Rules (No.1) S.I. No. 130 of 1977

Statutory Authority	Section	Statutory Instrument
Courts of Justice Act, No. 10 of 1924 (*Cont.*)		*Circuit Court Rules (No.2) S.I. No. 186 of 1977*
		Circuit Court Rules (No.1) S.I. No. 77 of 1978
		Circuit Court Rules (No.2) S.I. No. 138 of 1978
		Circuit Court Rules (No.3) S.I. No. 190 of 1978
		Circuit Court Rules (No.4) S.I. No. 205 of 1978
		Circuit Court Rules (No.5) S.I. No. 314 of 1978
		Circuit Court Rules (No.1) S.I. No. 10 of 1979
		Circuit Court Rules (No.2) S.I. No. 66 of 1979
		Circuit Court Rules (No.3) S.I. No. 360 of 1979
		Circuit Court Rules (No.1) S.I. No. 129 of 1980
		Circuit Court Rules (No.1) S.I. No. 20 of 1981
		Circuit Court Rules (No.2) S.I. No. 316 of 1981
		Circuit Court Rules (No.4) S.I. No. 318 of 1981
		Circuit Court Rules (No.3) S.I. No. 329 of 1981
		Circuit Court Rules (No.1) S.I. No. 34 of 1982
		Circuit Court Rules (No.2) S.I. No. 142 of 1982
		Circuit Court Rules (No.3) S.I. No. 152 of 1982
		Circuit Court Rules (No.5) S.I. No. 156 of 1982
		Circuit Court Rules (No.6) S.I. No. 158 of 1982
		Circuit Court Rules (No.4) S.I. No. 190 of 1982
		Circuit Court Rules (No.7) S.I. No. 244 of 1982
		Circuit Court Rules (No.1) S.I. No. 267 of 1983
		Circuit Court Rules (No.1) S.I. No. 118 of 1984
	91	**District Court Rules (No.2) S.I. No. 270 of 1948**
		District Court Rules (No.3) S.I. No. 431 of 1948
		District Court Rules, S.I. No. 83 of 1955
		District Court Rules (No.2) S.I. No. 84 of 1955
		District Court Rules, S.I. No. 277 of 1956
		District Court Rules (No.1) S.I. No. 7 of 1962
		District Court Rules (No.2) S.I. No. 8 of 1962
		District Court (Gaming and Lotteries Act, 1956) Rules, S.I. No. 9 of 1962
		District Court (Amending) Rules, S.I. No. 178 of 1962
		District Court (Costs) Rules, S.I. No. 206 of 1962
		District Court (Summary Judgment) Rules, S.I. No. .213 of 1963
		District Court (Hire-Purchase) Rules, S.I. No. 214 of 1963
		District Court (Costs) Rules, S.I. No. 279 of 1964
		District Court (Summons-Servers Fee) Rules, S.I. No. 211 of 1966
		District Court (Criminal Procedure Act, 1967) Rules, S.I. No. 181 of 1967
		District Court (Extradition Act, 1965) Rules, S.I. No. 279 of 1968

Court of Justice Act, No. 10 of 1924 (*Cont.*)		*District Court (Summons-Servers Fee) Rules, S.I. No. 35 of 1970*
		District Court (Costs) Rules, S.I. No. 315 of 1970
		District Court (Charge Sheet) Rules, S.I. No. 225 of 1971
		District Court (Extradition Act, 1965) Amending Rules, S.I. No. 275 of 1971
		District Court (Costs for Service of Documents) Rules, S.I. No. 351 of 1971
		District Court (Summons-Servers Fee) Rules, S.I. No. 352 of 1971
		District Court (Courts Act, 1971) Rules, S.I. No. 68 of 1972
		District Court (Costs) Rules, S.I. No. 175 of 1972
		District Court (Counsel's Fees) Rules, S.I. No. 39 of 1973
		District Court (Maintenance Orders Act, 1974) Rules, S.I. No. 58 of 1975
		District Court (Summons-Servers Fee) Rules, S.I. No. 99 of 1975
		District Court [Family Law (Maintenance of Spouses and Children) Act, 1976] Rules, S.I. No. 96 of 1976
		District Court (Summons-Servers Fee) Rules, S.I. No. 131 of 1977
		District Court (Costs) Rules, S.I. No. 370 of 1979
		District Court (Summons-Servers Fee) Rules, S.I. No. 128 of 1980
		District Court [Family Law (Maintenance of Spouses and Children) Act, 1976] (Amendment) Rules, S.I. No. 268 of 1980
		District Court [Family Law (Protection of Spouses and Children) Act, 1981] Rules, S.I. No. 246 of 1981
		District Court (Interest on Decrees and Lodgements) Rules, S.I. No. 140 of 1982
		District Court (Guardianship of Infants Act, 1964) Rules, S.I. No. 141 of 1982
		District Court (Malicious Injuries Act, 1981) Rules, S.I. No. 149 of 1982
		District Court [Fisheries (Consolidation) Act, 1959] Rules, S.I. No. 180 of 1982
		District Court (Costs) Rules, S.I. No. 218 of 1982
		District Court [Housing (Private Rented Dwellings) Act, 1982] Rules, S.I. No. 296 of 1982
		District Court (Costs) (Amendment) Rules, S.I. No. 173 of 1983
		District Court (Summons-Servers Fee) Rules, S.I. No. 119 of 1984
		District Court [Criminal Justice (Community Service) Act, 1983] Rules, S.I. No. 327 of 1984
		District Court (Gaming and Lotteries) Rules, (1984) S.I. No. 1 of 1985

Statutory Authority	Section	Statutory Instrument
Court of Justice Act, No. 10 of 1924 (*Cont.*)		**District Court (Air Navigation (Eurocontrol) Acts, 1963 to 1983) Rules, (1984) S.I. No. 2 of 1985**
		District Court (Third Party Procedure) Rules, (1984) S.I. No. 3 of 1985
		District Court (Criminal Procedure Act, 1967) Rules, S.I. No. 23 of 1985
Courts of Justice Act, No. 48 of 1936	4(5)	*Courts of Justice Act, 1936 (Commencement) Order [Vol. VIII p. 1203] S.R.& O. No. 380 of 1936*
	9(5)	*Courts of Justice Act, 1936, (Section 9) (Appointed Day) Order [Vol. VIII p. 1207] S.R.& O. No. 15 of 1937*
	13(1)	*Circuit Court (New Circuits) Order [Vol. VIII p. 1327] S.R.& O. No. 309 of 1937*
	28	*Courts of Justice Act, 1936 (Part IV) (Commencement) Order [Vol. VIII p. 1227] S.R.& O. No. 294 of 1937*
	33	**High Court Circuits (Amendment) Order, S.I. No. 51 of 1986**
	33(1)	**High Court Circuits Order [Vol. VIII p. 1231] S.R.& O. No. 295 of 1937**
	65	*Circuit Court (Fees) Order, S.I. No. 249 of 1956*
		District Court (Fees) Order, S.I. No. 250 of 1956
		Supreme Court and High Court (Fees) Order, S.I. No. 251 of 1956
		Courts (Fees) (Temporary Variation) Order, S.I. No. 258 of 1956
		Supreme Court and High Court (Fees) Order, S.I. No. 35 of 1963
		Circuit Court (Fees) Order, S.I. No. 53 of 1966
		District Court (Fees) Order, S.I. No. 54 of 1966
		Supreme Court and High Court (Fees) Order, S.I. No. 62 of 1966
		Circuit Court (Fees) (No.2) Order, S.I. No. 142 of 1966
		Circuit Court (Fees) (Amendment) Order, S.I. No. 153 of 1967
		Supreme Court and High Court (Fees) Order, S.I. No. 157 of 1968
		District Court (Fees) Order, S.I. No. 236 of 1970
		Circuit Court (Fees) Order, S.I. No. 237 of 1970
		Supreme Court and High Court (Fees) Order, S.I. No. 239 of 1970
		Courts (Guardianship of Infants) Order (Fees) S.I. No. 13 of 1974
		District Court (Fees) Order, S.I. No. 116 of 1976
		Supreme Court and High Court (Fees) Order, S.I. No. 42 of 1978
		Circuit Court (Fees) Order, S.I. No. 43 of 1978
		District Court (Fees) Order, S.I. No. 44 of 1978

Statutory Authority	Section	Statutory Instrument
Court of Justice Act, No. 48 of 1936 (*Cont.*)		*District Court (Fees) (No.2) Order, S.I. No. 56 of 1978*
		District Court (Fees) (No.3) Order, S.I. No. 152 of 1978
		Supreme Court and High Court (Fees) Order, S.I. No. 50 of 1980
		Circuit Court (Fees) Order, S.I. No. 51 of 1980
		District Court (Fees) Order, S.I. No. 52 of 1980
		Supreme Court and High Court (Fees) Order, S.I. No. 89 of 1981
		Circuit Court (Fees) Order, S.I. No. 90 of 1981
		District Court (Fees) Order, S.I. No. 91 of 1981
		Supreme Court and High Court (Fees) Order, S.I. No. 43 of 1982
		Circuit Court (Fees) Order, S.I. No. 44 of 1982
		District Court (Fees) Order, S.I. No. 45 of 1982
		District Court (Fees) (No.2) Order, S.I. No. 150 of 1982
		District Court (Fees) (Private Rented Dwellings) Order, S.I. No. 299 of 1982
		District Court (Fees) Order, S.I. No. 207 of 1983
		Circuit Court (Fees) Order, S.I. No. 208 of 1983
		Supreme Court and High Court (Fees) Order, S.I. No. 209 of 1983
		Supreme Court and High Court (Fees) Order, S.I. No. 19 of 1984
		Circuit Court (Fees) Order, S.I. No. 20 of 1984
		District Court (Fees) Order, S.I. No. 21 of 1984
		Supreme Court and High Court (Fees) Order, S.I. No. 36 of 1985
		Circuit Court (Fees) Order, S.I. No. 37 of 1985
		District Court (Fees) Order, S.I. No. 38 of 1985
		Supreme Court and High Court (Fees) Order, S.I. No. 375 of 1986
		Circuit Court (Fees) Order, S.I. No. 376 of 1986
		District Court (Fees) Order, S.I. No. 377 of 1986
	65(1)	*District Court (Fees) Order [Vol. VIII p. 1211] S.R.& O. No. 177 of 1937*
		District Court (Fees) Order [Vol. XXVIII p. 587] S.R.& O. No. 181 of 1939
		District Court (Fees) Order [Vol. XXVIII p. 581] S.R.& O. No. 343 of 1944
	68	*Auctioneers and House Agents Act, Rules [Vol. XXXVI p. 1073] S.R.& O. No. 319 of 1947*
		High Court Rules, S.I. No. 224 of 1951
		High Court Rules (No.1) Order, S.I. No. 97 of 1952
		High Court Rules (No.2) Order, S.I. No. 98 of 1952
		High Court Rules, S.I. No. 200 of 1953
		High Court Rules (No.2) S.I. No. 254 of 1953

Statutory Authority	Section	Statutory Instrument
Court of Justice Act, No. 48 of 1936 (*Cont.*)		*High Court (Social Welfare Act, 1952) Rules, S.I. No. 25 of 1954*
		Central Criminal Court Rules, S.I. No. 129 of 1954
		Rules of the High Court and Supreme Court, 1954 (Additional Rule in Order XVI of 1926 Rules) S.I. No. 131 of 1954
		High Court (Funds in Court) Rules, (1954) S.I. No. 2 of 1955
		High Court (Appeals from Circuit Court) Rules, (1954) S.I. No. 3 of 1955
		Solicitors Act Rules, S.I. No. 81 of 1955
		High Court Rules, S.I. No. 82 of 1956
		Criminal Appeal Rules, S.I. No. 252 of 1956
		High Court Rules (No.2) S.I. No. 282 of 1956
		High Court Rules, S.I. No. 12 of 1957
		High Court Rules, S.I. No. 159 of 1958
		High Court Rules, S.I. No. 139 of 1959
		High Court Rules (No.2) S.I. No. 189 of 1959
		High Court Rules, S.I. No. 92 of 1961
		Rules of the High Court and Supreme Court Mode of Address, S.I. No. 130 of 1961
		Rules of the Superior Courts, S.I. No. 72 of 1962
		Rules of the Superior Courts (No.1) S.I. No. 105 of 1963
		Rules of the Superior Courts (No.2) S.I. No. 224 of 1963
		Rules of the Superior Courts (No.1) S.I. No. 38 of 1964
		Rules of the Superior Courts (No.2) S.I. No. 96 of 1964
		Rules of the Superior Courts (No.3) S.I. No. 166 of 1964
		Rules of the Superior Courts (No.4) S.I. No. 168 of 1964
		Rules of the Superior Courts (No.5) (1964) S.I. No. 29 of 1965
		Rules of the Superior Courts (No.1) S.I. No. 28 of 1966
		Rules of the Superior Courts (No.2) S.I. No. 169 of 1966
		Rules of the Superior Courts (No.3) S.I. No. 185 of 1966
		Rules of the Superior Courts (No.1) S.I. No. 63 of 1967
		Rules of the Superior Courts (No.2) S.I. No. 219 of 1967
		Rules of the Superior Courts (No.1) S.I. No. 66 of 1968
		Rules of the Superior Courts (No.3) (1970) S.I. No. 27 of 1971
		Rules of the Superior Courts (No.1) (1970) S.I. No. 37 of 1971

Statutory Authority	Section	Statutory Instrument
Court of Justice Act, No. 48 of 1936 (*Cont.*)		*Rules of the Superior Courts (No.2) (1970) S.I. No. 38 of 1971*
		Rules of the Superior Courts (No.1) S.I. No. 129 of 1971
		Rules of the Superior Courts (No.2) S.I. No. 226 of 1971
		Rules of the Superior Courts (No.3) S.I. No. 284 of 1971
		Rules of the Superior Courts (No.1) S.I. No. 300 of 1972
		Rules of the Superior Courts (No.1) S.I. No. 220 of 1973
		Rules of the Superior Courts (No.1) S.I. No. 256 of 1974
		Rules of the Superior Courts (No.2) S.I. No. 261 of 1974
		Rules of the Superior Courts (No.1) S.I. No. 15 of 1975
		Rules of the Superior Courts (No.1) S.I. No. 286 of 1976
		Rules of the Superior Courts (No.1) S.I. No. 194 of 1977
		Rules of the Superior Courts (No.1) S.I. No. 295 of 1978
		Rules of the Superior Courts (No.1) S.I. No. 48 of 1980
		Rules of the Superior Courts (No.2) S.I. No. 127 of 1980
		Rules of the Superior Courts (No.3) S.I. No. 319 of 1980
		Rules of the Superior Courts (No.4) S.I. No. 384 of 1980
		Rules of the Superior Courts (No.1) S.I. No. 32 of 1981
		Rules of the Superior Courts (No.3) S.I. No. 124 of 1981
		Rules of the Superior Courts (No.2) S.I. No. 130 of 1981
		Rules of the Superior Courts (No.4) S.I. No. 237 of 1981
		Rules of the Superior Courts (No.5) S.I. No. 245 of 1981
		Rules of the Superior Courts (No.1) S.I. No. 125 of 1983
		Rules of the Superior Courts (No.2) S.I. No. 283 of 1983
		Rules of the Superior Courts (No.3) S.I. No. 370 of 1983
		Rules of the Superior Courts, S.I. No. 15 of 1986
	70	*Circuit Court Rules, S.I. No. 261 of 1948*
		Rules of the Circuit Court, S.I. No. 179 of 1950
		Circuit Court Rules, S.I. No. 212 of 1954

Statutory Authority	Section	Statutory Instrument
Courts of Justice Act, No. 48 of 1936 (*Cont.*)		**Circuit Court Rules, S.I. No. 1 of 1955**
		Circuit Court Rules, S.I. No. 270 of 1956
		Circuit Court Rules, S.I. No. 148 of 1961
		Circuit Court Rules, S.I. No. 84 of 1962
		Circuit Court Rules (No.2) S.I. No. 164 of 1962
		Circuit Court Rules, S.I. No. 3 of 1963
		Circuit Court Rules (No.1) S.I. No. 167 of 1964
		Circuit Court Rules (No.1) S.I. No. 202 of 1965
		Circuit Court Rules, S.I. No. 128 of 1966
		Circuit Court Rules, S.I. No. 37 of 1967
		Circuit Court Rules (No.2) S.I. No. 118 of 1967
		Circuit Court Rules (No.3) S.I. No. 215 of 1967
		Circuit Court Rules (No.1) S.I. No. 149 of 1970
		Circuit Court Rules (No.2) S.I. No. 308 of 1970
		Circuit Court Rules, S.I. No. 41 of 1971
		Circuit Court Rules (No.1) S.I. No. 129 of 1972
		Circuit Court Rules (No.2) S.I. No. 189 of 1972
		Circuit Court Rules (No.3), S.I. No. 322 of 1972
		Circuit Court Rules (No.1) S.I. No. 120 of 1975
		Circuit Court Rules (No.1) S.I. No. 266 of 1976
		Circuit Court Rules (No.1) S.I. No. 130 of 1977
		Circuit Court Rules (No.2) S.I. No. 186 of 1977
		Circuit Court Rules (No.1) S.I. No. 77 of 1978
		Circuit Court Rules (No.2) S.I. No. 138 of 1978
		Circuit Court Rules (No.3) S.I. No. 190 of 1978
		Circuit Court Rules (No.4) S.I. No. 205 of 1978
		Circuit Court Rules (No.5) S.I. No. 314 of 1978
		Circuit Court Rules (No.1) S.I. No. 10 of 1979
		Circuit Court Rules (No.2) S.I. No. 66 of 1979
		Circuit Court Rules (No.3) S.I. No. 360 of 1979
		Circuit Court Rules (No.1) S.I. No. 129 of 1980
		Circuit Court Rules (No.1) S.I. No. 20 of 1981
		Circuit Court Rules (No.2) S.I. No. 316 of 1981
		Circuit Court Rules (No.4) S.I. No. 318 of 1981
		Circuit Court Rules (No.3) S.I. No. 329 of 1981
		Circuit Court Rules (No.1) S.I. No. 34 of 1982
		Circuit Court Rules (No.2) S.I. No. 142 of 1982
		Circuit Court Rules (No.3) S.I. No. 152 of 1982
		Circuit Court Rules (No.5) S.I. No. 156 of 1982
		Circuit Court Rules (No.6) S.I. No. 158 of 1982
		Circuit Court Rules (No.4) S.I. No. 190 of 1982
		Circuit Court Rules (No.7) S.I. No. 244 of 1982
		Circuit Court Rules (No.1) S.I. No. 267 of 1983
		Circuit Court Rules (No.1) S.I. No. 118 of 1984
	72	**District Court Rules (No.2) S.I. No. 270 of 1948**
		District Court Rules (No.3) S.I. No. 431 of 1948

Statutory Authority	Section	Statutory Instrument
Court of Justice Act, No. 48 of 1936 (*Cont.*)		**District Court Rules, S.I. No. 83 of 1955**
		District Court Rules (No.2) S.I. No. 84 of 1955
		District Court Rules, S.I. No. 277 of 1956
		District Court Rules (No.1) S.I. No. 7 of 1962
		District Court Rules (No.2) S.I. No. 8 of 1962
		District Court (Gaming and Lotteries Act, 1956) Rules, S.I. No. 9 of 1962
		District Court (Amending) Rules, S.I. No. 178 of 1962
		District Court (Costs) Rules, S.I. No. 206 of 1962
		District Court (Summary Judgment) Rules, S.I. No. 213 of 1963
		District Court (Hire-Purchase) Rules, S.I. No. 214 of 1963
		District Court (Costs) Rules, S.I. No. 279 of 1964
		District Court (Summons-Servers Fee) Rules, S.I. No. 211 of 1966
		District Court (Criminal Procedure Act, 1967) Rules, S.I. No. 181 of 1967
		District Court (Extradition Act, 1965) Rules, S.I. No. 279 of 1968
		District Court (Summons-Servers Fee) Rules, S.I. No. 35 of 1970
		District Court (Costs) Rules, S.I. No. 315 of 1970
		District Court (Charge Sheet) Rules, S.I. No. 225 of 1971
		District Court (Extradition Act, 1965) Amending Rules, S.I. No. 275 of 1971
		District Court (Costs for Service of Documents) Rules, S.I. No. 351 of 1971
		District Court (Summons-Servers Fee) Rules, S.I. No. 352 of 1971
		District Court (Courts Act, 1971) Rules, S.I. No. 68 of 1972
		District Court (Costs) Rules, S.I. No. 175 of 1972
		District Court (Counsel's Fees) Rules, S.I. No. 39 of 1973
		District Court (Maintenance Orders Act, 1974) Rules, S.I. No. 58 of 1975
		District Court (Summons-Servers Fee) Rules, S.I. No. 99 of 1975
		District Court [Family Law (Maintenance of Spouses and Children) Act, 1976] Rules, S.I. No. 96 of 1976
		District Court (Summons-Servers Fee) Rules, S.I. No. 131 of 1977
		District Court (Costs) Rules, S.I. No. 370 of 1979
		District Court (Summons-Servers Fee) Rules, S.I. No. 128 of 1980
		District Court [Family Law (Maintenance of Spouses and Children) Act, 1976] (Amendment) Rules, S.I. No. 268 of 1980

Statutory Authority	Section	Statutory Instrument
Court of Justice Act, No. 48 of 1936 (*Cont.*)		**District Court [Family Law (Protection of Spouses and Children) Act, 1981] Rules, S.I. No. 246 of 1981**
		District Court (Interest on Decrees and Lodgements) Rules, S.I. No. 140 of 1982
		District Court (Malicious Injuries Act, 1981) Rules, S.I. No. 149 of 1982
		District Court [Fisheries (Consolidation) Act, 1959] Rules, S.I. No. 180 of 1982
		District Court (Costs) Rules, S.I. No. 218 of 1982
		District Court [Housing (Private Rented Dwellings) Act, 1982] Rules, S.I. No. 296 of 1982
		District Court (Costs) (Amendment) Rules, S.I. No. 173 of 1983
		District Court (Summons-Servers Fee) Rules, S.I. No. 119 of 1984
		District Court [Criminal Justice (Community Service) Act, 1983] Rules, S.I. No. 327 of 1984
		District Court (Gaming and Lotteries) Rules, (1984) S.I. No. 1 of 1985
		District Court (Air Navigation (Eurocontrol) Acts, 1963 to 1983) Rules, (1984) S.I. No. 2 of 1985
		District Court (Criminal Procedure Act, 1967) Rules, S.I. No. 23 of 1985
	74	*Land Registration (Solicitors' Costs) Rules, S.I. No. 180 of 1954*
		Land Registration Rules, S.I. No. 271 of 1956
		Land Registration Rules, S.I. No. 96 of 1959
		Land Registration (Solicitors' Costs) Rules, S.I. No. 148 of 1962
Courts of Justice Act, No. 32 of 1953	16	**Circuit Court (New Circuits) Order, S.I. No. 70 of 1960**
	21	**District Court (Areas) Order, S.I. No. 5 of 1961**
	22	**District Court (Districts) Order, S.I. No. 6 of 1961**
	26	**District Court Districts (Amendment) Order, S.I. No. 160 of 1970**
		District Court Areas (Amendment) Order, S.I. No. 161 of 1970
		District Court Districts (Dublin) (Amendment) Order, S.I. No. 300 of 1970
		District Court Areas (Amendment) (No.2) Order, S.I. No. 301 of 1970
		District Court Districts and Areas (Amendment) Order, S.I. No. 334 of 1973
		District Court Areas (Amendment) Order, S.I. No. 217 of 1977
		District Court Districts (Dublin) (Amendment) Order, S.I. No. 88 of 1982
		District Court Areas (Amendment) Order, S.I. No. 89 of 1982

Court of Justice Act, No. 32 of
1953 (*Cont.*)

**District Court Districts (Amendment) Order, S.I.
No. 90 of 1982**

**District Court Areas and Districts (Amendment)
Order, S.I. No. 233 of 1983**

**District Court Areas (Variation of Days and Hours)
Order, S.I. No. 234 of 1983**

**District Court Areas and Districts (Amendment)
Order, S.I. No. 53 of 1984**

**District Court Areas (Variation of Days) Order, S.I.
No. 54 of 1984**

**District Court Areas (Variation of Hours) Order,
S.I. No. 180 of 1984**

**District Court Areas (Variation of Days and Hours)
(No.3) Order, S.I. No. 216 of 1984**

**District Court Areas (Variation of Days, Hours,
Areas and Districts) Order, S.I. No. 232 of 1984**

**District Court (Variation of Days, Hours, Areas and
Districts) (Amendment) Order, S.I. No. 247 of
1984**

**District Court Areas (Variation of Hours) Order,
S.I. No. 42 of 1985**

**District Court Areas (Variation of Days and Hours)
Order, S.I. No. 43 of 1985**

**District Court Areas (Alteration of Place) Order,
S.I. No. 293 of 1986**

26(1)
**District Court Districts and Areas (Amendment) and
Variation of Days Order, S.I. No. 199 of 1978**

**District Court Areas (Variation of Place) Order, S.I.
No. 289 of 1978**

**District Court Areas (Variation of Days and Hours)
(No.5) Order, S.I. No. 303 of 1978**

**District Court Districts and Areas (Amendment)
Order, S.I. No. 311 of 1978**

**District Court Areas (Variation of Days and Hours)
Order, S.I. No. 13 of 1979**

**District Court Districts and Areas (Amendment)
Order, S.I. No. 20 of 1979**

**District Court Areas (Variation of Days and Hours)
(No.2) Order, S.I. No. 133 of 1979**

**District Court Areas (Variation of Days and Hours)
(No.4) Order, S.I. No. 184 of 1979**

**District Court Areas (Variation of Days and Hours)
(No.5) Order, S.I. No. 249 of 1979**

**District Court Areas and Districts (Variation of
Days, Hours and Districts) Order, S.I. No. 364 of
1979**

**District Court Districts and Areas (Amendment)
Order, S.I. No. 17 of 1980**

**District Court Areas (Variation of Hours) Order,
S.I. No. 18 of 1980**

**District Court Areas (Variation of Hours) (No.2)
Order, S.I. No. 149 of 1980**

District Court Areas (Variation of Days and Hours) (No.4) Order, S.I. No. 289 of 1982

District Court Areas (Variation of Days and Hours) (No.4) Order, S.I. No. 303 of 1984

District Court Areas (Variation of Days and Hours) (No.2) Order, S.I. No. 222 of 1985

District Court Districts and Areas (Amendment) and Variation of Days and Hours Order, S.I. No. 353 of 1985

District Court Areas (Amendment) and Variation of Days Order, S.I. No. 442 of 1985

District Court Areas (Amendment) (Variation of Days and Hours) Order, S.I. No. 294 of 1986

District Court Districts and Areas (Amendment) and Variation of Hours Order, S.I. No. 318 of 1986

26(1)(a) District Court Districts and Areas (Amendment) Order, S.I. No. 252 of 1965

District Court Districts and Areas (Amendment) Order, S.I. No. 13 of 1967

26(1)(c) District Court Districts and Areas (Amendment) Order, S.I. No. 252 of 1965

District Court Areas (Amendment) Order, S.I. No. 212 of 1966

District Court Districts and Areas (Amendment) Order, S.I. No. 13 of 1967

26(1)(d) District Court Districts and Areas (Amendment) Order, S.I. No. 252 of 1965

26(1)(f) District Court Areas (Alteration of Place) Order, S.I. No. 114 of 1962

District Court Areas (Variation of Days and Hours) Order, S.I. No. 165 of 1962

District Court Areas (Variation of Days) Order, S.I. No. 166 of 1962

District Court Areas (Variation of Days) Order, S.I. No. 3 of 1964

District Court Areas (Variation of Days) (No.2) Order, S.I. No. 175 of 1964

District Court Areas (Variation of Days) (No.3) Order, S.I..No. 237 of 1964

District Court Areas (Variation of Days) Order, S.I. No. 85 of 1965

District Court Areas (Variation of Hours) Order, S.I. No. 103 of 1965

District Court Areas (Amendment) Order, S.I. No. 106 of 1965

District Court Areas (Alteration of Place) Order, S.I. No. 134 of 1965

District Court Districts and Areas (Amendment) Order, S.I. No. 252 of 1965

District Court Areas (Variation of Hours) Order, S.I. No. 213 of 1966

Court of Justice Act, No. 32 of
1953 (*Cont.*)

District Court Areas (Variation of Hours) (No.2) Order, S.I. No. 254 of 1966

District Court Districts and Areas (Amendment) Order, S.I. No. 13 of 1967

District Court Areas (Variation of Hours) Order, S.I. No. 173 of 1967

District Court Areas (Amendment) (No.2) Order, S.I. No. 174 of 1967

District Court Areas (Variation of Days) Order, S.I. No. 226 of 1967

District Court Areas (Variation of Days and Hours) Order, S.I. No. 50 of 1968

District Court Areas (Variation of Days) Order, S.I. No. 74 of 1968

District Court Areas (Variation of Days and Hours) (No.2) Order, S.I. No. 204 of 1968

District Court Areas (Variation of Days and Hours) Order, S.I. No. 19 of 1969

District Court Areas (Variation of Days and Hours) (No.2) Order, S.I. No. 31 of 1969

District Court Areas (Variation of Days) Order, S.I. No. 145 of 1969

District Court Areas (Variation of Days and Hours) (No.2) Order, S.I. No. 117 of 1970

District Court Areas (Variation of Hours) Order, S.I. No. 124 of 1970

District Court Areas (Variation of Days and Hours) Order, S.I. No. 115 of 1971

District Court Areas (Variation of Days and Hours) (No.5) Order, S.I. No. 184 of 1971

District Court Areas (Variation of Hours) Order, S.I. No. 185 of 1971

District Court Areas (Variation of Hours) Order, S.I. No. 11 of 1972

District Court Areas (Variation of Days and Hours) (No.3) Order, S.I. No. 236 of 1972

District Court Areas (Variation of Place) Order, S.I. No. 17 of 1973

District Court Areas (Variation of Days) Order, S.I. No. 44 of 1973

District Court Areas (Variation of Hours) Order, S.I. No. 45 of 1973

District Court Areas (Variation of Hours) (No.2) Order, S.I. No. 46 of 1973

District Court Areas (Variation of Days and Hours) (No.3) Order, S.I. No. 260 of 1973

District Court Areas (Variation of Days and Hours) (No.4) Order, S.I. No. 288 of 1973

District Court Areas (Variation of Days and Hours) (No.5) Order, S.I. No. 308 of 1973

District Court Areas (Variation of Days and Hours) (No.8) Order, S.I. No. 344 of 1974

Statutory Authority	Section	Statutory Instrument
Courts of Justice Act, No. 48 of 1936 (*Cont.*)		**District Court Areas (Variation of Hours) (No.1) Order, S.I. No. 173 of 1975**
		District Court Areas (Variation of Days and Hours) (No.4) Order, S.I. No. 191 of 1975
		District Court Areas (Variation of Days and Hours) (No.2) Order, S.I. No. 114 of 1976
		District Court Areas (Variation of Days and Hours) (No.3) Order, S.I. No. 117 of 1976
		District Court Areas (Variation of Hours) (No.1) Order, S.I. No. 174 of 1976
		District Court Areas (Variation of Hours) (No.2) Order, S.I. No. 175 of 1976
		District Court Areas (Variation of Days and Hours) (No.5) Order, S.I. No. 217 of 1976
		District Court Areas (Variation of Days) Order, S.I. No. 75 of 1977
		District Court Areas (Variation of Days and Hours) (No.4) Order, S.I. No. 375 of 1977
		District Court Areas (Variation of Days and Hours) (No.3) Order, S.I. No. 269 of 1978
		District Court Areas (Variation of Days and Hours) (No.4) Order, S.I. No. 277 of 1978
Courts of Justice Acts, 1924 to 1936,		*District Court Rules (No.1) [Vol. XXVIII p. 533] S.R.& O. No. 296 of 1941*
		District Court Rules (No.2) [Vol. XXVIII p. 537] S.R.& O. No. 337 of 1941
		District Court Rules (No.2) [Vol. XXVIII p. 555] S.R.& O. No. 144 of 1942
		District Court Rules [Vol. XXVIII p. 503] S.R.& O. No. 299 of 1942
		District Court Rules (Amending Rule) [Vol. XXVIII p. 531] S.R.& O. No. 39 of 1943
		District Court Rules (No.1) [Vol. XXVIII p. 571] S.R.& O. No. 150 of 1945
Courts of Justice Acts, 1924 to 1946,		**District Court Rules (1948) [Vol. XXXVI p. 917] S.R.& O. No. 431 of 1947**
Courts of Justice and Court Officers (Superannuation) Act, No. 16 of 1961	6	**Courts of Justice and Court Officers (Adoption of Provisions and Allocation of Pensions) Regulations, S.I. No. 216 of 1961**
	7	**Courts of Justice and Court Officers (Adoption of Provisions and Allocation of Pensions) Regulations, S.I. No. 216 of 1961**
	7(2)(d)	*Courts of Justice and Court Officers (Superannuation) Act, 1961 (Section 7) (Appointed Day) Order, S.I. No. 173 of 1962*
Courts (Supplemental Provisions) Act, No. 39 of 1961	8(2)	*Courts (Establishment and Constitution) Act, 1961 (Commencement) Order, S.I. No. 217 of 1961*
	14	*Rules of the Superior Courts, S.I. No. 72 of 1962*
		Rules of the Superior Courts (No.2) S.I. No. 224 of 1963

Statutory Authority	Section	Statutory Instrument
Courts (Supplemental Provisions) Act, No. 39 of 1961 (*Cont.*)		*Rules of the Superior Courts (No.1) S.I. No. 38 of 1964*
		Rules of the Superior Courts (No.2) S.I. No. 96 of 1964
		Rules of the Superior Courts (No.3) S.I. No. 166 of 1964
		Rules of the Superior Courts (No.4) S.I. No. 168 of 1964
		Rules of the Superior Courts (No.5) (1964) S.I. No. 29 of 1965
		Rules of the Superior Courts (No.1) S.I. No. 28 of 1966
		Rules of the Superior Courts (No.2) S.I. No. 169 of 1966
		Rules of the Superior Courts (No.3) S.I. No. 185 of 1966
		Rules of the Superior Courts (No.1) S.I. No. 63 of 1967
		Rules of the Superior Courts (No.2) S.I. No. 219 of 1967
		Rules of the Superior Courts (No.1) S.I. No. 66 of 1968
		Rules of the Superior Courts (No.3) (1970) S.I. No. 27 of 1971
		Rules of the Superior Courts (No.1) (1970) S.I. No. 37 of 1971
		Rules of the Superior Courts (No.2) (1970) S.I. No. 38 of 1971
		Rules of the Superior Courts (No.1) S.I. No. 129 of 1971
		Rules of the Superior Courts (No.2) S.I. No. 226 of 1971
		Rules of the Superior Courts (No.3) S.I. No. 284 of 1971
		Rules of the Superior Courts (No.1) S.I. No. 300 of 1972
		Rules of the Superior Courts (No.1) S.I. No. 220 of 1973
		Rules of the Superior Courts (No.1) S.I. No. 256 of 1974
		Rules of the Superior Courts (No.2) S.I. No. 261 of 1974
		Rules of the Superior Courts (No.1) S.I. No. 15 of 1975
		Rules of the Superior Courts (No.1) S.I. No. 286 of 1976
		Rules of the Superior Courts (No.1) S.I. No. 194 of 1977
		Rules of the Superior Courts (No.1) S.I. No. 295 of 1978
		Rules of the Superior Courts (No.1) S.I. No. 48 of 1980

Courts (Supplemental Provisions)
Act, No. 39 of 1961 (*Cont.*)

Rules of the Superior Courts (No.2) S.I. No. 127 of 1980

Rules of the Superior Courts (No.3) S.I. No. 319 of 1980

Rules of the Superior Courts (No.4) S.I. No. 384 of 1980

Rules of the Superior Courts (No.1) S.I. No. 32 of 1981

Rules of the Superior Courts (No.3) S.I. No. 124 of 1981

Rules of the Superior Courts (No.2) S.I. No. 130 of 1981

Rules of the Superior Courts (No.4) S.I. No. 237 of 1981

Rules of the Superior Courts (No.5) S.I. No. 245 of 1981

Rules of the Superior Courts (No.1) S.I. No. 125 of 1983

Rules of the Superior Courts (No.2) S.I. No. 283 of 1983

Rules of the Superior Courts (No.3) S.I. No. 370 of 1983

Rules of the Superior Courts, S.I. No. 15 of 1986

27   **Circuit Court Rules, S.I. No. 84 of 1962**

Circuit Court Rules (No.2) S.I. No. 164 of 1962

Circuit Court Rules (No.1) S.I. No. 167 of 1964

Circuit Court Rules (No.1) S.I. No. 202 of 1965

Circuit Court Rules, S.I. No. 128 of 1966

Circuit Court Rules, S.I. No. 37 of 1967

Circuit Court Rules (No.2) S.I. No. 118 of 1967

Circuit Court Rules (No.3) S.I. No. 215 of 1967

Circuit Court Rules (No.1) S.I. No. 149 of 1970

Circuit Court Rules (No.2) S.I. No. 308 of 1970

Circuit Court Rules, S.I. No. 41 of 1971

Circuit Court Rules (No.1) S.I. No. 129 of 1972

Circuit Court Rules (No.2) S.I. No. 189 of 1972

Circuit Court Rules (No.3), S.I. No. 322 of 1972

Circuit Court Rules (No.1) S.I. No. 120 of 1975

Circuit Court Rules (No.1) S.I. No. 266 of 1976

Circuit Court Rules (No.2) S.I. No. 186 of 1977

Circuit Court Rules (No.1) S.I. No. 77 of 1978

Circuit Court Rules (No.2) S.I. No. 138 of 1978

Circuit Court Rules (No.3) S.I. No. 190 of 1978

Circuit Court Rules (No.4) S.I. No. 205 of 1978

Circuit Court Rules (No.5) S.I. No. 314 of 1978

Circuit Court Rules (No.1) S.I. No. 10 of 1979

Circuit Court Rules (No.2) S.I. No. 66 of 1979

Circuit Court Rules (No.3) S.I. No. 360 of 1979

Circuit Court Rules (No.1) S.I. No. 129 of 1980

Courts (Supplemental Provisions)
Act, No. 39 of 1961 (*Cont.*)

Circuit Court Rules (No.1) S.I. No. 20 of 1981

Circuit Court Rules (No.2) S.I. No. 316 of 1981

Circuit Court Rules (No.4) S.I. No. 318 of 1981

Circuit Court Rules (No.3) S.I. No. 329 of 1981

Circuit Court Rules (No.1) S.I. No. 34 of 1982

Circuit Court Rules (No.2) S.I. No. 142 of 1982

Circuit Court Rules (No.3) S.I. No. 152 of 1982

Circuit Court Rules (No.5) S.I. No. 156 of 1982

Circuit Court Rules (No.6) S.I. No. 158 of 1982

Circuit Court Rules (No.4) S.I. No. 190 of 1982

Circuit Court Rules (No.7) S.I. No. 244 of 1982

Circuit Court Rules (No.1) S.I. No. 267 of 1983

Circuit Court Rules (No.1) S.I. No. 118 of 1984

34   **District Court (Charge Sheet) Rules, S.I. No. 225 of 1971**

District Court (Extradition Act, 1965) Amending Rules, S.I. No. 275 of 1971

District Court (Costs for Service of Documents) Rules, S.I. No. 351 of 1971

District Court (Summons-Servers Fee) Rules, S.I. No. 352 of 1971

District Court (Courts Act, 1971) Rules, S.I. No. 68 of 1972

District Court (Costs) Rules, S.I. No. 175 of 1972

District Court (Counsel's Fees) Rules, S.I. No. 39 of 1973

District Court (Maintenance Orders Act, 1974) Rules, S.I. No. 58 of 1975

District Court (Summons-Servers Fee) Rules, S.I. No. 99 of 1975

District Court [Family Law (Maintenance of Spouses and Children) Act, 1976] Rules, S.I. No. 96 of 1976

District Court (Summons-Servers Fee) Rules, S.I. No. 131 of 1977

District Court (Costs) Rules, S.I. No. 370 of 1979

District Court (Summons-Servers Fee) Rules, S.I. No. 128 of 1980

District Court [Family Law (Maintenance of Spouses and Children) Act, 1976] (Amendment) Rules, S.I. No. 268 of 1980

District Court [Family Law (Protection of Spouses and Children) Act, 1981] Rules, S.I. No. 246 of 1981

District Court (Interest on Decrees and Lodgements) Rules, S.I. No. 140 of 1982

District Court (Malicious Injuries Act, 1981) Rules, S.I. No. 149 of 1982

District Court [Fisheries (Consolidation) Act, 1959] Rules, S.I. No. 180 of 1982

Courts (Supplemental Provisions)
Act, No. 39 of 1961 (*Cont.*)

District Court (Costs) Rules, S.I. No. 218 of 1982

District Court [Housing (Private Rented Dwellings) Act, 1982] Rules, S.I. No. 296 of 1982

District Court (Costs) (Amendment) Rules, S.I. No. 173 of 1983

District Court (Summons-Servers Fee) Rules, S.I. No. 119 of 1984

District Court [Criminal Justice (Community Service) Act, 1983] Rules, S.I. No. 327 of 1984

District Court (Gaming and Lotteries) Rules, (1984) S.I. No. 1 of 1985

District Court (Air Navigation (Eurocontrol) Acts, 1963 to 1983) Rules, (1984) S.I. No. 2 of 1985

District Court (Criminal Procedure Act, 1967) Rules, S.I. No. 23 of 1985

46

Courts (Supplemental Provisions) Act, 1961 (Section 46) Order, S.I. No. 186 of 1971

Courts (Supplemental Provisions) Act, 1961 (Section 46) Order, S.I. No. 226 of 1973

Courts (Supplemental Provisions) Act, 1961 (Section 46) Order, S.I. No. 193 of 1974

Courts (Supplemental Provisions) Act, 1961 (Section 46) Order, S.I. No. 106 of 1975

Courts (Supplemental Provisions) Act, 1961 (Section 46) Order, S.I. No. 62 of 1976

Courts (Supplemental Provisions) Act, 1961 (Section 46) Order, S.I. No. 141 of 1977

46(9)

Courts (Supplemental Provisions) Act, 1961 (Section 46) Order, S.I. No. 130 of 1978

Courts (Supplemental Provisions) Act, 1961 (Section 46) Order, S.I. No. 282 of 1979

Courts (Supplemental Provisions) Act, 1961 (Section 46) Order, S.I. No. 42 of 1980

Courts (Supplemental Provisions) Act, 1961 (Section 46) (No.2) Regulations, S.I. No. 363 of 1980

Courts (Supplemental Provisions) Act, 1961 (Section 46) Order, S.I. No. 383 of 1981

48

District Court Rules (No.1) S.I. No. 7 of 1962

District Court Rules (No.2) S.I. No. 8 of 1962

District Court (Gaming and Lotteries Act, 1956) Rules, S.I. No. 9 of 1962

District Court (Amending) Rules, S.I. No. 178 of 1962

District Court (Costs) Rules, S.I. No. 206 of 1962

District Court (Summary Judgment) Rules, S.I. No. 213 of 1963

District Court (Hire-Purchase) Rules, S.I. No. 214 of 1963

District Court (Costs) Rules, S.I. No. 279 of 1964

Circuit Court Rules (No.1) S.I. No. 202 of 1965

Statutory Authority	Section	Statutory Instrument
Courts (Supplemental Provisions) Act, No. 39 of 1961 (*Cont.*)		*District Court (Summons-Servers Fee) Rules, S.I. No. 211 of 1966*
		District Court (Criminal Procedure Act, 1967) Rules, S.I. No. 181 of 1967
		District Court (Extradition Act, 1965) Rules, S.I. No. 279 of 1968
		District Court (Summons-Servers Fee) Rules, S.I. No. 35 of 1970
		District Court (Costs) Rules, S.I. No. 315 of 1970
Courts-Martial Appeals Act, No. 19 of 1983	2	*Courts-Martial Appeals Act, 1983 (Commencement of Part III) Order, S.I. No. 426 of 1986*
	23	**Courts-Martial Appeal Court Rules, S.I. No. 206 of 1983**
	24	*Courts-Martial Appeals Act, 1983 (Application of Part II) Order, S.I. No. 201 of 1983*
	33	**Courts-Martial (Legal Aid) Regulations, S.I. No. 425 of 1986**
Creamery (Amendment) Act, No. 33 of 1934	5(1)	**Whey (Concentration or Condensation) Order [Vol. VIII p. 1245] S.R.& O. No. 644 of 1935**
		Processed Cheese Order [Vol. VIII p. 1249] S.R.& O. No. 382 of 1936
		Infant and Invalid Foods Order [Vol. VIII p. 1253] S.R.& O. No. 198 of 1937
		Artificial Horn Order [Vol. XXVIII p. 593] S.R.& O. No. 46 of 1939
		Creamery Butter (Packaging) Order, S.I. No. 40 of 1971
Credit Union Act, No. 19 of 1966	35	**Credit Union Regulations, S.I. No. 201 of 1973**
	35(1)(i)	*Industrial and Provident Societies (Financial Limits) Regulations, S.I. No. 124 of 1978*
		Industrial and Provident Societies (Financial Limit) Regulations, S.I. No. 254 of 1979
		Industrial and Provident Societies (Financial Limits) Regulations, S.I. No. 327 of 1979
		Industrial and Provident Societies (Financial Limits) Regulations, S.I. No. 392 of 1985
	39(2)	*Credit Union Act, 1966 (Commencement) Order, S.I. No. 29 of 1967*
Criminal Appeal Rules (1924) July 24		*Criminal Appeal (Fees and Expenses of Legal Aid) Regulations, S.I. No. 305 of 1950*
Criminal Justice Act, No. 27 of 1960	2	**Prisoners (Temporary Release) Rules, S.I. No. 167 of 1960**
		Temporary Release of Offenders (Shanganagh Castle) Rules, S.I. No. 312 of 1970
		Temporary Release of Offenders (Loughan House) Rules, S.I. No. 59 of 1973
		Temporary Release of Offenders (Training Unit) Rules, S.I. No. 250 of 1975

Statutory Authority	Section	Statutory Instrument
Criminal Justice Act, No. 27 of 1960 (*Cont.*)		**Temporary Release of Offenders (Shelton Abbey) Regulations, S.I. No. 294 of 1976**
		Temporary Release of Offenders (Fort Mitchel) Rules, S.I. No. 103 of 1985
	13	**Saint Patrick's Institution Regulations, S.I. No. 224 of 1960**
Criminal Justice Act, No. 22 of 1984	1(1)	*Criminal Justice Act, 1984 (Commencement) Order, S.I. No. 17 of 1985*
Criminal Justice Administration Act, No. 58 of 1914		**Rules for the Government of Prisons [Vol. XXXVI p. 1087] S.R.& O. No. 320 of 1947**
		Rules for the Government of Prisons, S.I. No. 127 of 1955
		Rules for the Government of Prisons, S.I. No. 135 of 1983
Criminal Justice (Community Service) Act, No. 23 of 1983	14	**Criminal Justice (Community Service) Regulations, S.I. No. 325 of 1984**
	16	*Criminal Justice (Community Service) Act, 1983 (Commencement) Order, S.I. No. 309 of 1984*
Criminal Justice (Legal Aid) Act, No. 12 of 1962	10	**Criminal Justice (Legal Aid) Regulations, S.I. No. 12 of 1965**
		Criminal Justice (Legal Aid) (Amendment) Regulations, S.I. No. 240 of 1970
		Criminal Justice (Legal Aid) (Amendment) Regulations, S.I. No. 100 of 1975
		Criminal Justice (Legal Aid) (Amendment) Regulations, S.I. No. 234 of 1976
		Criminal Justice (Legal Aid) (Amendment) Regulations, S.I. No. 202 of 1977
		Criminal Justice (Legal Aid) (Amendment) Regulations, S.I. No. 33 of 1978
		Criminal Justice (Legal Aid) (Amendment) (No.2) Regulations, S.I. No. 304 of 1978
		Criminal Justice (Legal Aid) (Amendment) Regulations, S.I. No. 357 of 1979
		Criminal Justice (Legal Aid) (Amendment) Regulations, S.I. No. 368 of 1981
		Criminal Justice (Legal Aid) (Amendment) Regulations, S.I. No. 305 of 1982
		Criminal Justice (Legal Aid) (Amendment) Regulations, S.I. No. 79 of 1983
		Criminal Justice (Legal Aid) (Amendment) (No.2) Regulations, S.I. No. 411 of 1983
		Criminal Justice (Legal Aid) (Amendment) Regulations, S.I. No. 297 of 1984
		Criminal Justice (Legal Aid) (Amendment) Regulations, S.I. No. 225 of 1985
		Criminal Justice (Legal Aid) (Amendment) Regulations, S.I. No. 36 of 1986
		Criminal Justice (Legal Aid) (Amendment) (No.2) Regulations, S.I. No. 248 of 1986

Statutory Authority	Section	Statutory Instrument
Criminal Justice (Legal Aid) Act, No. 12 of 1962 (*Cont.*)	12	*Criminal Justice (Legal Aid) Act, 1962 (Commencement) Order, S.I. No. 13 of 1965*
Criminal Law (Jurisdiction) Act, No. 14 of 1976	22(2)	*Criminal Law (Jurisdiction) Act, 1976 (Commencement) Order, S.I. No. 112 of 1976*
Criminal Procedure Act, No. 12 of 1967	2	*Criminal Procedure Act, 1967 (Commencement of Section 3 and Parts II and III) Order, S.I. No. 182 of 1967*
Curragh of Kildare Act, No. 35 of 1961	16	**Curragh Bye-Laws, S.I. No. 7 of 1964**
Currency Act, No. 32 of 1927	31(4)	**Currency Commission Pension Funds – Determination as a Public Fund [Vol. VIII p. 1265] S.R.& O. No. 13 of 1928**
	35	*Currency Commission (Form of Statement of Accounts) Regulations [Vol. VIII p. 1269] S.R.& O. No. 50 of 1928*
		Currency Commission (Form of Statement of Accounts) Regulations [Vol. VIII p. 1281] S.R.& O. No. 19 of 1931
		Central Bank of Ireland (Form of Statement of Accounts) Regulations [Vol. XXVIII p. 89] S.R.& O. No. 94 of 1943
		Central Bank of Ireland (Form of Statement of Accounts) (Amendment) Regulations, S.I. No. 86 of 1957
		Central Bank of Ireland (Form of Statement of Accounts) (Amendment) Regulations, S.I. No. 99 of 1959
		Central Bank of Ireland (Form of Statement of Accounts) (Amendment) Regulations, S.I. No. 103 of 1960
		Central Bank of Ireland (Form of Statement of Accounts) Regulations, S.I. No. 187 of 1961
		Central Bank of Ireland (Form of Statement of Accounts) (Amendment) Regulations, S.I. No. 120 of 1969
		Central Bank of Ireland (Form of Statement of Accounts) (Amendment) Regulations, S.I. No. 148 of 1970
		Central Bank of Ireland (Form of Statement of Accounts) (Amendment) Regulations, S.I. No. 121 of 1973
		Central Bank of Ireland (Form of Statement of Accounts) (Amendment) Regulations, S.I. No. 71 of 1975
		Central Bank of Ireland (Form of Statement of Accounts) (Amendment) Regulations, S.I. No. 97 of 1978
		Central Bank of Ireland (Form of Statement of Accounts) (Amendment) Regulations, S.I. No. 72 of 1980
		Central Bank of Ireland (Form of Statement of Accounts) (Amendment) Regulations, S.I. No. 95 of 1981

Statutory Authority	Section	Statutory Instrument
Currency Act, No. 32 of 1927 (*Cont.*)		**Central Bank of Ireland (Form of Statement of Accounts) (Amendment) Regulations, S.I. No. 83 of 1984**
	63(5)	*Currency Commission (Surplus Income) Regulations [Vol. VIII p. 1275] S.R.& O. No. 10 of 1929*
		Central Bank of Ireland (Surplus Income) Regulations [Vol. XXVIII p. 95] S.R.& O. No. 93 of 1943
Currency (Amendment) Act, No. 30 of 1930	3	**Currency (Amendment) Act, 1930 (Section 3) Order, S.I. No. 230 of 1956**
		Legal Tender Note Fund (Additional Form of Asset) Order, S.I. No. 92 of 1959
		Legal Tender Note Fund (Additional Form of Asset) Order, S.I. No. 186 of 1961
		Legal Tender Note Fund (Additional Form of Asset) Order, S.I. No. 119 of 1969
		Legal Tender Note Fund (Additional Form of Asset) Order, S.I. No. 204 of 1979
Customs Consolidation Act, No. 36 of 1876	139	*Exportation of Certain Articles (Prohibited to be exported to Italian Territory) (Entry) Order, (1935) [Vol. VIII p. 1347] S.R.& O. No. 304 of 1936*
		Exportation of Certain Articles (Prohibited to be exported to Italian Territory) (Entry) Order, 1935 (Revocation) Order [Vol. VIII p. 1355] S.R.& O. No. 305 of 1936
Customs Duties (Preferential Rates) Act, No. 19 of 1934	3	**Customs Duties (Preferential Rates) (Canned Fruit) Order [Vol. VIII p. 1405] S.R.& O. No. 513 of 1935**
		Customs Duties (Preferential Rates) (Fruit in Water) Order [Vol. VIII p. 1417] S.R.& O. No. 570 of 1935
		Customs Duties (Preferential Rates) (Canned Fruit) Order [Vol. VIII p. 1411] S.R.& O. No. 166 of 1938
		Customs Duties (Preferential Rates) (Fruit in Water) Order [Vol. VIII p. 1421] S.R.& O. No. 167 of 1938
Customs Duties (Provisional Imposition) Act, No. 38 of 1931	1	*Customs Duties (Bacon) (Provisional Imposition) Order [Vol. VIII p. 1427] S.R.& O. No. 88 of 1931*
		Customs Duties (Flowers) (Provisional Imposition) Order [Vol. VIII p. 1435] S.R.& O. No. 12 of 1932
		Customs Duties (Agricultural Machinery) (Provisional Imposition) Order [Vol. VIII p. 1441] S.R.& O. No. 21 of 1932
		Customs Duties (Potatoes) (Provisional Imposition) Order [Vol. VIII p. 1449] S.R.& O. No. 24 of 1932

Statutory Authority	Section	Statutory Instrument
Customs Duties (Provisional Imposition) Act, No. 38 of 1931 (*Cont.*)		*Customs Duties (Milk and Cream) (Provisional Imposition) Order [Vol. VIII p. 1455] S.R.& O. No. 28 of 1932*
		Customs Duties (Sweetened Condensed Milk) (Provisional Variation) Order [Vol. VIII p. 1503] S.R.& O. No. 29 of 1932
		Customs Duties (Boots and Shoes) (Provisional Variation) Order [Vol. VIII p. 1509] S.R.& O. No. 30 of 1932
		Customs Duties (Spades and Shovels) (Provisional Imposition) Order [Vol. VIII p. 1463] S.R.& O. No. 31 of 1932
		Customs Duties (Wool and Worsted) (Provisional Imposition) Order [Vol. VIII p. 1469] S.R.& O. No. 33 of 1932
		Customs Duties (Wool and Worsted) (Provisional Variation) Order [Vol. VIII p. 1517] S.R.& O. No. 34 of 1932
		Customs Duties (Clothing and Wearing Apparel) (Provisional Variation) Order [Vol. VIII p. 1523] S.R.& O. No. 35 of 1932
		Customs Duties (Brushes and Brooms) (Provisional Imposition) Order [Vol. VIII p. 1475] S.R.& O. No. 36 of 1932
		Customs Duties (Brushes and Brooms) (Provisional Variation) Order [Vol. VIII p. 1531] S.R.& O. No. 37 of 1932
		Customs Duties (Maize Meal) (Provisional Imposition) Order [Vol. VIII p. 1483] S.R.& O. No. 38 of 1932
		Customs Duties (Sugar Confectionery) (Provisional Variation) Order [Vol. VIII p. 1537] S.R.& O. No. 39 of 1932
		Customs Duties (Cocoa Preparations) (Provisional Variation) Order [Vol. VIII p. 1543] S.R.& O. No. 40 of 1932
		Customs Duties (Bedsteads and Furniture) (Provisional Variation) Order [Vol. VIII p. 1549] S.R.& O. No. 41 of 1932
		Customs Duties (Motor Car Bodies) (Provisional Variation) Order [Vol. VIII p. 1555] S.R.& O. No. 42 of 1932
		Customs Duties (Horse-drawn Vehicles) (Provisional Imposition) Order [Vol. VIII p. 1489] S.R.& O. No. 43 of 1932
		Customs Duties (Meat and Poultry) (Provisional Imposition) Order [Vol. VIII p. 1497] S.R.& O. No. 51 of 1932
Customs (Temporary Provisions) Act, No. 14 of 1945	11	*Textile Goods (Ascertainment of Weight) Regulations [Vol. XXVIII p. 597] S.R.& O. No. 200 of 1945*

Statutory Authority	Section	Statutory Instrument
Customs-free Airport Act, No. 5 of 1947	2	**Customs-free Airport Order [Vol. XXXVI p. 1141] S.R.& O. No. 114 of 1947**
		Customs-free Airport (Variation of Limits) Order, S.I. No. 258 of 1958
		Customs-free Airport (Variation of Limits) Order, S.I. No. 39 of 1967
		Customs-free Airport (Variation of Limits) Order, S.I. No. 181 of 1979
	12	**Customs-free Airport (Customs and Excise) Regulations [Vol. XXXVI p. 1149] S.R.& O. No. 137 of 1947**
		Customs-free Airport (Customs and Excise) (Amendment) Regulations, S.I. No. 364 of 1981
	13	**Customs-free Airport (Extension of Laws) Regulations [Vol. XXXVI p. 1159] S.R.& O. No. 115 of 1947**
		Customs-free Airport (Air Navigation) Regulations [Vol. XXXVI p. 1145] S.R.& O. No. 116 of 1947
		Customs-free Airport (Road Traffic) Regulations [Vol. XXXVI p. 1165] S.R.& O. No. 117 of 1947
		Customs-free Airport (Extension of Laws) Regulations, S.I. No. 4 of 1948
		Customs-free Airport (Extension of Laws) (No.2) Regulations, S.I. No. 339 of 1948
		Customs-free Airport (Extension of Laws) Regulations, S.I. No. 60 of 1951
		Customs-free Airport (Extension of Laws) (No.2) Regulations, S.I. No. 240 of 1951
		Customs-free Airport (Extension of Laws) Regulations, S.I. No. 226 of 1952
		Customs-free Airport (Extension of Laws) Regulations, S.I. No. 144 of 1953
		Customs-free Airport (Road Traffic) (Amendment) Regulations, S.I. No. 189 of 1953
		Customs-free Airport (Extension of Laws) Regulations, S.I. No. 17 of 1954
		Customs-free Airport (Extension of Laws) Regulations, S.I. No. 181 of 1955
		Customs-free Airport (Extension of Laws) (No.2) Regulations, S.I. No. 223 of 1955
		Customs-free Airport (Extension of Laws) Regulations, S.I. No. 76 of 1958
		Customs-free Airport (Extension of Laws) Regulations, S.I. No. 79 of 1959
		Customs-free Airport (Extension of Laws) (No.2) Regulations, S.I. No. 161 of 1959
		Customs-free Airport (Extension of Laws) Regulations, S.I. No. 109 of 1960
		Customs-free Airport (Road Traffic) Regulations, S.I. No. 120 of 1960
		Customs-free Airport (Extension of Laws) Regulations, S.I. No. 42 of 1961

Customs-free Airport Act, No. 5 of 1947 (*Cont.*)

Customs-free Airport (Extension of Laws) Regulations, S.I. No. 186 of 1962

Customs-free Airport (Extension of Laws) Regulations, S.I. No. 112 of 1964

Customs-free Airport (Extension of Laws) (No.2) Regulations, S.I. No. 245 of 1964

Customs-free Airport (Extension of Laws) Regulations, S.I. No. 36 of 1965

Customs-free Airport (Extension of Laws) (No.2) Regulations, S.I. No. 122 of 1965

Customs-free Airport (Extension of Laws) (No.3) Regulations, S.I. No. 196 of 1965

Customs-free Airport (Extension of Laws) (No.4) Regulations, S.I. No. 271 of 1965

Customs-free Airport (Extension of Laws) Regulations, S.I. No. 50 of 1966

Customs-free Airport (Extension of Laws) (No.2) Regulations, S.I. No. 279 of 1966

Customs-free Airport (Extension of Laws) Regulations, S.I. No. 25 of 1967

Customs-free Airport (Extension of Laws) (No.2) Regulations, S.I. No. 51 of 1967

Customs-free Airport (Extension of Laws) (No.3) Regulations, S.I. No. 167 of 1967

Customs-free Airport (Extension of Laws) Regulations, S.I. No. 71 of 1968

Customs-free Airport (Extension of Laws) Regulations, S.I. No. 9 of 1969

Customs-free Airport (Extension of Laws) (No.2) Regulations, S.I. No. 68 of 1969

Customs-free Airport (Extension of Laws) (No.3) Regulations, S.I. No. 127 of 1969

Customs-free Airport (Extension of Laws) Regulations, S.I. No. 56 of 1970

Customs-free Airport (Extension of Laws) Regulations, S.I. No. 294 of 1971

Customs-free Airport (Extension of Laws) Regulations, S.I. No. 186 of 1972

Customs-free Airport (Extension of Laws) Regulations, S.I. No. 192 of 1973

Customs-free Airport (Extension of Laws) Regulations, S.I. No. 245 of 1974

Customs-free Airport (Extension of Laws) Regulations, S.I. No. 169 of 1975

Customs-free Airport (Extension of Laws) Regulations, S.I. No. 238 of 1976

Customs-free Airport (Extension of Laws) Regulations, S.I. No. 304 of 1976

Customs-free Airport (Extension of Laws) Regulations, S.I. No. 203 of 1977

Customs-free Airport (Extension of Laws) (No.2) Regulations, S.I. No. 228 of 1977

Statutory Authority	Section	Statutory Instrument
Customs-free Airport Act, No. 5 of 1947 (*Cont.*)		**Customs-free Airport (Extension of Laws) (No.3) Regulations, S.I. No. 278 of 1977**
		Customs-free Airport (Extension of Laws) Regulations, S.I. No. 83 of 1978
		Customs-free Airport (Extension of Laws) (No.2) Regulations, S.I. No. 194 of 1978
		Customs-free Airport (Extension of Laws) (No.3) Regulations, S.I. No. 381 of 1978
		Customs-free Airport (Extension of Laws) Regulations, S.I. No. 174 of 1979
		Customs-free Airport (Extension of Laws) (No.2) Regulations, S.I. No. 281 of 1979
		Customs-free Airport (Extension of Laws) Regulations, S.I. No. 22 of 1980
		Customs-free Airport (Extension of Laws) (No.2) Regulations, S.I. No. 410 of 1980
		Customs-free Airport (Extension of Laws) Regulations, S.I. No. 436 of 1981
		Customs-free Airport (Extension of Laws) Regulations, S.I. No. 11 of 1983
		Customs-free Airport (Extension of Laws) (No.2) Regulations, S.I. No. 48 of 1983
		Customs-free Airport (Extension of Laws) (No.3) Regulations, S.I. No. 416 of 1983
		Customs-free Airport (Extension of Laws) Regulations, S.I. No. 360 of 1984
Customs-free Airport (Amendment) Act, No. 29 of 1958	7	*Customs-free Airport (Amendment) Act, 1958 (Commencement of Section 7) Order, S.I. No. 137 of 1963*
Dail Eireann Loans and Funds (Amendment) Act, No. 19 of 1933	4	**Dail Eireann External Loans (Form and Manner of Application) (No.2) Regulations [Vol. IX p. 17] S.R.& O. No. 190 of 1933**
Dail Finance Committee Resolution (1934) December 12		*Hydrocarbon Oil Regulations [Vol. XIX p. 539] S.R.& O. No. 28 of 1935*
Dail Finance Committee Resolution (1935) May 15		*Hydrocarbon Oil Regulations [Vol. XII p. 369] S.R.& O. No. 608 of 1935*
Dairy Produce Act, No. 58 of 1924		**Dairy Produce Act, 1924 (Regulations under Part III) (Amendment) Order [Vol. XXVIII p. 599] S.R.& O. No. 129 of 1939**
		Dairy Produce Act, 1924 (Regulations under Part III) (Amendment) Order, S.I. No. 129 of 1950
		Dairy Produce Act, 1924 (Regulations under Part III) (Amendment) (No.2) Order, S.I. No. 223 of 1950

Statutory Authority	Section	Statutory Instrument
Dairy Produce Act, No. 58 of 1924 *(Cont.)*	1(2)	*Dairy Produce Act, 1924 (Commencement) Order [Vol. IX p. 57] S.R.& O. No. 48 of 1925*
		Dairy Produce Act, 1924 (Commencement) Order No.2 [Vol. IX p. 61] S.R.& O. No. 49 of 1925
		Dairy Produce Act, 1924 (Commencement) Order No.3 [Vol. IX p. 65] S.R.& O. No. 16 of 1927
	11(1)	*Butter Exporting (Examination) Order [Vol. IX p. 131] S.R.& O. No. 25 of 1928*
		Butter Exporting (Examination) Order [Vol. IX p. 135] S.R.& O. No. 44 of 1931
		Butter Exporting (Examination) Order, 1931 (Amendment) Order [Vol. IX p. 145] S.R.& O. No. 83 of 1935
	27	**Dairy Produce Act, 1924 (Regulations under Part III) (Amendment) Order, S.I. No. 165 of 1955**
	27(1)	**Dairy Produce Act, 1924 (Regulations under Part III) (Amendment) Order [Vol. IX p. 103] S.R.& O. No. 22 of 1928**
		Churn Marks Order [Vol. IX p. 149] S.R.& O. No. 24 of 1928
		Dairy Produce Act, 1924 (Regulations under Part III) (Amendment) Order [Vol. IX p. 113] S.R.& O. No. 169 of 1936
		Dairy Produce Act, 1924 (Regulations under Part III) (Amendment) (No.2) Order [Vol. IX p. 117] S.R.& O. No. 394 of 1936
		Dairy Produce Act, 1924 (Regulations under Part III) (Amendment) (No.2) Order [Vol. XXVIII p. 611] S.R.& O. No. 400 of 1939
		Dairy Produce Act, 1924 (Regulations under Part III) (Amendment) Order [Vol. XXVIII p. 617] S.R.& O. No. 241 of 1940
	29	**Dairy Produce Act, 1924 (Regulations under Part III) (Amendment) Order, S.I. No. 165 of 1955**
	29(1)	**Churn Marks Order [Vol. IX p. 149] S.R.& O. No. 24 of 1928**
	30	**Pasteurising (Separated Milk) Regulations, S.I. No. 196 of 1957**
		Pasteurising (Separate Milk) (Temporary Amendment) Regulations, S.I. No. 112 of 1959
		Pasteurising (Separated Milk) (Temporary Amendment) Regulations, S.I. No. 92 of 1960
	32(1)	**Milk and Cream (Calculation of Price) Order [Vol. IX p. 157] S.R.& O. No. 23 of 1928**
	46	**Dairy Produce Act, 1924 (Regulations under Part I) Order [Vol. IX p. 69] S.R.& O. No. 28 of 1925**
		Dairy Produce Act, 1924 (Regulations under Part V) Order No.1 [Vol. IX p. 123] S.R.& O. No. 29 of 1925
		Dairy Produce Act, 1924 (Regulations under Part III) No.1 Order [Vol. IX p. 81] S.R.& O. No. 51 of 1925

Statutory Authority	Section	Statutory Instrument
Dairy Produce Act, No. 58 of 1924 (*Cont.*)		*Dairy Produce Act, 1924 (Regulations under Part V) Order No.2 [Vol. IX p. 127] S.R.& O. No. 15 of 1927*
		Dairy Produce Act, 1924 (Regulations under Part I) (Amendment) Order [Vol. IX p. 75] S.R.& O. No. 72 of 1933
		Dairy Produce Act, 1924 (Regulations under Part III) (Amendment) Order [Vol. IX p. 107] S.R.& O. No. 73 of 1933
	46(1)	**Licence to Export Butter (Form and Fees) Order [Vol. IX p. 153] S.R.& O. No. 26 of 1928**
Dairy Produce Act, No. 29 of 1931	8(1)	**Dairy Produce (Butter Returns) Regulations [Vol. IX p. 163] S.R.& O. No. 56 of 1931**
Dairy Produce (Amendment) Act, No. 10 of 1941	8	**Dairy Produce (Particulars of Appointments of Managers of Cream-Separating Stations) Regulations [Vol. XXVIII p. 623] S.R.& O. No. 376 of 1941**
Dairy Produce Marketing Act, No. 1 of 1961	1	*Dairy Produce Marketing Act, 1961 (Commencement) Order, S.I. No. 46 of 1961*
		Dairy Produce Marketing Act, 1961 (Commencement) (No.2) Order, S.I. No. 145 of 1961
	2(2)	**Milk Products Regulations, S.I. No. 24 of 1964**
	3	*Dairy Produce Marketing Act, 1961 (Establishment Day) Order, S.I. No. 48 of 1961*
	7	*Dairy Produce Marketing Act, 1961 (Nomination Day) Regulations, S.I. No. 47 of 1961*
		Dairy Produce Marketing Act, 1961 (Nomination Day) Regulations, S.I. No. 129 of 1965
		Dairy Produce Marketing Act, 1961 (Nomination Day) Regulations, S.I. No. 154 of 1969
	12	*Dairy Produce Marketing Act, 1961 (Nominations and Ballots) Regulations, S.I. No. 49 of 1961*
		Dairy Produce Marketing Act, 1961 (Nominations and Ballots) (Amendment) Regulations, S.I. No. 73 of 1961
		Dairy Produce Marketing Act, 1961 (Nomination and Ballots) (Amendment) Regulations, S.I. No. 155 of 1969
	36	*Dairy Produce Marketing Act, 1961 (Milk Levy) Order, S.I. No. 73 of 1962*
		Dairy Produce Marketing Act, 1961 (Milk Levy) Order, S.I. No. 72 of 1963
		Dairy Produce Marketing Act, 1961 (Milk Levy) Order, S.I. No. 124 of 1968
		Dairy Produce Marketing Act, 1961 (Milk Levy) Order, S.I. No. 23 of 1969
		Dairy Produce Marketing Act, 1961 (Milk Levy) Order, S.I. No. 299 of 1970

Statutory Authority	Section	Statutory Instrument
Dairy Produce Marketing Act, No. 1 of 1961 (*Cont.*)		*Dairy Produce Marketing Act, 1961 (Milk Levy) Order, S.I. No. 177 of 1971*
		Dairy Produce Marketing Act, 1961 (Milk Levy) (No.2.) Order, S.I. No. 327 of 1971
	37	*Dairy Produce Marketing Act, 1961 (Butter Levy) Order, S.I. No. 63 of 1964*
		Dairy Produce Marketing Act, 1961 (Butter Levy) Order, S.I. No. 124 of 1966
		Dairy Produce Marketing Act, 1961 (Butter Levy) Order, S.I. No. 319 of 1971
	38(3)(c)	*Dairy Produce Marketing Act, 1961 (Butter Stocks Levy) Order, S.I. No. 320 of 1971*
	40	*Dairy Produce Marketing Act, 1961 (Forms) Regulations, S.I. No. 97 of 1964*
		Dairy Produce Marketing Act, 1961 (Butter Levy Form) Regulations, S.I. No. 137 of 1966
		Dairy Produce Marketing Act, 1961 (Butter Levy Form) Regulations, S.I. No. 328 of 1971
	50	*Dairy Produce Marketing Act, 1961 (Transfer Day) Order, S.I. No. 146 of 1961*
	57	**Milk and Milk Products (Restriction of Exports) (Amendment) Order, S.I. No. 304 of 1971**
		Milk and Milk Products (Restriction of Exports) (Amendment) Order, S.I. No. 191 of 1982
	57(1)	**Milk and Milk Products (Restriction of Export) Order, S.I. No. 25 of 1964**
	57(2)	**Milk Products (Regulation of Import) Order, S.I. No. 149 of 1966**
	58(3)	**Dairy Produce (Price Stabilisation) Act, 1935 (Section 17 (1) (a) , (b) and (c)) (Suspending) Order, S.I. No. 66 of 1964**
		Dairy Produce (Price Stabilisation) Act, 1935 (Section 41) (Suspending) Order, S.I. No. 47 of 1965
		Dairy Produce (Price Stabilisation) Act, 1935 (Sections 24 and 29) (Suspending) Order, S.I. No. 150 of 1966
Dairy Produce (Miscellaneous Provisions) Act, No. 21 of 1973	2	*Dairy Produce (Miscellaneous Provisions) Act, 1973 (Transfer Day) Order, S.I. No. 21 of 1975*
	5	**An Bord Bainne (Dissolution) Order, S.I. No. 63 of 1975**
	7	**Dairy Produce (Miscellaneous Provisions) Act, 1973 (Section 7) (Transfer of Property) Order, S.I. No. 20 of 1975**
Dairy Produce (Price Stabilisation) Act, No. 10 of 1932	3	*Dairy Produce (Butter Traders' Records and Returns) Regulations [Vol. IX p. 277] S.R.& O. No. 210 of 1934*
		Dairy Produce (Form of Levy Undertaking) Regulations [Vol. IX p. 285] S.R.& O. No. 212 of 1934

Statutory Authority	Section	Statutory Instrument
Dairy Produce (Price Stabilisation) Act, No. 10 of 1932 (*Cont.*)	6	*Dairy Produce (Butter Levy and Bounty Rates) Regulations [Vol. IX p. 191] S.R.& O. No. 67 of 1932*
		Dairy Produce (Butter Levy and Bounty Rates) No.2 Regulations [Vol. IX p. 205] S.R.& O. No. 40 of 1933
		Dairy Produce (Butter Levy and Bounty Rates) No.3 Regulations [Vol. IX p. 213] S.R.& O. No. 90 of 1933
		Dairy Produce (Butter Levy and Bounty Rates) No.4 Regulations [Vol. IX p. 221] S.R.& O. No. 112 of 1933
		Dairy Produce (Butter Levy and Bounty Rates) No.5 Regulations [Vol. IX p. 229] S.R.& O. No. 138 of 1933
		Dairy Produce (Butter Levy and Bounty Rates) Regulations [Vol. IX p. 237] S.R.& O. No. 105 of 1934
		Dairy Produce (Butter Levy and Bounty Rates) No.2 Regulations [Vol. IX p. 245] S.R.& O. No. 137 of 1934
		Dairy Produce (Butter Levy and Bounty Rates) No.3 Regulations [Vol. IX p. 253] S.R.& O. No. 211 of 1934
		Dairy Produce (Butter Levy and Bounty Rates) No.4 Regulations [Vol. IX p. 261] S.R.& O. No. 246 of 1934
		Dairy Produce (Butter Levy and Bounty Rates) No.5 Regulations [Vol. IX p. 269] S.R.& O. No. 248 of 1934
	6(1)	*Dairy Produce (Butter Levy and Bounty Rates) Regulations [Vol. IX p. 197] S.R.& O. No. 35 of 1933*
	7	*Dairy Produce (Butter Levy and Bounty Rates) Regulations [Vol. IX p. 191] S.R.& O. No. 67 of 1932*
	7(1)	*Dairy Produce (Butter Levy and Bounty Rates) Regulations [Vol. IX p. 197] S.R.& O. No. 35 of 1933*
		Dairy Produce (Butter Levy and Bounty Rates) No.2 Regulations [Vol. IX p. 205] S.R.& O. No. 40 of 1933
		Dairy Produce (Butter Levy and Bounty Rates) No.3 Regulations [Vol. IX p. 213] S.R.& O. No. 90 of 1933
		Dairy Produce (Butter Levy and Bounty Rates) No.4 Regulations [Vol. IX p. 221] S.R.& O. No. 112 of 1933
		Dairy Produce (Butter Levy and Bounty Rates) No.5 Regulations [Vol. IX p. 229] S.R.& O. No. 138 of 1933
		Dairy Produce (Butter Levy and Bounty Rates) Regulations [Vol. IX p. 237] S.R.& O. No. 105 of 1934

Statutory Authority	Section	Statutory Instrument
Dairy Produce (Price Stabilisation) Act, No. 10 of 1932 (*Cont.*)		*Dairy Produce (Butter Levy and Bounty Rates) No.2 Regulations [Vol. IX p. 245] S.R.& O. No. 137 of 1934*
		Dairy Produce (Butter Levy and Bounty Rates) No.3 Regulations [Vol. IX p. 253] S.R.& O. No. 211 of 1934
		Dairy Produce (Butter Levy and Bounty Rates) No.4 Regulations [Vol. IX p. 261] S.R.& O. No. 246 of 1934
		Dairy Produce (Butter Levy and Bounty Rates) No.5 Regulations [Vol. IX p. 269] S.R.& O. No. 248 of 1934
	23	*Prohibition of Import (Cheese) Order [Vol. IX p. 303] S.R.& O. No. 65 of 1932*
	23(1)	*Prohibition of Import (Dried Milk and Powdered Milk) Order [Vol. IX p. 307] S.R.& O. No. 104 of 1932*
	27(1)	*Creamery Butter (Prohibition of Export) Order [Vol. IX p. 295] S.R.& O. No. 111 of 1933*
	27(2)	*Creamery Butter (Prohibition of Export) Order, 1933 (Revocation) Order [Vol. IX p. 299] S.R.& O. No. 57 of 1934*
	30	*Dairy Produce (Butter Levy and Bounty Rates) Regulations [Vol. IX p. 191] S.R.& O. No. 67 of 1932*
	30(1)	*Dairy Produce (Butter Levy and Bounty Rates) Regulations [Vol. IX p. 197] S.R.& O. No. 35 of 1933*
		Dairy Produce (Butter Levy and Bounty Rates) No.2 Regulations [Vol. IX p. 205] S.R.& O. No. 40 of 1933
		Dairy Produce (Butter Levy and Bounty Rates) No.3 Regulations [Vol. IX p. 213] S.R.& O. No. 90 of 1933
		Dairy Produce (Butter Levy and Bounty Rates) No.4 Regulations [Vol. IX p. 221] S.R.& O. No. 112 of 1933
		Dairy Produce (Butter Levy and Bounty Rates) No.5 Regulations [Vol. IX p. 229] S.R.& O. No. 138 of 1933
		Dairy Produce (Bounty Rates) Regulations [Vol. IX p. 175] S.R.& O. No. 10 of 1934
		Dairy Produce (Butter Levy and Bounty Rates) Regulations [Vol. IX p. 237] S.R.& O. No. 105 of 1934
		Dairy Produce (Butter Levy and Bounty Rates) No.2 Regulations [Vol. IX p. 245] S.R.& O. No. 137 of 1934
		Dairy Produce (Butter Levy and Bounty Rates) No.3 Regulations [Vol. IX p. 253] S.R.& O. No. 211 of 1934
		Dairy Produce (Butter Levy and Bounty Rates) No.4 Regulations [Vol. IX p. 261] S.R.& O. No. 246 of 1934

Statutory Authority	Section	Statutory Instrument
Dairy Produce (Price Stabilisation) Act, No. 10 of 1932 (*Cont.*)		*Dairy Produce (Butter Levy and Bounty Rates) No.5 Regulations [Vol. IX p. 269] S.R.& O. No. 248 of 1934*
		Dairy Produce (Bounty Rates) (Amendment) Regulations [Vol. IX p. 183] S.R.& O. No. 372 of 1934
	35(1)	*Milk Products (Cheese) Order [Vol. IX p. 291] S.R.& O. No. 137 of 1933*
	36	*Dairy Produce (Butter Levy and Bounty Rates) Regulations [Vol. IX p. 191] S.R.& O. No. 67 of 1932*
	36(1)	*Dairy Produce (Butter Levy and Bounty Rates) Regulations [Vol. IX p. 197] S.R.& O. No. 35 of 1933*
		Dairy Produce (Butter Levy and Bounty Rates) No.2 Regulations [Vol. IX p. 205] S.R.& O. No. 40 of 1933
		Dairy Produce (Butter Levy and Bounty Rates) No.3 Regulations [Vol. IX p. 213] S.R.& O. No. 90 of 1933
		Dairy Produce (Butter Levy and Bounty Rates) No.4 Regulations [Vol. IX p. 221] S.R.& O. No. 112 of 1933
		Dairy Produce (Butter Levy and Bounty Rates) No.5 Regulations [Vol. IX p. 229] S.R.& O. No. 138 of 1933
		Dairy Produce (Bounty Rates) Regulations [Vol. IX p. 175] S.R.& O. No. 10 of 1934
		Dairy Produce (Butter Levy and Bounty Rates) Regulations [Vol. IX p. 237] S.R.& O. No. 105 of 1934
		Dairy Produce (Butter Levy and Bounty Rates) No.2 Regulations [Vol. IX p. 245] S.R.& O. No. 137 of 1934
		Dairy Produce (Butter Levy and Bounty Rates) No.3 Regulations [Vol. IX p. 253] S.R.& O. No. 211 of 1934
		Dairy Produce (Butter Levy and Bounty Rates) No.4 Regulations [Vol. IX p. 261] S.R.& O. No. 246 of 1934
		Dairy Produce (Butter Levy and Bounty Rates) No.5 Regulations [Vol. IX p. 269] S.R.& O. No. 248 of 1934
		Dairy Produce (Bounty Rates) (Amendment) Regulations [Vol. IX p. 183] S.R.& O. No. 372 of 1934
	49(1)	*Dairy Produce (Butter Traders' Records and Returns) Regulations [Vol. IX p. 277] S.R.& O. No. 210 of 1934*
Dairy Produce (Price Stabilisation) Act, No. 21 of 1935		*Creamery Butter (Levy) (No.2) Order [Vol. XXVIII p. 747] S.R.& O. No. 184 of 1941*
		Creamery Butter (Levy) (Amending) Order [Vol. XXVIII p. 743] S.R.& O. No. 266 of 1941
		Creamery Butter (Levy) (No.3) Order [Vol. XXVIII p. 757] S.R.& O. No. 409 of 1941

Statutory Authority	Section	Statutory Instrument
Dairy Produce (Price Stabilisation) Act, No. 21 of 1935 (*Cont.*)		*Creamery Butter (Levy) (No.4) Order [Vol. XXVIII p. 753] S.R.& O. No. 582 of 1941*
		Creamery Butter (Levy) Order [Vol. XXVIII p. 761] S.R.& O. No. 385 of 1942
		Creamery Butter (Levy) (No.2) Order [Vol. XXVIII p. 765] S.R.& O. No. 414 of 1942
		Creamery Butter (Levy) Order [Vol. XXVIII p. 771] S.R.& O. No. 402 of 1943
		Creamery Butter (Levy) Order, 1943 (Amendment) Order [Vol. XXVIII p. 777] S.R.& O. No. 320 of 1944
		Creamery Butter (Levy) Order, S.I. No. 118 of 1951
		Creamery Butter (Levy) (No.2) Order, S.I. No. 175 of 1951
		Cheese (Levy) Order, S.I. No. 247 of 1951
		Creamery Butter (Levy) Order, S.I. No. 208 of 1952
		Creamery Butter (Levy) Order, S.I. No. 84 of 1953
		Cheese (Levy) Order, 1951 (Revocation) Order, S.I. No. 153 of 1953
		Non-Creamery Butter (Prohibition of Export) Order, 1952 (Revocation) Order, S.I. No. 199 of 1953
		Creamery Butter (Levy) (No.2) Order, S.I. No. 309 of 1953
	4(1)	**Dairy Produce (Butter Traders' Returns) Regulations [Vol. IX p. 695] S.R.& O. No. 177 of 1935**
		Dairy Produce (Forms) Regulations [Vol. IX p. 317] S.R.& O. No. 310 of 1935
		Dairy Produce (Forms) (Amendment) Regulations [Vol. IX p. 359] S.R.& O. No. 137 of 1936
		Dairy Produce (Forms) (Amendment) (No.2) Regulations [Vol. IX p. 365] S.R.& O. No. 267 of 1936
	11(5)	*Dairy Produce (Price Stabilisation) Act, 1935 (Appointed Days) Order [Vol. IX p. 311] S.R.& O. No. 318 of 1935*
	17(4)	*Dairy Produce (Price Stabilisation) Act, 1935 (Appointed Days) Order [Vol. IX p. 311] S.R.& O. No. 318 of 1935*
	18	*Cheese (Levy and Bounty) Order [Vol. IX p. 703] S.R.& O. No. 352 of 1935*
		Bulk Cream (Levy) (No.1) Order [Vol. IX p. 759] S.R.& O. No. 353 of 1935
		Butter (Levy and Bounty) (No.1) Order [Vol. IX p. 379] S.R.& O. No. 354 of 1935
		Butter (Levy and Bounty) (No.2) Order [Vol. IX p. 385] S.R.& O. No. 593 of 1935
		Butter (Levy and Bounty) (No.3) Order [Vol. IX p. 391] S.R.& O. No. 617 of 1935
		Bulk Cream (Levy) (No.2) Order [Vol. IX p. 763] S.R.& O. No. 670 of 1935
		Butter (Levy and Bounty) (No.4) Order [Vol. IX p. 397] S.R.& O. No. 671 of 1935

Statutory Authority	Section	Statutory Instrument
Dairy Produce (Price Stabilisation) Act, No. 21 of 1935 (*Cont.*)		*Butter (Levy and Bounty) (No.5) Order [Vol. IX p. 403] S.R.& O. No. 18 of 1936*
		Butter (Levy and Bounty) (No.6) Order [Vol. IX p. 409] S.R.& O. No. 44 of 1936
		Butter (Levy and Bounty) (No.7) Order [Vol. IX p. 417] S.R.& O. No. 45 of 1936
		Bulk Cream (Levy) (No.1) Order [Vol. IX p. 767] S.R.& O. No. 74 of 1936
		Cheese (Levy) Order [Vol. IX p. 713] S.R.& O. No. 106 of 1936
		Bulk Cream (Levy) (No.2) Order [Vol. IX p. 771] S.R.& O. No. 107 of 1936
		Non-Creamery Butter (Levy) Order [Vol. IX p. 617] S.R.& O. No. 108 of 1936
		Butter (Levy and Bounty) (No.7) Order, 1935 Revocation Order [Vol. IX p. 425] S.R.& O. No. 112 of 1936
		Creamery Butter (Levy) Order [Vol. IX p. 429] S.R.& O. No. 118 of 1936
		Condensed Milk (Levy) Order [Vol. IX p. 851] S.R.& O. No. 125 of 1936
		Cheese (Levy) (No.2) Order [Vol. IX p. 717] S.R.& O. No. 140 of 1936
		Non-Creamery Butter (Levy) (No.2) Order [Vol. IX p. 623] S.R.& O. No. 141 of 1936
		Non-Creamery Butter (Levy) (No.3) Order [Vol. IX p. 629] S.R.& O. No. 181 of 1936
		Creamery Butter (Levy) (No.2) Order [Vol. IX p. 435] S.R.& O. No. 188 of 1936
		Creamery Butter (Levy) (No.3) Order [Vol. IX p. 439] S.R.& O. No. 214 of 1936
		Non-Creamery Butter (Levy) (No.4) Order [Vol. IX p. 635] S.R.& O. No. 227 of 1936
		Condensed Milk (Levy) (No.2) Order [Vol. IX p. 855] S.R.& O. No. 228 of 1936
		Bulk Cream (Levy) (No.3) Order [Vol. IX p. 775] S.R.& O. No. 229 of 1936
		Creamery Butter (Levy) (No.4) Order [Vol. IX p. 443] S.R.& O. No. 271 of 1936
		Creamery Butter (Levy) (No.5) Order [Vol. IX p. 449] S.R.& O. No. 373 of 1936
		Non-Creamery Butter (Levy) (No.5) Order, S.R.& O. No. 375 of 1936
		Bulk Cream (Levy) (No.4) Order [Vol. IX p. 779] S.R.& O. No. 377 of 1936
		Condensed Milk (Levy) (No.3) Order [Vol. IX p. 859] S.R.& O. No. 378 of 1936
		Creamery Butter (Levy) Order [Vol. IX p. 455] S.R.& O. No. 85 of 1937
		Cheese (Levy) Order [Vol. IX p. 721] S.R.& O. No. 108 of 1937
		Creamery Butter (Levy) (No.2) Order [Vol. IX p. 461] S.R.& O. No. 109 of 1937

Statutory Authority	Section	Statutory Instrument

Dairy Produce (Price Stabilisation)
Act, No. 21 of 1935 (*Cont.*)

Creamery Butter (Levy) (No.3) Order [Vol. IX p. 465] S.R.& O. No. 166 of 1937

Cheese (Levy) (No.2) Order [Vol. IX p. 725] S.R.& O. No. 167 of 1937

Creamery Butter (Levy) Order [Vol. IX p. 473] S.R.& O. No. 157 of 1938

Cheese (Levy) Order [Vol. IX p. 729] S.R.& O. No. 159 of 1938

Creamery Butter (Levy) (No.2) Order [Vol. IX p. 477] S.R.& O. No. 195 of 1938

Condensed Milk (Levy) Order [Vol. IX p. 863] S.R.& O. No. 271 of 1938

Cheese (Levy) (No.2) Order [Vol. IX p. 733] S.R.& O. No. 272 of 1938

Creamery Butter (Levy) (No.3) Order [Vol. IX p. 481] S.R.& O. No. 332 of 1938

Condensed Milk (Levy) Order, 1938 (Revocation) Order [Vol. XXVIII p. 669] S.R.& O. No. 123 of 1939

Bulk Cream (Levy) (No.4) Order, 1936 (Revocation) Order [Vol. XXVIII p. 629] S.R.& O. No. 297 of 1941

Cheese (Levy) Order [Vol. XXVIII p. 657] S.R.& O. No. 415 of 1942

Creamery Butter (Levy) Order [Vol. XXXVII p. 11] S.R.& O. No. 155 of 1947

Cheese (Levy) Order [Vol. XXXVII p. 7] S.R.& O. No. 247 of 1947

Creamery Butter (Levy) Order, S.I. No. 101 of 1957

Creamery Butter (Levy) Regulations, S.I. No. 73 of 1958

Creamery Butter (Levy) (Amendment) Regulations, S.I. No. 133 of 1959

Creamery Butter (Levy) Regulations, S.I. No. 76 of 1960

18(1) *Cheese (Levy and Bounty) Order, 1935 (Revocation) Order [Vol. IX p. 709] S.R.& O. No. 120 of 1936*

Non-Creamery Butter (Levy) (No.5) Order, 1936 Revocation Order [Vol. IX p. 647] S.R.& O. No. 111 of 1937

Creamery Butter (Levy) Order [Vol. XXVIII p. 703] S.R.& O. No. 118 of 1939

Creamery Butter (Levy) (No.2) Order [Vol. XXVIII p. 709] S.R.& O. No. 177 of 1939

Creamery Butter (Levy) (No.3) Order [Vol. XXVIII p. 713] S.R.& O. No. 317 of 1939

Creamery Butter (Levy) (No.4) Order [Vol. XXVIII p. 719] S.R.& O. No. 398 of 1939

Cheese (Levy) (Amending) Order [Vol. XXVIII p. 651] S.R.& O. No. 26 of 1940

Creamery Butter (Levy) Order [Vol. XXVIII p. 723] S.R.& O. No. 109 of 1940

Statutory Authority	Section	Statutory Instrument
Dairy Produce (Price Stabilisation) Act, No. 21 of 1935 (*Cont.*)		*Creamery Butter (Levy) (No.2) Order [Vol. XXVIII p. 729] S.R.& O. No. 252 of 1940*
		Creamery Butter (Levy) (No.3) Order [Vol. XXVIII p. 733] S.R.& O. No. 369 of 1940
		Creamery Butter (Levy) Order [Vol. XXVIII p. 737] S.R.& O. No. 55 of 1941
	19	*Butter (Levy and Bounty) (No.7) Order [Vol. IX p. 417] S.R.& O. No. 45 of 1936*
		Non-Creamery Butter (Levy) Order [Vol. IX p. 617] S.R.& O. No. 108 of 1936
		Butter (Levy and Bounty) (No.7) Order, 1935 Revocation Order [Vol. IX p. 425] S.R.& O. No. 112 of 1936
		Non-Creamery Butter (Levy) (No.2) Order [Vol. IX p. 623] S.R.& O. No. 141 of 1936
		Non-Creamery Butter (Levy) (No.3) Order [Vol. IX p. 629] S.R.& O. No. 181 of 1936
		Non-Creamery Butter (Levy) (No.4) Order [Vol. IX p. 635] S.R.& O. No. 227 of 1936
		Non-Creamery Butter (Levy) (No.5) Order, S.R.& O. No. 375 of 1936
	19(1)	**Creamery Butter (Suspension of Levy) Order, (1937) [Vol. IX p. 469] S.R.& O. No. 46 of 1938**
	26	*Imported Butter (Levy) Order [Vol. IX p. 679] S.R.& O. No. 42 of 1937*
		Imported Butter (Levy) (No.2) Order [Vol. IX p. 683] S.R.& O. No. 50 of 1937
		Imported Butter (Levy) (No.3) Order [Vol. IX p. 687] S.R.& O. No. 62 of 1937
		Imported Butter (Levy) Order [Vol. XXVIII p. 837] S.R.& O. No. 47 of 1939
		Imported Butter (Levy) (No.2) Order [Vol. XXVIII p. 841] S.R.& O. No. 61 of 1939
		Imported Butter (Levy) Order, 1939 (Revocation) Order [Vol. XXVIII p. 845] S.R.& O. No. 121 of 1939
		Imported Butter (Levy) (No.2) Order, 1939 (Revocation) Order [Vol. XXVIII p. 849] S.R.& O. No. 122 of 1939
	26(1)	*Imported Butter (Levy) (No.3) Order, 1937 Revocation Order [Vol. IX p. 691] S.R.& O. No. 258 of 1937*
	29(1)	*Prohibition of Import (Cheese) Order [Vol. IX p. 755] S.R.& O. No. 643 of 1935*
		Prohibition of Import (Cheese) Order, S.I. No. 101 of 1949
		Prohibition of Import (Dried or Powdered Milk) Order, S.I. No. 65 of 1953
		Prohibition of Import (Dried or Powdered Milk) (No.2) Order, S.I. No. 313 of 1953
		Prohibition of Import (Cheese) Order, S.I. No. 119 of 1955

Statutory Authority	Section	Statutory Instrument
Dairy Produce (Price Stabilisation) Act, No. 21 of 1935 *(Cont.)*	31	*Bulk Cream (Prohibition of Export) Order [Vol. IX p. 839] S.R.& O. No. 256 of 1936*
		Creamery Butter (Prohibition of Export) Order [Vol. XXVIII p. 829] S.R.& O. No. 333 of 1939
		Cheese (Prohibition of Export) Order [Vol. XXVIII p. 661] S.R.& O. No. 19 of 1940
		Non-Creamery Butter (Prohibition of Export) Order [Vol. XXVIII p. 853] S.R.& O. No. 329 of 1940
		Creamery Butter (Prohibition of Export) Order, 1939 (Revocation) Order [Vol. XXVIII p. 833] S.R.& O. No. 28 of 1942
		Non-Creamery Butter (Prohibition of Export) Order, 1940 (Revocation) Order [Vol. XXVIII p. 857] S.R.& O. No. 29 of 1942
		Cheese (Prohibition of Export) Order, 1940 (Revocation) Order [Vol. XXVIII p. 665] S.R.& O. No. 230 of 1942
		Bulk Cream (Prohibition of Export) Order, 1936 (Revocation) Order [Vol. XXVIII p. 633] S.R.& O. No. 231 of 1942
		Creamery Butter (Prohibition of Export) Order, S.I. No. 176 of 1949
		Non-Creamery Butter (Prohibition of Export) Order, S.I. No. 267 of 1952
		Non-Creamery Butter (Prohibition of Export) Order, S.I. No. 101 of 1962
		Butter (Prohibition of Export) Orders (Revocation) Order, S.I. No. 27 of 1964
	31(2)	*Creamery Butter (Prohibition of Export) Order, 1949 (Partial Revocation) Order, S.I. No. 233 of 1956*
	34	*Cheese (Levy and Bounty) Order [Vol. IX p. 703] S.R.& O. No. 352 of 1935*
		Butter (Levy and Bounty) (No.1) Order [Vol. IX p. 379] S.R.& O. No. 354 of 1935
		Butter (Levy and Bounty) (No.2) Order [Vol. IX p. 385] S.R.& O. No. 593 of 1935
		Butter (Levy and Bounty) (No.3) Order [Vol. IX p. 391] S.R.& O. No. 617 of 1935
		Bulk Cream (Bounty) (No.1) Order [Vol. IX p. 783] S.R.& O. No. 642 of 1935
		Butter (Levy and Bounty) (No.4) Order [Vol. IX p. 397] S.R.& O. No. 671 of 1935
		Bulk Cream (Bounty) (No.2) Order [Vol. IX p. 787] S.R.& O. No. 683 of 1935
		Butter (Levy and Bounty) (No.5) Order [Vol. IX p. 403] S.R.& O. No. 18 of 1936
		Bulk Cream (Bounty) (No.3) Order [Vol. IX p. 793] S.R.& O. No. 37 of 1936
		Butter (Levy and Bounty) (No.6) Order [Vol. IX p. 409] S.R.& O. No. 44 of 1936
		Butter (Levy and Bounty) (No.7) Order [Vol. IX p. 417] S.R.& O. No. 45 of 1936
		Bulk Cream (Bounty) (No.1) Order [Vol. IX p. 799] S.R.& O. No. 73 of 1936

Dairy Produce (Price Stabilisation)
Act, No. 21 of 1935 (*Cont.*)

**Creamery Butter (Bounty) Order [Vol. IX p. 487]
S.R.& O. No. 110 of 1936**

*Bulk Cream (Bounty) (No.2) Order [Vol. IX
p. 805] S.R.& O. No. 111 of 1936*

*Butter (Levy and Bounty) (No.7) Order, 1935
Revocation Order [Vol. IX p. 425] S.R.& O.
No. 112 of 1936*

*Non-Creamery Butter (Bounty) Order [Vol. IX
p. 651] S.R.& O. No. 117 of 1936*

*Cheese (Bounty) Order [Vol. IX p. 739] S.R.& O.
No. 119 of 1936*

*Creamery Butter (Bounty) (No.2) Order [Vol. IX
p. 493] S.R.& O. No. 193 of 1936*

*Creamery Butter (Bounty) (No.3) Order [Vol. IX
p. 499] S.R.& O. No. 216 of 1936*

*Non-Creamery Butter (Bounty) (No.2) Order [Vol.
IX p. 655] S.R.& O. No. 226 of 1936*

*Bulk Cream (Bounty) (No.3) Order [Vol. IX
p. 811] S.R.& O. No. 230 of 1936*

*Creamery Butter (Bounty) (No.4) Order [Vol. IX
p. 505] S.R.& O. No. 281 of 1936*

*Non-Creamery Butter (Bounty) (No.3) Order [Vol.
IX p. 659] S.R.& O. No. 282 of 1936*

*Creamery Butter (Bounty) (No.5) Order [Vol. IX
p. 521] S.R.& O. No. 372 of 1936*

*Non-Creamery Butter (Bounty) (No.4) Order [Vol.
IX p. 663] S.R.& O. No. 374 of 1936*

*Bulk Cream (Bounty) (No.4) Order [Vol. IX
p. 817] S.R.& O. No. 393 of 1936*

*Creamery Butter (Bounty) (No.1) Order [Vol. IX
p. 517] S.R.& O. No. 86 of 1937*

*Creamery Butter (Bounty) (No.2) Order [Vol. IX
p. 523] S.R.& O. No. 110 of 1937*

*Cheese (Bounty) Order [Vol. IX p. 743] S.R.& O.
No. 114 of 1937*

*Bulk Cream (Bounty) (No.1) Order [Vol. IX
p. 823] S.R.& O. No. 115 of 1937*

*Dried or Powdered Milk (Bounty) Order [Vol. IX
p. 877] S.R.& O. No. 116 of 1937*

**Tinned Cream (Bounty) Order [Vol. IX p. 843]
S.R.& O. No. 117 of 1937**

*Condensed Milk (Bounty) Order [Vol. IX p. 869]
S.R.& O. No. 118 of 1937*

**Non-Creamery Butter (Bounty) Order [Vol. IX
p. 671] S.R.& O. No. 181 of 1937**

*Creamery Butter (Bounty) (No.3) Order [Vol. IX
p. 529] S.R.& O. No. 182 of 1937*

*Bulk Cream (Bounty) (No.2) Order [Vol. IX
p. 829] S.R.& O. No. 183 of 1937*

*Creamery Butter (Bounty) Order [Vol. IX p. 539]
S.R.& O. No. 158 of 1938*

*Cheese (Bounty) Order [Vol. IX p. 751] S.R.& O.
No. 160 of 1938*

Statutory Authority	Section	Statutory Instrument
Dairy Produce (Price Stabilisation) Act, No. 21 of 1935 (*Cont.*)		*Creamery Butter (Bounty) (No.2) Order [Vol. IX p. 545] S.R.& O. No. 288 of 1938*
		Cheese (Bounty) (Amending) Order [Vol. XXVIII p. 641] S.R.& O. No. 14 of 1939
		Creamery Butter (Bounty) (Amending) (No.2) Order [Vol. XXVIII p. 687] S.R.& O. No. 62 of 1939
		Creamery Butter (Bounty) Order [Vol. XXVIII p. 673] S.R.& O. No. 117 of 1939
		Cheese (Bounty) Order [Vol. XXVIII p. 637] S.R.& O. No. 119 of 1939
		Cheese (Bounty) Order, 1939 (Revocation) Order, (1939) [Vol. XXVIII p. 647] S.R.& O. No. 11 of 1940
	34(1)	*Cheese (Levy and Bounty) Order, 1935 (Revocation) Order [Vol. IX p. 709] S.R.& O. No. 120 of 1936*
		Non-Creamery Butter (Bounty) (No.4) Revocation Order [Vol. IX p. 667] S.R.& O. No. 112 of 1937
		Creamery Butter (Bounty) (Amending) (No.3) Order [Vol. XXVIII p. 697] S.R.& O. No. 328 of 1939
		Creamery Butter (Bounty) (Amending) Order [Vol. XXVIII p. 679] S.R.& O. No. 173 of 1940
		Creamery Butter (Bounty) (Amending) Order [Vol. XXVIII p. 683] S.R.& O. No. 71 of 1941
		Creamery Butter (Bounty) (Amending) (No.2) Order [Vol. XXVIII p. 693] S.R.& O. No. 328 of 1941
	35	*Butter (Levy and Bounty) (No.5) Order [Vol. IX p. 403] S.R.& O. No. 18 of 1936*
		Butter (Levy and Bounty) (No.6) Order [Vol. IX p. 409] S.R.& O. No. 44 of 1936
		Butter (Levy and Bounty) (No.7) Order [Vol. IX p. 417] S.R.& O. No. 45 of 1936
		Butter (Levy and Bounty) (No.7) Order, 1935 Revocation Order [Vol. IX p. 425] S.R.& O. No. 112 of 1936
		Bulk Cream Suspension of Bounty Order [Vol. IX p. 835] S.R.& O. No. 273 of 1937
		Creamery Butter (Suspension of Bounty) Order [Vol. IX p. 535] S.R.& O. No. 289 of 1937
		Non-Creamery Butter (Suspension of Bounty) Order, (1937) [Vol. IX p. 675] S.R.& O. No. 47 of 1938
		Condensed Milk (Suspension of Bounty) Order, (1937) [Vol. IX p. 873] S.R.& O. No. 48 of 1938
		Dried or Powdered Milk (Bounty) (Suspension) Order [Vol. IX p. 881] S.R.& O. No. 49 of 1938
		Tinned Cream (Suspension of Bounty) Order, (1937) [Vol. IX p. 847] S.R.& O. No. 50 of 1938
		Cheese (Bounty) Order, 1937 (Suspension) Order [Vol. IX p. 747] S.R.& O. No. 51 of 1938

Statutory Authority	Section	Statutory Instrument
Dairy Produce (Price Stabilisation) Act, No. 21 of 1935 (*Cont.*)	38	*Creamery Butter (Maximum Prices) Order, S.I. No. 54 of 1957*
		Creamery Butter (Maximum Prices) Order, 1957 (Revocation) Order, S.I. No. 99 of 1957
	39(2)	*Creamery Butter (Minimum Prices) Order [Vol. IX p. 551] S.R.& O. No. 647 of 1935*
		Creamery Butter (Minimum Prices) (No.2) Order [Vol. IX p. 557] S.R.& O. No. 682 of 1935
		Creamery Butter (Minimum Prices) Order [Vol. IX p. 563] S.R.& O. No. 138 of 1936
		Creamery Butter (Minimum Prices) (No.2) Order [Vol. IX p. 569] S.R.& O. No. 192 of 1936
		Creamery Butter (Minimum Prices) (No.3) Order [Vol. IX p. 575] S.R.& O. No. 272 of 1936
		Creamery Butter (Minimum Prices) (No.4) Order [Vol. IX p. 581] S.R.& O. No. 346 of 1936
		Creamery Butter (Minimum Prices) Order [Vol. IX p. 587] S.R.& O. No. 107 of 1937
		Creamery Butter (Minimum Prices) (No.2) Order [Vol. IX p. 593] S.R.& O. No. 165 of 1937
		Creamery Butter (Minimum Prices) Order [Vol. IX p. 599] S.R.& O. No. 156 of 1938
		Creamery Butter (Minimum Prices) (No.2) Order [Vol. IX p. 605] S.R.& O. No. 186 of 1938
		Creamery Butter (Minimum Prices) (No.3) Order [Vol. IX p. 611] S.R.& O. No. 326 of 1938
		Creamery Butter (Minimum Prices) (Amendment) Order [Vol. XXVIII p. 787] S.R.& O. No. 149 of 1939
		Creamery Butter (Minimum Prices) Order [Vol. XXVIII p. 781] S.R.& O. No. 176 of 1939
		Creamery Butter (Minimum Prices) (No.2) Order [Vol. XXVIII p. 793] S.R.& O. No. 335 of 1939
	39(2)(a)	*Creamery Butter (Minimum Prices) Order [Vol. XXVIII p. 799] S.R.& O. No. 93 of 1940*
		Creamery Butter (Minimum Prices) (Amendment) Order [Vol. XXVIII p. 805] S.R.& O. No. 124 of 1940
		Creamery Butter (Minimum Prices) (Amendment) (No.2) Order [Vol. XXVIII p. 809] S.R.& O. No. 213 of 1940
		Creamery Butter (Minimum Prices) (No.2) Order [Vol. XXVIII p. 815] S.R.& O. No. 247 of 1940
		Creamery Butter (Minimum Prices) (Amendment) (No.3) Order [Vol. XXVIII p. 821] S.R.& O. No. 286 of 1940
		Creamery Butter (Minimum Prices) (Revocation) Order [Vol. XXVIII p. 825] S.R.& O. No. 380 of 1940
	39(4)	*Creamery Butter (Minimum Prices) (No.2) Order [Vol. IX p. 557] S.R.& O. No. 682 of 1935*
		Creamery Butter (Minimum Prices) Order [Vol. IX p. 563] S.R.& O. No. 138 of 1936

Statutory Authority	Section	Statutory Instrument
Dairy Produce (Price Stabilisation) Act, No. 21 of 1935 (*Cont.*)		*Creamery Butter (Minimum Prices) (No.2) Order [Vol. IX p. 569] S.R.& O. No. 192 of 1936*
		Creamery Butter (Minimum Prices) (No.3) Order [Vol. IX p. 575] S.R.& O. No. 272 of 1936
		Creamery Butter (Minimum Prices) (No.4) Order [Vol. IX p. 581] S.R.& O. No. 346 of 1936
		Creamery Butter (Minimum Prices) Order [Vol. IX p. 587] S.R.& O. No. 107 of 1937
		Creamery Butter (Minimum Prices) (No.2) Order [Vol. IX p. 593] S.R.& O. No. 165 of 1937
		Creamery Butter (Minimum Prices) Order [Vol. IX p. 599] S.R.& O. No. 156 of 1938
		Creamery Butter (Minimum Prices) (No.2) Order [Vol. IX p. 605] S.R.& O. No. 186 of 1938
		Creamery Butter (Minimum Prices) (No.3) Order [Vol. IX p. 611] S.R.& O. No. 326 of 1938
		Creamery Butter (Minimum Prices) (Amendment) Order [Vol. XXVIII p. 787] S.R.& O. No. 149 of 1939
		Creamery Butter (Minimum Prices) Order [Vol. XXVIII p. 781] S.R.& O. No. 176 of 1939
		Creamery Butter (Minimum Prices) (No.2) Order [Vol. XXVIII p. 793] S.R.& O. No. 335 of 1939
	49	**Creamery Butter (Bounty) Order [Vol. XXVIII p. 673] S.R.& O. No. 117 of 1939**
Dairy Produce (Price Stabilisation) Acts, 1935 to 1941,		*Levy (Butter Stocks) (No.1) Order, 1943 (Amendment) Order [Vol. XXVIII p. 865] S.R.& O. No. 425 of 1943*
		Creamery Butter (Levy) Order, 1943 (Amendment) Order [Vol. XXVIII p. 861] S.R.& O. No. 432 of 1943
Dairy Produce (Price Stabilisation) (Amendment) Act, No. 30 of 1938	2(1)	**Dairy Produce (Price Stabilisation) Act, 1935 (Part II and Section 17(1)(d) and (e)) (Suspending) Order [Vol. IX p. 891] S.R.& O. No. 340 of 1938**
	2(2)	**Dairy Produce (Price Stabilisation) Act, 1935 (Section 17 (1) (a) , (b) and (c)) (Suspending) Order, S.I. No. 66 of 1964**
		Dairy Produce (Price Stabilisation) Act, 1935 (Section 41) (Suspending) Order, S.I. No. 47 of 1965
		Dairy Produce (Price Stabilisation) Act, 1935 (Sections 24 and 29) (Suspending) Order, S.I. No. 150 of 1966
	4(1)	*Butter Stocks (Levy) Order [Vol. IX p. 885] S.R.& O. No. 331 of 1938*
		Butter Stocks (Levy) Order [Vol. XXVIII p. 869] S.R.& O. No. 94 of 1940
	7	**Cheese (Levy) (Amending) Order [Vol. XXVIII p. 651] S.R.& O. No. 26 of 1940**
	10	*Creamery Butter (Levy) (Amending) Order [Vol. XXVIII p. 743] S.R.& O. No. 266 of 1941*

Statutory Authority	Section	Statutory Instrument
Dairy Produce (Price Stabilisation) (Amendment) Act, No. 30 of 1938 (*Cont.*)	11	**Creamery Butter (Bounty) (Amending) Order [Vol. XXVIII p. 679] S.R.& O. No. 173 of 1940** **Creamery Butter (Bounty) (Amending) Order [Vol. XXVIII p. 683] S.R.& O. No. 71 of 1941**
Dairy Produce (Price Stabilisation) (Amendment) Act, No. 9 of 1941	3	*Levy (Butter Stocks) (No.1) Order, S.I. No. 119 of 1951* *Levy (Butter Stocks) (No.3) Order, S.I. No. 176 of 1951* *Levy (Butter Stocks) (No.1) Order, S.I. No. 209 of 1952* *Levy (Butter Stocks) (No.1) Order, S.I. No. 85 of 1953* *Levy (Butter Stocks) (No.1) Order, S.I. No. 102 of 1957* *Levy (Butter Stocks) (No.1) Order, S.I. No. 77 of 1960*
	3(1)	*Levy (Butter Stocks) (No.1) Order [Vol. XXVIII p. 873] S.R.& O. No. 177 of 1942* *Levy (Butter Stocks) (No.3) Order [Vol. XXVIII p. 883] S.R.& O. No. 394 of 1942* *Levy (Butter Stocks) (No.1) Order [Vol. XXVIII p. 893] S.R.& O. No. 394 of 1943* *Levy (Butter Stocks) (No.1) Order [Vol. XXXVII p. 17] S.R.& O. No. 153 of 1947*
	4	*Levy (Butter Stocks) (No.2) Order, S.I. No. 120 of 1951* *Levy (Butter Stocks) (No.2) Order, S.I. No. 210 of 1952* *Levy (Butter Stocks) (No.3) Order, S.I. No. 211 of 1952* *Levy (Butter Stocks) (No.3) Order, S.I. No. 87 of 1953* *Levy (Butter Stocks) (No.2) Order, S.I. No. 103 of 1957* *Levy (Butter Stocks) (No.2) Order, S.I. No. 78 of 1960*
	4(2)	*Levy (Butter Stocks) (No.2) Order [Vol. XXVIII p. 877] S.R.& O. No. 178 of 1942* *Levy (Butter Stocks) (No.4) Order [Vol. XXVIII p. 887] S.R.& O. No. 395 of 1942* *Levy (Butter Stocks) (No.2) Order [Vol. XXVIII p. 897] S.R.& O. No. 395 of 1943* *Levy (Butter Stocks) (No.2) Order [Vol. XXXVII p. 23] S.R.& O. No. 154 of 1947* *Levy (Butter Stocks) (No.4) Order, S.I. No. 177 of 1951* *Levy (Butter Stocks) (No.2) Order, S.I. No. 86 of 1953*
Dairy Produce (Price Stabilisation) (Amendment) Act, No. 39 of 1956	4	*Butter (Control in Scheduled Area) Order, S.I. No. 53 of 1957*

Statutory Authority	Section	Statutory Instrument
Dairy Produce (Price Stabilisation) (Amendment) Act, No. 39 of 1956 (*Cont.*)		*Butter (Control in Scheduled Area) Order, 1957 (Revocation) Regulations, S.I. No. 146 of 1958*
	6	*Butter Boxes (Restriction on Sale) Regulations, S.I. No. 55 of 1957*
		Butter Boxes (Restriction on Sale) Regulations, 1957 (Revocation) Regulations, S.I. No. 100 of 1957
	11(2)	*Dairy Produce (Price Stabilisation) (Amendment) Act, 1956 (Commencement) Order, S.I. No. 30 of 1957*
Damage to Property (Compensation Act) No. 15 of 1923	11	**Damage to Property Scale of Compensation for Documents [Vol. IX p. 899] S.R.& O. No. 30 of 1924**
	13	**Damage to Property (Creation of Securities) Order [Vol. IX p. 903] S.R.& O. No. 159 of 1933**
	13(7)	**Damage to Property (Creation of Securities) Order, (1923) [Vol. IX p. 895] S.R.& O. No. 11 of 1924**
Damage to Property (Compensation) (Amendment) Act, No. 35 of 1933	3(2)	**Damage to Property (Notice of Application) Regulations [Vol. IX p. 913] S.R.& O. No. 172 of 1933**
Dangerous Drugs Act, No. 1 of 1934		*Dangerous Drugs (Fees) Regulations, S.I. No. 184 of 1954*
	1(2)	*Dangerous Drugs Act, 1934 (Commencement) Order [Vol. IX p. 923] S.R.& O. No. 40 of 1937*
	5	*Dangerous Drugs (Raw Opium, Coca Leaves and Indian Hemp) Regulations [Vol. IX p. 927] S.R.& O. No. 64 of 1937*
		Dangerous Drugs (Medicinal Opium, Tincture of Indian Hemp, Morphine, Cocaine, etc.) Regulations [Vol. IX p. 955] S.R.& O. No. 65 of 1937
		Dangerous Drugs (Methylmorphine and Ethylmorphine) Regulations [Vol. IX p. 1009] S.R.& O. No. 77 of 1937
		Dangerous Drugs Act, 1934 (Collection of Fees) Regulations [Vol. IX p. 1031] S.R.& O. No. 148 of 1937
		Dangerous Drugs (Medicinal Opium, Tincture of Indian Hemp, Morphine, Cocaine, etc.) (Amendment) Regulations, S.I. No. 273 of 1971
	14(1)	*Dangerous Drugs (Raw Opium, Coca Leaves and Indian Hemp) Regulations [Vol. IX p. 927] S.R.& O. No. 64 of 1937*
	17(2)	*Dangerous Drugs Act, 1934 (Application of Part IV to Preparations of Ecgonine, Morphine, Methylmorphine and Ethylmorphine) Order [Vol. IX p. 1063] S.R.& O. No. 275 of 1937*
		Dangerous Drugs Act, 1934 (Application of Part IV to Hydrochloride of 1-Methyl-4-Phenyl-Piperidine-4-Carboxylic Acid Athyl Ester) Order [Vol. XXXVII p. 1] S.R.& O. No. 171 of 1946
		Dangerous Drugs Act, 1934 Order, S.I. No. 125 of 1969

Statutory Authority	Section	Statutory Instrument
Dangerous Drugs Act, No. 1 of 1934 (*Cont.*)	17(3)	*Dangerous Drugs (Preparations containing Morphine, Cocaine, etc.) (Exemption) Order [Vol. IX p. 1037] S.R.& O. No. 160 of 1937*
	20	*Dangerous Drugs (Medicinal Opium, Tincture of Indian Hemp, Morphine, Cocaine, etc.) (Amendment) Regulations, S.I. No. 273 of 1971*
	20(1)	*Dangerous Drugs (Medicinal Opium, Tincture of Indian Hemp, Morphine, Cocaine, etc.) Regulations [Vol. IX p. 955] S.R.& O. No. 65 of 1937*
		Dangerous Drugs (Methylmorphine and Ethylmorphine) Regulations [Vol. IX p. 1009] S.R.& O. No. 77 of 1937
		Dangerous Drugs (Medicinal Opium, Tincture of Indian Hemp, Morphine, Cocaine, etc.) (Amendment) Regulations [Vol. IX p. 1053] S.R.& O. No. 257 of 1937
		Dangerous Drugs (Medicinal Opium, Tincture of Indian Hemp, Morphine, Cocaine, etc.) (Amendment) Regulations [Vol. XXVIII p. 903] S.R.& O. No. 88 of 1944
	22(1)	*Dangerous Drugs Act, 1934 (Application of Part IV to Methylmorphine and Ethylmorphine) Order [Vol. IX p. 1003] S.R.& O. No. 66 of 1937*
Dangerous Substances Act, No. 10 of 1972	1(2)	*Dangerous Substances Act, 1972 (Commencement) Order, S.I. No. 297 of 1979*
	4	**Dangerous Substances Act, 1972 (Part IV) (Declaration) Order, S.I. No. 267 of 1986**
	21(2)(b)	**Dangerous Substances (Retail and Private Petroleum Stores) Regulations, S.I. No. 311 of 1979**
	22	**Dangerous Substances (Oil Jetties) Regulations, S.I. No. 312 of 1979**
		Dangerous Substances (Conveyance of Petroleum by Road) Regulations, S.I. No. 314 of 1979
	22(2)	**Dangerous Substances (Retail and Private Petroleum Stores) Regulations, S.I. No. 311 of 1979**
		Dangerous Substances (Petroleum Bulk Stores) Regulations, S.I. No. 313 of 1979
	23	**Dangerous Substances (Retail and Private Petroleum Stores) Regulations, S.I. No. 311 of 1979**
		Dangerous Substances (Oil Jetties) Regulations, S.I. No. 312 of 1979
		Dangerous Substances (Petroleum Bulk Stores) Regulations, S.I. No. 313 of 1979
		Dangerous Substances (Conveyance of Petroleum by Road) Regulations, S.I. No. 314 of 1979
	24	*Dangerous Substances Act, 1972 (Part IV Declaration) Order, S.I. No. 236 of 1980*
		Dangerous Substances Act, 1972 (Part IV) (Declaration) Order, S.I. No. 267 of 1986
	36	**Dangerous Substances (Licensing Fees) Regulations, S.I. No. 301 of 1979**

Statutory Authority	Section	Statutory Instrument
Dangerous Substances Act, No. 10 of 1972 (*Cont.*)		**Dangerous Substances (Retail and Private Petroleum Stores) Regulations, S.I. No. 311 of 1979**
		Dangerous Substances (Oil Jetties) Regulations, S.I. No. 312 of 1979
		Dangerous Substances (Petroleum Bulk Stores) Regulations, S.I. No. 313 of 1979
		Dangerous Substances (Conveyance of Petroleum by Road) Regulations, S.I. No. 314 of 1979
	36(1)	**Dangerous Substances (Conveyance of Scheduled Substances by Road) (Trade or Business) Regulations, S.I. No. 235 of 1980**
		Dangerous Substances (Conveyance of Scheduled Substances by Road) (Trade or Business) (Amendment) Regulations, S.I. No. 268 of 1986
		Dangerous Substances (European Agreement Concerning Carriage of Dangerous Goods by Road (ADR)) Regulations, S.I. No. 269 of 1986
	37	**Dangerous Substances (Retail and Private Petroleum Stores) Regulations, S.I. No. 311 of 1979**
	38	**Dangerous Substances (Licensing Fees) Regulations, S.I. No. 301 of 1979**
	62	**Dangerous Substances (Oil Jetties) Regulations, S.I. No. 312 of 1979**
		Dangerous Substances (Conveyance of Petroleum by Road) Regulations, S.I. No. 314 of 1979
	62(2)	**Dangerous Substances (Retail and Private Petroleum Stores) Regulations, S.I. No. 311 of 1979**
		Dangerous Substances (Petroleum Bulk Stores) Regulations, S.I. No. 313 of 1979
		Dangerous Substances (Conveyance of Scheduled Substances by Road) (Trade or Business) Regulations, S.I. No. 235 of 1980
		Dangerous Substances (Conveyance of Scheduled Substances by Road) (Trade or Business) (Amendment) Regulations, S.I. No. 268 of 1986
		Dangerous Substances (European Agreement Concerning Carriage of Dangerous Goods by Road (ADR)) Regulations, S.I. No. 269 of 1986
	66	**Dangerous Substances (Retail and Private Petroleum Stores) Regulations, S.I. No. 311 of 1979**
		Dangerous Substances (Petroleum Bulk Stores) Regulations, S.I. No. 313 of 1979
Decimal Currency Act, No. 23 of 1969	2(2)	*Decimal Currency Act, 1969 (Appointment of Day for the Purposes of Section 2 (2)) Order, S.I. No. 203 of 1971*
	2(3)	*Decimal Currency Act, 1969 (Section 2 (3)) (Appointed Day) Order, S.I. No. 387 of 1985*
	3(6)	**Coinage (Dimensions and Designs) Regulations, S.I. No. 160 of 1969**
	4	**Coinage (Dimension and Design) Regulations, S.I. No. 112 of 1986**

Statutory Authority	Section	Statutory Instrument
Decimal Currency Act, No. 23 of 1969 (*Cont.*)	12	*Coinage (Calling In) Order, S.I. No. 204 of 1971* **Coinage (Calling In) Order, S.I. No. 113 of 1986**
	16	**Decimal Currency (Variation of Certain Payments) Regulations, S.I. No. 156 of 1969**
	34	**New Coinage (Twenty Pence) Order, S.I. No. 32 of 1986**
Decimal Currency Act, No. 21 of 1970	8	**Decimal Currency (Friendly Society and Industrial Assurance Contracts) Regulations, S.I. No. 64 of 1971**
	10	**Decimal Currency (Daily Rates of Disability Benefit, Unemployment Benefit, Unemployment Assistance and Occupational Injuries Benefit and Weekly Rates of Intermittent Unemployment Insurance Contributions) Order, S.I. No. 46 of 1971** **Decimal Currency (Amendment of References) Order, S.I. No. 54 of 1971** *Merchant Shipping (Fees) (Amendment) Order, S.I. No. 67 of 1971* **Harbours and Pilotage (Rates and Charges) (Decimal Currency) Order, S.I. No. 70 of 1971** **Decimal Currency (Amendment of References) (No.2) Order, S.I. No. 287 of 1971**
Defence Act, No. 18 of 1954	1	*Defence Act, 1954 (Commencement) Order, S.I. No. 233 of 1954*
	183	**Defence Forces (Summoning of Civilian Witnesses) Regulations, S.I. No. 297 of 1954**
	184	**Defence Forces (Summoning of Civilian Witnesses) Regulations, S.I. No. 297 of 1954**
	192	**Defence (Civil Authority with respect to Courts-Martial) Regulations, S.I. No. 250 of 1954**
	233	**Rules for Military Prisons and Detention Barracks, S.I. No. 203 of 1983**
	238	**Rules for Military Prisons and Detention Barracks, S.I. No. 291 of 1954**
	240	**Rules of Procedure (Defence Forces) S.I. No. 243 of 1954** **Rules of Procedure (Defence Forces) 1954 (Amendment) Rules, S.I. No. 58 of 1955** **Rules of Procedure (Defence Force) S.I. No. 22 of 1983** **Rules of Procedure (No.2) (Defence Forces) S.I. No. 72 of 1983** **Rules of Procedure (No.3) (Defence Forces) S.I. No. 202 of 1983**
	279	**Defence Act, 1954 (Control of Roads at Gormanston Aerodrome) Bye-Laws, S.I. No. 37 of 1959**

Statutory Authority	Section	Statutory Instrument
Defence (Amendment) (No.2) Act, No. 44 of 1960	6	**Defence Forces (Registration of Certain Births and Deaths Occurring Outside the State) Regulations, S.I. No. 188 of 1962**
Defence (Amendment) (No.2) Act, No. 28 of 1979	8(4)	*Defence (Amendment) (No.2) Act, 1979 (Commencement) Order, S.I. No. 19 of 1980*
Defence Forces (Pensions) Act, No. 26 of 1932	2	**Defence Forces (Pensions) (Amendment) Scheme, S.I. No. 35 of 1956**
		Defence Forces (Pensions) (Amendment) Scheme, S.I. No. 152 of 1957
		Defence Forces (Pensions) (Amendment) (No.2) Scheme, S.I. No. 194 of 1957
		Defence Forces (Pensions) (Amendment) Scheme, S.I. No. 66 of 1959
		Defence Forces (Pensions) (Amendment) Scheme, S.I. No. 135 of 1960
		Defence Forces (Pensions) (Amendment) Scheme, S.I. No. 42 of 1962
		Defence Forces (Pensions) (Amendment) (No.2) Scheme, S.I. No. 126 of 1962
		Defence Forces (Pensions) (Amendment) (No.3) Scheme, S.I. No. 204 of 1962
		Defence Forces (Pensions) (Amendment) Scheme, S.I. No. 247 of 1964
		Defence Forces (Pensions) (Amendment) Scheme, S.I. No. 154 of 1965
		Defence Forces (Pensions) (Amendment) Scheme, S.I. No. 105 of 1968
		Defence Forces (Pensions) (Amendment) Scheme, S.I. No. 34 of 1969
		Defence Forces (Pensions) (Amendment) (No.2) Scheme, S.I. No. 63 of 1969
		Defence Forces (Pensions) (Amendment) (No.3) Scheme, S.I. No. 144 of 1969
		Defence Forces (Pensions) (Amendment) (No.4) Scheme, S.I. No. 215 of 1969
		Defence Forces (Pensions) (Amendment) (No.5) Scheme, S.I. No. 247 of 1969
		Defence Forces (Pensions) (Amendment) Scheme, S.I. No. 143 of 1970
		Defence Forces (Pensions) (Amendment) (No.3) Scheme, S.I. No. 298 of 1970
		Defence Forces (Pensions) (Amendment) Scheme, S.I. No. 50 of 1971
		Defence Forces (Pensions) (Amendment) (No.2) Scheme, S.I. No. 52 of 1971
		Defence Forces (Pensions) (Amendment) Scheme, S.I. No. 100 of 1972
		Defence Forces (Pensions) (Amendment) (No.2) Scheme, S.I. No. 216 of 1972
		Defence Forces (Pensions) (Amendment) (No.3) Scheme, S.I. No. 306 of 1972

Statutory Authority	Section	Statutory Instrument
Defence Forces (Pensions) Act, No. 26 of 1932 (*Cont.*)		Defence Forces (Pensions) (Amendment) Scheme, S.I. No. 57 of 1973
		Defence Forces (Pensions) (Amendment) (No.2) Scheme, S.I. No. 205 of 1973
		Defence Forces (Pensions) (Amendment) (No.3) Scheme, S.I. No. 295 of 1973
		Defence Forces (Pensions) (Amendment) Scheme, S.I. No. 131 of 1974
		Defence Forces (Pensions) (Amendment) (No.2) Scheme, S.I. No. 223 of 1974
		Defence Forces (Pensions) (Amendment) (No.3) Scheme, S.I. No. 231 of 1974
		Defence Forces (Pensions) (Amendment) (No.4) Scheme, S.I. No. 236 of 1974
		Defence Forces (Pensions) (Amendment) (No.5) Scheme, S.I. No. 314 of 1974
		Defence Forces (Pensions) (Amendment) Scheme, S.I. No. 145 of 1975
		Defence Forces (Pensions) (Amendment) (No.2) Scheme, S.I. No. 171 of 1975
		Defence Forces (Pensions) (Amendment) (No.3) Scheme, S.I. No. 172 of 1975
		Defence Forces (Pensions) (Amendment) (No.4) Scheme, S.I. No. 309 of 1975
		Defence Forces (Pensions) (Amendment) Scheme, S.I. No. 218 of 1977
		Defence Forces (Pensions) (Amendment) (No.2) Scheme, S.I. No. 283 of 1977
		Defence Forces (Pensions) (Amendment) Scheme, S.I. No. 246 of 1978
		Defence Forces (Pensions) (Amendment) (No.2) Scheme, S.I. No. 274 of 1978
		Defence Forces (Pensions) (Amendment) (No.3) Scheme, S.I. No. 379 of 1978
		Defence Forces (Pensions) (Amendment) Scheme, S.I. No. 208 of 1979
		Defence Forces (Pensions) (Amendment) (No.2) Scheme, S.I. No. 245 of 1979
		Defence Forces (Pensions) (Amendment) (No.3) Scheme, S.I. No. 343 of 1979
		Defence Forces (Pensions) (Amendment) (No.4) Scheme, S.I. No. 398 of 1979
		Defence Forces (Pensions) (Amendment) (No.5) Scheme, S.I. No. 399 of 1979
		Defence Forces (Pensions) (Amendment) Scheme, S.I. No. 266 of 1980
		Defence Forces (Pensions) (Amendment) (No.2) Scheme, S.I. No. 366 of 1980
		Defence Forces (Pensions) (Amendment) Scheme, S.I. No. 174 of 1981
		Defence Forces (Pensions) (Amendment) (No.2) Scheme, S.I. No. 362 of 1981

Statutory Authority	Section	Statutory Instrument
Defence Forces (Pensions) Act, No. 26 of 1932 (*Cont.*)		Defence Forces (Pensions) (Amendment) Scheme, S.I. No. 137 of 1982
		Defence Forces (Pensions) (Amendment) (No.2) Scheme, S.I. No. 229 of 1982
		Defence Forces (Pensions) (Amendment) (No.3) Scheme, S.I. No. 247 of 1982
		Defence Forces (Pensions) (Amendment) (No.4) Scheme, S.I. No. 337 of 1982
		Defence Forces (Pensions) (Amendment) Scheme, S.I. No. 124 of 1983
		Defence Forces (Pensions) (Amendment) (No.2) Scheme, S.I. No. 190 of 1983
		Defence Forces (Pensions) (Amendment) (No.3) scheme, S.I. No. 214 of 1983
		Defence Forces (Pensions) (Amendment) Scheme, S.I. No. 55 of 1984
		Defence Forces (Pensions) (Amendment) (No.2) Scheme, S.I. No. 56 of 1984
		Defence Forces (Pensions) (Amendment) (No.3) Scheme, S.I. No. 113 of 1984
		Defence Forces (Pensions) (Amendment) (No.4) Scheme, S.I. No. 114 of 1984
		Defence Forces (Pensions) (Amendment) (No.5) Scheme, S.I. No. 172 of 1984
		Defence Forces (Pensions) (Amendment) (No.6) Scheme, S.I. No. 173 of 1984
		Defence Forces (Pensions) (Amendment) (No.7) Scheme, S.I. No. 235 of 1984
		Defence Forces (Pensions) (Amendment) (No.8) Scheme, S.I. No. 259 of 1984
		Defence Forces (Pensions) (Amendment) Scheme, S.I. No. 48 of 1985
		Defence Forces (Pensions) (Amendment) (No.2) Scheme, S.I. No. 221 of 1985
		Defence Forces (Pensions) (Amendment) (No.3) Scheme, S.I. No. 270 of 1985
		Defence Forces (Pensions) (Amendment) (No.4) Scheme, S.I. No. 300 of 1985
		Defence Forces (Pensions) (Amendment) (No.5) Scheme, S.I. No. 307 of 1985
		Defence Forces (Pensions) (Amendment) (No.6) Scheme, S.I. No. 360 of 1985
		Defence Forces (Pensions) (Amendment) (No.7) Scheme, S.I. No. 409 of 1985
		Defence Forces (Pensions) (Amendment) Scheme, S.I. No. 60 of 1986
	2(1)	Defence Forces (Pensions) Scheme [Vol. IX p. 1071] S.R.& O. No. 249 of 1937
		Defence Forces (Pensions) (Amendment) Scheme [Vol. XXVIII p. 909] S.R.& O. No. 299 of 1940
	3	Defence Forces (Pensions) (Amendment) Scheme, S.I. No. 35 of 1956

Statutory Authority	Section	Statutory Instrument
Defence Forces (Pensions) Act, No. 26 of 1932 (*Cont.*)		Defence Forces (Pensions) (Amendment) Scheme, S.I. No. 152 of 1957
		Defence Forces (Pensions) (Amendment) (No.2) Scheme, S.I. No. 194 of 1957
		Defence Forces (Pensions) (Amendment) Scheme, S.I. No. 66 of 1959
		Defence Forces (Pensions) (Amendment) Scheme, S.I. No. 135 of 1960
		Defence Forces (Pensions) (Amendment) Scheme, S.I. No. 42 of 1962
		Defence Forces (Pensions) (Amendment) (No.2) Scheme, S.I. No. 126 of 1962
		Defence Forces (Pensions) (Amendment) (No.3) Scheme, S.I. No. 204 of 1962
		Defence Forces (Pensions) (Amendment) Scheme, S.I. No. 247 of 1964
		Defence Forces (Pensions) (Amendment) Scheme, S.I. No. 154 of 1965
		Defence Forces (Pensions) (Amendment) Scheme, S.I. No. 105 of 1968
		Defence Forces (Pensions) (Amendment) Scheme, S.I. No. 34 of 1969
		Defence Forces (Pensions) (Amendment) (No.2) Scheme, S.I. No. 63 of 1969
		Defence Forces (Pensions) (Amendment) (No.3) Scheme, S.I. No. 144 of 1969
		Defence Forces (Pensions) (Amendment) (No.4) Scheme, S.I. No. 215 of 1969
		Defence Forces (Pensions) (Amendment) (No.5) Scheme, S.I. No. 247 of 1969
		Defence Forces (Pensions) (Amendment) Scheme, S.I. No. 143 of 1970
		Defence Forces (Pensions) (Amendment) (No.3) Scheme, S.I. No. 298 of 1970
		Defence Forces (Pensions) (Amendment) Scheme, S.I. No. 50 of 1971
		Defence Forces (Pensions) (Amendment) (No.2) Scheme, S.I. No. 52 of 1971
		Defence Forces (Pensions) (Amendment) Scheme, S.I. No. 100 of 1972
		Defence Forces (Pensions) (Amendment) (No.2) Scheme, S.I. No. 216 of 1972
		Defence Forces (Pensions) (Amendment) (No.3) Scheme, S.I. No. 306 of 1972
		Defence Forces (Pensions) (Amendment) Scheme, S.I. No. 57 of 1973
		Defence Forces (Pensions) (Amendment) (No.2) Scheme, S.I. No. 205 of 1973
		Defence Forces (Pensions) (Amendment) (No.3) Scheme, S.I. No. 295 of 1973
		Defence Forces (Pensions) (Amendment) Scheme, S.I. No. 131 of 1974
		Defence Forces (Pensions) (Amendment) (No.2) Scheme, S.I. No. 223 of 1974

Statutory Authority	Section	Statutory Instrument

Defence Forces (Pensions) Act,
No. 26 of 1932 (*Cont.*)

Defence Forces (Pensions) (Amendment) (No.3) Scheme, S.I. No. 231 of 1974

Defence Forces (Pensions) (Amendment) (No.4) Scheme, S.I. No. 236 of 1974

Defence Forces (Pensions) (Amendment) (No.5) Scheme, S.I. No. 314 of 1974

Defence Forces (Pensions) (Amendment) Scheme, S.I. No. 145 of 1975

Defence Forces (Pensions) (Amendment) (No.2) Scheme, S.I. No. 171 of 1975

Defence Forces (Pensions) (Amendment) (No.3) Scheme, S.I. No. 172 of 1975

Defence Forces (Pensions) (Amendment) (No.4) Scheme, S.I. No. 309 of 1975

Defence Forces (Pensions) (Amendment) Scheme, S.I. No. 218 of 1977

Defence Forces (Pensions) (Amendment) (No.2) Scheme, S.I. No. 283 of 1977

Defence Forces (Pensions) (Amendment) Scheme, S.I. No. 246 of 1978

Defence Forces (Pensions) (Amendment) (No.2) Scheme, S.I. No. 274 of 1978

Defence Forces (Pensions) (Amendment) (No.3) Scheme, S.I. No. 379 of 1978

Defence Forces (Pensions) (Amendment) Scheme, S.I. No. 208 of 1979

Defence Forces (Pensions) (Amendment) (No.2) Scheme, S.I. No. 245 of 1979

Defence Forces (Pensions) (Amendment) (No.3) Scheme, S.I. No. 343 of 1979

Defence Forces (Pensions) (Amendment) (No.4) Scheme, S.I. No. 398 of 1979

Defence Forces (Pensions) (Amendment) (No.5) Scheme, S.I. No. 399 of 1979

Defence Forces (Pensions) (Amendment) Scheme, S.I. No. 266 of 1980

Defence Forces (Pensions) (Amendment) (No.2) Scheme, S.I. No. 366 of 1980

Defence Forces (Pensions) (Amendment) Scheme, S.I. No. 174 of 1981

Defence Forces (Pensions) (Amendment) (No.2) Scheme, S.I. No. 362 of 1981

Defence Forces (Pensions) (Amendment) Scheme, S.I. No. 137 of 1982

Defence Forces (Pensions) (Amendment) (No.2) Scheme, S.I. No. 229 of 1982

Defence Forces (Pensions) (Amendment) (No.3) Scheme, S.I. No. 247 of 1982

Defence Forces (Pensions) (Amendment) (No.4) Scheme, S.I. No. 337 of 1982

Defence Forces (Pensions) (Amendment) Scheme, S.I. No. 124 of 1983

Defence Forces (Pensions) Act,
No. 26 of 1932 (*Cont.*)

Defence Forces (Pensions) (Amendment) (No.2) Scheme, S.I. No. 190 of 1983

Defence Forces (Pensions) (Amendment) (No.3) scheme, S.I. No. 214 of 1983

Defence Forces (Pensions) (Amendment) Scheme, S.I. No. 55 of 1984

Defence Forces (Pensions) (Amendment) (No.2) Scheme, S.I. No. 56 of 1984

Defence Forces (Pensions) (Amendment) (No.3) Scheme, S.I. No. 113 of 1984

Defence Forces (Pensions) (Amendment) (No.4) Scheme, S.I. No. 114 of 1984

Defence Forces (Pensions) (Amendment) (No.5) Scheme, S.I. No. 172 of 1984

Defence Forces (Pensions) (Amendment) (No.6) Scheme, S.I. No. 173 of 1984

Defence Forces (Pensions) (Amendment) (No.7) Scheme, S.I. No. 235 of 1984

Defence Forces (Pensions) (Amendment) (No.8) Scheme, S.I. No. 259 of 1984

Defence Forces (Pensions) (Amendment) Scheme, S.I. No. 48 of 1985

Defence Forces (Pensions) (Amendment) (No.2) Scheme, S.I. No. 221 of 1985

Defence Forces (Pensions) (Amendment) (No.3) Scheme, S.I. No. 270 of 1985

Defence Forces (Pensions) (Amendment) (No.4) Scheme, S.I. No. 300 of 1985

Defence Forces (Pensions) (Amendment) (No.5) Scheme, S.I. No. 307 of 1985

Defence Forces (Pensions) (Amendment) (No.6) Scheme, S.I. No. 360 of 1985

Defence Forces (Pensions) (Amendment) (No.7) Scheme, S.I. No. 409 of 1985

Defence Forces (Pensions) (Amendment) Scheme, S.I. No. 60 of 1986

5   Defence Forces (Pensions) (Amendment) Scheme [Vol. XXVIII p. 909] S.R.& O. No. 299 of 1940

Defence Forces (Pensions) (Amendment) Scheme, S.I. No. 35 of 1956

Defence Forces (Pensions) (Amendment) Scheme, S.I. No. 152 of 1957

Defence Forces (Pensions) (Amendment) (No.2) Scheme, S.I. No. 194 of 1957

Defence Forces (Pensions) (Amendment) Scheme, S.I. No. 66 of 1959

Defence Forces (Pensions) (Amendment) Scheme, S.I. No. 135 of 1960

Defence Forces (Pensions) (Amendment) Scheme, S.I. No. 42 of 1962

Defence Forces (Pensions) (Amendment) (No.2) Scheme, S.I. No. 126 of 1962

Statutory Authority	Section	Statutory Instrument
Defence Forces (Pensions) Act, No. 26 of 1932 (*Cont.*)		Defence Forces (Pensions) (Amendment) (No.3) Scheme, S.I. No. 204 of 1962
		Defence Forces (Pensions) (Amendment) Scheme, S.I. No. 247 of 1964
		Defence Forces (Pensions) (Amendment) Scheme, S.I. No. 154 of 1965
		Defence Forces (Pensions) (Amendment) Scheme, S.I. No. 105 of 1968
		Defence Forces (Pensions) (Amendment) Scheme, S.I. No. 34 of 1969
		Defence Forces (Pensions) (Amendment) Scheme, S.I. No. 63 of 1969
		Defence Forces (Pensions) (Amendment) (No.3) Scheme, S.I. No. 144 of 1969
		Defence Forces (Pensions) (Amendment) (No.4) Scheme, S.I. No. 215 of 1969
		Defence Forces (Pensions) (Amendment) (No.5) Scheme, S.I. No. 247 of 1969
		Defence Forces (Pensions) (Amendment) Scheme, S.I. No. 143 of 1970
		Defence Forces (Pensions) (Amendment) (No.3) Scheme, S.I. No. 298 of 1970
		Defence Forces (Pensions) (Amendment) Scheme, S.I. No. 50 of 1971
		Defence Forces (Pensions) (Amendment) (No.2) Scheme, S.I. No. 52 of 1971
		Defence Forces (Pensions) (Amendment) Scheme, S.I. No. 100 of 1972
		Defence Forces (Pensions) (Amendment) (No.2) Scheme, S.I. No. 216 of 1972
		Defence Forces (Pensions) (Amendment) (No.3) Scheme, S.I. No. 306 of 1972
		Defence Forces (Pensions) (Amendment) Scheme, S.I. No. 57 of 1973
		Defence Forces (Pensions) (Amendment) (No.2) Scheme, S.I. No. 205 of 1973
		Defence Forces (Pensions) (Amendment) (No.3) Scheme, S.I. No. 295 of 1973
		Defence Forces (Pensions) (Amendment) Scheme, S.I. No. 131 of 1974
		Defence Forces (Pensions) (Amendment) (No.2) Scheme, S.I. No. 223 of 1974
		Defence Forces (Pensions) (Amendment) (No.3) Scheme, S.I. No. 231 of 1974
		Defence Forces (Pensions) (Amendment) (No.4) Scheme, S.I. No. 236 of 1974
		Defence Forces (Pensions) (Amendment) (No.5) Scheme, S.I. No. 314 of 1974
		Defence Forces (Pensions) (Amendment) Scheme, S.I. No. 145 of 1975
		Defence Forces (Pensions) (Amendment) (No.2) Scheme, S.I. No. 171 of 1975
		Defence Forces (Pensions) (Amendment) (No.3) Scheme, S.I. No. 172 of 1975

Defence Forces (Pensions) Act,
No. 26 of 1932 (*Cont.*)

Defence Forces (Pensions) (Amendment) (No.4) Scheme, S.I. No. 309 of 1975

Defence Forces (Pensions) (Amendment) Scheme, S.I. No. 218 of 1977

Defence Forces (Pensions) (Amendment) (No.2) Scheme, S.I. No. 283 of 1977

Defence Forces (Pensions) (Amendment) Scheme, S.I. No. 246 of 1978

Defence Forces (Pensions) (Amendment) (No.2) Scheme, S.I. No. 274 of 1978

Defence Forces (Pensions) (Amendment) (No.3) Scheme, S.I. No. 379 of 1978

Defence Forces (Pensions) (Amendment) Scheme, S.I. No. 208 of 1979

Defence Forces (Pensions) (Amendment) (No.2) Scheme, S.I. No. 245 of 1979

Defence Forces (Pensions) (Amendment) (No.3) Scheme, S.I. No. 343 of 1979

Defence Forces (Pensions) (Amendment) (No.4) Scheme, S.I. No. 398 of 1979

Defence Forces (Pensions) (Amendment) (No.5) Scheme, S.I. No. 399 of 1979

Defence Forces (Pensions) (Amendment) Scheme, S.I. No. 266 of 1980

Defence Forces (Pensions) (Amendment) (No.2) Scheme, S.I. No. 366 of 1980

Defence Forces (Pensions) (Amendment) Scheme, S.I. No. 174 of 1981

Defence Forces (Pensions) (Amendment) (No.2) Scheme, S.I. No. 362 of 1981

Defence Forces (Pensions) (Amendment) Scheme, S.I. No. 137 of 1982

Defence Forces (Pensions) (Amendment) (No.2) Scheme, S.I. No. 229 of 1982

Defence Forces (Pensions) (Amendment) (No.3) Scheme, S.I. No. 247 of 1982

Defence Forces (Pensions) (Amendment) (No.4) Scheme, S.I. No. 337 of 1982

Defence Forces (Pensions) (Amendment) Scheme, S.I. No. 124 of 1983

Defence Forces (Pensions) (Amendment) (No.2) Scheme, S.I. No. 190 of 1983

Defence Forces (Pensions) (Amendment) (No.3) scheme, S.I. No. 214 of 1983

Defence Forces (Pensions) (Amendment) Scheme, S.I. No. 55 of 1984

Defence Forces (Pensions) (Amendment) (No.2) Scheme, S.I. No. 56 of 1984

Defence Forces (Pensions) (Amendment) (No.3) Scheme, S.I. No. 113 of 1984

Defence Forces (Pensions) (Amendment) (No.4) Scheme, S.I. No. 114 of 1984

Statutory Authority	Section	Statutory Instrument
Defence Forces (Pensions) Act, No. 26 of 1932 (*Cont.*)		Defence Forces (Pensions) (Amendment) (No.5) Scheme, S.I. No. 172 of 1984
		Defence Forces (Pensions) (Amendment) (No.6) Scheme, S.I. No. 173 of 1984
		Defence Forces (Pensions) (Amendment) (No.7) Scheme, S.I. No. 235 of 1984
		Defence Forces (Pensions) (Amendment) (No.8) Scheme, S.I. No. 259 of 1984
		Defence Forces (Pensions) (Amendment) Scheme, S.I. No. 48 of 1985
		Defence Forces (Pensions) (Amendment) (No.2) Scheme, S.I. No. 221 of 1985
		Defence Forces (Pensions) (Amendment) (No.3) Scheme, S.I. No. 270 of 1985
		Defence Forces (Pensions) (Amendment) (No.4) Scheme, S.I. No. 300 of 1985
		Defence Forces (Pensions) (Amendment) (No.5) Scheme, S.I. No. 307 of 1985
		Defence Forces (Pensions) (Amendment) (No.6) Scheme, S.I. No. 360 of 1985
		Defence Forces (Pensions) (Amendment) (No.7) Scheme, S.I. No. 409 of 1985
		Defence Forces (Pensions) (Amendment) Scheme, S.I. No. 60 of 1986
Defence Forces (Pensions) Acts, 1932 and 1938,		Defence Forces (Pensions) (Amendment) Scheme [Vol. XXXVI p. 29] S.R.& O. No. 81 of 1947
Defence Forces (Pensions) Acts, 1932 to 1949,		Defence Forces (Pensions) (Amendment) Scheme, S.I. No. 209 of 1949
		Defence Forces (Pensions) (Amendment) (No.2) Scheme, S.I. No. 291 of 1949
		Defence Forces (Pensions) (Amendment) Scheme, S.I. No. 259 of 1953
Defence Forces (Pensions) (Amendment) Act, No. 33 of 1938	4	Defence Forces (Pensions) (Amendment) Scheme, S.I. No. 35 of 1956
		Defence Forces (Pensions) (Amendment) Scheme, S.I. No. 152 of 1957
		Defence Forces (Pensions) (Amendment) (No.2) Scheme, S.I. No. 194 of 1957
		Defence Forces (Pensions) (Amendment) Scheme, S.I. No. 66 of 1959
		Defence Forces (Pensions) (Amendment) Scheme, S.I. No. 135 of 1960
		Defence Forces (Pensions) (Amendment) Scheme, S.I. No. 42 of 1962
		Defence Forces (Pensions) (Amendment) (No.2) Scheme, S.I. No. 126 of 1962
		Defence Forces (Pensions) (Amendment) (No.3) Scheme, S.I. No. 204 of 1962

Statutory Authority	Section	Statutory Instrument
Defence Forces (Pensions) (Amendment) Act, No. 33 of 1938 (*Cont.*)		Defence Forces (Pensions) (Amendment) Scheme, S.I. No. 247 of 1964
		Defence Forces (Pensions) (Amendment) Scheme, S.I. No. 154 of 1965
		Defence Forces (Pensions) (Amendment) Scheme, S.I. No. 105 of 1968
		Defence Forces (Pensions) (Amendment) Scheme, S.I. No. 34 of 1969
		Defence Forces (Pensions) (Amendment) (No.2) Scheme, S.I. No. 63 of 1969
		Defence Forces (Pensions) (Amendment) (No.3) Scheme, S.I. No. 144 of 1969
		Defence Forces (Pensions) (Amendment) (No.4) Scheme, S.I. No. 215 of 1969
		Defence Forces (Pensions) (Amendment) (No.5) Scheme, S.I. No. 247 of 1969
		Defence Forces (Pensions) (Amendment) Scheme, S.I. No. 143 of 1970
		Defence Forces (Pensions) (Amendment) Scheme, S.I. No. 50 of 1971
		Defence Forces (Pensions) (Amendment) (No.2) Scheme, S.I. No. 52 of 1971
		Defence Forces (Pensions) (Amendment) Scheme, S.I. No. 100 of 1972
		Defence Forces (Pensions) (Amendment) (No.2) Scheme, S.I. No. 216 of 1972
		Defence Forces (Pensions) (Amendment) (No.3) Scheme, S.I. No. 306 of 1972
		Defence Forces (Pensions) (Amendment) Scheme, S.I. No. 57 of 1973
		Defence Forces (Pensions) (Amendment) (No.2) Scheme, S.I. No. 205 of 1973
		Defence Forces (Pensions) (Amendment) Scheme, S.I. No. 131 of 1974
		Defence Forces (Pensions) (Amendment) (No.2) Scheme, S.I. No. 223 of 1974
		Defence Forces (Pensions) (Amendment) (No.3) Scheme, S.I. No. 231 of 1974
		Defence Forces (Pensions) (Amendment) (No.4) Scheme, S.I. No. 236 of 1974
		Defence Forces (Pensions) (Amendment) Scheme, S.I. No. 145 of 1975
		Defence Forces (Pensions) (Amendment) (No.2) Scheme, S.I. No. 171 of 1975
		Defence Forces (Pensions) (Amendment) (No.3) Scheme, S.I. No. 172 of 1975
		Defence Forces (Pensions) (Amendment) (No.4) Scheme, S.I. No. 309 of 1975
		Defence Forces (Pensions) (Amendment) Scheme, S.I. No. 218 of 1977
		Defence Forces (Pensions) (Amendment) (No.2) Scheme, S.I. No. 283 of 1977

Statutory Authority	Section	Statutory Instrument
Defence Forces (Pensions) (Amendment) Act, No. 33 of 1938 (*Cont.*)		**Defence Forces (Pensions) (Amendment) Scheme, S.I. No. 246 of 1978**
		Defence Forces (Pensions) (Amendment) (No.2) Scheme, S.I. No. 274 of 1978
		Defence Forces (Pensions) (Amendment) (No.3) Scheme, S.I. No. 379 of 1978
		Defence Forces (Pensions) (Amendment) Scheme, S.I. No. 208 of 1979
		Defence Forces (Pensions) (Amendment) (No.2) Scheme, S.I. No. 245 of 1979
		Defence Forces (Pensions) (Amendment) (No.4) Scheme, S.I. No. 398 of 1979
		Defence Forces (Pensions) (Amendment) (No.5) Scheme, S.I. No. 399 of 1979
		Defence Forces (Pensions) (Amendment) Scheme, S.I. No. 266 of 1980
		Defence Forces (Pensions) (Amendment) (No.2) Scheme, S.I. No. 366 of 1980
		Defence Forces (Pensions) (Amendment) Scheme, S.I. No. 174 of 1981
		Defence Forces (Pensions) (Amendment) (No.2) Scheme, S.I. No. 362 of 1981
		Defence Forces (Pensions) (Amendment) Scheme, S.I. No. 137 of 1982
		Defence Forces (Pensions) (Amendment) (No.2) Scheme, S.I. No. 229 of 1982
		Defence Forces (Pensions) (Amendment) (No.3) Scheme, S.I. No. 247 of 1982
		Defence Forces (Pensions) (Amendment) (No.4) Scheme, S.I. No. 337 of 1982
		Defence Forces (Pensions) (Amendment) Scheme, S.I. No. 124 of 1983
		Defence Forces (Pensions) (Amendment) (No.2) Scheme, S.I. No. 190 of 1983
		Defence Forces (Pensions) (Amendment) (No.3) scheme, S.I. No. 214 of 1983
		Defence Forces (Pensions) (Amendment) Scheme, S.I. No. 55 of 1984
		Defence Forces (Pensions) (Amendment) (No.2) Scheme, S.I. No. 56 of 1984
		Defence Forces (Pensions) (Amendment) (No.3) Scheme, S.I. No. 113 of 1984
		Defence Forces (Pensions) (Amendment) (No.4) Scheme, S.I. No. 114 of 1984
		Defence Forces (Pensions) (Amendment) (No.5) Scheme, S.I. No. 172 of 1984
		Defence Forces (Pensions) (Amendment) (No.6) Scheme, S.I. No. 173 of 1984
		Defence Forces (Pensions) (Amendment) (No.7) Scheme, S.I. No. 235 of 1984
		Defence Forces (Pensions) (Amendment) (No.8) Scheme, S.I. No. 259 of 1984

Statutory Authority	Section	Statutory Instrument

Defence Forces (Pensions)
(Amendment) Act, No. 33 of 1938
(*Cont.*)

Defence Forces (Pensions) (Amendment) Scheme, S.I. No. 48 of 1985

Defence Forces (Pensions) (Amendment) (No.2) Scheme, S.I. No. 221 of 1985

Defence Forces (Pensions) (Amendment) (No.3) Scheme, S.I. No. 270 of 1985

Defence Forces (Pensions) (Amendment) (No.4) Scheme, S.I. No. 300 of 1985

Defence Forces (Pensions) (Amendment) (No.5) Scheme, S.I. No. 307 of 1985

Defence Forces (Pensions) (Amendment) (No.6) Scheme, S.I. No. 360 of 1985

Defence Forces (Pensions) (Amendment) (No.7) Scheme, S.I. No. 409 of 1985

Defence Forces (Pensions) (Amendment) Scheme, S.I. No. 60 of 1986

Defence Forces (Temporary
Provisions) Act, No. 30 of 1923

Defence Forces (Requisitions of Emergency) Order, 1940 (Revocation) Order [Vol. XXXVI p. 63] S.R.& O. No. 283 of 1946

125 *Defence Forces Rules of Procedure [Vol. XXXVI p. 67] S.R.& O. No. 35 of 1946*

Rules of Procedure (Defence Forces) S.I. No. 112 of 1949

173(1) *Defence Forces (Billeting Requisitions) Order [Vol. XXVIII p. 925] S.R.& O. No. 223 of 1939*

Defence Forces (Billeting Requisitions) Order [Vol. XXVIII p. 929] S.R.& O. No. 104 of 1940

180(1) *Defence Forces (Requisitions of Emergency) Order [Vol. XXVIII p. 935] S.R.& O. No. 222 of 1939*

Defence Forces (Requisitions of Emergency) Order [Vol. XXVIII p. 941] S.R.& O. No. 103 of 1940

Defence Forces (Temporary
Provisions) (No.2) Act, No. 11 of
1940

4(1) *Defence Forces (Temporary Provisions) (No.2) Act, 1940 (State of Emergency) Order [Vol. XXVIII p. 975] S.R.& O. No. 163 of 1940*

4(2) *Defence Forces (Temporary Provisions) (No.2) Act, 1940 (State of Emergency) Order, 1940 (Revocation) Order [Vol. XXXVI p. 125] S.R.& O. No. 284 of 1946*

12 *Defence Forces (Billeting during a Period of Emergency) Regulations [Vol. XXVIII p. 947] S.R.& O. No. 267 of 1940*

Defence Forces (Billeting during a Period of Emergency) (Amendment) Regulations [Vol. XXVIII p. 965] S.R.& O. No. 79 of 1941

Defence Forces (Billeting during a Period of Emergency) (Amendment) (No.2) Regulations [Vol. XXVIII p. 971] S.R.& O. No. 194 of 1941

Statutory Authority	Section	Statutory Instrument
Defence Forces (Temporary Provisions) (No.2) Act, No. 11 of 1940 (*Cont.*)		*Defence Forces (Billeting during a Period of Emergency) Regulations, 1940 and 1941 (Revocation) Regulations [Vol. XXXVII p. 121] S.R. & O. No. 282 of 1946*
Dentists Act, No. 9 of 1985	3	*Dentists Act, 1985 (Commencement) Order, S.I. No. 149 of 1985*
		Dentists Act, 1985 (Commencement) (No.2) Order, S.I. No. 352 of 1985
	4	*Dentists Act, 1985 (Establishment Day) Order, S.I. No. 351 of 1985*
	11	**Dental Council (Election of Members) Regulations, S.I. No. 150 of 1985**
	63	**Dental Council (Election of Members) Regulations, S.I. No. 150 of 1985**
Derelict Sites Act, No. 3 of 1961	19	**Derelict Sites Act, 1961 Regulations, S.I. No. 105 of 1961**
	24(2)	*Derelict Sites Act, 1961 (Commencement) Order, S.I. No. 103 of 1961*
Destructive Insects Act, No. 68 of 1877	2	**Beet Eelworm Order, S.I. No. 313 of 1956**
Destructive Insects and Pests Act, No. 4 of 1907	1	**Beet Eelworm Order, S.I. No. 313 of 1956**
Destructive Insects and Pests Act, No. 7 of 1929	3	**Beet Eelworm Order, S.I. No. 313 of 1956**
Destructive Insects and Pests Acts, 1877 to 1929,		**Black Scab in Potatoes (Special Area) Order [Vol. XXVIII p. 979] S.R.& O. No. 36 of 1945**
		Colorado Beetle Order [Vol. XXV p. 83] S.R.& O. No. 228 of 1945
		Importation of Strawberry Plants and Blackcurrant and Gooseberry Bushes Order [Vol. XXXVII p. 133] S.R.& O. No. 358 of 1946
		Sale of Diseased Plants (Ireland) Order, 1922 (Second Amendment) Order [Vol. XXXVII p. 141] S.R.& O. No. 359 of 1946
		Black Scab in Potatoes (Special Area) Order, 1933 (Amendment) Order, S.I. No. 375 of 1948
		Importation of Forest Trees (Prohibition) Order, S.I. No. 292 of 1949
		Potato Root Eelworm Order, S.I. No. 372 of 1951
		Importation of Forest Trees (Prohibition) Order, 1949 (Amendment) Order, S.I. No. 371 of 1952
Destructive Insects and Pests (Consolidation) Act, No. 11 of 1958	2	**Colorado Beetle Order, S.I. No. 3 of 1962**

Statutory Authority	Section	Statutory Instrument
Destructive Insects and Pests (Consolidation) Act, No. 11 of 1958 (*Cont.*)		*Importation of Unbarked Coniferous Timber (Prohibition) Order, S.I. No. 5 of 1962*
		Stem and Bulb Eelworm Order, S.I. No. 2 of 1966
	3	**Fire Blight Disease Order, S.I. No. 19 of 1964**
		Hop Plant Diseases Order, S.I. No. 188 of 1965
		Sale of Diseased Plants (Ireland) Order, 1922 (Third Amendment) Order, S.I. No. 1 of 1966
		Stem and Bulb Eelworm Order, S.I. No. 2 of 1966
		Destructive Insects and Pests (Ireland) Order, 1922 (Amendment) Order, S.I. No. 227 of 1985
Diplomatic and Consular Fees Act, No. 31 of 1939		*Diplomatic and Consular Fees Regulations, S.I. No. 263 of 1956*
	2	*Diplomatic and Consular Fees (No.1) Regulations [Vol. XXVIII p. 997] S.R.& O. No. 224 of 1943*
		Diplomatic and Consular Fees (No.2) Regulations [Vol. XXVIII p. 1007] S.R.& O. No. 283 of 1943
		Diplomatic and Consular Fees (Amendment) Regulations [Vol. XXXVI p. 129] S.R.& O. No. 48 of 1946
		Diplomatic and Consular Fees (Amendment) r, S.I. No. 153 of 1950
		Diplomatic and Consular Fees (Amendment) Regulations, S.I. No. 205 of 1951
		Diplomatic and Consular Fees (Amendment) Regulations, S.I. No. 334 of 1974
		Diplomatic and Consular Fees (Amendment) Regulations, S.I. No. 268 of 1975
		Diplomatic and Consular Fees (Amendment) Regulations, S.I. No. 272 of 1976
		Diplomatic and Consular Fees (Amendment) Regulations, S.I. No. 95 of 1980
		Diplomatic and Consular Fees (Amendment) Regulations, S.I. No. 260 of 1981
		Diplomatic and Consular Fees (Amendment) Regulations, S.I. No. 6 of 1982
		Diplomatic and Consular Fees Regulations, S.I. No. 344 of 1982
		Diplomatic and Consular Fees (Amendment) Regulations, S.I. No. 14 of 1983
		Diplomatic and Consular Fees (Amendment) (No.2) Regulations, S.I. No. 43 of 1983
		Diplomatic and Consular Fees (Amendment) Regulations, S.I. No. 44 of 1984
		Diplomatic and Consular Fees (Amendment) (No.2) Regulations, S.I. No. 242 of 1984

Statutory Authority	Section	Statutory Instrument
Diplomatic Relations and Immunities Act, No. 8 of 1967	18	**Diplomatic Relations and Immunities Act (Section 18) Order, S.I. No. 255 of 1968**
	40	**International Atomic Energy Agency (Designation and Immunities) Order, S.I. No. 26 of 1972**
		Intelsat (Designation of Organisation and Immunities of Organisation and its Officers and Employees) Order, S.I. No. 39 of 1972
		International Tin Council (Designation) Order, S.I. No. 178 of 1973
		European University Institute (Designation of Organisation and Immunities of Organisation and its Offices and Servants) Order, S.I. No. 141 of 1974
		International Cocoa Organisation (Designation) Order, S.I. No. 380 of 1974
		International Coffee Organisation (Designation) Order, S.I. No. 79 of 1975
		Financial Support Fund of the Organisation for Economic Co-operation and Development (Designation of Organisation) Order, S.I. No. 275 of 1977
		International Fund for Agricultural Development (Designation of Organisation) Order, S.I. No. 329 of 1977
		European Space Agency (Designation of Organisation) Order, S.I. No. 291 of 1979
		International Tropical Timber Organisation (Designation of Organisation) Order, S.I. No. 276 of 1984
		Intergovernmental Organisation for International Carriage by Rail (OTIF) (Designation of Organisation) Order, S.I. No. 242 of 1986
		Eumetstat (Designation) Order, S.I. No. 290 of 1986
		International Centre for the Study of the Preservation and Restoration of Cultural Property (Designation of Organisation) Order, S.I. No. 370 of 1986
		International Fund for Ireland (Designation and Immunities) Order, S.I. No. 394 of 1986
	40(1)	**International Natural Rubber Organisation (Designation) Order, S.I. No. 274 of 1980**
		International Olive Oil Council (Designation and Immunities) Order, S.I. No. 321 of 1980
		Eurocontrol (Designation and Immunities) Order, S.I. No. 333 of 1980
		International Centre for Settlement of Investment Disputes (Designation and Immunities) Order, S.I. No. 339 of 1980
		Common Fund for Commodities (Designation of Organisation) Order, S.I. No. 235 of 1982

Statutory Authority	Section	Statutory Instrument

Diplomatic Relations and Immunities Act, No. 8 of 1967 (*Cont.*)

International Jute Organisation (Designation) Order, S.I. No. 184 of 1983

42A **ACP-EEC Convention of Lome Privileges and Immunities Order, S.I. No. 34 of 1976**

European Space Agency (Privileges and Immunities) Order, S.I. No. 324 of 1976

Second ACP-EEC Convention of Lome (Privileges and Immunities) Order, S.I. No. 105 of 1980

Intercountry Project for Statistical Computing (Privileges and Immunities) Order, S.I. No. 203 of 1982

ACP-EEC Convention of Lome (Privileges and Immunities) Order, S.I. No. 114 of 1985

43 **Council of Europe (Immunities of Persons participating in Proceedings of European Commission and Court of Human Rights) Order, S.I. No. 216 of 1971**

Diseases of Animals Act, No. 57 of 1894

22 **Anthrax (Counties of Cork, Kerry, Limerick, Tipperary North Riding and Tipperary South Riding (Temporary Provisions)) Order, S.I. No. 26 of 1956**

Live Pigeons (Prohibition of Export) Order, S.I. No. 222 of 1956

Bovine Tuberculosis (Clearance Area) (Sligo) Order, S.I. No. 217 of 1957

Bovine Tuberculosis (General Provisions) Order, S.I. No. 219 of 1957

Anti-Swine Fever Serum and Swine Fever Vaccine (Restriction on Importation) Order, S.I. No. 228 of 1957

Swine Fever (Controlled Area) Order, S.I. No. 255 of 1957

Bovine Tuberculosis (Clearance Area) (No.1) Order, S.I. No. 78 of 1958

Bovine Tuberculosis (14-Day Test) Order, S.I. No. 161 of 1958

Bovine Tuberculosis (Movement Control) (No.1) Order, S.I. No. 170 of 1958

Bovine Tuberculosis (Control of Certain Tests) Order, S.I. No. 102 of 1959

Bovine Tuberculosis (14 Day-Test) (Amendment) Order, S.I. No. 103 of 1959

Bovine Tuberculosis (Control of Public Sales of Cattle) (Counties of Sligo, Clare, Galway, Leitrim, Roscommon, Donegal and Mayo) Order, S.I. No. 110 of 1959

Bovine Tuberculosis (Movement Control) (Cavan and Monaghan) Order, S.I. No. 116 of 1959

Bovine Tuberculosis (Clearance Area) (Cavan and Monaghan) Order, S.I. No. 117 of 1959

Bovine Tuberculosis (Clearance Area) (Limerick) Order, S.I. No. 190 of 1959

Diseases of Animals Act, No. 57 of 1894 (*Cont.*)		*Bovine Tuberculosis (Movement Control) (Limerick) Order, S.I. No. 191 of 1959*
		Shipment of Livestock (Port of Dublin) Order, S.I. No. 221 of 1959
		Bovine Tuberculosis (14-Day Test) (Amendment) Order, S.I. No. 27 of 1960
		Bovine Tuberculosis (Clearance Area) (Longford) Order, S.I. No. 55 of 1960
		Bovine Tuberculosis (Clearance Area) (Westmeath) Order, S.I. No. 56 of 1960
		Bovine Tuberculosis (Movement Control) (Amendment) Order, S.I. No. 57 of 1960
		Bovine Tuberculosis (General Provisions) (Amendment) Order, S.I. No. 136 of 1960
		Bovine Tuberculosis (14-Day Test) Order, S.I. No. 176 of 1960
		Bovine Tuberculosis (Control of Certain Tests) Order, S.I. No. 177 of 1960
		Bovine Tuberculosis (Clearance Area) (Special Controls) Order, S.I. No. 178 of 1960
		Bovine Tuberculosis (Movement Control) Order, S.I. No. 179 of 1960
		Bovine Tuberculosis (Control of Public Sales of Cattle) Order, S.I. No. 180 of 1960
		Bovine Tuberculosis (Clearance Area) (Limerick) Order, S.I. No. 181 of 1960
		Bovine Tuberculosis (Places and Times for Movement into County Donegal) Order, S.I. No. 185 of 1960
		Bovine Tuberculosis (Movement Control) (No.2) Order, S.I. No. 186 of 1960
		Bovine Tuberculosis (Clearance Area) (Special Controls) (Amendment) Order, S.I. No. 218 of 1960
		Horses (Carriage by Sea) Order, S.I. No. 227 of 1960
		Bovine Tuberculosis (Attested Area) Order, S.I. No. 236 of 1960
		Bovine Tuberculosis (Control of Public Sales of Cattle) (No.2) Order, S.I. No. 247 of 1960
		Bovine Tuberculosis (Movement Control) (No.3) Order, S.I. No. 248 of 1960
		Bovine Tuberculosis (Attested Area) (Amendment) Order, S.I. No. 9 of 1961
		Bovine Tuberculosis (Attested Area) (Amendment) (No.2) Order, S.I. No. 17 of 1961
		Bovine Tuberculosis (Attested Area) (Amendment) (No.3) Order, S.I. No. 29 of 1961
		Bovine Tuberculosis (Clearance Area) Order, S.I. No. 38 of 1961
		Bovine Tuberculosis (Control of Movement and Public Sales of Cattle) Order, S.I. No. 39 of 1961

Statutory Authority	Section	Statutory Instrument
Diseases of Animals Act, No. 57 of 1894 (*Cont.*)		*Bovine Tuberculosis (Clearance Area) (Special Controls) Order, S.I. No. 65 of 1961*
		Bovine Tuberculosis (Restrictions on Further Tests) Order, S.I. No. 94 of 1961
		Bovine Tuberculosis (14-Day Test) (Amendment) Order, S.I. No. 125 of 1961
		Bovine Tuberculosis (Control of Certain Tests) (Amendment) Order, S.I. No. 126 of 1961
		Bovine Tuberculosis (Control of Movement and Public Sales of Cattle) (Amendment) Order, S.I. No. 136 of 1961
		Bovine Tuberculosis (Clearance Area) (No.2) Order, S.I. No. 137 of 1961
		Bovine Tuberculosis (Attested Area) (Amendment) (No.4) Order, S.I. No. 156 of 1961
		Bovine Tuberculosis (General Provisions) (Amendment) Order, S.I. No. 159 of 1961
		Bovine Tuberculosis (Movement Control) Order, S.I. No. 169 of 1961
		Bovine Tuberculosis (Attested Area) (Amendment) (No.5) Order, S.I. No. 228 of 1961
		Bovine Tuberculosis (Control of Movement and Public Sales of Cattle) (No.2) Order, S.I. No. 266 of 1961
		Bovine Tuberculosis (Control of Movement and Public Sales of Cattle) (No.2) (Amendment) Order, S.I. No. 43 of 1962
		Bovine Tuberculosis (Clearance Area) Order, S.I. No. 51 of 1962
		Bovine Tuberculosis (Control of Movement and Public Sales of Cattle) Order, S.I. No. 52 of 1962
		Bovine Tuberculosis (Control of Movement and Public Sales of Cattle) (No.2) (Amendment No.2) Order, S.I. No. 86 of 1962
		Bovine Tuberculosis (Clearance Area) (Special Controls) Order, S.I. No. 87 of 1962
		Bovine Tuberculosis (Clearance Area) (No.2) Order, S.I. No. 105 of 1962
		Bovine Tuberculosis (Control of Movement) Order, S.I. No. 106 of 1962
		Bovine Tuberculosis (Control of Movement and Public Sales of Cattle) (Dublin) Order, S.I. No. 150 of 1962
		Bovine Tuberculosis (Clearance Area) (Special Controls) (Amendment) Order, S.I. No. 152 of 1962
		Bovine Tuberculosis (Attested Area) (Amendment) (No.6) Order, S.I. No. 169 of 1962
		Bovine Tuberculosis (Clearance Area) (Special Controls) (Amendment) (No.2) Order, S.I. No. 191 of 1962
		Bovine Tuberculosis (Attested Area) (Amendment) (No.7) Order, S.I. No. 192 of 1962

Statutory Authority	Section	Statutory Instrument
Diseases of Animals Act, No. 57 of 1894 (*Cont.*)		*Bovine Tuberculosis (Special Controls) (Dublin) Order, S.I. No. 193 of 1962*
		Bovine Tuberculosis (Attested Area) (Amendment) (No.8) Order, S.I. No. 201 of 1962
		Bovine Tuberculosis (Attested Area) (Amendment) (No.9) Order, S.I. No. 23 of 1963
		Bovine Tuberculosis (Attested Area) (Amendment) (No.10) Order, S.I. No. 55 of 1963
		Bovine Tuberculosis (30-Day Test) Order, S.I. No. 76 of 1963
		Bovine Tuberculosis (Clearance Area) (Amendment) Order, S.I. No. 109 of 1963
		Bovine Tuberculosis (Control of Movement and Public Sales of Cattle) Order, S.I. No. 110 of 1963
		Importation of Meat and Animal Products Order, S.I. No. 186 of 1963
		Bovine Tuberculosis (General Provisions) (Amendment) Order, S.I. No. 238 of 1963
		Bovine Tuberculosis (Control of Movement) Order, S.I. No. 257 of 1963
		Bovine Tuberculosis (Control of Movement and Public Sales of Cattle) Order, S.I. No. 87 of 1964
		Bovine Tuberculosis (Control of Movement and Public Sales of Cattle) (Amendment) Order, S.I. No. 149 of 1964
		Importation of Meat and Animal Products (Amendment) Order, S.I. No. 197 of 1964
		Bovine Tuberculosis (Clearance Area) (Special Controls) Order, S.I. No. 26 of 1965
		Sheep Dipping Order, S.I. No. 105 of 1965
		Diseases of Animals (Control of Certain Vaccinations and Extension to Brucellosis) Order, S.I. No. 111 of 1965
		Importation of Meat and Animal Products (Amendment) Order, S.I. No. 148 of 1965
		Bovine Tuberculosis (Attestation of the State) Order, S.I. No. 211 of 1965
		Warble Fly Order, S.I. No. 246 of 1965
		Importation of Meat and Animal Products (Amendment) Order, S.I. No. 27 of 1966
		Sheep Dipping Order, 1965 (Amendment) Order, S.I. No. 98 of 1966
	25	**Importation of Wool Order, 1946 (Amendment) Order, S.I. No. 8 of 1960**
	49	*Swine Fever (Controlled Area) Order, S.I. No. 255 of 1957*
		Transit of Animals Order, 1927 (Swine Fever) (Amendment) Order, S.I. No. 65 of 1958
		Swine Fever (Controlled Area) Order, 1957 (Amendment) Order, S.I. No. 234 of 1958
		Swine Fever (Controlled Area) Order, 1957 (Revocation) Order, S.I. No. 45 of 1959

Statutory Authority	Section	Statutory Instrument
Diseases of Animals Act, No. 57 of 1894 (*Cont.*)		*Foot and Mouth Disease (Importation of Animals) Order, 1960 (Revocation) Order, S.I. No. 20 of 1961*
		Foot and Mouth Disease (Importation of Animals) Order, 1961 (Revocation) Order, S.I. No. 100 of 1961
		Shipment of Livestock (Port of Dublin) Order, 1959 (Revocation) Order, S.I. No. 123 of 1961
		Foot and Mouth Disease (Importation of Plants) Order, S.I. No. 4 of 1962
		Diseases of Animals (Licensing of Pig Dealers) Order, 1957 (Revocation) Order, S.I. No. 85 of 1962
		Importation of Meat and Animal Products (Amendment) Order, S.I. No. 197 of 1964
		Live Pigeons (Prohibition of Export) Order, 1956 (Revocation) Order, S.I. No. 232 of 1964
		Importation of Meat and Animal Products (Amendment) Order, S.I. No. 148 of 1965
		Importation of Meat and Animal Products (Amendment) Order, S.I. No. 27 of 1966
Diseases of Animals Act, No. 6 of 1954	2	*Live Pigeons (Prohibition of Export) Order, S.I. No. 222 of 1956*
Diseases of Animals Act, No. 26 of 1960	5(2)	*Diseases of Animals Act, 1960 (Section 5 (1)) (Commencement) Order, S.I. No. 175 of 1960*
Diseases of Animals Act, No. 6 of 1966	1(2)	*Diseases of Animals Act, 1966 (Commencement) Order, S.I. No. 119 of 1966*
		Diseases of Animals Act, 1966 (Section 27) (Commencement) Order, S.I. No. 209 of 1966
		Diseases of Animals Act, 1966 (Section 30) (Commencement) Order, S.I. No. 200 of 1966
		Diseases of Animals Act, 1966 (Section 56) (Commencement) Order, S.I. No. 228 of 1966
		Diseases of Animals Act, 1966 (Section 29) (Commencement) Order, S.I. No. 68 of 1967
		Diseases of Animals Act, 1966 (Section 28) (Commencement) Order, S.I. No. 256 of 1967
		Diseases of Animals Act, 1966 (Section 33) (Commencement) Order, S.I. No. 250 of 1969
		Diseases of Animals Act, 1966 (Commencement) Order, S.I. No. 213 of 1978
	2	*Dogs Order, S.I. No. 229 of 1966*
	3	*Brucellosis in Cattle (Clearance Area) (General Provisions) Order, S.I. No. 120 of 1966*
		Importation of Meat and Animal Products (Amendment) (No.2) Order, S.I. No. 194 of 1966

Statutory Authority	Section	Statutory Instrument

Diseases of Animals Act, No. 6 of 1966 (*Cont.*)

Importation of Carcases and Animal Products (Prohibition) Order, S.I. No. 201 of 1966

Warble Fly Order, S.I. No. 210 of 1966

Brucellosis in Cattle (Declaration of Clearance Area and Movement Control) (Amendment) Order, S.I. No. 249 of 1966

Brucellosis in Cattle (Clearance Area) (General Provisions) (Amendment) Order, S.I. No. 250 of 1966

Warble Fly Order, S.I. No. 6 of 1967

Brucellosis in Cattle (Movement Control) Order, S.I. No. 62 of 1967

Portal Inspection Order, 1924 (Amendment) Order, S.I. No. 69 of 1967

Warble Fly (Notification and Treatment) Order, S.I. No. 216 of 1967

Foot and Mouth Disease (Restriction of Import of Vehicles, Machinery and Other Equipment) Order, S.I. No. 243 of 1967

Importation of Carcases and Animal Products (Prohibition) (Amendment) Order, S.I. No. 246 of 1967

Importation of Wool (Amendment) Order, S.I. No. 247 of 1967

Foot and Mouth Disease (Restriction of Import of Vehicles, Machinery and Other Equipment) (Amendment) Order, S.I. No. 252 of 1967

Foot and Mouth Disease (Restriction of Sports and Sales) Order, S.I. No. 253 of 1967

Foot and Mouth Disease (Restriction of Exhibition and Sale of Bovine Animals) Order, S.I. No. 263 of 1967

Foot and Mouth Disease (Merchant Shipping) Order, S.I. No. 264 of 1967

Foot and Mouth Disease (Restriction on the Movement of Persons) Order, S.I. No. 266 of 1967

Foot and Mouth Disease (Restriction of Import of Vehicles, Machinery and Other Equipment) (Amendment) (No.2) Order, S.I. No. 267 of 1967

Foot and Mouth Disease (Regulation of Movement of Persons) Order, S.I. No. 271 of 1967

Foot and Mouth Disease (Restriction on the Movement of Persons) (Amendment) Order, S.I. No. 276 of 1967

Foot and Mouth Disease (Restriction of Sports and Sales) (Amendment) Order, S.I. No. 277 of 1967

Foot and Mouth Disease (Importation of Animals) (Amendment) Order, S.I. No. 282 of 1967

Diseases of Animals Act, No. 6 of 1966 (*Cont.*)

Diseases of Animals (Restriction of Movement of Cattle, Sheep and Swine) Order, S.I. No. 283 of 1967

Foot and Mouth Disease (Restriction of Entry of Persons into the State) Order, S.I. No. 287 of 1967

Foot and Mouth Disease (Restriction of Exhibition and Sale of Sheep and Pigs) Order, S.I. No. 295 of 1967

Foot and Mouth Disease (Restriction of Exhibition and Sale of Bovine Animals) (Amendment) Order, S.I. No. 296 of 1967

Foot and Mouth Disease Order, 1956 (Amendment) Order, S.I. No. 297 of 1967

Foot and Mouth Disease (Merchant Shipping) (Amendment) Order, S.I. No. 298 of 1967

Foot and Mouth Disease Order, 1956 (Amendment) (No.2) Order, S.I. No. 310 of 1967

Foot and Mouth Disease (Restriction on the Movement of Persons) Order, S.I. No. 25 of 1968

Foot and Mouth Disease (Restriction of Sports and Sales) Order, S.I. No. 30 of 1968

Foot and Mouth Disease (Restriction of Sports and Sales) (No.2) Order, S.I. No. 37 of 1968

Foot and Mouth Disease (Merchant Shipping) Order, S.I. No. 43 of 1968

Brucellosis in Cattle (Clearance Area) (General Provisions) (Amendment) Order, S.I. No. 44 of 1968

Brucellosis in Cattle (Movement Control) (Amendment) Order, S.I. No. 45 of 1968

Foot and Mouth Disease (Miscellaneous Orders) and Diseases of Animals (Restriction of Movement of Cattle, Sheep and Swine) Order, 1967 (Revocation) Order, S.I. No. 49 of 1968

Foot and Mouth Disease (Restriction on the Movement of Persons) Order (Amendment) Order, S.I. No. 59 of 1968

Foot and Mouth Disease (Restriction of Import of Vehicles, Machinery and other Equipment) Order (Revocation) Order, S.I. No. 60 of 1968

Foot and Mouth Disease (Restriction of Sports and Sales) Order (Revocation) Order, S.I. No. 61 of 1968

Foot and Mouth Disease (Merchant Shipping) Orders, (Revocation) Order, S.I. No. 62 of 1968

Foot and Mouth Disease Order, 1956 (Amendment) Order, S.I. No. 69 of 1968

Foot and Mouth Disease (Restriction of Entry of Persons into the State Order) (Revocation) Order, S.I. No. 78 of 1968

Foot and Mouth Disease (Restriction on the Movement of Persons) (No.2) Order, S.I. No. 79 of 1968

Diseases of Animals Act, No. 6 of
1966 (*Cont.*)

*Brucellosis in Cattle (Disease-Free Area) Order, S.I.
No. 112 of 1968*

Brucellosis in Cattle (Movement Control) (Amendment) (No.2) Order, S.I. No. 113 of 1968

*Foot and Mouth Disease (Importation of Animals)
Order (Revocation) Order, S.I. No. 149 of 1968*

*Brucellosis in Cattle (Control of Vaccination) Order,
S.I. No. 160 of 1968*

*Bovine Tuberculosis Order, 1926 (Revocation)
Order, S.I. No. 161 of 1968*

**Importation of Wool and Importation of Carcases
and Animal Products (Prohibition) Orders
(Amendment) Order, S.I. No. 165 of 1968**

Fowl Pest (Amendment) Order, S.I. No. 230 of 1968

*Brucellosis in Cattle (Clearance Area) (General
Provisions) (Amendment) Order, S.I. No. 20 of
1969*

Brucellosis in Cattle (Disease-Free Area) (Amendment) Order, S.I. No. 21 of 1969

*Brucellosis in Cattle (Movement Control) Order,
S.I. No. 22 of 1969*

*Importation of Dogs and Cats Order of 1929
(Amendment) Order, S.I. No. 204 of 1969*

*Importation of Dogs and Cats Order of 1929
(Amendment) (No.2) Order, S.I. No. 220 of 1969*

*Sheep Dipping (Tests of Dips) (Fees) Order, S.I.
No. 245 of 1969*

*Rabies (Importation and Landing of Animals)
Order, S.I. No. 248 of 1969*

**Importation of Dogs and Cats (Amendment) Order,
S.I. No. 249 of 1969**

Brucellosis in Cattle (Disease-Free Area) (Amendment) Order, S.I. No. 29 of 1970

**Importation of Dogs and Cats (Amendment) Order,
S.I. No. 65 of 1970**

Brucellosis in Cattle (Disease-Free Area) (Amendment) (No.2) Order, S.I. No. 82 of 1970

*Brucellosis in Cattle (Declaration of Clearance
Areas) Order, S.I. No. 134 of 1970*

*Brucellosis in Cattle (Movement Control) Order,
S.I. No. 135 of 1970*

*Brucellosis in Cattle (Clearance Area) (General
Provisions) (Amendment) Order, S.I. No. 136 of
1970*

*Brucellosis in Cattle (Declaration of Clearance
Areas) (Amendment) Order, S.I. No. 198 of 1970*

Brucellosis in Cattle (Movement Control) (Amendment) Order, S.I. No. 199 of 1970

**Importation of Dogs and Cats (Amendment) (No.2)
Order, S.I. No. 203 of 1970**

*Brucellosis in Cattle (Declaration of Clearance
Areas) (No.2) Order, S.I. No. 247 of 1970*

Statutory Authority	Section	Statutory Instrument

Diseases of Animals Act, No. 6 of 1966 *(Cont.)*

Brucellosis in Cattle (Movement Control) (Amendment) (No.2) Order, S.I. No. 248 of 1970

Importation of Dogs and Cats (Amendment) (No.3) Order, S.I. No. 280 of 1970

Importation of Livestock Order, S.I. No. 296 of 1970

Foreign Animals Order of 1931 (Amendment) Ordcr, S.I. No. 297 of 1970

Brucellosis in Cattle (Movement Control) (Amendment) Order, S.I. No. 10 of 1971

Brucellosis in Cattle (Declaration of Clearance Areas) Order, S.I. No. 11 of 1971

Brucellosis in Cattle (Movement Control) (Amendment) (No.2) Order, S.I. No. 65 of 1971

Brucellosis in Cattle (Declaration of Clearance Areas) (No.2) Order, S.I. No. 66 of 1971

Diseases of Animals Act, 1966 (First Schedule) (Amendment) Order, S.I. No. 137 of 1971

Live Pigeons (Prohibition of Export) Order, S.I. No. 138 of 1971

Poultry, Poultry Carcases, Poultry Eggs and Poultry Products (Restriction on Importation) Order, S.I. No. 139 of 1971

Importation of Fowl Pest Vaccine (Prohibition) Order, S.I. No. 140 of 1971

Brucellosis in Cattle (Movement Control) (Supplementary Provisions) Order, S.I. No. 176 of 1971

Warble Fly Order, S.I. No. 297 of 1971

Brucellosis in Cattle (Movement Control) (Supplementary Provisions) (Amendment) Order, S.I. No. 326 of 1971

Rabies (Importation, Landing and Movement of Animals) Order, S.I. No. 16 of 1972

Brucellosis in Cattle (Disease-Free Area) (Amendment) Order, S.I. No. 120 of 1972

Brucellosis in Cattle (Movement Control) (Supplementary Provisions) (Amendment) Order, S.I. No. 121 of 1972

Importation of Animal Semen (Prohibition) Order, S.I. No. 299 of 1972

Swine Vesicular Disease Order, S.I. No. 340 of 1972

Diseases of Animals Act, 1966 (First Schedule) (Amendment) Order, S.I. No. 343 of 1972

Transit of Animals (Amendment) Order, S.I. No. 11 of 1973

Brucellosis in Cattle (Declaration of Clearance Areas) Order, S.I. No. 131 of 1973

Brucellosis in Cattle (Movement Control) Order, S.I. No. 132 of 1973

Brucellosis in Cattle (Disease-Free Area) (Amendment) Order, S.I. No. 133 of 1973

Statutory Authority	Section	Statutory Instrument
Diseases of Animals Act, No. 6 of 1966 (*Cont.*)		*Brucellosis in Cattle (Movement Control) (Supplementary Provisions) (Amendment) Order, S.I. No. 134 of 1973*
		Brucellosis in Cattle (Clearance Area) (General Provisions) (Amendment) Order, S.I. No. 135 of 1973
		Warble Fly (Amendment) Order, S.I. No. 215 of 1973
		Transit of Animals (General) Order, S.I. No. 292 of 1973
		Diseases of Animals (Notification of Infectious Diseases) Order, S.I. No. 189 of 1975
		Diseases of Animals Act, 1966 (First Schedule) (Amendment) Order, S.I. No. 190 of 1975
		Warble Fly (Notification and Treatment) Order, S.I. No. 267 of 1975
		Diseases of Animals (Disinfectants) Order, S.I. No. 273 of 1975
		Rabies Order, S.I. No. 94 of 1976
		Rabies (Importation, Landing and Movement of Animals) (Amendment) Order, S.I. No. 95 of 1976
		Sheep Dipping Order, 1965 (Amendment) Order, S.I. No. 107 of 1976
		Brucellosis in Cattle (Movement Control) (Amendment) Order, S.I. No. 281 of 1976
		Brucellosis in Cattle (Declaration of Clearance Area) Order, S.I. No. 282 of 1976
		Warble Fly (Notification and Treatment) (Amendment) Order, S.I. No. 10 of 1977
		Sheep Dipping Order, 1965 (Amendment) Order, S.I. No. 158 of 1977
		Diseases of Animals Act, 1966 (First Schedule) (Amendment) Order, S.I. No. 326 of 1977
		Diseases of Animals (Bovine Leukosis) Order, S.I. No. 327 of 1977
		Brucellosis in Cattle (Movement Control) (Amendment) Order, S.I. No. 166 of 1978
		Brucellosis in Cattle (Declaration of Clearance Area) Order, S.I. No. 167 of 1978
		Warble Fly Order, S.I. No. 231 of 1978
		Brucellosis in Cattle (Movement Control) Order, S.I. No. 251 of 1978
		Brucellosis in Cattle (Movement Control) (No.2) Order, S.I. No. 252 of 1978
		Brucellosis in Cattle (Notification and Movement Control) Order, S.I. No. 253 of 1978
		Bovine Tuberculosis (Attestation of the State and General Provisions) Order, S.I. No. 256 of 1978
		Brucellosis in Cattle (General Provisions) Order, S.I. No. 251 of 1979
		Brucellosis in Cattle (Movement Control) (Amendment) Order, S.I. No. 252 of 1979

Statutory Authority	Section	Statutory Instrument

Diseases of Animals Act, No. 6 of
966 (*Cont.*)

*Brucellosis in Cattle (Declaration of Clearance Area)
Order, S.I. No. 253 of 1979*

Brucellosis in Cattle (Movement Control) (Amendment) (No.2) Order, S.I. No. 349 of 1979

**Portal Inspection Order, 1924 (Amendment) Order,
S.I. No. 155 of 1980**

**Diseases of Animals Act, 1966 (First Schedule)
(Amendment) Order, S.I. No. 165 of 1980**

Importation of Aujeszky's Disease Vaccine (Prohibition) Order, S.I. No. 166 of 1980

*Brucellosis in Cattle Orders (Amendment) Order,
S.I. No. 189 of 1980*

**Brucellosis in Cattle (General Provisions) Order,
S.I. No. 286 of 1980**

Warble Fly Order, S.I. No. 327 of 1980

Warble Fly Order, S.I. No. 338 of 1981

Brucellosis in Cattle (General Provisions) (Amendment) Order, S.I. No. 369 of 1981

**Sheep Dipping (Tests of Dips) (Fees) Order, S.I.
No. 438 of 1981**

Transit of Animals Order, S.I. No. 120 of 1982

**Bovine Tuberculosis (Attestation of the State and
General Provisions) (Amendment) Order, S.I.
No. 176 of 1982**

**Foot and Mouth Disease (Hay, Straw and Moss
Litter) Order, S.I. No. 201 of 1982**

Brucellosis in Cattle (General Provisions) (Amendment) Order, S.I. No. 306 of 1982

Brucellosis in Cattle (General Provisions) (Amendment) (No.2) Order, S.I. No. 312 of 1982

Brucellosis in Cattle (General Provisions) (Amendment) (No.3) Order, S.I. No. 336 of 1982

*Transit of Animals (No.2) Order, S.I. No. 385 of
1982*

**Bovine Tuberculosis (Movement Control) Order,
S.I. No. 188 of 1983**

**Bovine Tuberculosis (Attestation of the State and
General Provisions) (Amendment) Order, S.I.
No. 230 of 1983**

Transit of Animals Order, S.I. No. 409 of 1983

Parasitic Mange Order, S.I. No. 96 of 1984

Brucellosis in Cattle (General Provisions) (Amendment) Order, S.I. No. 121 of 1984

**Diseases of Animals (Feeding of and use of Swill)
Order, S.I. No. 153 of 1985**

**Bovine Tuberculosis (Attestation of the State and
General Provisions) (Amendment) Order, S.I.
No. 303 of 1985**

**Bovine Tuberculosis (Attestation of the State and
General Provisions) (Amendment) (No.2) Order,
S.I. No. 419 of 1985**

*Bovine Tuberculosis (Attestation of the State and
General Provisions) (Amendment) Order, S.I.
No. 82 of 1986*

Statutory Authority	Section	Statutory Instrument
Diseases of Animals Act, No. 6 of 1966 (*Cont.*)		**Diseases of Animals Act, 1966 (First Schedule) (Amendment) Order, S.I. No. 285 of 1986**
		Diseases of Animals Act, 1966 (First Schedule) (Amendment) (No.2) Order, S.I. No. 286 of 1986
		Diseases of Animals (Notification of Bluetongue and Vesicular Stomatitis) Order, S.I. No. 287 of 1986
		African Swine Fever Order, S.I. No. 288 of 1986
		Bovine Tuberculosis (Attestation of the State and General Provisions) Order, S.I. No. 430 of 1986
	3(2)	*Warble Fly (Notification and Treatment) Order, 1967 (Revocation) Order, S.I. No. 22 of 1971*
		Diseases of Animals (Disinfectants) Order, 1975 (Amendment) Order, S.I. No. 345 of 1978
	6	*Warble Fly (Notification and Treatment) Order, S.I. No. 216 of 1967*
		Sheep Dipping (Tests of Dips) (Fees) Order, S.I No. 245 of 1969
		Diseases of Animals (Disinfectants) Order, S.I No. 273 of 1975
		Sheep Dipping (Tests of Dips) (Fees) Order, S.I. No. 438 of 1981
		Transit of Animals Order, S.I. No. 120 of 1982
	10	*Importation of Meat and Animal Products (Amendment) (No.2) Order, S.I. No. 194 of 1966*
		Importation of Carcases and Animal Products (Prohibition) Order, S.I. No. 201 of 1966
		Warble Fly Order, S.I. No. 210 of 1966
		Dogs Order, S.I. No. 229 of 1966
		Portal Inspection Order, 1924 (Amendment) Order, S.I. No. 69 of 1967
		Warble Fly (Notification and Treatment) Order, S.I No. 216 of 1967
		Importation of Wool (Amendment) Order, S.I No. 247 of 1967
		Bovine Tuberculosis Order, 1926 (Revocation) Order, S.I. No. 161 of 1968
		Importation of Wool and Importation of Carcases and Animal Products (Prohibition) Orders (Amendment) Order, S.I. No. 165 of 1968
		Fowl Pest (Amendment) Order, S.I. No. 230 of 1968
		Poultry, Poultry Carcases, Poultry Eggs and Poultry Products (Restriction on Importation) Order, S.I No. 177 of 1969
		Importation of Dogs and Cats Order of 1929 (Amendment) Order, S.I. No. 204 of 1969
		Importation of Dogs and Cats Order of 1929 (Amendment) (No.2) Order, S.I. No. 220 of 1969

Statutory Authority	Section	Statutory Instrument

Diseases of Animals Act, No. 6 of 1966 (*Cont.*)

Sheep Dipping (Tests of Dips) (Fees) Order, S.I. No. 245 of 1969

Rabies (Importation and Landing of Animals) Order, S.I. No. 248 of 1969

Importation of Dogs and Cats (Amendment) Order, S.I. No. 249 of 1969

Importation of Dogs and Cats (Amendment) Order, S.I. No. 65 of 1970

Importation of Dogs and Cats (Amendment) (No.2) Order, S.I. No. 203 of 1970

Importation of Dogs and Cats (Amendment) (No.3) Order, S.I. No. 280 of 1970

Importation of Livestock Order, S.I. No. 296 of 1970

Foreign Animals Order of 1931 (Amendment) Order, S.I. No. 297 of 1970

Warble Fly Order, S.I. No. 297 of 1971

Rabies (Importation, Landing and Movement of Animals) Order, S.I. No. 16 of 1972

Transit of Animals (Amendment) Order, S.I. No. 11 of 1973

Rabies Order, S.I. No. 94 of 1976

Sheep Dipping Order, 1965 (Amendment) Order, S.I. No. 107 of 1976

Portal Inspection Order, 1924 (Amendment) Order, S.I. No. 155 of 1980

Parasitic Mange Order, S.I. No. 96 of 1984

Diseases of Animals (Feeding of and use of Swill) Order, S.I. No. 153 of 1985

11   *Foot and Mouth Disease (Importation of Animals) Order, S.I. No. 235 of 1967*

Diseases of Animals Act, 1966 (First Schedule) (Amendment) Order, S.I. No. 231 of 1968

Poultry, Poultry Carcases, Poultry Eggs and Poultry Products (Restriction on Importation) Order, S.I. No. 177 of 1969

Rabies (Importation and Landing of Animals) Order, S.I. No. 248 of 1969

Diseases of Animals Act, 1966 (First Schedule) (Amendment) Order, S.I. No. 137 of 1971

Rabies (Importation, Landing and Movement of Animals) Order, S.I. No. 16 of 1972

Diseases of Animals Act, 1966 (First Schedule) (Amendment) Order, S.I. No. 343 of 1972

Transit of Animals (General) Order, S.I. No. 292 of 1973

Diseases of Animals Act, 1966 (First Schedule) (Amendment) Order, S.I. No. 190 of 1975

Rabies (Importation, Landing and Movement of Animals) (Amendment) Order, S.I. No. 95 of 1976

Diseases of Animals Act, 1966 (First Schedule) (Amendment) Order, S.I. No. 326 of 1977

Diseases of Animals Act, No. 6 of 1966 (*Cont.*)		**Diseases of Animals Act, 1966 (First Schedule) (Amendment) Order, S.I. No. 165 of 1980**
		Diseases of Animals Act, 1966 (First Schedule) (Amendment) Order, S.I. No. 285 of 1986
		Diseases of Animals Act, 1966 (First Schedule) (Amendment) (No.2) Order, S.I. No. 286 of 1986
	12	*Brucellosis in Cattle (Clearance Area) (General Provisions) Order, S.I. No. 120 of 1966*
		Warble Fly (Notification and Treatment) Order, S.I. No. 216 of 1967
		Brucellosis in Cattle (Disease-Free Area) Order, S.I. No. 112 of 1968
		Diseases of Animals (Notification of Infectious Diseases) Order, S.I. No. 189 of 1975
		Warble Fly (Notification and Treatment) Order, S.I. No. 267 of 1975
		Rabies Order, S.I. No. 94 of 1976
		Warble Fly (Notification and Treatment) (Amendment) Order, S.I. No. 10 of 1977
		Diseases of Animals (Bovine Leukosis) Order, S.I. No. 327 of 1977
		Brucellosis in Cattle (Notification and Movement Control) Order, S.I. No. 253 of 1978
		Brucellosis in Cattle (General Provisions) Order, S.I. No. 251 of 1979
		Brucellosis in Cattle (General Provisions) Order, S.I. No. 286 of 1980
		Diseases of Animals (Notification of Bluetongue and Vesicular Stomatitis) Order, S.I. No. 287 of 1986
	13	*Brucellosis in Cattle (Clearance Area) (General Provisions) Order, S.I. No. 120 of 1966*
		Brucellosis in Cattle (Control of Vaccinations) Order, S.I. No. 199 of 1966
		Warble Fly Order, S.I. No. 210 of 1966
		Warble Fly (Notification and Treatment) Order, S.I. No. 216 of 1967
		Brucellosis in Cattle (Disease-Free Area) Order, S.I. No. 112 of 1968
		Brucellosis in Cattle (Control of Vaccination) Order, S.I. No. 160 of 1968
		Warble Fly Order, S.I. No. 297 of 1971
		Warble Fly (Amendment) Order, S.I. No. 215 of 1973
		Diseases of Animals (Notification of Infectious Diseases) Order, S.I. No. 189 of 1975
		Warble Fly (Notification and Treatment) Order, S.I. No. 267 of 1975
		Rabies Order, S.I. No. 94 of 1976
		Sheep Dipping Order, 1965 (Amendment) Order, S.I. No. 107 of 1976
		Warble Fly (Notification and Treatment) (Amendment) Order, S.I. No. 10 of 1977

Diseases of Animals Act, No. 6 of 1966 (*Cont.*)		**Diseases of Animals (Bovine Leukosis) Order, S.I. No. 327 of 1977**
		Warble Fly Order, S.I. No. 231 of 1978
		Brucellosis in Cattle (Movement Control) (No.2) Order, S.I. No. 252 of 1978
		Brucellosis in Cattle (Notification and Movement Control) Order, S.I. No. 253 of 1978
		Bovine Tuberculosis (Attestation of the State and General Provisions) Order, S.I. No. 256 of 1978
		Brucellosis in Cattle (General Provisions) Order, S.I. No. 251 of 1979
		Brucellosis in Cattle Orders (Amendment) Order, S.I. No. 189 of 1980
		Brucellosis in Cattle (General Provisions) Order, S.I. No. 286 of 1980
		Warble Fly Order, S.I. No. 338 of 1981
		Bovine Tuberculosis (Attestation of the State and General Provisions) (Amendment) Order, S.I. No. 176 of 1982
		Foot and Mouth Disease (Hay, Straw and Moss Litter) Order, S.I. No. 201 of 1982
		Bovine Tuberculosis (Attestation of the State and General Provisions) (Amendment) Order, S.I. No. 230 of 1983
		Diseases of Animals (Feeding of and use of Swill) Order, S.I. No. 153 of 1985
		Bovine Tuberculosis (Attestation of the State and General Provisions) (Amendment) Order, S.I. No. 303 of 1985
		Bovine Tuberculosis (Attestation of the State and General Provisions) (Amendment) (No.2) Order, S.I. No. 419 of 1985
		Bovine Tuberculosis (Attestation of the State and General Provisions) (Amendment) Order, S.I. No. 82 of 1986
		Diseases of Animals (Notification of Bluetongue and Vesicular Stomatitis) Order, S.I. No. 287 of 1986
		Bovine Tuberculosis (Attestation of the State and General Provisions) Order, S.I. No. 430 of 1986
	14	**Rabies Order, S.I. No. 94 of 1976**
		Diseases of Animals (Bovine Leukosis) Order, S.I. No. 327 of 1977
		Bovine Tuberculosis (Attestation of the State and General Provisions) Order, S.I. No. 256 of 1978
	15	**Foot and Mouth Disease (Regulation of Movement of Persons) Order, S.I. No. 271 of 1967**
		Rabies Order, S.I. No. 94 of 1976
		Diseases of Animals (Bovine Leukosis) Order, S.I. No. 327 of 1977

Statutory Authority	Section	Statutory Instrument
Diseases of Animals Act, No. 6 of 1966 (*Cont.*)	18	**Diseases of Animals (Disinfectants) Order, S.I. No. 273 of 1975**
		Diseases of Animals (Bovine Leukosis) Order, S.I. No. 327 of 1977
	19	*Brucellosis in Cattle (Declaration of Clearance Area and Movement Control) Order, S.I. No. 121 of 1966*
		Brucellosis in Cattle (Disease-Free Area) Order, S.I. No. 112 of 1968
		Brucellosis in Cattle (Disease-Free Area) (Amendment) Order, S.I. No. 29 of 1970
		Brucellosis in Cattle (Declaration of Clearance Areas) Order, S.I. No. 134 of 1970
		Brucellosis in Cattle (Declaration of Clearance Areas) (Amendment) Order, S.I. No. 198 of 1970
		Brucellosis in Cattle (Declaration of Clearance Areas) (No.2) Order, S.I. No. 247 of 1970
		Brucellosis in Cattle (Declaration of Clearance Areas) Order, S.I. No. 11 of 1971
		Brucellosis in Cattle (Declaration of Clearance Areas) (No.2) Order, S.I. No. 66 of 1971
		Brucellosis in Cattle (Declaration of Clearance Areas) Order, S.I. No. 131 of 1973
		Brucellosis in Cattle (Declaration of Clearance Area) Order, S.I. No. 282 of 1976
		Brucellosis in Cattle (Declaration of Clearance Area) Order, S.I. No. 167 of 1978
		Bovine Tuberculosis (Attestation of the State and General Provisions) Order, S.I. No. 256 of 1978
		Brucellosis in Cattle (Declaration of Clearance Area) Order, S.I. No. 253 of 1979
		Brucellosis in Cattle Orders (Amendment) Order, S.I. No. 189 of 1980
		Brucellosis in Cattle (General Provisions) Order, S.I. No. 286 of 1980
		Brucellosis in Cattle (General Provisions) (Amendment) Order, S.I. No. 369 of 1981
		Brucellosis in Cattle (General Provisions) (Amendment) (No.3) Order, S.I. No. 336 of 1982
		Brucellosis in Cattle (General Provisions) (Amendment) Order, S.I. No. 121 of 1984
	20	*Brucellosis in Cattle (Clearance Area) (General Provisions) Order, S.I. No. 120 of 1966*
		Brucellosis in Cattle (Declaration of Clearance Area and Movement Control) Order, S.I. No. 121 of 1966
		Brucellosis in Cattle (Movement Control) Order, S.I. No. 62 of 1967
		Brucellosis in Cattle (Movement Control) (Amendment) Order, S.I. No. 45 of 1968
		Brucellosis in Cattle (Disease-Free Area) Order, S.I. No. 112 of 1968

Statutory Authority	Section	Statutory Instrument
Diseases of Animals Act, No. 6 of 1966 (*Cont.*)		*Brucellosis in Cattle (Clearance Area) (General Provisions) (Amendment) Order, S.I. No. 20 of 1969*
		Brucellosis in Cattle (Disease-Free Area) (Amendment) Order, S.I. No. 21 of 1969
		Brucellosis in Cattle (Movement Control) Order, S.I. No. 22 of 1969
		Brucellosis in Cattle (Disease-Free Area) (Amendment) Order, S.I. No. 29 of 1970
		Brucellosis in Cattle (Disease-Free Area) (Amendment) (No.2) Order, S.I. No. 82 of 1970
		Brucellosis in Cattle (Movement Control) Order, S.I. No. 135 of 1970
		Brucellosis in Cattle (Clearance Area) (General Provisions) (Amendment) Order, S.I. No. 136 of 1970
		Brucellosis in Cattle (Movement Control) (Amendment) Order, S.I. No. 199 of 1970
		Brucellosis in Cattle (Movement Control) (Amendment) (No.2) Order, S.I. No. 248 of 1970
		Brucellosis in Cattle (Movement Control) (Amendment) Order, S.I. No. 10 of 1971
		Brucellosis in Cattle (Movement Control) (Amendment) (No.2) Order, S.I. No. 65 of 1971
		Brucellosis in Cattle (Movement Control) (Supplementary Provisions) Order, S.I. No. 176 of 1971
		Brucellosis in Cattle (Movement Control) (Supplementary Provisions) (Amendment) Order, S.I. No. 326 of 1971
		Brucellosis in Cattle (Disease-Free Area) (Amendment) Order, S.I. No. 120 of 1972
		Brucellosis in Cattle (Movement Control) (Supplementary Provisions) (Amendment) Order, S.I. No. 121 of 1972
		Brucellosis in Cattle (Movement Control) Order, S.I. No. 132 of 1973
		Brucellosis in Cattle (Disease-Free Area) (Amendment) Order, S.I. No. 133 of 1973
		Brucellosis in Cattle (Movement Control) (Supplementary Provisions) (Amendment) Order, S.I. No. 134 of 1973
		Brucellosis in Cattle (Clearance Area) (General Provisions) (Amendment) Order, S.I. No. 135 of 1973
		Brucellosis in Cattle (Movement Control) (Amendment) Order, S.I. No. 281 of 1976
		Brucellosis in Cattle (Movement Control) (Amendment) Order, S.I. No. 166 of 1978
		Brucellosis in Cattle (Movement Control) Order, S.I. No. 251 of 1978
		Bovine Tuberculosis (Attestation of the State and General Provisions) Order, S.I. No. 256 of 1978

Statutory Authority	Section	Statutory Instrument
Diseases of Animals Act, No. 6 of 1966 (*Cont.*)		*Brucellosis in Cattle (Movement Control) (Amendment) Order, S.I. No. 252 of 1979*
		Brucellosis in Cattle (Movement Control) (Amendment) (No.2) Order, S.I. No. 349 of 1979
		Brucellosis in Cattle Orders (Amendment) Order, S.I. No. 189 of 1980
		Brucellosis in Cattle (General Provisions) Order, S.I. No. 286 of 1980
		Bovine Tuberculosis (Movement Control) Order, S.I. No. 188 of 1983
	22	*Brucellosis in Cattle (Disease-Free Area) Order, S.I. No. 112 of 1968*
	25	*Warble Fly Order, S.I. No. 210 of 1966*
		Warble Fly (Notification and Treatment) Order, S.I. No. 216 of 1967
		Warble Fly Order, S.I. No. 297 of 1971
		Warble Fly (Notification and Treatment) Order, S.I. No. 267 of 1975
		Warble Fly (Notification and Treatment) (Amendment) Order, S.I. No. 10 of 1977
		Warble Fly Order, S.I. No. 231 of 1978
		Warble Fly Order, S.I. No. 338 of 1981
	26	**Rabies Order, S.I. No. 94 of 1976**
	27	*Warble Fly Order, S.I. No. 210 of 1966*
		Warble Fly (Notification and Treatment) Order, S.I. No. 216 of 1967
		Brucellosis in Cattle (Disease-Free Area) Order, S.I. No. 112 of 1968
		Brucellosis in Cattle (Clearance Area) (General Provisions) (Amendment) Order, S.I. No. 20 of 1969
		Brucellosis in Cattle (Disease-Free Area) (Amendment) Order, S.I. No. 21 of 1969
		Brucellosis in Cattle (Movement Control) Order, S.I. No. 22 of 1969
		Brucellosis in Cattle (Disease-Free Area) (Amendment) (No.2) Order, S.I. No. 82 of 1970
		Warble Fly Order, S.I. No. 297 of 1971
		Transit of Animals (Amendment) Order, S.I. No. 11 of 1973
		Diseases of Animals (Notification of Infectious Diseases) Order, S.I. No. 189 of 1975
		Warble Fly (Notification and Treatment) Order, S.I. No. 267 of 1975
		Rabies Order, S.I. No. 94 of 1976
		Warble Fly (Notification and Treatment) (Amendment) Order, S.I. No. 10 of 1977
		Warble Fly Order, S.I. No. 231 of 1978
		Brucellosis in Cattle (Movement Control) (No.2) Order, S.I. No. 252 of 1978

Statutory Authority	Section	Statutory Instrument
Diseases of Animals Act, No. 6 of 1966 (*Cont.*)		**Bovine Tuberculosis (Attestation of the State and General Provisions) Order, S.I. No. 256 of 1978**
		Brucellosis in Cattle Orders (Amendment) Order, S.I. No. 189 of 1980
		Brucellosis in Cattle (General Provisions) Order, S.I. No. 286 of 1980
		Warble Fly Order, S.I. No. 327 of 1980
		Warble Fly Order, S.I. No. 338 of 1981
		Brucellosis in Cattle (General Provisions) (Amendment) Order, S.I. No. 121 of 1984
		Diseases of Animals (Notification of Bluetongue and Vesicular Stomatitis) Order, S.I. No. 287 of 1986
	28	**Carriage of Pigs by Road Order, S.I. No. 257 of 1967**
		Transit of Animals (General) Order, S.I. No. 292 of 1973
		Rabies Order, S.I. No. 94 of 1976
		Protection of Animals (Marts, etc.) Order, S.I. No. 70 of 1984
	29	**Portal Inspection Order, 1924 (Amendment) Order, S.I. No. 69 of 1967**
		Transit of Animals (General) Order, S.I. No. 292 of 1973
		Transit of Animals Order, S.I. No. 120 of 1982
	30	**Importation of Carcases and Animal Products (Prohibition) Order, S.I. No. 201 of 1966**
		Warble Fly Order, S.I. No. 6 of 1967
		Warble Fly (Notification and Treatment) Order, S.I. No. 216 of 1967
		Foot and Mouth Disease (Importation of Animals) Order, S.I. No. 235 of 1967
		Importation of Milk and Cream (Prohibition) Order, S.I. No. 242 of 1967
		Foot and Mouth Disease (Restriction of Import of Vehicles, Machinery and Other Equipment) Order, S.I. No. 243 of 1967
		Foot and Mouth Disease (Restriction of Import of Vehicles, Machinery and Other Equipment) (Amendment) Order, S.I. No. 252 of 1967
		Foot and Mouth Disease (Restriction of Import of Vehicles, Machinery and Other Equipment) (Amendment) (No.2) Order, S.I. No. 267 of 1967
		Foot and Mouth Disease (Importation of Animals) (Amendment) Order, S.I. No. 282 of 1967
		Diseases of Animals (Restriction of Movement of Cattle, Sheep and Swine) Order, S.I. No. 283 of 1967
		Poultry, Poultry Carcases, Poultry Eggs and Poultry Products (Restriction on Importation) Order, S.I. No. 177 of 1969
		Importation of Dogs and Cats Order of 1929 (Amendment) Order, S.I. No. 204 of 1969

Statutory Authority	Section	Statutory Instrument
Diseases of Animals Act, No. 6 of 1966 (*Cont.*)		*Importation of Dogs and Cats Order of 1929 (Amendment) (No.2) Order, S.I. No. 220 of 1969*
		Rabies (Importation and Landing of Animals) Order, S.I. No. 248 of 1969
		Importation of Livestock Order, S.I. No. 296 of 1970
		Foreign Animals Order of 1931 (Amendment) Order, S.I. No. 297 of 1970
		Poultry, Poultry Carcases, Poultry Eggs and Poultry Products (Restriction on Importation) Order, S.I. No. 139 of 1971
		Importation of Fowl Pest Vaccine (Prohibition) Order, S.I. No. 140 of 1971
		Rabies (Importation, Landing and Movement of Animals) Order, S.I. No. 16 of 1972
		Importation of Animal Semen (Prohibition) Order, S.I. No. 299 of 1972
		Importation of Infectious Bursal Disease (Gumboro Disease) Vaccine (Prohibition) Order, S.I. No. 275 of 1978
		Importation of Aujeszky's Disease Vaccine (Prohibition) Order, S.I. No. 166 of 1980
		Foot and Mouth Disease (Hay, Straw and Moss Litter) Order, S.I. No. 201 of 1982
	33	**Importation of Dogs and Cats (Amendment) Order, S.I. No. 249 of 1969**
		Importation of Dogs and Cats (Amendment) Order, S.I. No. 65 of 1970
		Importation of Dogs and Cats (Amendment) (No.2) Order, S.I. No. 203 of 1970
		Importation of Dogs and Cats (Amendment) (No.3) Order, S.I. No. 280 of 1970
	35	*Sheep Dipping (Tests of Dips) (Fees) Order, S.I. No. 245 of 1969*
		Sheep Dipping Order, 1965 (Amendment) Order, S.I. No. 107 of 1976
		Sheep Dipping Order, 1965 (Amendment) Order, S.I. No. 158 of 1977
		Sheep Dipping (Tests of Dips) (Fees) Order, S.I. No. 438 of 1981
	36	**Foot and Mouth Disease (Hay, Straw and Moss Litter) Order, S.I. No. 201 of 1982**
	38	**Sheep Dipping Order, 1965 (Amendment) Order, S.I. No. 107 of 1976**
	48	*Foot and Mouth Disease (Restriction of Sports and Sales) Order, S.I. No. 253 of 1967*
		Carriage of Pigs by Road Order, S.I. No. 257 of 1967
		Foot and Mouth Disease (Importation of Animals) (Amendment) Order, S.I. No. 282 of 1967
		Diseases of Animals (Restriction of Movement of Cattle, Sheep and Swine) Order, S.I. No. 283 of 1967

Statutory Authority	Section	Statutory Instrument

Diseases of Animals Act, 1894 to 1914 (*Cont.*)

Importation of Carcases (Prohibition) (Amendment) Order [Vol. X p. 403] S.R.& O. No. 49 of 1927

Foot and Mouth Disease (Boiling of Animal Foodstuffs) Order [Vol. X p. 475] S.R.& O. No. 50 of 1927

Foreign Animals Order [Vol. X p. 495] S.R.& O. No. 62 of 1928

Transit of Animals Order of 1927 Amendment Order [Vol. X p. 459] S.R.& O. No. 61 of 1930

Foreign Animals Order [Vol. X p. 503] S.R.& O. No. 9 of 1931

Foreign Animals Order, 1931, Amendment Order [Vol. X p. 513] S.R.& O. No. 38 of 1931

Foot and Mouth Disease (Imported Packing) Order, 1923 Amendment Order [Vol. X p. 223] S.R.& O. No. 39 of 1931

Foreign Hay and Straw (Ireland) Order of 1912 Amendment Order [Vol. X p. 135] S.R.& O. No. 40 of 1931

Diseases of Animals (Disinfection) Order [Vol. X p. 587] S.R.& O. No. 59 of 1931

Exportation of Animals (Irish Free State) Order [Vol. X p. 181] S.R.& O. No. 63 of 1931

Foreign Animals Order [Vol. X p. 517] S.R.& O. No. 17 of 1932

Foot and Mouth Disease (Imported Packing) Order [Vol. X p. 227] S.R.& O. No. 18 of 1932

Foreign Hay and Straw Order [Vol. X p. 593] S.R.& O. No. 19 of 1932

Foreign Animals Order of 1932 No.2 [Vol. X p. 521] S.R.& O. No. 48 of 1932

Foreign Animals Order of 1932 No.2 Revocation Order [Vol. X p. 597] S.R.& O. No. 85 of 1932

Foot and Mouth Disease (Importation of Rodents and Insectivora) Order [Vol. X p. 601] S.R.& O. No. 10 of 1933

Diseases of Animals Act, 1894 (Extension to Rodents and Insectivora) Order [Vol. X p. 607] S.R.& O. No. 11 of 1933

Foreign Animals Order, 1931, Amendment Order [Vol. X p. 611] S.R.& O. No. 12 of 1933

Foot and Mouth Disease (Imported Packing) Order, 1923 Amendment Order [Vol. X p. 615] S.R.& O. No. 13 of 1933

Foreign Hay and Straw (Ireland) Order of 1912 Amendment Order [Vol. X p. 619] S.R.& O. No. 14 of 1933

Rabies Order [Vol. X p. 623] S.R.& O. No. 16 of 1933

Diseases of Animals Act, 1894 (Extension to Horses, Asses, Mules, Dogs and Cats) Order [Vol. X p. 645] S.R.& O. No. 17 of 1933

Statutory Authority	Section	Statutory Instrument

Diseases of Animals Act, 1894 to 1914 (*Cont.*)

Diseases of Animals Act, 1894 (Extension to Rabies) Order [Vol. X p. 649] S.R.& O. No. 18 of 1933

Foot and Mouth Disease and Swine Fever (Boiling of Animal Foodstuffs) Order [Vol. X p. 653] S.R.& O. No. 39 of 1933

Transit of Animals Order [Vol. X p. 659] S.R.& O. No. 42 of 1933

County Dublin (Special Dipping Area) Sheep Dipping Order [Vol. X p. 667] S.R.& O. No. 68 of 1933

Portal Inspection Order, 1924 (Revocation) Order [Vol. X p. 681] S.R.& O. No. 88 of 1933

County Dublin (Special Dipping Area) Sheep Dipping Order, 1933 Revocation Order [Vol. X p. 677] S.R.& O. No. 121 of 1933

Portal Inspection Order [Vol. X p. 685] S.R.& O. No. 175 of 1935

Portal Inspection Order of 1935, Amendment Order [Vol. X p. 689] S.R.& O. No. 651 of 1935

Warble Fly (Treatment of Cattle) Order [Vol. X p. 695] S.R.& O. No. 20 of 1936

Diseases of Animals Act, 1894 (Extension to Warble Fly Infestation) Order [Vol. X p. 717] S.R.& O. No. 43 of 1936

Warble Fly (Treatment of Cattle) (Amendment) Order [Vol. X p. 711] S.R.& O. No. 371 of 1936

Sheep Dipping Order [Vol. X p. 721] S.R.& O. No. 169 of 1937

Foot and Mouth Disease (Disposal of Swill) Order [Vol. X p. 741] S.R.& O. No. 337 of 1937

Diseases of Animals Act, 1894 (Extension to Poultry and Poultry Diseases) Order [Vol. X p. 745] S.R.& O. No. 23 of 1938

Importation of Carcases (Prohibition) (Amendment) Order [Vol. X p. 751] S.R.& O. No. 65 of 1938

Foreign Animals Order, 1931, Amendment Order [Vol. X p. 755] S.R.& O. No. 66 of 1938

Sheep Scab (Leitrim and Cavan) Order [Vol. X p. 759] S.R.& O. No. 99 of 1938

Dublin Swine Fever Orders, 1903 to 1928 (Revocation) Order [Vol. X p. 769] S.R.& O. No. 104 of 1938

Exportation of Animals (Irish Free State) Order [Vol. X p. 773] S.R.& O. No. 110 of 1938

Diseases of Animals Acts, 1894 to 1938,

Diseases of Animals Act, 1894 (Extension to Poultry and Poultry Diseases) (No.2) Order [Vol. X p. 779] S.R.& O. No. 125 of 1938

Poultry and Poultry Eggs (Importation) Order [Vol. X p. 785] S.R.& O. No. 126 of 1938

Hay, Straw and Peat Moss Litter Order [Vol. X p. 793] S.R.& O. No. 230 of 1938

Statutory Authority	Section	Statutory Instrument
Diseases of Animals Act, 1894 to 1938 (*Cont.*)		**Sheep Scab (Leitrim and Cavan) (Amendment) Order [Vol. X p. 801] S.R.& O. No. 231 of 1938**
		Sheep Dipping (Amendment) Order [Vol. X p. 805] S.R.& O. No. 232 of 1938
		Foot and Mouth Disease (Imported Carcases and Packing Materials) Order [Vol. X p. 811] S.R.& O. No. 273 of 1938
		Foot and Mouth Disease (Imported Carcases and Packing Materials) (Amendment) Order [Vol. X p. 821] S.R.& O. No. 287 of 1938
Diseases of Animals Acts, 1894 to 1945,		*Sheep Dipping Order, S.I. No. 157 of 1948*
		Diseases of Animals Act, 1894 (Extension to Certain Fur-Bearing Animals) Order, S.I. No. 57 of 1949
		Foot and Mouth Disease (Importation of Rodents and Insectivora Order, 1933 (Amendment) Order, S.I. No. 58 of 1949
Diseases of Animals Acts, 1894 to 1949,		*Poultry, Poultry Carcases and Poultry Eggs (Restriction on Importation) Order, S.I. No. 293 of 1949*
		Fowl Pest Order, S.I. No. 15 of 1950
		Diseases of Animals Act, 1894 (Extension to Poultry and Poultry Diseases) Order, S.I. No. 16 of 1950
		Diseases of Animals Act, 1894 (Extension to Poultry and Poultry Diseases) (Amendment) Order, S.I. No. 17 of 1950
		Fowl Pest (Amendment) Order, S.I. No. 18 of 1950
		Foot and Mouth Disease Order, S.I. No. 79 of 1950
		Foot and Mouth Disease (Importation of Animals) Order, S.I. No. 356 of 1951
		Foot and Mouth Disease (Importation of Plants) Order, S.I. No. 134 of 1952
		Foreign Animals Order, 1931 (Amendment) Order, S.I. No. 136 of 1952
		Foot and Mouth Disease Order, 1950 (Amendment) Order, S.I. No. 147 of 1952
		Foot and Mouth Disease (Importation of Animals) Order, 1951 (Revocation) Order, S.I. No. 268 of 1953
		Foreign Animals Order of 1931 (Amendment) Order, S.I. No. 39 of 1954
Diseases of Animals Acts, 1894 to 1954,		*Importation of Wool Order, 1946 (Amendment) Order, S.I. No. 113 of 1954*
		Rodents and Insectivora (Restriction on Importation) Order, S.I. No. 114 of 1954
		Diseases of Animals Act, 1894 (Extension to Rodents, Insectivora and Myxomatosis) Order, S.I. No. 115 of 1954
		Transit of Greyhounds Order, S.I. No. 121 of 1954
		Johne's Disease Order, S.I. No. 86 of 1955

Statutory Authority	Section	Statutory Instrument
Diseases of Animals Act, 1894 to 1954 (*Cont.*)		*Swine Fever Infected Area Order, S.I. No. 223 of 1956*
		Swine Fever (Dublin) Order, S.I. No. 242 of 1956
		Swine Fever Infected Area Order, 1956 (Amendment) Order, S.I. No. 276 of 1956
		Foot and Mouth Disease Order, S.I. No. 324 of 1956
		Swine Fever Infected Area Order, 1956 (Amendment) Order, S.I. No. 107 of 1957
		Swine Fever (Restriction of Movement of Pigs) Order, S.I. No. 128 of 1957
		Swine Fever (Restriction of Movement of Pigs) Order, 1957 (Amendment) Order, S.I. No. 166 of 1957
Diseases of Animals Acts, 1894 to 1957,		*Swine Fever (Restriction of Movement of Pigs) Order, 1957 (Amendment) (No.2) Order, S.I. No. 189 of 1957*
		Diseases of Animals (Licensing of Pig Dealers) Order, S.I. No. 202 of 1957
Diseases of Animals Acts, 1894 to 1960,		*Foot and Mouth Disease (Importation of Animals) Order, S.I. No. 225 of 1960*
		Foot and Mouth Disease (Importation of Animals) Order, S.I. No. 50 of 1961
Diseases of Animals (Bovine Tuberculosis) Act, No. 14 of 1957	2	**Bovine Tuberculosis (Clearance Area) (Sligo) Order, S.I. No. 217 of 1957**
		Bovine Tuberculosis (General Provisions) Order, S.I. No. 219 of 1957
		Bovine Tuberculosis (Clearance Area) (No.1) Order, S.I. No. 78 of 1958
		Bovine Tuberculosis (14-Day Test) Order, S.I. No. 161 of 1958
		Bovine Tuberculosis (Movement Control) (No.1) Order, S.I. No. 170 of 1958
		Bovine Tuberculosis (Control of Certain Tests) Order, S.I. No. 102 of 1959
		Bovine Tuberculosis (14 Day-Test) (Amendment) Order, S.I. No. 103 of 1959
		Bovine Tuberculosis (Control of Public Sales of Cattle) (Counties of Sligo, Clare, Galway, Leitrim, Roscommon, Donegal and Mayo) Order, S.I. No. 110 of 1959
		Bovine Tuberculosis (Movement Control) (Cavan and Monaghan) Order, S.I. No. 116 of 1959
		Bovine Tuberculosis (Clearance Area) (Cavan and Monaghan) Order, S.I. No. 117 of 1959
		Bovine Tuberculosis (Clearance Area) (Limerick) Order, S.I. No. 190 of 1959
		Bovine Tuberculosis (Movement Control) (Limerick) Order, S.I. No. 191 of 1959
		Bovine Tuberculosis (14-Day Test) (Amendment) Order, S.I. No. 27 of 1960

Statutory Authority	Section	Statutory Instrument

Diseases of Animals (Bovine
Tuberculosis) Act, No. 14 of 1957
(*Cont.*)

Bovine Tuberculosis (Clearance Area) (Longford) Order, S.I. No. 55 of 1960

Bovine Tuberculosis (Clearance Area) (Westmeath) Order, S.I. No. 56 of 1960

Bovine Tuberculosis (Movement Control) (Amendment) Order, S.I. No. 57 of 1960

Bovine Tuberculosis (General Provisions) (Amendment) Order, S.I. No. 136 of 1960

Bovine Tuberculosis (14-Day Test) Order, S.I. No. 176 of 1960

Bovine Tuberculosis (Control of Certain Tests) Order, S.I. No. 177 of 1960

Bovine Tuberculosis (Clearance Area) (Special Controls) Order, S.I. No. 178 of 1960

Bovine Tuberculosis (Movement Control) Order, S.I. No. 179 of 1960

Bovine Tuberculosis (Control of Public Sales of Cattle) Order, S.I. No. 180 of 1960

Bovine Tuberculosis (Clearance Area) (Limerick) Order, S.I. No. 181 of 1960

Bovine Tuberculosis (Places and Times for Movement into County Donegal) Order, S.I. No. 185 of 1960

Bovine Tuberculosis (Movement Control) (No.2) Order, S.I. No. 186 of 1960

Bovine Tuberculosis (Clearance Area) (Special Controls) (Amendment) Order, S.I. No. 218 of 1960

Bovine Tuberculosis (Attested Area) Order, S.I. No. 236 of 1960

Bovine Tuberculosis (Control of Public Sales of Cattle) (No.2) Order, S.I. No. 247 of 1960

Bovine Tuberculosis (Movement Control) (No.3) Order, S.I. No. 248 of 1960

Bovine Tuberculosis (Attested Area) (Amendment) Order, S.I. No. 9 of 1961

Bovine Tuberculosis (Attested Area) (Amendment) (No.2) Order, S.I. No. 17 of 1961

Bovine Tuberculosis (Attested Area) (Amendment) (No.3) Order, S.I. No. 29 of 1961

Bovine Tuberculosis (Clearance Area) Order, S.I. No. 38 of 1961

Bovine Tuberculosis (Control of Movement and Public Sales of Cattle) Order, S.I. No. 39 of 1961

Bovine Tuberculosis (Clearance Area) (Special Controls) Order, S.I. No. 65 of 1961

Bovine Tuberculosis (Restrictions on Further Tests) Order, S.I. No. 94 of 1961

Bovine Tuberculosis (14-Day Test) (Amendment) Order, S.I. No. 125 of 1961

Bovine Tuberculosis (Control of Certain Tests) (Amendment) Order, S.I. No. 126 of 1961

Statutory Authority	Section	Statutory Instrument
Diseases of Animals (Bovine Tuberculosis) Act, No. 14 of 1957 (*Cont.*)		*Bovine Tuberculosis (Control of Movement and Public Sales of Cattle) (Amendment) Order, S.I. No. 136 of 1961*
		Bovine Tuberculosis (Clearance Area) (No.2) Order, S.I. No. 137 of 1961
		Bovine Tuberculosis (Attested Area) (Amendment) (No.4) Order, S.I. No. 156 of 1961
		Bovine Tuberculosis (General Provisions) (Amendment) Order, S.I. No. 159 of 1961
		Bovine Tuberculosis (Movement Control) Order, S.I. No. 169 of 1961
		Bovine Tuberculosis (Attested Area) (Amendment) (No.5) Order, S.I. No. 228 of 1961
		Bovine Tuberculosis (Control of Movement and Public Sales of Cattle) (No.2) Order, S.I. No. 266 of 1961
		Bovine Tuberculosis (Control of Movement and Public Sales of Cattle) (No.2) (Amendment) Order, S.I. No. 43 of 1962
		Bovine Tuberculosis (Clearance Area) Order, S.I. No. 51 of 1962
		Bovine Tuberculosis (Control of Movement and Public Sales of Cattle) Order, S.I. No. 52 of 1962
		Bovine Tuberculosis (Control of Movement and Public Sales of Cattle) (No.2) (Amendment No.2) Order, S.I. No. 86 of 1962
		Bovine Tuberculosis (Clearance Area) (Special Controls) Order, S.I. No. 87 of 1962
		Bovine Tuberculosis (Clearance Area) (No.2) Order, S.I. No. 105 of 1962
		Bovine Tuberculosis (Control of Movement) Order, S.I. No. 106 of 1962
		Bovine Tuberculosis (Control of Movement and Public Sales of Cattle) (Dublin) Order, S.I. No. 150 of 1962
		Bovine Tuberculosis (Clearance Area) (Special Controls) (Amendment) Order, S.I. No. 152 of 1962
		Bovine Tuberculosis (Attested Area) (Amendment) (No.6) Order, S.I. No. 169 of 1962
		Bovine Tuberculosis (Clearance Area) (Special Controls) (Amendment) (No.2) Order, S.I. No. 191 of 1962
		Bovine Tuberculosis (Attested Area) (Amendment) (No.7) Order, S.I. No. 192 of 1962
		Bovine Tuberculosis (Special Controls) (Dublin) Order, S.I. No. 193 of 1962
		Bovine Tuberculosis (Attested Area) (Amendment) (No.8) Order, S.I. No. 201 of 1962
		Bovine Tuberculosis (Attested Area) (Amendment) (No.9) Order, S.I. No. 23 of 1963
		Bovine Tuberculosis (30-Day Test) Order, S.I. No. 76 of 1963

Statutory Authority	Section	Statutory Instrument
Diseases of Animals (Bovine Tuberculosis) Act, No. 14 of 1957 (*Cont.*)		*Bovine Tuberculosis (Clearance Area) (Amendment) Order, S.I. No. 109 of 1963*
		Bovine Tuberculosis (General Provisions) (Amendment) Order, S.I. No. 238 of 1963
		Bovine Tuberculosis (Control of Movement) Order, S.I. No. 257 of 1963
		Bovine Tuberculosis (Control of Movement and Public Sales of Cattle) Order, S.I. No. 87 of 1964
		Bovine Tuberculosis (Control of Movement and Public Sales of Cattle) (Amendment) Order, S.I. No. 149 of 1964
		Bovine Tuberculosis (Clearance Area) (Special Controls) Order, S.I. No. 26 of 1965
		Bovine Tuberculosis (Attestation of the State) Order, S.I. No. 211 of 1965
Documents and Pictures (Regulation of Export) Act, No. 29 of 1945	2(3)	**Documents and Pictures (Regulation of Export) Exclusion Order [Vol. XXXVII p. 145] S.R.& O. No. 334 of 1946**
Double Taxation (Relief) Act, No. 8 of 1923	2	**Double Taxation (Relief) Order [Vol. X p. 837] S.R.& O. No. 42 of 1926**
Dublin and Blessington Steam Tramway (Abandonment) Act, No. 13 of 1932	2	*Dublin and Blessington Steam Tramway (Abandonment) Order [Vol. X p. 855] S.R.& O. No. 73 of 1932*
Dublin and Blessington Steam Tramway Order, 1887		*Dublin and Blessington Tramway Order [Vol. X p. 843] S.R.& O. No. 43 of 1925*
	40	**Dublin and Blessington Steam Tramway (Committee of Management) Order [Vol. X p. 847] S.R.& O. No. 109 of 1927**
Dublin Carriage Act, No. 112 of 1853		**Dublin Carriage Bye-Laws [Vol. XXXVII p. 149] S.R.& O. No. 198 of 1946**
	49	**Dublin (Carriage Stands) Bye-Laws [Vol. XXVIII p. 1011] S.R.& O. No. 2 of 1944**
		Dublin (Carriage Stands) (Amendment) Bye-Laws, S.I. No. 2 of 1961
Dublin Port and Docks (Bridges) Act, No. 2 of 1929(Private)	8	*Dublin Port and Docks (Bridges) Act, 1929 (Extension of Time) Order [Vol. X p. 867] S.R.& O. No. 130 of 1936*
Dublin Transport Authority Act, No. 15 of 1986	3	*Dublin Transport Authority Act, 1986 (Commencement) Order, S.I. No. 357 of 1986*
	4	*Dublin Transport Authority Act, 1986 (Establishment Day) Order, S.I. No. 358 of 1986*
Dumping at Sea Act, No. 8 of 1981	12	*Dumping at Sea Act, 1981 (Commencement) Order, S.I. No. 268 of 1981*

Statutory Authority	Section	Statutory Instrument
Elections Act, No. 14 of 1960		*Dail Elections and Local Elections (Returning Officers' Charges and Accounts) Regulations, S.I. No. 128 of 1960*
	3	*Elections Order, S.I. No. 108 of 1960*
Electoral Act, No. 12 of 1923		*Electoral (Amendment) Order, S.I. No. 242 of 1951*
	11(2)	*Electoral Act (Alteration of Registration Rules) Order [Vol. XI p. 237] S.R.& O. No. 177 of 1933*
		Electoral (Amendment) Order [Vol. XI p. 135] S.R.& O. No. 17 of 1934
		Electoral Act (Alteration of Registration Rules) Order [Vol. XXIX p. 1] S.R.& O. No. 341 of 1940
		Electoral Act (Alteration of Registration Rules) Order, S.I. No. 342 of 1948
	12(3)	*Registration Expenses Order [Vol. XI p. 51] S.R.& O. No. 6 of 1924*
		Registration Expenses Order, 1924 (Amendment) Order, S.I. No. 76 of 1948
		Registration Expenses Order, 1924 (Amendment) Order, S.I. No. 91 of 1950
		Registration Expenses Scale, S.I. No. 19 of 1952
		Registration Expenses (Alteration) Scale, S.I. No. 96 of 1961
	18(1)(b)	*Dail Eireann (Sligo-Leitrim) Bye Election Order, S.I. No. 26 of 1961*
		Dail Eireann General Election Order, S.I. No. 202 of 1961
		Dail Eireann (Dublin North-East) Bye-Election Order, S.I. No. 75 of 1963
	21	*Electoral (Amendment) Order, S.I. No. 27 of 1961*
		Forms (Dail Elections, Presidential Elections and Referenda) Regulations, S.I. No. 246 of 1963
		Forms (Dail Elections, Presidential Elections and Referenda) (Amendment) Regulations, S.I. No. 115 of 1972
	22	**Local Elections Order [Vol. XXIX p. 5] S.R.& O. No. 123 of 1945**
		Forms (Dail Elections, Presidential Elections and Referenda) Regulations, S.I. No. 246 of 1963
	25	**Seanad Elections – Accounts of Constituency Returning Officers [Vol. XI p. 163] S.R.& O. No. 37 of 1925**
		Returning Officers' (Borough and County Constituencies) Charges Order [Vol. XXXVII p. 159] S.R.& O. No. 341 of 1947
		Returning Officers' (Borough and County Constituencies) Charges Order, S.I. No. 23 of 1948
		Returning Officers' (Borough and County Constituencies) Charges Order, S.I. No. 140 of 1951

Statutory Authority	Section	Statutory Instrument
Electoral Act, No. 12 of 1923 (*Cont.*)	25(5)	*University Constituency Returning Officers' Charges at Seanad Elections Order [Vol. XI p. 147] S.R.& O. No. 34 of 1925*
		Constituency Returning Officers' Charges at Seanad Elections [Vol. XI p. 151] S.R.& O. No. 35 of 1925
		Returning Officers' (Borough and County Constituencies) Charges Order [Vol. XI p. 177] S.R.& O. No. 40 of 1927
		Returning Officers' (Dail Elections) Accounts Regulations [Vol. XI p. 45] S.R.& O. No. 41 of 1927
		Returning Officers' (University Constituencies) Charges Order [Vol. XI p. 213] S.R.& O. No. 42 of 1927
		Returning Officers' (Borough and County Constituencies) Bye-Election Charges Order [Vol. XI p. 219] S.R.& O. No. 72 of 1927
		Returning Officers' (Borough and County Constituencies) Charges Order [Vol. XI p. 195] S.R.& O. No. 143 of 1937
		Returning Officers' (Borough and County Constituencies) Bye-Election Charges Order [Vol. XI p. 227] S.R.& O. No. 142 of 1938
		Returning Officers' (Borough and County Constituencies) Bye-Election Charges Order, S.I. No. 416 of 1948
		Returning Officers' (Borough and County Constituencies) Bye-Election Charges Order, S.I. No. 275 of 1952
		Returning Officers' (Borough and County Constituencies) Charges Order, S.I. No. 203 of 1961
		Returning Officers' (Borough and County Constituencies) Charges (No.2) Order, S.I. No. 278 of 1961
		Returning Officers' (Borough and County Constituencies) Charges Order, S.I. No. 134 of 1964
		Returning Officers' (Borough and County Constituencies) Charges Order, S.I. No. 60 of 1965
		Returning Officers' (Borough and County Constituencies) Bye-Election Charges Order, S.I. No. 262 of 1966
		Returning Officers' Charges (General Elections to Dail Eireann) Order, S.I. No. 95 of 1969
		Returning Officers' Charges (Bye-Elections to Dail Eireann) Order, S.I. No. 27 of 1970
		Returning Officers' Charges (Bye-Elections to Dail Eireann) (Amendment) Order, S.I. No. 70 of 1970
		Returning Officers' Charges (Bye-Elections to Dail Eireann) (Amendment) (No.2) Order, S.I. No. 256 of 1970
		Returning Officers' Charges (Bye-Elections to Dail Eireann) Order, S.I. No. 174 of 1972
		Returning Officers' Charges (General Elections to Dail Eireann) Order, S.I. No. 37 of 1973

Statutory Authority	Section	Statutory Instrument
Electoral Act, No. 12 of 1923 (*Cont.*)		*Polling Card (Dail Elections, Presidential Elections and Referenda) Regulations, S.I. No. 245 of 1961*
	Sch. I par. 16	*Electoral (Amendment) Order, S.I. No. 27 of 1961*
	Sch. IV par. 3(4)	**Forms (Dail Elections, Presidential Elections and Referenda) Regulations, S.I. No. 246 of 1963** **Forms (Dail Elections, Presidential Elections and Referenda) (Amendment) Regulations, S.I. No. 115 of 1972**
	Sch. V Part I par. 9(3)(a)	**Forms (Dail Elections, Presidential Elections and Referenda) Regulations, S.I. No. 246 of 1963**
	Sch. V Part I par. 28	**Forms (Dail Elections, Presidential Elections and Referenda) Regulations, S.I. No. 246 of 1963**
	Sch. V Part I par. 43	**Forms (Dail Elections, Presidential Elections and Referenda) Regulations, S.I. No. 246 of 1963**
Electoral Act, No. 43 of 1960	1(2)	*Electoral Act, 1960 (Commencement) Order, S.I. No. 265 of 1960*
Electoral Act, No. 19 of 1963	1(2)	*Electoral Act, 1963 (Commencement) Order, S.I. No. 121 of 1963* *Electoral Act, 1963 (Commencement) (No.2) Order, S.I. No. 245 of 1963* *Electoral Act, 1963 (Commencement) Order, S.I. No. 124 of 1965*
	3	**Dun Laoghaire Borough Electoral Areas Order, S.I. No. 83 of 1966**
	5	**Registration of Electors and Juries Acts (Specification of Dates) Regulations, S.I. No. 169 of 1963** **Registration of Electors (Amendment) Regulations, S.I. No. 402 of 1985**
	6	**Registration of Electors and Juries Acts (Specification of Dates) Regulations, S.I. No. 169 of 1963**
	7	**Registration of Electors and Juries Acts (Specification of Dates) Regulations, S.I. No. 169 of 1963** **Registration of Electors (Amendment) Regulations, S.I. No. 381 of 1977** **Registration of Electors (Amendment) Regulations, S.I. No. 402 of 1985**
	15	**Forms (Dail Elections, Presidential Elections and Referenda) Regulations, S.I. No. 246 of 1963**
	22	**Electoral (Polling Schemes) Regulations, S.I. No. 78 of 1964**
	23	**Forms (Dail Elections, Presidential Elections and Referenda) Regulations, S.I. No. 246 of 1963**
	44	**Forms (Dail Elections, Presidential Elections and Referenda) Regulations, S.I. No. 246 of 1963**

Statutory Authority	Section	Statutory Instrument
Electoral Act, No. 19 of 1963 (*Cont.*)	64	**Forms (Dail Elections, Presidential Elections and Referenda) Regulations, S.I. No. 246 of 1963**
	82	**Local Elections Regulations, S.I. No. 128 of 1965**
		Local Elections (Amendment) Regulations, S.I. No. 117 of 1974
		Local Elections (Postal Voting) Regulations, S.I. No. 118 of 1974
		Local Elections (Postal Voting) (Amendment) Regulations, S.I. No. 68 of 1985
	83	**Local Elections Regulations, S.I. No. 128 of 1965**
	86	**Local Elections Regulations, S.I. No. 128 of 1965**
	87	**Dun Laoghaire Borough Electoral Areas Order, S.I. No. 83 of 1966**
	88	*Waterford County Borough (Wards) Regulations, S.I. No. 1 of 1970*
		County Borough of Cork (Wards) Regulations, S.I. No. 246 of 1970
		County Borough of Dublin (Wards) Regulations, S.I. No. 269 of 1970
		County Borough of Limerick (Wards) Regulations, S.I. No. 279 of 1970
		Waterford County Borough (Wards) Regulations, S.I. No. 28 of 1983
		County Borough of Dublin (Wards) Regulations, S.I. No. 12 of 1986
		County Borough of Galway (Wards) Regulations, S.I. No. 34 of 1986
	89	*Dublin County (District Electoral Divisions) Regulations, S.I. No. 17 of 1971*
		Dublin County (District Electoral Divisions) Regulations, S.I. No. 13 of 1986
		Dublin County (District Electoral Divisions) (Amendment) Regulations, S.I. No. 69 of 1986
	91	*European Assembly and Local Elections Regulations, S.I. No. 138 of 1979*
		Returning Officers' Charges (European Assembly and Local Elections) Order, S.I. No. 163 of 1979
		Returning Officers' Charges (European Assembly and Local Elections) (Amendment) Order, S.I. No. 218 of 1979
		Returning Officers' and Local Returning Officers' Charges Regulations, S.I. No. 138 of 1984
		European Assembly Election, Dail Bye-Election and Referendum Regulations, S.I. No. 141 of 1984
	91(5)	**Referendum (Local Returning Officers' Charges) (No.2) Regulations, S.I. No. 229 of 1979**
	92	*European Assembly and Local Elections (Special Difficulty) Order, S.I. No. 166 of 1979*
		Referenda (Special Difficulty) Order, S.I. No. 205 of 1979

Statutory Authority	Section	Statutory Instrument
Electoral Acts, 1923 to 1935,		*Electoral Order [Vol. XI p. 243] S.R.& O. No. 21 of 1936*
		Electoral (Amendment) Order [Vol. XXIX p. 9] S.R.& O. No. 557 of 1942
		Electoral Order [Vol. XXXVII p. 163] S.R.& O. No. 96 of 1946
Electoral (Amendment) Act, No. 21 of 1927	3(1)	*Dail Eireann General Election Order, S.I. No. 206 of 1948*
		Dail Eireann General Election Order, S.I. No. 134 of 1951
		Dail Eireann General Election Order, S.I. No. 80 of 1954
		Dail Eireann General Election Order, S.I. No. 22 of 1957
Electoral (Amendment) Act, No. 31 of 1946	4	**Returning Officers' (Borough and County Constituencies) Charges Order [Vol. XXXVII p. 159] S.R.& O. No. 341 of 1947**
		Polling Card (Dail Elections, Presidential Elections and Referenda) Regulations, S.I. No. 245 of 1961
Electoral (Amendment) Act, No. 31 of 1947	7(1)	*Electoral (Amendment) Act, 1947 (Appointment of Returning Officer) Order, S.I. No. 71 of 1954*
	7(1)(d)	*Electoral (Amendment) Act, 1947 (Appointment of Returning Officer) Order, S.I. No. 67 of 1955*
Electoral (Amendment) Act, No. 19 of 1961	7(1)(b)	*Returning Officers' (Appointment) Order, S.I. No. 144 of 1961*
	7(1)(c)	*Returning Officers' (Appointment) Order, S.I. No. 144 of 1961*
Electoral (Amendment) Act, No. 12 of 1985	5	**Registration of Electors (Amendment) Regulations, S.I. No. 402 of 1985**
Electoral (Chairman of Dail Eireann) Act, No. 25 of 1937	4(b)	*Electoral (Chairman of Dail Eireann) Act, 1937 (Form of Certificate) Order [Vol. XXIX p. 15] S.R.& O. No. 180 of 1943*
Electoral (Dail Eireann and Local Authorities) Act, No. 6 of 1945		*Electoral Order [Vol. XXXVII p. 163] S.R.& O. No. 96 of 1946*
Electoral (Dublin Commercial) Act, No. 28 of 1930	18	*Electoral (Dublin Commercial) Order [Vol. XI p. 329] S.R.& O. No. 55 of 1930*
Electoral (University Constituencies) Act, No. 22 of 1936	1	*Electoral (University Electors Supplemental List) Order [Vol. XI p. 353] S.R.& O. No. 202 of 1936*
	2(2)(a)	*Electoral (University Electors Supplemental List) Order [Vol. XI p. 353] S.R.& O. No. 202 of 1936*
Electricity (Special Provisions) Act, No. 13 of 1966	1(2)	*Electricity (Special Provisions) Act, 1966 (Commencement) Order, S.I. No. 67 of 1968*

Statutory Authority	Section	Statutory Instrument
Electricity (Special Provisions) Act, No. 13 of 1966 (*Cont.*)	1(4)	*Electricity (Special Provisions) Act, 1966 (Commencement) Order, 1968 (Revocation) Order, S.I. No. 76 of 1968*
Electricity (Supply) Act, No. 27 of 1927	17(1)	**Shannon Works Transfer (No.1) Order [Vol. XI p. 361] S.R.& O. No. 13 of 1929**
		Shannon Works Transfer (No.2) Order [Vol. XI p. 365] S.R.& O. No. 32 of 1929
		Shannon Works Transfer (No.3) Order [Vol. XI p. 369] S.R.& O. No. 35 of 1929
		Shannon Works Transfer (No.4) Order [Vol. XI p. 373] S.R.& O. No. 49 of 1929
		Shannon Works Transfer (No.5) Order [Vol. XI p. 377] S.R.& O. No. 53 of 1929
		Shannon Works Transfer (No.6) Order [Vol. XI p. 381] S.R.& O. No. 55 of 1929
		Shannon Works Transfer (No.7) Order [Vol. XI p. 385] S.R.& O. No. 58 of 1929
		Shannon Works Transfer (No.8) Order [Vol. XI p. 389] S.R.& O. No. 70 of 1929
		Shannon Works Transfer (No.9) Order [Vol. XI p. 393] S.R.& O. No. 71 of 1929
		Shannon Works Transfer (No.10) Order [Vol. XI p. 397] S.R.& O. No. 72 of 1929
		Shannon Works Transfer (No.11) Order [Vol. XI p. 401] S.R.& O. No. 73 of 1929
		Shannon Works Transfer (No.12) Order [Vol. XI p. 405] S.R.& O. No. 15 of 1930
		Shannon Works Transfer (No.13) Order [Vol. XI p. 409] S.R.& O. No. 17 of 1930
		Shannon Works Transfer (No.16) Order [Vol. XI p. 421] S.R.& O. No. 25 of 1930
		Shannon Works Transfer (No.14) Order [Vol. XI p. 413] S.R.& O. No. 27 of 1930
		Shannon Works Transfer (No.15) Order [Vol. XI p. 417] S.R.& O. No. 30 of 1930
		Shannon Works Transfer (No.17) Order [Vol. XI p. 425] S.R.& O. No. 35 of 1930
		Shannon Works Transfer (No.18) Order [Vol. XI p. 429] S.R.& O. No. 40 of 1930
		Shannon Works Transfer (No.19) Order [Vol. XI p. 433] S.R.& O. No. 52 of 1930
		Shannon Works Transfer (No.20) Order [Vol. XI p. 437] S.R.& O. No. 60 of 1930
		Shannon Works Transfer (No.21) Order [Vol. XI p. 441] S.R.& O. No. 89 of 1931
		Shannon Works Transfer (No.22) Order [Vol. XXIX p. 25] S.R.& O. No. 93 of 1944
	104	**Relief from Obligation to Supply Gas (Sligo Area) Order, S.I. No. 168 of 1968**

Statutory Authority	Section	Statutory Instrument
Electricity Supply Board (Superannuation) Act, No. 17 of 1942 (*Cont.*)		*Electricity Supply Board (Confirmation of Manual Workers' Superannuation (Amendment) (No.1) Scheme) Order, S.I. No. 298 of 1952*
		Electricity Supply Board (Confirmation of General Employees Superannuation (Amendment) (No.1) Scheme) Order, S.I. No. 315 of 1952
	8	*Electricity Supply Board (General Employees Superannuation Fund) Regulations [Vol. XXIX p. 109] S.R.& O. No. 218 of 1943*
		Electricity Supply Board (Manual Workers' Superannuation Fund) Regulations [Vol. XXIX p. 115] S.R.& O. No. 219 of 1943
	9	*Electricity Supply Board (Appointment of Member of Tribunal) Regulations [Vol. XXIX p. 43] S.R.& O. No. 220 of 1943*
		Electricity Supply Board (Appointment of Member of Tribunal) Regulations [Vol. XXXVII p. 235] S.R.& O. No. 21 of 1947
Electricity (Temporary Provisions) Act, No. 42 of 1961	1(2)	*Electricity (Temporary Provisions) Act, 1961 (Termination) Order, S.I. No. 197 of 1961*
	4	*Electricity Supply Board (Commission of Inquiry) Order, S.I. No. 196 of 1961*
Emergency Imposition of Duties Act, No. 16 of 1932	1	*Emergency Imposition of Duties (No.1) Order [Vol. XI p. 445] S.R.& O. No. 60 of 1932*
		Emergency Imposition of Duties (No.2) Order [Vol. XI p. 467] S.R.& O. No. 70 of 1932
		Emergency Imposition of Duties (No.3) Order [Vol. XI p. 473] S.R.& O. No. 71 of 1932
		Emergency Imposition of Duties (No.1) (Amendment) Order [Vol. XI p. 461] S.R.& O. No. 75 of 1932
		Emergency Imposition of Duties (No.4) Order [Vol. XI p. 489] S.R.& O. No. 84 of 1932
		Emergency Imposition of Duties (No.4) (Amendment) Order [Vol. XI p. 507] S.R.& O. No. 103 of 1932
		Emergency Imposition of Duties (Miscellaneous Revocations) Order [Vol. XI p. 483] S.R.& O. No. 111 of 1932
		Emergency Imposition of Duties (No.5) Order [Vol. XI p. 515] S.R.& O. No. 112 of 1932
		Emergency Imposition of Duties (No.4) (Amendment) Order [Vol. XI p. 511] S.R.& O. No. 15 of 1933
		Emergency Imposition of Duties (No.6) Order [Vol. XI p. 533] S.R.& O. No. 24 of 1933
		Emergency Imposition of Duties (No.7) Order [Vol. XI p. 541] S.R.& O. No. 26 of 1933
		Emergency Imposition of Duties (No.8) Order [Vol. XI p. 545] S.R.& O. No. 31 of 1933

Statutory Authority	Section	Statutory Instrument
Emergency Imposition of Duties Act, No. 16 of 1932 (*Cont.*)		**Emergency Imposition of Duties (No.9) Order [Vol. XI p. 549] S.R.& O. No. 37 of 1933**
		Emergency Imposition of Duties (No.10) Order [Vol. XI p. 553] S.R.& O. No. 43 of 1933
		Emergency Imposition of Duties (No.11) Order [Vol. XI p. 559] S.R.& O. No. 44 of 1933
		Emergency Imposition of Duties (No.12) Order [Vol. XI p. 565] S.R.& O. No. 61 of 1933
		Emergency Imposition of Duties (No.13) Order [Vol. XI p. 569] S.R.& O. No. 62 of 1933
		Emergency Imposition of Duties (No.14) Order [Vol. XI p. 573] S.R.& O. No. 70 of 1933
		Emergency Imposition of Duties (No.15) Order [Vol. XI p. 577] S.R.& O. No. 110 of 1933
		Emergency Imposition of Duties (No.16) Order [Vol. XI p. 581] S.R.& O. No. 117 of 1933
		Emergency Imposition of Duties (No.17) Order [Vol. XI p. 587] S.R.& O. No. 123 of 1933
		Emergency Imposition of Duties (No.18) Order [Vol. XI p. 591] S.R.& O. No. 142 of 1933
		Emergency Imposition of Duties (No.19) Order [Vol. XI p. 595] S.R.& O. No. 155 of 1933
		Emergency Imposition of Duties (No.20) Order [Vol. XI p. 601] S.R.& O. No. 156 of 1933
		Emergency Imposition of Duties (No.21) Order [Vol. XI p. 607] S.R.& O. No. 166 of 1933
		Emergency Imposition of Duties (No.22) Order [Vol. XI p. 613] S.R.& O. No. 6 of 1934
		Emergency Imposition of Duties (No.23) Order [Vol. XI p. 621] S.R.& O. No. 13 of 1934
		Emergency Imposition of Duties (No.24) Order [Vol. XI p. 635] S.R.& O. No. 22 of 1934
		Emergency Imposition of Duties (No.25) Order [Vol. XI p. 643] S.R.& O. No. 27 of 1934
		Emergency Imposition of Duties (No.26) Order [Vol. XI p. 649] S.R.& O. No. 29 of 1934
		Emergency Imposition of Duties (No.27) Order [Vol. XI p. 655] S.R.& O. No. 30 of 1934
		Emergency Imposition of Duties (No.28) Order [Vol. XI p. 659] S.R.& O. No. 31 of 1934
		Emergency Imposition of Duties (No.29) Order [Vol. XI p. 665] S.R.& O. No. 42 of 1934
		Emergency Imposition of Duties (No.30) Order [Vol. XI p. 671] S.R.& O. No. 130 of 1934
		Emergency Imposition of Duties (No.31) Order [Vol. XI p. 677] S.R.& O. No. 135 of 1934
		Emergency Imposition of Duties (No.32) Order [Vol. XI p. 681] S.R.& O. No. 155 of 1934
		Emergency Imposition of Duties (No.33) Order [Vol. XI p. 687] S.R.& O. No. 156 of 1934
		Emergency Imposition of Duties (No.34) Order [Vol. XI p. 693] S.R.& O. No. 157 of 1934

Statutory Authority	Section	Statutory Instrument

Emergency Imposition of Duties
Act, No. 16 of 1932 (*Cont.*)

Emergency Imposition of Duties (No.35) Order [Vol. XI p. 699] S.R.& O. No. 158 of 1934

Emergency Imposition of Duties (No.36) Order [Vol. XI p. 705] S.R.& O. No. 159 of 1934

Emergency Imposition of Duties (No.37) Order [Vol. XI p. 711] S.R.& O. No. 160 of 1934

Emergency Imposition of Duties (No.38) Order [Vol. XI p. 717] S.R.& O. No. 161 of 1934

Emergency Imposition of Duties (No.39) Order [Vol. XI p. 723] S.R.& O. No. 162 of 1934

Emergency Imposition of Duties (No.40) Order [Vol. XI p. 729] S.R.& O. No. 163 of 1934

Emergency Imposition of Duties (No.41) Order [Vol. XI p. 735] S.R.& O. No. 164 of 1934

Emergency Imposition of Duties (No.42) Order [Vol. XI p. 739] S.R.& O. No. 184 of 1934

Emergency Imposition of Duties (No.43) Order [Vol. XI p. 745] S.R.& O. No. 198 of 1934

Emergency Imposition of Duties (No.44) Order [Vol. XI p. 751] S.R.& O. No. 218 of 1934

Emergency Imposition of Duties (No.45) Order [Vol. XI p. 757] S.R.& O. No. 219 of 1934

Emergency Imposition of Duties (No.46) Order [Vol. XI p. 763] S.R.& O. No. 235 of 1934

Emergency Imposition of Duties (No.47) Order [Vol. XI p. 769] S.R.& O. No. 236 of 1934

Emergency Imposition of Duties (No.48) Order [Vol. XI p. 773] S.R.& O. No. 237 of 1934

Emergency Imposition of Duties (No.49) Order [Vol. XI p. 779] S.R.& O. No. 250 of 1934

Emergency Imposition of Duties (No.50) Order [Vol. XI p. 785] S.R.& O. No. 266 of 1934

Emergency Imposition of Duties (No.51) Order [Vol. XI p. 789] S.R.& O. No. 267 of 1934

Emergency Imposition of Duties (No.52) Order [Vol. XI p. 809] S.R.& O. No. 290 of 1934

Emergency Imposition of Duties (No.53) Order [Vol. XI p. 813] S.R.& O. No. 330 of 1934

Emergency Imposition of Duties (No.54) Order [Vol. XI p. 819] S.R.& O. No. 331 of 1934

Emergency Imposition of Duties (No.55) Order [Vol. XI p. 823] S.R.& O. No. 332 of 1934

Emergency Imposition of Duties (No.56) Order [Vol. XI p. 829] S.R.& O. No. 333 of 1934

Emergency Imposition of Duties (No.57) Order [Vol. XI p. 835] S.R.& O. No. 349 of 1934

Emergency Imposition of Duties (No.58) Order [Vol. XI p. 839] S.R.& O. No. 356 of 1934

Emergency Imposition of Duties (No.59) Order [Vol. XI p. 843] S.R.& O. No. 364 of 1934

Emergency Imposition of Duties (No.60) Order [Vol. XI p. 847] S.R.& O. No. 1 of 1935

Statutory Authority	Section	Statutory Instrument

Emergency Imposition of Duties
Act, No. 16 of 1932 (*Cont.*)

*Emergency Imposition of Duties (No.61) Order
[Vol. XI p. 853] S.R.& O. No. 22 of 1935*

*Emergency Imposition of Duties (No.62) Order
[Vol. XI p. 859] S.R.& O. No. 23 of 1935*

*Emergency Imposition of Duties (No.63) Order
[Vol. XI p. 863] S.R.& O. No. 27 of 1935*

**Emergency Imposition of Duties (No.64) Order [Vol.
XI p. 869] S.R.& O. No. 32 of 1935**

*Emergency Imposition of Duties (No.65) Order
[Vol. XI p. 877] S.R.& O. No. 43 of 1935*

**Emergency Imposition of Duties (No.66) Order [Vol.
XI p. 883] S.R.& O. No. 81 of 1935**

*Emergency Imposition of Duties (No.67) Order
[Vol. XI p. 889] S.R.& O. No. 86 of 1935*

*Emergency Imposition of Duties (No.68) Order
[Vol. XI p. 895] S.R.& O. No. 91 of 1935*

*Emergency Imposition of Duties (No.69) Order
[Vol. XI p. 901] S.R.& O. No. 124 of 1935*

**Emergency Imposition of Duties (No.70) Order [Vol.
XI p. 907] S.R.& O. No. 257 of 1935**

*Emergency Imposition of Duties (No.71) Order
[Vol. XI p. 913] S.R.& O. No. 260 of 1935*

**Emergency Imposition of Duties (No.72) Order [Vol.
XI p. 917] S.R.& O. No. 404 of 1935**

**Emergency Imposition of Duties (No.73) Order [Vol.
XI p. 923] S.R.& O. No. 405 of 1935**

*Emergency Imposition of Duties (No.74) Order
[Vol. XI p. 929] S.R.& O. No. 406 of 1935*

*Emergency Imposition of Duties (No.75) Order
[Vol. XI p. 935] S.R.& O. No. 407 of 1935*

*Emergency Imposition of Duties (No.76) Order
[Vol. XI p. 939] S.R.& O. No. 543 of 1935*

**Emergency Imposition of Duties (No.77) Order [Vol.
XI p. 945] S.R.& O. No. 544 of 1935**

*Emergency Imposition of Duties (No.78) Order
[Vol. XI p. 953] S.R.& O. No. 561 of 1935*

*Emergency Imposition of Duties (No.79) Order
[Vol. XI p. 957] S.R.& O. No. 562 of 1935*

**Emergency Imposition of Duties (No.80) Order [Vol.
XI p. 963] S.R.& O. No. 571 of 1935**

**Emergency Imposition of Duties (No.81) Order [Vol.
XI p. 969] S.R.& O. No. 576 of 1935**

*Emergency Imposition of Duties (No.82) Order
[Vol. XI p. 975] S.R.& O. No. 623 of 1935*

*Emergency Imposition of Duties (No.83) Order
[Vol. XI p. 981] S.R.& O. No. 624 of 1935*

*Emergency Imposition of Duties (No.84) Order
[Vol. XI p. 985] S.R.& O. No. 625 of 1935*

*Emergency Imposition of Duties (No.85) Order
[Vol. XI p. 989] S.R.& O. No. 626 of 1935*

*Emergency Imposition of Duties (No.86) Order
[Vol. XI p. 993] S.R.& O. No. 630 of 1935*

Statutory Authority	Section	Statutory Instrument
Emergency Imposition of Duties Act, No. 16 of 1932 (*Cont.*)		*Emergency Imposition of Duties (No.87) Order [Vol. XI p. 997] S.R.& O. No. 633 of 1935*
		Emergency Imposition of Duties (No.88) Order [Vol. XI p. 1001] S.R.& O. No. 648 of 1935
		Emergency Imposition of Duties (No.89) Order [Vol. XI p. 1005] S.R.& O. No. 662 of 1935
		Emergency Imposition of Duties (No.90) Order [Vol. XI p. 1011] S.R.& O. No. 663 of 1935
		Emergency Imposition of Duties (No.91) Order [Vol. XI p. 1015] S.R.& O. No. 1 of 1936
		Emergency Imposition of Duties (No.92) Order [Vol. XI p. 1019] S.R.& O. No. 6 of 1936
		Emergency Imposition of Duties (No.93) Order [Vol. XI p. 1025] S.R.& O. No. 7 of 1936
		Emergency Imposition of Duties (No.94) Order [Vol. XI p. 1031] S.R.& O. No. 11 of 1936
		Emergency Imposition of Duties (No.95) Order [Vol. XI p. 1035] S.R.& O. No. 12 of 1936
		Emergency Imposition of Duties (No.96) Order [Vol. XI p. 1039] S.R.& O. No. 41 of 1936
		Emergency Imposition of Duties (No.97) Order [Vol. XI p. 1049] S.R.& O. No. 47 of 1936
		Emergency Imposition of Duties (No.98) Order [Vol. XI p. 1055] S.R.& O. No. 59 of 1936
		Emergency Imposition of Duties (No.99) Order [Vol. XI p. 1063] S.R.& O. No. 68 of 1936
		Emergency Imposition of Duties (No.100) Order [Vol. XI p. 1067] S.R.& O. No. 84 of 1936
		Emergency Imposition of Duties (No.101) Order [Vol. XI p. 1073] S.R.& O. No. 86 of 1936
		Emergency Imposition of Duties (No.102) Order [Vol. XI p. 1079] S.R.& O. No. 92 of 1936
		Emergency Imposition of Duties (No.103) Order [Vol. XI p. 1085] S.R.& O. No. 128 of 1936
		Emergency Imposition of Duties (No.104) Order [Vol. XI p. 1093] S.R.& O. No. 171 of 1936
		Emergency Imposition of Duties (No.105) Order [Vol. XI p. 1097] S.R.& O. No. 183 of 1936
		Emergency Imposition of Duties (No.106) Order [Vol. XI p. 1103] S.R.& O. No. 215 of 1936
		Emergency Imposition of Duties (No.107) Order [Vol. XI p. 1107] S.R.& O. No. 248 of 1936
		Emergency Imposition of Duties (No.108) Order [Vol. XI p. 1113] S.R.& O. No. 249 of 1936
		Emergency Imposition of Duties (No.109) Order [Vol. XI p. 1119] S.R.& O. No. 283 of 1936
		Emergency Imposition of Duties (No.110) Order [Vol. XI p. 1123] S.R.& O. No. 284 of 1936
		Emergency Imposition of Duties (No.111) Order [Vol. XI p. 1127] S.R.& O. No. 302 of 1936
		Emergency Imposition of Duties (No.112) Order [Vol. XI p. 1133] S.R.& O. No. 330 of 1936

Statutory Authority	Section	Statutory Instrument
Emergency Imposition of Duties Act, No. 16 of 1932 (*Cont.*)		**Emergency Imposition of Duties (No.113) Order** [Vol. XI p. 1139] S.R.& O. No. 357 of 1936
		Emergency Imposition of Duties (No.114) Order [Vol. XI p. 1145] S.R.& O. No. 358 of 1936
		Emergency Imposition of Duties (No.115) Order [Vol. XI p. 1153] S.R.& O. No. 368 of 1936
		Emergency Imposition of Duties (No.116) Order [Vol. XI p. 1159] S.R.& O. No. 381 of 1936
		Emergency Imposition of Duties (No.117) Order [Vol. XI p. 1165] S.R.& O. No. 3 of 1937
		Emergency Imposition of Duties (No.118) Order [Vol. XI p. 1171] S.R.& O. No. 11 of 1937
		Emergency Imposition of Duties (No.119) Order [Vol. XI p. 1177] S.R.& O. No. 12 of 1937
		Emergency Imposition of Duties (No.120) Order [Vol. XI p. 1181] S.R.& O. No. 13 of 1937
		Emergency Imposition of Duties (No.121) Order [Vol. XI p. 1187] S.R.& O. No. 14 of 1937
		Emergency Imposition of Duties (No.122) Order [Vol. XI p. 1193] S.R.& O. No. 22 of 1937
		Emergency Imposition of Duties (No.123) Order [Vol. XI p. 1197] S.R.& O. No. 31 of 1937
		Emergency Imposition of Duties (No.124) Order [Vol. XI p. 1203] S.R.& O. No. 69 of 1937
		Emergency Imposition of Duties (No.125) Order [Vol. XI p. 1207] S.R.& O. No. 132 of 1937
		Emergency Imposition of Duties (No.126) Order [Vol. XI p. 1213] S.R.& O. No. 140 of 1937
		Emergency Imposition of Duties (No.127) Order [Vol. XI p. 1219] S.R.& O. No. 194 of 1937
		Emergency Imposition of Duties (No.128) Order [Vol. XI p. 1225] S.R.& O. No. 218 of 1937
		Emergency Imposition of Duties (No.129) Order [Vol. XI p. 1231] S.R.& O. No. 219 of 1937
		Emergency Imposition of Duties (No.130) Order [Vol. XI p. 1237] S.R.& O. No. 243 of 1937
		Emergency Imposition of Duties (No.131) Order [Vol. XI p. 1243] S.R.& O. No. 315 of 1937
		Emergency Imposition of Duties (No.132) Order [Vol. XI p. 1253] S.R.& O. No. 321 of 1937
		Emergency Imposition of Duties (No.133) Order [Vol. XI p. 1259] S.R.& O. No. 322 of 1937
		Emergency Imposition of Duties (No.134) Order [Vol. XI p. 1263] S.R.& O. No. 327 of 1937
		Emergency Imposition of Duties (No.135) Order [Vol. XI p. 1269] S.R.& O. No. 328 of 1937
		Emergency Imposition of Duties (No.136) Order [Vol. XI p. 1275] S.R.& O. No. 329 of 1937
		Emergency Imposition of Duties (No.137) Order [Vol. XI p. 1281] S.R.& O. No. 20 of 1938
		Emergency Imposition of Duties (No.138) Order [Vol. XI p. 1287] S.R.& O. No. 89 of 1938

Statutory Authority	Section	Statutory Instrument

Emergency Imposition of Duties
Act, No. 16 of 1932 (*Cont.*)

Emergency Imposition of Duties (No.139) Order
[Vol. XI p. 1295] S.R.& O. No. 90 of 1938

Emergency Imposition of Duties (No.140) Order
[Vol. XI p. 1303] S.R.& O. No. 120 of 1938

Emergency Imposition of Duties (No.143) Order
[Vol. XI p. 1315] S.R.& O. No. 130 of 1938

Emergency Imposition of Duties (No.144) Order
[Vol. XI p. 1327] S.R.& O. No. 131 of 1938

Emergency Imposition of Duties (No.145) Order
[Vol. XI p. 1331] S.R.& O. No. 132 of 1938

Emergency Imposition of Duties (No.141) Order
[Vol. XI p. 1307] S.R.& O. No. 151 of 1938

Emergency Imposition of Duties (No.142) Order
[Vol. XI p. 1311] S.R.& O. No. 152 of 1938

Emergency Imposition of Duties (No.146) Order
[Vol. XI p. 1339] S.R.& O. No. 198 of 1938

Emergency Imposition of Duties (No.147) Order
[Vol. XI p. 1343] S.R.& O. No. 199 of 1938

Emergency Imposition of Duties (No.148) Order
[Vol. XI p. 1347] S.R.& O. No. 200 of 1938

Emergency Imposition of Duties (No.149) Order
[Vol. XI p. 1353] S.R.& O. No. 201 of 1938

Emergency Imposition of Duties (No.150) Order
[Vol. XI p. 1359] S.R.& O. No. 202 of 1938

Emergency Imposition of Duties (No.151) Order
[Vol. XI p. 1363] S.R.& O. No. 203 of 1938

Emergency Imposition of Duties (No.152) Order
[Vol. XI p. 1365] S.R.& O. No. 217 of 1938

Emergency Imposition of Duties (No.153) Order
[Vol. XI p. 1371] S.R.& O. No. 218 of 1938

Emergency Imposition of Duties (No.154) Order
[Vol. XI p. 1375] S.R.& O. No. 222 of 1938

Emergency Imposition of Duties (No.155) Order
[Vol. XI p. 1381] S.R.& O. No. 223 of 1938

Emergency Imposition of Duties (No.156) Order
[Vol. XI p. 1387] S.R.& O. No. 224 of 1938

Emergency Imposition of Duties (No.157) Order
[Vol. XI p. 1391] S.R.& O. No. 240 of 1938

Emergency Imposition of Duties (No.158) Order
[Vol. XI p. 1397] S.R.& O. No. 241 of 1938

Emergency Imposition of Duties (No.159) Order
[Vol. XI p. 1401] S.R.& O. No. 242 of 1938

Emergency Imposition of Duties (No.160) Order
[Vol. XI p. 1407] S.R.& O. No. 267 of 1938

Emergency Imposition of Duties (No.161) Order
[Vol. XI p. 1413] S.R.& O. No. 289 of 1938

Emergency Imposition of Duties (No.162) Order
[Vol. XI p. 1417] S.R.& O. No. 290 of 1938

Emergency Imposition of Duties (No.163) Order
[Vol. XI p. 1421] S.R.& O. No. 291 of 1938

Emergency Imposition of Duties (No.164) Order
[Vol. XI p. 1427] S.R.& O. No. 292 of 1938

Statutory Authority	Section	Statutory Instrument
Emergency Imposition of Duties Act, No. 16 of 1932 (*Cont.*)		**Emergency Imposition of Duties (No.165) Order** [Vol. XI p. 1433] S.R.& O. No. 323 of 1938
		Emergency Imposition of Duties (No.166) Order [Vol. XI p. 1439] S.R.& O. No. 324 of 1938
		Emergency Imposition of Duties (No.167) Order [Vol. XI p. 1445] S.R.& O. No. 325 of 1938
		Emergency Imposition of Duties (No.168) Order [Vol. XXIX p. 121] S.R.& O. No. 9 of 1939
		Emergency Imposition of Duties (No.169) Order [Vol. XXIX p. 127] S.R.& O. No. 11 of 1939
		Emergency Imposition of Duties (No.170) Order [Vol. XXIX p. 133] S.R.& O. No. 12 of 1939
		Emergency Imposition of Duties (No.171) Order [Vol. XXIX p. 139] S.R.& O. No. 13 of 1939
		Emergency Imposition of Duties (No.172) Order [Vol. XXIX p. 145] S.R.& O. No. 22 of 1939
		Emergency Imposition of Duties (No.173) Order [Vol. XXIX p. 151] S.R.& O. No. 43 of 1939
		Emergency Imposition of Duties (No.174) Order [Vol. XXIX p. 157] S.R.& O. No. 44 of 1939
		Emergency Imposition of Duties (No.175) Order [Vol. XXIX p. 161] S.R.& O. No. 50 of 1939
		Emergency Imposition of Duties (No.176) Order [Vol. XXIX p. 167] S.R.& O. No. 52 of 1939
		Emergency Imposition of Duties (No.177) Order [Vol. XXIX p. 173] S.R.& O. No. 65 of 1939
		Emergency Imposition of Duties (No.178) Order [Vol. XXIX p. 179] S.R.& O. No. 66 of 1939
		Emergency Imposition of Duties (No.179) Order [Vol. XXIX p. 187] S.R.& O. No. 67 of 1939
		Emergency Imposition of Duties (No.180) Order [Vol. XXIX p. 193] S.R.& O. No. 76 of 1939
		Emergency Imposition of Duties (No.181) Order [Vol. XXIX p. 201] S.R.& O. No. 77 of 1939
		Emergency Imposition of Duties (No.182) Order [Vol. XXIX p. 209] S.R.& O. No. 103 of 1939
		Emergency Imposition of Duties (No.183) Order [Vol. XXIX p. 213] S.R.& O. No. 104 of 1939
		Emergency Imposition of Duties (No.184) Order [Vol. XXIX p. 217] S.R.& O. No. 126 of 1939
		Emergency Imposition of Duties (No.185) Order [Vol. XXIX p. 223] S.R.& O. No. 127 of 1939
		Emergency Imposition of Duties (No.186) Order [Vol. XXIX p. 227] S.R.& O. No. 140 of 1939
		Emergency Imposition of Duties (No.187) Order [Vol. XXIX p. 233] S.R.& O. No. 141 of 1939
		Emergency Imposition of Duties (No.188) Order [Vol. XXIX p. 239] S.R.& O. No. 142 of 1939
		Emergency Imposition of Duties (No.189) Order [Vol. XXIX p. 243] S.R.& O. No. 143 of 1939
		Emergency Imposition of Duties (No.190) Order [Vol. XXIX p. 247] S.R.& O. No. 161 of 1939

Statutory Authority	Section	Statutory Instrument

Emergency Imposition of Duties
Act, No. 16 of 1932 (*Cont.*)

Emergency Imposition of Duties (No.191) Order
[Vol. XXIX p. 255] S.R.& O. No. 183 of 1939

Emergency Imposition of Duties (No.192) Order
[Vol. XXIX p. 261] S.R.& O. No. 189 of 1939

Emergency Imposition of Duties (No.193) Order
[Vol. XXIX p. 267] S.R.& O. No. 190 of 1939

Emergency Imposition of Duties (No.194) Order
[Vol. XXIX p. 277] S.R.& O. No. 209 of 1939

Emergency Imposition of Duties (No.195) Order
[Vol. XXIX p. 285] S.R.& O. No. 210 of 1939

Emergency Imposition of Duties (No.196) Order
[Vol. XXIX p. 291] S.R.& O. No. 211 of 1939

Emergency Imposition of Duties (No.197) Order
[Vol. XXIX p. 295] S.R.& O. No. 212 of 1939

Emergency Imposition of Duties (No.198) Order
[Vol. XXIX p. 301] S.R.& O. No. 213 of 1939

Emergency Imposition of Duties (No.199) Order
[Vol. XXIX p. 307] S.R.& O. No. 214 of 1939

Emergency Imposition of Duties (No.201) Order
[Vol. XXIX p. 321] S.R.& O. No. 232 of 1939

Emergency Imposition of Duties (No.200) Order
[Vol. XXIX p. 315] S.R.& O. No. 235 of 1939

Emergency Imposition of Duties (No.202) Order
[Vol. XXIX p. 327] S.R.& O. No. 289 of 1939

Emergency Imposition of Duties (No.203) Order
[Vol. XXIX p. 333] S.R.& O. No. 390 of 1939

Emergency Imposition of Duties (No.204) Order
[Vol. XXIX p. 339] S.R.& O. No. 73 of 1940

Emergency Imposition of Duties (No.205) Order
[Vol. XXIX p. 343] S.R.& O. No. 129 of 1940

Emergency Imposition of Duties (No.206) Order
[Vol. XXIX p. 351] S.R.& O. No. 154 of 1940

Emergency Imposition of Duties (No.207) Order
[Vol. XXIX p. 355] S.R.& O. No. 155 of 1940

Emergency Imposition of Duties (No.208) Order
[Vol. XXIX p. 359] S.R.& O. No. 189 of 1940

Emergency Imposition of Duties (No.209) Order
[Vol. XXIX p. 363] S.R.& O. No. 190 of 1940

Emergency Imposition of Duties (No.210) Order
[Vol. XXIX p. 373] S.R.& O. No. 191 of 1940

Emergency Imposition of Duties (No.211) Order
[Vol. XXIX p. 379] S.R.& O. No. 192 of 1940

Emergency Imposition of Duties (No.212) Order
[Vol. XXIX p. 387] S.R.& O. No. 193 of 1940

Emergency Imposition of Duties (No.213) Order
[Vol. XXIX p. 397] S.R.& O. No. 194 of 1940

Emergency Imposition of Duties (No.214) Order
[Vol. XXIX p. 407] S.R.& O. No. 195 of 1940

Emergency Imposition of Duties (No.215) Order
[Vol. XXIX p. 417] S.R.& O. No. 333 of 1940

Emergency Imposition of Duties (No.216) Order
[Vol. XXIX p. 423] S.R.& O. No. 70 of 1941

Emergency Imposition of Duties
Act, No. 16 of 1932 (*Cont.*)

Emergency Imposition of Duties (No.217) Order [Vol. XXIX p. 427] S.R.& O. No. 136 of 1941

Emergency Imposition of Duties (No.218) Order [Vol. XXIX p. 435] S.R.& O. No. 155 of 1941

Emergency Imposition of Duties (No.219) Order [Vol. XXIX p. 439] S.R.& O. No. 181 of 1941

Emergency Imposition of Duties (No.220) Order [Vol. XXIX p. 447] S.R.& O. No. 214 of 1941

Emergency Imposition of Duties (No.221) Order [Vol. XXIX p. 451] S.R.& O. No. 403 of 1941

Emergency Imposition of Duties (No.222) Order [Vol. XXIX p. 457] S.R.& O. No. 421 of 1941

Emergency Imposition of Duties (No.223) Order [Vol. XXIX p. 465] S.R.& O. No. 464 of 1941

Emergency Imposition of Duties (No.224) Order [Vol. XXIX p. 475] S.R.& O. No. 492 of 1941

Emergency Imposition of Duties (No.226) Order [Vol. XXXVII p. 245] S.R.& O. No. 129 of 1946

Emergency Imposition of Duties (No.227) Order [Vol. XXXVII p. 255] S.R.& O. No. 20 of 1947

Emergency Imposition of Duties (No.172) Order, 1939 (Revocation) Order [Vol. XXXVII p. 241] S.R.& O. No. 144 of 1947

Emergency Imposition of Duties (No.228) Order [Vol. XXXVII p. 259] S.R.& O. No. 285 of 1947

Emergency Imposition of Duties (No.229) Order, S.I. No. 52 of 1948

Emergency Imposition of Duties (No.230) Order, S.I. No. 68 of 1948

Emergency Imposition of Duties (No.231) Order, S.I. No. 69 of 1948

Emergency Imposition of Duties (No.232) Order, S.I. No. 70 of 1948

Emergency Imposition of Duties (No.233) Order, S.I. No. 241 of 1948

Emergency Imposition of Duties (No.234) Order, S.I. No. 284 of 1948

Emergency Imposition of Duties (No.235) Order, S.I. No. 285 of 1948

Emergency Imposition of Duties (No.236) Order, S.I. No. 286 of 1948

Emergency Imposition of Duties (No.237) Order, S.I. No. 3 of 1949

Emergency Imposition of Duties (No.238) Order, S.I. No. 12 of 1949

Emergency Imposition of Duties (No.239) Order, S.I. No. 69 of 1949

Emergency Imposition of Duties (No.240) Order, S.I. No. 127 of 1949

Emergency Imposition of Duties (No.241) Order, S.I. No. 189 of 1949

Emergency Imposition of Duties (No.242) Order, S.I. No. 194 of 1949

Emergency Imposition of Duties
Act, No. 16 of 1932 (*Cont.*)

Emergency Imposition of Duties (No.243) Order,
S.I. No. 243 of 1949

Emergency Imposition of Duties (No.244) Order,
S.I. No. 266 of 1949

Emergency Imposition of Duties (No.245) Order,
S.I. No. 273 of 1949

Emergency Imposition of Duties (No.246) Order,
S.I. No. 294 of 1949

Emergency Imposition of Duties (No.238) (Amendment) Order, S.I. No. 296 of 1949

Emergency Imposition of Duties (No.247) Order,
S.I. No. 305 of 1949

Emergency Imposition of Duties (No.248) Order,
S.I. No. 5 of 1950

Emergency Imposition of Duties (No.249) Order,
S.I. No. 14 of 1950

Emergency Imposition of Duties (No.250) Order,
S.I. No. 22 of 1950

Emergency Imposition of Duties (No.251) Order,
S.I. No. 64 of 1950

Emergency Imposition of Duties (No.252) Order,
S.I. No. 88 of 1950

Emergency Imposition of Duties (No.253) Order,
S.I. No. 94 of 1950

Emergency Imposition of Duties (No.254) Order,
S.I. No. 176 of 1950

Emergency Imposition of Duties (No.255) Order,
S.I. No. 192 of 1950

Emergency Imposition of Duties (No.256) Order,
S.I. No. 204 of 1950

Emergency Imposition of Duties (No.257) Order,
S.I. No. 234 of 1950

Emergency Imposition of Duties (No.258) Order,
S.I. No. 251 of 1950

Emergency Imposition of Duties (No.259) Order,
S.I. No. 284 of 1950

Emergency Imposition of Duties (No.260) Order,
S.I. No. 100 of 1951

*Emergency Imposition of Duties (No.262) Order,
S.I. No. 125 of 1951*

Emergency Imposition of Duties (No.261) Order,
S.I. No. 133 of 1951

Emergency Imposition of Duties (No.263) Order,
S.I. No. 304 of 1951

Emergency Imposition of Duties (No.264) (Cast Iron
Baths) Order, S.I. No. 313 of 1951

Emergency Imposition of Duties (No.265) (Pot
Scourers) Order, S.I. No. 317 of 1951

Emergency Imposition of Duties (No.266) (Cycle
Components) Order, S.I. No. 340 of 1951

Emergency Imposition of Duties (No.267) (Personal
Clothing and Wearing Apparel) Order, S.I.
No. 357 of 1951

Emergency Imposition of Duties (No.268) (Toilet
Seats and Covers) Order, S.I. No. 358 of 1951

Statutory Authority	Section	Statutory Instrument
Emergency Imposition of Duties Act, No. 16 of 1932 (*Cont.*)		Emergency Imposition of Duties (No.269) (Cotton Thread and Ply Yarn) Order, S.I. No. 27 of 1952
		Emergency Imposition of Duties (No.270) (Rain Gutters) Order, S.I. No. 29 of 1952
		Emergency Imposition of Duties (No.271) (Hard Floor Coverings) Order, S.I. No. 30 of 1952
		Emergency Imposition of Duties (No.272) (Sheep Skins) Order, S.I. No. 43 of 1952
		Emergency Imposition of Duties (No.273) (Forks and Wooden Handles) Order, S.I. No. 71 of 1952
		Emergency Imposition of Duties (No.274) (Razor Blades) Order, S.I. No. 99 of 1952
		Emergency Imposition of Duties (No.275) (Drinking Glasses) Order, S.I. No. 126 of 1952
		Emergency Imposition of Duties (No.276) (Crystal Glassware) Order, 1952:, S.I. No. 127 of 1952
		Emergency Imposition of Duties (No.277) (Knitted Woollen Fabric) Order, S.I. No. 152 of 1952
		Emergency Imposition of Duties (No.278) (Venetian Blinds) Order, S.I. No. 160 of 1952
		Emergency Imposition of Duties (No.280) (Lamp Shades) Order, S.I. No. 161 of 1952
		Emergency Imposition of Duties (No.279) (Woven Labels) Order, S.I. No. 162 of 1952
		Emergency Imposition of Duties (No.281) (Artificial Silk Piece Goods) Order, S.I. No. 163 of 1952
		Emergency Imposition of Duties (No.282) (Doll's Clothing and Components) Order, S.I. No. 185 of 1952
		Emergency Imposition of Duties (No.283) (Glue, Gelatine and Size) Order, S.I. No. 186 of 1952
		Emergency Imposition of Duties (No.284) (Abrasives) Order, S.I. No. 220 of 1952
		Emergency Imposition of Duties (No.285) (Hack Saw Blades) Order, S.I. No. 230 of 1952
		Emergency Imposition of Duties (No.286) (Leather) Order, S.I. No. 232 of 1952
		Emergency Imposition of Duties (No.287) (Tanks, Cisterns, etc.) Order, S.I. No. 253 of 1952
		Emergency Imposition of Duties (No.288) (Statues, Statuettes and Busts) Order, S.I. No. 254 of 1952
		Emergency Imposition of Duties (No.289) (Adhesive Gums) Order, S.I. No. 263 of 1952
		Emergency Imposition of Duties (No.290) (Malt Extract and Fish Liver Oil) Order, S.I. No. 264 of 1952
		Emergency Imposition of Duties (No.291) (Cotton Wool) Order, S.I. No. 281 of 1952
		Emergency Imposition of Duties (No.292) (Brace Elastic) Order, S.I. No. 285 of 1952
		Emergency Imposition of Duties (No.293) (Iron and Steel Wheelbarrows, Hand-Carts, etc.) Order, S.I. No. 297 of 1952

Emergency Imposition of Duties
Act, No. 16 of 1932 (*Cont.*)

Emergency Imposition of Duties (No.294) (Tanks, Cisterns, etc.) Order, S.I. No. 311 of 1952

Emergency Imposition of Duties (No.295) (Drinking Glasses) Order, S.I. No. 319 of 1952

Emergency Imposition of Duties (No.296) (Stainless Steel Couplings, etc.) Order, S.I. No. 347 of 1952

Emergency Imposition of Duties (No.297) (Television Sets) Order, S.I. No. 360 of 1952

Emergency Imposition of Duties (No.298) (Combs and Hair Slides) Order, S.I. No. 361 of 1952

Emergency Imposition of Duties (No.299) (Tarpaulins) Order, S.I. No. 57 of 1953

Emergency Imposition of Duties (No.300) (Woven Cotton Piece Goods) Order, S.I. No. 66 of 1953

Emergency Imposition of Duties (No.301) (Artificial Silk Piece Goods) Order, S.I. No. 67 of 1953

Emergency Imposition of Duties (No.302) (Sanitary Wear) Order, S.I. No. 68 of 1953

Emergency Imposition of Duties (No.303) (Cotton Ply Yarn) Order, S.I. No. 70 of 1953

Emergency Imposition of Duties (No.304) (Iron and Steel Bars and Sections) Order, S.I. No. 81 of 1953

Emergency Imposition of Duties (No.305) (Paper) Order, S.I. No. 125 of 1953

Emergency Imposition of Duties (No.306) (Root Crop Knives) Order, S.I. No. 127 of 1953

Emergency Imposition of Duties (No.307) (Iron and Steel Hexagonal Mesh Netting) Order, S.I. No. 197 of 1953

Emergency Imposition of Duties (No.308) (Iron and Steel Wire, Bars and Sections) Order, S.I. No. 198 of 1953

Emergency Imposition of Duties (No.309) (Single Cotton Yarns) Order, S.I. No. 217 of 1953

Emergency Imposition of Duties (No.310) (Handbags, etc) Order, S.I. No. 229 of 1953

Emergency Imposition of Duties (No.311) (Spectacle Frames) Order, S.I. No. 256 of 1953

Emergency Imposition of Duties (No.312) (Sheet and Plate Glass) Order, S.I. No. 271 of 1953

Emergency Imposition of Duties (No.313) (Asbestos Articles) Order, S.I. No. 277 of 1953

Emergency Imposition of Duties (No.314) (Table Ware) Order, S.I. No. 287 of 1953

Emergency Imposition of Duties (No.315) (Electric Wire and Cable) Order, S.I. No. 288 of 1953

Emergency Imposition of Duties (No.316) (Glass-Packed Sterile Liquids) Order, S.I. No. 302 of 1953

Emergency Imposition of Duties (No.317) (Toilet Paper) Order, S.I. No. 312 of 1953

Statutory Authority	Section	Statutory Instrument

Emergency Imposition of Duties
Act, No. 16 of 1932 (*Cont.*)

Emergency Imposition of Duties (No.340) (Woven Artificial Textile and Union Fabrics) Order, S.I. No. 228 of 1954

Emergency Imposition of Duties (No.341) (Rubber Solution) Order, S.I. No. 235 of 1954

Emergency Imposition of Duties (No.342) (Buttons and Button Blanks) Order, S.I. No. 237 of 1954

Emergency Imposition of Duties (No.343) (Woven Labels) Order, S.I. No. 281 of 1954

Emergency Imposition of Duties (No.344) (Electrical Accessories) Order, S.I. No. 35 of 1955

Emergency Imposition of Duties (No.345) (Gloves) Order, S.I. No. 46 of 1955

Emergency Imposition of Duties (No.346) (Slashers or Slash Hooks) Order, S.I. No. 61 of 1955

Emergency Imposition of Duties (No.347) (Silk and Artificial Silk) Order, S.I. No. 66 of 1955

Emergency Imposition of Duties (No.348) (Felting) Order, S.I. No. 101 of 1955

Emergency Imposition of Duties (No.350) (Gloves) (No.2) Order, S.I. No. 105 of 1955

Emergency Imposition of Duties (No.349) (Flexible Mirror Glass) Order, S.I. No. 106 of 1955

Emergency Imposition of Duties (No.351) (Woven Artificial Textile and Union Fabrics) Order, S.I. No. 131 of 1955

Emergency Imposition of Duties (No.352) (Display Shapes or Stands) (Plaster of Paris or Papier Mache) Order, S.I. No. 134 of 1955

Emergency Imposition of Duties (No.353) (Storage Water Heaters) , Order, S.I. No. 135 of 1955

Emergency Imposition of Duties (No.354) (Iron and Steel Fencing Material) Order, S.I. No. 166 of 1955

Emergency Imposition of Duties (No.355) (Milk Cans) Order, S.I. No. 169 of 1955

Emergency Imposition of Duties (No.356) (Iron and Steel Bolts) Order, S.I. No. 172 of 1955

Emergency Imposition of Duties (No.357) (Margarine) Order, S.I. No. 173 of 1955

Emergency Imposition of Duties (No.358) (Hoop or Strip of Iron, Steel or Aluminium, etc.) Order, S.I. No. 188 of 1955

Emergency Imposition of Duties (No.359) (Glucose) Order, S.I. No. 194 of 1955

Emergency Imposition of Duties (No.360) (Tableware) Order, S.I. No. 244 of 1955

Emergency Imposition of Duties (No.361) (Woven Artificial Textile and Union Fabrics) Order, S.I. No. 252 of 1955

Emergency Imposition of Duties (No.362) (Varnish, etc.) Order, S.I. No. 265 of 1955

Statutory Authority	Section	Statutory Instrument

Emergency Imposition of Duties
Act, No. 16 of 1932 (*Cont.*)

Emergency Imposition of Duties (No.363) (Power-take-off Units, Hydraulic Pumps and Hydraulic Lifting Mechanisms) Order, S.I. No. 14 of 1956

Emergency Imposition of Duties (No.264) (Block-board, etc.) Order, S.I. No. 16 of 1956

Emergency Imposition of Duties (No.365) (Plastic-Coated Fabric) Order, S.I. No. 22 of 1956

Emergency Imposition of Duties (No.366) (Knitted Fabric) Order, S.I. No. 32 of 1956

Emergency Imposition of Duties (No.367) (Printed Paper) Order, S.I. No. 38 of 1956

Emergency Imposition of Duties (No.368) (Religious Books) Order, S.I. No. 39 of 1956

Emergency Imposition of Duties (No.369) (Yarns) Order, S.I. No. 40 of 1956

Emergency Imposition of Duties (No.370) (Special Import Levy) Order, S.I. No. 45 of 1956

Emergency Imposition of Duties (No.371) (Catgut) Order, S.I. No. 62 of 1956

Emergency Imposition of Duties (No.372) (Golf Balls) Order, S.I. No. 63 of 1956

Emergency Imposition of Duties (No.373) (Gal-vanised Wrought Iron and Galvanised Steel Articles) Order, S.I. No. 64 of 1956

Emergency Imposition of Duties (No.374) (Scythe Mountings) Order, S.I. No. 65 of 1956

Emergency Imposition of Duties (No.375) (Alumi-nium Knitting Pins) Order, S.I. No. 66 of 1956

Emergency Imposition of Duties (No.376) (Miscell-aneous Revocations) Order, S.I. No. 67 of 1956

Emergency Imposition of Duties (No.377) (Manu-script Books) Order, S.I. No. 109 of 1956

Emergency Imposition of Duties (No.378) (Rosaries) Order, S.I. No. 130 of 1956

Emergency Imposition of Duties (No.379) (Special Import Levy) (Amendment) Order, S.I. No. 132 of 1956

Emergency Imposition of Duties (No.380) (Unglazed Clay Articles) Order, S.I. No. 187 of 1956

Emergency Imposition of Duties (No.381) (Saws and Saw Blades) Order, S.I. No. 191 of 1956

Emergency Imposition of Duties (No.382) (Fur-nishing Fabrics) Order, S.I. No. 197 of 1956

Emergency Imposition of Duties (No.383) (Special Import Levies) Order, S.I. No. 210 of 1956

Emergency Imposition of Duties (No.384) (Agricul-tural Machines) Order, S.I. No. 227 of 1956

Emergency Imposition of Duties (No.385) (Locks and Lock Fittings) Order, S.I. No. 229 of 1956

Emergency Imposition of Duties (No.346) (Lea-therboard) Order, S.I. No. 235 of 1956

Emergency Imposition of Duties
Act, No. 16 of 1932 (*Cont.*)

Emergency Imposition of Duties (No.387) (Preparations or Mixtures containing Malt Extract) Order, S.I. No. 241 of 1956

Emergency Imposition of Duties (No.388) (Wooden Clothes Pegs) Order, S.I. No. 243 of 1956

Emergency Imposition of Duties (No.389) (Television Sets) Order, S.I. No. 246 of 1956

Emergency Imposition of Duties (No.390) (Card Clothing) Order, S.I. No. 266 of 1956

Emergency Imposition of Duties (No.391) (Abrasives) Order, S.I. No. 267 of 1956

Emergency Imposition of Duties (No.392) (Mosaics) Order, S.I. No. 279 of 1956

Emergency Imposition of Duties (No.393) (Wheaten Breakfast Foods) Order, S.I. No. 28 of 1957

Emergency Imposition of Duties (No.395) (Powders containing Malt Extract) Order, S.I. No. 68 of 1957

Emergency Imposition of Duties (No.396) (Iron and Steel Bars, Rods and Sections) Order, S.I. No. 69 of 1957

Emergency Imposition of Duties (No.394) (Special Import Levies and Motor Car Duty) Order, S.I. No. 70 of 1957

Emergency Imposition of Duties (No.397) (Unprinted Paper Duty) Order, S.I. No. 77 of 1957

Emergency Imposition of Duties (No.398) (Special Import Levies) (Amendment) Order, S.I. No. 78 of 1957

Emergency Imposition of Duties (No.399) (Shirts) Order, S.I. No. 89 of 1957

Emergency Imposition of Duties (No.400) (Drags and Forks) Order, S.I. No. 91 of 1957

Emergency Imposition of Duties (No.401) (Agricultural Machines) Order, S.I. No. 108 of 1957

Emergency Powers Act, No. 28 of 1939

Emergency Powers Order, S.R.& O. No. 224 of 1939

Emergency Powers Order, S.R.& O. No. 224 of 1939

Emergency Powers (No.118) Order, S.R.& O. No. 456 of 1941

Emergency Powers (No.227) Order, S.R.& O. No. 417 of 1942

Emergency Powers (No.267) Order, S.R.& O. No. 102 of 1943

Emergency Powers (No.381) Order, S.R.& O. No. 179 of 1946

Candles (Maximum Prices) Order [Vol. XXXIX p. 47] S.R.& O. No. 390 of 1947

Distribution of Sugar to Manufacturing (Sugar) Consumers Order, S.I. No. 185 of 1948

Statutory Authority	Section	Statutory Instrument
Emergency Powers Order, S.R.& O. No. 224 of 1939 (*Cont.*)		*Emergency Powers (Orders Relating to Milling of Oats) (Revocation) Order, S.I. No. 340 of 1948*
		Biscuits (Maximum Prices) Order, 1948 (Revocation) Order, S.I. No. 430 of 1948
		Flour, Wheatenmeal and Bread Order, 1949 (Amendment) Order, S.I. No. 130 of 1949
		Flour, Wheatenmeal and Bread Order, 1949 (Amendment) Order, S.I. No. 150 of 1950
		Emergency Powers (Export of Beef, Mutton and Pork) Order, 1941 (Revocation) Order, S.I. No. 232 of 1953
	31	*Cheese (Levy) Order [Vol. IX p. 721] S.R.& O. No. 108 of 1937*
		Meat Extracts (Maximum Prices) Order [Vol. XXXIX p. 731] S.R.& O. No. 311 of 1946
		Cornflour (Maximum Prices) Order [Vol. XXXIX p. 337] S.R.& O. No. 326 of 1946
		Eggs (Maximum Prices) Order [Vol. XXXIX p. 383] S.R.& O. No. 327 of 1946
		Fertilisers (Maximum Prices) Order [Vol. XXXIX p. 419] S.R.& O. No. 330 of 1946
		Oatmeal (Maximum Prices) Order [Vol. XXXIX p. 775] S.R.& O. No. 353 of 1946
		Tomatoes (Maximum Prices) Order [Vol. XXXIX p. 1191] S.R.& O. No. 354 of 1946
		Dried Figs (Maximum Prices) Order [Vol. XXXIX p. 371] S.R.& O. No. 363 of 1946
		Oranges (Maximum Prices) Order [Vol. XXXIX p. 813] S.R.& O. No. 365 of 1946
		Grapefruit (Maximum Prices) Order [Vol. XXXIX p. 641] S.R.& O. No. 371 of 1946
		Cloth, Clothing and Knitting Wool (Maximum Prices) Order [Vol. XXXIX p. 147] S.R.& O. No. 381 of 1946
		Flour and Bread (Rationing) Order [Vol. XXXIX p. 443] S.R.& O. No. 388 of 1946
		Flour and Bread (Rationing) Order, 1946 (Supplemental Provisions) (No.1) Order [Vol. XXXIX p. 539] S.R.& O. No. 389 of 1946
		Sugar (Maximum Prices) Order [Vol. XXXIX p. 1011] S.R.& O. No. 393 of 1946
		Potatoes (Maximum Prices) Order [Vol. XXXIX p. 847] S.R.& O. No. 5 of 1947
		Prunes (Maximum Prices) Order [Vol. XXXIX p. 873] S.R.& O. No. 6 of 1947
		Raisins and Currants (Maximum Prices) Order [Vol. XXXIX p. 877] S.R.& O. No. 7 of 1947
		Onions (Maximum Prices) Order [Vol. XXXIX p. 795] S.R.& O. No. 10 of 1947
		Margarine (Maximum Prices) Order [Vol. XXXIX p. 719] S.R.& O. No. 17 of 1947
		Tyres and Tubes (Maximum Prices) Order [Vol. XXXIX p. 1203] S.R.& O. No. 22 of 1947

Statutory Authority	Section	Statutory Instrument

Emergency Powers Order, S.R.& O.
No. 224 of 1939 (*Cont.*)

Eggs (Maximum Prices) Order, 1946 (Revocation) Order [Vol. XXXIX p. 395] S.R.& O. No. 27 of 1947

Oatmeal (Maximum Prices) Order, 1946 (Amendment) (No.1) Order [Vol. XXXIX p. 791] S.R.& O. No. 38 of 1947

Firewood (Maximum Prices) Order [Vol. XXXIX p. 431] S.R.& O. No. 45 of 1947

Sulphate of Copper (Maximum Prices) Order [Vol. XXXIX p. 1035] S.R.& O. No. 46 of 1947

Canned Fish (Maximum Prices) Order [Vol. XXXIX p. 53] S.R.& O. No. 49 of 1947

Flour and Bread (Rationing) Order, 1946 (First Amendment) Order [Vol. XXXIX p. 507] S.R.& O. No. 56 of 1947

Flour and Bread (Rationing) Order, 1946 (Supplemental Provisions) (No.2) Order [Vol. XXXIX p. 545] S.R.& O. No. 57 of 1947

Bananas (Maximum Prices) Order [Vol. XXXIX p. 9] S.R.& O. No. 61 of 1947

Prohibition of Storage of Rabbits Order [Vol. XXXIX p. 867] S.R.& O. No. 64 of 1947

Footwear (Maximum Prices) Order [Vol. XXXIX p. 565] S.R.& O. No. 66 of 1947

Sewing Thread (Maximum Prices) Order [Vol. XXXIX p. 959] S.R.& O. No. 73 of 1947

Seed Oats (Importation from Scotland) (Maximum Prices) Order [Vol. XXXIX p. 951] S.R.& O. No. 75 of 1947

Seed Wheat (Importation from Sweden) (Maximum Prices) Order [Vol. XXXIX p. 955] S.R.& O. No. 80 of 1947

Prohibition of Storage of Ducks and Geese Order [Vol. XXXIX p. 861] S.R.& O. No. 96 of 1947

Fuel (Rationing for April and May, 1947) Order [Vol. XXXIX p. 609] S.R.& O. No. 99 of 1947

Scrap Lead (Maximum Prices) Order [Vol. XXXIX p. 947] S.R.& O. No. 108 of 1947

Butter (Maximum Prices) Order [Vol. XXXIX p. 43] S.R.& O. No. 111 of 1947

Milk (Maximum Prices to Retailers) Order [Vol. XXXIX p. 753] S.R.& O. No. 131 of 1947

Imported Timber (Maximum Prices) (No.6) Order [Vol. XXXIX p. 651] S.R.& O. No. 142 of 1947

Imported Timber (Maximum Prices) (No.7) Order [Vol. XXXIX p. 659] S.R.& O. No. 143 of 1947

Cigarettes (Maximum Prices) Order [Vol. XXXIX p. 123] S.R.& O. No. 150 of 1947

Tobaccos (Maximum Prices) Order [Vol. XXXIX p. 1141] S.R.& O. No. 151 of 1947

Roll Butter Order [Vol. XXXIX p. 943] S.R.& O. No. 156 of 1947

Creamery Butter and Butter Boxes Order [Vol. XXXIX p. 349] S.R.& O. No. 157 of 1947

Statutory Authority	Section	Statutory Instrument

Emergency Powers Order, S.R.& O.
No. 224 of 1939 (*Cont.*)

Sulphate of Copper (Maximum Prices) Order, 1947 (Amendment) (No.1) Order [Vol. XXXIX p. 1031] S.R.& O. No. 163 of 1947

Rationing of Yarn, Cloth and Clothing Order [Vol. XXXIX p. 895] S.R.& O. No. 172 of 1947

Rationing of Footwear Order [Vol. XXXIX p. 885] S.R.& O. No. 173 of 1947

Sugar (Maximum Prices) (No.2) Order [Vol. XXXIX p. 1017] S.R.& O. No. 180 of 1947

Binder Twine (Maximum Prices) Order [Vol. XXXIX p. 25] S.R.& O. No. 183 of 1947

Oranges (Maximum Prices) Order [Vol. XXXIX p. 819] S.R.& O. No. 189 of 1947

Fuel (Rationing for June and July, 1947) Order [Vol. XXXIX p. 615] S.R.& O. No. 191 of 1947

Biscuits (Maximum Prices) Order [Vol. XXXIX p. 33] S.R.& O. No. 196 of 1947

Cigarettes (Maximum Prices) Order, 1947 (Amendment) (No.1) Order [Vol. XXXIX p. 13] S.R.& O. No. 199 of 1947

Tea (Wholesale Distribution) Order [Vol. XXXIX p. 1047] S.R.& O. No. 201 of 1947

Condensed Milk (Maximum Prices) Order [Vol. XXXIX p. 327] S.R.& O. No. 204 of 1947

Tyres and Tubes (Maximum Prices) (No.2) Order [Vol. XXXIX p. 1211] S.R.& O. No. 206 of 1947

Cooling of Creamery Butter Order [Vol. XXXIX p. 333] S.R.& O. No. 220 of 1947

Raisins and Currants (Maximum Prices) (No.2) Order [Vol. XXXIX p. 881] S.R.& O. No. 221 of 1947

Cheese (Maximum Prices) Order [Vol. XXXIX p. 117] S.R.& O. No. 224 of 1947

Tea (Maximum Prices) Order [Vol. XXXIX p. 1039] S.R.& O. No. 226 of 1947

Importation of Pheasants and Partridges Order [Vol. XXXIX p. 645] S.R.& O. No. 233 of 1947

Cream Order [Vol. XXXIX p. 343] S.R.& O. No. 236 of 1947

Motor Spirit (Maximum Prices) Order [Vol. XXXIX p. 769] S.R.& O. No. 241 of 1947

Flour and Bread (Rationing) Order, 1946 (Second Amendment) Order [Vol. XXXIX p. 523] S.R.& O. No. 243 of 1947

Flour and Bread (Rationing) Order, 1946 (Supplemental Provisions) (No.3) Order [Vol. XXXIX p. 551] S.R.& O. No. 244 of 1947

Sligo Gas Charges Order [Vol. XXXIX p. 965] S.R.& O. No. 252 of 1947

Portable Threshing Mills Order [Vol. XXXIX p. 841] S.R.& O. No. 254 of 1947

Fuel (Rationing for August and September, 1947) Order [Vol. XXXIX p. 621] S.R.& O. No. 255 of 1947

Statutory Authority	Section	Statutory Instrument

Emergency Powers Order, S.R.& O.
No. 224 of 1939 *(Cont.)*

Bacon (Maximum Prices) Order [Vol. XXXIX p. 1] S.R.& O. No. 258 of 1947

Cereals Order [Vol. XXXIX p. 67] S.R.& O. No. 262 of 1947

Cobh Gas Charges Order [Vol. XXXIX p. 323] S.R.& O. No. 275 of 1947

Kilkenny Gas Charges Order [Vol. XXXIX p. 715] S.R.& O. No. 276 of 1947

Cigarettes (Maximum Prices) Order, 1947 (Amendment) (No.2) Order [Vol. XXXIX p. 143] S.R.& O. No. 277 of 1947

Rationing of Footwear Order, 1947 (Revocation) Order [Vol. XXXIX p. 891] S.R.& O. No. 286 of 1947

Enamelled Hollow-ware (Maximum Prices) Order [Vol. XXXIX p. 403] S.R.& O. No. 287 of 1947

Kerosene (Maximum Prices) Order [Vol. XXXIX p. 711] S.R.& O. No. 289 of 1947

Flour and Bread (Rationing) Order, 1946 (Supplemental Provisions) (Harvest Period) Order [Vol. XXXIX p. 555] S.R.& O. No. 294 of 1947

Onions (Maximum Prices) (No.2) Order [Vol. XXXIX p. 801] S.R.& O. No. 310 of 1947

Margarine (Maximum Prices) (No.2) Order [Vol. XXXIX p. 725] S.R.& O. No. 311 of 1947

Coal (Household) (Maximum Prices) Order [Vol. XXXIX p. 307] S.R.& O. No. 314 of 1947

Imported Timber (Maximum Prices) (No.8) Order [Vol. XXXIX p. 665] S.R.& O. No. 318 of 1947

Cloth, Clothing and Knitting Wool (Maximum Prices) Order [Vol. XXXIX p. 255] S.R.& O. No. 323 of 1947

Drogheda Gas Charges Order [Vol. XXXIX p. 379] S.R.& O. No. 331 of 1947

Intoxicating Liquor (Maximum Prices) Order [Vol. XXXIX p. 699] S.R.& O. No. 332 of 1947

Cigarettes (Maximum Prices) (No.2) Order [Vol. XXXIX p. 131] S.R.& O. No. 333 of 1947

Tobaccos (Maximum Prices) (No.2) Order [Vol. XXXIX p. 1167] S.R.& O. No. 334 of 1947

Flour and Bread (Rationing) Order, 1946 (Third Amendment) Order [Vol. XXXIX p. 533] S.R.& O. No. 335 of 1947

Tyres and Tubes (Maximum Prices) (No.3) Order [Vol. XXXIX p. 1219] S.R.& O. No. 336 of 1947

Soap (Maximum Prices) Order [Vol. XXXIX p. 1003] S.R.& O. No. 338 of 1947

Tea (Maximum Prices) (No.2) Order [Vol. XXXIX p. 1043] S.R.& O. No. 343 of 1947

Sugar (Maximum Prices) (No.3) Order [Vol. XXXIX p. 1025] S.R.& O. No. 344 of 1947

Dried Figs (Maximum Prices) Order, 1946 (Amendment) (No.1) Order [Vol. XXXIX p. 375] S.R.& O. No. 346 of 1947

Statutory Authority	Section	Statutory Instrument

Emergency Powers Order, S.R.& O. No. 224 of 1939 *(Cont.)*

Eggs (Maximum Prices) Order [Vol. XXXIX p. 389] S.R.& O. No. 348 of 1947

Milk (Maximum Prices to Retailers) (No.2) Order [Vol. XXXIX p. 757] S.R.& O. No. 357 of 1947

Fresh Meat (Maximum Prices) Order [Vol. XXXIX p. 581] S.R.& O. No. 361 of 1947

Mild Steel and Iron (Maximum Prices) Order [Vol. XXXIX p. 741] S.R.& O. No. 370 of 1947

Flour and Wheatenmeal (Importation) Order [Vol. XXXIX p. 561] S.R.& O. No. 377 of 1947

Fertilisers (Maximum Prices) Order [Vol. XXXIX p. 425] S.R.& O. No. 378 of 1947

Oranges (Maximum Prices) (No.2) Order [Vol. XXXIX p. 825] S.R.& O. No. 393 of 1947

Onions (Maximum Prices) (No.3) Order [Vol. XXXIX p. 807] S.R.& O. No. 397 of 1947

Intoxicating Liquor (Maximum Prices) Order, 1947 (Amendment) (No.1) Order [Vol. XXXIX p. 703] S.R.& O. No. 400 of 1947

Potatoes (Maximum Prices) (No.2) Order [Vol. XXXIX p. 853] S.R.& O. No. 403 of 1947

Imported Timber (Maximum Prices) (No.9) Order [Vol. XXXIX p. 673] S.R.& O. No. 404 of 1947

Imported Timber (Maximum Prices) (No.10) Order [Vol. XXXIX p. 683] S.R.& O. No. 405 of 1947

Imported Timber (Maximum Prices) (No.11) Order [Vol. XXXIX p. 691] S.R.& O. No. 406 of 1947

Firewood (Maximum Prices) Order, 1947 (Revocation) Order [Vol. XXXIX p. 439] S.R.& O. No. 423 of 1947

Coal (Household) (Maximum Prices) Order, 1947 (Revocation) Order [Vol. XXXIX p. 311] S.R.& O. No. 424 of 1947

Meat Extracts (Maximum Prices) Order, 1946 (Amendment) (No.1) Order [Vol. XXXIX p. 737] S.R.& O. No. 428 of 1947

Fuel Order [Vol. XXXIX p. 591] S.R.& O. No. 429 of 1947

Emergency Powers (Distribution of Butter) Order, 1944 (Exchange Value of Butter Coupons) Order, S.I. No. 1 of 1948

Sulphate of Ammonia (Maximum Prices) Order, S.I. No. 2 of 1948

Flour and Bread (Rationing) Order, 1946 (Supplemental Provisions) (No.4) Order, S.I. No. 5 of 1948

Rationing of Yarn, Cloth and Clothing Order, 1947 (Revocation) Order, S.I. No. 10 of 1948

Emergency Powers (Miscellaneous Revocations) Order, S.I. No. 11 of 1948

Cement Order, S.I. No. 12 of 1948

Woven Tissues of Wool or Worsted (Control of Importation) Order, S.I. No. 18 of 1948

Statutory Authority	Section	Statutory Instrument

Emergency Powers Order, S.R.& O. No. 224 of 1939 *(Cont.)*

Potatoes (Maximum Prices) (No.2) Order, 1947 (Amendment) (No.1) Order, S.I. No. 34 of 1948

Eggs (Maximum Prices) Order, 1947 (Revocation) Order, S.I. No. 35 of 1948

Fuel Order, 1947 (Supplemental Provisions) (No.1) Order, S.I. No. 37 of 1948

Canned Fish (Maximum Prices) Order, S.I. No. 48 of 1948

Emergency Powers (Returns Relating to Cargoes of Fuel) Order, 1944 (Amendment) Order, S.I. No. 53 of 1948

Emergency Powers (Wheaten Flour, Wheaten Meal and Manufacture of Bread) Order, 1946 (Third Amendment) Order, S.I. No. 56 of 1948

Maize Meal (Maximum Prices) Order, S.I. No. 67 of 1948

Emergency Powers (Kerosene Rationing) Order, 1943 (Monthly Ration of Domestic Users) Order, S.I. No. 71 of 1948

Emergency Powers (Export of Dead Poultry and Rabbits) Order, 1945 (Temporary Amendment) Order, S.I. No. 73 of 1948

Prohibition of Storage of Rabbits Order, S.I. No. 74 of 1948

Woven Tissues of Wool or Worsted (Control of Importation) Order, 1948 (Revocation) Order, S.I. No. 77 of 1948

Tobaccos (Maximum Prices) Order, S.I. No. 78 of 1948

Cigarettes (Maximum Prices) Order, S.I. No. 79 of 1948

Intoxicating Liquor (Maximum Prices) Order, S.I. No. 80 of 1948

Emergency Powers (Milling Offals) (Maximum Prices) Order, 1946 (Amendment) Order, S.I. No. 92 of 1948

Superphosphate 39% (Maximum Prices) Order, S.I. No. 93 of 1948

Fresh Meat (Maximum Prices) Order, S.I. No. 94 of 1948

Acid Calcium Phosphate (Maximum Prices) Order, S.I. No. 108 of 1948

Maize Meal (Maximum Prices) (No.2) Order, S.I. No. 109 of 1948

Emergency Powers (Fresh Bread and Prohibition of Returns) Order, 1946 (Temporary Amendment) (No.5) Order, S.I. No. 110 of 1948

Prohibition of Storage of Ducks and Geese Order, S.I. No. 112 of 1948

Emergency Powers (Restriction on Movement of Turf) Order, 1943 (Revocation) Order, S.I. No. 116 of 1948

Fuel Order, 1947 (Revocation) Order, S.I. No. 117 of 1948

Statutory Authority	Section	Statutory Instrument
Emergency Powers Order, S.R.& O. No. 224 of 1939 (*Cont.*)		*Emergency Powers (Turf) (Maximum Prices) Order, 1946 (Revocation) Order, S.I. No. 118 of 1948*
		Sulphate of Ammonia (Maximum Prices) Order, 1948 (Amendment) (No.1) Order, S.I. No. 120 of 1948
		Emergency Powers (Second-hand Agricultural Machinery) (Maximum Prices) Order, 1943 (Revocation) Order, S.I. No. 129 of 1948
		Binder Twine (Maximum Prices) Order, S.I. No. 132 of 1948
		Oatmeal (Maximum Prices) Order, S.I. No. 134 of 1948
		Motor Spirit (Maximum Prices) Order, S.I. No. 138 of 1948
		Kerosene (Maximum Prices) Order, S.I. No. 139 of 1948
		Emergency Powers (Control of Exports) (Amendment) (No.27) Order, S.I. No. 140 of 1948
		Cream Order, 1947 (Revocation) Order, S.I. No. 143 of 1948
		Milk (Maximum Prices to Retailers) Order, S.I. No. 147 of 1948
		Emergency Powers (Control of Exports) (Amendment) (No.28) Order, S.I. No. 152 of 1948
		Emergency Powers (Butter) (Licensing of Wholesalers and Retailers) Order, 1943 (Amendment) Order, S.I. No. 153 of 1948
		Emergency Powers (Distribution of Butter) Order, 1944 (Second Amendment) Order, S.I. No. 154 of 1948
		Butter (Maximum Prices) Order, 1947 (Amendment) Order, S.I. No. 155 of 1948
		Motor Spirit (Maximum Prices) (No.2) Order, S.I. No. 161 of 1948
		Margarine (Maximum Prices) Order, S.I. No. 162 of 1948
		Onions (Maximum Prices) Order, S.I. No. 171 of 1948
		Tea (Maximum Prices) (No.2) Order, 1947 (Amendment) (No.1) Order, S.I. No. 177 of 1948
		Sugar (Maximum Prices) (No.3) Order, 1947 (Amendment) (No.1) Order, S.I. No. 178 of 1948
		Emergency Powers (Fresh Bread and Prohibition of Returns) Order, 1946 (Temporary Amendment) (No.6) Order, S.I. No. 181 of 1948
		Distribution of Sugar to Catering Establishments and Institutions Order, S.I. No. 182 of 1948
		Emergency Powers (Distribution of Butter) Order, 1944 (Fifteenth Ration Period) Order, S.I. No. 183 of 1948

Statutory Authority	Section	Statutory Instrument

Emergency Powers Order, S.R.& O.
No. 224 of 1939 (*Cont.*)

Emergency Powers (Sugar) Order, 1943 (Thirteenth Ration Period) Order, S.I. No. 184 of 1948

Flour and Bread (Rationing) Orders (Suspension in Strike-affected Areas) Order, S.I. No. 186 of 1948

Emergency Powers (Retail Distribution of Tea) Order, 1943 (Exchange Value of Tea Coupons) Order, S.I. No. 188 of 1948

Distribution of Tea to Catering Establishments and Institutions Order, S.I. No. 189 of 1948

Tea (Wholesale Distribution) Order, 1947 (Amendment) Order, S.I. No. 190 of 1948

Oranges (Maximum Prices) Order, S.I. No. 191 of 1948

Onions (Maximum Prices) (No.2) Order, S.I. No. 194 of 1948

Rice (Maximum Prices) Order, S.I. No. 211 of 1948

Flour and Bread (Rationing) Orders (Suspension in Strike-affected Areas) Order, 1948 (Revocation) Order, S.I. No. 212 of 1948

Emergency Powers (Scutching of Flax) Orders (Revocation) Order, S.I. No. 215 of 1948

Biscuits (Maximum Prices) Order, S.I. No. 217 of 1948

Bacon (Maximum Prices) Order, S.I. No. 226 of 1948

Distribution of Tea to Catering Establishments (No.2) Order, S.I. No. 228 of 1948

Sugar (Maximum Prices) (No.3) Order, 1947 (Amendment) (No.2) Order, S.I. No. 231 of 1948

Emergency Powers (Sugar) Order, 1943 (Temporary Amendment) Order, S.I. No. 239 of 1948

Flour and Bread (Rationing) Order, 1946 (Supplemental Provisions) (No.5) Order, S.I. No. 242 of 1948

Emergency Powers (Unused Binder Twine) Order, 1942 (Revocation) Order, S.I. No. 244 of 1948

Emergency Powers (Rye-Grass Seeds) (Maximum and Minimum Prices) Order, 1944 (Revocation) Order, S.I. No. 246 of 1948

Creamery Butter (Prices for Catering Establishments) Order, S.I. No. 247 of 1948

Tea (Maximum Prices) (No.2) Order, 1947 (Amendment) (No.2) Order, S.I. No. 250 of 1948

Emergency Powers (Rationing of Soap) Order, 1944 (Amendment) Order, S.I. No. 257 of 1948

Emergency Powers (Fresh Bread and Prohibition of Returns) Order, 1946 (Revocation) Order, S.I. No. 258 of 1948

Cornflour (Maximum Prices) Order, S.I. No. 266 of 1948

Emergency Powers (Kerosene Rationing) Order, 1943 (Domestic Users) Order, S.I. No. 268 of 1948

Statutory Authority	Section	Statutory Instrument
Emergency Powers Order, S.R.& O. No. 224 of 1939 (*Cont.*)		*Cereals Order, S.I. No. 269 of 1948*
		Cream Order, S.I. No. 272 of 1948
		Emergency Powers (Distribution of Butter) Order, 1944 (Exchange Value of Butter Coupons) (No.1) Order, S.I. No. 274 of 1948
		Intoxicating Liquor (Maximum Prices) Order, 1948 (Amendment) (No.1) Order, S.I. No. 275 of 1948
		Emergency Powers (Rationing of Soap) Order, 1944 (Amendment) (No.2) Order, S.I. No. 291 of 1948
		Onions (Maximum Prices) (No.3) Order, S.I. No. 294 of 1948
		Tea (Maximum Prices) (No.2) Order, 1947 (Amendment) (No.3) Order, S.I. No. 295 of 1948
		Sugar (Maximum Prices) (No.3) Order, 1947 (Amendment) (No.3) Order, S.I. No. 296 of 1948
		Flour and Bread (Rationing) Order, 1946 (Supplemental Provisions) (Harvest Period) Order, S.I. No. 297 of 1948
		Tyres and Tubes (Maximum Prices) Order, S.I. No. 299 of 1948
		Sugar (Maximum Prices) (No.3) Order, 1947 (Amendment) (No.4) Order, S.I. No. 302 of 1948
		Emergency Powers (Orders Relating to Paper and Waste Paper) (Revocation) Order, S.I. No. 304 of 1948
		Tea and Sugar (Harvest Workers) Order, S.I. No. 305 of 1948
		Tea (Maximum Prices) (No.2) Order, 1947 (Amendment) (No.4) Order, S.I. No. 306 of 1948
		Sultanas and Currants (Maximum Prices) Order, S.I. No. 307 of 1948
		Flour and Bread (Rationing) Order, 1946 (Supplemental Provisions) (Harvest Period) (Amendment) Order, S.I. No. 312 of 1948
		Intoxicating Liquor (Maximum Prices) Order, 1948 (Amendment) (No.2) Order, S.I. No. 317 of 1948
		Tea (Maximum Prices) (No.2) Order, 1947 (Amendment) (No.5) Order, S.I. No. 320 of 1948
		Meat Extracts (Maximum Prices) Order, 1946 (Amendment) (No.1) Order, 1947 (Revocation) Order, S.I. No. 337 of 1948
		Oatmeal (Maximum Prices) Order, 1948 (Revocation) Order, S.I. No. 341 of 1948
		Flour and Bread (Rationing) Order, 1946 (Supplemental Provisions) (Harvest Period) (Amendment) (No.2) Order, S.I. No. 345 of 1948
		Margarine (Maximum Prices) (No.2) Order, S.I. No. 346 of 1948
		Fertilisers Orders (Revocation) Order, S.I. No. 347 of 1948
		Molasses Sugar Beet Pulp (Maximum Prices) Order, S.I. No. 348 of 1948
		Emergency Powers (Kerosene Rationing) Order, 1943 (Monthly Ration of Domestic Users) (No.2) Order, S.I. No. 349 of 1948

Statutory Authority	Section	Statutory Instrument
Emergency Powers Order, S.R.& O. No. 224 of 1939 (*Cont.*)		*Creamery Butter (Prices for Catering Establishments) (No.2) Order, S.I. No. 355 of 1948*
		Tea and Sugar (Harvest Workers) Order, 1948 (Extension) Order, S.I. No. 359 of 1948
		Emergency Powers (Distribution of Butter) Order, 1944 (Exchange Value of Butter Coupons) (No.2) Order, S.I. No. 360 of 1948
		Emergency Powers (Hides) Order, 1944 (Revocation) Order, S.I. No. 362 of 1948
		Emergency Powers (Importation of Wine) Order, 1942 (Revocation) Order, S.I. No. 363 of 1948
		Emergency Powers (Scutching of Flax) Order, S.I. No. 367 of 1948
		Imported Timber (Maximum Prices) (No.12) Order, S.I. No. 368 of 1948
		Emergency Powers (Export of Dead Poultry and Rabbits) Order, 1945 (Amendment) Order, S.I. No. 369 of 1948
		Wicklow Gas (Charges) Order, S.I. No. 372 of 1948
		Cheese (Maximum Prices) Order, 1947 (Amendment) (No.1) Order, S.I. No. 383 of 1948
		Emergency Powers (Sugar) Order, 1943 (Fourteenth Ration Period) Order, S.I. No. 384 of 1948
		Emergency Powers (Retail Distribution of Tea) Order, 1943 (Twelfth Ration Period) Order, S.I. No. 385 of 1948
		Emergency Powers (Distribution of Margarine) (No.2) Order, 1945 (Amendment) Order, S.I. No. 386 of 1948
		Emergency Powers (Distribution of Butter) Order, 1944 (Sixteenth Ration Period) Order, S.I. No. 387 of 1948
		Flour and Bread (Rationing) Order, 1946 (Supplemental Provisions) (No.6) Order, S.I. No. 388 of 1948
		Flour and Bread (Rationing) Order, 1946 (Fourth Amendment) Order, S.I. No. 389 of 1948
		Emergency Powers (Homespun) Order, 1943 (Revocation) Order, S.I. No. 390 of 1948
		Emergency Powers (Control of Exports) (Amendment) (No.29) Order, S.I. No. 391 of 1948
		Emergency Powers (Rationing of Soap) Order, 1944 (Amendment) (No.3) Order, S.I. No. 399 of 1948
		Bacon (Maximum Prices) Order, 1948 (Amendment) Order, S.I. No. 400 of 1948
		Bicycles (Maximum Prices) Order, S.I. No. 405 of 1948
		Kerosene (Maximum Prices) (No.2) Order, S.I. No. 410 of 1948
		Thurles Gas (Charges) Order, S.I. No. 417 of 1948
		Emergency Powers (Semolina) (Maximum Prices) Order, 1944 (Revocation) Order, S.I. No. 418 of 1948

Statutory Authority	Section	Statutory Instrument
Emergency Powers Order, S.R.& O. No. 224 of 1939 (*Cont.*)		*Emergency Powers (Control of Exports) Order, 1940 (Amendment) (No.30) Order, S.I. No. 427 of 1948*
		Cream Order, 1948 (Revocation) Order, S.I. No. 428 of 1948
		Maize Meal (Maximum Prices) (No.2) Order, 1948 (Revocation) Order, S.I. No. 5 of 1949
		Flour, Wheatenmeal and Bread Order, S.I. No. 8 of 1949
		Flour and Bread (Rationing) Order, 1946 (Fifth Amendment) Order, S.I. No. 10 of 1949
		Emergency Powers (Revocation of Orders relating to Flour, Wheatenmeal and Bread) Order, S.I. No. 11 of 1949
		Emergency Powers (Tallows and Greases) (Maximum Prices) Order, 1944 (Amendment) (No.2) Order, S.I. No. 14 of 1949
		Emergency Powers (Meat and Bone Meals) (Maximum Prices) Order, 1944 (Amendment) (No.1) Order, S.I. No. 15 of 1949
		Emergency Powers (Cocoa) Orders (Revocation) Order, S.I. No. 21 of 1949
		Soap (Maximum Prices) Order, S.I. No. 22 of 1949
		Binder Twine (Maximum Prices) Order, S.I. No. 30 of 1949
		Emergency Powers (Honey) (Maximum Prices) Order, 1944 (Revocation) Order, S.I. No. 34 of 1949
		Onions (Maximum Prices) (No.3) Order, 1948 (Revocation) Order, S.I. No. 35 of 1949
		Oranges (Maximum Prices) Order, S.I. No. 36 of 1949
		Emergency Powers (Jams and Marmalades) (Maximum Prices) Order, 1944 (Amendment) (No.4) Order, S.I. No. 37 of 1949
		Emergency Powers (Bakers) Orders (Revocation) Order, S.I. No. 46 of 1949
		Emergency Powers (Export of Dead Poultry and Rabbits) Order, 1945 (Temporary Amendment) Order, S.I. No. 48 of 1949
		Prohibition of Storage of Rabbits Order, S.I. No. 49 of 1949
		Margarine (Maximum Prices) Order, S.I. No. 53 of 1949
		Emergency Powers (Orders Relating to Soap) (Revocation) Order, S.I. No. 79 of 1949
		Prohibition of Storage of Ducks and Geese Order, S.I. No. 81 of 1949
		Sugar Order, S.I. No. 83 of 1949
		Motor Spirit (Maximum Prices) Order, S.I. No. 84 of 1949
		Kerosene (Maximum Prices) Order, S.I. No. 85 of 1949

Statutory Authority	Section	Statutory Instrument

Emergency Powers Order, S.R.& O.
No. 224 of 1939 (*Cont.*)

Sugar (Maximum Prices) Order, S.I. No. 86 of 1949

Fresh Meat (Maximum Prices) Order, 1948 (Amendment) Order, S.I. No. 87 of 1949

Imported Timber (Maximum Prices) (No.13) Order, S.I. No. 88 of 1949

Emergency Powers (Motor Spirit Rationing) Order, 1941 (Amendment) (No.10) Order, S.I. No. 91 of 1949

Emergency Powers (Wine in Bond) Order, 1944 (Revocation) Order, S.I. No. 99 of 1949

Emergency Powers (Kerosene and Fuel Oil) Orders (Revocation) Order, S.I. No. 102 of 1949

Horse-shoe Nails (Maximum Prices) Order, S.I. No. 116 of 1949

Milk (Maximum Prices to Retailers) Order, S.I. No. 119 of 1949

Emergency Powers (Distribution of Butter) Order, 1944 (Seventeenth Ration Period) Order, S.I. No. 131 of 1949

Sugar Order, 1949 (First Ration Period) Order, S.I. No. 132 of 1949

Emergency Powers (Retail Distribution of Tea) Order, 1943 (Fourth Amendment) Order, S.I. No. 133 of 1949

Flour and Bread (Rationing) Order, 1946 (Sixth Amendment) Order, S.I. No. 135 of 1949

Flour and Bread (Rationing) Order, 1946 (Supplemental Provisions) (No.7) Order, S.I. No. 136 of 1949

Emergency Powers (Export of Whiskey) Order, 1941 (Amendment) Order, S.I. No. 137 of 1949

Emergency Powers (Control of Exports) Order, 1940 (Amendment) (No.31) Order, (1946) S.I. No. 138 of 1949

Emergency Powers (Distribution of Butter) Order, 1944 (Exchange Value of Butter Coupons) (No.1) Order, S.I. No. 140 of 1949

Emergency Powers (Dried and Canned Peas) (Maximum Prices) Order, 1943 (No.2) Order, 1943 (Amendment) (No.2) Order, S.I. No. 145 of 1949

Candles (Maximum Prices) Order, S.I. No. 170 of 1949

Footwear (Maximum Prices) Orders (Revocation) Order, S.I. No. 177 of 1949

Emergency Powers (Control of Exports) Order, 1940 (Amendment) (No.32) Order, S.I. No. 178 of 1949

Fresh Meat (Maximum Prices) Order, 1948 (Amendment) (No.2) Order, S.I. No. 180 of 1949

Prunes (Maximum Prices) Order, S.I. No. 186 of 1949

Seedless Raisins (Maximum Prices) Order, S.I. No. 187 of 1949

Statutory Authority	Section	Statutory Instrument
Emergency Powers Order, S.R.& O. No. 224 of 1939 (*Cont.*)		*Oranges (Maximum Prices) Order, 1949 (Revocation) Order, S.I. No. 190 of 1949*
		Grapefruit (Maximum Prices) Order, 1946 (Revocation) Order, S.I. No. 191 of 1949
		Emergency Powers (Restrictions on Serving Butter at Catering Establishments) Order, 1942 (Revocation) Order, S.I. No. 192 of 1949
		Home-Grown Timber (Maximum Prices) Order, S.I. No. 210 of 1949
		Emergency Powers (Motor-Spirit Rationing) Order, 1941 (Amendment) (No.11) Order, S.I. No. 211 of 1949
		Canned Fish (Maximum Prices) Order, 1948 (Revocation) Order, S.I. No. 213 of 1949
		Emergency Powers (Distribution of Wheat and Maize) Orders (Revocation) Order, S.I. No. 217 of 1949
		Emergency Powers (Orders Relating to Margarine) (Revocation) Order, S.I. No. 218 of 1949
		Soap (Maximum Prices) (No.2) Order, S.I. No. 220 of 1949
		Tea Order, S.I. No. 223 of 1949
		Pork Sausages and Sausage Meat, Beef Sausages and Black and White Puddings (Maximum Prices) Orders (Revocation) Order, S.I. No. 227 of 1949
		Tea (Maximum Prices) Order, S.I. No. 228 of 1949
		Imported Timber (Maximum Prices) (No.14) Order, S.I. No. 233 of 1949
		Flour and Bread (Rationing) Order, 1946 (Supplemental Provisions) (Harvest Period) Order, S.I. No. 234 of 1949
		Bacon (Maximum Prices) Order, 1948 (Revocation) Order, S.I. No. 238 of 1949
		Wheat Order, S.I. No. 241 of 1949
		Candles (Maximum Prices) (No.2) Order, S.I. No. 248 of 1949
		Imported Timber (Maximum Prices) (No.15) Order, S.I. No. 249 of 1949
		Rice (Maximum Prices) Order, 1948 (Revocation) Order, S.I. No. 250 of 1949
		Acid Calcium Phosphates (Maximum Prices) Order, S.I. No. 253 of 1949
		Cloth, Clothing and Knitting Wool (Maximum Prices) Order, 1947 (Amendment) Order, S.I. No. 254 of 1949
		Emergency Powers (Motor-Spirit Rationing) Order, 1941 (Amendment) (No.12) Order, S.I. No. 262 of 1949
		Emergency Powers (Auctions) Order, 1943 (Revocation) Order, S.I. No. 263 of 1949
		Seedless Raisins (Maximum Prices) (No.2) Order, S.I. No. 264 of 1949

Emergency Powers Order, S.R.& O.
No. 224 of 1939 (*Cont.*)

Emergency Powers (Importation of Oils and Fats) Order, 1944 (Amendment) Order, S.I. No. 277 of 1949

Shotgun Cartridges (Maximum Prices) Order, S.I. No. 278 of 1949

Emergency Powers (Milling Offals) (Maximum Prices) Order, 1946 (Amendment) Order, S.I. No. 283 of 1949

Intoxicating Liquor (Maximum Prices) Order, 1948 (Amendment) (No.3) Order, S.I. No. 284 of 1949

Emergency Powers (Distribution of Duties) Order, 1944 (Eighteenth Ration Period) Order, S.I. No. 298 of 1949

Flour and Bread (Rationing) Order, 1946 (Seventh Amendment) Order, S.I. No. 299 of 1949

Sugar Order, 1949 (Second Ration Period) Order, S.I. No. 300 of 1949

Margarine (Maximum Prices) (No.2) Order, S.I. No. 301 of 1949

Sultanas and Currants (Maximum Prices) Order, 1948 (Amendment) (No.1) Order, S.I. No. 302 of 1949

Kerosene (Maximum Prices) (No.2) Order, S.I. No. 303 of 1949

Motor Spirit (Maximum Prices) (No.2) Order, S.I. No. 304 of 1949

Emergency Powers (Bicarbonate of Soda) (Maximum Prices) (No.2) Order, 1944 (Revocation) Order, S.I. No. 337 of 1949

Emergency Powers (Control of Prices) (No.123) Order, 1942 (Revocation) Order, S.I. No. 338 of 1949

Tyres and Tubes (Maximum Prices) Order, S.I. No. 4 of 1950

Emergency Powers (Control of Exports) Order, 1940 (Amendment) (No.33) Order, S.I. No. 9 of 1950

Live Pigeons (Prohibition of Export) Order, S.I. No. 10 of 1950

Motor Spirit Order, S.I. No. 12 of 1950

Margarine (Maximum Prices) Order, S.I. No. 19 of 1950

Tea Order, 1949 (Amendment) Order, S.I. No. 28 of 1950

Soap (Maximum Prices) (No.2) Order, 1949 (Revocation) Order, S.I. No. 31 of 1950

Importation of Pheasants and Partridges Order, 1947 (Revocation) Order, S.I. No. 32 of 1950

Emergency Powers (Tallows and Greases) Order, 1942 (Revocation) Order, S.I. No. 33 of 1950

Tea (Maximum Prices) Order, S.I. No. 45 of 1950

Importation of Tea Order, S.I. No. 51 of 1950

Statutory Authority	Section	Statutory Instrument

Emergency Powers Order, S.R.& O. No. 224 of 1939 (*Cont.*)

Emergency Powers (Importation of Timber) Orders (Revocation) Order, S.I. No. 59 of 1950

Emergency Powers (Export of Dead Poultry and Rabbits) Order, 1945 (Temporary Amendment) Order, S.I. No. 62 of 1950

Prohibition of Storage of Rabbits Order, S.I. No. 63 of 1950

Sugar (Maximum Prices) Order, 1949 (Amendment) (No.1) Order, S.I. No. 66 of 1950

Prohibition of Storage of Ducks and Geese Order, S.I. No. 72 of 1950

Fresh Meat (Maximum Prices) Order, 1948 (Amendment) Order, S.I. No. 76 of 1950

Maize (Maximum Prices) (Temporary Provisions) Order, S.I. No. 84 of 1950

Binder Twine (Maximum Prices) Order, S.I. No. 89 of 1950

Emergency Powers (Distribution of Butter) Order, 1944 (Third Amendment) Order, S.I. No. 100 of 1950

Milk (Maximum Prices to Retailers) Order, S.I. No. 103 of 1950

Emergency Powers (Sole Leather) (Maximum Prices) Order, 1946 (Revocation) Order, S.I. No. 120 of 1950

Sulphate of Copper (Maximum Prices) Orders, 1947 (Revocation) Order, S.I. No. 122 of 1950

Emergency Powers (Prices and Charges) (Standstill) Orders, 1944 (Revocation) Order, S.I. No. 123 of 1950

Flour and Bread (Rationing) Order, 1946 (Supplemental Provisions) (No.8) Order, S.I. No. 124 of 1950

Sugar Order, 1949 (Third Ration Period) Order, S.I. No. 125 of 1950

Emergency Powers (Distribution of Butter) Order, 1944 (Nineteenth Ration Period) Order, S.I. No. 126 of 1950

Creamery Butter (Prices for Catering Establishments) Order, S.I. No. 130 of 1950

Roll Butter Order, 1947 (Amendment) Order, S.I. No. 131 of 1950

Emergency Powers (Distribution of Butter) Order, 1944 (Fourth Amendment) Order, S.I. No. 133 of 1950

Emergency Powers (Butter) (Licensing of Wholesalers and Retailers) Order, 1943 (Amendment) Order, S.I. No. 134 of 1950

Butter (Maximum Prices) Order, S.I. No. 135 of 1950

Tea Order, S.I. No. 146 of 1950

Cornflour (Maximum Prices) Order, 1948 (Revocation) Order, S.I. No. 151 of 1950

Statutory Authority	Section	Statutory Instrument

Emergency Powers Order, S.R.& O. No. 224 of 1939 (*Cont.*)

Importation of Tea Order, 1950 (Amendment) (No.1) Order, S.I. No. 155 of 1950

Fresh Meat (Maximum Prices) Order, 1948 (Amendment) (No.2) Order, S.I. No. 160 of 1950

Meat and Bone Meal (Maximum Prices) Orders (Revocation) Order, S.I. No. 162 of 1950

Acid Calcium Phosphate (Maximum Prices) Order, S.I. No. 178 of 1950

Tyres and Tubes (Maximum Prices) (No.2) Order, S.I. No. 195 of 1950

Tallows and Greases (Maximum Prices) Orders (Revocation) Order, S.I. No. 196 of 1950

Enamelled Hollow-ware (Maximum Prices) Order, 1947 (Revocation) Order, S.I. No. 197 of 1950

Emergency Powers (Dried and Canned Peas) (Maximum Prices) Order, 1943 (No.2) Order, 1943 (Revocation) Order, S.I. No. 206 of 1950

Wheat Order, S.I. No. 208 of 1950

Flour and Bread (Rationing) Order, 1946 (Supplemental Provisions) (Harvest Period) Order, S.I. No. 211 of 1950

Emergency Powers (Milling Offals) (Maximum Prices) Order, 1946 (Amendment) Order, S.I. No. 217 of 1950

Emergency Powers (Feeding Stuffs) Order, 1944 (Amendment) Order, S.I. No. 237 of 1950

Sultanas and Currants (Maximum Prices) Order, 1948 (Revocation) Order, S.I. No. 245 of 1950

Flour and Bread (Rationing) Order, 1946 (Supplemental Provisions) (Harvest Period) (Amendment) Order, S.I. No. 246 of 1950

Sugar (Maximum Prices) Order, S.I. No. 249 of 1950

Emergency Powers (Export of Dead Poultry and Rabbits) Order, 1945 (Temporary Amendment) Order, S.I. No. 252 of 1950

Emergency Powers (Importation of Oils and Fats) Orders (Revocation) Order, S.I. No. 256 of 1950

Emergency Powers (Manufacture and Sale of Fertilizers) Order, 1944 (Amendment) Order, S.I. No. 263 of 1950

Imported Timber (Maximum Prices) (No.16) Order, S.I. No. 264 of 1950

Dried Figs (Maximum Prices) Order, 1946 (Revocation) Order, S.I. No. 271 of 1950

Sugar (Maximum Prices) (No.2) Order, S.I. No. 273 of 1950

Flour and Bread (Rationing) Order, 1946 (Eighth Amendment) Order, S.I. No. 283 of 1950

Margarine (Maximum Prices) (No.2) Order, S.I. No. 286 of 1950

Emergency Powers (Export of Live Poultry, Dead Poultry and Rabbits) Orders (Revocation) Order, S.I. No. 303 of 1950

Statutory Authority	Section	Statutory Instrument
Emergency Powers Order, S.R.& O. No. 224 of 1939 (*Cont.*)		*Prices and Charges (Standstill) Order, S.I. No. 3 of 1951*
		Tyres and Tubes (Maximum Prices) Order, S.I. No. 7 of 1951
		Prices and Charges (Standstill) Order, 1951 (Amendment) (No.1) Order, S.I. No. 22 of 1951
		Tea (Maximum Prices) Order, S.I. No. 24 of 1951
		Tea Order, 1950 (Second Ration Period) Order, S.I. No. 28 of 1951
		Sugar Order, 1949 (Fourth Ration Period) Order, S.I. No. 29 of 1951
		Emergency Powers (Distribution of Butter) Order, 1944 (Twentieth Ration Period) Order, S.I. No. 30 of 1951
		Emergency Powers (Restriction on use of Wheat and Wheaten Products) Orders (Revocation) Order, S.I. No. 39 of 1951
		Emergency Powers (Milling Offals) (Maximum Prices) Order, 1946 (Revocation) Order, S.I. No. 41 of 1951
		Prices and Charges (Standstill) Order, 1951 (Amendment) (No.2) Order, S.I. No. 42 of 1951
		Prices and Charges (Standstill) Order, 1951 (Amendment) (No.3) Order, S.I. No. 49 of 1951
		Emergency Powers (Control of Exports) Order, 1940 (Amendment) (No.34) Order, S.I. No. 51 of 1951
		Prices and Charges (Standstill) Order, 1951 (Amendment) (No.4) Order, S.I. No. 52 of 1951
		Candles (Maximum Prices) Order, S.I. No. 56 of 1951
		Imported Timber (Maximum Prices) (No.17) Order, S.I. No. 57 of 1951
		Binder Twine (Maximum Prices) Order, S.I. No. 62 of 1951
		Fresh Meat (Maximum Prices) Order, 1948 (Amendment) Order, S.I. No. 63 of 1951
		Acid Calcium Phosphate (Maximum Prices) Order, S.I. No. 72 of 1951
		Motor Spirit (Maximum Prices) Order, S.I. No. 75 of 1951
		Kerosene (Maximum Prices) Order, S.I. No. 76 of 1951
		Prices and Charges (Standstill) Order, 1951 (Amendment) (No.5) Order, S.I. No. 79 of 1951
		Prices and Charges (Standstill) Order, 1951 (Amendment) (No.6) Order, S.I. No. 80 of 1951
		Pork (Maximum Prices) Order, S.I. No. 81 of 1951
		Bacon (Maximum Prices) Order, S.I. No. 82 of 1951
		Prices and Charges (Standstill) Order, 1951 (Amendment) (No.7) Order, S.I. No. 86 of 1951

Statutory Authority	Section	Statutory Instrument

Emergency Powers Order, S.R.& O. No. 224 of 1939 (*Cont.*)

Potatoes (Maximum Prices) Order, S.I. No. 87 of 1951

Jams and Marmalades (Maximum Prices) Order, S.I. No. 91 of 1951

Margarine (Maximum Prices) Order, S.I. No. 93 of 1951

Oatmeal (Maximum Prices) Order, S.I. No. 94 of 1951

Binder Twine (Maximum Prices) Order, 1951 (Revocation) Order, S.I. No. 96 of 1951

Importation of Wheaten Flour Substitutes Order, S.I. No. 97 of 1951

Milk (Maximum Prices to Retailers) Order, S.I. No. 102 of 1951

Butter (Maximum Prices) Order, S.I. No. 108 of 1951

Prices and Charges (Standstill) Order, 1951 (Amendment) (No.8) Order, S.I. No. 109 of 1951

Prices and Charges (Standstill) Order, 1951 (Amendment) (No.9) Order, S.I. No. 110 of 1951

Creamery Butter and Butter Boxes Order, S.I. No. 115 of 1951

Roll Butter Order, S.I. No. 116 of 1951

Creamery Butter (Prices for Catering Establishments) Order, S.I. No. 117 of 1951

Motor Spirit (Maximum Prices) (No.2) Order, S.I. No. 122 of 1951

Flour, Wheatenmeal and Bread Order, 1949 (Amendment) Order, S.I. No. 124 of 1951

Butter (Prices for Butter Sold under Permit) Order, S.I. No. 130 of 1951

Bacon (Maximum Prices) Order, 1951 (Amendment) Order, S.I. No. 131 of 1951

Prices and Charges (Standstill) Order, 1951 (Amendment) (No.10) Order, S.I. No. 141 of 1951

Currants and Raisins (Maximum Prices) Order, S.I. No. 142 of 1951

Prices and Charges (Standstill) Order, 1951 (Amendment) (No.11) Order, S.I. No. 143 of 1951

Waste Paper (Maximum Prices) Order, S.I. No. 144 of 1951

Flour, Wheatenmeal and Bread Order, 1949 (Second Amendment) Order, S.I. No. 145 of 1951

Soda Crystals (Washing Soda) (Maximum Prices) Order, S.I. No. 151 of 1951

Scrap Lead (Maximum Prices) Order, S.I. No. 152 of 1951

Imported Timber (Maximum Prices) (No.18) Order, S.I. No. 160 of 1951

Sligo Gas Charges Order, S.I. No. 161 of 1951

Statutory Authority	Section	Statutory Instrument

Emergency Powers Order, S.R.& O.
No. 224 of 1939 (*Cont.*)

Prices and Charges (Standstill) Order, 1951 (Amendment) (No.12) Order, S.I. No. 165 of 1951

Soap and Detergents (Maximum Prices) Order, S.I. No. 166 of 1951

Creamery Butter and Butter Boxes (No.2) Order, S.I. No. 173 of 1951

Roll Butter (No.2) Order, S.I. No. 174 of 1951

Butter (Prices for Butter Sold under Permit) (No.2) Order, S.I. No. 178 of 1951

Butter (Maximum Prices) (No.2) Order, S.I. No. 179 of 1951

Prices and Charges (Standstill) Order, 1951 (Amendment) (No.13) Order, S.I. No. 184 of 1951

Packed and Canned Peas and Beans (Maximum Prices) Order, S.I. No. 185 of 1951

Condensed Milk (Maximum Prices) Order, S.I. No. 192 of 1951

Pigs (Unsuitable Types) Order, S.I. No. 193 of 1951

Sewing Thread (Maximum Prices) Order, S.I. No. 194 of 1951

Drogheda Gas Charges Order, S.I. No. 203 of 1951

Motor Spirit (Maximum Prices) (No.3) Order, S.I. No. 208 of 1951

Kerosene (Maximum Prices) (No.2) Order, S.I. No. 209 of 1951

Milk (Maximum Prices to Retailers) (No.2) Order, S.I. No. 215 of 1951

Fresh Meat (Maximum Prices) Order, 1948 (Revocation) Order, S.I. No. 216 of 1951

Prices and Charges (Standstill) Order, 1951 (Amendment) (No.14) Order, S.I. No. 217 of 1951

Oatmeal (Maximum Prices) (No.2) Order, S.I. No. 218 of 1951

Emergency Powers (Distribution of Butter) Order, 1944 (Fifth Amendment) Order, S.I. No. 221 of 1951

Cocoa (Maximum Prices) Order, S.I. No. 223 of 1951

Flour and Bread (Rationing) Order, 1946 (Supplemental Provisions) (Harvest Period) Order, S.I. No. 231 of 1951

Wheat Order, S.I. No. 233 of 1951

Intoxicating Liquor (Maximum Prices) Order, 1948 (Amendment) (No.4) Order, S.I. No. 234 of 1951

Miscellaneous Maximum Prices and Maximum Charges Orders (Revocation) Order, S.I. No. 244 of 1951

Cheese (Maximum Prices) Order, S.I. No. 246 of 1951

Statutory Authority	Section	Statutory Instrument
Emergency Powers Order, S.R.& O. No. 224 of 1939 (*Cont.*)		*Acid Calcium Phosphate (Maximum Prices) Order, 1951 (Revocation) Order, S.I. No. 249 of 1951*
		Home-grown Timber (Maximum Prices) Order, 1949 (Revocation) Order, S.I. No. 251 of 1951
		Coal (Maximum Prices) Order, S.I. No. 252 of 1951
		Prices and Charges (Standstill) Orders, 1951 (Revocation) Order, S.I. No. 253 of 1951
		Cinema Admission Charges Order, S.I. No. 254 of 1951
		Sugar (Maximum Prices) Order, S.I. No. 257 of 1951
		Kerosene (Maximum Prices) (No.3) Order, S.I. No. 264 of 1951
		Motor Spirit (Maximum Prices) (No.4) Order, S.I. No. 265 of 1951
		Flour and Bread (Rationing) Order, 1946 (Supplemental Provisions) (Harvest Period) (Amendment) Order, S.I. No. 268 of 1951
		Bacon and Pork (Maximum Prices) Orders (Revocation) Order, S.I. No. 269 of 1951
		Coal (Dublin and Dun Laoghaire) (Maximum Prices) Order, S.I. No. 272 of 1951
		Sewing Thread (Maximum Prices) Order, 1951 (Amendment) Order, S.I. No. 273 of 1951
		Emergency Powers (Pottery) (Maximum Prices) Order, 1943 (Revocation) Order, S.I. No. 275 of 1951
		Emergency Powers (Scutching of Flax) Order, 1948 (Revocation) Order, S.I. No. 278 of 1951
		Coal (Drogheda) (Maximum Prices) Order, S.I. No. 279 of 1951
		Coal (Waterford) (Maximum Prices) Order, S.I. No. 280 of 1951
		Coal (New Ross) (Maximum Prices) Order, S.I. No. 281 of 1951
		Emergency Powers (Distribution of Butter) Order, 1944 (Twenty-First Ration Period) Order, S.I. No. 289 of 1951
		Tea Order, 1950 (Third Ration Period) Order, S.I. No. 290 of 1951
		Sugar Order, 1949 (Fifth Ration Period) Order, S.I. No. 291 of 1951
		Sugar (Maximum Prices) (No.2) Order, S.I. No. 305 of 1951
		Jams and Marmalades (Maximum Prices) Order, 1951 (Revocation) Order, S.I. No. 306 of 1951
		Whiskey (Maximum Prices) Order, S.I. No. 309 of 1951
		Tobaccos (Maximum Prices) Order, S.I. No. 315 of 1951
		Cigarettes (Maximum Prices) Order, S.I. No. 316 of 1951

Statutory Authority	Section	Statutory Instrument

Emergency Powers Order, S.R.& O. No. 224 of 1939 (*Cont.*)

Currants and Raisins (Maximum Prices) Orders (Revocation) Order, S.I. No. 319 of 1951

Imported Timber (Maximum Prices) (No.10) Order, S.I. No. 320 of 1951

Margarine (Maximum Prices) (No.2) Order, S.I. No. 324 of 1951

Coal (Cork) (Maximum Prices) Order, S.I. No. 328 of 1951

Emergency Powers (Control of Prices) (No.120) Order, 1942 (Revocation) Order, S.I. No. 363 of 1951

Molasses Sugar Beet Pulp (Maximum Prices) Order, 1948 (Revocation) Order, S.I. No. 364 of 1951

Intoxicating Liquor (Maximum Prices) Order, S.I. No. 369 of 1951

Shotgun Cartridges (Maximum Prices) Order, 1949 (Revocation) Order, S.I. No. 382 of 1951

Coal (Galway) (Maximum Prices) Order, S.I. No. 4 of 1952

Packed and Canned Peas and Beans (Maximum Prices) Order, 1951 (Amendment) (No.1) Order, S.I. No. 5 of 1952

Matches (Maximum Prices) Order, S.I. No. 6 of 1952

Sweets and Chocolates (Maximum Prices) Orders (Revocation) Order, S.I. No. 7 of 1952

Margarine (Maximum Prices) Order, S.I. No. 11 of 1952

Motor Spirit Rationing Orders (Revocation) Order, (1951) S.I. No. 12 of 1952

Oatmeal (Maximum Prices) (No.2) Order, 1951 (Amendment) Order, S.I. No. 13 of 1952

Emergency Powers (Control of Exports) Order, 1940 (Amendment) (No.35) Order, S.I. No. 17 of 1952

Coal (Dundalk) (Maximum Prices) Order, S.I. No. 18 of 1952

Dripping, Lard and Raw Fats (Maximum Prices) Orders (Revocation) Order, S.I. No. 35 of 1952

Coal (Westport) (Maximum Prices) Order, S.I. No. 39 of 1952

Coal (Sligo) (Maximum Prices) Order, S.I. No. 40 of 1952

Coal (Ballina) (Maximum Prices) Order, S.I. No. 62 of 1952

Coal (Cork) (Maximum Prices) Order, S.I. No. 63 of 1952

Coal (Drogheda) (Maximum Prices) Order, S.I. No. 64 of 1952

Coal (Dublin and Dun Laoghaire) (Maximum Prices) Order, S.I. No. 65 of 1952

Coal (Dundalk) (Maximum Prices) (No.2) Order, S.I. No. 66 of 1952

Statutory Authority	Section	Statutory Instrument

Statutory Authority	Section	Statutory Instrument

Emergency Powers Order, S.R.& O.
No. 224 of 1939 (*Cont.*)

Sugar Orders (Revocation) Order, S.I. No. 178 of 1952

Flour and Wheatenmeal Order, S.I. No. 180 of 1952

Emergency Powers (Control of Exports) Order, 1940 (Amendment No.36) (Sugar and Sweetening Matter) Order, S.I. No. 182 of 1952

Flour and Wheatenmeal (Maximum Retail Prices) Order, S.I. No. 184 of 1952

Emergency Powers (Butter) Orders (Revocation) Order, S.I. No. 195 of 1952

Flour and Bread (Rationing) Orders (Revocation) Order, S.I. No. 196 of 1952

Tea (Maximum Prices) Order, 1951 (Revocation) Order, S.I. No. 198 of 1952

Butter (Maximum Prices) Order, S.I. No. 199 of 1952

Sugar (Maximum Prices) Order, S.I. No. 200 of 1952

Emergency Powers (Export of Eggs) Orders (Revocation) Order, S.I. No. 201 of 1952

Butter (Control in Scheduled Area) Order, S.I. No. 205 of 1952

Creamery Butter and Butter Boxes Order, S.I. No. 206 of 1952

Roll Butter Order, S.I. No. 207 of 1952

Cloth, Clothing and Knitting Wool (Maximum Prices) Order, 1947 (Amendment) Order, S.I. No. 213 of 1952

Tipperary Gas (Charges) Order, S.I. No. 225 of 1952

Wheat Order, S.I. No. 233 of 1952

Importation of Wheaten Flour Substitutes Order, 1952 (Revocation) Order, S.I. No. 234 of 1952

Margarine (Maximum Prices) (No.2) Order, 1952 (Revocation) Order, S.I. No. 255 of 1952

Condensed Milk (Maximum Prices) Order, S.I. No. 257 of 1952

Cocoa (Maximum Prices) Order, S.I. No. 259 of 1952

Emergency Powers (Wheat Flakes) (Maximum Prices) Order, 1946 (Revocation) Order, S.I. No. 261 of 1952

Flour and Wheatenmeal (Maximum Retail Prices) (No.2) Order, S.I. No. 269 of 1952

Flour and Wheatmeal Order, 1952 (Amendment) Order, S.I. No. 270 of 1952

Tobaccos (Maximum Prices) Order, 1952 (Amendment) (No.1) Order, S.I. No. 301 of 1952

American Coal (Cork) (Maximum Prices) Order, S.I. No. 302 of 1952

Coal (Dublin and Dun Laoghaire) (Maximum Prices) (No.2) Order, S.I. No. 321 of 1952

Emergency Powers Order, S.R.& O.
No. 224 of 1939 *(Cont.)*

Soap and Detergents and Candles (Maximum Prices) Orders (Revocation) Order, S.I. No. 322 of 1952

Oatmeal (Maximum Prices) Order, 1952 (Revocation) Order, S.I. No. 328 of 1952

Bananas (Maximum Prices) Order, 1947 (Revocation) Order, S.I. No. 342 of 1952

Emergency Powers (Fish) (Maximum Prices) Order, 1944 (Revocation) Order, S.I. No. 343 of 1952

Drogheda Gas Charges Order, S.I. No. 346 of 1952

Horse-shoe Nails (Maximum Prices) Order, 1949 (Revocation) Order, S.I. No. 353 of 1952

Bicycles (Maximum Prices) Order, 1948 (Revocation) Order, S.I. No. 354 of 1952

Imported Timber (Maximum Prices) (No.20) Order, S.I. No. 370 of 1952

Emergency Powers (Cast Iron Scrap) (Maximum Prices) Order, 1945 (Revocation) Order, S.I. No. 24 of 1953

Tyres and Tubes (Maximum Prices) Order, 1951 (Amendment) (No.2) Order, S.I. No. 29 of 1953

Cinema Admission Charges Order, 1951 (Revocation) Order, S.I. No. 30 of 1953

Packed and Canned Peas and Beans (Maximum Prices) Order, 1951 (Revocation) Order, S.I. No. 32 of 1953

Tomatoes (Maximum Prices) Order, 1946 (Revocation) Order, S.I. No. 34 of 1953

Coal (Maximum Prices) Orders (Revocation) Order, S.I. No. 36 of 1953

Reconstituted Whole Milk Order, S.I. No. 38 of 1953

Motor Spirit (Maximum Prices) Order, S.I. No. 40 of 1953

Reconstituted Whole Milk (Prices) Order, S.I. No. 43 of 1953

Emergency Powers (Maximum Charges for Footwear Repairs) (Display) Order, 1945 (Revocation) Order, S.I. No. 62 of 1953

Emergency Powers (Conditional and Part-Lot Sales) Order, 1944 (Revocation) Order, S.I. No. 75 of 1953

Scrap Lead (Maximum Prices) Order, 1951 (Revocation) Order, S.I. No. 78 of 1953

Creamery Butter and Butter Boxes Order, S.I. No. 82 of 1953

Roll Butter Order, S.I. No. 83 of 1953

Butter (Maximum Prices) Order, S.I. No. 88 of 1953

Emergency Powers (Export of Whiskey) Orders (Revocation) Order, S.I. No. 98 of 1953

Emergency Powers (Control of Exports) Order, 1940 (Amendment) (No.37) (Spirits) Order, S.I. No. 99 of 1953

Statutory Authority	Section	Statutory Instrument
Emergency Powers Order, S.R.& O. No. 224 of 1939 (*Cont.*)		*Emergency Powers (Spirits in Bond) Order, 1944 (Revocation) Order, S.I. No. 113 of 1953*
		Milk (Maximum Prices to Retailers) Order, 1952 (Amendment) Order, S.I. No. 115 of 1953
		Cement Order, 1948 (Revocation) Order, S.I. No. 119 of 1953
		Emergency Powers (Feeding Stuffs) Order, 1944 (Amendment) Order, S.I. No. 130 of 1953
		Reconstituted Whole Milk (Prices) Order, 1953 (Revocation) Order, S.I. No. 139 of 1953
		Cheese and Condensed Milk (Maximum Prices) Orders (Revocation) Order, S.I. No. 152 of 1953
		Sugar (Maximum Prices) Order, S.I. No. 160 of 1953
		Soda Crystals (Washing Soda) (Maximum Prices) Order, 1951 (Revocation) Order, S.I. No. 163 of 1953
		Tyres and Tubes (Maximum Prices) Order, 1951 (Revocation) Order, S.I. No. 164 of 1953
		Cocoa (Maximum Prices) Order, 1952 (Revocation) Order, S.I. No. 193 of 1953
		Control of Exports Order, S.I. No. 226 of 1953
		Wheat Order, S.I. No. 257 of 1953
		Imported Timber (Maximum Prices) (No.20) Order, 1952 (Revocation) Order, S.I. No. 289 of 1953
		Creamery Butter and Butter Boxes (No.2) Order, S.I. No. 307 of 1953
		Roll Butter (No.2) Order, S.I. No. 308 of 1953
		Control of Exports (Amendment) (No.1) Order, S.I. No. 314 of 1953
		Mild Steel and Iron (Maximum Prices) Order, 1947 (Revocation) Order, S.I. No. 319 of 1953
		Control of Exports (Amendment) (No.2) Order, S.I. No. 396 of 1953
		Emergency Powers (Milling Offals) Order, 1943 (Revocation) Order, S.I. No. 413 of 1953
		Imported Butter (Maximum Wholesale Prices) Order, S.I. No. 7 of 1954
		Butter (Maximum Prices) Order, S.I. No. 8 of 1954
		Emergency Powers (Restriction on Industrial Use of Potatoes) Order, 1943 (Revocation) Order, S.I. No. 14 of 1954
		Butter (Prices for Butter Sold under Permit) (No.2) Order, S.I. No. 16 of 1954
		Flour and Wheatenmeal Order, 1952 (Amendment) Order, S.I. No. 79 of 1954
		Flour and Wheatenmeal (Maximum Retail Prices) Order, S.I. No. 84 of 1954
		Wheat Order, S.I. No. 148 of 1954
		Waste Paper (Maximum Prices) Order, 1951 (Revocation) Order, S.I. No. 173 of 1954
		Roll Butter Order, S.I. No. 175 of 1954

Statutory Authority	Section	Statutory Instrument

Emergency Powers Order, S.R.& O.
No. 224 of 1939 (*Cont.*)

Creamery Butter and Butter Boxes Order, S.I. No. 176 of 1954

Butter (Maximum Prices) (No.2) Order, S.I. No. 177 of 1954

Importation of Knitted Woollen Wearing Apparel Order, 1952 (Revocation) Order, S.I. No. 186 of 1954

Control of Exports Order, S.I. No. 193 of 1954

Bacon (Maximum Prices) Order, S.I. No. 208 of 1954

Wheat Order, 1954 (Amendment) Order, S.I. No. 215 of 1954

Control of Exports (Amendment) (No.1) Order, S.I. No. 219 of 1954

Distribution of Hides and Skins Order, 1952 (Amendment) Order, S.I. No. 220 of 1954

Emergency Powers (Restriction on Use of Creamery Butter) Order, 1942 (Revocation) Order, S.I. No. 245 of 1954

Bacon (Maximum Prices) (No.2) Order, S.I. No. 248 of 1954

Emergency Powers (Feeding Stuffs) Order, 1944 (Revocation of Article 6) Order, S.I. No. 260 of 1954

Bacon (Maximum Prices) Order, S.I. No. 23 of 1955

Imported Butter (Maximum Wholesale Prices) Order, 1954 (Revocation) Order, S.I. No. 25 of 1955

Emergency Powers (Feeding Stuffs) Order, 1944 (Amendment) Order, S.I. No. 103 of 1955

Flour and Wheatenmeal Order, S.I. No. 104 of 1955

Wheat Order, S.I. No. 137 of 1955

Emergency Powers (Dundalk Gas Charges) Order, 1943 (Revocation) Order, S.I. No. 159 of 1955

Retail Prices (Display) Order, S.I. No. 183 of 1955

Drogheda Gas Charges Order, S.I. No. 192 of 1955

Distribution of Hides and Skins Orders (Revocation) Order, S.I. No. 202 of 1955

Intoxicating Liquor (Maximum Prices) Order, S.I. No. 207 of 1955

Tobaccos (Maximum Prices) Order, S.I. No. 208 of 1955

Cigarettes (Maximum Prices) Order, S.I. No. 209 of 1955

Sugar (Maximum Prices) Order, S.I. No. 212 of 1955

Sligo Gas Charges Order, S.I. No. 3 of 1956

Cork Gas Charges Order, S.I. No. 13 of 1956

Rabbits (Control) Order, S.I. No. 21 of 1956

Hiring, Hire-purchase and Credit Sale Order, S.I. No. 46 of 1956

Statutory Authority	Section	Statutory Instrument

Emergency Powers Order, S.R.& O.
No. 224 of 1939 (*Cont.*)

Gramophone Records (Maximum Prices) Order, S.I. No. 55 of 1956

Control of Exports Orders (Revocation) Order, S.I. No. 58 of 1956

Emergency Powers (Storage of Grain) Order, 1942 (Revocation) Order, S.I. No. 89 of 1956

Sugar (Maximum Prices) Order, 1955 (Amendment) Order, S.I. No. 106 of 1956

Motor Spirit (Maximum Prices) Order, S.I. No. 113 of 1956

Gramophone Records (Maximum Prices) Order, 1956 (Amendment) Order, S.I. No. 120 of 1956

Matches (Maximum Prices) Order, S.I. No. 124 of 1956

Tobaccos (Maximum Prices) Order, S.I. No. 125 of 1956

Cigarettes (Maximum Prices) Order, S.I. No. 126 of 1956

Hiring, Hire-purchase and Credit Sale Order, 1956 (Amendment) Order, S.I. No. 128 of 1956

Gramophone Records (Maximum Prices) Order, 1956 (Revocation) Order, S.I. No. 141 of 1956

Cork Gas Charges (No.2) Order, S.I. No. 149 of 1956

Tea Orders (Revocation) Order, S.I. No. 151 of 1956

Clonmel Gas Charges Order, S.I. No. 192 of 1956

Kilkenny Gas Charges Order, S.I. No. 193 of 1956

Cobh Gas Charges Order, S.I. No. 194 of 1956

Jams and Marmalades (Maximum Prices) Order, S.I. No. 199 of 1956

Bread Order, S.I. No. 214 of 1956

Jams and Marmalades (Maximum Prices) Order, 1956 (Revocation) Order, S.I. No. 219 of 1956

Live Pigeons (Prohibition of Export) Order, 1950 (Revocation) Order, S.I. No. 221 of 1956

Flour and Wheatenmeal (Importation) Order, 1947 (Revocation) Order, S.I. No. 239 of 1956

Flour and Wheatenmeal Order, 1955 (Amendment) Order, S.I. No. 240 of 1956

Drogheda Gas Charges Order, S.I. No. 275 of 1956

Motor Fuel Order, S.I. No. 288 of 1956

Motor Fuel (Retail Sale) Order, S.I. No. 289 of 1956

Motor Trials Prohibition Order, S.I. No. 290 of 1956

Pigs (Unsuitable Types) Order, 1951 (Revocation) Order, S.I. No. 312 of 1956

Hydrocarbon Oils Rationing Order, S.I. No. 330 of 1956

Petrol Rationing Order, S.I. No. 331 of 1956

Sugar (Maximum Prices) Order, 1955 (Second Amendment) Order, S.I. No. 3 of 1957

Statutory Authority	Section	Statutory Instrument

Emergency Powers Order, S.R.& O.
No. 224 of 1939 (*Cont.*)

Hiring, Hire-purchase and Credit Sale Order, 1956 (Amendment) Order, S.I. No. 4 of 1957

Hiring, Hire-purchase and Credit Sale Order, 1956 (Amendment) (No.2) Order, S.I. No. 25 of 1957

Motor Spirit (Maximum Prices) Order, S.I. No. 41 of 1957

Butter (Revocation of Orders) Order, S.I. No. 52 of 1957

Hiring, Hire-purchase and Credit Sale Order, 1956 (Amendment) (No.3) Order, S.I. No. 56 of 1957

Hydrocarbon Oils Rationing Order, 1956 (Revocation) Order, S.I. No. 61 of 1957

Emergency Powers (Returns Relating to Cargoes of Fuel) Orders (Revocation) Order, S.I. No. 62 of 1957

Motor Spirit (Maximum Prices) (No.2) Order, S.I. No. 65 of 1957

Hiring, Hire-purchase and Credit Sale Orders (Revocation) Order, S.I. No. 66 of 1957

Petrol Rationing Order, 1956 (Revocation) Order, S.I. No. 73 of 1957

Intoxicating Liquor (Maximum Prices) Order, 1955 (Amendment) Order, S.I. No. 75 of 1957

Sugar (Maximum Prices) Order, S.I. No. 83 of 1957

Butter (Maximum Prices) (No.2) Order, 1954 (Revocation) Order, S.I. No. 94 of 1957

Intoxicating Liquor (Maximum Prices) Order, S.I. No. 95 of 1957

Flour and Wheatenmeal (Maximum Retail Prices) Order, 1954 (Revocation) Order, S.I. No. 96 of 1957

Dublin and Cork Taximeter Areas Fare Order, S.I. No. 97 of 1957

Bread Order, 1956 (Revocation) Order, S.I. No. 98 of 1957

Cigarettes (Maximum Prices) Order, S.I. No. 104 of 1957

Tobaccos (Maximum Prices) Order, S.I. No. 105 of 1957

Flour and Wheatenmeal Orders (Partial Revocation) Order, S.I. No. 106 of 1957

Bread (Maximum Prices) Order, S.I. No. 111 of 1957

Bacon (Maximum Prices) Order, 1955 (Revocation) Order, S.I. No. 132 of 1957

Cloth, Clothing and Knitting Wool Maximum Prices Orders (Revocation) Order, S.I. No. 141 of 1957

Motor Spirit (Maximum Prices) (No.3) Order, S.I. No. 151 of 1957

Miscellaneous Maximum Prices Orders (Revocation) Order, S.I. No. 155 of 1957

Dublin and Cork Taximeter Areas Fare (No.2) Order, S.I. No. 159 of 1957

Statutory Authority	Section	Statutory Instrument
Emergency Powers Order, S.R.& O. No. 224 of 1939 (*Cont.*)		*Bread (Maximum Prices) Order, 1957 (Revocation) Order, S.I. No. 174 of 1957*
	32	*Dividends of Gas Undertakers Order [Vol. XXXVII p. 265] S.R.& O. No. 307 of 1946*
		Dividends of Gas Undertakers Order [Vol. XXXIX p. 367] S.R.& O. No. 270 of 1947
		Dividends of Gas Undertakers Order, S.I. No. 298 of 1948
		Dividends of Gas Undertakers Order, S.I. No. 247 of 1949
		Dividends of Gas Undertakers Order, S.I. No. 221 of 1950
		Dividends of Gas Undertakers Order, S.I. No. 238 of 1951
		Dividends of Gas Undertakers Order, S.I. No. 251 of 1952
		Dividends of Gas Undertakers Order, S.I. No. 274 of 1953
		Dividends of Gas Undertakers Order, S.I. No. 179 of 1954
		Dividends of Gas Undertakers Order, S.I. No. 36 of 1955
		Dividends of Gas Undertakers Order, S.I. No. 36 of 1956
		Dividends of Gas Undertakers Order, S.I. No. 48 of 1957
Emergency Powers Acts, 1939 to 1942,		*Bread (Regulation of Prices) Act, 1936 (Delegation of Powers and Duties) Order, 1940 (Revocation) Order [Vol. XXVIII p. 49] S.R.& O. No. 201 of 1945*
Emergency Powers (No.118) Order, S.R.& O. No. 456 of 1941		*Emergency Powers (No.118) Order, 1941 (Suspension of Section 5 of the Control of Imports Act, 1934) (No.14) Order, 1942 (Amendment) Order, S.I. No. 9 of 1948*
		Emergency Powers (No.118) Order, 1941 (Suspension of Section 5 of the Control of Imports Act, 1934) (Nos.8, 11, 12, 15, 16 and 18) Orders (Amendment) Order, S.I. No. 219 of 1948
		Emergency Powers (No.118) Order, 1941 (Suspension of Section 5 of the Control of Imports Act, 1934) (Nos.8, 11, 15, 16 and 18) Orders (Amendment) Order, S.I. No. 426 of 1948
		Emergency Powers (No.118) Order, 1941 (Suspension of Section 5 of the Control of Imports Act, 1934) (Nos.8, 11, 15, 16 and 18) Orders (Amendment) Order, S.I. No. 204 of 1949
		Emergency Powers (No.118) Order, 1941 (Suspension of Section 5 of the Control of Imports Act, 1934) (Nos.8, 15, 16 and 18) Orders (Amendment) Order, S.I. No. 356 of 1949
		Emergency Powers (No.118) Order, 1941 (Suspension of Section 5 of the Control of Imports Act, 1934) (Nos.8, 15, 16 and 18) Orders (Amendment) Order, S.I. No. 171 of 1950

Statutory Authority	Section	Statutory Instrument
Emergency Powers (No. 118) Order, S.R.& O. No. 456 of 1941 (*Cont.*)		*Emergency Powers (No.118) Order, 1941 (Suspension of Section 5 of the Control of Imports Act, 1934) (Nos.8, 15, 16 and 18) Orders (Second Amendment) Order, S.I. No. 313 of 1950*
		Import Quota No.16 (Fertilisers) Suspension Order, S.I. No. 404 of 1951
		Import Quota No.18 (Motor Cycles) Suspension Order, S.I. No. 405 of 1951
		Import Quota No.24 (Perambulators) Suspension Order, S.I. No. 406 of 1951
		Import Quota No.32 (Marble Chippings) Suspension Order, S.I. No. 407 of 1951
		Import Quota No.16 (Fertilizers) Suspension Order, S.I. No. 156 of 1952
		Import Quota No.18 (Motor Cycles) Suspension Order, S.I. No. 157 of 1952
		Import Quota No.24 (Perambulators) Suspension Order, S.I. No. 158 of 1952
		Import Quota No.32 (Marble Chippings) Suspension Order, S.I. No. 159 of 1952
		Import Quota No.16 (Fertilisers) Suspension Order, S.I. No. 208 of 1953
		Import Quota No.16 (Fertilisers) Suspension Order, S.I. No. 134 of 1954
		Import Quota No.16 (Fertilisers) Suspension Order, S.I. No. 50 of 1955
		Import Quota No.16 (Fertilisers) Suspension Order, S.I. No. 48 of 1956
Emergency Powers (No.227) Order, S.R.& O. No. 417 of 1942		*Emergency Powers (Orders Relating to Pigs, Pork and Bacon) (Revocation) Order, S.I. No. 5 of 1954*
	15	*Emergency Powers (Suspension Orders) (Revocation) Order, S.I. No. 4 of 1954*
Emergency Powers (No.267) Order, S.R.& O. No. 102 of 1943	15	*Emergency Powers (Suspension Orders) (Revocation) Order, S.I. No. 4 of 1954*
Emergency Powers (No.381) Order, S.R.& O. No. 179 of 1946		*Military Forces (International Arrangements) Insurance Fund (Appointed Day) Order [Vol. XXXIX p. 749] S.R.& O. No. 317 of 1946*
Employment Agency Act, No. 27 of 1971	1	**Employment Agency Regulations, S.I. No. 255 of 1972**
		Employment Agency Regulations, S.I. No. 318 of 1976
		Employment Agency Regulations, S.I. No. 288 of 1978
	6(2)	**Employment Agency (Exemption) Order, S.I. No. 257 of 1972**
	8	**Employment Agency Regulations, S.I. No. 255 of 1972**
		Employment Agency Regulations, S.I. No. 318 of 1976

Statutory Authority	Section	Statutory Instrument
Employment Agency Act, No. 27 of 1971 *(Cont.)*		**Employment Agency Regulations, S.I. No. 288 of 1978**
	14	*Employment Agency Act, 1971 (Commencement) Order, S.I. No. 256 of 1972*
Employment Equality Act, No. 16 of 1977	14(2)	**Employment Equality Act, 1977 (Employment of Females in Mines) Regulations, S.I. No. 176 of 1985**
	28	**Employment Equality Act, 1977 (Section 28) Regulations, S.I. No. 334 of 1977**
	34(1)	*Employment Equality Act, 1977 (Appointed Day) Order, S.I. No. 209 of 1977*
	53	*Employment Equality Act, 1977 Regulations, S.I. No. 222 of 1977*
	55	*Employment Equality Act, 1977 (Commencement) Order, S.I. No. 176 of 1977*
Enforcement of Court Orders Act, No. 18 of 1926	14(1)	**Under-sheriffs' Fees Order [Vol. XI p. 1463] S.R.& O. No. 47 of 1931**
		Under-sheriffs' Fees Order [Vol. XI p. 1469] S.R.& O. No. 9 of 1934
		Under-sheriffs' Fees Order [Vol. XI p. 1469] S.R.& O. No. 244 of 1934
		Under-sheriffs' Fees Order [Vol. XI p. 1475] S.R.& O. No. 269 of 1937
		Sheriffs' Fees Order, S.I. No. 1 of 1958
		Sheriffs' Fees Order, S.I. No. 230 of 1963
Erne Drainage and Development Act, No. 15 of 1950	6	**Lough and River Erne Drainage and Navigation Board (Dissolution) Order, S.I. No. 172 of 1950**
European Assembly Elections Act, No. 30 of 1977	3	**Registration of Electors (Amendment) Regulations, S.I. No. 402 of 1985**
	14(6)	*Returning Officers' and Local Returning Officers' Charges Regulations, S.I. No. 138 of 1984*
	19	**European Assembly Elections (Forms) Regulations, S.I. No. 162 of 1978**
		European Assembly Elections (Forms) Regulations, S.I. No. 120 of 1984
	Sch. I par. 18(1)	**European Assembly Elections Free Postage (Amendment) Scheme, S.I. No. 290 of 1984**
European Assembly (Irish Representatives) Act, No. 19 of 1979	4	**European Assembly (Irish Representatives) Pension Scheme, S.I. No. 387 of 1979**
European Communities Act, No. 27 of 1972	2	**European Communities (Cold Water Meters) Regulations, S.I. No. 320 of 1977**
	3	**European Communities (Motor Vehicles) Regulations, S.I. No. 311 of 1972**
		European Communities (Crystal Glass) Regulations, S.I. No. 312 of 1972

Statutory Authority	Section	Statutory Instrument

European Communities Act, No. 27 of 1972 (*Cont.*)

European Communities (Shipbuilding) Regulations, S.I. No. 314 of 1972

European Communities (Rules of Court) Regulations, S.I. No. 320 of 1972

European Communities (Textiles) Regulations, S.I. No. 325 of 1972

European Communities (State Financial Transactions) Regulations, S.I. No. 329 of 1972

European Communities (Enforcement of Community Judgments) Regulations, S.I. No. 331 of 1972

European Communities (Aliens) Regulations, S.I. No. 333 of 1972

European Communities (Customs) Regulations, S.I. No. 334 of 1972

European Communities (National Catalogue of Agricultural Plant Varieties) Regulations, S.I. No. 339 of 1972

European Communities (Judicial Notice and Documentary Evidence) Regulations, S.I. No. 341 of 1972

European Communities (Sea Fisheries) Regulations, S.I. No. 1 of 1973

European Communities (Cycle Tyres) Regulations, S.I. No. 14 of 1973

European Communities (Marketing of Eggs) Regulations, S.I. No. 15 of 1973

European Communities (Seeds of Perennial Ryegrass and Cereals) Regulations, S.I. No. 19 of 1973

European Communities (Fruit and Vegetables) Regulations, S.I. No. 20 of 1973

European Communities (Common Agricultural Policy) (Market Intervention) Regulations, S.I. No. 24 of 1973

European Communities (Bacon Levy Periods) Regulations, S.I. No. 30 of 1973

European Communities (An Bord Bainne) Regulations, S.I. No. 32 of 1973

European Communities (Names and Labelling of Textile Products) Regulations, S.I. No. 43 of 1973

European Communities (Measuring Instruments) Regulations, S.I. No. 67 of 1973

European Communities (Fishery Limits) Regulations, S.I. No. 127 of 1973

European Communities (Marketing Standards for Eggs) Regulations, S.I. No. 128 of 1973

European Communities (Fresh Poultry Meat) Regulations, S.I. No. 129 of 1973

European Communities (Companies) Regulations, S.I. No. 163 of 1973

European Communities (Forest Reproductive Material) Regulations, S.I. No. 165 of 1973

European Communities (Vegetable Seeds) Regulations, S.I. No. 173 of 1973

European Communities Act, No. 27 of 1972 (*Cont.*)

European Communities (Seeds) (Amendment) Regulations, S.I. No. 174 of 1973

European Communities (Avena fatua) Regulations, S.I. No. 285 of 1973

European Communities (Radio Interference from Vehicle Ignition Systems) Regulations, S.I. No. 331 of 1973

European Communities (Dairy Herds Conversion Premium) Regulations, S.I. No. 345 of 1973

European Communities (Road Transport) Regulations, S.I. No. 57 of 1974

European Communities (Italian Ryegrass Seeds) Regulations, S.I. No. 113 of 1974

European Communities (Retirement of Farmers) Regulations, S.I. No. 116 of 1974

European Communities (Classification of Wood in the Rough) Regulations, S.I. No. 119 of 1974

European Communities (Crystal Glass) (Amendment) Regulations, S.I. No. 122 of 1974

European Communities (Powers of the Central Bank in Relation to Certain Mutual Assistance by Member States) Regulations, S.I. No. 125 of 1974

European Communities (International Carriage of Passengers) Regulations, S.I. No. 133 of 1974

European Communities (Textiles) Regulations, S.I. No. 139 of 1974

European Communities (Proprietary Medicinal Products) Regulations, S.I. No. 187 of 1974

European Communities (Wine) Regulations, S.I. No. 195 of 1974

European Communities (Seeds) Regulations, S.I. No. 200 of 1974

European Communities (Feeding Stuffs) (Additives) Regulations, S.I. No. 302 of 1974

European Communities (Minimum Stocks of Petroleum Oils) Regulations, S.I. No. 325 of 1974

European Communities (Ancillary Equipment for Liquid Meters) Regulations, S.I. No. 32 of 1975

European Communities (Low-voltage Electrical Equipment) Regulations, S.I. No. 62 of 1975

European Communities (Detergents) Regulations, S.I. No. 102 of 1975

European Communities (Detergents) (No.2) Regulations, S.I. No. 107 of 1975

European Communities (Surveillance of Sisal Binder Twine Imports) Regulations, S.I. No. 111 of 1975

European Communities (Surveillance of Certain Footwear Imports) Regulations, S.I. No. 115 of 1975

European Communities (Surveillance of Certain Clothing and Footwear Imports) Regulations, S.I. No. 116 of 1975

Statutory Authority	Section	Statutory Instrument

European Communities Act, No. 27 of 1972 (*Cont.*)

European Communities (Statistical Surveys) Regulations, S.I. No. 160 of 1975

European Communities (Prohibition of Discrimination in Transport Rates and Conditions) Regulations, S.I. No. 175 of 1975

European Communities (Fresh Poultry Meat) Regulations, S.I. No. 176 of 1975

European Communities (Road Traffic) (Compulsory Insurance) Regulations, S.I. No. 178 of 1975

European Communities (Measuring Instruments) (Amendment) Regulations, S.I. No. 199 of 1975

European Communities (Weights and Measures of Length) Regulations, S.I. No. 200 of 1975

European Communities (An Bord Grain) Regulations, S.I. No. 203 of 1975

European Communities (International Carriage of Goods by Road and Rail) Regulations, S.I. No. 225 of 1975

European Communities (Seeds) Regulations, S.I. No. 252 of 1975

European Communities (Cattle Export Charges) Regulations, S.I. No. 259 of 1975

European Communities (Road Transport) Regulations, S.I. No. 260 of 1975

European Communities (Proprietary Medicinal Products) Regulations, S.I. No. 301 of 1975

European Communities (Textiles) Regulations, S.I. No. 323 of 1975

European Communities (Low-voltage Electrical Equipment) (No.2) Regulations, S.I. No. 11 of 1976

European Communities (Wine) Regulations, S.I. No. 12 of 1976

European Communities (Minimum Stocks of Petroleum Oils) Regulations, S.I. No. 59 of 1976

European Communities (Surveillance of Footwear Imports) Regulations, S.I. No. 61 of 1976

European Communities (Imports from State Trading Countries) Regulations, S.I. No. 74 of 1976

European Communities (Units of Measurement) Regulations, S.I. No. 102 of 1976

European Communities (Calibration of Tanks of Vessels) Regulations, S.I. No. 110 of 1976

European Communities (Standard Mass per Storage Volume of Grain) Regulations, S.I. No. 111 of 1976

European Communities (Non-life Insurance) Regulations, S.I. No. 115 of 1976

European Communities (State Financial Transactions) Regulations, S.I. No. 121 of 1976

European Communities (Retirement of Farmers) Regulations, S.I. No. 163 of 1976

European Communities Act, No. 27
of 1972 *(Cont.)*

European Communities (Statistical Surveys) Regulations, S.I. No. 223 of 1976

European Communities (Seed of Fodder Plants) Regulations, S.I. No. 228 of 1976

European Communities (Seed of Oil Plants and Fibre Plants) Regulations, S.I. No. 229 of 1976

European Communities (Beet Seed) Regulations, S.I. No. 230 of 1976

European Communities (Miscellaneous Seeds) Regulations (Revocation) Regulations, S.I. No. 231 of 1976

European Communities (Cereal Seed) Regulations, S.I. No. 232 of 1976

European Communities (Radio Interference from Tractor Ignition Systems) Regulations, S.I. No. 258 of 1976

European Communities (Non-life Insurance) (Amendment) Regulations, S.I. No. 276 of 1976

European Communities (Recognition of Medical Qualifications) Regulations, S.I. No. 288 of 1976

European Communities (Fresh Poultry Meat) Regulations, S.I. No. 317 of 1976

European Communities (Road Transport) (Amendment) Regulations, S.I. No. 34 of 1977

European Communities (Minimum Stocks of Petroleum Oils) Regulations, S.I. No. 78 of 1977

European Communities (Marketing of Fish) Regulations, S.I. No. 114 of 1977

European Communities (Cut Flowers, Flowering Bulbs and Ornamental Foliage) Regulations, S.I. No. 129 of 1977

European Communities (Aerosol Dispensers) Regulations, S.I. No. 144 of 1977

European Communities (Beet Seed) Regulations, S.I. No. 178 of 1977

European Communities (Miscellaneous Textiles) Regulations, S.I. No. 196 of 1977

European Communities (Miscellaneous Textile Piece Goods) Regulations, S.I. No. 197 of 1977

European Communities (Retirement of Farmers) Regulations, S.I. No. 206 of 1977

European Communities (Customs) Regulations, S.I. No. 216 of 1977

European Communities (Freedom of Establishment and Freedom to Provide Services) (Financial Institutions) Regulations, S.I. No. 221 of 1977

European Communities (Measuring Container Bottles) Regulations, S.I. No. 237 of 1977

European Communities (Feeding Stuffs) (Tolerances of Undesirable Substances and Products) Regulations, S.I. No. 246 of 1977

European Communities (Freedom of Establishment and Freedom to Provide Services) (Moneylenders) Regulations, S.I. No. 247 of 1977

European Communities Act, No. 27
of 1972 (*Cont.*)

European Communities (Termination of Fees on
Exported Butter) Regulations, S.I. No. 281 of
1977

European Communities (Co-responsibility Levy on
Milk and Milk Products) Regulations, S.I.
No. 297 of 1977

European Communities (Marketing Standards for
Eggs) Regulations, S.I. No. 325 of 1977

European Communities (Measuring Instruments)
Regulations, S.I. No. 328 of 1977

European Communities (Sulphur Content of Gas
Oil) Regulations, S.I. No. 361 of 1977

European Communities (Christmas Butter) Regulations, S.I. No. 362 of 1977

European Communities (Merchandise Road Transport) Regulations, S.I. No. 386 of 1977

European Communities (Road Passenger Transport)
Regulations, S.I. No. 388 of 1977

European Communities (Aliens) Regulations, S.I.
No. 393 of 1977

European Communities (Non-life Insurance Accounts) Regulations, S.I. No. 401 of 1977

European Communities (Sampling and Analysis of
Fertilisers) Regulations, S.I. No. 12 of 1978

European Communities (Marketing of Fertilisers)
Regulations, S.I. No. 13 of 1978

European Communities (Imposition of Provisional
Anti-dumping Duty on Iron and Steel Coils for
Re-rolling) Regulations, S.I. No. 59 of 1978

European Communities (Imposition of Provisional
Anti-dumping Duty on Certain Types of Haema-
tite Pig Iron and Cast Iron) Regulations, S.I.
No. 60 of 1978

European Communities (Imposition of Provisional
Anti-dumping Duty on Certain Galvanised Sheets
and Plates of Iron and Steel) Regulations, S.I.
No. 61 of 1978

European Communities (Imposition of Provisional
Anti-dumping Duty on Wire Rod) Regulations,
S.I. No. 62 of 1978

European Communities (Imposition of Provisional
Anti-Dumping Duty on Certain Sheets and Plates
of Iron or Steel) Regulations, S.I. No. 63 of 1978

European Communities (Imposition of Provisional
Anti-dumping Duty on Certain Sheets and Plates
of Iron or Steel) (No.2) Regulations, S.I. No. 64 of
1978

European Communities (Imposition of Provisional
Anti-dumping Duty on Certain Angles, Shapes
and U, I or H Sections of Iron or Steel) Regulations, S.I. No. 65 of 1978

European Communities (Imposition of Provisional
Anti-dumping Duty on Certain Sheets and Plates
of Iron or Steel) (No.3) Regulations, S.I. No. 66 of
1978

Statutory Authority	Section	Statutory Instrument

European Communities Act, No. 27 of 1972 (*Cont.*)

European Communities (Imposition of Provisional Anti-dumping Duty on Certain Sheets and Plates of Iron or Steel) (No.4) Regulations, S.I. No. 67 of 1978

European Communities (Imposition of Provisional Anti-dumping Duty on Iron and Steel Coils for Re-rolling) (No.2) Regulations, S.I. No. 68 of 1978

European Communities (Imposition of Provisional Anti-dumping Duty on Certain Sheets and Plates of Iron or Steel) (No.5) Regulations, S.I. No. 69 of 1978

European Communities (Imposition of Provisional Anti-dumping Duty on Certain Angles, Shapes and U, I or H Sections of Iron or Steel) (No.2) Regulations, S.I. No. 70 of 1978

European Communities (Imposition of Provisional Anti-Dumping Duty on Iron and Steel Coils for Re-rolling) (No.3) Regulations, S.I. No. 71 of 1978

European Communities (Imposition of Provisional Anti-dumping Duty on Certain Galvanised Steel Sheets and Plates) Regulations, S.I. No. 72 of 1978

European Communities (Natural Gas in Power Stations) Regulations, S.I. No. 73 of 1978

European Communities (Oil Fuels in Power Stations) Regulations, S.I. No. 75 of 1978

European Communities (Minimum Stocks of Fossil Fuel) Regulations, S.I. No. 76 of 1978

European Communities (Fresh Poultry Meat) Regulations, S.I. No. 109 of 1978

European Communities (Surveillance of Certain Motor Car Tyre Imports) Regulations, S.I. No. 111 of 1978

European Communities (Provisional Anti-dumping Duties) (Miscellaneous Suspensions) Regulations, S.I. No. 125 of 1978

European Communities (Wine) Regulations, S.I. No. 154 of 1978

European Communities (Surveillance of Certain Clothing and Footwear Imports) (Amendment) Regulations, S.I. No. 155 of 1978

European Communities (Insurance Agents and Brokers) Regulations, S.I. No. 178 of 1978

European Communities (Retirement of Farmers) Regulations, S.I. No. 223 of 1978

European Communities (Cattle Export Charges) (Revocation) Regulations, S.I. No. 233 of 1978

European Communities (Feeding Stuffs) (Methods of Analysis) Regulations, S.I. No. 250 of 1978

European Communities (Surveillance of Certain Clothing and Footwear Imports) Regulations, 1975 (Amendment) Regulations, S.I. No. 271 of 1978

European Communities (Reduced Price Butter) Regulations, S.I. No. 286 of 1978

European Communities Act, No. 27 of 1972 (*Cont.*)

European Communities (Motor Vehicles Type Approval) Regulations, S.I. No. 305 of 1978

European Communities (Imposition of Provisional Anti-dumping Duty on Certain Iron and Steel Goods) Regulations, S.I. No. 306 of 1978

European Communities (Imposition of Anti-dumping Duty on Certain Goods of Iron and Steel) Regulations, S.I. No. 307 of 1978

European Communities (Imposition of Provisional Anti-dumping Duty on Certain Iron and Steel Goods) (No.2) Regulations, S.I. No. 308 of 1978

European Communities (Provisional Anti-Dumping Duties) (Miscellaneous Suspensions) (No.2) Regulations, S.I. No. 309 of 1978

European Communities (Anti-dumping Duty on Certain Iron and Steel Goods) (Suspension) Regulations, S.I. No. 310 of 1978

European Communities (Taximeters) Regulations, S.I. No. 315 of 1978

European Communities (Electrical Energy Meters) Regulations, S.I. No. 320 of 1978

European Communities (Mutual Assistance in the Field of Direct Taxation) Regulations, S.I. No. 334 of 1978

European Communities (Anti-dumping Duty on Certain Iron and Steel Goods) (Suspension) (No.2) Regulations, S.I. No. 346 of 1978

European Communities (Insurance) (Non-life) Regulations, S.I. No. 382 of 1978

European Communities (Feeding Stuffs) (Additives) (Amendment) Regulations, S.I. No. 6 of 1979

European Communities (Road Transport) Regulations, S.I. No. 16 of 1979

European Communities (Imposition of Anti-dumping Duty on Certain Goods of Iron and Steel) (Amendment) Regulations, S.I. No. 18 of 1979

European Communities (Anti-dumping Duty on Certain Goods of Iron and Steel) (Suspension) Regulations, S.I. No. 48 of 1979

European Communities (Freedom to Provide Services) (Lawyers) Regulations, S.I. No. 58 of 1979

European Communities (Material Measures of Length) Regulations, S.I. No. 74 of 1979

European Communities (Imposition of Provisional Anti-dumping Duty on Certain Iron and Steel Goods) Regulations, S.I. No. 84 of 1979

European Communities (Low-voltage Electrical Equipment) Regulations, S.I. No. 123 of 1979

European Communities (Non-automatic Weighing Machines) Regulations, S.I. No. 128 of 1979

European Communities (Agricultural or Forestry Tractors Type Approval) Regulations, S.I. No. 137 of 1979

European Communities Act, No. 27
of 1972 (*Cont.*)

European Communities (Imposition of Provisional Anti-dumping Duty on Certain Iron and Steel Goods) (No.2) Regulations, S.I. No. 143 of 1979

European Communities (Surveillance of Certain Twine, Cordage, Ropes and Cables Imports) Regulations, S.I. No. 144 of 1979

European Communities (Labour Force Survey) Order, S.I. No. 151 of 1979

European Communities (Radio Interference from Electrical Household Appliances, Portable Tools and Similar Equipment) Regulations, S.I. No. 170 of 1979

European Communities (Radio Interference from Fluorescent Lighting Luminaires) Regulations, S.I. No. 171 of 1979

European Communities (Measuring Systems for Liquids Other than Water) Regulations, S.I. No. 173 of 1979

European Communities (Pesticide Residues) (Fruit and Vegetables) Regulations, S.I. No. 183 of 1979

European Communities (Measurement of Alcoholic Strength) Regulations, S.I. No. 187 of 1979

European Communities (Customs) Regulations, S.I. No. 188 of 1979

European Communities (Provisional Anti-dumping Duty on Certain Iron and Steel Goods) (Termination) Regulations, S.I. No. 191 of 1979

European Communities (Retirement of Farmers) Regulations, S.I. No. 198 of 1979

European Communities (Wire-ropes, Chains and Hooks) Regulations, S.I. No. 207 of 1979

European Communities (Road Transport) (Recording Equipment) Regulations, S.I. No. 214 of 1979

European Communities (Combined Road/Rail Carriage of Goods between Member States) Regulations, S.I. No. 227 of 1979

European Communities (Anti-dumping Duty on Certain Goods of Iron and Steel) Regulations, S.I. No. 234 of 1979

European Communities (Imposition of Provisional Anti-dumping Duty on Certain Iron and Steel Goods) (No.3) Regulations, S.I. No. 239 of 1979

European Communities (Gas Volume Meters) Regulations, S.I. No. 243 of 1979

European Communities (Miscellaneous Textiles) Regulations, S.I. No. 255 of 1979

European Communities (Miscellaneous Textile Piece Goods) Regulations, S.I. No. 256 of 1979

European Communities (Certification of Hops) Regulations, S.I. No. 267 of 1979

European Communities (Dangerous Substances and Preparations) (Marketing and Use) Regulations, S.I. No. 382 of 1979

European Communities Act, No. 27 of 1972 (*Cont.*)

European Communities (Dangerous Substances) (Classification, Packaging and Labelling) Regulations, S.I. No. 383 of 1979

European Communities (Waste) (No.2) Regulations, S.I. No. 388 of 1979

European Communities (Waste) Regulations, S.I. No. 390 of 1979

European Communities (Cosmetic Products) Regulations, S.I. No. 402 of 1979

European Communities (Sampling and Analysis of Fertilisers) Regulations, S.I. No. 409 of 1979

European Communities (Marketing of Fertilisers) Regulations, S.I. No. 411 of 1979

European Communities (Licensing and Supervision of Banks) Regulations, S.I. No. 414 of 1979

European Communities (Feeding Stuffs) (Methods of Analysis (Amendment) and Methods of Sampling) Regulations, S.I. No. 14 of 1980

European Communities (Dangerous Substances) (Classification, Packaging and Labelling) (Amendment) Regulations, S.I. No. 34 of 1980

European Communities (Vehicle Type Approval) Regulations, S.I. No. 41 of 1980

European Communities (Agriculture and Customs) (Mutual Assistance as Regards the Recovery of Claims) Regulations, S.I. No. 73 of 1980

European Communities (Recognition of Dental Qualifications) Regulations, S.I. No. 90 of 1980

European Communities (Agricultural or Forestry Tractors Type Approval) Regulations, S.I. No. 101 of 1980

European Communities (Introduction of Organisms Harmful to Plants or Plant Products) (Prohibition) Regulations, S.I. No. 125 of 1980

European Communities (Dehydrated Preserved Milk) Regulations, S.I. No. 152 of 1980

European Communities (Motor Vehicles Type Approval) Regulations, S.I. No. 169 of 1980

European Communities (Customs) (Amendment) Regulations, S.I. No. 211 of 1980

European Communities (Surveillance of Certain Motor Car Tyre Imports) Regulations, S.I. No. 228 of 1980

European Communities (Recognition of General Nursing Qualifications) Regulations, S.I. No. 237 of 1980

European Communities (Retirement of Farmers) Regulations, S.I. No. 238 of 1980

European Communities (Proprietary Medicinal Products) (Amendment) Regulations, S.I. No. 242 of 1980

European Communities (Feeding Stuffs) (Additives) (Amendment) Regulations, S.I. No. 250 of 1980

Statutory Authority	Section	Statutory Instrument

European Communities Act, No. 27 of 1972 (*Cont.*)

European Communities (International Carriage of Goods by Road) Regulations, S.I. No. 253 of 1980

European Communities (Surveillance of Certain Clothing and Textile Product Imports) Regulations, S.I. No. 256 of 1980

European Communities (Introduction of Organisms Harmful to Plants or Plant Products) (Prohibition) (Amendment) Regulations, S.I. No. 258 of 1980

European Communities (Surveillance of Certain Clothing and Textile Products Imports) (No.2) Regulations, S.I. No. 261 of 1980

European Communities (Common Agricultural Policy) (Scrutiny of Transactions) Regulations, S.I. No. 301 of 1980

European Communities (Safeguarding of Employees' Rights on Transfer of Undertaking) Regulations, S.I. No. 306 of 1980

European Communities (Seed Potatoes) Regulations, S.I. No. 343 of 1980

European Communities (Paints, etc.) (Classification, Packaging and Labelling) Regulations, S.I. No. 365 of 1980

European Communities (Lead Content of Petrol) Regulations, S.I. No. 372 of 1980

European Communities (Road Transport) (Exemptions) Regulations, S.I. No. 390 of 1980

European Communities (Recognition of Qualifications in Veterinary Medicine) Regulations, S.I. No. 391 of 1980

European Communities (Safety Signs at Places of Work) Regulations, S.I. No. 402 of 1980

European Communities (Deferred Payment of Excise Duty on Spirits and Imported Made Wine and Beer) Regulations, S.I. No. 405 of 1980

European Communities (Value-added Tax) (Mutual Assistance as Regards the Recovery of Claims) Regulations, S.I. No. 406 of 1980

European Communities (Value-added Tax) (Mutual Assistance in the Field of Value-added Tax) Regulations, S.I. No. 407 of 1980

European Communities (Beet Seed) Regulations, S.I. No. 37 of 1981

European Communities (Seed and Oil Plants and Fibre Plants) Regulations, S.I. No. 38 of 1981

European Communities (Cereal Seed) Regulations, S.I. No. 48 of 1981

European Communities (Electrical Equipment for use in Potentially Explosive Atmospheres) Regulations, S.I. No. 61 of 1981

European Communities (Vegetable Seeds) Regulations, S.I. No. 73 of 1981

European Communities Act, No. 27
of 1972 (*Cont.*)

European Communities (Introduction of Organisms Harmful to Plants or Plant Products) (Prohibition) (Amendment) Regulations, S.I. No. 98 of 1981

European Communities (Seed of Fodder Plants) Regulations, S.I. No. 112 of 1981

European Communities (Dangerous Substances and Preparations) (Marketing and Use) Regulations, S.I. No. 149 of 1981

European Communities (Automatic Checkweighing and Weight Grading Machines) Regulations, S.I. No. 150 of 1981

European Communities (Pesticide Residues) (Fruit and Vegetables) (Amendment) Regulations, S.I. No. 164 of 1981

European Communities (Aliens) (Amendment) Regulations, S.I. No. 165 of 1981

European Communities (Hot-water Meters) Regulations, S.I. No. 172 of 1981

European Communities (Antioxidant in Food) (Purity Criteria) Regulations, S.I. No. 183 of 1981

European Communities (Preservatives in Food) (Purity Criteria) Regulations, S.I. No. 184 of 1981

European Communities (Vehicle Testing) Regulations, S.I. No. 193 of 1981

European Communities (Freedom to Provide Services) (Lawyers) (Amendment) Regulations, S.I. No. 197 of 1981

European Communities (Retirement of Farmers) Regulations, S.I. No. 227 of 1981

European Communities (Feeding Stuffs) (Additives) (Amendment) Regulations, S.I. No. 262 of 1981

European Communities (Colouring of Medicinal Products) Regulations, S.I. No. 269 of 1981

European Communities (Restriction on Slaughter of Sheep) Regulations, S.I. No. 277 of 1981

European Communities (Entry Requirements for Tankers) Regulations, S.I. No. 301 of 1981

European Communities (Prohibition of Certain Active Substances in Plant Protection Products) Regulations, S.I. No. 320 of 1981

European Communities (New Wooden Furniture) Regulations, S.I. No. 345 of 1981

European Communities (Control of Stilbene and Thyrostatic Substances) Regulations, S.I. No. 366 of 1981

European Communities (Feeding Stuffs) (Additives) (Amendment) (No.2) Regulations, S.I. No. 372 of 1981

European Communities (Measurement of Alcoholic Strength) (Amendment) Regulations, S.I. No. 376 of 1981

European Communities Act, No. 27
of 1972 (*Cont.*)

European Communities (Non-automatic Weighing Machines) (Amendment) Regulations, S.I. No. 382 of 1981

European Communities (Potato Ring Rot) Regulations, S.I. No. 388 of 1981

European Communities (Agricultural or Forestry Tractors Type Approval) Regulations, S.I. No. 389 of 1981

European Communities (National Catalogue of Agricultural Plant Varieties) Regulations, S.I. No. 409 of 1981

European Communities (Marketing of Fertilisers) Regulations, S.I. No. 414 of 1981

European Communities (Motor Vehicles Type Approval) Regulations, S.I. No. 420 of 1981

European Communities (Merchandise Road Transport) Regulations, S.I. No. 431 of 1981

European Communities (Road Passenger Transport) Regulations, S.I. No. 432 of 1981

European Communities (Frozen and Deep Frozen Poultry) Regulations, S.I. No. 433 of 1981

European Communities (Cetacean Products) (Regulation of Import) Regulations, S.I. No. 7 of 1982

European Communities (Toxic and Dangerous Waste) Regulations, S.I. No. 33 of 1982

European Communities (Feeding Stuffs) (Tolerances of Aflatoxin B1) Regulations, S.I. No. 96 of 1982

European Communities (Motor Vehicles Type Approval) Regulations, S.I. No. 134 of 1982

European Communities (Customs) Regulations, S.I. No. 161 of 1982

European Communities (Surveillance of Certain Textile Products and Footwear Imports) Regulations, S.I. No. 189 of 1982

European Communities (Customs) (No.2) Regulations, S.I. No. 202 of 1982

European Communities (Labelling, Presentation and Advertising of Foodstuffs) Regulations, S.I. No. 205 of 1982

European Communities (Retirement of Farmers) Regulations, S.I. No. 225 of 1982

European Communities (Lead Content of Petrol) (Amendment) Regulations, S.I. No. 236 of 1982

European Communities (Imposition of Provisional Anti-dumping Duty on Certain Iron and Steel Goods) Regulations, S.I. No. 237 of 1982

European Communities (Wildbirds) (Gadwall and Goldeneye) Regulations, S.I. No. 241 of 1982

European Communities (Fruit Jams, Jellies and Marmalades and Chestnut Puree) Regulations, S.I. No. 250 of 1982

European Communities (Surveillance of Certain Copper Tube Imports) Regulations, S.I. No. 257 of 1982

European Communities Act, No. 27
of 1972 (*Cont.*)

European Communities (Dangerous Substances) (Classification, Packaging, Labelling and Notification) Regulations, S.I. No. 258 of 1982

European Communities (Feeding Stuffs) (Additives) (Amendment) Regulations, S.I. No. 260 of 1982

European Communities (Feeding Stuffs) (Methods of Analysis) (Amendment) Regulations, S.I. No. 261 of 1982

European Communities (Euric Acid in Food) (Method of Analysis) Regulations, S.I. No. 271 of 1982

European Communities (Fresh Poultry Meat) Regulations, S.I. No. 274 of 1982

European Communities (Control of Oestrogenic, Gestagenic and Thyrostatic Substances) Regulations, S.I. No. 282 of 1982

European Communities (Imposition of Provisional Anti-dumping Duty on Certain Iron and Steel Goods) (Amendment) Regulations, S.I. No. 292 of 1982

European Communities (Coffee Extracts and Chicory Extracts) Regulations, S.I. No. 295 of 1982

European Communities (Non-Automatic Weighing Machines) (Amendment) Regulations, S.I. No. 297 of 1982

European Communities (Employment Equality) Regulations, S.I. No. 302 of 1982

European Communities (Beef Carcase Classification) Regulations, S.I. No. 320 of 1982

European Communities (Recognition of Qualifications in Veterinary Medicine) (Amendment) Regulations, S.I. No. 323 of 1982

European Communities (Vehicle Testing) (Amendment) Regulations, S.I. No. 331 of 1982

European Communities (Cosmetic Products) Regulations, S.I. No. 341 of 1982

European Communities (Introduction of Organisms Harmful to Plants or Plant Products) (Prohibition) (Amendment) Regulations, S.I. No. 351 of 1982

European Communities (Combined Road/Rail Carriage of Goods between Member States) Regulations, S.I. No. 357 of 1982

European Communities (International Carriage of Goods by Road) Regulations, S.I. No. 358 of 1982

European Communities (Forest Reproductive Material) Regulations, S.I. No. 359 of 1982

European Communities (Surveillance of Certain Clothing and Textile Products Imports) Regulations, S.I. No. 364 of 1982

European Communities (Surveillance of Tableware) Regulations, S.I. No. 366 of 1982

European Communities (Distribution of Iron and Steel Products) Regulations, S.I. No. 371 of 1982

European Communities (Special Price Butter) Regulations, S.I. No. 6 of 1983

European Communities Act, No. 27
of 1972 (*Cont.*)

European Communities (Recognition of Midwifery Nursing Qualification) Regulations, S.I. No. 20 of 1983

European Communities (Dangerous Substances) (Classification, Packaging and Labelling) (Amendment) Regulations, S.I. No. 27 of 1983

European Communities (Feeding Stuffs) (Additives) Regulations, S.I. No. 29 of 1983

European Communities (Vehicle Testing) (Amendment) Regulations, S.I. No. 31 of 1983

European Communities (Proprietary Medicinal Products) (Amendment) Regulations, S.I. No. 57 of 1983

European Communities (Food Additives) (Purity Criteria Verification) Regulations, S.I. No. 60 of 1983

European Communities (Co-insurance) Regulations, S.I. No. 65 of 1983

European Communities (Motor Vehicles Type Approval) Regulations, S.I. No. 70 of 1983

European Communities (Customs) Regulations, S.I. No. 78 of 1983

European Communities (Measuring Systems for Liquids Other than Water) (Amendment) Regulations, S.I. No. 121 of 1983

European Communities (Gas Volume Metres) (Amendment) Regulations, S.I. No. 122 of 1983

European Communities (Measurement of Alcoholic Strength) (Amendment) Regulations, S.I. No. 123 of 1983

European Communities (Seed of Oil Plants and Fibre Plants) (Amendment) Regulations, S.I. No. 136 of 1983

European Communities (Imposition of Provisional Anti-dumping Duty on Certain Iron and Steel Goods) Regulations, S.I. No. 137 of 1983

European Communities (Feeding Stuffs) (Additives) (Amendment) (No.2) Regulations, S.I. No. 158 of 1983

European Communities (Aerosol Dispensers and Prepacked Goods) Regulations, S.I. No. 166 of 1983

European Communities (Broadcasting Authority Act, 1960) Regulations, S.I. No. 187 of 1983

European Communities (Dangerous Preparations) (Solvents) (Classification, Packaging and Labelling) Regulations, S.I. No. 189 of 1983

European Communities (Retirement of Farmers) Regulations, S.I. No. 197 of 1983

European Communities (Units of Measurement) Regulations, S.I. No. 235 of 1983

European Communities (Labelling, Presentation and Advertising of Foodstuffs) (Commencement) Regulations, S.I. No. 238 of 1983

European Communities Act, No. 27
of 1972 (*Cont.*)

European Communities (Anti-dumping Duty on Certain Iron and Steel Products) (No.2) Regulations, S.I. No. 240 of 1983

European Communities (Agricultural or Forestry Tractors Type Approval) Regulations, S.I. No. 270 of 1983

European Communities (Non-automatic Weighing Machines) (Amendment) Regulations, S.I. No. 287 of 1983

European Communities (Surveillance of Certain Motor Car Type Imports) Regulations, S.I. No. 323 of 1983

European Communities (Feeding Stuffs) (Additives) (Amendment) (No.3) Regulations, S.I. No. 325 of 1983

European Communities (Cereal Seed) Regulations, S.I. No. 329 of 1983

European Communities (Radio Interference from Electrical Household Appliances, Portable Tools and Similar Equipment) (Amendment) Regulations, S.I. No. 339 of 1983

European Communities (Radio Interference from Fluorescent Lighting Luminaires) (Amendment) Regulations, S.I. No. 340 of 1983

European Communities (Introduction of Organisms Harmful to Plants or Plant Products) (Prohibition) (Amendment) Regulations, S.I. No. 349 of 1983

European Communities (Indication of Prices of Food-stuffs) Regulations, S.I. No. 359 of 1983

European Communities (Surveillance of Certain Textile Products and Footwear Imports) Regulations, S.I. No. 393 of 1983

European Communities (Surveillance of Certain Clothing and Textile Products Imports) Regulations, S.I. No. 417 of 1983

European Communities (Exemption from Import Charges of Certain Vehicles) (Temporary Importation) Regulations, S.I. No. 422 of 1983

European Communities (Exemption from Import Charges of Certain Personal Property) Regulations, S.I. No. 423 of 1983

European Communities (Cosmetic Products) Regulations, S.I. No. 11 of 1984

European Communities (Restriction of Aeroplane Operations) Regulations, S.I. No. 14 of 1984

European Communities (Registration of Aeroplanes) Regulations, S.I. No. 16 of 1984

European Communities (Jewellery) Regulations, S.I. No. 28 of 1984

European Communities (Detergents) Regulations, S.I. No. 43 of 1984

European Communities (Life Assurance) Regulations, S.I. No. 57 of 1984

European Communities Act, No. 27
of 1972 (*Cont.*)

European Communities (Vehicle Testing) (Amendment) Regulations, S.I. No. 68 of 1984

European Communities (Introduction of Organisms Harmful to Plants or Plant Products) (Prohibition) (Amendment) Regulations, S.I. No. 84 of 1984

European Communities (Proprietary Medicinal Products) (Amendment) Regulations, S.I. No. 86 of 1984

European Communities (Introduction of Organisms Harmful to Plants or Plant Products) (Prohibition) Regulations, S.I. No. 89 of 1984

European Communities (Vinyl Chloride in Food) (Method of Analysis) Regulations, S.I. No. 92 of 1984

European Communities (Waste Oils) Regulations, S.I. No. 107 of 1984

European Communities (Waste) Regulations, S.I. No. 108 of 1984

European Communities (Introduction of Organisms Harmful to Plants or Plant Products) (Prohibition) (Amendment) (No.2) Regulations, S.I. No. 136 of 1984

European Communities (Surveillance of Certain Textile Imports) Regulations, S.I. No. 145 of 1984

European Communities (Retirement of Farmers) Regulations, S.I. No. 147 of 1984

European Communities (Non-Automatic Weighing Machines) (Amendment) Regulations, S.I. No. 165 of 1984

European Communities (Paints, etc.) Classification, Packaging and Labelling) (Amendment) Regulations, S.I. No. 170 of 1984

European Communities (Revocation of Certain Statutory Instruments) Regulations, S.I. No. 177 of 1984

European Communities (Imposition of Anti-dumping Duty on Certain Goods of Iron and Steel) Regulations, 1978 (Amendment) Regulations, S.I. No. 179 of 1984

European Communities (Marketing of Feeding Stuffs) Regulations, S.I. No. 200 of 1984

European Communities (Proprietary Medicinal Products) Regulations, 1975 (Revocation) Regulations, S.I. No. 209 of 1984

European Communities (Distribution of Iron and Steel Products) Regulations, 1982 (Amendment) Regulations, S.I. No. 225 of 1984

European Communities (Licensing of Drivers) Regulations, S.I. No. 234 of 1984

European Communities (Feeding Stuffs) (Additives) (Amendment) Regulations, S.I. No. 261 of 1984

European Communities (Prohibition of Certain Active Substances in Plant Protection Products) (Amendment) Regulations, S.I. No. 263 of 1984

European Communities Act, No. 27
of 1972 (*Cont.*)

European Communities (Motor Vehicles Type Approval) Regulations, S.I. No. 280 of 1984

European Communities (Stock Exchange) Regulations, S.I. No. 282 of 1984

European Communities (Special Price Butter) Regulations, S.I. No. 301 of 1984

European Communities (Dangerous Substances) (Classification, Packaging and Labelling) (Amendment) Regulations, S.I. No. 335 of 1984

European Communities (Customs) Regulations, S.I. No. 365 of 1984

European Communities (Motor Vehicles (Registration of Imports) Act, 1968) (Repeal) Regulations, S.I. No. 367 of 1984

European Communities (Surveillance of Sanitary Fixtures) Regulations, S.I. No. 5 of 1985

European Communities (Feeding Stuffs) (Methods of Analysis) (Amendment) Regulations, S.I. No. 16 of 1985

European Communities (Cereal Seed) Regulations, S.I. No. 25 of 1985

European Communities (Aliens) (Amendment) Regulations, S.I. No. 39 of 1985

European Communities (Surveillance of Certain Textile Imports) Regulations, S.I. No. 65 of 1985

European Communities (Pesticide Residues) (Fruit and Vegetables) Regulations, S.I. No. 67 of 1985

European Communities (Introduction of Organisms Harmful to Plants or Plant Products) (Prohibition) (Amendment) Regulations, S.I. No. 88 of 1985

European Communities (Dangerous Substances) (Classification, Packaging, Labelling and Notification) (Amendment) Regulations, S.I. No. 89 of 1985

European Communities (Retirement of Farmers) Regulations, S.I. No. 180 of 1985

European Communities (Exemption from Value-added Tax on the Permanent Importation of Certain Goods) Regulations, S.I. No. 183 of 1985

European Communities (Antioxidant in Food) (Purity Criteria) Regulations, S.I. No. 187 of 1985

European Communities (Units of Measurement) (Amendment) Regulations, S.I. No. 228 of 1985

European Communities (Prohibition of Certain Active Substances in Plant Protection Products) (Amendment) (No.2) Regulations, S.I. No. 237 of 1985

European Communities (Repeal and Revocation of Certain Statutory Provisions) Regulations, S.I. No. 238 of 1985

European Communities (Dangerous Substances and Preparations) (Marketing and Use) Regulations, S.I. No. 244 of 1985

European Communities Act, No. 27
of 1972 (*Cont.*)

European Communities (Caseins and Caseinates) Regulations, S.I. No. 248 of 1985

European Communities (Surveillance of Certain Motor Car Type Imports) Regulations, S.I. No. 262 of 1985

European Communities (Surveillance of Certain Textile Products and Footwear Imports) Regulations, S.I. No. 263 of 1985

European Communities (Surveillance of Certain Clothing and Textile Products Imports) Regulations, S.I. No. 264 of 1985

European Communities (Post Office) (Newspaper Registration) Regulations, S.I. No. 269 of 1985

European Communities (International Carriage of Goods by Road) Regulations, S.I. No. 283 of 1985

European Communities (Non-automatic Weighing Machines) (Amendment) Regulations, S.I. No. 285 of 1985

European Communities (Conservation of Wild Birds) Regulations, S.I. No. 291 of 1985

European Communities (Life Assurance) (Amendment) Regulations, S.I. No. 296 of 1985

European Communities (Non-life Insurance) (Amendment) Regulations, S.I. No. 297 of 1985

European Communities (Consolidated Supervision of Banks) Regulations, S.I. No. 302 of 1985

European Communities (Feeding Stuffs) (Additives) (Amendment) Regulations, S.I. No. 315 of 1985

European Communities (Motor Vehicles Type Approval) Regulations, S.I. No. 322 of 1985

European Communities (Sulphur Content of Gas Oil) (Amendment) Regulations, S.I. No. 326 of 1985

European Communities (Employment Equality) Regulations, S.I. No. 331 of 1985

European Communities (Vegetable Seeds) (Amendment) Regulations, S.I. No. 349 of 1985

European Communities (National Catalogue of Agricultural Plant Varieties) (Amendment) Regulations, S.I. No. 350 of 1985

European Communities (Diseases of Animals Acts, 1966 and 1979 Orders) (General Authorisation for Imports) Regulations, S.I. No. 365 of 1985

European Communities (Customs) (No.2) Regulations, S.I. No. 366 of 1984

European Communities (Removal of Restriction on Immature Spirits) Regulations, S.I. No. 368 of 1985

European Communities (International Carriage of Passengers) Regulations, S.I. No. 369 of 1985

European Communities (Classification, Packaging and Labelling of Pesticides) Regulations, S.I. No. 370 of 1985

European Communities (Lead Content of Petrol) Regulations, S.I. No. 378 of 1985

Statutory Authority	Section	Statutory Instrument

European Communities Act, No. 27 of 1972 (*Cont.*)

European Communities (Names and Labelling of Textile Products) (Amendment) Regulations, S.I. No. 388 of 1985

European Communities (Wildlife Act, 1976) (Amendment) Regulations, S.I. No. 397 of 1985

European Communities (Milk Levy) Regulations, S.I. No. 416 of 1985

European Communities (Non-automatic Weighing Machines) (Amendment) (No.2) Regulations, S.I. No. 440 of 1985

European Communities (Aliens) (Amendment) (No.2) Regulations, S.I. No. 441 of 1985

European Communities (Natural Mineral Waters) Regulations, S.I. No. 11 of 1986

European Communities (Veterinary Medicinal Products) Regulations, S.I. No. 22 of 1986

European Communities (Measuring Instruments) Regulations, S.I. No. 25 of 1986

European Communities (Cosmetic Products) Regulations, S.I. No. 35 of 1986

European Communities (Dangerous Substances and Preparations) (Marketing and Use) Regulations, S.I. No. 47 of 1986

European Communities (Conservation of Wild Birds) (Amendment) Regulations, S.I. No. 48 of 1986

European Communities (Concentrated Butter) (Maximum Prices) Regulations, S.I. No. 101 of 1986

European Communities (Vehicle Testing) (Amendment) Regulations, S.I. No. 214 of 1986

European Communities (Dangerous Substances) (Classification, Packaging and Labelling) (Amendment) Regulations, S.I. No. 224 of 1986

European Communities (Retirement of Farmers) Regulations, S.I. No. 225 of 1986

European Communities (Freedom to Provide Services) (Lawyers) (Amendment) Regulations, S.I. No. 226 of 1986

European Communities (Electrical Equipment for use in Potentially Explosive Atmospheres) (Amendment) Regulations, S.I. No. 244 of 1986

European Communities (Wildlife Act, 1976) (Amendment) Regulations, S.I. No. 254 of 1986

European Communities (Seed of Fodder Plants) (Amendment) Regulations, S.I. No. 259 of 1986

European Communities (Marketing of Feeding Stuffs) (Amendment) Regulations, S.I. No. 262 of 1986

European Communities (Value-added Tax) Exemption on Temporary Importation of Certain Goods) Regulations, 19868, S.I. No. 264 of 1986

Statutory Authority	Section	Statutory Instrument

European Communities Act, No. 27 of 1972 (*Cont.*)

European Communities (Introduction of Organisms Harmful to Plants or Plant Products) (Prohibition) (Amendment) Regulations, S.I. No. 277 of 1986

European Communities (Introduction of Organisms Harmful to Plants or Plant Products) (Prohibition) (Amendment) (No.2) Regulations, S.I. No. 278 of 1986

European Communities (Major Accident Hazards Of Certain Industrial Activities) Regulation, S.I. No. 292 of 1986

European Communities (Co-Responsibility Levy on Cereals) Regulations, S.I. No. 297 of 1986

European Communities (Material Measures of Length) Regulations, S.I. No. 299 of 1986

European Communities (Clinical Mercury-in-Glass Maximum Reading Thermometers) Regulations, S.I. No. 305 of 1986

European Communities (Non-life Insurance) (Amendment) Regulations, S.I. No. 309 of 1986

European Communities (Motor Vehicles Type Approval) Regulations, S.I. No. 320 of 1986

European Communities (Feeding Stuffs) (Tolerances of Undesirable Substances and Products) (Amendment) Regulations, S.I. No. 353 of 1986

European Communities (Lead Content of Petrol) Regulations, S.I. No. 374 of 1986

European Communities (Surveillance of Iron and Steel Products) Regulations, S.I. No. 378 of 1986

European Communities (Road Transport) Regulations, S.I. No. 392 of 1986

European Communities (Road Transport) (Recording Equipment) Regulations, S.I. No. 393 of 1986

European Communities (Concentrated Butter) (Maximum Prices) (Revocation) Regulations, S.I. No. 406 of 1986

European Communities (Protein Feeding Stuffs) Regulations, S.I. No. 433 of 1986

European Communities (Life Assurance Accounts Statements and Valuations) Regulations, S.I. No. 437 of 1986

European Communities (Fruit and Vegetables) Regulations, 1973 (Amendment) Regulations, S.I. No. 439 of 1986

European Communities (Non-automatic Weighing Machines) (Amendment) Regulations, S.I. No. 440 of 1986

3(2) **European Communities (Carnation Leaf Rollers) Regulations, S.I. No. 104 of 1976**

European Communities (Prohibition of Importation of Skins of Certain Seal Pups and Related Products) Regulations, S.I. No. 274 of 1983

Statutory Authority	Section	Statutory Instrument
European Communities (Amendment) Act, No. 32 of 1979	2(3)	*European Communities (Amendment) Act, 1979 (Commencement) Order, S.I. No. 392 of 1980*
European Communities (Amendment) Act, No. 1 of 1985	2(3)	*European Communities (Amendment) Act, 1985 (Commencement) Order, S.I. No. 34 of 1985*
European Communities (Major Accident Hazards Of Certain Industrial Activities) Regulation, S.I. No. 292 of 1986	5	**Major Accident Hazards (Local Competent Authorities) Order, S.I. No. 356 of 1986**
Exchange Control Act, No. 30 of 1954	2	*Exchange Control (Commencement) Order, S.I. No. 128 of 1955*
	4	*Exchange Control Regulations, S.I. No. 129 of 1955*
		Exchange Control (Amendment) Regulations, S.I. No. 186 of 1955
		Exchange Control (Amendment) Regulations, S.I. No. 40 of 1958
		Exchange Control Regulations, S.I. No. 44 of 1959
		Exchange Control Regulations, S.I. No. 121 of 1967
	27	*Exchange Control Regulations, S.I. No. 129 of 1955*
		Exchange Control (Amendment) Regulations, S.I. No. 40 of 1958
		Exchange Control (Amendment) (No.2) Regulations, S.I. No. 59 of 1958
		Exchange Control Regulations, S.I. No. 44 of 1959
		Exchange Control (Amendment) Regulations, S.I. No. 140 of 1959
		Exchange Control (Amendment) Regulations, S.I. No. 62 of 1960
		Exchange Control Regulations, S.I. No. 19 of 1961
		Exchange Control Regulations, S.I. No. 66 of 1965
		Exchange Control Regulations, S.I. No. 11 of 1966
		Exchange Control Regulations, S.I. No. 288 of 1971
		Exchange Control Regulations, S.I. No. 188 of 1975
		Exchange Control Regulations, S.I. No. 14 of 1978
		Exchange Control Regulations, S.I. No. 6 of 1980
	28	*Exchange Control Regulations, S.I. No. 129 of 1955*
		Exchange Control Regulations, S.I. No. 44 of 1959
	30	*Exchange Control Regulations, S.I. No. 129 of 1955*
		Exchange Control (Amendment) Regulations, S.I. No. 186 of 1955
		Exchange Control (Amendment) Regulations, S.I. No. 40 of 1958
		Exchange Control Regulations, S.I. No. 44 of 1959
		Exchange Control (Amendment) Regulations, S.I. No. 140 of 1959
		Exchange Control (Amendment) Regulations, S.I. No. 62 of 1960
		Exchange Control Regulations, S.I. No. 19 of 1961

Statutory Authority	Section	Statutory Instrument
Exchange Control Act, No. 30 of 1954 (*Cont.*)		Exchange Control Regulations, S.I. No. 205 of 1962
		Exchange Control Regulations, S.I. No. 51 of 1964
		Exchange Control (No.2) Regulations, S.I. No. 215 of 1964
		Exchange Control (No.3) Regulations, S.I. No. 266 of 1964
		Exchange Control Regulations, S.I. No. 66 of 1965
		Exchange Control (No.3) Regulations, S.I. No. 230 of 1965
		Exchange Control Regulations, S.I. No. 11 of 1966
		Exchange Control (No.2) Regulations, S.I. No. 252 of 1966
		Exchange Control Regulations, S.I. No. 121 of 1967
		Exchange Control Regulations, S.I. No. 253 of 1968
		Exchange Control Regulations, S.I. No. 288 of 1971
		Exchange Control (No.2) Regulations, S.I. No. 354 of 1971
		Exchange Control Regulations, S.I. No. 157 of 1972
		Exchange Control Regulations, S.I. No. 21 of 1973
		Exchange Control (No.5) Regulations, S.I. No. 349 of 1978
		Exchange Control Regulations, S.I. No. 6 of 1980
	31	Exchange Control Regulations, S.I. No. 19 of 1961
		Exchange Control (No.2) Regulations, S.I. No. 215 of 1964
		Exchange Control (No.3) Regulations, S.I. No. 266 of 1964
		Exchange Control (No.2) Regulations, S.I. No. 150 of 1965
		Exchange Control Regulations, S.I. No. 11 of 1966
		Exchange Control (No.2) Regulations, S.I. No. 252 of 1966
		Exchange Control Regulations, S.I. No. 121 of 1967
		Exchange Control Regulations, S.I. No. 253 of 1968
		Exchange Control Regulations, S.I. No. 62 of 1970
		Exchange Control Regulations, S.I. No. 288 of 1971
		Exchange Control (No.2) Regulations, S.I. No. 354 of 1971
		Exchange Control (No.2) Regulations, S.I. No. 234 of 1972
		Exchange Control (No.2) Regulations, S.I. No. 265 of 1973
		Exchange Control Regulations, S.I. No. 24 of 1974
		Exchange Control Regulations, S.I. No. 188 of 1975
		Exchange Control Regulations, S.I. No. 136 of 1977
		Exchange Control (No.2) Regulations, S.I. No. 114 of 1978
		Exchange Control (No.3) Regulations, S.I. No. 204 of 1978
		Exchange Control (No.4) Regulations, S.I. No. 257 of 1978

Exchange Control Act, No. 30 of 1954 (*Cont.*)

Exchange Control Regulations, S.I. No. 6 of 1980

Exchange Control Regulations, S.I. No. 176 of 1983

Exchange Control Regulations, S.I. No. 230 of 1986

Exchange Control Order [Vol. XXXIX p. 409] S.R.& O. No. 394 of 1947

Exchange Control Order, 1947 (Supplemental Provisions) (No.1) Order [Vol. XXXVII p. 269] S.R.& O. No. 395 of 1947

Exchange Control Order, 1947 (Supplemental Provisions) (No.1) Order, 1947 (Amendment) Order, S.I. No. 62 of 1948

Exchange Control Order, 1947 (Supplemental Provisions) (No.1) Order, 1947 (Amendment) (No.2) Order, S.I. No. 404 of 1948

Exchange Control Order, 1947 (Supplemental Provisions) (No.1) Order, 1947 (Amendment) Order, S.I. No. 268 of 1949

Exchange Control Order, 1947 (Supplemental Provisions) (No.1) Order, 1947 (Amendment) Order, S.I. No. 184 of 1950

Exchange Control Order, 1947 (Supplemental Provisions) (No.1) Order, 1947 (Amendment) (No.2) Order, S.I. No. 311 of 1950

Exchange Control Order, 1947 (Supplemental Provisions) (No.1) Order, 1947 (Amendment) Order, S.I. No. 162 of 1951

Exchange Control Order, 1947 (Supplemental Provisions) (No.1) Order, 1947 (Amendment) Order, S.I. No. 16 of 1952

Exchange Control Order, 1947 (Supplemental Provisions) (No.1) Order, 1947 (Amendment) (No.2) Order, S.I. No. 37 of 1952

Exchange Control Order, 1947 (Supplemental Provisions) (No.1) Order, 1947 (Amendment) Order, S.I. No. 368 of 1953

Exchange Control (Continuance and Amendment) Act, No. 24 of 1978

3(1)

Exchange Control (Scheduled Territories) Regulations, S.I. No. 350 of 1978

5(2)

Exchange Control (Continuance and Amendment) Act, 1978 (Commencement of Section 5 (1)) Order, S.I. No. 348 of 1978

Exchequer and Local Financial Years Act, No. 3 of 1974

5

Exchequer and Local Financial Years Act (Adaptation of Enactments and Statutory Instruments) Order, S.I. No. 215 of 1974

Exchequer and Local Financial Years Act (Adaptation of Enactments and Statutory Instruments) (No.2) Order, S.I. No. 293 of 1974

Exchequer and Local Financial Years Act, 1974 (Adaptation of Local Government Enactments and Statutory Instruments) Order, S.I. No. 323 of 1974

Exchequer and Local Financial Years Act, 1974 (Adaptation of the Rates of Agricultural Land (Relief) Acts) Order, S.I. No. 332 of 1974

Statutory Authority	Section	Statutory Instrument
Exchequer and Local Financial Years Act, No. 3 of 1974 (*Cont.*)		**Local Financial Year (Adaptation) Order, S.I. No. 179 of 1978**
		Local Financial Year (Adaptation) Order, S.I. No. 241 of 1979
		Local Financial Year (Adaptation) Order, S.I. No. 265 of 1984
		Local Financial Year (Adaptation) Order, S.I. No. 348 of 1986
Excise Transfer Order, S.R.& O. No. 197 of 1909		*Tobacco Growing Regulations [Vol. XII p. 89] S.R.& O. No. 3 of 1933*
		Tobacco Extract Regulations [Vol. XII p. 109] S.R.& O. No. 4 of 1933
		Spirits (Strength Ascertainment) Regulations, S.I. No. 417 of 1979
		Spirits and Wine (Amendment) Regulations, S.I. No. 419 of 1979
Executive Powers (Consequential Provisions) Act, No. 20 of 1937	2	**Solicitors' Remuneration General Order, 1957 (Disallowance) Order, S.I. No. 232 of 1957**
		Solicitors' Remuneration General Order, 1971 (Disallowance) Order, S.I. No. 61 of 1972
	5(1)	**Electoral Act, 1923, Adaptation Order [Vol. XI p. 1531] S.R.& O. No. 135 of 1937**
	6(1)	**Executive Powers (Convicts' Licences) Order [Vol. XI p. 1535] S.R.& O. No. 203 of 1937**
		Executive Powers (Remission of Sentences) Order [Vol. XI p. 1541] S.R.& O. No. 224 of 1937
Explosives Act, No. 17 of 1875	16	**Stores for Explosives Order, S.I. No. 42 of 1955**
	17	**Stores for Explosives Order, S.I. No. 42 of 1955**
	33	**Packing of Explosives for Conveyance Rules, S.I. No. 37 of 1955**
		Packing of Explosives for Conveyance (Amendment) Rules, S.I. No. 180 of 1974
		Packing of Explosives for Conveyance (Amendment) Rules, S.I. No. 274 of 1986
	37	**Conveyance of Explosives Bye-laws, S.I. No. 38 of 1955**
		Conveyance of Explosives (Amendment) Bye-laws, S.I. No. 151 of 1960
		Conveyance of Explosives (Amendment) Bye-laws, S.I. No. 309 of 1973
		Conveyance of Explosives (Amendment) Bye-laws, S.I. No. 317 of 1981
		Conveyance of Explosives (Amendment) Bye-laws, S.I. No. 275 of 1986
	39	**Conveyance of Explosives Bye-laws, S.I. No. 38 of 1955**
		Stores for Explosives Order, S.I. No. 42 of 1955
		Conveyance of Explosives (Amendment) Bye-laws, S.I. No. 151 of 1960

Statutory Authority	Section	Statutory Instrument
Explosives Act, No. 17 of 1875 (*Cont.*)		*Conveyance of Explosives (Amendment) Bye-laws, S.I. No. 309 of 1973*
		Conveyance of Explosives (Amendment) Bye-laws, S.I. No. 317 of 1981
		Conveyance of Explosives (Amendment) Bye-laws, S.I. No. 275 of 1986
	40	**Stores for Explosives Order, S.I. No. 42 of 1955**
		Keeping of Fireworks Order, S.I. No. 129 of 1984
		Packing of Explosives for Conveyance (Amendment) Rules, S.I. No. 274 of 1986
	40(3)	**Packing of Explosives for Conveyance Rules, S.I. No. 37 of 1955**
		Packing of Explosives for Conveyance (Amendment) Rules, S.I. No. 180 of 1974
	43	**Stores for Explosives Order, S.I. No. 42 of 1955**
		Sale of Explosives Order, S.I. No. 43 of 1955
	46	**Stores for Explosives Order, S.I. No. 42 of 1955**
	47	**Stores for Explosives Order, S.I. No. 42 of 1955**
	83	*Stores Licensed for Mixed Explosives (Amendment) Order [Vol. XXIX p. 479] S.R.& O. No. 73 of 1945*
		Keeping of Fireworks Order, S.I. No. 129 of 1984
	85	**Stores for Explosives Order, S.I. No. 42 of 1955**
	104	**Explosives (Ammonium Nitrate and Sodium Chlorate) Order, S.I. No. 191 of 1972**
		Explosives (Nitro-benzene) Order, S.I. No. 233 of 1972
		Explosives (Potassium Nitrate and Sodium Nitrate) Order, S.I. No. 273 of 1986
Export Promotion Act, No. 20 of 1959	2	*Export Promotion Act, 1959 (Establishment Day) Order, S.I. No. 147 of 1959*
	4(1)	**Export Promotion (Provision of Services) Order, S.I. No. 170 of 1983**
	21(3)	*Export Promotion Act, 1959 (Winding up of Coras Trachtala) (Appointed Day) Order, S.I. No. 148 of 1959*
Exported Live Stock (Insurance) Act, No. 25 of 1940	2(1)	*Exported Live Stock (Insurance) Act, 1940 (Establishment Date) Order [Vol. XXIX p. 495] S.R.& O. No. 265 of 1940*
	2(2)	*Exported Live Stock (Insurance) Act, 1940 (Appointed Day) Order [Vol. XXIX p. 483] S.R.& O. No. 264 of 1940*
	16(2)	*Exported Live Stock (Insurance) Act, 1940 (Appointed Percentage under Section 16) Order [Vol. XXIX p. 487] S.R.& O. No. 263 of 1940*
		Exported Live Stock (Insurance) Act, 1940 (Appointed Percentage under Section 16) Order [Vol. XXIX p. 491] S.R.& O. No. 15 of 1941

Statutory Authority	Section	Statutory Instrument
Exported Live Stock (Insurance) Act, No. 25 of 1940 (*Cont.*)		*Exported Live Stock (Insurance) Act, 1940 (Appointed Percentage under Section 16) Order, S.I. No. 232 of 1956*
		Exported Live Stock (Insurance) Act, 1940 (Appointed Percentage under Section 16) Order, S.I. No. 260 of 1958
		Exported Live Stock (Insurance) Act, 1940 (Appointed Percentage under Section 16) Order, S.I. No. 210 of 1963
		Exported Live Stock (Insurance) Act, 1940 (Appointed Percentage under Section 16) Order, S.I. No. 221 of 1965
		Exported Live Stock (Insurance) Act, 1940 (Appointed Percentage under Section 16) Order, S.I. No. 199 of 1967
		Exported Live Stock (Insurance) Act, 1940 (Appointed Percentage under Section 16) Order, S.I. No. 125 of 1977
Exported Live Stock (Insurance) Act, No. 2 of 1943	3	*Exported Live Stock (Insurance) Act, 1943 (Appointed Day) Order [Vol. XXIX p. 499] S.R.& O. No. 124 of 1943*
Exported Live Stock (Insurance) Act, No. 10 of 1950	7	*Exported Live Stock (Insurance) Act, 1940 (Appointed Percentage under Section 16) Order, S.I. No. 210 of 1963*
Extradition Act, No. 17 of 1965	2	*Extradition Act, 1965 (Commencement) Order, S.I. No. 161 of 1965*
	8	**Extradition Act, 1965 (Part II) (No.17) Order, S.I. No. 10 of 1983**
		Extradition Act, 1965 (Part II) (No.18) Order, S.I. No. 238 of 1984
		Extradition Act, 1965 (Part II) (No.20) Order, S.I. No. 300 of 1984
		Extradition Act, 1965 (Part II) (No.21) Order, S.I. No. 220 of 1986
	8(1)	*Extradition Act, 1965 (Part II) (No.1) Order, S.I. No. 161 of 1966*
		Extradition Act, 1965 (Part II) (No.2) Order, S.I. No. 52 of 1967
		Extradition Act, 1965 (Part II) (No.3) Order, S.I. No. 286 of 1967
		Extradition Act, 1965 (Part II) (No.4) Order, S.I. No. 76 of 1969
		Extradition Act, 1965 (Part II) (No.5) Order, S.I. No. 151 of 1969
		Extradition Act, 1965 (Part II) (No.6) Order, S.I. No. 33 of 1970
		Extradition Act, 1965 (Part II) (No.7) Order, S.I. No. 145 of 1971
		Extradition Act, 1965 (Part II) (No.8) Order, S.I. No. 229 of 1971

Statutory Authority	Section	Statutory Instrument

Extradition Act, No. 17 of 1965
(Cont.)

Extradition Act, 1965 (Part II) (No.9) Order, S.I. No. 334 of 1975

Extradition Act, 1965 (Part II) (No.10) Order, S.I. No. 251 of 1976

Extradition Act, 1965 (Part II) (No.11) Order, S.I. No. 322 of 1976

Extradition Act, 1965 (Part II) (No.12) Order, S.I. No. 323 of 1976

Extradition Act, 1965 (Part II) (No.13) Order, S.I. No. 62 of 1977

Extradition Act, 1965 (Part II) (No.14) Order, S.I. No. 102 of 1977

Extradition Act, 1965 (Part II) (No.15) Order, S.I. No. 47 of 1982

Extradition Act, 1965 (Part II) (No.16) Order, S.I. No. 349 of 1982

Extradition Act, 1965 (Part II) (No.19) Order, S.I. No. 271 of 1984

Factories Act, No. 10 of 1955

1(2) *Factories Act, 1955 (Commencement) Order, S.I. No. 160 of 1956*

1(3) *Factories Act, 1955 (Commencement of Sections 22 (2) and 33 (4) and (7)) Order, S.I. No. 161 of 1956*

Factories Act, 1955 (Commencement of Sections 34 and 35) Order, S.I. No. 162 of 1956

Factories Act, 1955 (Commencement of Sections 34 and 35) Order, S.I. No. 260 of 1957

2(1) *Factories Act, 1955 (Extension of Definition of Work of Engineering Construction) Regulations, S.I. No. 81 of 1972*

Factories Act, 1955 (Definition of Work of Engineering Construction) Regulations, S.I. No. 58 of 1981

6 **Factories Act, 1955 (Hygrometers) Regulations, S.I. No. 160 of 1958**

Factories (Electricity) Regulations, S.I. No. 3 of 1972

Factories Ionising Radiations (Sealed Sources) Regulations, S.I. No. 17 of 1972

Factories Act, 1955 (Extension of Definition of Work of Engineering Construction) Regulations, S.I. No. 81 of 1972

Factories (Asbestos Processes) Regulations, S.I. No. 188 of 1972

Factories (Carcinogenic Substances) (Processes) Regulations, S.I. No. 242 of 1972

Manufacture of Glass Bottles and Pressed Glass Articles (Welfare) Regulations, S.I. No. 243 of 1972

Factories Ionising Radiations (Unsealed Radioactive Substances) S.I. No. 249 of 1972

Statutory Authority	Section	Statutory Instrument
Factories Act, No. 10 of 1955 (*Cont.*)		**Factories Act, 1955 (Application of Section 76 to Certain Diseases) Regulations, S.I. No. 262 of 1972**
		Glass Bevelling Welfare Regulations, S.I. No. 103 of 1973
		Manufacture of Hollow-ware and the Process of Galvanising (Welfare) Regulations, S.I. No. 112 of 1973
		Factories (Preserving of Fruit) Regulations, S.I. No. 152 of 1973
		Laundries (Welfare) Regulations, S.I. No. 181 of 1973
		Factories (Spinning by Self-acting Mules) (Health) Regulations, S.I. No. 188 of 1973
		Factories (Bronzing) Regulations, S.I. No. 198 of 1973
		Factories (Welfare) (Use of Bichromates in Dyeing) Regulations, S.I. No. 252 of 1973
		Factories (Celluloid) Regulations, S.I. No. 277 of 1973
		Factories (Grinding of Metals) (Miscellaneous Industries) Regulations, S.I. No. 313 of 1973
		Factories (Grinding of Cutlery and Edge Tools) Regulations, S.I. No. 314 of 1973
		Factories (Gut and Tripe Preparation) Regulations, S.I. No. 145 of 1974
		Factories (Aerated Water) Regulations, S.I. No. 267 of 1974
		Factories (Abrasive Blasting of Surfaces) Regulations, S.I. No. 357 of 1974
		Factories (Chromium Plating) Regulations, S.I. No. 80 of 1975
		Factories (Oil Cake Mills) (Welfare) Regulations, S.I. No. 108 of 1975
		Factories (Chemical Factories) Regulations, S.I. No. 109 of 1975
		Factories (Non-ferrous Metals) (Melting and Founding) Regulations, S.I. No. 237 of 1975
		Factories (Asbestos Processes) Regulations, S.I. No. 238 of 1975
		Factories (Wool and Hair Processing) Regulations, S.I. No. 272 of 1975
		Construction (Safety, Health and Welfare) Regulations, S.I. No. 282 of 1975
		Shipbuilding and Ship-repairing (Safety, Health and Welfare) Regulations, S.I. No. 322 of 1975
		Factories (Lead Painting) Regulations, S.I. No. 2 of 1976
		Factories (Lead Painting of Vehicles) Regulations, S.I. No. 3 of 1976
		Factories (Heading of Yarn) Regulations, S.I. No. 28 of 1976

Statutory Authority	Section	Statutory Instrument
Factories Act, No. 10 of 1955 *(Cont.)*		**Factories (Indiarubber) Regulations, S.I. No. 29 of 1976**
		Factories (Manufacture of Lead Compounds) Regulations, S.I. No. 32 of 1976
		Factories (Electric Accumulators) Regulations, S.I. No. 33 of 1976
		Factories (Lead Processes) (Employment of Women and Young Persons) Regulations, S.I. No. 39 of 1976
		Factories (Vitreous Enamelling) Regulations, S.I. No. 40 of 1976
		Factories (Pottery) Regulations, S.I. No. 41 of 1976
		Factories (Tinning of Metal Hollow-ware, Iron Drums and Harness Furniture) Regulations, S.I. No. 42 of 1976
		Factories (Manufacture of Paints and Colours) Regulations, S.I. No. 43 of 1976
		Factories (Lead Smelting) Regulations, S.I. No. 44 of 1976
		Factories (Lead Processes) (Medical Examinations) Regulations, S.I. No. 45 of 1976
		Factories (Report of Examination of Air Receivers) (Amendment) Regulations, S.I. No. 357 of 1978
		Factories (Report of Examination of Steam Receivers) (Amendment) Regulations, S.I. No. 358 of 1978
		Factories (Report of Examination of Steam Boiler) (Amendment) Regulations, S.I. No. 359 of 1978
		Factories (Electricity) (Amendment) Regulations, S.I. No. 124 of 1979
		Factories Act, 1955 (Definition of Work of Engineering Construction) Regulations, S.I. No. 58 of 1981
		Safety in Industry (Diving Operations) Regulations, S.I. No. 422 of 1981
		Safety in Industry (Abrasive Wheels) Regulations, S.I. No. 30 of 1982
	8	**Home Work Order, 1911 (Variation) Order, S.I. No. 168 of 1956**
		Factories Act, 1955 (Extension of Section 74 to Dangerous Occurrences) Regulations, S.I. No. 169 of 1956
		Factories Act, 1955 (Application of Section 76 to Certain Diseases) Regulations, S.I. No. 170 of 1956
		Factories Act, 1955 (Hygrometers) Regulations, S.I. No. 160 of 1958
		Building (Safety, Health and Welfare) Regulations, S.I. No. 227 of 1959
		Docks (Safety, Health and Welfare) Regulations, S.I. No. 279 of 1960
		Factories (Adaptation of Regulations) Regulations, S.I. No. 247 of 1961

Factories Act, No. 10 of 1955
(*Cont.*)

Factories (Woodworking Machinery) Regulations, S.I. No. 203 of 1972

Factories (Miscellaneous Orders and Regulations) (Revocation) Order, S.I. No. 94 of 1973

Glass Bevelling Welfare Regulations, S.I. No. 103 of 1973

Manufacture of Hollow-ware and the Process of Galvanising (Welfare) Regulations, S.I. No. 112 of 1973

Factories (Preserving of Fruit) Regulations, S.I. No. 152 of 1973

Laundries (Welfare) Regulations, S.I. No. 181 of 1973

Factories (Spinning by Self-acting Mules) (Health) Regulations, S.I. No. 188 of 1973

Factories (Bronzing) Regulations, S.I. No. 198 of 1973

Factories (Refractory Materials) Regulations, S.I. No. 246 of 1973

Factories (Welfare) (Use of Bichromates in Dyeing) Regulations, S.I. No. 252 of 1973

Factories (Celluloid) Regulations, S.I. No. 277 of 1973

Factories (Hides and Skins) Regulations, S.I. No. 283 of 1973

Factories (Grinding of Cutlery and Edge Tools) Regulations, S.I. No. 314 of 1973

Factories (Gut and Tripe Preparation) Regulations, S.I. No. 145 of 1974

Factories (Aerated Water) Regulations, S.I. No. 267 of 1974

Factories (Chromium Plating) Regulations, S.I. No. 80 of 1975

Factories (Oil Cake Mills) (Welfare) Regulations, S.I. No. 108 of 1975

Factories (Chemical Factories) Regulations, S.I. No. 109 of 1975

Factories (Non-Ferrous Metals) (Melting and Founding) Regulations, S.I. No. 237 of 1975

Factories (Wool and Hair Processing) Regulations, S.I. No. 272 of 1975

Construction (Safety, Health and Welfare) Regulations, S.I. No. 282 of 1975

Factories (Lead Painting of Vehicles) Regulations, S.I. No. 3 of 1976

Factories (Heading of Yarn) Regulations, S.I. No. 28 of 1976

Factories (Indiarubber) Regulations, S.I. No. 29 of 1976

Factories (Manufacture of Lead Compounds) Regulations, S.I. No. 32 of 1976

Factories (Electric Accumulators) Regulations, S.I. No. 33 of 1976

Statutory Authority	Section	Statutory Instrument

Factories Act, No. 10 of 1955 (*Cont.*)

Factories (Vitreous Enamelling) Regulations, S.I. No. 40 of 1976

Factories (Pottery) Regulations, S.I. No. 41 of 1976

Factories (Tinning of Metal Hollow-ware, Iron Drums and Harness Furniture) Regulations, S.I. No. 42 of 1976

Factories (Manufacture of Paints and Colours) Regulations, S.I. No. 43 of 1976

Factories (Lead Smelting) Regulations, S.I. No. 44 of 1976

10   Factories (Grinding of Metals) (Miscellaneous Industries) Regulations, S.I. No. 313 of 1973

Factories (Grinding of Cutlery and Edge Tools) Regulations, S.I. No. 314 of 1973

10(4)   Factories (Cleanliness of Walls and Ceilings) Order, S.I. No. 175 of 1956

12   Factories (Woodworking Machinery) Regulations, S.I. No. 203 of 1972

17   Construction (Safety, Health and Welfare) Regulations, S.I. No. 282 of 1975

17(2)   Factories (Sanitary Accommodation) Regulations, S.I. No. 171 of 1956

20   Factories Ionising Radiations (Sealed Sources) Regulations, S.I. No. 17 of 1972

Factories (Carcinogenic Substances) (Processes) Regulations, S.I. No. 242 of 1972

Factories Ionising Radiations (Unsealed Radioactive Substances) S.I. No. 249 of 1972

Factories (Spinning by Self-acting Mules) (Health) Regulations, S.I. No. 188 of 1973

Factories (Refractory Materials) Regulations, S.I. No. 246 of 1973

Factories (Lead Painting) Regulations, S.I. No. 2 of 1976

Factories (Lead Painting of Vehicles) Regulations, S.I. No. 3 of 1976

Factories (Heading of Yarn) Regulations, S.I. No. 28 of 1976

Factories (Indiarubber) Regulations, S.I. No. 29 of 1976

Factories (Manufacture of Lead Compounds) Regulations, S.I. No. 32 of 1976

Factories (Electric Accumulators) Regulations, S.I. No. 33 of 1976

Factories (Vitreous Enamelling) Regulations, S.I. No. 40 of 1976

Factories (Pottery) Regulations, S.I. No. 41 of 1976

Factories (Tinning of Metal Hollow-ware, Iron Drums and Harness Furniture) Regulations, S.I. No. 42 of 1976

Statutory Authority	Section	Statutory Instrument
Factories Act, No. 10 of 1955 (*Cont.*)		**Factories (Manufacture of Paints and Colours) Regulations, S.I. No. 43 of 1976**
		Factories (Lead Smelting) Regulations, S.I. No. 44 of 1976
		Factories (Lead Processes) (Medical Examinations) Regulations, S.I. No. 45 of 1976
		Safety in Industry (Diving Operations) Regulations, S.I. No. 422 of 1981
	25	**Factories (Woodworking Machinery) Regulations, S.I. No. 203 of 1972**
	26	**Factories (Operations at Unfenced Machinery) Regulations, S.I. No. 173 of 1956**
	26(2)	**Safety in Industry (Operations at Unfenced Machinery) Regulations, S.I. No. 423 of 1981**
	27	**Factories (Operations at Unfenced Machinery) Regulations, S.I. No. 173 of 1956**
	32(2)	*Dangerous Machines (Training and Supervision of Persons) Regulations, S.I. No. 164 of 1956*
		Dangerous Machines (Training and Supervision of Persons) Regulations, S.I. No. 336 of 1971
	33(2)	**Factories (Report of Examination of Hoists and Lifts) Regulations, S.I. No. 182 of 1956**
	33(13)	**Factories Act, 1955 (Hoists and Lifts) (Exemption) Order, S.I. No. 80 of 1957**
		Factories Act, 1955 (Lifts) (Exemption) Order, S.I. No. 129 of 1960
		Factories Act, 1955 (Hoistways) (Exemption) Order, S.I. No. 211 of 1962
		Factories Act, 1955 (Hoistways) (Exemption) Order, S.I. No. 236 of 1976
		Factories Act, 1955 (Hoists) (Exemption) Order, S.I. No. 13 of 1977
		Safety in Industry Acts, 1955 and 1980 (Hoists and Hoistways) (Exemption) Order, S.I. No. 100 of 1985
	34(1)(g)	**Chains, Ropes and Lifting Tackle (Register) Regulations, S.I. No. 178 of 1956**
	35(2)	*Cranes and other Lifting Machines (Register of Examinations) Regulations, S.I. No. 179 of 1956*
		Safety in Industry (Vehicle Lifting Tables and Other Lifting Machines) (Register of Examinations) Regulations, S.I. No. 426 of 1981
	40(8)	**Factories (Preparation of Steam Boilers for Examination) Regulations, S.I. No. 174 of 1956**
	40(9)	**Factories (Report of Examination of Steam Boiler) Regulations, S.I. No. 183 of 1956**
	40(a)	**Factories (Report of Examination of Steam Boiler) (Amendment) Regulations, S.I. No. 359 of 1978**
	41(6)	**Factories (Report of Examination of Steam Receivers) Regulations, S.I. No. 184 of 1956**

Statutory Authority	Section	Statutory Instrument
Factories Act, No. 10 of 1955 (*Cont.*)		Factories (Report of Examination of Steam Receivers) (Amendment) Regulations, S.I. No. 358 of 1978
	42(7)	Factories (Report of Examination of Air Receivers) Regulations, S.I. No. 185 of 1956
		Factories (Report of Examination of Air Receivers) (Amendment) Regulations, S.I. No. 357 of 1978
	44(2)	Factories (Report of Examination of Gasholder) Regulations, S.I. No. 186 of 1956
	53	Glass Bevelling Welfare Regulations, S.I. No. 103 of 1973
		Factories (Bronzing) Regulations, S.I. No. 198 of 1973
		Factories (Hides and Skins) Regulations, S.I. No. 283 of 1973
		Factories (Gut and Tripe Preparation) Regulations, S.I. No. 145 of 1974
		Factories (Oil Cake Mills) (Welfare) Regulations, S.I. No. 108 of 1975
		Factories (Chemical Factories) Regulations, S.I. No. 109 of 1975
		Factories (Non-ferrous Metals) (Melting and Founding) Regulations, S.I. No. 237 of 1975
		Shipbuilding and Ship-repairing (Safety, Health and Welfare) Regulations, S.I. No. 322 of 1975
		Factories (Lead Painting of Vehicles) Regulations, S.I. No. 3 of 1976
		Factories (Heading of Yarn) Regulations, S.I. No. 28 of 1976
		Factories (Indiarubber) Regulations, S.I. No. 29 of 1976
		Factories (Manufacture of Lead Compounds) Regulations, S.I. No. 32 of 1976
		Factories (Electric Accumulators) Regulations, S.I. No. 33 of 1976
		Factories (Vitreous Enamelling) Regulations, S.I. No. 40 of 1976
		Factories (Tinning of Metal Hollow-ware, Iron Drums and Harness Furniture) Regulations, S.I. No. 42 of 1976
		Factories (Manufacture of Paints and Colours) Regulations, S.I. No. 43 of 1976
		Factories (Lead Smelting) Regulations, S.I. No. 44 of 1976
	54	Factories (Bronzing) Regulations, S.I. No. 198 of 1973
		Factories (Gut and Tripe Preparation) Regulations, S.I. No. 145 of 1974
		Factories (Oil Cake Mills) (Welfare) Regulations, S.I. No. 108 of 1975
		Factories (Chemical Factories) Regulations, S.I. No. 109 of 1975

Factories Act, No. 10 of 1955 (*Cont.*)

Section	Statutory Instrument
	Construction (Safety, Health and Welfare) Regulations, S.I. No. 282 of 1975
	Shipbuilding and Ship-repairing (Safety, Health and Welfare) Regulations, S.I. No. 322 of 1975
	Factories (Heading of Yarn) Regulations, S.I. No. 28 of 1976
	Factories (Indiarubber) Regulations, S.I. No. 29 of 1976
	Factories (Manufacture of Lead Compounds) Regulations, S.I. No. 32 of 1976
	Factories (Electric Accumulators) Regulations, S.I. No. 33 of 1976
	Factories (Vitreous Enamelling) Regulations, S.I. No. 40 of 1976
	Factories (Pottery) Regulations, S.I. No. 41 of 1976
	Factories (Tinning of Metal Hollow-ware, Iron Drums and Harness Furniture) Regulations, S.I. No. 42 of 1976
	Factories (Manufacture of Paints and Colours) Regulations, S.I. No. 43 of 1976
	Factories (Lead Smelting) Regulations, S.I. No. 44 of 1976
	Safety in Industry (Diving Operations) Regulations, S.I. No. 422 of 1981
59	Factories (Hides and Skins) Regulations, S.I. No. 283 of 1973
	Factories (Indiarubber) Regulations, S.I. No. 29 of 1976
60	*Factories (Protection of Eyes) Regulations, S.I. No. 172 of 1956*
	Factories (Protection of Eyes) Regulations, S.I. No. 280 of 1979
63	Factories Act, 1955 (Hygrometers) Regulations, S.I. No. 160 of 1958
67	Factories Act, 1955 (Manual Labour) (Maximum Weights and Transport) Regulations, S.I. No. 283 of 1972
70	Factories (Lead Processes) (Employment of Women and Young Persons) Regulations, S.I. No. 39 of 1976
	Factories (Lead Processes) (Medical Examinations) Regulations, S.I. No. 45 of 1976
71	*Building (Safety, Health and Welfare) Regulations, S.I. No. 227 of 1959*
	Docks (Safety, Health and Welfare) Regulations, S.I. No. 279 of 1960
	Docks (Safety, Health and Welfare) (Forms) Regulations, S.I. No. 63 of 1965
	Factories (Electricity) Regulations, S.I. No. 3 of 1972
	Factories Ionising Radiations (Sealed Sources) Regulations, S.I. No. 17 of 1972

Factories Act, No. 10 of 1955
(*Cont.*)

Factories (Lead Painting of Vehicles) Regulations, S.I. No. 3 of 1976

Factories (Heading of Yarn) Regulations, S.I. No. 28 of 1976

Factories (Indiarubber) Regulations, S.I. No. 29 of 1976

Factories (Manufacture of Lead Compounds) Regulations, S.I. No. 32 of 1976

Factories (Electric Accumulators) Regulations, S.I. No. 33 of 1976

Factories (Vitreous Enamelling) Regulations, S.I. No. 40 of 1976

Factories (Pottery) Regulations, S.I. No. 41 of 1976

Factories (Tinning of Metal Hollow-ware, Iron Drums and Harness Furniture) Regulations, S.I. No. 42 of 1976

Factories (Manufacture of Paints and Colours) Regulations, S.I. No. 43 of 1976

Factories (Lead Smelting) Regulations, S.I. No. 44 of 1976

Factories (Electricity) (Amendment) Regulations, S.I. No. 124 of 1979

Factories (Protection of Eyes) Regulations, S.I. No. 280 of 1979

Safety in Industry (Diving Operations) Regulations, S.I. No. 422 of 1981

Safety in Industry (Abrasive Wheels) Regulations, S.I. No. 30 of 1982

74 **Factories (Notification of Accidents) (Amendment) Regulations, S.I. No. 249 of 1981**

74(1) **Factories (Notification of Accidents) Regulations, S.I. No. 180 of 1956**

75 **Factories Act, 1955 (Extension of Section 74 to Dangerous Occurrences) Regulations, S.I. No. 169 of 1956**

76(3) **Factories (Notification of Industrial Diseases) Regulations, S.I. No. 181 of 1956**

76(6) *Factories Act, 1955 (Application of Section 76 to Certain Diseases) Regulations, S.I. No. 170 of 1956*

Factories Act, 1955 (Application of Section 76 to Certain Diseases) Regulations, S.I. No. 262 of 1972

80(8) **Factories (Certificates of Fitness of Young Persons) Regulations, S.I. No. 165 of 1956**

83 *Factories (Asbestos Processes) Regulations, S.I. No. 188 of 1972*

Factories Act, 1955 (Manual Labour) (Maximum Weights and Transport) Regulations, S.I. No. 283 of 1972

Factories (Noise) Regulations, S.I. No. 235 of 1975

Factories Act, No. 10 of 1955 (*Cont.*)		**Factories (Asbestos Processes) Regulations, S.I. No. 238 of 1975**
		Factories (Lead Painting) Regulations, S.I. No. 2 of 1976
		Factories (Protection of Eyes) Regulations, S.I. No. 280 of 1979
		Safety in Industry (Diving Operations) Regulations, S.I. No. 422 of 1981
	84	**Factories Act, 1955 (Manual Labour) (Maximum Weights and Transport) Regulations, S.I. No. 283 of 1972**
		Factories (Noise) Regulations, S.I. No. 235 of 1975
		Factories (Asbestos Processes) Regulations, S.I. No. 238 of 1975
		Factories (Protection of Eyes) Regulations, S.I. No. 280 of 1979
		Safety in Industry (Diving Operations) Regulations, S.I. No. 422 of 1981
	85	**Factories Act, 1955 (Manual Labour) (Maximum Weights and Transport) Regulations, S.I. No. 283 of 1972**
		Factories (Noise) Regulations, S.I. No. 235 of 1975
		Factories (Asbestos Processes) Regulations, S.I. No. 238 of 1975
		Factories (Lead Painting) Regulations, S.I. No. 2 of 1976
		Factories (Protection of Eyes) Regulations, S.I. No. 280 of 1979
		Safety in Industry (Diving Operations) Regulations, S.I. No. 422 of 1981
	86	**Docks (Safety, Health and Welfare) Regulations, S.I. No. 279 of 1960**
		Factories Act, 1955 (Manual Labour) (Maximum Weights and Transport) Regulations, S.I. No. 283 of 1972
		Factories (Noise) Regulations, S.I. No. 235 of 1975
		Factories (Asbestos Processes) Regulations, S.I. No. 238 of 1975
		Factories (Lead Painting) Regulations, S.I. No. 2 of 1976
		Factories (Protection of Eyes) Regulations, S.I. No. 280 of 1979
		Safety in Industry (Diving Operations) Regulations, S.I. No. 422 of 1981
	86(1)(l)	**Factories Act, 1955 (Building Operations, Engineering Works, Docks etc.) (Modification) Regulations, S.I. No. 163 of 1956**
	87	**Factories Act, 1955 (Manual Labour) (Maximum Weights and Transport) Regulations, S.I. No. 283 of 1972**
		Factories (Noise) Regulations, S.I. No. 235 of 1975

Statutory Authority	Section	Statutory Instrument
Factories Act, No. 10 of 1955 *(Cont.)*		**Factories (Asbestos Processes) Regulations, S.I. No. 238 of 1975**
		Factories (Lead Painting) Regulations, S.I. No. 2 of 1976
		Factories (Protection of Eyes) Regulations, S.I. No. 280 of 1979
		Safety in Industry (Diving Operations) Regulations, S.I. No. 422 of 1981
	88	*Building (Safety, Health and Welfare) Regulations, S.I. No. 227 of 1959*
		Factories Act, 1955 (Manual Labour) (Maximum Weights and Transport) Regulations, S.I. No. 283 of 1972
		Factories (Noise) Regulations, S.I. No. 235 of 1975
		Factories (Asbestos Processes) Regulations, S.I. No. 238 of 1975
		Factories (Lead Painting) Regulations, S.I. No. 2 of 1976
		Factories (Protection of Eyes) Regulations, S.I. No. 280 of 1979
		Safety in Industry (Diving Operations) Regulations, S.I. No. 422 of 1981
	88(2)	**Factories Act, 1955 (Building Operations, Engineering Works, Docks etc.) (Modification) Regulations, S.I. No. 163 of 1956**
	89	**Factories (Noise) Regulations, S.I. No. 235 of 1975**
		Factories (Asbestos Processes) Regulations, S.I. No. 238 of 1975
		Factories (Lead Painting) Regulations, S.I. No. 2 of 1976
		Factories (Protection of Eyes) Regulations, S.I. No. 280 of 1979
		Safety in Industry (Diving Operations) Regulations, S.I. No. 422 of 1981
	89(2)	**Factories Act, 1955 (Building Operations, Engineering Works, Docks etc.) (Modification) Regulations, S.I. No. 163 of 1956**
	91	**Factories (Home Work – Certain Bead Ornaments) Regulations, S.I. No. 167 of 1956**
	92	**Factories (Home Work – Certain Bead Ornaments) Regulations, S.I. No. 167 of 1956**
	97	*Factories (Fees of Certifying Doctors) Regulations, S.I. No. 253 of 1956*
		Factories (Fees of Certifying Doctors) Regulations, S.I. No. 205 of 1965
		Factories (Fees of Certifying Doctors) Regulations, S.I. No. 248 of 1971
		Factories (Fees of Certifying Doctors) Regulations, S.I. No. 196 of 1976
		Safety in Industry (Fees of Certifying Doctors) Regulations, S.I. No. 256 of 1983

Statutory Authority	Section	Statutory Instrument
Factories Act, No. 10 of 1955 (*Cont.*)	99	*Factories (Asbestos Processes) Regulations, S.I. No. 188 of 1972*
		Factories (Woodworking Machinery) Regulations, S.I. No. 203 of 1972
		Factories (Carcinogenic Substances) (Processes) Regulations, S.I. No. 242 of 1972
		Factories Ionising Radiations (Unsealed Radioactive Substances) S.I. No. 249 of 1972
		Factories Act, 1955 (Manual Labour) (Maximum Weights and Transport) Regulations, S.I. No. 283 of 1972
		Glass Bevelling Welfare Regulations, S.I. No. 103 of 1973
		Factories (Refractory Materials) Regulations, S.I. No. 246 of 1973
		Factories (Asbestos Processes) Regulations, S.I. No. 238 of 1975
		Factories (Lead Painting) Regulations, S.I. No. 2 of 1976
		Factories (Lead Painting of Vehicles) Regulations, S.I. No. 3 of 1976
		Factories (Heading of Yarn) Regulations, S.I. No. 28 of 1976
		Factories (Electric Accumulators) Regulations, S.I. No. 33 of 1976
		Factories (Vitreous Enamelling) Regulations, S.I. No. 40 of 1976
		Factories (Lead Processes) (Medical Examinations) Regulations, S.I. No. 45 of 1976
	114(2)	*Factories Act, 1955 (Birth Certificates) Regulations, S.I. No. 248 of 1956*
		Registration of Births, Deaths and Marriages (Reduced Fees) Regulations, S.I. No. 46 of 1982
		Registration of Births, Deaths and Marriages (Reduced Fees) (Amendment) Regulations, S.I. No. 148 of 1983
		Registration of Births, Deaths and Marriages (Reduced Fees) (Amendment) Regulations, S.I. No. 359 of 1984
	120(1)	**Factories Act, 1955 (Abstracts) Regulations, S.I. No. 176 of 1956**
	122	**Factories (General Register) Regulations, S.I. No. 177 of 1956**
		Safety in Industry (General Register) Regulations, S.I. No. 425 of 1981
	128(2)	*Quarries (General) Regulations, S.I. No. 274 of 1956*
Factory and Workshop Act, No. 22 of 1901	54(4)	**Night Employment of Young Persons in Sugar Beet Factories [Vol. XII p. 39] S.R.& O. No. 31 of 1929**
	79	*Chemical Works Regulations [Vol. XII p. 1] S.R.& O. No. 14 of 1923*

Statutory Authority	Section	Statutory Instrument
Factory and Workshop Act, No. 22 of 1901 (*Cont.*)		*Woodworking Machinery Regulations [Vol. XII p. 17] S.R.& O. No. 15 of 1923*
		Docks Regulations [Vol. XII p. 23] S.R.& O. No. 69 of 1928
		Vehicle Painting Regulations [Vol. XII p. 35] S.R.& O. No. 5 of 1929
		Building Regulations [Vol. XII p. 41] S.R.& O. No. 33 of 1930
		Electricity Regulations [Vol. XII p. 51] S.R.& O. No. 7 of 1932
		Cellulose Solutions Regulations [Vol. XXIX p. 503] S.R.& O. No. 385 of 1939
		First Aid Regulations [Vol. XXIX p. 563] S.R.& O. No. 139 of 1940
		Electric Accumulator Regulations [Vol. XXIX p. 545] S.R.& O. No. 19 of 1941
		Hide and Skin Regulations [Vol. XXIX p. 567] S.R.& O. No. 7 of 1942
		Chromium Plating Regulations [Vol. XXIX p. 529] S.R.& O. No. 8 of 1942
	124	**Certifying Surgeons (Fees) Order, S.I. No. 65 of 1950**
Family Law (Protection of Spouses and Children) Act, No. 21 of 1981	13	**Circuit Court Rules (No.3) S.I. No. 152 of 1982**
Farm Tax Act, No. 17 of 1985	3(3)	**Farm Tax (Adjusted Acreage) Regulations, S.I. No. 321 of 1986**
	9	**Farm Tax Regulations, S.I. No. 327 of 1986**
	12	**Farm Tax Regulations, S.I. No. 327 of 1986**
	27	**Farm Tax (Fees) Regulations, S.I. No. 331 of 1986**
Fertilisers, Feeding Stuffs and Mineral Mixtures Act, No. 8 of 1955	2	**Marketing of Non-EEC Fertilisers Regulations, S.I. No. 248 of 1978**
	3	**Marketing of Non-EEC Fertilisers Regulations, S.I. No. 248 of 1978**
		Marketing of Non-EEC Fertilisers Regulations, S.I. No. 410 of 1979
	4	**Marketing of Non-EEC Fertilisers Regulations, S.I. No. 248 of 1978**
	5	**Marketing of Non-EEC Fertilisers Regulations, S.I. No. 248 of 1978**
	6	**Animal and Poultry Feeding Stuffs and Mineral Mixtures (Control of Arsenic) Regulations, S.I. No. 124 of 1972**
		Animal and Poultry Feeding Stuffs (Control of Antibiotics) Regulations, S.I. No. 335 of 1972
	8	**Animal and Poultry Feeding Stuffs and Mineral Mixtures (Control of Arsenic) Regulations, S.I. No. 124 of 1972**

Statutory Authority	Section	Statutory Instrument
Fertilisers, Feeding Stuffs and Mineral Mixtures Act, No. 8 of 1955 (*Cont.*)		**Marketing of Non-EEC Fertilisers Regulations, S.I. No. 248 of 1978**
		Marketing of Non-EEC Fertilisers Regulations, S.I. No. 410 of 1979
		Feeding Stuffs and Mineral Mixtures (Methods of Sampling) and Fertilisers, Feeding Stuffs and Mineral Mixtures (Methods of Analysis (Amendment)) Regulations, S.I. No. 13 of 1980
	11	**Fertilisers, Feeding Stuffs and Mineral Mixtures Regulations, S.I. No. 264 of 1957**
		Animal and Poultry Feeding Stuffs and Mineral Mixtures (Control of Arsenic) Regulations, S.I. No. 124 of 1972
		Marketing of Non-EEC Fertilisers Regulations, S.I. No. 248 of 1978
		Fertilisers, Feeding Stuffs and Mineral Mixtures (Methods of Analysis) Regulations, S.I. No. 249 of 1978
		Marketing of Non-EEC Fertilisers Regulations, S.I. No. 410 of 1979
		Feeding Stuffs and Mineral Mixtures (Methods of Sampling) and Fertilisers, Feeding Stuffs and Mineral Mixtures (Methods of Analysis (Amendment)) Regulations, S.I. No. 13 of 1980
	16	*Fertilisers, Feeding Stuffs and Mineral Mixtures Act, 1955 (Commencement) Order, S.I. No. 265 of 1957*
Finance Act, No. 30 of 1894	20(3)	**Double Taxation (Federated Malay States) Relief Order [Vol. XII p. 59] S.R.& O. No. 18 of 1930**
		Double Taxation (Non-Federated Malay States) Relief Order [Vol. XII p. 63] S.R.& O. No. 93 of 1930
	20(4)	*Double Taxation (Province of Quebec) Revocation Order [Vol. XII p. 67] S.R.& O. No. 75 of 1931*
		Double Taxation (Yukon Territory) Revocation Order [Vol. XII p. 73] S.R.& O. No. 97 of 1933
		Double Taxation (Southern Rhodesia) Revocation Order [Vol. XII p. 79] S.R.& O. No. 98 of 1933
		Double Taxation (Province of Manitoba) Revocation Order [Vol. XXIX p. 583] S.R.& O. No. 208 of 1944
		Double Taxation (Province of Ontario) Revocation Order [Vol. XXIX p. 587] S.R.& O. No. 209 of 1944
Finance Act, No. 16 of 1895	6	**Spirits and Wine (Amendment) Regulations, S.I. No. 419 of 1979**
Finance Act, No. 13 of 1907	4	**Strength and Weight of Spirits Ascertainment Regulations [Vol. XII p. 85] S.R.& O. No. 205 of 1937**
		Spirits (Strength Ascertainment) Regulations, S.I. No. 417 of 1979

Statutory Authority	Section	Statutory Instrument
Finance Act, No. 13 of 1907 (*Cont.*)	8(2)	**Spirits and Wine (Amendment) Regulations, S.I. No. 419 of 1979**
Finance Act, No. 16 of 1908	3	*Tobacco Growing Regulations [Vol. XII p. 89] S.R.& O. No. 3 of 1933*
Finance Act, No. 48 of 1911	20	**Revenue and Post Office (Powers and Duties) Order [Vol. XII p. 97] S.R.& O. No. 30 of 1925**
		Revenue and Post Office (Powers and Duties) (No.2) Order [Vol. XII p. 103] S.R.& O. No. 31 of 1925
Finance Act, No. 8 of 1912	4	**Tobacco Extract Regulations [Vol. XII p. 109] S.R.& O. No. 4 of 1933**
Finance Act, No. 62 of 1915	8(2)	**Spirits and Wine (Amendment) Regulations, S.I. No. 419 of 1979**
Finance Act, No. 31 of 1917	37	**Government Stock (Management) Regulations [Vol. XII p. 157] S.R.& O. No. 237 of 1937**
Finance Act, No. 15 of 1918	4	**Spirits (Medical Purposes) Regulations [Vol. XII p. 165] S.R.& O. No. 14 of 1925**
		Spirits (Scientific Purposes) Regulations [Vol. XII p. 171] S.R.& O. No. 16 of 1925
	43	**Revenue and Post Office (Powers and Duties) Order [Vol. XII p. 97] S.R.& O. No. 30 of 1925**
Finance Act, No. 32 of 1919	8	**Finance Act, 1919 (Prescribed Proportion of Value of Artificial Silk) Regulations, (1938) [Vol. XXIX p. 591] S.R.& O. No. 38 of 1939**
	8(1)	**Customs Duties (Preferential Rates) Regulations [Vol. XII p. 177] S.R.& O. No. 81 of 1928**
Finance Act, No. 18 of 1920	13	*Road Vehicles (International Circulation) Regulations [Vol. XII p. 203] S.R.& O. No. 50 of 1932*
		Road Vehicles (International Circulation) Regulations [Vol. XII p. 233] S.R.& O. No. 119 of 1934
		Road Vehicles (International Circulation) (Amendment) Regulations [Vol. XII p. 265] S.R.& O. No. 98 of 1937
		Road Vehicles (International Circulation) (Amendment) Regulations [Vol. XII p. 269] S.R.& O. No. 190 of 1938
	13(3)	**Road Vehicles (Calculation of Horse-power) Regulations [Vol. XII p. 181] S.R.& O. No. 48 of 1926**
	56(7)	*Corporation Profits Tax Regulations, S.I. No. 130 of 1967*
Finance Act, No. 32 of 1921	16	**Power Methylated Spirits Regulations [Vol. XII p. 277] S.R.& O. No. 95 of 1937**
		Spirits and Wine (Amendment) Regulations, S.I. No. 419 of 1979

Statutory Authority	Section	Statutory Instrument
Finance Act, No. 17 of 1922	12	**Cinematograph: Imported Negative Cinematograph Films [Vol. XII p. 293] S.R.& O. No. 49 of 1930**
	15	**Road Vehicles (Registration and Licensing) Regulations, S.I. No. 13 of 1958**
Finance Act, No. 35 of 1926	25	*Betting Duty Regulations [Vol. XII p. 297] S.R.& O. No. 65 of 1926*
		Betting Duty (Certified Returns) Regulations [Vol. XII p. 303] S.R.& O. No. 113 of 1934
		Betting Duty (Official Sheets) Regulations [Vol. XII p. 309] S.R.& O. No. 114 of 1934
		Betting Duty (Certified Returns) (Amendment) Regulations, S.I. No. 46 of 1984
		Betting Duty (Official Sheets) (Amendment) Regulations, S.I. No. 47 of 1984
Finance Act, No. 18 of 1927	4	**Double Income Tax on Shipping (Norway) Relief Order [Vol. XII p. 319] S.R.& O. No. 92 of 1930**
		Double Income Tax on Shipping (Sweden) Relief Order [Vol. XII p. 323] S.R.& O. No. 83 of 1931
		Double Income Tax on Shipping (Denmark) Relief Order [Vol. XII p. 329] S.R.& O. No. 213 of 1934
	17	*Double Taxation (Northern Ireland) Relief Order [Vol. XII p. 315] S.R.& O. No. 85 of 1927*
Finance Act, No. 11 of 1928	3	*Income Tax Documents Service by Post [Vol. XIII p. 459] S.R.& O. No. 48 of 1929*
		Surtax Regulations, S.I. No. 155 of 1963
	14(2)	*Motor Cars (Temporary Importation) Regulations [Vol. p. 1930] S.R.& O. No. 72 of 1930*
Finance Act, No. 32 of 1929	30	**Betting Duty (Certified Returns) Regulations [Vol. XII p. 303] S.R.& O. No. 113 of 1934**
		Betting Duty (Official Sheets) Regulations [Vol. XII p. 309] S.R.& O. No. 114 of 1934
		Betting Duty (Certified Returns) (Amendment) Regulations, S.I. No. 46 of 1984
		Betting Duty (Official Sheets) (Amendment) Regulations, S.I. No. 47 of 1984
Finance Act, No. 20 of 1930	20	*Death Duties (Payment in Securities) Regulations, 1930 (Revocation) Regulations, S.I. No. 201 of 1951*
	20(1)	*Death Duties (Payment in Securities) Regulations [Vol. XII p. 347] S.R.& O. No. 78 of 1930*
Finance Act, No. 31 of 1934	12(4)	*Motor Cars (Temporary Importation) (Amendment) Regulations [Vol. XII p. 355] S.R.& O. No. 278 of 1938*
		Motor Cars (Temporary Importation) Regulations [Vol. XXIX p. 595] S.R.& O. No. 343 of 1945
		Motor Cars (Temporary Importation) Regulations, S.I. No. 227 of 1950

Statutory Authority	Section	Statutory Instrument
Finance Act, No. 31 of 1934 (*Cont.*)		*Motor Cars (Temporary Importation) Regulations, S.I. No. 14 of 1952*
		Motor Cars (Temporary Importation) Regulations, S.I. No. 3 of 1954
		Motor Cars (Temporary Importation) Regulations, S.I. No. 163 of 1955
		Motor Cars (Temporary Importation) Regulations, S.I. No. 253 of 1958
	12(5)	*Motor Cars (Temporary Importation) (Amendment) Regulations [Vol. XII p. 355] S.R.& O. No. 278 of 1938*
		Motor Cars (Temporary Importation) Regulations [Vol. XXIX p. 595] S.R.& O. No. 343 of 1945
Finance Act, No. 28 of 1935	21	*Hydrocarbon Oil (No.2) Regulations [Vol. XII p. 383] S.R.& O. No. 652 of 1935*
		Hydrocarbon Oil (Rebated Oil) Regulations, S.I. No. 122 of 1961
		Hydrocarbon (Heavy) Oil Regulations, S.I. No. 219 of 1965
		Hydrocarbon Oil (Amendment) Regulations, S.I. No. 382 of 1977
		Hydrocarbon Oil (Amendment) Regulations, S.I. No. 418 of 1979
		Hydrocarbon Oil (Rebated Oil) (Amendment) Regulations, S.I. No. 198 of 1982
Finance Act, No. 14 of 1940	10	**Cider Duty (No.2) Regulations, (1940) [Vol. XXIX p. 617] S.R.& O. No. 35 of 1941**
	17	*Hard Pressed Tobacco Rebate Regulations [Vol. XXIX p. 641] S.R.& O. No. 279 of 1940*
	18	**Hydrocarbon Oil Regulations [Vol. XXIX p. 695] S.R.& O. No. 490 of 1941**
	30	**Savings Certificates (Conversion to New Currency) Rules, S.I. No. 2 of 1971**
	30(2)	**Savings Certificates (Second Issue Extension) Rules [Vol. XXIX p. 663] S.R.& O. No. 169 of 1941**
		Savings Certificates (First Issue Extension) Rules [Vol. XXIX p. 657] S.R.& O. No. 305 of 1943
		Savings Certificates (Third Issue Extension) Rules [Vol. XXIX p. 669] S.R.& O. No. 192 of 1945
		Savings Certificates (Fourth Issue) Rules [Vol. XXXVII p. 285] S.R.& O. No. 220 of 1946
		Savings Certificates (Maximum Holdings) Rules [Vol. XXXVII p. 289] S.R.& O. No. 203 of 1947
		Savings Certificates (Maximum Holdings) Rules, S.I. No. 172 of 1948
		Savings Certificates (First Issue Extension) Rules, S.I. No. 322 of 1953
		Savings Certificates (Second Issue Extension) Rules, S.I. No. 323 of 1953

Statutory Authority	Section	Statutory Instrument
Finance Act, No. 14 of 1940 (*Cont.*)		**Savings Certificates (Sixth Issue) Rules, S.I. No. 101 of 1956**
		Savings Certificates (Fourth Issue Extension) Rules, S.I. No. 158 of 1957
		Savings Certificates (Savings Gift Tokens) Rules, S.I. No. 236 of 1957
		Savings Certificates (Third Issue Extension) Rules, S.I. No. 152 of 1958
		Savings Certificates (Fifth Issue) Rules, S.I. No. 153 of 1958
		Savings Certificates (Sixth Issue) (Amendment) Rules, S.I. No. 81 of 1961
		Savings Certificates (Fourth Issue Extension) Rules, S.I. No. 89 of 1962
		Savings Certificates (Sixth Issue Extension) Rules, S.I. No. 90 of 1962
		Savings Certificates (Sixth Issue) (Amendment) Rules, S.I. No. 99 of 1964
		Savings Certificates (Third Issue Extension) Rules, S.I. No. 142 of 1964
		Savings Certificates (Fifth Issue Extension) Rules, S.I. No. 143 of 1964
		Savings Certificates (Seventh Issue) Rules, S.I. No. 52 of 1966
		Savings Certificates (Third Issue Extension) Rules, S.I. No. 99 of 1968
		Savings Certificates (Fourth Issue Extension) Rules, S.I. No. 100 of 1968
		Savings Certificates (Fifth Issue Extension) Rules, S.I. No. 101 of 1968
		Savings Certificates (Sixth Issue Extension) Rules, S.I. No. 102 of 1968
		Savings Certificates (Seventh Issue) (Amendment) Rules, S.I. No. 247 of 1968
		Savings Certificates (Eighth Issue) Rules, S.I. No. 181 of 1971
		Savings Certificates (Ninth Issue) Rules, S.I. No. 291 of 1973
		Savings Certificates (Seventh Issue Extension) Rules, S.I. No. 56 of 1974
		Savings Certificates (First Issue Extension) Rules, S.I. No. 127 of 1974
		Savings Certificates (Second Issue Extension) Rules, S.I. No. 128 of 1974
		Savings Certificates (Fifth Issue Extension) Rules, S.I. No. 129 of 1974
		Savings Certificates (Sixth Issue Extension) Rules, S.I. No. 130 of 1974
		Savings Certificates (Third Issue Extension) Rules, S.I. No. 226 of 1974
		Savings Certificates (Fourth Issue Extension) Rules, S.I. No. 227 of 1974

Statutory Authority	Section	Statutory Instrument
Finance Act, No. 14 of 1940 (*Cont.*)		**Savings Certificates (Eighth Issue Extension) Rules, S.I. No. 178 of 1976**
		Savings Certificates (Ninth Issue) Amendment Rules, S.I. No. 27 of 1978
		Savings Certificates (Ninth Issue Extension) Rules, S.I. No. 290 of 1978
		Savings Certificates (Seventh Issue Extension) Rules, S.I. No. 56 of 1979
		Savings Certificates (Second Issue Extension) Rules, S.I. No. 103 of 1979
		Savings Certificates (Fifth Issue Extension) Rules, S.I. No. 104 of 1979
		Savings Certificates (Sixth Issue Extension) Rules, S.I. No. 105 of 1979
		Savings Certificates (First Issue Extension) Rules, S.I. No. 199 of 1979
		Savings Certificates (Third Issue Extension) Rules, S.I. No. 200 of 1979
		Savings Certificates (Eighth Issue Extension) Rules, S.I. No. 201 of 1979
		Savings Certificates (Fourth Issue Extension) Rules, S.I. No. 247 of 1979
		Savings Certificates (Ninth Issue) (Amendment) Rules, S.I. No. 64 of 1980
		Savings Certificates (Tenth Issue) Rules, S.I. No. 52 of 1981
		Savings Certificates (Tenth Issue) (Amendment) Rules, S.I. No. 263 of 1981
		Savings Certificates (Ninth Issue Extension) Rules, S.I. No. 371 of 1981
		Savings Certificates (Seventh Issue Extension) Rules, S.I. No. 53 of 1982
		Savings Certificates (Second Issue Extension) Rules, S.I. No. 105 of 1982
		Savings Certificates (Fifth Issue Extension) Rules, S.I. No. 106 of 1982
		Savings Certificates (Sixth Issue Extension) Rules, S.I. No. 107 of 1982
		Savings Certificates (First Issue Extension) Rules, S.I. No. 168 of 1982
		Savings Certificates (Third Issue Extension) Rules, S.I. No. 169 of 1982
		Savings Certificates (Fourth Issue Extension) Rules, S.I. No. 170 of 1982
		Savings Certificates (Eighth Issue Extension) Rules, S.I. No. 171 of 1982
		Savings Certificates (Ninth Issue Extension) Rules, S.I. No. 270 of 1984
		Savings Certificates (Seventh Issue Extension) Rules, S.I. No. 70 of 1985
		Savings Certificates (Second Issue Extension) Rules, S.I. No. 90 of 1985

Statutory Authority	Section	Statutory Instrument
Finance Act, No. 14 of 1940 (*Cont.*)		Savings Certificates (Fifth Issue Extension) Rules, S.I. No. 91 of 1985
		Savings Certificates (Sixth Issue Extension) Rules, S.I. No. 92 of 1985
		Savings Certificates (First Issue Extension) Rules, S.I. No. 168 of 1985
		Savings Certificates (Third Issue Extension) Rules, S.I. No. 169 of 1985
		Savings Certificates (Fourth Issue Extension) Rules, S.I. No. 170 of 1985
		Savings Certificates (Eighth Issue Extension) Rules, S.I. No. 171 of 1985
		Savings Certificates (Eleventh Issue) Rules, S.I. No. 58 of 1986
		Savings Certificates (Tenth Issue Extension) Rules, S.I. No. 59 of 1986
		Savings Certificates (Seventh Issue Extension) Rules, S.I. No. 66 of 1986
		Savings Certificates (Sixth Issue Extension) Rules, S.I. No. 84 of 1986
		Savings Certificates (Second Issue Extension) Rules, S.I. No. 85 of 1986
		Savings Certificates (Fifth Issue Extension) Rules, S.I. No. 86 of 1986
		Savings Certificates (First Issue Extension) Rules, S.I. No. 231 of 1986
		Savings Certificates (Third Issue Extension) Rules, S.I. No. 232 of 1986
		Savings Certificates (Fourth Issue Extension) Rules, S.I. No. 233 of 1986
		Savings Certificates (Eighth Issue Extension) Rules, S.I. No. 234 of 1986
		Savings Certificates (Ninth Issue Extension) Rules, S.I. No. 354 of 1986
	30(3)(f)	Savings Certificates (Fees on Determination of Disputes) Order [Vol. XXIX p. 651] S.R.& O. No. 363 of 1940
	31	Trustee Savings Banks Regulations [Vol. XXIX p. 673] S.R.& O. No. 336 of 1940
		Trustee Savings Banks Regulations, 1940 (Amendment) Regulations [Vol. XXXVII p. 293] S.R.& O. No. 377 of 1946
		Trustee Savings Banks Regulations, 1940 (Amendment) Regulations, S.I. No. 243 of 1948
		Trustee Savings Banks Regulations, 1940 (Amendment) Regulations, S.I. No. 150 of 1959
		Trustee Savings Banks Regulations, 1940 (Amendment) Regulations, S.I. No. 283 of 1966
	31(1)	*Finance Act, 1940 (Section 31) (Appointed Day) Order [Vol. XXIX p. 637] S.R.& O. No. 335 of 1940*

Statutory Authority	Section	Statutory Instrument
Finance Act, No. 14 of 1940 (*Cont.*)	31(4)	**Trustee Savings Banks Regulations, 1940 (Amendment) Regulations, S.I. No. 14 of 1969**
		Trustee Savings Banks Regulations, 1940 (Amendment) Regulations, S.I. No. 223 of 1971
Finance Act, No. 15 of 1946	28	*Post Office Savings Bank (Interest on Deposits) Order [Vol. XXXVII p. 297] S.R.& O. No. 368 of 1946*
Finance Act, No. 18 of 1950	9	**Customs and Excise (Aircraft) Regulations, S.I. No. 189 of 1964**
		Customs and Excise (Aircraft) (Amendment) Regulations, S.I. No. 131 of 1967
	12	**Relief of Double Taxation (Taxes on Income: Ireland-United States of America) Regulations, S.I. No. 381 of 1951**
		Relief of Double Taxation (Taxes on Income: Ireland-United States of America) Regulations, S.I. No. 87 of 1956
Finance Act, No. 15 of 1951	15	**Double Taxation Relief (Sea or Air Transport) (Kingdom of Denmark) Order, S.I. No. 97 of 1955**
		Double Taxation Relief (Sea or Air Transport) (Kingdom of Norway) Order, S.I. No. 98 of 1955
		Double Taxation Relief (Sea or Air Transport) (Kingdom of Sweden) Order, S.I. No. 99 of 1955
		Double Taxation Relief (Sea or Air Transport) (Union of South Africa) Order, S.I. No. 210 of 1959
		Double Taxation Relief (Sea or Air Transport) (Swiss Federal Council) Order, S.I. No. 211 of 1959
Finance Act, No. 14 of 1952	15(3)	*Valuation of Imported Goods Regulations, S.I. No. 123 of 1953*
Finance Act, No. 21 of 1953	16(2)	**Death Duties (Payment in Stock) Regulations, S.I. No. 15 of 1954**
Finance Act, No. 22 of 1954	22(5)	**Death Duties (Payment in Stock of the 4.5% National Loan 1973/78) Regulations, S.I. No. 146 of 1954**
		Death Duties (Payment in Stock of the 4.25% National Loan, 1975/80) Regulations, S.I. No. 7 of 1955
		Death Duties (Payment in Stock of the 5% National Savings Bonds, 1971/81) Regulations, S.I. No. 155 of 1956
		Death Duties (Payment in Stock of the 5.5% National Loan, 1966) Regulations, S.I. No. 38 of 1957
		Death Duties (Payment in Stock of the 6% National Loan, 1967) Regulations, S.I. No. 108 of 1958
		Death Duties (Payment in Stock of the 5.5% Exchequer Stock 1971–74) Regulations, S.I. No. 74 of 1959

Finance Act, No. 22 of 1954
(*Cont.*)

Death Duties (Payment in Stock of the 5.25% National Development Loan, 1979–1984) Regulations, S.I. No. 87 of 1960

Death Duties (Payment in Stock of the 6% Exchequer Stock 1980–1985) Regulations, S.I. No. 25 of 1961

Death Duties (Payment in Stock of the 5.75% National Loan 1982–1987) Regulations, S.I. No. 45 of 1963

Death Duties (Payment in Stock of the 4.5% Exchequer Stock 1984–1989) Regulations, S.I. No. 20 of 1964

Death Duties (Payment in Stock of the 5.75% Exchequer Stock 1984–1989) Regulations, S.I. No. 21 of 1964

Death Duties (Payment in Stock of the 6% Exchequer Loan 1985–1990) Regulations, S.I. No. 62 of 1965

Death Duties (Payment in Stock of the 6.25% National Loan, 1986–1991) Regulations, S.I. No. 82 of 1966

Death Duties (Payment in Stock of the 7.5% National Loan, 1981–1986) Regulations, S.I. No. 5 of 1967

Death Duties (Payment in Stock of the 7% National Loan 1987–1992) Regulations, S.I. No. 304 of 1967

Death Duties (Payment in Stock of the 6.5% Exchequer Stock, 2000–2005) Regulations, S.I. No. 309 of 1967

Death Duties (Payment in Stock of the 7.5% Exchequer Stock 1973) Regulations, S.I. No. 29 of 1968

Death Duties (Payment in Stock of the 6.5% Exchequer Stock, 1971) Regulations, S.I. No. 137 of 1968

Death Duties (Payment in Stock of the 7% Exchequer Stock, 1975) Regulations, S.I. No. 236 of 1968

Death Duties (Payment in Stock of the 7.5% Development Stock, 1988–1993) Regulations, S.I. No. 287 of 1968

Death Duties (Payment in Stock of the 8.5% Conversion Stock, 1971) Regulations, S.I. No. 12 of 1970

Death Duties (Payment in Stock of the 8.5% Conversion Stock, 1972) Regulations, S.I. No. 13 of 1970

Death Duties (Payment in Stock of the 8.25% Conversion Stock, 1970) Regulations, S.I. No. 14 of 1970

Death Duties (Payment in Stock of the 9.25% National Loan 1989–1994) Regulations, S.I. No. 25 of 1970

Death Duties (Payment in Stock of the 8.5% Conversion Stock, 1973) Regulations, S.I. No. 125 of 1970

Statutory Authority	Section	Statutory Instrument
Finance Act, No. 22 of 1954 (*Cont.*)		**Death Duties (Payment in Stock of the 8.75% Conversion Stock, 1976) Regulations, S.I. No. 124 of 1971**
		Death Duties (Payment in Stock of the 9.375% National Loan, 1984–1988) Regulations, S.I. No. 125 of 1971
		Death Duties (Payment in Stock of the 8% Exchequer Stock, 1972) Regulations, S.I. No. 126 of 1971
		Death Duties (Payment in Stock of the 7.75% Funding Loan, 1973) Regulations, S.I. No. 164 of 1971
		Death Duties (Payment in Stock of the 7.5% Funding Loan, 1974) Regulations, S.I. No. 167 of 1971
Finance Act, No. 25 of 1958	20	**Road Vehicles (Registration and Licensing) Regulations, S.I. No. 311 of 1982**
	44	**Double Taxation Relief (Taxes on Income and Capital) (Kingdom of Sweden) Order, S.I. No. 191 of 1960**
		Double Taxation Relief (Taxes on Income and Capital and Gewerbesteuer (Trade Tax)) (Federal Republic of Germany) Order, S.I. No. 212 of 1962
		Double Taxation Relief (Taxes on Income and Capital) (Royal Danish Government) Order, S.I. No. 203 of 1964
Finance Act, No. 18 of 1959	23	**Income Tax (Purchased Life Annuities) Regulations, S.I. No. 152 of 1959**
Finance Act, No. 19 of 1960	20	**Hydrocarbon Oil (Rebated Oil) Regulations, S.I. No. 122 of 1961**
	21	**Road Vehicles (Registration and Licensing) Regulations, S.I. No. 311 of 1982**
Finance Act, No. 23 of 1961	11	**Income Tax (Employments) (Surtax) Regulations, S.I. No. 231 of 1961**
	11(5)	**Income Tax (Employments) (Surtax) Regulations, S.I. No. 156 of 1963**
Finance Act, No. 15 of 1962	2	*Imposition of Duties (No.227) (Certain Processed Agricultural Products) Order, S.I. No. 97 of 1977*
	17(2)	*Finance Act, 1962 (Commencement of Section 17) Order, S.I. No. 130 of 1962*
	22	*Imposition of Duties (No.128) (Customs Duties and Form of Customs Tariff) Order, S.I. No. 163 of 1962*
		Imposition of Duties (No.134) (Wood) Order, S.I. No. 90 of 1963
		Imposition of Duties (No.135) (Tinplate) Order, S.I. No. 136 of 1963
		Imposition of Duties (No.136) (Drinking Glasses) Order, S.I. No. 182 of 1963
		Imposition of Duties (No.137) (Wooden Furniture) Order, S.I. No. 183 of 1963

Statutory Authority	Section	Statutory Instrument

Finance Act, No. 15 of 1962
(*Cont.*)

Imposition of Duties (No.139) (Clay Floor Tiles) Order, S.I. No. 259 of 1963

Imposition of Duties (No.140) (Floor Coverings) Order, S.I. No. 260 of 1963

Imposition of Duties (No.141) (Yarn of Flax) Order, S.I. No. 261 of 1963

Imposition of Duties (No.142) (Reduction of Rates of Customs Duties) Order, S.I. No. 262 of 1963

Imposition of Duties (No.143) (Miscellaneous Customs Duties) Order, S.I. No. 48 of 1964

Imposition of Duties (No.144) (Meat Preparations) Order, S.I. No. 223 of 1964

Imposition of Duties (No.147) (Miscellaneous Customs Duties) Order, S.I. No. 225 of 1965

Imposition of Duties (No.148) (Headgear) Order, S.I. No. 228 of 1965

Imposition of Duties (No.149) (Bedding) Order, S.I. No. 254 of 1965

Imposition of Duties (No.150) (Footwear) Order, S.I. No. 262 of 1965

Imposition of Duties (No.151) (Agricultural Machinery) Order, S.I. No. 34 of 1966

Imposition of Duties (No.152) (Ceramic Sanitary Ware) Order, S.I. No. 35 of 1966

Imposition of Duties (No.153) (Man-made Fibres) Order, S.I. No. 36 of 1966

Imposition of Duties (No.154) (Motor Vehicle Tyres) Order, S.I. No. 37 of 1966

Imposition of Duties (No.155) (Stockings of Man-made Fibres) Order, S.I. No. 38 of 1966

Imposition of Duties (No.156) (Twine etc.) Order, S.I. No. 39 of 1966

Imposition of Duties (No.158) (Matches) Order, S.I. No. 101 of 1966

Imposition of Duties (No.159) (Customs Duties and Form of Customs Tariff) Order, S.I. No. 132 of 1966

Imposition of Duties (Iron and Steel Products) Order, S.I. No. 152 of 1966

Imposition of Duties (Iron and Steel Products) (No.2) Order, S.I. No. 280 of 1966

Imposition of Duties (No.162) (Lawn-mowers) Order, S.I. No. 147 of 1967

Imposition of Duties (No.164) (Customs Duties and Form of Customs Tariff) Order, S.I. No. 156 of 1967

Imposition of Duties (No.166) (Customs Duties and Form of Customs Tariff) Order, S.I. No. 279 of 1967

Imposition of Duties (No.167) (Customs Duties and Form of Customs Tariff) Order, S.I. No. 290 of 1967

Imposition of Duties (No.171) (Polyurethane Foam and Solid Fuel Store Boilers) Order, S.I. No. 81 of 1968

Statutory Authority	Section	Statutory Instrument

Finance Act, No. 15 of 1962
(*Cont.*)

Imposition of Duties (No.172) (Customs Duties and Form of Customs Tariff) Order, S.I. No. 85 of 1968

Imposition of Duties (No.173) (Stockings) Order, S.I. No. 96 of 1968

Imposition of Duties (No.174) (Customs Duties and Form of Customs Tariff) Order, S.I. No. 135 of 1968

Imposition of Duties (Iron and Steel Products) Order, S.I. No. 144 of 1968

Imposition of Duties (No.177) (Crown Corks and Artificial Plastic Footballs) Order, S.I. No. 248 of 1968

Imposition of Duties (No.175) (Tufted Material) Order, S.I. No. 249 of 1968

Imposition of Duties (No.176) (Coated Copy-making Film) Order, S.I. No. 250 of 1968

Imposition of Duties (No.178) (Agricultural Machinery) Order, S.I. No. 7 of 1969

Imposition of Duties (Agricultural Machinery) Order, S.I. No. 11 of 1969

Imposition of Duties (No.179) (Customs Duties and Form of Customs Tariff) Order, S.I. No. 39 of 1969

Imposition of Duties (No.180) (Customs Duties and Forms of Customs Tariff) Order, S.I. No. 98 of 1969

Imposition of Duties (No.181) (Customs Duties and Form of Customs Tariff) (Wheat and Meslin) Order, S.I. No. 188 of 1969

Imposition of Duties (No.185) (Customs Duties and Form of Customs Tariff) Order, S.I. No. 133 of 1970

Imposition of Duties (Agricultural Machinery) Order, S.I. No. 241 of 1970

Imposition of Duties (No.189) (Customs and Excise Duties and Form of Tariff) Order, S.I. No. 191 of 1971

Imposition of Duties (No.191) (Customs Duties and Form of Customs Tariff) Order, S.I. No. 205 of 1971

Imposition of Duties (No.190) (Sugar Confectionery) Order, S.I. No. 206 of 1971

Imposition of Duties (No.192) (Metal Badges and Footwear Heels) Order, S.I. No. 221 of 1971

Imposition of Duties (No.193) (Pneumatic Tyres) Order, S.I. No. 305 of 1971

Imposition of Duties (No.194) (Customs Duties and Form of Customs Tariff) Order, S.I. No. 334 of 1971

Imposition of Duties (Iron and Steel Products) Order, S.I. No. 343 of 1971

Imposition of Duties (No.195) (Customs Duties and Form of Customs Tariff) Order, S.I. No. 349 of 1971

Statutory Authority	Section	Statutory Instrument

Finance Act, No. 15 of 1962
(*Cont.*)

Imposition of Duties (No.196) (Miscellaneous Customs Duties) Order, S.I. No. 353 of 1971

Imposition of Duties (No.197) (Outer Garments) Order, S.I. No. 355 of 1971

Imposition of Duties (No.198) (Customs Duties and Form of Customs Tariff) Order, S.I. No. 152 of 1972

Imposition of Duties (No.200) (Customs and Excise Duties and Form of Tariff) Order, S.I. No. 220 of 1972

Imposition of Duties (No.201) (Customs Duties and Form of Customs Tariff) Order, S.I. No. 4 of 1973

Imposition of Duties (No.202) (Customs and Excise Duties and Form of Tariff) (Amendment) Order, S.I. No. 68 of 1973

Imposition of Duties (No.203) (Customs Duties and Form of Customs Tariff) Order, S.I. No. 71 of 1973

Imposition of Duties (No.204) (Customs Duties and Form of Customs Tariff) Order, S.I. No. 72 of 1973

Imposition of Duties (No.205) (Beer, Spirits, Tobacco, Hydrocarbon Oils and Wine) Order, S.I. No. 83 of 1973

Imposition of Duties (No.206) (Stamp Duty on Certain Instruments) Order, S.I. No. 140 of 1973

Imposition of Duties (No.207) (Customs Duties and Form of Customs Tariff) Order, S.I. No. 158 of 1973

Imposition of Duties (No.208) (Beer, Spirits and Tobacco) Order, S.I. No. 249 of 1973

Imposition of Duties (No.210) (Stamp Duty on certain Instruments) Order, S.I. No. 273 of 1973

Imposition of Duties (No.212) (Customs Duties and Form of Customs Tariff) Order, S.I. No. 341 of 1973

Imposition of Duties (No.213) (Customs Duties and Form of Customs Tariff) Order, S.I. No. 174 of 1974

Imposition of Duties (No.215) (Customs Duties and Form of Customs Tariff) Order, S.I. No. 356 of 1974

Imposition of Duties (No.217) (Stamp Duty on Certain Instruments) Order, S.I. No. 27 of 1975

Imposition of Duties (No.218) (Customs Duties and Form of Customs Tariff) Order, S.I. No. 127 of 1975

Imposition of Duties (No.219) (Customs Duties and Form of Customs Tariff) Order, S.I. No. 131 of 1975

Imposition of Duties (No.220) (Footwear) Order, S.I. No. 157 of 1975

Imposition of Duties (No.221) (Excise Duties) Order, S.I. No. 307 of 1975

Statutory Authority	Section	Statutory Instrument

Finance Act, No. 15 of 1962
(*Cont.*)

Imposition of Duties (No.222) (Customs Duties and Form of Customs Tariff) Order, S.I. No. 320 of 1975

Imposition of Duties (No.223) (Footwear) Order, S.I. No. 324 of 1975

Imposition of Duties (No.224) (Customs Duties and Form of Customs Tariff) Order, S.I. No. 130 of 1976

Imposition of Duties (No.225) (Footwear) Order, S.I. No. 171 of 1976

Imposition of Duties (No.226) (Footwear) Order, S.I. No. 299 of 1976

Imposition of Duties (No.228) (Stamp Duty on Certain Instruments) Order, S.I. No. 101 of 1977

Imposition of Duties (No.230) (Certain Processed Agricultural Products) (No.2) Order, S.I. No. 150 of 1977

Imposition of Duties (No.233) (Rates of Excise Duty on Tobacco Products) Order, S.I. No. 384 of 1977

Imposition of Duties (No.235) (Beer) Order, S.I. No. 36 of 1978

Imposition of Duties (No.236) (Excise Duties on Motor Vehicles, Televisions and Gramophone Records) Order, S.I. No. 57 of 1979

Imposition of Duties (No.237) (Beer) Order, S.I. No. 67 of 1979

Imposition of Duties (No.238) (Exemption from Agreement as to Stamp Duty on Certain Transfers) Order, S.I. No. 121 of 1979

Imposition of Duties (No.239) (Agricultural Produce) (Cattle and Milk) Order, S.I. No. 152 of 1979

Imposition of Duties (No.240) (Agricultural Produce) (Cereals and Sugar Beet) Order, S.I. No. 153 of 1979

Imposition of Duties (No.241) (Limit on Stamp Duty in respect of Certain Transactions between Bodies Corporate) Order, S.I. No. 244 of 1979

Imposition of Duties (No.243) (Excise Duty on Tobacco Products) Order, S.I. No. 296 of 1979

Imposition of Duties (No.244) (Excise Duties on Spirits, Beer and Hydrocarbon Oils) Order, S.I. No. 415 of 1979

Imposition of Duties (No.246) (Beer) Order, S.I. No. 49 of 1980

Imposition of Duties (No.248) (Stamp Duty on Bills of Exchange and Promissory Notes) Order, S.I. No. 136 of 1980

Imposition of Duties (No.249) (Exemption of Certain Instruments from Stamp Duty) Order, S.I. No. 317 of 1980

Imposition of Duties (No.255) (Hydrocarbon Oils) Order, S.I. No. 367 of 1981

Statutory Authority	Section	Statutory Instrument

Finance Act, No. 15 of 1962 *(Cont.)*

Imposition of Duties (No.257) (Beer) Order, S.I. No. 22 of 1982

Imposition of Duties (No.258) (Beer) (No.2) Order, S.I. No. 37 of 1982

Imposition of Duties (No.259) (Excise Duties) Order, S.I. No. 48 of 1982

Imposition of Duties (No.260) (Excise Duty on Video Players) Order, S.I. No. 49 of 1982

Imposition of Duties (No.261) (Excise Duties) Order, S.I. No. 9 of 1983

Imposition of Duties (No.262) (Beer) Order, S.I. No. 12 of 1983

Imposition of Duties (No.263) (Excise Duties) (No.2) Order, S.I. No. 42 of 1983

Imposition of Duties (No.264) (Hydrocarbons) Order, S.I. No. 85 of 1983

Imposition of Duties (No.265) (Excise Duty on Hydrocarbon Oils) Order, S.I. No. 126 of 1983

Imposition of Duties (No.266) (Tobacco Products) Order, S.I. No. 213 of 1983

Imposition of Duties (No.266) (Beer) (No.2) Order, S.I. No. 398 of 1983

Imposition of Duties (No.268) (Stamp Duty on Bills of Exchange, Promissory Notes, Credit Cards and Charge Cards) Order, S.I. No. 34 of 1984

Imposition of Duties (No.269) (Exemption of Certain Instruments from Stamp Duty) , Order, S.I. No. 49 of 1984

Imposition of Duties (No.270) (Spirits) Order, S.I. No. 252 of 1984

Imposition of Duties (No.271) (Beer) Order, S.I. No. 352 of 1984

Imposition of Duties (No.272) (Excise Duties on Motor Vehicles) Order, S.I. No. 353 of 1984

Imposition of Duties (No.273) (Excise Duty on Motor-cycles) Order, S.I. No. 354 of 1984

Imposition of Duties (No.274) (Televisions) Order, S.I. No. 41 of 1985

Imposition of Duties (No.275) (Stamp Duties on Course Bets) Order, S.I. No. 60 of 1985

Imposition of Duties (No.276) (Stamp Duties on Conveyance and Transfers on Sale of Stocks and Marketable Securities) Order, S.I. No. 146 of 1985

Imposition of Duties (No.277) (Stamp Duty on Certain Instruments) Order, S.I. No. 151 of 1985

Imposition of Duties (No.278) (Stamp Duty on Certain Instruments) Order, (1983) S.I. No. 152 of 1985

Imposition of Duties (No.279) (Motor Vehicles and Motor-cycles) (Amendment) Order, S.I. No. 267 of 1985

Imposition of Duties (No.280) (Excise Duties) (Vehicles) Order, S.I. No. 304 of 1985

Statutory Authority	Section	Statutory Instrument
Finance Act, No. 15 of 1962 (*Cont.*)		**Imposition of Duties (No.281) (Hydrocarbons) Order, S.I. No. 3 of 1986**
		Imposition of Duties (No.282) (Stamp Duty on Statements of Interest) Order, S.I. No. 27 of 1986
		Imposition of Duties (Beer) (No.284) Order, S.I. No. 438 of 1986
	22(2)	**Imposition of Duties (Form of Customs Tariff) (Amendment) Order, S.I. No. 216 of 1965**
Finance Act, No. 23 of 1963	29	*Motor Vehicles (Temporary Importation) Regulations, S.I. No. 87 of 1965*
		Motor Vehicles (Temporary Importation) Regulations, S.I. No. 220 of 1967
		Motor Vehicles (Temporary Importation) Regulations, S.I. No. 54 of 1970
	31(1)	**Relief from Customs Duties (Fairs, Exhibitions and Similar Events) Order, S.I. No. 143 of 1965**
		Relief from Customs Duties (Professional Equipment) Order, S.I. No. 144 of 1965
		Relief from Customs Duties (Packings) Order, S.I. No. 223 of 1965
	48(2)(b)	*Turnover Tax (Exempted Activities) (No.1) Order, S.I. No. 163 of 1963*
		Turnover Tax (Exempted Activities) (No.2) Order, S.I. No. 164 of 1963
		Turnover Tax (Exempted Activities) (No.3) Order, S.I. No. 165 of 1963
		Turnover Tax (Exempted Activities) (No.4) Order, S.I. No. 202 of 1963
		Turnover Tax (Exempted Activities) (No.5) Order, S.I. No. 203 of 1963
		Turnover Tax (Exempted Activities) (No.6) Order, S.I. No. 204 of 1963
		Turnover Tax (Exempted Activities) (NO.7) Order, S.I. No. 205 of 1963
		Turnover Tax (Exempted Activities) (No.8) Order, S.I. No. 206 of 1963
		Turnover Tax (Exempted Activities) (No.9) Order, S.I. No. 207 of 1963
		Turnover Tax (Exempted Activities) (No.10) Order, S.I. No. 208 of 1963
		Turnover Tax (Exempted Activities) (No.11) Order, S.I. No. 1 of 1964
		Turnover Tax (Exempted Activities) (No.12) Order, S.I. No. 71 of 1964
		Turnover Tax (Exempted Activities) (No.13) Order, S.I. No. 144 of 1964
		Turnover Tax (Exempted Activities) (No.14) Order, S.I. No. 190 of 1966
		Turnover Tax (Exempted Activities) (No.15) Order, S.I. No. 218 of 1966

Statutory Authority	Section	Statutory Instrument
Finance Act, No. 23 of 1963 *(Cont.)*		*Turnover Tax (Exempted Activities) No.16 Order, S.I. No. 271 of 1966*
	49(5)	*Turnover Tax (Appointed Day) Order, S.I. No. 162 of 1963*
	52	*Turnover Tax Regulations, S.I. No. 157 of 1963*
		Turnover Tax (No.2) Regulations, S.I. No. 201 of 1963
		Turnover Tax (No.3) Regulations, S.I. No. 269 of 1963
		Turnover Tax (No.4) Regulations, S.I. No. 166 of 1965
		Turnover Tax (No.5) (Dances) Regulations, S.I. No. 77 of 1966
		Wholesale Tax Regulations, S.I. No. 195 of 1966
	64(2)(f)	*Turnover Tax (Exempted Imports) (No.1) Order, S.I. No. 216 of 1963*
		Turnover Tax (Exempted Imports) (No.2) Order, S.I. No. 9 of 1964
		Turnover Tax (Exempted Imports) (No.3) Order, S.I. No. 189 of 1966
		Turnover Tax (Exempted Imports) (No.4) Order, S.I. No. 215 of 1966
Finance Act, No. 15 of 1964	35(8)	*Finance Act, 1964 (Commencement of Section 28) Order, S.I. No. 58 of 1966*
Finance Act, No. 17 of 1966	15	**Wine Duty Regulations, S.I. No. 160 of 1966**
		Wine Duty (Amendment) Regulations, S.I. No. 180 of 1969
		Spirits and Wine (Amendment) Regulations, S.I. No. 419 of 1979
		Made Wine Duty Regulations, S.I. No. 398 of 1980
	15(2)(a)	*Agricultural Produce (Cattle and Milk) Regulations, S.I. No. 160 of 1979*
		Agricultural Produce (Cereals and Sugar Beet) Regulations, S.I. No. 266 of 1979
Finance Act, No. 33 of 1968	41	**Trustee Savings Banks Regulations, S.I. No. 228 of 1968**
		Trustee Savings Banks Regulations, S.I. No. 235 of 1971
		Trustee Savings Banks Regulations, S.I. No. 208 of 1973
		Trustee Savings Banks (No.2) Regulations, S.I. No. 241 of 1973
		Trustee Savings Banks Regulations, S.I. No. 269 of 1976
		Trustee Savings Banks Regulations, S.I. No. 352 of 1977
		Trustee Savings Banks Regulations, S.I. No. 168 of 1978
		Trustee Savings Banks (No.2) Regulations, S.I. No. 323 of 1978

Statutory Authority	Section	Statutory Instrument
Finance Act, No. 23 of 1963 (*Cont.*)		*Trustee Savings Banks Regulations, S.I. No. 361 of 1979*
		Trustee Savings Banks Regulations, S.I. No. 67 of 1980
		Trustee Savings Banks (No.2) Regulations, S.I. No. 132 of 1980
		Trustee Savings Banks Regulations, S.I. No. 12 of 1982
		Trustee Savings Banks (No.2) Regulations, S.I. No. 146 of 1982
		Trustee Savings Banks (No.3) Regulations, S.I. No. 316 of 1982
		Trustee Savings Banks Regulations, S.I. No. 244 of 1983
		Trustee Savings Banks (No.2) Regulations, S.I. No. 297 of 1983
		Trustee Savings Banks Regulations, S.I. No. 314 of 1984
		Trustee Savings Banks Regulations, S.I. No. 119 of 1985
		Trustee Savings Banks (No.2) Regulations, S.I. No. 251 of 1985
		Trustee Savings Banks (No.3) Regulations, S.I. No. 312 of 1985
		Trustee Savings Banks Regulations, S.I. No. 18 of 1986
		Trustee Savings Banks (No.2) Regulations, S.I. No. 205 of 1986
		Trustee Savings Banks (No.3) Regulations, S.I. No. 249 of 1986
		Trustee Savings Banks (No.4) Regulations, S.I. No. 336 of 1986
		Trustee Savings Banks (No.5) Regulations, S.I. No. 355 of 1986
Finance Act, No. 14 of 1970	17	**Income Tax (Construction Contracts) Regulations, S.I. No. 1 of 1971**
		Income Tax (Construction Contracts) Regulations, S.I. No. 274 of 1976
		Income Tax (Construction Contracts) Regulations, S.I. No. 239 of 1985
	17(11)	*Finance Act, 1970 (Commencement of Section 17) Order, S.I. No. 314 of 1970*
	55	*Government Loans (Postponement of Redemption) Order, S.I. No. 201 of 1970*
		Government Loans (Redemption) Order, S.I. No. 285 of 1970
Finance Act, No. 27 of 1974	85	*Finance Act, 1974 (Section 85) (Commencement) Order, S.I. No. 312 of 1974*
Finance Act, No. 6 of 1975	44(4)	*Finance Act, 1975 (Section 44) (Appointed Day) Order, S.I. No. 294 of 1975*

Statutory Authority	Section	Statutory Instrument
Finance Act, No. 6 of 1975 (*Cont.*)	46	**Imposition of Duties (No.221) (Excise Duties) Order, S.I. No. 307 of 1975**
		Imposition of Duties (No.236) (Excise Duties on Motor Vehicles, Televisions and Gramophone Records) Order, S.I. No. 57 of 1979
		Imposition of Duties (No.244) (Excise Duties on Spirits, Beer and Hydrocarbon Oils) Order, S.I. No. 415 of 1979
		Imposition of Duties (No.255) (Hydrocarbon Oils) Order, S.I. No. 367 of 1981
		Imposition of Duties (No.259) (Excise Duties) Order, S.I. No. 48 of 1982
		Imposition of Duties (No.260) (Excise Duty on Video Players) Order, S.I. No. 49 of 1982
		Imposition of Duties (No.261) (Excise Duties) Order, S.I. No. 9 of 1983
		Imposition of Duties (No.263) (Excise Duties) (No.2) Order, S.I. No. 42 of 1983
		Imposition of Duties (No.264) (Hydrocarbons) Order, S.I. No. 85 of 1983
		Imposition of Duties (No.265) (Excise Duty on Hydrocarbon Oils) Order, S.I. No. 126 of 1983
		Imposition of Duties (No.266) (Tobacco Products) Order, S.I. No. 213 of 1983
		Imposition of Duties (No.270) (Spirits) Order, S.I. No. 252 of 1984
		Imposition of Duties (No.272) (Excise Duties on Motor Vehicles) Order, S.I. No. 353 of 1984
		Imposition of Duties (No.273) (Excise Duty on Motor-cycles) Order, S.I. No. 354 of 1984
		Imposition of Duties (No.274) (Televisions) Order, S.I. No. 41 of 1985
		Imposition of Duties (No.279) (Motor Vehicles and Motor-cycles) (Amendment) Order, S.I. No. 267 of 1985
		Imposition of Duties (No.280) (Excise Duties) (Vehicles) Order, S.I. No. 304 of 1985
		Imposition of Duties (No.281) (Hydrocarbons) Order, S.I. No. 3 of 1986
Finance Act, No. 16 of 1976	42(7)	**Gaseous Hydrocarbons in Liquid Form Regulations, S.I. No. 283 of 1976**
	42(10)	*Finance Act, 1976 (Section 42) (Appointed Day) Order, S.I. No. 279 of 1976*
	64(3)	*Finance Act, 1976 (Part V) (Commencement) Order, S.I. No. 185 of 1976*
		Finance Act, 1976 (Part V) (Commencement) Order, S.I. No. 104 of 1977
	65	**Road Vehicles (Registration and Licensing) Regulations, S.I. No. 311 of 1982**
	67	**Road Vehicles (Registration and Licensing) Regulations, S.I. No. 311 of 1982**

Statutory Authority	Section	Statutory Instrument
Finance Act, No. 16 of 1976 (*Cont.*)	74	**Road Traffic Act, 1961 (Section 103) (Offences) (Amendment) Regulations, S.I. No. 255 of 1985**
	77	**Road Vehicles (Registration and Licensing) Regulations, S.I. No. 311 of 1982**
Finance Act, No. 21 of 1978	29(11)	*Finance Act, 1978 (Section 29) (Commencement) Order, S.I. No. 224 of 1978*
	50(4)	**Road Fund (Winding-up) Regulations, S.I. No. 230 of 1980**
Finance Act, No. 11 of 1979	5	*Finance Act, 1979 (Section 5) Order, S.I. No. 345 of 1979*
Finance Act, No. 14 of 1980	75(6)	**Mechanical Lighters Regulations, S.I. No. 221 of 1980**
Finance Act, No. 14 of 1982	65(10)	**Foreign Travel Duty Regulations, S.I. No. 265 of 1982**
Finance Act, No. 15 of 1983	73(4)	*Finance Act, 1983 (Subsection (4) of Section 73) (Commencement) Order, S.I. No. 172 of 1983*
Finance Act, No. 9 of 1984	73(4)	**Hydrocarbon Oil (Aviation Gasoline) Regulations, S.I. No. 140 of 1984**
	75	**Motor Vehicles Excise Duty Regulations, S.I. No. 361 of 1984**
		Motor-cycle Excise Duty Regulations, S.I. No. 362 of 1984
		Televisions and Gramophone Records Regulations, S.I. No. 363 of 1984
Finance (1909–10) Act, No. 8 of 1910	4	**Stamp Duty (Presentation of Instruments) Regulations, S.I. No. 181 of 1977**
	33	**Property Values (Arbitrations and Appeals) Rules, S.I. No. 91 of 1961**
Finance (Agreement with United Kingdom) Act, No. 12 of 1938	2	*Finance (Agreement with United Kingdom) Act, 1938 (Appointed Day) Order [Vol. XII p. 359] S.R.& O. No. 109 of 1938*
	16	*Agreement with United Kingdom (Prescribed Proportion of Value) (Amendment) Regulations [Vol. XXIX p. 685] S.R.& O. No. 21 of 1939*
		Prescribed Proportion of Value (Mirrors) Regulations [Vol. XXIX p. 689] S.R.& O. No. 242 of 1939
		Prescribed Proportion of Value (Silk and Artificial Silk) Regulations, S.I. No. 75 of 1955
		Agreement with United Kingdom (Prescribed Proportion of Value) Regulations, S.I. No. 209 of 1962
		Origin of Manufactured Goods Regulations, S.I. No. 202 of 1966
	16(1)	*Agreement with United Kingdom (Prescribed Proportion of Value) Regulations [Vol. XII p. 363] S.R.& O. No. 185 of 1938*

Statutory Authority	Section	Statutory Instrument
Finance (Excise Duties) (Vehicles) Act, No. 24 of 1952	1	**Road Vehicles (Registration and Licensing) Regulations, S.I. No. 13 of 1958**
		Road Vehicles (Registration and Licensing) (Amendment) Regulations, S.I. No. 198 of 1958
		Road Vehicles (Registration and Licensing) (Amendment) Regulations, S.I. No. 84 of 1960
		Mechanically Propelled Vehicles (International Circulation) Order, S.I. No. 269 of 1961
		Mechanically Propelled Vehicles (International Circulation) (Amendment) Order, S.I. No. 12 of 1962
		Road Vehicles (Registration and Licensing) (Amendment) Regulations, S.I. No. 13 of 1966
		Road Vehicles (Registration and Licensing) (Amendment) Regulations, S.I. No. 147 of 1968
		Road Vehicles (Registration and Licensing) (Amendment) Regulations, S.I. No. 205 of 1969
		Road Vehicles (Registration and Licensing) (Amendment) Regulations, S.I. No. 340 of 1974
		Road Vehicles (Registration and Licensing) (Amendment) Regulations, S.I. No. 38 of 1976
		Road Vehicles (Registration and Licensing) (Amendment) Regulations, S.I. No. 122 of 1977
		Road Vehicles (Registration and Licensing) (Amendment) (No.2) Regulations, S.I. No. 185 of 1977
		Road Vehicles (Registration and Licensing) (Amendment) (No.3) Regulations, S.I. No. 371 of 1977
		Road Vehicles (Registration and Licensing) Regulations, S.I. No. 311 of 1982
		Road Vehicles (Registration and Licensing) (Amendment) Regulations, S.I. No. 293 of 1985
	1(2)	*Road Vehicles (Miscellaneous Licensing Provisions) Regulations, S.I. No. 357 of 1952*
	1(3)	*Road Vehicles (Miscellaneous Licensing Provisions) Regulations, S.I. No. 357 of 1952*
	1(8)	*Mechanically Propelled Vehicles (International Circulation) Order, S.I. No. 94 of 1955*
		Public Service Vehicles (International Circulation) Order, S.I. No. 81 of 1958
	3	**Road Vehicles (Registration and Licensing) Regulations, S.I. No. 13 of 1958**
		Road Vehicles (Registration and Licensing) Order, S.I. No. 15 of 1958
		Road Vehicles (Registration and Licensing) (Amendment) Regulations, S.I. No. 198 of 1958
		Road Vehicles (Registration and Licensing) (Amendment) Regulations, S.I. No. 84 of 1960
		Road Vehicles (Registration and Licensing) (Amendment) (No.2) Regulations, S.I. No. 196 of 1960
		Mechanically Propelled Vehicles (International Circulation) Order, S.I. No. 269 of 1961
		Mechanically Propelled Vehicles (International Circulation) (Amendment) Order, S.I. No. 12 of 1962

Statutory Authority	Section	Statutory Instrument
Finance (Excise Duties) (Vehicles) Act, No. 24 of 1952 (*Cont.*)		*Road Vehicles (Registration and Licensing) (Amendment) Regulations, S.I. No. 147 of 1968*
		Road Vehicles (Registration and Licensing) (Amendment) Regulations, S.I. No. 205 of 1969
		Road Vehicles (Registration and Licensing) (Amendment) Regulations, S.I. No. 340 of 1974
		Road Vehicles (Registration and Licensing) (Amendment) Regulations, S.I. No. 122 of 1977
		Road Vehicles (Registration and Licensing) (Amendment) (No.3) Regulations, S.I. No. 371 of 1977
		Road Vehicles (Registration and Licensing) (Amendment) Regulations, S.I. No. 226 of 1980
		Road Vehicles (Registration and Licensing) (Amendment) Regulations, S.I. No. 103 of 1981
		Road Vehicles (Registration and Licensing) Regulations, S.I. No. 311 of 1982
		Road Vehicles (Registration and Licensing) (Amendment) Regulations, S.I. No. 293 of 1985
	4(1A)	**Driving Licences (Repayment of Excise Duties) Regulations, S.I. No. 88 of 1964**
		Driving Licences (Repayment of Excise Duties) Regulations, S.I. No. 119 of 1973
		Driving Licences (Repayment of Excise Duties) (Amendment) Regulations, S.I. No. 227 of 1980
		Driving Licences (Repayment of Excise Duties) (Amendment) Regulations, S.I. No. 50 of 1983
Finance (Excise Duties) (Vehicles) (Amendment) Act, No. 1 of 1960	4	*Road Vehicles (Registration and Licensing) (Amendment) Regulations, S.I. No. 84 of 1960*
		Road Vehicles (Registration and Licensing) Regulations, S.I. No. 311 of 1982
Finance (Excise Duty on Tobacco Products) Act, No. 32 of 1977		**Imposition of Duties (No.233) (Rates of Excise Duty on Tobacco Products) Order, S.I. No. 384 of 1977**
	2	**Imposition of Duties (No.243) (Excise Duty on Tobacco Products) Order, S.I. No. 296 of 1979**
	8	**Tobacco Products Regulations, S.I. No. 389 of 1977**
		Motor Vehicles Excise Duty Regulations, S.I. No. 60 of 1979
		Televisions and Gramaphone Records Regulations, S.I. No. 61 of 1979
		Motor Vehicles Excise Duty Regulations, S.I. No. 361 of 1984
		Televisions and Gramophone Records Regulations, S.I. No. 363 of 1984
Finance (Miscellaneous Provisions) Act, No. 7 of 1935	1	*Hydrocarbon Oil Regulations [Vol. XII p. 369] S.R.& O. No. 608 of 1935*
		Hydrocarbon Oil (No.2) Regulations [Vol. XII p. 383] S.R.& O. No. 652 of 1935
		Hydrocarbon Oil Regulations [Vol. XXIX p. 695] S.R.& O. No. 490 of 1941
		Hydrocarbon Oil (Amendment) Regulations, S.I. No. 418 of 1979

Statutory Authority	Section	Statutory Instrument
Finance (Miscellaneous Provisions) Act, No. 47 of 1956	23	**Prize Bonds Regulations, S.I. No. 40 of 1957**
		Prize Bonds (First Draw for Prizes) Regulations, S.I. No. 179 of 1957
		Prize Bonds (Draws for Prizes) Regulations, S.I. No. 60 of 1958
		Prize Bonds (Amendment) Regulations, S.I. No. 265 of 1964
		Prize Bonds (Draws for Prizes) Regulations, S.I. No. 92 of 1971
		Prize Bonds (Draws for Prizes) Regulations, S.I. No. 272 of 1972
		Prize Bonds Regulations, 1957 (Amendment) Regulations, S.I. No. 284 of 1972
Finance (New Duties) Act, No. 11 of 1916	2	**Entertainments Duty Regulations [Vol. XXIX p. 725] S.R.& O. No. 1 of 1944**
	3(4)	**Match Duty Regulations [Vol. XII p. 395] S.R.& O. No. 74 of 1928**
	6	**Table Waters (Amendment) Regulations, S.I. No. 218 of 1980**
		Table Waters (Amendment) Regulations, S.I. No. 200 of 1981
Finance (No.2) Act, No. 89 of 1915	13(6)	*Motor Cars (Temporary Importation) Regulations (1926) [Vol. XII p. 141] S.R.& O. No. 9 of 1927*
		Motor Cars (Temporary Importation) Regulations [Vol. XII p. 151] S.R.& O. No. 44 of 1927
	Sch. I Part III par. 3	*Manufacture of Sugar Regulations [Vol. XII p. 115] S.R.& O. No. 64 of 1926*
		Manufacture of Sugar Regulations [Vol. XII p. 121] S.R.& O. No. 85 of 1931
		Manufacture of Sugar Regulations [Vol. XII p. 127] S.R.& O. No. 117 of 1932
Finance (No.2) Act, No. 42 of 1959	6	**Income Tax (Employments) Rules, S.I. No. 28 of 1960**
		Income Tax (Employments) (No.2) Regulations, S.I. No. 166 of 1960
	9	**Income Tax (Employments) Rules, S.I. No. 28 of 1960**
		Income Tax (Employments) (No.2) Regulations, S.I. No. 166 of 1960
	11	**Income Tax (Employments) Rules, S.I. No. 28 of 1960**
		Income Tax (Employments) (No.2) Regulations, S.I. No. 166 of 1960
	14	**Income Tax (Employments) Rules, S.I. No. 28 of 1960**
		Income Tax (Employments) (No.2) Regulations, S.I. No. 166 of 1960
Finance (No.2) Act, No. 22 of 1966	3(5)(b)	*Wholesale Tax (Exempted Activities) (No.1) Order, S.I. No. 216 of 1966*

Statutory Authority	Section	Statutory Instrument
Finance (No. 2) Act, No. 22 of 1966 (*Cont.*)		*Wholesale Tax (Exempted Activities) (No.2) Order, S.I. No. 285 of 1966*
	4(3)	*Wholesale Tax (Appointed Day) Order, S.I. No. 196 of 1966*
	11(2)	*Wholesale Tax (Exempted Imports) (No.1) Order, S.I. No. 217 of 1966*
Finance (No.2) Act, No. 37 of 1968	9(1)	*Post Office Savings Bank (Interest on Deposits) Regulations, S.I. No. 16 of 1969*
		Post Office Savings Bank (Interest on Deposits) Regulations, S.I. No. 210 of 1973
		Post Office Savings Bank (Interest on Deposits) (No.2) Regulations, S.I. No. 239 of 1973
		Post Office Savings Bank (Interest on Deposits) Regulations, S.I. No. 350 of 1977
		Post Office Savings Bank (Interest on Deposits) Regulations, S.I. No. 321 of 1978
		Post Office Savings Bank (Interest on Deposits) Regulations, S.I. No. 65 of 1980
		Post Office Savings Bank (Interest on Deposits) (No.2) Regulations, S.I. No. 134 of 1980
		Post Office Savings Bank (Interest on Deposits) Regulations, S.I. No. 10 of 1982
		Post Office Savings Bank (Interest on Deposits) (No.2) Regulations, S.I. No. 148 of 1982
		Post Office Savings Bank (Interest on Deposits) (No.3) Regulations, S.I. No. 314 of 1982
		Post Office Savings Bank (Interest on Deposits) Regulations, S.I. No. 295 of 1983
		Post Office Savings Bank (Interest on Deposits) Regulations, S.I. No. 315 of 1984
		Post Office Savings Bank (Interest on Deposits) Regulations, S.I. No. 120 of 1985
		Post Office Savings Bank (Interest on Deposits) (No.2) Regulations, S.I. No. 250 of 1985
		Post Office Savings Bank (Interest on Deposits) (No.3) Regulations, S.I. No. 311 of 1985
		Post Office Savings Bank (Interest on Deposits) Regulations, S.I. No. 19 of 1986
		Post Office Savings Bank (Interest on Deposits) (No.2) Regulations, S.I. No. 203 of 1986
		Post Office Savings Bank (Interest on Deposits) (No.3) Regulations, S.I. No. 251 of 1986
		Post Office Savings Bank (Interest on Deposits) (No.4) Regulations, S.I. No. 337 of 1986
	9(2)	*Trustee Savings Banks (Interest on Deposits in Special Account) Regulations, S.I. No. 15 of 1969*
		Trustee Savings Banks (Interest on Deposits in Special Account) Regulations, S.I. No. 209 of 1973
		Trustee Savings Banks (Interest on Deposits in Special Account) (No.2) Regulations, S.I. No. 240 of 1973

Statutory Authority	Section	Statutory Instrument

Finance (No.2) Act, No. 37 of 1968
(*Cont.*)

Trustee Savings Banks (Interest on Deposits in Special Account) Regulations, S.I. No. 268 of 1976

Trustee Savings Banks (Interest on Deposits in Special Account) Regulations, S.I. No. 351 of 1977

Trustee Savings Banks (Interest on Deposits in Special Account) Regulations, S.I. No. 322 of 1978

Trustee Savings Banks (Interest on Deposits in Special Account) Regulations, S.I. No. 362 of 1979

Trustee Savings Banks (Interest on Deposits in Special Account) Regulations, S.I. No. 66 of 1980

Trustee Savings Banks (Interest on Deposits in Special Account) (No.2) Regulations, S.I. No. 133 of 1980

Trustee Savings Banks (Interest on Deposits in Special Account) Regulations, S.I. No. 11 of 1982

Trustee Savings Banks (Interest on Deposits in Special Account) (No.2) Regulations, S.I. No. 147 of 1982

Trustee Savings Banks (Interest on Deposits in Special Account) (No.3) Regulations, S.I. No. 315 of 1982

Trustee Savings Banks (Interest on Deposits in Special Account) Regulations, S.I. No. 296 of 1983

Trustee Savings Banks (Interest on Deposits in Special Account) Regulations, S.I. No. 316 of 1984

Trustee Savings Banks (Interest on Deposits in Special Account) Regulations, S.I. No. 121 of 1985

Trustee Savings Banks (Interest on Deposits in Special Account) (No.2) Regulations, S.I. No. 252 of 1985

Trustee Savings Banks (Interest on Deposits in Special Account) (No.3) Regulations, S.I. No. 313 of 1985

Trustee Savings Banks (Interest on Deposits in Special Account) Regulations, S.I. No. 20 of 1986

Trustee Savings Banks (Interest on Deposits in Special Account) (No.2) Regulations, S.I. No. 204 of 1986

Trustee Savings Banks (Interest on Deposits in Special Account) (No.3) Regulations, S.I. No. 250 of 1986

Trustee Savings Banks (Interest on Deposits in Special Account) (No.4) Regulations, S.I. No. 338 of 1986

Fire Brigades Act, No. 7 of 1940   19

Fire Brigades Act, 1940 (Date of Commencement) (No.1) Order [Vol. XXIX p. 753] S.R.& O. No. 233 of 1940

Statutory Authority	Section	Statutory Instrument
Fire Brigades Act, No. 7 of 1940 (*Cont.*)		*Fire Brigades Act, 1940 (Date of Commencement) (No.2) Order [Vol. XXIX p. 757] S.R.& O. No. 251 of 1940*
		Fire Brigades Act, 1940 (Date of Commencement) (No.3) Order [Vol. XXIX p. 761] S.R.& O. No. 326 of 1940
Fire Services Act, No. 30 of 1981	1	*Fire Services Act, 1981 (Commencement) Order, S.I. No. 430 of 1981*
	16	**Fire Services Council (Establishment) Order, S.I. No. 175 of 1983**
	37	**Fire Safety in Places of Assembly (Ease of Escape) Regulations, S.I. No. 249 of 1985**
Firearms Act, No. 17 of 1925	2(2B)	**Firearms (Dangerous Weapons) Order, S.I. No. 251 of 1972**
	27(1)	**Firearms Regulations, S.I. No. 239 of 1976**
Firearms Act, No. 1 of 1964	4(1)	*Firearms (Temporary Custody) Order, S.I. No. 187 of 1972*
Firearms (Proofing) Act, No. 20 of 1968	12	**Firearms (Shotguns) (Proofing Methods, Marks and Fees) Regulations, S.I. No. 65 of 1969**
	14	*Firearms (Proofing) Act, 1968 (Commencement) Order, S.I. No. 64 of 1969*
Fisheries Act, No. 32 of 1925		*Fisheries Act, 1925 (Regulations) Order [Vol. XII p. 445] S.R.& O. No. 55 of 1925*
		Fisheries Act, 1939 (Section 44) Regulations [Vol. XXIX p. 891] S.R.& O. No. 218 of 1940
		Fisheries Act, 1925 (Regulations) Order, S.I. No. 199 of 1951
	2	*Fisheries Act, 1925 (Commencement) Order [Vol. XII p. 441] S.R.& O. No. 32 of 1925*
	15(3)	**Fisheries Act, 1925 (Accounts and Audit) Order [Vol. XII p. 455] S.R.& O. No. 67 of 1927**
		Fisheries Act, 1925 (Accounts and Audit) Order [Vol. XII p. 491] S.R.& O. No. 54 of 1929
		Fisheries Act, 1925 (Accounts and Audit) Order [Vol. XXIX p. 875] S.R.& O. No. 341 of 1943
	36	**Fisheries Act, 1925 (Accounts and Audit) Order [Vol. XII p. 455] S.R.& O. No. 67 of 1927**
		Fisheries Act, 1925 (Accounts and Audit) Order [Vol. XII p. 491] S.R.& O. No. 54 of 1929
		Fisheries Act, 1925 (Accounts and Audit) Order [Vol. XXIX p. 875] S.R.& O. No. 341 of 1943
	36(1)	*Fisheries Act, 1925 (Regulations) Order [Vol. XXIX p. 885] S.R.& O. No. 393 of 1939*
Fisheries Act, No. 17 of 1939	2	*Fisheries Act, 1939 (Commencement) (No.1) Order [Vol. XXIX p. 901] S.R.& O. No. 269 of 1939*
		Fisheries Act, 1939 (Commencement) (No.2) Order [Vol. XXIX p. 905] S.R.& O. No. 58 of 1940

Statutory Authority	Section	Statutory Instrument
Fisheries Act, No. 17 of 1939 (*Cont.*)		*Fisheries Act, 1939 (Commencement) (No.3) Order [Vol. XXIX p. 909] S.R.& O. No. 48 of 1943*
		Fisheries Act, 1939 (Commencement) (No.4) Order [Vol. XXXVII p. 341] S.R.& O. No. 191 of 1946
	44	**Fisheries Act, 1939 (Section 44) Regulations [Vol. XXIX p. 891] S.R.& O. No. 218 of 1940**
	54	**River Foyle (Special Local Licence Duty) (Method of Payment) Order, S.I. No. 47 of 1951**
	54(1)	*River Foyle (Special Local Licence Duty) (Method of Payment) Order, S.I. No. 105 of 1949*
	54(6)	*River Erne (Special Local Licence Duty) (Method of Payment) (Amendment) Order, S.I. No. 91 of 1959*
Fisheries Act, No. 1 of 1980	3	*Fisheries Act, 1980 (Appointed Day) Order, S.I. No. 323 of 1980*
	4	**Fisheries (Alteration of Fishery Year) Order, S.I. No. 328 of 1982**
	5	**Fisheries Regions (Amendment) Order, S.I. No. 373 of 1981**
		Salmon Levy (Revocation) Order, S.I. No. 162 of 1982
	10	**Fisheries Regions Order, S.I. No. 324 of 1980**
		Fisheries Regions (Amendment) Order, S.I. No. 373 of 1981
	12(3)	**Elections to Regional Fisheries Boards Regulations, S.I. No. 361 of 1981**
		Elections to Regional Fisheries Boards (Amendment) Regulations, S.I. No. 352 of 1986
	12(5)	*Election of Members of Regional Fisheries Boards (First Election Year) Order, S.I. No. 360 of 1981*
	26	**Fisheries Act, 1980 (Section 26) Regulations, S.I. No. 71 of 1983**
	54	**Aquaculture (Achill Sound) Order, S.I. No. 116 of 1985**
		Aquaculture (Blacksod and Broadhaven Bays) Order, S.I. No. 117 of 1985
		Aquaculture (Killary Harbour) Order, S.I. No. 87 of 1986
		Aquaculture (Bertraghboy Bay) Order, S.I. No. 395 of 1986
		Aquaculture (Kilkieran Bay) Order, S.I. No. 396 of 1986
		Aquaculture (Mulroy Bay) Order, S.I. No. 397 of 1986
		Aquaculture (Carlingford Lough) Order, S.I. No. 398 of 1986
		Aquaculture (Ventry Harbour and Trabeg Bay) Order, S.I. No. 399 of 1986

Statutory Authority	Section	Statutory Instrument
Fisheries Act, No. 1 of 1980 (*Cont.*)		**Aquaculture (Ballynakill) Order, S.I. No. 400 of 1986**
		Aquaculture (Clew Bay) Order, S.I. No. 401 of 1986
		Aquaculture (Clifden Bay, Mannin Bay) Order, S.I. No. 402 of 1986
	54(18)	*Fisheries Act, 1980 (Section 54) (Commencement) Order, S.I. No. 261 of 1983*
	55	*Salmon Levy, Licensed Salmon Dealers' Registers and Salmon and Trout Records Regulations, S.I. No. 142 of 1980*
	55(2)	*Salmon Levy Order, S.I. No. 141 of 1980*
	55(3)	*Sales of Salmon (Attributable Price) Regulations, S.I. No. 143 of 1980*
	58(5)	**Register of Trout, Coarse Fish and Sea Anglers (Fixed Day) Regulations, S.I. No. 121 of 1982**
	69(4)	*Fisheries Act, 1980 (Section 69) (Commencement) Order, S.I. No. 414 of 1980*
Fisheries (Amendment) Act, No. 18 of 1949	2	*Fisheries (Amendment) Act, 1949 (Commencement) Order, S.I. No. 251 of 1949*
Fisheries (Amendment) Act, No. 16 of 1953	3	*Fishing Weir Operation (No.1) Order, S.I. No. 55 of 1954*
		Fishing Weir Operation (No.2) Order, S.I. No. 1 of 1957
		Fishing Weir Operation (No.1) Order, 1954, (Revocation) Order, S.I. No. 121 of 1958
		Fishing Weir Operation (No.3) Order, S.I. No. 88 of 1959
Fisheries (Amendment) Act, No. 15 of 1958	2(3)	*Fisheries (Amendment) Act, 1958 (Commencement) Order, S.I. No. 213 of 1958*
	14(2)(b)	**Salmon Rod (Late Season) (District) Ordinary Licences Order, S.I. No. 251 of 1958**
	15(1)	**Salmon Rod Ordinary Licences (Increase of Licence Duties) Order, S.I. No. 250 of 1958**
	15(2)	**Salmon Rod Ordinary Licences (Increase of Licence Duties) Order, S.I. No. 250 of 1958**
	15(3)	**Salmon Rod Ordinary Licences (Increase of Licence Duties) Order, S.I. No. 250 of 1958**
Fisheries (Amendment) Act, No. 31 of 1962	29	*Control of Fishing for Salmon (Lough Swilly) Order, S.I. No. 82 of 1972*
		Control of Fishing for Salmon Order, S.I. No. 298 of 1972
		Control of Fishing for Salmon (Amendment) Order, S.I. No. 108 of 1973
		Control of Fishing for Salmon Order, S.I. No. 330 of 1973
		Control of Fishing for Salmon Order, S.I. No. 353 of 1974

Statutory Authority	Section	Statutory Instrument

Fisheries (Amendment) Act, No. 31 of 1962 (*Cont.*)

Control of Fishing for Salmon Order, S.I. No. 310 of 1975

Control of Fishing for Salmon Order, S.I. No. 372 of 1977

Control of Fishing for Salmon (Amendment) Order, S.I. No. 346 of 1979

Control of Fishing for Salmon Order, S.I. No. 360 of 1980

Control of Fishing for Salmon by Drift Net (Kerry Fishery District) Order, S.I. No. 367 of 1982

Control of Fishing for Salmon (Amendment) Order, S.I. No. 368 of 1982

35   *Sea Fisheries (Rational Exploitation of Fisheries) Order, S.I. No. 259 of 1969*

Control of Fishing for Salmon at Sea Order, S.I. No. 309 of 1970

Purse Seine Prohibition Order, S.I. No. 262 of 1971

Control of Fishing for Salmon at Sea (Amendment) Order, S.I. No. 331 of 1971

Control of Fishing for Salmon at Sea (Amendment) Order, S.I. No. 296 of 1972

Control of Fishing for Salmon at Sea (Amendment) Order, S.I. No. 303 of 1975

Industrial Fishing for Mackerel (Minimum Size) Order, S.I. No. 167 of 1976

Sea Fisheries (Rational Exploitation of Fisheries) Order, S.I. No. 168 of 1976

Herring Fishing (Minimum Size) Order, S.I. No. 169 of 1976

Herring (Prohibition on Fishing) Order, S.I. No. 170 of 1976

Industrial Fishing for Herring (Prohibition) Order, S.I. No. 211 of 1976

Sea Fisheries (Conservation and Rational Exploitation) Order, S.I. No. 38 of 1977

Sea Fisheries (Conservation and Rational Exploitation) (No.2) Order, S.I. No. 39 of 1977

Sea Fisheries (Conservation and Rational Exploitation) (No.3) Order, S.I. No. 232 of 1977

Sea Fisheries (Conservation and Rational Exploitation) (No.4) Order, S.I. No. 233 of 1977

Sea Fisheries (Conservation and Rational Exploitation) (No.5) Order, S.I. No. 259 of 1977

Sea Fisheries (Conservation and Rational Exploitation) (No.6) Order, S.I. No. 260 of 1977

Sea Fisheries (Conservation and Rational Exploitation) (No.7) Order, S.I. No. 312 of 1977

Sea Fisheries (Conservation and Rational Exploitation) (No.8) Order, S.I. No. 402 of 1977

Sea Fisheries (Conservation and Rational Exploitation) (No.9) Order, S.I. No. 403 of 1977

Sea Fisheries (Conservation and Rational Exploitation) Order, S.I. No. 25 of 1978

Statutory Authority	Section	Statutory Instrument
Fisheries (Amendment) Act, No. 31 of 1962 (*Cont.*)		*Sea Fisheries (Conservation and Rational Exploitation) (No.2) Order, S.I. No. 163 of 1978*
	38(4)	*Fisheries (Amendment) Act, 1962 (Commencement) Order, S.I. No. 216 of 1962*
Fisheries (Amendment) Act, No. 25 of 1974	2(1)	*Elections of Conservators (Postponement) Order, S.I. No. 174 of 1975*
Fisheries (Amendment) Act, No. 23 of 1976	2(1)	*Elections of Conservators (Postponement) Order, S.I. No. 331 of 1977*
	2(2)	*Elections of Conservators (Postponement) Order, S.I. No. 302 of 1978*
		Elections of Conservators (Postponement) Order, S.I. No. 363 of 1979
Fisheries (Consolidation) Act, No. 14 of 1959	4	*Fisheries (Consolidation) Act, 1959 (Salmon Dealer's Licence) Regulations, S.I. No. 228 of 1963*
		Salmon Levy, Licensed Salmon Dealers' Registers and Salmon and Trout Records Regulations, S.I. No. 142 of 1980
		Fisheries (Salmon Dealers Licence) Regulations, S.I. No. 36 of 1981
		Fisheries Act, 1980 (Section 26) Regulations, S.I. No. 71 of 1983
	7	**Rivers Owenmore and Owenduff (Tidal Waters) Order, S.I. No. 33 of 1967**
	17	*Live Fish (Restriction on Import) Order, S.I. No. 39 of 1962*
		Live Fish (Restriction on Import) Order, S.I. No. 4 of 1972
	20	**Fishery Districts (Alteration of Boundaries) Regulations, S.I. No. 329 of 1982**
	27(5)	*Elections of Conservators of Fisheries Regulations, S.I. No. 190 of 1964*
	49	*Salmon Export Levy (Revocation) Order, S.I. No. 273 of 1974*
	49(4)	**Salmon Export Levy (Amendment) Regulations, S.I. No. 292 of 1964**
	51	*Cork Board of Conservators Dissolution Order, S.I. No. 281 of 1973*
		Drogheda Board of Conservators (Dissolution) Order, S.I. No. 14 of 1975
	68	**Salmon, Eel and Oyster (Miscellaneous Licences) (Alteration of Duties) Order, S.I. No. 386 of 1982**
		Salmon, Eel and Oyster Fishing Licences (Alteration of Licence Duties) Order, S.I. No. 343 of 1984
	68(1)	**Salmon, Eel and Oyster Fishing Licences (Alteration of Licence Duties) Order, S.I. No. 305 of 1976**
	68(2)	**Salmon, Eel and Oyster Fishing Licences (Alteration of Licence Duties) Order, S.I. No. 305 of 1976**

Statutory Authority	Section	Statutory Instrument
Fisheries (Consolidation) Act, No. 14 of 1959 (*Cont.*)	68(3)	**Salmon, Eel and Oyster Fishing Licences (Alteration of Licence Duties) Order, S.I. No. 305 of 1976**
	68(4)	**Salmon, Eel and Oyster Fishing Licences (Alteration of Licence Duties) Order, S.I. No. 305 of 1976**
	74	**Rivers Owenmore and Owenduff (Special Local Licences) Order, S.I. No. 34 of 1967**
		River Erne (Special Local Licences) (Amendment) Order, S.I. No. 193 of 1972
		River Erne (Special Local Licences) (Amendment) Order, S.I. No. 99 of 1976
		Special Tidal Waters (Special Local Licences) Order, S.I. No. 109 of 1977
		River Erne (Special Local Licences) (Amendment) Order, S.I. No. 219 of 1983
		Special Tidal Waters (Special Local Licences) Order, S.I. No. 26 of 1985
		River Erne (Special Local Licences) (Amendment) Order, S.I. No. 177 of 1985
		River Erne (Special Local Licences) (Amendment) Order, S.I. No. 212 of 1986
	74(6)	**River Erne (Special Local Licences) (Amendment) Order, S.I. No. 137 of 1960**
		River Erne (Special Local Licences) (Amendment) Order, S.I. No. 166 of 1961
		River Erne (Special Local Licences) (Amendment) Order, S.I. No. 111 of 1962
		River Erne (Special Local Licences) (Amendment) Order, S.I. No. 147 of 1963
		River Erne (Special Local Licences) (Amendment) Order, S.I. No. 163 of 1964
		River Erne (Special Local Licences) (Amendment) Order, S.I. No. 131 of 1965
		River Erne (Special Local Licences) (Amendment) Order, S.I. No. 88 of 1967
	77(3)	**River Erne (Special Local Licence Duty) (Method of Payment) (Amendment) Order, S.I. No. 138 of 1960**
		River Erne (Special Local Licence Duty) (Method of Payment) (Amendment) Order, S.I. No. 165 of 1961
		River Erne (Special Local Licences) (Amendment) Order, S.I. No. 88 of 1967
		River Erne (Special Local Licence Duty) (Method of Payment) (Amendment) Order, S.I. No. 194 of 1972
	108	**Fishing Weir Operation (No.4) Order, S.I. No. 164 of 1960**
	159	*Fisheries (Consolidation) Act, 1959 (Salmon Dealer's Licence) Regulations, S.I. No. 228 of 1963*

Fisheries (Consolidation) Act, No. 14 of 1959 (*Cont.*)

Fisheries (Salmon Dealers Licence) Regulations, S.I. No. 36 of 1981

159(6)(a)   **Salmon, Eel and Oyster (Miscellaneous Licences) (Alteration of Duties) Order, S.I. No. 386 of 1982**

160   **Fisheries (Salmon Dealers Licence) Regulations, S.I. No. 36 of 1981**

160(5)(a)   **Salmon, Eel and Oyster (Miscellaneous Licences) (Alteration of Duties) Order, S.I. No. 386 of 1982**

222B(4) (b)   **Licensing of Sea-Fishing Boats (Exemption) Regulations, S.I. No. 245 of 1983**

222C   *Sea-fishing Boats Regulations, S.I. No. 246 of 1983*

Sea-fishing Boats Regulations, S.I. No. 289 of 1986

223A   *Sea Fisheries (Conservation and Rational Exploitation) (No.3) Order, S.I. No. 187 of 1978*

Sea Fisheries (Conservation and Rational Exploitation) (No.4) Order, S.I. No. 218 of 1978

Sea Fisheries (Conservation and Rational Exploitation) (No.5) Order, S.I. No. 243 of 1978

Sea Fisheries (Conservation and Rational Exploitation) (No.6) Order, S.I. No. 280 of 1978

Sea Fisheries (Conservation and Rational Exploitation) (No.7) Order, S.I. No. 330 of 1978

Sea Fisheries (Conservation and Rational Exploitation) (No.8) Order, S.I. No. 372 of 1978

Sea Fisheries (Conservation and Rational Exploitation) Order, S.I. No. 212 of 1979

Sea Fisheries (Conservation and Rational Exploitation) (No.2) Order, S.I. No. 420 of 1979

Sea Fisheries (Conservation and Rational Exploitation) (No.3) Order, S.I. No. 421 of 1979

Sea Fisheries (Conservation and Rational Exploitation) (Revocation) Order, S.I. No. 47 of 1980

Mackerel Fishing (Licensing) Order, S.I. No. 326 of 1980

Sea Fisheries (Conservation and Rational Exploitation) Order, S.I. No. 404 of 1980

Sea Fisheries (Conservation and Rational Exploitation) Order, S.I. No. 285 of 1981

Sea Fisheries (Conservation and Rational Exploitation) (No.2) Order, S.I. No. 328 of 1981

Mackerel Fishing (Licensing) Order, S.I. No. 339 of 1981

Sea Fisheries (Conservation and Rational Exploitation) Order, S.I. No. 23 of 1982

Herring (Restriction of Fishing in the Celtic Sea) Order, S.I. No. 369 of 1982

Sea Fisheries (Conservation and Rational Exploitation) (No.2) Order, S.I. No. 388 of 1982

Herring (Restriction of Fishing in the North Irish Sea) Order, S.I. No. 18 of 1983

Statutory Authority	Section	Statutory Instrument

Fisheries (Consolidation) Act,
No. 14 of 1959 (*Cont.*)

Control of Fishing for Mackerel Order, S.I. No. 97 of 1983

Celtic Sea Herring Fishing (Licensing) Order, S.I. No. 280 of 1983

Herring (Restriction of Fishing in the Celtic Sea) Order, S.I. No. 281 of 1983

Control of Fishing for Mackerel Order, S.I. No. 52 of 1984

Sea Fisheries (Conservation and Rational Exploitation) Order, S.I. No. 87 of 1984

Salmon (Restriction of Fishing at Sea) Order, S.I. No. 117 of 1984

Herring (Restriction of Fishing in the Celtic Sea) (Revocation) Order, S.I. No. 167 of 1984

Celtic Sea Herring Fishing (Licensing) Order, S.I. No. 240 of 1984

Control of Fishing for Mackerel (No.2) Order, S.I. No. 260 of 1984

Sea Fishing (Enforcement of European Community Quotas) Order, S.I. No. 281 of 1984

Herring (Prohibition on Fishing) Order, S.I. No. 336 of 1984

Mackerel (Prohibition on Fishing) Order, S.I. No. 124 of 1985

Sea Fisheries (Conservation and Rational Exploitation) (Amendment) Order, S.I. No. 162 of 1985

Sea Fisheries (Control of Catches) Order, S.I. No. 163 of 1985

Sea Fishing (Enforcement of European Community Quotas) Order, S.I. No. 172 of 1985

Celtic Sea Herring Fishing (Licensing) Order, S.I. No. 308 of 1985

Fisheries (Control of Fish Processing Vessels) Order, S.I. No. 309 of 1985

Herring (Prohibition on Fishing in the Irish Sea) Order, S.I. No. 328 of 1985

Celtic Sea (Prohibition on Herring Fishing) Order, S.I. No. 329 of 1985

Mackerel (Prohibition on Fishing) (Revocation) Order, S.I. No. 332 of 1985

Herring (Prohibition on Fishing in the Celtic Sea) Order, S.I. No. 361 of 1985

Sole (Prohibition on Fishing in the Irish Sea) Order, S.I. No. 362 of 1985

Sea Fisheries (Conservation and Management of Fishery Resources) Order, S.I. No. 364 of 1985

Herring (Prohibition on Fishing in the Celtic Sea) (Revocation) Order, S.I. No. 385 of 1985

Mackerel (Prohibition on Fishing) (No.2) Order, S.I. No. 403 of 1985

Mackerel (Prohibition on Fishing) (No.2) Order, 1985 (Revocation) Order, S.I. No. 432 of 1985

Statutory Authority	Section	Statutory Instrument
Fisheries (Consolidation) Act, No. 14 of 1959 (*Cont.*)		*Herring (Prohibition on Fishing in the Celtic Sea) (No.2) Order, S.I. No. 433 of 1985*
		Herring (Prohibition on Fishing in the Celtic Sea) (No.2) Order, (1985) S.I. No. 1 of 1986
		Fisheries (Control of Fish Processing Vessels) (Amendment) Order, S.I. No. 28 of 1986
		Sole (Prohibition on Fishing in the Irish Sea) Order, 1985 (Revocation) Order, S.I. No. 29 of 1986
		Sea Fisheries (Conservation and Management of Fishery Resources) Order, S.I. No. 52 of 1986
		Sea Fisheries (Conservation and Management of Fishery Resources) (No.2) Order, S.I. No. 53 of 1986
		Sea Fisheries (Control of Catches) Order (Amendment) Order, S.I. No. 56 of 1986
		Sea Fishing (Enforcement of European Community Quotas) Order, S.I. No. 57 of 1986
		Fisheries (Control of Fish Processing Vessels) Order, S.I. No. 253 of 1986
		Irish Sea Herring Fishing (Licensing) Order, S.I. No. 258 of 1986
		Herring (Prohibition on Fishing in the Irish Sea) Order, S.I. No. 301 of 1986
		Celtic Sea (Prohibition on Herring Fishing) Order, 1985 (Revocation) Order, S.I. No. 322 of 1986
		Herring (Restriction of Fishing) Order, S.I. No. 359 of 1986
		Hake (Prohibition on Fishing) Order, S.I. No. 380 of 1986
		Herring (Restriction of Fishing) (Amendment) Order, S.I. No. 407 of 1986
		Sea Fisheries (Conservation and Management of Fishery Resources) (Amendment) Order, S.I. No. 456 of 1986
	224B	**Fishing Limits (European Communities) Regulations, S.I. No. 74 of 1984**
	225	*Undersized Sea-fish (Lobsters) Order, S.I. No. 52 of 1963*
		Undersized Sea-fish Order, S.I. No. 109 of 1976
		Undersized Sea-fish Order, S.I. No. 175 of 1978
		Undersized Sea-fish (Lobsters) Order, S.I. No. 299 of 1980
		Undersized Sea-fish Order, S.I. No. 341 of 1980
	226	*Fishing Nets (Regulation of Mesh) (Amendment) Order, S.I. No. 76 of 1961*
		Fishing Nets (Regulation of Mesh) (Amendment) Order, S.I. No. 47 of 1963
		Fishing Nets (Regulation of Mesh) Order, S.I. No. 16 of 1965
		Fishing Nets (Regulation of Mesh) (Amendment) Order, S.I. No. 231 of 1965

Statutory Authority	Section	Statutory Instrument
Fisheries (Consolidation) Act, No. 14 of 1959 (*Cont.*)		*Fishing Nets (Regulation of Mesh) (Amendment) Order, S.I. No. 254 of 1968*
		Fishing Nets (Regulation of Mesh) (Amendment) Order, S.I. No. 337 of 1971
		Fishing Nets (Regulation of Mesh) (Amendment) Order, S.I. No. 338 of 1973
		Fishing Nets (Regulation of Mesh) Order, S.I. No. 210 of 1976
		Fishing Nets (Regulation of Mesh) Order, S.I. No. 244 of 1978
		Sea Fisheries (Conservation and Rational Exploitation) Order, S.I. No. 285 of 1981
	230	*Fishing Nets (Regulation of Mesh) (Amendment) Order, S.I. No. 76 of 1961*
		Fishing Nets (Regulation of Mesh) (Amendment) Order, S.I. No. 47 of 1963
		Undersized Sea-fish (Lobsters) Order, S.I. No. 52 of 1963
		Fishing Nets (Regulation of Mesh) Order, S.I. No. 16 of 1965
		Fishing Nets (Regulation of Mesh) (Amendment) Order, S.I. No. 231 of 1965
		Fishing Nets (Regulation of Mesh) (Amendment) Order, S.I. No. 254 of 1968
		Fishing Nets (Regulation of Mesh) (Amendment) Order, S.I. No. 337 of 1971
		Fishing Nets (Regulation of Mesh) (Amendment) Order, S.I. No. 338 of 1973
		Fishing Nets (Regulation of Mesh) Order, S.I. No. 210 of 1976
		Undersized Sea-fish Order, S.I. No. 175 of 1978
		Fishing Nets (Regulation of Mesh) Order, S.I. No. 244 of 1978
		Undersized Sea-fish (Lobsters) Order, S.I. No. 299 of 1980
		Undersized Sea-fish Order, S.I. No. 341 of 1980
		Sea Fisheries (Conservation and Rational Exploitation) Order, S.I. No. 285 of 1981
		Sea Fisheries (Conservation and Rational Exploitation) Order, S.I. No. 87 of 1984
		Sea Fisheries (Conservation and Rational Exploitation) (Amendment) Order, S.I. No. 162 of 1985
	279	**Oyster Fishing Licences (Alteration of Licence Duty) Order, S.I. No. 247 of 1975**
	279(2)	**Salmon, Eel and Oyster Fishing Licences (Alteration of Licence Duties) Order, S.I. No. 305 of 1976**
		Salmon, Eel and Oyster (Miscellaneous Licences) (Alteration of Duties) Order, S.I. No. 386 of 1982
		Salmon, Eel and Oyster Fishing Licences (Alteration of Licence Duties) Order, S.I. No. 343 of 1984

Statutory Authority	Section	Statutory Instrument
Fisheries (Ireland) Act, No. 3 of 1846	70	**Pier at Clogherhead in the County of Louth Bye-laws, S.I. No. 125 of 1960**
		Bantry Pier Bye-laws, S.I. No. 183 of 1968
		Harbour at Burtonport, County Donegal (Bye-laws for the Regulation of the) S.I. No. 427 of 1986
		Harbour at Rathmullan, County Donegal (Bye-laws for the Regulation of the) S.I. No. 428 of 1986
		Harbour at Greencastle, County Donegal (Bye-laws for the Regulation of the) S.I. No. 429 of 1986
Fisheries (Ireland) Act, No. 92 of 1848	9	*Elections of Conservators of Fisheries Regulations [Vol. XXIX p. 913] S.R.& O. No. 240 of 1940*
Fisheries (Statute Law Revision) Act, No. 27 of 1949	2	*Fisheries (Statute Law Revision) Act, 1949 (Commencement) Order, S.I. No. 132 of 1950*
Fisheries (Tidal Waters) Act, No. 24 of 1934	2	**River Lackagh (Tidal Waters) Order [Vol. XXIX p. 929] S.R.& O. No. 14 of 1943**
	2(1)	**River Erne (Tidal Waters) Order [Vol. XII p. 501] S.R.& O. No. 177 of 1934**
		Owenea and Owentocker Rivers (Tidal Waters) Order [Vol. XII p. 523] S.R.& O. No. 38 of 1935
		River Foyle (Tidal Waters) Order, S.I. No. 103 of 1949
	4	**River Erne (Special Local Licences) Order [Vol. XII p. 507] S.R.& O. No. 178 of 1934**
		River Lackagh (Special Local Licences) Order [Vol. XXIX p. 923] S.R.& O. No. 15 of 1943
		River Foyle (Special Local Licences) Order, S.I. No. 104 of 1949
	4(1)	**Owenea and Owentocker Rivers (Special Local Licences) Order [Vol. XII p. 529] S.R.& O. No. 39 of 1935**
	4(5)	**River Lackagh (Special Local Licences) (Amendment) Regulations, S.I. No. 261 of 1958**
		River Erne (Special Local Licences) (Amendment) Order, S.I. No. 89 of 1959
	4(6)	**River Erne (Special Local Licences) (Amendment) Order [Vol. XII p. 513] S.R.& O. No. 40 of 1935**
		River Lackagh (Special Local Licences) (Amendment) Regulations, S.I. No. 261 of 1958
		River Erne (Special Local Licences) (Amendment) Order, S.I. No. 89 of 1959
	8	**River Erne (Fishing by Holders of Special Local Licences) Regulations, S.I. No. 90 of 1959**
	8(1)	**River Lackagh (Fishing by Holders of Special Local Licences) Regulations [Vol. XXIX p. 917] S.R.& O. No. 38 of 1943**
		River Foyle (Fishing by Holders of Special Local Licences) Regulations, S.I. No. 106 of 1949
	10(1)	**Fisheries (Returns by Holders of Special Local Licences) Regulations [Vol. XII p. 517] S.R.& O. No. 179 of 1934**

Statutory Authority	Section	Statutory Instrument
Fisheries (Tidal Waters) (Amendment) Act, No. 34 of 1937	2(1)	**River Erne (Special Local Licence Duty) (Method of Payment) Order [Vol. XII p. 535] S.R.& O. No. 15 of 1938**
Fishery Harbour Centres Act, No. 18 of 1968	2	**Fishery Harbour Centre (Killybegs) (Amendment) Order, S.I. No. 19 of 1983**
	2(1)	**Fishery Harbour Centre (Killybegs) Order, S.I. No. 210 of 1969**
		Fishery Harbour Centre (Castletownbere) Order, S.I. No. 57 of 1970
		Larionad Chuan Iascaigh Ros a' Mhil (An tOrdu um) S.I. No. 208 of 1981
	2(7)	*Fishery Harbour Centre (Killybegs) (Amendment) Order, S.I. No. 183 of 1974*
	4	**Killybegs Pier and Harbour (Amendment) Order, S.I. No. 90 of 1970**
		Killybegs Pier and Harbour (Amendment) Order, S.I. No. 376 of 1974
		Castletownbere Fishery Harbour Centre (Fish Auction Charges) Order, S.I. No. 56 of 1985
		Castletownbere Fishery Harbour Centre (Rates and Charges) Order, S.I. No. 57 of 1985
		Killybegs Fishery Harbour Centre (Rates and Charges) Order, S.I. No. 58 of 1985
		Larionad Chuan Iascaigh Ros a' Mhil (Ratai agus Muirir) (An tOrdu um) S.I. No. 59 of 1985
	4(2)(b)	*Castletownbere Fishery Harbour Centre (Fish Auction Charges) Order, S.I. No. 95 of 1974*
		Killybegs Fishery Harbour Centre (Rates and Charges) Order, S.I. No. 267 of 1978
		Castletownbere Fishery Harbour Centre (Rates and Charges) Order, S.I. No. 12 of 1979
	13(2)	*Fishery Harbour Centres Act, 1968 (Commencement) Order, S.I. No. 123 of 1969*
Flax Act, No. 20 of 1936	2(1)	*Flax Act (Appointed Area) Order [Vol. XII p. 543] S.R.& O. No. 201 of 1936*
	15	*Flax (Standard Price for Sale Season 1950–51) Order, S.I. No. 23 of 1950*
	15(1)	*Flax (Standard Price for Sale Season 1936–37) Order [Vol. XII p. 547] S.R.& O. No. 247 of 1936*
		Flax (Amount of Flax Bounty for Sale Season 1936–37) Order [Vol. XII p. 559] S.R.& O. No. 265 of 1936
		Flax (Amount of Flax Bounty for Sale Season 1937–38) Order [Vol. XII p. 563] S.R.& O. No. 4 of 1937
		Flax (Standard Price for Sale Season 1937–38) Order [Vol. XII p. 551] S.R.& O. No. 5 of 1937
		Flax (Standard Price for Sale Season 1938–39) Order [Vol. XII p. 555] S.R.& O. No. 2 of 1938

Statutory Authority	Section	Statutory Instrument
Flax Act, No. 20 of 1936 (*Cont.*)		*Flax (Amount of Flax Bounty for Sale Season 1938–39) Order [Vol. XII p. 567] S.R.& O. No. 3 of 1938*
		Flax (Standard Price for Sale Season 1939–40) Order [Vol. XXIX p. 943] S.R.& O. No. 2 of 1939
	18	*Flax (Amount of Flax Bounty for Sale Season 1939–40) Order [Vol. XXIX p. 935] S.R.& O. No. 1 of 1939*
		Flax (Amount of Flax Bounty for Sale Season 1950–51) Order, S.I. No. 24 of 1950
	20(1)	*Flax (Minimum Value for Sale Season 1936–37) Order [Vol. XII p. 591] S.R.& O. No. 280 of 1936*
		Flax (Minimum Value for Sale Season 1937–38) Order [Vol. XII p. 595] S.R.& O. No. 246 of 1937
		Flax (Minimum Value for Sale Season 1938–39) Order [Vol. XII p. 599] S.R.& O. No. 250 of 1938
		Flax (Minimum Value for Sale Season 1939–40) Order [Vol. XXIX p. 939] S.R.& O. No. 298 of 1939
	29	*Flax Act (Forms) Regulations [Vol. XII p. 571] S.R.& O. No. 270 of 1936*
Flour and Wheatenmeal Act, No. 40 of 1956	2	*Flour and Wheatenmeal Act, 1956 (Commencement) Order, S.I. No. 209 of 1957*
	4	*Flour and Wheatenmeal (Prescribed Prices) Regulations, S.I. No. 2 of 1967*
		Straight-run Flour (Prescribed Percentage of Wheat) Regulations, S.I. No. 3 of 1967
		Flour and Wheatenmeal (Prescribed Prices) Regulations, 1967 (Revocation) Regulations, S.I. No. 49 of 1967
		Straight-run Flour (Prescribed Percentage of Wheat) Regulations, 1967 (Revocation) Regulations, S.I. No. 50 of 1967
Foir Teoranta Act, No. 1 of 1972	19(9)	*Foir Teoranta Act, 1972 (Appointed Day for the Purposes of Section 19) Order, S.I. No. 80 of 1972*
Food Hygiene Regulations, S.I. No. 205 of 1950		*Food Hygiene Regulations, 1950 (Commencement of Part IV) Order, S.I. No. 270 of 1951*
		Food Hygiene (Official Certificate No.1) Order, S.I. No. 94 of 1952
		Food Hygiene (Official Certificate No.2) Order, S.I. No. 150 of 1952
		Food Hygiene (Official Certificate No.3) Order, S.I. No. 306 of 1953
		Food Hygiene (Official Certificate No.4) Order, S.I. No. 201 of 1954

Statutory Authority	Section	Statutory Instrument
Food Hygiene Regulations, S.I. No. 205 of 1950 (*Cont.*)		**Food Hygiene (Official Certificate No.5) Order, S.I. No. 20 of 1955**
		Food Hygiene Regulations Order, S.I. No. 21 of 1986
	55	**Food Hygiene Regulations, 1950 (Shellfish Controlled Areas) Order, S.I. No. 16 of 1951**
		Food Hygiene Regulations, 1950 (Shellfish Controlled Areas) Order, S.I. No. 273 of 1952
		Food Hygiene Regulations, 1950 (Shellfish Controlled Area) Order, S.I. No. 26 of 1971
		Food Hygiene Regulations, 1950 (Shellfish Controlled Area) Order, S.I. No. 113 of 1977
		Food Hygiene Regulations, 1950 (Shellfish Controlled Area) Order, S.I. No. 66 of 1984
Food Hygiene Regulations, 1950 to 1961,		**Food Hygiene (Official Certificates Nos.6 and 7) Order, S.I. No. 184 of 1963**
Food Standards Act, No. 11 of 1974	2	**Food Standards (Certain Sugars) (European Communities) Regulations, S.I. No. 118 of 1975**
		Food Standards (Cocoa and Chocolate Products) (European Communities) Regulations, S.I. No. 180 of 1975
		Food Standards (Honey) (European Communities) Regulations, S.I. No. 155 of 1976
		Food Standards (Potatoes) Regulations, S.I. No. 367 of 1977
		Food Standards (Potatoes) Regulations, S.I. No. 6 of 1978
		Food Standards (Fruit Juices and Fruit Nectars) (European Communities) Regulations, S.I. No. 173 of 1978
		Food Standards (Potatoes) (No.2) Regulations, S.I. No. 282 of 1978
		Food Standards (Certain Sugars) (European Communities) Regulations, S.I. No. 412 of 1981
		Food Standards (Fruit Juices and Fruit Nectars) (European Communities) Regulations, S.I. No. 266 of 1984
Foreshore Act, No. 12 of 1933	6	**Foreshore Act, 1933 Prohibitory Order No.1, S.I. No. 116 of 1950**
		Foreshore Act, 1933 Prohibitory Order No.2, S.I. No. 175 of 1950
Forestry Act, No. 34 of 1928	16	*Forestry Act, 1928 Regulations [Vol. XII p. 611] S.R.& O. No. 23 of 1930*
	20(2)	*Forestry Act, 1928 (Commencement) Order [Vol. XII p. 609] S.R.& O. No. 22 of 1930*
Forestry Act, No. 13 of 1946	1(2)	*Forestry Act, 1946 (Commencement) Order, S.I. No. 66 of 1949*
	5	**Forestry Act, 1946 (Part IV) Regulations, S.I. No. 67 of 1949**

Statutory Authority	Section	Statutory Instrument
Forestry Act, No. 13 of 1946 (*Cont.*)		**Forestry Act, 1946 (Part III) (Lay Commissioners) Regulations, S.I. No. 60 of 1959**
		Forestry Act, 1946 (Appeal Tribunal) Regulations, S.I. No. 61 of 1959
	5(1)	**Forestry Act, 1946 (Appeal Tribunal) Regulations, S.I. No. 214 of 1949**
		Forestry Act, 1946 (Part III) (Lay Commissioners) Regulations, S.I. No. 215 of 1949
		Forestry Act, 1946 (Part III) Regulations, S.I. No. 62 of 1959
	5(2)	**Forestry Act, 1946 (Part III) (Lay Commissioners) Regulations, S.I. No. 215 of 1949**
	5(3)	**Forestry Act, 1946 (Appeal Tribunal) Regulations, S.I. No. 214 of 1949**
	13	**Forestry Act, 1946 (Part III) Regulations, S.I. No. 62 of 1959**
Fowl Pest Order, S.I. No. 15 of 1950	11	**Fowl Pest Infected Area No.1 Order, S.I. No. 147 of 1956**
		Fowl Pest Infected Area No.1 Order, 1956 (Amendment) Order, S.I. No. 188 of 1956
	.	*Fowl Pest Infected Area No.1 Orders (Revocation) Order, S.I. No. 202 of 1956*
		Fowl Pest (Infected Area) Order, S.I. No. 212 of 1983
		Fowl Pest (Infected Area) Order, 1983 (Revocation) Order, S.I. No. 65 of 1984
Foyle Fisheries Act, No. 5 of 1952	10	*Foyle Fisheries Act, 1952 (Part III) (Commencement) Order, S.I. No. 75 of 1952*
Foyle Fisheries (Amendment) Act, No. 44 of 1961	11(3)	*Foyle Fisheries (Amendment) Act, 1961 (Commencement) Order, S.I. No. 24 of 1962*
Foyle Fisheries (Amendment) Act, No. 2 of 1983	7	*Foyle Fisheries (Amendment) Act, 1983 (Commencement) Order, S.I. No. 116 of 1983*
Friendly Societies Act, No. 25 of 1896	96	*Friendly Societies (Fees) Regulations, S.I. No. 87 of 1978*
		Friendly Societies (Fees) Regulations, S.I. No. 290 of 1983
Fuels (Control of Supplies) Act, No. 3 of 1971	2(1)	*Electricity (Control of Supply and Distribution) Order, S.I. No. 97 of 1972*
		Petroleum Oils (Control of Supply and Distribution) Order, S.I. No. 286 of 1973
		Electricity (Control of Supply and Distribution) Order, S.I. No. 296 of 1973
		Petroleum Oils (Control of Supply and Distribution) Order, 1975, S.I. No. 85 of 1975
		Electricity (Control of Supply and Distribution) Order, S.I. No. 4 of 1977
		Petroleum Oils (Control of Supply and Distribution) Order, S.I. No. 140 of 1979

Statutory Authority	Section	Statutory Instrument

Fuels (Control of Supplies) Act,
No. 3 of 1971 (*Cont.*)

Petroleum Oils (Regulation or Control of Acquisition, Supply, Distribution or Marketing) Order, S.I. No. 1 of 1983

2(4)   *Petroleum Oils (Control of Supply and Distribution) Order, 1973 (Continuance) Order, S.I. No. 81 of 1974*

Petroleum Oils (Control of Supply and Distribution) (Continuance) Order, S.I. No. 334 of 1979

Petroleum Oils (Control of Supply and Distribution) (Continuance) Order, S.I. No. 102 of 1980

Petroleum Oils (Control of Supply and Distribution) (Continuance) (No.2) Order, S.I. No. 320 of 1980

Petroleum Oils (Control of Supply and Distribution) (Continuance) Order, S.I. No. 132 of 1981

Petroleum Oils (Control of Supply and Distribution) (Continuance) (No.2) Order, S.I. No. 350 of 1981

Petroleum Oils (Control of Supply and Distribution) (Continuance) Order, S.I. No. 81 of 1982

Petroleum Oils (Control of the Acquisition, Supply, Distribution or Marketing) (Continuance) Order, S.I. No. 310 of 1982

Petroleum Oils (Regulation or Control of Acquisition, Supply, Distribution or Marketing) (Continuance) Order, S.I. No. 394 of 1983

Petroleum Oils (Regulation or Control of Acquisition, Supply, Distribution or Marketing) (Continuance) Order, S.I. No. 368 of 1984

Petroleum Oils (Regulation or Control of Acquisition, Supply, Distribution or Marketing) (Continuance) Order, S.I. No. 420 of 1985

Petroleum Oils (Regulation or Control of Acquisition, Supply, Distribution or Marketing) (Continuance) Order, S.I. No. 390 of 1986

3   *Petroleum Oils (Prohibition of Export) Order, S.I. No. 114 of 1971*

Petroleum Oils (Prohibition of Export) (Amendment) Order, S.I. No. 122 of 1971

Electricity (Restriction of Consumption) Order, S.I. No. 99 of 1972

Electricity (Restriction of Consumption) Order, 1972 (Revocation) Order, S.I. No. 117 of 1972

Petroleum Oils (Prohibition of Export) Order, S.I. No. 297 of 1973

Electricity (Restriction of Consumption) Order, S.I. No. 298 of 1973

Fuels (Control of Supplies) (Restriction on Deliveries of Motor Spirit) Order, S.I. No. 305 of 1973

Fuels (Control of Supplies) (Restriction on Deliveries of Gas Diesel Oil, Kerosene and Fuel Oil) Order, S.I. No. 306 of 1973

Electricity (Restriction of Consumption) (Amendment) Order, S.I. No. 321 of 1973

Fuels (Control of Supplies) (Restriction on Deliveries of Motor Spirit) (Amendment) Order, S.I. No. 346 of 1973

Statutory Authority	Section	Statutory Instrument

Fuels (Control of Supplies) Act,
No. 3 of 1971 (*Cont.*)

Fuels (Control of Supplies) (Restriction on Deliveries of Gas Diesel Oil, Kerosene and Fuel Oil) Order, S.I. No. 347 of 1973

Fuels (Control of Supplies) (Restriction on Deliveries of Motor Spirit) (Amendment) Order, S.I. No. 14 of 1974

Fuels (Control of Supplies) (Restriction on Deliveries of Gas Diesel Oil, Kerosene and Fuel Oil) (Amendment) Order, S.I. No. 15 of 1974

Electricity (Restriction of Consumption) Order, 1973 (Revocation) Order, S.I. No. 80 of 1974

Fuels (Control of Supplies) (Restriction on Deliveries of Motor Spirit) (No.2) Order, S.I. No. 84 of 1974

Fuels (Control of Supplies) (Restriction on Deliveries of Motor Spirit) (No.2) Order, 1974 (Revocation) Order, S.I. No. 121 of 1974

Petroleum Oils (Maintenance and Provision of Supplies) Order, S.I. No. 87 of 1975

Electricity (Restriction of Consumption) Order, S.I. No. 6 of 1977

Electricity (Restriction of Consumption) Order, 1977 (Revocation) Order, S.I. No. 123 of 1977

Fuels (Control of Supplies) (Regulation of Deliveries of Gas Diesel Oil) Order, S.I. No. 142 of 1979

Fuels (Regulation and Control of Supply and Distribution of Motor Spirit) Order, S.I. No. 172 of 1979

Fuels (Regulation and Control of Supply and Distribution of Motor Spirit) (Amendment) Order, S.I. No. 180 of 1979

Fuels (Control of Supplies) (Regulation of Deliveries of Gas Diesel Oil) (No.2) Order, S.I. No. 225 of 1979

Fuels (Control of Supplies) (Regulation of Deliveries of Gas Diesel Oil) (No.3) Order, S.I. No. 269 of 1979

Fuels (Control of Supplies) (Regulation of Deliveries of Gas Diesel Oil) (No.4) Order, S.I. No. 295 of 1979

Fuels (Regulation and Control of Supply and Distribution of Motor Spirit) (Revocation) Order, S.I. No. 321 of 1979

Fuels (Control of Supplies) (Regulation and Control of Supply and Distribution of Liquified Petroleum Gas) Order, S.I. No. 309 of 1980

Petroleum Oils (Maintenance and Provision of Supplies) Order, S.I. No. 328 of 1980

Fuels (Control of Supplies) Order, S.I. No. 280 of 1982

3(1)   **Fuels (Petroleum Oils) Order, S.I. No. 2 of 1983**

3(5)   *Fuels (Control of Supplies) (Regulation and Control of Supply and Distribution of Liquified Petroleum Gas) (Revocation) Order, S.I. No. 311 of 1980*

Statutory Authority	Section	Statutory Instrument
Fuels (Control of Supplies) Act, No. 3 of 1971 *(Cont.)*		**Fuels (Petroleum Oils) (Amendment) Order, S.I. No. 241 of 1986**
		Fuels (Petroleum Oils) (Amendment) (No.2) Order, S.I. No. 324 of 1986
Galway Harbour Act, No. 2 of 1935(Private)		*Galway Harbour Act, 1935 (Appointed Day) Order [Vol. XII p. 625] S.R.& O. No. 38 of 1936*
	38	*Galway Harbour Act, 1935 (Extension of Period for Completion of Works) Order, S.R.& O. No. 140 of 1945*
	47	*Galway Harbour Act, 1935 (Contributions) Order [Vol. XII p. 629] S.R.& O. No. 84 of 1937*
	49	**Galway Harbour Stock Regulations [Vol. XII p. 633] S.R.& O. No. 98 of 1938**
Game Preservation Act, No. 11 of 1930	6	*Game Birds Protection (No.1) Order [Vol. XII p. 677] S.R.& O. No. 75 of 1930*
		Game Birds Protection (No.1) Order [Vol. XII p. 693] S.R.& O. No. 11 of 1931
		Game Birds Protection (No.1) Order, 1930 (Continuing) Order [Vol. XII p. 681] S.R.& O. No. 51 of 1931
		Game Birds Protection (No.1) Order [Vol. XII p. 697] S.R.& O. No. 8 of 1932
		Game Birds Protection (No.2) Order [Vol. XII p. 701] S.R.& O. No. 9 of 1932
		Game Birds Protection (No.1) Order, 1930 (Continuing) Order [Vol. XII p. 685] S.R.& O. No. 62 of 1932
		Game Birds Protection (No.1) Order, 1930 (Continuing) Order [Vol. XII p. 689] S.R.& O. No. 99 of 1932
		Game Birds Protection (No.1) Order [Vol. XII p. 705] S.R.& O. No. 36 of 1933
		Game Birds Protection (No.2) Order [Vol. XII p. 709] S.R.& O. No. 87 of 1933
		Game Birds Protection (No.3) Order [Vol. XII p. 713] S.R.& O. No. 131 of 1933
		Game Birds Protection (No.1) Order [Vol. XII p. 723] S.R.& O. No. 24 of 1934
		Game Birds Protection (No.1) Order [Vol. XII p. 727] S.R.& O. No. 189 of 1934
		Game Birds Protection (No.2) Order [Vol. XII p. 731] S.R.& O. No. 214 of 1934
		Game Birds Protection (No.3) Order, 1933 (Varying) Order [Vol. XII p. 719] S.R.& O. No. 215 of 1934
		Game Birds Protection (No.1) Order [Vol. XII p. 735] S.R.& O. No. 55 of 1935
		Game Birds Protection (No.3) Order [Vol. XII p. 743] S.R.& O. No. 246 of 1935
		Game Birds Protection (No.4) Order [Vol. XII p. 747] S.R.& O. No. 313 of 1935

Statutory Authority	Section	Statutory Instrument
Game Preservation Act, No. 11 of 1930 (*Cont.*)		*Game Birds Protection Order, S.I. No. 56 of 1955*
		Game Birds Protection Order, S.I. No. 78 of 1959
		Game Birds Protection Order, S.I. No. 146 of 1960
		Game Birds Protection Order, S.I. No. 113 of 1961
		Game Birds Protection Order, S.I. No. 107 of 1962
		Game Birds Protection Order, S.I. No. 123 of 1963
		Game Birds Protection Order, S.I. No. 171 of 1964
		Game Birds Protection Order, S.I. No. 153 of 1965
		Game Birds Protection Order, S.I. No. 166 of 1966
		Game Birds Protection Order, S.I. No. 194 of 1967
		Game Birds Protection Order, S.I. No. 136 of 1968
		Game Birds Protection (Lough Carra, County Mayo) Order, S.I. No. 176 of 1968
		Game Birds Protection (Coosan Lough, County Westmeath) Order, S.I. No. 222 of 1968
		Game Birds Protection Order, S.I. No. 161 of 1969
		Game Birds Protection Order, S.I. No. 180 of 1970
		Game Birds Protection Order, S.I. No. 195 of 1971
		Game Birds Protection Order, S.I. No. 96 of 1972
		Game Birds Protection (Amendment) Order, S.I. No. 207 of 1972
		Game Birds Protection Order, S.I. No. 199 of 1973
		Game Birds Protection Order, S.I. No. 212 of 1974
		Game Birds Protection Order, S.I. No. 163 of 1975
		Game Birds Protection Order, S.I. No. 153 of 1976
	6(1)	*Game Birds Protection (No.2) Order [Vol. XII p. 739] S.R.& O. No. 186 of 1935*
		Game Birds Protection (No.1) Order [Vol. XII p. 751] S.R.& O. No. 199 of 1936
		Game Birds Protection (No.1) Order [Vol. XII p. 757] S.R.& O. No. 154 of 1937
		Game Birds Protection (No.1) Order [Vol. XII p. 763] S.R.& O. No. 112 of 1938
		Game Birds Protection (No.2) Order [Vol. XII p. 769] S.R.& O. No. 236 of 1938
		Game Birds Protection Order [Vol. XXX p. 5] S.R.& O. No. 109 of 1939
		Game Birds Protection Order [Vol. XXX p. 11] S.R.& O. No. 122 of 1940
		Game Birds Protection Order [Vol. XXX p. 17] S.R.& O. No. 225 of 1941
		Game Birds Protection Order [Vol. XXX p. 23] S.R.& O. No. 204 of 1942
		Game Birds Protection Order [Vol. XXX p. 29] S.R.& O. No. 172 of 1943
		Game Birds Protection Order [Vol. XXX p. 35] S.R.& O. No. 175 of 1944
		Game Birds Protection Order [Vol. XXX p. 41] S.R.& O. No. 139 of 1945
		Game Birds Protection Order [Vol. XXXVII p. 345] S.R.& O. No. 170 of 1946

Statutory Authority	Section	Statutory Instrument
Game Preservation Act, No. 11 of 1930 (*Cont.*)		*Game Birds Protection Order [Vol. XXXVII p. 351] S.R.& O. No. 68 of 1947*
		Game Birds Protection Order, S.I. No. 115 of 1948
		Game Birds Protection Order, S.I. No. 54 of 1949
		Game Birds Protection Order, S.I. No. 148 of 1950
		Game Birds Protection Order, S.I. No. 83 of 1951
		Game Birds Protection Order, S.I. No. 33 of 1952
		Game Birds Protection Order, S.I. No. 92 of 1953
		Game Birds Protection Order, S.I. No. 27 of 1954
		Game Birds Protection Order, S.I. No. 81 of 1956
		Game Birds Protection Order, S.I. No. 72 of 1957
		Game Birds Protection Order, S.I. No. 119 of 1958
	6(3)	*Game Birds Protection Order, 1944 (Variation) Order [Vol. XXX p. 47] S.R.& O. No. 295 of 1944*
	7	*Hares Protection (County Cork) Order, S.I. No. 209 of 1964*
		Hares Protection (County Cork) Order, S.I. No. 226 of 1966
		Hares Protection (County Meath) Order, S.I. No. 73 of 1967
		Hares Protection (County Waterford) Order, S.I. No. 87 of 1967
		Hares Protection (County Kerry) Order, S.I. No. 161 of 1967
		Hares Protection (County Clare) Order, S.I. No. 196 of 1967
		Hares Protection (County Tipperary) (South Riding) Order, S.I. No. 204 of 1967
		Hares Protection (County Cork) Order, S.I. No. 93 of 1968
		Hares Protection (County Clare) Order, S.I. No. 178 of 1969
	14	*Game Preservation Act, 1930 (Recognition of Coursing Clubs) Order, S.I. No. 311 of 1948*
		Game Preservation Act, 1930 (Recognition of Coursing Clubs) Order, S.I. No. 137 of 1950
		Game Preservation Act, 1930 (Recognition of Coursing Clubs) Order, S.I. No. 228 of 1951
		Game Preservation Act, 1930 (Recognition of Coursing Clubs) Order, S.I. No. 165 of 1952
		Game Preservation Act, 1930 (Recognition of Coursing Clubs) Order, S.I. No. 239 of 1954
		Game Preservation Act, 1930 (Recognition of Coursing Clubs) Order, S.I. No. 204 of 1956
		Game Preservation Act, 1930 (Recognition of Coursing Clubs) Order, S.I. No. 116 of 1958
		Game Preservation (Recognition of Coursing Clubs) Order, S.I. No. 198 of 1959
		Game Preservation (Recognition of Coursing Clubs) Order, S.I. No. 204 of 1960

Statutory Authority	Section	Statutory Instrument
Game Preservation Act, No. 11 of 1930 (*Cont.*)	14(1)	*Game Preservation (Recognition of Coursing Clubs) (No.1) Order [Vol. XII p. 811] S.R.& O. No. 2 of 1932*
		Game Preservation (Recognition of Coursing Clubs) (No.2) Order [Vol. XII p. 817] S.R.& O. No. 2 of 1933
		Game Preservation (Recognition of Coursing Clubs) (No.1) Order [Vol. XII p. 821] S.R.& O. No. 122 of 1934
		Game Preservation (Recognition of Coursing Clubs) (No.1) Order [Vol. XII p. 827] S.R.& O. No. 13 of 1935
		Game Preservation (Recognition of Coursing Clubs) (No.2) Order [Vol. XII p. 833] S.R.& O. No. 42 of 1935
		Game Preservation (Recognition of Coursing Clubs) (No.1) Order [Vol. XII p. 837] S.R.& O. No. 40 of 1936
		Game Preservation (Recognition of Coursing Clubs) (No.2) Order [Vol. XII p. 843] S.R.& O. No. 60 of 1936
		Game Preservation (Recognition of Coursing Clubs) (No.3) Order [Vol. XII p. 847] S.R.& O. No. 90 of 1936
		Game Preservation (Recognition of Coursing Clubs) (No.4) Order [Vol. XII p. 851] S.R.& O. No. 116 of 1936
		Game Preservation (Recognition of Coursing Clubs) (No.1) Order [Vol. XII p. 855] S.R.& O. No. 125 of 1937
	27	*Game Preservation (Prohibition of Export) Continuance Order [Vol. XII p. 777] S.R.& O. No. 38 of 1933*
		Game Preservation (Prohibition of Export) Continuance Order [Vol. XII p. 781] S.R.& O. No. 112 of 1934
		Game Preservation (Prohibition of Export) Continuance Order [Vol. XII p. 787] S.R.& O. No. 78 of 1935
		Game Preservation (Prohibition of Export) Continuance Order [Vol. XII p. 793] S.R.& O. No. 95 of 1936
		Game Preservation (Prohibition of Export) Continuance Order [Vol. XII p. 799] S.R.& O. No. 78 of 1937
		Game Preservation (Prohibition of Export) Continuance Order [Vol. XII p. 805] S.R.& O. No. 77 of 1938
	27(2)	*Game Preservation (Prohibition of Export) Continuance Order [Vol. XXX p. 69] S.R.& O. No. 101 of 1939*
		Game Preservation (Prohibition of Export) Continuance Order [Vol. XXX p. 75] S.R.& O. No. 130 of 1940

Statutory Authority	Section	Statutory Instrument
Game Preservation Act, No. 11 of 1930 (*Cont.*)		*Game Preservation (Prohibition of Export) Continuance Order [Vol. XXX p. 81] S.R.& O. No. 189 of 1941*
		Game Preservation (Prohibition of Export) Continuance Order [Vol. XXX p. 87] S.R.& O. No. 135 of 1942
		Game Preservation Act, 1930 (Period under Section 27) (Extension) Order [Vol. XXX p. 51] S.R.& O. No. 155 of 1943
		Game Preservation Act, 1930 (Period under Section 27) (Extension) Order [Vol. XXX p. 57] S.R.& O. No. 98 of 1944
		Game Preservation Act, 1930 (Period under Section 27) (Extension) Order [Vol. XXX p. 63] S.R.& O. No. 46 of 1945
		Game Preservation Act, 1930 (Period under Section 27) (Extension) Order [Vol. XXXVII p. 357] S.R.& O. No. 214 of 1946
		Game Preservation Act, 1930 (Period under Section 27) (Extension) Order [Vol. XXXVII p. 363] S.R.& O. No. 160 of 1947
		Game Preservation Act, 1930 (Period under Section 27) (Extension) Order, S.I. No. 141 of 1948
		Game Preservation Act, 1930 (Period under Section 27) (Extension) Order, S.I. No. 114 of 1949
		Game Preservation Act, 1930 (Period under Section 27) (Extension) Order, S.I. No. 101 of 1950
		Game Preservation Act, 1930 (Period under Section 27) (Extension) Order, S.I. No. 92 of 1951
		Game Preservation Act, 1930 (Period under Section 27) (Extension) Order, S.I. No. 76 of 1957
	27(5)	*Game Preservation Act, 1930 (Period under Section 27) (Extension) Order, S.I. No. 114 of 1952*
	32	*Game Preservation Regulations [Vol. XII p. 669] S.R.& O. No. 53 of 1930*
Gaming and Lotteries Act, No. 2 of 1956	1	*Gaming and Lotteries Act, 1956 (Commencement) Order, S.I. No. 18 of 1956*
	50	**Periodical Lotteries Regulations, S.I. No. 212 of 1961**
		Periodical Lotteries Regulations, S.I. No. 32 of 1966
Garda Siochana Act, No. 25 of 1924	8	**Garda Siochana Pensions Order [Vol. XII p. 873] S.R.& O. No. 63 of 1925**
	13	**Garda Siochana (Associations) Regulations, S.I. No. 135 of 1978**
		Garda Siochana (Associations) (Amendment) Regulations, S.I. No. 151 of 1983
Garda Siochana Act, No. 14 of 1958	1	**Garda Siochana (Appointments) Regulations, S.I. No. 176 of 1958**
		Garda Siochana (Retirement) (No.2) Regulations, S.I. No. 177 of 1958

Statutory Authority	Section	Statutory Instrument
Garda Siochana Act, No. 14 of 1958 (*Cont.*)		*Garda Siochana Pay Order, S.I. No. 51 of 1959*
		Garda Siochana (Appointments) Regulations, S.I. No. 38 of 1960
		Garda Siochana Pay Order, S.I. No. 102 of 1960
		Garda Siochana Pay and Allowances Order, S.I. No. 41 of 1961
		Garda Siochana Pay Order, S.I. No. 257 of 1961
		Garda Siochana Pay Order, S.I. No. 166 of 1963
		Garda Siochana Pay Order, S.I. No. 54 of 1964
		Garda Siochana Pensions Order, S.I. No. 149 of 1965
		Garda Siochana Allowances (Consolidation) Order, S.I. No. 218 of 1965
		Garda Siochana Pay (No.3) Order, S.I. No. 186 of 1966
		Garda Siochana Pensions Order, S.I. No. 236 of 1966
		Garda Siochana Pay (No.4) Order, S.I. No. 239 of 1966
		Garda Siochana Pay Order, S.I. No. 59 of 1967
		Garda Siochana Allowances Order, S.I. No. 220 of 1968
		Garda Siochana (No.2) Pay Order, S.I. No. 234 of 1968
		Garda Siochana Allowances (No.2) Order, S.I. No. 246 of 1968
		Garda Siochana Pensions Order, S.I. No. 136 of 1969
		Garda Siochana Pay Order, S.I. No. 214 of 1969
		Garda Siochana (Appointments) Regulations, S.I. No. 1 of 1977
		Garda Siochana (Appointments) Regulations, S.I. No. 308 of 1979
		Garda Siochana (Appointments) Regulations, S.I. No. 202 of 1981
		Garda Siochana (Appointments) Regulations, S.I. No. 108 of 1982
		Garda Siochana (Appointments) Regulations, S.I. No. 101 of 1984
	1(3)	**Garda Siochana (Promotion) Regulations, S.I. No. 203 of 1960**
Garda Siochana Act, No. 2 of 1972	1	**Garda Siochana (Ranks) Order, S.I. No. 67 of 1972**
		Garda Siochana (Ranks) Order, S.I. No. 114 of 1974
		Garda Siochana (Ranks) Order, S.I. No. 2 of 1977
		Garda Siochana (Ranks) Order, S.I. No. 28 of 1978
		Garda Siochana (Ranks) Order, S.I. No. 377 of 1979
		Garda Siochana (Ranks) Order, S.I. No. 220 of 1981
		Garda Siochana (Ranks) Order, S.I. No. 348 of 1982
Garda Siochana Act, No. 24 of 1977	1	*Garda Siochana Act, 1977 (Section 1) (Appointed Day) Order, S.I. No. 136 of 1978*

Statutory Authority	Section	Statutory Instrument
Garda Siochana (Compensation) Act, No. 19 of 1941	5	**Garda Siochana (Application for Compensation) Regulations [Vol. XXX p. 93] S.R.& O. No. 413 of 1941**
	13(1)	**Taca Siochana (Compensation) Order [Vol. XXX p. 103] S.R.& O. No. 484 of 1941**
	15	**Garda Siochana (Application for Compensation) Regulations [Vol. XXX p. 93] S.R.& O. No. 413 of 1941**
Gas Act, No. 30 of 1976	3	*Gas Act, 1976 (Establishment Day) Order, S.I. No. 209 of 1976*
Gas Regulation Act, No. 28 of 1920	1	**Gas (Charges Orders) Rules [Vol. XII p. 1023] S.R.& O. No. 18 of 1923**
		Gas (Amending Orders) Rules [Vol. XII p. 1027] S.R.& O. No. 19 of 1923
	1(1)	**Cork Gas Charges Order [Vol. XII p. 945] S.R.& O. No. 1 of 1922**
		Dundalk Gas Charges Order [Vol. XII p. 949] S.R.& O. No. 2 of 1922
		Fermoy Gas Charges Order [Vol. XII p. 953] S.R.& O. No. 3 of 1922
		Longford Gas Charges Order [Vol. XII p. 957] S.R.& O. No. 4 of 1922
		Thurles Gas Charges Order [Vol. XII p. 961] S.R.& O. No. 5 of 1922
		Tipperary Gas Charges Order [Vol. XII p. 965] S.R.& O. No. 6 of 1922
		Waterford Gas Charges Order [Vol. XII p. 969] S.R.& O. No. 7 of 1922
		Wicklow Gas Charges Order [Vol. XII p. 973] S.R.& O. No. 8 of 1922
		Mallow Gas Charges Order [Vol. XII p. 977] S.R.& O. No. 23 of 1923
		Limerick Gas Charges Order [Vol. XII p. 981] S.R.& O. No. 24 of 1923
		Drogheda Gas Charges Order [Vol. XII p. 985] S.R.& O. No. 2 of 1924
		Clonmel Gas Charges Order [Vol. XII p. 989] S.R.& O. No. 5 of 1924
		Sligo Gas Charges Order [Vol. XII p. 993] S.R.& O. No. 72 of 1926
		Kilkenny Gas (Charges) Order [Vol. XII p. 1019] S.R.& O. No. 71 of 1931
	7	*Gas Fund (Contribution) Order [Vol. XII p. 1029] S.R.& O. No. 118 of 1935*
		Gas Fund (Contribution) Order [Vol. XII p. 1033] S.R.& O. No. 198 of 1936
		Gas Fund (Contribution) Order [Vol. XII p. 1037] S.R.& O. No. 94 of 1937
		Gas Fund (Contribution) Order [Vol. XII p. 1041] S.R.& O. No. 154 of 1938

Gas Regulation Act, No. 28 of 1920
(*Cont.*)

Gas Fund (Contribution) Order [Vol. XXX p. 123]
S.R.& O. No. 60 of 1939

Gas Fund (Contribution) Order [Vol. XXX p. 127]
S.R.& O. No. 92 of 1940

Gas Fund (Contribution) Order [Vol. XXX p. 131]
S.R.& O. No. 137 of 1941

Gas Fund (Contribution) Order [Vol. XXX p. 135]
S.R.& O. No. 113 of 1942

Gas Fund (Contribution) Order [Vol. XXX p. 139]
S.R.& O. No. 243 of 1943

Gas Fund (Contribution) Order [Vol. XXX p. 143]
S.R.& O. No. 129 of 1944

Gas Fund (Contribution) Order [Vol. XXX p. 147]
S.R.& O. No. 72 of 1945

Gas Fund (Contribution) Order [Vol. XXXVII
p. 367] S.R.& O. No. 84 of 1946

Gas Fund (Contribution) Order [Vol. XXXVII
p. 371] S.R.& O. No. 147 of 1947

Gas Fund (Contribution) Order, S.I. No. 107 of
1948

Gas Fund (Contribution) Order, S.I. No. 65 of 1949

Gas Fund (Contribution) Order, S.I. No. 85 of 1950

Gas Fund (Contribution) Order, S.I. No. 78 of 1951

Gas Fund (Contribution) Order, S.I. No. 57 of 1952

Gas Fund (Contribution) Order, S.I. No. 100 of
1953

Gas Fund (Contribution) Order, S.I. No. 47 of 1954

Gas Fund (Contribution) Order, S.I. No. 41 of 1955

Gas Fund (Contribution) Order, S.I. No. 49 of 1956

Gas Fund (Contribution) Order, S.I. No. 57 of 1957

Gas Fund (Contribution) Order, S.I. No. 72 of 1958

Gas Fund (Contribution) Order, S.I. No. 54 of 1959

Gas Fund (Contribution) Order, S.I. No. 66 of 1960

Gas Fund (Contribution) Order, S.I. No. 50 of 1962

Gas Fund (Contribution) Order, S.I. No. 285 of
1980

Gas Fund (Contribution) Order, S.I. No. 134 of
1981

10   **Cobh (Queenstown) Gas Order [Vol. XII p. 997]**
S.R.& O. No. 21 of 1929

Cork Gas Order [Vol. XXX p. 107] S.R.& O.
No. 181 of 1940

Cork Gas Order, S.I. No. 422 of 1948

Waterford Gas Order, S.I. No. 80 of 1949

Limerick Gas Order, S.I. No. 58 of 1950

Alliance and Dublin Consumer's Gas Company
(General Meetings) Order, S.I. No. 177 of 1950

Dundalk Gas Order, S.I. No. 153 of 1952

Wexford Gas Order, S.I. No. 40 of 1954

Dublin Gas Order, S.I. No. 147 of 1954

Waterford Gas Order, S.I. No. 320 of 1956

Statutory Authority	Section	Statutory Instrument
Gas Regulation Act, No. 28 of 1920 (*Cont.*)		**Cork Gas Order, S.I. No. 179 of 1961**
		Dublin Gas Order, S.I. No. 135 of 1976
	12	**Weights and Measures (Departmental Fees) Order [Vol. XXII p. 333] S.R.& O. No. 78 of 1928**
	14	**Weights and Measures Fees Order [Vol. XXII p. 243] S.R.& O. No. 13 of 1924**
		Weights and Measures (Departmental Fees) Order [Vol. XXII p. 333] S.R.& O. No. 78 of 1928
	16(1)	**Gas Regulation (Special Orders) Rules [Vol. XXX p. 151] S.R.& O. No. 15 of 1940**
Gas Regulation Act, No. 24 of 1928	5(1)	**Gas Meters (Stamps) Regulations, S.I. No. 307 of 1949**
		Gas Meters (Stamps) Regulations, S.I. No. 138 of 1958
Gas Regulation Act, No. 26 of 1957	15	*Gas Fund (Contribution) Order, S.I. No. 285 of 1980*
Gas Regulation Act, No. 16 of 1982	7(3)	**Gas Regulation Act, 1982 (Section 7) Order, S.I. No. 110 of 1986**
	12	**Gas Regulation Act, 1982 (Removal of Difficulties) Order, S.I. No. 160 of 1985**
General Elections (Emergency Provisions) Act, No. 11 of 1943	7(a)	*General Elections (Emergency Provisions) (Polling) Order [Vol. XXX p. 171] S.R.& O. No. 178 of 1943*
	7(b)	*General Elections (Emergency Provisions) (Form of Writ) Order [Vol. XXX p. 165] S.R.& O. No. 181 of 1943*
General Prisons (Ireland) Act, No. 49 of 1877	12	**Rules for the Government of Prisons, S.I. No. 30 of 1976**
	13	**Rules for the Government of Prisons, S.I. No. 30 of 1976**
Gold and Silver Wares Act, No. 96 of 1854		*Gold Wares (Standard of Fineness) Order, S.I. No. 365 of 1951*
	1	*Gold Wares (Standard of Fineness) Order [Vol. XII p. 1063] S.R.& O. No. 255 of 1935*
Government Loans (Conversion) Act, No. 12 of 1951	9	*Government Loans (Conversion) Regulations, S.I. No. 191 of 1951*
		3% Transport Stock 1955–60 (Conversion) Regulations, S.I. No. 119 of 1960
		3.25% National Security Loan, 1956–61 (Conversion) Regulations, S.I. No. 249 of 1961
		5.5% National Loan, 1966 (Conversion) Regulations, S.I. No. 248 of 1966
		6% National Loan 1967 (Conversion) Regulations, S.I. No. 237 of 1967
		4.5% Exchequer Stock 1968 (Conversion) Regulations, S.I. No. 56 of 1968
		6% Funding Loan 1969 (Conversion) Regulations, S.I. No. 166 of 1969
		8.25% Conversion Stock 1970 (Conversion) Regulations, S.I. No. 44 of 1970

Government Loans (Conversion) Act, No. 12 of 1951 (*Cont.*)

Government Loans (Conversion) Regulations, S.I. No. 292 of 1970

8.5% Conversion Stock, 1971 (Conversion) Regulations, S.I. No. 89 of 1971

6.5% Exchequer Stock, 1971 (Conversion) Regulations, S.I. No. 252 of 1971

8.5% Conversion Stock 1972 (Conversion) Regulations, S.I. No. 40 of 1972

5% National Loan 1962–1972 (Conversion) Regulations, S.I. No. 195 of 1972

8% Exchequer Stock 1972 (Conversion) Regulations, S.I. No. 196 of 1972

7.75% Funding Loan 1973 (Conversion) Regulations, S.I. No. 236 of 1973

7.5% Exchequer Stock 1973 (Conversion) Regulations, S.I. No. 311 of 1973

7.5% Funding Loan, 1974 (Conversion) Regulations, S.I. No. 168 of 1974

5.5% Exchequer Stock, 1971–74 (Conversion) Regulations, S.I. No. 288 of 1974

5.5% Conversion Stock 1975 (Conversion) Regulations, S.I. No. 10 of 1975

7% Exchequer Stock 1975 (Conversion) Regulations, S.I. No. 211 of 1975

11% Conversion Stock, 1976 (Conversion) Regulations, S.I. No. 10 of 1976

8.75% Conversion Stock, 1976 (Conversion) Regulations, S.I. No. 162 of 1976

12% Convertible Stock 1979 (Conversion) Regulations, S.I. No. 293 of 1979

12% Convertible Stock 1979 (Closure of Register) Regulations, S.I. No. 294 of 1979

5% National Savings Bond 1971/81 (Closure of Register) Regulations, S.I. No. 46 of 1981

5% National Savings Bond 1971/81 (Conversion) Regulations, S.I. No. 47 of 1981

9% Conversion Stock, 1980/82 (Closure of Register) Regulations, S.I. No. 293 of 1982

9% Conversion Stock, 1980/82 (Conversion) Regulations, S.I. No. 294 of 1982

Great Northern Railway Act, No. 17 of 1953

6 — *Great Northern Railway Board Establishment Order, S.I. No. 261 of 1953*

24(7) — *Great Northern Railway Board (Dundalk-Clones, Glaslough-Cavan and Ballyhaise-Belturbet Railway Lines) (Termination of Passenger Services) Order, S.I. No. 188 of 1957*

Great Northern Railway Board (Drogheda-Oldcastle Railway Line) (Termination of Passenger Services) Order, S.I. No. 70 of 1958

49(1)(b) — *Great Northern Railway Company (Ireland) (Winding-up) Order, S.I. No. 55 of 1958*

Statutory Authority	Section	Statutory Instrument
Great Northern Railway Act, No. 20 of 1958	2	**Dundalk Engineering Works Limited (Designation of Successor) Order, S.I. No. 200 of 1958**
	15(10)	**Great Northern Railway Company (Ireland) Pension Fund (Amendment) Scheme for Wages Staff (Confirmation) Order, S.I. No. 53 of 1962**
		Great Northern Railway Company (Ireland) Pension Fund for Wages Staff (Amendment) Scheme (Confirmation) Order, S.I. No. 50 of 1965
		Great Northern Railway Company (Ireland) Pension Fund for Wages Staff (Amendment) Scheme (Confirmation) Order, S.I. No. 9 of 1967
		Great Northern Railway Company (Ireland) Pension Fund for Wages Staff (Amendment) Scheme (Confirmation) Order, S.I. No. 60 of 1969
		Great Northern Railway Company (Ireland) Wages Staff Pension Fund Reserves (Amendment) Scheme (Confirmation) Order, S.I. No. 79 of 1971
		Great Northern Railway Company (Ireland) Pension Fund (Amendment) Scheme for Wages Staff (Confirmation) Order, S.I. No. 81 of 1971
		Great Northern Railway Company (Ireland) Pension Fund (Amendment) Scheme for Wages Staff (Confirmation) Order, S.I. No. 251 of 1974
	20	*Great Northern Railway Board (Dissolution) Order, S.I. No. 17 of 1981*
Great Southern Railways (Superannuation Scheme) Act, No. 21 of 1947	Sch. par. 54(2)	**Coras Iompair Eireann Salaried Officers' and Clerks' (G. S. R.) Superannuation Scheme (Amendment) Scheme, 1962 (Confirmation) Order, S.I. No. 220 of 1963**
		Coras Iompair Eireann Salaried Officers' and Clerks' (G. S. R.) Superannuation Scheme (Amendment) Scheme, 1968 (Confirmation) Order, S.I. No. 76 of 1971
		Coras Iompair Eireann Salaried Officers' and Clerks' (G. S. R.) Superannuation Scheme (Amendment) Scheme, 1973 (Confirmation) Order, S.I. No. 253 of 1974
		Coras Iompair Eireann Salaried Officers' and Clerks' (G. S. R.) Superannuation Scheme (Amendment) Scheme, 1976 (Confirmation) Order, S.I. No. 46 of 1977
		Coras Iompair Eireann Salaried Officers' and Clerks' (G. S. R.) Superannuation Scheme (Amendment) Scheme, 1981 (Confirmation) Order, S.I. No. 127 of 1981
		Coras Iompair Eireann Salaried Officers' and Clerks' (G. S. R.) Superannuation Scheme (Amendment) Scheme, 1982 (Confirmation) (No.2) Order, S.I. No. 346 of 1982
Greyhound Industry Act, No. 12 of 1958	2	*Greyhound Race Track (Levy Collection) Regulations, S.I. No. 225 of 1958*

Statutory Authority	Section	Statutory Instrument

Greyhound Industry Act, No. 12 of 1958 (*Cont.*)

Greyhound Race Track (Totalisator) (Quinella Treble Forecast) Regulations, S.I. No. 90 of 1966

Greyhound Race Track (Admission Charges) Regulations, S.I. No. 31 of 1967

Greyhound Race Track (Racing) Regulations, S.I. No. 133 of 1967

Greyhound Race Track (Racing) (Amendment) Regulations, S.I. No. 52 of 1968

Authorised Coursing Meetings (Exemption from Levy) Regulations, S.I. No. 170 of 1968

Greyhound Race Track (Levy Collection) Regulations, S.I. No. 198 of 1968

Greyhound Trainers (Amendment) Regulations, S.I. No. 1 of 1969

Greyhound Race Track (Admission Charges) Regulations, S.I. No. 103 of 1970

Greyhound Race Track (Permits for Persons Performing Specified Functions) Regulations, S.I. No. 289 of 1970

Greyhound Race Track (Race Card Charges) Regulations, S.I. No. 119 of 1972

Authorised Coursing Meetings (Exemption from Levy) Regulations, S.I. No. 223 of 1973

Public Sales of Greyhounds (Amendment) Regulations, S.I. No. 53 of 1974

Greyhound Race Track (Admission Charges) Regulations, S.I. No. 304 of 1975

Greyhound Race Track (Admission Charges) (Amendment) Regulations, S.I. No. 299 of 1977

Greyhound Race Track (Racing) (Amendment) Regulations, S.I. No. 324 of 1977

Authorised Coursing Meetings (Exemption from Levy) Regulations, S.I. No. 254 of 1978

Greyhound Race Track (Admission Charges) Regulations, S.I. No. 54 of 1979

Greyhound Race Track (Admission Charges) Regulations, S.I. No. 32 of 1980

Greyhound Race Track (Race Card Charges) Regulations, S.I. No. 33 of 1980

Greyhound Race Track (Admission Charges) (Amendment) Regulations, S.I. No. 150 of 1980

Greyhound Race Track (Race Card Charges) (Amendment) Regulations, S.I. No. 151 of 1980

Greyhound Trainers (Amendment) Regulations, S.I. No. 371 of 1980

Greyhound Race Track (Bookmakers Admission Charges) Regulations, S.I. No. 92 of 1981

Public Sales of Greyhounds (Amendment) Regulations, S.I. No. 418 of 1981

Greyhound Race Track (Racing) (Amendment) Regulations, S.I. No. 138 of 1982

Greyhound Race Track (Bookmakers Admission Charges) Regulations, S.I. No. 303 of 1982

Greyhound Industry Act, No. 12 of 1958 (*Cont.*)		**Authorised Coursing Meetings (Exemption from Levy) Regulations, S.I. No. 345 of 1983**
		Greyhound Race Track (Bookmakers Admission Charges) (Revocation) Regulations, S.I. No. 77 of 1984
		Greyhound Race Track (Totalisator) (Operating) (Amendment) Regulations, S.I. No. 227 of 1984
	13	**Greyhound Race Track (Racing) Regulations, S.I. No. 133 of 1967**
		Greyhound Race Track (Racing) (Amendment) Regulations, S.I. No. 52 of 1968
	21	*Greyhound Race Track (Appointed Day) Order, S.I. No. 2 of 1959*
	25	*Greyhound Race Track (Permits for Persons Performing Specified Functions) Regulations, S.I. No. 10 of 1959*
		Greyhound Race Track (Racing) Regulations, S.I. No. 64 of 1960
		Greyhound Race Track (Special Exemption) Regulations, S.I. No. 73 of 1963
		Greyhound Race Track (Racing) (Amendment) Regulations, S.I. No. 111 of 1963
		Greyhound Race Track (Racing) (Amendment) Regulations, S.I. No. 133 of 1965
		Greyhound Race Track (Racing) Regulations, S.I. No. 133 of 1967
		Greyhound Race Track (Racing) (Amendment) Regulations, S.I. No. 52 of 1968
		Greyhound Race Track (Permits for Persons Performing Specified Functions) Regulations, S.I. No. 289 of 1970
		Greyhound Race Track (Racing) (Amendment) Regulations, S.I. No. 324 of 1977
		Greyhound Race Track (Racing) (Amendment) Regulations, S.I. No. 144 of 1980
		Greyhound Race Track (Racing) (Amendment) Regulations, S.I. No. 138 of 1982
	26	*Greyhound Industry Act, 1958 (Commencement of Section 26) Order, S.I. No. 259 of 1958*
	27	*Greyhound Industry Act, 1958 (Appointed Day for Purposes of Chapter I of Part V) Order, S.I. No. 226 of 1958*
	31	*Greyhound Industry Act, 1958 (Commencement of Sections 32, 33, 34 and 35) Order, S.I. No. 227 of 1958*
	32	*Greyhound Race Track (Levy) (Percentage) Regulations, S.I. No. 228 of 1958*
		Greyhound Race Track (Levy) (Percentage) Regulations, S.I. No. 131 of 1964
		Greyhound Race Track (Levy) (Percentage) Regulations, S.I. No. 91 of 1977

Statutory Authority	Section	Statutory Instrument
Greyhound Industry Act, No. 12 of 1958 (*Cont.*)		*Greyhound Race Track (Levy) (Percentage) Regulations, S.I. No. 183 of 1980*
		Greyhound Race Track (Levy) (Percentage) Regulations, S.I. No. 79 of 1985
	33(1)	*Greyhound Race Track (Levy Collection) Regulations, S.I. No. 225 of 1958*
		Greyhound Race Track (Levy Collection) (Amendment) Regulations, S.I. No. 170 of 1964
		Greyhound Race Track (Levy Collection) Regulations, S.I. No. 198 of 1968
		Greyhound Race Track (Levy Collection) (Amendment) Regulations, S.I. No. 48 of 1971
	37	**Greyhound Trainers Regulations, S.I. No. 58 of 1961**
		Greyhound Trainers (Amendment) Regulations, S.I. No. 1 of 1969
		Greyhound Trainers (Amendment) Regulations, S.I. No. 371 of 1980
	38	*Public Sales of Greyhounds Regulations, S.I. No. 34 of 1963*
		Public Sales of Greyhounds Regulations, S.I. No. 76 of 1966
		Public Sales of Greyhounds (Amendment) Regulations, S.I. No. 53 of 1974
		Public Sales of Greyhounds (Amendment) Regulations, S.I. No. 418 of 1981
	40	*Greyhound Race Track (Totalisator) (Percentage) Regulations, S.I. No. 69 of 1971*
		Greyhound Race Track (Totalisator) (Percentage) Regulations, S.I. No. 90 of 1977
	40(2)	*Greyhound Race Track (Totalisator) (Percentage) Regulations, S.I. No. 67 of 1960*
		Greyhound Race Track (Totalisator) (Percentage) Regulations, S.I. No. 132 of 1964
		Greyhound Race Track (Totalisator) (Percentage) Regulations, S.I. No. 192 of 1983
		Greyhound Race Track (Totalisator) (Percentage) Regulations, S.I. No. 24 of 1984
	40(3)	*Greyhound Race Track (Totalisator) (Operating) Regulations, S.I. No. 65 of 1960*
		Greyhound Race Track (Totalisator) (Operating) (Amendment) Regulations, S.I. No. 33 of 1963
		Greyhound Race Track (Totalisator) (Quinella Treble Forecast) Regulations, S.I. No. 40 of 1964
		Greyhound Race Track (Totalisator) (Twin Double) Regulations, S.I. No. 89 of 1966
		Greyhound Race Track (Totalisator) (Quinella Treble Forecast) Regulations, S.I. No. 90 of 1966
		Greyhound Race Track (Totalisator) (Jackpot) Regulations, S.I. No. 104 of 1969

Statutory Authority	Section	Statutory Instrument
Greyhound Industry Act, No. 12 of 1958 (*Cont.*)		**Greyhound Race Track (Totalisator) (Operating) Regulations, S.I. No. 47 of 1971**
		Greyhound Race Track (Totalisator) (Trio) Regulations, S.I. No. 135 of 1982
	40(iii)	**Greyhound Race Track (Totalisator) (Operating) (Amendment) Regulations, S.I. No. 227 of 1984**
	48	*Greyhound Race Track (Admission Charges) Regulations, S.I. No. 77 of 1964*
		Greyhound Race Track (Admission Charges) Regulations, S.I. No. 31 of 1967
		Greyhound Race Track (Racing) Regulations, S.I. No. 133 of 1967
		Greyhound Race Track (Racing) (Amendment) Regulations, S.I. No. 52 of 1968
		Greyhound Race Track (Admission Charges) Regulations, S.I. No. 103 of 1970
		Greyhound Race Track (Admission Charges) Regulations, S.I. No. 360 of 1974
		Greyhound Race Track (Admission Charges) Regulations, S.I. No. 304 of 1975
		Greyhound Race Track (Admission Charges) Regulations, S.I. No. 54 of 1977
		Greyhound Race Track (Admission Charges) (Amendment) Regulations, S.I. No. 299 of 1977
		Greyhound Race Track (Admission Charges) Regulations, S.I. No. 54 of 1979
		Greyhound Race Track (Admission Charges) Regulations, S.I. No. 32 of 1980
		Greyhound Race Track (Admission Charges) (Amendment) Regulations, S.I. No. 150 of 1980
	48(1)	*Greyhound Race Track (Bookmakers Admission Charges) Regulations, S.I. No. 92 of 1981*
		Greyhound Race Track (Admission Charges) (Revocation) Regulations, S.I. No. 100 of 1982
		Greyhound Race Track (Bookmakers Admission Charges) Regulations, S.I. No. 303 of 1982
		Greyhound Race Track (Bookmakers Admission Charges) (Revocation) Regulations, S.I. No. 77 of 1984
	48(5)	*Greyhound Race Track (Race Card Charges) Regulations, S.I. No. 119 of 1972*
		Greyhound Race Track (Race Card Charges) Regulations, S.I. No. 53 of 1977
		Greyhound Race Track (Race Card Charges) Regulations, S.I. No. 33 of 1980
		Greyhound Race Track (Race Card Charges) (Amendment) Regulations, S.I. No. 151 of 1980
		Greyhound Race Track (Race Card Charges) (Revocation) Regulations, S.I. No. 102 of 1982
Hallmarking Act, No. 18 of 1981	3	**Hallmarking (Approved Hallmarks) Regulations, S.I. No. 327 of 1983**

Statutory Authority	Section	Statutory Instrument
Hallmarking Act, No. 18 of 1981 (*Cont.*)	7	**Hallmarking (Irish Standards of Fineness) Regulations, S.I. No. 328 of 1983**
	18	*Hallmarking Act, 1981 (Commencement) Order, S.I. No. 326 of 1983*
Hallmarking of Foreign Plate Act, No. 6 of 1904	1(1)	**Hallmarking of Imported Plate Order [Vol. XIII p. 1] S.R.& O. No. 254 of 1935**
Harbours Act, No. 9 of 1946		**Harbour Authority (Elections) Regulations, S.I. No. 106 of 1948**
	4	**Harbour Rates Order (Application Form) Regulations [Vol. XXXVII p. 481] S.R.& O. No. 164 of 1946**
	6	*Harbours Act, 1946 (Commencement of Part II) Order [Vol. XXXVII p. 507] S.R.& O. No. 114 of 1946*
		Harbours Act, 1946 (Commencement of Part II) (Bantry Bay Harbour Commissioners) Order, S.I. No. 144 of 1976
	7(3)	**Harbours Act (Live Stock Members) Order [Vol. XXXVII p. 495] S.R.& O. No. 172 of 1946**
	7(4)	*Harbours Act (Labour Members) Order [Vol. XXXVII p. 491] S.R.& O. No. 166 of 1946*
		Harbour Authorities (Labour Members) Order, S.I. No. 154 of 1960
	8	**Waterford Harbour Commissioners (Additional Local Authority Members) Order, S.I. No. 120 of 1955**
		Limerick Harbour Commissioners (Additional Local Authority Members) Order, S.I. No. 100 of 1958
		Drogheda Harbour Commissioners (Additional Local Authority Members) Order, S.I. No. 194 of 1970
		Limerick Harbour Commissioners (Additional Local Authority Members) Order, S.I. No. 233 of 1979
	11	*Harbours Act (Section 11 Direction) Order [Vol. XXXVII p. 499] S.R.& O. No. 167 of 1946*
		Harbours Act (Section 11 Direction) Order, S.I. No. 156 of 1950
		Harbours Act (Section 11 Direction) Order, S.I. No. 112 of 1955
		Harbour Authorities (Miscellaneous) (Non-Holding of Elections) Order, S.I. No. 145 of 1960
		Harbour Authorities (Miscellaneous) (Non-Holding of Elections) Order, S.I. No. 151 of 1967
		Harbour Authorities (Miscellaneous) (Non-Holding of Elections) Order, S.I. No. 163 of 1974
		Harbour Authorities (Miscellaneous) (Non-Holding of Elections) Order, S.I. No. 210 of 1979
		Harbour Authorities (Miscellaneous) (Non-Holding of Elections) Order, S.I. No. 253 of 1985

Statutory Authority	Section	Statutory Instrument
Harbours Act, No. 9 of 1946 (*Cont.*)	45	**Harbours Act, 1946 (Section 45) (Wicklow Harbour) Order, S.I. No. 160 of 1948**
		Harbours Act, 1946 (Section 45) (Baltimore and Skibereen Harbour) Order, S.I. No. 166 of 1948
		Harbours Act, 1946 (Section 45) (Dingle Harbour) Order, S.I. No. 324 of 1950
		Harbours Act, 1946 (Section 45) (New Ross Harbour) Order, 1948 (Revocation) Order, S.I. No. 59 of 1955
	104	**Harbour Rates (Galway Harbour) Order [Vol. XXXVII p. 443] S.R.& O. No. 162 of 1947**
		Harbour Rates (Drogheda Harbour) Order [Vol. XXXVII p. 409] S.R.& O. No. 228 of 1947
		Harbour Rates (Arklow Harbour) Order [Vol. XXXVII p. 375] S.R.& O. No. 266 of 1947
		Harbour Rates (Cork Harbour) (Rates on Chocolate and Cocoa) Order, S.I. No. 218 of 1948
		Harbour Rates (Wicklow Harbour) Order, S.I. No. 172 of 1949
		Harbour Rates (New Ross Harbour) Order, S.I. No. 230 of 1949
		Harbour Rates (Dundalk Cranage Rates) Order, S.I. No. 252 of 1949
		Harbour Rates (Dublin Port and Docks Board) (Rates for Watching Dangerous or Combustible Goods) Order, S.I. No. 343 of 1949
		Harbour Rates (Wexford Harbour) Order, S.I. No. 238 of 1950
		Harbour Rates (Ballina Harbour) Order, S.I. No. 279 of 1950
		Harbour Rates (Kinsale Harbour) Order, S.I. No. 8 of 1951
		Harbour Rates (Drogheda Harbour) Order, 1947 (Amendment) Order, S.I. No. 18 of 1951
		Harbour Rates (Fishing Vessels – Wexford Harbour) Order, S.I. No. 282 of 1951
		Harbour Rates (Kilrush Pier) Order, S.I. No. 15 of 1952
		Harbour Rates (Limerick Harbour) Order, S.I. No. 356 of 1953
		Harbour Rates (Sligo Port and Harbour) Order, S.I. No. 369 of 1953
		Harbour Rates (Waterford Harbour) Order, S.I. No. 225 of 1954
		Harbour Rates (Tralee and Fenit Pier and Harbour) Order, S.I. No. 266 of 1954
		Harbour Rates (Drogheda Harbour) Order, 1947 (Amendment) Order, S.I. No. 16 of 1955
		Harbour Rates (Foynes Harbour) Order, S.I. No. 63 of 1955
		Harbour Rates (Cork Harbour) (Rates on Steel Sheet and Residual Fuel Oil) Order, S.I. No. 70 of 1955

Statutory Authority	Section	Statutory Instrument

Harbours Act, No. 9 of 1946
(Cont.)

Harbour Rates (Wexford Harbour) Order, 1950 (Amendment) Order, S.I. No. 91 of 1955

Harbour Rates (Limerick Harbour) Order, S.I. No. 198 of 1955

Harbour Rates (Tralee and Fenit Pier and Harbour) Order, S.I. No. 208 of 1956

Harbour Rates (Westport Harbour) (Rates on Fertiliser) Order, S.I. No. 209 of 1956

Harbour Rates (Buncrana Harbour) Order, S.I. No. 220 of 1956

Harbour Rates (Westport Harbour) Order, S.I. No. 305 of 1956

Harbour Rates (Dublin Port and Docks Board) (Rates for Watching Dangerous or Combustible Goods) Order, S.I. No. 143 of 1957

Harbour Rates (Drogheda Harbour) Order, 1947 (Amendment) Order, S.I. No. 156 of 1957

Harbour Rates (Cork Port and Harbour) Order, 1940 (Amendment) Order, S.I. No. 168 of 1957

Harbour Rates (Galway Harbour) Order, 1947 (Amendment) Order, S.I. No. 183 of 1957

Harbour Rates (Cork Harbour) (Rates on New Motor Cars and Motor Vehicles) Order, S.I. No. 7 of 1958

Harbour Rates (Wexford Harbour) Order, 1950 (Amendment) Order, S.I. No. 45 of 1958

Harbour Rates (Limerick Harbour) Order, S.I. No. 113 of 1958

Harbour Rates (Harbours of Dublin, Skerries and Balbriggan) Order, S.I. No. 188 of 1958

Harbour Rates (Cork Port and Harbour) Order, 1940 (Amendment) Order, S.I. No. 1 of 1959

Harbour Rates (Limerick Harbour) Order, S.I. No. 80 of 1959

Harbour Rates (Drogheda Harbour) Order, 1947 (Amendment) Order, S.I. No. 138 of 1959

Harbour Rates (Westport Harbour) (Rates of Seaweed Meal) Order, S.I. No. 162 of 1959

Harbour Rates (Arklow Harbour) (Amendment) Order, S.I. No. 71 of 1960

Harbour Rates (Waterford Harbour) (Amendment) Order, S.I. No. 81 of 1960

Harbour Rates (Galway Harbour) Order, 1947 (Amendment) Order, S.I. No. 260 of 1960

Harbour Rates (Waterford Harbour) Order, S.I. No. 7 of 1961

Harbour Rates (Limerick Harbour) Order, S.I. No. 191 of 1961

Harbour Rates (Drogheda Harbour) Order, S.I. No. 227 of 1961

Harbour Rates (Dundalk Harbour) Order, S.I. No. 69 of 1962

Statutory Authority	Section	Statutory Instrument

Harbours Act, No. 9 of 1946
(*Cont.*)

Harbour Rates (Cork Port and Harbour) (Rates on Containers) Order, S.I. No. 107 of 1963

Harbour Rates (Waterford Port and Harbour) (Rates on Containers) Order, S.I. No. 215 of 1963

Harbour Rates (Waterford Cranage Rates) Order, S.I. No. 172 of 1964

Harbour Rates (Cork Port and Harbour) (Rates on Refractory Materials) Order, S.I. No. 242 of 1964

Harbour Rates (Dublin Harbour) Order, S.I. No. 68 of 1965

Harbour Rates (Sligo Harbour) Order, S.I. No. 136 of 1965

Harbour Rates (New Ross Harbour) Order, S.I. No. 192 of 1965

Harbour Rates (Drogheda Harbour) Order, S.I. No. 78 of 1966

Harbour Rates (Dublin Port and Docks Board) (Rates for Watching Dangerous or Combustible Goods) Order, S.I. No. 130 of 1966

Harbour Rates (New Ross Harbour) Order, S.I. No. 270 of 1966

Harbour Rates (Dundalk Harbour) Order, S.I. No. 160 of 1967

Harbour Rates (Sligo Port and Harbour) Order, S.I. No. 244 of 1967

Harbour Rates (Harbours of Dublin, Skerries and Balbriggan) Order, S.I. No. 187 of 1968

Harbour Rates (Waterford Port and Harbour) (Amendment) Order, S.I. No. 213 of 1968

Harbour Rates (Dundalk Cranage Rates) Order, S.I. No. 53 of 1969

Harbour Rates (Kinsale Harbour) Order, S.I. No. 103 of 1969

Harbour Rates (Dundalk Harbour) Order, S.I. No. 126 of 1969

Harbour Rates (Drogheda Harbour) Order, S.I. No. 128 of 1969

Harbour Rates (Foynes Harbour) Order, S.I. No. 256 of 1969

Harbour Rates (Tralee and Fenit Pier and Harbour) Order, S.I. No. 83 of 1970

Harbour Rates (Drogheda Harbour) Order, S.I. No. 157 of 1970

Harbour Rates (Youghal Harbour) Order, S.I. No. 190 of 1970

Harbour Rates (Cork Port and Harbour) Order, S.I. No. 192 of 1970

Harbour Rates (Tralee and Fenit Pier and Harbour) Order, S.I. No. 74 of 1971

Harbour Rates (Wicklow Harbour) Order, S.I. No. 255 of 1971

Harbour Rates (New Ross Harbour) Order, S.I. No. 33 of 1972

Harbours Act, No. 9 of 1946 (*Cont.*)		**Harbour Rates (Foynes Harbour) Order, S.I. No. 98 of 1972**
		Harbour Rates (Limerick Harbour) Order, S.I. No. 145 of 1972
		Harbour Rates (Waterford Port and Harbour) Order, S.I. No. 149 of 1972
		Harbour Rates (Cork Port and Harbour) Order, S.I. No. 166 of 1972
		Harbour Rates (Buncrana Harbour) Order, S.I. No. 212 of 1972
		Harbour Rates (Limerick Harbour) Order, S.I. No. 239 of 1972
		Harbour Rates (Dundalk Harbour) Order, S.I. No. 247 of 1972
		Harbour Rates (Dundalk Harbour) Order, S.I. No. 48 of 1973
		Harbour Rates (Cork Port and Harbour) Order, S.I. No. 151 of 1973
		Harbour Rates (Galway Harbour) Order, S.I. No. 301 of 1973
		Harbour Rates (Foynes Harbour) Order, S.I. No. 304 of 1973
		Harbour Rates (Tralee and Fenit Pier and Harbour) Order, S.I. No. 325 of 1973
		Harbour Rates (Galway Harbour) (No.2) Order, S.I. No. 329 of 1973
		Harbour Rates (New Ross Harbour) Order, S.I. No. 337 of 1973
		Harbour Rates (Limerick Harbour) Order, S.I. No. 12 of 1974
		Harbour Rates (Dublin Harbour) Order, S.I. No. 126 of 1974
		Harbour Rates (Cork Port and Harbour) Order, S.I. No. 232 of 1974
		Harbour Rates (Harbours of Dublin, Skerries and Balbriggan) Order, S.I. No. 269 of 1974
		Harbour Rates (Drogheda Harbour) Order, S.I. No. 330 of 1974
		Harbour Rates (New Ross Harbour) Order, S.I. No. 359 of 1974
		Harbour Rates (Waterford Port and Harbour) Order, S.I. No. 374 of 1974
		Harbour Rates (Kinsale Harbour) Order, S.I. No. 30 of 1975
		Harbour Rates (Cork Port and Harbour) Order, S.I. No. 75 of 1975
		Harbour Rates (Limerick Harbour) Order, S.I. No. 134 of 1975
		Harbour Rates (Cork Port and Harbour) (No.2) Order, S.I. No. 227 of 1975
		Harbour Rates (Tralee and Fenit Pier and Harbour) Order, S.I. No. 245 of 1975

Statutory Authority	Section	Statutory Instrument

Harbours Act, No. 9 of 1946
(*Cont.*)

Harbour Rates (Waterford Port and Harbour) Order, S.I. No. 329 of 1975

Harbour Rates (Dublin Harbour) Order, S.I. No. 5 of 1976

Harbour Rates (Harbours of Dublin, Skerries and Balbriggan) Order, S.I. No. 6 of 1976

Harbour Rates (Limerick Harbour) Order, S.I. No. 13 of 1976

Harbour Rates (Galway Harbour) Order, S.I. No. 108 of 1976

Harbour Rates (Drogheda Harbour) Order, S.I. No. 150 of 1976

Harbour Rates (Kinsale Harbour) Order, S.I. No. 154 of 1976

Harbour Rates (Sligo Port and Harbour) Order, S.I. No. 173 of 1976

Harbour Rates (Tralee and Fenit Pier and Harbour) Order, S.I. No. 225 of 1976

Harbour Rates (Harbours of Dublin, Skerries and Balbriggan) (No.2) Order, S.I. No. 244 of 1976

Harbour Rates (Foynes Harbour) Order, S.I. No. 275 of 1976

Harbour Rates (New Ross Harbour) Order, S.I. No. 5 of 1977

Harbour Rates (Harbours of Dublin, Skerries and Balbriggan) Order, S.I. No. 8 of 1977

Harbour Rates (Dublin Harbour) Order, S.I. No. 9 of 1977

Harbour Rates (Cork Port and Harbour) Order, S.I. No. 20 of 1977

Harbour Rates (Limerick Harbour) Order, S.I. No. 37 of 1977

Harbour Rates (Waterford Port and Harbour) Order, S.I. No. 63 of 1977

Harbour Rates (Youghal Harbour) Order, S.I. No. 149 of 1977

Harbour Rates (Galway Harbour) Order, S.I. No. 153 of 1977

Harbour Rates (Dundalk Harbour) Order, S.I. No. 160 of 1977

Harbour Rates (Wicklow Harbour) Order, S.I. No. 262 of 1977

Harbour Rates (Cork Port and Harbour) Order, S.I. No. 22 of 1978

Harbour Rates (Tralee and Fenit Pier and Harbour) Order, S.I. No. 81 of 1978

Harbour Rates (Ballina Harbour) Order, S.I. No. 88 of 1978

Harbour Rates (Dublin Harbour) Order, S.I. No. 115 of 1978

Harbour Rates (Waterford Port and Harbour) Order, S.I. No. 157 of 1978

Harbours Act, No. 9 of 1946
(*Cont.*)

Harbour Rates (Dublin Port and Docks Board) (Rates for Watching Dangerous or Combustible Goods) Order, S.I. No. 191 of 1978

Harbour Rates (Galway Harbour) Order, S.I. No. 318 of 1978

Harbour Rates (Cappa Pier at Kilrush) Order, S.I. No. 353 of 1978

Harbour Rates (Drogheda Harbour) Order, S.I. No. 364 of 1978

Harbour Rates (Harbours of Dublin, Skerries and Balbriggan) Order, S.I. No. 19 of 1979

Harbour Rates (Tralee and Fenit Pier and Harbour) Order, S.I. No. 24 of 1979

Harbour Rates (Dublin Harbour) Order, S.I. No. 88 of 1979

Harbour Rates (Harbours of Dublin, Skerries and Balbriggan) (No.2) Order, S.I. No. 89 of 1979

Harbour Rates (Cork Port and Harbour) Order, S.I. No. 94 of 1979

Harbour Rates (New Ross Harbour) Order, S.I. No. 28 of 1980

Harbour Rates (Dundalk Harbour) Order, S.I. No. 43 of 1980

Harbour Rates (Waterford Port and Harbour) Order, S.I. No. 84 of 1980

Harbour Rates (Dublin Harbour) Order, S.I. No. 110 of 1980

Harbour Rates (Cork Port and Harbour) Order, S.I. No. 121 of 1980

Harbour Rates (Harbours of Dublin, Skerries and Balbriggan) Order, S.I. No. 130 of 1980

Harbour Rates (Tralee and Fenit Pier and Harbour) Order, S.I. No. 223 of 1980

Harbour Rates (Kinsale Harbour) Order, S.I. No. 281 of 1980

Harbour Rates (Foynes Harbour) Order, S.I. No. 342 of 1980

Harbour Rates (Limerick Harbour) Order, S.I. No. 409 of 1980

Harbour Rates (Harbours of Dublin, Skerries and Balbriggan) (No.2) Order, S.I. No. 411 of 1980

Harbour Rates (Cork Port and Harbour) Order, S.I. No. 18 of 1981

Harbour Rates (Wicklow Harbour) Order, S.I. No. 54 of 1981

Harbour Rates (Arklow Harbour) Order, S.I. No. 62 of 1981

Harbour Rates (Harbours in County Donegal) Order, S.I. No. 76 of 1981

Harbour Rates (Dublin Harbour) Order, S.I. No. 79 of 1981

Harbour Rates (Baltimore and Skibbereen Harbour) Order, S.I. No. 83 of 1981

Statutory Authority	Section	Statutory Instrument

Harbours Act, No. 9 of 1946
(*Cont.*)

Harbour Rates (Waterford Port and Harbour) Order, S.I. No. 128 of 1981

Harbour Rates (Dundalk Harbour) Order, S.I. No. 141 of 1981

Harbour Rates (Galway Harbour) Order, S.I. No. 182 of 1981

Harbour Rates (Cappa Pier at Kilrush) Order, S.I. No. 221 of 1981

Harbour Rates (Tralee and Fenit Pier and Harbour Order, S.I. No. 224 of 1981

Harbour Rates (Limerick Harbour) Order, S.I. No. 233 of 1981

Harbour Rates (New Ross Harbour) Order, S.I. No. 413 of 1981

Harbour Rates (Dublin Port and Docks Board) (Rates for Watching Dangerous or Combustible Goods) Order, S.I. No. 440 of 1981

Harbour Rates (Wicklow Harbour) (No.2) Order, S.I. No. 443 of 1981

Harbour Rates (Harbours of Dublin, Skerries and Balbriggan) Order, S.I. No. 444 of 1981

Harbour Rates (Dublin Harbour) (No.2) Order, S.I. No. 445 of 1981

Harbour Rates (Cork Port and Harbour) (No.2) Order, S.I. No. 446 of 1981

Harbour Rates (Foynes Harbour) Order, S.I. No. 447 of 1981

Harbour Rates (Limerick Harbour) Order, S.I. No. 25 of 1982

Harbour Rates (Kinsale Harbour) Order, S.I. No. 36 of 1982

Harbour Rates (New Ross Harbour) Order, S.I. No. 56 of 1982

Harbour Rates (Drogheda Harbour) Order, S.I. No. 110 of 1982

Harbour Rates (Tralee and Fenit Pier and Harbour) Order, S.I. No. 206 of 1982

Harbour Rates (Galway Harbour) Order, S.I. No. 262 of 1982

Harbour Rates (Wicklow Harbour) Order, S.I. No. 362 of 1982

Harbour Rates (Dublin Port and Docks Board) (Rates for Watching of Combustible Goods) Order, S.I. No. 363 of 1982

Harbour Rates (Arklow Harbour) Order, S.I. No. 384 of 1982

Harbour Rates (Limerick Harbour) (No.2) Order, S.I. No. 389 of 1982

Harbour Rates (Harbours of Dublin, Skerries and Balbriggan) Order, S.I. No. 8 of 1983

Harbour Rates (Dublin Harbour) Order, S.I. No. 16 of 1983

Statutory Authority	Section	Statutory Instrument
Harbours Act, No. 9 of 1946 (*Cont.*)		*Harbour Rates (Cork Port and Harbour) Order, S.I. No. 26 of 1983*
		Harbour Rates (Waterford Port and Harbour) Order, S.I. No. 69 of 1983
		Harbour Rates (Foynes Harbour) Order, S.I. No. 98 of 1983
		Harbour Rates (Galway Harbour) Order, S.I. No. 168 of 1983
		Harbour Rates (Dundalk Harbour) Order, S.I. No. 185 of 1983
		Harbour Rates (Cappa Pier at Kilrush) Order, S.I. No. 218 of 1983
		Harbour Rates (Wicklow Harbour) Order, S.I. No. 386 of 1983
		Harbour Rates (Cork Port and Harbour) (No.2) Order, S.I. No. 387 of 1983
		Harbour Rates (Dublin Harbour) (No.2) Order, S.I. No. 390 of 1983
		Harbour Rates (Youghal Harbour) Order, S.I. No. 395 of 1983
		Harbour Rates (Harbours of Dublin, Skerries and Balbriggan) (No.2) S.I. No. 404 of 1983
		Harbour Rates (Limerick Harbour) Order, S.I. No. 414 of 1983
		Harbour Rates (Foynes Harbour) Order, S.I. No. 58 of 1984
		Harbour Rates (Galway Harbour) Order, S.I. No. 174 of 1984
		Harbour Rates (Arklow Harbour) Order, S.I. No. 184 of 1984
		Harbour Rates (Sligo Port and Harbour) Order, S.I. No. 295 of 1984
		Harbour Rates (Waterford Port and Harbour) Order, S.I. No. 330 of 1984
		Harbour Rates (Limerick Harbour) Order, S.I. No. 30 of 1985
		Harbour Rates (Harbours of Dublin, Skerries and Balbriggan) Order, S.I. No. 53 of 1985
		Harbour Rates (Tralee and Fenit Pier and Harbour) Order, S.I. No. 54 of 1985
		Harbour Rates (Dublin Harbour) Order, S.I. No. 64 of 1985
		Harbour Rates (Cork Port and Harbour) Order, S.I. No. 73 of 1985
		Harbour Rates (Foynes Harbour) Order, S.I. No. 76 of 1985
		Harbour Rates (Dublin Port and Docks Board) (Rates for Watching Dangerous or Combustible Goods) Order, S.I. No. 83 of 1985
		Harbour Rates (Wicklow Harbour) Order, S.I. No. 97 of 1985
		Harbour Rates (Galway Harbour) Order, S.I. No. 191 of 1985

Statutory Authority	Section	Statutory Instrument
Harbours Act, No. 9 of 1946 (*Cont.*)		*Harbour Rates (Cork Port and Harbour) (No.2) Order, S.I. No. 339 of 1985*
		Harbour Rates (Harbours of Dublin, Skerries and Balbriggan) (No.2) Order, S.I. No. 413 of 1985
		Harbour Rates (Cork Port and Harbour) Order, S.I. No. 2 of 1986
		Harbour Rates (Dundalk Harbour) Order, S.I. No. 4 of 1986
		Harbour Rates (Limerick Harbour) Order, S.I. No. 54 of 1986
		Harbour Rates (Harbours of Dublin, Skerries and Balbriggan) Order, S.I. No. 209 of 1986
		Harbour Rates (Galway Harbour) Order, S.I. No. 247 of 1986
		Harbour Rates (Drogheda Harbour) Order, S.I. No. 304 of 1986
		Harbour Rates (Sligo Port and Harbour) Order, S.I. No. 328 of 1986
		Harbour Rates (Cork Port and Harbour) (No.2) Order, S.I. No. 458 of 1986
		Harbour Rates (Dublin Harbour) Order, S.I. No. 459 of 1986
		Harbour Rates (Harbours of Dublin, Skerries and Balbriggan) (No.2) Order, S.I. No. 460 of 1986
		Harbour Rates (Wicklow Harbour) Order, S.I. No. 461 of 1986
	126	**Harbour Authority (Mortgage) Regulations, S.I. No. 56 of 1949**
	134	**Arklow Harbour Works Order, S.I. No. 125 of 1957**
		Sligo Harbour Works Order, S.I. No. 175 of 1957
		Wicklow Harbour Works Order, 1956 (Amendment) Order, S.I. No. 159 of 1959
		Drogheda Harbour Works Order, S.I. No. 102 of 1961
		Limerick Harbour Works Order, 1951 (Amendment) Order, S.I. No. 115 of 1961
		Limerick Harbour Works Order, S.I. No. 135 of 1963
		Cork Harbour Works Order, S.I. No. 150 of 1963
		Galway Harbour Works Order, S.I. No. 151 of 1963
		Cork Harbour Works Order, S.I. No. 146 of 1964
		Limerick Harbour Works Order, 1951 (Amendment) Order, S.I. No. 182 of 1964
		New Ross Harbour Works Order, S.I. No. 199 of 1964
		Wicklow Harbour Works Order, S.I. No. 200 of 1964
		Foynes Harbour Works Order, S.I. No. 26 of 1966
		Dublin Harbour Works Order, S.I. No. 242 of 1966
		Dublin Harbour Works Order, S.I. No. 203 of 1967
		Waterford Harbour Works Order, S.I. No. 245 of 1967

Statutory Authority	Section	Statutory Instrument
Harbours Act, No. 9 of 1946 (*Cont.*)		Cork Harbour Works Order, S.I. No. 177 of 1968
		Wicklow Harbour Works Order, S.I. No. 184 of 1968
		Dublin Harbour Works Order, S.I. No. 82 of 1969
		River Moy Harbour Works Order, S.I. No. 124 of 1969
		New Ross Harbour Works Order, S.I. No. 187 of 1969
		Drogheda Harbour Works Order, S.I. No. 91 of 1970
		New Ross Harbour Works Order, S.I. No. 152 of 1971
		Dundalk Harbour Works Order, S.I. No. 303 of 1971
		Limerick Harbour Works Order, S.I. No. 335 of 1971
		Cork Harbour Works Order, S.I. No. 90 of 1972
		Wexford Harbour Works Order, S.I. No. 175 of 1974
		Dublin Harbour Works Order, S.I. No. 31 of 1975
		Cork Harbour Works Order, S.I. No. 61 of 1975
		Drogheda Harbour Works Order, S.I. No. 72 of 1975
		Arklow Harbour Works Order, S.I. No. 210 of 1975
		Cork Harbour Works Order, S.I. No. 90 of 1976
		Dublin Harbour Works Order, (North Side) S.I. No. 338 of 1977
		Wicklow Harbour Works Order, S.I. No. 342 of 1977
		Dublin Harbour Works Order, 1966 (Amendment) Order, S.I. No. 245 of 1978
		Cork Harbour Works Order, S.I. No. 352 of 1978
		Drogheda Harbour Works Order, S.I. No. 366 of 1978
		Wicklow Harbour Works Order, S.I. No. 203 of 1979
		New Ross Harbour Works Order, S.I. No. 71 of 1980
		Dublin Harbour Works (Bridge) Order, S.I. No. 251 of 1980
		Dublin Harbour Works Order, (South Side) S.I. No. 351 of 1980
		Foynes Harbour Works Order, S.I. No. 145 of 1982
		Dublin Harbour Works (Alexandra Basin) Order, S.I. No. 179 of 1982
		Cork Harbour Works Order, S.I. No. 100 of 1984
		Wicklow Harbour Works Order, S.I. No. 176 of 1984
	146	Harbours Act, 1946 (Tralee and Fenit Pier and Harbour Commissioners) Order, S.I. No. 28 of 1952

Statutory Authority	Section	Statutory Instrument
Harbours Act, No. 9 of 1946 (*Cont.*)		**Harbours Act, 1946 (Cork Harbour Commissioners) Order, S.I. No. 146 of 1952**
		Harbours Act, 1946 (Wicklow Harbour Commissioners) Order, S.I. No. 184 of 1960
	178(1)	**Harbours Act, 1946 (Section 178 (1)) (Pier Roadway) Order, S.I. No. 420 of 1948**
		Harbours Act, 1946 (Section 178 (1)) (Wexford Roads) (No.1) Order, S.I. No. 289 of 1949
		Harbours Act, 1946 (Section 178 (1)) (Wexford Roads) (No.2) Order, S.I. No. 290 of 1949
	181	**Waterford Harbour (Water Bailiff's Fees) (Abolition) Order, S.I. No. 226 of 1954**
	183	**Harbours Act, 1946 (Abolition of Cocket and Entry Tax at Cork Harbour) Order [Vol. XXXVII p. 503] S.R.& O. No. 274 of 1947**
	Part VIII	**Limerick Harbour Works Order, S.I. No. 168 of 1951**
		Cork Harbour Works Order, S.I. No. 48 of 1952
		Dublin Harbour Works Order, 1950 (Amendment) Order, S.I. No. 213 of 1955
		Waterford Harbour Works Order [Vol. XXXVII p. 511] S.R.& O. No. 141 of 1947
		Waterford Port and Harbour Works Order [Vol. XXXVII p. 517] S.R.& O. No. 432 of 1947
		Cork Harbour Works Order, S.I. No. 111 of 1948
		Tralee and Fenit Pier and Harbour Works Order, S.I. No. 300 of 1948
		Killybegs Harbour Works Order, S.I. No. 392 of 1948
		Arklow Harbour Works Order, S.I. No. 111 of 1949
		Dublin Harbour Works Order, S.I. No. 282 of 1950
		Cork Harbour Works Order, S.I. No. 32 of 1951
		Waterford (Extension of Harbour Limits) Harbour Works Order, S.I. No. 66 of 1951
		Sligo Harbour Works Order, S.I. No. 283 of 1951
		Arklow Harbour Works Order, S.I. No. 44 of 1952
		Dundalk Harbour Works Order, S.I. No. 58 of 1953
		Wexford Harbour Works Order, S.I. No. 192 of 1953
		New Ross Harbour Works Order, S.I. No. 275 of 1953
		Arklow Harbour Works Order, 1952 (Amendment) Order, S.I. No. 34 of 1954
		Waterford Harbour Works Order, S.I. No. 176 of 1955
		Cork Harbour Works Order, S.I. No. 239 of 1955
		Cork Harbour Works Order, S.I. No. 198 of 1956
		Wicklow Harbour Works Order, S.I. No. 255 of 1956

Statutory Authority	Section	Statutory Instrument
Harbours Act, No. 34 of 1947	7(4)	**Kerry County Council (Assistance to Harbour Authority) Order, S.I. No. 214 of 1948**
	9(7)	*Harbour Authorities (Allowances to Members) Rules, S.I. No. 75 of 1961*
		Harbour Authorities (Allowances to Members) Rules, S.I. No. 31 of 1970
		Harbour Authorities (Allowances to Members) Rules, S.I. No. 257 of 1973
		Harbour Authorities (Allowances to Members) Rules, S.I. No. 185 of 1975
		Harbour Authorities (Allowances to Members) Rules, S.I. No. 144 of 1978
		Harbour Authorities (Allowances to Members) Rules, S.I. No. 109 of 1980
		Harbour Authorities (Allowances to Members) Rules, S.I. No. 356 of 1982
		Harbour Authorities (Allowances to Members) Rules, S.I. No. 7 of 1984
Harbours Act, No. 5 of 1976	2(2)	**Harbours Act, 1946 (Commencement of Part IV) (Bantry Bay Harbour Commissioners) Order, S.I. No. 124 of 1977**
		Harbours Act, 1946 (Commencement of Part VII) (Bantry Bay Harbour Commissioners) Order, S.I. No. 155 of 1977
Harbours, Docks and Piers (Temporary Increase of Charges) Act, No. 21 of 1920		*Waterford Harbour (Temporary Increase of Charges) Order [Vol. XIII p. 13] S.R.& O. No. 62 of 1925*
		Wexford Harbour (Temporary Increase of Charges) Order [Vol. XIII p. 17] S.R.& O. No. 25 of 1926
		Youghal Harbour (Temporary Increase of Charges) Order [Vol. XIII p. 21] S.R.& O. No. 35 of 1926
		Galway Harbour (Temporary Increase of Charges) Order [Vol. XIII p. 25] S.R.& O. No. 40 of 1926
		Dungarvan Harbour (Temporary Increase of Charges) Order [Vol. XIII p. 29] S.R.& O. No. 44 of 1926
		Dingle Harbour (Temporary Increase of Charges) Order [Vol. XIII p. 33] S.R.& O. No. 104 of 1927
		Wicklow Harbour (Temporary Increase of Charges) Order [Vol. XIII p. 37] S.R.& O. No. 18 of 1928
Harbours (Regulation of Rates) Act, No. 2 of 1934	3	*Harbour Rates (Port of Dublin) Order [Vol. XXXVII p. 523] S.R.& O. No. 39 of 1946*
		Harbour Rates (Grand Canal Docks) Order, S.I. No. 131 of 1948
		Harbour Rates (Dungarvan Harbour) Order, S.I. No. 198 of 1951
		Harbour Rates (Clogherhead and Carlingford Harbours and Gyles Quay Pier) Order, S.I. No. 293 of 1952

Harbours (Regulation of Rates) Act, No. 2 of 1934 (*Cont.*)		**Harbour Rates (Bantry Pier) Order, S.I. No. 215 of 1968**
		Harbour Rates (Clare Castle Pier) Order, S.I. No. 5 of 1970
	3(1)	*Harbour Rates (Cork Harbour, Rates on Crude Petroleum, Sugar Beet And Sugar Beet Pulp) Order [Vol. XIII p. 49] S.R.& O. No. 126 of 1935*
		Harbour Rates (Cork Harbour, Rates on Raw Rubber) Order [Vol. XIII p. 55] S.R.& O. No. 592 of 1935
		Harbour Rates (Cork Harbour, Import and Export Duties on Horses) Order [Vol. XIII p. 67] S.R.& O. No. 376 of 1936
		Harbour Rates (Limerick Harbour, Export Rate on Cement) Order [Vol. XIII p. 73] S.R.& O. No. 265 of 1937
		Harbour Rates (Harbour of Balbriggan Tonnage Rates and Goods Rates) Order [Vol. XIII p. 79] S.R.& O. No. 285 of 1937
		Harbour Rates (Cork Harbour, Rates on Steel, Semi-Manufactured and Spelter) Order [Vol. XXX p. 197] S.R.& O. No. 55 of 1940
		Harbour Rates (New Ross Port and Harbour) Order [Vol. XXX p. 269] S.R.& O. No. 284 of 1940
		Harbour Rates (Westport Port and Harbour) Order [Vol. XXX p. 329] S.R.& O. No. 389 of 1940
		Harbour Rates (Cork Port and Harbour) Order [Vol. XXX p. 203] S.R.& O. No. 390 of 1940
		Harbour Rates (Port of Dublin) Order [Vol. XXX p. 291] S.R.& O. No. 565 of 1941
		Harbour Rates (Kinsale Port and Harbour) Order [Vol. XXX p. 231] S.R.& O. No. 200 of 1942
		Harbour Rates (Waterford Port and Harbour) Order [Vol. XXX p. 321] S.R.& O. No. 343 of 1942
		Harbour Rates (Limerick Harbour) Order [Vol. XXX p. 237] S.R.& O. No. 469 of 1942
		Harbour Rates (Sligo Port and Harbour) Order [Vol. XXX p. 297] S.R.& O. No. 43 of 1943
		Harbour Rates (Dingle Harbour) Order [Vol. XXX p. 221] S.R.& O. No. 83 of 1943
		Harbour Rates (Baltimore and Skibbereen Harbour) Order [Vol. XXX p. 181] S.R.& O. No. 208 of 1943
		Harbour Rates (Youghal Harbour) Order [Vol. XXX p. 335] S.R.& O. No. 346 of 1943
		Harbour Rates (Cork Harbour) (Rates on Dogs) Order [Vol. XXX p. 191] S.R.& O. No. 79 of 1945
		Harbour Rates (Rosslare Harbour) Order, S.I. No. 59 of 1956

Statutory Authority	Section	Statutory Instrument
Harbours (Regulation of Rates) Act, No. 2 of 1934 (*Cont.*)	3(2)	**Dungarvan Harbour (Temporary Increase of Charges) Order, 1926 (Amendment) Order [Vol. XIII p. 61] S.R.& O. No. 308 of 1936**
		Harbour Rates (Cork Port and Harbour) Order, 1940 (Amendment) Order [Vol. XXX p. 215] S.R.& O. No. 561 of 1941
	11	**Harbours (Regulation of Rates) Act, 1934, Order [Vol. XIII p. 41] S.R.& O. No. 147 of 1934**
Health Act, No. 28 of 1947		*Infectious Diseases Regulations, S.I. No. 99 of 1948*
		Infectious Diseases (Aircraft) Regulations, S.I. No. 136 of 1948
		Infectious Diseases (Shipping) Regulations, S.I. No. 170 of 1948
		Health (Compulsory Acquisition of Land) Regulations, S.I. No. 314 of 1948
		Infectious Diseases (Amendment) Regulations, S.I. No. 353 of 1948
		Prohibition from School Attendance (Notices) Regulations, S.I. No. 371 of 1948
		Infectious Diseases (Temporary Provisions) Regulations, S.I. No. 107 of 1949
		Infectious Diseases (Temporary Provisions) Regulations, 1949 (Revocation) Regulations, S.I. No. 149 of 1949
		Infectious Diseases (Amendment) Regulations, S.I. No. 351 of 1949
		Food Hygiene Regulations, S.I. No. 205 of 1950
		Infectious Diseases (Amendment) Regulations, S.I. No. 318 of 1951
		Infectious Diseases (Temporary Provisions) Regulations, S.I. No. 53 of 1952
		Infectious Diseases (Temporary Provisions) Regulations, 1952 (Revocation) Regulations, S.I. No. 166 of 1952
		Food Hygiene (Amendment) Regulations, S.I. No. 289 of 1952
		Infectious Diseases (Amendment) Regulations, S.I. No. 291 of 1952
	3	*Health Act, 1947 (Date of Commencement) Order [Vol. XXXVII p. 529] S.R.& O. No. 342 of 1947*
		Health Act, 1947 (Date of Commencement) (No.1) Order, S.I. No. 19 of 1948
		Health Act, 1947 (Date of Commencement) (No.2) Order, S.I. No. 98 of 1948
		Health Act, 1947 (Date of Commencement) Order, S.I. No. 14 of 1951
		Health (Vinyl Chloride in Food) Regulations, S.I. No. 95 of 1984
		Health (Emulsifiers, Stabilisers, Thickening and Gelling Agents in Food) Regulations, S.I. No. 186 of 1985

Statutory Authority	Section	Statutory Instrument
Health Act, No. 28 of 1947 *(Cont.)*	4	**Health Services (No.4) Regulations, S.I. No. 389 of 1983**
	5	**Food Standards (Ice-Cream) Regulations, S.I. No. 227 of 1952**
		Medical Preparations (Cortisone and A. C. T. H.) Regulations, S.I. No. 324 of 1952
		Maternity Cash Grants Regulations, S.I. No. 410 of 1953
		Medical Preparations (Barbiturates) Regulations, S.I. No. 30 of 1954
		Milk for Mothers and Children Regulations, S.I. No. 97 of 1954
		Disabled Persons (Maintenance Allowances) Regulations, S.I. No. 207 of 1954
		General Institutional and Specialist Services (Amendment) Regulations, S.I. No. 47 of 1955
		Maternity and Child Health Services (Amendment) Regulations, S.I. No. 48 of 1955
		General Medical Services (Amendment) Regulations, S.I. No. 49 of 1955
		General Institutional and Specialist Services (Amendment) Regulations, S.I. No. 43 of 1956
		Maternity and Child Health Services (Amendment) Regulations, S.I. No. 44 of 1956
		Maternity and Child Health Services (Amendment) (No.2) Regulations, S.I. No. 142 of 1956
		Medical Preparations (Oral Diabetic Treatments) Regulations, S.I. No. 203 of 1956
		Disabled Persons (Maintenance Allowances) (Amendment) Regulations, S.I. No. 51 of 1957
		Medical Preparations (Advertisement and Sale) Regulations, S.I. No. 135 of 1958
		Maternity and Child Health Services (Amendment) Regulations, S.I. No. 265 of 1958
		General Institutional and Specialist Services (Amendment) Regulations, S.I. No. 266 of 1958
		Disabled Persons (Maintenance Allowances) Regulations, S.I. No. 261 of 1960
		Infectious Diseases (Maintenance) Regulations, S.I. No. 132 of 1962
		Disabled Persons (Maintenance Allowances) (Amendment) Regulations, S.I. No. 133 of 1962
		Medical Preparations (Control of Sale) (Temporary) Regulations, S.I. No. 199 of 1962
		Medical Preparations (Control of Sale) Regulations, S.I. No. 82 of 1963
		Disabled Persons (Rehabilitation) Regulations, S.I. No. 141 of 1963
		Disabled Persons (Maintenance Allowances) Regulations, S.I. No. 142 of 1963
		Infectious Diseases (Maintenance) Regulations, S.I. No. 200 of 1963

Health Act, No. 28 of 1947
(*Cont.*)

Maternity and Child Health Services (Amendment) Regulations, S.I. No. 158 of 1964

Disabled Persons (Maintenance Allowances) (Amendment) Regulations, S.I. No. 192 of 1964

Infectious Diseases (Maintenance) Regulations, S.I. No. 193 of 1964

Infectious Diseases (Maintenance) Regulations, S.I. No. 175 of 1965

Disabled Persons (Maintenance Allowances) (Amendment) Regulations, S.I. No. 176 of 1965

Institutional Assistance Regulations, S.I. No. 177 of 1965

General Institutional and Specialist Services (Amendment) Regulations, S.I. No. 69 of 1966

Maternity and Child Health Services (Amendment) Regulations, S.I. No. 70 of 1966

Maternity and Child Health Services (Amendment) (No.2) Regulations, S.I. No. 105 of 1966

Infectious Diseases (Maintenance) (Amendment) Regulations, S.I. No. 243 of 1966

Medical Preparations (Control of Sale) Regulations, S.I. No. 261 of 1966

Disabled Persons (Maintenance Allowances) (Amendment) Regulations, S.I. No. 188 of 1967

Infectious Diseases (Maintenance) Regulations, S.I. No. 189 of 1967

Infectious Diseases (Amendment) Regulations, S.I. No. 258 of 1967

General Institutional and Specialist Services (Amendment) Regulations, S.I. No. 57 of 1968

Infectious Diseases (Amendment) Regulations, S.I. No. 114 of 1968

Infectious Diseases (Maintenance) Regulations, S.I. No. 154 of 1968

Disabled Persons (Maintenance Allowances) (Amendment) Regulations, S.I. No. 155 of 1968

Disabled Persons (Maintenance Allowances) (Amendment) Regulations, S.I. No. 142 of 1969

Infectious Diseases (Maintenance) Regulations, S.I. No. 143 of 1969

Medical Preparations (Control of Amphetamine) Regulations, S.I. No. 244 of 1969

Health (Cyclamate in Food) Regulations, S.I. No. 49 of 1970

Health (Sampling of Food) Regulations, S.I. No. 50 of 1970

Medical Preparations (Control of Amphetamine) (Amendment) Regulations, S.I. No. 137 of 1970

Infectious Diseases (Maintenance) Regulations, S.I. No. 168 of 1970

Disabled Persons (Maintenance Allowances) (Amendment) Regulations, S.I. No. 169 of 1970

Health Services Regulations, S.I. No. 105 of 1971

Disabled Persons (Maintenance Allowances) (Amendment) Regulations, S.I. No. 207 of 1971

Health Act, No. 28 of 1947
(*Cont.*)

Infectious Diseases (Maintenance) Regulations, S.I. No. 208 of 1971

Medical Preparations (Control of Sale) (Amendment) Regulations, S.I. No. 272 of 1971

Health Services (Amendment) Regulations, S.I. No. 277 of 1971

Food Hygiene (Amendment) Regulations, S.I. No. 322 of 1971

Health (Colouring Matter in Food) Regulations, S.I. No. 41 of 1972

Health (Antioxidant in Food) Regulations, S.I. No. 42 of 1972

Health (Preservatives in Food) Regulations, S.I. No. 43 of 1972

Health (Arsenic and Lead in Food) Regulations, S.I. No. 44 of 1972

Health (Mineral Hydrocarbons in Food) Regulations, S.I. No. 45 of 1972

Public Health (Preservatives, etc., in Food) Regulations 1928 and 1943 (Amendment) Regulations, S.I. No. 46 of 1972

Health Services Regulations, S.I. No. 88 of 1972

Disabled Persons (Maintenance Allowances) Regulations, S.I. No. 168 of 1972

Infectious Diseases (Maintenance) Regulations, S.I. No. 169 of 1972

Maternity Cash Grants Regulations, S.I. No. 241 of 1972

Health (Colouring in Food) (Amendment) Regulations, S.I. No. 301 of 1972

Health (Preservatives in Food) (Amendment) Regulations, S.I. No. 302 of 1972

Health (Antioxidant in Food) (Amendment) Regulations, S.I. No. 303 of 1972

Health (Solvents in Food) Regulations, S.I. No. 304 of 1972

Health (Preservatives in Food) Regulations, S.I. No. 147 of 1973

Health (Antioxidant in Food) Regulations, S.I. No. 148 of 1973

Health (Colouring Agents in Food) Regulations, S.I. No. 149 of 1973

Disabled Persons (Maintenance Allowances) Regulations, S.I. No. 160 of 1973

Infectious Diseases (Maintenance) Regulations, S.I. No. 161 of 1973

Health Services Regulations, S.I. No. 184 of 1973

Health Service Regulations, S.I. No. 90 of 1974

Disabled Persons (Maintenance Allowances) (Amendment) Regulations, S.I. No. 185 of 1974

Infectious Diseases (Maintenance) Regulations, S.I. No. 186 of 1974

Health Act, No. 28 of 1947
(*Cont.*)

Medical Preparations (Licensing of Manufacture) Regulations, S.I. No. 225 of 1974

Medical Preparations (Wholesale Licences) Regulations, S.I. No. 333 of 1974

Disabled Persons (Maintenance Allowances) (Amendment) Regulations, S.I. No. 39 of 1975

Infectious Diseases (Maintenance) Regulations, S.I. No. 40 of 1975

Health Services (Amendment) Regulations, S.I. No. 64 of 1975

Health Services Regulations, 1972 (Amendment) Regulations, S.I. No. 181 of 1975

Infectious Diseases (Maintenance) (Amendment) Regulations, S.I. No. 220 of 1975

Disabled Persons (Maintenance Allowances) (Amendment) (No.2) Regulations, S.I. No. 221 of 1975

Medical Preparations (Licensing of Manufacture) (Amendment) Regulations, S.I. No. 302 of 1975

Disabled Persons (Maintenance Allowances) (Amendment) Regulations, S.I. No. 67 of 1976

Infectious Diseases (Maintenance) Regulations, S.I. No. 68 of 1976

Medical Preparations (Control of Sale) (Amendment) Regulations, S.I. No. 82 of 1976

Health Services Regulations, S.I. No. 97 of 1976

Health Services (Amendment) Regulations, S.I. No. 142 of 1976

Health (Charges for In-patient Services) Regulations, S.I. No. 180 of 1976

Infectious Diseases (Amendment) Regulations, S.I. No. 214 of 1976

Disabled Persons (Maintenance Allowances) (Amendment) (No.2) Regulations, S.I. No. 260 of 1976

Infectious Diseases (Maintenance) (No.2) Regulations, S.I. No. 261 of 1976

Disabled Persons (Maintenance Allowances) (Amendment) Regulations, S.I. No. 79 of 1977

Infectious Diseases (Maintenance) Regulations, S.I. No. 80 of 1977

Disabled Persons (Maintenance Allowances) (Amendment) (No.2) Regulations, S.I. No. 314 of 1977

Infectious Diseases (Maintenance) (No.2) Regulations, S.I. No. 315 of 1977

Disabled Persons (Maintenance Allowances) (Amendment) Regulations, S.I. No. 54 of 1978

Infectious Diseases (Maintenance) Regulations, S.I. No. 55 of 1978

Health (Erucic Acid in Food) Regulations, S.I. No. 123 of 1978

Health Act, No. 28 of 1947
(*Cont.*)

Health (Colouring Agents in Food) (Amendment) Regulations, S.I. No. 140 of 1978

Health Services Regulations, S.I. No. 371 of 1978

Infectious Diseases (Maintenance) Regulations, S.I. No. 78 of 1979

Disabled Persons (Maintenance Allowances) (Amendment) Regulations, S.I. No. 79 of 1979

Health Services Regulations, S.I. No. 109 of 1979

Health Services (No.2) Regulations, S.I. No. 134 of 1979

Disabled Persons (Maintenance Allowances) (Amendment) (No.2) Regulations, S.I. No. 338 of 1979

Infectious Diseases (Maintenance) (No.2) Regulations, S.I. No. 339 of 1979

Health (Emulsifiers, Stabilisers, Thickening and Gelling Agents in Food) Regulations, S.I. No. 35 of 1980

Health Services Regulations, S.I. No. 61 of 1980

Infectious Diseases (Maintenance) Regulations, S.I. No. 91 of 1980

Disabled Persons (Maintenance Allowances) (Amendment) Regulations, S.I. No. 92 of 1980

Health Services (Amendment) Regulations, S.I. No. 93 of 1980

Medical Preparations (Amendment of Fees) Regulations, S.I. No. 241 of 1980

Infectious Diseases (Amendment) Regulations, S.I. No. 322 of 1980

Disabled Persons (Maintenance Allowances) (Amendment) (No.2) Regulations, S.I. No. 367 of 1980

Infectious Diseases (Maintenance) (Amendment) Regulations, S.I. No. 368 of 1980

Infectious Diseases (Maintenance) Regulations, S.I. No. 99 of 1981

Disabled Persons (Maintenance Allowances) (Amendment) Regulations, S.I. No. 100 of 1981

Health Services (Amendment) Regulations, S.I. No. 173 of 1981

Health Services Regulations, S.I. No. 267 of 1981

Health (Colouring Agents in Food) (Amendment) Regulations, S.I. No. 336 of 1981

Health (Preservatives in Food) Regulations, S.I. No. 337 of 1981

Disabled Persons (Maintenance Allowances) (Amendment) (No.2) Regulations, S.I. No. 341 of 1981

Infectious Diseases (Maintenance) (No.2) Regulations, S.I. No. 342 of 1981

Infectious Diseases Regulations, S.I. No. 390 of 1981

Disabled Persons (Maintenance Allowances) (Amendment) (No.3) Regulations, S.I. No. 407 of 1981

Statutory Authority	Section	Statutory Instrument

Health Act, No. 28 of 1947
(*Cont.*)

Infectious Diseases (Maintenance) (No.3) Regulations, S.I. No. 408 of 1981

Infectious Diseases (Maintenance) Regulations, S.I. No. 76 of 1982

Disabled Persons (Maintenance Allowances) (Amendment) Regulations, S.I. No. 77 of 1982

Health Services (Amendment) Regulations, S.I. No. 151 of 1982

Health (Foods for Particular Nutritional Uses) Regulations, S.I. No. 272 of 1982

Health (Emulsifiers, Stabilisers, Thickening and Gelling Agents) (Amendment) Regulations, S.I. No. 273 of 1982

Health Services Regulations, S.I. No. 283 of 1982

Infectious Diseases (Maintenance) (No.2) Regulations, S.I. No. 284 of 1982

Disabled Persons (Maintenance Allowances) (Amendment) (No.2) Regulations, S.I. No. 285 of 1982

Infectious Diseases (Maintenance) (No.3) Regulations, S.I. No. 339 of 1982

Disabled Persons (Maintenance Allowances) (Amendment) (No.3) Regulations, S.I. No. 340 of 1982

Health Services Regulations, S.I. No. 54 of 1983

Medical Preparations (Amendment of Fees) Regulations, S.I. No. 56 of 1983

Health (Antioxidant in Food) (Amendment) Regulations, S.I. No. 61 of 1983

Health Services (No.2) Regulations, S.I. No. 139 of 1983

Disabled Persons (Maintenance Allowances) (Amendment) Regulations, S.I. No. 154 of 1983

Infectious Diseases (Maintenance) Regulations, S.I. No. 155 of 1983

Disabled Persons (Maintenance Allowances) (Amendment) (No.2) Regulations, S.I. No. 361 of 1983

Health Services (No.3) Regulations, S.I. No. 381 of 1983

Disabled Persons (Maintenance Allowances) Regulations, S.I. No. 71 of 1984

Medical Preparations (Amendment of Fees) Regulations, S.I. No. 85 of 1984

Health (Hospital In-Patient Charges) Regulations, S.I. No. 94 of 1984

Health (Vinyl Chloride in Food) Regulations, S.I. No. 95 of 1984

Health Services (Amendment) Regulations, S.I. No. 123 of 1984

Infectious Diseases (Maintenance) Regulations, S.I. No. 135 of 1984

Health Act, No. 28 of 1947
(*Cont.*)

Medical Preparations (Licensing Advertisement and Sale) Regulations, S.I. No. 210 of 1984

Disabled Persons (Maintenance Allowances) (No.2) Regulations, S.I. No. 305 of 1984

Health Services (Amendment) Regulations, S.I. No. 145 of 1985

Medical Preparations (Amendment of Fees) Regulations, S.I. No. 159 of 1985

Health (Emulsifiers, Stabilisers, Thickening and Gelling Agents in Food) Regulations, S.I. No. 186 of 1985

Infectious Diseases (Maintenance) Regulations, S.I. No. 189 of 1985

Disabled Persons (Maintenance Allowances) (Amendment) Regulations, S.I. No. 190 of 1985

Infectious Diseases (Amendment) Regulations, 1985, S.I. No. 268 of 1985

Infectious Diseases (Maintenance) (No.2) Regulations, S.I. No. 372 of 1985

Disabled Persons (Maintenance Allowances) (No.2) Regulations, S.I. No. 373 of 1985

Medical Preparations (Amendment of Fees) Regulations, S.I. No. 49 of 1986

Health Services (Amendment) Regulations, S.I. No. 109 of 1986

Health (Hospital In-patient Charges) (Amendment) Regulations, S.I. No. 221 of 1986

Infectious Diseases (Maintenance) Regulations, S.I. No. 228 of 1986

Disabled Persons (Maintenance Allowances) (Amendment) Regulations, S.I. No. 252 of 1986

Disabled Persons (Maintenance Allowances) (No.2) Regulations, S.I. No. 403 of 1986

Infectious Diseases (Maintenance) (No.2) Regulations, S.I. No. 404 of 1986

7   **Dublin Public Assistance Authorities (Health Functions) Order, S.I. No. 72 of 1956**

South Cork Board of Public Assistance (Health Functions) Order, S.I. No. 73 of 1956

Waterford Board of Public Assistance (Health Functions) Order, S.I. No. 74 of 1956

Dublin Public Assistance Authorities (Health Functions) Order, S.I. No. 268 of 1958

South Cork Board of Public Assistance (Health Functions) Order, S.I. No. 269 of 1958

Waterford Board of Public Assistance (Health Functions) Order, S.I. No. 270 of 1958

15   *Bray Urban District Council (Transfer of Institution) Order, S.I. No. 102 of 1948*

16   *Hospital of Saint Margaret of Cortona Transfer Order, S.I. No. 77 of 1951*

Statutory Authority	Section	Statutory Instrument

Health Act, No. 28 of 1947
(*Cont.*)

Infectious Diseases (Maintenance) Regulations, S.I. No. 143 of 1969

Infectious Diseases (Maintenance) Regulations, S.I. No. 168 of 1970

Infectious Diseases (Maintenance) Regulations, S.I. No. 208 of 1971

Infectious Diseases (Maintenance) Regulations, S.I. No. 169 of 1972

Infectious Diseases (Maintenance) Regulations, S.I. No. 161 of 1973

Infectious Diseases (Maintenance) Regulations, S.I. No. 186 of 1974

Infectious Diseases (Maintenance) Regulations, S.I. No. 40 of 1975

Infectious Diseases (Maintenance) (Amendment) Regulations, S.I. No. 220 of 1975

Infectious Diseases (Maintenance) Regulations, S.I. No. 68 of 1976

Infectious Diseases (Maintenance) (No.2) Regulations, S.I. No. 261 of 1976

Infectious Diseases (Maintenance) Regulations, S.I. No. 80 of 1977

Infectious Diseases (Maintenance) (No.2) Regulations, S.I. No. 315 of 1977

Infectious Diseases (Maintenance) Regulations, S.I. No. 55 of 1978

Infectious Diseases (Maintenance) Regulations, S.I. No. 78 of 1979

Infectious Diseases (Maintenance) (No.2) Regulations, S.I. No. 339 of 1979

Infectious Diseases (Maintenance) Regulations, S.I. No. 91 of 1980

Infectious Diseases (Maintenance) (Amendment) Regulations, S.I. No. 368 of 1980

Infectious Diseases (Maintenance) Regulations, S.I. No. 99 of 1981

Infectious Diseases (Maintenance) (No.2) Regulations, S.I. No. 342 of 1981

Infectious Diseases (Maintenance) (No.3) Regulations, S.I. No. 408 of 1981

Infectious Diseases (Maintenance) Regulations, S.I. No. 76 of 1982

Infectious Diseases (Maintenance) (No.2) Regulations, S.I. No. 284 of 1982

Infectious Diseases (Maintenance) (No.3) Regulations, S.I. No. 339 of 1982

Infectious Diseases (Maintenance) Regulations, S.I. No. 155 of 1983

Infectious Diseases (Maintenance) (No.2) Regulations, S.I. No. 362 of 1983

Infectious Diseases (Maintenance) Regulations, S.I. No. 135 of 1984

Health Act, No. 28 of 1947
(*Cont.*)

Disabled Persons (Maintenance Allowances) (No.3) Regulations, S.I. No. 306 of 1984

Infectious Diseases (Maintenance) Regulations, S.I. No. 189 of 1985

Infectious Diseases (Maintenance) (No.2) Regulations, S.I. No. 372 of 1985

Infectious Diseases (Maintenance) Regulations, S.I. No. 228 of 1986

Infectious Diseases (Maintenance) (No.2) Regulations, S.I. No. 404 of 1986

54   **Food Hygiene (Amendment) Regulations, S.I. No. 24 of 1961**

Health (Cyclamate in Food) Regulations, S.I. No. 49 of 1970

Health (Sampling of Food) Regulations, S.I. No. 50 of 1970

Food Hygiene (Amendment) Regulations, S.I. No. 322 of 1971

Health (Colouring Matter in Food) Regulations, S.I. No. 41 of 1972

Health (Antioxidant in Food) Regulations, S.I. No. 42 of 1972

Health (Preservatives in Food) Regulations, S.I. No. 43 of 1972

Health (Arsenic and Lead in Food) Regulations, S.I. No. 44 of 1972

Health (Mineral Hydrocarbons in Food) Regulations, S.I. No. 45 of 1972

Public Health (Preservatives, etc., in Food) Regulations 1928 and 1943 (Amendment) Regulations, S.I. No. 46 of 1972

Health (Colouring in Food) (Amendment) Regulations, S.I. No. 301 of 1972

Health (Preservatives in Food) (Amendment) Regulations, S.I. No. 302 of 1972

Health (Antioxidant in Food) (Amendment) Regulations, S.I. No. 303 of 1972

Health (Solvents in Food) Regulations, S.I. No. 304 of 1972

Health (Preservatives in Food) Regulations, S.I. No. 147 of 1973

Health (Antioxidant in Food) Regulations, S.I. No. 148 of 1973

Health (Colouring Agents in Food) Regulations, S.I. No. 149 of 1973

Health (Erucic Acid in Food) Regulations, S.I. No. 123 of 1978

Health (Colouring Agents in Food) (Amendment) Regulations, S.I. No. 140 of 1978

Health (Emulsifiers, Stabilisers, Thickening and Gelling Agents in Food) Regulations, S.I. No. 35 of 1980

Statutory Authority	Section	Statutory Instrument

Health Act, No. 28 of 1947
(*Cont.*)

Health (Colouring Agents in Food) (Amendment) Regulations, S.I. No. 336 of 1981

Health (Preservatives in Food) Regulations, S.I. No. 337 of 1981

Health (Foods for Particular Nutritional Uses) Regulations, S.I. No. 272 of 1982

Health (Emulsifiers, Stabilisers, Thickening and Gelling Agents) (Amendment) Regulations, S.I. No. 273 of 1982

Health (Antioxidant in Food) (Amendment) Regulations, S.I. No. 61 of 1983

Health (Vinyl Chloride in Food) Regulations, S.I. No. 95 of 1984

Health (Emulsifiers, Stabilisers, Thickening and Gelling Agents in Food) Regulations, S.I. No. 186 of 1985

56 **Food Standards (Ice-cream) Regulations, S.I. No. 227 of 1952**

Health (Sampling of Food) Regulations, S.I. No. 50 of 1970

Health (Preservatives in Food) Regulations, S.I. No. 337 of 1981

58 **Health (Sampling of Food) Regulations, S.I. No. 50 of 1970**

Food Hygiene (Amendment) Regulations, S.I. No. 322 of 1971

Health (Preservatives in Food) Regulations, S.I. No. 147 of 1973

59 **Health (Cyclamate in Food) Regulations, S.I. No. 49 of 1970**

Health (Sampling of Food) Regulations, S.I. No. 50 of 1970

Food Hygiene (Amendment) Regulations, S.I. No. 322 of 1971

Health (Colouring Matter in Food) Regulations, S.I. No. 41 of 1972

Health (Antioxidant in Food) Regulations, S.I. No. 42 of 1972

Health (Preservatives in Food) Regulations, S.I. No. 43 of 1972

Health (Arsenic and Lead in Food) Regulations, S.I. No. 44 of 1972

Health (Mineral Hydrocarbons in Food) Regulations, S.I. No. 45 of 1972

Health (Colouring in Food) (Amendment) Regulations, S.I. No. 301 of 1972

Health (Preservatives in Food) (Amendment) Regulations, S.I. No. 302 of 1972

Health (Antioxidant in Food) (Amendment) Regulations, S.I. No. 303 of 1972

Health (Solvents in Food) Regulations, S.I. No. 304 of 1972

Health Act, No. 28 of 1947
(*Cont.*)

Health (Preservatives in Food) Regulations, S.I. No. 147 of 1973

Health (Antioxidant in Food) Regulations, S.I. No. 148 of 1973

Health (Colouring Agents in Food) Regulations, S.I. No. 149 of 1973

Health (Erucic Acid in Food) Regulations, S.I. No. 123 of 1978

Health (Colouring Agents in Food) (Amendment) Regulations, S.I. No. 140 of 1978

Health (Emulsifiers, Stabilisers, Thickening and Gelling Agents in Food) Regulations, S.I. No. 35 of 1980

Health (Colouring Agents in Food) (Amendment) Regulations, S.I. No. 336 of 1981

Health (Preservatives in Food) Regulations, S.I. No. 337 of 1981

Health (Foods for Particular Nutritional Uses) Regulations, S.I. No. 272 of 1982

Health (Vinyl Chloride in Food) Regulations, S.I. No. 95 of 1984

Health (Emulsifiers, Stabilisers, Thickening and Gelling Agents in Food) Regulations, S.I. No. 186 of 1985

65 *Medical Preparations (Cortisone and A. C. T. H.) Regulations, S.I. No. 324 of 1952*

Medical Preparations (Barbiturates) Regulations, S.I. No. 30 of 1954

Medical Preparations (Oral Diabetic Treatments) Regulations, S.I. No. 203 of 1956

Medical Preparations (Advertisement and Sale) Regulations, S.I. No. 135 of 1958

Medical Preparations (Control of Sale) (Temporary) Regulations, S.I. No. 199 of 1962

Medical Preparations (Control of Sale) Regulations, S.I. No. 82 of 1963

Medical Preparations (Control of Sale) Regulations, S.I. No. 261 of 1966

Medical Preparations (Control of Amphetamine) Regulations, S.I. No. 244 of 1969

Medical Preparations (Control of Amphetamine) (Amendment) Regulations, S.I. No. 137 of 1970

Medical Preparations (Control of Sale) (Amendment) Regulations, S.I. No. 272 of 1971

Medical Preparations (Licensing of Manufacture) Regulations, S.I. No. 225 of 1974

Medical Preparations (Wholesale Licences) Regulations, S.I. No. 333 of 1974

Medical Preparations (Licensing of Manufacture) (Amendment) Regulations, S.I. No. 302 of 1975

Medical Preparations (Control of Sale) (Amendment) Regulations, S.I. No. 82 of 1976

Medical Preparations (Amendment of Fees) Regulations, S.I. No. 241 of 1980

Statutory Authority	Section	Statutory Instrument
Health Act, No. 26 of 1953 *(Cont.)*		**Medical Preparations (Amendment of Fees) Regulations, S.I. No. 56 of 1983**
		Medical Preparations (Amendment of Fees) Regulations, S.I. No. 85 of 1984
		Medical Preparations (Licensing Advertisement and Sale) Regulations, S.I. No. 210 of 1984
		Medical Preparations (Amendment of Fees) Regulations, S.I. No. 159 of 1985
		Medical Preparations (Amendment of Fees) Regulations, S.I. No. 49 of 1986
	66	*Health (Restricted Article) Order, S.I. No. 429 of 1985*
	98	**National Health Council (Establishment) Order, S.I. No. 81 of 1948**
		Consultative Cancer Council (Establishment) Order, S.I. No. 125 of 1948
	98(4)	*National Health Council (Tenure of Office of Members) Order, S.I. No. 157 of 1950*
		National Health Council (Tenure of Office of Members) Order, S.I. No. 84 of 1952
	101	*Cork Port (Enforcement of Health Regulations) Order, S.I. No. 230 of 1948*
		Western Health Institutions Committee Order, S.I. No. 194 of 1952
	103	*Health Authorities (Borrowing Powers) Order, S.I. No. 211 of 1955*
		Health Authorities (Borrowing Powers) (Amendment) Order, S.I. No. 97 of 1958
	107	**Dublin Port Sanitary Authority (Dissolution) Order, S.I. No. 167 of 1948**
		Waterford and New Ross Port Sanitary Authority (Dissolution) Order, S.I. No. 168 of 1948
		Galway Port Sanitary Authority (Dissolution) Order, S.I. No. 169 of 1948
		Cork Port Sanitary Authority (Dissolution) Order, S.I. No. 229 of 1948
	109	**Health Act, 1947 (Adaptation) Order, S.I. No. 101 of 1948**
		Health Act, 1947 (Adaptation) Order, S.I. No. 15 of 1951
		Registration of Births and Deaths (Ireland) Act, 1863 and Adoption Act, 1952 (Adaptation) Order, S.I. No. 161 of 1954
Health Act, No. 26 of 1953	2	*Health Act, 1953 (Date of Commencement) Order, S.I. No. 377 of 1953*
		Health Act, 1953 (Date of Commencement) Order, S.I. No. 62 of 1954
	5	**Disabled Persons (Maintenance Allowances) (Amendment) Regulations, S.I. No. 244 of 1966**

Statutory Authority	Section	Statutory Instrument
Health Act, No. 26 of 1953 (*Cont.*)	15	*General Institutional and Specialist Services (Insured Persons) Order, S.I. No. 75 of 1956*
		Specialist Services (Charges) Order, S.I. No. 198 of 1957
		General Institutional and Specialist Services (Amendment) Regulations, S.I. No. 266 of 1958
		General Institutional and Specialist Services (Amendment) Regulations, S.I. No. 69 of 1966
	22	*General Medical Services (Amendment) Regulations, S.I. No. 159 of 1954*
		General Institutional and Specialist Services (Amendment) Regulations, S.I. No. 47 of 1955
		Maternity and Child Health Services (Amendment) Regulations, S.I. No. 48 of 1955
		General Institutional and Specialist Services (Amendment) Regulations, S.I. No. 43 of 1956
		Maternity and Child Health Services (Amendment) Regulations, S.I. No. 44 of 1956
		Maternity and Child Health Services (Amendment) (No.2) Regulations, S.I. No. 142 of 1956
		Maternity and Child Health Services (Amendment) Regulations, S.I. No. 265 of 1958
		General Institutional and Specialist Services (Amendment) Regulations, S.I. No. 266 of 1958
		Dental and Aural Appliances Regulations, S.I. No. 198 of 1961
		Maternity and Child Health Services (Amendment) Regulations, S.I. No. 158 of 1964
		Dental and Aural Appliances Regulations, S.I. No. 190 of 1965
		General Institutional and Specialist Services (Amendment) Regulations, S.I. No. 69 of 1966
		Maternity and Child Health Services (Amendment) Regulations, S.I. No. 70 of 1966
		Maternity and Child Health Services (Amendment) (No.2) Regulations, S.I. No. 105 of 1966
		General Institutional and Specialist Services (Amendment) Regulations, S.I. No. 57 of 1968
	23	*Maternity Cash Grants Regulations, S.I. No. 410 of 1953*
	25	*General Institutional and Specialist Services (Insured Persons) Order, S.I. No. 75 of 1956*
	38	**Food Hygiene (Amendment) Regulations, S.I. No. 322 of 1971**
	38(3)	*Health (Colouring Matter in Food) Regulations, S.I. No. 41 of 1972*
		Health (Antioxidant in Food) Regulations, S.I. No. 42 of 1972
		Health (Preservatives in Food) Regulations, S.I. No. 43 of 1972
		Health (Arsenic and Lead in Food) Regulations, S.I. No. 44 of 1972

Health Act, No. 26 of 1953
(*Cont.*)

Health (Mineral Hydrocarbons in Food) Regulations, S.I. No. 45 of 1972

Health (Colouring in Food) (Amendment) Regulations, S.I. No. 301 of 1972

Health (Preservatives in Food) (Amendment) Regulations, S.I. No. 302 of 1972

Health (Antioxidant in Food) (Amendment) Regulations, S.I. No. 303 of 1972

Health (Solvents in Food) Regulations, S.I. No. 304 of 1972

Health (Preservatives in Food) Regulations, S.I. No. 147 of 1973

Health (Antioxidant in Food) Regulations, S.I. No. 148 of 1973

Health (Colouring Agents in Food) Regulations, S.I. No. 149 of 1973

Health (Erucic Acid in Food) Regulations, S.I. No. 123 of 1978

Health (Colouring Agents in Food) (Amendment) Regulations, S.I. No. 140 of 1978

Health (Emulsifiers, Stabilisers, Thickening and Gelling Agents in Food) Regulations, S.I. No. 35 of 1980

Health (Colouring Agents in Food) (Amendment) Regulations, S.I. No. 336 of 1981

Health (Preservatives in Food) Regulations, S.I. No. 337 of 1981

Health (Foods for Particular Nutritional Uses) Regulations, S.I. No. 272 of 1982

Health (Vinyl Chloride in Food) Regulations, S.I. No. 95 of 1984

Health (Emulsifiers, Stabilisers, Thickening and Gelling Agents in Food) Regulations, S.I. No. 186 of 1985

39   **Medical Preparations (Control of Amphetamine) Regulations, S.I. No. 244 of 1969**

Medical Preparations (Licensing of Manufacture) Regulations, S.I. No. 225 of 1974

45   **Public Assistance Authorities (Health Functions) Order, S.I. No. 414 of 1953**

Western Health Institutions Board Order, S.I. No. 415 of 1953

Cork Sanatoria Board Order, S.I. No. 416 of 1953

Dublin Public Assistance Authorities (Health Functions) Order, S.I. No. 162 of 1954

South Cork Board of Public Assistance (Health Functions) Order, S.I. No. 163 of 1954

Waterford Board of Public Assistance (Health Functions) Order, S.I. No. 164 of 1954

Cork Sanatoria Board Order, 1953 (Amendment) Order, S.I. No. 165 of 1954

Western Health Institutions Board Order, 1953 (Amendment) Order, S.I. No. 166 of 1954

Statutory Authority	Section	Statutory Instrument
Health Act, No. 26 of 1953 (*Cont.*)		**South Cork Board of Public Assistance (Health Functions) Order, S.I. No. 17 of 1955**
		Waterford Board of Public Assistance (Health Functions) Order, S.I. No. 21 of 1955
		Dublin Public Assistance Authorities (Health Functions) Order, S.I. No. 72 of 1956
		South Cork Board of Public Assistance (Health Functions) Order, S.I. No. 73 of 1956
		Waterford Board of Public Assistance (Health Functions) Order, S.I. No. 74 of 1956
		Dublin Public Assistance Authorities (Health Functions) Order, S.I. No. 268 of 1958
		South Cork Board of Public Assistance (Health Functions) Order, S.I. No. 269 of 1958
		Waterford Board of Public Assistance (Health Functions) Order, S.I. No. 270 of 1958
		Mental Health Boards Order, S.I. No. 140 of 1960
	45(9)	**Joint Health Boards (Dissolution) Order, S.I. No. 118 of 1971**
	46	**Public Assistance Authorities (Health Functions) Order, S.I. No. 414 of 1953**
		Dublin Public Assistance Authorities (Health Functions) Order, S.I. No. 162 of 1954
		Dublin Public Assistance Authorities (Health Functions) Order, S.I. No. 72 of 1956
		Dublin Public Assistance Authorities (Health Functions) Order, S.I. No. 268 of 1958
	48	*Consultative Health Committees (Dublin, Cork and Waterford) Regulations, S.I. No. 73 of 1954*
		Consultative Health Committees (Dublin, Cork and Waterford) (Amendment) Regulations, S.I. No. 31 of 1955
	48(8)	**Consultative Health Committees (Dublin, Cork, Limerick and Waterford) Regulations, S.I. No. 241 of 1963**
	50(2)	*Disabled Persons (Rehabilitation) Regulations, S.I. No. 141 of 1963*
	50(5)	*Disabled Persons (Maintenance Allowances) (Amendment) Regulations, S.I. No. 51 of 1957*
		Disabled Persons (Maintenance Allowances) Regulations, S.I. No. 261 of 1960
		Disabled Persons (Maintenance Allowances) (Amendment) Regulations, S.I. No. 133 of 1962
		Disabled Persons (Maintenance Allowances) Regulations, S.I. No. 142 of 1963
		Disabled Persons (Maintenance Allowances) (Amendment) Regulations, S.I. No. 192 of 1964
		Disabled Persons (Maintenance Allowances) (Amendment) Regulations, S.I. No. 176 of 1965
		Disabled Persons (Maintenance Allowances) (Amendment) Regulations, S.I. No. 244 of 1966

Health Act, No. 26 of 1953
(*Cont.*)

Disabled Persons (Maintenance Allowances) (Amendment) Regulations, S.I. No. 188 of 1967

Disabled Persons (Maintenance Allowances) (Amendment) Regulations, S.I. No. 155 of 1968

Disabled Persons (Maintenance Allowances) (Amendment) Regulations, S.I. No. 142 of 1969

Disabled Persons (Maintenance Allowances) (Amendment) Regulations, S.I. No. 169 of 1970

Disabled Persons (Maintenance Allowances) (Amendment) Regulations, S.I. No. 207 of 1971

Disabled Persons (Maintenance Allowances) Regulations, S.I. No. 168 of 1972

51(2)   County Borough of Limerick (Dispensary Districts) Order, S.I. No. 293 of 1954

County Wateford (Dispensary Districts) Order, S.I. No. 167 of 1955

Dublin City and County Dispensary Districts Order, S.I. No. 111 of 1956

Wicklow County and Rathdown Public Assistance District (Dispensary Districts) Order, S.I. No. 225 of 1957

Waterford Public Assistance District (Dispensary Districts) Order, S.I. No. 107 of 1958

County Longford (Dispensary Districts) Order, S.I. No. 41 of 1959

Dublin Public Assistance District (Dispensary Districts) Order, S.I. No. 56 of 1959

Dublin Health Authority Area (Dispensary Districts) Order, S.I. No. 228 of 1960

Dublin Health Authority Area (Dispensary Districts) (No.2) Order, S.I. No. 253 of 1960

Cork Health Authority Area (Dispensary Districts) Order, S.I. No. 63 of 1961

Limerick Health Authority Area (Dispensary Districts) Order, S.I. No. 108 of 1961

County Wexford (Dispensary Districts) Order, S.I. No. 150 of 1961

County Kerry (Dispensary Districts) Order, S.I. No. 152 of 1961

County Wicklow (Dispensary Districts) Order, S.I. No. 172 of 1961

Dublin Health Authority Area (Dispensary Districts) Order, S.I. No. 193 of 1961

County Meath (Dispensary Districts) Order, S.I. No. 280 of 1961

County Kerry (Dispensary Districts) (No.2) Order, S.I. No. 281 of 1961

County Meath (Dispensary Districts) Order, S.I. No. 41 of 1962

County Kildare (Dispensary Districts) Order, S.I. No. 145 of 1962

County Laoighis (Dispensary Districts) Order, S.I. No. 213 of 1962

Statutory Authority	Section	Statutory Instrument
Health Act, No. 26 of 1953 *(Cont.)*		**County Galway (Dispensary Districts) Order, S.I. No. 61 of 1963**
		Dublin Health Authority Area (Dispensary Districts) Order, S.I. No. 74 of 1963
		County Clare (Dispensary Districts) Order, S.I. No. 84 of 1963
		Cork Health Authority Area (Dispensary Districts) Order, S.I. No. 211 of 1963
		County Wexford (Dispensary Districts) Order, S.I. No. 107 of 1964
		County Wexford (Dispensary Districts) (No.2) Order, S.I. No. 293 of 1964
		County Mayo (Dispensary Districts) Order, S.I. No. 51 of 1965
		County Mayo (Dispensary Districts) Order, S.I. No. 170 of 1967
	54	**Institutional Assistance Regulations, S.I. No. 177 of 1965**
	55	*Boarding Out of Children Regulations, S.I. No. 101 of 1954*
		Boarding Out of Children Regulations, S.I. No. 67 of 1983
Health Act, No. 23 of 1954	2	*General Institutional and Specialist Services (Amendment) Regulations, S.I. No. 43 of 1956*
	4(2)	*Health Act, 1954 (Date of Commencement) Order, S.I. No. 160 of 1954*
Health Act, No. 1 of 1970	1	*Health Act, 1970 (Commencement) Order, S.I. No. 47 of 1970*
		Health Act, 1970 (Commencement) Order, S.I. No. 90 of 1971
		Health Act, 1970 (Commencement) (No.2) Order, S.I. No. 271 of 1971
		Health Act, 1970 (Commencement) Order, S.I. No. 87 of 1972
		Health Act, 1970 (Commencement) (No.2) Order, S.I. No. 240 of 1972
		Health Act, 1970 (Commencement) Order, S.I. No. 159 of 1973
		Health Act, 1970 (Commencement) Order, S.I. No. 78 of 1976
	4	**Health Boards Regulations, S.I. No. 170 of 1970**
	6	**Food Hygiene (Amendment) Regulations, S.I. No. 322 of 1971**
		Health (Colouring Matter in Food) Regulations, S.I. No. 41 of 1972
		Health (Antioxidant in Food) Regulations, S.I. No. 42 of 1972
		Health (Preservatives in Food) Regulations, S.I. No. 43 of 1972

Statutory Authority	Section	Statutory Instrument
Health Act, No. 1 of 1970 (*Cont.*)		**Health (Arsenic and Lead in Food) Regulations, S.I. No. 44 of 1972**
		Health (Mineral Hydrocarbons in Food) Regulations, S.I. No. 45 of 1972
		Health (Colouring in Food) (Amendment) Regulations, S.I. No. 301 of 1972
		Health (Preservatives in Food) (Amendment) Regulations, S.I. No. 302 of 1972
		Health (Antioxidant in Food) (Amendment) Regulations, S.I. No. 303 of 1972
		Health (Solvents in Food) Regulations, S.I. No. 304 of 1972
		Health (Preservatives in Food) Regulations, S.I. No. 147 of 1973
		Health (Antioxidant in Food) Regulations, S.I. No. 148 of 1973
		Health (Colouring Agents in Food) Regulations, S.I. No. 149 of 1973
		Health (Erucic Acid in Food) Regulations, S.I. No. 123 of 1978
		Health (Colouring Agents in Food) (Amendment) Regulations, S.I. No. 140 of 1978
		Health (Emulsifiers, Stabilisers, Thickening and Gelling Agents in Food) Regulations, S.I. No. 35 of 1980
		Health (Colouring Agents in Food) (Amendment) Regulations, S.I. No. 336 of 1981
		Health (Preservatives in Food) Regulations, S.I. No. 337 of 1981
		Health (Foods for Particular Nutritional Uses) Regulations, S.I. No. 272 of 1982
		Health (Vinyl Chloride in Food) Regulations, S.I. No. 95 of 1984
		Health (Emulsifiers, Stabilisers, Thickening and Gelling Agents in Food) Regulations, S.I. No. 186 of 1985
	6(3)	**Health Boards (Functions of Chief Executive Officers) Order, S.I. No. 107 of 1971**
	7	**Health (Local Committees) Regulations, S.I. No. 31 of 1972**
		Health (Local Committees) Regulations, S.I. No. 68 of 1977
	8(2)	*Health (Disqualification of Officers and Servants) Order, S.I. No. 289 of 1971*
	11	**General Medical Services (Payments) Board (Establishment) Order, S.I. No. 184 of 1972**
	17(4)(e)	**Health Services Regulations, S.I. No. 88 of 1972**
	19	**Health (Officers Age Limit) Order, S.I. No. 109 of 1971**
	23(5)	**Health (Removal of Officers and Servants) Regulations, S.I. No. 110 of 1971**

Statutory Authority	Section	Statutory Instrument
Health Act, No. 1 of 1970 (*Cont.*)		**Social Welfare (Removal of Officers) Regulations, S.I. No. 200 of 1972**
	24(3)	**Health (Removal of Officers and Servants) Regulations, S.I. No. 110 of 1971**
		Health (Removal of Officers and Servants) (Amendment) Regulations, S.I. No. 165 of 1972
		Social Welfare (Removal of Officers) Regulations, S.I. No. 200 of 1972
		Health (Removal of Officers and Servants) (Amendment) Regulations, S.I. No. 180 of 1973
	24(8)	**Health (Removal of Officers and Servants) Regulations, S.I. No. 110 of 1971**
		Social Welfare (Removal of Officers) Regulations, S.I. No. 200 of 1972
	24(10)	**Health (Removal of Officers and Servants) Regulations, S.I. No. 110 of 1971**
		Social Welfare (Removal of Officers) Regulations, S.I. No. 200 of 1972
	34	**Health Authorities (Dissolution) Order, S.I. No. 117 of 1971**
	35	**Joint Health Boards (Dissolution) Order, S.I. No. 118 of 1971**
	41	**Health (Hospital Bodies) Regulations, S.I. No. 164 of 1972**
		Health (Hospital Bodies) Regulations, 1972 (Amendment) Regulations, S.I. No. 338 of 1978
	42	**Hospitals Commission (Dissolution) Order, S.I. No. 79 of 1976**
	44	**Central Mental Hospital Order, S.I. No. 236 of 1971**
	46	*Health Services (Limited Eligibility) Regulations, S.I. No. 276 of 1971*
		Health Services (Limited Eligibility) Regulations, S.I. No. 141 of 1976
		Health Services (Limited Eligibility) Regulations, S.I. No. 110 of 1979
	52	**Health Services (Amendment) Regulations, S.I. No. 277 of 1971**
		Health Services Regulations, S.I. No. 184 of 1973
	53	**Health Services Regulations, S.I. No. 105 of 1971**
		Health Services (Amendment) Regulations, S.I. No. 277 of 1971
		Health (Charges for In-Patient Services) Regulations, S.I. No. 180 of 1976
	53(2)	**Health (Hospital In-patient Charges) Regulations, S.I. No. 94 of 1984**
		Health (Hospital In-patient Charges) (Amendment) Regulations, S.I. No. 221 of 1986
	54	**Health Services Regulations, S.I. No. 105 of 1971**

Statutory Authority	Section	Statutory Instrument

Health Act, No. 1 of 1970
(*Cont.*)

56   **Health Services (Amendment) Regulations, S.I. No. 277 of 1971**

Health Services Regulations, S.I. No. 184 of 1973

58   **Health Services Regulations, S.I. No. 88 of 1972**

59   **Health Services (Amendment) Regulations, S.I. No. 277 of 1971**

Health Services Regulations, S.I. No. 88 of 1972

Health Services Regulations, S.I. No. 184 of 1973

Health Services (Amendment) Regulations, S.I. No. 64 of 1975

Health Services Regulations, 1972 (Amendment) Regulations, S.I. No. 181 of 1975

Health Services Regulations, S.I. No. 97 of 1976

Health Services Regulations, S.I. No. 61 of 1980

Health Services Regulations, S.I. No. 267 of 1981

Health Services Regulations, S.I. No. 283 of 1982

Health Services Regulations, S.I. No. 54 of 1983

Health Services (No.4) Regulations, S.I. No. 389 of 1983

64   **Maternity Cash Grants Regulations, S.I. No. 241 of 1972**

68   **Disabled Persons (Rehabilitation) Regulations, S.I. No. 186 of 1973**

69   **Disabled Persons (Maintenance Allowances) Regulations, S.I. No. 160 of 1973**

Disabled Persons (Rehabilitation) Regulations, S.I. No. 186 of 1973

Disabled Persons (Maintenance Allowances) (Amendment) Regulations, S.I. No. 39 of 1975

Disabled Persons (Maintenance Allowances) (Amendment) (No.2) Regulations, S.I. No. 221 of 1975

Disabled Persons (Maintenance Allowances) (Amendment) Regulations, S.I. No. 67 of 1976

Disabled Persons (Maintenance Allowances) (Amendment) (No.2) Regulations, S.I. No. 260 of 1976

Disabled Persons (Maintenance Allowances) (Amendment) Regulations, S.I. No. 79 of 1977

Disabled Persons (Maintenance Allowances) (Amendment) (No.2) Regulations, S.I. No. 314 of 1977

Disabled Persons (Maintenance Allowances) (Amendment) Regulations, S.I. No. 54 of 1978

Disabled Persons (Maintenance Allowances) (Amendment) Regulations, S.I. No. 79 of 1979

Disabled Persons (Maintenance Allowances) (Amendment) (No.2) Regulations, S.I. No. 338 of 1979

Disabled Persons (Maintenance Allowances) (Amendment) Regulations, S.I. No. 92 of 1980

Statutory Authority	Section	Statutory Instrument

Health Act, No. 1 of 1970
(*Cont.*)

Disabled Persons (Maintenance Allowances) (Amendment) (No.2) Regulations, S.I. No. 367 of 1980

Disabled Persons (Maintenance Allowances) (Amendment) Regulations, S.I. No. 100 of 1981

Disabled Persons (Maintenance Allowances) (Amendment) (No.2) Regulations, S.I. No. 341 of 1981

Disabled Persons (Maintenance Allowances) (Amendment) (No.3) Regulations, S.I. No. 407 of 1981

Disabled Persons (Maintenance Allowances) (Amendment) Regulations, S.I. No. 77 of 1982

Disabled Persons (Maintenance Allowances) (Amendment) (No.2) Regulations, S.I. No. 285 of 1982

Disabled Persons (Maintenance Allowances) (Amendment) (No.3) Regulations, S.I. No. 340 of 1982

Disabled Persons (Maintenance Allowances) (Amendment) Regulations, S.I. No. 154 of 1983

Disabled Persons (Maintenance Allowances) (Amendment) (No.2) Regulations, S.I. No. 361 of 1983

Disabled Persons (Maintenance Allowances) Regulations, S.I. No. 71 of 1984

Disabled Persons (Maintenance Allowances) (No.2) Regulations, S.I. No. 305 of 1984

Disabled Persons (Maintenance Allowances) (Amendment) Regulations, S.I. No. 190 of 1985

Disabled Persons (Maintenance Allowances) (No.2) Regulations, S.I. No. 373 of 1985

Disabled Persons (Maintenance Allowances) (Amendment) Regulations, S.I. No. 252 of 1986

Disabled Persons (Maintenance Allowances) (No.2) Regulations, S.I. No. 403 of 1986

70   **Disabled Persons (Maintenance Allowances) (Amendment) Regulations, S.I. No. 39 of 1975**

Disabled Persons (Maintenance Allowances) (Amendment) (No.2) Regulations, S.I. No. 221 of 1975

72   **Health Services Regulations, S.I. No. 105 of 1971**

Health Services (Amendment) Regulations, S.I. No. 277 of 1971

Health Services Regulations, S.I. No. 88 of 1972

Disabled Persons (Maintenance Allowances) Regulations, S.I. No. 160 of 1973

Disabled Persons (Rehabilitation) Regulations, S.I. No. 186 of 1973

Health Service Regulations, S.I. No. 90 of 1974

Health Services (Amendment) Regulations, S.I. No. 64 of 1975

Health Act, No. 1 of 1970
(*Cont.*)

Health Services Regulations, 1972 (Amendment) Regulations, S.I. No. 181 of 1975

Disabled Persons (Maintenance Allowances) (Amendment) Regulations, S.I. No. 67 of 1976

Health Services Regulations, S.I. No. 97 of 1976

Health Services (Amendment) Regulations, S.I. No. 142 of 1976

Disabled Persons (Maintenance Allowances) (Amendment) (No.2) Regulations, S.I. No. 260 of 1976

Disabled Persons (Maintenance Allowances) (Amendment) Regulations, S.I. No. 79 of 1977

Disabled Persons (Maintenance Allowances) (Amendment) (No.2) Regulations, S.I. No. 314 of 1977

Disabled Persons (Maintenance Allowances) (Amendment) Regulations, S.I. No. 54 of 1978

Health Services Regulations, S.I. No. 371 of 1978

Disabled Persons (Maintenance Allowances) (Amendment) Regulations, S.I. No. 79 of 1979

Health Services Regulations, S.I. No. 109 of 1979

Health Services (No.2) Regulations, S.I. No. 134 of 1979

Disabled Persons (Maintenance Allowances) (Amendment) (No.2) Regulations, S.I. No. 338 of 1979

Health Services Regulations, S.I. No. 61 of 1980

Disabled Persons (Maintenance Allowances) (Amendment) Regulations, S.I. No. 92 of 1980

Health Services (Amendment) Regulations, S.I. No. 93 of 1980

Disabled Persons (Maintenance Allowances) (Amendment) (No.2) Regulations, S.I. No. 367 of 1980

Disabled Persons (Maintenance Allowances) (Amendment) Regulations, S.I. No. 100 of 1981

Health Services (Amendment) Regulations, S.I. No. 173 of 1981

Health Services Regulations, S.I. No. 267 of 1981

Disabled Persons (Maintenance Allowances) (Amendment) (No.2) Regulations, S.I. No. 341 of 1981

Disabled Persons (Maintenance Allowances) (Amendment) (No.3) Regulations, S.I. No. 407 of 1981

Disabled Persons (Maintenance Allowances) (Amendment) Regulations, S.I. No. 77 of 1982

Health Services (Amendment) Regulations, S.I. No. 151 of 1982

Health Services Regulations, S.I. No. 283 of 1982

Disabled Persons (Maintenance Allowances) (Amendment) (No.2) Regulations, S.I. No. 285 of 1982

Health Act, No. 1 of 1970
(*Cont.*)

Disabled Persons (Maintenance Allowances) (Amendment) (No.3) Regulations, S.I. No. 340 of 1982

Health Services Regulations, S.I. No. 54 of 1983

Health Services (No.2) Regulations, S.I. No. 139 of 1983

Disabled Persons (Maintenance Allowances) (Amendment) Regulations, S.I. No. 154 of 1983

Disabled Persons (Maintenance Allowances) (Amendment) (No.2) Regulations, S.I. No. 361 of 1983

Health Services (No.3) Regulations, S.I. No. 381 of 1983

Health Services (No.4) Regulations, S.I. No. 389 of 1983

Disabled Persons (Maintenance Allowances) Regulations, S.I. No. 71 of 1984

Health Services (Amendment) Regulations, S.I. No. 123 of 1984

Disabled Persons (Maintenance Allowances) (No.2) Regulations, S.I. No. 305 of 1984

Health Services (Amendment) Regulations, S.I. No. 145 of 1985

Disabled Persons (Maintenance Allowances) (Amendment) Regulations, S.I. No. 190 of 1985

Disabled Persons (Maintenance Allowances) (No.2) Regulations, S.I. No. 373 of 1985

Health Services (Amendment) Regulations, S.I. No. 109 of 1986

Disabled Persons (Maintenance Allowances) (Amendment) Regulations, S.I. No. 252 of 1986

Disabled Persons (Maintenance Allowances) (No.2) Regulations, S.I. No. 403 of 1986

76 **Rotunda Hospital (Amendment of Charter) Order, S.I. No. 137 of 1972**

Royal Hospital for Incurables, Dublin (Charter Amendment) Order, S.I. No. 244 of 1974

Adelaide Hospital (Charter Amendment) Order, S.I. No. 374 of 1980

78 *Health (Possession of Controlled Substances) Regulations, S.I. No. 99 of 1970*

Health (Possession of Controlled Substances) (Amendment) Regulations, S.I. No. 55 of 1974

82 **Mental Treatment Acts (Adaptation) Order, S.I. No. 108 of 1971**

85 **Health Act, 1970 (Adaptation) Regulations, S.I. No. 106 of 1971**

Health Act, 1970 (Adaptation) Regulations, S.I. No. 65 of 1972

Health Act, 1970 (Adaptation) Regulations, S.I. No. 349 of 1973

Statutory Authority	Section	Statutory Instrument
Health Act, No. 1 of 1970 (*Cont.*)		**Health Act, 1970 (Adaptation) Regulations, S.I. No. 29 of 1975**
	Sch. II par. 5	**Health Boards (Election of Members) Regulations, S.I. No. 60 of 1972**
	Sch. II par. 8(2)	**Health (Disqualification of Officers and Servants) Order, S.I. No. 15 of 1985**
Health Acts, 1947 and 1953,		*Maternity and Child Health Services Regulations, S.I. No. 98 of 1954*
		General Institutional and Specialist Services Regulations, S.I. No. 100 of 1954
		General Medical Services Regulations, S.I. No. 102 of 1954
		Institutional Assistance Regulations, S.I. No. 103 of 1954
Health Acts, 1947 to 1954,		*General Institutional and Specialist Services (Temporary) Regulations, S.I. No. 157 of 1954*
		Maternity and Child Health Services (Amendment) Regulations, S.I. No. 158 of 1954
Health and Mental Treatment Act, No. 16 of 1957	3(4)	*Health and Mental Treatment Act, 1957 (Commencement) Order, S.I. No. 169 of 1957*
Health and Mental Treatment (Amendment) Act, No. 37 of 1958	3(4)	*Health and Mental Treatment (Amendment) Act, 1958 (Commencement) Order, S.I. No. 264 of 1958*
Health and Mental Treatment (Amendment) Act, No. 2 of 1966	3(4)	*Health and Mental Treatment (Amendment) Act, 1966 (Commencement) Order, S.I. No. 64 of 1966*
Health Authorities Act, No. 9 of 1960	2(6)(a)	*Health Authorities Act, 1960 (Wicklow Mental Hospital District) Order, S.I. No. 73 of 1964*
	10(2)(a)	*Dublin Health Authority (Local Committees) Regulations, S.I. No. 120 of 1962*
	11(9)	**Public Bodies (Temporary Provisions) Order, S.I. No. 174 of 1960**
	25(3)	*Health Authorities Act, 1960 (Wicklow Mental Hospital District) Regulations, S.I. No. 74 of 1964*
	30	*Health Authorities Act, 1960 (Commencement) Order, S.I. No. 134 of 1960*
		Health Authorities Act, 1960 (Commencement) (No.2) Order, S.I. No. 190 of 1960
		Health Authorities Act, 1960 (Commencement) Order, S.I. No. 83 of 1963
		Health Authorities Act, 1960 (Commencement) Order, S.I. No. 72 of 1964
Health Contributions Act, No. 21 of 1971	3	*Health Contributions Regulations, S.I. No. 278 of 1971*

Statutory Authority	Section	Statutory Instrument
Health Contributions Act, No. 21 of 1971 (*Cont.*)		*Health Contributions (Amendment) (No.2) Regulations, S.I. No. 373 of 1974*
		Health Contributions (Amendment) Regulations, S.I. No. 80 of 1976
		Health Contributions (Amendment) Regulations, S.I. No. 86 of 1977
		Health Contributions (Amendment) Regulations, S.I. No. 98 of 1978
	4	*Health Contributions Regulations, S.I. No. 278 of 1971*
		Health Contributions (Amendment) Regulations, S.I. No. 185 of 1973
		Health Contributions (Amendment) Regulations, S.I. No. 89 of 1974
	7	*Health Contributions Regulations, S.I. No. 278 of 1971*
		Health Contributions (Amendment) (No.2) Regulations, S.I. No. 373 of 1974
		Health Contributions (Amendment) Regulations, S.I. No. 80 of 1976
		Health Contributions (Amendment) Regulations, S.I. No. 86 of 1977
		Health Contributions (Amendment) Regulations, S.I. No. 98 of 1978
	8	*Health Contributions Regulations, S.I. No. 278 of 1971*
	12	*Health Contributions Regulations, S.I. No. 278 of 1971*
		Health Contributions (Amendment) Regulations, S.I. No. 185 of 1973
		Health Contributions (Amendment) Regulations, S.I. No. 89 of 1974
		Health Contributions (Amendment) (No.2) Regulations, S.I. No. 373 of 1974
		Health Contributions (Amendment) Regulations, S.I. No. 80 of 1976
		Health Contributions (Amendment) Regulations, S.I. No. 86 of 1977
		Health Contributions (Amendment) Regulations, S.I. No. 98 of 1978
	14	*Health Contributions Act, 1971 (Commencement) Order, S.I. No. 259 of 1971*
Health Contributions Act, No. 4 of 1979	2	**Health Contributions Regulations, S.I. No. 107 of 1979**
		Health Contributions (Amendment) Regulations, S.I. No. 87 of 1980
		Health Contributions (Amendment) Regulations, S.I. No. 55 of 1983
	9(1)	**Health Contributions (Rate of Contribution and Yearly Reckonable Income) (Confirmation and Variation) Regulations, S.I. No. 108 of 1979**

Statutory Authority	Section	Statutory Instrument
Health Contributions Act, No. 4 of 1979 (*Cont.*)	9(3)	**Health Contributions (Yearly Reckonable Income) (Variation) Regulations, S.I. No. 88 of 1980**
		Health Contributions (Yearly Reckonable Income) (Variation) Regulations, S.I. No. 113 of 1981
		Health Contributions (Yearly Reckonable Income) (Variation) Regulations, S.I. No. 79 of 1982
		Health Contributions (Yearly Reckonable Income) (Variation) Regulations, S.I. No. 86 of 1983
		Health Contributions (Yearly Reckonable Income) (Variation) Regulations, S.I. No. 88 of 1984
		Health Contributions (Yearly Reckonable Income) (Variation) Regulations, S.I. No. 93 of 1985
		Health Contributions (Yearly Reckonable Income) (Variation) Regulations, S.I. No. 71 of 1986
	10	**Health Contributions Regulations, S.I. No. 107 of 1979**
		Health Contributions (Amendment) Regulations, S.I. No. 55 of 1983
		Health Contributions (Amendment) Regulations, S.I. No. 73 of 1984
		Health Contributions (Amendment) Regulations, S.I. No. 233 of 1985
		Health Contributions (Amendment) Regulations, S.I. No. 102 of 1986
	13	**Health Contributions Regulations, S.I. No. 107 of 1979**
		Health Contributions (Amendment) Regulations, S.I. No. 233 of 1985
		Health Contributions (Amendment) Regulations, S.I. No. 102 of 1986
	19	*Health Contributions Act, 1979 (Commencement) Order, S.I. No. 106 of 1979*
Health (Corporate Bodies) Act, No. 27 of 1961	3	**Dublin Dental Hospital (Establishment) Order, S.I. No. 129 of 1963**
		Newcastle Hospital Board (Establishment) Order, S.I. No. 65 of 1964
		Mass-radiography Board (Establishment) Order, S.I. No. 152 of 1964
		Dublin Dental Hospital (Establishment) Order, 1963 (Amendment) Order, S.I. No. 260 of 1964
		Hospital Sterile Supplies Board (Establishment) Order, S.I. No. 1 of 1965
		Blood Transfusion Service Board (Establishment) Order, S.I. No. 78 of 1965
		Medico-social Research Board (Establishment) Order, S.I. No. 80 of 1965
		Hospital Sterile Supplies Board (Establishment) Order, 1965 (Amendment) Order, S.I. No. 157 of 1965
		Dublin Dental Hospital (Establishment) Order, 1963 (Amendment) Order, S.I. No. 3 of 1966

Statutory Authority	Section	Statutory Instrument
Health (Corporate Bodies) Act, No. 27 of 1961 (*Cont.*)		**Cork Hospitals Board (Establishment) Order, S.I. No. 133 of 1966**
		National Drugs Advisory Board (Establishment) Order, S.I. No. 163 of 1966
		Cork Hospitals Board (Establishment) Order, 1966 (Amendment) Order, S.I. No. 211 of 1967
		National Rehabilitation Board (Establishment) Order, S.I. No. 300 of 1967
		Cork Hospitals Board (Establishment) Order, 1966 (Amendment) Order, S.I. No. 235 of 1970
		Dublin Dental Hospital (Establishment) Order, 1963 (Amendment) Order, S.I. No. 23 of 1971
		James Connolly Memorial Hospital Board (Establishment) Order, S.I. No. 97 of 1971
		Cork Hospitals Board (Establishment) Order, 1966 (Amendment) Order, S.I. No. 104 of 1971
		National Rehabilitation Board (Establishment) Order, 1967 (Amendment) Order, S.I. No. 159 of 1971
		Saint James's Hospital Board (Establishment) Order, S.I. No. 187 of 1971
		Cork Hospitals Board (Establishment) Order, 1966 (Amendment) Order, S.I. No. 8 of 1973
		Hospital Bodies (Administrative Bureau) (Establishment) Order, S.I. No. 53 of 1973
		Medico-social Research Board (Establishment) Order, 1965 (Amendment) Order, S.I. No. 169 of 1974
		National Drugs Advisory Board (Establishment) Order, 1966 (Amendment) Order, S.I. No. 176 of 1974
		Health Education Bureau (Establishment) Order, S.I. No. 22 of 1975
		Dublin Dental Hospital (Establishment) Order, 1963 (Amendment) Order, S.I. No. 88 of 1975
		Cork Blood Transfusion Service Committee (Establishment) Order, S.I. No. 274 of 1975
		James Connolly Memorial Hospital Board (Establishment) Order, 1971 (Amendment) Order, S.I. No. 135 of 1977
		Beaumont Hospital Board (Establishment) Order, S.I. No. 255 of 1977
		Cork Voluntary Hospitals Board (Establishment) Order, S.I. No. 290 of 1977
		Erinville Hospital Board (Establishment) Order, S.I. No. 341 of 1977
		Leopardstown Park Hospital Board (Establishment) Order, S.I. No. 98 of 1979
		Tallaght Hospital Board (Establishment) Order, S.I. No. 38 of 1980
		Dublin Rheumatism Clinic Board (Establishment) Order, S.I. No. 135 of 1980

Health (Corporate Bodies) Act,
No. 27 of 1961 (*Cont.*)

National Rehabilitation Board (Establishment) Order, 1967 (Amendment) Order, S.I. No. 213 of 1980

National Drugs Advisory Board (Establishment) Order, 1966 (Amendment) Order, S.I. No. 335 of 1980

Dublin Dental Hospital (Establishment) Order, 1963 (Amendment) Order, S.I. No. 370 of 1980

Tallaght Hospital Board (Establishment) Order, 1980 (Amendment) Order, S.I. No. 313 of 1982

Beaumont Hospital Board (Establishment) Order, 1977 (Amendment) Order, S.I. No. 337 of 1983

Tallaght Hospital Board (Establishment) Order, 1980 (Amendment) Order, S.I. No. 162 of 1984

Saint James's Hospital Board (Establishment) Order, 1971 (Amendment) Order, S.I. No. 211 of 1984

National Drugs Advisory Board (Establishment) Order, 1966 (Amendment) Order, S.I. No. 220 of 1985

Dublin Dental Hospital (Establishment) Order, 1963 (Amendment) Order, S.I. No. 245 of 1985

Health Research Board (Establishment) Order, S.I. No. 279 of 1986

Medical Research Board (Establishment) Order, S.I. No. 371 of 1986

Health Research Board (Establishment) Order, 1986 (Amendment) Order, S.I. No. 452 of 1986

4   **Dublin Dental Hospital (Establishment) Order, S.I. No. 129 of 1963**

Newcastle Hospital Board (Establishment) Order, S.I. No. 65 of 1964

Mass-Radiography Board (Establishment) Order, S.I. No. 152 of 1964

Hospital Sterile Supplies Board (Establishment) Order, S.I. No. 1 of 1965

Blood Transfusion Service Board (Establishment) Order, S.I. No. 78 of 1965

Medico-Social Research Board (Establishment) Order, S.I. No. 80 of 1965

Hospital Sterile Supplies Board (Establishment) Order, 1965 (Amendment) Order, S.I. No. 157 of 1965

Dublin Dental Hospital (Establishment) Order, 1963 (Amendment) Order, S.I. No. 3 of 1966

Cork Hospitals Board (Establishment) Order, S.I. No. 133 of 1966

National Drugs Advisory Board (Establishment) Order, S.I. No. 163 of 1966

National Rehabilitation Board (Establishment) Order, S.I. No. 300 of 1967

Cork Hospitals Board (Establishment) Order, 1966 (Amendment) Order, S.I. No. 235 of 1970

Health (Corporate Bodies) Act, No. 27 of 1961 (*Cont.*)

Dublin Dental Hospital (Establishment) Order, 1963 (Amendment) Order, S.I. No. 23 of 1971

James Connolly Memorial Hospital Board (Establishment) Order, S.I. No. 97 of 1971

Cork Hospitals Board (Establishment) Order, 1966 (Amendment) Order, S.I. No. 104 of 1971

Saint James's Hospital Board (Establishment) Order, S.I. No. 187 of 1971

Cork Hospitals Board (Establishment) Order, 1966 (Amendment) Order, S.I. No. 8 of 1973

Hospital Bodies (Administrative Bureau) (Establishment) Order, S.I. No. 53 of 1973

Medico-Social Research Board (Establishment) Order, 1965 (Amendment) Order, S.I. No. 169 of 1974

National Drugs Advisory Board (Establishment) Order, 1966 (Amendment) Order, S.I. No. 176 of 1974

Health Education Bureau (Establishment) Order, S.I. No. 22 of 1975

Dublin Dental Hospital (Establishment) Order, 1963 (Amendment) Order, S.I. No. 88 of 1975

Cork Blood Transfusion Service Committee (Establishment) Order, S.I. No. 274 of 1975

James Connolly Memorial Hospital Board (Establishment) Order, 1971 (Amendment) Order, S.I. No. 135 of 1977

Beaumont Hospital Board (Establishment) Order, S.I. No. 255 of 1977

Cork Voluntary Hospitals Board (Establishment) Order, S.I. No. 290 of 1977

Leopardstown Park Hospital Board (Establishment) Order, S.I. No. 98 of 1979

Tallaght Hospital Board (Establishment) Order, S.I. No. 38 of 1980

Dublin Rheumatism Clinic Board (Establishment) Order, S.I. No. 135 of 1980

Dublin Dental Hospital (Establishment) Order, 1963 (Amendment) Order, S.I. No. 370 of 1980

Tallaght Hospital Board (Establishment) Order, 1980 (Amendment) Order, S.I. No. 313 of 1982

Beaumont Hospital Board (Establishment) Order, 1977 (Amendment) Order, S.I. No. 337 of 1983

Tallaght Hospital Board (Establishment) Order, 1980 (Amendment) Order, S.I. No. 162 of 1984

Saint James's Hospital Board (Establishment) Order, 1971 (Amendment) Order, S.I. No. 211 of 1984

National Drugs Advisory Board (Establishment) Order, 1966 (Amendment) Order, S.I. No. 220 of 1985

Dublin Dental Hospital (Establishment) Order, 1963 (Amendment) Order, S.I. No. 245 of 1985

Health (Corporate Bodies) Act, No. 27 of 1961 (*Cont.*)		**Health Research Board (Establishment) Order, S.I. No. 279 of 1986**
		Medical Research Board (Establishment) Order, S.I. No. 371 of 1986
		Health Research Board (Establishment) Order, 1986 (Amendment) Order, S.I. No. 452 of 1986
	5	**Dublin Dental Hospital (Establishment) Order, S.I. No. 129 of 1963**
		Newcastle Hospital Board (Establishment) Order, S.I. No. 65 of 1964
		Mass-Radiography Board (Establishment) Order, S.I. No. 152 of 1964
		Hospital Sterile Supplies Board (Establishment) Order, S.I. No. 1 of 1965
		Blood Transfusion Service Board (Establishment) Order, S.I. No. 78 of 1965
		Medico-Social Research Board (Establishment) Order, S.I. No. 80 of 1965
		Hospital Sterile Supplies Board (Establishment) Order, 1965 (Amendment) Order, S.I. No. 157 of 1965
		Dublin Dental Hospital (Establishment) Order, 1963 (Amendment) Order, S.I. No. 3 of 1966
		Cork Hospitals Board (Establishment) Order, S.I. No. 133 of 1966
		National Drugs Advisory Board (Establishment) Order, S.I. No. 163 of 1966
		National Rehabilitation Board (Establishment) Order, S.I. No. 300 of 1967
		Cork Hospitals Board (Establishment) Order, 1966 (Amendment) Order, S.I. No. 235 of 1970
		James Connolly Memorial Hospital Board (Establishment) Order, S.I. No. 97 of 1971
		Cork Hospitals Board (Establishment) Order, 1966 (Amendment) Order, S.I. No. 104 of 1971
		National Rehabilitation Board (Establishment) Order, 1967 (Amendment) Order, S.I. No. 159 of 1971
		Saint James's Hospital Board (Establishment) Order, S.I. No. 187 of 1971
		Cork Hospitals Board (Establishment) Order, 1966 (Amendment) Order, S.I. No. 8 of 1973
		Hospital Bodies (Administrative Bureau) (Establishment) Order, S.I. No. 53 of 1973
		National Drugs Advisory Board (Establishment) Order, 1966 (Amendment) Order, S.I. No. 176 of 1974
		Health Education Bureau (Establishment) Order, S.I. No. 22 of 1975
		Cork Blood Transfusion Service Committee (Establishment) Order, S.I. No. 274 of 1975
		James Connolly Memorial Hospital Board (Establishment) Order, 1971 (Amendment) Order, S.I. No. 135 of 1977

Statutory Authority	Section	Statutory Instrument
Health (Corporate Bodies) Act, No. 27 of 1961 (*Cont.*)		**Beaumont Hospital Board (Establishment) Order, S.I. No. 255 of 1977**
		Cork Voluntary Hospitals Board (Establishment) Order, S.I. No. 290 of 1977
		Leopardstown Park Hospital Board (Establishment) Order, S.I. No. 98 of 1979
		Tallaght Hospital Board (Establishment) Order, S.I. No. 38 of 1980
		Dublin Rheumatism Clinic Board (Establishment) Order, S.I. No. 135 of 1980
		National Rehabilitation Board (Establishment) Order, 1967 (Amendment) Order, S.I. No. 213 of 1980
		Saint James's Hospital Board (Establishment) Order, 1971 (Amendment) Order, S.I. No. 211 of 1984
		National Drugs Advisory Board (Establishment) Order, 1966 (Amendment) Order, S.I. No. 220 of 1985
		Health Research Board (Establishment) Order, S.I. No. 279 of 1986
		Medical Research Board (Establishment) Order, S.I. No. 371 of 1986
		Health Research Board (Establishment) Order, 1986 (Amendment) Order, S.I. No. 452 of 1986
	6	**Dublin Dental Hospital (Establishment) Order, S.I. No. 129 of 1963**
		Newcastle Hospital Board (Establishment) Order, S.I. No. 65 of 1964
		Mass-Radiography Board (Establishment) Order, S.I. No. 152 of 1964
		Dublin Dental Hospital (Establishment) Order, 1963 (Amendment) Order, S.I. No. 260 of 1964
		Hospital Sterile Supplies Board (Establishment) Order, S.I. No. 1 of 1965
		Blood Transfusion Service Board (Establishment) Order, S.I. No. 78 of 1965
		Medico-Social Research Board (Establishment) Order, S.I. No. 80 of 1965
		Hospital Sterile Supplies Board (Establishment) Order, 1965 (Amendment) Order, S.I. No. 157 of 1965
		Dublin Dental Hospital (Establishment) Order, 1963 (Amendment) Order, S.I. No. 3 of 1966
		Cork Hospitals Board (Establishment) Order, S.I. No. 133 of 1966
		National Drugs Advisory Board (Establishment) Order, S.I. No. 163 of 1966
		Cork Hospitals Board (Establishment) Order, 1966 (Amendment) Order, S.I. No. 211 of 1967
		National Rehabilitation Board (Establishment) Order, S.I. No. 300 of 1967

Health (Corporate Bodies) Act,
No. 27 of 1961 (*Cont.*)

Cork Hospitals Board (Establishment) Order, 1966 (Amendment) Order, S.I. No. 235 of 1970

Dublin Dental Hospital (Establishment) Order, 1963 (Amendment) Order, S.I. No. 23 of 1971

James Connolly Memorial Hospital Board (Establishment) Order, S.I. No. 97 of 1971

Cork Hospitals Board (Establishment) Order, 1966 (Amendment) Order, S.I. No. 104 of 1971

Saint James's Hospital Board (Establishment) Order, S.I. No. 187 of 1971

Cork Hospitals Board (Establishment) Order, 1966 (Amendment) Order, S.I. No. 8 of 1973

Hospital Bodies (Administrative Bureau) (Establishment) Order, S.I. No. 53 of 1973

National Drugs Advisory Board (Establishment) Order, 1966 (Amendment) Order, S.I. No. 176 of 1974

Health Education Bureau (Establishment) Order, S.I. No. 22 of 1975

Dublin Dental Hospital (Establishment) Order, 1963 (Amendment) Order, S.I. No. 88 of 1975

Cork Blood Transfusion Service Committee (Establishment) Order, S.I. No. 274 of 1975

James Connolly Memorial Hospital Board (Establishment) Order, 1971 (Amendment) Order, S.I. No. 135 of 1977

Beaumont Hospital Board (Establishment) Order, S.I. No. 255 of 1977

Cork Voluntary Hospitals Board (Establishment) Order, S.I. No. 290 of 1977

Erinville Hospital Board (Establishment) Order, S.I. No. 341 of 1977

Leopardstown Park Hospital Board (Establishment) Order, S.I. No. 98 of 1979

Tallaght Hospital Board (Establishment) Order, S.I. No. 38 of 1980

Dublin Rheumatism Clinic Board (Establishment) Order, S.I. No. 135 of 1980

National Drugs Advisory Board (Establishment) Order, 1966 (Amendment) Order, S.I. No. 335 of 1980

Tallaght Hospital Board (Establishment) Order, 1980 (Amendment) Order, S.I. No. 313 of 1982

Tallaght Hospital Board (Establishment) Order, 1980 (Amendment) Order, S.I. No. 162 of 1984

Saint James's Hospital Board (Establishment) Order, 1971 (Amendment) Order, S.I. No. 211 of 1984

National Drugs Advisory Board (Establishment) Order, 1966 (Amendment) Order, S.I. No. 220 of 1985

Health Research Board (Establishment) Order, S.I. No. 279 of 1986

Statutory Authority	Section	Statutory Instrument
Health (Corporate Bodies) Act, No. 27 of 1961 *(Cont.)*		*Medical Research Board (Establishment) Order, S.I. No. 371 of 1986*
		Health Research Board (Establishment) Order, 1986 (Amendment) Order, S.I. No. 452 of 1986
	7	**Newcastle Hospital Board (Establishment) Order, 1964 (Revocation) Order, S.I. No. 75 of 1964**
		Mass-Radiography Board (Establishment) Order, 1964 (Revocation) Order, S.I. No. 59 of 1975
		Cork Blood Transfusion Service Committee (Establishment) Order, 1975 (Revocation) Order, S.I. No. 287 of 1975
		Erinville Hospital Board (Establishment) Order, 1977 (Revocation) Order, S.I. No. 365 of 1977
		Dublin Rheumatism Clinic Board (Establishment) Order, 1980 (Revocation) Order, S.I. No. 153 of 1980
		Medico-social Research Board (Establishment) Orders (Revocation) Order, S.I. No. 450 of 1986
		Medical Research Board (Establishment) Order, 1986 (Revocation) Order, S.I. No. 451 of 1986
Health (Family Planning) Act, No. 20 of 1979	3	**Health (Family Planning) Regulations, S.I. No. 248 of 1980**
	4	**Health (Family Planning) Regulations, S.I. No. 248 of 1980**
	5	**Health (Family Planning) Regulations, S.I. No. 248 of 1980**
	7	**Health (Family Planning) Regulations, S.I. No. 248 of 1980**
	8	**Health (Family Planning) Regulations, S.I. No. 248 of 1980**
	16	**Health (Family Planning) Regulations, S.I. No. 248 of 1980**
	17(4)	*Health (Family Planning) Act, 1979 (Commencement) Order, S.I. No. 247 of 1980*
Health (Family Planning) (Amendment) Act, No. 4 of 1985	3(4)	*Health (Family Planning) (Amendment) Act, 1985 (Commencement) Order, S.I. No. 316 of 1985*
Health (Fluoridation of Water Supplies) Act, No. 46 of 1960		**Fluoridation of Water Supplies (Dublin) Regulations, S.I. No. 75 of 1962**
		Fluoridation of Water Supplies (Kildare) Regulations, S.I. No. 76 of 1962
		Fluoridation of Water Supplies (Wicklow) Regulations, S.I. No. 77 of 1962
		Fluoridation of Water Supplies (Kildare) (Amendment) Regulations, S.I. No. 273 of 1964
		Fluoridation of Water Supplies (Laoighis) Regulations, S.I. No. 274 of 1964
		Fluoridation of Water Supplies (Louth) Regulations, S.I. No. 275 of 1964

Statutory Authority	Section	Statutory Instrument

Health (Fluoridation of Water
Supplies) Act, No. 46 of 1960
(*Cont.*)

Fluoridation of Water Supplies (Offaly) Regulations, S.I. No. 276 of 1964

Fluoridation of Water Supplies (Tipperary South Riding) Regulations, S.I. No. 277 of 1964

Fluoridation of Water Supplies (Westmeath) Regulations, S.I. No. 278 of 1964

Fluoridation of Water Supplies (Donegal) Regulations, S.I. No. 69 of 1965

Fluoridation of Water Supplies (Mayo) Regulations, S.I. No. 70 of 1965

Fluoridation of Water Supplies (Meath) Regulations, S.I. No. 71 of 1965

Fluoridation of Water Supplies (Sligo) Regulations, S.I. No. 72 of 1965

Fluoridation of Water Supplies (Carlow) Regulations, S.I. No. 88 of 1965

Fluoridation of Water Supplies (Cavan) Regulations, S.I. No. 89 of 1965

Fluoridation of Water Supplies (Clare) Regulations, S.I. No. 90 of 1965

Fluoridation of Water Supplies (Galway) Regulations, S.I. No. 91 of 1965

Fluoridation of Water Supplies (Kerry) Regulations, S.I. No. 92 of 1965

Fluoridation of Water Supplies (Kilkenny) Regulations, S.I. No. 93 of 1965

Fluoridation of Water Supplies (Leitrim) Regulations, S.I. No. 94 of 1965

Fluoridation of Water Supplies (Limerick) Regulations, S.I. No. 95 of 1965

Fluoridation of Water Supplies (Longford) Regulations, S.I. No. 96 of 1965

Fluoridation of Water Supplies (Monaghan) Regulations, S.I. No. 97 of 1965

Fluoridation of Water Supplies (Roscommon) Regulations, S.I. No. 98 of 1965

Fluoridation of Water Supplies (Tipperary North Riding) Regulations, S.I. No. 99 of 1965

Fluoridation of Water Supplies (Waterford) Regulations, S.I. No. 100 of 1965

Fluoridation of Water Supplies (Wexford) Regulations, S.I. No. 101 of 1965

Fluoridation of Water Supplies (Wicklow) (Amendment) Regulations, S.I. No. 102 of 1965

Fluoridation of Water Supplies (Cork) Regulations, S.I. No. 130 of 1965

2 · **Fluoridation of Water Supplies (Cork) Regulations, S.I. No. 29 of 1963**

Fluoridation of Water Supplies (Limerick) Regulations, S.I. No. 30 of 1963

Fluoridation of Water Supplies (Waterford) Regulations, S.I. No. 31 of 1963

Statutory Authority	Section	Statutory Instrument
Health (Fluoridation of Water Supplies) Act, No. 46 of 1960 (*Cont.*)		**Fluoridation of Water Supplies (Dublin) (Amendment) Regulations, S.I. No. 268 of 1966**
		Fluoridation of Water Supplies (Kilkenny) (Amendment) Regulations, S.I. No. 269 of 1966
		Fluoridation of Water Supplies (Wicklow) (Amendment) Regulations, S.I. No. 287 of 1974
		Fluoridation of Water Supplies (Roscommon) (Amendment) Regulations, S.I. No. 338 of 1974
		Fluoridation of Water Supplies (Leitrim) (Amendment) Regulations, S.I. No. 339 of 1974
		Fluoridation of Water Supplies (Sligo) (Amendment) Regulations, S.I. No. 226 of 1975
		Fluoridation of Water Supplies (Cork) (Amendment) Regulations, S.I. No. 129 of 1979
		Fluoridation of Water Supplies (Tipperary South Riding) (Amendment) Regulations, S.I. No. 371 of 1984
		Fluoridation of Water Supplies (Limerick) (Amendment) Regulations, S.I. No. 242 of 1985
		Fluoridation of Water Supplies (Amendment) Regulations, S.I. No. 24 of 1986
	4	**Fluoridation of Water Supplies (Cork) Regulations, S.I. No. 29 of 1963**
		Fluoridation of Water Supplies (Limerick) Regulations, S.I. No. 30 of 1963
		Fluoridation of Water Supplies (Waterford) Regulations, S.I. No. 31 of 1963
		Fluoridation of Water Supplies (Dublin) (Amendment) Regulations, S.I. No. 268 of 1966
		Fluoridation of Water Supplies (Kilkenny) (Amendment) Regulations, S.I. No. 269 of 1966
		Health (Fluoridation of Water Supplies) Regulations, S.I. No. 119 of 1971
		Fluoridation of Water Supplies (Wicklow) (Amendment) Regulations, S.I. No. 287 of 1974
		Fluoridation of Water Supplies (Roscommon) (Amendment) Regulations, S.I. No. 338 of 1974
		Fluoridation of Water Supplies (Leitrim) (Amendment) Regulations, S.I. No. 339 of 1974
		Fluoridation of Water Supplies (Sligo) (Amendment) Regulations, S.I. No. 226 of 1975
		Fluoridation of Water Supplies (Cork) (Amendment) Regulations, S.I. No. 129 of 1979
		Fluoridation of Water Supplies (Tipperary South Riding) (Amendment) Regulations, S.I. No. 371 of 1984
		Fluoridation of Water Supplies (Limerick) (Amendment) Regulations, S.I. No. 242 of 1985
		Fluoridation of Water Supplies (Amendment) Regulations, S.I. No. 24 of 1986

Statutory Authority	Section	Statutory Instrument
Health (Homes for Incapacitated Persons) Act, No. 8 of 1964	2	*Homes for Incapacitated Persons Regulations, S.I. No. 44 of 1966* **Homes for Incapacitated Persons Regulations, S.I. No. 317 of 1985**
	9	*Health (Homes for Incapacitated Persons) Act, 1964 (Commencement) Order, S.I. No. 43 of 1966*
Higher Education Authority Act, No. 22 of 1971	1	**Higher Education Authority Act, 1971 (Designation of Institution of Higher Education) Regulations, S.I. No. 58 of 1973** **Higher Education Authority Act, 1971 (Designation of Institution of Higher Education) Regulations, S.I. No. 208 of 1976** **Higher Education Authority Act, 1971 (Designation of Institution of Higher Education) (No.2) Regulations, S.I. No. 295 of 1976** **Higher Education Authority Act, 1971 (Designation of Institution of Higher Education) Regulations, S.I. No. 287 of 1978** **Higher Education Authority Act, 1971 (Designation of Institution of Higher Education) Regulations, S.I. No. 423 of 1979**
	21(2)	*Higher Education Authority Act, 1971 (Commencement) Order, S.I. No. 116 of 1972*
Hire-purchase Act, No. 16 of 1946		*Hire-purchase Act, 1946 (Commencement) Order [Vol. XXXVII p. 533] S.R.& O. No. 237 of 1946*
Hire-purchase (Amendment) Act, No. 15 of 1960	2	*Hire-purchase (Amendment) Act, 1960 (Commencement) Order, S.I. No. 200 of 1960*
	6	**Hire-purchase and Credit Sale (Advertising) Order, S.I. No. 183 of 1961** *Hire-purchase and Credit Sale Order, S.I. No. 155 of 1965* *Hiring Order, S.I. No. 156 of 1965* **Hire-purchase and Credit Sale Order, S.I. No. 197 of 1966** **Hiring Order, S.I. No. 198 of 1966** *Hire-purchase and Credit Sale (Revocation) Order, S.I. No. 205 of 1967* *Hiring (Revocation) Order, S.I. No. 206 of 1967* *Hiring Order, S.I. No. 224 of 1968* *Hire-purchase and Credit Sale Order, S.I. No. 225 of 1968* *Hiring (No.2) Order, S.I. No. 275 of 1968* *Hire-purchase and Credit Sale (No.2) Order, S.I. No. 276 of 1968* *Hire-purchase and Credit Sale Order, S.I. No. 15 of 1970* *Hiring Order, S.I. No. 16 of 1970* *Hire-purchase and Credit Sale (Revocation) Order, S.I. No. 291 of 1971* *Hiring (Revocation) Order, S.I. No. 292 of 1971*

Statutory Authority	Section	Statutory Instrument
Holidays (Employees) Act, No. 1 of 1939	9(5)	*Holidays (Employees) Act, 1939 (Sections 9 and 10) Regulations [Vol. XXXVII p. 537] S.R.& O. No. 135 of 1946*
	10(4)	*Holidays (Employees) Act, 1939 (Sections 9 and 10) Regulations [Vol. XXXVII p. 537] S.R.& O. No. 135 of 1946*
		Holidays (Employees) Act, 1939 (Section 10) Regulations, S.I. No. 264 of 1948
	25(2)	*Holidays (Employees) Act, 1939 (Commencement) Order [Vol. XXX p. 345] S.R.& O. No. 100 of 1939*
Holidays (Employees) Act, No. 33 of 1961	1	*Holidays (Employees) Act, 1961 (Commencement) Order, S.I. No. 168 of 1961*
	3(3)	*Holidays (Employees) Act, 1961 (Section 3 (3)) Regulations, S.I. No. 139 of 1963*
	8(5)	*Holidays (Employees) Act, 1961 (Public Holiday) Order, S.I. No. 339 of 1973*
	8(6)	*Holidays (Employees) Act, 1961 (Church Holidays) Order, S.I. No. 265 of 1963*
	10(6)	*Holidays (Employees) Act, 1961 (Section 10) Regulations, S.I. No. 57 of 1963*
Holidays (Employees) Act, No. 25 of 1973	2	**Holidays (Agricultural Workers) Regulations, S.I. No. 64 of 1977**
	13	**Holidays (Agricultural Workers) Regulations, S.I. No. 64 of 1977**
	14	**Holidays (Employees) Act, 1973 (Public Holiday) Regulations, S.I. No. 341 of 1974**
		Holidays (Agricultural Workers) Regulations, S.I. No. 64 of 1977
		Holidays (Employees) Act, 1973 (Public Holidays) Regulations, S.I. No. 193 of 1977
	Sch. par. 1(e)	**Holidays (Employees) Act, 1973 (Public Holiday) Regulations, S.I. No. 341 of 1974**
		Holidays (Employees) Act, 1973 (Public Holidays) Regulations, S.I. No. 193 of 1977
Horse Breeding Act, No. 13 of 1918		*Horse Breeding (Ireland) Rules, 1920, Amendment Rules [Vol. XIII p. 85] S.R.& O. No. 59 of 1927*
Horse Breeding Act, No. 3 of 1934	2	*Horse Breeding Act, 1934 (Appointed Day) Order [Vol. XIII p. 117] S.R.& O. No. 381 of 1934*
	30	**Horse Breeding Regulations [Vol. XIII p. 89] S.R.& O. No. 224 of 1934**
Horse Industry Act, No. 19 of 1970	4	*Horse Industry Act, 1970 (Establishment Day) Order, S.I. No. 43 of 1971*
	22	**Bord na gCapall Widows' and Children's Contributory Pension Scheme, S.I. No. 427 of 1981**
		Bord na gCapall Staff Superannuation Scheme, S.I. No. 307 of 1984

Statutory Authority	Section	Statutory Instrument
Horse Industry Act, No. 19 of 1970 (*Cont.*)	33	**Bord na gCapall (Assignment of Additional Functions) Order, S.I. No. 25 of 1975**
Hospitals Federation and Amalgamation Act, No. 21 of 1961	2	*Hospitals Federation and Amalgamation Act, 1961 (Establishment Day) Order, S.I. No. 223 of 1961*
	8(7)	*Sir Patrick Dun's Hospital Board (Modification) Order, S.I. No. 241 of 1967*
		Sir Patrick Dun's Hospital Board (Modification) Order, S.I. No. 118 of 1969
	22	**Sir Patrick Dun's Hospital Board (Modification) Order, S.I. No. 118 of 1969**
Housing Act, No. 19 of 1921	5	**Small Dwellings (Rates of Interest on Advances) Order [Vol. XXXVII p. 541] S.R.& O. No. 74 of 1947**
Housing Act, No. 21 of 1966	1(2)	*Housing Act, 1966 (Commencement) Order, S.I. No. 277 of 1966*
		Housing Act, 1966 (Commencement) Order, S.I. No. 70 of 1967
	5	**Housing Act, 1966 (Acquisition of Land) Regulations, S.I. No. 278 of 1966**
		Housing Authorities (Loan Charges Contributions and Management) Regulations, S.I. No. 71 of 1967
		Housing Authorities (Loan Charges Contributions and Management) (Amendment) Regulations, S.I. No. 109 of 1969
		Housing Authorities (Loan Charges Contributions and Management) Regulations, 1967 (Amendment) Regulations, S.I. No. 42 of 1970
		Housing Authorities (Loan Charges Contributions and Management) (Amendment) Regulations, S.I. No. 111 of 1971
		Housing Authorities (Loans for Acquisition or Construction of Houses) Regulations, S.I. No. 29 of 1972
		Housing Authorities (Loan Charges Contributions and Management) Regulations, 1967 (Amendment) Regulations, S.I. No. 159 of 1972
		Housing Authorities (Loan Charges Contributions and Management) Regulations, 1967 (Amendment) Regulations (No.2) S.I. No. 294 of 1972
		Housing Authorities (Loans for Acquisition or Construction of Houses) (Amendment) Regulations, S.I. No. 250 of 1973
		Housing Act, 1970 (Supplementary Grants) Regulations, S.I. No. 259 of 1973
		Housing Act, 1970 (Supplementary Grants) (Amendment) Regulations, S.I. No. 132 of 1974

Statutory Authority	Section	Statutory Instrument
Housing Act, No. 21 of 1966 (*Cont.*)		*Housing Authorities (Borrowing and Management) Regulations, S.I. No. 276 of 1974*
		Housing Authorities (Borrowing and Management) Regulations, 1974 (Amendment) Regulations, S.I. No. 143 of 1976
		Housing Authorities (Loans for Acquisition and Construction of Houses) (Amendment) Regulations, S.I. No. 40 of 1977
		Housing Authorities (Loans for Acquisition or Construction of Houses) (Amendment) (No.2) Regulations, S.I. No. 293 of 1977
		Housing Authorities (Borrowing and Management) Regulations, 1974 (Amendment) Regulations, S.I. No. 270 of 1978
		Housing Authorities (Loans for Acquisition or Construction of Houses) (Amendment) Regulations, S.I. No. 337 of 1978
		Housing Regulations, S.I. No. 296 of 1980
		Housing Regulations, 1980 (Amendment) Regulations, S.I. No. 29 of 1981
		Housing Regulations, 1980 (Amendment) (No.2) Regulations, S.I. No. 185 of 1981
		Housing Regulations, 1980 (Amendment) (No.3) Regulations, S.I. No. 186 of 1981
		Finance Act, 1981 (Certificates of Reasonable Cost) Regulations, S.I. No. 300 of 1981
		Housing Regulations, 1980 (Amendment) Regulations, S.I. No. 177 of 1982
		Housing Regulations, 1980 Regulations, S.I. No. 38 of 1983
		Finance Act, 1981 (Certificate of Reasonable Cost) Regulations (Amendment) Regulations, S.I. No. 39 of 1983
		Housing (Improvement Grants) Regulations, S.I. No. 330 of 1983
		Housing Regulations, 1980 (Amendment) Regulations, S.I. No. 50 of 1984
		Housing (Improvement Grants) (Amendment) Regulations, S.I. No. 133 of 1984
		Housing Regulations, 1980 (Amendment) (No.2) Regulations, S.I. No. 203 of 1984
		Housing Regulations, 1980 (Amendment) Regulations, S.I. No. 223 of 1985
		Housing Regulations, 1980 (Amendment) Regulations, S.I. No. 386 of 1986
	26	**Housing Act, 1970 (Supplementary Grants) Regulations, S.I. No. 259 of 1973**
		Housing Act, 1970 (Supplementary Grants) (Amendment) Regulations, S.I. No. 132 of 1974
	39	*Housing Authorities (Loans for Acquisition or Construction of Houses) (Amendment) Regulations, S.I. No. 143 of 1968*

Statutory Authority	Section	Statutory Instrument
Housing Act, No. 21 of 1966 (*Cont.*)		*Housing Authorities (Loans for Acquisition or Construction of Houses) Regulations, S.I. No. 29 of 1972*
		Housing Authorities (Loans for Acquisition or Construction of Houses) (Amendment) Regulations, S.I. No. 250 of 1973
		Housing Authorities (Loans for Acquisition and Construction of Houses) (Amendment) Regulations, S.I. No. 40 of 1977
		Housing Authorities (Loans for Acquisition or Construction of Houses) (Amendment) (No.2) Regulations, S.I. No. 293 of 1977
		Housing Authorities (Loans for Acquisition or Construction of Houses) (Amendment) Regulations, S.I. No. 337 of 1978
		Housing Regulations, 1980 (Amendment) Regulations, S.I. No. 177 of 1982
		Housing Regulations, 1980 (Amendment) Regulations, S.I. No. 223 of 1985
		Housing Regulations, 1980 (Amendment) Regulations, S.I. No. 386 of 1986
	44	*Housing Authorities (Loan Charges Contributions and Management) Regulations, S.I. No. 71 of 1967*
		Housing Authorities (Loan Charges Contributions and Management) (Amendment) Regulations, S.I. No. 109 of 1969
		Housing Authorities (Loan Charges Contributions and Management) (Amendment) Regulations, S.I. No. 111 of 1971
		Housing Authorities (Loan Charges Contributions and Management) Regulations, 1967 (Amendment) Regulations, S.I. No. 159 of 1972
		Housing Authorities (Loan Charges Contributions and Management) Regulations, 1967 (Amendment) Regulations (No.2) S.I. No. 294 of 1972
		Housing Authorities (Borrowing and Management) Regulations, S.I. No. 276 of 1974
		Housing Authorities (Borrowing and Management) Regulations, 1974 (Amendment) Regulations, S.I. No. 270 of 1978
	58	*Housing Authorities (Loan Charges Contributions and Management) Regulations, S.I. No. 71 of 1967*
		Housing Authorities (Borrowing and Management) Regulations, S.I. No. 276 of 1974
		Housing Regulations, S.I. No. 296 of 1980
	76	**Housing Act, 1966 (Acquisition of Land) Regulations, S.I. No. 278 of 1966**
	78	**Housing Act, 1966 (Acquisition of Land) Regulations, S.I. No. 278 of 1966**

Statutory Authority	Section	Statutory Instrument
Housing (Amendment) Act, No. 1 of 1948 (*Cont.*)		**Housing (Reconstructed Houses) Regulations, S.I. No. 91 of 1948**
		Housing (New Houses) Regulations, S.I. No. 267 of 1950
		Housing (Reconstructed Houses) (Amendment) Regulations, S.I. No. 308 of 1950
	17	**Housing (New Houses) Regulations, S.I. No. 90 of 1948**
	19	**Housing (New Houses) Regulations, S.I. No. 90 of 1948**
		Housing (New Houses) Regulations, S.I. No. 267 of 1950
		Housing (New Houses) (Amendment) Regulations, S.I. No. 420 of 1953
	20	**Housing (New Houses) Regulations, S.I. No. 90 of 1948**
		Housing (New Houses) Regulations, S.I. No. 267 of 1950
		Housing (New Houses) (Amendment) Regulations, S.I. No. 420 of 1953
	21	**Housing (New Houses) Regulations, S.I. No. 90 of 1948**
	38(2)	**Small Dwellings Acquisition Act, 1899 (Maximum Sum) Order, S.I. No. 60 of 1948**
		Small Dwellings Acquisition Act, 1899 (Maximum Sum) (No.2) Order, S.I. No. 248 of 1948
	43	**Labourers (Acquisition of Land) (Forms) Order, S.I. No. 293 of 1948**
Housing (Amendment) Act, No. 25 of 1950		*Housing (Management and Letting) (Amendment) Regulations, S.I. No. 336 of 1953*
	6	**Housing (New Houses) Regulations, S.I. No. 267 of 1950**
	8	*Housing (Reconstruction Grants) Regulations, S.I. No. 243 of 1950*
		Housing (Reconstruction Grants) Regulations, S.I. No. 389 of 1952
Housing (Amendment) Act, No. 16 of 1952		*Housing (Management and Letting) (Amendment) Regulations, S.I. No. 336 of 1953*
	7	**Housing (Private Water Supply and Sewerage Facilities) Regulations, S.I. No. 313 of 1952**
	24	**Housing (Grants to Housing Authorities) Regulations, S.I. No. 174 of 1954**
Housing (Amendment) Act, No. 16 of 1954	12	**Housing (Repair and Improvement Works) Regulations, S.I. No. 200 of 1954**
		Housing (Repair and Improvement Works) Regulations, S.I. No. 75 of 1958
	13	**Housing (New Houses) Regulations, S.I. No. 261 of 1954**

Statutory Authority	Section	Statutory Instrument
Housing (Amendment) Act, No. 31 of 1956	11	**Housing (Private Water Supply and Sewerage Facilities) Regulations, S.I. No. 23 of 1957**
Housing (Amendment) Act, No. 27 of 1958	14	*Housing (Loan Charges Contributions) Regulations, S.I. No. 87 of 1959*
		Housing (Loan Charges Contributions) (Amendment) Regulations, S.I. No. 179 of 1962
	24	**Housing of the Working Classes Acts (Forms) Order, S.I. No. 230 of 1958**
		Local Government (No.2) Act, 1960 (Acquisition of Land Regulations) Order, S.I. No. 97 of 1961
Housing and Labourers Act, No. 42 of 1937	5	**Housing (Works in Urban Areas) Regulations [Vol. XIII p. 205] S.R.& O. No. 255 of 1938**
Housing (Financial and Miscellaneous Provisions) Act, No. 19 of 1932	6	*Housing (Loan Charges Contributions) (Amendment) Regulations, S.I. No. 179 of 1962*
	14	**Housing (Reconstructed Houses) Order [Vol. XIII p. 315] S.R.& O. No. 79 of 1932**
		Housing (New Houses) Order [Vol. XIII p. 325] S.R.& O. No. 80 of 1932
		Housing (Loan Charges Contributions) Regulations [Vol. XIII p. 353] S.R.& O. No. 96 of 1932
		Housing (New Houses) (Amendment) Order [Vol. XIII p. 363] S.R.& O. No. 331 of 1936
		Housing (New Houses) Order [Vol. XIII p. 341] S.R.& O. No. 19 of 1938
		Housing (Loan Charges Contributions) (Amendment) Regulations [Vol. XIII p. 359] S.R.& O. No. 26 of 1938
		Housing (Loan Charges Contributions) (Amendment) Regulations, S.I. No. 362 of 1951
		Housing (Loan Charges Contributions) (Amendment) Regulations, S.I. No. 149 of 1953
		Housing (Loan Charges Contributions) (Amendment) Regulations, S.I. No. 179 of 1962
	20	**Labourers (Acquisition of Land) (Forms) Order, S.I. No. 293 of 1948**
	Sch. III	**Labourers (Acquisition of Land) (Forms) Order, S.I. No. 293 of 1948**
Housing (Financial and Miscellaneous Provisions) Acts, 1932 to 1937,		**Housing (New Houses) (Amendment) Order [Vol. XIII p. 367] S.R.& O. No. 197 of 1938**
Housing (Gaeltacht) Act, No. 41 of 1929	8	*Tithe (Gaeltacht) (Airgeadais) (Rialachain na) [Vol. XIII p. 371] S.R.& O. No. 42 of 1931*
		Tithe (Gaeltacht) (Airgeadais) (Rialachain na), S.I. No. 91 of 1960
	16(1)	**Tithe (Gaeltacht) (Ginearalta) (Rialachain na) [Vol. XIII p. 383] S.R.& O. No. 43 of 1931**

Statutory Authority	Section	Statutory Instrument
Housing (Gaeltacht) Act, No. 41 of 1929 (*Cont.*)		**Tithe (Gaeltacht) (Ginearalta) (Rialachain na) [Vol. XIII p. 393] S.R.& O. No. 269 of 1934**
		Tithe (Gaeltacht) (Ginearalta) (Rialachain na) S.I. No. 185 of 1959
		Tithe (Gaeltacht) (Ginearalta) (Rialachain na) S.I. No. 41 of 1965
		Tithe (Gaeltacht) (Ginearalta) (Rialachain na) S.I. No. 227 of 1966
Housing (Gaeltacht) Acts, 1929 to 1949,		**Tithe (Gaeltacht) (Ginearalta) (Rialachain na) S.I. No. 175 of 1949**
Housing (Gaeltacht) Acts, 1929 to 1953,		**Tithe (Gaeltacht) (Ginearalta) (Rialachain na) S.I. No. 270 of 1953**
Housing (Ireland) Act, No. 45 of 1919		*Housing (Architects and Engineers) (Revocation) Order, S.I. No. 188 of 1950*
	30(1)	**Housing (Ireland) Act, 1919 (Application of Enactments) Order [Vol. XIII p. 121] S.R.& O. No. 70 of 1928**
	32	*Housing (Architects for Schemes) Rules [Vol. XIII p. 127] S.R.& O. No. 125 of 1935*
Housing (Loans and Grants) Act, No. 27 of 1962	11	*Housing Authorities (Loans for Acquisition or Construction of Houses) Regulations, S.I. No. 130 of 1964*
		Housing Authorities (Loans for Acquisition or Construction of Houses) (Amendment) Regulations, S.I. No. 137 of 1965
	11(11)	*Housing (Loans and Grants) Act, 1962 (Commencement of Section 11) Order, S.I. No. 129 of 1964*
Housing (Miscellaneous Provisions) Act, No. 50 of 1931	18	**Housing (Public Rights of Way) Order [Vol. XIII p. 429] S.R.& O. No. 614 of 1935**
	45	**Housing of the Working Classes Acts (Forms) Order [Vol. XIII p. 397] S.R.& O. No. 27 of 1932**
		Housing (Public Rights of Way) Order [Vol. XIII p. 429] S.R.& O. No. 614 of 1935
		Housing (Inspection of Districts) Regulations [Vol. XIII p. 445] S.R.& O. No. 5 of 1936
		Housing of the Working Classes Acts (Forms) Order [Vol. XXX p. 349] S.R.& O. No. 144 of 1943
		Housing of the Working Classes Acts (Forms) Order, S.I. No. 230 of 1958
		Housing of the Working Classes Acts (Forms) (Amendment) Order, S.I. No. 24 of 1959
		Local Government (No.2) Act, 1960 (Acquisition of Land Regulations) Order, S.I. No. 97 of 1961
	45(1)	**Housing (Scale of Maps) Regulations [Vol. XIII p. 437] S.R.& O. No. 629 of 1935**
Housing (Miscellaneous Provisions) Act, No. 27 of 1979	4	**Housing Regulations, S.I. No. 296 of 1980**
		Housing Regulations, 1980 (Amendment) Regulations, S.I. No. 29 of 1981

Statutory Authority	Section	Statutory Instrument
Housing (Miscellaneous Provisions) Act, No. 27 of 1979 (*Cont.*)		**Housing Regulations, 1980 (Amendment) Regulations, S.I. No. 177 of 1982**
		Housing Regulations, 1980 (Amendment) Regulations, S.I. No. 50 of 1984
		Housing Regulations, 1980 (Amendment) (No.2) Regulations, S.I. No. 203 of 1984
	5	**Housing Regulations, S.I. No. 296 of 1980**
		Housing Regulations, 1980 (Amendment) (No.2) Regulations, S.I. No. 185 of 1981
		Housing Regulations, 1980 (Amendment) (No.3) Regulations, S.I. No. 186 of 1981
		Housing (Improvement Grants) Regulations, S.I. No. 330 of 1983
		Housing (Improvement Grants) (Amendment) Regulations, S.I. No. 133 of 1984
	6	**Housing Regulations, S.I. No. 296 of 1980**
		Housing Regulations, 1980 (Amendment) Regulations, S.I. No. 177 of 1982
	7	**Housing Regulations, S.I. No. 296 of 1980**
	8	**Housing Regulations, S.I. No. 296 of 1980**
		Housing Regulations, 1980 (Amendment) Regulations, S.I. No. 177 of 1982
		Housing Regulations, 1980 (Amendment) Regulations, S.I. No. 223 of 1985
		Housing Regulations, 1980 (Amendment) Regulations, S.I. No. 386 of 1986
	9	**Housing Regulations, S.I. No. 296 of 1980**
		Housing Regulations, 1980 (Amendment) Regulations, S.I. No. 29 of 1981
		Housing Regulations, 1980 (Amendment) Regulations, S.I. No. 386 of 1986
	10	**Housing Regulations, S.I. No. 296 of 1980**
		Housing Regulations, 1980 (Amendment) Regulations, S.I. No. 29 of 1981
		Housing Regulations, 1980 (Amendment) Regulations, S.I. No. 223 of 1985
		Housing Regulations, 1980 (Amendment) Regulations, S.I. No. 386 of 1986
	11	**Housing Regulations, S.I. No. 296 of 1980**
	12	**Housing Regulations, S.I. No. 296 of 1980**
	13	**Housing Regulations, S.I. No. 296 of 1980**
	18	**Housing Regulations, S.I. No. 296 of 1980**
		Housing Regulations, 1980 (Amendment) Regulations, S.I. No. 29 of 1981
		Finance Act, 1981 (Certificates of Reasonable Cost) Regulations, S.I. No. 300 of 1981
		Housing Regulations, 1980 (Amendment) Regulations, S.I. No. 177 of 1982

Statutory Authority	Section	Statutory Instrument
Housing (Miscellaneous Provisions) Act, No. 27 of 1979 (*Cont.*)		**Housing Regulations, 1980 Regulations, S.I. No. 38 of 1983**
		Finance Act, 1981 (Certificate of Reasonable Cost) Regulations (Amendment) Regulations, S.I. No. 39 of 1983
		Housing Regulations, 1980 (Amendment) Regulations, S.I. No. 50 of 1984
	24(3)	*Housing (Miscellaneous Provisions) Act, 1979 (Commencement) Order, S.I. No. 276 of 1979*
		Housing (Miscellaneous Provisions) Act, 1979 (Commencement) Order, S.I. No. 297 of 1980
Housing (Private Rented Dwellings) Act, No. 6 of 1982	1(2)	*Housing (Private Rented Dwellings) Act (Commencement) Order, S.I. No. 216 of 1982*
	23	**Social Welfare (Rent Allowance) Regulations, S.I. No. 220 of 1982**
		Social Welfare (Rent Allowance) Regulations, S.I. No. 186 of 1983
		Social Welfare (Rent Allowance) (Amendment) Regulations, S.I. No. 352 of 1983
		Social Welfare (Rent Allowance) (Amendment) Regulations, S.I. No. 171 of 1984
		Social Welfare (Rent Allowance) (Amendment) Regulations, S.I. No. 236 of 1985
		Social Welfare (Rent Allowance) (Amendment) Regulations, S.I. No. 218 of 1986
	24	**Housing (Private Rented Dwellings) Regulations, S.I. No. 217 of 1982**
		Housing (Private Rented Dwellings) (Amendment) Regulations, S.I. No. 286 of 1983
	25	**Housing (Private Rented Dwellings) Regulations, S.I. No. 217 of 1982**
	26	**Housing (Private Rented Dwellings) (Standards) Regulations, S.I. No. 337 of 1984**
Housing (Private Rented Dwellings) (Amendment) Act, No. 22 of 1983	2	*Rent Tribunal (Date of Establishment) Order, S.I. No. 220 of 1983*
	15	**Housing (Rent Tribunal) Regulations, S.I. No. 222 of 1983**
	22(3)	*Housing (Private Rented Dwellings) (Amendment) Act, 1983 (Commencement) Order, S.I. No. 221 of 1983*
Imports (Miscellaneous Provisions) Act, No. 23 of 1966	4	**Origin of Manufactured Goods Regulations, S.I. No. 202 of 1966**
		Origin of Manufactured Goods (Developing Countries) Regulations, S.I. No. 62 of 1972
		Origin of Manufactured Goods (Amendment) Regulations, S.I. No. 92 of 1972
Imposition of Duties Act, No. 7 of 1957	1	**Imposition of Duties (No.1) (Glazed Fireclay Pipes and Connections) Order Connections) Order, S.I. No. 130 of 1957**

Statutory Authority	Section	Statutory Instrument

Imposition of Duties Act, No. 7 of 1957 (*Cont.*)

Imposition of Duties (No.2) (Iron and Steel Sheets) Order, S.I. No. 131 of 1957

Imposition of Duties (No.3) (Yarn of Man-made Fibres) Order, S.I. No. 148 of 1957

Imposition of Duties (No.4) (Cement Articles) Order, S.I. No. 149 of 1957

Imposition of Duties (No.5) (Special Import Levies and Miscellaneous Customs Duties) (Amendment) Order, S.I. No. 163 of 1957

Imposition of Duties (No.6) (Paper and Felt Flower Pots) Order, S.I. No. 172 of 1957

Imposition of Duties (No.7) (Iron and Steel Wire, Cable and Rope) Order, S.I. No. 182 of 1957

Imposition of Duties (No.8) (Malt Extract) Order, S.I. No. 185 of 1957

Imposition of Duties (No.9) (Coil Springs) Order, S.I. No. 187 of 1957

Imposition of Duties (No.10) (Gummed Paper) Order, S.I. No. 238 of 1957

Imposition of Duties (No.11) (Roofing Slates) Order, S.I. No. 275 of 1957

Imposition of Duties (No.12) (Unprinted Paper) Order, S.I. No. 17 of 1958

Imposition of Duties (No.13) (File Covers) Order, S.I. No. 18 of 1958

Imposition of Duties (No.14) (Silk and Artificial Silk) Order, S.I. No. 30 of 1958

Imposition of Duties (No.15) (Woven Artificial Textile and Union Fabrics) Order, S.I. No. 31 of 1958

Imposition of Duties (No.17) (Dried Peas) Order, S.I. No. 36 of 1958

Imposition of Duties (No.16) (Raw Tomatoes) Order, S.I. No. 37 of 1958

Imposition of Duties (No.18) (Sections for Beehives) Order, S.I. No. 38 of 1958

Imposition of Duties (No.19) (Glucose) Order, S.I. No. 39 of 1958

Imposition of Duties (No.20) (Berets) Order, S.I. No. 49 of 1958

Imposition of Duties (No.21) (Electrical Accessories) Order, S.I. No. 57 of 1958

Imposition of Duties (No.22) (Plastic Tubes and Pipes) Order, S.I. No. 58 of 1958

Imposition of Duties (Entertainment) (No.23) Order, S.I. No. 71 of 1958

Imposition of Duties (No.24) (Flypapers and Flycatchers) Order, S.I. No. 77 of 1958

Imposition of Duties (No.25) (Slide Fasteners) Order, S.I. No. 85 of 1958

Imposition of Duties Act, No. 7 of 1957 (*Cont.*)

Imposition of Duties (No.26) (Dyed Jute Yarns and Dyed or Bleached Jute Piece Goods) Order, S.I. No. 86 of 1958

Imposition of Duties (No.27) (Undyed and Unbleached Jute Piece Goods) Order, S.I. No. 87 of 1958

Imposition of Duties (No.28) (Special Import Levies and Miscellaneous Customs Duties) Order, S.I. No. 92 of 1958

Imposition of Duties (No.29) (Abrasives) Order, S.I. No. 109 of 1958

Imposition of Duties (No.30) (Bedding) Order, S.I. No. 110 of 1958

Imposition of Duties (No.31) (Floor Coverings) Order, S.I. No. 117 of 1958

Imposition of Duties (No.32) (Waxed Paper) Order, S.I. No. 118 of 1958

Imposition of Duties (No.33) (Door and Window Fittings) Order, S.I. No. 127 of 1958

Imposition of Duties (No.34) (Milk Cans) Order, S.I. No. 128 of 1958

Imposition of Duties (No.35) (Iron and Steel Bars, Rods and Sections) Order, S.I. No. 129 of 1958

Imposition of Duties (No.36) (Processed Fabrics) Order, S.I. No. 133 of 1958

Imposition of Duties (No.37) (Pot Scourers) Order, S.I. No. 158 of 1958

Imposition of Duties (No.38) (Woven Fabrics) Order, S.I. No. 166 of 1958

Imposition of Duties (No.39) (Bandages and Bandaging Material) Order, S.I. No. 183 of 1958

Imposition of Duties (No.40) (Flavouring Essences) Order, S.I. No. 187 of 1958

Imposition of Duties (No.41) (Cast Iron Pipe Connections) Order, S.I. No. 189 of 1958

Imposition of Duties (No.42) (Wire Webbing, Netting and Fencing) Order, S.I. No. 190 of 1958

Imposition of Duties (No.43) (Metal Fabric and Expanded Metal) Order, S.I. No. 192 of 1958

Imposition of Duties (No.44) (Oil Space Heaters) Order, S.I. No. 194 of 1958

Imposition of Duties (No.45) (Spectacles) Order, S.I. No. 201 of 1958

Imposition of Duties (No.46) (Adhesive Tape) Order, S.I. No. 205 of 1958

Imposition of Duties (No.47) (Cotton Wool) Order, S.I. No. 206 of 1958

Imposition of Duties (No.48) (Electric Motors) Order, S.I. No. 218 of 1958

Imposition of Duties (No.49) (Wheat) Order, S.I. No. 222 of 1958

Imposition of Duties (No.50) (Cast Iron Baths) Order, S.I. No. 235 of 1958

Statutory Authority	Section	Statutory Instrument
Imposition of Duties Act, No. 7 of 1957 (*Cont.*)		Imposition of Duties (No.51) (Gloves) Order, S.I. No. 245 of 1958
		Imposition of Duties (No.52) (Towels and Cloths) Order, S.I. No. 246 of 1958
		Imposition of Duties (No.53) (Yarn of Continuous Filaments of Man-made Fibres) Order, S.I. No. 3 of 1959
		Imposition of Duties (No.54) (Furnishing Fabrics) Order, S.I. No. 5 of 1959
		Imposition of Duties (No.55) (Polyethylene Film) Order, S.I. No. 6 of 1959
		Imposition of Duties (No.56) (Metal Containers) Order, S.I. No. 11 of 1959
		Imposition of Duties (No.57) (Aluminium Sheet, Strip and Foil) Order, S.I. No. 16 of 1959
		Imposition of Duties (No.58) (Hoods and Shapes for Hats) Order, S.I. No. 42 of 1959
		Imposition of Duties (No.59) (Aluminium Sections) Order, S.I. No. 59 of 1959
		Imposition of Duties (No.60) (Special Import Levies and Miscellaneous Customs Duties) Order, S.I. No. 63 of 1959
		Imposition of Duties (No.61) (Asbestos Pressure Pipes) Order, S.I. No. 67 of 1959
		Imposition of Duties (No.62) (Woven Tape) Order, S.I. No. 68 of 1959
		Imposition of Duties (No.63) (Electric Fluorescent Lighting Apparatus) Order, S.I. No. 82 of 1959
		Imposition of Duties (No.64) (Gloves) Order, S.I. No. 86 of 1959
		Imposition of Duties (No.65) (Iron and Steel Wool) Order, S.I. No. 94 of 1959
		Imposition of Duties (No.66) (Tip-up Chairs) Order, S.I. No. 97 of 1959
		Imposition of Duties (No.67) (Vitreous Enamelled Hollow-ware of Wrought Iron or Wrought Steel) Order, S.I. No. 98 of 1959
		Imposition of Duties (No.68) (Metal Containers for Brewing) Order, S.I. No. 101 of 1959
		Imposition of Duties (No.69) (Hydrocarbon Oils) (Excise Duties) Order, S.I. No. 104 of 1959
		Imposition of Duties (No.70) (Plumbers Fittings of Copper or Copper Alloy) Order, S.I. No. 105 of 1959
		Imposition of Duties (No.71) (Stainless Steel Butter Churns) Order, S.I. No. 108 of 1959
		Imposition of Duties (No.72) (Carrycots) Order, S.I. No. 121 of 1959
		Imposition of Duties (No.73) (Wheat) Order, S.I. No. 132 of 1959
		Imposition of Duties (No.74) (Cider and Perry) Order, S.I. No. 137 of 1959

Imposition of Duties Act, No. 7 of 1957 (*Cont.*)

Imposition of Duties (No.75) (Disinfectants) Order, S.I. No. 145 of 1959

Imposition of Duties (No.76) (Textile Floor Coverings) Order, S.I. No. 151 of 1959

Imposition of Duties (No.77) (Cardboard Tubes) Order, S.I. No. 154 of 1959

Imposition of Duties (No.78) (Medicinal Tablets) Order, S.I. No. 155 of 1959

Imposition of Duties (No.79) (Metallic Naphthenates, Paint and Varnish Driers) Order, S.I. No. 156 of 1959

Imposition of Duties (No.80) (Aluminium Capsules) Order, S.I. No. 165 of 1959

Imposition of Duties (No.81) (Iron and Steel Wire, Bars and Sections) Order, S.I. No. 183 of 1959

Imposition of Duties (No.82) (Iron and Steel Hexagonal Mesh Netting) Order, S.I. No. 184 of 1959

Imposition of Duties (No.83) (Fats and Oils) Order, S.I. No. 212 of 1959

Imposition of Duties (No.84) (Hydrocarbon Oils) (Customs Duties) Order, S.I. No. 219 of 1959

Imposition of Duties (No.85) (Toy Balloons) Order, S.I. No. 25 of 1960

Imposition of Duties (No.86) (Leatherboard) Order, S.I. No. 26 of 1960

Imposition of Duties (No.87) (Wool Wadding) Order, S.I. No. 44 of 1960

Imposition of Duties (No.88) (Electrical Accessories) Order, S.I. No. 54 of 1960

Imposition of Duties (No.89) (Special Import Levies and Miscellaneous Customs Duties) Order, S.I. No. 83 of 1960

Imposition of Duties (No.90) (Hats and Caps for Women and Girls) Order, S.I. No. 85 of 1960

Imposition of Duties (No.91) (Newspapers and Periodicals) Order, S.I. No. 106 of 1960

Imposition of Duties (No.92) (Ball-point Pens) Order, S.I. No. 115 of 1960

Imposition of Duties (No.93) (Heels for Boots and Shoes) Order, S.I. No. 133 of 1960

Imposition of Duties (No.94) (Watches) Order, S.I. No. 156 of 1960

Imposition of Duties (No.95) (Pillow Cases and Bolster Cases) Order, S.I. No. 182 of 1960

Imposition of Duties (No.96) (Silica Powder) Order, S.I. No. 183 of 1960

Imposition of Duties (No.97) (Wadding) Order, S.I. No. 187 of 1960

Imposition of Duties (No.98) (Structural Iron and Steel Manufactures) Order, S.I. No. 202 of 1960

Imposition of Duties (No.99) (Socks of Man-made Fibres) Order, S.I. No. 215 of 1960

Statutory Authority	Section	Statutory Instrument
Imposition of Duties Act, No. 7 of 1957 (*Cont.*)		**Imposition of Duties (No.100) (Shot Gun Cartridges) Order, S.I. No. 34 of 1961**
		Imposition of Duties (No.101) (Aluminium Ladders) Order, S.I. No. 40 of 1961
		Imposition of Duties (No.102) (Cider and Perry) Order, S.I. No. 60 of 1961
		Imposition of Duties (No.103) (Power-driven Pumps) Order, S.I. No. 72 of 1961
		Imposition of Duties (No.104) (Miscellaneous Customs Duties) Order, S.I. No. 77 of 1961
		Imposition of Duties (No.105) (Motor Vehicles) Order, S.I. No. 78 of 1961
		Imposition of Duties (No.106) (Material for Saw Blades) Order, S.I. No. 84 of 1961
		Imposition of Duties (No.107) (Aluminium for Beer Containers) Order, S.I. No. 106 of 1961
		Imposition of Duties (No.108) (Used Omnibuses) Order, S.I. No. 124 of 1961
		Imposition of Duties (No.109) (Spectacles) Order, S.I. No. 127 of 1961
		Imposition of Duties (No.110) (Towels and Towelling) Order, S.I. No. 142 of 1961
		Imposition of Duties (No.111) (Wheaten Breakfast Foods) Order, S.I. No. 143 of 1961
		Imposition of Duties (No.112) (Watches) Order, S.I. No. 151 of 1961
		Imposition of Duties (No.113) (Brassières) Order, S.I. No. 153 of 1961
		Imposition of Duties (No.114) (Miscellaneous Customs Duties) Order, S.I. No. 164 of 1961
		Imposition of Duties (No.115) (Tinned Meat and Vegetable Soups) Order, S.I. No. 177 of 1961
		Imposition of Duties (No.116) (Entertainments) Order, S.I. No. 182 of 1961
		Imposition of Duties (No.117) (Wheat Products) Order, S.I. No. 225 of 1961
		Imposition of Duties (No.118) (Chrome-tanned Leather) Order, S.I. No. 236 of 1961
		Imposition of Duties (No.119) (Polyurethane) Order, S.I. No. 252 of 1961
		Imposition of Duties (No.126) (Umbrellas) Order, S.I. No. 267 of 1961
		Imposition of Duties (No.121) (Braid) Order, S.I. No. 35 of 1962
		Imposition of Duties (No.122) (Iron and Steel Files) Order, S.I. No. 80 of 1962
		Imposition of Duties (No.123) (Tobacco) Order, S.I. No. 104 of 1962
		Imposition of Duties (No.124) (Overcoats for Men or Boys) Order, S.I. No. 116 of 1962
		Imposition of Duties (No.125) (Knitted Undergarments) Order, S.I. No. 146 of 1962

Statutory Authority	Section	Statutory Instrument

Imposition of Duties Act, No. 7 of 1957 (*Cont.*)

Imposition of Duties (No.151) (Agricultural Machinery) Order, S.I. No. 34 of 1966

Imposition of Duties (No.152) (Ceramic Sanitary Ware) Order, S.I. No. 35 of 1966

Imposition of Duties (No.153) (Man-made Fibres) Order, S.I. No. 36 of 1966

Imposition of Duties (No.154) (Motor Vehicle Tyres) Order, S.I. No. 37 of 1966

Imposition of Duties (No.155) (Stockings of Man-made Fibres) Order, S.I. No. 38 of 1966

Imposition of Duties (No.156) (Twine etc.) Order, S.I. No. 39 of 1966

Imposition of Duties (No.157) (Special Import Levy) Order, S.I. No. 59 of 1966

Imposition of Duties (No.158) (Matches) Order, S.I. No. 101 of 1966

Imposition of Duties (No.159) (Customs Duties and Form of Customs Tariff) Order, S.I. No. 132 of 1966

Imposition of Duties (No.160) (Special Import Levy) (No.2) Order, S.I. No. 145 of 1966

Imposition of Duties (No.161) (Pneumatic Tyres) Order, S.I. No. 135 of 1967

Imposition of Duties (No.162) (Lawn-mowers) Order, S.I. No. 147 of 1967

Imposition of Duties (No.163) (Duty on Wines) Order, S.I. No. 155 of 1967

Imposition of Duties (No.164) (Customs Duties and Form of Customs Tariff) Order, S.I. No. 156 of 1967

Imposition of Duties (No.165) (Customs Duties and Form of Customs Tariff) Order, S.I. No. 255 of 1967

Imposition of Duties (Miscellaneous Suspensions) (Amendment) Order, S.I. No. 265 of 1967

Imposition of Duties (No.166) (Customs Duties and Form of Customs Tariff) Order, S.I. No. 279 of 1967

Imposition of Duties (No.167) (Customs Duties and Form of Customs Tariff) Order, S.I. No. 290 of 1967

Imposition of Duties (Iron and Steel Products) (No.2) Order, S.I. No. 303 of 1967

Imposition of Duties (No.168) (Customs Duties and Form of Customs Tariff) (Wheat and Meslin) Order, S.I. No. 31 of 1968

Imposition of Duties (No.169) (Customs Duties and Form of Customs Tariff) Order, S.I. No. 55 of 1968

Imposition of Duties (No.170) (Excise Duties) (Vehicles) Order, S.I. No. 68 of 1968

Imposition of Duties (No.171) (Polyurethane Foam and Solid Fuel Stove Boilers) Order, S.I. No. 81 of 1968

Imposition of Duties Act, No. 7 of 1957 (*Cont.*)

Imposition of Duties (No.172) (Customs Duties and Form of Customs Tariff) Order, S.I. No. 85 of 1968

Imposition of Duties (No.173) (Stockings) Order, S.I. No. 96 of 1968

Imposition of Duties (No.174) (Customs Duties and Form of Customs Tariff) Order, S.I. No. 135 of 1968

Imposition of Duties (Iron and Steel Products) Order, S.I. No. 144 of 1968

Imposition of Duties (No.177) (Crown Corks and Artificial Plastic Footballs) Order, S.I. No. 248 of 1968

Imposition of Duties (No.175) (Tufted Material) Order, S.I. No. 249 of 1968

Imposition of Duties (No.176) (Coated Copy-making Film) Order, S.I. No. 250 of 1968

Imposition of Duties (No.178) (Agricultural Machinery) Order, S.I. No. 7 of 1969

Imposition of Duties (No.179) (Customs Duties and Form of Customs Tariff) Order, S.I. No. 39 of 1969

Imposition of Duties (No.180) (Customs Duties and Forms of Customs Tariff) Order, S.I. No. 98 of 1969

Imposition of Duties (No.181) (Customs Duties and Form of Customs Tariff) (Wheat and Meslin) Order, S.I. No. 188 of 1969

Imposition of Duties (No.182) (Immature Spirits) Order, S.I. No. 252 of 1969

Imposition of Duties (No.183) (Excise Duties) (Vehicles) Order, S.I. No. 263 of 1969

Imposition of Duties (No.184) (Wine) Order, S.I. No. 132 of 1970

Imposition of Duties (No.185) (Customs Duties and Form of Customs Tariff) Order, S.I. No. 133 of 1970

Imposition of Duties (No.186) (Mobile Structures) Order, S.I. No. 154 of 1970

Imposition of Duties (No.187) (Customs and Excise Duties and Form of Tariff) Order, S.I. No. 268 of 1970

Imposition of Duties (No.188) (Watches) Order, S.I. No. 307 of 1970

Imposition of Duties (No.189) (Customs and Excise Duties and Form of Tariff) Order, S.I. No. 191 of 1971

Imposition of Duties (No.191) (Customs Duties and Form of Customs Tariff) Order, S.I. No. 205 of 1971

Imposition of Duties (No.190) (Sugar Confectionery) Order, S.I. No. 206 of 1971

Imposition of Duties (No.192) (Metal Badges and Footwear Heels) Order, S.I. No. 221 of 1971

Imposition of Duties (No.193) (Pneumatic Tyres) Order, S.I. No. 305 of 1971

Statutory Authority	Section	Statutory Instrument

Imposition of Duties Act, No. 7 of 1957 (*Cont.*)

Imposition of Duties (No.194) (Customs Duties and Form of Customs Tariff) Order, S.I. No. 334 of 1971

Imposition of Duties (No.195) (Customs Duties and Form of Customs Tariff) Order, S.I. No. 349 of 1971

Imposition of Duties (No.196) (Miscellaneous Customs Duties) Order, S.I. No. 353 of 1971

Imposition of Duties (No.197) (Outer Garments) Order, S.I. No. 355 of 1971

Imposition of Duties (No.198) (Customs Duties and Form of Customs Tariff) Order, S.I. No. 152 of 1972

Imposition of Duties (No.199) (Excise Duties) (Firearm Certificates) Order, S.I. No. 162 of 1972

Imposition of Duties (No.200) (Customs and Excise Duties and Form of Tariff) Order, S.I. No. 220 of 1972

Imposition of Duties (No.201) (Customs Duties and Form of Customs Tariff) Order, S.I. No. 4 of 1973

Imposition of Duties (No.202) (Customs and Excise Duties and Form of Tariff) (Amendment) Order, S.I. No. 68 of 1973

Imposition of Duties (No.203) (Customs Duties and Form of Customs Tariff) Order, S.I. No. 71 of 1973

Imposition of Duties (No.204) (Customs Duties and Form of Customs Tariff) Order, S.I. No. 72 of 1973

Imposition of Duties (No.205) (Beer, Spirits, Tobacco, Hydrocarbon Oils and Wine) Order, S.I. No. 83 of 1973

Imposition of Duties (No.206) (Stamp Duty on Certain Instruments) Order, S.I. No. 140 of 1973

Imposition of Duties (No.207) (Customs Duties and Form of Customs Tariff) Order, S.I. No. 158 of 1973

Imposition of Duties (No.208) (Beer, Spirits and Tobacco) Order, S.I. No. 249 of 1973

Imposition of Duties (No.210) (Stamp Duty on Certain Instruments) Order, S.I. No. 273 of 1973

Imposition of Duties (No.212) (Customs Duties and Form of Customs Tariff) Order, S.I. No. 341 of 1973

Imposition of Duties (No.213) (Customs Duties and Form of Customs Tariff) Order, S.I. No. 174 of 1974

Imposition of Duties (No.214) (Mineral Hydrocarbon Light Oils) Order, S.I. No. 350 of 1974

Imposition of Duties (No.215) (Customs Duties and Form of Customs Tariff) Order, S.I. No. 356 of 1974

Imposition of Duties (No.216) (Excise Duties) (Vehicles) Order, S.I. No. 5 of 1975

Imposition of Duties Act, No. 7 of 1957 (*Cont.*)

Imposition of Duties (No.217) (Stamp Duty on Certain Instruments) Order, S.I. No. 27 of 1975

Imposition of Duties (No.218) (Customs Duties and Form of Customs Tariff) Order, S.I. No. 127 of 1975

Imposition of Duties (No.219) (Customs Duties and Form of Customs Tariff) Order, S.I. No. 131 of 1975

Imposition of Duties (No.220) (Footwear) Order, S.I. No. 157 of 1975

Imposition of Duties (No.221) (Excise Duties) Order, S.I. No. 307 of 1975

Imposition of Duties (No.222) (Customs Duties and Form of Customs Tariff) Order, S.I. No. 320 of 1975

Imposition of Duties (No.223) (Footwear) Order, S.I. No. 324 of 1975

Imposition of Duties (No.224) (Customs Duties and Form of Customs Tariff) Order, S.I. No. 130 of 1976

Imposition of Duties (No.225) (Footwear) Order, S.I. No. 171 of 1976

Imposition of Duties (No.226) (Footwear) Order, S.I. No. 299 of 1976

Imposition of Duties (No.227) (Certain Processed Agricultural Products) Order, S.I. No. 97 of 1977

Imposition of Duties (No.228) (Stamp Duty on Certain Instruments) Order, S.I. No. 101 of 1977

Imposition of Duties (No.229) (Excise Duties) (Vehicles) Order, S.I. No. 112 of 1977

Imposition of Duties (No.230) (Certain Processed Agricultural Products) (No.2) Order, S.I. No. 150 of 1977

Imposition of Duties (No.231) (Excise Duties) (Vehicles) Order, S.I. No. 241 of 1977

Imposition of Duties (No.232) (Hydrocarbon Oils) Order, S.I. No. 279 of 1977

Imposition of Duties (No.233) (Rates of Excise Duty on Tobacco Products) Order, S.I. No. 384 of 1977

Imposition of Duties (No.234) (Excise Duties on Hydrocarbon Oils and Beer) Order, S.I. No. 2 of 1978

Imposition of Duties (No.235) (Beer) Order, S.I. No. 36 of 1978

Imposition of Duties (No.236) (Excise Duties on Motor Vehicles, Televisions and Gramophone Records) Order, S.I. No. 57 of 1979

Imposition of Duties (No.237) (Beer) Order, S.I. No. 67 of 1979

Imposition of Duties (No.238) (Exemption from Agreement as to Stamp Duty on Certain Transfers) Order, S.I. No. 121 of 1979

Imposition of Duties (No.239) (Agricultural Produce) (Cattle and Milk) Order, S.I. No. 152 of 1979

Statutory Authority	Section	Statutory Instrument
Imposition of Duties Act, No. 7 of 1957 (*Cont.*)		*Imposition of Duties (No.240) (Agricultural Produce) (Cereals and Sugar Beet) Order, S.I. No. 153 of 1979*
		Imposition of Duties (No.241) (Limit on Stamp Duty in respect of Certain Transactions between Bodies Corporate) Order, S.I. No. 244 of 1979
		Imposition of Duties (No.242) (Agricultural Produce) (Amendment) Order, S.I. No. 250 of 1979
		Imposition of Duties (No.243) (Excise Duty on Tobacco Products) Order, S.I. No. 296 of 1979
		Imposition of Duties (No.244) (Excise Duties on Spirits, Beer and Hydrocarbon Oils) Order, S.I. No. 415 of 1979
		Imposition of Duties (No.245) (Excise Duty on Wine and Made Wine) Order, S.I. No. 416 of 1979
		Imposition of Duties (No.246) (Beer) Order, S.I. No. 49 of 1980
		Imposition of Duties (No.247) (Stamp Duty on Conveyances to Sub-Purchasers) Order, S.I. No. 123 of 1980
		Imposition of Duties (No.248) (Stamp Duty on Bills of Exchange and Promissory Notes) Order, S.I. No. 136 of 1980
		Imposition of Duties (No.249) (Exemption of Certain Instruments from Stamp Duty) Order, S.I. No. 317 of 1980
		Imposition of Duties (No.250) (Beer) Order, S.I. No. 10 of 1981
		Imposition of Duties (No.251) (Excise Duty on Wine) Order, S.I. No. 219 of 1981
		Imposition of Duties (No.252) (Stamp Duty on Bills of Exchange and Promissory Notes) Order, S.I. No. 271 of 1981
		Imposition of Duties (No.253) (Limit on Stamp Duty in respect of Certain Transactions between Bodies Corporate) Order, S.I. No. 272 of 1981
		Imposition of Duties (No.254) (Excise Duty on Tobacco Products) Order, S.I. No. 299 of 1981
		Imposition of Duties (No.255) (Hydrocarbon Oils) Order, S.I. No. 367 of 1981
		Imposition of Duties (No.256) (Excise Duty on Hydrocarbon Oils) Order, S.I. No. 404 of 1981
		Imposition of Duties (No.257) (Beer) Order, S.I. No. 22 of 1982
		Imposition of Duties (No.258) (Beer) (No.2) Order, S.I. No. 37 of 1982
		Imposition of Duties (No.259) (Excise Duties) Order, S.I. No. 48 of 1982
		Imposition of Duties (No.260) (Excise Duty on Video Players) Order, S.I. No. 49 of 1982
		Imposition of Duties (No.261) (Excise Duties) Order, S.I. No. 9 of 1983

Imposition of Duties Act, No. 7 of
1957 (*Cont.*)

*Imposition of Duties (No.262) (Beer) Order, S.I.
No. 12 of 1983*

**Imposition of Duties (No.263) (Excise Duties) (No.2)
Order, S.I. No. 42 of 1983**

**Imposition of Duties (No.264) (Hydrocarbons)
Order, S.I. No. 85 of 1983**

**Imposition of Duties (No.265) (Excise Duty on
Hydrocarbon Oils) Order, S.I. No. 126 of 1983**

**Imposition of Duties (No.266) (Tobacco Products)
Order, S.I. No. 213 of 1983**

**Imposition of Duties (No.266) (Beer) (No.2) Order,
S.I. No. 398 of 1983**

*Imposition of Duties (No.268) (Stamp Duty on Bills
of Exchange, Promissory Notes, Credit Cards and
Charge Cards) Order, S.I. No. 34 of 1984*

*Imposition of Duties (No.269) (Exemption of
Certain Instruments from Stamp Duty) , Order,
S.I. No. 49 of 1984*

**Imposition of Duties (No.270) (Spirits) Order, S.I.
No. 252 of 1984**

**Imposition of Duties (No.271) (Beer) Order, S.I.
No. 352 of 1984**

**Imposition of Duties (No.272) (Excise Duties on
Motor Vehicles) Order, S.I. No. 353 of 1984**

**Imposition of Duties (No.273) (Excise Duty on
Motor-cycles) Order, S.I. No. 354 of 1984**

**Imposition of Duties (No.274) (Televisions) Order,
S.I. No. 41 of 1985**

*Imposition of Duties (No.275) (Stamp Duties on
Course Bets) Order, S.I. No. 60 of 1985*

*Imposition of Duties (No.276) (Stamp Duties on
Conveyance and Transfers on Sale of Stocks and
Marketable Securities) Order, S.I. No. 146 of
1985*

*Imposition of Duties (No.277) (Stamp Duty on
Certain Instruments) Order, S.I. No. 151 of 1985*

*Imposition of Duties (No.278) (Stamp Duty on
Certain Instruments) Order, (1983) S.I. No. 152
of 1985*

**Imposition of Duties (No.279) (Motor Vehicles and
Motor-cycles) (Amendment) Order, S.I. No. 267
of 1985**

**Imposition of Duties (No.280) (Excise Duties)
(Vehicles) Order, S.I. No. 304 of 1985**

**Imposition of Duties (No.281) (Hydrocarbons)
Order, S.I. No. 3 of 1986**

*Imposition of Duties (No.282) (Stamp Duty on
Statements of Interest) Order, S.I. No. 27 of 1986*

**Imposition of Duties (No.283) (Value-added Tax)
Order, S.I. No. 412 of 1986**

**Imposition of Duties (Beer) (No.284) Order, S.I.
No. 438 of 1986**

Statutory Authority	Section	Statutory Instrument
Imposition of Duties Act, No. 7 of 1957 (*Cont.*)	3	Imposition of Duties (Miscellaneous Suspensions) Order, S.I. No. 268 of 1957
		Imposition of Duties (Yarn of Man-made Fibres) Order, S.I. No. 66 of 1958
		Imposition of Duties (Miscellaneous Suspensions) Order, 1957 (Amendment) Order, S.I. No. 136 of 1958
		Imposition of Duties (Woven Fabrics) Order, S.I. No. 151 of 1958
		Imposition of Duties (Gas Pressure Cylinders) Order, S.I. No. 252 of 1958
		Imposition of Duties (Yarn of Man-made Fibres) (No.2) Order, S.I. No. 262 of 1958
		Imposition of Duties (Raw Onions and Raw Shallots) Order, S.I. No. 4 of 1959
		Imposition of Duties (Aluminium Sheet, Strip and Foil) Order, S.I. No. 17 of 1959
		Suspension of Duty on Isinglass and Edible Gelatin Order, S.I. No. 65 of 1959
		Imposition of Duties (Aluminium Sheet, Strip and Foil) (Amendment) Order, S.I. No. 109 of 1959
		Imposition of Duties (Wooden Handles) Order, S.I. No. 170 of 1959
		Imposition of Duties (Isinglass and Edible Gelatine) Order, S.I. No. 180 of 1959
		Suspension of Duty on Electric Switches Order, S.I. No. 186 of 1959
		Imposition of Duties (Gas Pressure Cylinders) Order, S.I. No. 193 of 1959
		Imposition of Duties (Aluminium Sheet, Strip and Foil) (Amendment) (No.2) Order, S.I. No. 224 of 1959
		Imposition of Duties (Coated Aluminium Strip) Order, S.I. No. 13 of 1960
		Imposition of Duties (Iron and Steel Umbrella Shafts) Order, S.I. No. 118 of 1960
		Imposition of Duties (Isinglass and Edible Gelatine) Order, S.I. No. 216 of 1960
		Imposition of Duties (Gas Pressure Cylinders) Order, S.I. No. 229 of 1960
		Imposition of Duties (Aluminium Sheet, Strip and Foil) (Amendment) Order, S.I. No. 263 of 1960
		Imposition of Duties (Yarn of Man-made Fibres) Order, S.I. No. 273 of 1960
		Imposition of Duties (Shot Gun Cartridges) Order, S.I. No. 35 of 1961
		Imposition of Duties (Floor Coverings) Order, S.I. No. 85 of 1961
		Imposition of Duties (Aluminium Sheet, Strip and Foil) Order, S.I. No. 128 of 1961
		Imposition of Duties (Milk Cans) Order, S.I. No. 207 of 1961

Imposition of Duties Act, No. 7 of 1957 (*Cont.*)

Imposition of Duties (Coated Aluminium Strip) Order, S.I. No. 208 of 1961

Imposition of Duties (Isinglass and Edible Gelatine) Order, S.I. No. 234 of 1961

Imposition of Duties (Gas Pressure Cylinders) Order, S.I. No. 260 of 1961

Imposition of Duties (Yarn of Man-made Fibres) Order, S.I. No. 298 of 1961

Imposition of Duties (Flock) Order, S.I. No. 58 of 1962

Imposition of Duties (Floor Coverings) Order, S.I. No. 67 of 1962

Imposition of Duties (Inlaid Linoleum) Order, S.I. No. 88 of 1962

Imposition of Duties (Isinglass and Edible Gelatine) Order, S.I. No. 177 of 1962

Imposition of Duties (Miscellaneous Suspensions) Order, S.I. No. 228 of 1962

Imposition of Duties (Iron and Steel Products) Order, S.I. No. 19 of 1963

Imposition of Duties (Iron and Steel Products) (Amendment) Order, S.I. No. 70 of 1963

Imposition of Duties (Iron and Steel Products) (No.2) Order, S.I. No. 146 of 1963

Imposition of Duties (Beehive Sections of Wood) Order, S.I. No. 176 of 1963

Imposition of Duties (Iron and Steel Products) (No.3) Order, S.I. No. 271 of 1963

Imposition of Duties (Iron and Steel Products) Order, S.I. No. 157 of 1964

Imposition of Duties (Iron and Steel Products) (No.2) Order, S.I. No. 296 of 1964

Imposition of Duties (Iron and Steel Products) Order, S.I. No. 140 of 1965

Imposition of Duties (Form of Customs Tariff) (Amendment) Order, S.I. No. 216 of 1965

Imposition of Duties (Iron and Steel Products) (No.2) Order, S.I. No. 267 of 1965

Imposition of Duties (Agricultural Machinery) Order, S.I. No. 41 of 1966

Imposition of Duties (Ceramic Sanitary Ware) Order, S.I. No. 42 of 1966

Imposition of Duties (Ironing Boards of Wood) Order, S.I. No. 60 of 1966

Imposition of Duties (Iron and Steel Products) Order, S.I. No. 152 of 1966

Imposition of Duties (Miscellaneous Suspensions) Order, S.I. No. 153 of 1966

Imposition of Duties (Iron and Steel Products) (No.2) Order, S.I. No. 280 of 1966

Imposition of Duties (Imitation Parchment or Greaseproof Paper) Order, S.I. No. 86 of 1967

Statutory Authority	Section	Statutory Instrument
Imposition of Duties Act, No. 7 of 1957 (*Cont.*)		*Imposition of Duties (Iron and Steel Products) Order, S.I. No. 166 of 1967*
		Imposition of Duties (Agricultural Machinery) Order, S.I. No. 11 of 1969
		Imposition of Duties (Agricultural Machinery) Order, S.I. No. 241 of 1970
		Imposition of Duties (Iron and Steel Products) Order, S.I. No. 343 of 1971
		Imposition of Duties (Miscellaneous Suspensions) Order, S.I. No. 317 of 1972
Imposition of Duties (Dumping and Subsidies) Act, No. 11 of 1968	13	*Imposition of Duties (Dumping and Subsidies) (Provisional Duty on Pencils) Order, S.I. No. 48 of 1970*
		Imposition of Duties (Dumping and Subsidies) (Provisional Duty on Calcium Ammonium Nitrate) Order, S.I. No. 69 of 1970
		Imposition of Duties (Dumping and Subsidies) (Provisional Duty on Urea) Order, S.I. No. 230 of 1970
		Imposition of Duties (Dumping and Subsidies) (Provisional Duty on Reinforced Polyester Resin Sheets) Order, S.I. No. 86 of 1972
		Imposition of Duties (Dumping and Subsidies) (Provisional Duty on Paper Serviettes and Table Napkins) Order, S.I. No. 316 of 1972
		Imposition of Duties (Dumping and Subsidies) (Provisional Duty on Dog Foods) Order, S.I. No. 342 of 1972
		Imposition of Duties (Dumping and Subsidies) (Provisional Duty on Toilet Paper and Facial Tissues) Order, S.I. No. 117 of 1973
		Imposition of Duties (Dumping and Subsidies) (Provisional Duty on Calcium Ammonium Nitrate) Order, S.I. No. 168 of 1975
		Imposition of Duties (Dumping and Subsidies) (Provisional Duty on Electric Filament Lamps) Order, S.I. No. 113 of 1976
		Imposition of Duties (Dumping and Subsidies) (Provisional Duty on Steel Bars and Angles) Order, S.I. No. 16 of 1977
		Imposition of Duties (Dumping and Subsidies) (Provisional Duty on Steel Bars and Angles) (No.2) Order, S.I. No. 67 of 1977
		Imposition of Duties (Dumping and Subsidies) (Provisional Duty on Hardboard) Order, S.I. No. 84 of 1977
		Imposition of Duties (Dumping and Subsidies) (Provisional Duty on Refrigerators) Order, S.I. No. 85 of 1977
		Imposition of Duties (Dumping and Subsidies) (Provisional Duty on Refrigerators) (No.2) Order, S.I. No. 115 of 1977

Imposition of Duties (Dumping and Subsidies) Act, No. 11 of 1968 (*Cont.*)

Imposition of Duties (Dumping and Subsidies) (Provisional Duties on Wooden Louvre Doors) Order, S.I. No. 146 of 1977

Imposition of Duties (Dumping and Subsidies) (Provisional Duty on Bond Printing Paper) Order, S.I. No. 171 of 1977

14   *Imposition of Duties (Dumping and Subsidies) (Anti-dumping Duty on Pencils) Order, S.I. No. 208 of 1970*

Imposition of Duties (Dumping and Subsidies) (No.2) (Anti-dumping Duty on Calcium Ammonium Nitrate) Order, S.I. No. 217 of 1970

Imposition of Duties (Dumping and Subsidies) (No.3) (Anti-dumping Duty on Urea) Order, S.I. No. 121 of 1971

Imposition of Duties (Dumping and Subsidies) (Anti-dumping Duty on Slaked Lime) Order, S.I. No. 128 of 1972

Imposition of Duties (Dumping and Subsidies) (No.5) (Anti-dumping Duty on Reinforced Polyester Resin Sheets) Order, S.I. No. 235 of 1972

Imposition of Duties (Dumping and Subsidies) (No.6) (Anti-dumping Duty on Pencils) Order, S.I. No. 274 of 1972

Imposition of Duties (Dumping and Subsidies) (No.211) (Anti-dumping Duty on Toilet Paper and Facial Tissues) Order, S.I. No. 307 of 1973

Imposition of Duties (Dumping and Subsidies) (No.8) (Anti-dumping Duty on Footwear) Order, S.I. No. 328 of 1973

Imposition of Duties (Dumping and Subsidies) (No.10) (Anti-dumping Duty on Blouses) Order, S.I. No. 156 of 1975

Imposition of Duties (Dumping and Subsidies) (No.11) (Anti-dumping Duty on Pencils) Order, S.I. No. 180 of 1977

Imposition of Duties (Dumping and Subsidies) (No.12) (Anti-dumping Duty on Steel Bars and Angles) Order, S.I. No. 198 of 1977

Imposition of Duties (Dumping and Subsidies) (No.13) (Anti-dumping Duty on Hardboard) Order, S.I. No. 199 of 1977

Imposition of Duties (Dumping and Subsidies) (No.14) (Anti-dumping Duty on Wooden Louvre Doors) Order, S.I. No. 200 of 1977

Imposition of Duties (Dumping and Subsidies) (No.15) (Anti-dumping Duty on Bond Printing Paper) Order, S.I. No. 201 of 1977

Imposition of Duties (Dumping and Subsidies) (No.6) (Anti-dumping Duty on Pencils) Order, S.I. No. 274 of 1972

Imposition of Duties (Dumping and Subsidies) (No.7) (Miscellaneous Amendments) Order, S.I. No. 318 of 1972

Statutory Authority	Section	Statutory Instrument

Imposition of Duties (Dumping and Subsidies) Act, No. 11 of 1968 (*Cont.*)

Imposition of Duties (Dumping and Subsidies) (No.9) (Anti-dumping Duty on Slaked Lime) (Revocation) Order, S.I. No. 340 of 1973

Imposition of Duties (Dumping and Subsidies) (No.211) (Anti-dumping Duty on Toilet Paper and Facial Tissues) Order, 1973 (Revocation) Order, S.I. No. 58 of 1974

Imposition of Duties (Dumping and Subsidies) (Nos.2 and 3) Orders (Revocation) Order, S.I. No. 102 of 1974

Imposition of Duties (Dumping and Subsidies) (Provisional Duty on Steel Bars and Angles) (No.2) Order, 1977 (Revocation) Order, S.I. No. 161 of 1977

Imposition of Duties (Dumping and Subsidies) (Provisional Duty on Refrigerators) Order, 1977 (Revocation) Order, S.I. No. 207 of 1977

Imposition of Duties (Dumping and Subsidies) (Provisional Duty on Refrigerators) (No.2) Order, 1977 (Revocation) Order, S.I. No. 208 of 1977

Imposition of Duties (Dumping and Subsidies) (No.5) (Anti-dumping Duty on Reinforced Polyester Resin Sheets) Order, 1972 (Revocation) Order, S.I. No. 217 of 1974

Income Tax Act, No. 40 of 1918

7(8) **Income Tax Documents Service by Post [Vol. XIII p. 453] S.R.& O. No. 36 of 1925**

Income Tax Documents Service by Post [Vol. XIII p. 459] S.R.& O. No. 48 of 1929

Surtax Regulations, S.I. No. 155 of 1963

220(8) **Income Tax Documents Service by Post [Vol. XIII p. 453] S.R.& O. No. 36 of 1925**

Income Tax Documents Service by Post [Vol. XIII p. 459] S.R.& O. No. 48 of 1929

238(a) **Income Tax Documents Service by Post [Vol. XIII p. 453] S.R.& O. No. 36 of 1925**

Income Tax Documents Service by Post [Vol. XIII p. 459] S.R.& O. No. 48 of 1929

Income Tax Act, No. 6 of 1967

127 *Income Tax (Employments) Regulations, S.I. No. 223 of 1970*

Income Tax (Employments) Regulations, S.I. No. 182 of 1971

Income Tax (Employments) Regulations, S.I. No. 260 of 1972

Income Tax (Employments) Regulations, S.I. No. 86 of 1974

Income Tax (Employments) (No.2) Regulations, S.I. No. 292 of 1974

Income Tax (Employments) Regulations, S.I. No. 170 of 1975

Income Tax (Employments) Regulations, S.I. No. 368 of 1977

Statutory Authority	Section	Statutory Instrument
Income Tax Act, No. 6 of 1967 (*Cont.*)		Income Tax (Employments) Regulations, S.I. No. 377 of 1978
		Income Tax (Employments) Regulations, S.I. No. 284 of 1980
		Income Tax (Employments) Regulations, S.I. No. 67 of 1984
		Income Tax (Employments) Regulations, S.I. No. 148 of 1985
	142A	Income Tax (Rent Relief) Regulations, S.I. No. 318 of 1982
	361	Double Taxation Relief (Taxes on Income) (Government of Canada) Order, S.I. No. 212 of 1967
		Double Taxation Relief (Taxes on Income and Capital) (Swiss Confederation) Order, S.I. No. 240 of 1967
		Double Taxation Relief (Taxes on Income) (Republic of Austria) Order, S.I. No. 250 of 1967
		Double Taxation Relief (Taxes on Income and Capital) (Kingdom of the Netherlands) Order, S.I. No. 22 of 1970
		Double Taxation Relief (Taxes on Income) (Cyprus) Order, S.I. No. 79 of 1970
		Double Taxation Relief (Taxes on Income and Capital) (Kingdom of Norway) Order, S.I. No. 80 of 1970
		Double Taxation Relief (Taxes on Income and Capital) (Finland) Order, S.I. No. 81 of 1970
		Double Taxation Relief (Taxes on Income) (Republic of France) Order, S.I. No. 162 of 1970
		Double Taxation Relief (Taxes on Income) (Italy) Order, S.I. No. 64 of 1973
		Double Taxation Relief (Taxes on Income and on Capital) (Grand Duchy of Luxembourg) Order, S.I. No. 65 of 1973
		Double Taxation Relief (Taxes on Income) (Kingdom of Belgium) Order, S.I. No. 66 of 1973
		Double Taxation Relief (Taxes on Income) (Republic of Zambia) Order, S.I. No. 130 of 1973
		Double Taxation Relief (Taxes on Income) (Japan) Order, S.I. No. 259 of 1974
		Double Taxation Relief (Taxes on Income) (Pakistan) Order, S.I. No. 260 of 1974
		Double Taxation Relief (Taxes on Income) (United Kingdom) Order, S.I. No. 143 of 1975
		Double Taxation Relief (Taxes on Income and Capital Gains) (United Kingdom) Order, S.I. No. 319 of 1976
		Double Taxation Relief (Taxes on Income and Capital) (Australia) Order, S.I. No. 406 of 1983
		Double Taxation Relief (Taxes on Income and Capital) (Swiss Confederation) Order, S.I. No. 76 of 1984

Statutory Authority	Section	Statutory Instrument
Income Tax Act, No. 6 of 1967 (*Cont.*)	362	**Double Taxation Relief (Sea or Air Transport) (Finland) Order, S.I. No. 232 of 1967**
		Double Taxation Relief (Sea or Air Transport) (Belgium) Order, S.I. No. 89 of 1970
		Double Taxation Relief (Sea or Air Transport) (Spain) Order, S.I. No. 26 of 1977
	530	*Income Tax (Undistributed Income of Certain Companies) Regulations, S.I. No. 329 of 1974*
Industrial Alcohol Act, No. 40 of 1934	15	*Industrial Alcohol Act (Advisory Body) Order [Vol. XIII p. 495] S.R.& O. No. 58 of 1935*
Industrial Alcohol Act, No. 23 of 1938	3(1)	*Industrial Alcohol Act, 1938 (Appointed Day) Order [Vol. XXX p. 385] S.R.& O. No. 69 of 1939*
Industrial and Commercial Property (Protection) Act, No. 16 of 1927		**Industrial Property Rules [Vol. XIII p. 517] S.R.& O. No. 78 of 1927**
		Industrial Property (Amendment) Rules [Vol. XIII p. 581] S.R.& O. No. 14 of 1928
		Industrial Property (Amendment) (No.2) Rules [Vol. XIII p. 583] S.R.& O. No. 77 of 1928
		Industrial Property (Amendment) (No.3) Rules [Vol. XIII p. 585] S.R.& O. No. 50 of 1929
		Industrial Property Rules, 1927 (Amendment) Rules, S.I. No. 55 of 1950
		Industrial Property Rules, 1927 (Amendment) Rules, S.I. No. 116 of 1955
	2	*Industrial and Commercial Property (Protection) Act, 1927 (Commencement) Order [Vol. XIII p. 513] S.R.& O. No. 60 of 1927*
	9	**Industrial Property Rules, 1927 (Amendment) Rules, S.I. No. 315 of 1956**
		Industrial Property Rules, 1927 (Amendment) Rules, S.I. No. 155 of 1958
		Industrial Property Rules, 1927 (Amendment) Rules, S.I. No. 315 of 1980
	63	*Registers of Patent Agents and Clerks Rules [Vol. XIII p. 589] S.R.& O. No. 79 of 1927*
		Registers of Patent Agents and Clerks Rules, 1927 Amendment Rules [Vol. XIII p. 597] S.R.& O. No. 35 of 1928
		Registers of Patent Agents and Clerks Rules (Amendment) Rules, S.I. No. 56 of 1950
	152(2)	**Patents, Designs and Trade Marks (International Arrangements) Order, S.I. No. 22 of 1959**
	152(5)	*Patents, Designs and Trade Marks (International Convention) Order, (1938) [Vol. XIII p. 609] S.R.& O. No. 28 of 1928*

Statutory Authority	Section	Statutory Instrument

Industrial and Commercial Property (Protection) Act, No. 16 of 1927 *(Cont.)*

Patents, Designs and Trade Marks (Spanish Morocco) Order [Vol. XIII p. 627] S.R.& O. No. 75 of 1928

Patents, Designs and Trade Marks (International Arrangements) (Amendment) Order, S.I. No. 104 of 1960

Patents, Designs and Trade Marks (International Arrangements) (Amendment) Order, S.I. No. 23 of 1961

Patents, Designs and Trade Marks (International Arrangements) (Amendment) Order, S.I. No. 235 of 1962

Patents, Designs and Trade Marks (International Arrangements) (Amendment) Order, S.I. No. 275 of 1963

Patents, Designs and Trade Marks (International Arrangements) (Amendment) Order, S.I. No. 30 of 1966

Patents, Designs and Trade Marks (International Arrangements) (Amendment) Order, S.I. No. 32 of 1968

Industrial and Commercial Property (Protection) Act, 1927 (Section 152) (Declaration) Order, S.I. No. 315 of 1976

Patents, Designs and Trade Marks (International Arrangements) (Amendment) Order, S.I. No. 316 of 1976

152(6) *Patents, Designs and Trade Marks (United Kingdom) Order [Vol. XIII p. 605] S.R.& O. No. 27 of 1928*

Patents and Designs (South Africa and British India) Order [Vol. XIII p. 615] S.R.& O. No. 46 of 1928

Patents, Designs and Trade Marks (Canada) Order [Vol. XIII p. 619] S.R.& O. No. 47 of 1928

Patents, Designs and Trade Marks (New Zealand) Order [Vol. XIII p. 623] S.R.& O. No. 48 of 1928

Patents, Designs and Trade Marks (Commonwealth of Australia) Order, S.I. No. 256 of 1956

153 **Industrial Property (Amendment) Rules, S.I. No. 176 of 1964**

Industrial Property (Amendment) Rules, S.I. No. 190 of 1969

Industrial Property (Amendment) (No.2) Rules, S.I. No. 412 of 1980

154(2)(a) *Copyright (Irish Translations) (United States of America) Order [Vol. XIII p. 637] S.R.& O. No. 46 of 1929*

156 *Copyright Regulations [Vol. XIII p. 509] S.R.& O. No. 58 of 1927*

165 *Copyright (Importation of Infringing Works) [Vol. XIII p. 599] S.R.& O. No. 44 of 1928*

Statutory Authority	Section	Statutory Instrument
Industrial and Commercial Property (Protection) Act, No. 16 of 1927 (*Cont.*)	169	*Copyright Regulations [Vol. XIII p. 509] S.R.& O. No. 58 of 1927*
	175	*Copyright (United States of America) Order [Vol. XIII p. 631] S.R.& O. No. 45 of 1929*
		Copyright (Foreign Countries) Order [Vol. XIII p. 641] S.R.& O. No. 2 of 1930
		Copyright (United Kingdom and British Dominions) Order [Vol. XIII p. 651] S.R.& O. No. 73 of 1930
		Copyright (Union of South Africa) Order [Vol. XIII p. 663] S.R.& O. No. 74 of 1930
		Copyright (Federated Malay States) Order [Vol. XIII p. 671] S.R.& O. No. 111 of 1934
		Copyright (Commonwealth of Australia) Order [Vol. XIII p. 679] S.R.& O. No. 272 of 1937
		Copyright (Foreign Countries) Order, S.I. No. 50 of 1959
		Copyright (Foreign Countries) (Amendment) Order, S.I. No. 199 of 1960
		Copyright (Foreign Countries) (Amendment) Order, S.I. No. 5 of 1963
		Copyright (Foreign Countries) (Amendment) (No.2) Order, S.I. No. 274 of 1963
		Copyright (Foreign Countries) Order, S.I. No. 132 of 1978
		Copyright (Foreign Countries) (No.2) Order, S.I. No. 133 of 1978
	178	*Copyright Regulations [Vol. XIII p. 509] S.R.& O. No. 58 of 1927*
	181	*Register of Entertainments Regulations [Vol. XIII p. 505] S.R.& O. No. 57 of 1927*
Industrial and Commercial Property (Protection) Acts, 1927 and 1929,		*Industrial Property (Amendment) Rules (No.4) [Vol. XXX p. 365] S.R.& O. No. 7 of 1939*
		Industrial Property (Amendment) Rules (No.5) [Vol. XXX p. 379] S.R.& O. No. 51 of 1939
Industrial and Commercial Property (Protection) Acts, 1927 to 1949,		**Industrial Property (Amendment) Rules (No.7) S.I. No. 56 of 1954**
Industrial and Commercial Property (Protection) (Amendment) Act, No. 13 of 1957	11	*Copyright (Foreign Countries) (Amendment) Order, S.I. No. 199 of 1960*
		Copyright (Foreign Countries) (Amendment) Order, S.I. No. 5 of 1963
		Copyright (Foreign Countries) (Amendment) (No.2) Order, S.I. No. 274 of 1963
Industrial and Commercial Property (Protection) (Amendment) Act, No. 21 of 1958	5(3)	*Industrial and Commercial Property (Protection) (Amendment) Act, 1958 (Commencement) Order, S.I. No. 182 of 1958*
Industrial and Provident Societies Act, No. 39 of 1893	73	*Industrial and Provident Societies (Fees) Regulations, S.I. No. 84 of 1978*

Statutory Authority	Section	Statutory Instrument
Industrial and Provident Societies Act, No. 39 of 1893 (*Cont.*)		**Industrial and Provident Societies (Fees) Regulations, S.I. No. 291 of 1983**
	74	**Industrial and Provident Societies (Forms) Regulations, S.I. No. 351 of 1986**
Industrial and Provident Societies (Amendment) Act, No. 23 of 1978	5(3)	**Industrial and Provident Societies (Amendment) Act, 1978 (Section 5 (3)) Regulations, S.I. No. 338 of 1983**
	33(1)	*Industrial and Provident Societies (Financial Limit) Regulations, S.I. No. 254 of 1979*
		Industrial and Provident Societies (Financial Limits) Regulations, S.I. No. 327 of 1979
		Industrial and Provident Societies (Financial Limits) Regulations, S.I. No. 392 of 1985
Industrial Credit Act, No. 25 of 1933	11(2)	**Industrial Credit Company Ltd. (Accounts) Regulations [Vol. XIII p. 685] S.R.& O. No. 375 of 1934**
		Industrial Credit Company Ltd. (Accounts) Regulations [Vol. XIII p. 695] S.R.& O. No. 56 of 1938
Industrial Development Act, No. 32 of 1969	3	*Industrial Development Act, 1969 (Commencement) Order, S.I. No. 24 of 1970*
		Industrial Development Act, 1969 (Commencement) (No.2) Order, S.I. No. 63 of 1970
	6	*Industrial Development Act, 1969 (Designated Areas) Order, S.I. No. 287 of 1970*
		Industrial Development Act, 1969 (Designated Areas) Order, S.I. No. 330 of 1971
		Industrial Development Act, 1969 (Designated Areas) Order, S.I. No. 176 of 1972
		Industrial Development Act, 1969 (Designated Areas) (No.2) Order, S.I. No. 231 of 1972
		Industrial Development Act, 1969 (Designated Areas) (No.3) Order, S.I. No. 309 of 1972
		Industrial Development Act, 1969 (Designated Areas) (No.4) Order, S.I. No. 310 of 1972
		Industrial Development Act, 1969 (Designated Areas) Order, S.I. No. 272 of 1973
		Industrial Development Act, 1969 (Designated Areas) Order, S.I. No. 286 of 1974
		Industrial Development Act, 1969 (Designated Areas) Order, S.I. No. 216 of 1975
		Industrial Development Act, 1969 (Designated Areas) Order, S.I. No. 212 of 1976
		Industrial Development Act, 1969 (Designated Areas) Order, S.I. No. 298 of 1977
		Industrial Development Act, 1969 (Designated Areas) Order, S.I. No. 120 of 1978
		Industrial Development Act, 1969 (Designated Areas) Order, S.I. No. 139 of 1979
		Industrial Development Act, 1969 (Designated Areas) Order, S.I. No. 355 of 1982
		Industrial Development Act, 1969 (Designated Areas) Order, S.I. No. 273 of 1984

Statutory Authority	Section	Statutory Instrument
Industrial Development Act, No. 9 of 1986	1	*Industrial Development Act, 1986 (Commencement) Order, S.I. No. 105 of 1986*
Industrial Development (No.2) Act, No. 14 of 1981	3	**Industrial Development (Service Industries) Order, S.I. No. 321 of 1981**
Industrial Grants Act, No. 26 of 1959	15(2)	*Industrial Grants Act, 1959 (Commencement) Order, S.I. No. 144 of 1959*
Industrial Relations Act, No. 26 of 1946		*Industrial Relations Act, 1946 Regulations [Vol. XXXVII p. 629] S.R.& O. No. 320 of 1946*
		Industrial Relations Act, 1946 Regulations, S.I. No. 258 of 1950
	2	*Industrial Relations Act, 1946 (Commencement) Order [Vol. XXXVII p. 625] S.R.& O. No. 304 of 1946*
	10(5)	*Labour Court (Appointment of First Workers' Members) Regulations [Vol. XXXVII p. 639] S.R.& O. No. 292 of 1946*
		Labour Court (Appointment of Workers' Members) Regulations, S.I. No. 195 of 1951
		Labour Court (Appointment of Workers' Members) Regulations, S.I. No. 231 of 1956
	35	**Messengers (Cork City Area) Joint Labour Committee Establishment Order [Vol. XXXVII p. 655] S.R.& O. No. 298 of 1947**
		Law Clerks Joint Labour Committee (Establishment) Order [Vol. XXXVII p. 643] S.R.& O. No. 308 of 1947
		Creameries Joint Labour Committee Establishment Order, S.I. No. 173 of 1948
		Messengers (Dublin City and Dun Laoghaire) Joint Labour Committee Establishment Order, S.I. No. 128 of 1950
		Messengers (Waterford City) Joint Labour Committee Establishment Order, S.I. No. 118 of 1957
		Messengers (Limerick City) Joint Labour Committee Establishment Order, S.I. No. 119 of 1957
		Provender Milling Joint Labour Committee Establishment Order, S.I. No. 223 of 1960
		Hairdressing Joint Labour Committee Establishment Order, S.I. No. 212 of 1964
		Hotels Joint Labour Committee Establishment Order, S.I. No. 81 of 1965
		Catering Joint Labour Committee Establishment Order, S.I. No. 225 of 1977
		Hairdressing (Cork County Borough) Joint Labour Committee Establishment Order, S.I. No. 226 of 1977
		Contract Cleaning (City and County of Dublin) Joint Labour Committee Establishment Order, S.I. No. 105 of 1984

Industrial Relations Act, No. 26 of 1946 (*Cont.*)

39

Messengers (Cork City Area) Joint Labour Committee Establishment Order [Vol. XXXVII p. 655] S.R.& O. No. 298 of 1947

Law Clerks Joint Labour Committee (Establishment) Order [Vol. XXXVII p. 643] S.R.& O. No. 308 of 1947

Creameries Joint Labour Committee Establishment Order, S.I. No. 173 of 1948

Messengers (Dublin City and Dun Laoghaire) Joint Labour Committee Establishment Order, S.I. No. 128 of 1950

Messengers (Waterford City) Joint Labour Committee Establishment Order, S.I. No. 118 of 1957

Messengers (Limerick City) Joint Labour Committee Establishment Order, S.I. No. 119 of 1957

Provender Milling Joint Labour Committee Establishment Order, S.I. No. 223 of 1960

Hairdressing Joint Labour Committee Establishment Order, S.I. No. 212 of 1964

Hotels Joint Labour Committee Establishment Order, S.I. No. 81 of 1965

Catering Joint Labour Committee Establishment Order, S.I. No. 225 of 1977

Hairdressing (Cork County Borough) Joint Labour Committee Establishment Order, S.I. No. 226 of 1977

Contract Cleaning (City and County of Dublin) Joint Labour Committee Establishment Order, S.I. No. 105 of 1984

40

Button-Making Joint Labour Committee (Amendment) Establishment Order [Vol. XXXVII p. 649] S.R.& O. No. 412 of 1947

Establishment Order (Tailoring Joint Labour Committee) Amendment Order, S.I. No. 203 of 1948

Establishment Order (Women's Clothing and Millinery Joint Labour Committee) Amendment Order, S.I. No. 333 of 1953

Establishment Order (Tailoring Joint Labour Committee) Amendment Order, S.I. No. 334 of 1953

Establishment Order (Aerated Waters Joint Labour Committee) Amendment Order, S.I. No. 158 of 1956

Provender Milling Joint Labour Committee Establishment Order (Amendment Order) S.I. No. 102 of 1962

Establishment Order (Sugar Confectionery and Food Preserving Joint Labour Committee) Amendment Order, S.I. No. 147 of 1962

Paper Box Joint Labour Committee (Abolition) Order, S.I. No. 113 of 1963

Industrial Relations Act, No. 26 of 1946 (*Cont.*)

Creameries Joint Labour Committee (Abolition) Order, S.I. No. 340 of 1978

Hand Embroidery Joint Labour Committee (Abolition) Order, S.I. No. 341 of 1978

Rope, Twine and Net Joint Labour Committee (Abolition) Order, S.I. No. 342 of 1978

Tobacco Joint Labour Committee (Abolition) Order, S.I. No. 343 of 1978

Sugar Confectionery Joint Labour Committee (Abolition) Order, S.I. No. 344 of 1978

Packing Joint Labour Committee (Abolition) Order, S.I. No. 186 of 1979

Button-Making Joint Labour Committee (Abolition) Order, S.I. No. 39 of 1984

Messengers (Cork City) Joint Labour Committee (Abolition) Order, S.I. No. 40 of 1984

Messengers (Limerick City) Joint Labour Committee (Abolition) Order, S.I. No. 41 of 1984

Messengers (Waterford City) Joint Labour Committee (Abolition) Order, S.I. No. 42 of 1984

43   *Tobacco Joint Labour Committee Employment Regulation Order [Vol. XXXVII p. 727] S.R.& O. No. 90 of 1947*

Packing Joint Labour Committee Employment Regulation Order [Vol. XXXVII p. 661] S.R.& O. No. 136 of 1947

Sugar Confectionery and Food Preserving Joint Labour Committee Employment Regulation Order [Vol. XXXVII p. 697] S.R.& O. No. 171 of 1947

Paper Box Joint Labour Committee Employment Regulation Order [Vol. XXXVII p. 667] S.R.& O. No. 197 of 1947

Aerated Waters Joint Labour Committee Employment Regulation Order [Vol. XXXVII p. 577] S.R.& O. No. 209 of 1947

Women's Clothing and Millinery Joint Labour Committee Employment Regulation Order [Vol. XXXVII p. 735] S.R.& O. No. 210 of 1947

Tailoring Joint Labour Committee Employment Regulation Order [Vol. XXXVII p. 705] S.R.& O. No. 229 of 1947

General Waste Materials Reclamation Joint Labour Committee Employment Regulation Order [Vol. XXXVII p. 613] S.R.& O. No. 269 of 1947

Button-making Joint Labour Committee Employment Regulation Order [Vol. XXXVII p. 605] S.R.& O. No. 292 of 1947

Shirtmaking Joint Labour Committee Employment Regulation Order [Vol. XXXVII p. 673] S.R.& O. No. 372 of 1947

Boot and Shoe Repairing Joint Labour Committee Employment Regulation Order [Vol. XXXVII p. 583] S.R.& O. No. 454 of 1947

Industrial Relations Act, No. 26 of 1946 (*Cont.*)		*Employment Regulation Order (Handkerchief and Household Piece Goods Joint Labour Committee) S.I. No. 57 of 1948*
		Employment Regulation Order (Sugar Confectionery and Food Preserving Joint Labour Committee) S.I. No. 82 of 1948
		Employment Regulation Order (Paper Box Joint Labour Committee) S.I. No. 83 of 1948
		Employment Regulation Order (Tobacco Joint Labour Committee) S.I. No. 84 of 1948
		Employment Regulation Order (Brush and Broom Joint Labour Committee) S.I. No. 96 of 1948
		Employment Regulation Order (Aerated Waters Joint Labour Committee) S.I. No. 113 of 1948
		Employment Regulation Order (Tailoring Joint Labour Committee) S.I. No. 114 of 1948
		Employment Regulation Order (Messengers (Cork City Area) Joint Labour Committee) S.I. No. 163 of 1948
		Employment Regulation Order (Packing Joint Labour Committee) S.I. No. 179 of 1948
		Employment Regulation Order (Law Clerks Joint Labour Committee) S.I. No. 180 of 1948
		Employment Regulation Order (Women's Clothing and Millinery Joint Labour Committee) S.I. No. 251 of 1948
		Employment Regulation Order (Button-making Joint Labour Committee) S.I. No. 252 of 1948
		Employment Regulation Order (General Waste Materials Reclamation Joint Labour Committee) S.I. No. 253 of 1948
		Employment Regulation Order (Creameries Joint Labour Committee) S.I. No. 260 of 1948
		Emergency Powers (No.157) Order, 1942 (Sixth Amendment) Order, S.I. No. 277 of 1948
		Employment Regulation Order (Shirtmaking Joint Labour Committee) S.I. No. 303 of 1948
		Employment Regulation (No.2) Order (Law Clerks Joint Labour Committee) S.I. No. 374 of 1948
		Employment Regulation Order (Tailoring Joint Labour Committee) S.I. No. 38 of 1949
		Employment Regulation Order (Aerated Waters Joint Labour Committee) S.I. No. 39 of 1949
		Employment Regulation Order (Handkerchief and Household Piece Goods Joint Labour Committee) S.I. No. 59 of 1949
		Employment Regulation Order (Paper Box Joint Labour Committee) (Male Workers) S.I. No. 60 of 1949
		Employment Regulation Order (Brush and Broom Joint Labour Committee) S.I. No. 61 of 1949
		Employment Regulation Order (Law Clerks Joint Labour Committee) S.I. No. 265 of 1949

Statutory Authority	Section	Statutory Instrument
Industrial Relations Act, No. 26 of 1946 (*Cont.*)		*Employment Regulation Order (Creameries Joint Labour Committee) S.I. No. 271 of 1949*
		Employment Regulation (Holidays) Order (Shirt-making Joint Labour Committee) S.I. No. 332 of 1949
		Employment Regulation (Holidays) Order (Cream-eries Joint Labour Committee) S.I. No. 333 of 1949
		Employment Regulation Order (Creameries Joint Labour Committee) S.I. No. 191 of 1950
		Employment Regulation Order (Tobacco Joint Labour Committee) S.I. No. 314 of 1950
		Employment Regulation Order (Handkerchief and Household Piece Goods Joint Labour Committee) , 1951,, S.I. No. 36 of 1951
		Employment Regulation Order (Paper Box Joint Labour Committee) (Female Workers) S.I. No. 68 of 1951
		Employment Regulation Order (Button-making Joint Labour Committee) S.I. No. 126 of 1951
		Employment Regulation Order (Aerated Waters Joint Labour Committee) S.I. No. 127 of 1951
		Employment Regulation Order (Women's Clothing and Millinery Joint Labour Committee) S.I. No. 128 of 1951
		Employment Regulation Order (Messengers (Cork City Area) Joint Labour Committee) S.I. No. 129 of 1951
		Employment Regulation Order (Shirtmaking Joint Labour Committee) S.I. No. 136 of 1951
		Employment Regulation Order (Sugar Confectionery and Food Preserving Joint Labour Committee) S.I. No. 139 of 1951
		Employment Regulation (No.2) Order (Paper Box Joint Labour Committee) S.I. No. 153 of 1951
		Employment Regulation Order (Brush and Broom Joint Labour Committee) S.I. No. 163 of 1951
		Employment Regulation Order (Tailoring Joint Labour Committee) S.I. No. 167 of 1951
		Employment Regulation Order (Packing Joint Labour Committee) S.I. No. 189 of 1951
		Employment Regulation Order (General Waste Materials Reclamation Joint Labour Committee) S.I. No. 190 of 1951
		Employment Regulation Order (Messengers (Dublin City and Dun Laoghaire) Joint Labour Committee) S.I. No. 204 of 1951
		Employment Regulation Order (Law Clerks Joint Labour Committee) S.I. No. 230 of 1951
		Employment Regulation Order (Creameries Joint Labour Committee) S.I. No. 239 of 1951
		Employment Regulation (No.2) Order (Messengers (Dublin City and Dun Laoghaire) Joint Labour Committee) S.I. No. 354 of 1951

Statutory Authority	Section	Statutory Instrument

Industrial Relations Act, No. 26 of
1946 (*Cont.*)

Employment Regulation Order (Paper Box Joint Labour Committee) S.I. No. 181 of 1952

Employment Regulation Order (Boot and Shoe Repairing Joint Labour Committee) S.I. No. 187 of 1952

Employment Regulation Order (Aerated Waters Joint Labour Committee) S.I. No. 238 of 1952

Employment Regulation Order (Sugar Confectionery and Food Preserving Joint Labour Committee) S.I. No. 247 of 1952

Employment Regulation Order (Creameries Joint Labour Committee) S.I. No. 276 of 1952

Employment Regulation Order (Packing Joint Labour Committee) S.I. No. 292 of 1952

Employment Regulation Order (Brush and Broom Joint Labour Committee) S.I. No. 299 of 1952

Employment Regulation Order (Tobacco Joint Labour Committee) S.I. No. 310 of 1952

Employment Regulation Order (Law Clerks Joint Labour Committee) S.I. No. 325 of 1952

Employment Regulation Order (Handkerchief and Household Piece Goods Joint Labour Committee) S.I. No. 348 of 1952

Employment Regulation Order (General Waste Materials Reclamation Joint Labour Committee) S.I. No. 369 of 1952

Employment Regulation Order (Women's Clothing and Millinery Joint Labour Committee) S.I. No. 45 of 1953

Employment Regulation Order (Shirtmaking Joint Labour Committee) S.I. No. 46 of 1953

Employment Regulation Order (Messengers (Dublin City and Dun Laoghaire) Joint Labour Committee) S.I. No. 89 of 1953

Employment Regulation Order (Tailoring Joint Labour Committee) S.I. No. 90 of 1953

Employment Regulation Order (Button-making Joint Labour Committee) S.I. No. 118 of 1953

Employment Regulation Order (Creameries Joint Labour Committee) S.I. No. 132 of 1953

Employment Regulation Order (Messengers (Cork City Area) Joint Labour Committee) S.I. No. 154 of 1953

Employment Regulation (Female Workers) Order (Paper Box Joint Labour Committee) S.I. No. 190 of 1953

Employment Regulation (Male Workers) Order (Paper Box Joint Labour Committee) S.I. No. 244 of 1953

Employment Regulation Order (Messengers (Dublin City and Dun Laoghaire) Joint Labour Committee) S.I. No. 38 of 1954

Employment Regulation Order (Messengers (Cork City Area) Joint Labour Committee) S.I. No. 54 of 1954

Industrial Relations Act, No. 26 of 1946 (*Cont.*)

Employment Regulation Order (Creameries Joint Labour Committee) S.I. No. 202 of 1954

Employment Regulation Order (Women's Clothing and Millinery Joint Labour Committee) S.I. No. 276 of 1954

Employment Regulation Order (Packing Joint Labour Committee) S.I. No. 9 of 1955

Employment Regulation Order (Handkerchief and Household Piece Goods Joint Labour Committee) S.I. No. 11 of 1955

Employment Regulation Order (Shirtmaking Joint Labour Committee) S.I. No. 110 of 1955

Employment Regulation Order (Aerated Waters Joint Labour Committee) S.I. No. 111 of 1955

Employment Regulation (Waiting Time) Order (Shirtmaking Joint Labour Committee) S.I. No. 139 of 1955

Employment Regulation Order (Tobacco Joint Labour Committee) S.I. No. 148 of 1955

Employment Regulation Order (Messengers (Cork City Area) Joint Labour Committee) S.I. No. 158 of 1955

Employment Regulation Order (Boot and Shoe Repairing Joint Labour Committee) S.I. No. 179 of 1955

Employment Regulation Order (Law Clerks Joint Labour Committee) S.I. No. 184 of 1955

Employment Regulation Order (Sugar Confectionery and Food Preserving Joint Labour Committee) S.I. No. 189 of 1955

Employment Regulation Order (Tailoring Joint Labour Committee) S.I. No. 193 of 1955

Employment Regulation (Male Workers) Order (Packing Joint Labour Committee) S.I. No. 230 of 1955

Employment Regulation Order (Button-making Joint Labour Committee) S.I. No. 231 of 1955

Employment Regulation Order (General Waste Materials Reclamation Joint Labour Committee) S.I. No. 232 of 1955

Employment Regulation Order (Messengers (Dublin City and Dun Laoghaire) Joint Labour Committee) S.I. No. 261 of 1955

Employment Regulation Order (Brush and Broom Joint Labour Committee) S.I. No. 8 of 1956

Employment Regulation Order (Women's Clothing and Millinery Joint Labour Committee) S.I. No. 9 of 1956

Employment Regulation Order (Paper Box Joint Labour Committee) S.I. No. 11 of 1956

Employment Regulation Order (Aerated Waters Joint Labour Committee) S.I. No. 27 of 1956

Employment Regulation Order (Handkerchief and Household Piece Goods Joint Labour Committee) S.I. No. 28 of 1956

Statutory Authority	Section	Statutory Instrument

Industrial Relations Act, No. 26 of
1946 (*Cont.*)

Employment Regulation Order (Shirtmaking Joint Labour Committee) S.I. No. 105 of 1956

Employment Regulation (Female Workers) Order (Packing Joint Labour Committee) S.I. No. 137 of 1956

Employment Regulation Order (Boot and Shoe Repairing Joint Labour Committee) S.I. No. 138 of 1956

Employment Regulation Order (Tobacco Joint Labour Committee) S.I. No. 144 of 1956

Employment Regulation Order (Sugar Confectionery and Food Preserving Joint Labour Committee) S.I. No. 195 of 1956

Employment Regulation Order (Creameries Joint Labour Committee) S.I. No. 260 of 1956

Employment Regulation Order (Aerated Waters and Wholesale Bottling Joint Labour Committee) S.I. No. 322 of 1956

Employment Regulation Order (Women's Clothing and Millinery Joint Labour Committee) S.I. No. 87 of 1957

Employment Regulation (Waiting Time) Order (Boot and Shoe Repairing Joint Labour Committee) S.I. No. 88 of 1957

Employment Regulation Order (Creameries Joint Labour Committee) S.I. No. 176 of 1957

Employment Regulation Order (Messengers (Waterford City) Joint Labour Committee) S.I. No. 192 of 1957

Employment Regulation Order (Messengers (Limerick City) Joint Labour Committee) S.I. No. 195 of 1957

Employment Regulation Order (Tailoring Joint Labour Committee) S.I. No. 250 of 1957

Employment Regulation Order (Sugar Confectionery and Food Preserving Joint Labour Committee) S.I. No. 2 of 1958

Employment Regulation Order (General Waste Materials Reclamation Joint Labour Committee) S.I. No. 3 of 1958

Employment Regulation Order (Tobacco Joint Labour Committee) S.I. No. 4 of 1958

Employment Regulation Order (Brush and Broom Joint Labour Committee) S.I. No. 9 of 1958

Employment Regulation Order (Law Clerks Joint Labour Committee) S.I. No. 10 of 1958

Employment Regulation Order (Packing Joint Labour Committee) S.I. No. 11 of 1958

Employment Regulation Order (Handkerchief and Household Piece Goods Joint Labour Committee) S.I. No. 19 of 1958

Employment Regulation Order (Aerated Waters and Wholesale Bottling Joint Labour Committee) S.I. No. 23 of 1958

Industrial Relations Act, No. 26 of 1946 (*Cont.*)

Employment Regulation Order (Button-making Joint Labour Committee) S.I. No. 24 of 1958

Employment Regulation Order (Paper Box Joint Labour Committee) S.I. No. 25 of 1958

Employment Regulation Order (Shirtmaking Joint Labour Committee) S.I. No. 26 of 1958

Employment Regulation Order (Women's Clothing and Millinery Joint Labour Committee) S.I. No. 27 of 1958

Employment Regulation Order (Creameries Joint Labour Committee) S.I. No. 41 of 1958

Employment Regulation Order (Messengers (Dublin City and Dun Laoghaire) Joint Labour Committee) S.I. No. 42 of 1958

Employment Regulation Order (Boot and Shoe Repairing Joint Labour Committee) S.I. No. 68 of 1958

Employment Regulation Order (Messengers (Cork City Area) Joint Labour Committee) S.I. No. 99 of 1958

Employment Regulation Order (Paper Box Joint Labour Committee) S.I. No. 168 of 1959

Employment Regulation Order (Aerated Waters and Wholesale Bottling Joint Labour Committee) S.I. No. 181 of 1959

Employment Regulation Order (Packing Joint Labour Committee) S.I. No. 194 of 1959

Employment Regulation Order (Sugar Confectionery and Food Preserving Joint Labour Committee) S.I. No. 195 of 1959

Employment Regulation Order (Brush and Broom Joint Labour Committee) S.I. No. 199 of 1959

Employment Regulation Order (Women's Clothing and Millinery Joint Labour Committee) S.I. No. 215 of 1959

Employment Regulation Order (Tobacco Joint Labour Committee) S.I. No. 216 of 1959

Employment Regulation Order (Button-making Joint Labour Committee) S.I. No. 229 of 1959

Employment Regulation Order (Handkerchief and Household Piece Goods Joint Labour Committee) S.I. No. 230 of 1959

Employment Regulation Order (General Waste Materials Reclamation Joint Labour Committee) S.I. No. 231 of 1959

Employment Regulation Order (Shirtmaking Joint Labour Committee) S.I. No. 232 of 1959

Employment Regulation Order (Tailoring Joint Labour Committee) S.I. No. 233 of 1959

Employment Regulation Order (Messengers (Dublin City and Dun Laoghaire) Joint Labour Committee) S.I. No. 12 of 1960

Employment Regulation Order (Creameries Joint Labour Committee) S.I. No. 24 of 1960

Industrial Relations Act, No. 26 of
1946 (*Cont.*)

Employment Regulation Order (Boot and Shoe Repairing Joint Labour Committee) S.I. No. 31 of 1960

Employment Regulation Order (Law Clerks Joint Labour Committee) S.I. No. 58 of 1960

Employment Regulation Order (Messengers (Cork City Area) Joint Labour Committee) S.I. No. 143 of 1960

Employment Regulation Order (Messengers (Waterford City) Joint Labour Committee) S.I. No. 152 of 1960

Employment Regulation Order (Messengers (Limerick City) Joint Labour Committee) S.I. No. 192 of 1960

Employment Regulation Order (Brush and Broom Joint Labour Committee) S.I. No. 205 of 1960

Employment Regulation Order (Aerated Waters and Wholesale Bottling Joint Labour Committee) S.I. No. 1 of 1961

Employment Regulation Order (Sugar Confectionery and Food Preserving Joint Labour Committee) S.I. No. 18 of 1961

Employment Regulation Order (Provender Milling Joint Labour Committee) S.I. No. 111 of 1961

Employment Regulation Order (Tailoring Joint Labour Committee) S.I. No. 112 of 1961

Employment Regulation Order (Women's Clothing and Millinery Joint Labour Committee) S.I. No. 132 of 1961

Employment Regulation Order (Shirtmaking Joint Labour Committee) S.I. No. 149 of 1961

Employment Regulation Order (Brush and Broom Joint Labour Committee) S.I. No. 180 of 1961

Employment Regulation Order (Messengers (Dublin City and Dun Laoghaire) Joint Labour Committee) S.I. No. 239 of 1961

Employment Regulation Order (General Waste Materials Reclamation Joint Labour Committee) S.I. No. 240 of 1961

Employment Regulation Order (Packing Joint Labour Committee) S.I. No. 241 of 1961

Employment Regulation Order (Messengers (Cork City Area) Joint Labour Committee) S.I. No. 250 of 1961

Employment Regulation Order (Messengers (Waterford City) Joint Labour Committee) S.I. No. 251 of 1961

Employment Regulation Order (Button-making Joint Labour Committee) S.I. No. 254 of 1961

Employment Regulation Order (Handkerchief and Household Piece Goods Joint Labour Committee) S.I. No. 255 of 1961

Employment Regulation Order (Tobacco Joint Labour Committee) S.I. No. 256 of 1961

Statutory Authority	Section	Statutory Instrument

Industrial Relations Act, No. 26 of 1946 (*Cont.*)

Employment Regulation Order (Creameries Joint Labour Committee) S.I. No. 262 of 1961

Employment Regulation (No.2) Order (Aerated Waters and Wholesale Bottling Joint Labour Committee) S.I. No. 300 of 1961

Employment Regulation Order (Paper Box Joint Labour Committee) S.I. No. 17 of 1962

Employment Regulation Order (Provender Milling Joint Labour Committee) S.I. No. 18 of 1962

Employment Regulation Order (Sugar Confectionery and Food Preserving Joint Labour Committee) S.I. No. 19 of 1962

Employment Regulation Order (Tailoring Joint Labour Committee) S.I. No. 20 of 1962

Employment Regulation Order (Brush and Broom Joint Labour Committee) S.I. No. 40 of 1962

Employment Regulation Order (Boot and Shoe Repairing Joint Labour Committee) S.I. No. 47 of 1962

Employment Regulation Order (Shirtmaking Joint Labour Committee) S.I. No. 48 of 1962

Employment Regulation Order (Law Clerks Joint Labour Committee) S.I. No. 54 of 1962

Employment Regulation Order (Women's Clothing and Millinery Joint Labour Committee) S.I. No. 55 of 1962

Employment Regulation Order (Creameries Joint Labour Committee) S.I. No. 108 of 1962

Employment Regulation Order (Packing Joint Labour Committee) S.I. No. 109 of 1962

Employment Regulation Order (Aerated Waters and Wholesale Bottling Joint Labour Committee) S.I. No. 159 of 1962

Employment Regulation (No.2) Order (Paper Box Joint Labour Committee) S.I. No. 208 of 1962

Employment Regulation Order (Provender Milling Joint Labour Committee) S.I. No. 22 of 1963

Employment Regulation Order (Creameries Joint Labour Committee) S.I. No. 134 of 1963

Employment Regulation Order (Sugar Confectionery and Food Preserving Joint Labour Committee) S.I. No. 264 of 1963

Employment Regulation Order (Brush and Broom Joint Labour Committee) (Apprentices) S.I. No. 39 of 1964

Employment Regulation Order (Aerated Waters and Wholesale Bottling Joint Labour Committee) S.I. No. 52 of 1964

Employment Regulation Order (Button-making Joint Labour Committee) S.I. No. 67 of 1964

Employment Regulation Order (Handkerchief and Household Piece Goods Joint Labour Committee) S.I. No. 68 of 1964

Industrial Relations Act, No. 26 of 1946 (*Cont.*)		*Employment Regulation Order (Packing Joint Labour Committee) S.I. No. 69 of 1964*
		Employment Regulation Order (Women's Clothing and Millinery Joint Labour Committee) S.I. No. 70 of 1964
		Employment Regulation Order (Shirtmaking Joint Labour Committee) S.I. No. 79 of 1964
		Employment Regulation Order (Provender Milling Joint Labour Committee) S.I. No. 83 of 1964
		Employment Regulation Order (Messengers (Dublin City and Dun Laoghaire) Joint Labour Committee) S.I. No. 84 of 1964
		Employment Regulation Order (Boot and Shoe Repairing Joint Labour Committee) S.I. No. 85 of 1964
		Employment Regulation Order (Creameries Joint Labour Committee) S.I. No. 86 of 1964
		Employment Regulation Order (Brush and Broom Joint Labour Committee) S.I. No. 90 of 1964
		Employment Regulation Order (Messengers (Waterford City) Joint Labour Committee) S.I. No. 100 of 1964
		Employment Regulation Order (Messengers (Cork City Area) Joint Labour Committee) S.I. No. 101 of 1964
		Employment Regulation Order (Law Clerks Joint Labour Committee) S.I. No. 109 of 1964
		Employment Regulation Order (General Waste Materials Reclamation Joint Labour Committee) S.I. No. 116 of 1964
		Employment Regulation Order (Messengers (Limerick City) Joint Labour Committee) S.I. No. 117 of 1964
		Employment Regulation Order (Tailoring Joint Labour Committee) S.I. No. 151 of 1964
		Employment Regulation Order (Sugar Confectionery and Food Preserving Joint Labour Committee) S.I. No. 227 of 1964
		Employment Regulation Order (Tobacco Joint Labour Committee) S.I. No. 255 of 1964
		Employment Regulation Order (Provender Milling Joint Labour Committee) S.I. No. 2 of 1965
		Employment Regulation Order (Messengers (Dublin City and Dun Laoghaire) Joint Labour Committee) S.I. No. 110 of 1965
		Employment Regulation Order (Women's Clothing and Millinery Joint Labour Committee) S.I. No. 17 of 1966
		Employment Regulation Order (Brush and Broom Joint Labour Committee) S.I. No. 156 of 1966
		Employment Regulation Order (Handkerchief and Household Piece Goods Joint Labour Committee) S.I. No. 157 of 1966

Statutory Authority	Section	Statutory Instrument

Industrial Relations Act, No. 26 of 1946 (*Cont.*)

Employment Regulation Order (Shirtmaking Joint Labour Committee) S.I. No. 158 of 1966

Employment Regulation Order (Tailoring Joint Labour Committee) S.I. No. 159 of 1966

Employment Regulation Order (Aerated Waters and Wholesale Bottling Joint Labour Committee) S.I. No. 171 of 1966

Employment Regulation Order (Button-making Joint Labour Committee) S.I. No. 172 of 1966

Employment Regulation Order (General Waste Materials Reclamation Joint Labour Committee) S.I. No. 173 of 1966

Employment Regulation Order (Hairdressing Joint Labour Committee) S.I. No. 174 of 1966

Employment Regulation Order (Law Clerks Joint Labour Committee) S.I. No. 175 of 1966

Employment Regulation Order (Messengers (Dublin City and Dun Laoghaire) Joint Labour Committee) S.I. No. 176 of 1966

Employment Regulation Order (Packing Joint Labour Committee) S.I. No. 177 of 1966

Employment Regulation Order (Provender Milling Joint Labour Committee) S.I. No. 178 of 1966

Employment Regulation Order (Sugar Confectionery and Food Preserving Joint Labour Committee) S.I. No. 203 of 1966

Employment Regulation Order (Messengers (Waterford City) Joint Labour Committee) S.I. No. 204 of 1966

Employment Regulation Order (Messengers (Cork City Area) Joint Labour Committee) S.I. No. 205 of 1966

Employment Regulation Order (Boot and Shoe Repairing Joint Labour Committee) S.I. No. 219 of 1966

Employment Regulation (No.2) Order (Women's Clothing and Millinery Joint Labour Committee) S.I. No. 220 of 1966

Employment Regulation Order (Tobacco Joint Labour Committee) S.I. No. 240 of 1966

Employment Regulation Order (Messengers (Limerick City) Joint Labour Committee) S.I. No. 256 of 1966

Employment Regulation Order (Creameries Joint Labour Committee) S.I. No. 10 of 1967

Employment Regulation Order (Hotels Joint Labour Committee) S.I. No. 284 of 1967

Employment Regulation Order (Button-Making Joint Labour Committee) S.I. No. 13 of 1968

Employment Regulation Order (Tailoring Joint Labour Committee) S.I. No. 22 of 1968

Employment Regulation Order (Women's Clothing and Millinery Joint Labour Committee) S.I. No. 88 of 1968

Statutory Authority	Section	Statutory Instrument
Industrial Relations Act, No. 26 of 1946 (*Cont.*)		*Employment Regulation Order (Handkerchief and Household Piece Goods Joint Labour Committee) S.I. No. 89 of 1968*
		Employment Regulation Order (General Waste Materials Reclamation Joint Labour Committee) S.I. No. 90 of 1968
		Employment Regulation Order (Shirtmaking Joint Labour Committee) S.I. No. 138 of 1968
		Employment Regulation Order (Provender Milling Joint Labour Committee) S.I. No. 139 of 1968
		Employment Regulation Order (Messengers (Dublin City and Dun Laoghaire) Joint Labour Committee) S.I. No. 146 of 1968
		Employment Regulation Order (Aerated Waters and Wholesale Bottling Joint Labour Committee) S.I. No. 156 of 1968
		Employment Regulation Order (Packing Joint Labour Committee) S.I. No. 171 of 1968
		Employment Regulation Order (Boot and Shoe Repairing Joint Labour Committee) S.I. No. 172 of 1968
		Employment Regulation Order (Messengers (Cork City Area) Joint Labour Committee) S.I. No. 181 of 1968
		Employment Regulation Order (Brush and Broom Joint Labour Committee) S.I. No. 190 of 1968
		Employment Regulation (No.2) Order (Buttermaking Joint Labour Committee) S.I. No. 193 of 1968
		Employment Regulation Order (Messengers (Waterford City) Joint Labour Committee) S.I. No. 194 of 1968
		Employment Regulation Order (Hairdressing Joint Labour Committee) S.I. No. 5 of 1969
		Employment Regulation Order (Messengers (Limerick City) Joint Labour Committee) S.I. No. 56 of 1969
		Employment Regulation Order (Law Clerks Joint Labour Committee) S.I. No. 73 of 1969
		Employment Regulation Order (Hotels Joint Labour Committee) S.I. No. 194 of 1969
		Employment Regulation Order (Tailoring Joint Labour Committee) S.I. No. 213 of 1969
		Employment Regulation Order (Handkerchief and Household Piece Goods Joint Labour Committee) S.I. No. 223 of 1969
		Employment Regulation Order (Shirtmaking Joint Labour Committee) S.I. No. 254 of 1969
		Employment Regulation Order (Brush and Broom Joint Labour Committee) S.I. No. 71 of 1970
		Employment Regulation Order (Packing Joint Labour Committee) S.I. No. 88 of 1970
		Employment Regulation Order (General Waste Materials Reclamation Joint Labour Committee) S.I. No. 98 of 1970

Statutory Authority	Section	Statutory Instrument

Industrial Relations Act, No. 26 of
1946 (*Cont.*)

Employment Regulation Order (Women's Clothing and Millinery Joint Labour Committee) S.I. No. 119 of 1970

Employment Regulation Order (Messengers (Dublin City and Dun Laoghaire) Joint Labour Committee) S.I. No. 120 of 1970

Employment Regulation Order (Aerated Waters and Wholesale Bottling Joint Labour Committee) S.I. No. 130 of 1970

Employment Regulation Order (Button-making Joint Labour Committee) S.I. No. 144 of 1970

Employment Regulation Order (Tailoring Joint Labour Committee) S.I. No. 145 of 1970

Employment Regulation Order (Messengers (Cork City Area) Joint Labour Committee) S.I. No. 151 of 1970

Employment Regulation Order (Provender Milling Joint Labour Committee) S.I. No. 152 of 1970

Employment Regulation Order (Boot and Shoe Repairing Joint Labour Committee) S.I. No. 171 of 1970

Employment Regulation Order (Handkerchief and Household Piece Goods Joint Labour Committee) S.I. No. 175 of 1970

Employment Regulation Order (Messengers (Waterford City) Joint Labour Committee) S.I. No. 184 of 1970

Employment Regulation Order (Law Clerks Joint Labour Committee) S.I. No. 185 of 1970

Employment Regulation Order (Messengers (Limerick City) Joint Labour Committee) S.I. No. 189 of 1970

Employment Regulation Order (Shirtmaking Joint Labour Committee) S.I. No. 207 of 1970

Employment Regulation Order (Hairdressing Joint Labour Committee) S.I. No. 254 of 1970

Employment Regulation (No.2) Order (General Waste Materials Reclamation Joint Labour Committee) S.I. No. 265 of 1970

Employment Regulation (No.2) Order (Aerated Waters and Wholesale Bottling Joint Labour Committee) 267, S.I. No. 266 of 1970

Employment Regulation (No.2) Order (Provender Milling Joint Labour Committee) S.I. No. 267 of 1970

Employment Regulation Order (Hotels Joint Labour Committee) S.I. No. 13 of 1971

Employment Regulation Order (Messengers (Dublin City and Dun Laoghaire) Joint Labour Committee) S.I. No. 88 of 1971

Employment Regulation Order (Women's Clothing and Millinery Joint Labour Committee) S.I. No. 161 of 1971

Industrial Relations Act, No. 26 of
1946 (*Cont.*)

Employment Regulation Order (Law Clerks Joint Labour Committee) S.I. No. 162 of 1971

Employment Regulation Order (Shirtmaking Joint Labour Committee) S.I. No. 197 of 1971

Employment Regulation Order (Provender Milling Joint Labour Committee) S.I. No. 265 of 1971

Employment Regulation Order (Brush and Broom Joint Labour Committee) S.I. No. 309 of 1971

Employment Regulation (No.2) Order (Messengers (Dublin City and Dun Laoghaire) Joint Labour Committee) S.I. No. 310 of 1971

Employment Regulation Order (Tailoring Joint Labour Committee) S.I. No. 332 of 1971

Employment Regulation Order (Aerated Waters and Wholesale Bottling Joint Labour Committee) S.I. No. 333 of 1971

Employment Regulation Order (Packing Joint Labour Committee) S.I. No. 338 of 1971

Employment Regulation Order (Messengers (Cork City Area) Joint Labour Committee) S.I. No. 346 of 1971

Employment Regulation Order (Messengers (Limerick City) Joint Labour Committee) S.I. No. 347 of 1971

Employment Regulation Order (Messengers (Waterford City) Joint Labour Committee) S.I. No. 348 of 1971

Employment Regulation Order (Button-making Joint Labour Committee) S.I. No. 13 of 1972

Employment Regulation Order (Women's Clothing and Millinery Joint Labour Committee) S.I. No. 14 of 1972

Employment Regulation Order (Handkerchief and Household Piece Goods Joint Labour Committee) S.I. No. 36 of 1972

Employment Regulation Order (Law Clerks Joint Labour Committee) S.I. No. 37 of 1972

Employment Regulation Order (General Waste Materials Reclamation Joint Labour Committee) S.I. No. 47 of 1972

Employment Regulation Order (Shirtmaking Joint Labour Committee) S.I. No. 48 of 1972

Employment Regulation Order (Hairdressing Joint Labour Committee) S.I. No. 72 of 1972

Employment Regulation Order (Provender Milling Joint Labour Committee) S.I. No. 151 of 1972

Employment Regulation Order (Boot and Shoe Repairing Joint Labour Committee) S.I. No. 161 of 1972

Employment Regulation Order (Brush and Broom Joint Labour Committee) S.I. No. 224 of 1972

Employment Regulation (No.2) Order (Button-making Joint Labour Committee) S.I. No. 253 of 1972

Statutory Authority	Section	Statutory Instrument

Industrial Relations Act, No. 26 of 1946 (*Cont.*)

Employment Regulation Order (Hotels Joint Labour Committee) S.I. No. 281 of 1972

Employment Regulation Order (Tailoring Joint Labour Committee) S.I. No. 323 of 1972

Employment Regulation Order No.2 (Women's Clothing and Millinery Joint Labour Committee) S.I. No. 346 of 1972

Employment Regulation Order (Handkerchief and Household Piece Goods Joint Labour Committee) S.I. No. 33 of 1973

Employment Regulation Order (Law Clerks Joint Labour Committee) S.I. No. 40 of 1973

Employment Regulation Order (Hairdressing Joint Labour Committee) S.I. No. 41 of 1973

Employment Regulation Order (Aerated Waters and Wholesale Bottling Joint Labour Committee) S.I. No. 63 of 1973

Employment Regulation Order (Provender Milling Joint Labour Committee) S.I. No. 76 of 1973

Employment Regulation Order (Packing Joint Labour Committee) S.I. No. 139 of 1973

Employment Regulation Order (Shirtmaking Joint Labour Committee) S.I. No. 164 of 1973

Employment Regulation Order (General Waste Materials Reclamation Joint Labour Committee) S.I. No. 176 of 1973

Employment Regulation Order (Boot and Shoe Repairing Joint Labour Committee) S.I. No. 179 of 1973

Employment Regulation Order (Messengers (Waterford City) Joint Labour Committee) S.I. No. 229 of 1973

Employment Regulation Order (Messengers (Dublin City and Dun Laoghaire) Joint Labour Committee) S.I. No. 230 of 1973

Employment Regulation Order (Button-making Joint Labour Committee) S.I. No. 269 of 1973

Employment Regulation Order (Messengers (Limerick City) Joint Labour Committee) S.I. No. 279 of 1973

Employment Regulation Order (Messengers (Cork City Area) Joint Labour Committee) S.I. No. 280 of 1973

Employment Regulation Order (No.2) (Hairdressing Joint Labour Committee) S.I. No. 299 of 1973

Employment Regulation Order (Hotels Joint Labour Committee) S.I. No. 7 of 1974

Employment Regulation Order (Tailoring Joint Labour Committee) S.I. No. 140 of 1974

Employment Regulation Order (Hairdressing Joint Labour Committee) S.I. No. 150 of 1974

Employment Regulation Order (Women's Clothing and Millinery Joint Labour Committee) S.I. No. 151 of 1974

Industrial Relations Act, No. 26 of
1946 (*Cont.*)

Employment Regulation Order (Packing Joint Labour Committee) S.I. No. 161 of 1974

Employment Regulation Order (Handkerchief and Household Piece Goods Joint Labour Committee) S.I. No. 173 of 1974

Employment Regulation Order (Law Clerks Joint Labour Committee) S.I. No. 184 of 1974

Employment Regulation Order (Messengers (Dublin City and Dun Laoghaire) Joint Labour Committee) S.I. No. 203 of 1974

Employment Regulation Order (Shirtmaking Joint Labour Committee) S.I. No. 204 of 1974

Employment Regulation Order (Button-making Joint Labour Committee) S.I. No. 205 of 1974

Employment Regulation Order (General Waste Materials Reclamation Joint Labour Committee) S.I. No. 206 of 1974

Employment Regulation Order (Brush and Broom Joint Labour Committee) S.I. No. 265 of 1974

Employment Regulation Order (Aerated Waters and Wholesale Bottling Joint Labour Committee) S.I. No. 285 of 1974

Employment Regulation Order (Messengers (Limerick City) Joint Labour Committee) S.I. No. 317 of 1974

Employment Regulation Order (Messengers (Waterford City) Joint Labour Committee) S.I. No. 318 of 1974

Employment Regulation Order (Messengers (Cork City Area) Joint Labour Committee) S.I. No. 319 of 1974

Employment Regulation Order (Boot and Shoe Repairing Joint Labour Committee) S.I. No. 328 of 1974

Employment Regulation Order (Provender Milling Joint Labour Committee) S.I. No. 2 of 1975

Employment Regulation Order (Hotels Joint Labour Committee) S.I. No. 38 of 1975

Employment Regulation Order (Messengers (Waterford City) Joint Labour Committee) S.I. No. 239 of 1975

Employment Regulation Order (Messengers (Cork City Area) Joint Labour Committee) S.I. No. 240 of 1975

Employment Regulation Order (Messengers (Limerick City) Joint Labour Committee) S.I. No. 241 of 1975

Employment Regulation Order (Messengers (Dublin City and Dun Laoghaire) Joint Labour Committee) S.I. No. 248 of 1975

Employment Regulation Order (Tailoring Joint Labour Committee) S.I. No. 254 of 1975

Employment Regulation Order (Boot and Shoe Repairing Joint Labour Committee) S.I. No. 258 of 1975

Statutory Authority	Section	Statutory Instrument

Industrial Relations Act, No. 26 of 1946 (*Cont.*)

Employment Regulation Order (Women's Clothing and Millinery Joint Labour Committee) S.I. No. 263 of 1975

Employment Regulation Order (Hairdressing Joint Labour Committee) S.I. No. 264 of 1975

Employment Regulation Order (Law Clerks Joint Labour Committee) S.I. No. 269 of 1975

Employment Regulation Order (Shirtmaking Joint Labour Committee) S.I. No. 270 of 1975

Employment Regulation Order (Handkerchief and Household Piece Goods Joint Labour Committee) S.I. No. 271 of 1975

Employment Regulation Order (Packing Joint Labour Committee) S.I. No. 275 of 1975

Employment Regulation Order No.2 (Provender Milling Joint Labour Committee) S.I. No. 276 of 1975

Employment Regulation Order (Aerated Waters and Wholesale Bottling Joint Labour Committee) S.I. No. 292 of 1975

Employment Regulation Order (General Waste Materials Reclamation Joint Labour Committee) S.I. No. 296 of 1975

Employment Regulation Order (Button-making Joint Labour Committee) S.I. No. 297 of 1975

Employment Regulation Order (Brush and Broom Joint Labour Committee) S.I. No. 69 of 1976

Employment Regulation Order (Hotels Joint Labour Committee) S.I. No. 133 of 1976

Employment Regulation Order (Hairdressing Joint Labour Committee) S.I. No. 27 of 1977

Employment Regulation Order (Messengers (Dublin City and Dun Laoghaire) Joint Labour Committee) S.I. No. 36 of 1977

Employment Regulation Order (Handkerchief and Household Piece Goods Joint Labour Committee) S.I. No. 44 of 1977

Employment Regulation Order (Agricultural Workers Joint Labour Committee) S.I. No. 61 of 1977

Employment Regulation Order (Boot and Shoe Repairing Joint Labour Committee) S.I. No. 69 of 1977

Employment Regulation Order (Law Clerks Joint Labour Committee) S.I. No. 70 of 1977

Employment Regulation Order (Tailoring Joint Labour Committee) S.I. No. 163 of 1977

Employment Regulation Order (Shirtmaking Joint Labour Committee) S.I. No. 224 of 1977

Employment Regulation Order (Button-making Joint Labour Committee) S.I. No. 231 of 1977

Employment Regulation Order (Brush and Broom Joint Labour Committee) S.I. No. 261 of 1977

Employment Regulation Order (Hotels Joint Labour Committee) S.I. No. 273 of 1977

Statutory Authority	Section	Statutory Instrument

Industrial Relations Act, No. 26 of 1946 (*Cont.*)

Employment Regulation Order (Agricultural Workers Joint Labour Committee) S.I. No. 302 of 1977

Employment Regulation Order (Women's Clothing and Millinery Joint Labour Committee) S.I. No. 309 of 1977

Employment Regulation Order (Provender Milling Joint Labour Committee) S.I. No. 310 of 1977

Employment Regulation Order No.2 (Boot and Shoe Repairing Joint Labour Committee) S.I. No. 339 of 1977

Employment Regulation Order No.2 (Provender Milling Joint Labour Committee) S.I. No. 340 of 1977

Employment Regulation Order (Aerated Waters and Wholesale Bottling Joint Labour Committee) S.I. No. 345 of 1977

Employment Regulation Order (Messengers (Cork City Area) Joint Labour Committee) S.I. No. 346 of 1977

Employment Regulation Order (Messengers (Limerick City) Joint Labour Committee) S.I. No. 347 of 1977

Employment Regulation Order (Agricultural Workers Joint Labour Committee) S.I. No. 17 of 1978

Employment Regulation Order (Hairdressing (Cork County Borough) Joint Labour Committee) S.I. No. 116 of 1978

Employment Regulation Order (Messengers (Dublin City and Dun Laoghaire) Joint Labour Committee) S.I. No. 150 of 1978

Employment Regulation Order (Hotels Joint Labour Committee) S.I. No. 156 of 1978

Employment Regulation Order (Law Clerks Joint Labour Committee) S.I. No. 169 of 1978

Employment Regulation Order (Brush and Broom Joint Labour Committee) S.I. No. 217 of 1978

Employment Regulation Order (Provender Milling Joint Labour Committee) S.I. No. 235 of 1978

Employment Regulation Order (Boot and Shoe Repairing Joint Labour Committee) S.I. No. 236 of 1978

Employment Regulation Order (Handkerchief and Household Piece Goods Joint Labour Committee) S.I. No. 255 of 1978

Employment Regulation Order (Shirtmaking Joint Labour Committee) S.I. No. 263 of 1978

Employment Regulation Order No.2 (Agricultural Workers' Joint Labour Committee) S.I. No. 264 of 1978

Employment Regulation Order (Tailoring Joint Labour Committee) S.I. No. 265 of 1978

Employment Regulation Order (Women's Clothing and Millinery Joint Labour Committee) S.I. No. 266 of 1978

Statutory Authority	Section	Statutory Instrument
Industrial Relations Act, No. 26 of 1946 (*Cont.*)		*Employment Regulation Order (Catering Joint Labour Committee) S.I. No. 281 of 1978*
		Employment Regulation Order (Messengers (Cork City Area) Joint Labour Committee) S.I. No. 361 of 1978
		Employment Regulation Order (Messengers (Limerick City) Joint Labour Committee) S.I. No. 362 of 1978
		Employment Regulation Order (Aerated Waters and Wholesale Bottling Joint Labour Committee) S.I. No. 4 of 1979
		Employment Regulation Order (Hairdressing (Cork County Borough) Joint Labour Committee) S.I. No. 258 of 1979
		Employment Regulation Order (Law Clerks Joint Labour Committee) S.I. No. 277 of 1979
		Employment Regulation Order (Hotels Joint Labour Committee) S.I. No. 288 of 1979
		Employment Regulation Order (Hairdressing Joint Labour Committee) S.I. No. 298 of 1979
		Employment Regulation Order (Agricultural Workers Joint Labour Committee) S.I. No. 353 of 1979
		Employment Regulation Order No.2 (Aerated Waters and Wholesale Bottling Joint Labour Committee) S.I. No. 374 of 1979
		Employment Regulation Order (Boot and Shoe Repairing Joint Labour Committee) S.I. No. 375 of 1979
		Employment Regulation Order (Brush and Broom Joint Labour Committee) S.I. No. 391 of 1979
		Employment Regulation Order (Shirtmaking Joint Labour Committee) S.I. No. 392 of 1979
		Employment Regulation Order (Tailoring Joint Labour Committee) S.I. No. 393 of 1979
		Employment Regulation Order (Catering Joint Labour Committee) S.I. No. 405 of 1979
		Employment Regulation Order (Provender Milling Joint Labour Committee) S.I. No. 406 of 1979
		Employment Regulation Order (Women's Clothing and Millinery Joint Labour Committee) S.I. No. 426 of 1979
		Employment Regulation Order (Messengers (Dublin City and Dun Laoghaire) Joint Labour Committee) S.I. No. 29 of 1980
		Employment Regulation Order (Hairdressing (Cork County Borough) Joint Labour Committee) S.I. No. 116 of 1980
		Employment Regulation Order (Handkerchief and Household Piece Goods Joint Labour Committee) S.I. No. 117 of 1980
		Employment Regulation Order (Hairdressing Joint Labour Committee) S.I. No. 118 of 1980
		Employment Regulation Order (Law Clerks Joint Labour Committee) S.I. No. 140 of 1980

Industrial Relations Act, No. 26 of 1946 (*Cont.*)

Employment Regulation Order (Messengers (Cork City Area) Joint Labour Committee) S.I. No. 157 of 1980

Employment Regulation Order (Hotels Joint Labour Committee) S.I. No. 179 of 1980

Employment Regulation Order (Messengers (Limerick City) Joint Labour Committee) S.I. No. 192 of 1980

Employment Regulation Order (Agricultural Workers Joint Labour Committee) S.I. No. 396 of 1980

Employment Regulation Order (Women's Clothing and Millinery Joint Labour Committee) S.I. No. 397 of 1980

Employment Regulation Order (Aerated Waters and Wholesale Bottling Joint Labour Committee) S.I. No. 28 of 1981

Employment Regulation Order (Shirtmaking Joint Labour Committee) S.I. No. 44 of 1981

Employment Regulation Order (Tailoring Joint Labour Committee) S.I. No. 45 of 1981

Employment Regulation Order (Provender Milling Joint Labour Committee) S.I. No. 80 of 1981

Employment Regulation Order (Hairdressing Joint Labour Committee) S.I. No. 81 of 1981

Employment Regulation Order (Law Clerks Joint Labour Committee) S.I. No. 122 of 1981

Employment Regulation Order (Hotels Joint Labour Committee) S.I. No. 146 of 1981

Employment Regulation Order (Catering Joint Labour Committee) S.I. No. 147 of 1981

Employment Regulation Order (Hairdressing (Cork County Borough) Joint Labour Committee) S.I. No. 155 of 1981

Employment Regulation Order (Handkerchief and Household Piece Goods Joint Labour Committee) S.I. No. 156 of 1981

Employment Regulation Order (Boot and Shoe Repairing Joint Labour Committee) S.I. No. 179 of 1981

Employment Regulation Order (General Waste Materials Reclamation Joint Labour Committee) S.I. No. 180 of 1981

Employment Regulation Order (Messengers (Dublin City and Dun Laoghaire) Joint Labour Committee) S.I. No. 181 of 1981

Employment Regulation Order (Aerated Waters and Wholesale Bottling Joint Labour Committee) No.2, S.I. No. 287 of 1981

Employment Regulation Order (Hairdressing (Cork County Borough) Joint Labour Committee) S.I. No. 13 of 1982

Employment Regulation Order (Handkerchief and Household Piece Goods Joint Labour Committee) S.I. No. 57 of 1982

Statutory Authority	Section	Statutory Instrument

Industrial Relations Act, No. 26 of 1946 (*Cont.*)

Employment Regulation Order (Tailoring Joint Labour Committee) S.I. No. 85 of 1982

Employment Regulation Order (Law Clerks Joint Labour Committee) S.I. No. 86 of 1982

Employment Regulation Order (Hairdressing Joint Labour Committee) S.I. No. 87 of 1982

Employment Regulation Order (Brush and Broom Joint Labour Committee) S.I. No. 101 of 1982

Employment Regulation Order (Shirtmaking Joint Labour Committee) S.I. No. 126 of 1982

Employment Regulation Order (Provender Milling Joint Labour Committee) S.I. No. 127 of 1982

Employment Regulation Order (Aerated Waters and Wholesale Bottling Joint Labour Committee) S.I. No. 128 of 1982

Employment Regulation Order (Women's Clothing and Millinery Joint Labour Committee) S.I. No. 129 of 1982

Employment Regulation Order (Boot and Shoe Repairing Joint Labour Committee) S.I. No. 155 of 1982

Employment Regulation Order (General Waste Materials Reclamation Joint Labour Committee) S.I. No. 160 of 1982

Employment Regulation Order (Hotels Joint Labour Committee) S.I. No. 196 of 1982

Employment Regulation Order (Catering Joint Labour Committee) S.I. No. 197 of 1982

Employment Regulation Order (Agricultural Workers Joint Labour Committee) S.I. No. 222 of 1982

Employment Regulation Order (Hairdressing (Cork County Borough) Joint Labour Committee) No.2, S.I. No. 278 of 1982

Employment Regulation Order (Agricultural Workers Joint Labour Committee) S.I. No. 62 of 1983

Employment Regulation Order (Tailoring Joint Labour Committee) S.I. No. 130 of 1983

Employment Regulation Order (Shirtmaking Joint Labour Committee) S.I. No. 131 of 1983

Employment Regulation Order (General Waste Materials Reclamation Joint Labour Committee) S.I. No. 150 of 1983

Employment Regulation Order (Women's Clothing and Millinery Joint Labour Committee) S.I. No. 159 of 1983

Employment Regulation Order (Handkerchief and Household Piece Goods Joint Labour Committee) S.I. No. 191 of 1983

Employment Regulation Order (Boot and Shoe Repairing Joint Labour Committee) S.I. No. 194 of 1983

Employment Regulation Order (Hairdressing Joint Labour Committee) S.I. No. 228 of 1983

Statutory Authority	Section	Statutory Instrument

Industrial Relations Act, No. 26 of
1946 (*Cont.*)

Employment Regulation Order (Law Clerks Joint Labour Committee) S.I. No. 229 of 1983

Employment Regulation Order (Hairdressing (Cork County Borough) Joint Labour Committee) S.I. No. 241 of 1983

Employment Regulation Order (Messengers (Dublin City and Dun Laoghaire) Joint Labour Committee) S.I. No. 242 of 1983

Employment Regulation Order (Aerated Waters and Wholesale Bottling Joint Labour Committee) S.I. No. 252 of 1983

Employment Regulation Order (Catering Joint Labour Committee) S.I. No. 269 of 1983

Employment Regulation Order (Agricultural Workers Joint Labour Committee) No.2, S.I. No. 336 of 1983

Employment Regulation Order (Brush and Broom Joint Labour Committee) S.I. No. 372 of 1983

Employment Regulation Order (Hotels Joint Labour Committee) S.I. No. 373 of 1983

Employment Regulation Order (General Waste Materials Reclamation Joint Labour Committee) S.I. No. 17 of 1984

Employment Regulation Order (Provender Milling Joint Labour Committee) S.I. No. 30 of 1984

Employment Regulation Order (Catering Joint Labour Committee) S.I. No. 128 of 1984

Employment Regulation Order (Women's Clothing and Millinery Joint Labour Committee) S.I. No. 262 of 1984

Employment Regulation Order (Shirtmaking Joint Labour Committee) S.I. No. 267 of 1984

Employment Regulation Order (Tailoring Joint Labour Committee) S.I. No. 268 of 1984

Employment Regulation Order (Hairdressing (Cork County Borough) Joint Labour Committee) S.I. No. 292 of 1984

Employment Regulation Order (Handkerchief and Household Piece Goods Joint Labour Committee) S.I. No. 293 of 1984

Employment Regulation Order No.2 (Provender Milling Joint Labour Committee) S.I. No. 294 of 1984

Employment Regulation Order (Law Clerks Joint Labour Committee) S.I. No. 312 of 1984

Employment Regulation Order (Hairdressing Joint Labour Committee) S.I. No. 313 of 1984

Employment Regulation (No.2) Order (General Waste Materials Reclamation Joint Labour Committee) S.I. No. 338 of 1984

Employment Regulation Order (Aerated Waters and Wholesale Bottling Joint Labour Committee) S.I. No. 339 of 1984

Industrial Relations Act, No. 26 of
1946 (*Cont.*)

Employment Regulation Order (Messengers (Dublin City and Dun Laoghaire) Joint Labour Committee) S.I. No. 8 of 1985

Employment Regulation Order (Catering Joint Labour Committee) S.I. No. 13 of 1985

Employment Regulation Order (Contract Cleaning (City and County of Dublin) Joint Labour Committee) S.I. No. 14 of 1985

Employment Regulation Order (Hotels Joint Labour Committee) S.I. No. 72 of 1985

Employment Regulation Order (Agricultural Workers Joint Labour Committee) S.I. No. 107 of 1985

Employment Regulation Order (Law Clerks Joint Labour Committee) S.I. No. 342 of 1985

Employment Regulation Order (Tailoring Joint Labour Committee) S.I. No. 354 of 1985

Employment Regulation Order (Women's Clothing and Millinery Joint Labour Committee) S.I. No. 355 of 1985

Employment Regulation Order (Shirtmaking Joint Labour Committee) S.I. No. 356 of 1985

Employment Regulation Order (Handkerchief and Household Piece Goods Joint Labour Committee) S.I. No. 357 of 1985

Employment Regulation Order (Provender Milling Joint Labour Committee) S.I. No. 390 of 1985

Employment Regulation Order (Aerated Waters and Wholesale Bottling Joint Labour Committee) S.I. No. 391 of 1985

Employment Regulation Order (Contract Cleaning (City and County of Dublin) Joint Labour Committee) S.I. No. 16 of 1986

Employment Regulation Order (Hairdressing Joint Labour Committee) S.I. No. 17 of 1986

Employment Regulation Order (Catering Joint Labour Committee) S.I. No. 44 of 1986

Employment Regulation Order (Hotels Joint Labour Committee) S.I. No. 65 of 1986

Employment Regulation Order (Brush and Broom Joint Labour Committee) S.I. No. 256 of 1986

Employment Regulation Order (Hairdressing (Cork County Borough) Joint Labour Committee) S.I. No. 271 of 1986

Employment Regulation Order (Agricultural Workers Joint Labour Committee) S.I. No. 311 of 1986

Employment Regulation Order (Law Clerks Joint Labour Committee) S.I. No. 408 of 1986

Employment Regulation Order (Handkerchief and Household Piece Goods Joint Labour Committee) S.I. No. 409 of 1986

Employment Regulation Order (Tailoring Joint Labour Committee) S.I. No. 410 of 1986

Employment Regulation Order (Women's Clothing and Millinery Joint Labour Committee) S.I. No. 411 of 1986

Statutory Authority	Section	Statutory Instrument
Industrial Relations Act, No. 26 of 1946 (*Cont.*)	74(2)	*Industrial Relations Act, 1946 (Continuance of Part VII) Regulations [Vol. XXXVII p. 635] S.R.& O. No. 309 of 1947*
Industrial Relations Act, No. 14 of 1969	5(2)	**Labour Court (Members) Superannuation Scheme (Amendment) Scheme, S.I. No. 268 of 1979**
		Labour Court (Members) Superannuation Scheme (Amendment) Scheme, S.I. No. 216 of 1983
Industrial Relations Act, No. 15 of 1976	4	**Agricultural Wages Joint Labour Committee Establishment Order, S.I. No. 198 of 1976**
	8(1)	**Labour Court (Fourth Division) Order, S.I. No. 161 of 1979**
Industrial Relations (Amendment) Act, No. 19 of 1955	2(2)	*Industrial Relations Act, 1946 (Part VI, Extension) Order, S.I. No. 92 of 1956*
Industrial Research and Standards Act, No. 25 of 1946	20(3)	**Standard Specification (Turpentine) Order, S.I. No. 150 of 1949**
		Standard Specification (White Spirit) Order, S.I. No. 151 of 1949
		Standard Specification (Concrete Plain Roofing Tiles and Fittings) Order, S.I. No. 152 of 1949
		Standard Specification (Concrete Cylindrical Pipes) Order, S.I. No. 153 of 1949
		Standard Specification (Ready Mixed Oil Paints) Order, S.I. No. 154 of 1949
		Standard Specification (White Pigments for Paints) Order, S.I. No. 155 of 1949
		Standard Specification (Cotton Bed Sheetings and Cotton Bed Sheets) Order, S.I. No. 156 of 1949
		Standard Specification (Galvanised Cisterns and Cisterns for Domestic Water Supply) Order, S.I. No. 157 of 1949
		Standard Specification (Liquid Driers for Paints) Order, S.I. No. 158 of 1949
		Standard Specification (Linseed Oil for Paints) Order, S.I. No. 159 of 1949
		Standard Specification (Gold Size) Order, S.I. No. 160 of 1949
		Standard Specification (Knotting) Order, S.I. No. 161 of 1949
		Standard Specification (Portland Cement) Order, S.I. No. 162 of 1949
		Standard Specification (Hydrated Lime for Building Purposes) Order, S.I. No. 286 of 1949
		Standard Specification (Extenders for Paints) Order, S.I. No. 287 of 1949
		Standard Specification (Solid Concrete Building Blocks made with Natural Aggregate) Order, S.I. No. 288 of 1949

Statutory Authority	Section	Statutory Instrument

Industrial Research and Standards
Act, No. 25 of 1946 (*Cont.*)

Standard Specification (Coarse and Fine Aggregates from Natural Sources for Concrete) Order, S.I. No. 354 of 1949

Standard Specification (Water Paints and Distempers for Interior Use) Order, S.I. No. 355 of 1949

Standard Specification (Concrete Interlocking Roofing Tiles) Order, S.I. No. 29 of 1950

Standard Specification (Electrical Plugs and Socket-outlets) (10 Ampere Continental Type) Order, S.I. No. 30 of 1950

Standard Specification (Varnish) Order, S.I. No. 43 of 1950

Standard Specification (Asbestos-cement Slates and Sheets) Order, S.I. No. 44 of 1950

Standard Specification (Woollen Blankets) Order, S.I. No. 109 of 1950

Standard Specification (Gypsum Plasters) Order, S.I. No. 240 of 1950

Standard Specification (Linseed Oil Putty) Order, S.I. No. 241 of 1950

Standard Specification (Tungsten Filament General Service Electric Lamps) Order, S.I. No. 242 of 1950

Standard Specification (Test Sieves) Order, S.I. No. 293 of 1950

Standard Specification (Concrete Land Drainage Pipes) Order, S.I. No. 46 of 1951

Standard Specification (Pickled Herrings) Order, S.I. No. 314 of 1951

Standard Specification (Zinc Chromate Primers for use in Aluminium and Light Alloys) Order, S.I. No. 321 of 1951

Standard Specification (Bituminous Roofing Felt) Order, S.I. No. 330 of 1951

Standard Specification (Writing Ink) Order, S.I. No. 81 of 1952

Standard Specification (Coal Tar Creosote for the Preservation of Timber) Order, S.I. No. 286 of 1952

Standard Specification (Wrapping Paper) Order, S.I. No. 314 of 1952

Standard Specification (Irish Handwoven Tweed) Order, S.I. No. 351 of 1952

Standard Specification (Gypsum Plasterboard) Order, S.I. No. 352 of 1952

Standard Specification (Flush Wood Doors) Order, S.I. No. 31 of 1953

Standard Specification (Portland Cement) Order, S.I. No. 35 of 1953

Standard Specification (Hollow Concrete Building Blocks made with Natural Aggregate) Order, S.I. No. 50 of 1953

Standard Specification (Men's Heavy Boots) Order, S.I. No. 51 of 1953

Statutory Authority	Section	Statutory Instrument

Industrial Research and Standards
Act, No. 25 of 1946 (*Cont.*)

Standard Specification (Edible Gelatine) Order, S.I. No. 63 of 1953

Standard Specification (Hard Gloss Paints and Enamels) Order, S.I. No. 71 of 1953

Standard Specification (Heavy Duty Shovels) Order, S.I. No. 91 of 1953

Standard Specification (Cast Iron Rainwater Goods) Order, S.I. No. 93 of 1953

Standard Specification (School Paper Stationery) Order, S.I. No. 170 of 1953

Standard Specification (Panelled Wood Doors) Order, S.I. No. 252 of 1953

Standard Specification (Ground Limestone) Order, S.I. No. 260 of 1953

Standard Specification (Men's Heavy Boots) (No.2) Order, S.I. No. 317 of 1953

Standard Specification (Irish Homespun Tweed) Order, S.I. No. 383 of 1953

Standard Specification (Cotton Dungaree Cloth) Order, S.I. No. 384 of 1953

Standard Specification (Clayware Land Drainage Pipes) Order, S.I. No. 385 of 1953

Standard Specification (Clayware Flue Liners for Open Fires) Order, S.I. No. 386 of 1953

Standard Specification (Pressed Steel Rainwater Goods) Order, S.I. No. 388 of 1953

Standard Specification (Finished Wallpaper) Order, S.I. No. 389 of 1953

Standard Specification (Wallpaper Base) Order, S.I. No. 390 of 1953

Standard Specification (Bitumen Damp-proof Courses) Order, S.I. No. 391 of 1953

Standard Specification (Sparking Plugs) Order, S.I. No. 19 of 1954

22(1) Standard Mark (Portland Cement) Order, S.I. No. 384 of 1951

Standard Mark (Cotton Bed Sheetings and Cotton Bed Sheets) Order, S.I. No. 385 of 1951

Standard Mark (Gypsum Plasters) Order, S.I. No. 386 of 1951

Standard Mark (Linseed Oil Putty) Order, S.I. No. 387 of 1951

Standard Mark (Concrete Plain Roofing Tiles and Fittings) Order, S.I. No. 388 of 1951

Standard Mark (Concrete Interlocking Roofing Tiles) Order, S.I. No. 389 of 1951

Standard Mark (Concrete Cylindrical Pipes) Order, S.I. No. 390 of 1951

Standard Mark (Asbestos Cement Slates and Sheets) Order, S.I. No. 391 of 1951

Standard Mark (Hydrated Lime for Building Purposes) Order, S.I. No. 392 of 1951

Statutory Authority	Section	Statutory Instrument

Industrial Research and Standards
Act, No. 25 of 1946 (*Cont.*)

Standard Mark (Galvanised Cisterns and Cylinders for Domestic Water Supply) Order, S.I. No. 393 of 1951

Standard Mark (Varnish) Order, S.I. No. 394 of 1951

Standard Mark (Ready Mixed Oil Paints) Order, S.I. No. 395 of 1951

Standard Mark (Solid Concrete Building Blocks made with Natural Aggregate) Order, S.I. No. 396 of 1951

Standard Mark (Water Paints and Distempers for Interior Use) Order, S.I. No. 397 of 1951

Standard Mark (Tunsten Filament General Service Electric Lamps) Order, S.I. No. 398 of 1951

Standard Mark (Woollen Blankets) Order, S.I. No. 399 of 1951

Standard Mark (Electric Plugs and Socket Outlets (10 Ampere Continental Type)) Order, S.I. No. 400 of 1951

Standard Mark (Test Sieves) Order, S.I. No. 401 of 1951

Standard Mark (Concrete Land Drainage Pipes) Order, S.I. No. 402 of 1951

Standard Mark (Bituminous Roofing Felt) Order, S.I. No. 115 of 1952

Standard Mark (Zinc Chromate Primers for use on Aluminium and Light Alloys) Order, S.I. No. 116 of 1952

Standard Mark (Flush Wood Doors) Order, S.I. No. 102 of 1953

Standard Mark (Irish Handwoven Tweed) Order, S.I. No. 103 of 1953

Standard Mark (Men's Heavy Boots) Order, S.I. No. 135 of 1953

Standard Mark (Gypsum Plasterboard) Order, S.I. No. 136 of 1953

Standard Mark (Turpentine) Order, S.I. No. 177 of 1953

Standard Mark (Portland Cement) Order, S.I. No. 178 of 1953

Standard Mark (Liquid Driers for Paints) Order, S.I. No. 179 of 1953

Standard Mark (Knotting) Order, S.I. No. 180 of 1953

Standard Mark (Gold Size) Order, S.I. No. 181 of 1953

Standard Mark (Linseed Oil for Paints) Order, S.I. No. 182 of 1953

Standard Mark (Heavy Duty Shovels) Order, S.I. No. 183 of 1953

Standard Mark (Coal Tar Creosote for the Preservation of Timber) Order, S.I. No. 184 of 1953

Industrial Research and Standards Act, No. 25 of 1946 (*Cont.*)		**Standard Mark (Wrapping Paper) Order, S.I. No. 185 of 1953**
		Standard Mark (Writing Ink) Order, S.I. No. 186 of 1953
		Standard Mark (Cast Iron Rainwater Goods) Order, S.I. No. 187 of 1953
		Standard Mark (White Spirit) Order, S.I. No. 188 of 1953
		Standard Mark (Panelled Wood Doors) Order, S.I. No. 253 of 1953
		Standard Mark (Hard Gloss Paints and Enamels) Order, S.I. No. 269 of 1953
		Standard Mark (Men's Heavy Boots) (No.2) Order, S.I. No. 326 of 1953
		Standard Mark (School Paper Stationery) Order, S.I. No. 367 of 1953
		Standard Mark (Irish Homespun Tweed) Order, S.I. No. 378 of 1953
		Standard Mark (Clayware Flue Liners for Open Fires) Order, S.I. No. 379 of 1953
		Standard Mark (Clayware Land Drainage Pipes) Order, S.I. No. 380 of 1953
		Standard Mark (Cotton Dungaree Cloth) Order, S.I. No. 381 of 1953
		Standard Mark (Pressed Steel Rainwater Goods) Order, S.I. No. 392 of 1953
		Standard Mark (Bitumen Damp-proof Courses) Order, S.I. No. 393 of 1953
		Standard Mark (Finished Wallpaper) Order, S.I. No. 394 of 1953
Industrial Research and Standards Act, No. 20 of 1961	1	*Industrial Research and Standards Act, 1961 (Commencement) Order, S.I. No. 210 of 1961*
	24	**Standard Mark (General) Order, S.I. No. 81 of 1964**
	24(4)	*Standard Mark (Men's Heavy Boots) (Revocation) Order, S.I. No. 199 of 1974*
		Standard Mark (Gypsum Plasters) (Revocation) Order, S.I. No. 266 of 1975
		Standard Mark (Gypsum Plasterboard) (Revocation) Order, S.I. No. 298 of 1975
		Standard Mark (Galvanised Cisterns and Cylinders for Domestic Water Supply) (Revocation) Order, S.I. No. 86 of 1976
	44	*Industrial Research and Standards (Section 44) (Children's Nightdresses) Order, S.I. No. 4 of 1967*
		Industrial Research and Standards (Section 44) (Children's Toys) Order, S.I. No. 75 of 1969
		Industrial Research and Standards (Section 44) (Electrical Appliances) Order, S.I. No. 222 of 1969
		Industrial Research and Standards (Section 44) (Hood Cord for Children's Clothes) Order, S.I. No. 140 of 1976

Statutory Authority	Section	Statutory Instrument
Industrial Research and Standards Act, No. 20 of 1961 (*Cont.*)		**Industrial Research and Standards (Section 44) (Children's Nightwear) Order, S.I. No. 3 of 1979**
		Industrial Research and Standards (Section 44) (Children's Nightdresses) (Amendment) Order, S.I. No. 215 of 1979
		Industrial Research and Standards (Fire Safety Requirements for Upholstered Furniture) Order, S.I. No. 298 of 1980
		Industrial Research and Standards (Section 44) (Perambulators and Pushchairs) Order, S.I. No. 212 of 1981
		Industrial Research and Standards (Section 44) (Toxicity of Pencils and Graphic Instruments) Order, S.I. No. 231 of 1983
		Industrial Research and Standards (Section 44) (Children's Cots) Order, S.I. No. 232 of 1983
		Industrial Research and Standards (Section 44) (Babies' Dummies) Order, S.I. No. 236 of 1983
		Industrial Research and Standards (Section 44) (Gas Operated Ovens) Order, S.I. No. 237 of 1983
		Industrial Research and Standards (Section 44) (Resemblance to Food of Non-food Products Used by Children) Order, S.I. No. 368 of 1983
		Industrial Research and Standards (Section 44) (Gas Catalytic Heaters) Order, S.I. No. 125 of 1984
		Industrial Research and Standards (Section 44) (Babies' Dummies) Order, S.I. No. 284 of 1984
		Industrial Research and Standards (Section 44) (Children's Toys) Order, S.I. No. 44 of 1985
	44(1)	**Industrial Research and Standards Act (Section 44) (Electrical Mains Socket-outlets) Order, S.I. No. 322 of 1973**
		Industrial Research and Standards (Section 44) (Caravans and Mobile Homes) Order, S.I. No. 111 of 1974
		Industrial Research and Standards (Section 44) (Children's Toys) (Amendment) Order, S.I. No. 33 of 1975
		Industrial Research and Standards (Section 44) (Electrical Plugs and Sockets) Order, S.I. No. 178 of 1983
Industrial Training Act, No. 5 of 1967	3	*Industrial Training Act, 1967 (Establishment Day) Order, S.I. No. 117 of 1967*
	21	*Industrial Training Levy (Textiles Industry) Order, S.I. No. 131 of 1970*
		Industrial Training Levy (Clothing and Footwear Industry) Order, S.I. No. 270 of 1970
		Industrial Training Levy (Food, Drink and Tobacco Industry) Order, S.I. No. 9 of 1971
		Industrial Training Levy (Engineering Industry) Order, S.I. No. 220 of 1971
		Industrial Training Levy (Textiles Industry) Order, S.I. No. 266 of 1971

Statutory Authority	Section	Statutory Instrument

Industrial Training Act, No. 5 of 1967 (*Cont.*)

Industrial Training Levy (Construction Industry) Order, S.I. No. 299 of 1971

Industrial Training Levy (Textiles Industry) Order, 1971 (Amendment) Order, S.I. No. 197 of 1972

Industrial Training Levy (Engineering Industry) Order, 1971 (Amendment) Order, S.I. No. 198 of 1972

Industrial Training Levy (Construction Industry) Order, 1971 (Amendment) Order, S.I. No. 199 of 1972

Industrial Training Levy (Clothing and Footwear Industry) Order, S.I. No. 205 of 1972

Industrial Training Levy (Food, Drink and Tobacco Industry) Order, S.I. No. 206 of 1972

Industrial Training Levy (Printing and Paper Industry) Order, S.I. No. 305 of 1972

Industrial Training Levy (Textiles Industry) Order, S.I. No. 321 of 1972

Industrial Training Levy (Engineering Industry) Order, S.I. No. 75 of 1973

Industrial Training Levy (Construction Industry) Order, S.I. No. 79 of 1973

Industrial Training Levy (Textiles Industry) Order, 1970 (Amendment) Order, S.I. No. 80 of 1973

Industrial Training Levy (Food, Drink and Tobacco Industry) Order, 1971 (Amendment) Order, S.I. No. 81 of 1973

Industrial Training Levy (Clothing and Footwear Industry) Order, 1970 (Amendment) Order, S.I. No. 82 of 1973

Industrial Training Levy (Clothing and Footwear Industry) Order, S.I. No. 253 of 1973

Industrial Training Levy (Food, Drink and Tobacco Industry) Order, S.I. No. 264 of 1973

Industrial Training Levy (Engineering Industry) Order, S.I. No. 336 of 1973

Industrial Training Levy (Chemical and Allied Products Industry) Order, S.I. No. 72 of 1974

Industrial Training Levy (Textiles Industry) Order, S.I. No. 73 of 1974

Industrial Training Levy (Printing and Paper Industry) Order, S.I. No. 100 of 1974

Industrial Training Levy (Construction Industry) Order, S.I. No. 101 of 1974

Industrial Training Levy (Clothing and Footwear Industry) Order, S.I. No. 255 of 1974

Industrial Training Levy (Food, Drink and Tobacco Industry) Order, S.I. No. 289 of 1974

Industrial Training Levy (Engineering Industry) Order, S.I. No. 1 of 1975

Industrial Training Levy (Printing and Paper Industry) Order, S.I. No. 49 of 1975

Statutory Authority	Section	Statutory Instrument
Industrial Training Act, No. 5 of 1967 (*Cont.*)		*Industrial Training Levy (Textiles Industry) Order, S.I. No. 50 of 1975*
		Industrial Training Levy (Chemical and Allied Products Industry) Order, S.I. No. 51 of 1975
		Industrial Training Levy (Construction Industry) Order, S.I. No. 129 of 1975
		Industrial Training Levy (Food, Drink and Tobacco Industry) Order, S.I. No. 183 of 1975
		Industrial Training Levy (Clothing and Footwear Industry) Order, S.I. No. 184 of 1975
		Industrial Training Levy (Engineering Industry) Order, S.I. No. 242 of 1975
		Industrial Training Levy (Chemical and Allied Products Industry) Order, S.I. No. 25 of 1976
		Industrial Training Levy (Printing and Paper Industry) Order, S.I. No. 54 of 1976
		Industrial Training Levy (Textiles Industry) Order, S.I. No. 55 of 1976
		Industrial Training Levy (Construction Industry) Order, S.I. No. 179 of 1976
		Industrial Training Levy (Food, Drink and Tobacco Industry) Order, S.I. No. 202 of 1976
		Industrial Training Levy (Clothing and Footwear Industry) Order, S.I. No. 203 of 1976
		Industrial Training Levy (Engineering Industry) Order, S.I. No. 298 of 1976
		Industrial Training Levy (Chemical and Allied Products Industry) Order, S.I. No. 81 of 1977
		Industrial Training Levy (Textiles Industry) Order, S.I. No. 87 of 1977
		Industrial Training Levy (Printing and Paper Industry) Order, S.I. No. 179 of 1977
		Industrial Training Levy (Construction Industry) Order, S.I. No. 236 of 1977
		Industrial Training Levy (Clothing and Footwear Industry) Order, S.I. No. 300 of 1977
		Industrial Training Levy (Food, Drink and Tobacco Industry) Order, S.I. No. 301 of 1977
		Industrial Training Levy (Engineering Industry) Order, S.I. No. 364 of 1977
		Industrial Training Levy (Chemical and Allied Products Industry) Order, S.I. No. 58 of 1978
		Industrial Training Levy (Textiles Industry) Order, S.I. No. 80 of 1978
		Industrial Training Levy (Printing and Paper Industry) Order, S.I. No. 177 of 1978
		Industrial Training Levy (Construction Industry) Order, S.I. No. 222 of 1978
		Industrial Training Levy (Clothing and Footwear Industry) Order, S.I. No. 260 of 1978
		Industrial Training Levy (Food, Drink and Tobacco Industry) Order, S.I. No. 261 of 1978

Statutory Authority	Section	Statutory Instrument

Industrial Training Act, No. 5 of
1967 (*Cont.*)

*Industrial Training Levy (Engineering Industry)
Order, S.I. No. 354 of 1978*

*Industrial Training Levy (Textiles Industry) Order,
S.I. No. 82 of 1979*

*Industrial Training Levy (Chemical and Allied
Products Industry) Order, S.I. No. 83 of 1979*

*Industrial Training Levy (Printing and Paper
Industry) Order, S.I. No. 226 of 1979*

*Industrial Training Levy (Construction Industry)
Order, S.I. No. 230 of 1979*

*Industrial Training Levy (Clothing and Footwear
Industry) Order, S.I. No. 309 of 1979*

*Industrial Training Levy (Food, Drink and Tobacco
Industry) Order, S.I. No. 310 of 1979*

*Industrial Training Levy (Engineering Industry)
Order, S.I. No. 376 of 1979*

*Industrial Training Levy (Chemical and Allied
Products Industry) Order, S.I. No. 77 of 1980*

*Industrial Training Levy (Textiles Industry) Order,
S.I. No. 86 of 1980*

*Industrial Training Levy (Construction Industry)
Order, S.I. No. 180 of 1980*

*Industrial Training Levy (Printing and Paper
Industry) Order, S.I. No. 207 of 1980*

*Industrial Training Levy (Clothing and Footwear
Industry) Order, S.I. No. 288 of 1980*

*Industrial Training Levy (Food, Drink and Tobacco
Industry) Order, S.I. No. 289 of 1980*

*Industrial Training Levy (Engineering Industry)
Order, S.I. No. 380 of 1980*

*Industrial Training Levy (Chemical and Allied
Products Industry) Order, S.I. No. 97 of 1981*

*Industrial Training Levy (Textiles Industry) Order,
S.I. No. 111 of 1981*

*Industrial Training Levy (Printing and Paper
Industry) Order, S.I. No. 244 of 1981*

*Industrial Training Levy (Construction Industry)
Order, S.I. No. 251 of 1981*

*Industrial Training Levy (Food, Drink and Tobacco
Industry) Order, S.I. No. 305 of 1981*

*Industrial Training Levy (Clothing and Footwear
Industry) Order, S.I. No. 315 of 1981*

*Industrial Training Levy (Textiles Industry) (No.2)
Order, S.I. No. 411 of 1981*

*Industrial Training Levy (Engineering Industry)
(No.2) Order, S.I. No. 419 of 1981*

*Industrial Training Levy (Chemical and Allied
Products Industry) Order, S.I. No. 175 of 1982*

*Industrial Training Levy (Printing and Paper
Industry) Order, S.I. No. 213 of 1982*

*Industrial Training Levy (Construction Industry)
Order, S.I. No. 214 of 1982*

Statutory Authority	Section	Statutory Instrument
Industrial Training Act, No. 5 of 1967 (*Cont.*)		*Industrial Training Levy (Clothing and Footwear Industry) Order, S.I. No. 290 of 1982*
		Industrial Training Levy (Food, Drink and Tobacco Industry) Order, S.I. No. 291 of 1982
		Industrial Training Levy (Engineering Industry) Order, S.I. No. 326 of 1982
		Industrial Training Levy (Textiles Industry) Order, S.I. No. 353 of 1982
		Industrial Training Levy (Chemical and Allied Products Industry) Order, S.I. No. 118 of 1983
		Industrial Training Levy (Construction Industry) Order, S.I. No. 195 of 1983
		Industrial Training Levy (Printing and Paper Industry) Order, S.I. No. 196 of 1983
		Industrial Training Levy (Food, Drink and Tobacco Industry) Order, S.I. No. 250 of 1983
		Industrial Training Levy (Clothing and Footwear Industry) Order, S.I. No. 251 of 1983
		Industrial Training Levy (Textiles Industry) Order, S.I. No. 356 of 1983
		Industrial Training Levy (Engineering Industry) Order, S.I. No. 357 of 1983
		Industrial Training Levy (Chemical and Allied Products Industry) Order, S.I. No. 79 of 1984
		Industrial Training Levy (Printing and Paper Industry) Order, S.I. No. 164 of 1984
		Industrial Training Levy (Construction Industry) Order, S.I. No. 195 of 1984
		Industrial Training Levy (Clothing and Footwear Industry) Order, S.I. No. 212 of 1984
		Industrial Training Levy (Food, Drink and Tobacco Industry) Order, S.I. No. 226 of 1984
		Industrial Training Levy (Textiles Industry) Order, S.I. No. 274 of 1984
		Industrial Training Levy (Engineering Industry) Order, (1985) S.I. No. 302 of 1984
		Industrial Training Levy (Chemical and Allied Products Industry) Order, S.I. No. 74 of 1985
		Industrial Training Levy (Printing and Paper Industry) Order, S.I. No. 164 of 1985
		Industrial Training Levy (Construction Industry) Order, S.I. No. 173 of 1985
		Industrial Training Levy (Clothing and Footwear Industry) Order, S.I. No. 298 of 1985
		Industrial Training Levy (Food, Drink and Tobacco Industry) Order, S.I. No. 299 of 1985
		Industrial Training Levy (Textiles Industry) Order, S.I. No. 389 of 1985
		Industrial Training Levy (Chemical and Allied Products Industry) Order, S.I. No. 39 of 1986
		Industrial Training Levy (Engineering Industry) Order, S.I. No. 64 of 1986

Statutory Authority	Section	Statutory Instrument
Industrial Training Act, No. 5 of 1967 (*Cont.*)		Industrial Training Levy (Printing and Paper Industry) Order, S.I. No. 219 of 1986
		Industrial Training Levy (Construction Industry) Order, S.I. No. 245 of 1986
		Industrial Training Levy (Food, Drink and Tobacco Industry) Order, S.I. No. 282 of 1986
		Industrial Training Levy (Clothing and Footwear Industry) Order, S.I. No. 360 of 1986
		Industrial Training Levy (Textiles Industry) Order, S.I. No. 361 of 1986
	22	Industrial Training Levy (Appeal Tribunal) Regulations, S.I. No. 166 of 1970
	23	Industrial Training (Textiles Industry) Order, S.I. No. 278 of 1968
		Industrial Training (Engineering Industry) Order, S.I. No. 40 of 1969
		Industrial Training (Clothing and Footwear Industry) Order, S.I. No. 44 of 1969
		Industrial Training (Construction Industry) Order, S.I. No. 47 of 1969
		Industrial Training (Food, Drink and Tobacco Industry) Order, S.I. No. 260 of 1969
		Industrial Training (Printing and Paper Industry) Order, S.I. No. 21 of 1970
		Industrial Training (Textiles Industry) (Amendment) Order, S.I. No. 97 of 1970
		Industrial Training (Chemical and Allied Products Industry) Order, S.I. No. 181 of 1972
		Industrial Training Order, S.I. No. 312 of 1978
	24	Industrial Training (Engineering Committee) Order, S.I. No. 121 of 1969
		Industrial Training (Textiles Committee) Order, S.I. No. 171 of 1969
		Industrial Training (Construction Committee) Order, S.I. No. 172 of 1969
		Industrial Training (Clothing and Footwear Committee) Order, S.I. No. 219 of 1969
		Industrial Training (Food, Drink and Tobacco Committee) Order, S.I. No. 3 of 1970
		Industrial Training (Printing and Paper Committee) Order, S.I. No. 87 of 1970
		Industrial Training (Textiles Industry) (Amendment) Order, S.I. No. 97 of 1970
		Industrial Training (Construction Committee) (Amendment) Order, S.I. No. 106 of 1972
		Industrial Training (Textiles Committee) (Amendment) Order, S.I. No. 107 of 1972
		Industrial Training (Chemical and Allied Products Committee) Order, S.I. No. 259 of 1972
		Industrial Training (Food, Drink and Tobacco Committee) (Amendment) Order, S.I. No. 297 of 1972

Statutory Authority	Section	Statutory Instrument
Industrial Training Act, No. 5 of 1967 (*Cont.*)		**Industrial Training (Chemical and Allied Products Committee) (Amendment) Order, S.I. No. 203 of 1973**
		Industrial Training (Engineering Committee) (Amendment) Order, S.I. No. 104 of 1975
		Industrial Training (Printing and Paper Committee) (Amendment) Order, S.I. No. 136 of 1976
		Industrial Training (Engineering Committee) (Amendment) Order, S.I. No. 378 of 1981
		Industrial Training (Construction Committee) (Amendment) Order, S.I. No. 113 of 1982
		Industrial Training (Printing and Paper Committee) (Amendment) Order, S.I. No. 114 of 1982
		Industrial Training (Chemical and Allied Products Committee) (Amendment) Order, S.I. No. 115 of 1982
		Industrial Training (Engineering Committee) (Amendment) Order, S.I. No. 116 of 1982
		Industrial Training (Food, Drink and Tobacco Committee) (Amendment) Order, S.I. No. 117 of 1982
		Industrial Training (Clothing and Footwear Committee) (Amendment) Order, S.I. No. 118 of 1982
		Industrial Training (Textiles Committee) (Amendment) Order, S.I. No. 119 of 1982
		Industrial Training Chemical and Allied Products Committee) (Amendment) Order, S.I. No. 97 of 1984
	49	*Industrial Training Act (Revocation of Initial Registration Fee) Order, S.I. No. 131 of 1976*
		Apprenticeship Educational Qualifications Amendment Order, S.I. No. 204 of 1976
		Period of Apprenticeship Amendment Order, S.I. No. 205 of 1976
		Period of Apprenticeship Amendment Order, S.I. No. 57 of 1977
		Apprenticeship Act (Designated Trade) (Printing Trade) Amendment Order, S.I. No. 379 of 1981
Infectious Diseases (Aircraft) Regulations, S.I. No. 136 of 1948	6(4)	**Infectious Diseases (Aircraft) Regulations, 1948 (Specified Areas) Order, S.I. No. 232 of 1948**
Institute for Advanced Studies Act, No. 13 of 1940		**Institute for Advanced Studies (School of Cosmic Physics) Establishment Order [Vol. XXXVII p. 747] S.R.& O. No. 77 of 1947**
	4(1)	**Institute for Advanced Studies (School of Celtic Studies) Establishment Order [Vol. XXX p. 389] S.R.& O. No. 308 of 1940**
		Institute for Advanced Studies (School of Theoretical Physics) Establishment Order [Vol. XXX p. 409] S.R.& O. No. 309 of 1940
	6	*Institute for Advanced Studies (Establishment Orders) (Amendment) Order, S.I. No. 105 of 1975*

Statutory Authority	Section	Statutory Instrument
Institute for Advanced Studies Act, No. 13 of 1940 (*Cont.*)	6(1)	**Institute for Advanced Studies (School of Celtic Studies) Establishment Order [Vol. XXX p. 389] S.R.& O. No. 308 of 1940**
		Institute for Advanced Studies (School of Theoretical Physics) Establishment Order [Vol. XXX p. 409] S.R.& O. No. 309 of 1940
	6(3)	**Institute for Advanced Studies (School of Celtic Studies) Establishment Order, 1940 (Amendment) Order [Vol. XXXVII p. 743] S.R.& O. No. 327 of 1947**
		Institute for Advanced Studies (School of Theoretical Physics) Establishment Order, 1940 (Amendment) Order [Vol. XXXVII p. 767] S.R.& O. No. 328 of 1947
Institute of Chartered Accountants in Ireland (Charter Amendment) Act, No. 2 of 1966(Private)	9	*Institute of Chartered Accountants in Ireland (Charter Amendment) Act, 1966 (Commencement) Order, S.I. No. 180 of 1966*
Insurance Act, No. 45 of 1936	2	*Insurance Act, 1936 (Parts I, III and IV) (Commencement) Order [Vol. XIII p. 705] S.R.& O. No. 17 of 1937*
		Insurance Act, 1936 (Parts II, V and VII) (Commencement) Order [Vol. XXX p. 445] S.R.& O. No. 77 of 1940
	5	**Actuary (Qualification) Regulations [Vol. XXX p. 429] S.R.& O. No. 75 of 1940**
		Insurance Regulations [Vol. XXX p. 449] S.R.& O. No. 80 of 1940
	62(1)	**Industrial Assurance (Contents of Policies) Order [Vol. XXX p. 433] S.R.& O. No. 76 of 1940**
	72	**Industrial Assurance (Fees for Determination of Disputes) Regulations [Vol. XXX p. 439] S.R.& O. No. 81 of 1940**
Insurance Act, No. 7 of 1953	2(1)	**Insurance (Provision of Services) Order, S.I. No. 171 of 1983**
Insurance (Amendment) Act, No. 31 of 1938	2(1)	*Insurance (Amendment) Act, 1938 (Transfer Date) Order [Vol. XXX p. 479] S.R.& O. No. 250 of 1939*
	18(2)	**Insurance (Amendment) Act, 1938 (Amendment of Section 18) Order [Vol. XXX p. 475] S.R.& O. No. 367 of 1939**
Insurance (Intermittent Unemployment) Act, No. 7 of 1942		**Insurance (Intermittent Unemployment) (Contributions) Regulations [Vol. XXX p. 491] S.R.& O. No. 33 of 1943**
		Insurance (Intermittent Unemployment) (Determination of Questions) Regulations [Vol. XXX p. 509] S.R.& O. No. 34 of 1943
		Insurance (Intermittent Unemployment) (Supplementary Benefit) Regulations [Vol. XXX p. 527] S.R.& O. No. 109 of 1943

Statutory Authority	Section	Statutory Instrument
Insurance (Intermittent Unemployment Act, No. 7 of 1942 (*Cont.*)		**Insurance (Intermittent Unemployment) (Insurance Year) Regulations, S.I. No. 274 of 1952**
		Insurance (Intermittent Unemployment) (Contributions) Amendment Regulations, S.I. No. 1 of 1953
		Insurance (Intermittent Unemployment) (Supplementary Benefit) (Amendment) Regulations, S.I. No. 15 of 1953
		Insurance (Intermittent Unemployment) Act, 1942 (Amendment of Rates of Weekly Contributions) Regulations, S.I. No. 134 of 1953
	1(3)	*Insurance (Intermittent Unemployment) Act, 1942 (Sections 18 and 28) (Amendment) Order [Vol. XXX p. 487] S.R.& O. No. 85 of 1943*
	1(4)	*Insurance (Intermittent Unemployment) Act, 1942 (Sections 18 and 28) (Amendment) Order [Vol. XXX p. 487] S.R.& O. No. 85 of 1943*
	12	**Insurance (Intermittent Unemployment) Regulations, S.I. No. 80 of 1979**
	15	**Insurance (Intermittent Unemployment) (Extension) Order, S.I. No. 82 of 1955**
	24	**Insurance (Intermittent Unemployment) Regulations, S.I. No. 80 of 1979**
	25	**Intermittent Unemployment (Supplementary Insurance Stamps) Regulations [Vol. XXX p. 557] S.R.& O. No. 434 of 1943**
	26(1)	**Insurance (Intermittent Unemployment) (Powers in Relation to Supplementary Insurance Stamps) Order [Vol. XXX p. 523] S.R.& O. No. 152 of 1943**
	42	**Insurance (Intermittent Unemployment) Regulations, S.I. No. 80 of 1979**
	46	**Insurance (Intermittent Unemployment) Act, 1942 (Amendment of Rates of Weekly Contributions) Regulations, S.I. No. 228 of 1956**
		Insurance (Intermittent Unemployment) Act, 1942 (Amendment of Rates of Weekly Contributions and Supplementary Benefit) Regulations, S.I. No. 128 of 1963
		Insurance (Intermittent Unemployment) Act, 1942 (Amendment of Rates of Supplementary Benefit) Regulations, S.I. No. 188 of 1966
		Insurance (Intermittent Unemployment) Act, 1942 (Amendment of Rates of Supplementary Benefit) Regulations, S.I. No. 7 of 1971
		Insurance (Intermittent Unemployment) Act, 1942 (Amendment of Rates of Weekly Contributions and Supplementary Benefit) Regulations, S.I. No. 279 of 1975
		Insurance (Intermittent Unemployment) Act, 1942 (Amendment of Rates of Weekly Contributions and Supplementary Benefit) Regulations, S.I. No. 159 of 1977

Statutory Authority	Section	Statutory Instrument
Insurance (Intermittent Unemployment Act, No. 7 of 1942 (*Cont.*)		**Insurance (Intermittent Unemployment) Act, 1942 (Amendment of Rates of Weekly Contributions and Supplementary Benefit) Regulations, S.I. No. 139 of 1978**
		Insurance (Intermittent Unemployment) Act, 1942 (Amendment of Rates of Weekly Contributions) Regulations, S.I. No. 347 of 1978
	46(1)	**Insurance (Intermittent Unemployment) Act, 1942 (Amendment of Rates of Weekly Contributions) Regulations [Vol. XXX p. 483] S.R.& O. No. 163 of 1945**
		Insurance (Intermittent Unemployment) Act, 1942 (Amendment of Rates of Supplementary Benefit) Regulations [Vol. XXXVII p. 771] S.R.& O. No. 92 of 1947
		Insurance (Intermittent Unemployment) Act, 1942 (Amendment of Rates of Supplementary Benefit) Regulations, S.I. No. 366 of 1951
		Insurance (Intermittent Unemployment) Act, 1942 (Amendment of Rates of Supplementary Benefit) Regulations, S.I. No. 290 of 1954
Insurance (Intermittent Unemployment) (Powers in Relation to Supplementary Insurance Stamps) Order [Vol. XXX p. 523] S.R.& O. No. 152 of 1943		**Intermittent Unemployment (Supplementary Insurance Stamps) Regulations [Vol. XXX p. 557] S.R.& O. No. 434 of 1943**
Insurance (No.2) Act, No. 29 of 1983	3(6)	*Insurance (No.2) Act, 1983 (Section 3) (Accounting Period) Order, S.I. No. 5 of 1986*
	3(6)(a)	*Insurance (No.2) Act, 1983 (Section 3) Order, S.I. No. 201 of 1984*
		Insurance (No.2) Act, 1983 (Section 3) Order, S.I. No. 226 of 1985
	3(6)(b)	*Insurance (No.2) Act, 1983 (Section 3) (Amendment) Order, S.I. No. 241 of 1984*
		Insurance (No.2) Act, 1983 (Section 3) (Amendment) Order, S.I. No. 330 of 1985
Intermediate Education (Ireland) Act, No. 41 of 1914	1	**Registration Council (Constitution and Procedure) Rules, S.I. No. 197 of 1959**
		Registration Council (Constitution and Procedure) (Amendment) Rules, S.I. No. 200 of 1962
		Registration Council (Constitution and Procedure) (Amendment) Rules, S.I. No. 140 of 1968
		Registration Council (Constitution and Procedure) (Amendment) Rules, S.I. No. 162 of 1974
		Registration Council (Constitution and Procedure) (Amendment) Rules, S.I. No. 26 of 1986
	3	**Registration Council (Constitution and Procedure) Rules [Vol. XIII p. 709] S.R.& O. No. 17 of 1926**
		Registration Council (Constitution and Procedure) Rules, S.I. No. 197 of 1959

Statutory Authority	Section	Statutory Instrument
Intermediate Education (Ireland) Act, No. 41 of 1914 (*Cont.*)		**Registration Council (Constitution and Procedure) (Amendment) Rules, S.I. No. 200 of 1962**
		Registration Council (Constitution and Procedure) (Amendment) Rules, S.I. No. 140 of 1968
		Registration Council (Constitution and Procedure) (Amendment) Rules, S.I. No. 162 of 1974
		Registration Council (Constitution and Procedure) (Amendment) Rules, S.I. No. 26 of 1986
International Health Bodies (Corporate Status) Act, No. 1 of 1971	3(1)	**International Federation of Voluntary Health Service Funds (Corporate Status) Order, S.I. No. 308 of 1971**
		European Association of Programmes in Health Services Studies (Corporate Status) Order, S.I. No. 164 of 1982
Interpretation Act, No. 46 of 1923	11(3)	**Moneylenders Act Rules [Vol. XVI p. 1197] S.R.& O. No. 160 of 1933**
Interpretation Act, No. 38 of 1937	17	**District Court (Counsel's Fees) Rules, S.I. No. 39 of 1973**
		District Court [Family Law (Maintenance of Spouses and Children) Act, 1976] Rules, S.I. No. 96 of 1976
		District Court (Summons-Servers Fee) Rules, S.I. No. 131 of 1977
		District Court [Family Law (Maintenance of Spouses and Children) Act, 1976] (Amendment) Rules, S.I. No. 268 of 1980
		District Court (Costs) (Amendment) Rules, S.I. No. 173 of 1983
		District Court (Summons-Servers Fee) Rules, S.I. No. 119 of 1984
		District Court [Criminal Justice (Community Service) Act, 1983] Rules, S.I. No. 327 of 1984
		District Court (Gaming and Lotteries) Rules, (1984) S.I. No. 1 of 1985
		District Court (Air Navigation (Eurocontrol) Acts, 1963 to 1983) Rules, (1984) S.I. No. 2 of 1985
		District Court (Criminal Procedure Act, 1967) Rules, S.I. No. 23 of 1985
Intoxicating Liquor Act, No. 15 of 1927	53	*Intoxicating Liquor (Reduction of Licences) Rules [Vol. XIII p. 717] S.R.& O. No. 66 of 1928*
		Intoxicating Liquor (Reduction of Licences) Rules [Vol. XIII p. 721] S.R.& O. No. 15 of 1929
Intoxicating Liquor (General) Act, No. 62 of 1924	9	*Intoxicating Liquor (Standardisation of Bottles) No.2 Order [Vol. XIII p. 733] S.R.& O. No. 42 of 1925*
		Intoxicating Liquor (Standardisation of Bottles) No.1 Order [Vol. XIII p. 729] S.R.& O. No. 56 of 1925
		Intoxicating Liquor (Standardisation of Bottles) No.3 Order [Vol. XIII p. 737] S.R.& O. No. 66 of 1925

Statutory Authority	Section	Statutory Instrument
Intoxicating Liquor (General) Act, No. 62 of 1924 (*Cont.*)		*Intoxicating Liquor (Standardisation of Bottles) (No.3) (Revocation) Order, S.I. No. 399 of 1983*
	26(6)	**Prevention of Illicit Distillation Order [Vol. XXXVII p. 777] S.R.& O. No. 211 of 1947**
Intoxicating Liquor Act, No. 21 of 1962	9(2)	**Intoxicating Liquor Act, 1962 (Section 9) Order, S.I. No. 211 of 1979**
Irish Film Board Act, No. 36 of 1980	2	*Irish Film Board (Establishment Day) Order, S.I. No. 282 of 1981*
Irish Land Act, No. 37 of 1903	41	**Irish Land (Finance) Rules, 1912 (Amendment) Regulations, S.I. No. 49 of 1979**
	52(15)	**Public Trustee Rules [Vol. XIV p. 267] S.R.& O. No. 14 of 1927**
		Public Trustee Rules [Vol. XXXVII p. 781] S.R.& O. No. 94 of 1947
		Public Trustee Rules, S.I. No. 29 of 1973
Irish Land Act, No. 42 of 1909	14	**Irish Land (Finance) Rules, 1912 (Amendment) Regulations, S.I. No. 49 of 1979**
	30	**Land (Finance) Rules, S.I. No. 83 of 1956**
		Land (Finance) (No.2) Rules, S.I. No. 335 of 1956
Irish Nationality and Citizenship Act, No. 26 of 1956	3	**Irish Nationality and Citizenship Regulations, S.I. No. 216 of 1956**
		Irish Nationality and Citizenship (Fees) Regulations, S.I. No. 137 of 1980
		Irish Nationality and Citizenship (Fees) Regulations, S.I. No. 279 of 1983
		Irish Nationality and Citizenship (Fees) Regulations, S.I. No. 260 of 1986
		Irish Nationality and Citizenship Regulations, S.I. No. 261 of 1986
	27(5)	**Foreign Births Regulations, S.I. No. 224 of 1956**
		Foreign Births (Amendment) Regulations, S.I. No. 349 of 1974
		Foreign Births (Amendment) Regulations, S.I. No. 273 of 1976
		Foreign Births (Amendment) Regulations, S.I. No. 94 of 1980
		Foreign Births (Amendment) Regulations, S.I. No. 259 of 1981
		Foreign Births (Amendment) Regulations, S.I. No. 363 of 1985
Irish Nationality and Citizenship Act, No. 13 of 1935		**Irish Nationality and Citizenship Regulations [Vol. XXX p. 585] S.R.& O. No. 16 of 1939**
		Irish Nationality and Citizenship (Amendment of Fees) Regulations, S.I. No. 366 of 1948
		New Zealand Citizens (Irish Citizenship Rights) Order, S.I. No. 2 of 1949

Statutory Authority	Section	Statutory Instrument
Irish Nationality and Citizenship Act, No. 13 of 1935 (*Cont.*)		**Australian Citizens (Irish Citizenship Rights) Order, S.I. No. 18 of 1949**
		Irish Nationality and Citizenship Regulations, 1939 (Amendment) Regulations, S.I. No. 188 of 1949
		South African Citizens (Irish Citizenship Rights) Order, S.I. No. 198 of 1950
		Southern Rhodesian Citizens (Irish Citizenship Rights) Order, S.I. No. 11 of 1951
		Canadian Citizens (Irish Citizenship Rights) Order, S.I. No. 89 of 1951
		Irish Nationality and Citizenship Regulations, 1939 (Amendment) Regulations, S.I. No. 173 of 1952
	24(5)	*Foreign Births Entry Book Regulations [Vol. XIII p. 799] S.R.& O. No. 147 of 1935*
		Foreign Births Entry Book (Amendment) Regulations [Vol. XIII p. 809] S.R.& O. No. 87 of 1938
	24(6)	*Northern Ireland Births Register Regulations [Vol. XIII p. 815] S.R.& O. No. 148 of 1935*
		Northern Ireland Births Register (Amendment) Regulations [Vol. XIII p. 825] S.R.& O. No. 88 of 1938
	25(6)	*Foreign Births Register Regulations [Vol. XIII p. 831] S.R.& O. No. 149 of 1935*
		Foreign Births Register (Amendment) Regulations [Vol. XIII p. 841] S.R.& O. No. 86 of 1938
	26(5)	*Register of Nationals Regulations [Vol. XIII p. 847] S.R.& O. No. 150 of 1935*
		Register of Nationals (Amendment) Regulations [Vol. XIII p. 857] S.R.& O. No. 85 of 1938
	27(5)	*General Register of Nationals Regulations [Vol. XIII p. 863] S.R.& O. No. 151 of 1935*
		General Register of Nationals (Amendment) Regulations [Vol. XIII p. 873] S.R.& O. No. 84 of 1938
	28(1)	*Irish Nationality and Citizenship Regulations [Vol. XIII p. 879] S.R.& O. No. 555 of 1935*
		Irish Nationality and Citizenship Regulations [Vol. XIII p. 931] S.R.& O. No. 220 of 1937
	89	**Citizens of United Kingdom and Colonies (Irish Citizenship Rights) Order, S.I. No. 1 of 1949**
Irish Shipping Limited Act, No. 37 of 1947	13	*Irish Shipping Limited Act, 1947 (Commencement) Order [Vol. XXXVII p. 787] S.R.& O. No. 427 of 1947*
Irish Steel Holdings Limited (Amendment) Act, No. 13 of 1979	2	*Irish Steel Holdings Limited (Amendment) Act, 1979 (Section 2) (Commencement) Order, S.I. No. 292 of 1979*
Johnstown Castle Agricultural College (Amendment) Act, No. 30 of 1959	14(2)	*Johnstown Castle Agricultural College (Amendment) Act, 1959 (Commencement) Order, S.I. No. 6 of 1960*

Statutory Authority	Section	Statutory Instrument
Juries Act, No. 23 of 1927		*Electoral Order [Vol. XI p. 243] S.R.& O. No. 21 of 1936*
		Electoral (Amendment) Order [Vol. XXIX p. 9] S.R.& O. No. 557 of 1942
	1	*Jury Districts (County Kildare) Order, S.I. No. 173 of 1963*
	1(3)	*Jury Districts Order [Vol. XIII p. 939] S.R.& O. No. 61 of 1927*
		Jury Districts (No.2) Order [Vol. XIII p. 951] S.R.& O. No. 86 of 1927
		Jury Districts (No.3) Order [Vol. XIII p. 963] S.R.& O. No. 99 of 1927
		Jury Districts (County Wicklow) Order [Vol. XIII p. 965] S.R.& O. No. 27 of 1929
	1(4)	*Jury Districts (No.2) Order [Vol. XIII p. 951] S.R.& O. No. 86 of 1927*
		Jury Districts (No.2) Order, 1927 (Variation No.1) Order, S.I. No. 100 of 1949
		Jury Districts Order (No.2) 1927 (Variation No.2) Order, S.I. No. 200 of 1961
		Jury Districts (No.2) Order, 1927 (Variation) Order, S.I. No. 102 of 1964
		Jury Districts (No.2) Order, 1927 (Variation No.3) Order, S.I. No. 266 of 1965
	2(1)	*Jurors (Minimum Rating Qualification) Order [Vol. XIII p. 977] S.R.& O. No. 92 of 1927*
		Jurors (Minimum Rating Qualification) (County Galway) Order [Vol. XIII p. 981] S.R.& O. No. 56 of 1928
	2(2)	*Jurors (Minimum Rating Qualification) Order [Vol. XIII p. 977] S.R.& O. No. 92 of 1927*
		Jurors (Minimum Rating Qualification) (County Galway) Order [Vol. XIII p. 981] S.R.& O. No. 56 of 1928
	33(3)	*Juries (Panels for Trial of Criminal Issues) Order [Vol. XIII p. 967] S.R.& O. No. 87 of 1927*
		Juries (Panels for Trial of Criminal Issues) Order [Vol. XIII p. 971] S.R.& O. No. 1 of 1928
		Juries (Panels for Trial of Criminal Issues in County Wicklow) Order [Vol. XIII p. 975] S.R.& O. No. 28 of 1929
	50(3)	*Juries (Copies of Panels) Order [Vol. XIII p. 937] S.R.& O. No. 51 of 1927*
	69	*Jury Summonses Order, S.I. No. 30 of 1955*
Juries Act, No. 11 of 1961	2(2)(b)	*Juries (County Borough of Cork) Order, S.I. No. 201 of 1961*
	4	*Jury (Panels for Trial of Criminal Issues) Order, S.I. No. 84 of 1970*
		Jury (Panels for Trial of Criminal Issues) (County Louth) Order, S.I. No. 114 of 1973

Statutory Authority	Section	Statutory Instrument
Juries Act, No. 11 of 1961 (*Cont.*)	4(2)	*Juries for Circuit Court (Criminal Issues) (County Kildare) Order, S.I. No. 174 of 1963*
	9(3)	*Juries Act, 1961 (Commencement) Order, S.I. No. 199 of 1961*
Juries Act, No. 4 of 1976	5	**Jury Districts Order, S.I. No. 59 of 1977**
		Jury Districts Order, S.I. No. 262 of 1983
	5(2)	**Jury Districts Order, S.I. No. 57 of 1976**
	12	**Jury Summons Regulations, S.I. No. 56 of 1976**
Juries Acts, 1927 to 1945,		*Electoral Order [Vol. XXXVII p. 163] S.R.& O. No. 96 of 1946*
Labourers Act, No. 24 of 1936		*Labourers Cottage (Purchase) Regulations, S.R.& O. No. 52 of 1937*
		Labourers Cottage (Purchase) Regulations [Vol. XIV p. 31] S.R.& O. No. 97 of 1938
		Labourers Cottage (Purchase) (Amendment) Regulations, S.I. No. 171 of 1954
Labourers Acts, 1883 to 1948,		*Housing (Architects and Engineers) (Revocation) Order, S.I. No. 188 of 1950*
Labourers Acts, 1883 to 1950,		*Labourers (Ireland) Order, 1912, Rule 47 (Revocation) Order, S.I. No. 202 of 1951*
Labourers (Ireland) Act, No. 37 of 1906	31	**Labourers Order, S.I. No. 90 of 1954**
		Labourers Acts (Solicitors' Remuneration) Order, S.I. No. 144 of 1957
Land Act, No. 42 of 1923		**Land Registry Rules [Vol. XIV p. 377] S.R.& O. No. 14 of 1926**
	1	**Land Bond (Drawing) Regulations [Vol. XXX p. 629] S.R.& O. No. 245 of 1940**
		Land Bond (Drawing) (Amendment) Regulations [Vol. XXX p. 647] S.R.& O. No. 294 of 1943
		Land Bond (Drawings) Regulations, S.I. No. 72 of 1970
		Land Bond (Drawings) Regulations, S.I. No. 103 of 1972
		Land Bond (Drawings of 9.75% Land Bonds) Regulations, S.I. No. 108 of 1974
		Land Bond (Drawings of 12.5% Land Bonds) Regulations, S.I. No. 85 of 1976
		Land Bond (Drawings of 16% Land Bonds) Regulations, S.I. No. 128 of 1977
		Land Bond (Drawings of 15% Land Bonds) Regulations, S.I. No. 118 of 1978
		Land Bond (Drawings of 14.75% Land Bonds) Regulations, S.I. No. 159 of 1979
		Land Bond (Drawings of 13.75% Land Bonds) Regulations, S.I. No. 157 of 1981

Statutory Authority	Section	Statutory Instrument
Land Act, No. 42 of 1923 (*Cont.*)		**Land Bond (Drawings of 16.5% Land Bonds) Regulations, S.I. No. 132 of 1982**
		Land Bonds (Drawings of 16.25% Land Bonds) Regulations, S.I. No. 115 of 1983
		Land Bond (Drawings of 18.25% Land Bonds) Regulations, S.I. No. 110 of 1984
	1(3)	*Land Bond (Drawing) Regulations [Vol. XIV p. 387] S.R.& O. No. 254 of 1934*
	12	**Purchase of Land (Ireland) Act, 1891 (Guarantee Fund Apportionment) (Amendment) Regulations [Vol. XXXII p. 811] S.R.& O. No. 142 of 1945**
	12(3)	*Purchase Annuities Fund Rules [Vol. XIV p. 313] S.R.& O. No. 10 of 1924*
	17	*Purchase Annuities Fund Rules [Vol. XIV p. 313] S.R.& O. No. 10 of 1924*
		Land (Finance) Rules, 1925 (Amendment) Rules [Vol. XIV p. 353] S.R.& O. No. 81 of 1927
		Land (Finance) Rules [Vol. XIV p. 359] S.R.& O. No. 136 of 1933
		Land (Finance) (No.2) Rules [Vol. XIV p. 367] S.R.& O. No. 209 of 1934
		Land (Finance) Rules, S.I. No. 83 of 1956
		Land (Finance) (No.2) Rules, S.I. No. 335 of 1956
Land Act, No. 19 of 1927	40	**Land (Finance) (No.2) Rules [Vol. XIV p. 367] S.R.& O. No. 209 of 1934**
	57	**Land (Finance) Rules, S.I. No. 83 of 1956**
		Land (Finance) (No.2) Rules, S.I. No. 335 of 1956
	57(2)	*Land (Finance) Rules [Vol. XIV p. 399] S.R.& O. No. 82 of 1927*
Land Act, No. 11 of 1931	53	**Land (Finance) Rules, S.I. No. 83 of 1956**
		Land (Finance) (No.2) Rules, S.I. No. 335 of 1956
Land Act, No. 38 of 1933	3	**Land Act, 1933 (Rules and Orders under Section 3) [Vol. XIV p. 411] S.R.& O. No. 18 of 1934**
		Land (Finance) Rules [Vol. XIV p. 433] S.R.& O. No. 25 of 1934
		Land Purchase Acts Rules [Vol. XIV p. 453] S.R.& O. No. 361 of 1936
		Land Purchase Acts Rules [Vol. XXX p. 657] S.R.& O. No. 341 of 1939
		Land Purchase Acts Rules [Vol. XXX p. 687] S.R.& O. No. 292 of 1940
		Land Purchase Acts Rules [Vol. XXX p. 705] S.R.& O. No. 70 of 1942
		Land Purchase Acts Rules [Vol. XXX p. 689] S.R.& O. No. 40 of 1945
		Land Purchase Acts Rules [Vol. XXXVII p. 797] S.R.& O. No. 124 of 1947
		Land Purchase Acts Rules, S.I. No. 50 of 1951
		Land (Finance) Rules, S.I. No. 83 of 1956
		Land (Finance) (No.2) Rules, S.I. No. 335 of 1956

Statutory Authority	Section	Statutory Instrument
Land Act, No. 38 of 1933 (*Cont.*)		**Land Purchase Acts Rules, S.I. No. 20 of 1960**
		Land Purchase Acts Rules, S.I. No. 230 of 1964
		Land Purchase Acts Rules, S.I. No. 147 of 1965
		Land Purchase Acts Rules, S.I. No. 216 of 1974
		Land Purchase Acts Rules, S.I. No. 253 of 1984
	5	*Land Act, 1933 (Appointed Day for Part II) [Vol. XIV p. 405] S.R.& O. No. 12 of 1934*
	7	**Appeal Tribunal Rules [Vol. XIV p. 447] S.R.& O. No. 26 of 1934**
		Appeal Tribunal (Amendment) Rules [Vol. XXX p. 653] S.R.& O. No. 113 of 1944
		Appeal Tribunal (Amendment) Rules [Vol. XXXVII p. 791] S.R.& O. No. 159 of 1947
	28	**County Registrars (Land Commission) Regulations [Vol. XIV p. 407] S.R.& O. No. 16 of 1934**
	28(3)	**County Registrars (Land Commission) Regulations, 1934 (Amendment) Regulations, S.I. No. 52 of 1955**
Land Act, No. 41 of 1936	4	**Land Bond (Drawing) Regulations [Vol. XXX p. 763] S.R.& O. No. 69 of 1941**
		Land Bond Order [Vol. XXX p. 727] S.R.& O. No. 20 of 1942
		Land Bond Order [Vol. XXX p. 737] S.R.& O. No. 547 of 1942
		Land Bond Order [Vol. XXX p. 743] S.R.& O. No. 407 of 1943
		Land Bond Order [Vol. XXX p. 749] S.R.& O. No. 365 of 1944
		Land Bond Order [Vol. XXX p. 755] S.R.& O. No. 352 of 1945
		Land Bond Order [Vol. XXXVII p. 807] S.R.& O. No. 396 of 1946
		Land Bond Order [Vol. XXXVII p. 813] S.R.& O. No. 438 of 1947
		Land Bond Order, S.I. No. 433 of 1948
		Land Bond Order, S.I. No. 352 of 1949
		Land Bond Order, S.I. No. 317 of 1950
		Land Bond Order, S.I. No. 261 of 1951
		Land Bond (No.2) Order, S.I. No. 368 of 1951
		Land Bond Order, S.I. No. 246 of 1953
		Land Bond (No.2) Order, S.I. No. 417 of 1953
		Land Bond Order, S.I. No. 296 of 1954
		Land Bond Order, S.I. No. 268 of 1955
		Land Bond Order, S.I. No. 306 of 1956
		Land Bond Order, S.I. No. 230 of 1957
		Land Bond (No.2) Order, S.I. No. 253 of 1957
		Land Bond Order, S.I. No. 276 of 1958
		Land Bond Order, S.I. No. 228 of 1959
		Land Bond Order, S.I. No. 235 of 1960
		Land Bond Order, S.I. No. 10 of 1961
		Land Bond (No.2) Order, S.I. No. 131 of 1961

Statutory Authority	Section	Statutory Instrument
Land Act, No. 41 of 1936 (*Cont.*)		**Land Bond (No.3) Order, S.I. No. 307 of 1961**
		Land Bond Order, S.I. No. 231 of 1962
		Land Bond Order, S.I. No. 272 of 1963
		Land Bond Order, S.I. No. 253 of 1964
		Land Bond Order, S.I. No. 7 of 1965
		Land Bond Order, S.I. No. 18 of 1966
		Land Bond Order, S.I. No. 28 of 1967
		Land Bond Order, S.I. No. 20 of 1968
		Land Bond Order, S.I. No. 10 of 1969
		Land Bond (No.2) Order, S.I. No. 112 of 1969
		Land Bond (No.3) Order, S.I. No. 225 of 1969
		Land Bond (No.4) Order, S.I. No. 270 of 1969
		Land Bond Order, S.I. No. 8 of 1971
		Land Bond Order, S.I. No. 19 of 1972
		Land Bond (No.2) Order, S.I. No. 345 of 1972
		Land Bond Order, S.I. No. 6 of 1974
		Land Bonds (No.2) Order, S.I. No. 316 of 1974
		Land Bond Order, S.I. No. 26 of 1975
		Land Bond (No.2) Order, S.I. No. 159 of 1975
		Land Bond (No.3) Order, S.I. No. 326 of 1975
		Land Bond Order, S.I. No. 26 of 1976
		Land Bond (No.2) Order, S.I. No. 245 of 1976
		Land Bond (No.3) Order, S.I. No. 246 of 1976
		Land Bond Order, S.I. No. 42 of 1977
		Land Bond (No.2) Order, S.I. No. 43 of 1977
		Land Bond (No.3) Order, S.I. No. 336 of 1977
		Land Bond Order, S.I. No. 50 of 1978
		Land Bond (No.2) Order, S.I. No. 51 of 1978
		Land Bond (No.3) Order, S.I. No. 214 of 1978
		Land Bond (No.4) Order, S.I. No. 215 of 1978
		Land Bond (No.2) Order, S.I. No. 22 of 1979
		Land Bond Order, S.I. No. 23 of 1979
		Land Bond Order, S.I. No. 21 of 1980
		Land Bond (No.2) Order, S.I. No. 173 of 1980
		Land Bond Order, S.I. No. 24 of 1981
		Land Bond (No.2) Order, S.I. No. 25 of 1981
		Land Bond Order, S.I. No. 18 of 1982
		Land Bond Order, S.I. No. 193 of 1983
		Land Bond (No.2) Order, S.I. No. 204 of 1983
		Land Bond Order, S.I. No. 102 of 1984
		Land Bond (No.2) Order, S.I. No. 103 of 1984
		Land Bond Order, S.I. No. 155 of 1985
	4(1)	**New Land Bond (Drawing) Regulations [Vol. XIV p. 477] S.R.& O. No. 59 of 1938**
Land Act, No. 26 of 1939		**Land (Finance) Rules [Vol. XXX p. 693] S.R.& O. No. 201 of 1944**
	3	**Land (Finance) Rules, S.I. No. 83 of 1956**
		Land (Finance) (No.2) Rules, S.I. No. 335 of 1956

Statutory Authority	Section	Statutory Instrument
Land Act, No. 16 of 1950	3	**Land (Finance) Rules, S.I. No. 83 of 1956**
		Land (Finance) (No.2) Rules, S.I. No. 335 of 1956
	14	*Land Act, 1950, Section 14, Appointed Day, S.I. No. 163 of 1950*
Land Act, No. 18 of 1953	2	**Land (Finance) Rules, S.I. No. 83 of 1956**
		Land (Finance) (No.2) Rules, S.I. No. 335 of 1956
	4	**Land Bond Order, S.I. No. 246 of 1953**
		Land Bond (No.2) Order, S.I. No. 417 of 1953
		Land Bond Order, S.I. No. 296 of 1954
		Land Bond Order, S.I. No. 268 of 1955
		Land Bond Order, S.I. No. 306 of 1956
		Land Bond Order, S.I. No. 230 of 1957
		Land Bond (No.2) Order, S.I. No. 253 of 1957
		Land Bond Order, S.I. No. 276 of 1958
		Land Bond Order, S.I. No. 228 of 1959
		Land Bond Order, S.I. No. 235 of 1960
		Land Bond Order, S.I. No. 10 of 1961
		Land Bond (No.2) Order, S.I. No. 131 of 1961
		Land Bond (No.3) Order, S.I. No. 307 of 1961
		Land Bond Order, S.I. No. 231 of 1962
		Land Bond Order, S.I. No. 272 of 1963
		Land Bond Order, S.I. No. 253 of 1964
		Land Bond Order, S.I. No. 7 of 1965
		Land Bond Order, S.I. No. 18 of 1966
		Land Bond Order, S.I. No. 28 of 1967
		Land Bond Order, S.I. No. 20 of 1968
		Land Bond Order, S.I. No. 10 of 1969
		Land Bond (No.2) Order, S.I. No. 112 of 1969
		Land Bond (No.3) Order, S.I. No. 225 of 1969
		Land Bond (No.4) Order, S.I. No. 270 of 1969
		Land Bond Order, S.I. No. 8 of 1971
		Land Bond Order, S.I. No. 19 of 1972
		Land Bond (No.2) Order, S.I. No. 345 of 1972
		Land Bond Order, S.I. No. 6 of 1974
		Land Bond (No.2) Order, S.I. No. 316 of 1974
		Land Bond Order, S.I. No. 26 of 1975
		Land Bond (No.2) Order, S.I. No. 159 of 1975
		Land Bond (No.3) Order, S.I. No. 326 of 1975
		Land Bond Order, S.I. No. 26 of 1976
		Land Bond (No.2) Order, S.I. No. 245 of 1976
		Land Bond (No.3) Order, S.I. No. 246 of 1976
		Land Bond Order, S.I. No. 42 of 1977
		Land Bond (No.2) Order, S.I. No. 43 of 1977
		Land Bond (No.3) Order, S.I. No. 336 of 1977
		Land Bond Order, S.I. No. 509 of 1978
		Land Bond (No.2) Order, S.I. No. 51 of 1978
		Land Bond (No.3) Order, S.I. No. 214 of 1978
		Land Bond (No.4) Order, S.I. No. 215 of 1978

Statutory Authority	Section	Statutory Instrument
Land Act, No. 18 of 1953 (*Cont.*)		Land Bond (No.2) Order, S.I. No. 22 of 1979
		Land Bond Order, S.I. No. 23 of 1979
		Land Bond Order, S.I. No. 21 of 1980
		Land Bond (No.2) Order, S.I. No. 173 of 1980
		Land Bond Order, S.I. No. 24 of 1981
		Land Bond (No.2) Order, S.I. No. 25 of 1981
		Land Bond Order, S.I. No. 18 of 1982
		Land Bond Order, S.I. No. 193 of 1983
		Land Bond (No.2) Order, S.I. No. 204 of 1983
		Land Bond Order, S.I. No. 102 of 1984
		Land Bond (No.2) Order, S.I. No. 103 of 1984
		Land Bond Order, S.I. No. 155 of 1985
	8	Land Bond Order, S.I. No. 246 of 1953
		Land Bond (No.2) Order, S.I. No. 417 of 1953
		Land Bond Order, S.I. No. 296 of 1954
		Land Bond Order, S.I. No. 268 of 1955
		Land Bond Order, S.I. No. 306 of 1956
		Land Bond Order, S.I. No. 230 of 1957
		Land Bond (No.2) Order, S.I. No. 253 of 1957
		Land Bond Order, S.I. No. 276 of 1958
		Land Bond Order, S.I. No. 228 of 1959
		Land Bond Order, S.I. No. 235 of 1960
		Land Bond Order, S.I. No. 10 of 1961
		Land Bond (No.2) Order, S.I. No. 131 of 1961
		Land Bond (No.3) Order, S.I. No. 307 of 1961
		Land Bond Order, S.I. No. 231 of 1962
		Land Bond Order, S.I. No. 272 of 1963
		Land Bond Order, S.I. No. 253 of 1964
		Land Bond Order, S.I. No. 7 of 1965
		Land Bond Order, S.I. No. 18 of 1966
		Land Bond Order, S.I. No. 28 of 1967
		Land Bond Order, S.I. No. 20 of 1968
		Land Bond Order, S.I. No. 10 of 1969
		Land Bond (No.2) Order, S.I. No. 112 of 1969
		Land Bond (No.3) Order, S.I. No. 225 of 1969
		Land Bond (No.4) Order, S.I. No. 270 of 1969
		Land Bond Order, S.I. No. 8 of 1971
		Land Bond Order, S.I. No. 19 of 1972
		Land Bond (No.2) Order, S.I. No. 345 of 1972
		Land Bond Order, S.I. No. 6 of 1974
		Land Bonds (No.2) Order, S.I. No. 316 of 1974
		Land Bond Order, S.I. No. 26 of 1975
		Land Bond (No.2) Order, S.I. No. 159 of 1975
		Land Bond (No.3) Order, S.I. No. 326 of 1975
		Land Bond Order, S.I. No. 26 of 1976
		Land Bond (No.2) Order, S.I. No. 245 of 1976
		Land Bond (No.3) Order, S.I. No. 246 of 1976
		Land Bond Order, S.I. No. 42 of 1977
		Land Bond (No.2) Order, S.I. No. 43 of 1977

Statutory Authority	Section	Statutory Instrument
Land Act, No. 18 of 1953 (*Cont.*)		**Land Bond (No.3) Order, S.I. No. 336 of 1977**
		Land Bond Order, S.I. No. 509 of 1978
		Land Bond (No.2) Order, S.I. No. 51 of 1978
		Land Bond (No.3) Order, S.I. No. 214 of 1978
		Land Bond (No.4) Order, S.I. No. 215 of 1978
		Land Bond (No.2) Order, S.I. No. 22 of 1979
		Land Bond Order, S.I. No. 23 of 1979
		Land Bond Order, S.I. No. 21 of 1980
		Land Bond (No.2) Order, S.I. No. 173 of 1980
		Land Bond Order, S.I. No. 24 of 1981
		Land Bond (No.2) Order, S.I. No. 25 of 1981
		Land Bond Order, S.I. No. 18 of 1982
		Land Bond Order, S.I. No. 193 of 1983
		Land Bond (No.2) Order, S.I. No. 204 of 1983
		Land Bond Order, S.I. No. 102 of 1984
		Land Bond (No.2) Order, S.I. No. 103 of 1984
		Land Bond Order, S.I. No. 155 of 1985
Land Act, No. 2 of 1965	4(1)(b)	**Land Act, 1965 (Congested Areas) Order, S.I. No. 284 of 1973**
	5(2)(a)	**Purchase of Land (Advances by Land Commission) Regulations, S.I. No. 26 of 1967**
	6(5)	*Life Annuity (Sale of Land to Land Commission) Regulations, S.I. No. 27 of 1967*
		Life Annuity (Sale of Land to Land Commission) (Amendment) Regulations, S.I. No. 67 of 1969
		Life Annuity (Sale of Land to Land Commission) (Revocation) Regulations, S.I. No. 16 of 1973
	45	**Land Act, 1965 (Additional Categories of Qualified Persons) Regulations, S.I. No. 332 of 1972**
	45(1)(x)	**Land Act, 1965 (Additional Category of Qualified Persons) Regulations, S.I. No. 40 of 1970**
		Land Act, 1965 (Additional Category of Qualified Person) Regulations, S.I. No. 144 of 1983
Land Bond Act, No. 25 of 1925	7	**Land (Finance) Rules, S.I. No. 83 of 1956**
		Land (Finance) (No.2) Rules, S.I. No. 335 of 1956
Land Bond Act, No. 33 of 1933	4	**Land Bond (Drawings) Regulations, S.I. No. 72 of 1970**
		Land Bond (Drawings) Regulations, S.I. No. 103 of 1972
		Land Bond (Drawings of 9.75% Land Bonds) Regulations, S.I. No. 108 of 1974
		Land Bond (Drawings of 12.5% Land Bonds) Regulations, S.I. No. 85 of 1976
		Land Bond (Drawings of 16% Land Bonds) Regulations, S.I. No. 128 of 1977
		Land Bond (Drawings of 15% Land Bonds) Regulations, S.I. No. 118 of 1978
		Land Bond (Drawings of 13.75% Land Bonds) Regulations, S.I. No. 157 of 1981

Statutory Authority	Section	Statutory Instrument
Land Bond Act, No. 33 of 1933 (*Cont.*)		Land Bond (Drawings of 16.5% Land Bonds) Regulations, S.I. No. 132 of 1982
		Land Bonds (Drawings of 16.25% Land Bonds) Regulations, S.I. No. 115 of 1983
		Land Bond (Drawings of 18.25% Land Bonds) Regulations, S.I. No. 110 of 1984
	4(4)	New Land Bond (Drawing) Regulations [Vol. XIV p. 477] S.R.& O. No. 59 of 1938
	11	Land (Finance) Rules [Vol. XIV p. 359] S.R.& O. No. 136 of 1933
		Land (Finance) Rules, S.I. No. 83 of 1956
		Land (Finance) (No.2) Rules, S.I. No. 335 of 1956
Land Bond Act, No. 11 of 1934	4	Land Bond Order [Vol. XXX p. 709] S.R.& O. No. 389 of 1939
		Land Bond Order [Vol. XXX p. 715] S.R.& O. No. 372 of 1940
		Land Bond Order [Vol. XXX p. 721] S.R.& O. No. 583 of 1941
		Land Bond Order [Vol. XXX p. 727] S.R.& O. No. 20 of 1942
		Land Bond (No.2) Order [Vol. XXX p. 737] S.R.& O. No. 547 of 1942
		Land Bond Order [Vol. XXX p. 743] S.R.& O. No. 407 of 1943
		Land Bond Order [Vol. XXX p. 749] S.R.& O. No. 365 of 1944
		Land Bond Order [Vol. XXX p. 755] S.R.& O. No. 352 of 1945
		Land Bond Order [Vol. XXXVII p. 807] S.R.& O. No. 396 of 1946
		Land Bond Order [Vol. XXXVII p. 813] S.R.& O. No. 438 of 1947
		Land Bond Order, S.I. No. 433 of 1948
		Land Bond (No.2) Order, S.I. No. 434 of 1948
		Land Bond Order, S.I. No. 352 of 1949
		Land Bond Order, S.I. No. 317 of 1950
		Land Bond Order, S.I. No. 261 of 1951
		Land Bond (No.2) Order, S.I. No. 368 of 1951
		Land Bond Order, S.I. No. 246 of 1953
		Land Bond (No.2) Order, S.I. No. 417 of 1953
		Land Bond Order, S.I. No. 296 of 1954
		Land Bond Order, S.I. No. 268 of 1955
		Land Bond Order, S.I. No. 306 of 1956
		Land Bond Order, S.I. No. 230 of 1957
		Land Bond (No.2) Order, S.I. No. 253 of 1957
		Land Bond Order, S.I. No. 276 of 1958
		Land Bond Order, S.I. No. 228 of 1959
		Land Bond Order, S.I. No. 235 of 1960
		Land Bond Order, S.I. No. 10 of 1961
		Land Bond (No.2) Order, S.I. No. 131 of 1961
		Land Bond (No.3) Order, S.I. No. 307 of 1961

Statutory Authority	Section	Statutory Instrument
Land Bond Act, No. 11 of 1934 (*Cont.*)		Land Bond Order, S.I. No. 231 of 1962
		Land Bond Order, S.I. No. 272 of 1963
		Land Bond Order, S.I. No. 253 of 1964
		Land Bond Order, S.I. No. 7 of 1965
		Land Bond Order, S.I. No. 18 of 1966
		Land Bond Order, S.I. No. 28 of 1967
		Land Bond Order, S.I. No. 20 of 1968
		Land Bond Order, S.I. No. 10 of 1969
		Land Bond (No.2) Order, S.I. No. 112 of 1969
		Land Bond (No.3) Order, S.I. No. 225 of 1969
		Land Bond (No.4) Order, S.I. No. 270 of 1969
		Land Bond Order, S.I. No. 8 of 1971
		Land Bond Order, S.I. No. 19 of 1972
		Land Bond (No.2) Order, S.I. No. 345 of 1972
		Land Bond Order, S.I. No. 6 of 1974
		Land Bonds (No.2) Order, S.I. No. 316 of 1974
		Land Bond Order, S.I. No. 26 of 1975
		Land Bond (No.2) Order, S.I. No. 159 of 1975
		Land Bond (No.3) Order, S.I. No. 326 of 1975
		Land Bond Order, S.I. No. 26 of 1976
		Land Bond (No.2) Order, S.I. No. 245 of 1976
		Land Bond (No.3) Order, S.I. No. 246 of 1976
		Land Bond Order, S.I. No. 42 of 1977
		Land Bond (No.2) Order, S.I. No. 43 of 1977
		Land Bond (No.3) Order, S.I. No. 336 of 1977
		Land Bond Order, S.I. No. 50 of 1978
		Land Bond (No.2) Order, S.I. No. 51 of 1978
		Land Bond (No.3) Order, S.I. No. 214 of 1978
		Land Bond (No.4) Order, S.I. No. 215 of 1978
		Land Bond (No.2) Order, S.I. No. 22 of 1979
		Land Bond Order, S.I. No. 23 of 1979
		Land Bond Order, S.I. No. 21 of 1980
		Land Bond (No.2) Order, S.I. No. 173 of 1980
		Land Bond Order, S.I. No. 24 of 1981
		Land Bond (No.2) Order, S.I. No. 25 of 1981
		Land Bond Order, S.I. No. 18 of 1982
		Land Bond Order, S.I. No. 193 of 1983
		Land Bond (No.2) Order, S.I. No. 204 of 1983
		Land Bond Order, S.I. No. 102 of 1984
		Land Bond Order, S.I. No. 155 of 1985
	4(1)	Land Bond Order [Vol. XIV p. 495] S.R.& O. No. 181 of 1934
		Land Bond Order [Vol. XIV p. 503] S.R.& O. No. 680 of 1935
		Land Bond Order [Vol. XIV p. 509] S.R.& O. No. 386 of 1936
		Land Bond Order [Vol. XIV p. 515] S.R.& O. No. 324 of 1937

Statutory Authority	Section	Statutory Instrument
Land Bond Act, No. 11 of 1934 (*Cont.*)		**Land Bond Order [Vol. XIV p. 521] S.R.& O. No. 329 of 1938**
	7	**Land Bond (Drawing) Regulations [Vol. XXX p. 763] S.R.& O. No. 69 of 1941**
		Land Bond (Drawing) Regulations, S.I. No. 3 of 1948
		Land Bond (Drawing) Regulations, S.I. No. 97 of 1953
		Land Bond (Drawing) Regulations, S.I. No. 21 of 1959
		Land Bond (Drawings of 5% Land Bonds) Regulations, S.I. No. 52 of 1961
		Land Bond (Drawings of 5.75% Land Bonds) Regulations, S.I. No. 53 of 1961
		Land Bond (Drawings of 5.5% Land Bonds) Regulations, S.I. No. 13 of 1963
		Land Bond (Drawings of 6% Land Bonds) Regulations, S.I. No. 14 of 1963
		Land Bond (Drawings) Regulations, S.I. No. 72 of 1970
		Land Bond (Drawings of 9.75% Land Bonds) Regulations, S.I. No. 108 of 1974
		Land Bond (Drawings of 12.5% Land Bonds) Regulations, S.I. No. 85 of 1976
		Land Bond (Drawings of 16% Land Bonds) Regulations, S.I. No. 128 of 1977
		Land Bond (Drawings of 15% Land Bonds) Regulations, S.I. No. 118 of 1978
		Land Bond (Drawings of 13.75% Land Bonds) Regulations, S.I. No. 157 of 1981
		Land Bond (Drawings of 16.5% Land Bonds) Regulations, S.I. No. 132 of 1982
		Land Bonds (Drawings of 16.25% Land Bonds) Regulations, S.I. No. 115 of 1983
		Land Bond (Drawings of 18.25% Land Bonds) Regulations, S.I. No. 110 of 1984
	10	**Land (Finance) (No.2) Rules [Vol. XIV p. 367] S.R.& O. No. 209 of 1934**
		Land (Finance) Rules, S.I. No. 83 of 1956
		Land (Finance) (No.2) Rules, S.I. No. 335 of 1956
	34	**Land Bond (Drawings) Regulations, S.I. No. 103 of 1972**
Land Bond Act, No. 24 of 1969	2(2)	*Land Bond Act, 1969 (Section 2) (Commencement) Order, S.I. No. 269 of 1969*
	3(2)	*Land Bond Act, 1969 (Section 3) (Commencement) Order, S.I. No. 168 of 1969*
Land Purchase Acts,		**Land (Finance) Rules, S.I. No. 78 of 1954**
Land Reclamation Act, No. 25 of 1949	7	**Land (Finance) Rules, S.I. No. 83 of 1956**
		Land (Finance) (No.2) Rules, S.I. No. 335 of 1956

Statutory Authority	Section	Statutory Instrument
Land Reclamation Act, No. 25 of 1949 (*Cont.*)	7(1)	**Land Reclamation Act (Finance) Regulations, S.I. No. 87 of 1952**
		Land Reclamation Act (Finance) Regulations, S.I. No. 77 of 1954
	7(2)	**Land Reclamation Act Rules, S.I. No. 187 of 1950**
		Land Reclamation Act Rules, S.I. No. 308 of 1951
Land Transfer (Ireland) Act, No. 120 of 1848	9	**Registry of Deeds (Fees) Order, S.I. No. 287 of 1956**
		Registry of Deeds (Fees) Order, S.I. No. 195 of 1962
		Registry of Deeds (Fees) Order, S.I. No. 238 of 1970
		Registry of Deeds (Fees) Order, S.I. No. 363 of 1981
		Registry of Deeds (Fees) Order, S.I. No. 304 of 1982
Landlord and Tenant Act, No. 55 of 1931	7	*Landlord and Tenant Regulations [Vol. XIV p. 531] S.R. & O. No. 10 of 1932*
	26(3)	*Landlord and Tenant (Finance) Regulations [Vol. XIV p. 575] S.R. & O. No. 162 of 1933*
	30(2)	*Landlord and Tenant (Finance) Regulations [Vol. XIV p. 575] S.R. & O. No. 162 of 1933*
	49(2)	*Landlord and Tenant (Finance) Regulations [Vol. XIV p. 575] S.R. & O. No. 162 of 1933*
Landlord and Tenant (Amendment) Act, No. 10 of 1980	2	*Landlord and Tenant (Amendment) Act, 1980 (Commencement) Order, S.I. No. 271 of 1980*
	9	**Landlord and Tenant Regulations, S.I. No. 272 of 1980**
Landlord and Tenant (Ground Rents) Act, No. 3 of 1967	1	*Landlord and Tenant (Ground Rents) Act, 1967 (Commencement) Regulations, S.I. No. 42 of 1967*
	34	**Landlord and Tenant (Ground Rents) Act, 1967 (Forms) Regulations, S.I. No. 43 of 1967**
		Ground Rents Registers Regulations, S.I. No. 152 of 1967
		Ground Rents Registers (Amendment) Regulations, S.I. No. 355 of 1983
		Ground Rents Registers (Amendment) Regulations, S.I. No. 296 of 1984
Landlord and Tenant (Ground Rents) (No. 2) Act, No. 16 of 1978	5	**Landlord and Tenant (Ground Rents) (No.2) Act, 1978 Regulations, S.I. No. 219 of 1978**
	23	*Landlord and Tenant (Ground Rents) (No.2) Act, 1978 (Fees) Order, S.I. No. 220 of 1978*
	23(2)	*Landlord and Tenant (Ground Rents) (No.2) Act, 1978 (Fees) Order, S.I. No. 205 of 1983*
		Landlord and Tenant (Ground Rents) (No.2) Act, 1978 (Fees) Order, S.I. No. 194 of 1984

Statutory Authority	Section	Statutory Instrument
Law Reform Commission Act, No. 3 of 1975	2	*Law Reform Commission (Establishment Day) Order, S.I. No. 214 of 1975*
League of Nations (Obligations of Membership) Act, No. 40 of 1935	2(1)	*League of Nations (Obligations of Membership) Order [Vol. XIV p. 583] S.R.& O. No. 635 of 1935*
	2(2)	*League of Nations (Obligations of Membership) Order [Vol. XIV p. 583] S.R.& O. No. 635 of 1935*
	3	*League of Nations (Obligations of Membership) (Revocation) Order [Vol. XIV p. 597] S.R.& O. No. 196 of 1936*
Legitimacy Act, No. 13 of 1931	Sch. par. (1)	**Legitimacy Act (Alteration of Registration Fee) Regulations, S.I. No. 224 of 1954**
	Sch. par. (5)	**Legitimacy Act (Alteration of Registration Fee) Regulations, S.I. No. 224 of 1954**
Limerick City Management Act, No. 35 of 1934	7(2)	*Limerick County Borough Electoral Areas Order, S.I. No. 11 of 1967*
		Limerick County Borough (Electoral Areas) Order, S.I. No. 112 of 1985
	12(2)	**Cork and Limerick City Management (Reserved Functions) Order, S.I. No. 43 of 1986**
Limerick Harbour Tramways Act, No. 1 of 1931(Private)	9	*Limerick Harbour Tramways Act, 1931 (Extension of Time) Order [Vol. XIV p. 605] S.R.& O. No. 129 of 1936*
Litter Act, No. 11 of 1982	5(4)	**Litter Act, 1982 (Section 5) (Payments) Regulations, S.I. No. 176 of 1986**
	14	**Litter Regulations, S.I. No. 233 of 1982**
	18	**Litter Regulations, S.I. No. 233 of 1982**
	20	*Litter Act, 1982 (Commencement) Order, S.I. No. 232 of 1982*
Live Stock (Artificial Insemination) Act, No. 32 of 1947	3	**Live Stock (Artificial Insemination) Regulations, S.I. No. 55 of 1948**
		Live Stock (Artificial Insemination) (Pigs) Regulations, S.I. No. 255 of 1965
Live Stock Breeding Act, No. 3 of 1925		*Live Stock (Bulls) Breeding Regulations [Vol. XIV p. 639] S.R.& O. No. 70 of 1931*
	5(1)	*Live Stock Breeding Regulations [Vol. XIV p. 613] S.R.& O. No. 27 of 1925*
		Live Stock (Boars) (Unsuitable Types) Regulations [Vol. XIV p. 643] S.R.& O. No. 628 of 1935
		Live Stock (Boars) (Unsuitable Types) Regulations [Vol. XIV p. 649] S.R.& O. No. 176 of 1936
		Live Stock (Boars) (Unsuitable Types) Regulations, S.I. No. 94 of 1958
		Live Stock (Boars) (Unsuitable Types) Regulations, 1958 (Amendment) Regulations, S.I. No. 221 of 1972

Statutory Authority	Section	Statutory Instrument
Live Stock Breeding Act, No. 3 of 1925 (*Cont.*)	20	Live Stock Breeding Regulations [Vol. XIV p. 613] S.R.& O. No. 27 of 1925
		Live Stock Breeding Regulations [Vol. XIV p. 623] S.R.& O. No. 66 of 1927
		Live Stock (Boars) Breeding Regulations [Vol. XIV p. 629] S.R.& O. No. 71 of 1930
	20(1)	Live Stock Breeding (Amendment) Regulations, S.I. No. 271 of 1970
		Live Stock (Boars) Breeding (Amendment) Regulations, S.I. No. 272 of 1970
	21(2)	Live Stock Breeding Act, 1925 (Application to Boars) Order [Vol. XIV p. 627] S.R.& O. No. 70 of 1930
		Live Stock Breeding Act, 1925 (Application to Boars) Order, S.I. No. 93 of 1958
Livestock Marts Act, No. 20 of 1967	2(3)	Livestock Marts Act (Section 2) (Commencement) Order, S.I. No. 197 of 1967
	6	**Livestock Marts Regulations, S.I. No. 251 of 1968**
Local Authorities (Combined Purchasing) Act, No. 20 of 1925	3	Local Authorities (Combined Purchasing) Regulations [Vol. XIV p. 655] S.R.& O. No. 11 of 1926
		Local Authorities (Combined Purchasing) Regulations [Vol. XIV p. 669] S.R.& O. No. 37 of 1929
		Local Authorities (Combined Purchasing) (Amendment) Regulations [Vol. XIV p. 677] S.R.& O. No. 170 of 1933
		Local Authorities (Combined Purchasing) Regulations [Vol. XXX p. 139] S.R.& O. No. 358 of 1942
	12	Local Authorities (Combined Purchasing) Regulations [Vol. XIV p. 655] S.R.& O. No. 11 of 1926
		Local Authorities (Combined Purchasing) Regulations [Vol. XIV p. 669] S.R.& O. No. 37 of 1929
		Local Authorities (Combined Purchasing) (Road Surfacing) Regulations [Vol. XIV p. 681] S.R.& O. No. 34 of 1930
		Local Authorities (Combined Purchasing) (Supply in Bulk) Regulations [Vol. XIV p. 689] S.R.& O. No. 5 of 1933
		Local Authorities (Combined Purchasing) (Amendment) Regulations [Vol. XIV p. 677] S.R.& O. No. 170 of 1933
		Local Authorities (Combined Purchasing) Regulations [Vol. XXX p. 139] S.R.& O. No. 358 of 1942
		Local Authorities (Combined Purchasing) (Amendment) Regulations, S.I. No. 292 of 1950

Statutory Authority	Section	Statutory Instrument
Local Authorities (Combined Purchasing) Act, No. 14 of 1939	1(2)	*Local Authorities (Combined Purchasing) Act, 1939 (Commencement) Order, S.I. No. 271 of 1960*
	3	**Local Authorities (Combined Purchasing) Act, 1939 (Extension of Application) Order, S.I. No. 24 of 1971**
	8	**Local Authorities (Combined Purchasing Regulations) Order, S.I. No. 37 of 1961**
	14	**Local Authorities (Combined Purchasing Regulations) Order, S.I. No. 37 of 1961**
	15	**Local Authorities (Combined Purchasing Regulations) Order, S.I. No. 37 of 1961**
	19	**Local Authorities (Combined Purchasing Regulations) Order, S.I. No. 37 of 1961**
		Local Government (Combined Purchasing Regulations) (Amendment) Order, S.I. No. 74 of 1969
Local Authorities (Education Scholarships) (Amendment) Act, No. 34 of 1961	5	*Local Authorities (Education Scholarships) (Amendment) Act, 1961 (Commencement) Order, S.I. No. 34 of 1962*
Local Authorities (Miscellaneous Provisions) Act, No. 55 of 1936	10	**Urban Districts (Alteration of Boundaries) Regulations [Vol. XIV p. 699] S.R.& O. No. 221 of 1937**
		Castleblaney Urban District (Alteration of Boundary) Order, S.I. No. 63 of 1948
		Killarney Urban District (Alteration of Boundary) Order, S.I. No. 64 of 1948
		Clones Urban District (Alteration of Boundary) Order, S.I. No. 65 of 1948
Local Authorities (Officers and Employees) Act, No. 39 of 1926	2	**Local Appointments (Sanitary Inspectors) Order [Vol. XIV p. 723] S.R.& O. No. 105 of 1932**
	2(1)	**Local Appointments Commissioners (Declaration of Offices) Order [Vol. XIV p. 719] S.R.& O. No. 46 of 1927**
		Local Appointments Commissioners (Declaration of Offices) Order [Vol. XIV p. 727] S.R.& O. No. 58 of 1933
	2(1)(c)	**Local Authorities (Officers and Employees) Act, 1926 (Health Inspectors) Order, S.I. No. 351 of 1948**
Local Authorities (Officers and Employees) Act, No. 1 of 1983	9	*Local Authorities (Officers and Employees) Act, 1983 (Commencement) Order, S.I. No. 371 of 1983*
Local Authorities (Officers and Employees) (Amendment) Act, No. 15 of 1940	2	*Local Authorities (Officers and Employees) (Amendment) Act, 1940 (Date of Commencement) Order [Vol. XXX p. 1179] S.R.& O. No. 475 of 1941*
	4(1)	*Local Appointments Commissioners (Declaration of Office) Order, 1933 (Revocation) Order, S.I. No. 376 of 1948*

Statutory Authority	Section	Statutory Instrument
Local Authorities (Officers and Employees) (Amendment) Act, No. 15 of 1940 (*Cont.*)		*Local Authorities (Officers and Employees) Act, 1926 (Revocation of Declaration) Order, S.I. No. 143 of 1949*
Local Authorities (Traffic Wardens) Act, No. 14 of 1975	3(1)	**Local Authorities (Traffic Wardens) Act, 1975 (Section 3) (Offences) Regulations, S.I. No. 261 of 1975**
		Local Authorities (Traffic Wardens) Act, 1975 (Section 3) (Offences) (Amendment) Regulations, S.I. No. 168 of 1979
		Local Authorities (Traffic Wardens) Act, 1975 (Section 3) (Offences) (Amendment) Regulations, S.I. No. 256 of 1985
		Local Authorities (Traffic Wardens) Act, 1975 (Section 3) (Offences) (Amendment) Regulations, S.I. No. 444 of 1986
	3(6)	**Local Authorities (Traffic Wardens) Act, 1975 (Section 3) (Offences) Regulations, S.I. No. 261 of 1975**
		Local Authorities (Traffic Wardens) Act, 1975 (Section 3) (Offences) (Amendment) Regulations, S.I. No. 168 of 1979
		Local Authorities (Traffic Wardens) Act, 1975 (Section 3) (Offences) (Amendment) Regulations, S.I. No. 256 of 1985
		Local Authorities (Traffic Wardens) Act, 1975 (Section 3) (Offences) (Amendment) Regulations, S.I. No. 444 of 1986
	3(8)	**Local Authorities (Traffic Wardens) Act, 1975 (Disposal of Monies) Regulations, S.I. No. 262 of 1975**
	6	**Local Authorities (Traffic Wardens) Act, 1975 (Section 3) (Offences) Regulations, S.I. No. 261 of 1975**
		Local Authorities (Traffic Wardens) Act, 1975 (Disposal of Monies) Regulations, S.I. No. 262 of 1975
		Local Authorities (Traffic Wardens) Act, 1975 (Section 3) (Offences) (Amendment) Regulations, S.I. No. 168 of 1979
		Local Authorities (Traffic Wardens) Act, 1975 (Section 3) (Offences) (Amendment) Regulations, S.I. No. 256 of 1985
		Local Authorities (Traffic Wardens) Act, 1975 (Section 3) (Offences) (Amendment) Regulations, S.I. No. 444 of 1986
Local Elections Act, No. 39 of 1927	14(1)	*Local Elections (Polling Districts and Polling Places) Rules [Vol. XIV p. 731] S.R.& O. No. 2 of 1928*
Local Elections Act, No. 8 of 1948		*Local Elections (Date of Elections) Order, S.I. No. 49 of 1950*
	3	*Dublin and Kerry County Councils (Elections) Order, S.I. No. 281 of 1948*

Statutory Authority	Section	Statutory Instrument
Local Elections Act, No. 8 of 1948 (*Cont.*)	4	*Tramore Town Commissioners (Election) Order, S.I. No. 280 of 1948*
Local Elections Act, No. 19 of 1965	5	**Local Elections Act, 1965 (Section 5) Regulations, S.I. No. 258 of 1974**
		Local Elections Act, 1965 (Section 5) Regulations, S.I. No. 223 of 1975
Local Elections Act, No. 7 of 1973	2	*Local Elections (Specification of Local Election Year) Order, S.I. No. 6 of 1984*
Local Elections and Meetings (Postponement) Act, No. 17 of 1931	2	*Local Elections (Date of Election) Order [Vol. XIV p. 743] S.R.& O. No. 102 of 1933*
		Local Elections (Postponement) Order [Vol. XIV p. 749] S.R.& O. No. 116 of 1933
		Local Elections (Postponement) Order [Vol. XIV p. 755] S.R.& O. No. 104 of 1934
Local Elections (Petitions and Disqualifications) Act, No. 8 of 1974	25	**Local Elections (Petitions and Disqualifications) Act, 1974 (Section 25) (Amendment) Order, S.I. No. 16 of 1976**
	25(1)	**Local Elections (Petitions and Disqualifications) Act, 1974 (Section 25) Order, S.I. No. 135 of 1974**
	25(2)	**Local Elections (Petitions and Disqualifications) Act, 1974 (Section 25) (No.3) Order, S.I. No. 137 of 1974**
	25(3)	**Local Elections (Petitions and Disqualifications) Act, 1974 (Section 25) (No.2) Order, S.I. No. 136 of 1974**
Local Government Act, No. 5 of 1925		*Public Bodies Order [Vol. XIV p. 973] S.R.& O. No. 46 of 1925*
		Public Bodies (Transitory Provisions) Order [Vol. XIV p. 1133] S.R.& O. No. 61 of 1925
		Public Bodies (Temporary Provisions) Order [Vol. XIV p. 1135] S.R.& O. No. 30 of 1927
		Public Bodies Order [Vol. XIV p. 1157] S.R.& O. No. 91 of 1927
		Public Bodies Order [Vol. XIV p. 1181] S.R.& O. No. 43 of 1929
	24(3)	*Urban Districts (Transferred Road Duties) Regulations [Vol. XIV p. 1269] S.R.& O. No. 4 of 1926*
	36(1)(b), (c),(d),(e)	**Road Signs and Traffic Signals Regulations [Vol. XIV p. 1279] S.R.& O. No. 55 of 1926**
	36(2)	**Road Signs and Traffic Signals Regulations [Vol. XIV p. 1279] S.R.& O. No. 55 of 1926**
	74	**Belturbet Urban District (De-Urbanisation) Order, S.I. No. 74 of 1950**

Statutory Authority	Section	Statutory Instrument
Local Government Act, No. 5 of 1925 (*Cont.*)		**Cootehill Urban District (De-Urbanisation) Order, S.I. No. 75 of 1950**
	86	**Rating of New Buildings Order [Vol. XIV p. 1245] S.R.& O. No. 57 of 1925**
		Public Bodies (Amendment) Order, S.I. No. 173 of 1977
	86(1)	**Local Government (Application and Adaptation of Enactments) Order [Vol. XIV p. 1219] S.R.& O. No. 47 of 1925**
		Local Government (Application and Adaptation of Enactments) (Dublin) Order [Vol. XIV p. 1229] S.R.& O. No. 25 of 1933
	86(1)(c)	*County Rate (1926 to 1927) Adjustment Rules [Vol. XIV p. 1263] S.R.& O. No. 2 of 1926*
	86(1)(d)	**Public Bodies (Amendment) Order, S.I. No. 27 of 1979**
Local Government Act, No. 23 of 1941		*Public Assistance (Medical Assistance in Dispensary Districts) Order [Vol. XXXII p. 597] S.R.& O. No. 1 of 1942*
		Public Assistance (General Regulations) Order [Vol. XXXII p. 491] S.R.& O. No. 83 of 1942
		Mental Hospitals (Officers and Servants) Order [Vol. XXXVII p. 1045] S.R.& O. No. 203 of 1946
		Mental Hospitals (Officers and Servants) (Amendment) Order, S.I. No. 213 of 1948
		Public Assistance Orders (Revocation) Order, S.I. No. 116 of 1954
		Mental Hospitals (Officers and Servants) Order, 1946 (Amendment) Order, S.I. No. 149 of 1954
	3	*Local Government Act, 1941 (Date of Commencement) (No.1) Order [Vol. XXX p. 967] S.R.& O. No. 474 of 1941*
		Local Government Act, 1941 (Date of Commencement) (No.2) Order [Vol. XXX p. 973] S.R.& O. No. 303 of 1942
		Local Government Act, 1941 (Date of Commencement) (No.3) Order [Vol. XXX p. 977] S.R.& O. No. 357 of 1942
	4	**Local Government (Civil Defence Offices) Regulations, S.I. No. 213 of 1973**
	5	*Dublin and Kerry County Councils (Elections) Order, S.I. No. 281 of 1948*
	8	*Local Officers (Removal by Local Authority) Regulations [Vol. XXX p. 1071] S.R.& O. No. 106 of 1943*
	8(1)	*Mental Hospitals Officers (General Trained Nurses) Order [Vol. XXX p. 1083] S.R.& O. No. 509 of 1942*

<table>
<tr><td>Local Government Act, No. 23 of 1941 (Cont.)</td><td></td><td>Local Government (Minor Officers) Order [Vol. XXX p. 981] S.R.& O. No. 46 of 1943

Mental Hospitals (Assistant Medical Officers) Order [Vol. XXX p. 1075] S.R.& O. No. 165 of 1943

Local Government (Minor Officers) (Amendment) Order [Vol. XXX p. 989] S.R.& O. No. 16 of 1944

Mental Hospitals Officers (Attendants) Order [Vol. XXX p. 1079] S.R.& O. No. 17 of 1944

Local Government (Minor Officers) (Amendment) (No.2) Order [Vol. XXX p. 1031] S.R.& O. No. 291 of 1944

Local Government (Minor Officers) (Amendment) Order, S.I. No. 352 of 1948</td></tr>
</table>

Statutory Authority	Section	Statutory Instrument
Local Government Act, No. 23 of 1941 (*Cont.*)		*Local Government (Minor Officers) Order [Vol. XXX p. 981] S.R.& O. No. 46 of 1943*
		Mental Hospitals (Assistant Medical Officers) Order [Vol. XXX p. 1075] S.R.& O. No. 165 of 1943
		Local Government (Minor Officers) (Amendment) Order [Vol. XXX p. 989] S.R.& O. No. 16 of 1944
		Mental Hospitals Officers (Attendants) Order [Vol. XXX p. 1079] S.R.& O. No. 17 of 1944
		Local Government (Minor Officers) (Amendment) (No.2) Order [Vol. XXX p. 1031] S.R.& O. No. 291 of 1944
		Local Government (Minor Officers) (Amendment) Order, S.I. No. 352 of 1948
	8(2)	**Local Government Act, 1941 (Appropriate Minister for Office of Civil Defence Officer) Order, S.I. No. 67 of 1951**
		Local Government Act, 1941 (Appropriate Minister for Civil Defence Offices) Order, S.I. No. 43 of 1963
	9	*Local Government (Minor Officers) Order [Vol. XXX p. 981] S.R.& O. No. 46 of 1943*
		Local Government (Minor Officers) (Amendment) Order [Vol. XXX p. 989] S.R.& O. No. 16 of 1944
		Local Government (Minor Officers) (Amendment) (No.2) Order [Vol. XXX p. 1031] S.R.& O. No. 291 of 1944
		Local Government (Minor Officers) (Amendment) Order, S.I. No. 352 of 1948
		Health (Officers) Order, S.I. No. 47 of 1958
		Health (Officers) Order, 1958 (Amendment) Order, S.I. No. 100 of 1960
	10(5)	**Health Officers (Reclassification) Order, S.I. No. 46 of 1958**
	11	*Local Government (Minor Officers) Order [Vol. XXX p. 981] S.R.& O. No. 46 of 1943*
		Local Government (Minor Officers) (Amendment) Order [Vol. XXX p. 989] S.R.& O. No. 16 of 1944
		Galway County Council (Medical Officers) Order, S.I. No. 80 of 1956
		Mental Hospitals (Officers and Servants) Order, 1946 (Amendment) Order, S.I. No. 254 of 1960
		Galway County Council (Medical Officers) Order, 1956 (Revocation) Order, S.I. No. 111 of 1968
	13	*Local Government (Officers Age Limit) Order, 1948 (Revocation) Order, S.I. No. 44 of 1949*
		Local Offices (Irish Language) (Amendment) Regulations, S.I. No. 225 of 1951
		Local Offices (Gaeltacht) (Amendment) Order, S.I. No. 227 of 1951

Statutory Authority	Section	Statutory Instrument
Local Government Act, No. 23 of 1941 (*Cont.*)		*Local Offices (Gaeltacht) (Amendment) Order, S.I. No. 50 of 1952*
		Local Officers (Irish Language) (Amendment) Regulations, S.I. No. 51 of 1952
		Local Offices (Gaeltacht) (Amendment) Order, S.I. No. 52 of 1953
		Local Officers (Irish Language) (Amendment) Regulations, S.I. No. 53 of 1953
		Local Officers (Irish Language) (Amendment) Regulations, S.I. No. 20 of 1954
		Local Offices (Gaeltacht) (Amendment) Order, S.I. No. 21 of 1954
		Local Officers (Irish Language) (Amendment) Regulations, S.I. No. 18 of 1955
		Local Offices (Gaeltacht) (Amendment) Order, S.I. No. 19 of 1955
		Local Officers (Irish Language) (Amendment) Regulations, S.I. No. 7 of 1956
		Local Offices (Gaeltacht) (Amendment) Order, S.I. No. 10 of 1956
		Mental Hospitals (Assistant Medical Officers) Order, 1943 (Amendment) Order, S.I. No. 314 of 1956
		Health (Officers Age Limit) (Amendment) Order, S.I. No. 11 of 1957
		Local Officers (Irish Language) (Amendment) Regulations, S.I. No. 13 of 1957
		Local Offices (Gaeltacht) (Amendment) Order, S.I. No. 14 of 1957
		Local Government (Officers Age Limit) Order, S.I. No. 140 of 1957
		Local Officers (Irish Language) (Amendment) (No.2) Regulations, S.I. No. 184 of 1957
		Local Offices (Gaeltacht) (Amendment) Order, S.I. No. 32 of 1958
		Local Officers (Irish Language) (Amendment) Regulations, S.I. No. 33 of 1958
		Health (Officers) Order, S.I. No. 47 of 1958
		Local Offices (Gaeltacht) (Amendment) Order, S.I. No. 14 of 1959
		Local Officers (Irish Language) (Amendment) Order, S.I. No. 15 of 1959
		Health (Officers Age Limit) Declaration, S.I. No. 1 of 1960
		Social Welfare (Age Limit for Offices) Declaration, S.I. No. 2 of 1960
		Local Offices (Gaeltacht) (Amendment) Order, S.I. No. 21 of 1960
		Local Officers (Irish Language) (Amendment) Regulations, S.I. No. 22 of 1960
		Mental Hospitals Officers (Registration in Register of Nurses) Regulations, S.I. No. 99 of 1960

Local Government Act, No. 23 of 1941 (*Cont.*)

Health (Officers) Order, 1958 (Amendment) Order, S.I. No. 100 of 1960

Health (Age Limit for Office of District Medical Officer) Declaration, S.I. No. 141 of 1960

Mental Hospitals (Officers and Servants) Order, 1946 (Amendment) Order, S.I. No. 254 of 1960

Local Offices (Gaeltacht) (Amendment) Order, S.I. No. 15 of 1961

Local Officers (Irish Language) (Amendment) Regulations, S.I. No. 16 of 1961

Local Offices (Gaeltacht) (Amendment) Order, S.I. No. 15 of 1962

Local Officers (Irish Language) (Amendment) Regulations, S.I. No. 16 of 1962

Health (Age Limit for Office of District Medical Officer) Declaration, S.I. No. 21 of 1962

Local Officers (Irish Language) (Amendment) Regulations, S.I. No. 15 of 1963

Local Offices (Gaeltacht) (Amendment) Regulations, S.I. No. 16 of 1963

Health (Age Limit for Office of District Medical Officer) Declaration, S.I. No. 119 of 1963

Local Offices (Gaeltacht) (Amendment) Order, S.I. No. 15 of 1964

Local Officers (Irish Language) (Amendment) Regulations, S.I. No. 16 of 1964

Local Offices (Gaeltacht) (Amendment) S.I. No. 20 of 1965

Local Officers (Irish Language) (Amendment) Regulations, S.I. No. 21 of 1965

Health (Age Limit for Office of District Medical Officer) Declaration, S.I. No. 40 of 1965

Local Officers (Irish Language) (Amendment) Regulations, S.I. No. 21 of 1966

Local Offices (Gaeltacht) (Amendment) Order, S.I. No. 22 of 1966

Oifigi Aitiuila (An Ghaeilge) (Rialachain na) S.I. No. 221 of 1966

Galway County Council (Medical Officers) Order, 1956 (Revocation) Order, S.I. No. 111 of 1968

14   *Local Offices (Gaeltacht) (Amendment) Order [Vol. XXX p. 1035] S.R.& O. No. 97 of 1943*

Local Offices (Gaeltacht) (Amendment) Order, 1943 Amending Order [Vol. XXX p. 1093] S.R.& O. No. 300 of 1943

Local Offices (Gaeltacht) (Amendment) Order [Vol. XXX p. 1043] S.R.& O. No. 75 of 1944

Local Offices (Gaeltacht) (Amendment) Order [Vol. XXX p. 1047] S.R.& O. No. 27 of 1945

Local Offices (Gaeltacht) (Amendment) (No.2) Order [Vol. XXX p. 1051] S.R.& O. No. 203 of 1945

Local Offices (Gaeltacht) (Amendment) Order [Vol. XXXVII p. 1033] S.R.& O. No. 72 of 1946

Statutory Authority	Section	Statutory Instrument
Local Government Act, No. 23 of 1941 (*Cont.*)		*Local Offices (Gaeltacht) (Amendment) (No.2) Order [Vol. XXXVII p. 1037] S.R.& O. No. 248 of 1946*
		Local Offices (Gaeltacht) (Amendment) Order [Vol. XXXVII p. 1041] S.R.& O. No. 78 of 1947
		Local Offices (Gaeltacht) (Amendment) Order, S.I. No. 227 of 1951
		Local Offices (Gaeltacht) (Amendment) Order, S.I. No. 50 of 1952
		Local Offices (Gaeltacht) (Amendment) Order, S.I. No. 52 of 1953
		Local Offices (Gaeltacht) (Amendment) Order, S.I. No. 21 of 1954
		Local Offices (Gaeltacht) (Amendment) Order, S.I. No. 19 of 1955
		Local Offices (Gaeltacht) (Amendment) Order, S.I. No. 10 of 1956
		Local Offices (Gaeltacht) (Amendment) Order, S.I. No. 14 of 1957
		Local Offices (Gaeltacht) (Amendment) Order, S.I. No. 32 of 1958
		Local Offices (Gaeltacht) (Amendment) Order, S.I. No. 14 of 1959
		Local Offices (Gaeltacht) (Amendment) Order, S.I. No. 21 of 1960
		Local Offices (Gaeltacht) (Amendment) Order, S.I. No. 15 of 1961
		Local Offices (Gaeltacht) (Amendment) Order, S.I. No. 15 of 1962
		Local Offices (Gaeltacht) (Amendment) Regulations, S.I. No. 16 of 1963
		Local Offices (Gaeltacht) (Amendment) Order, S.I. No. 15 of 1964
		Local Offices (Gaeltacht) (Amendment) S.I. No. 20 of 1965
		Local Offices (Gaeltacht) (Amendment) Order, S.I. No. 22 of 1966
	19	*Local Offices (Gaeltacht) (Amendment) Order [Vol. XXX p. 1035] S.R.& O. No. 97 of 1943*
		Local Offices (Gaeltacht) (Amendment) Order, 1943 Amending Order [Vol. XXX p. 1093] S.R.& O. No. 300 of 1943
		Local Offices (Gaeltacht) (Amendment) Order [Vol. XXX p. 1043] S.R.& O. No. 75 of 1944
		Local Offices (Gaeltacht) (Amendment) Order [Vol. XXX p. 1047] S.R.& O. No. 27 of 1945
		Local Offices (Gaeltacht) (Amendment) (No.2) Order [Vol. XXX p. 1051] S.R.& O. No. 203 of 1945
		Local Offices (Gaeltacht) (Amendment) Order [Vol. XXXVII p. 1033] S.R.& O. No. 72 of 1946
		Local Offices (Gaeltacht) (Amendment) (No.2) Order [Vol. XXXVII p. 1037] S.R.& O. No. 248 of 1946

Statutory Authority	Section	Statutory Instrument

Local Government Act, No. 23 of 1941 (*Cont.*)

Local Offices (Gaeltacht) (Amendment) Order [Vol. XXXVII p. 1041] S.R.& O. No. 78 of 1947

Local Offices (Gaeltacht) (Amendment) Order, S.I. No. 227 of 1951

Local Offices (Gaeltacht) (Amendment) Order, S.I. No. 50 of 1952

Local Offices (Gaeltacht) (Amendment) Order, S.I. No. 52 of 1953

Local Offices (Gaeltacht) (Amendment) Order, S.I. No. 21 of 1954

Local Offices (Gaeltacht) (Amendment) Order, S.I. No. 19 of 1955

Local Offices (Gaeltacht) (Amendment) Order, S.I. No. 10 of 1956

Local Offices (Gaeltacht) (Amendment) Order, S.I. No. 14 of 1957

Local Offices (Gaeltacht) (Amendment) Order, S.I. No. 32 of 1958

Local Offices (Gaeltacht) (Amendment) Order, S.I. No. 14 of 1959

Local Offices (Gaeltacht) (Amendment) Order, S.I. No. 21 of 1960

Local Offices (Gaeltacht) (Amendment) Order, S.I. No. 15 of 1961

Local Offices (Gaeltacht) (Amendment) Order, S.I. No. 15 of 1962

Local Offices (Gaeltacht) (Amendment) Regulations, S.I. No. 16 of 1963

Local Offices (Gaeltacht) (Amendment) Order, S.I. No. 15 of 1964

Local Offices (Gaeltacht) (Amendment) S.I. No. 20 of 1965

Local Offices (Gaeltacht) (Amendment) Order, S.I. No. 22 of 1966

Local Government (Civil Defence Offices) Regulations, S.I. No. 213 of 1973

Local Government (Appointment of Officers) Regulations, S.I. No. 61 of 1974

Local Government (Officers) Regulations, S.I. No. 263 of 1983

Local Government (Officers) Regulations, S.I. No. 69 of 1984

19(1)(a) *Local Government (Minor Officers) Order [Vol. XXX p. 981] S.R.& O. No. 46 of 1943*

Local Government (Minor Officers) (Amendment) Order [Vol. XXX p. 989] S.R.& O. No. 16 of 1944

Local Government (Minor Officers) (Amendment) (No.2) Order [Vol. XXX p. 1031] S.R.& O. No. 291 of 1944

Local Government (Minor Officers) (Amendment) Order, S.I. No. 352 of 1948

19(1)(g) **Dispensary (Medical Officers) (Appointment) Regulations, S.I. No. 169 of 1949**

Statutory Authority	Section	Statutory Instrument
Local Government Act, No. 23 of 1941 (*Cont.*)	19(1)	*Mental Hospitals Officers (General Trained Nurses) Order [Vol. XXX p. 1083] S.R.& O. No. 509 of 1942*
		Mental Hospitals (Assistant Medical Officers) Order [Vol. XXX p. 1075] S.R.& O. No. 165 of 1943
		Mental Hospitals Officers (Attendants) Order [Vol. XXX p. 1079] S.R.& O. No. 17 of 1944
		Local Officers (Irish Language) Regulations [Vol. XXX p. 1055] S.R.& O. No. 76 of 1944
		Local Offices (Irish Language) (Amendment) Regulations, S.I. No. 225 of 1951
		Local Officers (Irish Language) (Amendment) Regulations, S.I. No. 51 of 1952
		Local Officers (Irish Language) (Amendment) Regulations, S.I. No. 53 of 1953
		Local Officers (Irish Language) (Amendment) Regulations, S.I. No. 20 of 1954
		Local Officers (Irish Language) (Amendment) Regulations, S.I. No. 18 of 1955
		Local Officers (Irish Language) (Amendment) Regulations, S.I. No. 7 of 1956
		Mental Hospitals (Assistant Medical Officers) Order, 1943 (Amendment) Order, S.I. No. 314 of 1956
		Local Officers (Irish Language) (Amendment) Regulations, S.I. No. 13 of 1957
		Local Officers (Irish Language) (Amendment) (No. 2) Regulations, S.I. No. 184 of 1957
		Local Officers (Irish Language) (Amendment) Regulations, S.I. No. 33 of 1958
		Local Officers (Irish Language) (Amendment) Order, S.I. No. 15 of 1959
		Local Officers (Irish Language) (Amendment) Regulations, S.I. No. 22 of 1960
		Mental Hospitals Officers (Tutors) Regulations, S.I. No. 95 of 1960
		Mental Hospitals Officers (Registration in Register of Nurses) Regulations, S.I. No. 99 of 1960
		Local Officers (Irish Language) (Amendment) Regulations, S.I. No. 16 of 1961
		Local Officers (Irish Language) (Amendment) Regulations, S.I. No. 16 of 1962
		Local Officers (Irish Language) (Amendment) Regulations, S.I. No. 15 of 1963
		Local Officers (Irish Language) (Amendment) Regulations, S.I. No. 16 of 1964
		Local Officers (Irish Language) (Amendment) Regulations, S.I. No. 21 of 1965

Statutory Authority	Section	Statutory Instrument
Local Government Act, No. 23 of 1941 (*Cont.*)		*Local Officers (Irish Language) (Amendment) Regulations, S.I. No. 21 of 1966*
		Oifigi Aitiuila (An Ghaeilge) (Rialachain na) S.I. No. 221 of 1966
	20	*Health (Duties of Officers) (Temporary Provisions) Order, S.I. No. 103 of 1948*
		Health (Duties of Officers) Order, S.I. No. 128 of 1949
		Health (Duties of District Medical Officers) Order, S.I. No. 168 of 1954
		Health (Duties of Midwives) Order, S.I. No. 169 of 1954
		Health (Duties of Midwives) Order, S.I. No. 76 of 1956
		Mental Hospitals (Officers and Servants) Order, 1946 (Amendment) Order, S.I. No. 254 of 1960
	21	**Mental Nurses (Qualification) Order [Vol. XXX p. 1087] S.R.& O. No. 290 of 1944**
		Mental Nurses (Qualification) (Amendment) Order, S.I. No. 249 of 1948
	23	**Local Government (Officers Age Limit) Order [Vol. XXXVII p. 1025] S.R.& O. No. 333 of 1946**
		Local Government (Officers Age Limit) Order, S.I. No. 370 of 1948
		Local Government (Officers Age Limit) Order, 1948 (Revocation) Order, S.I. No. 44 of 1949
		Health (Officers Age Limit) Order, S.I. No. 92 of 1950
		Local Government (Officers Age Limit) Order, S.I. No. 310 of 1951
		Health (Officers Age Limit) (Amendment) Order, S.I. No. 11 of 1957
		Health (Age Limit for Specified Office) Order, S.I. No. 47 of 1957
		Local Government (Officers Age Limit) Order, S.I. No. 140 of 1957
		Health (Officers Age Limit) Declaration, S.I. No. 1 of 1960
		Social Welfare (Age Limit for Offices) Declaration, S.I. No. 2 of 1960
		Health (Age Limit for Office of District Medical Officer) Declaration, S.I. No. 141 of 1960
		Health (Age Limit for Office of District Medical Officer) Declaration, S.I. No. 21 of 1962
		Health (Age Limit for Office of District Medical Officer) Declaration, S.I. No. 119 of 1963
		Health (Age Limit for Office of District Medical Officer) Declaration, S.I. No. 40 of 1965
		Local Government (Civil Defence Offices Age Limit) Order, S.I. No. 212 of 1973

| | 26 | *Local Officers (Removal by Local Authority) Regulations [Vol. XXX p. 1071] S.R.& O. No. 106 of 1943* |

Local Government (Civil Defence Offices) Regulations, S.I. No. 213 of 1973

| | 33(7) | *Dublin County Council Order, S.I. No. 267 of 1948* |

Donegal County Council (Amendment) Order, S.I. No. 214 of 1950

Dublin County Council (Amendment) Order, S.I. No. 263 of 1953

Kildare County Council (Amendment) Order, S.I. No. 29 of 1954

Longford County Council (Amendment) Order, S.I. No. 63 of 1954

Clare (County Electoral Areas) Order, S.I. No. 200 of 1956

Dublin County Council (Amendment) Order, S.I. No. 101 of 1960

Kildare County Council (Amendment) Order, S.I. No. 48 of 1966

Roscommon County Council (Amendment) Order, S.I. No. 11 of 1974

Leitrim County Council (Amendment) Order, S.I. No. 21 of 1974

Longford County Council (Amendment) Order, S.I. No. 22 of 1974

Sligo County Council (Amendment) Order, S.I. No. 23 of 1974

Dublin County Council (Amendment) Order, S.I. No. 29 of 1974

Kerry County Council (Amendment) Order, S.I. No. 30 of 1974

Limerick County Council (Amendment) Order, S.I. No. 31 of 1974

Louth County Council (Amendment) Order, S.I. No. 32 of 1974

Meath County Council (Amendment) Order, S.I. No. 33 of 1974

Westmeath County Council (Amendment) Order, S.I. No. 34 of 1974

Mayo County Council (Amendment) Order, S.I. No. 40 of 1974

Wicklow County Council (Amendment) Order, S.I. No. 41 of 1974

Carlow County Council (Amendment) Order, S.I. No. 46 of 1974

Galway County Council (Amendment) Order, S.I. No. 47 of 1974

Clare County Council (Amendment) Order, S.I. No. 48 of 1974

Kildare County Council (Amendment) Order, S.I. No. 49 of 1974

Longford County Council (Amendment) (No.2) Order, S.I. No. 50 of 1974

Local Government Act, No. 23 of 1941 (*Cont.*)

Donegal County Council (Amendment) Order, S.I. No. 51 of 1974

Waterford County Council (Amendment) Order, S.I. No. 52 of 1974

Clare County Council (Amendment) (No.2) Order, S.I. No. 83 of 1974

Donegal County Council (Amendment) (No.2) Order, S.I. No. 123 of 1974

Dublin County Council Order, S.I. No. 40 of 1979

County Electoral Areas (Amendment) (No.2) Order, S.I. No. 110 of 1985

Galway County Council (Amendment) Order, S.I. No. 127 of 1985

Kildare County Council (Amendment) Order, S.I. No. 144 of 1985

34   **Constitution of Urban Authorities Order [Vol. XXX p. 947] S.R.& O. No. 272 of 1942**

Constitution of Urban Authorities Order, 1942 (Amendment) Order, S.I. No. 398 of 1981

Constitution of Urban Authorities Order, 1942 (Amendment) Order, S.I. No. 163 of 1983

35   **Dun Laoghaire Borough Electoral Areas Order, S.I. No. 83 of 1966**

Bray Urban District Local Electoral Areas Order, S.I. No. 19 of 1967

Borough of Sligo Local Electoral Areas Order, S.I. No. 20 of 1967

Borough of Galway Local Electoral Areas Order, S.I. No. 21 of 1967

Borough of Drogheda Local Electoral Areas Order, S.I. No. 22 of 1967

Dundalk Urban District Local Electoral Areas Order, S.I. No. 23 of 1967

Dundalk Urban District Local Electoral Areas Order, 1967 (Revocation) Order, S.I. No. 39 of 1974

Borough of Sligo Local Electoral Areas Order, 1967 (Revocation) Order, S.I. No. 42 of 1974

Borough of Drogheda Local Electoral Areas Order, 1967 (Revocation) Order, S.I. No. 43 of 1974

Bray Urban District Local Electoral Areas Order, 1967 (Revocation) Order, S.I. No. 44 of 1974

Borough of Galway Local Electoral Areas Order, 1967 (Revocation) Order, S.I. No. 45 of 1974

Bray Urban District Local Electoral Areas Order, S.I. No. 42 of 1979

Dundalk Urban District Local Electoral Areas Order, S.I. No. 43 of 1979

Borough of Drogheda Local Electoral Areas Order, S.I. No. 44 of 1979

Borough of Galway Local Electoral Areas Order, S.I. No. 45 of 1979

Statutory Authority	Section	Statutory Instrument
Local Government Act, No. 23 of 1941 (*Cont.*)		**Borough of Sligo Local Electoral Areas Order, S.I. No. 46 of 1979**
		Borough of Galway Local Electoral Areas Order, S.I. No. 125 of 1985
	51	*Dublin and Kerry County Councils (Elections) Order, S.I. No. 281 of 1948*
	52	**Dublin County Council (University College, Dublin, Elections) Order [Vol. XXX p. 951] S.R.& O. No. 430 of 1943**
	53	**Dublin County Council (University College, Dublin, Elections) Order [Vol. XXX p. 951] S.R.& O. No. 430 of 1943**
	54(1)	**Dublin Fever Hospital Act, 1936 (Adaptation) Order [Vol. XXX p. 957] S.R.& O. No. 299 of 1944**
		Dublin Fever Hospital Act, 1936 (Adaptation) Order [Vol. XXX p. 961] S.R.& O. No. 144 of 1945
		Dublin Fever Hospital Act, 1936 (Adaptation) Order, S.I. No. 122 of 1948
	80(2)	**Local Authorities (Travelling Expenses of Members) Order [Vol. XXXVII p. 1021] S.R.& O. No. 59 of 1947**
		Local Authorities (Travelling Expenses of Members) Order, S.I. No. 201 of 1960
		Local Authorities (Travelling Expenses of Members) Order, S.I. No. 255 of 1973
	81(3)	*County Limerick (District Electoral Divisions) Order, S.I. No. 1 of 1950*
		Wicklow County (District Electoral Divisions) Order, S.I. No. 216 of 1957
	Part II	**Local Government (Officers) Regulations [Vol. XXX p. 993] S.R.& O. No. 161 of 1943**
		Local Government (Officers) Order, S.I. No. 170 of 1952
		Health (Officers) Regulations, S.I. No. 158 of 1953
Local Government Act, No. 24 of 1946	3	*Local Government Act, 1946 (Date of Commencement) (No.1) Order [Vol. XXXVII p. 1101] S.R.& O. No. 315 of 1946*
	4	**Local Authorities (Allowances to Members) Order [Vol. XXXVII p. 1095] S.R.& O. No. 316 of 1946**
		Local Elections (Scale of Expenses) Order, S.I. No. 344 of 1948
		Local Government (Changing of Place Names) Regulations, S.I. No. 126 of 1949
		Local Elections (Scale of Expenses) Order, S.I. No. 213 of 1950
		Local Elections (Scale of Expenses) Regulations, S.I. No. 96 of 1955
		Local Government (Changing of Place Names) Regulations, S.I. No. 31 of 1956

Statutory Authority	Section	Statutory Instrument
Local Government Act, No. 24 of 1946 (*Cont.*)		**County Councils and Mental Hospital Boards (Allowances to Members) Order, S.I. No. 34 of 1956**
	67	**County Councils and Mental Hospital Boards (Allowances to Members) Order, S.I. No. 34 of 1956**
	67(7)	**Local Authorities (Allowances to Members) Order [Vol. XXXVII p. 1095] S.R.& O. No. 316 of 1946**
	67(8)	**Local Authorities (Allowances to Members) Order [Vol. XXXVII p. 1095] S.R.& O. No. 316 of 1946**
	69	*Traffic Signs Regulations, S.I. No. 284 of 1956*
		Traffic Signs (Temporary Authorisations) Order, S.I. No. 285 of 1956
		Traffic Signs (Temporary Authorisations) Order, 1956 (Amendment) Order, S.I. No. 254 of 1958
		Traffic Signs (Amendment) Regulations, S.I. No. 57 of 1959
		Traffic Signals (Temporary Authorisation) Order, 1956 (Amendment) Order, S.I. No. 275 of 1960
		Traffic Signs (Amendment) Regulations, S.I. No. 67 of 1961
		Traffic Signs (Temporary Authorisation) Order, S.I. No. 71 of 1961
		Traffic Signs (Temporary Authorisations) Order, S.I. No. 306 of 1961
	72	*Local Elections (Scale of Expenses) Order, S.I. No. 344 of 1948*
		Local Elections (Scale of Expenses) Order, S.I. No. 213 of 1950
		Local Elections (Scale of Expenses) Regulations, S.I. No. 96 of 1955
	76	*Local Government (Changing of Place Names) Regulations, S.I. No. 126 of 1949*
		Local Government (Changing of Place Names) Regulations, S.I. No. 31 of 1956
		Local Government (Change of Name of Urban District) Order, S.I. No. 200 of 1971
	77	*Local Government (Changing of Place Names) Regulations, S.I. No. 126 of 1949*
		Local Government (Change of Name of Townland) Order, S.I. No. 170 of 1950
		Local Government (Change of Name of Non-Municipal Town) Order, S.I. No. 281 of 1950
		Local Government (Change of Name of Townland) Order, S.I. No. 138 of 1951
		Local Government (Changing of Place Names) Regulations, S.I. No. 31 of 1956
		Local Government (Change of Name of Non-Municipal Town) Order, S.I. No. 201 of 1971

Statutory Authority	Section	Statutory Instrument
Local Government Act, No. 24 of 1946 (*Cont.*)		**Local Government (Change of Name of Townland) Order, S.I. No. 300 of 1971**
		Local Government (Change of Name of Non-Municipal Town) Order, S.I. No. 166 of 1974
	78	*Local Government (Changing of Place Names) Regulations, S.I. No. 126 of 1949*
		Local Government (Changing of Place Names) Regulations, S.I. No. 31 of 1956
	79	*Local Government (Changing of Place Names) Regulations, S.I. No. 126 of 1949*
		Local Government (Changing of Place Names) Regulations, S.I. No. 31 of 1956
Local Government Act, No. 9 of 1955	3	*Local Government Act, 1955 (Date of Commencement) (No.1) Order, S.I. No. 100 of 1955*
		Local Government Act, 1955 (Date of Commencement) (No.2) Order, S.I. No. 269 of 1955
		Local Government Act, 1955 (Commencement) Order, S.I. No. 212 of 1956
		Local Government Act, 1955 (Commencement) Order, S.I. No. 268 of 1961
		Local Government Act, 1955 (Commencement) Order, S.I. No. 60 of 1974
		Local Government Act, 1955 (Commencement) Order, S.I. No. 264 of 1983
	4	*Traffic Wardens Regulations, S.I. No. 246 of 1955*
		Temporary Closing of Roads Regulations, S.I. No. 30 of 1956
	8	**Health Officers (Reclassification) Order, S.I. No. 46 of 1958**
	14	**Local Government (Appointment of Officers) Regulations, S.I. No. 61 of 1974**
	24	**Local Government (Officers Age Limit) Order, S.I. No. 140 of 1957**
		Vocational Education Committees (Age Limit for Officers) Declaration, S.I. No. 56 of 1958
	35	**Temporary Closing of Roads Regulations, S.I. No. 30 of 1956**
	37	*Traffic Wardens Regulations, S.I. No. 246 of 1955*
	38	*Mechanically Propelled Vehicles (International Circulation) Order, S.I. No. 94 of 1955*
		Public Service Vehicles (International Circulation) Order, S.I. No. 81 of 1958
		Mechanically Propelled Vehicles (International Circulation) Order, S.I. No. 269 of 1961
		Mechanically Propelled Vehicles (International Circulation) (Amendment) Order, S.I. No. 12 of 1962
		Mechanically Propelled Vehicles (International Circulation) (Amendment) Order, S.I. No. 193 of 1963

Statutory Authority	Section	Statutory Instrument
Local Government Act, No. 9 of 1955 (*Cont.*)		**Mechanically Propelled Vehicles (International Circulation) (Amendment) Order, S.I. No. 59 of 1964**
		Mechanically Propelled Vehicles (International Circulation) (Amendment) Order, S.I. No. 99 of 1966
		Mechanically Propelled Vehicles (International Circulation) (Amendment) Order, S.I. No. 71 of 1976
		Mechanically Propelled Vehicles (International Circulation) (Amendment) Order, S.I. No. 346 of 1980
		Mechanically Propelled Vehicles (International Circulation) (Amendment) Order, S.I. No. 215 of 1983
	50	**Public Bodies (Temporary Provisions) Order, S.I. No. 155 of 1955**
Local Government Acts, 1925 and 1927,		**Notice of Rates Order [Vol. XIV p. 1299] S.R.& O. No. 15 of 1928**
		Public Health (Saorstat Eireann) (Preservatives, etc., in Food) Regulations [Vol. XVIII p. 867] S.R.& O. No. 54 of 1928
		Public Bodies (Dublin) Order [Vol. XIV p. 1209] S.R.& O. No. 85 of 1930
		Public Bodies (Dublin) Order [Vol. XIV p. 1215] S.R.& O. No. 34 of 1931
Local Government Acts, 1925 to 1941,		*Public Bodies Order [Vol. XXX p. 779] S.R.& O. No. 191 of 1942*
		Public Health (Preservatives, etc., in Food) (Amendment) Regulations [Vol. XXXII p. 739] S.R.& O. No. 74 of 1943
Local Government Acts, 1925 to 1946,		**Public Bodies Order [Vol. XXXVII p. 835] S.R.& O. No. 273 of 1946**
		Public Bodies (Temporary Provisions) Order [Vol. XXXVII p. 1013] S.R.& O. No. 367 of 1947
Local Government Acts, 1925 to 1953,		**Public Roads (Notice of Declaration) Regulations, S.I. No. 166 of 1953**
Local Government (Application of Enactments) Order, S.R.& O. No. 1120 of 1898		*Local Elections Order [Vol. XIV p. 759] S.R.& O. No. 19 of 1925*
		Local Elections Order [Vol. XIV p. 803] S.R.& O. No. 29 of 1928
		Local Elections (Amendment) Order [Vol. XIV p. 849] S.R.& O. No. 7 of 1929
		Heavy Motor Car (Amendment) Order [Vol. XVI p. 1219] S.R.& O. No. 9 of 1929
		Local Elections (Temporary Amendment) Order [Vol. XXX p. 1135] S.R.& O. No. 283 of 1942
		Local Elections (Amendment) Order [Vol. XXX p. 1131] S.R.& O. No. 284 of 1942

Statutory Authority	Section	Statutory Instrument
Local Government (Application of Enactments) Order, S.R.& O. No. 1120 of 1898 (*Cont.*)	Sch. par. 5	*Local Elections Order [Vol. XXX p. 1097] S.R.& O. No. 255 of 1942*
		Local Elections (Amendment) (No.2) Order [Vol. XXX p. 1175] S.R.& O. No. 301 of 1942
		Local Elections (Amendment) Order, S.I. No. 343 of 1948
		Local Elections (Amendment) Order, S.I. No. 95 of 1955
		Local Elections (Amendment) (No.2) Order, S.I. No. 118 of 1955
	Sch. par. 25	*Dublin County Council Order, S.I. No. 267 of 1948*
		Dublin County Council Order, S.I. No. 40 of 1979
	Sch. par. 26	**Bray Urban District (Alteration of Boundary) Order, S.I. No. 42 of 1952**
		Letterkenny Urban District (Alteration of Boundary) Order, S.I. No. 79 of 1953
		Urban District of Ceannanus Mor (Alteration of Boundary) Order, S.I. No. 35 of 1957
		Urban District of Enniscorthy (Alteration of Boundary) Order, S.I. No. 36 of 1957
		Urban District of Bray (Alteration of Boundary) Order, S.I. No. 48 of 1958
		Urban District of An Uaimh (Alteration of Boundary) Order, S.I. No. 34 of 1960
		Urban District of Trim (Alteration of Boundary) Order, S.I. No. 168 of 1965
		Urban District of Ceannanus Mor (Alteration of Boundary) Order, S.I. No. 169 of 1965
		Urban District of Monaghan (Alteration of Boundary) Order, S.I. No. 50 of 1969
		Urban District of Ceanannus Mor (Alteration of Boundary) Order, S.I. No. 51 of 1969
		Urban District of Carlow (Alteration of Boundary) Order, S.I. No. 264 of 1969
		Urban District of Tralee (Alteration of Boundary) Order, S.I. No. 222 of 1973
		Urban District of Navan (Alteration of Boundary) Order, S.I. No. 162 of 1975
		Urban District of Youghal (Alteration of Boundary) Order, S.I. No. 102 of 1978
		Urban District of Bray (Alteration of Boundary) Order, S.I. No. 370 of 1978
		Urban District of Tralee (Alteration of Boundary) Order, S.I. No. 408 of 1979
		Urban District of Longford (Alteration of Boundary) Order, S.I. No. 377 of 1985
	Sch. par. 26(2)	**Urban Districts (Alteration of Boundaries) Regulations [Vol. XIV p. 699] S.R.& O. No. 221 of 1937**
	Sch. par. 26(8)	**Urban Districts (Alteration of Boundaries) Regulations [Vol. XIV p. 699] S.R.& O. No. 221 of 1937**

Statutory Authority	Section	Statutory Instrument
Local Government (Application of Enactments) Order, S.R.& O. No. 1120 of 1898 (*Cont.*)	Sch. par. 31(1)	*County Borough of Dublin (Number of Wards) Order, S.I. No. 2 of 1954*
	Sch. par. 31(3)	*County Borough of Dublin (Number of Wards) Order, S.I. No. 2 of 1954*
Local Government (Collection of Rates) Act, No. 11 of 1924	7	**County Kerry (Jurors Lists and Register of Electors) Order, S.I. No. 204 of 1961**
Local Government (Dublin) Act, No. 27 of 1930	33	**Dublin City (Borough Electoral Areas) Order [Vol. XIV p. 1363] S.R.& O. No. 54 of 1930**
	51(2)	**Dublin City Management (Reserved Functions) Order, S.I. No. 14 of 1986**
	102(2)	**Dublin Local Acts (Extension) Order [Vol. XIV p. 1373] S.R.& O. No. 33 of 1933**
	103(1)	**Dublin Local Acts (Annulment) Order [Vol. XIV p. 1385] S.R.& O. No. 34 of 1933**
Local Government (Dublin) Act, No. 8 of 1945	3	*Dublin County Borough (Electoral Areas) Order, S.I. No. 133 of 1953*
		Dublin County Borough (Electoral Areas) Order, S.I. No. 143 of 1954
		Dublin County Borough (Electoral Areas) Order, S.I. No. 47 of 1967
		Dublin County Borough (Electoral Areas) Order, S.I. No. 28 of 1974
		Dublin County Borough (Electoral Areas) Order, S.I. No. 41 of 1979
		Dublin County Borough (Electoral Areas) Order, S.I. No. 134 of 1985
	3(1)	*Dublin County Borough (Local Electoral Areas) Order [Vol. XXX p. 1147] S.R.& O. No. 57 of 1945*
Local Government (Dublin) (Amendment) Act, No. 21 of 1940	3(1)	*Local Government (Dublin) (Amendment) Act, 1940 (Appointed Day) Order [Vol. XXX p. 1159] S.R.& O. No. 372 of 1942*
Local Government (Dublin) (Temporary) Act, No. 15 of 1948	3(2)	*Local Government (Dublin) (Temporary) Act, 1948 (Continuance) Order, S.I. No. 203 of 1949*
		Local Government (Dublin) (Temporary) Act, 1948 (Continuance No.2) Order, S.I. No. 353 of 1949
		Local Government (Dublin) (Temporary) Act, 1948 (Continuance) Order, S.I. No. 161 of 1950
		Local Government (Dublin) (Temporary) Act, 1948 (Continuance No.2) Order, S.I. No. 316 of 1950
		Local Government (Dublin) (Temporary) Act, 1948 (Continuance No.1) Order, S.I. No. 170 of 1951
		Local Government (Dublin) (Temporary) Act, 1948 (Continuance No.2) Order, S.I. No. 367 of 1951
		Local Government (Dublin) (Temporary) Act, 1948 (Continuance No.1) Order, S.I. No. 188 of 1952
		Local Government (Dublin) (Temporary) Act, 1948 (Continuance No.2) Order, S.I. No. 377 of 1952

Statutory Authority	Section	Statutory Instrument
Local Government (Dublin) (Temporary) Act, No. 15 of 1948 (*Cont.*)		*Local Government (Dublin) (Temporary) Act, 1948 (Continuance No.1) Order, S.I. No. 236 of 1953*
		Local Government (Dublin) (Temporary) Act, 1948 (Continuance No.2) Order, S.I. No. 376 of 1953
		Local Government (Dublin) (Temporary) Act, 1948 (Continuance No.1) Order, S.I. No. 142 of 1954
		Local Government (Dublin) (Temporary) Act, 1948 (Continuance No.2) Order, S.I. No. 295 of 1954
		Local Government (Dublin) (Temporary) Act, 1948 (Continuance) Order, S.I. No. 122 of 1955
		Local Government (Dublin) (Temporary) Act, 1948 (Continuance No.2) Order, S.I. No. 267 of 1955
		Local Government (Dublin) (Temporary) Act, 1948 (Continuance) Order, S.I. No. 154 of 1956
		Local Government (Dublin) (Temporary) Act, 1948 (Continuance No.2) Order, S.I. No. 333 of 1956
Local Government Electors Registration Act 1924, No. 7 of 1924		*Electoral Order [Vol. XI p. 243] S.R.& O. No. 21 of 1936*
		Electoral (Amendment) Order [Vol. XXIX p. 9] S.R.& O. No. 557 of 1942
		Electoral Order [Vol. XXXVII p. 163] S.R.& O. No. 96 of 1946
	4	*Electoral (Amendment) Order [Vol. XI p. 135] S.R.& O. No. 17 of 1934*
Local Government (Ireland) Act, No. 37 of 1898	33(2)	**Boards of Health Urban Lighting Powers [Vol. XIV p. 853] S.R.& O. No. 96 of 1930**
		Boards of Health (Urban Powers) Order [Vol. XIV p. 857] S.R.& O. No. 4 of 1931
		Rural Roads (Planting of Trees) Order [Vol. XXX p. 1163] S.R.& O. No. 166 of 1943
		County Councils (Purchase of Markets and Fairs) Order, S.I. No. 216 of 1948
	36	**Local Government (Ireland) Act, 1898, (Section 36) (Wicklow County Council) Order, S.I. No. 26 of 1957**
	42(3)	**Castleblaney Urban District (Alteration of Boundary) Order, S.I. No. 63 of 1948**
		Clones Urban District (Alteration of Boundary) Order, S.I. No. 65 of 1948
		Bray Urban District (Alteration of Boundary) Order, S.I. No. 42 of 1952
		Letterkenny Urban District (Alteration of Boundary) Order, S.I. No. 79 of 1953
		Urban District of Ceannanus Mor (Alteration of Boundary) Order, S.I. No. 35 of 1957
		Urban District of Enniscorthy (Alteration of Boundary) Order, S.I. No. 36 of 1957
		Urban District of Trim (Alteration of Boundary) Order, S.I. No. 168 of 1965
		Urban District of Ceannanus Mor (Alteration of Boundary) Order, S.I. No. 169 of 1965

Local Government (Ireland) Act, No. 37 of 1898 (*Cont.*)		**Urban District of Monaghan (Alteration of Boundary) Order, S.I. No. 50 of 1969**
		Urban District of Ceanannus Mor (Alteration of Boundary) Order, S.I. No. 51 of 1969
		Urban District of Carlow (Alteration of Boundary) Order, S.I. No. 264 of 1969
		Urban District of Tralee (Alteration of Boundary) Order, S.I. No. 222 of 1973
		Urban District of Navan (Alteration of Boundary) Order, S.I. No. 162 of 1975
		Urban District of Youghal (Alteration of Boundary) Order, S.I. No. 102 of 1978
		Urban District of Bray (Alteration of Boundary) Order, S.I. No. 370 of 1978
		Urban District of Longford (Alteration of Boundary) Order, S.I. No. 377 of 1985
	54(10)	**Local Government (Certificate of Rateable Value) (Amendment) Order, S.I. No. 408 of 1980**
	58(2)(a) (ii)	**Relief of the Poor (Trained Nurses) Regulations [Vol. XVIII p. 471] S.R.& O. No. 31 of 1935**
Local Government (Ireland) Act, No. 38 of 1902	22	**Public Bodies (Temporary Provisions) Order, S.I. No. 232 of 1954**
		Public Bodies (Temporary Provisions) Order, S.I. No. 155 of 1955
		Public Bodies (Temporary Provisions) Order, S.I. No. 174 of 1960
		Public Bodies (Amendment) Order, S.I. No. 173 of 1977
		Public Bodies (Amendment) Order, S.I. No. 340 of 1985
Local Government (Ireland) Act, No. 19 of 1919		**Local Elections (Amendment) Order [Vol. XIV p. 849] S.R.& O. No. 7 of 1929**
		Local Elections (Amendment) (No.2) Order, S.I. No. 118 of 1955
	10	*Local Elections (Temporary Amendment) Order [Vol. XXX p. 1135] S.R.& O. No. 283 of 1942*
		Local Elections (Amendment) Order [Vol. XXX p. 1131] S.R.& O. No. 284 of 1942
		Local Elections (Amendment) Order, S.I. No. 95 of 1955
	10(2)	*Local Elections (Adaptation) Order [Vol. XXX p. 1169] S.R.& O. No. 253 of 1944*
	19	*Local Elections Order [Vol. XIV p. 759] S.R.& O. No. 19 of 1925*
Local Government (No.2) Act, No. 40 of 1960	4	*Housing Authorities (Borrowing and Management) Regulations, S.I. No. 276 of 1974*
Local Government (Planning and Development) Act, No. 28 of 1963	1(3)(a)	*Local Government (Planning and Development) Act, 1963 (Appointed Day) Order, S.I. No. 211 of 1964*

Statutory Authority	Section	Statutory Instrument
Local Government (Planning and Development) Act, No. 28 of 1963 (*Cont.*)	4	*Local Government (Planning and Development) Act, 1963 (Exempted Development) Regulations, S.I. No. 236 of 1964*
		Local Government (Planning and Development) Act, 1963 (Exempted Development) Regulations, S.I. No. 176 of 1967
		Local Government (Planning and Development) Act, 1963 (Exempted Development) (Amendment) Regulations, S.I. No. 260 of 1968
		Local Government (Planning and Development) Act, 1963 (Exempted Development) (Amendment) Regulations, S.I. No. 219 of 1976
		Local Government (Planning and Development) Regulations, S.I. No. 65 of 1977
		Local Government (Planning and Development) (Amendment) Regulations, S.I. No. 154 of 1981
		Local Government (Planning and Development) (Postal and Telecommunications) Exempted Development Regulations, S.I. No. 403 of 1983
		Local Government (Planning and Development) (Exempted Development and Amendment) Regulations, S.I. No. 348 of 1984
		Local Government (Planning and Development) (Exempted Development) Regulations, S.I. No. 130 of 1985
	8	*Local Government (Planning and Development) (Fees and Amendment) Regulations, S.I. No. 30 of 1983*
		Local Government (Planning and Development) (Fees) Regulations, S.I. No. 358 of 1984
	10	*Local Government (Planning and Development) Act, 1963 (Appeals and References) Regulations, S.I. No. 216 of 1964*
		Local Government (Planning and Development) Act, 1963 (Compensation) Regulations, S.I. No. 217 of 1964
		Local Government (Planning and Development) Act, 1963 (Licensing) Regulations, S.I. No. 218 of 1964
		Local Government (Planning and Development) Act, 1963 (Miscellaneous) Regulations, S.I. No. 219 of 1964
		Local Government (Planning and Development) Act, 1963 (Permission) Regulations, S.I. No. 221 of 1964
		Local Government (Planning and Development) Act, 1963 (Exempted Development) Regulations, S.I. No. 236 of 1964
		Local Government (Planning and Development) Act, 1963 (Licensing) Regulations, S.I. No. 76 of 1965
		Local Government (Planning and Development) Act, 1963 (Miscellaneous and Licensing) Regulations, S.I. No. 72 of 1966

Local Government (Planning and Development) Act, No. 28 of 1963 (*Cont.*)

Local Government (Planning and Development) Act, 1963 (Copies of Development Plans) Regulations, S.I. No. 154 of 1967

Local Government (Planning and Development) Act, 1963 (Exempted Development) Regulations, S.I. No. 176 of 1967

Local Government (Planning and Development) Act, 1963 (Miscellaneous) (Amendment) Regulations, S.I. No. 230 of 1967

Local Government (Planning and Development) Act, 1963 (Licensing) (Amendment) Regulations, S.I. No. 210 of 1968

Local Government (Planning and Development) Act, 1963 (Exempted Development) (Amendment) Regulations, S.I. No. 260 of 1968

Local Government (Planning and Development) Act, 1963 (Exempted Development) (Amendment) Regulations, S.I. No. 219 of 1976

Local Government (Planning and Development) Act, 1976 (Section 25) Regulations, S.I. No. 226 of 1976

Local Government (Planning and Development) Regulations, S.I. No. 65 of 1977

Local Government (Planning and Development) (Amendment) Regulations, S.I. No. 231 of 1980

Local Government (Planning and Development) (Amendment) Regulations, S.I. No. 154 of 1981

Local Government (Planning and Development) (Amendment) Regulations, S.I. No. 342 of 1982

Local Government (Planning and Development) (Fees and Amendment) Regulations, S.I. No. 30 of 1983

Local Government (Planning and Development) (An Bord Pleanala) Regulations, S.I. No. 285 of 1983

Local Government (Planning and Development) (Postal and Telecommunications) Exempted Development Regulations, S.I. No. 403 of 1983

Local Government (Planning and Development) (Exemption from Fees) Regulations, S.I. No. 1 of 1984

Local Government (Planning and Development) (Exempted Development and Amendment) Regulations, S.I. No. 348 of 1984

Local Government (Planning and Development) (Fees) Regulations, S.I. No. 358 of 1984

Local Government (Planning and Development) (Exempted Development) Regulations, S.I. No. 130 of 1985

19   *Local Government (Planning and Development) Act, 1963 (Copies of Development Plans) Regulations, S.I. No. 154 of 1967*

Local Government (Planning and Development) Regulations, S.I. No. 65 of 1977

Statutory Authority	Section	Statutory Instrument
Local Government (Planning and Development) Act, No. 28 of 1963 (*Cont.*)	21	*Local Government (Planning and Development) Act, 1963 (Miscellaneous) Regulations, S.I. No. 219 of 1964*
		Local Government (Planning and Development) Act, 1963 (Miscellaneous) (Amendment) Regulations, S.I. No. 230 of 1967
		Local Government (Planning and Development) Regulations, S.I. No. 65 of 1977
	25	*Local Government (Planning and Development) Act, 1963 (Permission) Regulations, S.I. No. 221 of 1964*
		Local Government (Planning and Development) Regulations, S.I. No. 65 of 1977
		Local Government (Planning and Development) (Amendment) Regulations, S.I. No. 342 of 1982
		Local Government (Planning and Development) (Fees and Amendment) Regulations, S.I. No. 30 of 1983
		Local Government (Planning and Development) (Exempted Development and Amendment) Regulations, S.I. No. 348 of 1984
		Local Government (Planning and Development) (Fees) Regulations, S.I. No. 358 of 1984
	26	**Local Government (Planning and Development) Regulations, S.I. No. 65 of 1977**
	43(3)	**Dublin Bay Special Amenity Area Order (Refusal of Confirmation) Order, S.I. No. 384 of 1981**
		Ballyvelly/Lohercannan Special Amenity Area Order (Refusal of Confirmation) Order, S.I. No. 319 of 1982
		Donegal County Council (Knockalla Coast Road) Special Amenity Area Order (Refusal of Confirmation) Order, S.I. No. 250 of 1984
	46	*Local Government (Planning and Development) Act, 1963 (Miscellaneous and Licensing) Regulations, S.I. No. 72 of 1966*
		Local Government (Planning and Development) Regulations, S.I. No. 65 of 1977
	67	*Local Government (Planning and Development) Act, 1963 (Compensation) Regulations, S.I. No. 217 of 1964*
		Local Government (Planning and Development) Regulations, S.I. No. 65 of 1977
	76	*Local Government (Planning and Development) Act, 1963 (Miscellaneous) Regulations, S.I. No. 219 of 1964*
		Local Government (Planning and Development) Regulations, S.I. No. 65 of 1977
	82	*Local Government (Planning and Development) Act, 1963 (Appeals and References) Regulations, S.I. No. 216 of 1964*

Statutory Authority	Section	Statutory Instrument
Local Government (Planning and Development) Act, No. 28 of 1963 (*Cont.*)		**Local Government (Planning and Development) Regulations, S.I. No. 65 of 1977**
	89	*Local Government (Planning and Development) Act, 1963 (Licensing) Regulations, S.I. No. 218 of 1964*
		Local Government (Planning and Development) Act, 1963 (Licensing) Regulations, S.I. No. 76 of 1965
		Local Government (Planning and Development) Act, 1963 (Miscellaneous and Licensing) Regulations, S.I. No. 72 of 1966
		Local Government (Planning and Development) Act, 1963 (Licensing) (Amendment) Regulations, S.I. No. 210 of 1968
		Local Government (Planning and Development) Regulations, S.I. No. 65 of 1977
		Local Government (Planning and Development) (Amendment) Regulations, S.I. No. 231 of 1980
Local Government (Planning and Development) Act, No. 20 of 1976	2	*Local Government (Planning and Development) Act, 1976 (Establishment of An Bord Pleanala) Order, S.I. No. 307 of 1976*
	5	**Local Government (Planning and Development) Regulations, S.I. No. 65 of 1977**
	20	**Local Government (Planning and Development) Regulations, S.I. No. 65 of 1977**
		Local Government (Planning and Development) (Amendment) Regulations, S.I. No. 342 of 1982
	25	*Local Government (Planning and Development) Act, 1976 (Section 25) Regulations, S.I. No. 226 of 1976*
		Local Government (Planning and Development) Regulations, S.I. No. 65 of 1977
	29	**Local Government (Planning and Development) Regulations, S.I. No. 65 of 1977**
	32	**Local Government (Planning and Development) Regulations, S.I. No. 65 of 1977**
	35	**Local Government (Planning and Development) Regulations, S.I. No. 65 of 1977**
		Local Government (Planning and Development) (Amendment) Regulations, S.I. No. 342 of 1982
	46(3)	*Local Government (Planning and Development) Act, 1976 (Commencement) Order, S.I. No. 166 of 1976*
		Local Government (Planning and Development) Act, 1976 (Commencement) (No.2) Order, S.I. No. 227 of 1976
		Local Government (Planning and Development) Act, 1976 (Commencement) (No.3) Order, S.I. No. 308 of 1976
		Local Government (Planning and Development) Act, 1976 (Commencement) Order, S.I. No. 56 of 1977

Statutory Authority	Section	Statutory Instrument
Local Government (Planning and Development) Act, No. 20 of 1976 (*Cont.*)	Sch. par. 17	*Local Government (Planning and Development) Act, 1976 (Establishment of An Bord Pleanala) Order, S.I. No. 307 of 1976*
	Sch. par. 18	*Local Government (Planning and Development) Act, 1976 (Establishment of An Bord Pleanala) Order, S.I. No. 307 of 1976*
Local Government (Planning and Development) Act, No. 21 of 1982	7	**Local Government (Planning and Development) General Policy Directive, S.I. No. 264 of 1982**
	10	*Local Government (Planning and Development) (Fees and Amendment) Regulations, S.I. No. 30 of 1983*
		Local Government (Water Pollution) Regulations, S.I. No. 36 of 1983
		Local Government (Planning and Development) (Exemption from Fees) Regulations, S.I. No. 1 of 1984
		Local Government (Water Pollution) (Fees) Regulations, S.I. No. 115 of 1985
	11	**Local Government (Planning and Development) (Amendment) Regulations, S.I. No. 342 of 1982**
	15(3)	*Local Government (Planning and Development) Act, 1982 (Commencement) Order, S.I. No. 34 of 1983*
Local Government (Planning and Development) Act, No. 28 of 1983	5(9)	**Local Government (Planning and Development) (An Bord Pleanala) Regulations, S.I. No. 285 of 1983**
	7	**Local Government (Planning and Development) (An Bord Pleanala) Regulations, S.I. No. 285 of 1983**
	26(3)	*Local Government (Planning and Development) Act, 1983 (Commencement) Order, S.I. No. 284 of 1983*
		Local Government (Planning and Development) Act, 1983 (Commencement) Order, S.I. No. 45 of 1984
Local Government (Rates) Act, No. 2 of 1970	5	**Local Government (Rates) (Instalments) Regulations, S.I. No. 34 of 1970**
		Local Government (Rates) (Waiver) Regulations, S.I. No. 41 of 1970
Local Government (Rates on Small Dwellings) Act, No. 4 of 1928	2	*Local Government (Rates on Small Dwellings) Act, 1928 (Cork County Borough) Order, S.I. No. 97 of 1956*
Local Government (Reorganisation) Act, No. 7 of 1985	1(6)	*Local Government (Reorganisation) Act, 1985 (Commencement) Order, S.I. No. 98 of 1985*
		Local Government (Reorganisation) Act, 1985 (Commencement) (No.2) Order, S.I. No. 129 of 1985

Statutory Authority	Section	Statutory Instrument
Local Government (Reorganisation) Act, No. 7 of 1985 (*Cont.*)		*Local Government (Reorganisation) Act, 1985 (Commencement) (No.3) Order, S.I. No. 175 of 1985*
	5(1)	*Local Government (Reorganisation) Act, 1985 (County Borough of Galway) (Appointed Day) Order, S.I. No. 425 of 1985*
	8	**Local Government (Reorganisation) Act, 1985 (County Borough of Galway) Order, S.I. No. 426 of 1985**
	14	**Dublin Electoral Counties Order, S.I. No. 133 of 1985**
	16	**Dublin Electoral Counties Order, S.I. No. 133 of 1985**
	18	**Local Government (Reorganisation) (Supplementary Provisions) (Dublin) Regulations, S.I. No. 128 of 1985**
		Local Government (Reorganisation) (Supplementary Provisions) (Dublin) (Amendment) Regulations, S.I. No. 418 of 1985
		Local Government (Reorganisation) (Supplementary Provisions) (Dublin) (Amendment) Regulations, S.I. No. 70 of 1986
		Local Government (Reorganisation) (Supplementary Provisions) (Dublin) (Amendment) (No.2) Regulations, S.I. No. 270 of 1986
	19(1)(b)	*Borough of Galway (Alteration of Boundary) S.I. No. 126 of 1985*
	19(2)	**Borough of Galway (Alteration of Boundary) (Implementation) Order, S.I. No. 410 of 1985**
	19(4)	**Borough of Galway (Alteration of Boundary) (Implementation) Order, S.I. No. 410 of 1985**
	20	**Galway County Council (Amendment) Order, S.I. No. 127 of 1985**
	21	**County Electoral Areas (Amendment) (No.2) Order, S.I. No. 110 of 1985**
		Galway County Council (Amendment) Order, S.I. No. 127 of 1985
	24	**Local Government (Reorganisation) Act, 1985 (County Borough of Galway) Order, S.I. No. 426 of 1985**
	25	**Dublin Electoral Counties Order, S.I. No. 133 of 1985**
	26	**Local Government (Reorganisation) Act, 1985 (Committee of Agriculture) Order, S.I. No. 131 of 1985**
	28(3)	**Local Government (Reorganisation) (Supplementary Provisions) (Cork) Order, S.I. No. 174 of 1985**

Statutory Authority	Section	Statutory Instrument
Local Government (Roads and Motorways) Act, No. 6 of 1974	2	**Local Government (Roads and Motorways) Act, 1974 (Declaration of National Roads) Order, S.I. No. 164 of 1977**
		Local Government (Roads and Motorways) Act, 1974 (Declaration of National Roads) Order, S.I. No. 277 of 1980
		Local Government (Roads and Motorways) Act, 1974 (Declaration of National Roads) Order, S.I. No. 108 of 1986
	4	**Local Government (Roads and Motorways) Act, 1974 (Prescribed Forms) Regulations, S.I. No. 395 of 1977**
	9	**Local Government (Roads and Motorways) Act, 1974 (Prescribed Traffic) General Regulations, S.I. No. 396 of 1977**
	14	**Local Government (Roads and Motorways) Act, 1974 (Prescribed Forms) Regulations, S.I. No. 395 of 1977**
		Local Government (Roads and Motorways) Act, 1974 (Prescribed Traffic) General Regulations, S.I. No. 396 of 1977
	15	*Local Government (Roads and Motorways) Act, 1974 (Commencement) Order, S.I. No. 147 of 1974*
Local Government (Sanitary Services) Act, No. 3 of 1948	3	*Local Government (Sanitary Services) Act, 1948 (Date of Commencement) Order, S.I. No. 72 of 1948*
	34(2)	**Local Government (Sanitary Services) Act, 1948 (Section 34) (County Health District of Wicklow) Order, S.I. No. 8 of 1950**
		Local Government (Sanitary Services) Act, 1948 (Section 34) (Urban District of Arklow) Order, S.I. No. 97 of 1950
		Local Government (Sanitary Services) Act, 1948 (Section 34) (County Health District of Dublin) Order, S.I. No. 250 of 1952
		Local Government (Sanitary Services) Act, 1948 (Section 34) (Urban District of Bray) Order, S.I. No. 260 of 1952
		Local Government (Sanitary Services) Act, 1948 (Section 34) (Borough of Galway) Order, S.I. No. 324 of 1953
		Local Government (Sanitary Services) Act, 1948 (Section 34) (Urban District of Wicklow) Order, S.I. No. 335 of 1953
		Local Government (Sanitary Services) Act, 1948 (Section 34) (County Health District of Wexford) Order, S.I. No. 233 of 1955
		Local Government (Sanitary Services) Act, 1948 (Section 34) (Town of Kilkee) Order, S.I. No. 114 of 1957
		Local Government (Sanitary Services) Act, 1948 (Section 34) (Part of County of Cork) Order, S.I. No. 220 of 1957

Statutory Authority	Section	Statutory Instrument

Local Government (Sanitary
Services) Act, No. 3 of 1948
(*Cont.*)

Local Government (Sanitary Services) Act, 1948
(Section 34) (County Health District of Galway)
Order, S.I. No. 234 of 1957

Local Government (Sanitary Services) Act, 1948
(Section 34) (Part of County of Cork) Order, S.I.
No. 145 of 1958

Local Government (Sanitary Services) Act, 1948
(Section 34) (Part of Urban District of Youghal)
Order, S.I. No. 164 of 1958

Local Government (Sanitary Services) Act, 1948
(Section 34) (Urban District of Bundoran) Order,
S.I. No. 20 of 1959

Local Government (Sanitary Services) Act, 1948
(Section 34) (Part of County of Waterford) Order,
S.I. No. 141 of 1959

Local Government (Sanitary Services) Act, 1948
(Section 34) (Part of County of Cork) Order, S.I.
No. 142 of 1959

Local Government (Sanitary Services) Act, 1948
(Section 34) (Part of County of Donegal) Order,
S.I. No. 173 of 1960

Local Government (Sanitary Services) Act, 1948
(Section 34) Order, S.I. No. 220 of 1960

Local Government (Sanitary Services) Act, 1948
(Section 34) Order, S.I. No. 22 of 1961

Local Government (Sanitary Services) Act, 1948
(Section 34) (County Health District of Meath)
Order, S.I. No. 90 of 1961

Local Government (Sanitary Services) Act, 1948
(Section 34) (County of Sligo and Part of County
of Donegal) Order, S.I. No. 93 of 1961

Local Government (Sanitary Services) Act, 1948
(Section 34) (Part of County of Donegal) Order,
S.I. No. 295 of 1961

Local Government (Sanitary Services) Act, 1948
(Section 34) (Urban District of Buncrana) Order,
S.I. No. 26 of 1962

Local Government (Sanitary Services) Act, 1948
(Section 34) (Borough of Dun Laoghaire) Order,
S.I. No. 144 of 1962

Local Government (Sanitary Services) Act, 1948
(Section 34) (Urban District of Listowel) Order,
S.I. No. 51 of 1963

Local Government (Sanitary Services) Act, 1948
(Section 34) (County Health District of Kerry)
Order, S.I. No. 54 of 1963

Local Government (Sanitary Services) Act, 1948
(Section 34) (Part of County of Donegal) Order,
S.I. No. 144 of 1963

Local Government (Sanitary Services) Act, 1948
(Section 34) (Urban District of Killarney) Order,
S.I. No. 237 of 1963

Local Government (Sanitary Services) Act, 1948
(Section 34) (Urban District of An Uaimh) Order,
S.I. No. 49 of 1964

Statutory Authority	Section	Statutory Instrument
Local Government (Sanitary Services) Act, No. 3 of 1948 (*Cont.*)		**Local Government (Sanitary Services) Act, 1948 (Section 34) (Urban District of Dungarvan) Order, S.I. No. 173 of 1964**
		Local Government (Sanitary Services) Act, 1948 (Section 34) (Urban District of Ceanannus Mor) Order, S.I. No. 246 of 1964
		Local Government (Sanitary Services) Act, 1948 (Section 34) (Part of County of Donegal) Order, S.I. No. 158 of 1965
		Local Government (Sanitary Services) Act, 1948 (Section 34) (Part of County Cork) Order, S.I. No. 253 of 1966
		Local Government (Sanitary Services) Act, 1948 (Section 34) (Part of County of Cork) Order, S.I. No. 208 of 1978
		Local Government (Sanitary Services) Act, 1948 (Section 34) (Part of County of Donegal) Order, S.I. No. 209 of 1978
		Local Government (Sanitary Services) Act, 1948 (Section 34) (Urban District of Westport) Order, S.I. No. 285 of 1979
		Local Government (Sanitary Services) Act, 1948 (Section 34) (County Health District of Kildare) Order, S.I. No. 228 of 1984
		Local Government (Sanitary Services) Act, 1948 (Section 34) (Part of County of Donegal) Order, S.I. No. 217 of 1986
		Local Government (Sanitary Services) Act, 1948 (Section 34) (Part of County of Donegal) Order, S.I. No. 317 of 1986
	34(3)	**Local Government (Sanitary Services) Act, 1948 (Section 34) (No.2) Order, S.I. No. 232 of 1960**
Local Government (Sanitary Services) Act, No. 26 of 1962	2	*Private Water Supplies and Sewerage Facilities Regulations, S.I. No. 117 of 1963*
		Private Water Supplies and Sewerage Facilities (Amendment) Regulations, S.I. No. 30 of 1972
		Private Water Supplies and Sewerage Facilities (Amendment) Regulations, S.I. No. 185 of 1978
	3	*Private Water Supplies and Sewerage Facilities Regulations, S.I. No. 117 of 1963*
		Private Water Supplies and Sewerage Facilities (Amendment) Regulations, S.I. No. 30 of 1972
		Private Water Supplies and Sewerage Facilities (Amendment) Regulations, S.I. No. 185 of 1978
	10	**Control of Atmospheric Pollution Regulations, S.I. No. 156 of 1970**
		Control of Atmospheric Pollution (Licensing) Regulations, S.I. No. 178 of 1985
	14	*Local Government (Sanitary Services) Act, 1962 (Commencement) Order, S.I. No. 180 of 1962*
		Local Government (Sanitary Services) Act, 1962 (Commencement) Order, S.I. No. 116 of 1963

Statutory Authority	Section	Statutory Instrument
Local Government (Sanitary Services) Act, No. 26 of 1962 *(Cont.)*		*Local Government (Sanitary Services) Act, 1962 (Commencement) Order, S.I. No. 155 of 1970*
Local Government (Sanitary Services) Act, No. 29 of 1964	19	**Local Government (Sanitary Services) Act, 1964 Regulations, S.I. No. 222 of 1964**
Local Government Services (Corporate Bodies) Act, No. 6 of 1971	3	**Local Government Staff Negotiations Board (Establishment) Order, S.I. No. 217 of 1971**
		National Road Safety Association (Establishment) Order, S.I. No. 103 of 1974
		Local Government Staff Negotiations Board (Establishment) (Amendment) Order, S.I. No. 54 of 1975
		Local Government Computer Services Board (Establishment) Order, S.I. No. 212 of 1975
		Fire Prevention Council (Establishment) Order, S.I. No. 206 of 1978
		Local Government Staff Negotiations Board (Establishment) (Amendment) Order, S.I. No. 15 of 1979
		Irish Water Safety Association (Establishment) Order, S.I. No. 244 of 1980
		Fire Prevention Council (Establishment) (Amendment) Order, S.I. No. 246 of 1980
		Fire Prevention Council (Establishment) Order, 1978 (Amendment) Order, S.I. No. 23 of 1984
		Fire Services Council (Establishment) Order, 1983 (Amendment) Order, S.I. No. 344 of 1984
		Local Government Services (Establishment) (Orders) (Amendment) Order, S.I. No. 345 of 1984
		Fire Prevention Council (Establishment) Order, 1978 (Amendment) Order, S.I. No. 239 of 1986
	3(2)	**Local Government Services (Corporate Bodies) Act, 1971 (Designation of Bodies) Order, S.I. No. 197 of 1976**
		Local Government Services (Corporate Bodies) Act, 1971 (Designation of Bodies) Order, S.I. No. 207 of 1978
		Local Government Services (Corporate Bodies) Act, 1971 (Designation of Bodies) Order, S.I. No. 77 of 1981
		Local Government Services (Corporate Bodies) Act, 1971 (Designation of Bodies) Order, S.I. No. 325 of 1986
	4	**Fire Services Council (Establishment) Order, 1983 (Amendment) Order, S.I. No. 344 of 1984**
		Local Government Services (Establishment) (Orders) (Amendment) Order, S.I. No. 345 of 1984
Local Government (Superannuation) Act, No. 4 of 1948	4	*Local Government (Superannuation) Act, 1948 (Date of Commencement) Order, S.I. No. 105 of 1948*

Statutory Authority	Section	Statutory Instrument
Local Government (Superannuation) Act, No. 4 of 1948 (*Cont.*)	71	**Local Government (Superannuation) Act, 1948 (Fire Brigade and Officers and Servants) Regulations, S.I. No. 356 of 1948**
Local Government (Superannuation) Act, No. 10 of 1956	4	*Local Government (Superannuation) Act, 1956 (Commencement) Order, S.I. No. 78 of 1956*
	13	**Local Government (Superannuation) Act, 1956 (Addition to Service) Regulations, S.I. No. 79 of 1956**
Local Government (Superannuation) Act, No. 8 of 1980	2	*Local Government (Superannuation Revision) Scheme, S.I. No. 33 of 1984*
		Local Government (Transfer of Service) Scheme, S.I. No. 298 of 1984
		Local Government Employees (Widows and Orphans Contributory Pension) Scheme, S.I. No. 318 of 1984
		Local Government Employees (Widows and Orphans Ex-gratia Pension) Scheme, S.I. No. 319 of 1984
		Local Government Officers (Widows and Orphans Ex-gratia Pension) Scheme, S.I. No. 320 of 1984
		Local Government Officers (Widows and Orphans Contributory Pension) Scheme, S.I. No. 321 of 1984
		Local Government (Superannuation Revision) (Amendment) Scheme, S.I. No. 404 of 1985
		Local Government (Superannuation Revision) (Job-sharing) (Amendment) Scheme, S.I. No. 406 of 1985
		Local Government Employees (Spouses and Children's Contributory Pension) Scheme, S.I. No. 363 of 1986
		Local Government Officers (Spouses and Children's Contributory Pension) Scheme, S.I. No. 364 of 1986
		Local Government (Superannuation Revision) (Consolidation) Scheme, S.I. No. 391 of 1986
		Local Government (Superannuation) (Purchase) Scheme, S.I. No. 421 of 1986
	3	**Local Government (Superannuation) Regulations, S.I. No. 32 of 1984**
		Local Government (Superannuation) (Job-sharing) Regulations, 1985, S.I. No. 405 of 1985
		Local Government (Superannuation) Regulations, S.I. No. 407 of 1985
	4	**Local Government (Superannuation) (Gratuities) Regulations, S.I. No. 346 of 1984**
	5	**Local Government (Superannuation) Regulations, S.I. No. 32 of 1984**
		Local Government (Superannuation Revision) Scheme, S.I. No. 33 of 1984
		Local Government (Transfer of Service) Scheme, S.I. No. 298 of 1984

Local Government (Superannuation)
Act, No. 8 of 1980 (*Cont.*)

Local Government Employees (Widows and Orphans Contributory Pension) Scheme, S.I. No. 318 of 1984

Local Government Employees (Widows and Orphans Ex-gratia Pension) Scheme, S.I. No. 319 of 1984

Local Government Officers (Widows and Orphans Ex-gratia Pension) Scheme, S.I. No. 320 of 1984

Local Government Officers (Widows and Orphans Contributory Pension) Scheme, S.I. No. 321 of 1984

Local Government (Superannuation) (Gratuities) Regulations, S.I. No. 346 of 1984

Local Government (Superannuation Revision) (Amendment) Scheme, S.I. No. 404 of 1985

Local Government (Superannuation) (Job-sharing) Regulations, 1985, S.I. No. 405 of 1985

Local Government (Superannuation Revision) (Job-sharing) (Amendment) Scheme, S.I. No. 406 of 1985

Local Government (Superannuation) Regulations, S.I. No. 407 of 1985

Local Government Employees (Spouses and Children's Contributory Pension) Scheme, S.I. No. 363 of 1986

Local Government Officers (Spouses and Children's Contributory Pension) Scheme, S.I. No. 364 of 1986

Local Government (Superannuation Revision) (Consolidation) Scheme, S.I. No. 391 of 1986

Local Government (Superannuation) (Purchase) Scheme, S.I. No. 421 of 1986

12(2)(b) *Local Government (Superannuation) Act, 1980 (Sections 2, 3, 4, 9 and 10) (Commencement) Order, S.I. No. 31 of 1984*

Local Government (Temporary
Provisions) Act, No. 9 of 1923

County Schemes (Officers of District Hospitals) (Amendment) Order [Vol. XXXII p. 337] S.R.& O. No. 147 of 1939

5 *Limerick County Borough Scheme (Amendment) Order [Vol. XV p. 409] S.R.& O. No. 25 of 1929*

Clare County Scheme (Amendment) Order [Vol. XV p. 97] S.R.& O. No. 25 of 1932

Cork County Scheme (Amendment) Order [Vol. XV p. 143] S.R.& O. No. 72 of 1932

Laoighis County Scheme (Amendment) Order [Vol. XV p. 347] S.R.& O. No. 87 of 1932

Limerick County Borough Scheme (Amendment) Order [Vol. XV p. 415] S.R.& O. No. 109 of 1933

Monaghan County Scheme (Amendment) Order [Vol. XV p. 615] S.R.& O. No. 82 of 1935

Louth County Scheme (Amendment) Order [Vol. XV p. 513] S.R.& O. No. 135 of 1936

Statutory Authority	Section	Statutory Instrument
Local Government (Temporary Provisions) Act, No. 9 of 1923 (*Cont.*)		*Westmeath County Scheme (Amendment) Order [Vol. XV p. 825] S.R.& O. No. 232 of 1936*
		County Schemes (General Amendment) Order [Vol. XXX p. 1183] S.R.& O. No. 99 of 1939
		Leitrim County Scheme (Amendment) Order [Vol. XXX p. 1205] S.R.& O. No. 170 of 1939
		Kildare County Scheme (Amendment) Order [Vol. XXX p. 1199] S.R.& O. No. 553 of 1941
	15	*Local Offices and Employments (Gaeltacht) Order [Vol. XV p. 917] S.R.& O. No. 33 of 1928*
		Local Offices and Employments (Gaeltacht) Order [Vol. XV p. 933] S.R.& O. No. 61 of 1931
		Local Offices and Employments (Gaeltacht) (Amendment) Order [Vol. XV p. 939] S.R.& O. No. 46 of 1932
		Old Age Pensions Committees (Clerks) Order [Vol. XV p. 1097] S.R.& O. No. 81 of 1932
		Local Offices and Employments (Gaeltacht) (Amendment) Order [Vol. XV p. 945] S.R.& O. No. 2 of 1934
		Local Offices and Employments (Gaeltacht) (Amendment) Order [Vol. XV p. 949] S.R.& O. No. 165 of 1935
		Local Offices and Employments (Gaeltacht) (Amendment) Order [Vol. XV p. 955] S.R.& O. No. 10 of 1936
		Old Age Pensions Committees (Clerks) Order [Vol. XV p. 1105] S.R.& O. No. 80 of 1936
		Local Offices and Employments (Amendment) Order [Vol. XV p. 913] S.R.& O. No. 136 of 1936
		Local Offices and Employments (Gaeltacht) (Amendment) Order [Vol. XV p. 961] S.R.& O. No. 331 of 1937
		Local Offices and Employments (Gaeltacht) (Amendment) Order [Vol. XV p. 967] S.R.& O. No. 54 of 1938
		Local Offices and Employments (Gaeltacht) (Amendment) (No.2) Order [Vol. XV p. 973] S.R.& O. No. 207 of 1938
		Local Offices and Employments (Gaeltacht) (Amendment) Order [Vol. XXX p. 1223] S.R.& O. No. 45 of 1939
		Local Offices and Employments (Gaeltacht) (Amendment) (No.2) Order [Vol. XXX p. 1229] S.R.& O. No. 205 of 1939
		Local Offices and Employments (Gaeltacht) (Amendment) Order [Vol. XXX p. 1233] S.R.& O. No. 84 of 1940
		Local Offices and Employments (Amendment) Order [Vol. XXX p. 1211] S.R.& O. No. 98 of 1940
		Local Offices and Employments (Gaeltacht) (Amendment) (No.2) Order [Vol. XXX p. 1239] S.R.& O. No. 217 of 1940

Statutory Authority	Section	Statutory Instrument
Local Government (Temporary Provisions) Act, No. 9 of 1923 (*Cont.*)		*Local Offices and Employments (Gaeltacht) (Amendment) Order [Vol. XXX p. 1243] S.R.& O. No. 62 of 1941*
		Local Offices and Employments (Amendment) Order [Vol. XXX p. 1215] S.R.& O. No. 260 of 1941
		Local Offices and Employments (Gaeltacht) (Amendment) (No.2) Order [Vol. XXX p. 1249] S.R.& O. No. 346 of 1941
		Local Offices and Employments (Gaeltacht) (Amendment) Order [Vol. XXX p. 1253] S.R.& O. No. 81 of 1942
		Local Offices and Employments (Gaeltacht) (Amendment) (No.2) Order [Vol. XXX p. 1259] S.R.& O. No. 317 of 1942
	20	*Prisons (Ireland) Act, 1826, (Adaptation) Order [Vol. XV p. 1091] S.R.& O. No. 5 of 1932*
Local Government (Temporary Provisions) Acts, 1923 and 1924,		**County Boards of Health (Assistance) (Amendment) Order [Vol. XVIII p. 373] S.R.& O. No. 3 of 1926**
		County Schemes (Officers of District Hospitals) Order [Vol. XVIII p. 417] S.R.& O. No. 100 of 1927
		Boards of Public Assistance (General Regulations) (Amendment) Order [Vol. XVIII p. 427] S.R.& O. No. 17 of 1928
		County Boards of Health (Assistance) (Amendment) Order [Vol. XVIII p. 379] S.R.& O. No. 86 of 1931
		Boards of Public Assistance (General Regulations) (Amendment) Order [Vol. XVIII p. 437] S.R.& O. No. 312 of 1938
		Boards of Public Assistance (General Regulations) (Amendment) Order [Vol. XXXII p. 333] S.R.& O. No. 208 of 1939
		Boarded Out Children (Contracts) (Amendment) Order [Vol. XXXII p. 125] S.R.& O. No. 99 of 1940
Local Government (Water Pollution) Act, No. 1 of 1977	2	**Water Pollution Advisory Council Order, S.I. No. 172 of 1977**
	4	**Local Government (Water Pollution) Regulations, S.I. No. 108 of 1978**
	4(1)	*Local Government (Water Pollution) Act, 1977 (Sections 4 and 16) (Fixing of Dates) Order, S.I. No. 16 of 1978*
	6	**Local Government (Water Pollution) Regulations, S.I. No. 108 of 1978**
		Local Government (Water Pollution) (Fees) Regulations, S.I. No. 115 of 1985
		Local Government (Water Pollution) Act, 1977 (Control of Cadmium Discharges) Regulations, S.I. No. 294 of 1985

Statutory Authority	Section	Statutory Instrument
Local Government (Water Pollution) Act, No. 1 of 1977 (*Cont.*)		**Local Government (Water Pollution) Act, 1977 (Control of Hexachlorocyclohexane and Mercury Discharges) Regulations, S.I. No. 55 of 1986**
	7	**Local Government (Water Pollution) Regulations, S.I. No. 108 of 1978**
		Local Government (Water Pollution) Act, 1977 (Control of Cadmium Discharges) Regulations, S.I. No. 294 of 1985
		Local Government (Water Pollution) Act, 1977 (Control of Hexachlorocyclohexane and Mercury Discharges) Regulations, S.I. No. 55 of 1986
	8	**Local Government (Water Pollution) Regulations, S.I. No. 108 of 1978**
	9	**Local Government (Water Pollution) Regulations, S.I. No. 108 of 1978**
		Local Government (Water Pollution) Regulations, S.I. No. 36 of 1983
		Local Government (Water Pollution) (Fees) Regulations, S.I. No. 115 of 1985
	15	**Local Government (Water Pollution) Regulations, S.I. No. 108 of 1978**
	16	**Local Government (Water Pollution) Regulations, S.I. No. 108 of 1978**
	16(1)	*Local Government (Water Pollution) Act, 1977 (Sections 4 and 16) (Fixing of Dates) Order, S.I. No. 16 of 1978*
	17	**Local Government (Water Pollution) Regulations, S.I. No. 108 of 1978**
		Local Government (Water Pollution) Act, 1977 (Control of Cadmium Discharges) Regulations, S.I. No. 294 of 1985
		Local Government (Water Pollution) Act, 1977 (Control of Hexachlorocyclohexane and Mercury Discharges) Regulations, S.I. No. 55 of 1986
	19	**Local Government (Water Pollution) Regulations, S.I. No. 108 of 1978**
		Local Government (Water Pollution) (Fees) Regulations, S.I. No. 115 of 1985
		Local Government (Water Pollution) Act, 1977 (Control of Cadmium Discharges) Regulations, S.I. No. 294 of 1985
		Local Government (Water Pollution) Act, 1977 (Control of Hexachlorocyclohexane and Mercury Discharges) Regulations, S.I. No. 55 of 1986
	20	**Local Government (Water Pollution) Regulations, S.I. No. 108 of 1978**
	21	**Local Government (Water Pollution) Act, 1977 (Transfer of Appeals) Order, S.I. No. 96 of 1978**
		Local Government (Water Pollution) Act, 1977 (Transfer of Appeals) Order, 1978, (Amendment) Order, S.I. No. 37 of 1983

Statutory Authority	Section	Statutory Instrument
Local Government (Water Pollution) Act, No. 1 of 1977 (*Cont.*)	26	**Local Government (Water Pollution) Act, 1977 (Control of Cadmium Discharges) Regulations, S.I. No. 294 of 1985**
		Local Government (Water Pollution) Act, 1977 (Control of Hexachlorocyclohexane and Mercury Discharges) Regulations, S.I. No. 55 of 1986
	30	**Local Government (Water Pollution) Regulations, S.I. No. 108 of 1978**
		Local Government (Water Pollution) Regulations, S.I. No. 36 of 1983
		Local Government (Water Pollution) (Fees) Regulations, S.I. No. 115 of 1985
		Local Government (Water Pollution) Act, 1977 (Control of Cadmium Discharges) Regulations, S.I. No. 294 of 1985
		Local Government (Water Pollution) Act, 1977 (Control of Hexachlorocyclohexane and Mercury Discharges) Regulations, S.I. No. 55 of 1986
	33	*Local Government (Water Pollution) Act, 1977 (Commencement) Order, S.I. No. 117 of 1977*
		Local Government (Water Pollution) Act, 1977 (Commencement) (No.2) Order, S.I. No. 296 of 1977
Local Loans Fund Act, No. 16 of 1935		**Local Loans Fund (Rate of Interest) Direction [Vol. XXXVII p. 1113] S.R.& O. No. 183 of 1946**
		Local Loans Fund (Rate of Interest) Direction, S.I. No. 158 of 1948
	2(1)	*Local Loans Fund Act, 1935 (Appointed Day) Order [Vol. XV p. 1111] S.R.& O. No. 94 of 1935*
	17	**Local Loans Fund (Fees and Expenses) Regulations [Vol. XXXVII p. 1107] S.R.& O. No. 182 of 1946**
	17(1)	**Local Loans Fund Regulations [Vol. XV p. 1117] S.R.& O. No. 119 of 1937**
Local Services (Temporary Economies) Act, No. 16 of 1934	15	*Variation of the Scales of Expenses in Relation to the Draft Jurors' Lists (1934) [Vol. XV p. 1267] S.R.& O. No. 17 of 1935*
	16	*Variation of the Scale of Registration Expenses [Vol. XV p. 1259] S.R.& O. No. 382 of 1934*
Locomotives on Highways Act, No. 36 of 1896	6	*Heavy Motor Car (Amendment) Order [Vol. XVI p. 1207] S.R.& O. No. 50 of 1925*
		Motor Car (Public Service Vehicles) Order [Vol. XVI p. 1223] S.R.& O. No. 67 of 1928
		Heavy Motor Car (Amendment) Order [Vol. XVI p. 1219] S.R.& O. No. 9 of 1929
		Heavy Motor Car (Speed) Order [Vol. XVI p. 1233] S.R.& O. No. 41 of 1930
Lough Corrib Navigation Act, No. 37 of 1945	2	*Lough Corrib Navigation Act, 1945 (Appointed Day) Order [Vol. XXXVII p. 1117] S.R.& O. No. 30 of 1946*

Statutory Authority	Section	Statutory Instrument
Lough Corrib Navigation Act, No. 37 of 1945 (*Cont.*)	13	**Lough Corrib Navigation Act, 1945 (Section 13) Order, S.I. No. 31 of 1949**
		Lough Corrib Navigation Act, 1945 (Section 13) Order, S.I. No. 232 of 1958
		Lough Corrib Navigation Act, 1945 (Section 13) Order, S.I. No. 6 of 1963
Lunacy (Ireland) Acts, 1821 to 1901,		**Louth Mental Hospital District Order [Vol. XV p. 1273] S.R.& O. No. 31 of 1930**
		Louth Mental Hospital District (Adjustment) Order [Vol. XV p. 1279] S.R.& O. No. 31 of 1931
Maintenance Orders Act, No. 16 of 1974	2	*Maintenance Orders Act, 1974 (Commencement) Order, S.I. No. 23 of 1975*
Malicious Injuries Act, No. 9 of 1981	8	**Malicious Injuries (Preliminary Notice) Regulations, S.I. No. 319 of 1981**
	15(2)	**District Court (Malicious Injuries Act, 1981) (Costs and Fees) Regulations, S.I. No. 103 of 1982**
Maritime Jurisdiction Act, No. 22 of 1959	4(2)	**Maritime Jurisdiction Act, 1959 (Straight Base Lines) Order, S.I. No. 173 of 1959**
	6	**Maritime Jurisdiction (Exclusive Fisheries Limits) Order, S.I. No. 320 of 1976**
	13	**Maritime Jurisdiction Act, 1959 (Charts) Order, S.I. No. 174 of 1959**
Maritime Jurisdiction (Amendment) Act, No. 32 of 1964	3	**Maritime Jurisdiction (Amendment) Act, 1964 (Specified States) Order, S.I. No. 198 of 1965**
		Maritime Jurisdiction (Amendment) Act, 1964 (Specified States) (Amendment) Order, S.I. No. 14 of 1967
	5(2)	*Maritime Jurisdiction (Amendment) Act, 1964 (Commencement) Order, S.I. No. 197 of 1965*
Marriages Act, No. 30 of 1972	19	*Marriages Act, 1972 (Commencement) Order, S.I. No. 12 of 1973*
		Marriages Act, 1972 (Commencement) (No.2) Order, S.I. No. 105 of 1973
		Marriages Act, 1972 (Commencement) Order, S.I. No. 324 of 1974
Maternity Protection of Employees Act, No. 2 of 1981	16	**Maternity Protection (Time Off for Ante-natal and Post-natal Care) Regulations, S.I. No. 358 of 1981**
	27(4)	**Maternity Protection (Disputes and Appeals) Regulations, S.I. No. 357 of 1981**
Medical Act, No. 4 of 1926	3	*Medical Act, 1925 (First Continuance) Order [Vol. XVI p. 1] S.R.& O. No. 41 of 1926*
		Medical Act, 1925 (Second Continuance) Order [Vol. XVI p. 5] S.R.& O. No. 47 of 1926

Statutory Authority	Section	Statutory Instrument
Medical Act, No. 4 of 1926 (*Cont.*)		*Medical Act, 1925 (Third Continuance) Order [Vol. XVI p. 9] S.R.& O. No. 62 of 1926*
		Medical Act, 1925 (Fourth Continuance) Order [Vol. XVI p. 13] S.R.& O. No. 70 of 1926
		Medical Act, 1925 (Fifth Continuance) Order [Vol. XVI p. 17] S.R.& O. No. 73 of 1926
		Medical Act, 1925 (Sixth Continuance) Order [Vol. XVI p. 21] S.R.& O. No. 6 of 1927
		Medical Act, 1925 (Seventh Continuance) Order [Vol. XVI p. 25] S.R.& O. No. 17 of 1927
Medical Act, No. 2 of 1927	2	*Medical Act, 1925 (Eighth Continuance) Order [Vol. XVI p. 29] S.R.& O. No. 27 of 1927*
		Medical Act, 1925 (Ninth Continuance) Order [Vol. XVI p. 33] S.R.& O. No. 33 of 1927
		Medical Act, 1925 (Tenth Continuance) Order [Vol. XVI p. 37] S.R.& O. No. 37 of 1927
Medical Practitioners Act, No. 25 of 1927	11(4)	*Medical Registration Council Election Rules [Vol. XVI p. 41] S.R.& O. No. 56 of 1927*
		Medical Registration Council Election (Amendment) Rules, S.I. No. 118 of 1962
		Medical Registration Council Election (Amendment) Rules, S.I. No. 5 of 1974
	12(2)	*Medical Registration Council Election Rules [Vol. XVI p. 41] S.R.& O. No. 56 of 1927*
		Medical Registration Council Election (Amendment) Rules, S.I. No. 118 of 1962
		Medical Registration Council Election (Amendment) Rules, S.I. No. 5 of 1974
	26	**Medical Practitioners Act, 1927 (Application of Section 26) Order [Vol. XXXI p. 1] S.R.& O. No. 82 of 1944**
		Medical Practitioners Act, 1927 (Application of Section 26) Order, S.I. No. 272 of 1953
		Medical Practitioners Act, 1927 (Application of Section 26) (No.2) Order, S.I. No. 99 of 1961
	26(2)	**Medical Practitioners Act, 1927 (Application of Section 26) Order, S.I. No. 212 of 1958**
		Medical Practitioners Act, 1927 (Application of Section 26) Order, S.I. No. 206 of 1960
		Medical Practitioners Act, 1927 (Application of Section 26) Order, S.I. No. 31 of 1961
Medical Practitioners Act, No. 29 of 1951	1(1)	*Medical Practitioners Act, 1952 (Appointed Day) Order, S.I. No. 228 of 1952*
Medical Practitioners Act, No. 4 of 1978	3	*Medical Practitioners Act, 1978 (Commencement) Order, S.I. No. 196 of 1978*
		Medical Practitioners Act, 1978 (Commencement) Order, S.I. No. 132 of 1979
	4	*Medical Practitioners Act, 1978 (Establishment Day) Order, S.I. No. 131 of 1979*

Statutory Authority	Section	Statutory Instrument
Medical Practitioners Act, No. 4 of 1978 (*Cont.*)	11	**Medical Council (Election of Members) Regulations, S.I. No. 197 of 1978**
	65	**Medical Council (Election of Members) Regulations, S.I. No. 197 of 1978**
	68	**Medical Practitioners (Termination of Agreement) Order, S.I. No. 158 of 1979**
Mental Treatment Act, No. 19 of 1945		*Mental Treatment (Regulations) Order [Vol. XXXVII p. 1121] S.R.& O. No. 202 of 1946*
		Mental Hospitals (Officers and Servants) Order [Vol. XXXVII p. 1045] S.R.& O. No. 203 of 1946
		Mental Hospitals (Officers and Servants) (Amendment) Order, S.I. No. 213 of 1948
		Mental Treatment Regulations, S.I. No. 99 of 1954
		Mental Treatment Regulations, S.I. No. 261 of 1961
	2	*Mental Treatment Act, 1945 (Date of Commencement) Order [Vol. XXXVII p. 1293] S.R.& O. No. 329 of 1946*
	8	*Mental Treatment (Registration of Private Institutions) Order [Vol. XXXVII p. 1313] S.R.& O. No. 373 of 1946*
		Mental Treatment (Amendment) Regulations, S.I. No. 17 of 1949
		Mental Treatment (Amendment) Regulations, S.I. No. 267 of 1958
		Mental Treatment (Amendment) Regulations, S.I. No. 68 of 1966
	17	*Mental Treatment (Election of Joint Boards) Order [Vol. XXXVII p. 1297] S.R.& O. No. 392 of 1946*
	17(a)	*Mental Treatment (Names of Joint Bodies) Order [Vol. XXXVII p. 1307] S.R.& O. No. 207 of 1946*
	40	**Mental Treatment (Amendment) Regulations, S.I. No. 17 of 1949**
	110	*Mental Treatment (Examination by Authorised Medical Officers) Order [Vol. XXXVII p. 1301] S.R.& O. No. 293 of 1946*
	115	*Mental Treatment (Registration of Private Institutions) Order [Vol. XXXVII p. 1313] S.R.& O. No. 373 of 1946*
	162	**Western Health Board (District Mental Hospitals) Order, S.I. No. 53 of 1975**
	165	**Western Health Board (District Mental Hospitals) Order, S.I. No. 53 of 1975**
	166	**Western Health Board (District Mental Hospitals) Order, S.I. No. 53 of 1975**
	184	**Western Health Board (District Mental Hospitals) Order, S.I. No. 53 of 1975**

Statutory Authority	Section	Statutory Instrument
Mental Treatment Act, No. 19 of 1945 (*Cont.*)	231A	*Mental Treatment (Amendment) Regulations, S.I. No. 267 of 1958*
		Mental Treatment (Amendment) Regulations, S.I. No. 68 of 1966
	234	*Mental Treatment Act, 1945 (Section 234) (Savings Certificates) Rules [Vol. XXXVII p. 1323] S.R.& O. No. 303 of 1947*
		Mental Treatment Act, 1945 (Section 234) (Post Office Savings Bank) Regulations [Vol. XXXVII p. 1317] S.R.& O. No. 304 of 1947
	281(2)	**Mental Treatment Act, 1945 (Adaptation of Enactments) Order [Vol. XXXVII p. 1287] S.R.& O. No. 216 of 1946**
Mental Treatment Act, No. 7 of 1961	43	*Mental Treatment Act, 1961 (Commencement) Order, S.I. No. 70 of 1961*
		Mental Treatment Act, 1961 (Commencement) (No.2) Order, S.I. No. 264 of 1961
Mercantile Marine Act, No. 29 of 1955	4	*Merchant Shipping (Fees) Order, 1954 (Amendment) Order, S.I. No. 200 of 1957*
		Merchant Shipping (Fees) Order, S.I. No. 266 of 1963
		Merchant Shipping (Fees) Order, S.I. No. 185 of 1968
		Merchant Shipping (Fees) Order, S.I. No. 42 of 1981
		Merchant Shipping (Fees) Order, S.I. No. 402 of 1983
	8	**Mercantile Marine (Ships' Names) Regulations, S.I. No. 119 of 1959**
	19	**Mercantile Marine Act, 1955 (Reciprocating States) (New Zealand and Pakistan) Order, S.I. No. 189 of 1968**
	19(1)	**Mercantile Marine Act, 1955 (Reciprocating State) (United Kingdom and Colonies) Order, S.I. No. 263 of 1955**
		Mercantile Marine Act, 1955 (Reciprocating States) (Union of South Africa, New Zealand and Pakistan) Order, S.I. No. 184 of 1958
		Mercantile Marine Act, 1955 (Reciprocating State) (Canada) Order, S.I. No. 299 of 1961
	62	**Mercantile Marine Act, 1955 (Section 62) Regulations, S.I. No. 77 of 1963**
	76	**Mercantile Marine Act, 1955 (Section 76) Regulations, S.I. No. 78 of 1963**
	91	*Merchant Shipping (Tonnage) Regulations, S.I. No. 213 of 1967*
		Merchant Shipping (Tonnage) Regulations, S.I. No. 369 of 1984

Statutory Authority	Section	Statutory Instrument
Merchandise Marks Act, No. 28 of 1887	8(2)	Merchandise Marks (Watch Case Marks and Declaration) Order [Vol. XVI p. 65] S.R.& O. No. 256 of 1935
Merchandise Marks Act, No. 48 of 1931	3	Merchandise Marks Commission (Proceedings) Regulations [Vol. XVI p. 73] S.R.& O. No. 49 of 1932
		Merchandise Marks Commission (Proceedings) Regulations, S.I. No. 157 of 1967
	8	Merchandise Marks (Restriction on Importation of Ceramic Ware) Order, S.I. No. 137 of 1969
		Merchandise Marks (Restriction on Importation of Vitreous Enamelled Ware) Order, S.I. No. 257 of 1970
		Merchandise Marks (Restriction on Sale of Imported Biscuits) Order, S.I. No. 258 of 1970
		Merchandise Marks (Restriction on Sale of Imported Men's and Boys' Outer Garments) Order, S.I. No. 262 of 1970
		Merchandise Marks (Restriction on Importation of Plumbers' Brass-foundry and Compression Couplings) Order, S.I. No. 263 of 1970
		Merchandise Marks (Restriction on Importation of Men's and Boys' Outer Garments) Order, S.I. No. 264 of 1970
		Merchandise Marks (Restriction on Importation of Electric Kettles and Aluminium Hollowware) Order, S.I. No. 282 of 1970
		Merchandise Marks (Restriction on Sale of Imported Hosiery) Order, S.I. No. 283 of 1970
		Merchandise Marks (Restriction on Importation of Hosiery) Order, S.I. No. 284 of 1970
		Merchandise Marks (Restriction on Importation of Carpets) Order, S.I. No. 130 of 1971
		Merchandise Marks (Restriction on Sale of Imported Carpets) Order, S.I. No. 131 of 1971
		Merchandise Marks (Restriction on Importation of Footwear) Order, S.I. No. 132 of 1971
		Merchandise Marks (Restriction on Importation of Knitted and Crocheted Clothing) Order, S.I. No. 133 of 1971
		Merchandise Marks (Restriction on Sale of Imported Knitted and Crocheted Clothing) Order, S.I. No. 134 of 1971
		Merchandise Marks (Restriction on Sale of Imported Jewellery) Order, S.I. No. 306 of 1971
		Merchandise Marks (Restriction on Importation of Jewellery) Order, S.I. No. 307 of 1971
		Merchandise Marks (Restriction on Importation of Lead Acid Accumulators) Order, S.I. No. 130 of 1972
	8(1)	Merchandise Marks (Restriction on Sale of New Imported Wooden Furniture) Order [Vol. XVI p. 93] S.R.& O. No. 400 of 1935

Statutory Authority	Section	Statutory Instrument
Merchandise Marks Act, No. 48 of 1931 (*Cont.*)	8(2)	*Merchandise Marks (Restriction on Importation of New Wooden Furniture) Order [Vol. XVI p. 101] S.R.& O. No. 401 of 1935*
	12	*Merchandise Marks (Restriction on Importation of Ceramic Ware) (Amendment) Order, S.I. No. 6 of 1970*
	12(1)	*Merchandise Marks (Restriction on Importation of Ceramic Ware) (Amendment) Order, S.I. No. 93 of 1972*
	20	*Merchandise Marks Act, 1931 (Section 20) (Exemption) Order [Vol. XXXVII p. 1329] S.R.& O. No. 225 of 1947*
		Merchandise Marks Act, 1931 (Section 20) (Air Mail Postage Stamps Exemption) Order, S.I. No. 61 of 1948
	20(2)	*Merchandise Marks Act, 1931 (Exemption No.1 under Section 20) Order [Vol. XVI p. 91] S.R.& O. No. 86 of 1932*
	30(1)	**Merchandise Marks Acts (Prosecutions by the Minister for Industry and Commerce) Regulations [Vol. XVI p. 87] S.R.& O. No. 74 of 1932**
	31(1)	**Merchandise Marks Acts (Prosecutions by the Minister for Agriculture) Regulations [Vol. XVI p. 83] S.R.& O. No. 59 of 1932**
Merchandise Marks Act, No. 10 of 1970	2	**Merchandise Marks (Prepacked Goods) (Marking and Quantities) Order, S.I. No. 28 of 1973**
		Merchandise Marks (Prepacked Goods) (Marking and Quantities) (Amendment) Order, S.I. No. 267 of 1973
		Merchandise Marks (Prepacked Goods) (Marking and Quantities) (Amendment) Order, S.I. No. 222 of 1979
		Merchandise Marks (Prepacked Goods) (Marking and Quantities) (Amendment) Order, S.I. No. 394 of 1981
		Merchandise Marks (Prepacked Goods) (Marking and Quantities) (Amendment) Order, S.I. No. 367 of 1983
		Merchandise Marks (Prepacked Goods) (Marking and Quantities) (Amendment) Order, S.I. No. 295 of 1985
		Merchandise Marks (Prepacked Goods) (Marking and Quantities) (Amendment) Order, S.I. No. 100 of 1986
	7(1)	*Merchandise Marks (Restriction of Importation of Ceramic Ware) (Amendment) Order, S.I. No. 204 of 1973*
Merchant Shipping Act, No. 60 of 1894	4	**Merchant Shipping (Safety Convention) (Countries of Application) Order, S.I. No. 343 of 1953**
	18	*Merchant Shipping (Direction-Finders) Rules, S.I. No. 342 of 1953*

Statutory Authority	Section	Statutory Instrument
Merchant Shipping Act, No. 60 of 1894 (*Cont.*)	369	**Merchant Shipping Act, 1894 (Exemption of Certain Trawlers from Section 413 (1)) Order, S.I. No. 124 of 1960**
	373(5)	**Merchant Shipping (Registry, Lettering and Numbering of Fishing Boats) (Regulations) Order [Vol. XVI p. 113] S.R.& O. No. 105 of 1927**
	418	*Collision Regulations (Ships and Seaplanes on the Water) Order, S.I. No. 399 of 1953*
		Collision Regulations (Ships and Seaplanes on the Water) Order, S.I. No. 185 of 1965
		Collision Regulations (Ships and Water Craft on the Water) Order, S.I. No. 229 of 1977
		Collision Regulations (Ships and Water Craft on the Water) Order, S.I. No. 29 of 1984
	424	*Collision Regulations (Ships and Seaplanes on the Water) Order, S.I. No. 185 of 1965*
		Collision Regulations (Ships and Seaplanes on the Water) (Amendment) Order, S.I. No. 18 of 1968
		Collision Regulations (Ships and Seaplanes on the Water) (Amendment) Order, S.I. No. 253 of 1975
		Collision Regulations (Ships and Water Craft on the Water) Order, S.I. No. 29 of 1984
	427	*Merchant Shipping (Life-Saving Appliances) Rules [Vol. XVI p. 145] S.R.& O. No. 155 of 1938*
		Merchant Shipping (Life-Saving Appliances) (Amendment) Rules [Vol. XXXVII p. 1333] S.R.& O. No. 267 of 1947
		Merchant Shipping (Life-saving and Fire Appliances) Rules, S.I. No. 341 of 1953
		Merchant Shipping (Life-saving Appliances) Rules, S.I. No. 29 of 1960
		Merchant Shipping (Life-saving Appliances) Rules, S.I. No. 100 of 1967
		Merchant Shipping (Fire Appliances) Rules, S.I. No. 101 of 1967
		Merchant Shipping (Musters) Rules, S.I. No. 106 of 1967
		Merchant Shipping (Pilot Ladders) Rules, S.I. No. 107 of 1967
		Merchant Shipping (Life-saving Appliances) (Amendment) Rules, S.I. No. 178 of 1972
		Merchant Shipping (Pilot Ladders) (Amendment) Rules, S.I. No. 223 of 1972
		Merchant Shipping (Life-saving Appliances) (Amendment) Rules, S.I. No. 216 of 1978
		Merchant Shipping (Life-saving Appliances) Rules, S.I. No. 302 of 1983
		Merchant Shipping (Fire Appliance) (Post-1980 Ships) Rules, S.I. No. 303 of 1983
		Merchant Shipping (Fire Appliances) (Amendment) Rules, S.I. No. 304 of 1983

Statutory Authority	Section	Statutory Instrument
Merchant Shipping Act, No. 60 of 1894 (*Cont.*)		**Merchant Shipping (Fire Appliances – Application to other Ships) Rules, S.I. No. 305 of 1983**
		Merchant Shipping (Cargo Ship Safety Equipment Survey) Rules, S.I. No. 312 of 1983
		Merchant Shipping (Pilot Ladders and Hoists) Rules, S.I. No. 314 of 1983
		Merchant Shipping (Musters) Rules, S.I. No. 316 of 1983
		Merchant Shipping (Certificates of Proficiency in Survival Craft) Regulations, S.I. No. 191 of 1984
		Merchant Shipping (Fire Appliances) (Amendment) Rules, S.I. No. 277 of 1985
		Merchant Shipping (Fire Appliances) (Post-1980 Ships) (Amendment) Rules, S.I. No. 278 of 1985
		Merchant Shipping (Fire Protection) Rules, S.I. No. 279 of 1985
	428	*Collision Regulations (Ships and Water Craft on the Water) Order, S.I. No. 229 of 1977*
	443(2)	*Merchant Shipping (Load Line) Regulations [Vol. XVI p. 141] S.R.& O. No. 84 of 1930*
	738	*Collision Regulations (Ships and Seaplanes on the Water) (Amendment) Order, S.I. No. 18 of 1968*
		Collision Regulations (Ships and Seaplanes on the Water) (Amendment) Order, S.I. No. 253 of 1975
Merchant Shipping Act, No. 48 of 1906	25(4)	**Merchant Shipping Act, 1906 (Variation of Seamen's Provisions) Order [Vol. XXI p. 29] S.R. & O. No. 432 of 1941**
	50	*Merchant Shipping (Ships' Names) Amendment Regulations [Vol. XVI p. 247] S.R.& O. No. 345 of 1936*
Merchant Shipping Act, No. 46 of 1947	7	**Merchant Shipping (Recognition of British Certificates of Competency) Order, S.I. No. 47 of 1949**
		Merchant Shipping (Recognition of Miscellaneous Foreign Certificates of Competency) Order, S.I. No. 223 of 1957
		Merchant Shipping (Recognition of Australian Certificates of Competency) Order, S.I. No. 195 of 1958
		Merchant Shipping (Recognition of Canadian Certificates of Competency) Order, S.I. No. 180 of 1963
		Merchant Shipping (Recognition of New Zealand Certificates of Competency) Order, S.I. No. 169 of 1964
		Merchant Shipping (Recognition of Miscellaneous Foreign Certificates of Competency) Order, 1957 (Amendment) Order, S.I. No. 188 of 1968
	9	*Merchant Shipping Act, 1947 (Section 9) Regulations, S.I. No. 38 of 1948*

Statutory Authority	Section	Statutory Instrument
Merchant Shipping Act, No. 46 of 1947 (*Cont.*)		*Merchant Shipping Act, 1947 (Section 9) Regulations, S.I. No. 270 of 1954*
	10	*Merchant Shipping Act, 1947 (Section 10) Regulations, S.I. No. 39 of 1948*
		Merchant Shipping Act, 1947 (Section 10) Regulations, S.I. No. 271 of 1954
	12	**Merchant Shipping (Certification of Ships Cooks) Regulations, S.I. No. 281 of 1949**
		Merchant Shipping (Crew Accommodation on Board Ship) Regulations, S.I. No. 95 of 1951
		Merchant Shipping (Certification of Able Seamen) Regulations, S.I. No. 109 of 1957
		Merchant Shipping (Certification of Able Seamen) Regulations, S.I. No. 91 of 1973
		Merchant Shipping (Certification and Watch-keeping) Regulations, S.I. No. 187 of 1984
		Merchant Shipping (Navigational Watch Ratings) Regulations, S.I. No. 188 of 1984
		Merchant Shipping (Engine Room Watch Ratings) Regulations, S.I. No. 189 of 1984
		Merchant Shipping (Tankers – Officers and Ratings) Regulations, S.I. No. 190 of 1984
		Merchant Shipping (Certificates of Proficiency in Survival Craft) Regulations, S.I. No. 191 of 1984
		Merchant Shipping (Medical Examinations) Regulations, S.I. No. 193 of 1984
	13(6)	*Merchant Shipping Act, 1947 (Section 13) Order, S.I. No. 51 of 1948*
	15	*Merchant Shipping Act, 1947 (Commencement) Order, S.I. No. 33 of 1948*
Merchant Shipping Act, No. 20 of 1966	3	*Merchant Shipping (Cargo Ship Construction and Survey) Rules, S.I. No. 99 of 1967*
		Merchant Shipping (Cargo Ship Survey Fees) Order, S.I. No. 150 of 1967
		Merchant Shipping (Cargo Ship Construction and Survey) Rules, S.I. No. 301 of 1983
		Merchant Shipping (Cargo Ship Construction and Survey) Rules, 1983 (Amendment) Rules, S.I. No. 275 of 1985
		Merchant Shipping (Cargo Ship Construction and Survey) Rules, S.I. No. 276 of 1985
	11(1)	**Merchant Shipping (Radio Installations Survey) Rules, S.I. No. 313 of 1983**
	17	*Merchant Shipping (Navigational Warnings) Rules, S.I. No. 108 of 1967*
		Merchant Shipping (Navigational Warnings) Rules, S.I. No. 310 of 1983
	20(3)	*Merchant Shipping (Safety Convention) (Transitional Provisions) Regulations, S.I. No. 110 of 1967*

Statutory Authority	Section	Statutory Instrument
Merchant Shipping Act, No. 20 of 1966 (*Cont.*)	21(2)	*Merchant Shipping Act, 1966 (Commencement) Order, S.I. No. 54 of 1967*
Merchant Shipping Act, No. 33 of 1981	3	**Merchant Shipping Act, 1952 (Section 15) (Amendment) Order, S.I. No. 271 of 1985**
	5	*Merchant Shipping (Carriage of Nautical Publications) Regulations, S.I. No. 311 of 1983*
		Merchant Shipping (Carriage of Nautical Publications) Regulations, S.I. No. 282 of 1985
	13	**Merchant Shipping (Safety Convention) (Transitional Provisions) Regulations, S.I. No. 319 of 1983**
	15(2)	*Merchant Shipping Act, 1981 (Commencement) Order, S.I. No. 15 of 1983*
Merchant Shipping Acts, 1894 to 1939,		*Merchant Shipping (Fees) Order [Vol. XXXI p. 9] S.R.& O. No. 36 of 1940*
Merchant Shipping Acts, 1894 to 1947,		*Merchant Shipping (Fees) Order, 1940 (Amendment) Order, S.I. No. 236 of 1949*
Merchant Shipping Acts, 1894 to 1952,		*Merchant Shipping (Fees) Order, S.I. No. 267 of 1954*
Merchant Shipping (Amendment) Act, No. 12 of 1939	4	*Merchant Shipping (Life-Saving Appliances) (Amendment) Rules [Vol. XXXVII p. 1333] S.R.& O. No. 267 of 1947*
	5	*Merchant Shipping (Fees) Order, S.I. No. 266 of 1963*
		Merchant Shipping (Fees) (Amendment) Order, S.I. No. 265 of 1966
		Merchant Shipping (Fees) Order, S.I. No. 185 of 1968
		Merchant Shipping (Fees) (Amendment) Order, S.I. No. 212 of 1969
		Merchant Shipping (Fees) Order, S.I. No. 42 of 1981
		Merchant Shipping (Fees) Order, S.I. No. 402 of 1983
Merchant Shipping (Certification of Seamen) Act, No. 37 of 1979	3	**Merchant Shipping (Certification of Marine Engineer Officers) Regulations, S.I. No. 12 of 1981**
		Merchant Shipping (Certification of Deck Officers) Regulations, S.I. No. 13 of 1981
		Merchant Shipping (Fees) Order, S.I. No. 402 of 1983
		Merchant Shipping (Certification and Watchkeeping) Regulations, S.I. No. 187 of 1984
		Merchant Shipping (Engine Room Watch Ratings) Regulations, S.I. No. 189 of 1984
	8	**Merchant Shipping (Certification of Marine Engineer Officers) Regulations, S.I. No. 12 of 1981**
		Merchant Shipping (Certification of Deck Officers) Regulations, S.I. No. 13 of 1981

Statutory Authority	Section	Statutory Instrument
Merchant Shipping (Certification of Seamen) Act, No. 37 of 1979 (*Cont.*)		**Merchant Shipping (Certification and Watchkeeping) Regulations, S.I. No. 187 of 1984**
		Merchant Shipping (Navigational Watch Ratings) Regulations, S.I. No. 188 of 1984
		Merchant Shipping (Tankers – Officers and Ratings) Regulations, S.I. No. 190 of 1984
		Merchant Shipping (Certificates of Proficiency in Survival Craft) Regulations, S.I. No. 191 of 1984
	15(4)	*Merchant Shipping (Certification of Seamen) Act, 1979 (Commencement) Order, S.I. No. 11 of 1981*
Merchant Shipping (Light Dues) Act, No. 18 of 1983	2	**Merchant Shipping (Light Dues) Order, S.I. No. 247 of 1983**
		Merchant Shipping (Light Dues) Order, S.I. No. 316 of 1986
Merchant Shipping (Load Lines) Act, No. 17 of 1968	1(6)	**Merchant Shipping (Load Lines) (Length of Ship) Regulations, S.I. No. 208 of 1968**
	3	**Merchant Shipping (Load Line) Rules, S.I. No. 205 of 1968**
		Merchant Shipping (Load Lines) (Amendment) Rules, S.I. No. 71 of 1971
	11	**Merchant Shipping (Load Lines) (Particulars of Depth of Loading) Regulations, S.I. No. 331 of 1974**
	19(2)	**Merchant Shipping (Load Lines) (Exemption) Order, S.I. No. 237 of 1968**
	25	**Merchant Shipping (Load Lines) (Deck Cargo) Regulations, S.I. No. 238 of 1968**
	26	*Merchant Shipping (Load Lines) (Fees) Regulations, S.I. No. 257 of 1968*
		Merchant Shipping (Fees) Order, S.I. No. 42 of 1981
		Merchant Shipping (Fees) Order, S.I. No. 402 of 1983
	29	**Merchant Shipping (Load Line) Rules, S.I. No. 205 of 1968**
		Merchant Shipping (Load Lines) (Amendment) Rules, S.I. No. 71 of 1971
	30(1)	*Merchant Shipping (International Convention on Load Lines) (Convention Countries) Order, S.I. No. 133 of 1969*
		Merchant Shipping (International Convention on Load Lines) (Convention Countries) Order, S.I. No. 10 of 1970
		Merchant Shipping (International Convention on Load Lines) (Convention Countries) Order, S.I. No. 282 of 1971
		Merchant Shipping (International Convention on Load Lines) (Convention Countries) Order, S.I. No. 308 of 1977

Statutory Authority	Section	Statutory Instrument
Merchant Shipping (Load Lines) Act, No. 17 of 1968 (*Cont.*)		**Merchant Shipping (International Convention on Load Lines) (Convention Countries) Order, S.I. No. 319 of 1986**
	31(2)	*Merchant Shipping (Load Lines) (Transitional Provisions) Regulations, S.I. No. 207 of 1968*
	32(4)	*Merchant Shipping (Load Lines) Act, 1968 (Commencement) Order, S.I. No. 206 of 1968*
Merchant Shipping (Safety and Load Line Conventions) Act, No. 42 of 1933		*Merchant Shipping (Wireless Telegraphy) Rules [Vol. XXXI p. 37] S.R.& O. No. 318 of 1939*
	15(3)	*Merchant Shipping (Forms of Safety Convention Certificates) Rules [Vol. XVI p. 327] S.R.& O. No. 141 of 1935*
	16(2)	*Merchant Shipping (Validity of Safety Convention and Load Line Convention Certificates) Regulations [Vol. XVI p. 253] S.R.& O. No. 175 of 1933*
	24(2)	*Merchant Shipping (Distress and Urgency Signals and Danger Warnings) Order [Vol. XVI p. 347] S.R.& O. No. 298 of 1936*
	25	*Merchant Shipping (Distress and Urgency Signals) Order [Vol. XVI p. 341] S.R.& O. No. 277 of 1936*
	25(2)	*Merchant Shipping (Distress and Urgency Signals and Danger Warnings) Order [Vol. XVI p. 347] S.R.& O. No. 298 of 1936*
	36	*Merchant Shipping (Safety and Load Line Conventions) Order [Vol. XVI p. 251] S.R.& O. No. 174 of 1933*
	37(2)(c)	*Merchant Shipping (Load Line Exemption) Order, (1933) [Vol. XVI p. 257] S.R.& O. No. 4 of 1934*
	39	*Load Line Rules [Vol. XVI p. 259] S.R.& O. No. 14 of 1935*
	44	*Load Line Rules [Vol. XVI p. 259] S.R.& O. No. 14 of 1935*
	45	*Load Line Rules [Vol. XVI p. 259] S.R.& O. No. 14 of 1935*
	47	*Merchant Shipping (Particulars of Depth of Loading, etc.) Regulations [Vol. XVI p. 357] S.R.& O. No. 322 of 1936*
	49(2)	*Merchant Shipping (Validity of Safety Convention and Load Line Convention Certificates) Regulations [Vol. XVI p. 253] S.R.& O. No. 175 of 1933*
	57	*Merchant Shipping (Timber Cargo) Regulations [Vol. XVI p. 331] S.R.& O. No. 189 of 1936*
	61	*Merchant Shipping (Safety and Load Line Conventions) Order [Vol. XVI p. 251] S.R.& O. No. 174 of 1933*

Statutory Authority	Section	Statutory Instrument
Merchant Shipping (Safety and Load Line Conventions) Act, No. 42 of 1933 *(Cont.)*	62	*Load Line Rules [Vol. XVI p. 259] S.R.& O. No. 14 of 1935*
Merchant Shipping (Safety Convention) Act, No. 29 of 1952	2	*Merchant Shipping (Safety Convention) Act, 1952 (Commencement) Order, S.I. No. 338 of 1953*
	4	**Merchant Shipping (Safety Convention) (Countries of Application) Order, S.I. No. 130 of 1954**
		Merchant Shipping (Safety Convention) (Countries of Application) Order, S.I. No. 197 of 1955
		Merchant Shipping (Safety Convention) (Countries of Application) Order, S.I. No. 224 of 1958
		Merchant Shipping (Safety Convention) (Countries of Application) Order, S.I. No. 10 of 1960
		Merchant Shipping (Safety Convention) (Countries of Application) Order, S.I. No. 167 of 1961
		Merchant Shipping (Safety Convention) (Countries of Application) Order, S.I. No. 239 of 1963
		Merchant Shipping (Safety Convention) (Countries of Application) Order, S.I. No. 161 of 1964
		Merchant Shipping (Countries of Acceptance) Order, S.I. No. 112 of 1967
		Merchant Shipping (Safety Convention) (Countries of Acceptance) Order, S.I. No. 34 of 1968
		Merchant Shipping (Safety Convention) (Countries of Acceptance) (No.2) Order, S.I. No. 94 of 1968
		Merchant Shipping (Safety Convention) (Countries of Acceptance) (No.3) Order, S.I. No. 178 of 1968
		Merchant Shipping (Safety Convention) (Countries of Acceptance) Order, S.I. No. 13 of 1969
		Merchant Shipping (Safety Convention) (Countries of Acceptance) (No.2) Order, S.I. No. 211 of 1969
		Merchant Shipping (Safety Convention) (Countries of Acceptance) Order, S.I. No. 179 of 1972
		Merchant Shipping (Safety Convention) (Countries of Acceptance) Order, S.I. No. 320 of 1983
		Merchant Shipping (Safety Convention) (Countries of Acceptance) Order, S.I. No. 272 of 1985
	5	*Merchant Shipping (Fees) Order, S.I. No. 266 of 1963*
		Merchant Shipping (Cargo Ship Survey Fees) Order, S.I. No. 150 of 1967
		Merchant Shipping (Fees) Order, S.I. No. 185 of 1968
		Merchant Shipping (Fees) Order, S.I. No. 42 of 1981
		Merchant Shipping (Fees) Order, S.I. No. 402 of 1983
	9	*Merchant Shipping (Safety Convention) (Transitional Provisions) Regulations, S.I. No. 344 of 1953*

Statutory Authority	Section	Statutory Instrument
Merchant Shipping (Safety Convention) Act, No. 29 of 1952 (*Cont.*)	10	*Merchant Shipping (Construction) Rules, S.I. No. 339 of 1953*
		Merchant Shipping (Passenger Ship Construction) Rules, S.I. No. 98 of 1967
		Merchant Shipping (Passenger Ship Construction) Rules, S.I. No. 300 of 1983
		Merchant Shipping (Passenger Ship Construction) (Amendment) Rules, S.I. No. 273 of 1985
		Merchant Shipping (Passenger Ship Construction and Survey) Rules, S.I. No. 274 of 1985
	15	*Merchant Shipping (Radio) Rules, S.I. No. 340 of 1953*
		Merchant Shipping (Radio) Rules, S.I. No. 103 of 1967
		Merchant Shipping (Radio Installations) Rules, S.I. No. 308 of 1983
		Merchant Shipping (Radio Installations Survey) Rules, S.I. No. 313 of 1983
		Merchant Shipping (Radio Installations) (Amendment) Rules, S.I. No. 192 of 1984
		Merchant Shipping (Radio Installations) (Amendment No.2) Rules, S.I. No. 281 of 1985
	18	*Merchant Shipping (Direction-finders) Rules, S.I. No. 104 of 1967*
		Merchant Shipping (Cargo Ship Safety Equipment Survey) Rules, S.I. No. 312 of 1983
	19	**Merchant Shipping (Cargo Ship Safety Equipment Survey) Rules, S.I. No. 312 of 1983**
	19(1A)	*Merchant Shipping (Navigational Equipment) Rules, S.I. No. 309 of 1983*
		Merchant Shipping (Automatic Pilot and Testing of Steering Gear) Rules, S.I. No. 317 of 1983
		Merchant Shipping (Navigational Equipment) Rules, S.I. No. 280 of 1985
	28(2)	**Merchant Shipping (Accepted Safety Convention Certificates) Regulations, S.I. No. 345 of 1953**
		Merchant Shipping (Accepted Safety Convention Certificates) Regulations, S.I. No. 111 of 1967
		Merchant Shipping (Accepted Safety Convention Certificates) Regulations, S.I. No. 318 of 1983
	33	*Merchant Shipping (Closing of Openings in Hulls and in Watertight Bulkheads) Rules, S.I. No. 346 of 1953*
		Merchant Shipping (Closing of Openings in Hulls and in Watertight Bulkheads) Rules, S.I. No. 109 of 1967
		Merchant Shipping (Closing of Openings in Hulls and in Watertight Bulkheads) Rules, S.I. No. 315 of 1983
	35	*Merchant Shipping (Navigational Warnings) Rules, S.I. No. 108 of 1967*

Statutory Authority	Section	Statutory Instrument
Merchant Shipping (Safety Convention) Act, No. 29 of 1952 (*Cont.*)		**Merchant Shipping (Navigational Warnings) Rules, S.I. No. 310 of 1983**
	36	*Signals of Distress (Ships and Seaplanes on the Water) Rules, S.I. No. 395 of 1953*
		Signals of Distress (Ships and Seaplanes on the Water) Order, S.I. No. 186 of 1965
		Signals of Distress (Ships and Water Craft on the Water) Rules, S.I. No. 234 of 1977
	38	*Merchant Shipping (Dangerous Goods) Rules, S.I. No. 347 of 1953*
		Merchant Shipping (Dangerous Goods) Rules, S.I. No. 105 of 1967
		Merchant Shipping (Dangerous Goods) (Amendment) Rules, S.I. No. 179 of 1968
		Merchant Shipping (Dangerous Goods) Rules, S.I. No. 306 of 1983
	39(3)	*Merchant Shipping (Grain) Rules, S.I. No. 348 of 1953*
		Merchant Shipping (Grain) Rules, S.I. No. 102 of 1967
		Merchant Shipping (Grain) Rules, S.I. No. 307 of 1983
	Sch. II par. 3	*Merchant Shipping (Safety Convention) (Transitional Provisions) Regulations, S.I. No. 344 of 1953*
Merchant Shipping (Spanish Civil War) Act, No. 9 of 1937	2(1)	*Merchant Shipping (Spanish Civil War) Act, 1937 (Commencement) Order [Vol. XVI p. 367] S.R.& O. No. 51 of 1937*
	2(2)	*Merchant Shipping (Spanish Civil War) Act, 1937 (Continuation) Order [Vol. XVI p. 399] S.R.& O. No. 245 of 1937*
		Merchant Shipping (Spanish Civil War) Act, 1937 (Continuation) Order [Vol. XVI p. 403] S.R.& O. No. 30 of 1938
		Merchant Shipping (Spanish Civil War) Act, 1937 (Continuation) (No.2) Order [Vol. XVI p. 407] S.R.& O. No. 226 of 1938
		Merchant Shipping (Spanish Civil War) Act, 1937 (Continuation) Order [Vol. XXXI p. 69] S.R.& O. No. 49 of 1939
	4(1)	*Merchant Shipping (Spanish Civil War) Order [Vol. XVI p. 371] S.R.& O. No. 76 of 1937*
		Merchant Shipping (Spanish Civil War) (No.2) Order [Vol. XVI p. 381] S.R.& O. No. 104 of 1937
	4(3)	*Merchant Shipping (Spanish Civil War) (No.3) Order [Vol. XVI p. 389] S.R.& O. No. 255 of 1937*
		Merchant Shipping (Spanish Civil War) (Revocation) Order [Vol. XXXI p. 73] S.R.& O. No. 102 of 1939

Statutory Authority	Section	Statutory Instrument
Merchant Shipping (Wireless Telegraphy) Act, No. 38 of 1919		*Merchant Shipping (Wireless Telegraphy) Rules [Vol. XXXI p. 37] S.R.& O. No. 318 of 1939*
	1(2)	*Merchant Shipping (Wireless Telegraphy) Rules Amendment Rules [Vol. XVI p. 411] S.R.& O. No. 28 of 1926*
Mergers, Take-overs and Monopolies (Control) Act, No. 17 of 1978	2(4)	**Mergers, Take-overs and Monopolies (Control) Act, 1978 (Section 2) Order, S.I. No. 230 of 1985**
	2(5)	**Mergers, Take-overs and Monopolies (Newspapers) Order, S.I. No. 17 of 1979**
	9	*Proposed Merger or Take-over Conditional Order, S.I. No. 331 of 1981*
		Proposed Merger or Take-over Conditional Order, S.I. No. 130 of 1982
		Proposed Merger or Take-over Conditional Order, 1981 (Revocation) Order, S.I. No. 317 of 1982
		Proposed Merger or Take-over Conditional Order, S.I. No. 217 of 1984
Midwives Act, No. 10 of 1944	1(2)	*Midwives Act, 1944 (Date of Commencement) Order [Vol. XXXVII p. 1343] S.R.& O. No. 294 of 1946*
	10(3)	*Central Midwives Board (Elections) Order, S.I. No. 174 of 1948*
Military Service Pensions Act, No. 48 of 1924	9	*Military Service Pensions Regulations (No.2) [Vol. XVI p. 425] S.R.& O. No. 54 of 1925*
		Military Service Pensions Regulations (No.1) [Vol. XVI p. 435] S.R.& O. No. 37 of 1926
		Military Service Pensions Regulations (No.1) [Vol. XVI p. 445] S.R.& O. No. 13 of 1927
		Military Service Pensions Regulations (No.1) 1927 (Amendment) Regulations, S.I. No. 119 of 1950
		Military Service Pensions Regulations (No.1) 1927 (Amendment) Regulations, S.I. No. 286 of 1951
		Military Service Pensions Regulations (No.1) 1927 (Amendment) Regulations, S.I. No. 117 of 1953
		Military Service Pensions Regulations (No.1) 1927 (Amendment) Regulations, S.I. No. 120 of 1954
Military Service Pensions Act, No. 43 of 1934		*Military Service Pensions Act, 1934 Regulations [Vol. XXXI p. 77] S.R.& O. No. 23 of 1939*
		Military Service Pensions Act, 1934 Regulations [Vol. XXXI p. 81] S.R.& O. No. 134 of 1940
		Military Service Pensions Act, 1934 Regulations [Vol. XXXI p. 85] S.R.& O. No. 46 of 1941
		Military Service Pensions Act, 1934 Regulations, S.I. No. 52 of 1950
		Military Service Pensions Act, 1934 (No.2) Regulations, S.I. No. 255 of 1950
		Military Service Pensions Act, 1934 Regulations, S.I. No. 285 of 1951

Statutory Authority	Section	Statutory Instrument
Military Service Pensions Act, No. 43 of 1934 (*Cont.*)	5(5)	*Referee (Military Service Pensions) Rules [Vol. XV. p. 517] S.R.& O. No. 354 of 1934*
		Referee (Military Service Pensions) Rules [Vol. XV. p. 523] S.R.& O. No. 70 of 1935
		Referee (Military Service Pensions) (No.2) Rule. [Vol. XVI p. 527] S.R.& O. No. 71 of 1935
		Referee (Military Service Pensions) (Amendment, Rules [Vol. XVI p. 531] S.R.& O. No. 61 of 1936
		Referee (Military Service Pensions) (Amendment, Rules [Vol. XVI p. 537] S.R.& O. No. 58 of 1938
		Referee (Military Service Pensions) Rules, S.I. No. 269 of 1950
	21	*Military Service Pensions Act, 1934 Regulations [Vol. XVI p. 455] S.R.& O. No. 355 of 1934*
		Military Service Pensions Act, 1934 Regulations [Vol. XVI p. 505] S.R.& O. No. 165 of 1936
		Military Service Pensions Act, 1934 Regulations [Vol. XVI p. 509] S.R.& O. No. 99 of 1937
		Military Service Pensions Act, 1934 Regulations [Vol. XVI p. 513] S.R.& O. No. 57 of 1938
		Military Service Pensions Act, 1934 Regulations, S.I. No. 116 of 1953
		Military Service Pensions Act, 1934 Regulations, S.I. No. 119 of 1954
Military Service Pensions (Amendment) Act, No. 29 of 1949	6(3)	**Board of Assessors (Military Service Pensions) Rules, S.I. No. 270 of 1950**
	11(3)	**Referee (Military Service Pensions) Rules, S.I. No. 269 of 1950**
Milk and Dairies Act, No. 22 of 1935	2	*Milk and Dairies Regulations, S.I. No. 274 of 1949*
		Milk and Dairies Act, 1935 (Date of Commencement) (No.1) Order [Vol. XVI p. 615] S.R.& O. No. 360 of 1936
		Milk and Dairies Act, 1935 (Date of Commencement) (No.2) Order [Vol. XVI p. 619] S.R.& O. No. 1 of 1938
		Milk and Dairies Act, 1935 (Date of Commencement) (No.3) Order [Vol. XVI p. 623] S.R.& O. No. 313 of 1938
	6	**Milk and Dairies (Bacteriological Examination) Regulations, (1936) [Vol. XVI p. 639] S.R.& O. No. 37 of 1937**
	15	**Registration of Dairymen Regulations [Vol. XVI p. 545] S.R.& O. No. 299 of 1936**
		Milk and Dairies (Prohibition Order) Regulations [Vol. XVI p. 561] S.R.& O. No. 300 of 1936
		Milk and Dairies (Milk Sampling) Regulations [Vol. XVI p. 647] S.R.& O. No. 38 of 1937
		Milk and Dairies (Special Designations) Regulations [Vol. XVI p. 687] S.R.& O. No. 148 of 1938
		Milk and Dairies (Application for Restriction on Sale) (Form of Notice) Regulations, S.I. No. 39 of 1950

Milk and Dairies (Special Designations) (Amendment) Regulations, S.I. No. 136 of 1955

Milk and Dairies (Fees for Bacteriological Examination) (Amendment) Regulations, S.I. No. 293 of 1956

Milk and Dairies (Fees for Bacteriological Examination) (Amendment) Regulations, S.I. No. 233 of 1962

Milk and Dairies (Fees for Bacteriological Examination) (Amendment) Regulations, S.I. No. 31 of 1982

15(1) **Milk and Dairies Act, 1935 (Appeals to District Court under Section 41) Regulations [Vol. XVI p. 627] S.R.& O. No. 363 of 1936**

15(2) **Milk and Dairies (Bacteriological Examination) Regulations, (1936) [Vol. XVI p. 639] S.R.& O. No. 37 of 1937**

31 **Milk and Dairies Regulations [Vol. XVI p. 567] S.R.& O. No. 310 of 1936**

Milk and Dairies (Special Designations) Regulations [Vol. XVI p. 687] S.R.& O. No. 148 of 1938

Milk and Dairies (Special Designations) (Amendment) Regulations [Vol. XXXI p. 95] S.R.& O. No. 20 of 1939

Milk and Dairies (Amendment) Regulations [Vol. XXXI p. 89] S.R.& O. No. 234 of 1941

Milk and Dairies Regulations, 1936 (Amendment) Regulations, S.I. No. 108 of 1953

Milk and Dairies Regulations, S.I. No. 138 of 1957

32 *Milk and Dairies (Sale of Heated Milk) (Restrictions) Regulations [Vol. XVI p. 683] S.R.& O. No. 147 of 1938*

33(1) **Milk and Dairies Act, 1935 (Sale of Milk in County Borough of Dublin) Order, S.I. No. 121 of 1962**

Milk and Dairies Act, 1935 (Sale of Milk in County Borough of Limerick) Order, S.I. No. 91 of 1968

Milk and Dairies Act, 1935 (Sale of Milk) Order, S.I. No. 134 of 1977

Milk and Dairies Act, 1935 (Sale of Milk in Urban District of Cobh) Order, S.I. No. 126 of 1978

Milk and Dairies Act, 1935 (Sale of Milk in South Cork County Health District) Order, S.I. No. 127 of 1978

Milk and Dairies Act, 1935 (Sale of Milk in Borough of Dun Laoghaire) Order, S.I. No. 128 of 1978

Milk and Dairies Act, 1935 (Sale of Milk in County Health District of Dublin) Order, S.I. No. 64 of 1979

Milk and Dairies Act, 1935 (Sale of Milk in Urban District of Enniscorthy) Order, S.I. No. 75 of 1979

Milk and Dairies Act, 1935 (Sale of Milk in County Health District of Wexford) Order, S.I. No. 149 of 1979

Milk and Dairies Act, 1935 (Sale of Milk in Urban District of Nenagh) Order, S.I. No. 319 of 1979

Statutory Authority	Section	Statutory Instrument
Milk and Dairies Act, No. 22 of 1935 (*Cont.*)		Milk and Dairies Act, 1935 (Sale of Milk in County Health District of Tipperary (North Riding) Order, S.I. No. 352 of 1979
		Milk and Dairies Act, 1935 (Sale of Milk in Urban District of Templemore) Order, S.I. No. 7 of 1980
		Milk and Dairies Act, 1935 (Sale of Milk in County Health District of North Cork) Order, S.I. No. 15 of 1980
		Milk and Dairies Act, 1935 (Sale of Milk in Borough of Drogheda) Order, S.I. No. 68 of 1980
		Milk and Dairies Act, 1935 (Sale of Milk in Borough of Galway) Order, S.I. No. 182 of 1980
		Milk and Dairies Act, 1935 (Sale of Milk in County Borough of Cork) Order, S.I. No. 249 of 1980
		Milk and Dairies Act, 1935 (Sale of Milk in Urban District of Tralee) Order, S.I. No. 74 of 1981
		Milk and Dairies Act, 1935 (Sale of Milk in Urban District of Ballinasloe) Order, S.I. No. 75 of 1981
		Milk and Dairies Act, 1935 (Sale of Milk in Urban District of Killarney) Order, S.I. No. 188 of 1981
		Milk and Dairies Act, 1935 (Sale of Milk in Urban District of Listowel) Order, S.I. No. 356 of 1981
		Milk and Dairies Act, 1935 (Sale of Milk in County Health District of Kildare) Order, S.I. No. 442 of 1981
		Milk and Dairies Act, 1935 (Sale of Milk in Borough of Wexford) Order, S.I. No. 143 of 1982
		Milk and Dairies Act, 1935 (Sale of Milk in Urban District of Youghal) Order, S.I. No. 144 of 1982
		Milk and Dairies Act, 1935 (Sale of Milk in County Health District of Kilkenny) Order, S.I. No. 193 of 1982
		Milk and Dairies Act, 1935 (Sale of Milk in Urban District of Monaghan) Order, S.I. No. 194 of 1982
		Milk and Dairies Act, 1935 (Sale of Milk in Urban District of Carrickmacross) Order, S.I. No. 195 of 1982
		Milk and Dairies Act, 1935 (Sale of Milk in County Health District of Tipperary South Riding) Order, S.I. No. 227 of 1982
		Milk and Dairies Act, 1935 (Sale of Milk) Order, S.I. No. 352 of 1982
		Milk and Dairies Act, 1935 (Sale of Milk in County Health District of Monaghan) Order, S.I. No. 25 of 1983
		Milk and Dairies Act, 1935 (Sale of Milk in Borough of Kilkenny) Order, S.I. No. 146 of 1983
		Milk and Dairies Act, 1935 (Sale of Milk in Urban District of Clones) Order, S.I. No. 147 of 1983
		Milk and Dairies Act, 1935 (Sale of Milk) Order, S.I. No. 78 of 1984
		Milk and Dairies Act, 1935 (Sale of Milk in Urban Districts of Birr and Carlow) Order, S.I. No. 124 of 1984
		Milk and Dairies Act, 1935 (Sale of Milk in Urban District of Kilrush) Order, S.I. No. 28 of 1985

<table>
<tr><td>Milk and Dairies Act, No. 22 of 1935 (Cont.)</td><td></td><td>Milk and Dairies Act, 1935 (Sale of Milk in Urban District of Ennis) Order, S.I. No. 156 of 1985</td></tr>
</table>

Statutory Authority	Section	Statutory Instrument
Milk and Dairies Act, No. 22 of 1935 (*Cont.*)		**Milk and Dairies Act, 1935 (Sale of Milk in Urban District of Ennis) Order, S.I. No. 156 of 1985**
		Milk and Dairies Act, 1935 (Sale of Milk in County Health District of Offaly) Order, S.I. No. 347 of 1986
	33(3)(a)	**Milk and Dairies (Application for Restriction on Sale) (Form of Notice) Regulations, S.I. No. 39 of 1950**
	34	**Milk and Dairies Regulations [Vol. XVI p. 567] S.R.& O. No. 310 of 1936**
		Milk and Dairies (Amendment) Regulations [Vol. XXXI p. 89] S.R.& O. No. 234 of 1941
		Milk and Dairies Regulations, 1936 (Amendment) Regulations, S.I. No. 162 of 1957
	35	**Milk and Dairies (Special Designations) Regulations [Vol. XVI p. 687] S.R.& O. No. 148 of 1938**
		Milk and Dairies (Special Designations) (Amendment) Regulations [Vol. XXXI p. 95] S.R.& O. No. 20 of 1939
		Milk and Dairies (Special Designations) (Amendment) Regulations, S.I. No. 136 of 1955
	36	**Milk and Dairies (Special Designations) Regulations [Vol. XVI p. 687] S.R.& O. No. 148 of 1938**
	38	**Milk and Dairies (General Designations) Regulations [Vol. XVI p. 679] S.R.& O. No. 146 of 1938**
	40(2)	**Milk and Dairies (Infectious Diseases) Order [Vol. XXXVII p. 1489] S.R.& O. No. 169 of 1947**
		Milk and Dairies (Infectious Diseases) Order, S.I. No. 321 of 1948
	41(3)	**Milk and Dairies (Prohibition Order) Regulations [Vol. XVI p. 561] S.R.& O. No. 300 of 1936**
	41(7)	**Milk and Dairies Act, 1935 (Appeals to District Court under Section 41) Regulations [Vol. XVI p. 627] S.R.& O. No. 363 of 1936**
	47(2)	*Milk and Dairies Act, 1935 (Application of Part VI) Order, S.I. No. 354 of 1948*
		Milk and Dairies Act, 1935 (Application of Part VI) Order, 1948 (Revocation) Order, S.I. No. 137 of 1957
	50	**Milk and Dairies (Fees for Bacteriological Examination) Regulations, (1936) [Vol. XVI p. 633] S.R.& O. No. 16 of 1937**
		Milk and Dairies (Fees for Bacteriological Examination) (Amendment) Regulations, S.I. No. 293 of 1956
		Milk and Dairies (Fees for Bacteriological Examination) (Amendment) Regulations, S.I. No. 233 of 1962
		Milk and Dairies (Fees for Bacteriological Examination) (Amendment) Regulations, S.I. No. 31 of 1982

Statutory Authority	Section	Statutory Instrument
Milk and Dairies Act, No. 22 of 1935 (Cont.)	52	**Milk and Dairies (Bacteriological Examination) Regulations, (1936) [Vol. XVI p. 639] S.R.& O. No. 37 of 1937**
	59	**Milk and Dairies (Bacteriological Examination) Regulations, (1936) [Vol. XVI p. 639] S.R.& O. No. 37 of 1937**
	Part II	**Registration of Dairymen Regulations [Vol. XVI p. 545] S.R.& O. No. 299 of 1936**
Milk and Dairies (Amendment) Act, 1956, No. 42 of 1956	1	*Milk and Dairies (Amendment) Act, 1956 (Commencement) Order, S.I. No. 135 of 1957*
		Milk and Dairies (Amendment) Act, 1956 (Commencement) (No.2) Order, S.I. No. 177 of 1957
		Milk and Dairies (Amendment) Act, 1956 (Commencement) (No.3) Order, S.I. No. 212 of 1957
	14	**Milk and Dairies (Temporary Special Designation Licence) Regulations, S.I. No. 161 of 1957**
Milk (Miscellaneous Provisions) Act, No. 24 of 1979	3	**Milk (Miscellaneous Provisions) Act, 1979 (Section 3) Regulations, S.I. No. 29 of 1982**
		Milk (Miscellaneous Provisions) Act, 1979 (Section 3) Regulations, S.I. No. 343 of 1982
	4	**Milk (Miscellaneous Provisions) Act, 1979 (Section 4) Regulations, S.I. No. 286 of 1979**
	10	**Milk (Miscellaneous Provisions) Act, 1979 (Section 4) Regulations, S.I. No. 286 of 1979**
Milk (Regulation of Supply and Price) Act, No. 43 of 1936		**Dublin District Milk Board (Registration and Records) Regulations [Vol. XVI p. 765] S.R.& O. No. 294 of 1936**
		Dublin District Milk Board (Levy) (Amendment) Regulations, S.I. No. 114 of 1950
		Cork District Milk Board (Levy) (Amendment) Regulations, S.I. No. 210 of 1951
	4	**Dublin District Milk Board (Levy) Regulations [Vol. XVI p. 821] S.R.& O. No. 317 of 1936**
		Cork District Milk Board (Levy) Regulations [Vol. XVI p. 907] S.R.& O. No. 124 of 1937
		Cork District Milk Board (Registration and Records) Regulations [Vol. XVI p. 855] S.R.& O. No. 155 of 1937
		Cork District Milk Board (Levy) (Amendment) Regulations [Vol. XVI p. 919] S.R.& O. No. 260 of 1937
		Dublin District Milk Board (Levy) (Amendment) Regulations [Vol. XVI p. 829] S.R.& O. No. 254 of 1938
		Dublin District Milk Board (Levy) (Amendment) Regulations [Vol. XXXI p. 221] S.R.& O. No. 126 of 1940

Statutory Authority	Section	Statutory Instrument

Milk (Regulation of Supply and Price) Act, No. 43 of 1936 (*Cont.*)

Cork District Milk Board (Levy) (Amendment) Regulations [Vol. XXXI p. 109] S.R.& O. No. 128 of 1940

Cork District Milk Board (Levy) (Amendment) (No.2) Regulations [Vol. XXXI p. 119] S.R.& O. No. 273 of 1940

Dublin District Milk Board (Levy) (Amendment) (No.2) Regulations [Vol. XXXI p. 227] S.R.& O. No. 274 of 1940

Cork District Milk Board (Levy) (Amendment) Regulations [Vol. XXXI p. 115] S.R.& O. No. 205 of 1941

Dublin Joint District (Form of Contract) Regulations [Vol. XXXI p. 347] S.R.& O. No. 470 of 1941

Dublin District Milk Board (Levy) (Amendment) Regulations, S.I. No. 54 of 1968

Dublin District Milk Board (Levy) (Amendment) Regulations, S.I. No. 2 of 1969

Cork District Milk Board (Levy) (Amendment) Regulations, S.I. No. 19 of 1970

Dublin District Milk Board (Levy) (Amendment) Regulations, S.I. No. 20 of 1970

Cork District Milk Board (Levy) (Amendment) (No.2) Regulations, S.I. No. 281 of 1970

Dublin District Milk Board (Levy) (Amendment) Regulations, S.I. No. 16 of 1971

Cork District Milk Board (Levy) (Amendment) Regulations, S.I. No. 106 of 1973

Dublin District Milk Board (Levy) (Amendment) Regulations, S.I. No. 107 of 1973

Dublin District Milk Board (Levy) (Amendment) Regulations, S.I. No. 314 of 1981

Cork District Milk Board (Levy) (Amendment) Regulations, S.I. No. 231 of 1985

6(1)   **Dublin District Milk Board Order [Vol. XVI p. 751] S.R.& O. No. 254 of 1936**

Cork District Milk Board Order [Vol. XVI p. 837] S.R.& O. No. 91 of 1937

6(3)   **Dublin District Milk Board (Amendment) Order [Vol. XVI p. 755] S.R.& O. No. 301 of 1936**

Dublin District Milk Board (Amendment) (No.2) Order [Vol. XVI p. 757] S.R.& O. No. 316 of 1936

Dublin District Milk Board (Amendment) Order [Vol. XVI p. 761] S.R.& O. No. 45 of 1937

Cork District Milk Board (Amendment) Order [Vol. XVI p. 847] S.R.& O. No. 199 of 1937

Cork District Milk Board (Amendment) (No.2) Order [Vol. XVI p. 851] S.R.& O. No. 286 of 1937

Dublin District Milk Board (Amendment) Order [Vol. XXXI p. 203] S.R.& O. No. 256 of 1940

Milk (Regulation of Supply and Price) Act, No. 43 of 1936 (*Cont.*)

Dublin District Milk Board (Amendment) Order [Vol. XXXI p. 213] S.R.& O. No. 424 of 1943

Dublin District Milk Board (Amendment) Order [Vol. XXXI p. 207] S.R.& O. No. 234 of 1944

Dublin District Milk Board (Amendment) Order [Vol. XXXVII p. 1369] S.R.& O. No. 207 of 1947

Dublin District Milk Board (Amendment) Order, S.I. No. 133 of 1948

Dublin District Milk Board (Amendment) (No.2) Order, S.I. No. 380 of 1948

Dublin District Milk Board (Amendment) Order, S.I. No. 57 of 1955

11(1) *Dublin District Milk Board (Election Day, 1937) Order [Vol. XVI p. 835] S.R.& O. No. 179 of 1937*

Cork District Milk Board (Election Day, 1938) Order [Vol. XVI p. 925] S.R.& O. No. 61 of 1938

11(2) *Dublin District Milk Board (Election Day, 1940) Order [Vol. XXXI p. 217] S.R.& O. No. 197 of 1940*

Cork District Milk Board (Election Day, 1941) Order [Vol. XXXI p. 101] S.R.& O. No. 381 of 1940

Cork District Milk Board (Election Day, 1944) Order [Vol. XXXI p. 105] S.R.& O. No. 40 of 1944

Dublin District Milk Board (Election Day, 1946) Order [Vol. XXXVII p. 1375] S.R.& O. No. 305 of 1946

Cork District Milk Board (Election Day, 1947) Order [Vol. XXXVII p. 1374] S.R.& O. No. 8 of 1947

Dublin District Milk Board (Election Day, 1949) Order, S.I. No. 219 of 1949

Cork District Milk Board (Election Day, 1950) Order, S.I. No. 158 of 1950

Dublin District Milk Board (Election Day, 1952) Order, S.I. No. 219 of 1952

Cork District Milk Board (Election Day, 1953) Order, S.I. No. 242 of 1953

Dublin District Milk Board (Election Day, 1955) Order, S.I. No. 153 of 1955

Cork District Milk Board (Election Day, 1956) Order, S.I. No. 121 of 1956

Dublin District Milk Board (Election Day, 1958) Order, S.I. No. 126 of 1958

Cork District Milk Board (Election Day, 1959) Order, S.I. No. 76 of 1959

Dublin District Milk Board (Election Day, 1961) Order, S.I. No. 133 of 1961

Cork District Milk Board (Election Day, 1962) Order, S.I. No. 57 of 1962

Statutory Authority	Section	Statutory Instrument
Milk (Regulation of Supply and Price) Act, No. 43 of 1936 (*Cont.*)		*Dublin District Milk Board (Election Day, 1964) Order, S.I. No. 224 of 1964*
		Cork District Milk Board (Election Day, 1965) Order, S.I. No. 104 of 1965
		Dublin District Milk Board (Election Day, 1967) Order, S.I. No. 238 of 1967
		Dublin District Milk Board (Election Day Order, 1967) (Revocation) Order, S.I. No. 275 of 1967
		Dublin District Milk Board (Election Day, 1968) Order, S.I. No. 119 of 1968
		Cork District Milk Board (Election Day, 1968) Order, S.I. No. 167 of 1968
		Dublin District Milk Board (Election Day, 1970) Order, S.I. No. 167 of 1970
		Cork District Milk Board (Election Day, 1971) Order, S.I. No. 72 of 1971
		Dublin District Milk Board (Election Day, 1973) Order, S.I. No. 248 of 1973
		Cork District Milk Board (Election Day, 1974) Order, S.I. No. 88 of 1974
		Dublin District Milk Board (Election Day, 1976) Order, S.I. No. 218 of 1976
		Cork District Milk Board (Election Day, 1977) Order, S.I. No. 148 of 1977
		Dublin District Milk Board (Election Day, 1979) Order, S.I. No. 331 of 1979
		Cork District Milk Board (Election Day, 1980) Order, S.I. No. 232 of 1980
		Dublin District Milk Board (Election Day, 1982) Order, S.I. No. 298 of 1982
		Cork District Milk Board (Election Day, 1983) Order, S.I. No. 282 of 1983
		Dublin District Milk Board (Election Day, 1985) Order, S.I. No. 327 of 1985
		Cork District Milk Board (Election Day, 1986) Order, S.I. No. 326 of 1986
	13	*Milk Boards (Elections) Regulations, S.I. No. 122 of 1956*
	13(2)	*Milk Boards (Elections) Regulations [Vol. XVI p. 659] S.R.& O. No. 178 of 1937*
		Milk Boards (Elections) Regulations, S.I. No. 239 of 1967
		Milk Boards (Elections) Regulations, S.I. No. 120 of 1968
	41	*Dublin District Milk Board (Levy) (Amendment) Regulations, S.I. No. 54 of 1968*
		Dublin District Milk Board (Levy) (Amendment) Regulations, S.I. No. 2 of 1969
		Cork District Milk Board (Levy) (Amendment) Regulations, S.I. No. 19 of 1970
		Dublin District Milk Board (Levy) (Amendment) Regulations, S.I. No. 20 of 1970

Milk (Regulation of Supply and
Price) Act, No. 43 of 1936 (*Cont.*)

**Cork District Milk Board (Levy) (Amendment)
(No.2) Regulations, S.I. No. 281 of 1970**

**Dublin District Milk Board (Levy) (Amendment)
Regulations, S.I. No. 16 of 1971**

**Cork District Milk Board (Levy) (Amendment)
Regulations, S.I. No. 231 of 1985**

43   *Dublin District Milk Board (Minimum Prices for
Milk) Order, S.I. No. 79 of 1960*

*Cork District Milk Board (Minimum Prices for
Milk) Order, S.I. No. 80 of 1960*

*Cork District Milk Board (Minimum Prices for
Milk) Order, S.I. No. 66 of 1963*

*Dublin District Milk Board (Minimum Prices for
Milk) Order, S.I. No. 67 of 1963*

*Cork District Milk Board (Minimum Prices for
Milk) Order, S.I. No. 93 of 1964*

*Dublin District Milk Board (Minimum Prices for
Milk) Order, S.I. No. 94 of 1964*

*Dublin District Milk Board (Minimum Prices for
Milk) Order, S.I. No. 138 of 1965*

*Cork District Milk Board (Minimum Prices for
Milk) Order, S.I. No. 139 of 1965*

*Dublin District Milk Board (Minimum Prices for
Milk) Order, S.I. No. 122 of 1966*

*Cork District Milk Board (Minimum Prices for
Milk) Order, S.I. No. 123 of 1966*

*Dublin District Milk Board (Minimum Prices for
Milk) Order, S.I. No. 94 of 1967*

*Cork District Milk Board (Minimum Prices for
Milk) Order, S.I. No. 95 of 1967*

*Cork District Milk Board (Minimum Prices for
Milk) Order, S.I. No. 17 of 1970*

*Dublin District Milk Board (Minimum Prices for
Milk) Order, S.I. No. 18 of 1970*

*Dublin District Milk Board (Minimum Prices for
Milk) (No.2) Order, S.I. No. 66 of 1970*

*Cork District Milk Board (Minimum Prices for
Milk) (No.2) Order, S.I. No. 67 of 1970*

*Dublin District Milk Board (Minimum Prices for
Milk) Order, S.I. No. 29 of 1971*

*Cork District Milk Board (Minimum Prices for
Milk) Order, S.I. No. 30 of 1971*

*Cork District Milk Board (Minimum Prices for
Milk) (No.2) Order, S.I. No. 155 of 1971*

*Dublin District Milk Board (Minimum Prices for
Milk) (No.2) Order, S.I. No. 156 of 1971*

*Dublin District Milk Board (Minimum Prices for
Milk) Order, S.I. No. 78 of 1972*

*Cork District Milk Board (Minimum Prices for
Milk) Order, S.I. No. 79 of 1972*

*Dublin District Milk Board (Minimum Prices for
Milk) Order, S.I. No. 85 of 1973*

Milk (Regulation of Supply and
Price) Act, No. 43 of 1936 (*Cont.*)

*Cork District Milk Board (Minimum Prices for
Milk) Order, S.I. No. 86 of 1973*

*Cork District Milk Board (Minimum Prices for
Milk) (No.2) Order, S.I. No. 156 of 1973*

*Dublin District Milk Board (Minimum Prices for
Milk) (No.2) Order, S.I. No. 157 of 1973*

*Cork District Milk Board (Minimum Prices for
Milk) Order, S.I. No. 62 of 1974*

*Dublin District Milk Board (Minimum Prices for
Milk) Order, S.I. No. 64 of 1974*

*Dublin District Milk Board (Minimum Prices for
Milk) (No.2) Order, S.I. No. 91 of 1974*

*Cork District Milk Board (Minimum Prices for
Milk) (No.2) Order, S.I. No. 92 of 1974*

*Cork District Milk Board (Minimum Prices for
Milk) (No.3) Order, S.I. No. 307 of 1974*

*Dublin District Milk Board (Minimum Prices for
Milk) (No.3) Order, S.I. No. 308 of 1974*

*Cork District Milk Board (Minimum Prices for
Milk) Order, S.I. No. 44 of 1975*

*Dublin District Milk Board (Minimum Prices for
Milk) Order, S.I. No. 45 of 1975*

*Cork District Milk Board (Minimum Prices for
Milk) (No.2) Order, S.I. No. 196 of 1975*

*Dublin District Milk Board (Minimum Prices for
Milk) (No.2) Order, S.I. No. 197 of 1975*

*Cork District Milk Board (Minimum Prices for
Milk) (No.3) Order, S.I. No. 218 of 1975*

*Dublin District Milk Board (Minimum Prices for
Milk) (No.3) Order, S.I. No. 219 of 1975*

*Dublin District Milk Board (Minimum Prices for
Milk) Order, S.I. No. 148 of 1976*

*Cork District Milk Board (Minimum Prices for
Milk) Order, S.I. No. 149 of 1976*

*Dublin District Milk Board (Minimum Prices for
Milk) Order, S.I. No. 17 of 1977*

*Cork District Milk Board (Minimum Prices for
Milk) Order, S.I. No. 18 of 1977*

*Cork District Milk Board (Minimum Prices for
Milk) (No.2) Order, S.I. No. 142 of 1977*

*Dublin District Milk Board (Minimum Prices for
Milk) (No.2) Order, S.I. No. 143 of 1977*

*Dublin District Milk Board (Minimum Prices for
Milk) Order, S.I. No. 183 of 1978*

*Cork District Milk Board (Minimum Prices for
Milk) Order, S.I. No. 184 of 1978*

*Cork District Milk Board (Minimum Prices for
Milk) Order, S.I. No. 96 of 1979*

*Dublin District Milk Board (Minimum Prices for
Milk) Order, S.I. No. 97 of 1979*

*Cork District Milk Board (Minimum Prices for
Milk) Order, S.I. No. 208 of 1980*

Statutory Authority	Section	Statutory Instrument
Milk (Regulation of Supply and Price) Act, No. 43 of 1936 (*Cont.*)		*Dublin District Milk Board (Minimum Prices for Milk) Order, S.I. No. 209 of 1980*
		Dublin District Milk Board (Minimum Prices for Milk) Order, S.I. No. 158 of 1981
		Cork District Milk Board (Minimum Prices for Milk) Order, S.I. No. 159 of 1981
		Dublin District Milk Board (Minimum Prices for Milk) Order, S.I. No. 165 of 1982
		Cork District Milk Board (Minimum Prices for Milk) Order, S.I. No. 166 of 1982
		Cork District Milk Board (Minimum Prices for Milk) Order, S.I. No. 142 of 1983
		Dublin District Milk Board (Minimum Prices for Milk) Order, S.I. No. 143 of 1983
		Cork District Milk Board (Minimum Prices for Milk) (No.2) Order, S.I. No. 164 of 1983
		Dublin District Milk Board (Minimum Prices for Milk) (No.2) Order, S.I. No. 165 of 1983
		Dublin District Milk Board (Minimum Prices for Milk) Order, S.I. No. 111 of 1984
		Cork District Milk Board (Minimum Prices for Milk) Order, S.I. No. 112 of 1984
		Dublin District Milk Board (Minimum Prices for Milk) Order, S.I. No. 184 of 1985
		Cork District Milk Board (Minimum Prices for Milk) Order, S.I. No. 185 of 1985
		Dublin District Milk Board (Minimum Prices for Milk) Order, S.I. No. 210 of 1986
		Cork District Milk Board (Minimum Prices for Milk) Order, S.I. No. 211 of 1986
	43(1)	*Dublin District Milk Board (Minimum Prices for Milk) Order [Vol. XVI p. 777] S.R.& O. No. 273 of 1936*
		Cork District Milk Board (Minimum Prices for Milk) Order [Vol. XVI p. 883] S.R.& O. No. 101 of 1937
		Dublin District Milk Board (Minimum Prices for Milk) Order [Vol. XVI p. 781] S.R.& O. No. 106 of 1937
		Dublin District Milk Board (Minimum Prices for Milk) (No.2) Order [Vol. XVI p. 787] S.R.& O. No. 238 of 1937
		Dublin District Milk Board (Minimum Prices for Milk) Order [Vol. XVI p. 793] S.R.& O. No. 123 of 1938
		Dublin District Milk Board (Minimum Prices for Milk (No.2) Order [Vol. XVI p. 809] S.R.& O. No. 215 of 1938
	43(1)(b) (i)	*Cork District Milk Board (Minimum Prices for Milk) (No.2) Order [Vol. XVI p. 889] S.R.& O. No. 259 of 1937*
		Cork District Milk Board (Minimum Prices for Milk) Order [Vol. XVI p. 895] S.R.& O. No. 124 of 1938

Statutory Authority	Section	Statutory Instrument
Milk (Regulation of Supply and Price) Act, No. 43 of 1936 (*Cont.*)		*Cork District Milk Board (Minimum Prices for Milk) (No.2) Order [Vol. XVI p. 901] S.R.& O. No. 249 of 1938*
		Cork District Milk Board (Minimum Prices for Milk) Order [Vol. XXXI p. 125] S.R.& O. No. 84 of 1939
		Dublin District Milk Board (Minimum Prices for Milk) Order [Vol. XXXI p. 233] S.R.& O. No. 91 of 1939
		Cork District Milk Board (Minimum Prices for Milk) (No.2) Order [Vol. XXXI p. 169] S.R.& O. No. 307 of 1939
		Dublin District Milk Board (Minimum Prices for Milk) Order [Vol. XXXI p. 249] S.R.& O. No. 125 of 1940
		Cork District Milk Board (Minimum Prices for Milk) Order [Vol. XXXI p. 131] S.R.& O. No. 127 of 1940
		Dublin District Milk Board (Minimum Prices for Milk) (No.2) Order [Vol. XXXI p. 321] S.R.& O. No. 253 of 1940
		Cork District Milk Board (Minimum Prices for Milk) (No.2) Order [Vol. XXXI p. 175] S.R.& O. No. 394 of 1940
		Cork District Milk Board (Minimum Prices for Milk) Order [Vol. XXXI p. 137] S.R.& O. No. 135 of 1941
		Dublin District Milk Board (Minimum Prices for Milk) Order [Vol. XXXI p. 257] S.R.& O. No. 193 of 1941
		Cork District Milk Board (Minimum Prices for Milk) (No.2) Order [Vol. XXXI p. 181] S.R.& O. No. 206 of 1941
		Dublin District Milk Board (Minimum Prices for Milk) Order [Vol. XXXI p. 273] S.R.& O. No. 131 of 1942
		Cork District Milk Board (Minimum Prices for Milk) Order [Vol. XXXI p. 143] S.R.& O. No. 132 of 1942
		Dublin District Milk Board (Minimum Prices for Milk) Order [Vol. XXXI p. 289] S.R.& O. No. 147 of 1943
		Cork District Milk Board (Minimum Prices for Milk) Order [Vol. XXXI p. 149] S.R.& O. No. 148 of 1943
		Dublin District Milk Board (Minimum Prices for Milk) Order [Vol. XXXI p. 305] S.R.& O. No. 96 of 1944
		Cork District Milk Board (Minimum Prices for Milk) Order [Vol. XXXI p. 157] S.R.& O. No. 97 of 1944
		Dublin District Milk Board (Minimum Prices for Milk) Order [Vol. XXXVII p. 1379] S.R.& O. No. 122 of 1947

Statutory Authority	Section	Statutory Instrument
Milk (Regulation of Supply and Price) Act, No. 43 of 1936 (*Cont.*)		*Cork District Milk Board (Minimum Prices for Milk) Order [Vol. XXXVII p. 1357] S.R.& O. No. 123 of 1947*
		Dublin District Milk Board (Minimum Prices for Milk) Order, S.I. No. 145 of 1948
		Cork District Milk Board (Minimum Prices for Milk) Order, S.I. No. 146 of 1948
		Dublin District Milk Board (Minimum Prices for Milk) Order, S.I. No. 108 of 1949
		Cork District Milk Board (Minimum Prices for Milk) Order, S.I. No. 109 of 1949
		Dublin District Milk Board (Minimum Prices for Milk) Order, S.I. No. 99 of 1950
		Dublin District Milk Board (Minimum Prices for Milk) Order, S.I. No. 98 of 1951
		Cork District Milk Board (Minimum Prices for Milk) Order, S.I. No. 99 of 1951
		Dublin District Milk Board (Minimum Prices for Milk) Order, S.I. No. 106 of 1952
	43(1)(b)(ii)	*Cork District Milk Board (Minimum Prices for Milk) Order, 1943 (Amendment) Order [Vol. XXXI p. 165] S.R.& O. No. 331 of 1943*
		Cork District Milk Board (Minimum Prices for Milk) Order, 1944 (Amendment) Order [Vol. XXXVII p. 1351] S.R.& O. No. 356 of 1946
		Cork District Milk Board (Minimum Prices for Milk) Order, 1947 (Amendment) Order [Vol. XXXVII p. 1363] S.R.& O. No. 351 of 1947
		Dublin District Milk Board (Minimum Prices for Milk) Order, 1947 (Amendment) Order [Vol. XXXVII p. 1395] S.R.& O. No. 352 of 1947
	47(4)	**Dublin Joint District (Form of Contract) Regulations [Vol. XXXI p. 347] S.R.& O. No. 470 of 1941**
	52	*Milk (Retail Price) (Dublin Sale District) Order [Vol. XXXI p. 401] S.R.& O. No. 201 of 1941*
		Milk (Retail Price) Order [Vol. XXXI p. 429] S.R.& O. No. 203 of 1941
		Milk (Retail Price) (Cork Sale District) Order [Vol. XXXI p. 367] S.R.& O. No. 204 of 1941
		Milk (Retail Price) (County Louth) Order [Vol. XXXI p. 371] S.R.& O. No. 446 of 1941
		Milk (Retail Price) Order, 1941 (Amendment) Order [Vol. XXXI p. 455] S.R.& O. No. 449 of 1941
		Milk (Retail Price) (County Louth) (No.2) Order [Vol. XXXI p. 375] S.R.& O. No. 558 of 1941
		Milk (Retail Price) (Dublin Sale District) Order [Vol. XXXI p. 407] S.R.& O. No. 148 of 1942
		Milk (Retail Price) Order [Vol. XXXI p. 433] S.R.& O. No. 149 of 1942
		Milk (Retail Price) (County Louth) Order [Vol. XXXI p. 379] S.R.& O. No. 150 of 1942
		Milk (Retail Price) (No.2) Order [Vol. XXXI p. 467] S.R.& O. No. 245 of 1942

Statutory Authority	Section	Statutory Instrument

Milk (Regulation of Supply and
Price) Act, No. 43 of 1936 (*Cont.*)

*Milk (Retail Price) (County Louth) (No.2) Order
[Vol. XXXI p. 395] S.R.& O. No. 246 of 1942*

*Milk (Retail Price) Order [Vol. XXXI p. 437]
S.R.& O. No. 136 of 1943*

*Milk (Retail Price) Order, 1943 Amendment (No.1)
Order [Vol. XXXI p. 459] S.R.& O. No. 323 of
1943*

*Milk (Retail Price) Order, 1943 Amendment (No.2)
Order [Vol. XXXI p. 463] S.R.& O. No. 87 of
1944*

*Milk (Retail Price) (Dublin Sale District) Order
[Vol. XXXI p. 413] S.R.& O. No. 115 of 1944*

*Milk (Retail Price) (County Louth) Order [Vol.
XXXI p. 383] S.R.& O. No. 116 of 1944*

*Milk (Retail Price) Order [Vol. XXXI p. 443]
S.R.& O. No. 117 of 1944*

*Milk (Retail Price) (County Louth) Order [Vol.
XXXI p. 389] S.R.& O. No. 69 of 1945*

*Milk (Retail Price) Order [Vol. XXXI p. 449]
S.R.& O. No. 70 of 1945*

*Milk (Retail Price) (Dublin Sale District) Order
[Vol. XXXI p. 419] S.R.& O. No. 71 of 1945*

*Milk (Retail Price) (Dublin Sale District) Order,
1945 (Amendment) (No.1) Order [Vol. XXXI
p. 425] S.R.& O. No. 232 of 1945*

*Milk (Retail Price) (Dublin Sale District) Order
[Vol. XXXVII p. 1465] S.R.& O. No. 103 of
1946*

*Milk (Retail Price) (County Louth) Order [Vol.
XXXVII p. 1447] S.R.& O. No. 104 of 1946*

*Milk (Retail Price) Order [Vol. XXXVII p. 1411]
S.R.& O. No. 105 of 1946*

*Milk (Retail Price) (Cork Sale District) Order [Vol.
XXXVII p. 1429] S.R.& O. No. 362 of 1946*

*Milk (Retail Price) Order [Vol. XXXVII p. 1417]
S.R.& O. No. 127 of 1947*

*Milk (Retail Price) (County Louth) Order [Vol.
XXXVII p. 1453] S.R.& O. No. 128 of 1947*

*Milk (Retail Price) (Cork Sale District) Order [Vol.
XXXVII p. 1435] S.R.& O. No. 129 of 1947*

*Milk (Retail Price) (Dublin Sale District) Order
[Vol. XXXVII p. 1471] S.R.& O. No. 130 of
1947*

*Milk (Retail Price) (Cork Sale District) (No.2)
Order [Vol. XXXVII p. 1441] S.R.& O. No. 353
of 1947*

*Milk (Retail Price) (County Louth) (No.2) Order
[Vol. XXXVII p. 1459] S.R.& O. No. 354 of
1947*

*Milk (Retail Price) (No.2) Order [Vol. XXXVII
p. 1423] S.R.& O. No. 355 of 1947*

*Milk (Retail Price) (Dublin Sale District) (No.2)
Order [Vol. XXXVII p. 1479] S.R.& O. No. 356
of 1947*

Statutory Authority	Section	Statutory Instrument
Milk (Regulation of Supply and Price) Act, No. 43 of 1936 (*Cont.*)		*Milk (Retail Price) Order, S.I. No. 148 of 1948*
		Milk (Retail Price) (County Louth) Order, S.I. No. 149 of 1948
		Milk (Retail Price) (Cork Sale District) Order, S.I. No. 150 of 1948
		Milk (Retail Price) (Dublin Sale District) Order, S.I. No. 151 of 1948
		Milk (Retail Price) Order, S.I. No. 117 of 1949
		Milk (Retail Price) (Dublin Sale District) Order, S.I. No. 118 of 1949
		Milk (Retail Price) (County Louth) Order, S.I. No. 120 of 1949
		Milk (Retail Price) (Cork Sale District) Order, S.I. No. 121 of 1949
		Milk (Retail Price) Order, S.I. No. 104 of 1950
		Milk (Retail Price) (County Louth) Order, S.I. No. 105 of 1950
		Milk (Retail Price) (Dublin Sale District) Order, S.I. No. 106 of 1950
		Milk (Retail Price) (Cork Sale District) Order, S.I. No. 107 of 1950
		Milk (Retail Price) (Cork Sale District) Order, S.I. No. 12 of 1951
		Milk (Retail Price) Order, S.I. No. 101 of 1951
		Milk (Retail Price) (Dublin Sale District) Order, S.I. No. 103 of 1951
		Milk (Retail Price) (Cork Sale District) (No.2) Order, S.I. No. 104 of 1951
		Milk (Retail Price) (County Louth) Order, S.I. No. 105 of 1951
		Milk (Retail Price) (Dublin Sale District) (No.2) Order, S.I. No. 211 of 1951
		Milk (Retail Price) (County Louth) (No.2) Order, S.I. No. 212 of 1951
		Milk (Retail Price) (Cork Sale District) (No.3) Order, S.I. No. 213 of 1951
		Milk (Retail Price) (No.2) Order, S.I. No. 214 of 1951
		Milk (Retail Price) Orders (Revocation) Order, S.I. No. 10 of 1952
		Milk (Retail Price) (Cork Sale District) Order, S.I. No. 108 of 1952
		Milk (Retail Price) (Dublin Sale District) Order, S.I. No. 109 of 1952
		Milk (Retail Price) (Dublin Sale District) (No.2) Order, S.I. No. 349 of 1952
		Milk (Retail Price) (Dublin Sale District) (No.2) Order, 1952 (Amendment) Order, S.I. No. 114 of 1953
		Milk (Retail Price) (Dublin Sale District) Order, S.I. No. 140 of 1953
		Milk (Retail Price) (Cork Sale District) Order, S.I. No. 141 of 1953

Statutory Authority	Section	Statutory Instrument
Milk (Regulation of Supply and Price) Act, No. 43 of 1936 (*Cont.*)		*Milk (Retail Price) (Cork Sale District) Order, S.I. No. 81 of 1954*
		Milk (Retail Price) (Dublin Sale District) Order, S.I. No. 82 of 1954
		Milk (Retail Price) (Cork Sale District) Order, S.I. No. 72 of 1955
		Milk (Retail Price) (Dublin Sale District) Order, S.I. No. 73 of 1955
		Milk (Retail Price) (Cork Sale District) Order, 1955 (Amendment) Order, S.I. No. 245 of 1955
		Milk (Retail Price) (Cork Sale District) Order, S.I. No. 99 of 1956
		Milk (Retail Price) (Dublin Sale District) Order, S.I. No. 100 of 1956
		Milk (Retail Price) (Dublin Sale District) Order, S.I. No. 81 of 1957
		Milk (Retail Price) (Cork Sale District) Order, S.I. No. 82 of 1957
		Milk (Retail Price) (Dublin Sale District) Order, S.I. No. 103 of 1958
		Milk (Retail Price) (Cork Sale District) Order, S.I. No. 104 of 1958
		Milk (Retail Price) (Dublin Sale District) Order, S.I. No. 72 of 1959
		Milk (Retail Price) (Cork Sale District) Order, S.I. No. 73 of 1959
		Milk (Retail Price) (Dublin Sale District) Order, S.I. No. 86 of 1960
		Milk (Retail Price) (Dublin Sale District) Order, S.I. No. 80 of 1961
		Milk (Retail Price) (Dublin Sale District) (Amendment) Order, S.I. No. 233 of 1961
		Milk (Retail Price) (Dublin Sale District) Order, S.I. No. 25 of 1962
		Milk (Retail Price) (Dublin Sale District) Order, S.I. No. 27 of 1963
		Milk (Retail Price) (Dublin Sale District) (No.2) Order, S.I. No. 64 of 1963
		Milk (Retail Price) (Dublin Sale District) (No.3) Order, S.I. No. 143 of 1963
		Milk (Retail Price) (Dublin Sale District) Order, S.I. No. 91 of 1964
		Milk (Retail Price) (Dublin Sale District) Order, S.I. No. 82 of 1965
		Milk (Retail Price) (Dublin Sale District) Order, S.I. No. 85 of 1966
		Milk (Retail Price) (Dublin Sale District) (No.2) Order, S.I. No. 170 of 1966
		Milk (Retail Price) (Dublin Sale District) Order, S.I. No. 76 of 1967
		Milk (Retail Price) (Dublin Sale District) Order, S.I. No. 70 of 1968

Statutory Authority	Section	Statutory Instrument
Milk (Regulation of Supply and Price) Act, No. 43 of 1936 (*Cont.*)		*Milk (Retail Price) (Dublin Sale District) (No.2) Order, S.I. No. 87 of 1968*
		Milk (Retail Price) (Dublin Sale District) Order, S.I. No. 33 of 1969
		Milk (Retail Price) (Dublin Sale District) (No.2) Order, S.I. No. 69 of 1969
		Milk (Retail Price) (Dublin Sale District) Order, S.I. No. 59 of 1970
		Milk (Retail Price) (Dublin Sale District) (No.2) Order, S.I. No. 255 of 1970
		Milk (Retail Price) (Dublin Sale District) Order, S.I. No. 147 of 1971
		Milk (Retail Prices) (Dublin Sale District) (No.2) Order, S.I. No. 244 of 1971
		Milk (Retail Price) (Dublin Sale District) Order, S.I. No. 6 of 1972
		Milk (Retail Price) (Dublin Sale District) (No.2) Order, S.I. No. 55 of 1972
		Milk (Retail Price) (Dublin Sale District) (No.3) Order, S.I. No. 113 of 1972
	52(2)(e)	*Milk (Retail Price) (Dublin Sale District) (Amendment) Order, S.I. No. 127 of 1959*
Milk (Regulation of Supply and Price) Acts, 1936 and 1941,		**Dublin District Milk Board Regulations [Vol. XXXI p. 333] S.R.& O. No. 526 of 1941**
		Cork District Milk Board Regulations [Vol. XXXI p. 187] S.R.& O. No. 543 of 1941
		Milk Boards (Elections) Regulations [Vol. XXXI p. 361] S.R.& O. No. 38 of 1944
		Milk Boards (Elections) Regulations [Vol. XXXVII p. 1485] S.R.& O. No. 306 of 1946
Milk (Regulation of Supply and Price) Acts, 1936 to 1952,		**Cork District Milk Board (Levy) (Amendment) Regulations, S.I. No. 137 of 1953**
Milk (Regulation of Supply and Price) (Amendment) Act, No. 11 of 1941	22	*Dublin District Milk Board (Minimum Prices for Milk) Order, S.I. No. 79 of 1960*
		Cork District Milk Board (Minimum Prices for Milk) Order, S.I. No. 80 of 1960
		Cork District Milk Board (Minimum Prices for Milk) Order, S.I. No. 66 of 1963
		Dublin District Milk Board (Minimum Prices for Milk) Order, S.I. No. 67 of 1963
		Cork District Milk Board (Minimum Prices for Milk) Order, S.I. No. 93 of 1964
		Dublin District Milk Board (Minimum Prices for Milk) Order, S.I. No. 94 of 1964
		Dublin District Milk Board (Minimum Prices for Milk) Order, S.I. No. 138 of 1965
		Cork District Milk Board (Minimum Prices for Milk) Order, S.I. No. 139 of 1965
		Dublin District Milk Board (Minimum Prices for Milk) Order, S.I. No. 122 of 1966

Statutory Authority	Section	Statutory Instrument
Milk (Regulation of Supply and Price) (Amendment) Act, No. 11 of 1941 (*Cont.*)		*Cork District Milk Board (Minimum Prices for Milk) Order, S.I. No. 123 of 1966*
		Dublin District Milk Board (Minimum Prices for Milk) Order, S.I. No. 94 of 1967
		Cork District Milk Board (Minimum Prices for Milk) Order, S.I. No. 95 of 1967
		Cork District Milk Board (Minimum Prices for Milk) Order, S.I. No. 17 of 1970
		Dublin District Milk Board (Minimum Prices for Milk) Order, S.I. No. 18 of 1970
		Dublin District Milk Board (Minimum Prices for Milk) (No.2) Order, S.I. No. 66 of 1970
		Cork District Milk Board (Minimum Prices for Milk) (No.2) Order, S.I. No. 67 of 1970
		Dublin District Milk Board (Minimum Prices for Milk) Order, S.I. No. 29 of 1971
		Cork District Milk Board (Minimum Prices for Milk) Order, S.I. No. 30 of 1971
		Cork District Milk Board (Minimum Prices for Milk) (No.2) Order, S.I. No. 155 of 1971
		Dublin District Milk Board (Minimum Prices for Milk) (No.2) Order, S.I. No. 156 of 1971
		Dublin District Milk Board (Minimum Prices for Milk) Order, S.I. No. 78 of 1972
		Cork District Milk Board (Minimum Prices for Milk) Order, S.I. No. 79 of 1972
		Dublin District Milk Board (Minimum Prices for Milk) Order, S.I. No. 85 of 1973
		Cork District Milk Board (Minimum Prices for Milk) Order, S.I. No. 86 of 1973
		Cork District Milk Board (Minimum Prices for Milk) (No.2) Order, S.I. No. 156 of 1973
		Cork District Milk Board (Minimum Prices for Milk) Order, S.I. No. 62 of 1974
		Dublin District Milk Board (Minimum Prices for Milk) Order, S.I. No. 64 of 1974
		Dublin District Milk Board (Minimum Prices for Milk) (No.2) Order, S.I. No. 91 of 1974
		Cork District Milk Board (Minimum Prices for Milk) (No.2) Order, S.I. No. 92 of 1974
		Cork District Milk Board (Minimum Prices for Milk) (No.3) Order, S.I. No. 307 of 1974
		Cork District Milk Board (Minimum Prices for Milk) Order, S.I. No. 44 of 1975
		Dublin District Milk Board (Minimum Prices for Milk) Order, S.I. No. 45 of 1975
		Cork District Milk Board (Minimum Prices for Milk) (No.2) Order, S.I. No. 196 of 1975
		Dublin District Milk Board (Minimum Prices for Milk) (No.2) Order, S.I. No. 197 of 1975
		Cork District Milk Board (Minimum Prices for Milk) (No.3) Order, S.I. No. 218 of 1975

Statutory Authority	Section	Statutory Instrument
Milk (Regulation of Supply and Price) (Amendment) Act, No. 11 of 1941 (*Cont.*)		*Dublin District Milk Board (Minimum Prices for Milk) (No.3) Order, S.I. No. 219 of 1975*
		Dublin District Milk Board (Minimum Prices for Milk) Order, S.I. No. 148 of 1976
		Cork District Milk Board (Minimum Prices for Milk) Order, S.I. No. 149 of 1976
		Dublin District Milk Board (Minimum Prices for Milk) Order, S.I. No. 17 of 1977
		Cork District Milk Board (Minimum Prices for Milk) Order, S.I. No. 18 of 1977
		Cork District Milk Board (Minimum Prices for Milk) (No.2) Order, S.I. No. 142 of 1977
		Dublin District Milk Board (Minimum Prices for Milk) (No.2) Order, S.I. No. 143 of 1977
		Dublin District Milk Board (Minimum Prices for Milk) Order, S.I. No. 183 of 1978
		Cork District Milk Board (Minimum Prices for Milk) Order, S.I. No. 184 of 1978
		Cork District Milk Board (Minimum Prices for Milk) Order, S.I. No. 96 of 1979
		Dublin District Milk Board (Minimum Prices for Milk) Order, S.I. No. 97 of 1979
		Cork District Milk Board (Minimum Prices for Milk) Order, S.I. No. 208 of 1980
		Dublin District Milk Board (Minimum Prices for Milk) Order, S.I. No. 209 of 1980
		Dublin District Milk Board (Minimum Prices for Milk) Order, S.I. No. 158 of 1981
		Cork District Milk Board (Minimum Prices for Milk) Order, S.I. No. 159 of 1981
		Dublin District Milk Board (Minimum Prices for Milk) Order, S.I. No. 165 of 1982
		Cork District Milk Board (Minimum Prices for Milk) Order, S.I. No. 166 of 1982
		Cork District Milk Board (Minimum Prices for Milk) Order, S.I. No. 142 of 1983
		Dublin District Milk Board (Minimum Prices for Milk) Order, S.I. No. 143 of 1983
		Cork District Milk Board (Minimum Prices for Milk) (No.2) Order, S.I. No. 164 of 1983
		Dublin District Milk Board (Minimum Prices for Milk) Order, S.I. No. 111 of 1984
		Cork District Milk Board (Minimum Prices for Milk) Order, S.I. No. 112 of 1984
		Dublin District Milk Board (Minimum Prices for Milk) Order, S.I. No. 184 of 1985
		Cork District Milk Board (Minimum Prices for Milk) Order, S.I. No. 185 of 1985
		Dublin District Milk Board (Minimum Prices for Milk) Order, S.I. No. 210 of 1986
		Cork District Milk Board (Minimum Prices for Milk) Order, S.I. No. 211 of 1986

Statutory Authority	Section	Statutory Instrument
Milk (Regulation of Supply and Price) (Amendment) Act, No. 11 of 1941 (*Cont.*)	22(1)	*Dublin District Milk Board (Minimum Prices for Milk) (No.2) Order, S.I. No. 171 of 1951*
		Cork District Milk Board (Minimum Prices for Milk) (No.2) Order, S.I. No. 172 of 1951
		Cork District Milk Board (Minimum Prices for Milk) Order, S.I. No. 107 of 1952
		Dublin District Milk Board (Minimum Prices for Milk) Order, S.I. No. 109 of 1953
		Cork District Milk Board (Minimum Prices for Milk) Order, S.I. No. 121 of 1953
	28(1)	**Dublin Joint District (Commencement of Provision for Yearly Contracts) Order [Vol. XXXI p. 473] S.R.& O. No. 398 of 1941**
	41	*Cork District Milk Board (Levy) (Amendment) Regulations, S.I. No. 106 of 1973*
		Dublin District Milk Board (Levy) (Amendment) Regulations, S.I. No. 314 of 1981
Milk (Regulation of Supply and Price) (Amendment) Act, No. 9 of 1952	2	*Milk (Regulation of Supply and Price) (Amendment) Act, 1952 (Commencement) Order, S.I. No. 272 of 1952*
Minerals Development Act, No. 31 of 1940		*Minerals Development Regulations [Vol. XXXI p. 477] S.R.& O. No. 28 of 1941*
	80	**Minerals Development Regulations, S.I. No. 340 of 1979**
Minerals Development Act, No. 12 of 1979	9	**Minerals Development Regulations, S.I. No. 340 of 1979**
Minerals Exploration and Development Company Act, No. 13 of 1941	23(2)	**Minerals Exploration and Development (Application for Compensation) Regulations [Vol. XXXI p. 497] S.R.& O. No. 397 of 1941**
Mines and Minerals Act, No. 54 of 1931	7	*Mines and Minerals Act (Mining Board Regulations) Order [Vol. XVI p. 977] S.R.& O. No. 29 of 1933*
	54	*Mines and Minerals Act Regulations [Vol. XVI p. 929] S.R.& O. No. 82 of 1932*
		Mines and Minerals Act Regulations [Vol. XVI p. 955] S.R.& O. No. 28 of 1933
		Mines and Minerals Act (Fees) Regulations [Vol. XVI p. 965] S.R.& O. No. 30 of 1933
Mines and Quarries Act, No. 7 of 1965	2	*Mines and Quarries Act, 1965 (Section 151) (Commencement) Order, S.I. No. 183 of 1966*
		Mines and Quarries Act, 1965 (Commencement) Order, S.I. No. 73 of 1970
	11	**Mines (Managers and Officials) Regulations, S.I. No. 74 of 1970**
		Mines and Quarries (References) Rules, S.I. No. 75 of 1970

Statutory Authority	Section	Statutory Instrument
Mines and Quarries Act, No. 7 of 1965 (*Cont.*)		**Quarries (Explosives) Regulations, S.I. No. 237 of 1971**
		Mines (Locomotives) Regulations, S.I. No. 238 of 1971
		Quarries (Electricity) Regulations, S.I. No. 50 of 1972
		Mines (Electricity) Regulations, S.I. No. 51 of 1972
		Mines (Explosives) Regulations, S.I. No. 123 of 1972
		Mines (Fire and Rescue) Regulations, S.I. No. 226 of 1972
		Quarries (General) Regulations, S.I. No. 146 of 1974
	15	**Mines (Managers and Officials) Regulations, S.I. No. 74 of 1970**
	17	**Mines (Managers and Officials) Regulations, S.I. No. 74 of 1970**
	18	**Mines (Managers and Officials) Regulations, S.I. No. 74 of 1970**
		Mines (Surveyors and Plans) Regulations, S.I. No. 78 of 1970
		Mines (Locomotives) Regulations, S.I. No. 238 of 1971
		Mines (Electricity) Regulations, S.I. No. 51 of 1972
		Mines (Explosives) Regulations, S.I. No. 123 of 1972
		Mines (Mechanically Propelled Vehicles) Regulations, S.I. No. 153 of 1973
		Mines (General) Regulations, S.I. No. 331 of 1975
	21	**Mines (Surveyors and Plans) Regulations, S.I. No. 78 of 1970**
	29	**Quarries (Explosives) Regulations, S.I. No. 237 of 1971**
		Quarries (Electricity) Regulations, S.I. No. 50 of 1972
		Quarries (General) Regulations, S.I. No. 146 of 1974
	41	**Mines (Mechanically Propelled Vehicles) Regulations, S.I. No. 153 of 1973**
		Mines (General) Regulations, S.I. No. 331 of 1975
	46	**Mines (General) Regulations, S.I. No. 331 of 1975**
	48	**Tynagh Mine (Winding) Regulations, S.I. No. 330 of 1975**
		Tara Mine (Winding) Regulations, S.I. No. 14 of 1977
	65	**Mines (Electricity) (Amendment) Regulations, S.I. No. 125 of 1979**
		Quarries (Electricity) (Amendment) Regulations, S.I. No. 126 of 1979
	65(1)	**Mines (Electricity) Regulations, S.I. No. 51 of 1972**
	66	**Mines (Explosives) Regulations, S.I. No. 123 of 1972**
	68	**Mines (Fire and Rescue) Regulations, S.I. No. 226 of 1972**

Statutory Authority	Section	Statutory Instrument
Mines and Quarries Act, No. 7 of 1965 (*Cont.*)	70	**Mines (General) Regulations, S.I. No. 331 of 1975**
	76	**Mines (Locomotives) Regulations, S.I. No. 238 of 1971**
		Mines (Mechanically Propelled Vehicles) Regulations, S.I. No. 153 of 1973
		Quarries (General) Regulations, S.I. No. 146 of 1974
		Mines (General) Regulations, S.I. No. 331 of 1975
	77	**Quarries (General) Regulations, S.I. No. 146 of 1974**
		Mines (General) Regulations, S.I. No. 331 of 1975
	78	**Quarries (General) Regulations, S.I. No. 146 of 1974**
	79	**Quarries (General) Regulations, S.I. No. 146 of 1974**
		Mines (General) Regulations, S.I. No. 331 of 1975
	85	**Quarries (General) Regulations, S.I. No. 146 of 1974**
		Mines (General) Regulations, S.I. No. 331 of 1975
	90	**Quarries (General) Regulations, S.I. No. 146 of 1974**
		Mines (General) Regulations, S.I. No. 331 of 1975
	96	**Quarries (Electricity) Regulations, S.I. No. 50 of 1972**
		Quarries (General) Regulations, S.I. No. 146 of 1974
	96(1)(b)	**Quarries (Explosives) Regulations, S.I. No. 237 of 1971**
		Quarries (Explosives) (Amendment) Regulations, S.I. No. 1 of 1976
	97	**Quarries (General) Regulations, S.I. No. 146 of 1974**
	98	**Mines and Quarries (Notification of Dangerous Occurrences) Order, S.I. No. 76 of 1970**
	100(1)	**Mines and Quarries (Notification of Diseases) Order, S.I. No. 61 of 1971**
	112	**Quarries (General) Regulations, S.I. No. 146 of 1974**
		Mines (General) Regulations, S.I. No. 331 of 1975
		Mines (General) (Amendment) Regulations, S.I. No. 279 of 1979
	122	**Quarries (General) Regulations, S.I. No. 146 of 1974**
	127	**Mines (Managers and Officials) Regulations, S.I. No. 74 of 1970**
		Mines and Quarries (Notification of Accidents) Regulations, S.I. No. 77 of 1970
		Mines (Surveyors and Plans) Regulations, S.I. No. 78 of 1970
		Quarries (Explosives) Regulations, S.I. No. 237 of 1971
		Mines (Locomotives) Regulations, S.I. No. 238 of 1971
		Quarries (Electricity) Regulations, S.I. No. 50 of 1972
		Mines (Electricity) Regulations, S.I. No. 51 of 1972
		Mines (Explosives) Regulations, S.I. No. 123 of 1972

Statutory Authority	Section	Statutory Instrument
Mines and Quarries Act, No. 7 of 1965 (*Cont.*)		**Mines (Fire and Rescue) Regulations, S.I. No. 226 of 1972**
		Mines (Mechanically Propelled Vehicles) Regulations, S.I. No. 153 of 1973
		Mines and Quarries (General Register) Regulations, S.I. No. 97 of 1974
		Quarries (General) Regulations, S.I. No. 146 of 1974
		Tynagh Mine (Winding) Regulations, S.I. No. 330 of 1975
		Mines (General) Regulations, S.I. No. 331 of 1975
		Quarries (Explosives) (Amendment) Regulations, S.I. No. 1 of 1976
		Tara Mine (Winding) Regulations, S.I. No. 14 of 1977
		Mines (Electricity) (Amendment) Regulations, S.I. No. 125 of 1979
		Quarries (Electricity) (Amendment) Regulations, S.I. No. 126 of 1979
		Mines (General) (Amendment) Regulations, S.I. No. 279 of 1979
	146	**Quarries (Explosives) Regulations, S.I. No. 237 of 1971**
		Mines (Electricity) Regulations, S.I. No. 51 of 1972
		Mines (Explosives) Regulations, S.I. No. 123 of 1972
		Mines (General) Regulations, S.I. No. 331 of 1975
	146(8)(b)	**Mines and Quarries (References) Rules, S.I. No. 75 of 1970**
	147	*Mines (Employment of Women) (Exemption) Regulations, S.I. No. 356 of 1978*
		Mines (Employment of Women) (Exemption) Regulations, S.I. No. 369 of 1983
	150(2)	*Mines and Quarries Act, 1965 (Birth Certificates) Regulations, S.I. No. 110 of 1970*
		Registration of Births, Deaths and Marriages (Reduced Fees) Regulations, S.I. No. 46 of 1982
		Registration of Births, Deaths and Marriages (Reduced Fees) (Amendment) Regulations, S.I. No. 148 of 1983
		Registration of Births, Deaths and Marriages (Reduced Fees) (Amendment) Regulations, S.I. No. 359 of 1984
	Sch. II par. 8	**Mines and Quarries (Inquiries) (Draft Regulations) Rules, S.I. No. 219 of 1971**
Minimum Notice and Terms of Employment Act, No. 4 of 1973	2	*Minimum Notice and Terms of Employment Act, 1973 (Commencement) Order, S.I. No. 242 of 1973*
	11	**Minimum Notice and Terms of Employment (Reference of Disputes) Regulations, S.I. No. 243 of 1973**
	14	**Minimum Notice and Terms of Employment (Reference of Disputes) Regulations, S.I. No. 243 of 1973**

Statutory Authority	Section	Statutory Instrument
Minister for Supplies (Transfer of Functions) Act, No. 21 of 1945	2	*Minister for Supplies (Transfer of Functions) Act, 1945 (Appointed Day) Order [Vol. XXXI p. 623] S.R.& O. No. 171 of 1945*
Ministerial and Parliamentary Offices Act, No. 38 of 1938	8A	**Ministerial and Parliamentary Offices (Salaries) Order, S.I. No. 103 of 1977**
		Members of the Oireachtas (Allowances) Order, S.I. No. 167 of 1977
		Members of the Oireachtas and Ministerial and Parliamentary Offices (Allowances and Salaries) Order, S.I. No. 129 of 1978
		Parliamentary Offices (Allowances) Order, S.I. No. 365 of 1978
		Members of the Oireachtas and Ministerial and Parliamentary Offices (Allowances and Salaries) Order, S.I. No. 299 of 1979
		Members of the Oireachtas and Ministerial and Parliamentary Offices (Allowances and Salaries) Order, S.I. No. 46 of 1980
		Members of the Oireachtas and Ministerial and Parliamentary Offices (Allowances and Salaries) (No.2) Order, S.I. No. 369 of 1980
		Parliamentary Offices (Allowances) Order, S.I. No. 137 of 1981
		Members of the Oireachtas and Ministerial and Parliamentary Offices (Allowances and Salaries) Order, S.I. No. 386 of 1981
Ministers and Secretaries Act, No. 16 of 1924		**Boards of Guardians (Minor Officers) Order [Vol. XVIII p. 441] S.R.& O. No. 38 of 1928**
		Postal Order (Inland) Amendment (No.4) Regulations, S.I. No. 294 of 1951
	2(3)	*Civil Service (Stabilisation of Bonus) Regulations [Vol. XXVIII p. 203] S.R.& O. No. 177 of 1940*
		Civil Service (Stabilisation of Bonus) (Amendment) Regulations [Vol. XXVIII p. 211] S.R.& O. No. 258 of 1942
		Civil Service (Emergency Bonus) Regulations [Vol. XXVIII p. 175] S.R.& O. No. 1 of 1943
		Civil Service (Emergency Bonus) Regulations [Vol. XXVIII p. 185] S.R.& O. No. 43 of 1944
		Civil Service (Bonus) Regulations [Vol. XXVIII p. 169] S.R.& O. No. 364 of 1944
		Civil Service (Emergency Bonus) Regulations [Vol. XXVIII p. 195] S.R.& O. No. 345 of 1945
	9	**Saorstat Eireann Forestry Commissioners (Transfer of Functions) Order [Vol. XVI p. 1073] S.R.& O. No. 69 of 1927**
		Royal Hospital Kilmainham (Dissolution of Governors and Revocation of Charters) Order, S.I. No. 260 of 1955
	9(1)	**Intermediate Education Commissioners (Transfer of Functions) Order [Vol. XVI p. 1015] S.R.& O. No. 17 of 1925**

Statutory Authority	Section	Statutory Instrument

Ministers and Secretaries Act,
No. 16 of 1924 (*Cont.*)

Commissioners of Education (Ireland) (Transfer of Functions) Order [Vol. XVI p. 1043] S.R.& O. No. 22 of 1925

General Prisons Board (Transfer of Functions) Order [Vol. XVI p. 1119] S.R.& O. No. 79 of 1928

Irish Insurance Commissioners (Transfer of Functions) Order [Vol. XVI p. 1139] S.R.& O. No. 1 of 1933

National Education Commissioners (Transfer of Functions) Order [Vol. XVI p. 1171] S.R.& O. No. 264 of 1935

9(2)

Department of Agriculture and Technical Instruction (Fisheries) (Transfer of Functions) Order [Vol. XVI p. 1059] S.R.& O. No. 5 of 1927

Department of Agriculture and Technical Instruction (Education) (Transfer of Functions) Order [Vol. XVI p. 1085] S.R.& O. No. 101 of 1927

Irish Land Commission (Fisheries and Rural Industries) (Transfer of Functions) Order [Vol. XVI p. 1107] S.R.& O. No. 60 of 1928

10

Endowment Fund (First Apportionment and Winding-up) Order [Vol. XVI p. 995] S.R.& O. No. 12 of 1925

Endowment Fund (Second Apportionment and Winding-up) Order [Vol. XVI p. 1003] S.R.& O. No. 13 of 1925

Development Fund (Winding-up) Order [Vol. XVI p. 1009] S.R.& O. No. 15 of 1925

Intermediate Education Commissioners (Statutory Funds Winding-up) Order [Vol. XVI p. 1023] S.R.& O. No. 18 of 1925

Endowment Fund (Final Winding-up) Order [Vol. XVI p. 1029] S.R.& O. No. 20 of 1925

Department of Agriculture and Technical Instruction (Winding-up of a Fund for Congested Districts) Order [Vol. XVI p. 1037] S.R.& O. No. 21 of 1925

Forestry Fund (Winding-up) Order [Vol. XVI p. 1079] S.R.& O. No. 70 of 1927

General Cattle Diseases Fund (Cattle Pleuro-pneumonia Account) (Winding-up) Order [Vol. XVI p. 1101] S.R.& O. No. 11 of 1928

National School Teachers' Pension Fund (Winding-up) Order [Vol. XVI p. 1159] S.R.& O. No. 43 of 1934

Sea Fisheries Fund (Winding-up) Order [Vol. XXXI p. 531] S.R.& O. No. 276 of 1941

11

Minister for Local Government and Public Health (Agency) Order [Vol. XXXI p. 519] S.R.& O. No. 115 of 1939

Minister for Local Government and Public Health (Agency) (No.2) Order [Vol. XXXI p. 525] S.R.& O. No. 132 of 1939

Ministers and Secretaries Act, No. 16 of 1924 (*Cont.*)		*Minister for Finance (Agency) Order [Vol. XXXI p. 507] S.R.& O. No. 184 of 1939*
		Minister for Industry and Commerce (Agency) Order [Vol. XXXI p. 513] S.R.& O. No. 194 of 1939
	12(2)	*Registrar of Friendly Societies (Re-distribution of Public Services) Order [Vol. XVI p. 1055] S.R.& O. No. 12 of 1926*
		Irish Land Commission (Re-distribution of Public Services) Order [Vol. XVI p. 1067] S.R.& O. No. 55 of 1927
		Geological Survey (Re-distribution of Public Services) Order [Vol. XVI p. 1095] S.R.& O. No. 4 of 1928
		Forestry (Re-distribution of Public Services) Order [Vol. XVI p. 1145] S.R.& O. No. 158 of 1933
		Fisheries (Re-distribution of Public Services) Order [Vol. XVI p. 1151] S.R.& O. No. 40 of 1934
		Forestry (Re-distribution of Public Services) Consequential Order [Vol. XVI p. 1165] S.R.& O. No. 117 of 1934
		Meteorological Services (Re-distribution of Public Services) Order [Vol. XVI p. 1177] S.R.& O. No. 276 of 1936
Ministers and Secretaries Act, No. 6 of 1928	4(2)	*Fisheries (Re-distribution of Public Services) Order [Vol. XVI p. 1151] S.R.& O. No. 40 of 1934*
		Ministers and Secretaries (Amendment) Act, 1928 (Commencement) Order [Vol. XVI p. 1183] S.R.& O. No. 49 of 1928
Ministers and Secretaries Act, No. 38 of 1946	2(1)	*Ministers and Secretaries (Amendment) Act, 1946 (Section 2) (Commencement) Order [Vol. XXXVII p. 1599] S.R.& O. No. 14 of 1947*
	3(1)	*Ministers and Secretaries (Amendment) Act, 1946 (Section 3) (Commencement) Order [Vol. XXXVII p. 1603] S.R.& O. No. 15 of 1947*
Ministers and Secretaries (Amendment) Act, No. 36 of 1939	6	**Wheat and Flour (Transfer of Ministerial Functions) Order, S.I. No. 284 of 1951**
	6(1)	**Minister for Supplies (Transfer of Functions under Control of Prices Act, 1937) Order [Vol. XXXI p. 555] S.R.& O. No. 142 of 1940**
		Minister for Supplies (Transfer of Functions under Section 52 of the Milk (Regulation of Supply and Price) Act, 1936) Order [Vol. XXXI p. 561] S.R.& O. No. 29 of 1941
		Transfer of Administration and Functions (Turf) Order [Vol. XXXI p. 569] S.R.& O. No. 285 of 1941
		Minister for Supplies (Transfer of Functions under the Scrap Iron (Control of Export) Act, 1938) Order [Vol. XXXI p. 565] S.R.& O. No. 369 of 1941
		Transfer of Administration and Functions (Turf) Order [Vol. XXXI p. 575] S.R.& O. No. 54 of 1943

Ministers and Secretaries
(Amendment) Act, No. 36 of 1939
(*Cont.*)

Allocation of Administration (Genealogical Office) Order [Vol. XXXI p. 537] S.R.& O. No. 267 of 1943

Departments and Ministers (Alteration of Irish Names and Titles) Order [Vol. XXXI p. 541] S.R.& O. No. 218 of 1944

Local Government and Public Health (Alteration of Name of Department and Title of Minister) Order [Vol. XXXVII p. 1553] S.R.& O. No. 16 of 1947

Social Welfare (Transfer of Departmental Administration and Ministerial Functions) (No.1) Order [Vol. XXXVII p. 1563] S.R.& O. No. 18 of 1947

Minister for Local Government (Transfer of Functions under subsection (3) of Section 16 of the Barrow Drainage Act, 1927) Order [Vol. XXXVII p. 1549] S.R.& O. No. 41 of 1947

Health (Transfer of Departmental Administration and Ministerial Functions) Order [Vol. XXXVII p. 1515] S.R.& O. No. 58 of 1947

Workmen's Compensation Act, 1934 (Transfer of Ministerial Functions) Order [Vol. XXXVII p. 1595] S.R.& O. No. 161 of 1947

National Health Insurance (Termination of Sanatorium Benefit and Abolition of Insurance Committees) Regulations, 1934 (Transfer of Ministerial Functions) Order [Vol. XXXVII p. 1559] S.R. & O. No. 288 of 1947

Social Welfare (Transfer of Departmental Administration and Ministerial Functions) (No.2) Order [Vol. XXXVII p. 1573] S.R.& O. No. 329 of 1947

Agriculture and Health (Transfer of Departmental Administration and Ministerial Functions) Order [Vol. XXXVII p. 1493] S.R.& O. No. 417 of 1947

Agriculture (Transfer of Departmental Administration and Ministerial Functions) (Wheat and Flour Subsidy) Order, S.I. No. 78 of 1949

Statistics Acts, 1926 and 1946 (Transfer of Ministerial Functions) Order, S.I. No. 142 of 1949

Health (Transfer of Departmental Administration and Ministerial Functions) Order, S.I. No. 256 of 1949

Health (Transfer of Departmental Administration and Ministerial Functions) Order, S.I. No. 138 of 1950

Riarachan a Dhaileadh (Oifig na Gaeltachta agus na gCeantar gCung) (An tOrdu chun) S.I. No. 125 of 1954

Gaeltachta (Riarachan Roinne agus Feidhmeanna Aire d'Aistriu) (Ordu na) S.I. No. 257 of 1956

Gaeltachta (Riarachan Roinne agus Feidhmeanna Aire d'Aistriu) (Uimh.2) (Ordu na) S.I. No. 304 of 1956

Gaeltachta (Riarachan Roinne agus Feidhmeanna Aire d'Aistriu) (Ordu na) S.I. No. 16 of 1957

<table>
<tr><td>Ministers and Secretaries
(Amendment) Act, No. 36 of 1939
(Cont.)</td><td></td><td>

Fisheries (Transfer of Departmental Administration and Ministerial Functions) Order, S.I. No. 67 of 1957

Education (Transfer of Departmental Administration and Ministerial Functions) Order, S.I. No. 193 of 1957

Game Preservation Act, 1930 (Transfer of Departmental Administration and Ministerial Functions) Order, S.I. No. 186 of 1958

Health (Transfer of Departmental Administration and Ministerial Functions) Order, S.I. No. 202 of 1958

Transport, Fuel and Power (Transfer of Departmental Administration and Ministerial Functions) Order, S.I. No. 125 of 1959

Transport, Fuel and Power (Transfer of Departmental Administration and Ministerial Functions) Order, S.I. No. 198 of 1960

Transport, Fuel and Power (Transfer of Departmental Administration and Ministerial Functions) Order, S.I. No. 62 of 1961

Wheat (Transfer of Ministerial Functions) Order, S.I. No. 158 of 1961

Transport, Fuel and Power (Transfer of Departmental Administration and Ministerial Functions) (No.2) Order, S.I. No. 246 of 1961

Wild Birds Protection Act, 1930 (Transfer of Departmental Administration and Ministerial Functions) Order, S.I. No. 259 of 1961

Fisheries (Transfer of Departmental Administration and Ministerial Functions) Order, S.I. No. 83 of 1965

Transport, Fuel and Power (Transfer of Departmental Administration and Ministerial Functions) Order, S.I. No. 125 of 1965

Agriculture (Alteration of Name of Department and Title of Minister) Order, S.I. No. 146 of 1965

Labour (Transfer of Departmental Administration and Ministerial Functions) Order, S.I. No. 164 of 1966

Labour (Transfer of Departmental Administration and Ministerial Functions) (No.2) Order, S.I. No. 214 of 1966

Labour (Transfer of Departmental Administration and Ministerial Functions) Order, S.I. No. 175 of 1967

Hire-Purchase (Transfer of Departmental Administration and Ministerial Functions) Order, S.I. No. 158 of 1968

Wheat Milling (Transfer of Departmental Administration and Ministerial Functions) S.I. No. 217 of 1968

Shannon Free Airport Development Company Limited (Transfer of Departmental Administration and Ministerial Functions) Order, S.I. No. 219 of 1968

</td></tr>
</table>

Ministers and Secretaries (Amendment) Act, No. 36 of 1939 (*Cont.*)		External Affairs (Alteration of Name of Department and Title of Minister) Order, S.I. No. 158 of 1971
		Health (Transfer of Departmental Administration and Ministerial Functions) Order, S.I. No. 83 of 1972
		Social Welfare (Transfer of Departmental Administration and Ministerial Functions) Order, S.I. No. 183 of 1972
		Air-Raid Precautions Services (Compensation for Personal Injuries) (Transfer of Departmental Administration and Ministerial Functions) Order, S.I. No. 78 of 1973
		Public Service (Transfer of Departmental Administration and Ministerial Functions) Order, S.I. No. 294 of 1973
		Lands (Transfer of Departmental Administration and Ministerial Functions) Order, S.I. No. 28 of 1977
		Lands (Alteration of Name of Department and Title of Minister) Order, S.I. No. 29 of 1977
		Fisheries (Transfer of Departmental Administration and Ministerial Functions) Order, S.I. No. 30 of 1977
		Fisheries (Alteration of Name of Department and Title of Minister) Order, S.I. No. 31 of 1977
		Local Government (Alteration of Name of Department and Title of Minister) Order, S.I. No. 269 of 1977
		Energy (Transfer of Departmental Administration and Ministerial Functions) Order, S.I. No. 295 of 1977
		Transport and Power (Alteration of Name of Department and Title of Minister) Order, S.I. No. 305 of 1977
		Industry and Commerce (Alteration of Name of Department and Title of Minister) Order, S.I. No. 306 of 1977
		Fisheries (Alteration of Name of Department and Title of Minister) Order, S.I. No. 195 of 1978
		Wine (Transfer of Departmental Administration and Ministerial Functions) Order, S.I. No. 232 of 1978
		Economic Planning and Development (Transfer of Departmental Administration and Ministerial Functions) Order, S.I. No. 1 of 1980
		Tourism (Transfer of Departmental Administration and Ministerial Functions) Order, S.I. No. 8 of 1980
		Energy (Transfer of Departmental Administration and Ministerial Functions) Order, S.I. No. 9 of 1980
		Industry, Commerce and Energy (Alteration of Name of Department and Title of Minister) Order, S.I. No. 10 of 1980
		Tourism and Transport (Alteration of Name of Department and Title of Minister) Order, S.I. No. 11 of 1980

Statutory Authority	Section	Statutory Instrument

Ministers and Secretaries
(Amendment) Act, No. 36 of 1939
(*Cont.*)

Economic Planning and Development (Alteration of Name of Department and Title of Minister) Order, S.I. No. 12 of 1980

National Board for Science and Technology (Transfer of Departmental Administration and Ministerial Functions) Order, S.I. No. 37 of 1980

Sugar Manufacture (Transfer of Departmental Administration and Ministerial Functions) Order, S.I. No. 55 of 1980

Racing Board and Racecourses (Transfer of Departmental Administration and Ministerial Functions) Order, S.I. No. 56 of 1980

Rent Restrictions (Transfer of Departmental Administration and Ministerial Functions) Order, S.I. No. 257 of 1980

Shannon Free Airport Development Company Limited (Transfer of Departmental Administration and Ministerial Functions) Order, S.I. No. 225 of 1981

Industry (Transfer of Departmental Administration and Ministerial Functions) Order, S.I. No. 288 of 1981

Energy (Alteration of Name of Department and Title of Minister) Order, S.I. No. 289 of 1981

Industry, Commerce and Tourism (Alteration of Name of Department and Title of Minister) Order, S.I. No. 290 of 1981

Road Traffic Regulations (Transfer of Departmental Administration and Ministerial Functions) Order, S.I. No. 417 of 1981

Justice (Transfer of Departmental Administration and Ministerial Functions) Order, S.I. No. 327 of 1982

Industry and Energy (Transfer of Departmental Administration and Ministerial Functions) Order, S.I. No. 21 of 1983

National Board for Science and Technology (Transfer of Departmental Administration and Ministerial Functions) Order, S.I. No. 80 of 1983

Education (Transfer of Departmental Administration and Ministerial Functions) Order, S.I. No. 358 of 1983

Industry (Transfer of Departmental Administration and Ministerial Functions) Order, S.I. No. 383 of 1983

Trade, Commerce and Tourism (Alteration of Name of Department and Title of Minister) Order, S.I. No. 384 of 1983

Industry and Energy (Alteration of Name of Department and Title of Minister) Order, S.I. No. 385 of 1983

Arts and Culture (Transfer of Departmental Administration and Ministerial Functions) Order, S.I. No. 27 of 1984

Statutory Authority	Section	Statutory Instrument
Ministers and Secretaries (Amendment) Act, No. 36 of 1939 (*Cont.*)		*Minister for Agriculture (Agency) Order, S.I. No. 326 of 1951*
		Minister for Justice (Agency) Order, S.I. No. 337 of 1951
		Minister for Finance (Agency) Order, S.I. No. 338 of 1951
		Minister for Industry and Commerce (Agency) Order, S.I. No. 88 of 1952
		Minister for Justice (Agency) Order, S.I. No. 262 of 1952
		Minister for Local Government (Agency) Order, S.I. No. 278 of 1952
		Minister for Justice (Agency) Order, S.I. No. 28 of 1953
		Minister for Justice (Agency) (No.2) Order, S.I. No. 155 of 1953
		Minister for Finance (Agency) Order, S.I. No. 206 of 1953
		Minister for Finance (Agency) (No.2) Order, S.I. No. 225 of 1953
		Minister for Finance (Agency) (No.3) Order, S.I. No. 243 of 1953
		Minister for Finance (Agency) (No.4) Order, S.I. No. 247 of 1953
		Minister for Finance (Agency) (No.5) Order, S.I. No. 294 of 1953
		Minister for Industry and Commerce (Agency) Order, S.I. No. 295 of 1953
		Minister for Agriculture (Agency) Order, S.I. No. 296 of 1953
		Minister for Justice (Agency) (No.3) Order, S.I. No. 297 of 1953
		Minister for Finance (Agency) (No.6) Order, S.I. No. 337 of 1953
		Minister for Finance (Agency) (No.7) Order, S.I. No. 373 of 1953
		Minister for Finance (Agency) (No.8) Order, S.I. No. 409 of 1953
		Minister for Finance (Agency) Order, S.I. No. 18 of 1954
		Minister for Finance (Agency) (No.2) Order, S.I. No. 41 of 1954
		Minister for Justice (Agency) Order, S.I. No. 123 of 1954
		Minister for Justice (Agency) (No.2) Order, S.I. No. 132 of 1954
		Minister for Justice (Agency) (No.3) Order, S.I. No. 140 of 1954
		Minister for Justice (Agency) (No.4) Order, S.I. No. 150 of 1954
		Minister for Justice (Agency) (No.5) Order, S.I. No. 170 of 1954

Statutory Authority	Section	Statutory Instrument
Ministers and Secretaries (Amendment) Act, No. 36 of 1939 (*Cont.*)		*Minister for Defence (Agency) Order, S.I. No. 192 of 1954*
		Minister for Defence (Agency) (No.2) Order, S.I. No. 222 of 1954
		Minister for Health (Agency) Order, S.I. No. 268 of 1954
		Minister for Defence (Agency) Order, S.I. No. 22 of 1955
		Minister for Posts and Telegraphs (Agency) Order, S.I. No. 143 of 1955
		Minister for Health (Agency) Order, S.I. No. 152 of 1955
		Minister for Defence (Agency) (No.2) Order, S.I. No. 170 of 1955
		Minister for Defence (Agency) (No.3) Order, S.I. No. 191 of 1955
		Minister for Local Government (Agency) Order, S.I. No. 238 of 1955
		Minister for Industry and Commerce (Agency) Order, S.I. No. 253 of 1955
		Minister for Lands (Agency) Order, S.I. No. 1 of 1956
		Minister for Industry and Commerce (Agency) Order, S.I. No. 12 of 1956
		Minister for Education (Agency) Order, S.I. No. 19 of 1956
		Minister for Education (Agency) (No.2) Order, S.I. No. 53 of 1956
		Minister for Finance (Agency) Order, S.I. No. 284 of 1968
		Minister for Finance (Agency) (No.2) Order, S.I. No. 285 of 1968
	7(2)	*Minister for Local Government (Agency) Order, 1947 (Revocation of Nomination) Order [Vol. XXXVII p. 95] S.R.& O. No. 95 of 1947*
		Minister for Justice (Agency) Order, 1949 (Revocation of Nomination) Order, S.I. No. 269 of 1949
		Minister for Local Government (Agency) Order, 1955 (Revocation of Nomination) Order, S.I. No. 240 of 1955
	9	*Gaeltachta (Feidhmeanna Aire a Tharmligean) (Ordu na), S.I. No. 421 of 1953*
	9(1)	*Turf (Use and Development) Act, 1936 (Delegation of Ministerial Functions) Order [Vol. XXXI p. 581] S.R.& O. No. 298 of 1941*
		Local Government and Public Health (Delegation of Ministerial Functions) Order [Vol. XXXI p. 585] S.R.& O. No. 103 of 1944
		Local Government and Public Health (Delegation of Ministerial Functions) (No.2) Order [Vol. XXXI p. 611] S.R.& O. No. 188 of 1944

Ministers and Secretaries
Amendment) Act, No. 36 of 1939
(Cont.)

Local Government and Public Health (Delegation of Ministerial Functions) Order [Vol. XXXI p. 597] S.R.& O. No. 58 of 1945

Fisheries (Delegation of Ministerial Functions) Order, S.I. No. 292 of 1951

Gaeltachta (Feidhmeanna Aire a Tharmligean) (Ordu na), S.I. No. 21 of 1952

Fisheries (Delegation of Ministerial Functions) Order, S.I. No. 179 of 1952

Fisheries (Delegation of Ministerial Functions) Order, S.I. No. 281 of 1953

Fisheries (Delegation of Ministerial Functions) Order, S.I. No. 43 of 1954

Fisheries (Delegation of Ministerial Functions) Order, S.I. No. 258 of 1961

Fisheries (Delegation of Ministerial Functions) Order, S.I. No. 40 of 1963

Fisheries (Delegation of Ministerial Functions) (No.2) Order, S.I. No. 187 of 1963

Justice (Delegation of Ministerial Functions) Order, S.I. No. 248 of 1964

Fisheries (Delegation of Ministerial Functions) Order, S.I. No. 256 of 1964

Gaeltachta (Feidhmeanna Aire a Tharmligean) (Ordu na) S.I. No. 108 of 1965

Gaeltachta (Feidhmeanna Aire a Tharmligean) (Ordu na) S.I. No. 258 of 1966

Local Government (Delegation of Ministerial Functions) Order, S.I. No. 41 of 1967

Posts and Telegraphs (Delegation of Ministerial Functions) Order, S.I. No. 158 of 1967

Local Government (Delegation of Ministerial Functions) Order, S.I. No. 117 of 1969

Local Government (Delegation of Ministerial Functions) (No.2) Order, S.I. No. 146 of 1969

Local Government (Delegation of Ministerial Functions) Order, S.I. No. 109 of 1970

Fisheries (Delegation of Ministerial Functions) Order, S.I. No. 123 of 1970

Local Government (Delegation of Ministerial Functions) Order, S.I. No. 52 of 1973

Local Government (Delegation of Ministerial Functions) (No.2) Order, S.I. No. 84 of 1973

Fisheries (Delegation of Ministerial Functions) Order, S.I. No. 93 of 1973

Social Welfare (Delegation of Ministerial Functions) Order, S.I. No. 193 of 1975

Local Government (Delegation of Ministerial Functions) Order, S.I. No. 236 of 1975

Fisheries (Delegation of Ministerial Functions) Order, S.I. No. 263 of 1976

Local Government (Delegation of Ministerial Functions) Order, S.I. No. 306 of 1976

Statutory Authority	Section	Statutory Instrument
Ministers and Secretaries (Amendment) Act, No. 36 of 1939 (*Cont.*)		*Posts and Telegraphs (Delegation of Ministerial Functions) Order, S.I. No. 274 of 1977*
	9(2)	*Social Welfare (Delegation of Ministerial Functions (Revocation) Order, S.I. No. 209 of 1975*
	9(2)(a)	*Local Government and Public Health (Delegation o Ministerial Functions) Order [Vol. XXXI p. 597 S.R.& O. No. 58 of 1945*
Ministers and Secretaries (Amendment) Act, No. 21 of 1956	1	*Ministers and Secretaries (Amendment) Act, 1956 (Appointed Day) Order, S.I. No. 152 of 1956*
	2	**Limistear Gaeltachta (Ordu na) S.I. No. 245 of 1956** **Limistear Gaeltachta (Ordu na) S.I. No. 200 of 1967** **Limistear Gaeltachta (Ordu na) S.I. No. 192 of 1974** **Limistear Gaeltachta (Ordu na) S.I. No. 350 of 1982**
Ministers and Secretaries (Amendment) Act, No. 17 of 1959	1	*Ministers and Secretaries (Amendment) Act, 1959 (Appointed Day) Order, S.I. No. 124 of 1959*
Ministers and Secretaries (Amendment) Act, No. 18 of 1966	1	*Ministers and Secretaries (Amendment) Act, 1966 (Appointed Day) Order, S.I. No. 162 of 1966*
Ministers and Secretaries (Amendment) Act, No. 14 of 1973	1	**Public Service (Designation of Bodies) Regulations S.I. No. 387 of 1981**
	2	*Ministers and Secretaries (Amendment) Act, 1973 (Appointed Day) Order, S.I. No. 293 of 1973*
Ministers and Secretaries (Amendment) Act, No. 27 of 1977	1	*Ministers and Secretaries (Amendment) Act, 1977 (Appointed Day) Order, S.I. No. 377 of 1977*
Ministers and Secretaries (Amendment) (No. 2) Act, No. 28 of 1977	2	*Agriculture (Delegation of Ministerial Functions, Order, S.I. No. 148 of 1978*
		Agriculture (Delegation of Ministerial Functions, Order, S.I. No. 79 of 1980
		Agriculture (Delegation of Ministerial Functions, (No.2) Order, S.I. No. 80 of 1980
		Agriculture (Delegation of Ministerial Functions, Order, S.I. No. 82 of 1981
		Agriculture (Delegation of Ministerial Functions, (No.2) Order, S.I. No. 359 of 1981
	2(1)	*Air-raid Precautions (Delegation of Ministerial Functions) Order, S.I. No. 385 of 1977*
		Posts and Telegraphs (Delegation of Ministerial Functions) Order, S.I. No. 3 of 1978
		Public Service (Delegation of Ministerial Functions) Order, S.I. No. 117 of 1978
		Statistics (Delegation of Powers and Duties) Order, S.I. No. 148 of 1979
		Statistics (Delegation of Powers and Duties) (No.2) Order, S.I. No. 228 of 1979
		Justice (Delegation of Powers and Duties) Order, S.I. No. 237 of 1979
		Air-raid Precautions (Delegation of Ministerial Functions) Order, S.I. No. 278 of 1979

Statutory Authority	Section	Statutory Instrument
Ministers and Secretaries (Amendment) (No. 2) Act, No. 28 of 1977 (*Cont.*)		*Posts and Telegraphs (Delegation of Ministerial Functions) Order, S.I. No. 20 of 1980*
		Air-raid Precautions (Delegation of Ministerial Functions) Order, S.I. No. 27 of 1980
		Statistics (Delegation of Powers and Duties) Order, S.I. No. 36 of 1980
		Education (Delegation of Ministerial Functions) Order, S.I. No. 44 of 1980
		Air-raid Precautions (Delegation of Ministerial Functions) (No.2) Order, S.I. No. 373 of 1980
		Posts and Telegraphs (Delegation of Ministerial Functions) Order, S.I. No. 278 of 1981
		Air-raid Precautions (Delegation of Ministerial Functions) Order, S.I. No. 298 of 1981
		Statistics (Delegation of Powers and Duties) Order, S.I. No. 395 of 1981
		Statistics (Delegation of Powers and Duties) Order, S.I. No. 97 of 1982
		Air-raid Precautions (Delegation of Ministerial Functions) Order, S.I. No. 125 of 1982
		Posts and Telegraphs (Delegation of Ministerial Functions) Order, S.I. No. 211 of 1982
		Statistics (Delegation of Ministerial Functions) Order, S.I. No. 13 of 1983
		Posts and Telegraphs (Delegation of Ministerial Functions) Order, S.I. No. 59 of 1983
		Air-raid Precautions (Delegation of Ministerial Functions) Order, S.I. No. 94 of 1983
		Posts and Telegraphs (Delegation of Ministerial Functions) (No.2) Order, S.I. No. 106 of 1983
		Environment (Delegation of Functions) Order, S.I. No. 272 of 1983
		Health (Delegation of Functions) Order, S.I. No. 322 of 1983
		Health (Delegation of Functions) Order, S.I. No. 4 of 1984
		Taoiseach (Delegation of Ministerial Functions) Order, S.I. No. 36 of 1984
		Communications (Delegation of Ministerial Functions) Order, S.I. No. 146 of 1984
		Air-raid Precautions (Delegation of Ministerial Functions) Order, S.I. No. 284 of 1986
	7(3)	*Ministers and Secretaries (Amendment) (No.2) Act, 1977 (Commencement) Order, S.I. No. 378 of 1977*
Ministry of Transport Act, No. 50 of 1919	1	**Pier at Clogherhead in the County of Louth Bye-Laws, S.I. No. 125 of 1960**
		Bantry Pier Bye-Laws, S.I. No. 183 of 1968
		Harbour at Burtonport, County Donegal (Bye-Laws for the Regulation of the) S.I. No. 427 of 1986
		Harbour at Rathmullan, County Donegal (Bye-Laws for the Regulation of the) S.I. No. 428 of 1986

Statutory Authority	Section	Statutory Instrument
Ministry of Transport Act, No. 50 of 1919 (*Cont.*)		**Harbour at Greencastle, County Donegal (Bye-laws for the Regulation of the) S.I. No. 429 of 1986**
Misuse of Drugs Act, No. 12 of 1977	3	**Misuse of Drugs (Exemption) Order, S.I. No. 29 of 1979**
	4	**Misuse of Drugs Regulations, S.I. No. 32 of 1979**
		Misuse of Drugs (Safe Custody) Regulations, S.I. No. 321 of 1982
	5	**Misuse of Drugs Regulations, S.I. No. 32 of 1979**
		Misuse of Drugs (Safe Custody) Regulations, S.I. No. 321 of 1982
	8	*Misuse of Drugs (Committees of Enquiry, Advisory Committees and Advisory Panels) Regulations, S.I. No. 31 of 1979*
		Misuse of Drugs (Committees of Inquiry) Regulations, S.I. No. 264 of 1984
	9	*Misuse of Drugs (Committees of Enquiry, Advisory Committees and Advisory Panels) Regulations, S.I. No. 31 of 1979*
	10	*Misuse of Drugs (Committees of Enquiry, Advisory Committees and Advisory Panels) Regulations, S.I. No. 31 of 1979*
	12	*Misuse of Drugs (Committees of Enquiry, Advisory Committees and Advisory Panels) Regulations, S.I. No. 31 of 1979*
		Misuse of Drugs (Committees of Inquiry) Regulations, S.I. No. 264 of 1984
	13	**Misuse of Drugs (Designation) Order, S.I. No. 30 of 1979**
	14	**Misuse of Drugs (Licence Fees) Regulations, S.I. No. 164 of 1979**
		Misuse of Drugs (Licence Fees) (Amendment) Regulations, S.I. No. 29 of 1985
		Misuse of Drugs (Licence Fees) (Amendment) Regulations, S.I. No. 172 of 1986
	18	**Misuse of Drugs Regulations, S.I. No. 32 of 1979**
	28(10)	**Misuse of Drugs (Custodial Treatment Centre) Order, S.I. No. 30 of 1980**
	38	*Misuse of Drugs (Committees of Enquiry, Advisory Committees and Advisory Panels) Regulations, S.I. No. 31 of 1979*
		Misuse of Drugs Regulations, S.I. No. 32 of 1979
		Misuse of Drugs (Licence Fees) Regulations, S.I. No. 164 of 1979
		Misuse of Drugs (Safe Custody) Regulations, S.I. No. 321 of 1982
		Misuse of Drugs (Committees of Inquiry) Regulations, S.I. No. 264 of 1984
		Misuse of Drugs (Licence Fees) (Amendment) Regulations, S.I. No. 29 of 1985

Statutory Authority	Section	Statutory Instrument
Misuse of Drugs Act, No. 12 of 1977 (*Cont.*)		**Misuse of Drugs (Licence Fees) (Amendment) Regulations, S.I. No. 172 of 1986**
	42	**Misuse of Drugs Regulations, S.I. No. 32 of 1979**
	43(2)	*Misuse of Drugs Act, 1977 (Commencement) Order, S.I. No. 28 of 1979*
Misuse of Drugs Act, No. 18 of 1984	16(2)	*Misuse of Drugs Act, 1984 (Commencement) Order, S.I. No. 205 of 1984*
Moneylenders Act, No. 51 of 1900	6(e)	**Moneylenders (Exemption of Bodies Corporate) Regulations [Vol. XVI p. 1187] S.R.& O. No. 11 of 1934**
	6(f)	**Moneylenders Act, 1900 (Section 6(f)) Order, S.I. No. 344 of 1983**
Moneylenders Act, No. 36 of 1933	6(6)	**Moneylenders Act Rules [Vol. XVI p. 1197] S.R.& O. No. 160 of 1933**
Motor Car Act, No. 36 of 1903	12	*Heavy Motor Car (Amendment) Order [Vol. XVI p. 1207] S.R.& O. No. 50 of 1925*
		Heavy Motor Car (Amendment) Order [Vol. XVI p. 1213] S.R.& O. No. 34 of 1928
		Heavy Motor Car (Speed) Order [Vol. XVI p. 1233] S.R.& O. No. 41 of 1930
Motor Car (International Circulation) Act, No. 37 of 1909	1(1)	*Motor Car (International Circulation) Order [Vol. XVI p. 1239] S.R.& O. No. 67 of 1931*
		Motor Car (International Circulation) (Amendment) Order [Vol. XVI p. 1255] S.R.& O. No. 116 of 1934
Motor Car (International Circulation) Order [Vol. XVI p. 1239] S.R.& O. No. 67 of 1931		*Road Vehicles (International Circulation) Regulations [Vol. XII p. 203] S.R.& O. No. 50 of 1932*
		Road Vehicles (International Circulation) Regulations [Vol. XII p. 233] S.R.& O. No. 119 of 1934
		Road Vehicles (International Circulation) (Amendment) Regulations [Vol. XII p. 265] S.R.& O. No. 98 of 1937
		Road Vehicles (International Circulation) (Amendment) Regulations [Vol. XII p. 269] S.R.& O. No. 190 of 1938
		Public Service Vehicles (International Circulation) Order, S.I. No. 81 of 1958
Motor Car (International Circulation) (Amendment) Order [Vol. XVI p. 1255] S.R.& O. No. 116 of 1934		*Road Vehicles (International Circulation) Regulations [Vol. XII p. 233] S.R.& O. No. 119 of 1934*
		Road Vehicles (International Circulation) (Amendment) Regulations [Vol. XII p. 265] S.R.& O. No. 98 of 1937
		Road Vehicles (International Circulation) (Amendment) Regulations [Vol. XII p. 269] S.R.& O. No. 190 of 1938
Motor Vehicles (Registration of Importers) Act, No. 15 of 1968	1(2)	*Motor Vehicles (Registration of Importers) Act, 1968 (Definition of Motor Vehicle) Regulations, S.I. No. 2 of 1973*

Statutory Authority	Section	Statutory Instrument
Motor Vehicles (Registration of Importers) Act, No. 15 of 1968 (*Cont.*)	10	*Motor Vehicles (Registration of Importers) Act, 1968 (Commencement) Order, S.I. No. 163 of 1968*
Musk Rats Act, No. 16 of 1933	6	**Musk Rats (Notification by Occupiers of Land and Returns) Regulations, (1933) [Vol. XVI p. 1275] S.R.& O. No. 5 of 1934**
	38	**Musk Rats Act, 1933 (Application to Mink) Order, S.I. No. 199 of 1965**
National Agricultural Advisory, Education and Research Authority Act, No. 13 of 1977	1(2)	*National Agricultural Advisory, Education and Research Authority Act, 1977 (Commencement) Order, S.I. No. 184 of 1977*
		National Agricultural Advisory, Education and Research Authority Act, 1977 (Commencement) (No.2) Order, S.I. No. 204 of 1977
		National Agricultural Advisory, Education and Research Authority Act, 1977 (Commencement) Order, S.I. No. 190 of 1980
	3(2)	*An Chomhairle Oiliuna Talmhaiochta (Nomination of Members of the Board) (Amendment) (No.2) Order, S.I. No. 329 of 1980*
		An Chomhairle Oiliuna Talmhaiochta (Nomination of Members of the Board) (Amendment) Order, S.I. No. 178 of 1982
	13(2)	**An Chomhairle Oiliuna Talmhaiochta (Nomination of Members of the Board) (Amendment) Order, S.I. No. 62 of 1980**
	26(3)	**National Agricultural Authority (Nomination of Members of the Board) Order, S.I. No. 183 of 1977**
		An Chomhairle Oiliuna Talmhaiochta (Nomination of Members of the Board) Order, S.I. No. 270 of 1979
		An Chomhairle Oiliuna Talmhaiochta (Nomination of Members of the Board) (Amendment) (No.2) Order, S.I. No. 329 of 1980
		An Chomhairle Oiliuna Talmhaiochta (Nomination of Members of the Board) (Amendment) Order, S.I. No. 178 of 1982
	39	**National Agricultural Advisory, Education and Research Authority Act, 1977 (Section 39) (Prescribed Forms) Order, S.I. No. 33 of 1986**
	Sch. II par. 6	**National Agricultural Authority (Nomination of Members of the Board) Order, S.I. No. 183 of 1977**
National Bank Transfer Act, No. 8 of 1966	9(2)	*National Bank Transfer Act, 1966 (Commencement) Order, S.I. No. 63 of 1966*
National Board for Science and Technology Act, No. 25 of 1977	2	*National Board for Science and Technology Act, 1977 (Establishment Day) Order, S.I. No. 78 of 1978*

Statutory Authority	Section	Statutory Instrument
National Board for Science and Technology Act, No. 25 of 1977 (*Cont.*)	28(1)	**National Board for Science and Technology Staff Superannuation Scheme, S.I. No. 344 of 1980** **National Board for Science and Technology Widows' and Children's Contributory Pension Scheme, S.I. No. 345 of 1980**
National College of Art and Design Act, No. 28 of 1971	3	*National College of Art and Design Act, 1971 (Establishment Day) Order, S.I. No. 108 of 1972*
National Community Development Agency, No. 20 of 1982	2	*National Community Development Agency Act, 1982 (Establishment Day) Order, S.I. No. 354 of 1982*
National Council for Educational Awards Act, No. 30 of 1979	20	**National Council for Educational Awards Act, 1979 (Designation of Institutions) Order, S.I. No. 252 of 1980** **National Council for Educational Awards Act, 1979 (Designation of Institutions) Order, S.I. No. 245 of 1984** **National Council for Educational Awards Act, 1979 (Designation of Institutions) Order, S.I. No. 147 of 1985** **National Council for Educational Awards Act, 1979 (Designation of Institutions) Regulations, S.I. No. 358 of 1985**
	22(2)	*National Council for Educational Awards Act, 1979 (Commencement) Order, S.I. No. 224 of 1980*
National Development Corporation Act, No. 5 of 1986	7	*National Development Corporation Limited (Vesting Day) Order, S.I. No. 208 of 1986*
National Health Insurance Act, No. 62 of 1918 (sess. 1)		*National Health Insurance (Women's Equalisation Fund) Regulations, S.R.& O. No. 7 of 1923* *National Health Insurance (Small Societies Valuation Deficiencies) Regulations, S.R.& O. No. 8 of 1923* *National Health Insurance (Unclaimed proceeds of Stamp Sales) Regulations, S.R.& O. No. 15 of 1926* *National Health Insurance (Small Societies Valuation Deficiencies) Regulations, S.R.& O. No. 93 of 1927* *National Health Insurance (Assistant Teachers) Exclusion Order, S.R.& O. No. 201 of 1934*
National Health Insurance Act, No. 10 of 1920	16	*National Health Insurance (Payments to Insurance Committees) (Persons over 70) Regulations [Vol. XVII p. 83] S.R.& O. No. 32 of 1927*
	Sch. II	*National Health Insurance (Payments to Insurance Committees) (Persons over 70) Regulations [Vol. XVII p. 83] S.R.& O. No. 32 of 1927*
National Health Insurance Act, No. 20 of 1923	17	*National Health Insurance (Great Britain Reciprocal Arrangements) Order [Vol. XVII p. 29] S.R.& O. No. 7 of 1924* *National Health Insurance (Great Britain Reciprocal Arrangements) Order [Vol. XVII p. 41] S.R.& O. No. 296 of 1938*

Statutory Authority	Section	Statutory Instrument
National Health Insurance Act, No. 20 of 1923 (*Cont.*)		*National Health Insurance (Great Britain Reciprocal Arrangement) Order [Vol. XXXI p. 681] S.R.& O. No. 405 of 1939*
		National Health Insurance (Great Britain Reciprocal Arrangements) Order [Vol. XXXVIII p. 43] S.R.& O. No. 148 of 1946
National Health Insurance Act, No. 42 of 1929	Sch. I par. 2(1)	*National Health Insurance (Appeal from Approved Society Audit) Regulations [Vol. XVII p. 145] S.R.& O. No. 46 of 1930*
National Health Insurance Act, No. 13 of 1933	2	*National Health Insurance (Appointed Day) Order [Vol. XVII p. 157] S.R.& O. No. 109 of 1936*
	27	*National Health Insurance (Valuation) Regulations [Vol. XVII p. 259] S.R.& O. No. 258 of 1936*
	29	*National Health Insurance (Removal of Difficulties) Order [Vol. XVII p. 153] S.R.& O. No. 171 of 1933*
National Health Insurance Act, No. 5 of 1942	4(5)	*National Health Insurance (Additional Benefits) Regulations [Vol. XXXI p. 689] S.R.& O. No. 431 of 1942*
National Health Insurance Act, No. 9 of 1947	19	*National Health Insurance (Remuneration Limit for Insurance) Order [Vol. XXXVIII p. 53] S.R.& O. No. 134 of 1947*
National Health Insurance Acts, 1911 to 1921,		*National Health Insurance (Arrears) Amendment Regulations [Vol. XVII p. 1] S.R.& O. No. 6 of 1923*
National Health Insurance Acts, 1911 to 1923,		*National Health Insurance (Insurance Committees) Amendment Regulations (No.3) [Vol. XVII p. 13] S.R.& O. No. 17 of 1923*
		National Health Insurance (Reserve and Transfer Values) Regulations [Vol. XVII p. 15] S.R.& O. No. 20 of 1923
		National Health Insurance (Arrears) Amendment Regulations [Vol. XVII p. 25] S.R.& O. No. 1 of 1924
		National Health Insurance (Irish Migratory Labourers Benefits) Amendment Regulations [Vol. XVII p. 27] S.R.& O. No. 17 of 1924
National Health Insurance Acts, 1911 to 1924,		*National Health Insurance (Arrears) Amendment Regulations (No.2) [Vol. XVII p. 49] S.R.& O. No. 32 of 1924*
		National Health Insurance (Military Forces) (International Arrangements) Insurance Fund Regulations [Vol. XVII p. 51] S.R.& O. No. 24 of 1925
National Health Insurance Acts, 1911 to 1925,		*National Health Insurance (Approved Societies) Amendment Regulations [Vol. XVII p. 63] S.R.& O. No. 39 of 1925*
		National Health Insurance (Arrears) Amendment Regulations [Vol. XVII p. 73] S.R.& O. No. 7 of 1926

Statutory Authority	Section	Statutory Instrument
National Health Insurance Acts, 1911 to 1925 *(Cont.)*		*National Health Insurance (Approved Societies) Amendment Regulations [Vol. XVII p. 69] S.R.& O. No. 31 of 1926*
		National Health Insurance (Additional Benefits) Regulations [Vol. XVII p. 75] S.R.& O. No. 50 of 1926
		National Health Insurance (Additional Benefits) (No.2) Regulations [Vol. XVII p. 77] S.R.& O. No. 61 of 1926
National Health Insurance Acts, 1911 to 1926,		*National Health Insurance (Arrears) Amendment Regulations (No.2) [Vol. XVII p. 79] S.R.& O. No. 75 of 1926*
		National Health Insurance (Reserve Suspense Fund) Regulations [Vol. XVII p. 85] S.R.& O. No. 73 of 1927
		National Health Insurance (Additional Benefits) Regulations [Vol. XVII p. 89] S.R.& O. No. 95 of 1927
		National Health Insurance (Arrears) Amendment Regulations . [Vol. XVII p. 81] S.R.& O. No. 96 of 1927
		National Health Insurance (Approved Societies) Amendment Regulations [Vol. XVII p. 91] S.R.& O. No. 110 of 1927
National Health Insurance Acts, 1911 to 1927,		*National Health Insurance (Collection of Contributions) Amendment Regulations [Vol. XVII p. 93] S.R.& O. No. 39 of 1928*
		National Health Insurance (Arrears) Amendment Regulations [Vol. XVII p. 95] S.R.& O. No. 1 of 1929
		National Health Insurance (Additional Benefits) Regulations [Vol. XVII p. 97] S.R.& O. No. 3 of 1929
National Health Insurance Acts, 1911 to 1928,		*National Health Insurance (Approved Societies) Amendment Regulations [Vol. XVII p. 99] S.R.& O. No. 17 of 1929*
		National Health Insurance (Arrears) Amendment Regulations (No.2) [Vol. XVII p. 101] S.R.& O. No. 39 of 1929
		National Health Insurance (Collection of Contributions) Amendment Regulations, (1929) [Vol. XVII p. 103] S.R.& O. No. 1 of 1930
National Health Insurance Acts, 1911 to 1929,		*National Health Insurance (Exempt Persons) (Discontinuance) Regulations [Vol. XVII p. 105] S.R.& O. No. 21 of 1930*
		National Health Insurance (Marriage Benefit) Regulations [Vol. XVII p. 113] S.R.& O. No. 36 of 1930
		National Health Insurance (Additional Benefits) Regulations [Vol. XVII p. 117] S.R.& O. No. 37 of 1930
		National Health Insurance (Approved Societies) Amendment Regulations [Vol. XVII p. 119] S.R.& O. No. 47 of 1930

Statutory Authority	Section	Statutory Instrument
National Health Insurance Acts, 1911 to 1929 *(Cont.)*		*National Health Insurance (Deposit Contributors) (Abolition) Regulations [Vol. XVII p. 127] S.R.& O. No. 67 of 1930*
		National Health Insurance (Termination of Sanatorium Benefit and Abolition of Insurance Committee) Regulations [Vol. XVII p. 135] S.R.& O. No. 28 of 1934
		National Health Insurance (Reserve and Transfer Values) Regulations [Vol. XVII p. 139] S.R.& O. No. 646 of 1935
National Health Insurance Acts, 1911 to 1930,		*National Health Insurance (Approved Societies) Amendment Regulations [Vol. XVII p. 123] S.R.& O. No. 6 of 1932*
National Health Insurance Acts, 1911 to 1936,		*National Health Insurance (Committee of Management) Regulations [Vol. XVII p. 175] S.R.& O. No. 166 of 1936*
		National Health Insurance (Repayment of Compensation Loan) Regulations [Vol. XVII p. 193] S.R.& O. No. 246 of 1936
		National Health Insurance (Unclaimed Proceeds of Stamp Sales) Regulations [Vol. XVII p. 197] S.R.& O. No. 291 of 1936
		National Health Insurance (Collection of Contributions) Amendment Regulations [Vol. XVII p. 203] S.R.& O. No. 44 of 1937
		National Health Insurance (Approved Societies) Amendment Regulations [Vol. XVII p. 215] S.R.& O. No. 79 of 1938
		National Health Insurance (Repayment of Compensation Loan) Regulations [Vol. XXXI p. 627] S.R.& O. No. 85 of 1939
		National Health Insurance (Unclaimed Proceeds of Stamp Sales) Amendment Regulations [Vol. XXXI p. 639] S.R.& O. No. 86 of 1939
		National Health Insurance (Repayment of Compensation Loan) Regulations [Vol. XXXI p. 631] S.R.& O. No. 228 of 1940
		National Health Insurance (Repayment of Compensation Loan) Regulations [Vol. XXXI p. 635] S.R.& O. No. 384 of 1941
		National Health Insurance (Repayment of Compensation Loan) Regulations [Vol. XXXI p. 647] S.R.& O. No. 454 of 1942
		National Health Insurance (Repayment of Compensation Loan) Regulations [Vol. XXXI p. 651] S.R.& O. No. 321 of 1943
		National Health Insurance (Approved Societies) (Amendment) Regulations [Vol. XXXI p. 643] S.R.& O. No. 212 of 1944
		National Health Insurance (Repayment of Compensation Loan) Regulations [Vol. XXXI p. 657] S.R.& O. No. 363 of 1944
		National Health Insurance (Repayment of Compensation Loan) Regulations [Vol. XXXI p. 661] S.R.& O. No. 274 of 1945

National Health Insurance Acts,
1911 to 1942,

National Health Insurance (Unclaimed Proceeds of Stamp Sales) Regulations [Vol. XXXVIII p. 33] S.R.& O. No. 37 of 1946

National Health Insurance (Arrears) (Amendment) Regulations [Vol. XXXVIII p. 17] S.R.& O. No. 98 of 1946

National Health Insurance (Repayment of Compensation Loan) Regulations [Vol. XXXVIII p. 29] S.R.& O. No. 107 of 1946

National Health Insurance (Approved Societies) (Amendment) Regulations [Vol. XXXVIII p. 1] S.R.& O. No. 222 of 1946

National Health Insurance (Arrears) Regulations [Vol. XXXVIII p. 5] S.R.& O. No. 223 of 1946

National Health Insurance (Collection of Contributions) (Amendment) Regulations [Vol. XXX-VIII p. 21] S.R.& O. No. 224 of 1946

National Health Insurance (Marriage Benefit) Regulations [Vol. XXXVIII p. 25] S.R.& O. No. 226 of 1946

National Health Insurance (Additional Benefits) Regulations [Vol. XXXVIII p. 39] S.R.& O. No. 112 of 1947

National Health Insurance Acts,
1911 to 1948,

National Health Insurance (Approved Societies) (Amendment) Regulations, S.I. No. 224 of 1949

National Health Insurance Acts,
1911 to 1950,

National Health Insurance (Additional Benefits) Regulations, S.I. No. 55 of 1952

National Health Insurance Acts,
1911 to 1952,

National Health Insurance (Approved Societies) (Amendment) Regulations, S.I. No. 217 of 1952

National Health Insurance (Arrears) (Amendment) Regulations, S.I. No. 223 of 1952

National Health Insurance (Arrears) (Amendment) (No.2) Regulations, S.I. No. 241 of 1952

National Health Insurance (Collection of Contributions) Amendment Regulations, S.I. No. 294 of 1952

National Institute for Higher
Education, Dublin Act, No. 30 of
1980

17(2)

National Institute for Higher Education, Dublin, Act, 1980 (Commencement) Order, S.I. No. 213 of 1981

National Institute for Higher
Education, Limerick Act, No. 25 of
1980

17(2)

National Institute for Higher Education, Limerick, Act, 1980 (Commencement) Order, S.I. No. 215 of 1981

National Insurance Act, No. 55 of
1911

1(2)

National Health Insurance (Subsidiary Employments) Order [Vol. XVII p. 131] S.R.& O. No. 50 of 1931

National Health Insurance (Subsidiary Employments) Order [Vol. XVII p. 209] S.R.& O. No. 141 of 1937

National Health Insurance (Subsidiary Employments) Consolidated Order [Vol. XXXI p. 665] S.R.& O. No. 277 of 1944

Statutory Authority	Section	Statutory Instrument
National Insurance Act, No. 55 of 1911 (*Cont.*)	1(2) Proviso	*National Health Insurance (Subsidiary Employments) Special Order, S.I. No. 358 of 1949*
		National Health Insurance (Subsidiary Employments) Consolidated Order [Vol. XVII p. 161] S.R.& O. No. 150 of 1936
	35(2)	*National Health Insurance (Approved Societies) Amendment Regulations [Vol. XVII p. 233] S.R.& O. No. 18 of 1924*
	36	*National Health Insurance (Valuation) Regulations [Vol. XVII p. 235] S.R.& O. No. 33 of 1925*
		National Health Insurance (Valuation) Regulations [Vol. XVII p. 247] S.R.& O. No. 95 of 1930
	36(2)	*National Health Insurance (Valuation) Regulations [Vol. XVII p. 259] S.R.& O. No. 258 of 1936*
	38(2)	*National Health Insurance (Valuation) Regulations [Vol. XVII p. 235] S.R.& O. No. 33 of 1925*
		National Health Insurance (Valuation) Regulations [Vol. XVII p. 247] S.R.& O. No. 95 of 1930
		National Health Insurance (Valuation) Regulations [Vol. XVII p. 259] S.R.& O. No. 258 of 1936
	59(4)	*National Health Insurance (Insurance Committees) Amendment Regulations (No.2) [Vol. XVII p. 221] S.R.& O. No. 16 of 1923*
		National Health Insurance (Insurance Committees) Amendment Regulations [Vol. XVII p. 223] S.R.& O. No. 21 of 1924
		National Health Insurance (Insurance Committees) Amendment Regulations [Vol. XVII p. 225] S.R.& O. No. 71 of 1927
		National Health Insurance (Insurance Committees) Amendment Regulations [Vol. XVII p. 227] S.R.& O. No. 41 of 1928
		National Health Insurance (Insurance Committees) Amendment Regulations [Vol. XVII p. 229] S.R.& O. No. 33 of 1929
	60(1)(c)	*National Health Insurance (Accounts of Insurance Committees) Regulations [Vol. XVII p. 219] S.R.& O. No. 9 of 1923*
	65	*National Health Insurance (Women's Equalisation Fund) Regulations [Vol. XVII p. 5] S.R.& O. No. 7 of 1923*
		National Health Insurance (Accounts of Insurance Committees) Regulations [Vol. XVII p. 219] S.R.& O. No. 9 of 1923
		National Health Insurance (Payments to Insurance Committees) Amendment Regulations [Vol. XVII p. 231] S.R.& O. No. 22 of 1923
	81(8)	*National Health Insurance (Insurance Committees) Amendment Regulations (No.2) [Vol. XVII p. 221] S.R.& O. No. 16 of 1923*

Statutory Authority	Section	Statutory Instrument
National Insurance Act, No. 55 of 1911 (*Cont.*)		*National Health Insurance (Insurance Committees) Amendment Regulations [Vol. XVII p. 223] S.R.& O. No. 21 of 1924*
		National Health Insurance (Insurance Committees) Amendment Regulations [Vol. XVII p. 225] S.R.& O. No. 71 of 1927
		National Health Insurance (Insurance Committees) Amendment Regulations [Vol. XVII p. 227] S.R.& O. No. 41 of 1928
		National Health Insurance (Insurance Committees) Amendment Regulations [Vol. XVII p. 229] S.R.& O. No. 33 of 1929
	83	*National Health Insurance (Valuation) Regulations [Vol. XVII p. 235] S.R.& O. No. 33 of 1925*
		National Health Insurance (Valuation) Regulations [Vol. XVII p. 247] S.R.& O. No. 95 of 1930
	Sch. I	*National Health Insurance (Subsidiary Employments) Order [Vol. XVII p. 209] S.R.& O. No. 141 of 1937*
	Sch. I Part II par. (i)	*National Health Insurance (Subsidiary Employments) Consolidated Order [Vol. XVII p. 161] S.R.& O. No. 150 of 1936*
		National Health Insurance (Subsidiary Employments) Consolidated Order [Vol. XXXI p. 665] S.R.& O. No. 277 of 1944
		National Health Insurance (Subsidiary Employments) Special Order, S.I. No. 358 of 1949
		National Health Insurance (Subsidiary Employments) Order [Vol. XVII p. 131] S.R.& O. No. 50 of 1931
National Insurance Act, No. 37 of 1913	28	*National Health Insurance (Payments to Insurance Committees) Amendment Regulations [Vol. XVII p. 231] S.R.& O. No. 22 of 1923*
	Sch. I par. (f)	*National Health Insurance (Payments to Insurance Committees) Amendment Regulations [Vol. XVII p. 231] S.R.& O. No. 22 of 1923*
National Loan (Conversion) Act, No. 39 of 1935	7	**National Loan (Conversion) Regulations [Vol. XVII p. 283] S.R.& O. No. 676 of 1935**
National Monuments Act, No. 2 of 1930	17	**Sheepstown Church National Monument (Prohibition of Burials) Order [Vol. XVII p. 293] S.R.& O. No. 389 of 1936**
		Drumacoo Church National Monument (Prohibition of Burials) Order [Vol. XVII p. 297] S.R.& O. No. 276 of 1937
		Claregalway Abbey National Monument (Prohibition of Burials) Order [Vol. XVII p. 301] S.R.& O. No. 116 of 1938
		Hore Abbey National Monument (Prohibition of Burials) Order [Vol. XXXI p. 697] S.R.& O. No. 74 of 1942

Statutory Authority	Section	Statutory Instrument
National Monuments Act, No. 2 of 1930 (*Cont.*)		**Aghowle National Monument Order [Vol. XXXI p. 693] S.R.& O. No. 78 of 1944**
		Killeshin National Monument (Prohibition of Burials) Order [Vol. XXXVIII p. 57] S.R.& O. No. 17 of 1946
National Monuments (Amendment) Act, No. 37 of 1954	15(1)	*National Monuments (Amendment) Act, 1954 (Appointed Day) Order, S.I. No. 39 of 1955*
National School Teachers (Ireland) Act, No. 74 of 1879	11	**Teachers' Pension Rules [Vol. XVII p. 305] S.R.& O. No. 34 of 1924**
		Teachers' Pension (No.2) Rules [Vol. XVII p. 311] S.R.& O. No. 35 of 1924
		Teachers' Pension Rules [Vol. XVII p. 315] S.R.& O. No. 52 of 1925
		Teachers' Pension Rules [Vol. XVII p. 321] S.R.& O. No. 45 of 1926
		Teachers' Pension Rules [Vol. XVII p. 323] S.R.& O. No. 14 of 1934
		Teachers' Pension (No.2) Rules [Vol. XVII p. 329] S.R.& O. No. 338 of 1934
National Social Service Board Act, No. 2 of 1984	2	*National Social Service Board Act, 1984 (Establishment Day) Order, S.I. No. 185 of 1984*
National Stud Act, No. 31 of 1945	4	*National Stud Act, 1945 (Appointment of Transfer Date) Order [Vol. XXXVIII p. 61] S.R.& O. No. 289 of 1946*
Nelson Pillar Act, No. 9 of 1969	5(2)	*Nelson Pillar Act, 1969 (Commencement) Order, S.I. No. 97 of 1969*
Neutrality (War Damage to Property) Act, No. 24 of 1941	4	**Neutrality (War Damage to Property) Act, 1941 (Form of Application) Regulations [Vol. XXXI p. 717] S.R.& O. No. 435 of 1941**
	8	**Neutrality (War Damage to Property) Act, 1941 (Compensation for Documents) Order [Vol. XXXI p. 701] S.R.& O. No. 458 of 1941**
	24	**Neutrality (War Damage to Property) Act, 1941 (Form of Application) Regulations [Vol. XXXI p. 717] S.R.& O. No. 435 of 1941**
	Sch. par. 8	**Neutrality (War Damage to Property) (Acquisition of Land) Regulations [Vol. XXXI p. 711] S.R.& O. No. 368 of 1941**
Night Work (Bakeries) Act, No. 42 of 1936	4(1)	**Night Work (Bakeries) (The Period of Night) Order [Vol. XVII p. 343] S.R.& O. No. 9 of 1937**
	5(1)	*Night Work (Bakeries) (Exceptional Work) Order [Vol. XVII p. 337] S.R.& O. No. 7 of 1937*
		Night Work (Bakeries) (Exceptional Work) Order, S.I. No. 93 of 1955
	5(2)	*Night Work (Bakeries) (Exceptional Work for a Limited Period) (No.1) Order [Vol. XVII p. 349] S.R.& O. No. 8 of 1937*

Statutory Authority	Section	Statutory Instrument
Night Work (Bakeries) Act, No. 42 of 1936 (*Cont.*)		*Night Work (Bakeries) (Exceptional Work for a Limited Period) (No.2) Order [Vol. XVII p. 355] S.R.& O. No. 70 of 1937*
		Night Work (Bakeries) (Exceptional Work for a Limited Period) (No.3) Order [Vol. XVII p. 361] S.R.& O. No. 136 of 1937
		Night Work (Bakeries) (Exceptional Work for a Limited Period) (No.4) Order [Vol. XVII p. 367] S.R.& O. No. 223 of 1937
		Night Work (Bakeries) (Exceptional Work for a Limited Period) (No.5) Order [Vol. XVII p. 373] S.R.& O. No. 290 of 1937
		Night Work (Bakeries) (Exceptional Work for a Limited Period) (No.6) Order [Vol. XVII p. 379] S.R.& O. No. 317 of 1937
		Night Work (Bakeries) (Exceptional Work for a Limited Period) (No.7) Order [Vol. XVII p. 385] S.R.& O. No. 318 of 1937
		Night Work (Bakeries) (Exceptional Work for a Limited Period) (No.8) Order [Vol. XVII p. 391] S.R.& O. No. 36 of 1938
		Night Work (Bakeries) (Exceptional Work for Limited Periods) Regulations [Vol. XVII p. 397] S.R.& O. No. 121 of 1938
		Night Work (Bakeries) (Exceptional Work for Limited Periods) Regulations [Vol. XXXI p. 731] S.R.& O. No. 54 of 1939
		Night Work (Bakeries) (Exceptional Work for Limited Periods) Regulations [Vol. XXXI p. 737] S.R.& O. No. 60 of 1940
		Night Work (Bakeries) (Exceptional Work for Limited Periods) Regulations [Vol. XXXI p. 743] S.R.& O. No. 130 of 1941
		Night Work (Bakeries) (Exceptional Work for Limited Periods) Regulations [Vol. XXXI p. 749] S.R.& O. No. 54 of 1942
		Night Work (Bakeries) (Exceptional Work for Limited Periods) Regulations [Vol. XXXI p. 755] S.R.& O. No. 132 of 1943
		Night Work (Bakeries) (Exceptional Work for Limited Periods) Regulations [Vol. XXXI p. 761] S.R.& O. No. 72 of 1944
		Night Work (Bakeries) (Exceptional Work for Limited Periods) Regulations [Vol. XXXI p. 767] S.R.& O. No. 34 of 1945
		Night Work (Bakeries) (Exceptional Work for Limited Periods) Regulations [Vol. XXXVIII p. 65] S.R.& O. No. 19 of 1946
		Night Work (Bakeries) (Exceptional Work for Limited Periods) Regulations [Vol. XXXVIII p. 71] S.R.& O. No. 30 of 1947
		Night Work (Bakeries) (Exceptional Work for Limited Periods) Regulations, S.I. No. 43 of 1948
	11(2)	*Night Work (Bakeries) Act, 1936 (Date of Commencement) Order [Vol. XVII p. 333] S.R.& O. No. 6 of 1937*

Statutory Authority	Section	Statutory Instrument
Noxious Weeds Act, No. 38 of 1936	2	**Noxious Weeds (Common Barberry) Order, S.I. No. 120 of 1958**
		Noxious Weeds (Male Wild Hop Plant) Order, S.I. No. 189 of 1965
		Noxious Weeds (Wild Oat) Order, S.I. No. 194 of 1973
	2(1)	**Noxious Weeds (Thistle, Ragwort and Dock) Order [Vol. XVII p. 403] S.R.& O. No. 103 of 1937**
Nuclear Energy (An Bord Fuinnimh Nuicleigh) Act, No. 12 of 1971	2	*Nuclear Energy (An Bord Fuinnimh Nuicleigh) Act, 1971 (Commencement) Order, S.I. No. 319 of 1973*
	6	**Nuclear Energy (General Control of Fissile Fuels, Radio-active Substances and Irradiating Apparatus) Order, S.I. No. 166 of 1977**
Nurses Act, No. 27 of 1950	3	*Nurses Act, 1950 (Establishment of An Bord Altranais) Order, S.I. No. 164 of 1951*
	11	*Nurses Act, 1950 (Establishment of An Bord Altranais) Order, S.I. No. 164 of 1951*
	12	*Nurses Act, 1950 (Establishment of An Bord Altranais) Order, S.I. No. 164 of 1951*
	28	*Nurses Act, 1950 (Establishment of An Bord Altranais) Order, S.I. No. 164 of 1951*
	29	*Nurses Act, 1950 (Establishment of An Bord Altranais) Order, S.I. No. 164 of 1951*
	80	*Nurses Act, 1950 (Adaptation of Rules) Order, S.I. No. 222 of 1951*
Nurses Act, No. 18 of 1985	3	*Nurses Act, 1985 (Commencement) Order, S.I. No. 438 of 1985*
		Nurses Act, 1985 (Commencement) Order, S.I. No. 265 of 1986
	4	*Nurses Act, 1985 (Establishment Day) Order, S.I. No. 266 of 1986*
	11	*An Bord Altranais (First Election of Members) Rules, S.I. No. 439 of 1985*
	55	*An Bord Altranais (First Election of Members) Rules, S.I. No. 439 of 1985*
Occasional Trading Act, No. 35 of 1979	2(3)	**Occasional Trading Act (Section 2 (2)) (Amendment) Regulations, S.I. No. 19 of 1981**
	13	*Occasional Trading Act, 1979 (Commencement) Order, S.I. No. 404 of 1979*
Offences Against the State Act, No. 13 of 1939	19(1)	**Unlawful Organisation (Suppression) Order [Vol. XXXII p. 109] S.R.& O. No. 162 of 1939**
		Unlawful Organisation (Suppression) Order, S.I. No. 7 of 1983
	36	**Offences Against the State (Scheduled Offences) Order [Vol. XXXII p. 69] S.R.& O. No. 339 of 1939**

Offences Against the State Act, No. 13 of 1939 (*Cont.*)

Offences Against the State (Scheduled Offences) (No.2) Order [Vol. XXXII p. 73] S.R.& O. No. 343 of 1939

Offences Against the State (Scheduled Offences) (No.3) Order, (1939) [Vol. XXXII p. 77] S.R.& O. No. 334 of 1940

Offences Against the State (Scheduled Offences) (No.4) Order [Vol. XXXVIII p. 77] S.R.& O. No. 205 of 1947

Offences Against the State (Scheduled Offences) (No.5) Order [Vol. XXXVIII p. 83] S.R.& O. No. 212 of 1947

Offences Against the State (Scheduled Offences) (No.6) Order [Vol. XXXVIII p. 87] S.R.& O. No. 282 of 1947

Offences Against the State (Scheduled Offences) (No.7) Order [Vol. XXXVIII p. 91] S.R.& O. No. 326 of 1947

Offences Against the State (Scheduled Offences) Order, S.I. No. 142 of 1972

Offences Against the State (Scheduled Offences) (No.2) Order, S.I. No. 282 of 1972

36(3)   Offences Against the State (Scheduled Offences) (Cessation) Order, S.I. No. 192 of 1948

41(1)   Special Criminal Court Rules [Vol. XXXII p. 81] S.R.& O. No. 266 of 1939

Special Criminal Court Additional Rules [Vol. XXXII p. 99] S.R.& O. No. 346 of 1939

Special Criminal Court Additional Rules [Vol. XXXII p. 103] S.R.& O. No. 441 of 1942

Rules of the Special Criminal Court, S.I. No. 147 of 1972

Special Criminal Court Rules, S.I. No. 234 of 1975

50(4)   Offences Against the State Act, 1939 (Military Custody) Regulations [Vol. XXXII p. 1] S.R.& O. No. 288 of 1939

Offences Against the State Act, 1939 (Military Custody) (Amendment) Regulations [Vol. XXXII p. 33] S.R.& O. No. 106 of 1940

Offences Against the State Act, 1939 (Military Custody) (Amendment) (No.2) Regulations [Vol. XXXII p. 37] S.R.& O. No. 178 of 1940

Offences Against the State Act, 1939 (Military Custody) (Amendment) (No.3) Regulations [Vol. XXXII p. 41] S.R.& O. No. 297 of 1940

Offences Against the State Act, 1939 (Military Custody) (Amendment) (No.4) Regulations [Vol. XXXII p. 45] S.R.& O. No. 182 of 1942

Offences Against the State Act, 1939 (Military Custody) (Amendment) (No.5) Regulations [Vol. XXXII p. 49] S.R.& O. No. 338 of 1942

Offences Against the State Act, 1939 (Military Custody) (Amendment) (No.6) Regulations [Vol. XXXVIII p. 95] S.R.& O. No. 279 of 1946

Statutory Authority	Section	Statutory Instrument
Offences Against the State Act, No. 13 of 1939 (*Cont.*)	58	*Offences Against the State Act, 1939 (Part VI) (Detention) Regulations [Vol. XXXII p. 55] S.R.& O. No. 249 of 1939*
	59	*Offences Against the State (Internment Commission) Order [Vol. XXXII p. 67] S.R.& O. No. 344 of 1939*
Offences Against the State (Amendment) Act, No. 2 of 1940	7	**Offences Against the State (Amendment) Act, 1940 (Detention) Regulations, S.I. No. 146 of 1957**
		Offences Against the State (Amendment) Act, 1940 (Detention) (Amendment) Regulations, S.I. No. 154 of 1957
		Offences Against the State (Amendment) Act, 1940 (Detention) (Amendment) Regulations, S.I. No. 16 of 1958
	8	**Offences Against the State (Amendment) Act, 1940 (Internment Commission) Order [Vol. XXXII p. 113] S.R.& O. No. 182 of 1945**
		Offences Against the State (Amendment) Act, 1940 (Commission for Inquiring into Detentions) Order, S.I. No. 157 of 1957
Office Premises Act, No. 3 of 1958	1(2)	*Office Premises Act, 1958 (Commencement) Order, S.I. No. 29 of 1959*
	9(2)	**Office Premises (Overcrowding) Regulations, S.I. No. 30 of 1959**
		Office Premises (Overcrowding) (Amendment) Regulations, S.I. No. 175 of 1963
	10(2)	**Office Premises (Minimum Temperature in Workrooms and Cloakrooms) Regulations, S.I. No. 31 of 1959**
	12(2)	**Office Premises (Standards of Lighting) Regulations, S.I. No. 196 of 1959**
	13(2)	**Office Premises (Sanitary Conveniences) Regulations, S.I. No. 32 of 1959**
	20(2)	**Office Premises (Washing Facilities) Regulations, S.I. No. 33 of 1959**
	23	**Office Premises (Clothing Accommodation) Regulations, S.I. No. 34 of 1959**
Official Secrets Act, No. 28 of 1911	3	*Shannon Electricity Works (Declaration of Prohibited Place) Order [Vol. XVII p. 407] S.R.& O. No. 73 of 1935*
Oil Burners (Standards) Act, No. 24 of 1960	2	**Oil Heaters Regulations, S.I. No. 9 of 1963**
		Oil Heaters (Amendment) Regulations, S.I. No. 178 of 1963
Oil in Navigable Waters Act, No. 5 of 1926	6	*Oil in Navigable Waters (Records) Order [Vol. XVII p. 413] S.R.& O. No. 21 of 1926*

Statutory Authority	Section	Statutory Instrument
Oil Pollution of the Sea Act, No. 25 of 1956	2	*Oil Pollution of the Sea Act, 1956 (Commencement) Order, S.I. No. 203 of 1957*
		Oil Pollution of the Sea Act, 1956 (Commencement) (No.2) Order, S.I. No. 165 of 1958
	4(2)	*Oil Pollution of the Sea Act, 1956 (Exceptions and Exemptions) Regulations, S.I. No. 205 of 1957*
		Oil Pollution of the Sea Act, 1956 (Exceptions and Exemptions) (Amendment) Regulations, S.I. No. 126 of 1967
	9	*Oil Pollution of the Sea Act, 1956 (Extension of Prohibited Zones) Order, S.I. No. 104 of 1961*
	10	*Oil Pollution of the Sea Act, 1956 (Application of Section 10) Regulations, S.I. No. 125 of 1967*
		Oil Pollution of the Sea Act, 1956 (Application of Section 10) Regulations, S.I. No. 353 of 1980
	10(2)	*Oil Pollution of the Sea Act, 1956 (Application of Section 10) Regulations, S.I. No. 204 of 1957*
	10(5)	*Oil Pollution of the Sea Act, 1956 (Exceptions and Exemptions) Regulations, S.I. No. 205 of 1957*
		Oil Pollution of the Sea Act, 1956 (Exception from Section 10 (3)) Regulations, S.I. No. 244 of 1958
		Oil Pollution of the Sea Act, 1956 (Exceptions and Exemptions) (Amendment) Regulations, S.I. No. 126 of 1967
		Oil Pollution of the Sea Act, 1956 (Exceptions) Regulations, S.I. No. 354 of 1980
	16(1)	*Oil Pollution of the Sea (Ships' Equipment) Regulations, S.I. No. 208 of 1957*
		Oil Pollution of the Sea (Ships' Equipment) Regulations, S.I. No. 352 of 1980
	17	*Oil Pollution of the Sea (Records) (Amendment) Regulations, S.I. No. 124 of 1967*
	17(1)	*Oil Pollution of the Sea (Records) Regulations, S.I. No. 206 of 1957*
		Oil Pollution of the Sea (Records) Regulations, S.I. No. 119 of 1980
	17(2)	**Oil Pollution of the Sea (Transfer Records) Regulations, S.I. No. 207 of 1957**
	17(3)	*Oil Pollution of the Sea (Records) Regulations, S.I. No. 206 of 1957*
		Oil Pollution of the Sea (Records) Regulations, S.I. No. 119 of 1980
	19(1)	**Oil Pollution of the Sea (Convention Countries) (Miscellaneous) Order, S.I. No. 69 of 1959**
		Oil Pollution of the Sea (Convention Countries) (Finland and Poland) Order, S.I. No. 154 of 1961
		Oil Pollution of the Sea (Convention Countries) (United States of America) Order, S.I. No. 302 of 1961

Statutory Authority	Section	Statutory Instrument
Oil Pollution of the Sea Act, No. 25 of 1956 (*Cont.*)		**Oil Pollution of the Sea (Convention Countries) (Ghana, Iceland, Kuwait and Liberia) Order, S.I. No. 158 of 1962**
		Oil Pollution of the Sea (Convention Countries) (Australia and the Netherlands Antilles) Order, S.I. No. 8 of 1963
		Oil Pollution of the Sea (Convention Countries) (Miscellaneous) Order, S.I. No. 240 of 1963
		Oil Pollution of the Sea (Convention Countries) (Miscellaneous) Order, S.I. No. 119 of 1964
		Oil Pollution of the Sea (Convention Countries) (Italy and Malagasy Republic) Order, S.I. No. 126 of 1965
		Oil Pollution of the Sea (Convention Amendment Countries) Order, S.I. No. 127 of 1967
		Oil Pollution of the Sea (Convention Countries and Convention Amendment Countries) Order, S.I. No. 305 of 1967
		Oil Pollution of the Sea (Convention Countries and Convention Amendment Countries) Order, S.I. No. 123 of 1968
		Oil Pollution of the Sea (Convention Countries and Convention Amendment Countries) Order, S.I. No. 224 of 1969
		Oil Pollution of the Sea (Convention Countries and Convention Amendment Countries) Order, S.I. No. 323 of 1971
		Oil Pollution of the Sea (Intervention Convention Countries) Order, S.I. No. 369 of 1979
		Oil Pollution of the Sea (Convention Countries and Convention Amendment Countries) Order, S.I. No. 222 of 1981
		Oil Pollution of the Sea (Intervention Convention Countries) Order, S.I. No. 223 of 1981
Oil Pollution of the Sea (Amendment) Act, No. 1 of 1965	1	*Oil Pollution of the Sea (Amendment) Act, 1965 (Commencement) Order, S.I. No. 122 of 1967*
	9	*Oil Pollution of the Sea (Extension of Prohibited Zones) Order, S.I. No. 123 of 1967*
Oil Pollution of the Sea (Amendment) Act, No. 15 of 1977	5	**Oil Pollution of the Sea (Amendment) Act, 1977 (Application of Section 2) Order, S.I. No. 318 of 1979**
	19	*Oil Pollution of the Sea (Amendment) Act, 1977 (Commencement) Order, S.I. No. 9 of 1978*
Oireachtas (Allowances to Members) Act, No. 34 of 1938	3A	**Members of the Oireachtas (Allowances) Order, S.I. No. 167 of 1977**
		Members of the Oireachtas and Ministerial and Parliamentary Offices (Allowances and Salaries) Order, S.I. No. 129 of 1978
		Members of the Oireachtas and Ministerial and Parliamentary Offices (Allowances and Salaries) Order, S.I. No. 299 of 1979

Statutory Authority	Section	Statutory Instrument
Oireachtas (Allowances to Members) Act, No. 34 of 1938 (*Cont.*)		**Members of the Oireachtas and Ministerial and Parliamentary Offices (Allowances and Salaries) Order, S.I. No. 46 of 1980**
		Members of the Oireachtas and Ministerial and Parliamentary Offices (Allowances and Salaries) (No.2) Order, S.I. No. 369 of 1980
		Members of the Oireachtas and Ministerial and Parliamentary Offices (Allowances and Salaries) Order, S.I. No. 386 of 1981
	4	**Oireachtas (Travelling Facilities to Members) Regulations, S.I. No. 46 of 1948**
		Oireachtas (Travelling Facilities to Members) (Amendment) Regulations, S.I. No. 174 of 1983
	6A	**Houses of the Oireachtas (Members) Pensions (Amendment) Scheme, S.I. No. 431 of 1986**
		Houses of the Oireachtas (Members) Pensions (Amendment) (No.2) Scheme, S.I. No. 432 of 1986
	6A(3)	**Houses of the Oireachtas (Members) Pension Scheme (Deduction of Contributions) Regulations, S.I. No. 269 of 1960**
Oireachtas (Allowances to Members) Act, No. 32 of 1962	3	**Oireachtas (Allowances to Members) Regulations, S.I. No. 4 of 1963**
		Oireachtas (Allowances to Members) (Amendment) Regulations, S.I. No. 276 of 1963
		Oireachtas (Allowances to Members) (Amendment) Regulations, S.I. No. 50 of 1964
		Oireachtas (Allowances to Members) (Amendment) Regulations, S.I. No. 180 of 1965
		Oireachtas (Allowances to Members) (Amendment) Regulations, S.I. No. 112 of 1975
		Oireachtas (Allowances to Members) (Amendment) Regulations, S.I. No. 119 of 1978
		Oireachtas (Allowances to Members) (Amendment) Regulations, S.I. No. 126 of 1984
Oireachtas (Allowances to Members) and Ministerial and Parliamentary and Judicial Offices (Amendment) Act, No. 29 of 1977	1(2)	*Oireachtas (Allowances to Members) and Ministerial, Parliamentary and Judicial Offices (Amendment) Act, 1977 (Commencement) Order, S.I. No. 379 of 1977*
Oireachtas (Allowances to Members) and Ministerial and Parliamentary Offices (Amendment) Act, No. 12 of 1960	2	*Oireachtas (Allowances to Members) and Ministerial and Parliamentary Offices (Amendment) Act, 1960 (Commencement) Order, S.I. No. 82 of 1960*
Oireachtas (Allowances to Members) and Ministerial and Parliamentary Offices (Amendment) Act, No. 14 of 1964	5(1)	*Oireachtas (Allowances to Members) (Travelling Facilities) Regulations, S.I. No. 281 of 1964*
		Oireachtas (Allowances to Members) (Travelling Facilities) (Amendment) Regulations, S.I. No. 100 of 1971
		Oireachtas (Allowances to Members) (Travelling Facilities) (Amendment) Regulations, S.I. No. 156 of 1972

Statutory Authority	Section	Statutory Instrument
Oireachtas (Allowances to Members) and Ministerial and Parliamentary Offices (Amendment) Act, No. 14 of 1964 (*Cont.*)		*Oireachtas (Allowances to Members) (Travelling Facilities) (Amendment) Regulations, S.I. No. 167 of 1974*
		Oireachtas (Allowances to Members) (Travelling Facilities) (Amendment) Regulations, S.I. No. 84 of 1976
		Oireachtas (Allowances to Members) (Travelling Facilities) (Amendment) Regulations, S.I. No. 162 of 1977
		Oireachtas (Allowances to Members) (Travelling Facilities) (Amendment) (No.2) Regulations, S.I. No. 227 of 1977
		Oireachtas (Allowances to Members) (Travelling Facilities) (Amendment) Regulations, S.I. No. 112 of 1978
		Oireachtas (Allowances to Members) (Travelling Facilities) (Amendment) (No.2) Regulations, S.I. No. 278 of 1978
		Oireachtas (Allowances to Members) (Travelling Facilities) (Amendment) Regulations, S.I. No. 210 of 1980
		Oireachtas (Allowances to Members) (Travelling Facilities) (Amendment) (No.2) Regulations, S.I. No. 378 of 1980
		Oireachtas (Allowances to Members) (Travelling Facilities) (Amendment) Regulations, S.I. No. 341 of 1983
	5(3)	*Oireachtas (Allowances to Members) and Ministerial and Parliamentary Offices (Amendment) Act, 1964 (Commencement of Section 5) Order, S.I. No. 280 of 1964*
Old Age Pensions Act, No. 18 of 1932	10(3)	*Old Age Pensions Act, 1932, (Commencement) Order [Vol. XVII p. 415] S.R.& O. No. 68 of 1932*
Old Age Pensions Acts, 1908 to 1938,		*Old Age Pensions (Amendment) Regulations [Vol. XXXVIII p. 99] S.R.& O. No. 23 of 1947*
Ombudsman Act, No. 26 of 1980	4(10)	**Ombudsman Act, 1980 (First Schedule) (Amendment) Order, S.I. No. 332 of 1984**
		Ombudsman Act, 1980 (First Schedule) (Amendment) Order, S.I. No. 66 of 1985
		Ombudsman Act, 1980 (Second Schedule) (Amendment) Order, S.I. No. 69 of 1985
	12(2)	*Ombudsman Act, 1980 (Appointed Day) Order, S.I. No. 424 of 1983*
Opticians Act, No. 17 of 1956	3	*Opticians Act, 1956 (Establishment Day) Order, S.I. No. 286 of 1956*
	3(2)	*Opticians Act, 1956 (Appointed Day) Order, S.I. No. 172 of 1959*
	23(5)	*Opticians Registers (Certification) Order, S.I. No. 143 of 1959*

Statutory Authority	Section	Statutory Instrument
Opticians Act, No. 17 of 1956 (*Cont.*)	32(5)	*Opticians Registers (Certification) Order, S.I. No. 143 of 1959*
Organisation for Economic Co-operation and Development (Financial Support Fund) (Amendment) Act, No. 21 of 1976	7	*Organisation for Economic Co-operation and Development (Financial Support Fund) (Agreement) Act, 1976 (Commencement) Order, S.I. No. 282 of 1977*
Oyster Cultivation (Ireland) Act, No. 48 of 1884	2	**Oyster Fishery (River Shannon) Order [Vol. XXXII p. 117] S.R.& O. No. 159 of 1939**
Packaged Goods (Quantity Control) Act, No. 11 of 1980	1	*Packaged Goods (Quantity Control) Act, 1980 (Commencement) Order, S.I. No. 41 of 1981*
	3	**Packaged Goods (Quantity Control) Regulations, S.I. No. 39 of 1981**
	8	**Packaged Goods (Quantity Control) Regulations, S.I. No. 39 of 1981**
	9	**Packaged Goods (Quantity Control) Regulations, S.I. No. 39 of 1981**
	10	**Packaged Goods (Quantity Control) Regulations, S.I. No. 39 of 1981**
	11	**Packaged Goods (Quantity Control) Regulations, S.I. No. 39 of 1981**
Patents Act, No. 12 of 1964	1	*Patents Act, 1964 (Commencement) Order, S.I. No. 91 of 1966*
	80	**Patents Rules, S.I. No. 268 of 1965**
		Patents (Amendment) Rules, S.I. No. 159 of 1970
		Patents (Amendment) Rules, S.I. No. 20 of 1974
		Patents (Amendment) Rules, S.I. No. 165 of 1976
		Patents (Amendment) Rules, S.I. No. 110 of 1978
		Patents (Amendment) Rules, S.I. No. 186 of 1980
		Patents (Amendment) Rules, S.I. No. 199 of 1982
		Patents (Amendment) Rules, S.I. No. 198 of 1983
		Patents (Amendment) Rules, S.I. No. 45 of 1985
		Patents (Amendment) Rules, S.I. No. 76 of 1986
	86	**Register of Patents Agents and Clerks Rules, S.I. No. 139 of 1966**
	93	**Patents, Designs and Trade Marks (International Arrangements) (Amendment) Order, S.I. No. 32 of 1968**
	93(1)	**Patents Act, 1964 (Section 93) (Declaration) Order, S.I. No. 314 of 1976**
	96	**Patents Rules, S.I. No. 268 of 1965**
		Register of Patents Agents and Clerks Rules, S.I. No. 139 of 1966
		Patents (Amendment) Rules, S.I. No. 159 of 1970
		Patents (Amendment) Rules, S.I. No. 20 of 1974
		Patents (Amendment) Rules, S.I. No. 165 of 1976
		Patents (Amendment) Rules, S.I. No. 110 of 1978
		Patents (Amendment) (No.2) Rules, S.I. No. 241 of 1978

Statutory Authority	Section	Statutory Instrument
Patents Act, No. 12 of 1964 (*Cont.*)		**Patents (Amendment) Rules, S.I. No. 52 of 1979**
		Patents (Amendment) (No.2) Rules, S.I. No. 300 of 1979
		Patents (Amendment) Rules, S.I. No. 186 of 1980
		Patents (Amendment) Rules, S.I. No. 199 of 1982
		Patents (Amendment) Rules, S.I. No. 198 of 1983
		Patents (Amendment) Rules, S.I. No. 45 of 1985
		Patents (Amendment) Rules, S.I. No. 76 of 1986
Pauper Children (Ireland) Act, 1898 and 1902,		**Boarded Out Children (Contracts) (Amendment) Order [Vol. XXXII p. 125] S.R.& O. No. 99 of 1940**
Pawnbrokers Act, No. 31 of 1964	1(2)	*Pawnbrokers Act, 1964 (Commencement) Order, S.I. No. 290 of 1964*
Payment of Wages Act, No. 40 of 1979	5(5)	*Payment of Wages Act, 1979 (Section 5) (Commencement) Order, S.I. No. 401 of 1980*
Penal Servitude Act, No. 69 of 1891		**Rules for the Government of Prisons [Vol. XXXVI p. 1087] S.R.& O. No. 320 of 1947**
		Measuring and Photographing of Prisoners, S.I. No. 114 of 1955
		Rules for the Government of Prisons, S.I. No. 127 of 1955
		Rules for the Government of Prisons, S.I. No. 135 of 1983
Pensions (Increase) Act, No. 3 of 1950	7	**Pensions (Increase) (Dublin Port and Docks Board) Regulations, S.I. No. 215 of 1950**
		Pensions (Increase) (Limerick Harbour Commissioners) Regulations, S.I. No. 216 of 1950
		Pensions (Increase) (Waterford Harbour Commissioners) Regulations, S.I. No. 280 of 1950
		Pensions (Increase) (Dundalk Harbour Commissioners) Regulations, S.I. No. 304 of 1950
		Pensions (Increase) (Dublin Port and Docks Board) Regulations, S.I. No. 21 of 1951
Pensions (Increase) Act, No. 10 of 1964	29	**Pensions (Increase) Regulations, S.I. No. 4 of 1966**
		Pensions (Increase) (No.2) Regulations, S.I. No. 147 of 1966
		Pensions (Increase) Regulations, S.I. No. 139 of 1967
		Pensions (Increase) Regulations, S.I. No. 103 of 1968
		Pensions (Increase) Regulations, S.I. No. 25 of 1969
		Pensions (Increase) Regulations, S.I. No. 181 of 1970
		Pensions (Increase) Regulations, S.I. No. 280 of 1971
		Pensions (Increase) Regulations, S.I. No. 76 of 1974
		Pensions (Increase) Regulations, S.I. No. 83 of 1975
		Pensions (Increase) (No.2) Regulations, S.I. No. 119 of 1975

Statutory Authority	Section	Statutory Instrument
Pensions (Increase) Act, No. 10 of 1964 (*Cont.*)		**Pensions (Increase) Regulations, S.I. No. 35 of 1976**
		Pensions (Increase) Regulations, S.I. No. 55 of 1977
		Pensions (Increase) (No.2) Regulations, S.I. No. 398 of 1977
		Pensions (Increase) Regulations, S.I. No. 331 of 1978
		Pensions (Increase) Regulations, S.I. No. 413 of 1980
		Pensions (Increase) Regulations, S.I. No. 330 of 1981
		Pensions (Increase) Regulations, S.I. No. 263 of 1982
		Pensions (Increase) Regulations, S.I. No. 254 of 1983
		Pensions (Increase) (No.1) Regulations, S.I. No. 255 of 1984
Pensions (Increase) Act, 1956, No. 44 of 1956	6	**Pensions (Increase) (Dublin Port and Docks Board) Regulations, S.I. No. 84 of 1957**
		Pensions (Increase) (Waterford Harbour Commissioners) Regulations, S.I. No. 122 of 1957
		Pensions (Increase) (Limerick Harbour Commissioners) Regulations, S.I. No. 150 of 1957
		Pensions (Increase) (Galway Harbour Commissioners) Regulations, S.I. No. 167 of 1957
Performers' Protection Act, No. 19 of 1968	12	**Performers' Protection (Foreign Countries) Order, S.I. No. 134 of 1978**
	13(2)	*Performers' Protection Act, 1968 (Commencement) Order, S.I. No. 201 of 1968*
Perpetual Funds (Registration) Act, No. 22 of 1933	15	*Perpetual Funds (Registration) Act, 1933 (Fees) Order, S.I. No. 85 of 1978*
		Perpetual Funds (Registration) Act, 1933 (Fees) Order, S.I. No. 293 of 1983
	15(1)	**Perpetual Funds (Registration) Act, 1933 (Regulations) Order [Vol. XVIII p. 17] S.R.& O. No. 308 of 1935**
	15(2)	*Perpetual Funds (Registration) Act (Fees Regulations) Order [Vol. XVIII p. 9] S.R.& O. No. 247 of 1935*
	16(2)	*Perpetual Funds (Registration) Act, 1933 (Commencement) Order [Vol. XVIII p. 13] S.R.& O. No. 248 of 1935*
Pharmacy Act, No. 30 of 1951	8(3)	*Pharmacy Act, 1951 (Date of Commencement) Order, S.I. No. 54 of 1952*
Pharmacy Act, No. 14 of 1962	11(3)	*Pharmacy Act, 1962 (Commencement) Order, S.I. No. 154 of 1962*
		Pharmacy Act, 1962 (Commencement) Order, S.I. No. 186 of 1982

Statutory Authority	Section	Statutory Instrument
Pharmacy (Ireland) Act, No. 57 of 1875	17	**Pharmaceutical Society Regulations (Amendment) (No.1) S.I. No. 164 of 1948**
		Pharmaceutical Society Regulations (Amendment) (No.2) S.I. No. 165 of 1948
		Pharmaceutical Society Regulations (Amendment) (No.3) S.I. No. 373 of 1948
		Pharmaceutical Society Regulations (Amendment) (No.4) S.I. No. 412 of 1948
		Pharmaceutical Society Regulations (Amendment) (No.1) Order, S.I. No. 32 of 1949
		Pharmaceutical Society Regulations (Amendment) (No.1) Order, S.I. No. 60 of 1950
		Pharmaceutical Society Regulations (Amendment) (No.2) Order, S.I. No. 61 of 1950
Phoenix Park Act, No. 31 of 1925		**Phoenix Park Dublin, Bye-laws [Vol. XVIII p. 33] S.R.& O. No. 6 of 1926**
Pigs and Bacon Act, No. 24 of 1935	1(2)	*Pigs and Bacon Act, 1935 (Parts I and II) (Commencement) Order [Vol. XVIII p. 41] S.R.& O. No. 187 of 1935*
		Pigs and Bacon Act, 1935 (Part III) (Commencement) Order [Vol. XVIII p. 45] S.R.& O. No. 262 of 1935
		Pigs and Bacon Act, 1935 (Part IV) (Commencement) Order [Vol. XVIII p. 49] S.R.& O. No. 409 of 1935
	6	*Pigs and Bacon Act, 1935 (Part II) (Appointed Day) Order [Vol. XVIII p. 53] S.R.& O. No. 43 of 1937*
	8	*Pigs and Bacon Act, 1935 (Part II) (No.3) Regulations, S.I. No. 37 of 1964*
		Pigs and Bacon Act, 1935 (Part II) Regulations, S.I. No. 113 of 1965
		Pigs and Bacon Act, 1935 (Part II) (No.4) Regulations, S.I. No. 217 of 1973
		Pigs and Bacon Act, 1935 (Part II) (No.5) Regulations, S.I. No. 105 of 1976
		Pigs and Bacon Act, 1935 (Part II) (No.6) Regulations, S.I. No. 52 of 1978
		Pigs and Bacon Act, 1935 (Part II) (Amendment) Regulations, S.I. No. 154 of 1980
		Pigs and Bacon Act, 1935 (Part II) (No.7) Regulations, S.I. No. 394 of 1980
		Pigs and Bacon Act, 1935 (Part II) (No.8) Regulations, S.I. No. 153 of 1982
		Pigs and Bacon Act, 1935 (Part II) (No.9) Regulations, S.I. No. 382 of 1982
		Pigs and Bacon Act, 1935 (Part II) (No.10) Regulations, S.I. No. 410 of 1983
		Pigs and Bacon Act, 1935 (Part II) (No.11) Regulations, S.I. No. 247 of 1985

Statutory Authority	Section	Statutory Instrument
Pigs and Bacon Act, No. 24 of 1935 (*Cont.*)	8(1)	**Pigs and Bacon Act, 1935 (Part II) (No.1) Regulations [Vol. XVIII p. 57] S.R.& O. No. 245 of 1935**
		Pigs and Bacon Act, 1935 (Part II) (No.2) Regulations [Vol. XVIII p. 71] S.R.& O. No. 311 of 1936
	11	**Pigs and Bacon Act, 1935 (Part II) Regulations, S.I. No. 113 of 1965**
	15	**Pigs and Bacon Act, 1935 (Part II) Regulations, S.I. No. 113 of 1965**
	17	**Pigs and Bacon Act, 1935 (Part II) Regulations, S.I. No. 113 of 1965**
	28	*Pigs and Bacon Act, 1935 (Part II) (No.8) Regulations, S.I. No. 153 of 1982*
		Pigs and Bacon Act, 1935 (Part II) (No.9) Regulations, S.I. No. 382 of 1982
		Pigs and Bacon Act, 1935 (Part II) (No.10) Regulations, S.I. No. 410 of 1983
		Pigs and Bacon Act, 1935 (Part II) (No.11) Regulations, S.I. No. 247 of 1985
	28(1)	*Pigs and Bacon Act, 1935 (Part II) (No.3) Regulations, S.I. No. 37 of 1964*
		Pigs and Bacon Act, 1935 (Part II) (No.4) Regulations, S.I. No. 217 of 1973
		Pigs and Bacon Act, 1935 (Part II) (No.5) Regulations, S.I. No. 105 of 1976
		Pigs and Bacon Act, 1935 (Part II) (No.6) Regulations, S.I. No. 52 of 1978
		Pigs and Bacon Act, 1935 (Part II) (No.7) Regulations, S.I. No. 394 of 1980
	32	**Pigs and Bacon Act, 1935 (Part II) Regulations, S.I. No. 113 of 1965**
	41	**Pigs and Bacon Act, 1935 (Part II) Regulations, S.I. No. 113 of 1965**
	42	**Pigs and Bacon Act, 1935 (Part II) Regulations, S.I. No. 113 of 1965**
	43	**Pigs and Bacon Act, 1935 (Part II) Regulations, S.I. No. 113 of 1965**
		Pigs and Bacon Act, 1935 (Part II) (Amendment) Regulations, S.I. No. 154 of 1980
	44	**Pigs and Bacon Act, 1935 (Part II) Regulations, S.I. No. 113 of 1965**
	45	**Pigs and Bacon Act, 1935 (Part II) Regulations, S.I. No. 113 of 1965**
	46	**Pigs and Bacon Act, 1935 (Part II) Regulations, S.I. No. 113 of 1965**
	51	**Bacon (Production from Carcases of Pigs Slaughtered in Licensed Slaughtering Premises) Order [Vol. XVIII p. 119] S.R.& O. No. 142 of 1936**

Statutory Authority	Section	Statutory Instrument
Pigs and Bacon Act, No. 24 of 1935 (*Cont.*)	52	**Pigs and Bacon Act, 1935 (Part II) Regulations, S.I. No. 113 of 1965**
		Pigs and Bacon Act, 1935 (Part II) (Amendment) Regulations, S.I. No. 259 of 1985
	54	**Pigs and Bacon Act, 1935 (Part II) Regulations, S.I. No. 113 of 1965**
	54(1)	*Pigs and Bacon Act, 1935 (Part II) (Amendment) Regulations [Vol. XXXII p. 129] S.R.& O. No. 82 of 1939*
	77(3)	*Bacon Marketing Board (Ordinary Members) Election Order [Vol. XVIII p. 103] S.R.& O. No. 317 of 1935*
		Bacon Marketing Board (Ordinary Members) Election Order, S.R.& O. No. 290 of 1936
Pigs and Bacon Act, No. 23 of 1937	12(1)	*Pigs and Bacon Act, 1937 (Part III) (Appointed Day) Order [Vol. XVIII p. 123] S.R.& O. No. 175 of 1937*
	30	*External-Sales (No.1) Order, S.I. No. 44 of 1958*
		External-Sales (No.2) Order, S.I. No. 69 of 1958
		External-Sales (No.3) Order, S.I. No. 96 of 1958
		External-Sales (No.4) Order, S.I. No. 105 of 1958
		External-Sales (No.5) Order, S.I. No. 111 of 1958
		External-Sales (No.6) Order, S.I. No. 122 of 1958
	42(1)	*Pigs and Bacon Act, 1937 (Part IV) (Appointed Day) Order [Vol. XVIII p. 127] S.R.& O. No. 176 of 1937*
	58	*Pigs and Bacon Acts, 1935 to 1956 (Pigs and Bacon Commission) Insurance Allowance (No.1) Order, S.I. No. 178 of 1958*
		Pigs and Bacon Acts, 1935 to 1956 (Pigs and Bacon Commission) Insurance Allowance (No.1) Order, S.I. No. 60 of 1960
		Pigs and Bacon Acts, 1935 to 1961 (Pigs and Bacon Commission) Insurance Allowance (No.1) Order, S.I. No. 218 of 1967
		Pigs and Bacon Acts, 1935 to 1961 (Pigs and Bacon Commission) Insurance Allowance (No.1) Order, S.I. No. 164 of 1969
		Pigs and Bacon Acts, 1935 to 1961 (Pigs and Bacon Commission) Insurance Allowance (No.1) Order, S.I. No. 39 of 1971
		Pigs And Bacon Acts, 1935 to 1961 (Pigs and Bacon Commission) Insurance Allowance (No.2) Order, S.I. No. 231 of 1971
		Pigs and Bacon Acts, 1935 to 1961 (Pigs and Bacon Commission) Insurance Allowance (No.1) Order, S.I. No. 282 of 1973
		Pigs and Bacon Acts, 1935 to 1961 (Pigs and Bacon Commission) Insurance Allowance (No.1) Order, S.I. No. 149 of 1974
		Pigs and Bacon Acts, 1935 to 1961 (Pigs and Bacon Commission) Insurance Allowance (No.1) Order, S.I. No. 93 of 1975

Statutory Authority	Section	Statutory Instrument
Pigs and Bacon Act, No. 23 of 1937 (*Cont.*)	58(1)	*Pigs and Bacon Acts, 1935 to 1961 (Pigs and Bacon Commission) Insurance Allowance (No.1) Order, S.I. No. 113 of 1964*
		Pigs and Bacon Acts, 1935 to 1961 (Pigs and Bacon Commission) Insurance Allowance (No.2) Order, S.I. No. 240 of 1964
	59	*Pigs and Bacon Acts, 1935 to 1961 (Pigs and Bacon Commission) Damage Allowance (No.1) Order, S.I. No. 96 of 1967*
		Pigs and Bacon Acts, 1935 to 1961 (Pigs and Bacon Commission) Damage Allowance (No.1) Order, S.I. No. 207 of 1974
	62(1)	*Pigs and Bacon Acts, 1935 to 1956 (Pigs and Bacon Commission) Grading (No.1) Order, S.I. No. 144 of 1958*
		Pigs and Bacon Acts, 1935 to 1956 (Pigs and Bacon Commission) Grading (No.1) Order, S.I. No. 88 of 1960
		Pigs and Bacon Acts, 1935 to 1956 (Pigs and Bacon Commission) Grading (No.1) (Amendment) Order, S.I. No. 209 of 1960
		Pigs and Bacon Acts, 1935 to 1961 (Pigs and Bacon Commission) Grading (No.1) Order, S.I. No. 61 of 1962
		Pigs and Bacon Acts, 1935 to 1961 (Pigs and Bacon Commission) Grading (No.1) Order, S.I. No. 1 of 1963
		Pigs and Bacon Acts, 1935 to 1961 (Pigs and Bacon Commission) Grading (No.2) Order, S.I. No. 48 of 1963
		Pigs and Bacon Acts, 1935 to 1961 (Pigs and Bacon Commission) Grading (No.3) Order, S.I. No. 132 of 1963
		Pigs and Bacon Acts, 1935 to 1961 (Pigs and Bacon Commission) Grading (No.4) Order, S.I. No. 152 of 1963
		Pigs and Bacon Acts, 1935 to 1961 (Pigs and Bacon Commission) Grading (No.5) Order, S.I. No. 194 of 1963
		Pigs and Bacon Acts, 1935 to 1961 (Pigs and Bacon Commission) Grading (No.6) Order, S.I. No. 267 of 1963
		Pigs and Bacon Acts, 1935 to 1961 (Pigs and Bacon Commission) Grading (No.1) Order, S.I. No. 10 of 1964
		Pigs and Bacon Acts, 1935 to 1961 (Pigs and Bacon Commission) Grading (No.2) Order, S.I. No. 12 of 1964
		Pigs and Bacon Acts, 1935 to 1961 (Pigs and Bacon Commission) Grading (No.3) Order, S.I. No. 60 of 1964
		Pigs and Bacon Acts, 1935 to 1961 (Pigs and Bacon Commission) Grading (No.4) Order, S.I. No. 145 of 1964

Statutory Authority	Section	Statutory Instrument
Pigs and Bacon Act, No. 23 of 1937 (*Cont.*)		*Pigs and Bacon Acts, 1935 to 1961 (Pigs and Bacon Commission) Grading (No.5) Order, S.I. No. 160 of 1964*
		Pigs and Bacon Acts, 1935 to 1961 (Pigs and Bacon Commission) Grading (No.1) Order, S.I. No. 74 of 1966
		Pigs and Bacon Acts, 1935 to 1961 (Pigs and Bacon Commission) Grading (No.1) Order, S.I. No. 135 of 1969
		Pigs and Bacon Acts, 1935 to 1961 (Pigs and Bacon Commission) Grading (No.2) Order, S.I. No. 198 of 1969
		Pigs and Bacon Acts, 1935 to 1961 (Pigs and Bacon Commission) Grading (No.1) Order, S.I. No. 257 of 1971
Pigs and Bacon (Amendment) Act, No. 35 of 1939	4(3)(b)(i)	**Pigs and Bacon Commission (Nominating Bodies) (Pig Producers) Order, S.I. No. 118 of 1961**
	4(3)(b)(ii)	**Pigs and Bacon Commission (Nominating Body) (Curers of Bacon) Order, S.I. No. 117 of 1961**
	4(3)(d)	**Pigs and Bacon Commission (Nominating Bodies) (Pig Producers) (Amendment) Order, S.I. No. 159 of 1964**
		Pigs and Bacon Commission (Nominating Bodies) (Pig Producers) (Amendment) Order, S.I. No. 177 of 1973
	5	*Pigs and Bacon Commission (Appointed Day) Order, S.I. No. 135 of 1961*
	13	*Bacon Export Subsidy (No.1) Order, S.I. No. 64 of 1958*
	34	*Pigs and Bacon Acts, 1935 to 1956 (Pigs and Bacon Commission) Bacon Pig Production Levy (No.2) Order, S.I. No. 136 of 1957*
		Pigs and Bacon Acts, 1935 to 1956 (Pigs and Bacon Commission) Bacon Pig Production Levy (No.3) Order, S.I. No. 191 of 1957
		Pigs and Bacon Acts, 1935 to 1956 (Pigs and Bacon Commission) Bacon Pig Production Levy (No.1) Order, S.I. No. 143 of 1958
		Pigs and Bacon Acts, 1935 to 1956 (Pigs and Bacon Commission) Bacon Pig Production Levy (No.2) Order, S.I. No. 235 of 1959
		Pigs and Bacon Acts, 1935 to 1961 (Pigs and Bacon Commission) Bacon Pig Production Levy (No.1) Order, S.I. No. 206 of 1965
		Pigs and Bacon Acts, 1935 to 1961 (Pigs and Bacon Commission) Bacon Pig Production Levy (No.2) Order, S.I. No. 270 of 1965
		Pigs and Bacon Acts, 1935 to 1961 (Pigs and Bacon Commission) Bacon Pig Production Levy (No.1) Order, S.I. No. 61 of 1967
		Pigs and Bacon Acts, 1935 to 1961 (Pigs and Bacon Commission) Bacon Pig Production Levy (No.1) Order, S.I. No. 95 of 1972

Statutory Authority	Section	Statutory Instrument

igs and Bacon (Amendment) Act,
Io. 35 of 1939 *(Cont.)*

Pigs and Bacon Acts, 1935 to 1961 (Pigs and Bacon Commission and European Communities Act, 1972) Bacon Pig Production Levy (No.1) Order, S.I. No. 31 of 1973

Pigs and Bacon Acts, 1935 to 1961 (Pigs and Bacon Commission) Bacon Pig Production Levy (No.1) Order, S.I. No. 299 of 1974

Pigs and Bacon Acts, 1935 to 1961 (Pigs and Bacon Commission) Bacon Pig Production Levy (No.1) Order, S.I. No. 70 of 1975

Pigs and Bacon Acts, 1935 to 1961 (Pigs and Bacon Commission) Bacon Pig Production Levy (No.2) Order, S.I. No. 141 of 1975

Pigs and Bacon Acts, 1935 to 1961 (Pigs and Bacon Commission) Bacon Pig Production Levy (No.3) Order, S.I. No. 217 of 1975

Pigs and Bacon Acts, 1935 to 1961 (Pigs and Bacon Commission) Bacon Pig Production Levy (No.1) Order, S.I. No. 303 of 1976

Pigs and Bacon Acts, 1935 to 1961 (Pigs and Bacon Commission) Bacon Pig Production Levy (No.1) Order, S.I. No. 400 of 1977

Pigs and Bacon Acts, 1935 to 1961 (Pigs and Bacon Commission) Bacon Pig Production Levy (No.1) Order, S.I. No. 176 of 1978

Pigs and Bacon Acts, 1935 to 1961 (Pigs and Bacon Commission) Bacon Pig Production Levy (No.1) Order, S.I. No. 93 of 1979

Pigs and Bacon Acts, 1935 to 1961 (Pigs and Bacon Commission) Bacon Pig Production Levy (No.2) Order, S.I. No. 259 of 1979

34(1) *Pigs and Bacon Acts, 1935 to 1956 (Pigs and Bacon Commission) Bacon Pig Production Levy (No.1) Order, S.I. No. 55 of 1959*

Pigs and Bacon Acts, 1935 to 1961 (Pigs and Bacon Commission) Bacon Pig Production Levy (No.1) Order, S.I. No. 56 of 1962

34(3) *Pigs and Bacon Acts, 1935 to 1956 (Pigs and Bacon Commission) Bacon Pig Production Levy (No.1) Order, S.I. No. 258 of 1960*

Pigs and Bacon Acts, 1935 to 1961 (Pigs and Bacon Commission) Bacon Pig Production Levy (No.1) Order, S.I. No. 145 of 1968

Pigs and Bacon Acts, 1935 to 1961 (Pigs and Bacon Commission) Bacon Pig Production Levy (No.2) Order, S.I. No. 202 of 1968

Pigs and Bacon Acts, 1935 to 1961 (Pigs and Bacon Commission) Bacon Pig Production Levy (No.1) Order, S.I. No. 49 of 1969

Pigs and Bacon Acts, 1935 to 1961 (Pigs and Bacon Commission) Bacon Pig Production Levy (No.1) Order, S.I. No. 215 of 1970

Pigs and Bacon Acts, 1935 to 1961 (Pigs and Bacon Commission) Bacon Pig Production Levy (No.2) Order, S.I. No. 306 of 1970

Statutory Authority	Section	Statutory Instrument
Pigs and Bacon (Amendment) Act, No. 35 of 1939 *(Cont.)*		*Pigs and Bacon Acts, 1935 to 1961 (Pigs and Bacon Commission) Bacon Pig Production Levy (No.1) Order, S.I. No. 123 of 1971*
		Pigs and Bacon Acts, 1935 to 1961 (Pigs and Bacon Commission) Bacon Pig Production Levy (No.2) Order, S.I. No. 194 of 1971
		Pigs and Bacon Acts, 1935 to 1961 (Pigs and Bacon Commission) Bacon Pig Production Levy (No.1) Order, S.I. No. 395 of 1980
	35(2)	*Pigs and Bacon Acts, 1935 to 1956 Bacon Sales Levy (Home Consumption) Suspending (No.8) Order, S.I. No. 170 of 1957*
		Pigs and Bacon Acts, 1935 to 1956 Bacon Sales Levy (Home Consumption) Suspending (No.9) Order, S.I. No. 186 of 1957
		Bacon Sales Levy (Home Consumption) Suspending (No.10) Order, S.I. No. 201 of 1957
		Bacon Sales Levy (Home Consumption) Suspending (No.11) Order, S.I. No. 233 of 1957
		Bacon Sales Levy (Home Consumption) Suspending (No.12) Order, S.I. No. 251 of 1957
		Bacon Sales Levy (Home Consumption) Suspending (No.1) Order, S.I. No. 8 of 1958
		Bacon Sales Levy (Home Consumption) Suspending (No.2) Order, S.I. No. 43 of 1958
		Bacon Sales Levy (Home Consumption) Suspending (No.3) Order, S.I. No. 61 of 1958
		Bacon Sales Levy (Home Consumption) Suspending (No.4) Order, S.I. No. 95 of 1958
		Bacon Sales Levy (Home Consumption) Suspending (No.5) Order, S.I. No. 112 of 1958
		Bacon Sales Levy (Home Consumption) Suspending (No.6) Order, S.I. No. 131 of 1958
		Bacon Sales Levy (Home Consumption) Suspending (No.7) Order, S.I. No. 149 of 1958
		Bacon Sales Levy (Home Consumption) Suspending (No.8) Order, S.I. No. 172 of 1958
		Bacon Sales Levy (Home Consumption) Suspending (No.9) Order, S.I. No. 191 of 1958
		Bacon Sales Levy (Home Consumption) Suspending (No.10) Order, S.I. No. 207 of 1958
		Bacon Sales Levy (Home Consumption) Suspending (No.11) Order, S.I. No. 219 of 1958
		Bacon Sales Levy (Home Consumption) Suspending (No.12) Order, S.I. No. 257 of 1958
		Bacon Sales Levy (Home Consumption) Suspending (No.1) Order, S.I. No. 7 of 1959
		Bacon Sales Levy (Home Consumption) Suspending (No.2) Order, S.I. No. 23 of 1959
		Bacon Sales Levy (Home Consumption) Suspending (No.3) Order, S.I. No. 39 of 1959
		Bacon Sales Levy (Home Consumption) Suspending (No.4) Order, S.I. No. 71 of 1959

Statutory Authority	Section	Statutory Instrument
igs and Bacon (Amendment) Act, o. 35 of 1939 (*Cont.*)		*Bacon Sales Levy (Home Consumption) Suspending (No.5) Order, S.I. No. 85 of 1959*
		Bacon Sales Levy (Home Consumption) Suspending (No.6) Order, S.I. No. 106 of 1959
		Bacon Sales Levy (Home Consumption) Suspending (No.7) Order, S.I. No. 113 of 1959
		Bacon Sales Levy (Home Consumption) Suspending (No.8) Order, S.I. No. 134 of 1959
		Bacon Sales Levy (Home Consumption) Suspending (No.9) Order, S.I. No. 153 of 1959
		Bacon Sales Levy (Home Consumption) Suspending (No.10) Order, S.I. No. 163 of 1959
		Bacon Sales Levy (Home Consumption) Suspending (No.11) Order, S.I. No. 187 of 1959
		Bacon Sales Levy (Home Consumption) Suspending (No.12) Order, S.I. No. 213 of 1959
		Bacon Sales Levy (Home Consumption) Suspending (No.1) Order, S.I. No. 7 of 1960
		Bacon Sales Levy (Home Consumption) Suspending (No.2) Order, S.I. No. 30 of 1960
		Bacon Sales Levy (Home Consumption) Suspending (No.3) Order, S.I. No. 47 of 1960
		Bacon Sales Levy (Home Consumption) Suspending (No.4) Order, S.I. No. 73 of 1960
		Bacon Sales Levy (Home Consumption) Suspending (No.5) Order, S.I. No. 105 of 1960
		Bacon Sales Levy (Home Consumption) Suspending (No.6) Order, S.I. No. 127 of 1960
		Bacon Sales Levy (Home Consumption) Suspending (No.7) Order, S.I. No. 150 of 1960
		Bacon Sales Levy (Home Consumption) Suspending (No.8) Order, S.I. No. 171 of 1960
		Bacon Sales Levy (Home Consumption) Suspending (No.9) Order, S.I. No. 197 of 1960
		Bacon Sales Levy (Home Consumption) Suspending (No.10) Order, S.I. No. 214 of 1960
		Bacon Sales Levy (Home Consumption) Suspending (No.11) Order, S.I. No. 230 of 1960
		Bacon Sales Levy (Home Consumption) Suspending (No.12) Order, S.I. No. 257 of 1960
		Bacon Sales Levy (Home Consumption) Suspending (No.1) Order, S.I. No. 8 of 1961
		Bacon Sales Levy (Home Consumption) Suspending (No.2) Order, S.I. No. 28 of 1961
		Bacon Sales Levy (Home Consumption) Suspending (No.3) Order, S.I. No. 61 of 1961
		Bacon Sales Levy (Home Consumption) Suspending (No.4) Order, S.I. No. 83 of 1961
		Bacon Sales Levy (Home Consumption) Suspending (No.5) Order, S.I. No. 101 of 1961
		Bacon Sales Levy (Home Consumption) Suspending (No.6) Order, S.I. No. 120 of 1961

Statutory Authority	Section	Statutory Instrument
Pigs and Bacon (Amendment) Act, No. 35 of 1939 *(Cont.)*	40	*Bacon Export Subsidy (No.3) Order, S.I. No. 18 of 1957*
		Bacon Export Subsidy (No.1) Order, S.I. No. 64 o 1958
		Bacon Export Subsidy (No.1) Order, S.I. No. 16 of 1959
		Bacon Export Subsidy (No.1) Order, S.I. No. 79 o 1961
		Bacon Export Subsidy (No.1) Order, S.I. No. 18 of 1963
		Bacon Export Subsidy (No.1) Order, S.I. No. 15 of 1964
	42	*Pigs and Bacon Acts, 1935 to 1956 (Pigs and Baco Commission) Regulations (No.2) Order, S.I No. 171 of 1957*
		Pigs and Bacon Acts, 1935 to 1961 (Pigs and Baco Commission) Regulations (No.1) Order, S.I No. 177 of 1963
	50(1)	**Pigs and Bacon Act, 1939 (Suspension of Section 98 Order [Vol. XXXII p. 135] S.R.& O. No. 74 o 1940**
Pigs and Bacon (Amendment) Act, No. 37 of 1956	2	*Pigs and Bacon (Amendment) Act, 1956 (Com mencement) Order, S.I. No. 311 of 1956*
	3	**Pigs and Bacon Acts, 1935 to 1961 (Pigs and Baco Commission) Minimum Prices (No.3) Order, S.I No. 293 of 1972**
	3(1)	*Pigs and Bacon Acts, 1935 to 1956 (Pigs and Baco Commission) Minimum Prices (No.1) Order, S.I No. 142 of 1958*
		Pigs and Bacon Acts, 1935 to 1956 (Pigs and Baco Commission) Minimum Prices (No.1) Order, S.I No. 90 of 1960
		Pigs and Bacon Acts, 1935 to 1961 (Pigs and Baco Commission) Minimum Prices (No.1) Order, S.I No. 2 of 1963
		Pigs and Bacon Acts, 1935 to 1961 (Pigs and Baco Commission) Minimum Prices (No.2) Order, S.I No. 49 of 1963
		Pigs and Bacon Acts, 1935 to 1961 (Pigs and Baco Commission) Minimum Prices (No.3) Order, S.I No. 131 of 1963
		Pigs and Bacon Acts, 1935 to 1961 (Pigs and Baco Commission) Minimum Prices (No.4) Order, S.I No. 196 of 1963
		Pigs and Bacon Acts, 1935 to 1961 (Pigs and Baco Commission) Minimum Prices (No.5) Order, S.I No. 273 of 1963
		Pigs and Bacon Acts, 1935 to 1961 (Pigs and Baco Commission) Minimum Prices (No.1) Order, S.I No. 110 of 1964
		Pigs and Bacon Acts, 1935 to 1961 (Pigs and Baco Commission) Minimum Prices (No.2) Order, S.I No. 120 of 1964

Pigs and Bacon (Amendment) Act, No. 37 of 1956 (*Cont.*)

Pigs and Bacon Acts, 1935 to 1961 (Pigs and Bacon Commission) Minimum Prices (No.1) Order, S.I. No. 200 of 1965

Pigs and Bacon Acts, 1935 to 1961 (Pigs and Bacon Commission) Minimum Prices (No.1) Order, S.I. No. 65 of 1966

Pigs and Bacon Acts, 1935 to 1961 (Pigs and Bacon Commission) Minimum Prices (No.1) Order, S.I. No. 84 of 1967

Pigs and Bacon Acts, 1935 to 1961 (Pigs and Bacon Commission) Minimum Prices (No.2) Order, S.I. No. 233 of 1967

Pig and Bacon Acts, 1935 to 1961 (Pigs and Bacon Commission) Minimum Prices (No.1) Order, S.I. No. 92 of 1968

Pigs and Bacon Acts, 1935 to 1961 (Pigs and Bacon Commission) Minimum Prices (No.1) Order, S.I. No. 130 of 1969

Pigs and Bacon Acts, 1935 to 1961 (Pigs and Bacon Commission) Minimum Prices (No.2) Order, S.I. No. 199 of 1969

Pigs and Bacon Acts, 1935 to 1961 (Pigs and Bacon Commission) Minimum Prices (No.1) Order, S.I. No. 93 of 1970

Pigs and Bacon Acts, 1935 to 1961 (Pigs and Bacon Commission) Minimum Prices (No.2) Order, S.I. No. 288 of 1970

Pigs and Bacon Acts, 1935 to 1961 (Pigs and Bacon Commission) Minimum Prices (No.1) Order, S.I. No. 157 of 1971

Pigs and Bacon Acts, 1935 to 1961 (Pigs and Bacon Commission) Minimum Prices (No.2) Order, S.I. No. 258 of 1971

Pigs and Bacon Acts, 1935 to 1961 (Pigs and Bacon Commission) Minimum Prices (No.1) Order, S.I. No. 94 of 1972

Pigs and Bacon Acts, 1935 to 1961 (Pigs and Bacon Commission) Minimum Prices (No.2) Order, S.I. No. 109 of 1972

4(3) **Pigs and Bacon Acts, 1935 to 1956 (Pigs and Bacon Commission) Freight Allowance (No.1) Order, S.I. No. 141 of 1958**

4(3)(a) **Pigs and Bacon Acts, 1935 to 1956 (Pigs and Bacon Commission) Freight Allowance (No.1) Order, S.I. No. 89 of 1960**

13 *Bacon Export Subsidy (No.3) Order, S.I. No. 180 of 1957*

Bacon Export Subsidy (No.1) Order, S.I. No. 164 of 1959

Bacon Export Subsidy (No.1) Order, S.I. No. 79 of 1961

Bacon Export Subsidy (No.1) Order, S.I. No. 181 of 1963

Bacon Export Subsidy (No.1) Order, S.I. No. 150 of 1964

Statutory Authority	Section	Statutory Instrument
Pigs and Bacon (Amendment) Act, No. 14 of 1961	2	*Pigs and Bacon (Amendment) Act, 1961 (Commencement of Sections 7, 8, 9 and 31) Order, S.I. No. 116 of 1961*
		Pigs and Bacon (Amendment) Act, 1961 (Commencement) (No.2) Order, S.I. No. 134 of 1961
		Pigs and Bacon (Amendment) Act, 1961 (Commencement of Section 16) Order, S.I. No. 26 of 1963
		Pigs and Bacon (Amendment) Act, 1961 (Commencement of Section 17) Order, S.I. No. 80 of 1963
	22	**Pigs and Bacon Commission Superannuation Scheme, S.I. No. 239 of 1971**
	24	**Pigs and Bacon Acts, 1935 to 1961 (Pigs and Bacon Commission) Regulations (No.1) S.I. No. 123 of 1965**
Pilotage Act, No. 31 of 1913 (sess. 2)		**Pilotage Orders (Applications) Rules, S.R.& O. No. 82 of 1928**
		Drogheda Pilotage Order, 1920 (Amendment) Order, S.I. No. 306 of 1950
		Dublin Pilotage Order, 1925 (Amendment) Order, S.I. No. 24 of 1963
		Dundalk Pilotage Order, 1920 (Amendment) Order, S.I. No. 100 of 1966
		Dublin Pilotage Order, 1925 (Amendment) Order, S.I. No. 32 of 1982
		Cork Pilotage District (Amendment) Order, S.I. No. 141 of 1983
		Limerick Pilotage (Amendment) Order, S.I. No. 88 of 1986
Pilotage (Amendment) Act, No. 2 of 1962	6	*Pilotage (Amendment) Act, 1962 (Commencement) Order, S.I. No. 25 of 1963*
Place Names (Irish Forms) Act, No. 24 of 1973	2(1)	**Logainmneacha (Foirmeacha Gaeilge) (Uimh.1) (Postbhailte) (An tOrdu) S.I. No. 133 of 1975**
Plant Varieties (Proprietary Rights) Act, No. 24 of 1980	2	**Plant Varieties (Proprietary Rights) Act, 1980 (Convention Countries) Order, S.I. No. 190 of 1981**
		Plant Varieties (Proprietary Rights) Act, 1980 (Convention Countries) Order, S.I. No. 284 of 1985
	4	**Plant Varieties (Proprietary Rights) Regulations, S.I. No. 23 of 1981**
		Plant Varieties (Proprietary Rights) (Amendment) Regulations, S.I. No. 137 of 1984
		Plant Varieties (Proprietary Rights) (Amendment) Regulations, S.I. No. 46 of 1986
	4(3)	**Plant Breeders' Rights (Form of Certificate) Regulations, S.I. No. 19 of 1982**
	11	**Plant Varieties (Proprietary Rights) Regulations, S.I. No. 23 of 1981**
	12	**Plant Varieties (Proprietary Rights) Regulations, S.I. No. 23 of 1981**

Statutory Authority	Section	Statutory Instrument
Plant Varieties (Proprietary Rights) Act, No. 24 of 1980 (*Cont.*)		**Plant Varieties (Proprietary Rights) (Amendment) Regulations, S.I. No. 137 of 1984**
		Plant Varieties (Proprietary Rights) (Amendment) Regulations, S.I. No. 46 of 1986
	15	**Plant Varieties (Proprietary Rights) Regulations, S.I. No. 23 of 1981**
	21	**Plant Varieties (Proprietary Rights) Regulations, S.I. No. 23 of 1981**
	25 Sch. I par. 2(d)	**Plant Varieties (Proprietary Rights) Regulations, S.I. No. 23 of 1981**
	26	**Plant Varieties (Proprietary Rights) (Amendment) Regulations, S.I. No. 137 of 1984**
		Plant Varieties (Proprietary Rights) (Amendment) Regulations, S.I. No. 46 of 1986
	28(2)	*Plant Varieties (Proprietary Rights) Act, 1980 (Commencement) Order, S.I. No. 22 of 1981*
Plebiscite (Draft Constitution) Act, No. 16 of 1937	11(5)	*Plebiscite (Accounts) Regulations [Vol. XVIII p. 141] S.R.& O. No. 142 of 1937*
		Plebiscite (Returning Officers' Charges) Order [Vol. XVIII p. 147] S.R.& O. No. 145 of 1937
Poblacht na hEireann (Acht um) No. 22 of 1948	4	*Poblacht na hEireann, 1948 (Tosach Feidhme) (An tOrdu um Acht) S.I. No. 27 of 1949*
Poisons Act, No. 12 of 1961	2	**Comhairle na Nimheanna Order, S.I. No. 44 of 1962**
	7	**Comhairle na Nimheanna Order, S.I. No. 44 of 1962**
	14	*Poisons Act, 1961 (Paraquat) Regulations, S.I. No. 95 of 1968*
		Poisons Act, 1961 (Paraquat) Regulations, S.I. No. 146 of 1975
		Poisons Regulations, S.I. No. 188 of 1982
		Poisons (Amendment) Regulations, S.I. No. 51 of 1983
		Poisons (Amendment) Regulations, S.I. No. 349 of 1984
		Poisons (Amendment) Regulations, S.I. No. 424 of 1986
	15	**Poisons (Control of Residues in Foods of Animal Origin) Regulations, S.I. No. 257 of 1985**
		Poisons (Control of Residues in Foods of Animal Origin) (Amendment) Regulations, S.I. No. 236 of 1986
	15A	**Poisons (Control of Residues in Foods of Animal Origin) Regulations, S.I. No. 257 of 1985**
		Poisons (Control of Residues in Foods of Animal Origin) (Amendment) Regulations, S.I. No. 236 of 1986
	16	*Poisons Act, 1961 (Paraquat) Regulations, S.I. No. 95 of 1968*
	22	*Poisons Act, 1961 (Date of Commencement) Order, S.I. No. 121 of 1961*

Statutory Authority	Section	Statutory Instrument
Poisons (Ireland) Act, No. 26 of 1870	1	*Poisons (Ireland) Act, 1870 (Additional Poison) Order [Vol. XVIII p. 163] S.R.& O. No. 109 of 1934*
		Poisons (Ireland) Act, 1870 (Additional Poisons) Order [Vol. XXXII p. 143] S.R.& O. No. 254 of 1939
		Poisons (Ireland) Act, 1870 (Additional Poisons) Order [Vol. XXXII p. 139] S.R.& O. No. 97 of 1942
		Poisons (Ireland) Act, 1870 (Additional Poisons) Order [Vol. XXXII p. 149] S.R.& O. No. 28 of 1944
		Poisons (Ireland) Act, 1870 (Additional Poisons) Order, S.I. No. 55 of 1951
Police Forces Amalgamation Act, No. 7 of 1925	12	*Garda Siochana Allowances Order [Vol. XVIII p. 199] S.R.& O. No. 62 of 1938*
		Garda Siochana Pay Order [Vol. XXXVIII p. 129] S.R.& O. No. 9 of 1946
		Garda Siochana Allowances (Consolidation) Order [Vol. XXXVIII p. 103] S.R.& O. No. 167 of 1947
		Garda Siochana Pay (No.2) Order [Vol. XXXVIII p. 135] S.R.& O. No. 281 of 1947
		Garda Siochana Pay Order, S.I. No. 205 of 1949
		Garda Siochana Allowances Order, S.I. No. 344 of 1949
		Garda Siochana Allowances Order, S.I. No. 174 of 1950
		Garda Siochana Pay Order, S.I. No. 196 of 1951
		Garda Siochana Allowances Order, S.I. No. 206 of 1951
		Garda Siochana Pay (No.2) Order, S.I. No. 408 of 1951
		Garda Siochana Allowances (No.2) Order, S.I. No. 409 of 1951
		Garda Siochana Allowances Order, S.I. No. 279 of 1952
		Garda Siochana Pay Order, S.I. No. 235 of 1953
		Garda Siochana Allowances Order, S.I. No. 258 of 1953
		Garda Siochana Pay Order, S.I. No. 182 of 1954
		Garda Siochana Pay (No.2) Order, S.I. No. 278 of 1954
		Garda Siochana Allowances Order, S.I. No. 294 of 1954
		Garda Siochana Allowances Order, S.I. No. 271 of 1955
		Garda Siochana Pay Order, S.I. No. 272 of 1955
		Garda Siochana Pay Order, S.I. No. 15 of 1956
		Garda Siochana Allowances Order, S.I. No. 323 of 1956
		Garda Siochana Pay Order, S.I. No. 51 of 1958
		Garda Siochana Allowances Order, S.I. No. 52 of 1958
		Garda Siochana Pay (No.2) Order, S.I. No. 156 of 1958

Police Forces Amalgamation Act,
No. 7 of 1925 (*Cont.*)

Garda Siochana Pay Order, S.I. No. 51 of 1959

Garda Siochana Pay (No.2) Order, S.I. No. 146 of 1959

Garda Siochana Pay Order, S.I. No. 102 of 1960

Garda Siochana Pay (No.2) Order, S.I. No. 264 of 1960

Garda Siochana Pay and Allowances Order, S.I. No. 41 of 1961

Garda Siochana Pay Order, S.I. No. 257 of 1961

Garda Siochana Pay Order, S.I. No. 45 of 1962

Garda Siochana Pay (No.2) Order, S.I. No. 103 of 1962

Garda Siochana Pay Order, S.I. No. 166 of 1963

Garda Siochana Pay (No.2) Order, S.I. No. 222 of 1963

Garda Siochana Pay Order, S.I. No. 54 of 1964

Garda Siochana Allowances (Consolidation) Order, S.I. No. 218 of 1965

Garda Siochana Pay Order, S.I. No. 88 of 1966

Garda Siochana Pay (No.2) Order, S.I. No. 92 of 1966

Garda Siochana Pay (No.3) Order, S.I. No. 186 of 1966

Garda Siochana Pay (No.4) Order, S.I. No. 239 of 1966

Garda Siochana Pay Order, S.I. No. 59 of 1967

Garda Siochana Pay Order, S.I. No. 75 of 1968

Garda Siochana Allowances Order, S.I. No. 220 of 1968

Garda Siochana (No.2) Pay Order, S.I. No. 234 of 1968

Garda Siochana Allowances (No.2) Order, S.I. No. 246 of 1968

Garda Siochana Pay (No.3) Order, S.I. No. 286 of 1968

Garda Siochana Pay Order, S.I. No. 214 of 1969

Garda Siochana Pay Order, S.I. No. 146 of 1971

Garda Siochana Pay Order, S.I. No. 155 of 1975

12(1)   *Garda Siochana Pay Order [Vol. XXXII p. 257] S.R.& O. No. 27 of 1940*

Garda Siochana Allowances Order [Vol. XXXII p. 205] S.R.& O. No. 44 of 1940

Garda Siochana Pay Order [Vol. XXXII p. 265] S.R.& O. No. 136 of 1942

Garda Siochana Allowances Order [Vol. XXXII p. 217] S.R.& O. No. 110 of 1943

Garda Siochana Pay Order [Vol. XXXII p. 273] S.R.& O. No. 111 of 1943

Garda Siochana Allowances (Consolidation) Order [Vol. XXXII p. 235] S.R.& O. No. 167 of 1943

Garda Siochana Pay Order [Vol. XXXII p. 289] S.R.& O. No. 90 of 1944

Garda Siochana Allowances Order [Vol. XXXII p. 223] S.R.& O. No. 91 of 1944

Statutory Authority	Section	Statutory Instrument
Police Forces Amalgamation Act, No. 7 of 1925 (*Cont.*)		*Garda Siochana Pay Order [Vol. XXXII p. 295] S.R.& O. No. 25 of 1945*
		Garda Siochana Allowances Order [Vol. XXXII p. 229] S.R.& O. No. 220 of 1945
		Garda Siochana Pay Order, S.I. No. 265 of 1952
	13	**Garda Siochana Pensions Order [Vol. XII p. 873] S.R.& O. No. 63 of 1925**
		Garda Siochana Pensions Order [Vol. XVIII p. 257] S.R.& O. No. 82 of 1938
		Garda Siochana Pensions (No.2) Order [Vol. XVIII p. 265] S.R.& O. No. 234 of 1938
		Garda Siochana Pensions Order [Vol. XXXII p. 311] S.R.& O. No. 301 of 1941
		Garda Siochana Pensions (No.2) Order [Vol. XXXII p. 317] S.R.& O. No. 530 of 1941
		Garda Siochana Pensions Order [Vol. XXXII p. 327] S.R.& O. No. 257 of 1942
		Garda Siochana Pensions Order, S.I. No. 154 of 1950
		Garda Siochana Pensions Order, S.I. No. 410 of 1951
		Garda Siochana Pensions Order, S.I. No. 266 of 1952
		Garda Siochana Pensions Order, S.I. No. 251 of 1953
		Garda Siochana Pensions Order, S.I. No. 115 of 1955
		Garda Siochana Pensions Order, S.I. No. 231 of 1957
		Garda Siochana Pensions Order, S.I. No. 149 of 1965
		Garda Siochana Pensions Order, S.I. No. 236 of 1966
		Garda Siochana Pensions Order, S.I. No. 136 of 1969
		Garda Siochana Pensions Order, S.I. No. 146 of 1972
		Garda Siochana Pensions Order, S.I. No. 164 of 1975
		Garda Siochana Pensions Order, S.I. No. 120 of 1976
		Garda Siochana Pensions Order, S.I. No. 199 of 1981
	14	*Garda Siochana (Promotion) Regulations [Vol. XVIII p. 301] S.R.& O. No. 187 of 1936*
		Garda Siochana (Promotion) (No.2) Regulations [Vol. XVIII p. 305] S.R.& O. No. 242 of 1936
		Garda Siochana (Appointments) Regulations [Vol. XXXII p. 153] S.R.& O. No. 107 of 1942
		Garda Siochana (Discipline) Regulations [Vol. XXXII p. 181] S.R.& O. No. 254 of 1942
		Garda Siochana (Promotion) Regulations [Vol. XXXII p. 185] S.R.& O. No. 339 of 1942
		Garda Siochana (Appointments) Regulations [Vol. XXXII p. 159] S.R.& O. No. 168 of 1943

Police Forces Amalgamation Act, No. 7 of 1925 (*Cont.*)

Garda Siochana (Promotion) Regulations [Vol. XXXII p. 189] S.R.& O. No. 303 of 1943

Garda Siochana (Appointments) (No.2) Regulations [Vol. XXXII p. 165] S.R.& O. No. 410 of 1943

Garda Siochana (Appointments) Regulations [Vol. XXXII p. 171] S.R.& O. No. 173 of 1945

Garda Siochana (Appointments) Regulations, 1945 (Amendment) Regulations [Vol. XXXVIII p. 125] S.R.& O. No. 69 of 1947

Garda Siochana (Promotion) Regulations [Vol. XXXVIII p. 149] S.R.& O. No. 70 of 1947

Garda Siochana (Promotion) Regulations, S.I. No. 325 of 1951

Garda Siochana (Appointments) Regulations, 1945 (Amendment) Regulations, S.I. No. 334 of 1951

Garda Siochana (Retirement) (No.2) Regulations, S.I. No. 335 of 1951

Garda Siochana (Promotion) Regulations, S.I. No. 32 of 1952

Garda Siochana (Appointments) Regulations, 1945 (Amendment) Regulations, S.I. No. 291 of 1953

Garda Siochana (Appointments) Regulations, 1945 (Amendment) Regulations, S.I. No. 28 of 1954

Garda Siochana (Promotion) Regulations, S.I. No. 141 of 1955

Garda Siochana (Retirement) Regulations, S.I. No. 157 of 1955

Garda Siochana (Promotion) (No.2) Regulations, S.I. No. 185 of 1955

Garda Siochana (Appointments) Regulations, 1945 (Amendment) Regulations, S.I. No. 259 of 1956

Garda Siochana (Promotion) Regulations, S.I. No. 276 of 1957

Garda Siochana (Retirement) Regulations, S.I. No. 50 of 1958

Garda Siochana (Appointments) Regulations, S.I. No. 176 of 1958

Garda Siochana (Retirement) (No.2) Regulations, S.I. No. 177 of 1958

Garda Siochana (Appointments) Regulations, 1945 (Amendment) Regulations, S.I. No. 234 of 1959

Garda Siochana (Appointments) Regulations, S.I. No. 38 of 1960

Garda Siochana (Retirement) Regulations, S.I. No. 68 of 1960

Garda Siochana (Promotion) Regulations, S.I. No. 203 of 1960

Garda Siochana (Representative Bodies) Regulations, 1927 (Amendment) Regulations, S.I. No. 6 of 1962

Garda Siochana (Representative Bodies) Regulations, S.I. No. 64 of 1962

Garda Siochana (Promotion) Regulations, S.I. No. 97 of 1962

Garda Siochana (Retirement) Regulations, S.I. No. 34 of 1965

Statutory Authority	Section	Statutory Instrument
Police Forces Amalgamation Act, No. 7 of 1925 *(Cont.)*		**Garda Siochana (Representative Bodies) Regulations, 1962 (Amendment) Regulations, S.I. No. 42 of 1965**
		Garda Siochana (Promotion) (Amendment) Regulations, S.I. No. 222 of 1966
		Garda Siochana (Retirement) Regulations, S.I. No. 275 of 1966
		Garda Siochana (Promotion) (Amendment) Regulations, S.I. No. 43 of 1970
		Garda Siochana (Retirement) Regulations, S.I. No. 234 of 1970
		Garda Siochana (Retirement) Regulations, S.I. No. 298 of 1971
		Garda Siochana (Discipline) Regulations, S.I. No. 316 of 1971
		Garda Siochana (Appointments) Regulations, S.I. No. 18 of 1972
		Garda Siochana (Retirement) Regulations, S.I. No. 258 of 1972
		Garda Siochana (Retirement) Regulations, S.I. No. 61 of 1973
		Garda Siochana (Retirement) (No.2) Regulations, 1958 (Revocation) Regulations, S.I. No. 8 of 1974
		Garda Siochana (Retirement) Regulations, S.I. No. 54 of 1974
		Garda Siochana (Retirement) (No.2) Regulations, S.I. No. 266 of 1974
		Garda Siochana (Retirement) (No.3) Regulations, S.I. No. 345 of 1974
		Garda Siochana (Retirement) Regulations, S.I. No. 78 of 1975
		Garda Siochana (Representative Bodies) (Amendment) Regulations, S.I. No. 118 of 1976
		Garda Siochana (Appointments) Regulations, S.I. No. 1 of 1977
		Garda Siochana (Representative Bodies) (Amendment) Regulations, S.I. No. 94 of 1977
		Garda Siochana (Representative Bodies) (Amendment) (No.2) Regulations, S.I. No. 187 of 1977
		Garda Siochana (Representative Bodies) (Amendment) (No.3) Regulations, S.I. No. 380 of 1977
		Garda Siochana (Associations) Regulations, S.I. No. 135 of 1978
		Garda Siochana (Appointments) Regulations, S.I. No. 308 of 1979
		Garda Siochana (Appointments) Regulations, S.I. No. 202 of 1981
		Garda Siochana (Appointments) Regulations, S.I. No. 108 of 1982
		Garda Siochana (Associations) (Amendment) Regulations, S.I. No. 151 of 1983
		Garda Siochana (Promotion) (Amendment) Regulations, S.I. No. 180 of 1983
		Garda Siochana (Appointments) Regulations, S.I. No. 101 of 1984

Statutory Authority	Section	Statutory Instrument
Police Forces Amalgamation Act, No. 7 of 1925 (*Cont.*)	14(1)	*Garda Siochana (Appointments) Regulations [Vol. XVIII p. 205] S.R.& O. No. 59 of 1937*
	14(1)(b)	**Garda Siochana (Retirement) Regulations [Vol. XVIII p. 317] S.R.& O. No. 146 of 1934**
		Garda Siochana (Retirement) Regulations [Vol. XXXII p. 195] S.R.& O. No. 309 of 1941
		Garda Siochana (Retirement) (No.2) Regulations [Vol. XXXII p. 201] S.R.& O. No. 310 of 1941
		Garda Siochana (Retirement) Regulations, S.I. No. 132 of 1951
Poor Relief (Ireland) Act, No. 68 of 1851		**Dispensary and Vaccination (Rules and Regulations) Order [Vol. XVIII p. 561] S.R.& O. No. 38 of 1934**
Poor Relief (Ireland) Acts, 1838 to 1914,		**County Boards of Health (Assistance) (Amendment) Order [Vol. XVIII p. 373] S.R.& O. No. 3 of 1926**
		County Schemes (Officers of District Hospitals) Order [Vol. XVIII p. 417] S.R.& O. No. 100 of 1927
		Boards of Public Assistance (General Regulations) (Amendment) Order [Vol. XVIII p. 427] S.R.& O. No. 17 of 1928
		Boards of Guardians (Minor Officers) Order [Vol. XVIII p. 441] S.R.& O. No. 38 of 1928
		Union Committees (Dublin, Balrothery and Rathdown) Order [Vol. XVIII p. 449] S.R.& O. No. 80 of 1930
		Dublin Boards of Assistance (Annual Meetings) Order [Vol. XVIII p. 459] S.R.& O. No. 68 of 1931
		Boards of Public Health and Public Assistance (Procedure) Order [Vol. XVIII p. 465] S.R.& O. No. 76 of 1932
		Relief of the Poor (Trained Nurses) Regulations [Vol. XVIII p. 471] S.R.& O. No. 31 of 1935
		Public Assistance Contracts (Fair Wages) Order [Vol. XVIII p. 477] S.R.& O. No. 169 of 1938
		Boards of Guardians (Officers) Order [Vol. XVIII p. 483] S.R.& O. No. 311 of 1938
		Boards of Public Assistance (General Regulations) (Amendment) Order [Vol. XVIII p. 437] S.R.& O. No. 312 of 1938
		County Schemes (Officers of District Hospitals) (Amendment) Order [Vol. XXXII p. 337] S.R.& O. No. 147 of 1939
		Boards of Public Assistance (General Regulations) (Amendment) Order [Vol. XXXII p. 333] S.R.& O. No. 208 of 1939
		Boarded Out Children (Contracts) (Amendment) Order [Vol. XXXII p. 125] S.R.& O. No. 99 of 1940
Post Office Act, No. 48 of 1908	2	**Inland Post Amendment (No.8) Warrant, S.I. No. 116 of 1956**

Statutory Authority	Section	Statutory Instrument
Post Office Act, No. 48 of 1908 (*Cont.*)		Foreign Post Amendment (No.4) Warrant, S.I. No. 148 of 1956
		Foreign Parcel Post Amendment (No.3) Warrant, S.I. No. 49 of 1957
		Foreign Post Amendment (No.5) Warrant, S.I. No. 58 of 1957
		Inland Post Amendment (No.9) Warrant, S.I. No. 46 of 1959
		Foreign Post Amendment (No.6) Warrant, S.I. No. 47 of 1959
		Foreign Post Amendment (No.4) Warrant, S.I. No. 48 of 1959
		Inland Post Amendment (No.10) Warrant, S.I. No. 48 of 1960
		Inland Post Amendment (No.11) Warrant, S.I. No. 66 of 1962
		Inland Post Amendment (No.12) Warrant, S.I. No. 153 of 1963
		Inland Post Amendment (No.13) Warrant, S.I. No. 122 of 1964
		Foreign Post Amendment (No.7) Warrant, S.I. No. 123 of 1964
		Foreign Parcel Post Amendment (No.5) Warrant, S.I. No. 124 of 1964
		Foreign Post Amendment (No.8) Warrant, S.I. No. 253 of 1965
		Inland Post Amendment (No.14) Warrant, S.I. No. 262 of 1968
		Foreign Post Amendment (No.9) Warrant, S.I. No. 263 of 1968
		Foreign Parcel Post Amendment (No.6) Warrant, S.I. No. 264 of 1968
	4	*Foreign Parcel Post Amendment (No.3) Warrant, S.I. No. 49 of 1957*
		Foreign Post Amendment (No.6) Warrant, S.I. No. 47 of 1959
		Foreign Post Amendment (No.4) Warrant, S.I. No. 48 of 1959
		Inland Post Amendment (No.11) Warrant, S.I. No. 66 of 1962
		Foreign Post Amendment (No.7) Warrant, S.I. No. 123 of 1964
		Foreign Parcel Post Amendment (No.5) Warrant, S.I. No. 124 of 1964
		Foreign Post Amendment (No.8) Warrant, S.I. No. 253 of 1965
		Foreign Post Amendment (No.9) Warrant, S.I. No. 263 of 1968
		Foreign Parcel Post Amendment (No.6) Warrant, S.I. No. 264 of 1968
	12	Foreign Post Amendment (No.4) Warrant, S.I. No. 148 of 1956
		Foreign Post Amendment (No.5) Warrant, S.I. No. 58 of 1957

Statutory Authority	Section	Statutory Instrument
Post Office Act, No. 48 of 1908 (*Cont.*)		Inland Post Amendment (No.9) Warrant, S.I. No. 46 of 1959
		Foreign Post Amendment (No.6) Warrant, S.I. No. 47 of 1959
		Foreign Post Amendment (No.4) Warrant, S.I. No. 48 of 1959
		Inland Post Amendment (No.10) Warrant, S.I. No. 48 of 1960
		Inland Post Amendment (No.11) Warrant, S.I. No. 66 of 1962
		Inland Post Amendment (No.12) Warrant, S.I. No. 153 of 1963
		Inland Post Amendment (No.13) Warrant, S.I. No. 122 of 1964
		Foreign Post Amendment (No.7) Warrant, S.I. No. 123 of 1964
		Foreign Parcel Post Amendment (No.5) Warrant, S.I. No. 124 of 1964
		Foreign Post Amendment (No.8) Warrant, S.I. No. 253 of 1965
		Inland Post Amendment (No.14) Warrant, S.I. No. 262 of 1968
		Foreign Post Amendment (No.9) Warrant, S.I. No. 263 of 1968
		Foreign Parcel Post Amendment (No.6) Warrant, S.I. No. 264 of 1968
	14	Newspapers (Special Service for Conveyance by Post Office Mail Vans) Warrant, S.I. No. 37 of 1957
		Newspapers (Special Service for Conveyance by Post Office Mail Vans) Amendment (No.1) Warant, S.I. No. 127 of 1964
		Newspapers (Special Service for Conveyance by Post Office Mail Vans) Amendment (No.2) Warrant, S.I. No. 267 of 1968
	23	Money Order Amendment (No.15) Regulations, S.I. No. 114 of 1956
		Postal Order (Inland) Amendment (No.6) Regulations, S.I. No. 115 of 1956
		Money Order Amendment (No.16) Regulations, S.I. No. 49 of 1960
		Postal Order (Inland) Amendment (No.7) Regulations, S.I. No. 50 of 1960
		Money Order Amendment (No.17) Regulations, S.I. No. 125 of 1964
		Postal Order (Inland) Amendment (No.8) Regulations, S.I. No. 126 of 1964
		Postal Order (Inland) Amendment (No.9) Warrant, S.I. No. 265 of 1968
		Money Order Amendment (No.18) Regulations, S.I. No. 266 of 1968
		Postal Order (Inland) Amendment (No.10) Regulations, S.I. No. 34 of 1971
		Money Order Amendment (No.19) Regulations, S.I. No. 35 of 1971

Post Office Act, No. 48 of 1908
(*Cont.*)

Postal Order (Inland) Amendment (No.11) Regulations, S.I. No. 277 of 1974

Money Order Amendment (No.20) Regulations, S.I. No. 283 of 1974

Money Order Amendment (No.21) Regulations, S.I. No. 317 of 1975

Postal Order (Inland) Amendment (No.12) Regulations, S.I. No. 318 of 1975

Money Order Amendment (No.22) Regulations, S.I. No. 51 of 1977

Postal Order (Inland) Amendment (No.13) Regulations, S.I. No. 52 of 1977

Postal Order (Inland) Amendment (No.14) Regulations, S.I. No. 263 of 1979

Money Order Amendment (No.23) Regulations, S.I. No. 264 of 1979

Money Order Amendment (No.24) Regulations, S.I. No. 204 of 1980

Postal Order (Inland) Amendment (No.15) Regulations, S.I. No. 205 of 1980

Money Order Amendment (No.25) Regulations, S.I. No. 119 of 1981

Postal Order (Inland) Amendment (No.16) Regulations, S.I. No. 120 of 1981

Postal Order (Inland) Amendment (No.17) Regulations, S.I. No. 309 of 1981

Money Order Amendment (No.26) Regulations, S.I. No. 310 of 1981

Money Order Amendment (No.27) Regulations, S.I. No. 61 of 1982

Postal Order (Inland) Amendment (No.18) Regulations, S.I. No. 62 of 1982

24 **Postal Order (Inland) Amendment (No.7) Regulations, S.I. No. 50 of 1960**

Postal Order (Inland) Amendment (No.8) Regulations, S.I. No. 126 of 1964

Postal Order (Inland) Amendment (No.9) Warrant, S.I. No. 265 of 1968

Postal Order (Inland) Amendment (No.10) Regulations, S.I. No. 34 of 1971

Postal Order (Inland) Amendment (No.11) Regulations, S.I. No. 277 of 1974

Postal Order (Inland) Amendment (No.12) Regulations, S.I. No. 318 of 1975

Postal Order (Inland) Amendment (No.13) Regulations, S.I. No. 52 of 1977

Postal Order (Inland) Amendment (No.14) Regulations, S.I. No. 263 of 1979

Postal Order (Inland) Amendment (No.15) Regulations, S.I. No. 205 of 1980

Postal Order (Inland) Amendment (No.16) Regulations, S.I. No. 120 of 1981

Postal Order (Inland) Amendment (No.17) Regulations, S.I. No. 309 of 1981

Statutory Authority	Section	Statutory Instrument
Post Office Act, No. 48 of 1908 (*Cont.*)		Postal Order (Inland) Amendment (No.18) Regulations, S.I. No. 62 of 1982
	82	Money Order Amendment (No.15) Regulations, S.I. No. 114 of 1956
		Postal Order (Inland) Amendment (No.6) Regulations, S.I. No. 115 of 1956
		Foreign Post Amendment (No.4) Warrant, S.I. No. 148 of 1956
		Newspapers (Special Service for Conveyance by Post Office Mail Vans) Warrant, S.I. No. 37 of 1957
		Foreign Post Amendment (No.5) Warrant, S.I. No. 58 of 1957
		Inland Post Amendment (No.9) Warrant, S.I. No. 46 of 1959
		Foreign Post Amendment (No.6) Warrant, S.I. No. 47 of 1959
		Foreign Post Amendment (No.4) Warrant, S.I. No. 48 of 1959
		Inland Post Amendment (No.10) Warrant, S.I. No. 48 of 1960
		Money Order Amendment (No.16) Regulations, S.I. No. 49 of 1960
		Postal Order (Inland) Amendment (No.7) Regulations, S.I. No. 50 of 1960
		Inland Post Amendment (No.11) Warrant, S.I. No. 66 of 1962
		Inland Post Amendment (No.12) Warrant, S.I. No. 153 of 1963
		Inland Post Amendment (No.13) Warrant, S.I. No. 122 of 1964
		Foreign Post Amendment (No.7) Warrant, S.I. No. 123 of 1964
		Foreign Parcel Post Amendment (No.5) Warrant, S.I. No. 124 of 1964
		Money Order Amendment (No.17) Regulations, S.I. No. 125 of 1964
		Postal Order (Inland) Amendment (No.8) Regulations, S.I. No. 126 of 1964
		Newspapers (Special Service for Conveyance by Post Office Mail Vans) Amendment (No.1) Warant, S.I. No. 127 of 1964
		Foreign Post Amendment (No.8) Warrant, S.I. No. 253 of 1965
		Inland Post Amendment (No.14) Warrant, S.I. No. 262 of 1968
		Foreign Post Amendment (No.9) Warrant, S.I. No. 263 of 1968
		Foreign Parcel Post Amendment (No.6) Warrant, S.I. No. 264 of 1968
		Postal Order (Inland) Amendment (No.9) Warrant, S.I. No. 265 of 1968
		Money Order Amendment (No.18) Regulations, S.I. No. 266 of 1968

Statutory Authority	Section	Statutory Instrument

Post Office Act, No. 48 of 1908
(*Cont.*)

Newspapers (Special Service for Conveyance by Post Office Mail Vans) Amendment (No.2) Warrant, S.I. No. 267 of 1968

Post Office Acts, 1908 to 1920,

Foreign and Colonial Parcel Post Amendment (No.1) Warrant [Vol. XVIII p. 729] S.R.& O. No. 8 of 1924

Inland Post Amendment (No.25) Warrant [Vol. XVIII p. 573] S.R.& O. No. 27 of 1924

Foreign and Colonial Parcel Post Amendment (No.2) Warrant [Vol. XVIII p. 733] S.R.& O. No. 28 of 1924

Money Order Amendment (No.11) Regulations [Vol. XVIII p. 717] S.R.& O. No. 29 of 1924

Inland Post Amendment (No.26) Warrant [Vol. XVIII p. 679] S.R.& O. No. 33 of 1924

Inland Post Amendment (No.27) Warrant [Vol. XVIII p. 685] S.R.& O. No. 25 of 1925

Inland Post Amendment (No.28) Warrant [Vol. XVIII p. 691] S.R.& O. No. 64 of 1925

Foreign and Colonial Parcel Post Amendment (No.3) Warrant [Vol. XVIII p. 739] S.R.& O. No. 68 of 1926

Foreign and Colonial Post Amendment (No.3) Warrant [Vol. XVIII p. 753] S.R.& O. No. 69 of 1926

Money Order Amendment (No.12) Regulations [Vol. XVIII p. 721] S.R.& O. No. 71 of 1926

Inland Post Amendment (No.29) Warrant [Vol. XVIII p. 695] S.R.& O. No. 9 of 1928

Inland Post Amendment (No.30) Warrant [Vol. XVIII p. 705] S.R.& O. No. 30 of 1928

Foreign and Colonial Parcel Post Amendment (No.4) Warrant [Vol. XVIII p. 745] S.R.& O. No. 31 of 1928

Money Order Amendment (No.13) Regulations [Vol. XVIII p. 725] S.R.& O. No. 14 of 1929

Foreign and Colonial Parcel Post Amendment (No.5) Warrant [Vol. XVIII p. 749] S.R.& O. No. 185 of 1934

Inland Post Amendment (No.31) Warrant [Vol. XVIII p. 709] S.R.& O. No. 203 of 1936

Post Office Acts, 1908 to 1937,

Inland Post Amendment (No.32) Warrant [Vol. XVIII p. 759] S.R.& O. No. 134 of 1937

Inland Post Amendment (No.33) Warrant [Vol. XVIII p. 763] S.R.& O. No. 113 of 1938

Foreign and Colonial Parcel Post Amendment (No.6) Warrant [Vol. XVIII p. 769] S.R.& O. No. 114 of 1938

Inland Post Warrant [Vol. XXXII p. 347] S.R.& O. No. 202 of 1939

Inland Post Amendment (No.1) Warrant [Vol. XXXII p. 421] S.R.& O. No. 235 of 1941

Statutory Authority	Section	Statutory Instrument

Post Office Acts, 1908 to 1937
(*Cont.*)

Foreign and Colonial Post Amendment (No.4) Warrant [Vol. XXXII p. 341] S.R.& O. No. 317 of 1943

Inland Post Amendment (No.2) Warrant, S.I. No. 224 of 1948

Foreign Post Warrant, S.I. No. 267 of 1949

Foreign Post Amendment (No.1) Warrant, S.I. No. 59 of 1951

Inland Post Amendment (No.3) Warrant, S.I. No. 293 of 1951

Postal Order (Inland) Amendment (No.4) Regulations, S.I. No. 294 of 1951

Money Order Amendment (No.14) Regulations, S.I. No. 295 of 1951

Post Office Acts, 1908 to 1951,

Foreign Parcel Post Amendment (No.7) Warrant, S.I. No. 300 of 1951

Inland Post Amendment (No.5) Warrant, S.I. No. 248 of 1953

Postal Order (Inland) Amendment (No.5) Regulations, S.I. No. 249 of 1953

Inland Post Amendment (No.4) Warrant, S.I. No. 279 of 1953

Foreign Post Amendment (No.2) Warrant, S.I. No. 280 of 1953

Foreign Parcel Post Warrant, S.I. No. 418 of 1953

Inland Post Amendment (No.6) Warrant, S.I. No. 23 of 1954

Inland Post Amendment (No.7) Warrant, S.I. No. 65 of 1954

Foreign Parcel Post Amendment (No.1) Warrant, S.I. No. 66 of 1954

Foreign Post Amendment (No.3) Warrant, S.I. No. 67 of 1954

Foreign Parcel Post Amendment (No.2) Warrant, S.I. No. 221 of 1955

Post Office (Amendment) Act, No. 17 of 1951

5

Postal Order (Inland) Amendment (No.7) Regulations, S.I. No. 50 of 1960

Postal Order (Inland) Amendment (No.8) Regulations, S.I. No. 126 of 1964

Postal Order (Inland) Amendment (No.9) Warrant, S.I. No. 265 of 1968

Postal Order (Inland) Amendment (No.10) Regulations, S.I. No. 34 of 1971

Postal Order (Inland) Amendment (No.11) Regulations, S.I. No. 277 of 1974

Postal Order (Inland) Amendment (No.12) Regulations, S.I. No. 318 of 1975

Postal Order (Inland) Amendment (No.13) Regulations, S.I. No. 52 of 1977

Postal Order (Inland) Amendment (No.14) Regulations, S.I. No. 263 of 1979

Statutory Authority	Section	Statutory Instrument
Post Office (Amendment) Act, No. 17 of 1951 (*Cont.*)		Postal Order (Inland) Amendment (No.15) Regulations, S.I. No. 205 of 1980
		Postal Order (Inland) Amendment (No.16) Regulations, S.I. No. 120 of 1981
		Postal Order (Inland) Amendment (No.17) Regulations, S.I. No. 309 of 1981
		Postal Order (Inland) Amendment (No.18) Regulations, S.I. No. 62 of 1982
Post Office (Amendment) Act, No. 18 of 1969	2	Foreign Post Amendment (No.10) Warrant, S.I. No. 152 of 1969
		Inland Post Amendment (No.15) Warant, S.I. No. 153 of 1969
		Inland Post Amendment (No.16) Warrant, S.I. No. 204 of 1970
		Foreign Post Amendment (No.11) Warrant, S.I. No. 205 of 1970
		Inland Post Amendment (No.17) Warrant, S.I. No. 31 of 1971
		Foreign Post Amendment (No.12) Warrant, S.I. No. 32 of 1971
		Foreign Parcel Post Amendment (No.7) Warrant, S.I. No. 33 of 1971
		Foreign Post Amendment (No.13) Warrant, S.I. No. 198 of 1971
		Foreign Parcel Post Amendment (No.8) Warrant, S.I. No. 199 of 1971
		Foreign Post Amendment (No.14) Warrant, S.I. No. 154 of 1973
		Inland Post Amendment (No.18) Warrant, S.I. No. 155 of 1973
		Newspapers (Special Service for Conveyance by Post Office Mail Vans) Amendment (No.3) Warrant, S.I. No. 278 of 1974
		Foreign Parcel Post Amendment (No.9) Warrant, S.I. No. 279 of 1974
		Inland Post Amendment (No.19) Warrant, S.I. No. 280 of 1974
		Foreign Post Amendment (No.15) Warrant, S.I. No. 281 of 1974
		Inland Post Amendment (No.20) Warrant, S.I. No. 314 of 1975
		Foreign Post Amendment (No.16) Warrant, S.I. No. 315 of 1975
		Foreign Parcel Post Amendment (No.10) Warrant, S.I. No. 316 of 1975
		Inland Post Amendment (No.21) Warrant, S.I. No. 48 of 1977
		Foreign Post Amendment (No.17) Warrant, S.I. No. 49 of 1977
		Foreign Parcel Post Amendment (No.11) Warrant, S.I. No. 50 of 1977

Post Office (Amendment) Act,
No. 18 of 1969 (*Cont.*)

Inland Post Amendment (No.22) Warrant, S.I. No. 212 of 1977

Foreign Post Amendment (No.18) Warrant, S.I. No. 213 of 1977

Foreign Parcel Post Amendment (No.12) Warrant, S.I. No. 214 of 1977

Newspapers (Special Service for Conveyance by Post Office Mail Vans) Amendment (No.4) Warrant, S.I. No. 215 of 1977

Foreign Post Amendment (No.19) Warrant, S.I. No. 174 of 1978

Inland Post Amendment (No.23) Warrant, S.I. No. 260 of 1979

Foreign Post Amendment (No.20) Warrant, S.I. No. 261 of 1979

Foreign Parcel Post Amendment (No.13) Warrant, S.I. No. 262 of 1979

Newspapers (Special Service for Conveyance by Post Office Mail Vans) Amendment (No.5) Warrant, S.I. No. 265 of 1979

Inland Post Amendment (No.24) Warrant, S.I. No. 201 of 1980

Foreign Post Amendment (No.21) Warrant, S.I. No. 202 of 1980

Foreign Parcel Post Amendment (No.14) Warrant, S.I. No. 203 of 1980

Newspapers (Special Service for Conveyance by Post Office Mail Vans) Amendment (No.6) Warrant, S.I. No. 206 of 1980

Inland Post Amendment (No.25) Warrant, S.I. No. 116 of 1981

Foreign Post Amendment (No.22) Warrant, S.I. No. 117 of 1981

Foreign Parcel Post Amendment (No.15) Warrant, S.I. No. 118 of 1981

Newspapers (Special Service for Conveyance by Post Office Mail Vans) Amendment (No.7) Warrant, S.I. No. 121 of 1981

Inland Post Amendment (No.26) Warrant, S.I. No. 306 of 1981

Foreign Post Amendment (No.23) Warrant, S.I. No. 307 of 1981

Foreign Parcel Post Amendment (No.16) Warrant, S.I. No. 308 of 1981

Money Order Amendment (No.26) Regulations, S.I. No.310 of 1981

Newspapers (Special Service for Conveyance by Post Office Mail Vans) Amendment (No.8) Warrant, S.I. No. 311 of 1981

Inland Post Amendment (No.27) Warrant, S.I. No. 58 of 1982

Foreign Post Amendment (No.24) Warrant, S.I. No. 59 of 1982

Foreign Parcel Post Amendment (No.17) Warrant, S.I. No. 60 of 1982

Post Office (Amendment) Act,
No. 18 of 1969 (*Cont.*)

Newspapers (Special Service for Conveyance by Post Office Mail Vans) Amendment (No.9) Warrant, S.I. No. 63 of 1982

Foreign Parcel Post Amendment (No.18) Warrant, S.I. No. 257 of 1983

3 Foreign Post Amendment (No.10) Warrant, S.I. No. 152 of 1969

Inland Post Amendment (No.15) Warant, S.I. No. 153 of 1969

Inland Post Amendment (No.16) Warrant, S.I. No. 204 of 1970

Foreign Post Amendment (No.11) Warrant, S.I. No. 205 of 1970

Inland Post Amendment (No.17) Warrant, S.I. No. 31 of 1971

Foreign Post Amendment (No.12) Warrant, S.I. No. 32 of 1971

Foreign Parcel Post Amendment (No.7) Warrant, S.I. No. 33 of 1971

Postal Order (Inland) Amendment (No.10) Regulations, S.I. No. 34 of 1971

Money Order Amendment (No.19) Regulations, S.I. No. 35 of 1971

Foreign Post Amendment (No.13) Warrant, S.I. No. 198 of 1971

Foreign Parcel Post Amendment (No.8) Warrant, S.I. No. 199 of 1971

Foreign Post Amendment (No.14) Warrant, S.I. No. 154 of 1973

Inland Post Amendment (No.18) Warrant, S.I. No. 155 of 1973

Postal Order (Inland) Amendment (No.11) Regulations, S.I. No. 277 of 1974

Newspapers (Special Service for Conveyance by Post Office Mail Vans) Amendment (No.3) Warrant, S.I. No. 278 of 1974

Foreign Parcel Post Amendment (No.9) Warrant, S.I. No. 279 of 1974

Inland Post Amendment (No.19) Warrant, S.I. No. 280 of 1974

Foreign Post Amendment (No.15) Warrant, S.I. No. 281 of 1974

Money Order Amendment (No.20) Regulations, S.I. No. 283 of 1974

Inland Post Amendment (No.20) Warrant, S.I. No. 314 of 1975

Foreign Post Amendment (No.16) Warrant, S.I. No. 315 of 1975

Foreign Parcel Post Amendment (No.10) Warrant, S.I. No. 316 of 1975

Money Order Amendment (No.21) Regulations, S.I. No. 317 of 1975

Postal Order (Inland) Amendment (No.12) Regulations, S.I. No. 318 of 1975

Statutory Authority	Section	Statutory Instrument
Post Office (Amendment) Act, No. 18 of 1969 (*Cont.*)		Inland Post Amendment (No.21) Warrant, S.I. No. 48 of 1977
		Foreign Post Amendment (No.17) Warrant, S.I. No. 49 of 1977
		Foreign Parcel Post Amendment (No.11) Warrant, S.I. No. 50 of 1977
		Money Order Amendment (No.22) Regulations, S.I. No. 51 of 1977
		Postal Order (Inland) Amendment (No.13) Regulations, S.I. No. 52 of 1977
		Inland Post Amendment (No.22) Warrant, S.I. No. 212 of 1977
		Foreign Post Amendment (No.18) Warrant, S.I. No. 213 of 1977
		Foreign Parcel Post Amendment (No.12) Warrant, S.I. No. 214 of 1977
		Newspapers (Special Service for Conveyance by Post Office Mail Vans) Amendment (No.4) Warrant, S.I. No. 215 of 1977
		Foreign Post Amendment (No.19) Warrant, S.I. No. 174 of 1978
		Inland Post Amendment (No.23) Warrant, S.I. No. 260 of 1979
		Foreign Post Amendment (No.20) Warrant, S.I. No. 261 of 1979
		Foreign Parcel Post Amendment (No.13) Warrant, S.I. No. 262 of 1979
		Postal Order (Inland) Amendment (No.14) Regulations, S.I. No. 263 of 1979
		Money Order Amendment (No.23) Regulations, S.I. No. 264 of 1979
		Newspapers (Special Service for Conveyance by Post Office Mail Vans) Amendment (No.5) Warrant, S.I. No. 265 of 1979
		Inland Post Amendment (No.24) Warrant, S.I. No. 201 of 1980
		Foreign Post Amendment (No.21) Warrant, S.I. No. 202 of 1980
		Foreign Parcel Post Amendment (No.14) Warrant, S.I. No. 203 of 1980
		Money Order Amendment (No.24) Regulations, S.I. No. 204 of 1980
		Postal Order (Inland) Amendment (No.15) Regulations, S.I. No. 205 of 1980
		Newspapers (Special Service for Conveyance by Post Office Mail Vans) Amendment (No.6) Warrant, S.I. No. 206 of 1980
		Inland Post Amendment (No.25) Warrant, S.I. No. 116 of 1981
		Foreign Post Amendment (No.22) Warrant, S.I. No. 117 of 1981
		Foreign Parcel Post Amendment (No.15) Warrant, S.I. No. 118 of 1981
		Money Order Amendment (No.25) Regulations, S.I. No. 119 of 1981

Post Office (Amendment) Act,
No. 18 of 1969 (*Cont.*)

Postal Order (Inland) Amendment (No.16) Regulations, S.I. No. 120 of 1981

Newspapers (Special Service for Conveyance by Post Office Mail Vans) Amendment (No.7) Warrant, S.I. No. 121 of 1981

Inland Post Amendment (No.26) Warrant, S.I. No. 306 of 1981

Foreign Post Amendment (No.23) Warrant, S.I. No. 307 of 1981

Foreign Parcel Post Amendment (No.16) Warrant, S.I. No. 308 of 1981

Postal Order (Inland) Amendment (No.17) Regulations, S.I. No. 309 of 1981

Newspapers (Special Service for Conveyance by Post Office Mail Vans) Amendment (No.8) Warrant, S.I. No. 311 of 1981

Inland Post Amendment (No.27) Warrant, S.I. No. 58 of 1982

Foreign Post Amendment (No.24) Warrant, S.I. No. 59 of 1982

Foreign Parcel Post Amendment (No.17) Warrant, S.I. No. 60 of 1982

Money Order Amendment (No.27) Regulations, S.I. No. 61 of 1982

Postal Order (Inland) Amendment (No.18) Regulations, S.I. No. 62 of 1982

Newspapers (Special Service for Conveyance by Post Office Mail Vans) Amendment (No.9) Warrant, S.I. No. 63 of 1982

6   **Foreign Post Amendment (No.10) Warrant, S.I. No. 152 of 1969**

Inland Post Amendment (No.15) Warant, S.I. No. 153 of 1969

Inland Post Amendment (No.16) Warrant, S.I. No. 204 of 1970

Foreign Post Amendment (No.11) Warrant, S.I. No. 205 of 1970

Inland Post Amendment (No.17) Warrant, S.I. No. 31 of 1971

Foreign Post Amendment (No.12) Warrant, S.I. No. 32 of 1971

Foreign Parcel Post Amendment (No.7) Warrant, S.I. No. 33 of 1971

Foreign Post Amendment (No.13) Warrant, S.I. No. 198 of 1971

Foreign Parcel Post Amendment (No.8) Warrant, S.I. No. 199 of 1971

Foreign Post Amendment (No.14) Warrant, S.I. No. 154 of 1973

Inland Post Amendment (No.18) Warrant, S.I. No. 155 of 1973

Newspapers (Special Service for Conveyance by Post Office Mail Vans) Amendment (No.3) Warrant, S.I. No. 278 of 1974

Foreign Parcel Post Amendment (No.9) Warrant, S.I. No. 279 of 1974

Statutory Authority	Section	Statutory Instrument
Post Office (Amendment) Act, No. 18 of 1969 (*Cont.*)		Inland Post Amendment (No.19) Warrant, S.I. No. 280 of 1974
		Foreign Post Amendment (No.15) Warrant, S.I. No. 281 of 1974
		Inland Post Amendment (No.20) Warrant, S.I. No. 314 of 1975
		Foreign Post Amendment (No.16) Warrant, S.I. No. 315 of 1975
		Foreign Parcel Post Amendment (No.10) Warrant, S.I. No. 316 of 1975
		Inland Post Amendment (No.21) Warrant, S.I. No. 48 of 1977
		Foreign Post Amendment (No.17) Warrant, S.I. No. 49 of 1977
		Foreign Parcel Post Amendment (No.11) Warrant, S.I. No. 50 of 1977
		Inland Post Amendment (No.22) Warrant, S.I. No. 212 of 1977
		Foreign Post Amendment (No.18) Warrant, S.I. No. 213 of 1977
		Foreign Parcel Post Amendment (No.12) Warrant, S.I. No. 214 of 1977
		Newspapers (Special Service for Conveyance by Post Office Mail Vans) Amendment (No.4) Warrant, S.I. No. 215 of 1977
		Foreign Post Amendment (No.19) Warrant, S.I. No. 174 of 1978
		Inland Post Amendment (No.23) Warrant, S.I. No. 260 of 1979
		Foreign Post Amendment (No.20) Warrant, S.I. No. 261 of 1979
		Foreign Parcel Post Amendment (No.13) Warrant, S.I. No. 262 of 1979
		Newspapers (Special Service for Conveyance by Post Office Mail Vans) Amendment (No.5) Warrant, S.I. No. 265 of 1979
		Inland Post Amendment (No.24) Warrant, S.I. No. 201 of 1980
		Foreign Post Amendment (No.21) Warrant, S.I. No. 202 of 1980
		Foreign Parcel Post Amendment (No.14) Warrant, S.I. No. 203 of 1980
		Newspapers (Special Service for Conveyance by Post Office Mail Vans) Amendment (No.6) Warrant, S.I. No. 206 of 1980
		Inland Post Amendment (No.25) Warrant, S.I. No. 116 of 1981
		Foreign Post Amendment (No.22) Warrant, S.I. No. 117 of 1981
		Foreign Parcel Post Amendment (No.15) Warrant, S.I. No. 118 of 1981
		Newspapers (Special Service for Conveyance by Post Office Mail Vans) Amendment (No.7) Warrant, S.I. No. 121 of 1981
		Inland Post Amendment (No.26) Warrant, S.I. No. 306 of 1981

Statutory Authority	Section	Statutory Instrument
Post Office (Amendment) Act, No. 18 of 1969 (*Cont.*)		**Foreign Post Amendment (No.23) Warrant, S.I. No. 307 of 1981**
		Foreign Parcel Post Amendment (No.16) Warrant, S.I. No. 308 of 1981
		Newspapers (Special Service for Conveyance by Post Office Mail Vans) Amendment (No.8) Warrant, S.I. No. 311 of 1981
		Inland Post Amendment (No.27) Warrant, S.I. No. 58 of 1982
		Foreign Post Amendment (No.24) Warrant, S.I. No. 59 of 1982
		Foreign Parcel Post Amendment (No.17) Warrant, S.I. No. 60 of 1982
		Newspapers (Special Service for Conveyance by Post Office Mail Vans) Amendment (No.9) Warrant, S.I. No. 63 of 1982
		Foreign Parcel Post Amendment (No.18) Warrant, S.I. No. 257 of 1983
Post Office Savings Bank Act, No. 14 of 1861	1	**Post Office Savings Bank (Savings Gift Tokens) Regulations, S.I. No. 237 of 1957**
		Post Office Savings Bank Regulations, 1921 (Amendment) Regulations, S.I. No. 91 of 1958
		Post Office Savings Bank Regulations, 1921 (Amendment) Regulations, S.I. No. 57 of 1969
	2	**Post Office Savings Bank (Savings Gift Tokens) Regulations, S.I. No. 237 of 1957**
		Post Office Savings Bank Regulations, 1921 (Amendment) Regulations, S.I. No. 91 of 1958
		Post Office Savings Bank Regulations, 1921 (Amendment) Regulations, S.I. No. 64 of 1959
		Post Office Savings Bank Regulations, 1921 (Amendment) Regulations, S.I. No. 57 of 1969
		Post Office Savings Bank Regulations, 1921 (Amendment) Regulations, S.I. No. 204 of 1982
Post Office Savings Bank Acts, 1861 to 1920,		**Post Office Savings Bank Regulations, 1921 (Amendment) Regulations [Vol. XXXVIII p. 153] S.R.& O. No. 378 of 1946**
		Post Office Savings Bank Regulations, 1921 (Amendment) Regulations, S.I. No. 277 of 1954
		Post Office Savings Bank Regulations, 1921 (Amendment) Regulations, S.I. No. 121 of 1955
Postal and Telecommunications Services Act, No. 24 of 1983	9(2)	*Postal and Telecommunications Services Act, 1983 (An Post) (Vesting Day) Order, S.I. No. 407 of 1983*
		Postal and Telecommunications Services Act, 1983 (Bord Telecom Eireann) (Vesting Day) Order, S.I. No. 408 of 1983

Postal and Telecommunications Services Act, No. 24 of 1983 (*Cont.*)	70	Inland Post Amendment (No.28) Scheme, S.I. No. 257 of 1984
		Inland Post Amendment (No.31) Scheme, S.I. No. 94 of 1985
		Foreign Post Amendment (No.27) Scheme, S.I. No. 95 of 1985
		Foreign Parcel Post Amendment (No.20) Scheme, S.I. No. 96 of 1985
		Newspapers (Special Service for Conveyance by Post Office Mail Vans) (Amendment) (No.10) Scheme, S.I. No. 135 of 1985
		Postal Order (Inland) Amendment (No.19) Scheme, S.I. No. 136 of 1985
		Inland Post Amendment (No.29) Scheme, S.I. No. 137 of 1985
		Money Order Amendment (No.28) Scheme, S.I. No. 138 of 1985
		Foreign Post Amendment (No.26) Scheme, S.I. No. 139 of 1985
		Foreign Parcel Post Amendment (No.19) Scheme, S.I. No. 140 of 1985
		Inland Post Amendment (No.32) Scheme, S.I. No. 141 of 1985
		Account Payment Scheme, S.I. No. 394 of 1985
		Foreign Post Amendment (No.25) Scheme, S.I. No. 395 of 1985
		Inland Post Amendment (No.30) Scheme, S.I. No. 396 of 1985
		Inland Post Amendment (No.33) Scheme, S.I. No. 444 of 1985
		Inland Post Amendment (No.34) Scheme, S.I. No. 445 of 1985
		Inland Post Amendment (No.35) Section, S.I. No. 89 of 1986
		Foreign Post Amendment (No.28) Scheme, S.I. No. 90 of 1986
		Foreign Post Amendment (No.29) Scheme, S.I. No. 91 of 1986
		Inland Post Amendment (No.37) Scheme, S.I. No. 92 of 1986
		Inland Post Amendment (No.38) Scheme, S.I. No. 93 of 1986
		Foreign Parcel Post Amendment (No.21) Scheme, S.I. No. 94 of 1986
		Money Order Amendment (No.29) Scheme, S.I. No. 95 of 1986
		Foreign Parcel Post Amendment (No.22) Scheme, S.I. No. 96 of 1986
		Newspapers (Special Service for Conveyance by Post Office Mail Vans) Amendment (No.11) Scheme, S.I. No. 314 of 1986
		Inland Post Amendment (No.36) Scheme, S.I. No. 362 of 1986

Statutory Authority	Section	Statutory Instrument
Postal and Telecommunications Services Act, No. 24 of 1983 (*Cont.*)		**Inland Post Amendment (No.39) Scheme, S.I. No. 463 of 1986**
	74	**Presidential Elections Free Postage (Amendment) Scheme, S.I. No. 288 of 1984**
		Seanad Elections (University Members) Free Postage (Amendment) Scheme, S.I. No. 289 of 1984
		European Assembly Elections Free Postage (Amendment) Scheme, S.I. No. 290 of 1984
		Dail Elections Free Postage (Amendment) Scheme, S.I. No. 291 of 1984
	76(1)	**Postal and Telecommunications Services Act, 1983 (Wireless Telegraphy) (No.1) Order, S.I. No. 419 of 1983**
	76(3)	**Postal and Telecommunications Services Act, 1983 (Wireless Telegraphy) (No.2) Order, S.I. No. 420 of 1983**
	76(4)	**Postal and Telecommunications Services Act, 1983 (Wireless Telegraphy) (No.3) Order, S.I. No. 421 of 1983**
	90	**Telex (Amendment) Scheme, S.I. No. 82 of 1984**
		Telephone (Amendment) Scheme, S.I. No. 244 of 1984
		Telephone (Amendment) (No.2) Scheme, S.I. No. 310 of 1984
		Eirpac (Irish National Packet Switched Data Network) Scheme, S.I. No. 311 of 1984
		Telex (Amendment) Scheme, S.I. No. 80 of 1985
		Telephone (Amendment) Scheme, S.I. No. 81 of 1985
		Telegraph (Inland Written Telegram) (Amendment) Scheme, S.I. No. 82 of 1985
		Telex (Amendment) (No.2) Scheme, S.I. No. 188 of 1985
		Eirmail (Computer Messaging Service) Scheme, S.I. No. 323 of 1985
		Telephone (Amendment) (No.2) Scheme, S.I. No. 324 of 1985
		Telephone (Amendment) (No.3) Scheme, S.I. No. 325 of 1985
		Eircell Scheme, S.I. No. 414 of 1985
		Telephone (Amendment) (No.4) Scheme, S.I. No. 415 of 1985
		Telephone (Amendment) Scheme, S.I. No. 78 of 1986
		Telex (Amendment) Scheme, S.I. No. 79 of 1986
		Eircell (Amendment) Scheme, S.I. No. 80 of 1986
Poultry Hatcheries Act, No. 49 of 1947		**Poultry Hatcheries Regulations, S.I. No. 378 of 1948**
		Poultry and Hatcheries Regulations, S.I. No. 275 of 1949
		Poultry Hatcheries Regulations, S.I. No. 186 of 1951
		Poultry Hatcheries Regulations, S.I. No. 33 of 1953

Statutory Authority	Section	Statutory Instrument
Poultry Hatcheries Act, No. 49 of 1947 (*Cont.*)	2	*Poultry Hatcheries Act, 1947 (Commencement) (No.1) Order, S.I. No. 377 of 1948*
	22	*Poultry Hatcheries Regulations, S.I. No. 229 of 1957* **Poultry Hatcheries Regulations, S.I. No. 122 of 1959**
Pounds (Provision and Maintenance) Act, No. 17 of 1935	8	*Pounds (Amendment) Regulations, S.I. No. 35 of 1959* *Pounds (Amendment) Regulations, S.I. No. 28 of 1968* *Pounds (Amendment) Regulations, S.I. No. 12 of 1972* *Pounds (Amendment) Regulations, S.I. No. 289 of 1975* *Pounds (Amendment) Regulations, S.I. No. 349 of 1977* *Pounds (Amendment) Regulations, S.I. No. 215 of 1980* *Pounds (Amendment) Regulations, S.I. No. 20 of 1982* *Pounds (Amendment) Regulations, S.I. No. 114 of 1983* *Pounds (Amendment) Regulations, S.I. No. 181 of 1984* **Pounds Regulations, S.I. No. 306 of 1985**
	8(1)	*Pounds Regulations [Vol. XVIII p. 773] S.R.& O. No. 149 of 1938*
Presidential and Local Elections Act, No. 15 of 1945	14	*Presidential and Local Elections Regulations [Vol. XXXII p. 439] S.R.& O. No. 96 of 1945*
Presidential Elections Act, No. 32 of 1937	4	*Presidential Elections (Forms) Regulations [Vol. XVIII p. 787] S.R.& O. No. 4 of 1938* *Presidential Elections (Polling Cards) Regulations, S.I. No. 212 of 1950* *Polling Card (Dail Elections, Presidential Elections and Referenda) Regulations, S.I. No. 245 of 1961* **Forms (Dail Elections, Presidential Elections and Referenda) Regulations, S.I. No. 246 of 1963** **Forms (Dail Elections, Presidential Elections and Referenda) (Amendment) Regulations, S.I. No. 115 of 1972**
	12	**Forms (Dail Elections, Presidential Elections and Referenda) (Amendment) Regulations, S.I. No. 115 of 1972**
	21(5)	**Presidential and Local Elections (Local Returning Officers' Charges and Accounts) Regulations [Vol. XXXII p. 427] S.R.& O. No. 102 of 1945** *Referendum and Presidential Elections (Local Returning Officers' Charges and Accounts) Regulations, S.I. No. 81 of 1959* *Presidential Elections (Local Returning Officers' Charges and Accounts) Regulations, S.I. No. 97 of 1966*

Statutory Authority	Section	Statutory Instrument
Presidential Elections Act, No. 32 of 1937 (*Cont.*)		*Presidential Elections (Local Returning Officers' Charges and Accounts) Regulations, S.I. No. 115 of 1973*
		Presidential Elections (Local Returning Officers' Charges and Accounts) Regulations, S.I. No. 45 of 1977
		Presidential Elections (Local Returning Officers' Charges and Accounts) Regulations, S.I. No. 64 of 1984
	29	**Forms (Dail Elections, Presidential Elections and Referenda) Regulations, S.I. No. 246 of 1963**
	34	**Presidential Elections Free Postage (Amendment) Scheme, S.I. No. 288 of 1984**
	Sch. I par. 22	**Forms (Dail Elections, Presidential Elections and Referenda) Regulations, S.I. No. 246 of 1963**
Presidential Elections (Amendment) Act, No. 29 of 1946	4(1)	*Presidential Elections (Polling Cards) Regulations, S.I. No. 212 of 1950*
		Polling Card (Dail Elections, Presidential Elections and Referenda) Regulations, S.I. No. 245 of 1961
Prevention of Crime Act, No. 59 of 1908	4	**Saint Patrick's Institution Regulations, S.I. No. 224 of 1960**
Prevention of Electoral Abuses Act, No. 38 of 1923	38	*Seanad Election Expenses Order [Vol. XVIII p. 803] S.R.& O. No. 58 of 1925*
	42	*Seanad Election Expenses Order [Vol. XVIII p. 803] S.R.& O. No. 58 of 1925*
	50	**Dail Elections Free Postage Regulations, S.I. No. 195 of 1961**
		Dail Elections Free Postage (Amendment) Scheme, S.I. No. 291 of 1984
Prices Act, No. 4 of 1958	1(2)	*Prices Act, 1958 (Commencement) Order, S.I. No. 98 of 1958*
	13	*Maximum Prices (Intoxicating Liquor and Non-alcoholic Beverages) Order, S.I. No. 233 of 1965*
	17	*Maximum Prices (Bread) Order, S.I. No. 228 of 1972*
		Maximum Prices (Bread) Order, S.I. No. 234 of 1973
		Maximum Prices (Bread) Order, S.I. No. 3 of 1974
		Maximum Prices (Bread) (No.2) Order, S.I. No. 70 of 1974
		Maximum Prices (Bread) (No.3) Order, S.I. No. 190 of 1974
		Maximum Prices (Bread) (No.4) Order, S.I. No. 275 of 1974
		Maximum Prices (Bread) (No.5) Order, S.I. No. 321 of 1974
		Maximum Prices (Bread) Order, S.I. No. 42 of 1975

Statutory Authority	Section	Statutory Instrument
Prices Act, No. 4 of 1958 *(Cont.)*		*Maximum Prices (Bread) (No.2) Order, S.I. No. 166 of 1975*
		Maximum Prices (Bread) Order, S.I. No. 9 of 1976
		Maximum Prices (Bread) (No.2) Order, S.I. No. 128 of 1976
		Maximum Prices (Bread) (No.3) Order, S.I. No. 207 of 1976
		Maximum Prices (Bread) Order, S.I. No. 58 of 1977
		Maximum Prices (Bread) (No.2) Order, S.I. No. 254 of 1977
		Maximum Prices (Bread) Order, S.I. No. 38 of 1978
		Maximum Prices (Bread) (No.2) Order, S.I. No. 160 of 1978
		Maximum Prices (Bread) (No.3) Order, S.I. No. 221 of 1978
		Maximum Prices (Bread) (No.4) Order, S.I. No. 376 of 1978
		Maximum Prices (Bread) Order, S.I. No. 287 of 1979
		Maximum Prices (Bread) Order, S.I. No. 26 of 1980
		Maximum Prices (Bread) (No.2) Order, S.I. No. 220 of 1980
		Maximum Prices (Bread) Order, S.I. No. 14 of 1981
		Maximum Prices (Bread) (No.2) Order, S.I. No. 162 of 1981
		Maximum Prices (Bread) (No.3) Order, S.I. No. 284 of 1981
		Maximum Prices (Bread) Order, S.I. No. 4 of 1982
	18	*Maximum Prices (Bread) Order, S.I. No. 228 of 1972*
		Maximum Prices (Bread) Order, S.I. No. 9 of 1976
		Maximum Prices (Bread) (No.2) Order, S.I. No. 128 of 1976
		Maximum Prices (Bread) (No.3) Order, S.I. No. 207 of 1976
		Maximum Prices (Bread) Order, S.I. No. 58 of 1977
		Maximum Prices (Bread) (No.2) Order, S.I. No. 254 of 1977
		Maximum Prices (Bread) Order, S.I. No. 38 of 1978
		Maximum Prices (Bread) (No.2) Order, S.I. No. 160 of 1978
		Maximum Prices (Bread) (No.3) Order, S.I. No. 221 of 1978
		Maximum Prices (Bread) (No.4) Order, S.I. No. 376 of 1978
		Maximum Prices (Bread) Order, S.I. No. 287 of 1979
		Maximum Prices (Bread) Order, S.I. No. 26 of 1980
		Maximum Prices (Bread) (No.2) Order, S.I. No. 220 of 1980
		Maximum Prices (Bread) Order, S.I. No. 14 of 1981

Statutory Authority	Section	Statutory Instrument
Prices Act, No. 4 of 1958 (*Cont.*)		*Maximum Prices (Bread) (No.3) Order, S.I. No. 190 of 1974*
		Maximum Prices (Bread) (No.4) Order, S.I. No. 275 of 1974
		Maximum Prices (Bread) (No.5) Order, S.I. No. 321 of 1974
		Maximum Prices (Bread) Order, S.I. No. 42 of 1975
		Maximum Prices (Bread) (No.2) Order, S.I. No. 166 of 1975
		Maximum Prices (Bread) Order, S.I. No. 9 of 1976
		Maximum Prices (Bread) (No.2) Order, S.I. No. 128 of 1976
		Maximum Prices (Bread) (No.3) Order, S.I. No. 207 of 1976
		Charges (Medical and Veterinary Services) Display Order (Revocation) Order, S.I. No. 309 of 1976
		Maximum Prices (Bread) Order, S.I. No. 58 of 1977
		Retail Prices (Food) Display Order, S.I. No. 127 of 1977
		Maximum Prices (Bread) (No.2) Order, S.I. No. 254 of 1977
		Maximum Prices (Bread) Order, S.I. No. 38 of 1978
		Maximum Prices (Bread) (No.2) Order, S.I. No. 160 of 1978
		Maximum Prices (Bread) (No.3) Order, S.I. No. 221 of 1978
		Maximum Prices (Bread) (No.4) Order, S.I. No. 376 of 1978
		Maximum Prices (Bread) Order, S.I. No. 287 of 1979
		Maximum Prices (Bread) Order, S.I. No. 26 of 1980
		Maximum Prices (Bread) (No.2) Order, S.I. No. 220 of 1980
		Maximum Prices (Bread) Order, S.I. No. 14 of 1981
		Maximum Prices (Bread) (No.2) Order, S.I. No. 162 of 1981
		Maximum Prices (Bread) (No.3) Order, S.I. No. 284 of 1981
		Maximum Prices (Bread) Order, S.I. No. 4 of 1982
		Maximum Prices (Bread) (Revocation) Order, S.I. No. 243 of 1982
	22	*Maximum Prices (Petroleum Products) (No.6) Order, S.I. No. 255 of 1983*
	22A	*Prices Stabilisation Order, S.I. No. 208 of 1965*
		Prices Stabilisation (Continuance) Order, S.I. No. 73 of 1966
		Prices Stabilisation (Continuance) (No.2) Order, S.I. No. 223 of 1966
		Maximum Prices (Flour) Order, S.I. No. 264 of 1966
		Prices Stabilisation (Continuance) Order, S.I. No. 64 of 1967

Statutory Authority	Section	Statutory Instrument

Prices Act, No. 4 of 1958
(*Cont.*)

Prices Stabilisation (Continuance) (No.2) Order, S.I. No. 209 of 1967

Maximum Prices (Milk) (Ballinasloe) Order, S.I. No. 227 of 1967

Prices Stabilisation (Continuance) Order, S.I. No. 72 of 1968

Prices Stabilisation (Continuance) (No.2) Order, S.I. No. 203 of 1968

Prices Stabilisation (Continuance) Order, S.I. No. 46 of 1969

Prices Stabilisation (Commencement) (No.2) Order, S.I. No. 184 of 1969

Prices Stabilisation (Continuance) Order, S.I. No. 55 of 1970

Prices Stabilisation (Continuance) (No.2) Order, S.I. No. 216 of 1970

Prices Stabilisation (Continuance) Order, S.I. No. 103 of 1971

Maximum Prices (Milk) (Donegal) Order, S.I. No. 135 of 1971

Minimum Prices (Milk) (Ballinasloe) Order, S.I. No. 193 of 1971

Maximum Prices (Milk) (Mayo) Order, S.I. No. 209 of 1971

Maximum Prices (Milk) (Donegal) (No.2) Order, S.I. No. 243 of 1971

Maximum Prices (Milk) (Ballinasloe) (No.2) Order, S.I. No. 245 of 1971

Maximum Prices (Milk) (Mayo) (No.2) Order, S.I. No. 246 of 1971

Prices Stabilisation (Continuance) (No.2) Order, S.I. No. 268 of 1971

Maximum Prices (Milk) (Mayo) Order, S.I. No. 7 of 1972

Maximum Prices (Milk) (Donegal) Order, S.I. No. 8 of 1972

Maximum Prices (Milk) (Ballinasloe) Order, S.I. No. 9 of 1972

Maximum Prices (Milk) (Mayo) (No.2) Order, S.I. No. 52 of 1972

Maximum Prices (Milk) (Ballinasloe) (No.2) Order, S.I. No. 53 of 1972

Maximum Prices (Milk) (Donegal) (No.2) Order, S.I. No. 54 of 1972

Prices Stabilisation (Continuance) Order, S.I. No. 91 of 1972

Maximum Prices (Milk) (Donegal) (No.3) Order, S.I. No. 111 of 1972

Maximum Prices (Milk) (Mayo) (No.3) Order, S.I. No. 112 of 1972

Maximum Prices (Milk) (Ballinasloe) (No.3) Order, S.I. No. 114 of 1972

Statutory Authority	Section	Statutory Instrument

ices Act, No. 4 of 1958
Cont.)

Maximum Prices (Bread) Order, S.I. No. 228 of 1972

Maximum Prices (Intoxicating Liquor) Order, S.I. No. 229 of 1972

Maximum Prices (Milk) (Mayo) (No.4) Order, S.I. No. 263 of 1972

Maximum Prices (Milk) (Donegal) (No.4) Order, S.I. No. 264 of 1972

Maximum Prices (Milk) (Dublin Sale District) Order, S.I. No. 265 of 1972

Maximum Prices (Milk) (Ballinasloe) (No.4) Order, S.I. No. 266 of 1972

Maximum Prices (Intoxicating Liquor) (No.2) Order, S.I. No. 275 of 1972

Prices Stabilisation Order, S.I. No. 96 of 1973

Maximum Prices (Milk) Order, S.I. No. 97 of 1973

Prices and Charges (Notification of Increases) Order, S.I. No. 98 of 1973

Maximum Prices (Intoxicating Liquor) Order, S.I. No. 99 of 1973

Maximum Prices (Intoxicating Liquor) (No.2) Order, S.I. No. 116 of 1973

Maximum Prices (Intoxicating Liquor) (No.3) Order, S.I. No. 136 of 1973

Maximum Prices (Household Goods) Order, S.I. No. 169 of 1973

Maximum Prices (Intoxicating Liquor) (No.4) Order, S.I. No. 200 of 1973

Maximum Prices (Intoxicating Liquor) (No.5) Order, S.I. No. 228 of 1973

Maximum Prices (Household Goods) (No.3) Order, S.I. No. 235 of 1973

Maximum Prices (Milk) (No.2) Order, S.I. No. 270 of 1973

Maximum Prices (Intoxicating Liquor) (No.6) Order, S.I. No. 278 of 1973

Maximum Prices (Household Goods) Order, S.I. No. 2 of 1974

Maximum Prices (Pre-packaged Coal) Order, S.I. No. 65 of 1974

Maximum Prices (Milk) Order, S.I. No. 85 of 1974

Maximum Prices (Intoxicating Liquor) Order, S.I. No. 98 of 1974

Maximum Prices (Cigarettes) Order, S.I. No. 104 of 1974

Maximum Prices (Petrol) Order, S.I. No. 109 of 1974

Maximum Prices (Household Goods) (No.4) Order, S.I. No. 189 of 1974

Maximum Prices (Milk) (No.2) Order, S.I. No. 191 of 1974

Maximum Prices (Sugar) Order, S.I. No. 241 of 1974

Statutory Authority	Section	Statutory Instrument
Prices Act, No. 4 of 1958 *(Cont.)*		*Maximum Prices (Milk) (No.3) Order, S.I. No. 242 of 1974*
		Maximum Prices (Household Goods) (No.5) Order, S.I. No. 274 of 1974
		Maximum Prices (Butter) Order, S.I. No. 306 of 1974
		Maximum Prices (Milk) (No.4) Order, S.I. No. 311 of 1974
		Maximum Prices (Household Goods) (No.6) Order, S.I. No. 320 of 1974
		Maximum Prices (Cigarettes) (No.2) Order, S.I. No. 335 of 1974
		Maximum Prices (Household Goods) (No.7) Order, S.I. No. 337 of 1974
		Maximum Prices (Sugar) (No.2) Order, S.I. No. 343 of 1974
		Maximum Prices (Butter) (No.2) Order, S.I. No. 358 of 1974
		Maximum Prices (Intoxicating Liquor) (No.2) Order, S.I. No. 362 of 1974
		Maximum Prices (Petrol) Order, S.I. No. 4 of 1975
		Maximum Prices (Intoxicating Liquor) Order, S.I. No. 11 of 1975
		Maximum Prices (Cigarettes) Order, S.I. No. 12 of 1975
		Maximum Prices (Household Goods) Order, S.I. No. 13 of 1975
		Maximum Prices (Milk) Order, S.I. No. 17 of 1975
		Maximum Prices (Turf Briquettes) Order, S.I. No. 18 of 1975
		Prices and Charges (Notification of Increases) Order, No. 19 of 1975
		Maximum Prices (Household Goods) (No.2) Order, S.I. No. 24 of 1975
		Maximum Prices (Milk) (No.2) Order, S.I. No. 37 of 1975
		Maximum Prices (Flour) Order, S.I. No. 41 of 1975
		Maximum Prices (Household Goods) (No.3) Order, S.I. No. 43 of 1975
		Maximum Prices (Butter) Order, S.I. No. 46 of 1975
		Maximum Prices (Milk) (No.3) Order, S.I. No. 47 of 1975
		Maximum Prices (Sugar) Order, S.I. No. 60 of 1975
		Maximum Prices (Margarine and Cooking Fats) Order, S.I. No. 77 of 1975
		Maximum Prices (Milk) (No.4) Order, S.I. No. 91 of 1975
		Maximum Prices (Household Goods) (No.4) Order, S.I. No. 94 of 1975
		Maximum Prices (Kerosene) Order, S.I. No. 123 of 1975
		Maximum Prices (Milk) (No.5) Order, S.I. No. 136 of 1975

Statutory Authority	Section	Statutory Instrument

Prices Act, No. 4 of 1958
(*Cont.*)

Maximum Prices (Turf Briquettes) (No.2) Order, S.I. No. 137 of 1975

Maximum Prices (Bottled Gas) Order, S.I. No. 138 of 1975

Maximum Prices (Butter) (No.2) Order, S.I. No. 139 of 1975

Maximum Prices (Pre-packaged Coal) (No.3) Order, S.I. No. 140 of 1975

Maximum Prices (Cigarettes) (No.2) Order, S.I. No. 147 of 1975

Maximum Prices (Margarine and Cooking Fats) (No.2) Order, S.I. No. 154 of 1975

Maximum Prices (Flour) (No.2) Order, S.I. No. 165 of 1975

Maximum Prices (Milk) (No.6) Order, S.I. No. 187 of 1975

Maximum Prices (Cigarettes) (No.3) Order, S.I. No. 201 of 1975

Maximum Prices (Intoxicating Liquor) (No.2) Order, S.I. No. 202 of 1975

Maximum Prices (Margarine and Cooking Fats) (No.3) Order, S.I. No. 207 of 1975

Maximum Prices (Bottled Gas) (No.2) Order, S.I. No. 213 of 1975

Maximum Prices (Milk) (No.7) Order, S.I. No. 222 of 1975

Maximum Prices (Butter) (No.3) Order, S.I. No. 224 of 1975

Maximum Prices (Margarine and Cooking Fats) (No.4) Order, S.I. No. 228 of 1975

Maximum Prices (Household Goods) (No.5) Order, S.I. No. 229 of 1975

Maximum Prices (Pre-packaged Coal) (No.4) Order, S.I. No. 230 of 1975

Maximum Prices (Intoxicating Liquor) (No.3) Order, S.I. No. 243 of 1975

Maximum Prices (Butter) (No.4) Order, S.I. No. 265 of 1975

Maximum Prices (Household Goods) (No.6) Order, S.I. No. 295 of 1975

Maximum Prices (Kerosene) (No.2) Order, S.I. No. 299 of 1975

Maximum Prices (Petrol) (No.2) Order, S.I. No. 300 of 1975

Maximum Prices (Milk) (No.8) Order, S.I. No. 321 of 1975

Maximum Prices (Bottled Gas) Order, S.I. No. 7 of 1976

Maximum Prices (Household Goods) Order, S.I. No. 8 of 1976

Maximum Prices (Cigarettes) Order, S.I. No. 17 of 1976

Statutory Authority	Section	Statutory Instrument
Prices Act, No. 4 of 1958 (*Cont.*)		*Maximum Prices (Petrol) Order, S.I. No. 18 of 1976*
		Maximum Prices (Kerosene) Order, S.I. No. 19 of 1976
		Maximum Prices (Intoxicating Liquor) Order, S.I. No. 20 of 1976
		Maximum Prices (Bottled Gas) (No.2) Order, S.I. No. 21 of 1976
		Maximum Prices (Flour) Order, S.I. No. 22 of 1976
		Maximum Prices (Household Goods) (No.2) Order, S.I. No. 36 of 1976
		Maximum Prices (Intoxicating Liquor) (No.2) Order, S.I. No. 46 of 1976
		Maximum Prices (Cigarettes) (No.2) Order, S.I. No. 49 of 1976
		Maximum Prices (Pre-packaged Coal) Order, S.I. No. 50 of 1976
		Maximum Prices (Petrol) (No.2) Order, S.I. No. 51 of 1976
		Maximum Prices (Bottled Gas) (No.3) Order, S.I. No. 52 of 1976
		Maximum Prices (Household Goods) (No.3) Order, S.I. No. 65 of 1976
		Maximum Prices (Butter) Order, S.I. No. 66 of 1976
		Maximum Prices (Household Goods) (No.4) Order, S.I. No. 93 of 1976
		Prices and Charges (Notification of Increases) Order, S.I. No. 100 of 1976
		Maximum Prices (Household Goods) (No.5) Order, S.I. No. 103 of 1976
		Maximum Prices (Household Goods) (No.6) Order, S.I. No. 127 of 1976
		Maximum Prices (Kerosene) (No.2) Order, S.I. No. 129 of 1976
		Maximum Prices (Flour) (No.2) Order, S.I. No. 147 of 1976
		Maximum Prices (Petrol) (No.3) Order, S.I. No. 181 of 1976
		Maximum Prices (Kerosene) (No.3) Order, S.I. No. 182 of 1976
		Maximum Prices (Cigarettes) (No.3) Order, S.I. No. 189 of 1976
		Maximum Prices (Margarine and Cooking Fats) Order, S.I. No. 191 of 1976
		Maximum Prices (Household Goods) (No.7) Order, S.I. No. 192 of 1976
		Maximum Prices (Bottled Gas) (No.4) Order, S.I. No. 206 of 1976
		Maximum Prices (Butter) (No.2) Order, S.I. No. 213 of 1976
		Maximum Prices (Milk) Order, S.I. No. 221 of 1976
		Maximum Prices (Margarine and Cooking Fats) (No.2) Order, S.I. No. 224 of 1976

Statutory Authority	Section	Statutory Instrument

Prices Act, No. 4 of 1958
(*Cont.*)

Maximum Prices (Sugar) Order, S.I. No. 235 of 1976

Maximum Prices (Butter) (No.3) Order, S.I. No. 241 of 1976

Maximum Prices (Household Goods) (No.8) Order, S.I. No. 254 of 1976

Maximum Prices (Intoxicating Liquor) (No.3) Order, S.I. No. 255 of 1976

Maximum Prices (Petrol) (No.4) Order, S.I. No. 265 of 1976

Maximum Prices (Kerosene) (No.4) Order, S.I. No. 267 of 1976

Maximum Prices (Margarine and Cooking Fats) (No.3) Order, S.I. No. 277 of 1976

Maximum Prices (Household Goods) (No.9) Order, S.I. No. 278 of 1976

Maximum Prices (Turf Briquettes) Order, S.I. No. 280 of 1976

Maximum Prices (Bottled Gas) (No.5) Order, S.I. No. 297 of 1976

Maximum Prices (Household Goods) (No.10) Order, S.I. No. 310 of 1976

Maximum Prices (Margarine and Cooking Fats) (No.4) Order, S.I. No. 311 of 1976

Maximum Prices (Petrol) Order, S.I. No. 3 of 1977

Maximum Prices (Household Goods) Order, S.I. No. 12 of 1977

Maximum Prices (Kerosene) Order, S.I. No. 19 of 1977

Maximum Prices (Flour) Order, S.I. No. 32 of 1977

Maximum Prices (Pre-packaged Coal) Order, S.I. No. 35 of 1977

Maximum Prices (Cigarettes) Order, S.I. No. 60 of 1977

Retail Prices (Intoxicating Liquor) Order, S.I. No. 77 of 1977

Maximum Prices (Household Goods) (No.2) Order, S.I. No. 88 of 1977

Maximum Prices (Bottled Gas) Order, S.I. No. 120 of 1977

Maximum Prices (Margarine and Cooking Fats) Order, S.I. No. 121 of 1977

Maximum Prices (Petrol) (No.2) Order, S.I. No. 137 of 1977

Maximum Prices (Household Goods) (No.3) Order, S.I. No. 152 of 1977

Maximum Prices (Petrol) (No.3) Order, S.I. No. 230 of 1977

Maximum Prices (Flour) (No.2) Order, S.I. No. 248 of 1977

Maximum Prices (Sugar) Order, S.I. No. 249 of 1977

Statutory Authority	Section	Statutory Instrument
Prices Act, No. 4 of 1958 (*Cont.*)		*Maximum Prices (Margarine and Cooking Fats) (No.2) Order, S.I. No. 250 of 1977*
		Maximum Prices (Household Goods) (No.4) Order, S.I. No. 251 of 1977
		Maximum Prices (Turf Briquettes) Order, S.I. No. 252 of 1977
		Maximum Prices (Intoxicating Liquor) Order, S.I. No. 294 of 1977
		Maximum Prices (Margarine and Cooking Fats) (No.3) Order, S.I. No. 311 of 1977
		Maximum Prices (Bottled Gas) (No.2) Order, S.I. No. 332 of 1977
		Maximum Prices (Household Goods) (No.5) Order, S.I. No. 333 of 1977
		Maximum Prices (Pre-packaged Coal) (No.2) Order, S.I. No. 363 of 1977
		Maximum Prices (Cigarettes) (No.2) Order, S.I. No. 383 of 1977
		Maximum Prices (Household Goods) (No.6) Order, S.I. No. 387 of 1977
		Maximum Prices (Margarine and Cooking Fats) Order, S.I. No. 1 of 1978
		Maximum Prices (Butter) Order, S.I. No. 18 of 1978
		Maximum Prices (Petrol) Order, S.I. No. 21 of 1978
		Maximum Prices (Petrol) (No.2) Order, S.I. No. 26 of 1978
		Maximum Prices (Bottled Gas) Order, S.I. No. 32 of 1978
		Maximum Prices (Petrol) (No.3) Order, S.I. No. 34 of 1978
		Maximum Prices (Flour) Order, S.I. No. 37 of 1978
		Maximum Prices (Petrol) (No.4) Order, S.I. No. 39 of 1978
		Maximum Prices (Household Goods) Order, S.I. No. 57 of 1978
		Maximum Prices (Cigarettes) Order, S.I. No. 99 of 1978
		Maximum Prices (Household Goods) (No.2) Order, S.I. No. 107 of 1978
		Maximum Prices (Household Goods) (No.3) Order, S.I. No. 149 of 1978
		Maximum Prices (Butter) (No.2) Order, S.I. No. 159 of 1978
		Maximum Prices (Petrol) (No.5) Order, S.I. No. 161 of 1978
		Maximum Prices (Margarine and Cooking Fats) (No.2) Order, S.I. No. 171 of 1978
		Maximum Prices (Household Goods) (No.4) Order, S.I. No. 172 of 1978
		Maximum Prices (Milk) Order, S.I. No. 182 of 1978
		Maximum Prices (Petrol) (No.6) Order, S.I. No. 200 of 1978

Statutory Authority	Section	Statutory Instrument
Prices Act, No. 4 of 1958 (*Cont.*)		*Maximum Prices (Flour) (No.2) Order, S.I. No. 211 of 1978*
		Maximum Prices (Intoxicating Liquor) Order, S.I. No. 212 of 1978
		Maximum Prices (Household Goods) (No.5) Order, S.I. No. 242 of 1978
		Maximum Prices (Breakfast Cereals) Order, S.I. No. 276 of 1978
		Maximum Prices (Sugar) Order, S.I. No. 283 of 1978
		Maximum Prices (Turf Briquettes) Order, S.I. No. 284 of 1978
		Maximum Prices (Household Goods) (No.6) Order, S.I. No. 298 of 1978
		Maximum Prices (Margarine and Cooking Fats) (No.3) Order, S.I. No. 299 of 1978
		Maximum Prices (Petroleum Products) Order, S.I. No. 301 of 1978
		Maximum Prices (Milk) (No.2) Order, S.I. No. 326 of 1978
		Maximum Prices (Household Goods) (No.7) Order, S.I. No. 332 of 1978
		Maximum Prices (Bottled Gas) (No.2) Order, S.I. No. 335 of 1978
		Maximum Prices (Butter) (No.3) Order, S.I. No. 373 of 1978
		Maximum Prices (Milk) (No.3) Order, S.I. No. 374 of 1978
		Maximum Prices (Flour) (No.3) Order, S.I. No. 375 of 1978
		Maximum Prices (Margarine and Cooking Fats) Order, S.I. No. 5 of 1979
		Maximum Prices (Pre-packaged Coal) Order, S.I. No. 14 of 1979
		Maximum Prices (Chickens) Order, S.I. No. 21 of 1979
		Prices and Charges (Notification of Increases) Order, S.I. No. 33 of 1979
		Maximum Prices (Intoxicating Liquor) Order, S.I. No. 37 of 1979
		Maximum Prices (Cigarettes) Order, S.I. No. 38 of 1979
		Maximum Prices (Household Goods) Order, S.I. No. 47 of 1979
		Maximum Prices (Household Goods) (No.2) Order, S.I. No. 68 of 1979
		Maximum Prices (Pre-packaged Coal) (No.2) Order, S.I. No. 71 of 1979
		Maximum Prices (Petroleum Products) Order, S.I. No. 73 of 1979
		Maximum Prices (Bottled Gas) Order, S.I. No. 85 of 1979
		Maximum Prices (Margarine and Cooking Fats) (No.2) Order, S.I. No. 145 of 1979

Statutory Authority	Section	Statutory Instrument
Prices Act, No. 4 of 1958 (*Cont.*)		*Maximum Prices (Household Goods) (No.3) Order, S.I. No. 146 of 1979*
		Maximum Prices (Petroleum Products) (No.2) Order, S.I. No. 147 of 1979
		Maximum Prices (Petroleum Products) (No.3) Order, S.I. No. 182 of 1979
		Maximum Prices (Chickens) (No.2) Order, S.I. No. 206 of 1979
		Maximum Prices (Flour) Order, S.I. No. 216 of 1979
		Maximum Prices (Household Goods) (No.4) Order, S.I. No. 220 of 1979
		Maximum Prices (Butter) Order, S.I. No. 221 of 1979
		Maximum Prices (Margarine and Cooking Fats) (No.3) Order, S.I. No. 231 of 1979
		Maximum Prices (Bottled Gas) (No.2) Order, S.I. No. 240 of 1979
		Maximum Prices (Intoxicating Liquor) (No.2) Order, S.I. No. 246 of 1979
		Maximum Prices (Petroleum Products) (No.4) Order, S.I. No. 273 of 1979
		Maximum Prices (Household Goods) (No.5) Order, S.I. No. 290 of 1979
		Maximum Prices (Cigarettes) (No.2) Order, S.I. No. 302 of 1979
		Maximum Prices (Household Goods) (No.6) Order, S.I. No. 303 of 1979
		Maximum Prices (Sugar) Order, S.I. No. 304 of 1979
		Maximum Prices (Intoxicating Liquor) (No.3) Order, S.I. No. 305 of 1979
		Maximum Prices (Breakfast Cereals) Order, S.I. No. 306 of 1979
		Maximum Prices (Milk) Order, S.I. No. 307 of 1979
		Maximum Prices (Bottled Gas) (No.3) Order, S.I. No. 333 of 1979
		Maximum Prices (Margarine and Cooking Fats) (No.4) Order, S.I. No. 336 of 1979
		Maximum Prices (Milk) (No.2) Order, S.I. No. 344 of 1979
		Maximum Prices (Turf Briquettes) Order, S.I. No. 347 of 1979
		Maximum Prices (Pre-packaged Coal) (No.3) Order, S.I. No. 348 of 1979
		Maximum Prices (Butter) (No.2) Order, S.I. No. 351 of 1979
		Maximum Prices (Breakfast Cereals) (No.2) Order, S.I. No. 380 of 1979
		Maximum Prices (Bottled Gas) (No.4) Order, S.I. No. 395 of 1979
		Maximum Prices (Chickens) (No.3) Order, S.I. No. 400 of 1979
		Maximum Prices (Household Goods) (No.7) Order, S.I. No. 422 of 1979

Statutory Authority	Section	Statutory Instrument
Prices Act, No. 4 of 1958 (*Cont.*)		*Maximum Prices (Cigarettes) Order, S.I. No. 2 of 1980*
		Maximum Prices (Pre-packaged Coal) Order, S.I. No. 3 of 1980
		Maximum Prices (Bottled Gas) Order, S.I. No. 4 of 1980
		Maximum Prices (Flour) Order, S.I. No. 5 of 1980
		Maximum Prices (Milk) Order, S.I. No. 25 of 1980
		Maximum Prices (Intoxicating Liquor) Order, S.I. No. 31 of 1980
		Maximum Prices (Petroleum Products) Order, S.I. No. 39 of 1980
		Maximum Prices (Household Goods) Order, S.I. No. 45 of 1980
		Maximum Prices (Cigarettes) (No.2) Order, S.I. No. 57 of 1980
		Maximum Prices (Petroleum Products) (No.2) Order, S.I. No. 58 of 1980
		Maximum Prices (Intoxicating Liquor) (No.2) Order, S.I. No. 59 of 1980
		Maximum Prices (Bottled Gas) (No.2) Order, S.I. No. 60 of 1980
		Maximum Prices (Chickens) Order, S.I. No. 96 of 1980
		Maximum Prices (Pre-packaged Coal) (No.2) Order, S.I. No. 97 of 1980
		Maximum Prices (Processed Peas and Beans) Order, S.I. No. 111 of 1980
		Maximum Prices (Frozen Foods) Order, S.I. No. 112 of 1980
		Maximum Prices (Babyfoods) Order, S.I. No. 113 of 1980
		Maximum Prices (Turf Briquettes) Order, S.I. No. 122 of 1980
		Maximum Prices (Margarine and Cooking Fats) Order, S.I. No. 126 of 1980
		Maximum Prices (Processed Peas and Beans) (No.2) Order, S.I. No. 147 of 1980
		Maximum Prices (Babyfoods) (No.2) Order, S.I. No. 158 of 1980
		Maximum Prices (Pre-packaged Coal) (No.3) Order, S.I. No. 168 of 1980
		Maximum Prices (Petroleum Products) (No.3) Order, S.I. No. 170 of 1980
		Maximum Prices (Breakfast Cereals) Order, S.I. No. 171 of 1980
		Maximum Prices (Cigarettes) (No.3) Order, S.I. No. 176 of 1980
		Maximum Prices (Butter) Order, S.I. No. 219 of 1980
		Maximum Prices (Margarine and Cooking Fats) (No.2) Order, S.I. No. 222 of 1980

Statutory Authority	Section	Statutory Instrument

Prices Act, No. 4 of 1958
(Cont.)

Maximum Prices (Breakfast Cereals) (No.2) Order, S.I. No. 234 of 1980

Maximum Prices (Sugar) Order, S.I. No. 243 of 1980

Maximum Prices (Petroleum Products) (No.4) Order, S.I. No. 245 of 1980

Maximum Prices (Pre-packaged Coal) (No.4) Order, S.I. No. 259 of 1980

Maximum Prices (Bottled Gas) (No.3) Order, S.I. No. 260 of 1980

Maximum Prices (Frozen Foods) (No.2) Order, S.I. No. 265 of 1980

Maximum Prices (Milk) (No.2) Order, S.I. No. 273 of 1980

Maximum Prices (Turf Briquettes) (No.2) Order, S.I. No. 290 of 1980

Maximum Prices (Babyfoods) (No.3) Order, S.I. No. 291 of 1980

Maximum Prices (Frozen Foods) (No.3) Order, S.I. No. 293 of 1980

Maximum Prices (Processed Peas and Beans) (No.3) Order, S.I. No. 294 of 1980

Maximum Prices (Margarine and Cooking Fats) (No.3) Order, S.I. No. 300 of 1980

Maximum Prices (Intoxicating Liquor) (No.3) Order, S.I. No. 302 of 1980

Maximum Prices (Pre-packaged Coal) (No.5) Order, S.I. No. 318 of 1980

Maximum Prices (Milk) (No.3) Order, S.I. No. 325 of 1980

Maximum Prices (Pre-packaged Coal) (No.6) Order, S.I. No. 347 of 1980

Maximum Prices (Frozen Foods) (No.4) Order, S.I. No. 357 of 1980

Maximum Prices (Breakfast Cereals) (No.3) Order, S.I. No. 364 of 1980

Maximum Prices (Cigarettes) (No.4) Order, S.I. No. 382 of 1980

Maximum Prices (Margarine and Cooking Fats) Order, S.I. No. 1 of 1981

Maximum Prices (Intoxicating Liquor) Order, S.I. No. 2 of 1981

Maximum Prices (Pre-packaged Coal) Order, S.I. No. 5 of 1981

Maximum Prices (Petroleum Products) Order, S.I. No. 6 of 1981

Maximum Prices (Bottled Gas) Order, S.I. No. 8 of 1981

Maximum Prices (Processed Peas and Beans) Order, S.I. No. 9 of 1981

Maximum Prices (Flour) Order, S.I. No. 15 of 1981

Maximum Prices (Babyfoods) Order, S.I. No. 26 of 1981

Statutory Authority	Section	Statutory Instrument
Prices Act, No. 4 of 1958 (*Cont.*)		*Maximum Prices (Petroleum Products) (No.2) Order, S.I. No. 31 of 1981*
		Maximum Prices (Cigarettes) Order, S.I. No. 33 of 1981
		Maximum Prices (Intoxicating Liquor) (No.2) Order, S.I. No. 34 of 1981
		Maximum Prices (Milk) Order, S.I. No. 35 of 1981
		Maximum Prices (Intoxicating Liquor) (No.3) Order, S.I. No. 57 of 1981
		Maximum Prices (Pre-packaged Coal) (No.2) Order, S.I. No. 68 of 1981
		Maximum Prices (Cigarettes) (No.2) Order, S.I. No. 86 of 1981
		Maximum Prices (Petroleum Products) (No.3) Order, S.I. No. 87 of 1981
		Maximum Prices (Bottled Gas) (No.2) Order, S.I. No. 88 of 1981
		Maximum Prices (Milk) (No.2) Order, S.I. No. 93 of 1981
		Maximum Prices (Margarine and Cooking Fats) (No.2) Order, S.I. No. 140 of 1981
		Maximum Prices (Frozen Foods) Order, S.I. No. 142 of 1981
		Maximum Prices (Pre-packaged Coal) (No.3) Order, S.I. No. 143 of 1981
		Maximum Prices (Turf Briquettes) Order, S.I. No. 144 of 1981
		Maximum Prices (Butter) Order, S.I. No. 145 of 1981
		Maximum Prices (Chickens) Order, S.I. No. 151 of 1981
		Maximum Prices (Butter) (No.2) Order, S.I. No. 161 of 1981
		Maximum Prices (Flour) (No.2) Order, S.I. No. 163 of 1981
		Maximum Prices (Babyfoods) (No.2) Order, S.I. No. 217 of 1981
		Maximum Prices (Frozen Foods) (No.2) Order, S.I. No. 218 of 1981
		Maximum Prices (Processed Peas and Beans) (No.2) Order, S.I. No. 232 of 1981
		Maximum Prices (Chickens) (No.2) Order, S.I. No. 238 of 1981
		Maximum Prices (Petroleum Products) (No.4) Order, S.I. No. 239 of 1981
		Maximum Prices (Cigarettes) (No.3) Order, S.I. No. 240 of 1981
		Maximum Prices (Breakfast Cereals) Order, S.I. No. 241 of 1981
		Maximum Prices (Intoxicating Liquor) (No.4) Order, S.I. No. 242 of 1981
		Maximum Prices (Pre-packaged Coal) (No.4) Order, S.I. No. 243 of 1981
		Maximum Prices (Petroleum Products) (No.5) Order, S.I. No. 250 of 1981

Statutory Authority	Section	Statutory Instrument
Prices Act, No. 4 of 1958 (*Cont.*)		*Maximum Prices (Petroleum Products) (No.6) Order, S.I. No. 255 of 1981*
		Maximum Prices (Cigarettes) (No.4) Order, S.I. No. 256 of 1981
		Maximum Prices (Intoxicating Liquor) (No.5) Order, S.I. No. 257 of 1981
		Maximum Prices (Sugar) Order, S.I. No. 275 of 1981
		Maximum Prices (Turf Briquettes) (No.2) Order, S.I. No. 279 of 1981
		Maximum Prices (Bottled Gas) (No.3) Order, S.I. No. 280 of 1981
		Maximum Prices (Frozen Foods) (No.3) Order, S.I. No. 281 of 1981
		Maximum Prices (Breakfast Cereals) (No.2) Order, S.I. No. 283 of 1981
		Maximum Prices (Margarine and Cooking Fats) (No.3) Order, S.I. No. 286 of 1981
		Maximum Prices (Cigarettes) (No.5) Order, S.I. No. 302 of 1981
		Maximum Prices (Intoxicating Liquor) (No.6) Order, S.I. No. 303 of 1981
		Maximum Prices (Petroleum Products) (No.7) Order, S.I. No. 304 of 1981
		Maximum Prices (Pre-packaged Coal) (No.5) Order, S.I. No. 352 of 1981
		Maximum Prices (Bottled Gas) (No.4) Order, S.I. No. 353 of 1981
		Maximum Prices (Petroleum Products) (No.8) Order, S.I. No. 354 of 1981
		Maximum Prices (Babyfoods) (No.3) Order, S.I. No. 355 of 1981
		Maximum Prices (Frozen Foods) (No.4) Order, S.I. No. 374 of 1981
		Maximum Prices (Breakfast Cereals) (No.3) Order, S.I. No. 375 of 1981
		Maximum Prices (Processed Peas and Beans) (No.3) Order, S.I. No. 380 of 1981
		Maximum Prices (Turf Briquettes) (No.3) Order, S.I. No. 381 of 1981
		Maximum Prices (Margarine and Cooking Fats) (No.4) Order, S.I. No. 392 of 1981
		Maximum Prices (Babyfoods) (No.4) Order, S.I. No. 393 of 1981
		Maximum Prices (Petroleum Products) (No.9) Order, S.I. No. 410 of 1981
		Maximum Prices (Babyfoods) (No.5) Order, S.I. No. 441 of 1981
		Maximum Prices (Butter) Order, S.I. No. 1 of 1982
		Maximum Prices (Flour) Order, S.I. No. 5 of 1982
		Maximum Prices (Breakfast Cereals) Order, S.I. No. 50 of 1982

Statutory Authority	Section	Statutory Instrument
Prices Act, No. 4 of 1958 (*Cont.*)		*Maximum Prices (Margarine and Cooking Fats) Order, S.I. No. 51 of 1982*
		Maximum Prices (Frozen Foods) Order, S.I. No. 52 of 1982
		Maximum Prices (Intoxicating Liquor) Order, S.I. No. 54 of 1982
		Maximum Prices (Cigarettes) Order, S.I. No. 55 of 1982
		Maximum Prices (Petroleum Products) Order, S.I. No. 71 of 1982
		Maximum Prices (Margarine and Cooking Fats) (No.2) Order, S.I. No. 98 of 1982
		Maximum Prices (Petroleum Products) (No.2) Order, S.I. No. 99 of 1982
		Maximum Prices (Frozen Foods) (No.2) Order, S.I. No. 111 of 1982
		Maximum Prices (Cigarettes) (No.2) Order, S.I. No. 112 of 1982
		Maximum Prices (Intoxicating Liquor) (No.2) Order, S.I. No. 122 of 1982
		Maximum Prices (Cigarettes) (No.3) Order, S.I. No. 123 of 1982
		Maximum Prices (Petroleum Products) (No.3) Order, S.I. No. 124 of 1982
		Maximum Prices (Bottled Gas) Order, S.I. No. 139 of 1982
		Maximum Prices (Butter) (No.2) Order, S.I. No. 159 of 1982
		Maximum Prices (Milk) Order, S.I. No. 167 of 1982
		Maximum Prices (Processed Peas and Beans) Order, S.I. No. 174 of 1982
		Maximum Prices (Babyfoods) Order, S.I. No. 185 of 1982
		Maximum Prices (Pre-packaged Coal) Order, S.I. No. 192 of 1982
		Maximum Prices (Butter) (No.3) Order, S.I. No. 207 of 1982
		Maximum Prices (Turf Briquettes) Order, S.I. No. 208 of 1982
		Maximum Prices (Milk) (No.2) Order, S.I. No. 209 of 1982
		Maximum Prices (Cornflakes) Order, S.I. No. 210 of 1982
		Maximum Prices (Margarine and Cooking Fats) (No.3) Order, S.I. No. 221 of 1982
		Maximum Prices (Flakemeal) Order, S.I. No. 224 of 1982
		Maximum Prices (Intoxicating Liquor) (No.3) Order, S.I. No. 238 of 1982
		Maximum Prices (Petroleum Products) (No.4) Order, S.I. No. 239 of 1982
		Maximum Prices (Butter) (No.4) Order, S.I. No. 252 of 1982

Statutory Authority	Section	Statutory Instrument
Prices Act, No. 4 of 1958 *(Cont.)*		*Maximum Prices (Flour) (No.2) Order, S.I. No. 253 of 1982*
		Maximum Prices (Margarine and Cooking Fats) (No.4) Order, S.I. No. 254 of 1982
		Maximum Prices (Sugar) Order, S.I. No. 275 of 1982
		Maximum Prices (Frozen Foods) (No.3) Order, S.I. No. 276 of 1982
		Maximum Prices (Babyfoods) (No.2) Order, S.I. No. 286 of 1982
		Maximum Prices (Cigarettes) (No.4) Order, S.I. No. 300 of 1982
		Maximum Prices (Petroleum Products) (No.5) Order, S.I. No. 301 of 1982
		Maximum Prices (Frozen Foods) (No.4) Order, S.I. No. 338 of 1982
		Maximum Prices (Pre-packaged Coal) (No.2) Order, S.I. No. 373 of 1982
		Maximum Prices (Bottled Gas) (No.2) Order, S.I. No. 374 of 1982
		Maximum Prices (Intoxicating Liquor) (No.4) Order, S.I. No. 375 of 1982
		Maximum Prices (Babyfoods) (No.3) Order, S.I. No. 376 of 1982
		Maximum Prices (Margarine and Cooking Fats) (No.5) Order, S.I. No. 377 of 1982
		Maximum Prices (Intoxicating Liquor) Order, S.I. No. 3 of 1983
		Maximum Prices (Cigarettes) Order, S.I. No. 4 of 1983
		Maximum Prices (Petroleum Products) Order, S.I. No. 5 of 1983
		Maximum Prices (Bottled Gas) Order, S.I. No. 32 of 1983
		Maximum Prices (Petroleum Products) (No.2) Order, S.I. No. 33 of 1983
		Maximum Prices (Frozen Foods) Order, S.I. No. 35 of 1983
		Maximum Prices (Petroleum Products) (No.3) Order, S.I. No. 53 of 1983
		Maximum Prices (Petroleum Products) (No.4) Order, S.I. No. 93 of 1983
		Maximum Prices (Margarine and Cooking Fats) Order, S.I. No. 107 of 1983
		Maximum Prices (Bottled Gas) (No.2) Order, S.I. No. 109 of 1983
		Maximum Prices (Pre-packaged Coal) Order, S.I. No. 110 of 1983
		Maximum Prices (Turf Briquettes) Order, S.I. No. 111 of 1983
		Maximum Prices (Petroleum Products) (No.5) Order, S.I. No. 112 of 1983
		Maximum Prices (Cornflakes) Order, S.I. No. 128 of 1983

Statutory Authority	Section	Statutory Instrument
Prices Act, No. 4 of 1958 (*Cont.*)		*Maximum Prices (Butter) Order, S.I. No. 134 of 1983*
		Maximum Prices (Frozen Foods) (No.2) Order, S.I. No. 138 of 1983
		Maximum Prices (Cigarettes) (No.2) Order, S.I. No. 140 of 1983
		Maximum Prices (Milk) Order, S.I. No. 145 of 1983
		Maximum Prices (Margarine and Cooking Fats) (No.2) Order, S.I. No. 153 of 1983
		Maximum Prices (Butter) (No.2) Order, S.I. No. 167 of 1983
		Maximum Prices (Bottled Gas) (No.3) Order, S.I. No. 183 of 1983
		Maximum Prices (Intoxicating Liquor) (No.2) Order, S.I. No. 210 of 1983
		Maximum Prices (Cigarettes) (No.3) Order, S.I. No. 211 of 1983
		Maximum Prices (Milk) (No.2) Order, S.I. No. 224 of 1983
		Maximum Prices (Sugar) Order, S.I. No. 227 of 1983
		Maximum Prices (Babyfoods) Order, S.I. No. 239 of 1983
		Maximum Prices (Flakemeal) Order, S.I. No. 248 of 1983
		Maximum Prices (Margarine and Cooking Fats) (No.3) Order, S.I. No. 249 of 1983
		Maximum Prices (Bottled Gas) (No.4) Order, S.I. No. 294 of 1983
		Maximum Prices (Cigarettes) (No.4) Order, S.I. No. 299 of 1983
		Maximum Prices (Chickens) Order, S.I. No. 321 of 1983
		Maximum Prices (Margarine and Cooking Fats) (No.4) Order, S.I. No. 333 of 1983
		Maximum Prices (Intoxicating Liquor) (No.3) Order, S.I. No. 335 of 1983
		Maximum Prices (Pre-packaged Coal) (No.2) Order, S.I. No. 360 of 1983
		Maximum Prices (Cornflakes) (Revocation) Order, S.I. No. 382 of 1983
		Maximum Prices (Processed Peas and Beans) (Frozen Foods) (Revocation) Order, S.I. No. 401 of 1983
		Maximum Prices (Petroleum Products) Order, S.I. No. 5 of 1984
		Maximum Prices (Babyfoods) Order, S.I. No. 9 of 1984
		Maximum Prices (Petroleum Products) (No.2) Order, S.I. No. 22 of 1984
		Maximum Prices (Cigarettes) Order, S.I. No. 25 of 1984
		Maximum Prices (Intoxicating Liquor) Order, S.I. No. 26 of 1984

Statutory Authority	Section	Statutory Instrument
Prices Act, No. 4 of 1958 *(Cont.)*		*Maximum Prices (Pre-packaged Coal) Order, S.I. No. 35 of 1984*
		Maximum Prices (Margarine and Cooking Fats) Order, S.I. No. 37 of 1984
		Maximum Prices (Flakemeal) Order, S.I. No. 51 of 1984
		Maximum Prices (Babyfoods) (No.2) Order, S.I. No. 61 of 1984
		Maximum Prices (Butter) Order, S.I. No. 93 of 1984
		Maximum Prices (Milk) Order, S.I. No. 115 of 1984
		Maximum Prices (Cigarettes) (No.2) Order, S.I. No. 122 of 1984
		Maximum Prices (Chickens) Order, S.I. No. 127 of 1984
		Maximum Prices (Margarine and Cooking Fats) (No.2) Order, S.I. No. 131 of 1984
		Maximum Prices (Bottled Gas) Order, S.I. No. 142 of 1984
		Maximum Prices (Petroleum Products) (No.3) Order, S.I. No. 156 of 1984
		Maximum Prices (Babyfoods) (No.3) Order, S.I. No. 160 of 1984
		Maximum Prices (Intoxicating Liquor) (No.2) Order, S.I. No. 175 of 1984
		Maximum Prices (Petroleum Products) (No.4) Order, S.I. No. 183 of 1984
		Maximum Prices (Butter) (No.2) Order, S.I. No. 206 of 1984
		Maximum Prices (Milk) (No.2) Order, S.I. No. 207 of 1984
		Maximum Prices (Pre-packaged Coal) (No.2) Order, S.I. No. 208 of 1984
		Maximum Prices (Petroleum Products) (No.5) Order, S.I. No. 215 of 1984
		Maximum Prices (Margarine and Cooking Fats) (Revocation) Order, S.I. No. 218 of 1984
		Maximum Prices (Petroleum Products) (No.6) Order, S.I. No. 237 of 1984
		Maximum Prices (Turf Briquettes) (Revocation) Order, S.I. No. 246 of 1984
		Maximum Prices (Pre-packaged Coal) (No.3) Order, S.I. No. 251 of 1984
		Maximum Prices (Petroleum Products) (No.7) O, S.I. No. 254 of 1984
		Maximum Prices (Sugar) (Revocation) Order, S.I. No. 256 of 1984
		Maximum Prices (Intoxicating Liquor) (No.3) Order, S.I. No. 258 of 1984
		Maximum Prices (Flakemeal) (Revocation) Order, S.I. No. 269 of 1984
		Maximum Prices (Petroleum Products) (No.8) Order, S.I. No. 285 of 1984

Statutory Authority	Section	Statutory Instrument
Prices Act, No. 4 of 1958 *(Cont.)*		*Maximum Prices (Milk) (No.3) Order, S.I. No. 287 of 1984*
		Maximum Prices (Cigarettes) (Revocation) Order, S.I. No. 326 of 1984
		Maximum Prices (Petroleum Products) (No.9) Order, S.I. No. 331 of 1984
		Maximum Prices (Petroleum Products) Order, S.I. No. 9 of 1985
		Petroleum Products (Petroleum Products) (No.2) Order, S.I. No. 18 of 1985
		Maximum Prices (Pre-packaged Coal) Order, S.I. No. 21 of 1985
		Maximum Prices (Babyfoods) (Revocation) Order, S.I. No. 22 of 1985
		Maximum Prices (Petroleum Products) (No.3) Order, S.I. No. 35 of 1985
		Maximum Prices (Petroleum Products) (No.4) Order, S.I. No. 50 of 1985
		Maximum Prices (Pre-packaged Coal) (No.2) Order, S.I. No. 51 of 1985
		Maximum Prices (Bottled Gas) Order, S.I. No. 52 of 1985
		Maximum Prices (Petroleum Products) (No.5) Order, S.I. No. 71 of 1985
		Maximum Prices (Bottled Gas) (No.2) Order, S.I. No. 99 of 1985
		Maximum Prices (Flour) (Revocation) Order, S.I. No. 105 of 1985
		Maximum Prices (Butter) (Revocation) Order, S.I. No. 106 of 1985
		Maximum Prices (Petroleum Products) (No.6) Order, S.I. No. 108 of 1985
		Maximum Prices (Pre-packaged Coal) (No.3) Order, S.I. No. 142 of 1985
		Maximum Prices (Petroleum Products) (No.7) Order, S.I. No. 143 of 1985
		Maximum Prices (Petroleum Products) (No.8) Order, S.I. No. 179 of 1985
		Maximum Prices (Petroleum Products) (No.9) Order, S.I. No. 234 of 1985
		Maximum Prices (Intoxicating Liquor) Order, S.I. No. 235 of 1985
		Maximum Prices (Petroleum Products) (No.10) Order, S.I. No. 265 of 1985
		Maximum Prices (Petroleum Products) (Revocation) Order, S.I. No. 301 of 1985
		Maximum Prices (Bottled Gas) (Revocation) Order, S.I. No. 314 of 1985
		Maximum Prices (Pre-packaged Coal) (Revocation) Order, S.I. No. 333 of 1985
		Maximum Prices (Intoxicating Liquor) (No.2) Order, S.I. No. 345 of 1985

Statutory Authority	Section	Statutory Instrument
Prices Act, No. 4 of 1958 *(Cont.)*		*Maximum Prices (Milk) Order, 1985, S.I. No. 386 of 1985*
		Maximum Prices (Intoxicating Liquor) (Revocation) Order, S.I. No. 408 of 1985
		Maximum Prices (Milk) Order, S.I. No. 73 of 1986
		Maximum Prices (Milk) (No.2) Order, S.I. No. 449 of 1986
		Maximum Prices (Milk) (No.3) Order, S.I. No. 455 of 1986
	22A(1) (b)	**Prices and Charges (Notification of Increases) Order, S.I. No. 271 of 1972**
	22A(3)	*Prices Stabilisation (Amendment) Order, S.I. No. 246 of 1972*
	22B	*Prices Advisory Body (Fertilisers) Order, S.I. No. 226 of 1965*
		Prices Advisory Body (Brewing) Order, S.I. No. 265 of 1965
		Prices Advisory Body (Flour and Bread) Order, S.I. No. 224 of 1966
		Prices Advisory Body (Electricity) Order, S.I. No. 232 of 1966
		Prices Advisory Body (Flour and Bread) Order, S.I. No. 49 of 1971
		National Prices Commission (Establishment) Order, S.I. No. 285 of 1971
		Prices Advisory Body (Coal) Order, S.I. No. 66 of 1974
		Prices Advisory Body (Fertilisers) Order, S.I. No. 68 of 1974
		Prices Advisory Body (Meat) Order, S.I. No. 69 of 1974
		Motor Insurance Advisory Board (Establishment) Order, S.I. No. 299 of 1984
	22C	**Prices Advisory Body (Flour and Bread) Order, S.I. No. 49 of 1971**
		National Prices Commission (Establishment) Order, S.I. No. 285 of 1971
		Maximum Prices (Intoxicating Liquor) Order, S.I. No. 229 of 1972
		Maximum Prices (Milk) (Mayo) (No.4) Order, S.I. No. 263 of 1972
		Maximum Prices (Milk) (Donegal) (No.4) Order, S.I. No. 264 of 1972
		Maximum Prices (Milk) (Dublin Sale District) Order, S.I. No. 265 of 1972
		Maximum Prices (Milk) (Ballinasloe) (No.4) Order, S.I. No. 266 of 1972
		Maximum Prices (Intoxicating Liquor) (No.2) Order, S.I. No. 275 of 1972
		Maximum Prices (Milk) Order, S.I. No. 97 of 1973
		Prices and Charges (Notification of Increases) Order, S.I. No. 98 of 1973

Statutory Authority	Section	Statutory Instrument

Prices Act, No. 4 of 1958
(*Cont.*)

Maximum Prices (Intoxicating Liquor) Order, S.I. No. 99 of 1973

Maximum Prices (Intoxicating Liquor) (No.2) Order, S.I. No. 116 of 1973

Maximum Prices (Intoxicating Liquor) (No.3) Order, S.I. No. 136 of 1973

Maximum Prices (Household Goods) Order, S.I. No. 169 of 1973

Prices and Charges (Notification of Increases) (Amendment) Order, S.I. No. 171 of 1973

Maximum Prices (Intoxicating Liquor) (No.4) Order, S.I. No. 200 of 1973

Maximum Prices (Intoxicating Liquor) (No.5) Order, S.I. No. 228 of 1973

Maximum Prices (Household Goods) (No.3) Order, S.I. No. 235 of 1973

Maximum Prices (Milk) (No.2) Order, S.I. No. 270 of 1973

Maximum Prices (Intoxicating Liquor) (No.6) Order, S.I. No. 278 of 1973

Maximum Prices (Household Goods) Order, S.I. No. 2 of 1974

Maximum Prices (Pre-packaged Coal) Order, S.I. No. 65 of 1974

Prices Advisory Body (Coal) Order, S.I. No. 66 of 1974

Prices Advisory Body (Fertilisers) Order, S.I. No. 68 of 1974

Prices Advisory Body (Meat) Order, S.I. No. 69 of 1974

Maximum Prices (Milk) Order, S.I. No. 85 of 1974

Maximum Prices (Intoxicating Liquor) Order, S.I. No. 98 of 1974

Maximum Prices (Cigarettes) Order, S.I. No. 104 of 1974

Maximum Prices (Petrol) Order, S.I. No. 109 of 1974

Maximum Prices (Household Goods) (No.4) Order, S.I. No. 189 of 1974

Maximum Prices (Milk) (No.2) Order, S.I. No. 191 of 1974

Maximum Prices (Sugar) Order, S.I. No. 241 of 1974

Maximum Prices (Milk) (No.3) Order, S.I. No. 242 of 1974

Maximum Prices (Pre-packaged Coal) (No.2) Order, S.I. No. 262 of 1974

Maximum Prices (Household Goods) (No.5) Order, S.I. No. 274 of 1974

Maximum Prices (Butter) Order, S.I. No. 306 of 1974

Maximum Prices (Milk) (No.4) Order, S.I. No. 311 of 1974

Statutory Authority	Section	Statutory Instrument
Prices Act, No. 4 of 1958 (*Cont.*)		*Maximum Prices (Household Goods) (No.6) Order, S.I. No. 320 of 1974*
		Maximum Prices (Cigarettes) (No.2) Order, S.I. No. 335 of 1974
		Maximum Prices (Household Goods) (No.7) Order, S.I. No. 337 of 1974
		Maximum Prices (Sugar) (No.2) Order, S.I. No. 343 of 1974
		Maximum Prices (Petrol) (No.2) Order, S.I. No. 351 of 1974
		Maximum Prices (Butter) (No.2) Order, S.I. No. 358 of 1974
		Maximum Prices (Intoxicating Liquor) (No.2) Order, S.I. No. 362 of 1974
		Maximum Prices (Petrol) Order, S.I. No. 4 of 1975
		Maximum Prices (Pre-packaged Coal) Order, S.I. No. 6 of 1975
		Maximum Prices (Intoxicating Liquor) Order, S.I. No. 11 of 1975
		Maximum Prices (Cigarettes) Order, S.I. No. 12 of 1975
		Maximum Prices (Household Goods) Order, S.I. No. 13 of 1975
		Maximum Prices (Milk) Order, S.I. No. 17 of 1975
		Maximum Prices (Turf Briquettes) Order, S.I. No. 18 of 1975
		Prices and Charges (Notification of Increases) Order, S.I. No. 19 of 1975
		Maximum Prices (Household Goods) (No.2) Order, S.I. No. 24 of 1975
		Maximum Prices (Milk) (No.2) Order, S.I. No. 37 of 1975
		Maximum Prices (Flour) Order, S.I. No. 41 of 1975
		Maximum Prices (Household Goods) (No.3) Order, S.I. No. 43 of 1975
		Maximum Prices (Butter) Order, S.I. No. 46 of 1975
		Maximum Prices (Milk) (No.3) Order, S.I. No. 47 of 1975
		Maximum Prices (Pre-packaged Coal) (No.2) Order, S.I. No. 52 of 1975
		Maximum Prices (Sugar) Order, S.I. No. 60 of 1975
		National Prices Commission (Establishment) (Amendment) Order, S.I. No. 74 of 1975
		Maximum Prices (Margarine and Cooking Fats) Order, S.I. No. 77 of 1975
		Prices (Stabilisation of Profit Margins of Retailers of Motor Vehicles) Order, S.I. No. 86 of 1975
		Maximum Prices (Milk) (No.4) Order, S.I. No. 91 of 1975
		Maximum Prices (Household Goods) (No.4) Order, S.I. No. 94 of 1975
		Maximum Prices (Kerosene) Order, S.I. No. 123 of 1975

Statutory Authority	Section	Statutory Instrument
Prices Act, No. 4 of 1958 (*Cont.*)		*Maximum Prices (Milk) (No.5) Order, S.I. No. 136 of 1975*
		Maximum Prices (Turf Briquettes) (No.2) Order, S.I. No. 137 of 1975
		Maximum Prices (Bottled Gas) Order, S.I. No. 138 of 1975
		Maximum Prices (Butter) (No.2) Order, S.I. No. 139 of 1975
		Maximum Prices (Pre-packaged Coal) (No.3) Order, S.I. No. 140 of 1975
		Maximum Prices (Cigarettes) (No.2) Order, S.I. No. 147 of 1975
		Maximum Prices (Margarine and Cooking Fats) (No.2) Order, S.I. No. 154 of 1975
		Maximum Prices (Flour) (No.2) Order, S.I. No. 165 of 1975
		Maximum Prices (Milk) (No.6) Order, S.I. No. 187 of 1975
		Maximum Prices (Cigarettes) (No.3) Order, S.I. No. 201 of 1975
		Maximum Prices (Intoxicating Liquor) (No.2) Order, S.I. No. 202 of 1975
		Maximum Prices (Margarine and Cooking Fats) (No.3) Order, S.I. No. 207 of 1975
		Maximum Prices (Bottled Gas) (No.2) Order, S.I. No. 213 of 1975
		Maximum Prices (Milk) (No.7) Order, S.I. No. 222 of 1975
		Maximum Prices (Butter) (No.3) Order, S.I. No. 224 of 1975
		Maximum Prices (Margarine and Cooking Fats) (No.4) Order, S.I. No. 228 of 1975
		Maximum Prices (Household Goods) (No.5) Order, S.I. No. 229 of 1975
		Maximum Prices (Pre-packaged Coal) (No.4) Order, S.I. No. 230 of 1975
		Maximum Prices (Intoxicating Liquor) (No.3) Order, S.I. No. 243 of 1975
		Maximum Prices (Butter) (No.4) Order, S.I. No. 265 of 1975
		Maximum Prices (Household Goods) (No.6) Order, S.I. No. 295 of 1975
		Maximum Prices (Kerosene) (No.2) Order, S.I. No. 299 of 1975
		Maximum Prices (Petrol) (No.2) Order, S.I. No. 300 of 1975
		Maximum Prices (Milk) (No.8) Order, S.I. No. 321 of 1975
		Maximum Prices (Bottled Gas) Order, S.I. No. 7 of 1976
		Maximum Prices (Household Goods) Order, S.I. No. 8 of 1976

Statutory Authority	Section	Statutory Instrument
Prices Act, No. 4 of 1958 *(Cont.)*		*Maximum Prices (Cigarettes) Order, S.I. No. 17 of 1976*
		Maximum Prices (Petrol) Order, S.I. No. 18 of 1976
		Maximum Prices (Kerosene) Order, S.I. No. 19 of 1976
		Maximum Prices (Intoxicating Liquor) Order, S.I. No. 20 of 1976
		Maximum Prices (Bottled Gas) (No.2) Order, S.I. No. 21 of 1976
		Maximum Prices (Flour) Order, S.I. No. 22 of 1976
		Maximum Prices (Household Goods) (No.2) Order, S.I. No. 36 of 1976
		Maximum Prices (Intoxicating Liquor) (No.2) Order, S.I. No. 46 of 1976
		Maximum Prices (Cigarettes) (No.2) Order, S.I. No. 49 of 1976
		Maximum Prices (Pre-packaged Coal) Order, S.I. No. 50 of 1976
		Maximum Prices (Petrol) (No.2) Order, S.I. No. 51 of 1976
		Maximum Prices (Bottled Gas) (No.3) Order, S.I. No. 52 of 1976
		Maximum Prices (Household Goods) (No.3) Order, S.I. No. 65 of 1976
		Maximum Prices (Butter) Order, S.I. No. 66 of 1976
		Maximum Prices (Household Goods) (No.4) Order, S.I. No. 93 of 1976
		Prices and Charges (Notification of Increases) Order, S.I. No. 100 of 1976
		Maximum Prices (Household Goods) (No.5) Order, S.I. No. 103 of 1976
		Maximum Prices (Household Goods) (No.6) Order, S.I. No. 127 of 1976
		Maximum Prices (Kerosene) (No.2) Order, S.I. No. 129 of 1976
		Maximum Prices (Flour) (No.2) Order, S.I. No. 147 of 1976
		Maximum Prices (Petrol) (No.3) Order, S.I. No. 181 of 1976
		Maximum Prices (Kerosene) (No.3) Order, S.I. No. 182 of 1976
		Maximum Prices (Cigarettes) (No.3) Order, S.I. No. 189 of 1976
		Maximum Prices (Margarine and Cooking Fats) Order, S.I. No. 191 of 1976
		Maximum Prices (Household Goods) (No.7) Order, S.I. No. 192 of 1976
		Maximum Prices (Bottled Gas) (No.4) Order, S.I. No. 206 of 1976
		Maximum Prices (Butter) (No.2) Order, S.I. No. 213 of 1976
		Maximum Prices (Milk) Order, S.I. No. 221 of 1976

Statutory Authority	Section	Statutory Instrument

Prices Act, No. 4 of 1958
(*Cont.*)

Maximum Prices (Margarine and Cooking Fats) (No.2) Order, S.I. No. 224 of 1976

Maximum Prices (Sugar) Order, S.I. No. 235 of 1976

Maximum Prices (Butter) (No.3) Order, S.I. No. 241 of 1976

Maximum Prices (Household Goods) (No.8) Order, S.I. No. 254 of 1976

Maximum Prices (Intoxicating Liquor) (No.3) Order, S.I. No. 255 of 1976

Maximum Prices (Petrol) (No.4) Order, S.I. No. 265 of 1976

Maximum Prices (Kerosene) (No.4) Order, S.I. No. 267 of 1976

Maximum Prices (Margarine and Cooking Fats) (No.3) Order, S.I. No. 277 of 1976

Maximum Prices (Household Goods) (No.9) Order, S.I. No. 278 of 1976

Maximum Prices (Turf Briquettes) Order, S.I. No. 280 of 1976

Maximum Prices (Bottled Gas) (No.5) Order, S.I. No. 297 of 1976

Maximum Prices (Household Goods) (No.10) Order, S.I. No. 310 of 1976

Maximum Prices (Margarine and Cooking Fats) (No.4) Order, S.I. No. 311 of 1976

Maximum Prices (Petrol) Order, S.I. No. 3 of 1977

Maximum Prices (Household Goods) Order, S.I. No. 12 of 1977

Maximum Prices (Kerosene) Order, S.I. No. 19 of 1977

Maximum Prices (Flour) Order, S.I. No. 32 of 1977

Maximum Prices (Pre-packaged Coal) Order, S.I. No. 35 of 1977

Maximum Prices (Cigarettes) Order, S.I. No. 60 of 1977

Retail Prices (Intoxicating Liquor) Order, S.I. No. 77 of 1977

Maximum Prices (Household Goods) (No.2) Order, S.I. No. 88 of 1977

Maximum Prices (Bottled Gas) Order, S.I. No. 120 of 1977

Maximum Prices (Margarine and Cooking Fats) Order, S.I. No. 121 of 1977

Maximum Prices (Petrol) (No.2) Order, S.I. No. 137 of 1977

Maximum Prices (Household Goods) (No.3) Order, S.I. No. 152 of 1977

Maximum Prices (Petrol) (No.3) Order, S.I. No. 230 of 1977

Maximum Prices (Flour) (No.2) Order, S.I. No. 248 of 1977

Statutory Authority	Section	Statutory Instrument
Prices Act, No. 4 of 1958 (*Cont.*)		*Maximum Prices (Sugar) Order, S.I. No. 249 of 1977*
		Maximum Prices (Margarine and Cooking Fats) (No.2) Order, S.I. No. 250 of 1977
		Maximum Prices (Household Goods) (No.4) Order, S.I. No. 251 of 1977
		Maximum Prices (Turf Briquettes) Order, S.I. No. 252 of 1977
		Maximum Prices (Intoxicating Liquor) Order, S.I. No. 294 of 1977
		Maximum Prices (Margarine and Cooking Fats) (No.3) Order, S.I. No. 311 of 1977
		Maximum Prices (Bottled Gas) (No.2) Order, S.I. No. 332 of 1977
		Maximum Prices (Household Goods) (No.5) Order, S.I. No. 333 of 1977
		Maximum Prices (Pre-packaged Coal) (No.2) Order, S.I. No. 363 of 1977
		Maximum Prices (Cigarettes) (No.2) Order, S.I. No. 383 of 1977
		Maximum Prices (Household Goods) (No.6) Order, S.I. No. 387 of 1977
		Maximum Prices (Margarine and Cooking Fats) Order, S.I. No. 1 of 1978
		Maximum Prices (Butter) Order, S.I. No. 18 of 1978
		Maximum Prices (Petrol) Order, S.I. No. 21 of 1978
		Maximum Prices (Petrol) (No.2) Order, S.I. No. 26 of 1978
		Maximum Prices (Bottled Gas) Order, S.I. No. 32 of 1978
		Maximum Prices (Petrol) (No.3) Order, S.I. No. 34 of 1978
		Maximum Prices (Flour) Order, S.I. No. 37 of 1978
		Maximum Prices (Petrol) (No.4) Order, S.I. No. 39 of 1978
		Maximum Prices (Household Goods) Order, S.I. No. 57 of 1978
		Maximum Prices (Cigarettes) Order, S.I. No. 99 of 1978
		Maximum Prices (Household Goods) (No.2) Order, S.I. No. 107 of 1978
		Maximum Prices (Household Goods) (No.3) Order, S.I. No. 149 of 1978
		Maximum Prices (Butter) (No.2) Order, S.I. No. 159 of 1978
		Maximum Prices (Petrol) (No.5) Order, S.I. No. 161 of 1978
		Maximum Prices (Margarine and Cooking Fats) (No.2) Order, S.I. No. 171 of 1978
		Maximum Prices (Household Goods) (No.4) Order, S.I. No. 172 of 1978
		Maximum Prices (Milk) Order, S.I. No. 182 of 1978

Statutory Authority	Section	Statutory Instrument

Prices Act, No. 4 of 1958
(*Cont.*)

Maximum Prices (Petrol) (No.6) Order, S.I. No. 200 of 1978

Maximum Prices (Flour) (No.2) Order, S.I. No. 211 of 1978

Maximum Prices (Intoxicating Liquor) Order, S.I. No. 212 of 1978

Maximum Prices (Household Goods) (No.5) Order, S.I. No. 242 of 1978

Maximum Prices (Breakfast Cereals) Order, S.I. No. 276 of 1978

Maximum Prices (Sugar) Order, S.I. No. 283 of 1978

Maximum Prices (Turf Briquettes) Order, S.I. No. 284 of 1978

Maximum Prices (Household Goods) (No.6) Order, S.I. No. 298 of 1978

Maximum Prices (Margarine and Cooking Fats) (No.3) Order, S.I. No. 299 of 1978

Maximum Prices (Petroleum Products) Order, S.I. No. 301 of 1978

Maximum Prices (Milk) (No.2) Order, S.I. No. 326 of 1978

Maximum Prices (Household Goods) (No.7) Order, S.I. No. 332 of 1978

Maximum Prices (Bottled Gas) (No.2) Order, S.I. No. 335 of 1978

Maximum Prices (Butter) (No.3) Order, S.I. No. 373 of 1978

Maximum Prices (Milk) (No.3) Order, S.I. No. 374 of 1978

Maximum Prices (Flour) (No.3) Order, S.I. No. 375 of 1978

Maximum Prices (Margarine and Cooking Fats) Order, S.I. No. 5 of 1979

Maximum Prices (Pre-packaged Coal) Order, S.I. No. 14 of 1979

Maximum Prices (Chickens) Order, S.I. No. 21 of 1979

Prices and Charges (Notification of Increases) Order, S.I. No. 33 of 1979

Maximum Prices (Intoxicating Liquor) Order, S.I. No. 37 of 1979

Maximum Prices (Cigarettes) Order, S.I. No. 38 of 1979

Maximum Prices (Household Goods) Order, S.I. No. 47 of 1979

Maximum Prices (Household Goods) (No.2) Order, S.I. No. 68 of 1979

Maximum Prices (Pre-packaged Coal) (No.2) Order, S.I. No. 71 of 1979

Maximum Prices (Petroleum Products) Order, S.I. No. 73 of 1979

Maximum Prices (Bottled Gas) Order, S.I. No. 85 of 1979

Prices Act, No. 4 of 1958
(*Cont.*)

Maximum Prices (Margarine and Cooking Fats) (No.2) Order, S.I. No. 145 of 1979

Maximum Prices (Household Goods) (No.3) Order, S.I. No. 146 of 1979

Maximum Prices (Petroleum Products) (No.2) Order, S.I. No. 147 of 1979

Maximum Prices (Petroleum Products) (No.3) Order, S.I. No. 182 of 1979

Maximum Prices (Chickens) (No.2) Order, S.I. No. 206 of 1979

Maximum Prices (Flour) Order, S.I. No. 216 of 1979

Maximum Prices (Household Goods) (No.4) Order, S.I. No. 220 of 1979

Maximum Prices (Butter) Order, S.I. No. 221 of 1979

Maximum Prices (Margarine and Cooking Fats) (No.3) Order, S.I. No. 231 of 1979

Maximum Prices (Bottled Gas) (No.2) Order, S.I. No. 240 of 1979

Maximum Prices (Intoxicating Liquor) (No.2) Order, S.I. No. 246 of 1979

Maximum Prices (Petroleum Products) (No.4) Order, S.I. No. 273 of 1979

Maximum Prices (Household Goods) (No.5) Order, S.I. No. 290 of 1979

Maximum Prices (Cigarettes) (No.2) Order, S.I. No. 302 of 1979

Maximum Prices (Household Goods) (No.6) Order, S.I. No. 303 of 1979

Maximum Prices (Sugar) Order, S.I. No. 304 of 1979

Maximum Prices (Intoxicating Liquor) (No.3) Order, S.I. No. 305 of 1979

Maximum Prices (Breakfast Cereals) Order, S.I. No. 306 of 1979

Maximum Prices (Milk) Order, S.I. No. 307 of 1979

Maximum Prices (Bottled Gas) (No.3) Order, S.I. No. 333 of 1979

Maximum Prices (Margarine and Cooking Fats) (No.4) Order, S.I. No. 336 of 1979

Maximum Prices (Milk) (No.2) Order, S.I. No. 344 of 1979

Maximum Prices (Turf Briquettes) Order, S.I. No. 347 of 1979

Maximum Prices (Pre-packaged Coal) (No.3) Order, S.I. No. 348 of 1979

Maximum Prices (Butter) (No.2) Order, S.I. No. 351 of 1979

Maximum Prices (Breakfast Cereals) (No.2) Order, S.I. No. 380 of 1979

Maximum Prices (Bottled Gas) (No.4) Order, S.I. No. 395 of 1979

Maximum Prices (Chickens) (No.3) Order, S.I. No. 400 of 1979

Statutory Authority	Section	Statutory Instrument
Prices Act, No. 4 of 1958 (*Cont.*)		*Maximum Prices (Household Goods) (No.7) Order, S.I. No. 422 of 1979*
		Maximum Prices (Cigarettes) Order, S.I. No. 2 of 1980
		Maximum Prices (Pre-packaged Coal) Order, S.I. No. 3 of 1980
		Maximum Prices (Bottled Gas) Order, S.I. No. 4 of 1980
		Maximum Prices (Flour) Order, S.I. No. 5 of 1980
		Maximum Prices (Milk) Order, S.I. No. 25 of 1980
		Maximum Prices (Intoxicating Liquor) Order, S.I. No. 31 of 1980
		Maximum Prices (Petroleum Products) Order, S.I. No. 39 of 1980
		Maximum Prices (Household Goods) Order, S.I. No. 45 of 1980
		Maximum Prices (Cigarettes) (No.2) Order, S.I. No. 57 of 1980
		Maximum Prices (Petroleum Products) (No.2) Order, S.I. No. 58 of 1980
		Maximum Prices (Intoxicating Liquor) (No.2) Order, S.I. No. 59 of 1980
		Maximum Prices (Bottled Gas) (No.2) Order, S.I. No. 60 of 1980
		Maximum Prices (Chickens) Order, S.I. No. 96 of 1980
		Maximum Prices (Pre-packaged Coal) (No.2) Order, S.I. No. 97 of 1980
		Maximum Prices (Processed Peas and Beans) Order, S.I. No. 111 of 1980
		Maximum Prices (Frozen Foods) Order, S.I. No. 112 of 1980
		Maximum Prices (Babyfoods) Order, S.I. No. 113 of 1980
		Maximum Prices (Turf Briquettes) Order, S.I. No. 122 of 1980
		Maximum Prices (Margarine and Cooking Fats) Order, S.I. No. 126 of 1980
		Maximum Prices (Processed Peas and Beans) (No.2) Order, S.I. No. 147 of 1980
		Maximum Prices (Babyfoods) (No.2) Order, S.I. No. 158 of 1980
		Maximum Prices (Pre-packaged Coal) (No.3) Order, S.I. No. 168 of 1980
		Maximum Prices (Petroleum Products) (No.3) Order, S.I. No. 170 of 1980
		Maximum Prices (Breakfast Cereals) Order, S.I. No. 171 of 1980
		Maximum Prices (Cigarettes) (No.3) Order, S.I. No. 176 of 1980
		Maximum Prices (Butter) Order, S.I. No. 219 of 1980

Statutory Authority	Section	Statutory Instrument
Prices Act, No. 4 of 1958 *(Cont.)*		*Maximum Prices (Margarine and Cooking Fats) (No.2) Order, S.I. No. 222 of 1980*
		Maximum Prices (Breakfast Cereals) (No.2) Order, S.I. No. 234 of 1980
		Maximum Prices (Sugar) Order, S.I. No. 243 of 1980
		Maximum Prices (Petroleum Products) (No.4) Order, S.I. No. 245 of 1980
		Maximum Prices (Pre-packaged Coal) (No.4) Order, S.I. No. 259 of 1980
		Maximum Prices (Bottled Gas) (No.3) Order, S.I. No. 260 of 1980
		Maximum Prices (Frozen Foods) (No.2) Order, S.I. No. 265 of 1980
		Maximum Prices (Milk) (No.2) Order, S.I. No. 273 of 1980
		Maximum Prices (Turf Briquettes) (No.2) Order, S.I. No. 290 of 1980
		Maximum Prices (Babyfoods) (No.3) Order, S.I. No. 291 of 1980
		Maximum Prices (Frozen Foods) (No.3) Order, S.I. No. 293 of 1980
		Maximum Prices (Processed Peas and Beans) (No.3) Order, S.I. No. 294 of 1980
		Maximum Prices (Margarine and Cooking Fats) (No.3) Order, S.I. No. 300 of 1980
		Maximum Prices (Intoxicating Liquor) (No.3) Order, S.I. No. 302 of 1980
		Maximum Prices (Pre-packaged Coal) (No.5) Order, S.I. No. 318 of 1980
		Maximum Prices (Milk) (No.3) Order, S.I. No. 325 of 1980
		Maximum Prices (Pre-packaged Coal) (No.6) Order, S.I. No. 347 of 1980
		Maximum Prices (Frozen Foods) (No.4) Order, S.I. No. 357 of 1980
		Maximum Prices (Breakfast Cereals) (No.3) Order, S.I. No. 364 of 1980
		Maximum Prices (Cigarettes) (No.4) Order, S.I. No. 382 of 1980
		Maximum Prices (Margarine and Cooking Fats) Order, S.I. No. 1 of 1981
		Maximum Prices (Intoxicating Liquor) Order, S.I. No. 2 of 1981
		Maximum Prices (Pre-packaged Coal) Order, S.I. No. 5 of 1981
		Maximum Prices (Petroleum Products) Order, S.I. No. 6 of 1981
		Maximum Prices (Bottled Gas) Order, S.I. No. 8 of 1981
		Maximum Prices (Processed Peas and Beans) Order, S.I. No. 9 of 1981
		Maximum Prices (Flour) Order, S.I. No. 15 of 1981

Statutory Authority	Section	Statutory Instrument
Prices Act, No. 4 of 1958 *(Cont.)*		*Maximum Prices (Babyfoods) Order, S.I. No. 26 of 1981*
		Maximum Prices (Petroleum Products) (No.2) Order, S.I. No. 31 of 1981
		Maximum Prices (Cigarettes) Order, S.I. No. 33 of 1981
		Maximum Prices (Intoxicating Liquor) (No.2) Order, S.I. No. 34 of 1981
		Maximum Prices (Milk) Order, S.I. No. 35 of 1981
		Maximum Prices (Intoxicating Liquor) (No.3) Order, S.I. No. 57 of 1981
		Maximum Prices (Pre-packaged Coal) (No.2) Order, S.I. No. 68 of 1981
		Maximum Prices (Cigarettes) (No.2) Order, S.I. No. 86 of 1981
		Maximum Prices (Petroleum Products) (No.3) Order, S.I. No. 87 of 1981
		Maximum Prices (Bottled Gas) (No.2) Order, S.I. No. 88 of 1981
		Maximum Prices (Milk) (No.2) Order, S.I. No. 93 of 1981
		Maximum Prices (Margarine and Cooking Fats) (No.2) Order, S.I. No. 140 of 1981
		Maximum Prices (Frozen Foods) Order, S.I. No. 142 of 1981
		Maximum Prices (Pre-packaged Coal) (No.3) Order, S.I. No. 143 of 1981
		Maximum Prices (Turf Briquettes) Order, S.I. No. 144 of 1981
		Maximum Prices (Butter) Order, S.I. No. 145 of 1981
		Maximum Prices (Chickens) Order, S.I. No. 151 of 1981
		Maximum Prices (Butter) (No.2) Order, S.I. No. 161 of 1981
		Maximum Prices (Flour) (No.2) Order, S.I. No. 163 of 1981
		Maximum Prices (Babyfoods) (No.2) Order, S.I. No. 217 of 1981
		Maximum Prices (Frozen Foods) (No.2) Order, S.I. No. 218 of 1981
		Maximum Prices (Processed Peas and Beans) (No.2) Order, S.I. No. 232 of 1981
		Maximum Prices (Chickens) (No.2) Order, S.I. No. 238 of 1981
		Maximum Prices (Petroleum Products) (No.4) Order, S.I. No. 239 of 1981
		Maximum Prices (Cigarettes) (No.3) Order, S.I. No. 240 of 1981
		Maximum Prices (Breakfast Cereals) Order, S.I. No. 241 of 1981
		Maximum Prices (Intoxicating Liquor) (No.4) Order, S.I. No. 242 of 1981
		Maximum Prices (Pre-packaged Coal) (No.4) Order, S.I. No. 243 of 1981

Statutory Authority	Section	Statutory Instrument
Prices Act, No. 4 of 1958 (*Cont.*)		*Maximum Prices (Petroleum Products) (No.5) Order, S.I. No. 250 of 1981*
		Maximum Prices (Petroleum Products) (No.6) Order, S.I. No. 255 of 1981
		Maximum Prices (Cigarettes) (No.4) Order, S.I. No. 256 of 1981
		Maximum Prices (Intoxicating Liquor) (No.5) Order, S.I. No. 257 of 1981
		Maximum Prices (Sugar) Order, S.I. No. 275 of 1981
		Maximum Prices (Turf Briquettes) (No.2) Order, S.I. No. 279 of 1981
		Maximum Prices (Bottled Gas) (No.3) Order, S.I. No. 280 of 1981
		Maximum Prices (Frozen Foods) (No.3) Order, S.I. No. 281 of 1981
		Maximum Prices (Breakfast Cereals) (No.2) Order, S.I. No. 283 of 1981
		Maximum Prices (Margarine and Cooking Fats) (No.3) Order, S.I. No. 286 of 1981
		Maximum Prices (Cigarettes) (No.5) Order, S.I. No. 302 of 1981
		Maximum Prices (Intoxicating Liquor) (No.6) Order, S.I. No. 303 of 1981
		Maximum Prices (Petroleum Products) (No.7) Order, S.I. No. 304 of 1981
		Maximum Prices (Pre-packaged Coal) (No.5) Order, S.I. No. 352 of 1981
		Maximum Prices (Bottled Gas) (No.4) Order, S.I. No. 353 of 1981
		Maximum Prices (Petroleum Products) (No.8) Order, S.I. No. 354 of 1981
		Maximum Prices (Babyfoods) (No.3) Order, S.I. No. 355 of 1981
		Maximum Prices (Frozen Foods) (No.4) Order, S.I. No. 374 of 1981
		Maximum Prices (Breakfast Cereals) (No.3) Order, S.I. No. 375 of 1981
		Maximum Prices (Processed Peas and Beans) (No.3) Order, S.I. No. 380 of 1981
		Maximum Prices (Turf Briquettes) (No.3) Order, S.I. No. 381 of 1981
		Maximum Prices (Margarine and Cooking Fats) (No.4) Order, S.I. No. 392 of 1981
		Maximum Prices (Babyfoods) (No.4) Order, S.I. No. 393 of 1981
		Maximum Prices (Petroleum Products) (No.9) Order, S.I. No. 410 of 1981
		Maximum Prices (Babyfoods) (No.5) Order, S.I. No. 441 of 1981
		Maximum Prices (Butter) Order, S.I. No. 1 of 1982
		Maximum Prices (Flour) Order, S.I. No. 5 of 1982

Statutory Authority	Section	Statutory Instrument

Prices Act, No. 4 of 1958
Cont.)

Maximum Prices (Breakfast Cereals) Order, S.I. No. 50 of 1982

Maximum Prices (Margarine and Cooking Fats) Order, S.I. No. 51 of 1982

Maximum Prices (Frozen Foods) Order, S.I. No. 52 of 1982

Maximum Prices (Intoxicating Liquor) Order, S.I. No. 54 of 1982

Maximum Prices (Cigarettes) Order, S.I. No. 55 of 1982

Maximum Prices (Petroleum Products) Order, S.I. No. 71 of 1982

Maximum Prices (Margarine and Cooking Fats) (No.2) Order, S.I. No. 98 of 1982

Maximum Prices (Petroleum Products) (No.2) Order, S.I. No. 99 of 1982

Maximum Prices (Frozen Foods) (No.2) Order, S.I. No. 111 of 1982

Maximum Prices (Cigarettes) (No.2) Order, S.I. No. 112 of 1982

Maximum Prices (Intoxicating Liquor) (No.2) Order, S.I. No. 122 of 1982

Maximum Prices (Cigarettes) (No.3) Order, S.I. No. 123 of 1982

Maximum Prices (Petroleum Products) (No.3) Order, S.I. No. 124 of 1982

Maximum Prices (Bottled Gas) Order, S.I. No. 139 of 1982

Maximum Prices (Butter) (No.2) Order, S.I. No. 159 of 1982

Maximum Prices (Milk) Order, S.I. No. 167 of 1982

Maximum Prices (Processed Peas and Beans) Order, S.I. No. 174 of 1982

Maximum Prices (Babyfoods) Order, S.I. No. 185 of 1982

Maximum Prices (Pre-packaged Coal) Order, S.I. No. 192 of 1982

Maximum Prices (Butter) (No.3) Order, S.I. No. 207 of 1982

Maximum Prices (Turf Briquettes) Order, S.I. No. 208 of 1982

Maximum Prices (Milk) (No.2) Order, S.I. No. 209 of 1982

Maximum Prices (Cornflakes) Order, S.I. No. 210 of 1982

Maximum Prices (Margarine and Cooking Fats) (No.3) Order, S.I. No. 221 of 1982

Maximum Prices (Flakemeal) Order, S.I. No. 224 of 1982

Maximum Prices (Intoxicating Liquor) (No.3) Order, S.I. No. 238 of 1982

Maximum Prices (Petroleum Products) (No.4) Order, S.I. No. 239 of 1982

Statutory Authority	Section	Statutory Instrument
Prices Act, No. 4 of 1958 (*Cont.*)		*Maximum Prices (Butter) (No.4) Order, S.I. No. 252 of 1982*
		Maximum Prices (Flour) (No.2) Order, S.I. No. 253 of 1982
		Maximum Prices (Margarine and Cooking Fats) (No.4) Order, S.I. No. 254 of 1982
		Maximum Prices (Sugar) Order, S.I. No. 275 of 1982
		Maximum Prices (Frozen Foods) (No.3) Order, S.I. No. 276 of 1982
		Maximum Prices (Babyfoods) (No.2) Order, S.I. No. 286 of 1982
		Maximum Prices (Cigarettes) (No.4) Order, S.I. No. 300 of 1982
		Maximum Prices (Petroleum Products) (No.5) Order, S.I. No. 301 of 1982
		Maximum Prices (Frozen Foods) (No.4) Order, S.I. No. 338 of 1982
		Maximum Prices (Pre-packaged Coal) (No.2) Order, S.I. No. 373 of 1982
		Maximum Prices (Bottled Gas) (No.2) Order, S.I. No. 374 of 1982
		Maximum Prices (Intoxicating Liquor) (No.4) Order, S.I. No. 375 of 1982
		Maximum Prices (Babyfoods) (No.3) Order, S.I. No. 376 of 1982
		Maximum Prices (Margarine and Cooking Fats) (No.5) Order, S.I. No. 377 of 1982
		Maximum Prices (Intoxicating Liquor) Order, S.I. No. 3 of 1983
		Maximum Prices (Cigarettes) Order, S.I. No. 4 of 1983
		Maximum Prices (Petroleum Products) Order, S.I. No. 5 of 1983
		Maximum Prices (Bottled Gas) Order, S.I. No. 32 of 1983
		Maximum Prices (Petroleum Products) (No.2) Order, S.I. No. 33 of 1983
		Maximum Prices (Frozen Foods) Order, S.I. No. 35 of 1983
		Maximum Prices (Petroleum Products) (No.3) Order, S.I. No. 53 of 1983
		Maximum Prices (Petroleum Products) (No.4) Order, S.I. No. 93 of 1983
		Maximum Prices (Margarine and Cooking Fats) Order, S.I. No. 107 of 1983
		Maximum Prices (Bottled Gas) (No.2) Order, S.I. No. 109 of 1983
		Maximum Prices (Turf Briquettes) Order, S.I. No. 111 of 1983
		Maximum Prices (Petroleum Products) (No.5) Order, S.I. No. 112 of 1983

Statutory Authority	Section	Statutory Instrument
Prices Act, No. 4 of 1958 (Cont.)		*Maximum Prices (Cornflakes) Order, S.I. No. 128 of 1983*
		Maximum Prices (Butter) Order, S.I. No. 134 of 1983
		Maximum Prices (Frozen Foods) (No.2) Order, S.I. No. 138 of 1983
		Maximum Prices (Cigarettes) (No.2) Order, S.I. No. 140 of 1983
		Maximum Prices (Milk) Order, S.I. No. 145 of 1983
		Maximum Prices (Margarine and Cooking Fats) (No.2) Order, S.I. No. 153 of 1983
		Maximum Prices (Butter) (No.2) Order, S.I. No. 167 of 1983
		Prices (Stabilisation of Profit Margins of Retailers of Motor Cars) Order, S.I. No. 181 of 1983
		Maximum Prices (Bottled Gas) (No.3) Order, S.I. No. 183 of 1983
		Maximum Prices (Intoxicating Liquor) (No.2) Order, S.I. No. 210 of 1983
		Maximum Prices (Cigarettes) (No.3) Order, S.I. No. 211 of 1983
		Maximum Prices (Milk) (No.2) Order, S.I. No. 224 of 1983
		Maximum Prices (Sugar) Order, S.I. No. 227 of 1983
		Maximum Prices (Babyfoods) Order, S.I. No. 239 of 1983
		Maximum Prices (Flakemeal) Order, S.I. No. 248 of 1983
		Maximum Prices (Margarine and Cooking Fats) (No.3) Order, S.I. No. 249 of 1983
		Maximum Prices (Petroleum Products) (No.6) Order, S.I. No. 255 of 1983
		Maximum Prices (Bottled Gas) (No.4) Order, S.I. No. 294 of 1983
		Maximum Prices (Cigarettes) (No.4) Order, S.I. No. 299 of 1983
		Maximum Prices (Chickens) Order, S.I. No. 321 of 1983
		Maximum Prices (Margarine and Cooking Fats) (No.4) Order, S.I. No. 333 of 1983
		Maximum Prices (Intoxicating Liquor) (No.3) Order, S.I. No. 335 of 1983
		Maximum Prices (Pre-packaged Coal) (No.2) Order, S.I. No. 360 of 1983
		Maximum Prices (Cornflakes) (Revocation) Order, S.I. No. 382 of 1983
		Maximum Prices (Processed Peas and Beans) (Frozen Foods) (Revocation) Order, S.I. No. 401 of 1983
		Maximum Prices (Petroleum Products) Order, S.I. No. 5 of 1984
		Maximum Prices (Babyfoods) Order, S.I. No. 9 of 1984

Statutory Authority	Section	Statutory Instrument

Prices Act, No. 4 of 1958
(*Cont.*)

Maximum Prices (Petroleum Products) (No.2) Order, S.I. No. 22 of 1984

Maximum Prices (Cigarettes) Order, S.I. No. 25 of 1984

Maximum Prices (Intoxicating Liquor) Order, S.I. No. 26 of 1984

Maximum Prices (Pre-packaged Coal) Order, S.I. No. 35 of 1984

Maximum Prices (Margarine and Cooking Fats) Order, S.I. No. 37 of 1984

Maximum Prices (Flakemeal) Order, S.I. No. 51 of 1984

Maximum Prices (Babyfoods) (No.2) Order, S.I. No. 61 of 1984

Maximum Prices (Butter) Order, S.I. No. 93 of 1984

Maximum Prices (Milk) Order, S.I. No. 115 of 1984

Maximum Prices (Cigarettes) (No.2) Order, S.I. No. 122 of 1984

Maximum Prices (Chickens) Order, S.I. No. 127 of 1984

Maximum Prices (Margarine and Cooking Fats) (No.2) Order, S.I. No. 131 of 1984

Maximum Prices (Bottled Gas) Order, S.I. No. 142 of 1984

Maximum Prices (Petroleum Products) (No.3) Order, S.I. No. 156 of 1984

Maximum Prices (Babyfoods) (No.3) Order, S.I. No. 160 of 1984

Maximum Prices (Intoxicating Liquor) (No.2) Order, S.I. No. 175 of 1984

Maximum Prices (Petroleum Products) (No.4) Order, S.I. No. 183 of 1984

Maximum Prices (Butter) (No.2) Order, S.I. No. 206 of 1984

Maximum Prices (Milk) (No.2) Order, S.I. No. 207 of 1984

Maximum Prices (Pre-packaged Coal) (No.2) Order, S.I. No. 208 of 1984

Maximum Prices (Petroleum Products) (No.5) Order, S.I. No. 215 of 1984

Maximum Prices (Margarine and Cooking Fats) (Revocation) Order, S.I. No. 218 of 1984

Prices (Stabilisation of Profit Margins of Retailers of Motor Cars) Order, S.I. No. 223 of 1984

Maximum Prices (Petroleum Products) (No.6) Order, S.I. No. 237 of 1984

Maximum Prices (Turf Briquettes) (Revocation) Order, S.I. No. 246 of 1984

Maximum Prices (Pre-packaged Coal) (No.3) Order, S.I. No. 251 of 1984

Maximum Prices (Petroleum Products) (No.7) O, S.I. No. 254 of 1984

Statutory Authority	Section	Statutory Instrument
Prices Act, No. 4 of 1958 *(Cont.)*		*Maximum Prices (Sugar) (Revocation) Order, S.I. No. 256 of 1984*
		Maximum Prices (Intoxicating Liquor) (No.3) Order, S.I. No. 258 of 1984
		Maximum Prices (Flakemeal) (Revocation) Order, S.I. No. 269 of 1984
		Maximum Prices (Petroleum Products) (No.8) Order, S.I. No. 285 of 1984
		Maximum Prices (Milk) (No.3) Order, S.I. No. 287 of 1984
		Maximum Prices (Cigarettes) (Revocation) Order, S.I. No. 326 of 1984
		Maximum Prices (Petroleum Products) (No.9) Order, S.I. No. 331 of 1984
		Maximum Prices (Petroleum Products) Order, S.I. No. 9 of 1985
		Petroleum Products (Petroleum Products) (No.2) Order, S.I. No. 18 of 1985
		Maximum Prices (Pre-packaged Coal) Order, S.I. No. 21 of 1985
		Maximum Prices (Babyfoods) (Revocation) Order, S.I. No. 22 of 1985
		Maximum Prices (Petroleum Products) (No.3) Order, S.I. No. 35 of 1985
		Maximum Prices (Petroleum Products) (No.4) Order, S.I. No. 50 of 1985
		Maximum Prices (Pre-packaged Coal) (No.2) Order, S.I. No. 51 of 1985
		Maximum Prices (Bottled Gas) Order, S.I. No. 52 of 1985
		Maximum Prices (Petroleum Products) (No.5) Order, S.I. No. 71 of 1985
		Maximum Prices (Bottled Gas) (No.2) Order, S.I. No. 99 of 1985
		Maximum Prices (Flour) (Revocation) Order, S.I. No. 105 of 1985
		Maximum Prices (Butter) (Revocation) Order, S.I. No. 106 of 1985
		Maximum Prices (Petroleum Products) (No.6) Order, S.I. No. 108 of 1985
		Maximum Prices (Pre-packaged Coal) (No.3) Order, S.I. No. 142 of 1985
		Maximum Prices (Petroleum Products) (No.7) Order, S.I. No. 143 of 1985
		Maximum Prices (Petroleum Products) (No.8) Order, S.I. No. 179 of 1985
		Maximum Prices (Petroleum Products) (No.9) Order, S.I. No. 234 of 1985
		Maximum Prices (Intoxicating Liquor) Order, S.I. No. 235 of 1985
		Maximum Prices (Petroleum Products) (No.10) Order, S.I. No. 265 of 1985

Statutory Authority	Section	Statutory Instrument
Prices Act, No. 4 of 1958 (*Cont.*)		*Maximum Prices (Petroleum Products) (Revocation) Order, S.I. No. 301 of 1985*
		Maximum Prices (Bottled Gas) (Revocation) Order, S.I. No. 314 of 1985
		Maximum Prices (Pre-packaged Coal) (Revocation) Order, S.I. No. 333 of 1985
		Maximum Prices (Intoxicating Liquor) (No.2) Order, S.I. No. 345 of 1985
		Maximum Prices (Milk) Order, 1985, S.I. No. 386 of 1985
		Maximum Prices (Intoxicating Liquor) (Revocation) Order, S.I. No. 408 of 1985
		Maximum Prices (Milk) Order, S.I. No. 73 of 1986
		Maximum Prices (Milk) (No.2) Order, S.I. No. 449 of 1986
		Maximum Prices (Milk) (No.3) Order, S.I. No. 455 of 1986
	22C(3)	*Maximum Prices (Flour) Order, 1966 (Revocation) Order, S.I. No. 48 of 1967*
		Maximum Prices (Milk) (Ballinasloe) (Revocation) Order, S.I. No. 167 of 1969
		Maximum Prices (Household Goods) (No.2) Order, S.I. No. 211 of 1973
		Maximum Prices (Household Goods) (No.4) Order, S.I. No. 289 of 1973
		Maximum Prices (Household Goods) (No.5) Order, S.I. No. 320 of 1973
		Maximum Prices (Household Goods) (No.2) Order, S.I. No. 71 of 1974
		Maximum Prices (Household Goods) (No.3) Order, S.I. No. 105 of 1974
	22F	*Prices (Stabilisation of Profit Margins of Importers and Wholesalers) Order, S.I. No. 167 of 1973*
		Prices (Stabilisation of Profit Margins of Retailers) Order, S.I. No. 168 of 1973
		Prices (Stabilisation of Profit Margins of Retailers of Motor Vehicles) Order, S.I. No. 86 of 1975
		Prices (Stabilisation of Profit Margins of Retailers of Motor Cars) Order, S.I. No. 181 of 1983
		Prices (Stabilisation of Profit Margins of Retailers of Motor Cars) Order, S.I. No. 223 of 1984
Prices (Amendment) Act, No. 20 of 1972	6	**Prices Acts, 1958 to 1972 (Retail Prices of Milk) (Transfer of Functions) Order, S.I. No. 281 of 1986**

Statutory Authority	Section	Statutory Instrument
Prices and Charges (Standstill) Order, S.I. No. 3 of 1951	10	*Coal Prices (Dublin and Dun Laoghaire) Direction, S.I. No. 9 of 1951*
Prison Act, No. 41 of 1898		**Rules for the Government of Prisons [Vol. XXXVI p. 1087] S.R.& O. No. 320 of 1947**
		Rules for the Government of Prisons, S.I. No. 127 of 1955
		Rules for the Government of Prisons, S.I. No. 135 of 1983
Prisons Act, No. 51 of 1933	2(1)	*Galway Prison Closing Order [Vol. XXXII p. 451] S.R.& O. No. 87 of 1939*
		Waterford Prison Closing Order [Vol. XXXII p. 455] S.R.& O. No. 349 of 1939
		Cork Prison Closing Order, S.I. No. 20 of 1956
		Sligo Prison Closing Order, S.I. No. 98 of 1956
Prisons Act, No. 11 of 1970	2	**Detention of Offenders (Training Unit) Regulations, S.I. No. 251 of 1975**
	3	**Detention of Offenders (Shanganagh Castle) Regulations, S.I. No. 313 of 1970**
		Detention of Offenders (Loughan House) Regulations, S.I. No. 60 of 1973
		Detention of Offenders (Shelton Abbey) Regulations, S.I. No. 293 of 1976
		Detention of Offenders (Loughan House) (Amendment) Regulations, 1983, S.I. No. 132 of 1983
		Detention of Offenders (Fort Mitchel) Regulations, S.I. No. 104 of 1985
	7(1)	**Prisons Act, 1970 (Section 7) Order, S.I. No. 118 of 1985**
		Prisons Act, 1970 (Section 7) (No.2) Order, S.I. No. 348 of 1985
		Prisons Act, 1970 (Section 7) Order, S.I. No. 97 of 1986
Prisons Act, No. 7 of 1972	2(9)	**Prisons Act, 1972 (Military Custody) Regulations, S.I. No. 138 of 1972**
		Prisons Act, 1972 (Military Custody) Regulations, S.I. No. 87 of 1976
Prisons (Ireland) Acts, 1826 to 1907,		**Rules for the Government of Prisons [Vol. XXXVI p. 1087] S.R.& O. No. 320 of 1947**
		Rules for the Government of Prisons, S.I. No. 127 of 1955
		Rules for the Government of Prisons, S.I. No. 135 of 1983
Prisons (Visiting Committees) Act, No. 11 of 1925	5	**Prisons (Visiting Committees) Order, S.I. No. 217 of 1972**

Statutory Authority	Section	Statutory Instrument
Prohibition of Forcible Entry and Occupation Act, No. 25 of 1971	10	*Prohibition of Forcible Entry and Occupation Act, 1971 (Commencement) Order, S.I. No. 250 of 1971*
Property Values (Arbitrations and Appeals) Act, No. 45 of 1960	3	**Property Values (Arbitrations and Appeals) Rules, S.I. No. 91 of 1961**
	4	**Property Values (Arbitrations and Appeals) Rules, S.I. No. 91 of 1961**
Prosecution of Offences Act, No. 22 of 1974	2(7)(d)	**Prosecution of Offences Act (Section 2) Regulations, S.I. No. 304 of 1974**
	14(2)	*Prosecution of Offences Act, 1974 (Commencement) Order, S.I. No. 272 of 1974*
		Prosecution of Offences Act, 1974 (Commencement) Order, S.I. No. 3 of 1975
Protection of Animals (Amendment) Act, No. 10 of 1965	8	*Protection of Animals (Approved Spring Traps) Order, S.I. No. 116 of 1968*
Protection of Employees (Employers' Insolvency) Act, No. 21 of 1984	4(3)	**Protection of Employees (Employers' Insolvency) (Specification of Date) Regulations, S.I. No. 232 of 1985**
		Protection of Employees (Employers' Insolvency) (Specification of Date) Regulations, S.I. No. 50 of 1986
	6	**Protection of Employees (Employers' Insolvency) (Forms and Procedure) Regulations, S.I. No. 356 of 1984**
	7	**Protection of Employees (Employers' Insolvency) (Occupational Pension Scheme) (Forms and Procedure) Regulations, S.I. No. 123 of 1985**
	16	**Protection of Employees (Employers' Insolvency) (Forms and Procedure) Regulations, S.I. No. 356 of 1984**
		Protection of Employees (Employers' Insolvency) (Occupational Pension Scheme) (Forms and Procedure) Regulations, S.I. No. 123 of 1985
Protection of Employment Act, No. 7 of 1977	1(2)	*Protection of Employment Act, 1977 (Commencement) Order, S.I. No. 139 of 1977*
	12	**Protection of Employment Act, 1977 (Notification of Proposed Collective Redundancies) Regulations, S.I. No. 140 of 1977**
Protection of Young Persons (Employment) Act, No. 9 of 1977	4(5)	*Protection of Young Persons (Employment) (Section 4) Order, S.I. No. 224 of 1979*
		Protection of Young Persons (Employment) (Section 4) Order, S.I. No. 175 of 1980
	4(6)(b)	**Protection of Young Persons (Prohibition on Employment of Children) Order, S.I. No. 429 of 1981**

Statutory Authority	Section	Statutory Instrument
Protection of Young Persons (Employment) Act, No. 9 of 1977 (*Cont.*)	5(3)	**Registration of Births, Deaths and Marriages (Reduced Fees) Regulations, S.I. No. 46 of 1982** *Registration of Births, Deaths and Marriages (Reduced Fees) (Amendment) Regulations, S.I. No. 148 of 1983* **Registration of Births, Deaths and Marriages (Reduced Fees) (Amendment) Regulations, S.I. No. 359 of 1984**
	17(1)	**Protection of Young Persons (Employment) (Agricultural Workers) Regulations, S.I. No. 220 of 1977** **Protection of Young Persons (Employment) (Exclusion of Close Relatives) Regulations, S.I. No. 303 of 1977**
	25	**Protection of Young Persons (Employment) (Prescribed Abstract) Regulations, S.I. No. 348 of 1977**
	31(2)	*Protection of Young Persons (Employment) Act, 1977 (Commencement) Order, S.I. No. 219 of 1977*
Provisional Collection of Taxes Act, No. 7 of 1927		**Dail Finance Committee Resolution (1934) December 12** **Dail Finance Committee Resolution (1935) May 15**
Public Assistance Act, No. 27 of 1939		*Public Assistance (Medical Assistance in Dispensary Districts) Order [Vol. XXXII p. 597] S.R.& O. No. 1 of 1942* **Public Assistance (Acquisition of Land) Regulations [Vol. XXXII p. 459] S.R.& O. No. 18 of 1942** **Public Assistance (General Regulations) Order [Vol. XXXII p. 491] S.R.& O. No. 83 of 1942** **Public Assistance (General Regulations) (Amendment) Order, S.I. No. 69 of 1951** **Public Assistance Orders (Revocation) Order, S.I. No. 116 of 1954**
	2	*Public Assistance Act, 1939 (Date of Commencement) Order [Vol. XXXII p. 657] S.R.& O. No. 413 of 1942*
	5	*Public Assistance (Footwear Regulations) Order [Vol. XXXII p. 481] S.R.& O. No. 339 of 1944* *Home Assistance Order, S.I. No. 85 of 1955* *Public Assistance (Footwear Regulations) (Amendment) Order, S.I. No. 9 of 1970*
	7	*Dublin and Balrothery Public Assistance Districts (Boundaries) Order, S.I. No. 112 of 1956* *Rathdown and Wicklow Public Assistance Districts (Alteration of Boundaries) Order, S.I. No. 215 of 1957*
	7(3)	*Public Assistance (Names of Districts) Regulations [Vol. XXXII p. 645] S.R.& O. No. 312 of 1942*
	9	*Dublin Public Assistance Authorities (Constitution) Order, S.I. No. 350 of 1948*

Statutory Authority	Section	Statutory Instrument
Public Assistance Act, No. 27 of 1939 (*Cont.*)	9(1)(f)	*Dublin Public Assistance Authorities (Meetings) Order, S.I. No. 361 of 1948*
	26	*Public Assistance (Cost) Order [Vol. XXXII p. 475] S.R.& O. No. 216 of 1944*
	30	*Public Assistance Act, 1939 (Section 30) (Savings Certificates) Rules [Vol. XXXII p. 667] S.R.& O. No. 134 of 1944*
		Public Assistance Act, 1939 (Section 30) (Post Office Savings Bank) Regulations [Vol. XXXII p. 661] S.R.& O. No. 135 of 1944
	31	*Louth Public Assistance District (District Institutions) Order, S.I. No. 46 of 1950*
	39	*Home Assistance Order, S.I. No. 85 of 1955*
	39(2)	*Public Assistance (Footwear Regulations) Order [Vol. XXXII p. 481] S.R.& O. No. 339 of 1944*
		Public Assistance (Footwear Regulations) (Amendment) Order, S.I. No. 9 of 1970
	40(2)	*Sligo Public Assistance District (Dispensary Districts) Order, S.I. No. 222 of 1950*
		Limerick City Public Assistance District (Dispensary Districts) Order, S.I. No. 332 of 1951
		Limerick Public Assistance District (Dispensary Districts) Order, S.I. No. 333 of 1951
		Kildare Public Assistance District (Dispensary Districts) Order, S.I. No. 36 of 1952
		Donegal Public Assistance District (Dispensary Districts) Order, S.I. No. 298 of 1953
		Wexford Public Assistance District (Dispensary Districts) Order, S.I. No. 325 of 1953
	86	**Limerick County Infirmary (Abolition) Order, S.I. No. 204 of 1958**
		Meath County Infirmary (Abolition) Order, S.I. No. 284 of 1946
	89	*Public Assistance (Midwives (Ireland) Act, 1918) Adaptation Order [Vol. XXXII p. 641] S.R.& O. No. 483 of 1942*
	89(1)	*Public Assistance (State Grants) (Adaptation) Order [Vol. XXXII p. 651] S.R.& O. No. 82 of 1945*
Public Assistance (Acquisition of Land) Act, No. 23 of 1934	15	*Public Assistance (Acquisition of Land) Regulations [Vol. XVIII p. 815] S.R.& O. No. 183 of 1934*
Public Health Act, No. 19 of 1896		*Public Health (Saorstat Eireann) (Preservatives, etc., in Food) Regulations [Vol. XVIII p. 867] S.R.& O. No. 54 of 1928*
		Public Health (Louth and Meath Shellfish Layings) Regulations [Vol. XVIII p. 903] S.R.& O. No. 4 of 1930

Statutory Authority	Section	Statutory Instrument

Public Health Act, No. 19 of 1896 (*Cont.*)

Public Health (Deratisation of Ships) Regulations [Vol. XVIII p. 843] S.R.& O. No. 76 of 1930

Public Health (Preservatives, etc., in Food) (Amendment) Regulations [Vol. XXXII p. 739] S.R.& O. No. 74 of 1943

Public Health Act, No. 16 of 1904

Public Health (Deratisation of Ships) Regulations [Vol. XVIII p. 843] S.R.& O. No. 76 of 1930

Public Health Acts, 1878 to 1931,

Public Health (Waterford Shellfish Layings) Regulations [Vol. XXXII p. 745] S.R.& O. No. 28 of 1940

Public Health (Galway Shellfish Layings) Regulations [Vol. XXXII p. 673] S.R.& O. No. 135 of 1940

Public Health (Preservatives, etc., in Food) (Amendment) Regulations [Vol. XXXII p. 739] S.R.& O. No. 74 of 1943

Public Health (Infectious Diseases) (Amendment) Regulations [Vol. XXXII p. 711] S.R.& O. No. 122 of 1945

Importation of Parrots Regulations [Vol. XXXVIII p. 163] S.R.& O. No. 348 of 1946

Public Health (Infectious Diseases) (Amendment) Regulations [Vol. XXXVIII p. 171] S.R.& O. No. 349 of 1946

Public Health (Infectious Diseases) (Amendment) Regulations [Vol. XXXVIII p. 175] S.R.& O. No. 297 of 1947

Public Health Acts Amendment Act, No. 59 of 1890

Urban Stock (Amendment) Regulations, 1928, Confirmation Order [Vol. XVIII p. 925] S.R.& O. No. 29 of 1930

Public Health Acts Amendment Act, No. 53 of 1907

Public Health Acts Amendment Act, 1907 (Application of Part VII to County Health District of Waterford) Order, S.I. No. 125 of 1952

3 **Public Health Acts Amendment Act, 1907 (Application of Section 82 to County Health District of Kerry) Order, S.I. No. 182 of 1959**

Public Health Acts Amendment Act, 1907 (Application of Section 82 to County Health Districts of South Cork and West Cork) Order, S.I. No. 82 of 1968

Public Health Acts Amendment Act, 1907 (Application of Section 82 to County Health District of Sligo) Order, S.I. No. 327 of 1981

Public Health Acts Amendment Act, 1907 (Application of Section 82 to County Health District of Meath) Order, S.I. No. 132 of 1984

Public Health (Ireland) Act, No. 52 of 1878

2 **Public Health (Ireland) Act, 1878 (Sections 128, 129 and 130) (County Health District of Galway) Order, S.I. No. 198 of 1962**

11 **Public Health (Veterinary Inspection) Order [Vol. XVIII p. 835] S.R.& O. No. 22 of 1929**

Statutory Authority	Section	Statutory Instrument
Public Health (Ireland) Act, No. 52 of 1878 (*Cont.*)		**Public Health (Urban Sanitary Inspectors) Order [Vol. XVIII p. 851] S.R.& O. No. 89 of 1930**
		Milk and Dairies Regulations [Vol. XVI p. 567] S.R.& O. No. 310 of 1936
	128	**Public Health (Ireland) Act, 1878 (Sections 128, 129 and 130) (County Health District of Galway) Order, S.I. No. 198 of 1962**
	129	**Public Health (Ireland) Act, 1878 (Sections 128, 129 and 130) (County Health District of Galway) Order, S.I. No. 198 of 1962**
	130	**Public Health (Ireland) Act, 1878 (Sections 128, 129 and 130) (County Health District of Galway) Order, S.I. No. 198 of 1962**
	148	*Public Health (Infectious Diseases) Regulations [Vol. XVIII p. 891] S.R.& O. No. 12 of 1929*
		Importation of Parrots (Temporary) Regulations [Vol. XVIII p. 919] S.R.& O. No. 42 of 1930
		Public Health (Deratisation of Ships) Regulations [Vol. XVIII p. 843] S.R.& O. No. 76 of 1930
		Public Health (Infectious Diseases) Regulations [Vol. XXXII p. 683] S.R.& O. No. 13 of 1941
		Public Health (Influenza) Regulations [Vol. XXXVIII p. 157] S.R.& O. No. 413 of 1947
	149	**Vaccination Regulations [Vol. XXXIV p. 517] S.R.& O. No. 127 of 1942**
	191	**Returns of Burials (Amendment) Order, S.I. No. 263 of 1957**
Public Health (Ireland) Act, No. 54 of 1896	1	**Public Health (Ireland) Act, 1878 (Section 103) County Health District of Galway Order, S.I. No. 203 of 1953**
		Public Health (Ireland) Act, 1878 (Section 103) (County Health District of Kildare) Order, S.I. No. 216 of 1954
		Public Health (Ireland) Act, 1878 (Sections 128, 129 and 130) (County Health Districts of Cork) Order, S.I. No. 211 of 1958
		Public Health (Ireland) Act, 1878 (Sections 128, 129 and 130) (County Health District of Galway) Order, S.I. No. 198 of 1962
		Public Health (Ireland) Act, 1878 (Section 103) County Health District of Limerick Order, S.I. No. 13 of 1964
		Public Health (Ireland) Act, 1878 (Section 52) (County Health District of Dublin) Order, S.I. No. 83 of 1967
		Public Health (Ireland) Act, 1878 (Section 54) (County Health District of Dublin) Order, S.I. No. 310 of 1970
Public Health (Ireland) Acts, 1878 to 1919,		*Smallpox (Importation of Clothing etc.) Temporary Regulations [Vol. XVIII p. 857] S.R.& O. No. 62 of 1927*

Statutory Authority	Section	Statutory Instrument
Public Health (Ireland) Acts, 1878 to 1919 (*Cont.*)		*Public Health (Saorstat Eireann) (Preservatives, etc., in Food) Regulations [Vol. XVIII p. 867] S.R.& O. No. 54 of 1928*
		Public Health (Louth and Meath Shellfish Layings) Regulations [Vol. XVIII p. 903] S.R.& O. No. 4 of 1930
		Public Health (Infectious Diseases) (Amendment) Regulations [Vol. XXXII p. 755] S.R.& O. No. 126 of 1942
		Public Health (Infectious Diseases) (Amendment) Regulations [Vol. XXXII p. 761] S.R.& O. No. 258 of 1943
		Public Health (Infectious Diseases) (Amendment) (No.2) Regulations [Vol. XXXII p. 767] S.R.& O. No. 350 of 1943
Public Health (Regulations as to Food) Act, No. 32 of 1907		*Public Health (Saorstat Eireann) (Preservatives, etc., in Food) Regulations [Vol. XVIII p. 867] S.R.& O. No. 54 of 1928*
		Public Health (Louth and Meath Shellfish Layings) Regulations [Vol. XVIII p. 903] S.R.& O. No. 4 of 1930
		Public Health (Preservatives, etc., in Food) (Amendment) Regulations [Vol. XXXII p. 739] S.R.& O. No. 74 of 1943
		Public Health (Louth and Meath Shellfish Layings) Regulations, 1939 (Amendment) Regulations, S.I. No. 246 of 1949
	1	*Public Health (Louth and Meath Shellfish Layings) Regulations [Vol. XVIII p. 911] S.R.& O. No. 22 of 1931*
		Public Health (Louth and Meath Shellfish Layings) Regulations [Vol. XXXII p. 727] S.R.& O. No. 4 of 1939
		Public Health (Kerry Shellfish Layings) Regulations [Vol. XXXII p. 715] S.R.& O. No. 342 of 1942
Public Hospitals (Amendment) Act, No. 21 of 1938	10(2)	*Public Hospitals (Amendment) Act (Commencement) Order [Vol. XVIII p. 967] S.R.& O. No. 210 of 1938*
Public Hospitals (Amendment) Act, No. 9 of 1940	2(1)	*Dublin Hospital Bureau Order [Vol. XXXII p. 771] S.R.& O. No. 330 of 1940*
	2(3)	*Hospitals Commission (Dublin Hospitals Bureau) Regulations [Vol. XXXII p. 777] S.R.& O. No. 236 of 1941*
Public Libraries Act, No. 40 of 1947	16	**Public Libraries Act, 1947 (Grants) Regulations, S.I. No. 265 of 1961**
		Public Libraries Act, 1947 (Grants) (Amendment) Regulations, S.I. No. 321 of 1977
Public Offices Fees Act, No. 58 of 1879	2	**Censorship of Films (Collection of Fees) Order, (1923) [Vol. XVIII p. 971] S.R.& O. No. 14 of 1924**
		Censorship of Films (Collection of Fees) Order [Vol. XVIII p. 975] S.R.& O. No. 38 of 1925

Statutory Authority	Section	Statutory Instrument
Public Offices Fees Act, No. 58 of 1879 (*Cont.*)		**Civil Service Examination Fees Order [Vol. XVIII p. 981] S.R.& O. No. 45 of 1925**
		Local Appointments Commissioners (Collection of Fees) Order [Vol. XVIII p. 985] S.R.& O. No. 10 of 1927
		Tariff Commission (Collection of Fees) Order [Vol. XVIII p. 993] S.R.& O. No. 22 of 1927
		Railway Tribunal (Collection of Fees) Order [Vol. XVIII p. 1003] S.R.& O. No. 43 of 1927
		Industrial and Commercial Property Registration Office (Collection of Fees) Order [Vol. XVIII p. 1013] S.R.& O. No. 88 of 1927
		Registration of Chattel Mortgages (Collection of Fees) Order [Vol. XVIII p. 1023] S.R.& O. No. 42 of 1928
		Agricultural Produce (Fresh Meat) Act (Collection of Fees) Order [Vol. XVIII p. 1033] S.R.& O. No. 81 of 1930
		Live Stock Breeding Act (Collection of Fees) Order [Vol. XVIII p. 1041] S.R.& O. No. 87 of 1930
		Agricultural Produce (Eggs) Acts (Collection of Fees) Order [Vol. XVIII p. 1049] S.R.& O. No. 76 of 1931
		Agricultural Produce (Potatoes) Act (Collection of Fees) Order [Vol. XVIII p. 1050] S.R.& O. No. 13 of 1932
		Merchandise Marks Commission (Collection of Fees) Order [Vol. XVIII p. 1069] S.R.& O. No. 44 of 1932
		Dairy Produce Act (Collection of Fees) Order [Vol. XVIII p. 1081] S.R.& O. No. 113 of 1932
		District Probate Registries (Collection of Fees) Order [Vol. XVIII p. 1091] S.R.& O. No. 115 of 1932
		Agricultural Produce (Cereals) Act (Collection of Fees) Order [Vol. XVIII p. 1107] S.R.& O. No. 76 of 1933
		Irish Land Commission (Collection of Office Fees) Order [Vol. XVIII p. 1117] S.R.& O. No. 139 of 1934
		Air Navigation (Collection of Fees) Order [Vol. XVIII p. 1121] S.R.& O. No. 360 of 1934
		Town and Regional Planning (Collection of Fees) Order [Vol. XVIII p. 1131] S.R.& O. No. 152 of 1935
		Railway Tribunal (Collection of Fees) Order [Vol. XVIII p. 1141] S.R.& O. No. 618 of 1935
		Cement Act (Collection of Fees on Import Licences) Order [Vol. XVIII p. 1153] S.R.& O. No. 681 of 1935
		Perpetual Funds (Registration) Act (Collection of Fees) Order, (1935) [Vol. XVIII p. 1157] S.R.& O. No. 22 of 1936

Public Offices Fees Act, No. 58 of 1879 (*Cont.*)

Landlord and Tenant Act (Collection of Fees) Order [Vol. XVIII p. 1167] S.R.& O. No. 148 of 1936

Local Registration of Title (Collection of Fees) Order [Vol. XVIII p. 1177] S.R.& O. No. 10 of 1938

Ballina District Probate Registry (Collection of Fees) Order [Vol. XXXII p. 791] S.R.& O. No. 16 of 1941

Castlebar District Probate Registry (Collection of Fees) Order [Vol. XXXII p. 801] S.R.& O. No. 253 of 1945

Mullingar District Probate Registry (Collection of Fees) Order, S.I. No. 287 of 1948

Censorship of Films (Collection of Fees) Order, S.I. No. 252 of 1976

Local Appointments Commissioners (Collection of Fees) Order, S.I. No. 64 of 1983

3   **Censorship of Films (Collection of Fees) Order, (1923)** [Vol. XVIII p. 971] S.R.& O. No. 14 of 1924

Censorship of Films (Collection of Fees) Order [Vol. XVIII p. 975] S.R.& O. No. 38 of 1925

Civil Service Examination Fees Order [Vol. XVIII p. 981] S.R.& O. No. 45 of 1925

Local Appointments Commissioners (Collection of Fees) Regulations [Vol. XVIII p. 989] S.R.& O. No. 11 of 1927

Tariff Commission (Collection of Fees) Regulations [Vol. XVIII p. 997] S.R.& O. No. 23 of 1927

Railway Tribunal (Collection of Fees) Regulations [Vol. XVIII p. 1007] S.R.& O. No. 53 of 1927

Industrial and Commercial Property Registration Office (Collection of Fees) Regulations [Vol. XVIII p. 1017] S.R.& O. No. 89 of 1927

Registration of Chattel Mortgages (Collection of Fees) Regulations [Vol. XVIII p. 1027] S.R.& O. No. 51 of 1928

Agricultural Produce (Fresh Meat) Act (Collection of Fees) Regulations [Vol. XVIII p. 1037] S.R.& O. No. 82 of 1930

Live Stock Breeding Act (Collection of Fees) Regulations [Vol. XVIII p. 1045] S.R.& O. No. 88 of 1930

Agricultural Produce (Eggs) Acts (Collection of Fees) Regulations [Vol. XVIII p. 1053] S.R.& O. No. 77 of 1931

Agricultural Produce (Potatoes) Act (Collection of Fees) Regulations [Vol. XVIII p. 1063] S.R.& O. No. 14 of 1932

Merchandise Marks Commission (Collection of Fees) Order [Vol. XVIII p. 1069] S.R.& O. No. 44 of 1932

Merchandise Marks Commission (Collection of Fees) Regulations [Vol. XVIII p. 1073] S.R.& O. No. 45 of 1932

Statutory Authority	Section	Statutory Instrument
Public Offices Fees Act, No. 58 of 1879 (*Cont.*)		**Dairy Produce Act (Collection of Fees) Regulations [Vol. XVIII p. 1085] S.R.& O. No. 114 of 1932**
		District Probate Registries (Collection of Fees) Regulations [Vol. XVIII p. 1095] S.R.& O. No. 116 of 1932
		Agricultural Produce (Cereals) Act (Collection of Fees) Regulations [Vol. XVIII p. 1111] S.R.& O. No. 77 of 1933
		District Probate Registries (Collection of Fees) (Amendment) Regulations [Vol. XVIII p. 1101] S.R.& O. No. 118 of 1933
		Air Navigation (Collection of Fees) Regulations [Vol. XVIII p. 1125] S.R.& O. No. 361 of 1934
		Town and Regional Planning (Collection of Fees) Regulations [Vol. XVIII p. 1135] S.R.& O. No. 153 of 1935
		Railway Tribunal (Collection of Fees) Regulations [Vol. XVIII p. 1145] S.R.& O. No. 619 of 1935
		Perpetual Funds (Registration) Act (Collection of Fees) Regulations, (1935) [Vol. XVIII p. 1161] S.R.& O. No. 23 of 1936
		Landlord and Tenant Act (Collection of Fees) Regulations [Vol. XVIII p. 1171] S.R.& O. No. 149 of 1936
		Local Registration of Title (Collection of Fees) Regulations [Vol. XVIII p. 1181] S.R.& O. No. 11 of 1938
		Ballina District Probate Registry (Collection of Fees) Regulations [Vol. XXXII p. 795] S.R.& O. No. 17 of 1941
		Castlebar District Probate Registry (Collection of Fees) Regulations [Vol. XXXII p. 805] S.R.& O. No. 254 of 1945
		Mullingar District Probate Registry (Collection of Fees) Regulations, S.I. No. 289 of 1948
		Local Appointments Commissioners (Collection of Fees) Regulations, S.I. No. 63 of 1983
	4	**Railway Tribunal (Collection of Fees) Regulations [Vol. XVIII p. 1007] S.R.& O. No. 53 of 1927**
Public Records (Ireland) Act, No. 70 of 1867	17	*Public Records (Fees) Order, S.I. No. 53 of 1955*
		Public Records Office (Times of Opening) Rules, S.I. No. 165 of 1964
		Public Records (Fees) Order, S.I. No. 254 of 1980
		Public Records (Fees) Order, S.I. No. 38 of 1982
Public Works Loans Act, No. 29 of 1906	4	*Kilrush Pier, County Clare Order [Vol. XX p. 391] S.R.& O. No. 161 of 1933*
Purchase of Land (Ireland) Act, No. 48 of 1891	6	**Purchase of Land (Ireland) Act, 1891 (Guarantee Fund Apportionment) (Amendment) Regulations [Vol. XXXII p. 811] S.R.& O. No. 142 of 1945**
Pyramid Selling Act, No. 27 of 1980	9	*Pyramid Selling Act, 1980 (Commencement) Order, S.I. No. 340 of 1980*

Statutory Authority	Section	Statutory Instrument
Racing Board and Racecourses Act, No. 16 of 1945	3(1)	*Racing Board and Racecourses Act, 1945 (Appointment of Establishment Date) Order [Vol. XXXIII p. 1] S.R.& O. No. 145 of 1945*
	3(2)	*Racing Board and Racecourses Act, 1945 (Appointment of Transfer Date) Order [Vol. XXXIII p. 5] S.R.& O. No. 185 of 1945*
	21	*Racing Board and Racecourses Act, 1945 (Commencement of Chapters II and III of Part III) Order [Vol. XXXIII p. 9] S.R.& O. No. 243 of 1945*
	27	*Racecourse (Levy) (Percentage) Regulations, S.I. No. 121 of 1964*
		Racecourse (Levy) (Percentage) Regulations, S.I. No. 130 of 1975
		Racecourse (Levy) (Percentage) Regulations, S.I. No. 181 of 1980
		Racecourse (Levy) (Percentage) Regulations, S.I. No. 86 of 1985
	28	**Racecourse (Levy Collection) (Amendment) Regulations, S.I. No. 323 of 1986**
	28(1)	**Racecourse (Levy Collection) Regulations, S.I. No. 404 of 1977**
Racing Board and Racecourses (Amendment) Act, No. 11 of 1975	4(10)	*Racing Board and Racecourses (Amendment) Act (Commencement of Sections 4 and 5) Order, S.I. No. 144 of 1975*
Railway and Canal Traffic Act, No. 25 of 1888		**Royal Canal (Longford) (Abandonment) Warrant, S.I. No. 172 of 1954**
		Grand Canal (Blackwood Branch) (Abandonment) Warrant, S.I. No. 107 of 1955
	45	**Grand Canal (Blackwood Branch) (Cesser of Maintenance) Order, S.I. No. 180 of 1955**
		Royal Canal (Longford) (Cesser of Maintenance) Order, S.I. No. 264 of 1956
		Abandonment Order for Part of the Athlone Canal, S.I. No. 228 of 1982
Railway Employment (Prevention of Accidents) Act, No. 27 of 1900	1(1)	**Prevention of Accidents Rules, 1911 Amendment Rules [Vol. XIX p. 1] S.R.& O. No. 30 of 1926**
Railways Act, No. 29 of 1924		**Railways (Great Southern) Preliminary Amalgamation Scheme [Vol. XIX p. 23] S.R.& O. No. 31 of 1924**
		Great Southern Railways Amalgamation Scheme [Vol. XIX p. 41] S.R.& O. No. 1 of 1925
		Great Southern Railways Supplemental Amalgamation Scheme [Vol. XIX p. 61] S.R.& O. No. 4 of 1925
		Great Southern Railway Company Schedule of Standard Charges [Vol. XIX p. 159] S.R.& O. No. 5 of 1930
		Railway Tribunal (Additional) Rules [Vol. XIX p. 295] S.R.& O. No. 659 of 1935

Statutory Authority	Section	Statutory Instrument
Railways Act, No. 29 of 1924 (*Cont.*)	5	**Great Southern Railways Absorption (No.1) Scheme [Vol. XIX p. 67] S.R.& O. No. 5 of 1925**
		Great Southern Railways Absorption (No.2) Scheme [Vol. XIX p. 77] S.R.& O. No. 6 of 1925
		Great Southern Railways Absorption (No.3) Scheme [Vol. XIX p. 83] S.R.& O. No. 7 of 1925
		Great Southern Railways Absorption (No.4) Scheme [Vol. XIX p. 93] S.R.& O. No. 8 of 1925
		Great Southern Railways Absorption (No.5) Scheme [Vol. XIX p. 103] S.R.& O. No. 59 of 1925
	19	*Railway Tribunal Rules [Vol. XIX p. 107] S.R.& O. No. 23 of 1926*
	19(2)	*Railway Tribunal Fees Order [Vol. XIX p. 155] S.R.& O. No. 24 of 1926*
	33	**Great Southern Railway Company (Modification of Standard Charges) [Vol. XIX p. 289] S.R.& O. No. 56 of 1930**
		Railways (Carriage of Damageable Merchandise, Reductions from Standard Charges) [Vol. XIX p. 273] S.R.& O. No. 1 of 1932
	41	**Standard Terms and Conditions of Carriage [Vol. XIX p. 211] S.R.& O. No. 13 of 1930**
	44(1)	*Railways (Carriage of Damageable Merchandise, Reductions from Standard Charges) [Vol. XIX p. 255] S.R.& O. No. 14 of 1930*
	54	*Great Southern Railways Company Modification of Standard Charges [Vol. XIX p. 301] S.R.& O. No. 319 of 1937*
	59	**Coras Iompair Eireann (Acquisition of Land at Limerick) Order [Vol. XXXVIII p. 179] S.R.& O. No. 110 of 1947**
Railways Act, No. 9 of 1933	3(2)	*Railways Act, 1933, (Appointed Day under Section 3) Order [Vol. XIX p. 317] S.R.& O. No. 80 of 1933*
	5(2)	*Railways Act, 1933 (Appointed Day under Section 5) Order [Vol. XIX p. 359] S.R.& O. No. 176 of 1933*
	6(2)	**Great Southern Railways Company Postal Voting Scheme, 1933 (Confirming and Appointed Day) Order [Vol. XIX p. 341] S.R.& O. No. 163 of 1933**
	9	**Great Southern Railways (Tralee – Castlegregory) Termination of Railway Services Order [Vol. XXXIII p. 13] S.R.& O. No. 80 of 1939**
		Great Southern Railways (Tralee – Dingle) Termination of Passenger Train Services Order [Vol. XXXIII p. 19] S.R.& O. No. 81 of 1939
		Londonderry and Lough Swilly Railway (Letterkenny-Burtonport) Termination of Railway Services Order [Vol. XXXIII p. 31] S.R.& O. No. 164 of 1940

Railways Act, No. 9 of 1933
(*Cont.*)

Londonderry and Lough Swilly (Letterkenny-Bridge End) Termination of Passenger Train Services Order [Vol. XXXIII p. 25] S.R.& O. No. 165 of 1940

Donegal County Railways (Stranorlar-Glenties) Reduction of Railway Services Order [Vol. XXXVIII p. 185] S.R.& O. No. 368 of 1947

County Donegal Railways (Stranorlar-Glenties) Termination of Railway Services Order, S.I. No. 49 of 1952

Londonderry and Lough Swilly Railway (Bridge End-Buncrana; Tooban Junction-Farland Point) Termination of Railway Services Order, S.I. No. 350 of 1952

Letterkenny Railway (Letterkenny-Farland Point) Termination of Train Services Order, S.I. No. 239 of 1953

County Donegal Railways (Donegal, Ballyshannon) Termination of Railway Services Order, S.I. No. 178 of 1959

County Donegal Railways (Killybegs-Strabane, Letterkenny-Strabane) Termination of Railway Services Order, S.I. No. 179 of 1959

9(2) **Great Northern Railway Company (Ireland) (Dromin Junction – Ardee) Termination of Railway Services Order [Vol. XIX p. 361] S.R.& O. No. 143 of 1934**

Great Southern Railways (Ballina – Killala) Termination of Railway Services Order [Vol. XIX p. 367] S.R.& O. No. 176 of 1934

Great Southern Railways (Patrick's Well – Charleville) Termination of Railway Services Order [Vol. XIX p. 373] S.R.& O. No. 385 of 1934

Great Southern Railways (Cork – Coachford) Termination of Railway Services Order [Vol. XIX p. 379] S.R.& O. No. 386 of 1934

Great Southern Railways (Cork – Donoughmore) Termination of Railway Services Order [Vol. XIX p. 385] S.R.& O. No. 387 of 1934

Great Southern Railways (Tralee – Fenit) Termination of Railway Services Order [Vol. XIX p. 391] S.R.& O. No. 388 of 1934

Great Southern Railways (Westport – Achill) Termination of Railway Services Order [Vol. XIX p. 397] S.R.& O. No. 389 of 1934

Great Southern Railways (Galway – Clifden) Termination of Railway Services Order [Vol. XIX p. 409] S.R.& O. No. 119 of 1935

Great Southern Railways (Cork – Macroom) Termination of Railway Services Order [Vol. XIX p. 415] S.R.& O. No. 568 of 1935

Londonderry and Lough Swilly Railway (Buncrana-Carndonagh) Termination of Railway Services Order [Vol. XIX p. 421] S.R.& O. No. 672 of 1935

Statutory Authority	Section	Statutory Instrument
Railways Act, No. 9 of 1933 (*Cont.*)		**Londonderry and Lough Swilly Railway (Tooban Junction-Buncrana) Termination of Railway Services Order [Vol. XIX p. 427] S.R.& O. No. 673 of 1935**
		Great Southern Railways (Westport – Achill) Termination of Railway Services Order [Vol. XIX p. 403] S.R.& O. No. 266 of 1937
	12	*Uniform Rate (Peat Fuel) Order [Vol. XIX p. 321] S.R.& O. No. 84 of 1933*
		Uniform Rate (Peat Fuel) Order [Vol. XIX p. 325] S.R.& O. No. 208 of 1934
	12(12)	*Uniform Rate (Peat Fuel) (Revocation) Order [Vol. XIX p. 333] S.R.& O. No. 358 of 1934*
		Uniform Rate (Peat Fuel) (Revocation) Order [Vol. XIX p. 337] S.R.& O. No. 309 of 1936
Railways (Amendment) Act, No. 23 of 1929	3(1)	*Railway Tribunal – Reduction of Membership [Vol. XIX p. 433] S.R.& O. No. 49 of 1931*
Railways (Ireland) Act, No. 34 of 1896	2(d)	**Londonderry and Lough Swilly (Carndonagh Extension) Light Railway Order, 1898, Amendment Order [Vol. XIX p. 13] S.R.& O. No. 24 of 1931**
		Londonderry and Lough Swilly (Letterkenny to Burtonport Extension) Railway Order, 1898, Amendment Order [Vol. XIX p. 3] S.R.& O. No. 25 of 1931
		Londonderry and Lough Swilly (Carndonagh Extension) Light Railway Order, 1898, Amendment Order, (1935) [Vol. XIX p. 17] S.R.& O. No. 27 of 1936
		Londonderry and Lough Swilly (Letterkenny to Burtonport Extension) Railway Order, 1898, Amendment Order, (1935) [Vol. XIX p. 7] S.R.& O. No. 28 of 1936
Railways (Miscellaneous) Act, No. 3 of 1932	7	*Ballina to Killala Railway (Modification of Obligatory Service of Trains) Order [Vol. XIX p. 437] S.R.& O. No. 16 of 1932*
		Railways (Modification of Service) (Drimoleague and Bantry Line) Order [Vol. XIX p. 441] S.R.& O. No. 89 of 1932
		Railways (Modification of Service) (Baltinglass and Tullow Line) Order [Vol. XIX p. 445] S.R.& O. No. 90 of 1932
		Railways (Modification of Service) (Clonakilty Junction and Clonakilty Line) Order [Vol. XIX p. 449] S.R.& O. No. 91 of 1932
		Railways (Modification of Service) (Headford Junction and Kenmare Line) Order [Vol. XIX p. 453] S.R.& O. No. 92 of 1932
		Railways (Modification of Service) (Ennis and Kilrush and Kilkee Line) Order [Vol. XIX p. 457] S.R.& O. No. 93 of 1932
		Railways (Modification of Service) (Goold's Cross and Cashel Line) Order [Vol. XIX p. 461] S.R.& O. No. 94 of 1932

Statutory Authority	Section	Statutory Instrument
Railways (Miscellaneous) Act, No. 3 of 1932 (*Cont.*)		*Railways (Modification of Service) (Fermoy and Michelstown Line) Order [Vol. XIX p. 465] S.R.& O. No. 95 of 1932*
		Railways (Modification of Service) (Letterkenny and Burtonport Line) Order [Vol. XIX p. 469] S.R.& O. No. 106 of 1932
		Railways (Modification of Service) (Buncrana and Carndonagh Line) Order [Vol. p. XIX473] S.R.& O. No. 107 of 1932
Rates on Agricultural Land (Relief) Act, No. 1 of 1935	5	*Rates on Agricultural Land (Certificate) Order [Vol. XIX p. 477] S.R.& O. No. 35 of 1935*
Rates on Agricultural Land (Relief) Act, No. 9 of 1978	1(3)	*Rates on Agricultural Land (Application of Relief) Order, S.I. No. 198 of 1978*
		Rates on Agricultural Land (Application of Relief) Order, S.I. No. 7 of 1979
Red Cross Act, No. 32 of 1938	1	**Irish Red Cross Society Order [Vol. XXXIII p. 37] S.R.& O. No. 206 of 1939**
	1(3)	**Irish Red Cross Society Order, 1939 (Amendment) Order [Vol. XXXVIII p. 189] S.R.& O. No. 184 of 1947**
Red Cross Act, No. 28 of 1954	1	*Red Cross Act, 1954 (Commencement) Order, S.I. No. 216 of 1955*
	6	**Irish Red Cross Society (Directions as to Ambulance Service) Order, S.I. No. 251 of 1955**
Redundancy Payments Act, No. 21 of 1967	3	*Redundancy Payments Act (Appointed Day) Order, S.I. No. 302 of 1967*
	17	*Redundancy (Notice of Dismissal) Regulations, S.I. No. 2 of 1968*
		Redundancy (Notice of Dismissal) Regulations, S.I. No. 111 of 1979
		Redundancy (Notice of Dismissal) Regulations, S.I. No. 220 of 1984
	18	*Redundancy Certificate Regulations, S.I. No. 3 of 1968*
		Redundancy Certificate Regulations, S.I. No. 112 of 1979
		Redundancy Certificate Regulations, S.I. No. 221 of 1984
	19	*Redundancy Payments (Weekly Payments and Lump Sum) Order, S.I. No. 82 of 1974*
	28	**Redundancy Contributions (Variation of Rates) Order, S.I. No. 36 of 1971**

Statutory Authority	Section	Statutory Instrument
Redundancy Payments Act, No. 21 of 1967 (*Cont.*)		**Redundancy Contributions (Variation of Rates) Order, S.I. No. 172 of 1972**
		Redundancy Contributions (Variation of Rates) Order, S.I. No. 172 of 1973
		Redundancy Contributions (Variation of Rates) Order, S.I. No. 65 of 1975
		Redundancy Contributions (Variation of Rates) Order, S.I. No. 81 of 1976
	28(3)	*Redundancy Payments (Variation of Employer's Redundancy Contribution) Regulations, S.I. No. 94 of 1981*
		Redundancy Payments (Variation of Employer's Redundancy Contribution) Regulations, S.I. No. 75 of 1982
		Redundancy Payments (Employer's Redundancy Contributions) Regulations, S.I. No. 84 of 1983
		Redundancy Payments (Variation of Employee's Redundancy Contribution) Regulations, S.I. No. 63 of 1984
		Redundancy Payments (Variation of Employer's Redundancy Contribution) Regulations, S.I. No. 75 of 1985
		Redundancy Payments (Variation of Employer's Redundancy Contribution) Regulations, S.I. No. 67 of 1986
	28(5)	*Redundancy (Collection of Contributions) Regulations, S.I. No. 4 of 1968*
		Redundancy (Collection of Contributions) (Revocation) Regulations, S.I. No. 271 of 1968
	30	*Redundancy Payments (Weekly Payments and Lump Sum) Order, S.I. No. 82 of 1974*
		Redundancy Payments (Weekly Payments) Order, S.I. No. 126 of 1976
	33(1)	*Redundancy (Collection of Contributions) Regulations, S.I. No. 4 of 1968*
		Redundancy (Collection of Contributions) (Revocation) Regulations, S.I. No. 271 of 1968
	33(2)	*Redundancy (Collection of Contributions) Regulations, S.I. No. 4 of 1968*
		Redundancy (Collection of Contributions) (Revocation) Regulations, S.I. No. 271 of 1968
		Redundancy Contributions (Method of Payment) Regulations, S.I. No. 272 of 1968
		Redundancy Contributions (Method of Payment) (Revocation) Regulations, S.I. No. 116 of 1979
	35	**Redundancy Payments (Dublin Port Dockers) Regulations, S.I. No. 301 of 1971**
		Redundancy Payments (Dublin Port Dockers) Regulations, S.I. No. 42 of 1973
		Redundancy Payments (Dundalk Port Dockers) Regulations, S.I. No. 95 of 1973

Statutory Authority	Section	Statutory Instrument
Redundancy Payments Act, No. 21 of 1967 (*Cont.*)		**Redundancy Payments (Galway Port Dockers) Regulations, S.I. No. 261 of 1973**
		Redundancy Payments (Limerick Port Dockers) Regulations, S.I. No. 59 of 1974
		Redundancy Payments (Waterford Port Dockers) Regulations, S.I. No. 73 of 1975
	35(1)	*Redundancy (Collection of Contributions) Regulations, S.I. No. 4 of 1968*
		Redundancy (Collection of Contributions) (Revocation) Regulations, S.I. No. 271 of 1968
	36	**Redundancy (Rebates and Weekly Payments) Regulations, S.I. No. 11 of 1968**
		Redundancy (Rebates and Weekly Payments) (Amendment) Regulations, S.I. No. 134 of 1969
		Redundancy (Rebates and Weekly Payments) Regulations, S.I. No. 113 of 1979
		Redundancy (Rebates) Regulations, S.I. No. 222 of 1984
	39(19)	**Redundancy (Redundancy Appeals Tribunal) Regulations, S.I. No. 24 of 1968**
		Redundancy (Redundancy Appeals Tribunal) (Amendment) Regulations, S.I. No. 26 of 1969
		Minimum Notice and Terms of Employment (Reference of Disputes) Regulations, S.I. No. 243 of 1973
		Redundancy (Employment Appeals Tribunal) Regulations, S.I. No. 114 of 1979
	41	**Redundancy (Repayment and Recovery of Payments) Regulations, S.I. No. 5 of 1968**
	46	*Redundancy (Resettlement Assistance) Regulations, S.I. No. 8 of 1968*
		Redundancy (Resettlement Assistance) Regulations, S.I. No. 286 of 1971
		Redundancy (Resettlement Assistance) (Revocation) Regulations, S.I. No. 251 of 1982
	46(1)	*Redundancy (Resettlement Assistance) Regulations, S.I. No. 271 of 1974*
		Redundancy (Resettlement Assistance) Regulations, S.I. No. 322 of 1979
		Redundancy (Resettlement Assistance) Regulations, S.I. No. 248 of 1982
	55	**Redundancy Payments Act (Authorised Officers) Order, S.I. No. 106 of 1968**
	57	**Redundancy (Inspector of Records) Regulations, S.I. No. 12 of 1968**
	58	*Redundancy (Notice of Dismissal) Regulations, S.I. No. 2 of 1968*
		Redundancy Certificate Regulations, S.I. No. 3 of 1968
		Redundancy (Collection of Contributions) Regulations, S.I. No. 4 of 1968

Statutory Authority	Section	Statutory Instrument
Redundancy Payments Act, No. 21 of 1967 (*Cont.*)		**Redundancy (Inspector of Records) Regulations, S.I. No. 12 of 1968**
		Redundancy (Collection of Contributions) (Revocation) Regulations, S.I. No. 271 of 1968
		Redundancy (Notice of Dismissal) Regulations, S.I. No. 111 of 1979
		Redundancy Certificate Regulations, S.I. No. 112 of 1979
		Redundancy (Inspection of Records) Regulations, S.I. No. 115 of 1979
		Redundancy (Notice of Dismissal) Regulations, S.I. No. 220 of 1984
		Redundancy Certificate Regulations, S.I. No. 221 of 1984
Redundancy Payments Act, No. 20 of 1971	20(3)	*Redundancy Payments Act, 1971 (Commencement) Order, S.I. No. 230 of 1971*
Redundancy Payments Act, No. 11 of 1973	2(3)	*Redundancy Payments Act, 1973 (Commencement) Order, S.I. No. 175 of 1973*
Redundancy Payments Act, No. 7 of 1979	4(2)(a)	*Redundancy Payments (Lump Sum) Regulations, S.I. No. 191 of 1981*
		Redundancy Payments (Lump Sum) Regulations, S.I. No. 104 of 1982
		Redundancy Payments (Lump Sum) Regulations, S.I. No. 108 of 1983
	21	*Redundancy Payments Act, 1979 (Commencement) Order, S.I. No. 95 of 1979*
Referendum Act, No. 8 of 1942	3	*Referendum (Prescribed Forms) Regulations, S.I. No. 83 of 1959*
		Polling Card (Dail Elections, Presidential Elections and Referenda) Regulations, S.I. No. 245 of 1961
		Forms (Dail Elections, Presidential Elections and Referenda) Regulations, S.I. No. 246 of 1963
		Forms (Dail Elections, Presidential Elections and Referenda) (Amendment) Regulations, S.I. No. 115 of 1972
	12(5)	*Referendum and Presidential Elections (Local Returning Officers' Charges and Accounts) Regulations, S.I. No. 81 of 1959*
		Referendum (Local Returning Officers' Charges and Accounts) Regulations, S.I. No. 195 of 1968
		Referendum (Local Returning Officers' Charges and Accounts) Regulations, S.I. No. 104 of 1972
		Referendum (Local Returning Officers' Charges and Accounts) (No.2) Regulations, S.I. No. 279 of 1972
		Referendum (Local Returning Officers' Charges) Regulations, S.I. No. 209 of 1979
		Referendum (Local Returning Officers' Charges) (No.2) Regulations, S.I. No. 229 of 1979

Referendum Act, No. 8 of 1942 (*Cont.*)		*Referendum (Local Returning Officers' Charges) Regulations, S.I. No. 243 of 1983*
		Returning Officers' and Local Returning Officers' Charges Regulations, S.I. No. 138 of 1984
		Referendum (Local Returning Officers' Charges) Regulations, S.I. No. 175 of 1986
	20	**Forms (Dail Elections, Presidential Elections and Referenda) Regulations, S.I. No. 246 of 1963**
		Forms (Dail Elections, Presidential Elections and Referenda) (Amendment) Regulations, S.I. No. 115 of 1972
	Sch. I par. 3	**Forms (Dail Elections, Presidential Elections and Referenda) Regulations, S.I. No. 246 of 1963**
	Sch. I par. 23	**Forms (Dail Elections, Presidential Elections and Referenda) Regulations, S.I. No. 246 of 1963**
	Sch. I par. 31	**Forms (Dail Elections, Presidential Elections and Referenda) Regulations, S.I. No. 246 of 1963**
	Sch. I par. 32	**Forms (Dail Elections, Presidential Elections and Referenda) Regulations, S.I. No. 246 of 1963**
Referendum (Amendment) Act, No. 30 of 1946	4(1)	*Polling Card (Dail Elections, Presidential Elections and Referenda) Regulations, S.I. No. 245 of 1961*
Referendum (Amendment) Act, No. 5 of 1959	5	*Referendum and Presidential Elections (Local Returning Officers' Charges and Accounts) Regulations, S.I. No. 81 of 1959*
Register of Population Order [Vol. XXXIX p. 937] S.R.& O. No. 295 of 1947	2	*Register of Population Order, 1947, Regulations [Vol. XXXVIII p. 193] S.R.& O. No. 299 of 1947*
		Register of Population Order, 1947 (Appointed Time) Order [Vol. XXXVIII p. 201] S.R.& O. No. 300 of 1947
Registration of Births and Deaths (Ireland) Act, No. 11 of 1863	18	**Dublin Public Assistance District (Registrar's Districts) Order, S.I. No. 214 of 1959**
		Dublin Health Authority Area (Registrars' Districts) Order, S.I. No. 246 of 1960
		Dublin Health Authority Area (Registrars' Districts) (No.2) Order, S.I. No. 276 of 1960
		Cork Health Authority Area (Registrars' Districts) Order, S.I. No. 89 of 1961
		Dublin Health Authority Area (Registrars' Districts) Order, S.I. No. 213 of 1961
		County Wexford (Registrars' Districts) Order, S.I. No. 214 of 1961
		County Wicklow (Registrars' Districts) Order, S.I. No. 215 of 1961
		County Meath (Registrars' Districts) Order, S.I. No. 293 of 1961
		County Meath (Registrars' Districts) Order, S.I. No. 142 of 1962
		County Kildare (Registrars' Districts) No.1 Order, S.I. No. 155 of 1962

Statutory Authority	Section	Statutory Instrument

Registration of Births and Deaths
(Ireland) Act, No. 11 of 1863
(*Cont.*)

County Kildare (Registrars' Districts) (No.2) Order, S.I. No. 160 of 1962

County Laoighis (Registrars' Districts) Order, S.I. No. 232 of 1962

County Galway (Registrars' Districts) Order, S.I. No. 81 of 1963

County Galway (Registrars' Districts) Order, S.I. No. 89 of 1963

Cork Health Authority Area (Registrars' Districts) Order, S.I. No. 227 of 1963

County Kerry (Registrars' Districts) Order, S.I. No. 61 of 1964

County Louth (Registrars' Districts) Order, S.I. No. 243 of 1964

Limerick Health Authority Area (Registrars' Districts) Order, S.I. No. 286 of 1964

County Donegal (Registrars' Districts) Order, S.I. No. 4 of 1965

Dublin Health Authority Area (Registrars' Districts) Order, S.I. No. 5 of 1965

County Longford (Registrars' Districts) Order, S.I. No. 6 of 1965

Waterford Health Authority Area (Registrars' Districts) Order, S.I. No. 9 of 1965

Wicklow County and Dublin Health Authority Area (Registrars' Districts) Order, S.I. No. 10 of 1965

Dublin Health Authority Area (Registrars' Districts) (No.2) Order, S.I. No. 23 of 1965

County Mayo (Registrars' Districts) Order, S.I. No. 57 of 1965

Waterford Health Authority Area and Kilkenny County (Registrars' Districts) Order, S.I. No. 73 of 1965

Dublin Health Authority Area (Registrars' Districts) (No.3) Order, S.I. No. 77 of 1965

Amalgamation of Registrars' Districts Order, S.I. No. 258 of 1973

County Dublin (Registrars' Districts) Order, S.I. No. 164 of 1974

City and County of Cork (Registrars' Districts) Order, S.I. No. 272 of 1978

Registration of Business Names Act,
No. 30 of 1963 — 1 — *Registration of Business Names Act, 1963 (Commencement) Order, S.I. No. 46 of 1964*

17 — Business Names Regulations, S.I. No. 47 of 1964

Business Names Regulations, S.I. No. 63 of 1976

Business Names Regulations, S.I. No. 399 of 1980

Business Names Regulations, S.I. No. 260 of 1983

Registration of Marriages (Ireland)
Act, No. 90 of 1863 — 8 — Dublin Public Assistance District (Registrar's Districts) Order, S.I. No. 214 of 1959

Dublin Health Authority Area (Registrars' Districts) Order, S.I. No. 246 of 1960

Statutory Authority	Section	Statutory Instrument

Registration of Marriages (Ireland)
Act, No. 90 of 1863 (*Cont.*)

Dublin Health Authority Area (Registrars' Districts) (No.2) Order, S.I. No. 276 of 1960

Cork Health Authority Area (Registrars' Districts) Order, S.I. No. 89 of 1961

Dublin Health Authority Area (Registrars' Districts) Order, S.I. No. 213 of 1961

County Wexford (Registrars' Districts) Order, S.I. No. 214 of 1961

County Wicklow (Registrars' Districts) Order, S.I. No. 215 of 1961

County Meath (Registrars' Districts) Order, S.I. No. 293 of 1961

County Meath (Registrars' Districts) Order, S.I. No. 142 of 1962

County Kildare (Registrars' Districts) No.1 Order, S.I. No. 155 of 1962

County Kildare (Registrars' Districts) (No.2) Order, S.I. No. 160 of 1962

County Laoighis (Registrars' Districts) Order, S.I. No. 232 of 1962

County Galway (Registrars' Districts) Order, S.I. No. 81 of 1963

County Galway (Registrars' Districts) Order, S.I. No. 89 of 1963

Cork Health Authority Area (Registrars' Districts) Order, S.I. No. 227 of 1963

County Kerry (Registrars' Districts) Order, S.I. No. 61 of 1964

County Louth (Registrars' Districts) Order, S.I. No. 243 of 1964

Limerick Health Authority Area (Registrars' Districts) Order, S.I. No. 286 of 1964

County Donegal (Registrars' Districts) Order, S.I. No. 4 of 1965

Dublin Health Authority Area (Registrars' Districts) Order, S.I. No. 5 of 1965

County Longford (Registrars' Districts) Order, S.I. No. 6 of 1965

Waterford Health Authority Area (Registrars' Districts) Order, S.I. No. 9 of 1965

Wicklow County and Dublin Health Authority Area (Registrars' Districts) Order, S.I. No. 10 of 1965

Dublin Health Authority Area (Registrars' Districts) (No.2) Order, S.I. No. 23 of 1965

County Mayo (Registrars' Districts) Order, S.I. No. 57 of 1965

Waterford Health Authority Area and Kilkenny County (Registrars' Districts) Order, S.I. No. 73 of 1965

Dublin Health Authority Area (Registrars' Districts) (No.3) Order, S.I. No. 77 of 1965

Amalgamation of Registrars' Districts Order, S.I. No. 258 of 1973

Statutory Authority	Section	Statutory Instrument
Registration of Marriages (Ireland) Act, No. 90 of 1863 (*Cont.*)		**County Dublin (Registrars' Districts) Order, S.I. No. 164 of 1974**
		City and County of Cork (Registrars' Districts) Order, S.I. No. 272 of 1978
Registration of Potato Growers and Potato Packers Act, No. 25 of 1984	5	**Registration of Potato Growers and Potato Packers Regulations, S.I. No. 336 of 1985**
	11(2)	*Registration of Potato Growers and Potato Packers Act, 1984 (Commencement) Order, S.I. No. 335 of 1985*
Registration of Title Act, No. 66 of 1891		**Land Registry Rules [Vol. XIV p. 377] S.R.& O. No. 14 of 1926**
	8(1)	*Land Registration Fee Order [Vol. XV p. 1247] S.R.& O. No. 292 of 1937*
		Land Registration Fee Order [Vol. XXXIII p. 61] S.R.& O. No. 132 of 1944
		Land Registration Fee Order, S.I. No. 128 of 1954
		Land Registration Fees Order, S.I. No. 157 of 1959
		Land Registration Fees Order, S.I. No. 57 of 1966
	94	*Land Registration (Solicitors' Costs) Rules, S.I. No. 180 of 1954*
		Land Registration Rules, S.I. No. 271 of 1956
		Land Registration Rules, S.I. No. 96 of 1959
		Land Registration (Solicitors' Costs) Rules, S.I. No. 148 of 1962
	94(1)	*Land Registration Rules [Vol. XV p. 1123] S.R.& O. No. 264 of 1937*
		Land Registration Rules [Vol. XXXIII p. 75] S.R.& O. No. 89 of 1944
		Land Registration Rules [Vol. XXXVI p. 1081] S.R.& O. No. 4 of 1946
		Land Registration (Solicitors' Costs) Rules [Vol. XXXVI p. 1085] S.R.& O. No. 62 of 1947
		Land Registration Rules, S.I. No. 7 of 1949
		Land Registration Rules, 1949 (Solicitors Costs) S.I. No. 334 of 1949
		Land Registration Rules, S.I. No. 226 of 1951
Registration of Title Act, No. 16 of 1964	2	*Registration of Title Act, 1964 (Commencement) Order, S.I. No. 167 of 1966*
	14(1)	*Land Registration Fees (No.2) Order, S.I. No. 276 of 1966*
		Land Registration Fees Order, S.I. No. 315 of 1974
		Land Registration Fees Order, S.I. No. 40 of 1978
		Land Registration Fees (No.2) Order, S.I. No. 74 of 1978
		Land Registration Fees Order, S.I. No. 255 of 1980
		Land Registration Fees Order, S.I. No. 370 of 1981
		Land Registration Fees Order, S.I. No. 388 of 1983

Statutory Authority	Section	Statutory Instrument
Registration of Title Act, No. 16 of 1964 (*Cont.*)	24	**Compulsory Registration of Ownership (Carlow, Laoighis and Meath) Order, S.I. No. 87 of 1969**
	126	*Land Registration Rules, S.I. No. 266 of 1966*
		Land Registration (Solicitors' Costs) Rules, (1970) S.I. No. 28 of 1971
		Land Registration Rules, S.I. No. 230 of 1972
		Land Registration Rules, S.I. No. 246 of 1975
		Land Registration Rules, S.I. No. 89 of 1977
		Land Registration Rules, S.I. No. 258 of 1981
		Land Registration Rules, S.I. No. 310 of 1986
	126(4)	**Land Registry and Registry of Deeds (Hours of Business) Order, S.I. No. 164 of 1964**
		Land Registry and Registry of Deeds (Hours of Business) (Amendment) Order, S.I. No. 75 of 1967
		Land Registry and Registry of Deeds (Hours of Business) (Amendment) Order, S.I. No. 358 of 1973
Registrations of Maternity Homes Act, No. 14 of 1934	14	**Maternity Homes Regulations [Vol. XIX p. 483] S.R.& O. No. 167 of 1934**
Registry of Deeds (Ireland) Act, No. 87 of 1832	35	**Registry of Deeds (Fees) Order, S.I. No. 287 of 1956**
		Registry of Deeds (Fees) Order, S.I. No. 195 of 1962
		Registry of Deeds (Fees) Order, S.I. No. 238 of 1970
		Registry of Deeds (Fees) Order, S.I. No. 160 of 1974
		Registry of Deeds (Fees) Order, S.I. No. 200 of 1980
		Registry of Deeds (Fees) Order, S.I. No. 363 of 1981
		Registry of Deeds (Fees) Order, S.I. No. 304 of 1982
Regulation of Banks (Remuneration and Conditions of Employment) (Temporary Provisions) Act, No. 12 of 1973	1	*Regulation of Banks (Remuneration and Conditions of Employment) (Temporary Provisions) Act, 1973 (Commencement) Order, S.I. No. 195 of 1973*
		Regulation of Banks (Remuneration and Conditions of Employment) (Temporary Provisions) Act, 1973 (Expiration) Order, S.I. No. 335 of 1973
	3	*Regulation of Banks (Remuneration and Conditions of Employment) (Temporary Prohibition of Increases and Amendments) Order, S.I. No. 196 of 1973*
Regulation of Banks (Remuneration and Conditions of Employment) (Temporary Provisions) Act, No. 27 of 1975	1	*Regulation of Banks (Remuneration and Conditions of Employment) (Temporary Provisions) Act, 1975 (Commencement) Order, S.I. No. 305 of 1975*
		Regulation of Banks (Remuneration and Conditions of Employment) (Temporary Provisions) Act, 1975 (Expiration) Order, S.I. No. 137 of 1976
	3	*Regulation of Banks (Remuneration and Conditions of Employment) (Temporary Prohibition of Increases and Amendments) Order, S.I. No. 306 of 1975*

Statutory Authority	Section	Statutory Instrument
Regulation of Banks (Remuneration and Conditions of Employment) (Temporary Provisions) Act, No. 18 of 1976	1	*Regulation of Banks (Remuneration and Conditions of Employment) (Temporary Provisions) Act, 1976 (Expiration) Order, S.I. No. 237 of 1976*
	1(1)	*Regulation of Banks (Remuneration and Conditions of Employment) (Temporary Provisions) Act, 1976 (Commencement) Order, S.I. No. 138 of 1976*
	3	*Regulation of Banks (Remuneration and Conditions of Employment) (Temporary Prohibition of Increases and Amendments) Order, S.I. No. 139 of 1976*
		Regulation of Banks (Remuneration and Conditions of Employment) (Temporary Prohibition of Increases and Amendments) (No.2) Order, S.I. No. 176 of 1976
		Regulation of Banks (Remuneration and Conditions of Employment) (Temporary Prohibition of Increases and Amendments) (No.2) Order, 1976 (Revocation) Order, S.I. No. 184 of 1976
Rent Restrictions Act, No. 4 of 1946		*Rent Restrictions Act, 1946 (Notice under Section 32 (2)) Regulations [Vol. XXXVIII p. 239] S.R.& O. No. 398 of 1947*
	49	*Rent Restrictions Act, 1946 (Valuation Fee) Regulations [Vol. XXXVIII p. 243] S.R.& O. No. 158 of 1947*
	53	*Rent Restrictions Act, 1946 (Forms) Regulations [Vol. XXXVIII p. 205] S.R.& O. No. 68 of 1946*
Rent Restrictions Act, No. 42 of 1960	48	*Rent Restrictions Act, 1960 (Forms) Regulations, S.I. No. 270 of 1960*
		Rent Restrictions Act, 1930 and 1967 (Forms) Regulations, S.I. No. 115 of 1967
Restriction of Imports Act, No. 20 of 1962	2	*Restriction of Imports (Goods from Southern Rhodesia) Order, S.I. No. 10 of 1966*
		Restriction of Imports (Fertilisers from East Germany) Order, S.I. No. 254 of 1967
		Restriction of Imports (Fertilisers from East Germany) (Amendment) Order, S.I. No. 13 of 1973
		Restriction of Imports (Footwear from Czechoslovakia and Taiwan) Order, S.I. No. 262 of 1976
		Restriction of Imports (Motor Car Tyres from the German Democratic Republic) Order, S.I. No. 376 of 1977
		Restriction of Imports (Goods from Southern Rhodesia) (Revocation) Order, S.I. No. 23 of 1980
		Restriction of Imports (Copper Tubes from Spain) Order, S.I. No. 133 of 1983
		Restriction of Imports (Tableware from Rumania) Order, S.I. No. 163 of 1984

Statutory Authority	Section	Statutory Instrument
Restriction of Imports Act, No. 20 of 1962 (*Cont.*)		**Restriction of Imports (Iron and Steel Products from the German Democratic Republic) Order, S.I. No. 223 of 1986**
		Restriction of Imports (Agricultural Produce from South Africa) Order, S.I. No. 291 of 1986
Restriction of Imports (Fertilisers from East Germany) Order, S.I. No. 254 of 1967	3	**Restriction of Imports (Origin of Fertilisers) Regulations, S.I. No. 269 of 1967**
Restrictive Practices Act, No. 11 of 1972	8	*Restrictive Practices (Groceries) Order, S.I. No. 49 of 1973*
		Restrictive Practices (Groceries) (Amendment) Order, S.I. No. 287 of 1973
		Restrictive Practices (Groceries) (Amendment) Order, S.I. No. 82 of 1978
		Restrictive Practices (Groceries) (Amendment) (No.2) Order, S.I. No. 336 of 1978
		Restrictive Practices (Groceries) Order, S.I. No. 69 of 1981
		Restrictive Practices (Motor Spirits and Motor Vehicle Lubricating Oil) Order, S.I. No. 70 of 1981
	8(2)	*Restrictive Practices (Motor Spirit) Order, S.I. No. 121 of 1975*
		Restrictive Practices (Motor Spirit) Order, S.I. No. 153 of 1978
		Restrictive Practices (Motor Spirit) Order, S.I. No. 202 of 1979
		Restrictive Practices (Motor Spirit) Order, S.I. No. 156 of 1980
		Restrictive Practices (Motor Spirit) (No.2) Order, S.I. No. 376 of 1980
		Restrictive Practices (Groceries) Order, 1981 (Amendment) Order, S.I. No. 329 of 1986
Restrictive Trade Practices Act, No. 14 of 1953	7	*Restrictive Trade Practices (Motor Cars) Order, S.I. No. 86 of 1956*
	9	**Restrictive Trade Practices (Radios) Order, S.I. No. 102 of 1955**
		Restrictive Trade Practices (Building Materials) Order, S.I. No. 187 of 1955
		Restrictive Trade Practices (Groceries) Order, S.I. No. 332 of 1956
		Restrictive Trade Practices (Carpets) Order, S.I. No. 59 of 1960
		Restrictive Trade Practices (Motor Spirit and Motor Vehicle Lubricating Oil) Order, S.I. No. 294 of 1961
		Restrictive Trade Practices (Cookers and Ranges) Order, S.I. No. 117 of 1962
		Restrictive Trade Practices (Hand Knitting Yarns) Order, S.I. No. 197 of 1962

809

Statutory Authority	Section	Statutory Instrument
Restrictive Trade Practices Act, No. 14 of 1953 (*Cont.*)		**Restrictive Trade Practices (Intoxicating Liquor and Non-Alcoholic Beverages) Order, S.I. No. 232 of 1965**
		Restrictive Trade Practices (Jewellery, Watches and Clocks) Order, S.I. No. 80 of 1968
		Restrictive Trade Practices (Electrical Appliances and Equipment) Order, S.I. No. 151 of 1971
		Restrictive Trade Practices (Electrical Appliances and Equipment) (Amendment) Order, S.I. No. 313 of 1971
		Restrictive Trade Practices (Motor Spirit) Order, S.I. No. 150 of 1972
	9(2)	*Restrictive Trade Practices (Groceries) Order, 1956 (Amendment) Order, S.I. No. 163 of 1958*
		Restrictive Trade Practices (Motor Spirit and Motor Vehicle Lubricating Oil) Order, 1961 (Amendment) Order, S.I. No. 62 of 1962
Revenue Act, No. 20 of 1906	3	**Spirits and Wine (Amendment) Regulations, S.I. No. 419 of 1979**
	7	**Wine Duty Regulations, S.I. No. 160 of 1966**
		Spirits and Wine (Amendment) Regulations, S.I. No. 419 of 1979
Revenue Commissioners Order (Executive Council Order No.2), 1923		*Tobacco Growing Regulations [Vol. XII p. 89] S.R.& O. No. 3 of 1933*
		Strength and Weight of Spirits Ascertainment Regulations [Vol. XII p. 85] S.R.& O. No. 205 of 1937
		Entertainments Duty Regulations [Vol. XXIX p. 725] S.R.& O. No. 1 of 1944
		Spirits (Strength Ascertainment) Regulations, S.I. No. 417 of 1979
		Spirits and Wine (Amendment) Regulations, S.I. No. 419 of 1979
Road Traffic Act, No. 11 of 1933	2	*Road Traffic Act, 1933 (Date of Commencement) No.1 Order [Vol. XIX p. 587] S.R.& O. No. 94 of 1933*
		Road Traffic Act, 1933 (Date of Commencement) No.2 Order [Vol. XIX p. 593] S.R.& O. No. 127 of 1933
		Road Traffic Act, 1933 (Date of Commencement) No.3 Order [Vol. XIX p. 597] S.R.& O. No. 132 of 1933
		Road Traffic Act, 1933 (Date of Commencement) No.4 Order [Vol. XIX p. 601] S.R.& O. No. 179 of 1933
		Road Traffic Act, 1933 (Date of Commencement) No.5 Order [Vol. XIX p. 605] S.R.& O. No. 108 of 1934
		Road Traffic Act, 1933 (Date of Commencement) No.6 Order [Vol. XIX p. 611] S.R.& O. No. 49 of 1935
		Road Traffic Act, 1933 (Date of Commencement) No.7 Order [Vol. XIX p. 615] S.R.& O. No. 87 of 1937

Statutory Authority	Section	Statutory Instrument
Road Traffic Act, No. 11 of 1933 (*Cont.*)	3	*Public Service Vehicles (Licences and Vehicle Plates) Order [Vol. XIX p. 857] S.R.& O. No. 88 of 1937*
	4	*Mechanically Propelled Vehicles (Construction, Equipment and Use) Order [Vol. XIX p. 693] S.R.& O. No. 150 of 1934*
	5	*Mechanically Propelled Vehicles (Construction, Equipment and Use) Order [Vol. XIX p. 693] S.R.& O. No. 150 of 1934*
	6	*Small Public Service Vehicles (Amendment) Regulations, S.I. No. 189 of 1956*
	8(1)	**Road Traffic (Bye-laws) Order [Vol. XIX p. 791] S.R.& O. No. 326 of 1934**
	8(3)	**Road Traffic (Bye-laws) Order [Vol. XIX p. 791] S.R.& O. No. 326 of 1934**
	12	*Road Traffic (Third Party Risks) Regulations [Vol. XIX p. 645] S.R.& O. No. 130 of 1933*
		Road Traffic (Third Party Risks) Regulations [Vol. XIX p. 667] S.R.& O. No. 81 of 1934
	15	*Large Public Service Vehicles Regulations [Vol. XIX p. 797] S.R.& O. No. 259 of 1935*
		Small Public Service Vehicles Regulations [Vol. XIX p. 841] S.R.& O. No. 269 of 1936
		Mechanically Propelled Vehicles (Construction, Equipment and Use) Order [Vol. XIX p. 741] S.R.& O. No. 330 of 1938
		Mechanically Propelled Vehicles (Construction, Equipment and Use) Order [Vol. XXXIII p. 535] S.R.& O. No. 404 of 1939
		Mechanically Propelled Vehicles (Construction, Equipment and Use) Order [Vol. XXXIII p. 539] S.R.& O. No. 392 of 1940
		Mechanically Propelled Vehicles (Construction, Equipment and Use) Order [Vol. XXXIII p. 543] S.R.& O. No. 581 of 1941
		Large Public Service Vehicles (Amendment) Regulations [Vol. XXXIII p. 413] S.R.& O. No. 206 of 1944
		Large Public Service Vehicles (Special Roads) Order [Vol. XXXVIII p. 355] S.R.& O. No. 122 of 1946
		Mechanically Propelled Vehicles (Construction, Equipment and Use) (Amendment) Order [Vol. XXXVIII p. 359] S.R.& O. No. 218 of 1946
		Mechanically Propelled Vehicles (Construction, Equipment and Use) (Amendment) Order, S.I. No. 240 of 1948
		Small Public Service Vehicles (Amendment) Regulations, S.I. No. 189 of 1956
		Small Public Service Vehicles (Amendment) Regulations, S.I. No. 117 of 1960
	16	*Large Public Service Vehicles Regulations [Vol. XIX p. 797] S.R.& O. No. 259 of 1935*

Statutory Authority	Section	Statutory Instrument
Road Traffic Act, No. 11 of 1933 (*Cont.*)		*Large Public Service Vehicles (Special Roads) Order [Vol. XXXVIII p. 355] S.R.& O. No. 122 of 1946*
	17	*Mechanically Propelled Vehicles (Construction, Equipment and Use) Order [Vol. XIX p. 693] S.R.& O. No. 150 of 1934*
		Mechanically Propelled Vehicles (Construction, Equipment and Use) Order [Vol. XIX p. 741] S.R.& O. No. 330 of 1938
		Mechanically Propelled Vehicles (Construction, Equipment and Use) Order [Vol. XXXIII p. 535] S.R.& O. No. 404 of 1939
		Mechanically Propelled Vehicles (Construction, Equipment and Use) Order [Vol. XXXIII p. 539] S.R.& O. No. 392 of 1940
		Mechanically Propelled Vehicles (Construction, Equipment and Use) Order [Vol. XXXIII p. 543] S.R.& O. No. 581 of 1941
	19	*Road Traffic (Weighbridges) Order [Vol. XIX p. 835] S.R.& O. No. 200 of 1936*
	20	*Large Public Service Vehicles Regulations [Vol. XIX p. 797] S.R.& O. No. 259 of 1935*
		Small Public Service Vehicles Regulations [Vol. XIX p. 841] S.R.& O. No. 269 of 1936
	42	*Road Traffic (Driving Licence) (Non-residents) Regulations [Vol. XIX p. 785] S.R.& O. No. 216 of 1934*
		Mechanically Propelled Vehicles (International Circulation) Order, S.I. No. 269 of 1961
		Mechanically Propelled Vehicles (International Circulation) (Amendment) Order, S.I. No. 12 of 1962
	48	*Bray Special Speed Limit Regulations, S.I. No. 69 of 1950*
	53	**Road Traffic (Exemption from Speed Limits) Regulations [Vol. XIX p. 769] S.R.& O. No. 154 of 1934**
	61(4)	**Road Traffic Act (Deposits by Vehicle Guarantors and Exempted Persons) Order [Vol. XIX p. 677] S.R.& O. No. 178 of 1933**
	67	**Road Vehicles (Registration and Licensing) Regulations, S.I. No. 13 of 1958**
		Mechanically Propelled Vehicles (International Circulation) Order, S.I. No. 269 of 1961
	80	*Road Traffic (Third Party Risks) (Visiting Motorists) Regulations, S.I. No. 383 of 1952*
		Road Traffic (Third Party Risks) (Visiting Motorists) Regulations, S.I. No. 82 of 1958
		Mechanically Propelled Vehicles (International Circulation) Order, S.I. No. 269 of 1961
	81	*Road Traffic Act (Parts VI and VII) (Fees) Regulations [Vol. XIX p. 869] S.R.& O. No. 92 of 1937*

Statutory Authority	Section	Statutory Instrument
Road Traffic Act, No. 11 of 1933 (Cont.)	82	Road Traffic Act (Parts VI and VII) (Fees) Regulations [Vol. XIX p. 869] S.R.& O. No. 92 of 1937
	84	Public Service Vehicles (Licences and Vehicle Plates) Order [Vol. XIX p. 857] S.R.& O. No. 88 of 1937
	88	Road Traffic Act (Parts VI and VII) (Fees) Regulations [Vol. XIX p. 869] S.R.& O. No. 92 of 1937
	95	Public Service Vehicles (Licences and Vehicle Plates) Order [Vol. XIX p. 857] S.R.& O. No. 88 of 1937
		Road Traffic Act (Parts VI and VII) (Fees) Regulations [Vol. XIX p. 869] S.R.& O. No. 92 of 1937
	96	Public Service Vehicles (Licences and Vehicle Plates) Order [Vol. XIX p. 857] S.R.& O. No. 88 of 1937
	109	Road Traffic Act (Parts VI and VII) (Fees) Regulations [Vol. XIX p. 869] S.R.& O. No. 92 of 1937
	113	Road Traffic Act (Parts VI and VII) (Fees) Regulations [Vol. XIX p. 869] S.R.& O. No. 92 of 1937
	118(1)	**Dublin Large Public Service Vehicles Bye-laws [Vol. XXXIII p. 215] S.R.& O. No. 10 of 1939**
		Cork Large Public Service Vehicles Bye-laws [Vol. XXXIIII p. 103] S.R.& O. No. 108 of 1939
		Limerick Large Public Service Vehicles Bye-laws [Vol. XXXIII p. 449] S.R.& O. No. 166 of 1939
		Waterford Large Public Service Vehicles Bye-laws [Vol. XXXIII p. 547] S.R.& O. No. 320 of 1941
		Kilkenny Large Public Service Vehicles Bye-laws [Vol. XXXIII p. 349] S.R.& O. No. 323 of 1941
	121	Large Public Service Vehicles Regulations [Vol. XIX p. 797] S.R.& O. No. 259 of 1935
	121(2)	Large Public Service Vehicles (Amendment) Regulations [Vol. XXXIII p. 407] S.R.& O. No. 98 of 1942
		Large Public Service Vehicles (Amendment) Regulations [Vol. XXXIII p. 417] S.R.& O. No. 351 of 1945
		Large Public Service Vehicles (Amendment) Regulations, S.I. No. 5 of 1957
	123	Large Public Service Vehicles (Conduct) Regulations [Vol. XIX p. 879] S.R.& O. No. 187 of 1937
		Large Public Service Vehicles (Conduct) Regulations [Vol. XXXIII p. 423] S.R.& O. No. 66 of 1942
	127	Dublin Street Service Vehicles (Lost Property) Bye-laws, S.I. No. 259 of 1948

Statutory Authority	Section	Statutory Instrument
Road Traffic Act, No. 11 of 1933 (*Cont.*)		*Dublin Street Service Vehicles (Lost Property) Bye-laws, S.I. No. 169 of 1959*
	132	*Dublin Metropolitan Taximeter Area Order [Vol. XIX p. 875] S.R.& O. No. 162 of 1937*
		City of Cork Taximeter Area Order [Vol. XXXVIII p. 99] S.R.& O. No. 89 of 1939
	134	*Small Public Service Vehicles Regulations [Vol. XIX p. 841] S.R.& O. No. 269 of 1936*
	136(3)(b)	**Special Inspector (Taximeter) (Grant of Certificate) Regulations, (1937) [Vol. XIX p. 1067] S.R.& O. No. 285 of 1938**
	136(3)(g)	*Taximeter (Fees on Verification and Stamping by Special Inspectors) Regulations [Vol. XIX p. 1063] S.R.& O. No. 284 of 1938*
	136(5)	**Weights and Measures (Taximeter: Section 136 of the Road Traffic Act, 1933) Regulations [Vol. XIX p. 1073] S.R.& O. No. 286 of 1938**
	137(1)	*Dublin Appointed Standings (Street Service Vehicles) Bye-laws [Vol. XIX p. 1031] S.R.& O. No. 105 of 1938*
		Limerick Appointed Standings (Street Service Vehicles) Bye-laws [Vol. XXXIII p. 427] S.R.& O. No. 165 of 1939
		Ennis Appointed Standings (Street Service Vehicles) Bye-laws [Vol. XXXIII p. 307] S.R.& O. No. 144 of 1940
		Cork Appointed Standings (Street Service Vehicles) Bye Laws [Vol. XXXVIII p. 287] S.R.& O. No. 140 of 1947
		Tralee Appointed Standings (Street Service Vehicles) Bye-laws [Vol. XXXVIII p. 365] S.R.& O. No. 235 of 1947
		Drogheda Appointed Standings (Street Service Vehicles) Bye-laws, S.I. No. 19 of 1951
		Dublin Appointed Standings (Street Service Vehicles) Bye-laws, 1938 (Amendment) Bye-laws, S.I. No. 185 of 1954
	139	*Cork Taximeter Area Fare Bye-laws [Vol. XXXIII p. 139] S.R.& O. No. 107 of 1939*
		Dublin Taximeter Area Fare Bye-laws [Vol. XXXVIII p. 319] S.R.& O. No. 228 of 1946
		Cork Taximeter Area Fare Bye-laws [Vol. XXXVIII p. 307] S.R.& O. No. 229 of 1946
		Dublin Taximeter Area Fare Bye-laws [Vol. XXXVIII p. 325] S.R.& O. No. 436 of 1947
		Cork Taximeter Area Fare Bye-laws [Vol. XXXVIII p. 313] S.R.& O. No. 437 of 1947
		Dublin Taximeter Area Fare Bye-laws, S.I. No. 316 of 1952
		Dublin Taximeter Area Fare Bye-laws, S.I. No. 132 of 1955

Statutory Authority	Section	Statutory Instrument
Road Traffic Act, No. 11 of 1933 (*Cont.*)		*Cork Taximeter Area Fare Bye-laws, S.I. No. 133 of 1955*
		Dublin Taximeter Area Fare Bye-laws, S.I. No. 258 of 1957
		Cork Taximeter Area Fare Bye-laws, S.I. No. 259 of 1957
	139(1)	*Dublin Taximeter Area Fare Bye-laws [Vol. XIX p. 897] S.R.& O. No. 192 of 1937*
	140	*Cork Taximeter Area Fare Bye-laws [Vol. XXXIII p. 139] S.R.& O. No. 107 of 1939*
		Dublin Taximeter Area Fare Bye-laws [Vol. XXXVIII p. 319] S.R.& O. No. 228 of 1946
		Cork Taximeter Area Fare Bye-laws [Vol. XXXVIII p. 307] S.R.& O. No. 229 of 1946
		Dublin Taximeter Area Fare Bye-laws [Vol. XXXVIII p. 325] S.R.& O. No. 436 of 1947
		Cork Taximeter Area Fare Bye-laws [Vol. XXXVIII p. 313] S.R.& O. No. 437 of 1947
		Dublin Taximeter Area Fare Bye-laws, S.I. No. 316 of 1952
		Dublin Taximeter Area Fare Bye-laws, S.I. No. 132 of 1955
		Cork Taximeter Area Fare Bye-laws, S.I. No. 133 of 1955
		Dublin Taximeter Area Fare Bye-laws, S.I. No. 258 of 1957
		Cork Taximeter Area Fare Bye-laws, S.I. No. 259 of 1957
	147(1)	*General Bye-laws for the Control of Traffic [Vol. XIX p. 905] S.R.& O. No. 222 of 1937*
		General Bye-laws for the Control of Traffic, 1937 (Amendment) Bye-laws, S.I. No. 316 of 1956
		General Bye-laws for the Control of Traffic, 1937 (Amendment) Bye-laws, S.I. No. 58 of 1959
	149(1)	*Dublin Traffic Bye-laws [Vol. XIX p. 949] S.R.& O. No. 241 of 1937*
		Cork Traffic Bye-laws [Vol. XXXIII p. 151] S.R.& O. No. 134 of 1939
		Limerick Traffic Bye-laws [Vol. XXXIII p. 467] S.R.& O. No. 167 of 1939
		Dublin Traffic (Amendment) Bye-laws [Vol. XXXIII p. 255] S.R.& O. No. 127 of 1941
		Waterford Traffic Bye-laws [Vol. XXXIII p. 569] S.R.& O. No. 318 of 1941
		Kilkenny Traffic Bye-laws [Vol. XXXIII p. 363] S.R.& O. No. 321 of 1941
		Bray Traffic Bye-laws [Vol. XXXVIII p. 247] S.R.& O. No. 148 of 1947
		Clonmel Traffic Bye-laws, S.I. No. 159 of 1948
		Cork Traffic (Amendment) Bye-laws, S.I. No. 173 of 1949

Statutory Authority	Section	Statutory Instrument
Road Traffic Act, No. 11 of 1933 (*Cont.*)		*Dublin Traffic (Amendment) Bye-laws, S.I. No. 201 of 1953*
		Cork Traffic (Amendment) Bye-laws, S.I. No. 317 of 1956
		Cork Traffic (Amendment) Bye-laws, S.I. No. 28 of 1958
	150	*Dublin Traffic (Parking and Waiting) Bye-laws, S.I. No. 70 of 1949*
		Monaghan Traffic (Parking and Waiting) Bye-laws, S.I. No. 71 of 1949
		Galway Traffic (Parking and Waiting) Bye-laws, 1946 (Amendment) Bye-laws, S.I. No. 78 of 1952
		Athy Traffic (Parking and Waiting) Bye-laws, S.I. No. 266 of 1955
	150(1)	*Dublin Traffic (Parking and Waiting) Bye-laws [Vol. XIX p. 987] S.R.& O. No. 242 of 1937*
		Cork Traffic (Parking and Waiting) Bye-laws [Vol. XXXIII p. 175] S.R.& O. No. 112 of 1939
		Limerick Traffic (Parking and Waiting) Bye-laws [Vol. XXXIII p. 487] S.R.& O. No. 168 of 1939
		Ennis Traffic (Parking and Waiting) Bye-laws [Vol. XXXIII p. 323] S.R.& O. No. 145 of 1940
		Dublin Traffic (Parking and Waiting) (Amendment) Bye-laws [Vol. XXXIII p. 263] S.R.& O. No. 128 of 1941
		Waterford Traffic (Parking and Waiting) Bye-laws [Vol. XXXIII p. 591] S.R.& O. No. 319 of 1941
		Kilkenny Traffic (Parking and Waiting) Bye-laws [Vol. XXXIII p. 385] S.R.& O. No. 322 of 1941
		Galway Traffic (Parking and Waiting) Bye-laws [Vol. XXXVIII p. 256] S.R.& O. No. 256 of 1946
		Bray Traffic (Parking and Waiting) Bye-laws [Vol. XXXVIII p. 259] S.R.& O. No. 149 of 1947
		Tralee Traffic (Parking) Bye-laws [Vol. XXXVIII p. 379] S.R.& O. No. 234 of 1947
		Sligo Traffic (Parking and Waiting) Bye-laws, S.I. No. 437 of 1948
		Drogheda Traffic (Parking and Waiting) Bye-laws, S.I. No. 438 of 1948
		Athlone Traffic (Parking and Waiting) Bye-laws, S.I. No. 439 of 1948
		Cork Traffic (Parking and Waiting) (Amendment) Bye-laws, S.I. No. 174 of 1949
		Dublin Traffic (Parking and Waiting) (Amendment) Bye-laws, S.I. No. 98 of 1950
		Mallow Traffic (Parking and Waiting) Bye-laws, S.I. No. 168 of 1950
		Portarlington (Parking and Waiting) Bye-laws, S.I. No. 169 of 1950
		Athlone Traffic (Parking and Waiting) (Amendment) Bye-laws, S.I. No. 181 of 1950

Statutory Authority	Section	Statutory Instrument
Road Traffic Act, No. 11 of 1933 (*Cont.*)		*Dundalk Traffic (Parking and Waiting) Bye-laws, S.I. No. 218 of 1950*
		Carlow Traffic (Parking and Waiting) Bye-laws, S.I. No. 228 of 1950
		Cork Traffic (Parking and Waiting) (Amendment) Bye-laws, S.I. No. 331 of 1951
		Sligo Traffic (Parking and Waiting) Bye-laws, 1948 (Amendment) Bye-laws, S.I. No. 361 of 1951
		Dublin Traffic (Parking and Waiting) (Amendment) Bye-laws, S.I. No. 202 of 1953
		Athlone Traffic (Parking and Waiting) Bye-laws, S.I. No. 301 of 1954
		Wexford Traffic (Parking and Waiting) Bye-laws, S.I. No. 243 of 1955
		Sligo Traffic (Parking and Waiting) Bye-laws, 1948 (Amendment) Bye-laws, S.I. No. 54 of 1956
		Cork Traffic (Parking and Waiting) (Amendment) Bye-laws, S.I. No. 318 of 1956
	158	**Road Traffic (Bridge Notice) Order [Vol. XIX p. 631] S.R.& O. No. 108 of 1933**
	163	*Lighting of Vehicles Regulations [Vol. XIX p. 773] S.R.& O. No. 166 of 1934*
	163(1)(e)	*Lighting of Vehicles (Amendment) Regulations, S.I. No. 334 of 1956*
	169(5)(b)	**Road Traffic Act (Advisory Body Regulations) Order [Vol. XIX p. 637] S.R.& O. No. 129 of 1933**
	169(7)	**Road Traffic Act (Variation of Excessive Periods of Driving) (No. l) Order [Vol. XIX p. 685] S.R.& O. No. 128 of 1934**
		Road Traffic Act (Variation of Excessive Periods of Driving) Order [Vol. XIX p. 829] S.R.& O. No. 72 of 1936
	179	*Road Traffic (Petroleum Spirit) Regulations [Vol. XIX p. 621] S.R.& O. No. 93 of 1933*
	Part III	*Road Traffic (Driving Licence) Regulations [Vol. XIX p. 747] S.R.& O. No. 151 of 1934*
Road Traffic Act, No. 24 of 1961	2	*Road Traffic Act, 1961 (Commencement) Order, S.I. No. 173 of 1961*
		Road Traffic Act, 1961 (Commencement) Order, S.I. No. 11 of 1962
		Road Traffic Act, 1961 (Commencement) Order, S.I. No. 17 of 1963
		Road Traffic Act, 1961 (Commencement) (No.2) Order, S.I. No. 188 of 1963
		Road Traffic Act, 1961 (Commencement) Order, S.I. No. 28 of 1964
	5	**Road Traffic (Bye-laws and Temporary Rules) Regulations, S.I. No. 219 of 1961**
		Road Traffic (Compulsory Insurance) Regulations, S.I. No. 14 of 1962

Statutory Authority	Section	Statutory Instrument
Road Traffic Act, No. 24 of 1961 (*Cont.*)		**Road Traffic (Bye-laws and Temporary Rules) (Amendment) Regulations, S.I. No. 60 of 1962**
		Road Traffic Act, 1961 (Section 103) (Offences) Regulations, S.I. No. 91 of 1962
		Road Traffic (Passenger Accommodation of Mechanically Propelled Vehicles) Regulations, S.I. No. 143 of 1962
		Road Traffic (Signs) Regulations, S.I. No. 171 of 1962
		Road Traffic (Speed Limits) Regulations, S.I. No. 18 of 1963
		Road Traffic (Lighting of Vehicles) Regulations, S.I. No. 189 of 1963
		Road Traffic (Construction, Equipment and Use of Vehicles) Regulations, S.I. No. 190 of 1963
		Road Traffic (Public Service Vehicles) Regulations, S.I. No. 191 of 1963
		Road Traffic (Weighbridges) Regulations, S.I. No. 192 of 1963
		Road Traffic (Licensing of Drivers) Regulations, S.I. No. 29 of 1964
		Road Traffic (Signs) (Amendment) Regulations, S.I. No. 56 of 1964
		Road Traffic (Compulsory Insurance) (Amendment) Regulations, S.I. No. 58 of 1964
		Mechanically Propelled Vehicles (International Circulation) (Amendment) Order, S.I. No. 59 of 1964
		Road Traffic (Public Service Vehicles) (Amendment) Regulations, S.I. No. 106 of 1964
		Road Traffic (Petroleum) Regulations, S.I. No. 174 of 1964
		Road Traffic Act, 1961 (Section 103) (Offences) (Amendment) Regulations, S.I. No. 191 of 1964
		Road Traffic (Construction, Equipment and Use of Vehicles) (Amendment) Regulations, S.I. No. 79 of 1965
		Road Traffic (Speed Limits) (Amendment) Regulations, S.I. No. 86 of 1965
		Road Traffic (Speed Limits) (Amendment) (No.2) Regulations, S.I. No. 116 of 1965
		Road Traffic (Speed Limits) (Amendment) (No.3) Regulations, S.I. No. 142 of 1965
		Road Traffic (Licensing of Drivers) (Amendment) Regulations, S.I. No. 47 of 1966
		Road Traffic (Speed Limits) (County Borough of Limerick and County of Limerick) Regulations, S.I. No. 80 of 1966
		Mechanically Propelled Vehicles (International Circulation) (Amendment) Order, S.I. No. 99 of 1966
		Road Traffic (Speed Limits) (County of Carlow) Regulations, S.I. No. 127 of 1966

Statutory Authority	Section	Statutory Instrument
Road Traffic Act, No. 24 of 1961 (*Cont.*)		*Road Traffic (Speed Limits) (County of Offaly) Regulations, S.I. No. 132 of 1968*
		Road Traffic (Speed Limits) (County of Wexford) Regulations, S.I. No. 153 of 1968
		Road Traffic (Speed Limits) (County of Tipperary North Riding) Regulations, S.I. No. 173 of 1968
		Road Traffic (Speed Limits) (County of Cavan) Regulations, S.I. No. 196 of 1968
		Road Traffic (Speed Limits) (County of Clare) Regulations, S.I. No. 199 of 1968
		Road Traffic (Speed Limits) (County of Wicklow) Regulations, S.I. No. 212 of 1968
		Road Traffic (Speed Limits) (County of Tipperary South Riding) Regulations, S.I. No. 214 of 1968
		Road Traffic (Public Service Vehicles) (Amendment) Regulations, S.I. No. 273 of 1968
		Road Traffic (Speed Limits) (County Borough of Cork and County of Cork) Regulations, S.I. No. 282 of 1968
		Road Traffic (Speed Limits) (County of Kildare) Regulations, S.I. No. 27 of 1969
		Road Traffic (Speed Limits) (County Borough of Limerick and County of Limerick) (Amendment) Regulations, S.I. No. 28 of 1969
		Road Traffic (Speed Limits) (County of Mayo) Regulations, S.I. No. 36 of 1969
		Road Traffic (General Speed Limit) Regulations, S.I. No. 45 of 1969
		Road Traffic (Speed Limits) (County of Sligo) (Amendment) Regulations, S.I. No. 52 of 1969
		Road Traffic (Construction, Equipment and Use of Vehicles) (Amendment) Regulations, S.I. No. 94 of 1969
		Road Traffic (Construction, Equipment and Use of Vehicles) (Amendment) (No.2) Regulations, S.I. No. 138 of 1969
		Road Traffic (Licensing of Drivers) (Amendment) Regulations, S.I. No. 140 of 1969
		Road Traffic (Parking Fees) Regulations, S.I. No. 169 of 1969
		Road Traffic Act, 1968 (Part V) Regulations, S.I. No. 196 of 1969
		Road Traffic (Signs) (Amendment) Regulations, S.I. No. 217 of 1969
		Road Traffic Act, 1961 (Section 103) (Offences) (Amendment) Regulations, S.I. No. 4 of 1970
		Road Traffic (Speed Limits) (County Borough of Dublin and County of Dublin) Regulations, S.I. No. 100 of 1970
		Road Traffic (Speed Limits) (County Galway) (Amendment) Regulations, S.I. No. 126 of 1970
		Road Traffic (Lighting of Vehicles) (Amendment) Regulations, S.I. No. 128 of 1970

Statutory Authority	Section	Statutory Instrument

Road Traffic Act, No. 24 of 1961
(*Cont.*)

Road Traffic (Public Service Vehicles) (Amendment) Regulations, S.I. No. 138 of 1970

Road Traffic (Speed Limits) (County of Carlow) Regulations, S.I. No. 142 of 1970

Road Traffic (Signs) (Amendment) Regulations, S.I. No. 164 of 1970

Road Traffic (Speed Limits) (County of Monaghan) Regulations, S.I. No. 174 of 1970

Road Traffic (Public Service Vehicles) (Amendment) (No.2) Regulations, S.I. No. 200 of 1970

Road Traffic (Construction, Equipment and Use of Vehicles) (Amendment) Regulations, S.I. No. 211 of 1970

Road Traffic (Public Service Vehicles) (Amendment) (No.3) Regulations, S.I. No. 252 of 1970

Road Traffic (Speed Limits) (County of Meath) Regulations, S.I. No. 259 of 1970

Road Traffic (Speed Limits) (County Borough of Waterford and County of Waterford) Regulations, S.I. No. 275 of 1970

Road Traffic (Removal, Storage and Disposal of Vehicles) Regulations, S.I. No. 5 of 1971

Road Traffic Act, 1961 (Section 103) (Offences) (Amendment) Regulations, S.I. No. 12 of 1971

Road Traffic (Speed Limits) (County of Cavan) (Amendment) Regulations, S.I. No. 14 of 1971

Road Traffic (Speed Limits) (County of Leitrim) (Amendment) Regulations, S.I. No. 15 of 1971

Road Traffic (Speed Limits) (County of Longford) (Amendment) Regulations, S.I. No. 56 of 1971

Road Traffic (Construction, Equipment and Use of Vehicles) (Amendment) Regulations, S.I. No. 96 of 1971

Road Traffic (Signs) (Amendment) Regulations, S.I. No. 127 of 1971

Road Traffic (Speed Limits) (County of Roscommon) (Amendment) Regulations, S.I. No. 136 of 1971

Road Traffic (Speed Limits) (County of Westmeath) (Amendment) Regulations, S.I. No. 150 of 1971

Road Traffic (Signs) (Amendment) (No.2) Regulations, (1970) S.I. No. 188 of 1971

Road Traffic (Speed Limits) (County of Kerry) (Amendment) Regulations, S.I. No. 242 of 1971

Road Traffic (Signs) (Amendment) (No.3) Regulations, S.I. No. 256 of 1971

Road Traffic (Speed Limits) (County of Donegal) (Amendment) Regulations, S.I. No. 263 of 1971

Road Traffic (Speed Limits) (County of Clare) (Amendment) Regulations, S.I. No. 279 of 1971

Road Traffic (Speed Limits) (County of Offaly) (Amendment) Regulations, S.I. No. 27 of 1972

Statutory Authority	Section	Statutory Instrument

Road Traffic Act, No. 24 of 1961
(*Cont.*)

Road Traffic (Speed Limits) (County of Laoighis) (Amendment) Regulations, S.I. No. 28 of 1972

Road Traffic (Speed Limits) (County of Galway) (Amendment) Regulations, S.I. No. 225 of 1972

Road Traffic (Speed Limits) (County Borough of Limerick and County of Limerick) Regulations, S.I. No. 273 of 1972

Road Traffic (Licensing of Drivers) (Amendment) Regulations, S.I. No. 120 of 1973

Road Traffic Act, 1968 (Part V) (Amendment) Regulations, S.I. No. 138 of 1973

Road Traffic Act, 1968 (Part V) (Amendment) (No.2) Regulations, S.I. No. 221 of 1973

Road Traffic (Public Service Vehicles) (Amendment) Regulations, S.I. No. 225 of 1973

Road Traffic (Speed Limits) (County Borough of Cork and County of Cork) (Amendment) Regulations, S.I. No. 263 of 1973

Road Traffic (Speed Limits) (County of Mayo) (Amendment) Regulations, S.I. No. 300 of 1973

Road Traffic (General Speed Limit) Regulations, S.I. No. 348 of 1973

Road Traffic (Speed Limits) (County Borough of Dublin and County of Dublin) (Amendment) Regulations, S.I. No. 350 of 1973

Road Traffic (Speed Limits) (County of Kildare) (Amendment) Regulations, S.I. No. 351 of 1973

Road Traffic (Speed Limits) (County of Tipperary North Riding) (Amendment) Regulations, S.I. No. 115 of 1974

Road Traffic (General Speed Limit) Regulations, S.I. No. 134 of 1974

Road Traffic (Speed Limits) (County of Kilkenny) (Amendment) Regulations, S.I. No. 148 of 1974

Road Traffic (Speed Limits) (County of Meath) (Amendment) Regulations, S.I. No. 230 of 1974

Road Traffic Act, 1961 (Section 103) (Offences) (Amendment) Regulations, S.I. No. 246 of 1974

Road Traffic (Signs) (Amendment) Regulations, S.I. No. 247 of 1974

Road Traffic (Speed Limits) (County of Wicklow) (Amendment) Regulations, S.I. No. 263 of 1974

Road Traffic (Licensing of Drivers) (Amendment) Regulations, S.I. No. 295 of 1974

Road Traffic (Public Service Vehicles) (Amendment) Regulations, S.I. No. 296 of 1974

Road Traffic (Construction, Equipment and Use of Vehicles) (Amendment) Regulations, S.I. No. 297 of 1974

Road Traffic (Speed Limits) (County Borough of Cork and County of Cork) Regulations, S.I. No. 310 of 1974

Road Traffic Act, 1968 (Part V) (Amendment) Regulations, S.I. No. 336 of 1974

Road Traffic Act, No. 24 of 1961
(*Cont.*)

Road Traffic (Speed Limits) (County Borough of Dublin and County of Dublin) (Amendment) Regulations, S.I. No. 342 of 1974

Road Traffic (General Speed Limit) (No.2) Regulations, S.I. No. 352 of 1974

Road Traffic (Public Service Vehicles) (Amendment) Regulations, S.I. No. 35 of 1975

Road Traffic (General Speed Limit) Regulations, S.I. No. 55 of 1975

Road Traffic (Public Service Vehicles) (Amendment) (No.2) Regulations, S.I. No. 101 of 1975

Road Traffic (Public Service Vehicles) (Amendment) (No.3) Regulations, S.I. No. 113 of 1975

Road Traffic Act, 1961 (Section 103) (Offences) (Amendment) Regulations, S.I. No. 158 of 1975

Road Traffic (Licensing of Drivers) (Amendment) Regulations, S.I. No. 277 of 1975

Road Traffic (Signs) (Amendment) Regulations, S.I. No. 280 of 1975

Road Traffic General Bye-laws (Amendment) Regulations, S.I. No. 281 of 1975

Road Traffic (Public Service Vehicles) (Amendment) Regulations, S.I. No. 24 of 1976

Road Traffic (Speed Limits) (County Borough of Dublin and County of Dublin) (Amendment) Regulations, S.I. No. 151 of 1976

Road Traffic (Public Service Vehicles) (Amendment) (No.2) Regulations, S.I. No. 160 of 1976

Road Traffic (Speed Limits) (County of Tipperary South Riding) Regulations, S.I. No. 172 of 1976

Road Traffic Act, 1961 (Section 103) (Offences) Regulations, S.I. No. 188 of 1976

Road Traffic Act, 1968 (Part V) (Amendment) Regulations, S.I. No. 240 of 1976

Road Traffic (Speed Limits) (County of Roscommon) Regulations, S.I. No. 285 of 1976

Road Traffic (Speed Limits) (County of Meath) Regulations, S.I. No. 300 of 1976

Road Traffic (Speed Limits) (County of Tipperary North Riding) Regulations, S.I. No. 312 of 1976

Road Traffic (Signs) (Amendment) Regulations, S.I. No. 66 of 1977

Road Traffic (Removal, Storage and Disposal of Vehicles) (Amendment) Regulations, S.I. No. 95 of 1977

Road Traffic (Speed Limits) (County of Kildare) Regulations, S.I. No. 105 of 1977

Road Traffic (Speed Limits) (County of Monaghan) Regulations, S.I. No. 110 of 1977

Road Traffic (Public Service Vehicles) (Amendment) Regulations, S.I. No. 111 of 1977

Statutory Authority	Section	Statutory Instrument

Road Traffic Act, No. 24 of 1961
(*Cont.*)

Road Traffic (Speed Limits) (County of Kerry) Regulations, S.I. No. 145 of 1977

Road Traffic (Speed Limits) (County Borough of Limerick and County of Limerick) Regulations, S.I. No. 157 of 1977

Road Traffic (Public Service Vehicles) (Amendment) (No.2) Regulations, S.I. No. 177 of 1977

Road Traffic (Speed Limits) (County of Wexford) Regulations, S.I. No. 238 of 1977

Road Traffic (Public Service Vehicles) (Amendment) (No.3) Regulations, S.I. No. 268 of 1977

Road Traffic (Speed Limits) (County of Westmeath) Regulations, S.I. No. 270 of 1977

Road Traffic (Public Service Vehicles) (Amendment) (No.4) Regulations, S.I. No. 284 of 1977

Road Traffic (Speed Limits) (County of Clare) Regulations, S.I. No. 292 of 1977

Road Traffic (Speed Limits) (County Borough of Dublin and County of Dublin) Regulations, S.I. No. 358 of 1977

Road Traffic (Compulsory Insurance) (Amendment) Regulations, S.I. No. 359 of 1977

Road Traffic (Speed Limits) (County Borough of Cork and County of Cork) Regulations, S.I. No. 370 of 1977

Road Traffic (Speed Limits) (County of Laoighis) Regulations, S.I. No. 394 of 1977

Road Traffic (Speed Limits) (County of Kilkenny) Regulations, S.I. No. 399 of 1977

Road Traffic (Public Service Vehicles) (Amendment) Regulations, S.I. No. 15 of 1978

Road Traffic (Speed Limits) (County of Wicklow) Regulations, S.I. No. 31 of 1978

Road Traffic (Speed Limits) (County of Offaly) Regulations, S.I. No. 41 of 1978

Road Traffic (Speed Limits) (County of Carlow) Regulations, S.I. No. 121 of 1978

Road Traffic (Speed Limits) (County of Longford) Regulations, S.I. No. 122 of 1978

Road Traffic (Amendment) Act, 1978 (Part III) Regulations, S.I. No. 193 of 1978

Road Traffic (Public Service Vehicles) (Amendment) (No.2) Regulations, S.I. No. 226 of 1978

Road Traffic (Public Service Vehicles) (Amendment) (No.3) Regulations, S.I. No. 247 of 1978

Road Traffic (Public Service Vehicles) (Amendment) (No.4) Regulations, S.I. No. 259 of 1978

Statutory Authority	Section	Statutory Instrument
Road Traffic Act, No. 24 of 1961 (*Cont.*)		**Road Traffic (Construction, Equipment and Use of Vehicles) (Amendment) Regulations, S.I. No. 291 of 1978**
		Road Traffic (Public Service Vehicles) (Licensing) Regulations, S.I. No. 292 of 1978
		Road Traffic (Speed Limits) (County Borough of Dublin and County of Dublin) (Amendment) Regulations, S.I. No. 328 of 1978
		Road Traffic (Construction, Equipment and Use of Vehicles) (Amendment) (No.2) Regulations, S.I. No. 360 of 1978
		Road Traffic (Speed Limits) (County Borough of Waterford and County of Waterford) Regulations, S.I. No. 50 of 1979
		Road Traffic (Signs) (Amendment) Regulations, S.I. No. 51 of 1979
		Road Traffic Act, 1961 (Section 103) (Offences) (Amendment) Regulations, S.I. No. 167 of 1979
		Road Traffic (General Speed Limit) Regulations, S.I. No. 176 of 1979
		Road Traffic (Speed Limits) (County of Galway) Regulations, S.I. No. 189 of 1979
		Road Traffic (Public Service Vehicles) (Amendment) Regulations, S.I. No. 242 of 1979
		Road Traffic (Speed Limits) (County of Cavan) Regulations, S.I. No. 283 of 1979
		Road Traffic (Speed Limits) (County of Sligo) Regulations, S.I. No. 284 of 1979
		Road Traffic (Lighting of Vehicles) (Amendment) Regulations, S.I. No. 328 of 1979
		Road Traffic (Signs) (Amendment) (No.2) Regulations, S.I. No. 329 of 1979
		Road Traffic (Licensing of Drivers) (Amendment) Regulations, S.I. No. 337 of 1979
		Road Traffic (Licensing of Drivers) (Amendment) (No.2) Regulations, S.I. No. 342 of 1979
		Road Traffic (Speed Limits) (County of Louth) Regulations, S.I. No. 378 of 1979
		Road Traffic (Signs) (Bus Lane) Regulations, S.I. No. 413 of 1979
		Road Traffic (Public Service Vehicles) (Amendment) Regulations, S.I. No. 54 of 1980
		Road Traffic (Speed Limits) (County of Mayo) Regulations, S.I. No. 216 of 1980
		Road Traffic (Licensing of Drivers) (Amendment) Regulations, S.I. No. 225 of 1980
		Road Traffic (Speed Limits) (County of Leitrim) Regulations, S.I. No. 278 of 1980
		Road Traffic (Speed Limits) (County of Cavan) (Amendment) Regulations, S.I. No. 279 of 1980
		Road Traffic (Licensing of Drivers) (Amendment) (No.2) Regulations, S.I. No. 334 of 1980

Road Traffic Act, No. 24 of 1961
(*Cont.*)

Road Traffic (Licensing of Trailers and Semi-trailers) (Amendment) Regulations, S.I. No. 127 of 1983

Road Traffic (Speed Limits) (County Borough of Cork and County of Cork) (Amendment) Regulations, S.I. No. 161 of 1983

Road Traffic (Speed Limits) (County Borough of Dublin and County of Dublin) (Amendment) Regulations, S.I. No. 217 of 1983

Road Traffic (Public Service Vehicles) (Amendment) Regulations, S.I. No. 273 of 1983

Road Traffic General Bye-laws (Amendment) Regulations, S.I. No. 275 of 1983

Road Traffic (Signs) (Amendment) Regulations, S.I. No. 276 of 1983

Road Traffic (Speed Limits) (County of Kildare) Regulations, S.I. No. 277 of 1983

Road Traffic (Construction, Equipment and Use of Vehicles) (Amendment) Regulations, S.I. No. 278 of 1983

Road Traffic (Speed Limits) (County of Kildare) (Amendment) Regulations, S.I. No. 298 of 1983

Road Traffic (Speed Limits) (County of Kerry) Regulations, S.I. No. 334 of 1983

Road Traffic (Amendment) Act, 1978 (Part III) Regulations, S.I. No. 363 of 1983

Road Traffic (Licensing of Drivers) (Amendment) Regulations, S.I. No. 18 of 1984

Road Traffic (Speed Limits) (County Borough of Limerick and County of Limerick) Regulations, S.I. No. 104 of 1984

Road Traffic (Speed Limits) (County of Longford) Regulations, S.I. No. 229 of 1984

Road Traffic (Licensing of Drivers) (Amendment) (No.2) Regulations, S.I. No. 233 of 1984

Road Traffic (Insurance Disc) Regulations, S.I. No. 355 of 1984

Road Traffic (Licensing of Drivers) (Amendment) Regulations, S.I. No. 20 of 1985

Road Traffic (Speed Limits) (County of Cavan) Regulations, S.I. No. 63 of 1985

Road Traffic (Lighting of Vehicles) (Amendment) Regulations, S.I. No. 157 of 1985

Road Traffic (Construction, Equipment and Use of Vehicles) (Amendment) Regulations, S.I. No. 158 of 1985

Road Traffic (Signs) (Amendment) Regulations, S.I. No. 182 of 1985

Road Traffic (Licensing of Drivers) (Amendment) (No.2) Regulations, S.I. No. 254 of 1985

Road Traffic Act, 1961 (Section 103) (Offences) (Amendment) Regulations, S.I. No. 255 of 1985

Road Traffic (Speed Limits) (County of Meath) Regulations, S.I. No. 318 of 1985

Road Traffic Act, No. 24 of 1961
(*Cont.*)

Road Traffic (Lighting of Vehicles) (Amendment) Regulations, S.I. No. 128 of 1970

Road Traffic (Construction, Equipment and Use of Vehicles) (Amendment) Regulations, S.I. No. 211 of 1970

Road Traffic (Construction, Equipment and Use of Vehicles) (Amendment) Regulations, S.I. No. 96 of 1971

Road Traffic (Construction, Equipment and Use of Vehicles) (Amendment) Regulations, S.I. No. 297 of 1974

Road Traffic (Construction, Equipment and Use of Vehicles) (Amendment) Regulations, S.I. No. 291 of 1978

Road Traffic (Construction, Equipment and Use of Vehicles) (Amendment) (No.2) Regulations, S.I. No. 360 of 1978

Road Traffic (Lighting of Vehicles) (Amendment) Regulations, S.I. No. 328 of 1979

Road Traffic (Construction, Equipment and Use of Vehicles) (Amendment) Regulations, S.I. No. 270 of 1981

Road Traffic (Construction, Equipment and Use of Vehicles) (Amendment) Regulations, S.I. No. 119 of 1983

Road Traffic (Construction, Equipment and Use of Vehicles) (Amendment) Regulations, S.I. No. 278 of 1983

Road Traffic (Insurance Disc) Regulations, S.I. No. 355 of 1984

Road Traffic (Lighting of Vehicles) (Amendment) Regulations, S.I. No. 157 of 1985

Road Traffic (Construction, Equipment and Use of Vehicles) (Amendment) Regulations, S.I. No. 158 of 1985

Road Traffic (Insurance Disc) (Amendment) Regulations, S.I. No. 227 of 1986

Road Traffic (Construction, Equipment and Use of Vehicles) (Amendment) Regulations, S.I. No. 442 of 1986

12

Road Traffic (Construction, Equipment and Use of Vehicles) Regulations, S.I. No. 190 of 1963

Road Traffic (Construction, Equipment and Use of Vehicles) (Amendment) Regulations, S.I. No. 119 of 1983

Road Traffic (Construction, Equipment and Use of Vehicles) (Amendment) Regulations, S.I. No. 278 of 1983

Road Traffic (Construction, Equipment and Use of Vehicles) (Amendment) Regulations, S.I. No. 442 of 1986

Statutory Authority	Section	Statutory Instrument
Road Traffic Act, No. 24 of 1961 (*Cont.*)	13	**Road Traffic (Construction, Equipment and Use of Vehicles) Regulations, S.I. No. 190 of 1963**
		Road Traffic (Construction, Equipment and Use of Vehicles) (Amendment) Regulations, S.I. No. 158 of 1985
	15	**Road Traffic (Weighbridges) Regulations, S.I. No. 192 of 1963**
	22	**Road Traffic (Licensing of Drivers) (Amendment) Regulations, S.I. No. 337 of 1979**
		Road Traffic (Licensing of Drivers) (Amendment) (No.2) Regulations, S.I. No. 342 of 1979
	22(3)	**Road Traffic (Licensing of Drivers) Regulations, S.I. No. 29 of 1964**
		Road Traffic (Licensing of Drivers) (Amendment) Regulations, S.I. No. 120 of 1973
		Road Traffic (Licensing of Drivers) (Amendment) Regulations, S.I. No. 198 of 1981
	23(2)	**Road Traffic (Licensing of Drivers) Regulations, S.I. No. 29 of 1964**
	31	**Road Traffic (Licensing of Drivers) Regulations, S.I. No. 29 of 1964**
		Road Traffic (Licensing of Drivers) (Amendment) Regulations, S.I. No. 198 of 1981
	32	**Road Traffic (Licensing of Drivers) (Amendment) (No.2) Regulations, S.I. No. 340 of 1986**
	33 42	**Road Traffic (Licensing of Drivers) (Amendment) (No.2) Regulations, S.I. No. 276 of 1981**
	33	**Road Traffic (Licensing of Drivers) Regulations, S.I. No. 29 of 1964**
		Road Traffic (Licensing of Drivers) (Amendment) Regulations, S.I. No. 47 of 1966
		Road Traffic (Licensing of Drivers) (Amendment) Regulations, S.I. No. 140 of 1969
		Road Traffic (Licensing of Drivers) (Amendment) Regulations, S.I. No. 120 of 1973
		Road Traffic (Licensing of Drivers) (Amendment) Regulations, S.I. No. 295 of 1974
		Road Traffic (Licensing of Drivers) (Amendment) Regulations, S.I. No. 277 of 1975
		Road Traffic (Licensing of Drivers) (Amendment) Regulations, S.I. No. 337 of 1979
		Road Traffic (Licensing of Drivers) (Amendment) (No.2) Regulations, S.I. No. 342 of 1979
		Road Traffic (Licensing of Drivers) (Amendment) (No.2) Regulations, S.I. No. 334 of 1980
		Road Traffic (Licensing of Drivers) (Amendment) Regulations, S.I. No. 198 of 1981
		Road Traffic (Licensing of Drivers) (Amendment) Regulations, S.I. No. 27 of 1982
		Road Traffic (Licensing of Drivers) (Amendment) Regulations, S.I. No. 49 of 1983

Statutory Authority	Section	Statutory Instrument
Road Traffic Act, No. 24 of 1961 (*Cont.*)		Road Traffic (Licensing of Drivers) (Amendment) Regulations, S.I. No. 18 of 1984
		Road Traffic (Licensing of Drivers) (Amendment) (No.2) Regulations, S.I. No. 233 of 1984
		Road Traffic (Licensing of Drivers) (Amendment) Regulations, S.I. No. 20 of 1985
		Road Traffic (Licensing of Drivers) (Amendment) Regulations, S.I. No. 23 of 1986
		Road Traffic (Licensing of Drivers) (Amendment) (No.2) Regulations, S.I. No. 340 of 1986
	34	Road Traffic (Licensing of Drivers) Regulations, S.I. No. 29 of 1964
		Road Traffic (Licensing of Drivers) (Amendment) Regulations, S.I. No. 47 of 1966
		Road Traffic (Licensing of Drivers) (Amendment) Regulations, S.I. No. 120 of 1973
		Road Traffic (Licensing of Drivers) (Amendment) Regulations, S.I. No. 198 of 1981
		Road Traffic (Licensing of Drivers) (Amendment) (No.2) Regulations, S.I. No. 340 of 1986
	35	Road Traffic (Licensing of Drivers) Regulations, S.I. No. 29 of 1964
		Road Traffic (Licensing of Drivers) (Amendment) Regulations, S.I. No. 47 of 1966
		Road Traffic (Licensing of Drivers) (Amendment) Regulations, S.I. No. 140 of 1969
		Road Traffic (Licensing of Drivers) (Amendment) Regulations, S.I. No. 295 of 1974
		Road Traffic (Licensing of Drivers) (Amendment) Regulations, S.I. No. 337 of 1979
		Road Traffic (Licensing of Drivers) (Amendment) (No.2) Regulations, S.I. No. 342 of 1979
		Road Traffic (Licensing of Drivers) (Amendment) Regulations, S.I. No. 198 of 1981
		Road Traffic (Licensing of Drivers) (Amendment) (No.2) Regulations, S.I. No. 254 of 1985
	35(2)	Road Traffic (Licensing of Drivers) (Amendment) Regulations, S.I. No. 120 of 1973
	38(7)	Road Traffic (Licensing of Drivers) Regulations, S.I. No. 29 of 1964
	42	Road Traffic (Licensing of Drivers) Regulations, S.I. No. 29 of 1964
		Mechanically Propelled Vehicles (International Circulation) (Amendment) Order, S.I. No. 59 of 1964
		Road Traffic (Licensing of Drivers) (Amendment) Regulations, S.I. No. 47 of 1966
		Mechanically Propelled Vehicles (International Circulation) (Amendment) Order, S.I. No. 99 of 1966
		Road Traffic (Licensing of Drivers) (Amendment) Regulations, S.I. No. 24 of 1967

Road Traffic Act, No. 24 of 1961
(*Cont.*)

Road Traffic (Speed Limits) (Amendment) (No.3) Regulations, S.I. No. 142 of 1965

Road Traffic (Speed Limits) (County Borough of Limerick and County of Limerick) Regulations, S.I. No. 80 of 1966

Road Traffic (Speed Limits) (County of Carlow) Regulations, S.I. No. 127 of 1966

Road Traffic (Speed Limits) (County of Monaghan) Regulations, S.I. No. 30 of 1967

Road Traffic (Speed Limits) (Amendment) Regulations, S.I. No. 65 of 1967

Road Traffic (Speed Limits) (County Borough of Waterford and County of Waterford) Regulations, S.I. No. 74 of 1967

Road Traffic (Speed Limits) (County Borough of Dublin and County of Dublin) Regulations, S.I. No. 93 of 1967

Road Traffic (Speed Limits) (County of Sligo) Regulations, S.I. No. 172 of 1967

Road Traffic (Speed Limits) (County of Kerry) Regulations, S.I. No. 208 of 1967

Road Traffic (Speed Limits) (County of Meath) Regulations, S.I. No. 222 of 1967

Road Traffic (Speed Limits) (County of Roscommon) Regulations, S.I. No. 306 of 1967

Road Traffic (Speed Limits) (County of Westmeath) Regulations, S.I. No. 307 of 1967

Road Traffic (Speed Limits) (County of Leitrim) Regulations, S.I. No. 9 of 1968

Road Traffic (Speed Limits) (County of Louth) Regulations, S.I. No. 16 of 1968

Road Traffic (Speed Limits) (County of Longford) Regulations, S.I. No. 27 of 1968

Road Traffic (Speed Limits) (County of Laoighis) Regulations, S.I. No. 42 of 1968

Road Traffic (Speed Limits) (County of Donegal) Regulations, S.I. No. 73 of 1968

Road Traffic (Speed Limits) (County of Kilkenny) Regulations, S.I. No. 107 of 1968

Road Traffic (Speed Limits) (County of Galway) Regulations, S.I. No. 110 of 1968

Road Traffic (Speed Limits) (County of Offaly) Regulations, S.I. No. 132 of 1968

Road Traffic (Speed Limits) (County of Wexford) Regulations, S.I. No. 153 of 1968

Road Traffic (Speed Limits) (County of Tipperary North Riding) Regulations, S.I. No. 173 of 1968

Road Traffic (Speed Limits) (County of Cavan) Regulations, S.I. No. 196 of 1968

Road Traffic (Speed Limits) (County of Clare) Regulations, S.I. No. 199 of 1968

Road Traffic (Speed Limits) (County of Wicklow) Regulations, S.I. No. 212 of 1968

Statutory Authority	Section	Statutory Instrument
Road Traffic Act, No. 24 of 1961 (*Cont.*)		*Road Traffic (Speed Limits) (County of Tipperary South Riding) Regulations, S.I. No. 214 of 1968*
		Road Traffic (Speed Limits) (County Borough of Cork and County of Cork) Regulations, S.I. No. 282 of 1968
		Road Traffic (Speed Limits) (County of Kildare) Regulations, S.I. No. 27 of 1969
		Road Traffic (Speed Limits) (County Borough of Limerick and County of Limerick) (Amendment) Regulations, S.I. No. 28 of 1969
		Road Traffic (Speed Limits) (County of Mayo) Regulations, S.I. No. 36 of 1969
		Road Traffic (Speed Limits) (County of Sligo) (Amendment) Regulations, S.I. No. 52 of 1969
		Road Traffic (Speed Limits) (County Borough of Dublin and County of Dublin) Regulations, S.I. No. 100 of 1970
		Road Traffic (Speed Limits) (County Galway) (Amendment) Regulations, S.I. No. 126 of 1970
		Road Traffic (Speed Limits) (County of Carlow) Regulations, S.I. No. 142 of 1970
		Road Traffic (Speed Limits) (County of Monaghan) Regulations, S.I. No. 174 of 1970
		Road Traffic (Speed Limits) (County of Meath) Regulations, S.I. No. 259 of 1970
		Road Traffic (Speed Limits) (County Borough of Waterford and County of Waterford) Regulations, S.I. No. 275 of 1970
		Road Traffic (Speed Limits) (County of Cavan) (Amendment) Regulations, S.I. No. 14 of 1971
		Road Traffic (Speed Limits) (County of Leitrim) (Amendment) Regulations, S.I. No. 15 of 1971
		Road Traffic (Speed Limits) (County of Longford) (Amendment) Regulations, S.I. No. 56 of 1971
		Road Traffic (Speed Limits) (County of Roscommon) (Amendment) Regulations, S.I. No. 136 of 1971
		Road Traffic (Speed Limits) (County of Westmeath) (Amendment) Regulations, S.I. No. 150 of 1971
		Road Traffic (Speed Limits) (County of Kerry) (Amendment) Regulations, S.I. No. 242 of 1971
		Road Traffic (Speed Limits) (County of Donegal) (Amendment) Regulations, S.I. No. 263 of 1971
		Road Traffic (Speed Limits) (County of Clare) (Amendment) Regulations, S.I. No. 279 of 1971
		Road Traffic (Speed Limits) (County of Offaly) (Amendment) Regulations, S.I. No. 27 of 1972
		Road Traffic (Speed Limits) (County of Laoighis) (Amendment) Regulations, S.I. No. 28 of 1972
		Road Traffic (Speed Limits) (County of Galway) (Amendment) Regulations, S.I. No. 225 of 1972
		Road Traffic (Speed Limits) (County Borough of Limerick and County of Limerick) Regulations, S.I. No. 273 of 1972

Statutory Authority	Section	Statutory Instrument

Road Traffic Act, No. 24 of 1961
(*Cont.*)

Road Traffic (Speed Limits) (County Borough of Cork and County of Cork) (Amendment) Regulations, S.I. No. 263 of 1973

Road Traffic (Speed Limits) (County of Mayo) (Amendment) Regulations, S.I. No. 300 of 1973

Road Traffic (Speed Limits) (County of Tipperary North Riding) (Amendment) Regulations, S.I. No. 115 of 1974

Road Traffic (Speed Limits) (County of Kilkenny) (Amendment) Regulations, S.I. No. 148 of 1974

Road Traffic (Speed Limits) (County of Wicklow) (Amendment) Regulations, S.I. No. 263 of 1974

Road Traffic (Speed Limits) (County Borough of Cork and County of Cork) Regulations, S.I. No. 310 of 1974

Road Traffic (Speed Limits) (County Borough of Dublin and County of Dublin) (Amendment) Regulations, S.I. No. 342 of 1974

Road Traffic (Speed Limits) (County Borough of Dublin and County of Dublin) (Amendment) Regulations, S.I. No. 151 of 1976

Road Traffic (Speed Limits) (County of Tipperary South Riding) Regulations, S.I. No. 172 of 1976

Road Traffic (Speed Limits) (County of Roscommon) Regulations, S.I. No. 285 of 1976

Road Traffic (Speed Limits) (County of Meath) Regulations, S.I. No. 300 of 1976

Road Traffic (Speed Limits) (County of Tipperary North Riding) Regulations, S.I. No. 312 of 1976

Road Traffic (Speed Limits) (County of Kildare) Regulations, S.I. No. 105 of 1977

Road Traffic (Speed Limits) (County of Monaghan) Regulations, S.I. No. 110 of 1977

Road Traffic (Speed Limits) (County of Kerry) Regulations, S.I. No. 145 of 1977

Road Traffic (Speed Limits) (County Borough of Limerick and County of Limerick) Regulations, S.I. No. 157 of 1977

Road Traffic (Speed Limits) (County of Wexford) Regulations, S.I. No. 238 of 1977

Road Traffic (Speed Limits) (County of Westmeath) Regulations, S.I. No. 270 of 1977

Road Traffic (Speed Limits) (County of Clare) Regulations, S.I. No. 292 of 1977

Road Traffic (Speed Limits) (County Borough of Dublin and County of Dublin) Regulations, S.I. No. 358 of 1977

Road Traffic (Speed Limits) (County Borough of Cork and County of Cork) Regulations, S.I. No. 370 of 1977

Road Traffic (Speed Limits) (County of Laoighis) Regulations, S.I. No. 394 of 1977

Road Traffic (Speed Limits) (County of Kilkenny) Regulations, S.I. No. 399 of 1977

Road Traffic Act, No. 24 of 1961
(*Cont.*)

Road Traffic (Speed Limits) (County of Wicklow) Regulations, S.I. No. 31 of 1978

Road Traffic (Speed Limits) (County of Offaly) Regulations, S.I. No. 41 of 1978

Road Traffic (Speed Limits) (County of Carlow) Regulations, S.I. No. 121 of 1978

Road Traffic (Speed Limits) (County of Longford) Regulations, S.I. No. 122 of 1978

Road Traffic (Speed Limits) (County Borough of Dublin and County of Dublin) (Amendment) Regulations, S.I. No. 328 of 1978

Road Traffic (Speed Limits) (County Borough of Waterford and County of Waterford) Regulations, S.I. No. 50 of 1979

Road Traffic (Speed Limits) (County of Galway) Regulations, S.I. No. 189 of 1979

Road Traffic (Speed Limits) (County of Cavan) Regulations, S.I. No. 283 of 1979

Road Traffic (Speed Limits) (County of Sligo) Regulations, S.I. No. 284 of 1979

Road Traffic (Speed Limits) (County of Louth) Regulations, S.I. No. 378 of 1979

Road Traffic (Speed Limits) (County of Mayo) Regulations, S.I. No. 216 of 1980

Road Traffic (Speed Limits) (County of Leitrim) Regulations, S.I. No. 278 of 1980

Road Traffic (Speed Limits) (County of Cavan) (Amendment) Regulations, S.I. No. 279 of 1980

Road Traffic (Speed Limits) (County of Roscommon) Regulations, S.I. No. 355 of 1980

Road Traffic (Speed Limits) (County Borough of Dublin and County of Dublin) (Amendment) Regulations, S.I. No. 169 of 1981

Road Traffic (Speed Limits) (County of Monaghan) Regulations, S.I. No. 170 of 1981

Road Traffic (Speed Limits) (County of Tipperary North Riding) Regulations, S.I. No. 176 of 1981

Road Traffic (Speed Limits) (County Borough of Cork and County of Cork) Regulations, S.I. No. 211 of 1981

Road Traffic (Speed Limits) (County of Kilkenny) Regulations, S.I. No. 332 of 1981

Road Traffic (Speed Limits) (County of Westmeath) Regulations, S.I. No. 365 of 1981

Road Traffic (Speed Limits) (County of Carlow) (Amendment) Regulations, S.I. No. 72 of 1982

Road Traffic (Speed Limits) (County Borough of Dublin and County of Dublin) (Amendment) Regulations, S.I. No. 330 of 1982

Road Traffic (Speed Limits) (County of Wexford) Regulations, S.I. No. 45 of 1983

Road Traffic (Speed Limits) (County of Clare) Regulations, S.I. No. 46 of 1983

Statutory Authority	Section	Statutory Instrument

Road Traffic Act, No. 24 of 1961
(*Cont.*)

Road Traffic (Speed Limits) (County of Kerry) (Amendment) Regulations, S.I. No. 77 of 1983

Road Traffic (Speed Limits) (County of Offaly) Regulations, S.I. No. 81 of 1983

Road Traffic (Speed Limits) (County Borough of Cork and County of Cork) (Amendment) Regulations, S.I. No. 161 of 1983

Road Traffic (Speed Limits) (County Borough of Dublin and County of Dublin) (Amendment) Regulations, S.I. No. 217 of 1983

Road Traffic (Speed Limits) (County of Kildare) Regulations, S.I. No. 277 of 1983

Road Traffic (Speed Limits) (County of Kildare) (Amendment) Regulations, S.I. No. 298 of 1983

Road Traffic (Speed Limits) (County of Kerry) Regulations, S.I. No. 334 of 1983

Road Traffic (Speed Limits) (County Borough of Limerick and County of Limerick) Regulations, S.I. No. 104 of 1984

Road Traffic (Speed Limits) (County of Longford) Regulations, S.I. No. 229 of 1984

Road Traffic (Speed Limits) (County of Cavan) Regulations, S.I. No. 63 of 1985

Road Traffic (Speed Limits) (County of Meath) Regulations, S.I. No. 318 of 1985

Road Traffic (Speed Limits) (County of Carlow) Regulations, S.I. No. 398 of 1985

Road Traffic (Speed Limits) (County Borough of Waterford and County of Waterford) Regulations, S.I. No. 8 of 1986

Road Traffic (Speed Limits) (County Borough of Limerick and County of Limerick) (Amendment) Regulations, S.I. No. 38 of 1986

Road Traffic (Speed Limits) (County of Laoighis) Regulations, S.I. No. 72 of 1986

Road Traffic (Speed Limits) (County of Donegal) Regulations, S.I. No. 103 of 1986

Road Traffic (Speed Limits) (County of Tipperary North Riding) Regulations, S.I. No. 206 of 1986

Road Traffic (Speed Limits) (County Borough of Cork and County of Cork) Regulations, S.I. No. 457 of 1986

46 **Road Traffic (Speed Limits) Regulations, S.I. No. 18 of 1963**

Road Traffic (Speed Limits) (Amendment) Regulations, S.I. No. 86 of 1965

Road Traffic (Speed Limits) (Amendment) (No.2) Regulations, S.I. No. 116 of 1965

Road Traffic (Speed Limits) (Amendment) (No.3) Regulations, S.I. No. 142 of 1965

Road Traffic (Speed Limits) (County Borough of Limerick and County of Limerick) Regulations, S.I. No. 80 of 1966

Road Traffic Act, No. 24 of 1961
(*Cont.*)

Road Traffic (Speed Limits) (County of Carlow) Regulations, S.I. No. 127 of 1966

Road Traffic (Speed Limits) (County of Monaghan) Regulations, S.I. No. 30 of 1967

Road Traffic (Speed Limits) (Amendment) Regulations, S.I. No. 65 of 1967

Road Traffic (Speed Limits) (County Borough of Waterford and County of Waterford) Regulations, S.I. No. 74 of 1967

Road Traffic (Speed Limits) (County Borough of Dublin and County of Dublin) Regulations, S.I. No. 93 of 1967

Road Traffic (Speed Limits) (County of Sligo) Regulations, S.I. No. 172 of 1967

Road Traffic (Speed Limits) (County of Kerry) Regulations, S.I. No. 208 of 1967

Road Traffic (Speed Limits) (County of Meath) Regulations, S.I. No. 222 of 1967

Road Traffic (Speed Limits) (Amendment) (No.2) Regulations, S.I. No. 224 of 1967

Road Traffic (Speed Limits) (County Borough of Dublin and County of Dublin) (Amendment) Regulations, S.I. No. 225 of 1967

Road Traffic (Speed Limits) (County of Roscommon) Regulations, S.I. No. 306 of 1967

Road Traffic (Speed Limits) (County of Westmeath) Regulations, S.I. No. 307 of 1967

Road Traffic (Speed Limits) (County of Leitrim) Regulations, S.I. No. 9 of 1968

Road Traffic (Speed Limits) (County of Louth) Regulations, S.I. No. 16 of 1968

Road Traffic (Speed Limits) (County of Longford) Regulations, S.I. No. 27 of 1968

Road Traffic (Speed Limits) (County of Laoighis) Regulations, S.I. No. 42 of 1968

Road Traffic (Speed Limits) (County of Donegal) Regulations, S.I. No. 73 of 1968

Road Traffic (Speed Limits) (County of Kilkenny) Regulations, S.I. No. 107 of 1968

Road Traffic (Speed Limits) (County of Galway) Regulations, S.I. No. 110 of 1968

Road Traffic (Speed Limits) (County of Offaly) Regulations, S.I. No. 132 of 1968

Road Traffic (Speed Limits) (County of Wexford) Regulations, S.I. No. 153 of 1968

Road Traffic (Speed Limits) (County of Tipperary North Riding) Regulations, S.I. No. 173 of 1968

Road Traffic (Speed Limits) (County of Cavan) Regulations, S.I. No. 196 of 1968

Road Traffic (Speed Limits) (County of Clare) Regulations, S.I. No. 199 of 1968

Road Traffic (Speed Limits) (County of Wicklow) Regulations, S.I. No. 212 of 1968

Statutory Authority	Section	Statutory Instrument
Road Traffic Act, No. 24 of 1961 (*Cont.*)		*Road Traffic (Speed Limits) (County of Tipperary South Riding) Regulations, S.I. No. 214 of 1968*
		Road Traffic (Speed Limits) (County Borough of Cork and County of Cork) Regulations, S.I. No. 282 of 1968
		Road Traffic (Speed Limits) (County of Kildare) Regulations, S.I. No. 27 of 1969
		Road Traffic (Speed Limits) (County Borough of Limerick and County of Limerick) (Amendment) Regulations, S.I. No. 28 of 1969
		Road Traffic (Speed Limits) (County of Mayo) Regulations, S.I. No. 36 of 1969
		Road Traffic (Speed Limits) (County of Sligo) (Amendment) Regulations, S.I. No. 52 of 1969
		Road Traffic (Speed Limits) (County Borough of Dublin and County of Dublin) Regulations, S.I. No. 100 of 1970
		Road Traffic (Speed Limits) (County Galway) (Amendment) Regulations, S.I. No. 126 of 1970
		Road Traffic (Speed Limits) (County of Carlow) Regulations, S.I. No. 142 of 1970
		Road Traffic (Speed Limits) (County of Monaghan) Regulations, S.I. No. 174 of 1970
		Road Traffic (Speed Limits) (County of Meath) Regulations, S.I. No. 259 of 1970
		Road Traffic (Speed Limits) (County Borough of Waterford and County of Waterford) Regulations, S.I. No. 275 of 1970
		Road Traffic (Speed Limits) (County of Longford) (Amendment) Regulations, S.I. No. 56 of 1971
		Road Traffic (Speed Limits) (County of Roscommon) (Amendment) Regulations, S.I. No. 136 of 1971
		Road Traffic (Speed Limits) (County of Westmeath) (Amendment) Regulations, S.I. No. 150 of 1971
		Road Traffic (Speed Limits) (County of Kerry) (Amendment) Regulations, S.I. No. 242 of 1971
		Road Traffic (Speed Limits) (County of Donegal) (Amendment) Regulations, S.I. No. 263 of 1971
		Road Traffic (Speed Limits) (County of Clare) (Amendment) Regulations, S.I. No. 279 of 1971
		Road Traffic (Speed Limits) (County of Offaly) (Amendment) Regulations, S.I. No. 27 of 1972
		Road Traffic (Speed Limits) (County of Laoighis) (Amendment) Regulations, S.I. No. 28 of 1972
		Road Traffic (Speed Limits) (County of Galway) (Amendment) Regulations, S.I. No. 225 of 1972
		Road Traffic (Speed Limits) (County Borough of Limerick and County of Limerick) Regulations, S.I. No. 273 of 1972
		Road Traffic (Speed Limits) (County Borough of Cork and County of Cork) (Amendment) Regulations, S.I. No. 263 of 1973

Statutory Authority	Section	Statutory Instrument

Road Traffic Act, No. 24 of 1961
(*Cont.*)

Road Traffic (Speed Limits) (County of Mayo) (Amendment) Regulations, S.I. No. 300 of 1973

Road Traffic (Speed Limits) (County Borough of Dublin and County of Dublin) (Amendment) Regulations, S.I. No. 350 of 1973

Road Traffic (Speed Limits) (County of Kildare) (Amendment) Regulations, S.I. No. 351 of 1973

Road Traffic (Speed Limits) (County of Tipperary North Riding) (Amendment) Regulations, S.I. No. 115 of 1974

Road Traffic (Speed Limits) (County of Kilkenny) (Amendment) Regulations, S.I. No. 148 of 1974

Road Traffic (Speed Limits) (County of Meath) (Amendment) Regulations, S.I. No. 230 of 1974

Road Traffic (Speed Limits) (County of Wicklow) (Amendment) Regulations, S.I. No. 263 of 1974

Road Traffic (Speed Limits) (County Borough of Cork and County of Cork) Regulations, S.I. No. 310 of 1974

Road Traffic (Speed Limits) (County Borough of Dublin and County of Dublin) (Amendment) Regulations, S.I. No. 342 of 1974

Road Traffic (Speed Limits) (County Borough of Dublin and County of Dublin) (Amendment) Regulations, S.I. No. 151 of 1976

Road Traffic (Speed Limits) (County of Tipperary South Riding) Regulations, S.I. No. 172 of 1976

Road Traffic (Speed Limits) (County of Roscommon) Regulations, S.I. No. 285 of 1976

Road Traffic (Speed Limits) (County of Meath) Regulations, S.I. No. 300 of 1976

Road Traffic (Speed Limits) (County of Tipperary North Riding) Regulations, S.I. No. 312 of 1976

Road Traffic (Speed Limits) (County of Kildare) Regulations, S.I. No. 105 of 1977

Road Traffic (Speed Limits) (County of Monaghan) Regulations, S.I. No. 110 of 1977

Road Traffic (Speed Limits) (County of Kerry) Regulations, S.I. No. 145 of 1977

Road Traffic (Speed Limits) (County Borough of Limerick and County of Limerick) Regulations, S.I. No. 157 of 1977

Road Traffic (Speed Limits) (County of Wexford) Regulations, S.I. No. 238 of 1977

Road Traffic (Speed Limits) (County of Westmeath) Regulations, S.I. No. 270 of 1977

Road Traffic (Speed Limits) (County of Clare) Regulations, S.I. No. 292 of 1977

Road Traffic (Speed Limits) (County Borough of Dublin and County of Dublin) Regulations, S.I. No. 358 of 1977

Road Traffic (Speed Limits) (County Borough of Cork and County of Cork) Regulations, S.I. No. 370 of 1977

Road Traffic Act, No. 24 of 1961
(*Cont.*)

Road Traffic (Speed Limits) (County of Laoighis) Regulations, S.I. No. 394 of 1977

Road Traffic (Speed Limits) (County of Kilkenny) Regulations, S.I. No. 399 of 1977

Road Traffic (Speed Limits) (County of Wicklow) Regulations, S.I. No. 31 of 1978

Road Traffic (Speed Limits) (County of Offaly) Regulations, S.I. No. 41 of 1978

Road Traffic (Speed Limits) (County of Carlow) Regulations, S.I. No. 121 of 1978

Road Traffic (Speed Limits) (County of Longford) Regulations, S.I. No. 122 of 1978

Road Traffic (Speed Limits) (County Borough of Dublin and County of Dublin) (Amendment) Regulations, S.I. No. 328 of 1978

Road Traffic (Speed Limits) (County Borough of Waterford and County of Waterford) Regulations, S.I. No. 50 of 1979

Road Traffic (Speed Limits) (County of Galway) Regulations, S.I. No. 189 of 1979

Road Traffic (Speed Limits) (County of Cavan) Regulations, S.I. No. 283 of 1979

Road Traffic (Speed Limits) (County of Sligo) Regulations, S.I. No. 284 of 1979

Road Traffic (Speed Limits) (County of Louth) Regulations, S.I. No. 378 of 1979

Road Traffic (Speed Limits) (County of Mayo) Regulations, S.I. No. 216 of 1980

Road Traffic (Speed Limits) (County of Leitrim) Regulations, S.I. No. 278 of 1980

Road Traffic (Speed Limits) (County of Cavan) (Amendment) Regulations, S.I. No. 279 of 1980

Road Traffic (Speed Limits) (County of Roscommon) Regulations, S.I. No. 355 of 1980

Road Traffic (Speed Limits) (County Borough of Dublin and County of Dublin) (Amendment) Regulations, S.I. No. 169 of 1981

Road Traffic (Speed Limits) (County of Monaghan) Regulations, S.I. No. 170 of 1981

Road Traffic (Speed Limits) (County of Tipperary North Riding) Regulations, S.I. No. 176 of 1981

Road Traffic (Speed Limits) (County Borough of Cork and County of Cork) Regulations, S.I. No. 211 of 1981

Road Traffic (Speed Limits) (County of Kilkenny) Regulations, S.I. No. 332 of 1981

Road Traffic (Speed Limits) (County of Westmeath) Regulations, S.I. No. 365 of 1981

Road Traffic (Speed Limits) (County of Carlow) (Amendment) Regulations, S.I. No. 72 of 1982

Road Traffic (Speed Limits) (County Borough of Dublin and County of Dublin) (Amendment) Regulations, S.I. No. 330 of 1982

Road Traffic Act, No. 24 of 1961
(*Cont.*)

Road Traffic (Speed Limits) (County of Wexford) Regulations, S.I. No. 45 of 1983

Road Traffic (Speed Limits) (County of Clare) Regulations, S.I. No. 46 of 1983

Road Traffic (Speed Limits) (County of Kerry) (Amendment) Regulations, S.I. No. 77 of 1983

Road Traffic (Speed Limits) (County of Offaly) Regulations, S.I. No. 81 of 1983

Road Traffic (Speed Limits) (County Borough of Cork and County of Cork) (Amendment) Regulations, S.I. No. 161 of 1983

Road Traffic (Speed Limits) (County Borough of Dublin and County of Dublin) (Amendment) Regulations, S.I. No. 217 of 1983

Road Traffic (Speed Limits) (County of Kildare) Regulations, S.I. No. 277 of 1983

Road Traffic (Speed Limits) (County of Kerry) Regulations, S.I. No. 334 of 1983

Road Traffic (Speed Limits) (County Borough of Limerick and County of Limerick) Regulations, S.I. No. 104 of 1984

Road Traffic (Speed Limits) (County of Longford) Regulations, S.I. No. 229 of 1984

Road Traffic (Speed Limits) (County of Cavan) Regulations, S.I. No. 63 of 1985

Road Traffic (Speed Limits) (County of Meath) Regulations, S.I. No. 318 of 1985

Road Traffic (Speed Limits) (County of Carlow) Regulations, S.I. No. 398 of 1985

Road Traffic (Speed Limits) (County Borough of Waterford and County of Waterford) Regulations, S.I. No. 8 of 1986

Road Traffic (Speed Limits) (County Borough of Limerick and County of Limerick) (Amendment) Regulations, S.I. No. 38 of 1986

Road Traffic (Speed Limits) (County of Laoighis) Regulations, S.I. No. 72 of 1986

Road Traffic (Speed Limits) (County of Donegal) Regulations, S.I. No. 103 of 1986

Road Traffic (Speed Limits) (County of Tipperary North Riding) Regulations, S.I. No. 206 of 1986

Road Traffic (Speed Limits) (County Borough of Cork and County of Cork) Regulations, S.I. No. 457 of 1986

62(1)(c) Road Traffic (Compulsory Insurance) Regulations, S.I. No. 14 of 1962

Road Traffic (Compulsory Insurance) (Amendment) Regulations, S.I. No. 58 of 1964

Road Traffic (Compulsory Insurance) (Amendment) Regulations, S.I. No. 359 of 1977

63(1)(c) Road Traffic (Compulsory Insurance) Regulations, S.I. No. 14 of 1962

Statutory Authority	Section	Statutory Instrument
Road Traffic Act, No. 24 of 1961 (Cont.)		**Road Traffic (Compulsory Insurance) (Amendment) Regulations, S.I. No. 58 of 1964**
	65(1)(a)	**Road Traffic (Compulsory Insurance) Regulations, S.I. No. 14 of 1962**
	66	**Road Traffic (Compulsory Insurance) Regulations, S.I. No. 14 of 1962**
	68(1)	**Road Traffic (Compulsory Insurance) Regulations, S.I. No. 14 of 1962**
	75	**Road Traffic (Compulsory Insurance) Regulations, S.I. No. 14 of 1962**
	79	**Road Traffic (Compulsory Insurance) Regulations, S.I. No. 14 of 1962**
	80	**Mechanically Propelled Vehicles (International Circulation) (Amendment) Order, S.I. No. 12 of 1962**
	82	**Road Traffic (Public Service Vehicles) Regulations, S.I. No. 191 of 1963**
		Road Traffic (Public Service Vehicles) (Amendment) Regulations, S.I. No. 106 of 1964
		Road Traffic (Public Service Vehicles) (Amendment) Regulations, S.I. No. 274 of 1967
		Road Traffic (Public Service Vehicles) (Amendment) Regulations, S.I. No. 273 of 1968
		Road Traffic (Public Service Vehicles) (Amendment) Regulations, S.I. No. 138 of 1970
		Road Traffic (Public Service Vehicles) (Amendment) (No.2) Regulations, S.I. No. 200 of 1970
		Road Traffic (Public Service Vehicles) (Amendment) (No.3) Regulations, S.I. No. 252 of 1970
		Road Traffic (Public Service Vehicles) (Amendment) Regulations, S.I. No. 225 of 1973
		Road Traffic (Public Service Vehicles) (Amendment) Regulations, S.I. No. 296 of 1974
		Road Traffic (Public Service Vehicles) (Amendment) Regulations, S.I. No. 35 of 1975
		Road Traffic (Public Service Vehicles) (Amendment) (No.2) Regulations, S.I. No. 101 of 1975
		Road Traffic (Public Service Vehicles) (Amendment) (No.3) Regulations, S.I. No. 113 of 1975
		Road Traffic (Public Service Vehicles) (Amendment) Regulations, S.I. No. 24 of 1976
		Road Traffic (Public Service Vehicles) (Amendment) (No.2) Regulations, S.I. No. 160 of 1976
		Road Traffic (Public Service Vehicles) (Amendment) Regulations, S.I. No. 111 of 1977
		Road Traffic (Public Service Vehicles) (Amendment) (No.2) Regulations, S.I. No. 177 of 1977
		Road Traffic (Public Service Vehicles) (Amendment) (No.3) Regulations, S.I. No. 268 of 1977

Statutory Authority	Section	Statutory Instrument

Road Traffic Act, No. 24 of 1961
(*Cont.*)

Road Traffic (Public Service Vehicles) (Amend-ment) (No.4) Regulations, S.I. No. 284 of 1977

Road Traffic (Public Service Vehicles) (Amendment) Regulations, S.I. No. 15 of 1978

Road Traffic (Public Service Vehicles) (Amend-ment) (No.2) Regulations, S.I. No. 226 of 1978

Road Traffic (Public Service Vehicles) (Amend-ment) (No.3) Regulations, S.I. No. 247 of 1978

Road Traffic (Public Service Vehicles) (Amendment) (No.4) Regulations, S.I. No. 259 of 1978

Road Traffic (Public Service Vehicles) (Licensing) Regulations, S.I. No. 292 of 1978

Road Traffic (Public Service Vehicles) (Amendment) Regulations, S.I. No. 242 of 1979

Road Traffic (Public Service Vehicles) (Amendment) Regulations, S.I. No. 54 of 1980

Road Traffic (Public Service Vehicles) (Amendment) Regulations, S.I. No. 66 of 1981

Road Traffic (Public Service Vehicles) (Amendment) Regulations, S.I. No. 273 of 1983

Road Traffic (Public Service Vehicles) (Amendment) Regulations, S.I. No. 300 of 1986

83   *Taximeters (Fees on Verification and Stamping by Special Inspectors) Regulations, S.I. No. 158 of 1978*

Taximeter (Fees on Verification and Stamping by Special Inspectors) Regulations, S.I. No. 436 of 1986

84   *Dublin Appointed Stands (Street Service Vehicles) Bye-laws, S.I. No. 50 of 1963*

Galway Appointed Stands (Street Service Vehicles) Bye-laws, S.I. No. 109 of 1965

Ennis Appointed Stands (Street Service Vehicles) Bye-laws, S.I. No. 162 of 1965

Dundalk Appointed Stands (Street Service Vehicles) Bye-laws, S.I. No. 171 of 1965

Cork Appointed Stands (Street Service Vehicles) Bye-laws, S.I. No. 179 of 1965

Tralee Appointed Stands (Street Service Vehicles) Bye-laws, S.I. No. 203 of 1965

Drogheda Appointed Stands (Street Service Vehicles) Bye-laws, S.I. No. 132 of 1967

Donegal Appointed Stands (Street Service Vehicles) Bye-laws, S.I. No. 3 of 1971

Dublin Appointed Stands (Street Service Vehicles) Temporary Rules, S.I. No. 142 of 1973

Dublin Appointed Stands (Street Service Vehicles) Temporary Rules, S.I. No. 170 of 1974

Road Traffic Act, No. 24 of 1961 *(Cont.)*		**Drogheda Appointed Stands (Street Service Vehicles) Bye-laws, S.I. No. 171 of 1974**
		Dublin Appointed Stands (Street Service Vehicles) Temporary Rules, S.I. No. 103 of 1975
		Dublin Appointed Stands (Street Service Vehicles) Bye-laws, S.I. No. 53 of 1979
		Galway Appointed Stands (Street Service Vehicles) Bye-laws, S.I. No. 199 of 1980
		Killarney Appointed Stands (Street Service Vehicles) Bye-laws, (1980) S.I. No. 71 of 1981
		Waterford Appointed Stands (Street Service Vehicles) Bye-laws, (1979) S.I. No. 72 of 1981
		Limerick Appointed Stands (Street Service Vehicles) Bye-laws, (1980) S.I. No. 102 of 1981
		Waterford Appointed Stands (Steel Service Vehicles) Bye-laws, S.I. No. 288 of 1982
		Dublin Appointed Stands (Street Service Vehicles) Bye-laws, S.I. No. 104 of 1986
		Donegal Appointed Stands (Street Service Vehicles) Bye-laws, (1985) S.I. No. 243 of 1986
		Galway Appointed Stands (Street Service Vehicles) Bye-laws, S.I. No. 303 of 1986
	84(3)	**Road Traffic (Bye-laws and Temporary Rules) Regulations, S.I. No. 219 of 1961**
	84(4)	**Road Traffic (Bye-laws and Temporary Rules) Regulations, S.I. No. 219 of 1961**
	86	**Omnibus (Stopping Places and Stands) General Bye-laws, S.I. No. 122 of 1962**
		Road Traffic (Signs) Regulations, S.I. No. 171 of 1962
		Road Traffic (Signs) (Amendment) Regulations, S.I. No. 233 of 1966
	87	*Street Service Vehicles (Dublin) (Lost Property) Bye-laws, S.I. No. 32 of 1963*
		Street Service Vehicles (Dublin) (Lost Property) Amendment Bye-laws, S.I. No. 63 of 1968
		Street Service Vehicles (Dublin) (Lost Property) Bye-laws, S.I. No. 365 of 1983
	88	**Omnibus (Stopping Places and Stands) General Bye-laws, S.I. No. 122 of 1962**
		Road Traffic General Bye-laws, S.I. No. 294 of 1964
	89	*Limerick Traffic Bye-laws, S.I. No. 110 of 1962*
		Wexford Traffic and Parking Bye-laws, S.I. No. 210 of 1964
		Galway Traffic and Parking Bye-laws, S.I. No. 235 of 1964
		Drogheda Traffic and Parking Bye-laws, S.I. No. 267 of 1964
		Cavan Traffic and Parking Bye-laws (1964) S.I. No. 28 of 1965

Statutory Authority	Section	Statutory Instrument
Road Traffic Act, No. 24 of 1961 (*Cont.*)		*Bray Traffic and Parking Bye-laws, S.I. No. 59 of 1965*
		Cavan Traffic and Parking Bye-laws (1965) S.I. No. 8 of 1966
		Clonmel Traffic and Parking Bye-laws, S.I. No. 3 of 1966
		Waterford Traffic and Parking Bye-laws, S.I. No. 8 of 1966
		Loughrea Traffic and Parking Bye-laws, S.I. No. 1 of 1967
		Sligo Traffic and Parking Temporary Rules, S.I. No. 107 of 1969
		Castlebar Traffic and Parking Temporary Rules, S.I. No. 114 of 1969
		Kilkee Traffic and Parking Temporary Rules, S.I. No. 116 of 1969
		Newcastle West Traffic and Parking Temporary Rules, S.I. No. 157 of 1969
		Greystones Traffic and Parking Temporary Rules S.I. No. 158 of 1969
		Longford Traffic and Parking Bye-laws, S.I. No. 173 of 1969
		Enniscorthy Traffic and Parking Bye-laws, S.I. No. 174 of 1969
		Tuam Traffic and Parking Bye-laws, S.I. No. 175 of 1969
		Drogheda Traffic Temporary Rules, S.I. No. 193 of 1969
		Carlow Traffic and Parking Bye-laws, S.I. No. 200 of 1969
		Thurles Traffic and Parking Bye-laws, S.I. No. 200 of 1969
		New Ross Traffic and Parking (No.2) Temporary Rules, S.I. No. 218 of 1969
		Ennis Traffic and Parking Bye-laws, S.I. No. 246 of 1969
		Dundalk Traffic Temporary Rules, S.I. No. 253 of 1969
		Limerick Traffic (No.2) Temporary Rules, S.I. No. 7 of 1970
		Cork Traffic Temporary Rules, S.I. No. 11 of 1970
		Cork Traffic and Parking Temporary Rules, S.I. No. 46 of 1970
		Limerick Traffic and Parking Temporary Rules, S.I. No. 51 of 1970
		Dublin and Dun Laoghaire Traffic Temporary Rules, S.I. No. 52 of 1970
		Mallow Traffic and Parking Bye-laws, S.I. No. 60 of 1970
		Tralee Traffic and Parking Bye-laws, S.I. No. 95 of 1970
		Cork Traffic (No.2) Temporary Rules, S.I. No. 104 of 1970
		Carrickmacross Traffic and Parking Bye-laws, S.I. No. 118 of 1970

Statutory Authority	Section	Statutory Instrument
Road Traffic Act, No. 24 of 1961 (*Cont.*)		*Sligo Traffic and Parking Temporary Rules, S.I. No. 146 of 1970*
		Youghal Traffic and Parking Temporary Rules, S.I. No. 158 of 1970
		Waterford Suburbs Traffic Temporary Rules, S.I. No. 172 of 1970
		Kilkee Traffic and Parking Bye-laws, S.I. No. 173 of 1970
		Castlebar Traffic and Parking Bye-laws, S.I. No. 182 of 1970
		Salterstown, County Louth Traffic Temporary Rules, S.I. No. 183 of 1970
		Newcastle West Traffic and Parking Bye-laws, S.I. No. 249 of 1970
		Greystones Traffic and Parking Bye-laws, S.I. No. 260 of 1970
		Dundalk Traffic Temporary Rules, S.I. No. 304 of 1970
		Drogheda Traffic and Parking Bye-laws, S.I. No. 18 of 1971
		Cork Traffic Temporary Rules, S.I. No. 25 of 1971
		Limerick Traffic Temporary Rules, S.I. No. 42 of 1971
		Dublin Traffic and Parking Bye-laws, S.I. No. 59 of 1971
		Dublin Traffic and Parking Temporary Rules, 1970 (Revocation) Rules, S.I. No. 91 of 1971
		Cork Traffic and Parking Temporary Rules, S.I. No. 94 of 1971
		Dublin and Dun Laoghaire Traffic Temporary Rules, S.I. No. 95 of 1971
		New Ross Traffic and Parking Bye-laws, S.I. No. 101 of 1971
		Galway Traffic and Parking Temporary Rules, S.I. No. 141 of 1971
		Killarney Traffic and Parking Temporary Rules, S.I. No. 153 of 1971
		Limerick Traffic and Parking (Clearway) Bye-laws, S.I. No. 160 of 1971
		Ballina Traffic and Parking Bye-laws, S.I. No. 165 of 1971
		Kilkenny Traffic and Parking Temporary Rules, S.I. No. 168 of 1971
		Mullingar Traffic and Parking Bye-laws, (1970) S.I. No. 178 of 1971
		Letterkenny Traffic and Parking Bye-laws, (1970) S.I. No. 179 of 1971
		Sligo Traffic and Parking Temporary Rules, S.I. No. 189 of 1971
		Arklow Traffic and Parking Bye-laws, S.I. No. 213 of 1971
		Youghal Traffic and Parking Bye-laws, S.I. No. 214 of 1971
		Midleton Traffic and Parking Bye-laws, S.I. No. 215 of 1971

Statutory Authority	Section	Statutory Instrument
Road Traffic Act, No. 24 of 1961 (*Cont.*)		*Loughrea Traffic and Parking Bye-laws, S.I. No. 224 of 1971*
		Callan Traffic and Parking Bye-laws, S.I. No. 281 of 1971
		Dundalk Traffic and Parking Bye-laws, S.I. No. 340 of 1971
		Athlone Traffic and Parking Bye-laws, S.I. No. 2 of 1972
		Cork Traffic Bye-laws (1971) S.I. No. 32 of 1972
		Dublin Traffic Temporary Rules, S.I. No. 73 of 1972
		Limerick Traffic Bye-laws, S.I. No. 102 of 1972
		Galway Traffic and Parking Temporary Rules, S.I. No. 110 of 1972
		Cork Traffic and Parking (Clearway) Bye-laws, S.I. No. 118 of 1972
		Naas Traffic and Parking Bye-laws, S.I. No. 126 of 1972
		Kilkenny Traffic and Parking Temporary Rules, S.I. No. 127 of 1972
		Killarney Traffic and Parking Temporary Rules, S.I. No. 140 of 1972
		Waterford Traffic and Parking Bye-laws, S.I. No. 144 of 1972
		Sligo Traffic and Parking Bye-laws, S.I. No. 154 of 1972
		Dungarvan Traffic and Parking Bye-laws, S.I. No. 336 of 1972
		Letterkenny Traffic and Parking Bye-laws, S.I. No. 337 of 1972
		Carrick-on-Suir Traffic and Parking Bye-laws (1972) S.I. No. 6 of 1973
		Dublin Traffic Temporary Rules, S.I. No. 62 of 1973
		Dublin Traffic and Parking (Pedestrianisation) Temporary Rules, S.I. No. 92 of 1973
		Galway Traffic and Parking Temporary Rules, S.I. No. 101 of 1973
		Leixlip Traffic and Parking Bye-laws, S.I. No. 110 of 1973
		Kilkenny Traffic and Parking Temporary Rules, S.I. No. 118 of 1973
		Killarney Traffic and Parking Temporary Rules, S.I. No. 137 of 1973
		Cashel Traffic and Parking Bye-laws, S.I. No. 145 of 1973
		Listowel Traffic and Parking Bye-laws, S.I. No. 146 of 1973
		Waterford Suburbs Traffic Temporary Rules, S.I. No. 266 of 1973
		Collooney Traffic and Parking Bye-laws, S.I. No. 323 of 1973

Statutory Authority	Section	Statutory Instrument
Road Traffic Act, No. 24 of 1961 (*Cont.*)		*Kilmallock Traffic and Parking Bye-laws, S.I. No. 324 of 1973*
		Monaghan Traffic and Parking Bye-laws, S.I. No. 352 of 1973
		Dublin Traffic and Parking (Pedestrianisation) (No.2) Temporary Rules, (1973) S.I. No. 1 of 1974
		Dublin Traffic Bye-laws, S.I. No. 63 of 1974
		Tubbercurry Traffic and Parking Bye-laws, S.I. No. 99 of 1974
		Galway Traffic and Parking Bye-laws, S.I. No. 124 of 1974
		Tramore Traffic and Parking Bye-laws, S.I. No. 142 of 1974
		Killarney Traffic and Parking Temporary Rules, S.I. No. 143 of 1974
		Bray Traffic and Parking Bye-laws, S.I. No. 152 of 1974
		Kilkenny Traffic and Parking Bye-laws, S.I. No. 153 of 1974
		Crosshaven Traffic and Parking Bye-laws, S.I. No. 154 of 1974
		Wexford Traffic and Parking Bye-laws, S.I. No. 165 of 1974
		Birr Traffic and Parking Bye-laws, S.I. No. 172 of 1974
		Lahinch Traffic and Parking Bye-laws, S.I. No. 177 of 1974
		Waterford Suburbs Traffic Temporary Rules, S.I. No. 268 of 1974
		Tuam Traffic and Parking Bye-laws, S.I. No. 291 of 1974
		Cavan Traffic and Parking Bye-laws, (1973) S.I. No. 326 of 1974
		Dingle Traffic and Parking Bye-laws, S.I. No. 9 of 1975
		Dublin Traffic and Parking (Pedestrianisation) Temporary Rules, S.I. No. 16 of 1975
		Fermoy Traffic and Parking Bye-laws, S.I. No. 56 of 1975
		Trim Traffic and Parking Bye-laws, S.I. No. 57 of 1975
		Ballinrobe Traffic and Parking Bye-laws, S.I. No. 82 of 1975
		Clifden Traffic and Parking Bye-laws, S.I. No. 89 of 1975
		Manorhamilton Traffic and Parking Bye-laws, S.I. No. 90 of 1975
		Killarney Traffic and Parking Bye-laws, S.I. No. 132 of 1975
		Limerick Traffic and Parking Bye-laws, S.I. No. 204 of 1975

Road Traffic Act, No. 24 of 1961
(*Cont.*)

Portumna Traffic and Parking Bye-laws, S.I. No. 208 of 1975

Droichead Nua Traffic and Parking Bye-laws, S.I. No. 293 of 1975

Athy Traffic and Parking Bye-laws, (1975) S.I. No. 37 of 1976

Dublin Traffic and Parking Bye-laws, S.I. No. 83 of 1976

Athlone Traffic and Parking Bye-laws, (1975) S.I. No. 134 of 1976

Wicklow Traffic and Parking Bye-laws, S.I. No. 193 of 1976

Cork Traffic and Parking (Pedestrianisation) Temporary Rules, S.I. No. 194 of 1976

Clonmel Traffic and Parking Bye-laws, S.I. No. 248 of 1976

Mountrath Traffic and Parking Bye-laws, S.I. No. 249 of 1976

Castlerea Traffic and Parking Bye-laws, S.I. No. 256 of 1976

Ballyshannon Traffic and Parking Bye-laws, S.I. No. 257 of 1976

Clones Traffic and Parking Bye-laws, S.I. No. 271 of 1977

Tullamore Traffic and Parking Bye-laws, S.I. No. 272 of 1977

Dublin Traffic and Parking Bye-laws, S.I. No. 82 of 1980

Dublin Traffic and Parking (No.2) Bye-laws, (1980) S.I. No. 49 of 1981

Dublin Traffic and Parking Temporary Rules, S.I. No. 148 of 1981

Dublin Traffic and Parking (No.2) Temporary Rules, S.I. No. 401 of 1981

Dublin Traffic and Parking Temporary Rules, S.I. No. 109 of 1982

Dublin Traffic and Parking (No.2) Temporary Rules, S.I. No. 287 of 1982

Dublin Traffic and Parking Temporary Rules, S.I. No. 105 of 1983

Cork (County Borough and County) Traffic and Parking Temporary Rules, S.I. No. 3 of 1984

Dublin Traffic and Parking Temporary Rules, S.I. No. 38 of 1984

County of Carlow Traffic and Parking Temporary Rules, S.I. No. 148 of 1984

County of Clare Traffic and Parking Temporary Rules, S.I. No. 149 of 1984

County of Galway Traffic and Parking Temporary Rules, S.I. No. 150 of 1984

County of Laois Traffic and Parking Temporary Rules, S.I. No. 151 of 1984

Statutory Authority	Section	Statutory Instrument
Road Traffic Act, No. 24 of 1961 (*Cont.*)		*Limerick (County Borough and County) Traffic and Parking Temporary Rules, S.I. No. 152 of 1984*
		County of Louth Traffic and Parking Temporary Rules, S.I. No. 153 of 1984
		County of Tipperary North Riding and County of Tipperary South Riding Traffic and Parking Temporary Rules, S.I. No. 154 of 1984
		Dublin Traffic and Parking (No.2) Temporary Rules, S.I. No. 329 of 1984
		Cork (County Borough and County) Traffic and Parking Temporary Rules, S.I. No. 4 of 1985
		County of Carlow Traffic and Parking Temporary Rules, S.I. No. 193 of 1985
		County of Cavan Traffic and Parking Temporary Rules, S.I. No. 194 of 1985
		County of Clare Traffic and Parking Temporary Rules, S.I. No. 195 of 1985
		Cork (County Borough and County) Traffic and Parking (No.2) Temporary Rules, S.I. No. 196 of 1985
		County of Donegal Traffic and Parking Temporary Rules, S.I. No. 197 of 1985
		Dublin Area Traffic and Parking Temporary Rules, S.I. No. 198 of 1985
		County of Galway Traffic and Parking Temporary Rules, S.I. No. 199 of 1985
		County of Kerry Traffic and Parking Temporary Rules, S.I. No. 200 of 1985
		County of Kildare Traffic and Parking Temporary Rules, S.I. No. 201 of 1985
		County of Kilkenny Traffic and Parking Temporary Rules, S.I. No. 202 of 1985
		County of Laois Traffic and Parking Temporary Rules, S.I. No. 203 of 1985
		County of Leitrim Traffic and Parking Temporary Rules, S.I. No. 204 of 1985
		Limerick (County Borough and County) Traffic and Parking Temporary Rules, S.I. No. 205 of 1985
		County of Longford Traffic and Parking Temporary Rules, S.I. No. 206 of 1985
		County of Louth Traffic and Parking Temporary Rules, S.I. No. 207 of 1985
		County of Mayo Traffic and Parking Temporary Rules, S.I. No. 208 of 1985
		County of Meath Traffic and Parking Temporary Rules, S.I. No. 209 of 1985
		County of Monaghan Traffic and Parking Temporary Rules, S.I. No. 210 of 1985
		County of Offaly Traffic and Parking Temporary Rules, S.I. No. 211 of 1985
		County of Roscommon Traffic and Parking Temporary Rules, S.I. No. 212 of 1985

Statutory Authority	Section	Statutory Instrument
Road Traffic Act, No. 24 of 1961 (*Cont.*)		*County of Sligo Traffic and Parking Temporary Rules, S.I. No. 213 of 1985*
		County of Tipperary North Riding and County of Tipperary South Riding Traffic and Parking Temporary Rules, S.I. No. 214 of 1985
		Waterford (County Borough and County) Traffic and Parking Temporary Rules, S.I. No. 215 of 1985
		County of Westmeath Traffic and Parking Temporary Rules, S.I. No. 216 of 1985
		County of Wexford Traffic and Parking Temporary Rules, S.I. No. 217 of 1985
		County of Wicklow Traffic and Parking Temporary Rules, S.I. No. 218 of 1985
		Limerick (County Borough and County) Traffic and Parking (No.2) Temporary Rules, S.I. No. 240 of 1985
		Waterford (County Borough and County) Traffic and Parking (No.2) Temporary Rules, S.I. No. 241 of 1985
		County of Carlow Traffic and Parking Bye-laws, S.I. No. 177 of 1986
		County of Cavan Traffic and Parking Bye-laws, S.I. No. 178 of 1986
		County of Clare Traffic and Parking Bye-laws, S.I. No. 179 of 1986
		Cork (County Borough and County) Traffic and Parking Bye-laws, S.I. No. 180 of 1986
		County of Donegal Traffic and Parking Bye-laws, S.I. No. 181 of 1986
		Dublin Area Traffic and Parking Bye-laws, S.I. No. 182 of 1986
		Galway (County Borough and County) Traffic and Parking Bye-laws, S.I. No. 183 of 1986
		County of Kerry Traffic and Parking Bye-laws, S.I. No. 184 of 1986
		County of Kildare Traffic and Parking Bye-laws, S.I. No. 185 of 1986
		County of Kilkenny Traffic and Parking Bye-laws, S.I. No. 186 of 1986
		County of Laois Traffic and Parking Bye-laws, S.I. No. 187 of 1986
		County of Leitrim Traffic and Parking Bye-laws, S.I. No. 188 of 1986
		Limerick (County Borough and County) Traffic and Parking Bye-laws, S.I. No. 189 of 1986
		County of Longford Traffic and Parking Bye-laws, S.I. No. 190 of 1986
		County of Louth Traffic and Parking Bye-laws, S.I. No. 191 of 1986
		County of Mayo Traffic and Parking Bye-laws, S.I. No. 192 of 1986

Road Traffic Act, No. 24 of 1961
(*Cont.*)

County of Meath Traffic and Parking Bye-laws, S.I. No. 193 of 1986

County of Monaghan Traffic and Parking Bye-laws, S.I. No. 194 of 1986

County of Offaly Traffic and Parking Bye-laws, S.I. No. 195 of 1986

County of Roscommon Traffic and Parking Bye-laws, S.I. No. 196 of 1986

County of Sligo Traffic and Parking Bye-laws, S.I. No. 197 of 1986

County of Tipperary North Riding and County of Tipperary South Riding Traffic and Parking Bye-laws, S.I. No. 198 of 1986

Waterford (County Borough and County) Traffic and Parking Bye-laws, S.I. No. 199 of 1986

County of Westmeath Traffic and Parking Bye-laws, 19868, S.I. No. 200 of 1986

County of Wexford Traffic and Parking Bye-laws, S.I. No. 201 of 1986

County of Wicklow Traffic and Parking Bye-laws, S.I. No. 202 of 1986

89(3) *Dublin and Dun Laoghaire Traffic (One-way Streets) Temporary Rules, S.I. No. 55 of 1964*

Dublin and Dun Laoghaire Traffic (One-way Streets) (Amendment) Temporary Rules, S.I. No. 259 of 1964

Dublin and Dun Laoghaire Traffic (One-way Streets) Temporary Rules, S.I. No. 44 of 1965

Cork Traffic (One-way Streets) Temporary Rules, S.I. No. 245 of 1965

Cork Traffic (One-way Streets) Temporary Rules, S.I. No. 15 of 1966

Dublin and Dun Laoghaire Traffic (One-way Streets) Temporary Rules, S.I. No. 51 of 1966

Dublin and Dun Laoghaire Traffic (One-way Streets) (Amendment) Temporary Rules, (1965) S.I. No. 104 of 1966

Dublin and Dun Laoghaire Traffic (One-way Streets) (Amendment) (No.2) Temporary Rules, S.I. No. 192 of 1966

Dublin Traffic and Parking Temporary Rules, S.I. No. 257 of 1966

Cork Traffic (One-way Streets) Temporary Rules, S.I. No. 15 of 1967

Dublin and Dun Laoghaire Traffic (One-way Streets) Temporary Rules, S.I. No. 53 of 1967

Dublin and Dun Laoghaire Traffic (One-way Streets) (Amendment) Temporary Rules, S.I. No. 149 of 1967

Carlow Traffic and Parking Temporary Rules, S.I. No. 214 of 1967

Dublin Traffic and Parking (Amendment) Temporary Rules, S.I. No. 221 of 1967

Statutory Authority	Section	Statutory Instrument
Road Traffic Act, No. 24 of 1961 (*Cont.*)		*Dublin Traffic and Parking Temporary Rules, S.I. No. 259 of 1967*
		Dundalk Traffic (One-way Streets) Temporary Rules, S.I. No. 289 of 1967
		Cork Traffic (One-way Streets) Temporary Rules, S.I. No. 21 of 1968
		Limerick Traffic and Parking Temporary Rules, S.I. No. 38 of 1968
		Dublin and Dun Laoghaire Traffic (One-way Streets) Temporary Rules, S.I. No. 58 of 1968
		Limerick Traffic Temporary Rules, S.I. No. 77 of 1968
		Carlow Traffic and Parking Temporary Rules, S.I. No. 211 of 1968
		Dublin Traffic and Parking Temporary Rules, S.I. No. 242 of 1968
		Dundalk Traffic (One-way Streets) Temporary Rules, S.I. No. 269 of 1968
		Cork Traffic (One-way Streets) Temporary Rules, S.I. No. 6 of 1969
		Drogheda Traffic (One-way Streets) Temporary Rules, S.I. No. 29 of 1969
		Limerick Traffic and Parking Temporary Rules, S.I. No. 30 of 1969
		New Ross Traffic and Parking Temporary Rules, S.I. No. 37 of 1969
		Dublin and Dun Laoghaire Traffic (One-way Streets) Temporary Rules, S.I. No. 38 of 1969
		Limerick Traffic Temporary Rules, S.I. No. 54 of 1969
		Dublin Traffic and Parking Temporary Rules, S.I. No. 239 of 1969
		Dublin Traffic and Parking Temporary Rules, S.I. No. 290 of 1970
	89(4)	*Carlow Traffic and Parking Temporary Rules, S.I. No. 214 of 1967*
		Carlow Traffic and Parking Temporary Rules, S.I. No. 211 of 1968
		New Ross Traffic and Parking Temporary Rules, S.I. No. 37 of 1969
	90	*Dublin Parking Bye-laws (1962) S.I. No. 11 of 1963*
		Limerick Parking Bye-laws, S.I. No. 62 of 1963
		Tralee Parking Bye-laws, S.I. No. 79 of 1963
		Cork Parking Bye-laws, S.I. No. 158 of 1963
		Mallow Parking Bye-laws, S.I. No. 159 of 1963
		Castlebar Parking Bye-laws, S.I. No. 11 of 1964
		Wexford Traffic and Parking Bye-laws, S.I. No. 210 of 1964
		Galway Traffic and Parking Bye-laws, S.I. No. 235 of 1964
		Monaghan Parking Bye-laws, S.I. No. 252 of 1964

Statutory Authority	Section	Statutory Instrument

Road Traffic Act, No. 24 of 1961
(*Cont.*)

Drogheda Traffic and Parking Bye-laws, S.I. No. 267 of 1964

Mullingar Parking Bye-laws (1964) S.I. No. 8 of 1965

Athlone Parking Bye-laws (1964) S.I. No. 17 of 1965

Ballina Parking Bye-laws (1964) S.I. No. 27 of 1965

Cavan Traffic and Parking Bye-laws (1964) S.I. No. 28 of 1965

An Uaimh Parking Bye-laws (1964) S.I. No. 31 of 1965

Bray Traffic and Parking Bye-laws, S.I. No. 59 of 1965

Tullamore Parking Bye-laws, S.I. No. 127 of 1965

Killarney Parking Bye-laws, S.I. No. 165 of 1965

Clones Parking Bye-laws, S.I. No. 170 of 1965

Nenagh Parking Bye-laws, S.I. No. 182 of 1965

Dungarvan Parking Bye-laws, S.I. No. 210 of 1965

Dundalk Parking Bye-laws, S.I. No. 212 of 1965

Youghal Parking Bye-laws, S.I. No. 256 of 1965

Cavan Traffic and Parking Bye-laws (1965) S.I. No. 8 of 1966

Athy Parking Bye-laws (1965) S.I. No. 9 of 1966

Clonmel Traffic and Parking Bye-laws, S.I. No. 31 of 1966

Carrick-on-Suir Parking Bye-laws, S.I. No. 79 of 1966

Waterford Traffic and Parking Bye-laws, S.I. No. 87 of 1966

Portlaoighise Parking Bye-laws, S.I. No. 179 of 1966

Loughrea Traffic and Parking Bye-laws, S.I. No. 16 of 1967

Tullamore Parking Bye-laws, (1966) S.I. No. 38 of 1967

Sligo Traffic and Parking Temporary Rules, S.I. No. 107 of 1969

Castlebar Traffic and Parking Temporary Rules, S.I. No. 114 of 1969

Kilkee Traffic and Parking Temporary Rules, S.I. No. 116 of 1969

Newcastle West Traffic and Parking Temporary Rules, S.I. No. 157 of 1969

Greystones Traffic and Parking Temporary Rules, S.I. No. 158 of 1969

Road Traffic (Parking Fees) Regulations, S.I. No. 169 of 1969

Dublin Parking Bye-laws, S.I. No. 170 of 1969

Longford Traffic and Parking Bye-laws, S.I. No. 173 of 1969

Road Traffic Act, No. 24 of 1961
(*Cont.*)

Enniscorthy Traffic and Parking Bye-laws, S.I. No. 174 of 1969

Tuam Traffic and Parking Bye-laws, S.I. No. 175 of 1969

Ballinasloe Parking Bye-laws, S.I. No. 176 of 1969

Belturbet Parking Bye-laws, S.I. No. 181 of 1969

Nenagh Parking Bye-laws, S.I. No. 186 of 1969

Carlow Traffic and Parking Bye-laws, S.I. No. 200 of 1969

Thurles Traffic and Parking Bye-laws, S.I. No. 206 of 1969

Tipperary Parking Bye-laws, S.I. No. 209 of 1969

New Ross Traffic and Parking (No.2) Temporary Rules, S.I. No. 218 of 1969

Ennis Traffic and Parking Bye-laws, S.I. No. 246 of 1969

Dublin Parking Temporary Rules, 1969 (Revocation) Rules, S.I. No. 2 of 1970

Ceanannus Mor Parking Temporary Rules, S.I. No. 23 of 1970

Boyle Parking Bye-laws (1969) S.I. No. 30 of 1970

Ballybay Parking Bye-laws, S.I. No. 39 of 1970

Cork Traffic and Parking Temporary Rules, S.I. No. 46 of 1970

Limerick Traffic and Parking Temporary Rules, S.I. No. 51 of 1970

Mallow Traffic and Parking Bye-laws, S.I. No. 60 of 1970

Thomastown Parking Bye-laws, S.I. No. 61 of 1970

Tralee Traffic and Parking Bye-laws, S.I. No. 95 of 1970

Graiguenamanagh Parking Bye-laws, S.I. No. 102 of 1970

Carrickmacross Traffic and Parking Bye-laws, S.I. No. 118 of 1970

Sligo Traffic and Parking Temporary Rules, S.I. No. 146 of 1970

Youghal Traffic and Parking Temporary Rules, S.I. No. 158 of 1970

Kilkee Traffic and Parking Bye-laws, S.I. No. 173 of 1970

Castlebar Traffic and Parking Bye-laws, S.I. No. 182 of 1970

Portarlington Parking Bye-laws, S.I. No. 187 of 1970

Donegal Parking Bye-laws, S.I. No. 197 of 1970

Carrick-on-Shannon Parking Bye-laws, S.I. No. 209 of 1970

Bundoran Parking Bye-laws, S.I. No. 210 of 1970

Newcastle West Traffic and Parking Bye-laws, S.I. No. 249 of 1970

Statutory Authority	Section	Statutory Instrument
Road Traffic Act, No. 24 of 1961 (*Cont.*)		*Castleblayney Parking Bye-laws, S.I. No. 250 of 1970*
		Greystones Traffic and Parking Bye-laws, S.I. No. 260 of 1970
		Skibbereen Parking Bye-laws, S.I. No. 276 of 1970
		Roscommon Parking Bye-laws, S.I. No. 303 of 1970
		An Uaimh Parking Bye-laws, S.I. No. 305 of 1970
		Drogheda Traffic and Parking Bye-laws, S.I. No. 18 of 1971
		Dublin Traffic and Parking Bye-laws, S.I. No. 59 of 1971
		Dublin Parking Temporary Rules, S.I. No. 60 of 1971
		Dublin Traffic and Parking Temporary Rules, 1970 (Revocation) Rules, S.I. No. 91 of 1971
		Cork Traffic and Parking Temporary Rules, S.I. No. 94 of 1971
		New Ross Traffic and Parking Bye-laws, S.I. No. 101 of 1971
		Castlerea Parking Bye-laws, S.I. No. 102 of 1971
		Macroom Parking Bye-laws, S.I. No. 112 of 1971
		Ceanannus Mor Parking Bye-laws, S.I. No. 113 of 1971
		Galway Traffic and Parking Temporary Rules, S.I. No. 141 of 1971
		Killarney Traffic and Parking Temporary Rules, S.I. No. 153 of 1971
		Limerick Traffic and Parking (Clearway) Bye-laws, S.I. No. 160 of 1971
		Ballina Traffic and Parking Bye-laws, S.I. No. 165 of 1971
		Kilkenny Traffic and Parking Temporary Rules, S.I. No. 168 of 1971
		Mullingar Traffic and Parking Bye-laws, (1970) S.I. No. 178 of 1971
		Letterkenny Traffic and Parking Bye-laws, (1970) S.I. No. 179 of 1971
		Sligo Traffic and Parking Temporary Rules, S.I. No. 189 of 1971
		Arklow Traffic and Parking Bye-laws, S.I. No. 213 of 1971
		Youghal Traffic and Parking Bye-laws, S.I. No. 214 of 1971
		Midleton Traffic and Parking Bye-laws, S.I. No. 215 of 1971
		Loughrea Traffic and Parking Bye-laws, S.I. No. 224 of 1971
		Dublin Parking (No.2) Temporary Rules, S.I. No. 251 of 1971
		Rathkeale Parking Bye-laws, S.I. No. 260 of 1971

Statutory Authority	Section	Statutory Instrument
Road Traffic Act, No. 24 of 1961 (*Cont.*)		*Callan Traffic and Parking Bye-laws, S.I. No. 281 of 1971*
		Ballybunion Parking Bye-laws, S.I. No. 318 of 1971
		Dundalk Traffic and Parking Bye-laws, S.I. No. 340 of 1971
		Dublin Parking (Pedestrianisation) Temporary Rules, S.I. No. 1 of 1972
		Athlone Traffic and Parking Bye-laws, S.I. No. 2 of 1972
		Dublin Parking Temporary Rules, S.I. No. 58 of 1972
		Galway Traffic and Parking Temporary Rules, S.I. No. 110 of 1972
		Cork Traffic and Parking (Clearway) Bye-laws, S.I. No. 118 of 1972
		Naas Traffic and Parking Bye-laws, S.I. No. 126 of 1972
		Kilkenny Traffic and Parking Temporary Rules, S.I. No. 127 of 1972
		Killarney Traffic and Parking Temporary Rules, S.I. No. 140 of 1972
		Waterford Traffic and Parking Bye-laws, S.I. No. 144 of 1972
		Sligo Traffic and Parking Bye-laws, S.I. No. 154 of 1972
		Dungarvan Traffic and Parking Bye-laws, S.I. No. 336 of 1972
		Letterkenny Traffic and Parking Bye-laws, S.I. No. 337 of 1972
		Dublin Parking (Pedestrianisation) Temporary Rules (1972) S.I. No. 3 of 1973
		Newmarket-on-Fergus Parking Bye-laws (1972) S.I. No. 5 of 1973
		Carrick-on-Suir Traffic and Parking Bye-laws (1972) S.I. No. 6 of 1973
		Clarecastle Parking Bye-laws (1972) S.I. No. 7 of 1973
		Ballyhaunis Parking Bye-laws, S.I. No. 38 of 1973
		Dublin Parking Temporary Rules, S.I. No. 50 of 1973
		Dublin Traffic and Parking (Pedestrianisation) Temporary Rules, S.I. No. 92 of 1973
		Galway Traffic and Parking Temporary Rules, S.I. No. 101 of 1973
		Leixlip Traffic and Parking Bye-laws, S.I. No. 110 of 1973
		Newmarket-on-Fergus Parking Bye-laws, S.I. No. 113 of 1973
		Kilkenny Traffic and Parking Temporary Rules, S.I. No. 118 of 1973
		Killarney Traffic and Parking Temporary Rules, S.I. No. 137 of 1973

Statutory Authority	Section	Statutory Instrument
Road Traffic Act, No. 24 of 1961 (*Cont.*)		*Cashel Traffic and Parking Bye-laws, S.I. No. 145 of 1973*
		Listowel Traffic and Parking Bye-laws, S.I. No. 146 of 1973
		Collooney Traffic and Parking Bye-laws, S.I. No. 323 of 1973
		Kilmallock Traffic and Parking Bye-laws, S.I. No. 324 of 1973
		Monaghan Traffic and Parking Bye-laws, S.I. No. 352 of 1973
		Dublin Traffic and Parking (Pedestrianisation) (No.2) Temporary Rules, (1973) S.I. No. 1 of 1974
		Dublin Parking Temporary Rules, S.I. No. 35 of 1974
		Tubbercurry Traffic and Parking Bye-laws, S.I. No. 99 of 1974
		Galway Traffic and Parking Bye-laws, S.I. No. 124 of 1974
		Tramore Traffic and Parking Bye-laws, S.I. No. 142 of 1974
		Killarney Traffic and Parking Temporary Rules, S.I. No. 143 of 1974
		Bray Traffic and Parking Bye-laws, S.I. No. 152 of 1974
		Kilkenny Traffic and Parking Bye-laws, S.I. No. 153 of 1974
		Crosshaven Traffic and Parking Bye-laws, S.I. No. 154 of 1974
		Wexford Traffic and Parking Bye-laws, S.I. No. 165 of 1974
		Birr Traffic and Parking Bye-laws, S.I. No. 172 of 1974
		Lahinch Traffic and Parking Bye-laws, S.I. No. 177 of 1974
		Cork Parking Bye-laws, S.I. No. 249 of 1974
		Tuam Traffic and Parking Bye-laws, S.I. No. 291 of 1974
		Cavan Traffic and Parking Bye-laws, (1973) S.I. No. 326 of 1974
		Dingle Traffic and Parking Bye-laws, S.I. No. 9 of 1975
		Dublin Traffic and Parking (Pedestrianisation) Temporary Rules, S.I. No. 16 of 1975
		Dublin Parking Temporary Rules, S.I. No. 28 of 1975
		Fermoy Traffic and Parking Bye-laws, S.I. No. 56 of 1975
		Trim Traffic and Parking Bye-laws, S.I. No. 57 of 1975
		Ballinrobe Traffic and Parking Bye-laws, S.I. No. 82 of 1975

Statutory Authority	Section	Statutory Instrument
Road Traffic Act, No. 24 of 1961 *(Cont.)*		*Clifden Traffic and Parking Bye-laws, S.I. No. 89 of 1975*
		Manorhamilton Traffic and Parking Bye-laws, S.I. No. 90 of 1975
		Killarney Traffic and Parking Bye-laws, S.I. No. 132 of 1975
		Limerick Traffic and Parking Bye-laws, S.I. No. 204 of 1975
		Portumna Traffic and Parking Bye-laws, S.I. No. 208 of 1975
		Droichead Nua Traffic and Parking Bye-laws, S.I. No. 293 of 1975
		Athy Traffic and Parking Bye-laws, (1975) S.I. No. 37 of 1976
		Dublin Traffic and Parking Bye-laws, S.I. No. 83 of 1976
		Athlone Traffic and Parking Bye-laws, (1975) S.I. No. 134 of 1976
		Wicklow Traffic and Parking Bye-laws, S.I. No. 193 of 1976
		Cork Traffic and Parking (Pedestrianisation) Temporary Rules, S.I. No. 194 of 1976
		Clonmel Traffic and Parking Bye-laws, S.I. No. 248 of 1976
		Mountrath Traffic and Parking Bye-laws, S.I. No. 249 of 1976
		Castlerea Traffic and Parking Bye-laws, S.I. No. 256 of 1976
		Ballyshannon Traffic and Parking Bye-laws, S.I. No. 257 of 1976
		Clones Traffic and Parking Bye-laws, S.I. No. 271 of 1977
		Tullamore Traffic and Parking Bye-laws, S.I. No. 272 of 1977
		Knock Parking Temporary Rules, S.I. No. 165 of 1979
		Cork Parking Bye-laws, S.I. No. 195 of 1979
		Dublin Traffic and Parking Bye-laws, S.I. No. 82 of 1980
		Knock Parking Temporary Rules, S.I. No. 172 of 1980
		Dublin Traffic and Parking (No.2) Bye-laws, (1980) S.I. No. 49 of 1981
		Dublin Traffic and Parking Temporary Rules, S.I. No. 148 of 1981
		Knock Parking Temporary Rules, S.I. No. 210 of 1981
		Dublin Traffic and Parking (No.2) Temporary Rules, S.I. No. 401 of 1981
		Dublin Traffic and Parking Temporary Rules, S.I. No. 109 of 1982
		Knock Parking Temporary Rules, S.I. No. 223 of 1982

Statutory Authority	Section	Statutory Instrument
Road Traffic Act, No. 24 of 1961 *(Cont.)*		*Dublin Traffic and Parking (No.2) Temporary Rules, S.I. No. 287 of 1982*
		Dublin Traffic and Parking Temporary Rules, S.I. No. 105 of 1983
		Cork (County Borough and County) Traffic and Parking Temporary Rules, S.I. No. 3 of 1984
		Dublin Traffic and Parking Temporary Rules, S.I. No. 38 of 1984
		County of Carlow Traffic and Parking Temporary Rules, S.I. No. 148 of 1984
		County of Clare Traffic and Parking Temporary Rules, S.I. No. 149 of 1984
		County of Galway Traffic and Parking Temporary Rules, S.I. No. 150 of 1984
		County of Laois Traffic and Parking Temporary Rules, S.I. No. 151 of 1984
		Limerick (County Borough and County) Traffic and Parking Temporary Rules, S.I. No. 152 of 1984
		County of Louth Traffic and Parking Temporary Rules, S.I. No. 153 of 1984
		County of Tipperary North Riding and County of Tipperary South Riding Traffic and Parking Temporary Rules, S.I. No. 154 of 1984
		Dublin Traffic and Parking (No.2) Temporary Rules, S.I. No. 329 of 1984
		Cork (County Borough and County) Traffic and Parking Temporary Rules, S.I. No. 4 of 1985
		County of Carlow Traffic and Parking Temporary Rules, S.I. No. 193 of 1985
		County of Cavan Traffic and Parking Temporary Rules, S.I. No. 194 of 1985
		County of Clare Traffic and Parking Temporary Rules, S.I. No. 195 of 1985
		Cork (County Borough and County) Traffic and Parking (No.2) Temporary Rules, S.I. No. 196 of 1985
		County of Donegal Traffic and Parking Temporary Rules, S.I. No. 197 of 1985
		Dublin Area Traffic and Parking Temporary Rules, S.I. No. 198 of 1985
		County of Galway Traffic and Parking Temporary Rules, S.I. No. 199 of 1985
		County of Kerry Traffic and Parking Temporary Rules, S.I. No. 200 of 1985
		County of Kildare Traffic and Parking Temporary Rules, S.I. No. 201 of 1985
		County of Kilkenny Traffic and Parking Temporary Rules, S.I. No. 202 of 1985
		County of Laois Traffic and Parking Temporary Rules, S.I. No. 203 of 1985
		County of Leitrim Traffic and Parking Temporary Rules, S.I. No. 204 of 1985

Statutory Authority	Section	Statutory Instrument
Road Traffic Act, No. 24 of 1961 *(Cont.)*		*Limerick (County Borough and County) Traffic and Parking Temporary Rules, S.I. No. 205 of 1985*
		County of Longford Traffic and Parking Temporary Rules, S.I. No. 206 of 1985
		County of Louth Traffic and Parking Temporary Rules, S.I. No. 207 of 1985
		County of Mayo Traffic and Parking Temporary Rules, S.I. No. 208 of 1985
		County of Meath Traffic and Parking Temporary Rules, S.I. No. 209 of 1985
		County of Monaghan Traffic and Parking Temporary Rules, S.I. No. 210 of 1985
		County of Offaly Traffic and Parking Temporary Rules, S.I. No. 211 of 1985
		County of Roscommon Traffic and Parking Temporary Rules, S.I. No. 212 of 1985
		County of Sligo Traffic and Parking Temporary Rules, S.I. No. 213 of 1985
		County of Tipperary North Riding and County of Tipperary South Riding Traffic and Parking Temporary Rules, S.I. No. 214 of 1985
		Waterford (County Borough and County) Traffic and Parking Temporary Rules, S.I. No. 215 of 1985
		County of Westmeath Traffic and Parking Temporary Rules, S.I. No. 216 of 1985
		County of Wexford Traffic and Parking Temporary Rules, S.I. No. 217 of 1985
		County of Wicklow Traffic and Parking Temporary Rules, S.I. No. 218 of 1985
		Limerick (County Borough and County) Traffic and Parking (No.2) Temporary Rules, S.I. No. 240 of 1985
		Waterford (County Borough and County) Traffic and Parking (No.2) Temporary Rules, S.I. No. 241 of 1985
		County of Carlow Traffic and Parking Bye-laws, S.I. No. 177 of 1986
		County of Cavan Traffic and Parking Bye-laws, S.I. No. 178 of 1986
		County of Clare Traffic and Parking Bye-laws, S.I. No. 179 of 1986
		Cork (County Borough and County) Traffic and Parking Bye-laws, S.I. No. 180 of 1986
		County of Donegal Traffic and Parking Bye-laws, S.I. No. 181 of 1986
		Dublin Area Traffic and Parking Bye-laws, S.I. No. 182 of 1986
		Galway (County Borough and County) Traffic and Parking Bye-laws, S.I. No. 183 of 1986
		County of Kerry Traffic and Parking Bye-laws, S.I. No. 184 of 1986

Road Traffic Act, No. 24 of 1961
(*Cont.*)

County of Kildare Traffic and Parking Bye-laws, S.I. No. 185 of 1986

County of Kilkenny Traffic and Parking Bye-laws, S.I. No. 186 of 1986

County of Laois Traffic and Parking Bye-laws, S.I. No. 187 of 1986

County of Leitrim Traffic and Parking Bye-laws, S.I. No. 188 of 1986

Limerick (County Borough and County) Traffic and Parking Bye-laws, S.I. No. 189 of 1986

County of Longford Traffic and Parking Bye-laws, S.I. No. 190 of 1986

County of Louth Traffic and Parking Bye-laws, S.I. No. 191 of 1986

County of Mayo Traffic and Parking Bye-laws, S.I. No. 192 of 1986

County of Meath Traffic and Parking Bye-laws, S.I. No. 193 of 1986

County of Monaghan Traffic and Parking Bye-laws, S.I. No. 194 of 1986

County of Offaly Traffic and Parking Bye-laws, S.I. No. 195 of 1986

County of Roscommon Traffic and Parking Bye-laws, S.I. No. 196 of 1986

County of Sligo Traffic and Parking Bye-laws, S.I. No. 197 of 1986

County of Tipperary North Riding and County of Tipperary South Riding Traffic and Parking Bye-laws, S.I. No. 198 of 1986

Waterford (County Borough and County) Traffic and Parking Bye-laws, S.I. No. 199 of 1986

County of Westmeath Traffic and Parking Bye-laws, 19868, S.I. No. 200 of 1986

County of Wexford Traffic and Parking Bye-laws, S.I. No. 201 of 1986

County of Wicklow Traffic and Parking Bye-laws, S.I. No. 202 of 1986

90(3)(b)   *Dublin Meter Parking Places Rules, S.I. No. 261 of 1969*

Dublin Meter Parking Places Rules, S.I. No. 26 of 1979

Dublin Meter Parking Places Rules, S.I. No. 265 of 1983

Dublin Meter Parking Places Rules, S.I. No. 27 of 1985

90(7)   **Road Traffic (Bye-laws and Temporary Rules) Regulations, S.I. No. 219 of 1961**

Dublin Parking Temporary Rules, S.I. No. 30 of 1964

Limerick Parking Temporary Rules, S.I. No. 181 of 1966

Statutory Authority	Section	Statutory Instrument
Road Traffic Act, No. 24 of 1961 (*Cont.*)		*Dublin Traffic and Parking Temporary Rules, S.I. No. 257 of 1966*
		Arklow Parking Temporary Rules, S.I. No. 148 of 1967
		Cork Parking Temporary Rules, S.I. No. 164 of 1967
		Carrick-on-Shannon Parking Temporary Rules, S.I. No. 168 of 1967
		Drogheda Parking Temporary Rules, S.I. No. 171 of 1967
		Limerick Parking Temporary Rules, S.I. No. 185 of 1967
		Skibbereen Parking Temporary Rules, S.I. No. 207 of 1967
		Carlow Traffic and Parking Temporary Rules, S.I. No. 214 of 1967
		Dublin Traffic and Parking (Amendment) Temporary Rules, S.I. No. 221 of 1967
		Dublin Traffic and Parking Temporary Rules, S.I. No. 259 of 1967
		Ballybay Parking Temporary Rules (1967) S.I. No. 6 of 1968
		Ceanannus Mor Parking Temporary Rules (1967) S.I. No. 7 of 1968
		Limerick Traffic and Parking Temporary Rules, S.I. No. 38 of 1968
		Mullingar Parking Temporary Rules, S.I. No. 83 of 1968
		Dublin Parking Temporary Rules, S.I. No. 86 of 1968
		Kilkenny Parking Temporary Rules, S.I. No. 108 of 1968
		Arklow Parking Temporary Rules, S.I. No. 118 of 1968
		Loughrea Parking Temporary Rules, S.I. No. 122 of 1968
		Cork Parking Temporary Rules, S.I. No. 141 of 1968
		Carrick-on-Shannon Parking Temporary Rules, S.I. No. 150 of 1968
		Drogheda Parking Temporary Rules, S.I. No. 152 of 1968
		Limerick Parking Temporary Rules, S.I. No. 162 of 1968
		Skibbereen Parking Temporary Rules, S.I. No. 200 of 1968
		Carlow Traffic and Parking Temporary Rules, S.I. No. 211 of 1968
		Dublin Traffic and Parking Temporary Rules, S.I. No. 242 of 1968
		Dublin Parking (Amendment) Temporary Rules, S.I. No. 268 of 1968

Statutory Authority	Section	Statutory Instrument
Road Traffic Act, No. 24 of 1961 (*Cont.*)		*Ceanannus Mor Parking Temporary Rules, S.I. No. 4 of 1969*
		Ballybay Parking Temporary Rules, S.I. No. 24 of 1969
		Limerick Traffic and Parking Temporary Rules, S.I. No. 30 of 1969
		New Ross Traffic and Parking Temporary Rules, S.I. No. 37 of 1969
		Dublin Parking Temporary Rules, S.I. No. 71 of 1969
		Kilkenny Parking Temporary Rules, S.I. No. 78 of 1969
		Mullingar Parking Temporary Rules, S.I. No. 79 of 1969
		Loughrea Parking Temporary Rules, S.I. No. 99 of 1969
		Arklow Parking Temporary Rules, S.I. No. 100 of 1969
		Cork Parking Temporary Rules, S.I. No. 115 of 1969
		Carrick-on-Shannon Parking Temporary Rules, S.I. No. 131 of 1969
		Drogheda Parking Temporary Rules, S.I. No. 132 of 1969
		Bundoran Parking Temporary Rules, S.I. No. 148 of 1969
		Limerick Parking Temporary Rules, S.I. No. 149 of 1969
		Skibbereen Parking Temporary Rules, S.I. No. 179 of 1969
		Dublin Traffic and Parking Temporary Rules, S.I. No. 239 of 1969
		Mullingar Parking Temporary Rules, S.I. No. 105 of 1970
		Kilkenny Parking Temporary Rules, S.I. No. 106 of 1970
		Arklow Parking Temporary Rules, S.I. No. 122 of 1970
		Loughrea Parking Temporary Rules, S.I. No. 129 of 1970
		Cork Parking Temporary Rules, S.I. No. 147 of 1970
		Limerick Parking Temporary Rules, S.I. No. 193 of 1970
		Dublin Traffic and Parking Temporary Rules, S.I. No. 290 of 1970
		Cork Parking Temporary Rules, S.I. No. 190 of 1971
		Limerick Parking Temporary Rules, S.I. No. 240 of 1971
		Cork Parking Temporary Rules, S.I. No. 155 of 1972

Statutory Authority	Section	Statutory Instrument
Road Traffic Act, No. 24 of 1961 (*Cont.*)		*Limerick Parking Temporary Rules, S.I. No. 208 of 1972*
		Cork Parking Temporary Rules, S.I. No. 166 of 1973
		Limerick Parking Temporary Rules, S.I. No. 247 of 1973
		Cork Parking Temporary Rules, S.I. No. 188 of 1974
		Limerick Parking Temporary Rules, S.I. No. 257 of 1974
		Cork Parking Temporary Rules, 1974 (Revocation) Rules, S.I. No. 34 of 1975
		Cork Parking Temporary Rules, S.I. No. 225 of 1983
		Knock Parking Temporary Rules, S.I. No. 226 of 1983
	90(8)	*Arklow Parking Temporary Rules, S.I. No. 148 of 1967*
		Carrick-on-Shannon Parking Temporary Rules, S.I. No. 168 of 1967
		Drogheda Parking Temporary Rules, S.I. No. 171 of 1967
		Skibbereen Parking Temporary Rules, S.I. No. 207 of 1967
		Carlow Traffic and Parking Temporary Rules, S.I. No. 214 of 1967
		Ballybay Parking Temporary Rules (1967) S.I. No. 6 of 1968
		Ceanannus Mor Parking Temporary Rules (1967) S.I. No. 7 of 1968
		Kilkenny Parking Temporary Rules, S.I. No. 108 of 1968
		Arklow Parking Temporary Rules, S.I. No. 118 of 1968
		Loughrea Parking Temporary Rules, S.I. No. 122 of 1968
		Carrick-on-Shannon Parking Temporary Rules, S.I. No. 150 of 1968
		Drogheda Parking Temporary Rules, S.I. No. 152 of 1968
		Skibbereen Parking Temporary Rules, S.I. No. 200 of 1968
		Carlow Traffic and Parking Temporary Rules, S.I. No. 211 of 1968
		Ceanannus Mor Parking Temporary Rules, S.I. No. 4 of 1969
		Ballybay Parking Temporary Rules, S.I. No. 24 of 1969
		New Ross Traffic and Parking Temporary Rules, S.I. No. 37 of 1969
	91	**Road Traffic (Signs) (Amendment) Regulations, S.I. No. 217 of 1969**

Statutory Authority	Section	Statutory Instrument
Road Traffic Act, No. 24 of 1961 (*Cont.*)	103	*Road Traffic Act, 1961 (Section 103) (Offences) (Amendment) Regulations, S.I. No. 191 of 1964*
		Road Traffic Act, 1961 (Section 103) (Offences) (Amendment) Regulations, S.I. No. 4 of 1970
		Road Traffic Act, 1961 (Section 103) (Offences) (Amendment) Regulations, S.I. No. 12 of 1971
		Road Traffic Act, 1961 (Section 103) (Offences) (Amendment) Regulations, S.I. No. 246 of 1974
		Road Traffic Act, 1961 (Section 103) (Offences) (Amendment) Regulations, S.I. No. 158 of 1975
		Road Traffic Act, 1961 (Section 103) (Offences) Regulations, S.I. No. 188 of 1976
		Road Traffic Act, 1961 (Section 103) (Offences) (Amendment) Regulations, S.I. No. 167 of 1979
		Road Traffic Act, 1961 (Section 103) (Offences) (Amendment) Regulations, S.I. No. 90 of 1983
		Road Traffic Act, 1961 (Section 103) (Offences) (Amendment) Regulations, S.I. No. 255 of 1985
		Road Traffic Act, 1961 (Section 103) (Offences) (Amendment) Regulations, S.I. No. 443 of 1986
	103(1)	*Road Traffic Act, 1961 (Section 103) (Offences) Regulations, S.I. No. 91 of 1962*
	103(2)	*Road Traffic Act, 1961 (Section 103) (Offences) Regulations, S.I. No. 91 of 1962*
	103(3)	*Road Traffic Act, 1961 (Section 103) (Offences) Regulations, S.I. No. 91 of 1962*
	121	**Road Traffic (Passenger Accommodation of Mechanically Propelled Vehicles) Regulations, S.I. No. 143 of 1962**
	122	*Road Traffic (Petroleum) Regulations, S.I. No. 174 of 1964*
	123	**Mechanically Propelled Vehicles (International Circulation) (Amendment) Order, S.I. No. 12 of 1962**
		Road Vehicles (Registration and Licensing) Regulations, S.I. No. 311 of 1982
Road Traffic Act, No. 25 of 1968	3	*Road Traffic Act, 1968 (Commencement) Order, S.I. No. 169 of 1968*
	4	*Road Traffic Act, 1968 (Commencement) (No.2) Order, S.I. No. 195 of 1969*
		Road Traffic Act, 1968 (Commencement) Order, S.I. No. 244 of 1970
		Road Traffic Act, 1968 (Commencement) Order, S.I. No. 6 of 1971
	5	*Road Traffic Act, 1968 (Commencement) Order, S.I. No. 169 of 1968*
		Road Traffic (Speed Limits) (County of Louth) (Amendment) Regulations, S.I. No. 83 of 1971
		Road Traffic (Speed Limits) (County of Donegal) Regulations, S.I. No. 267 of 1977

Statutory Authority	Section	Statutory Instrument
Road Traffic Act, No. 25 of 1968 (*Cont.*)	10	**Road Traffic (Licensing of Trailers and Semi-trailers) Regulations, S.I. No. 35 of 1982**
		Road Traffic (Licensing of Trailers and Semi-trailers) (Amendment) Regulations, S.I. No. 127 of 1983
	28	*Road Traffic Act, 1968 (Part V) Regulations, S.I. No. 196 of 1969*
		Road Traffic Act, 1968 (Part V) (Amendment) (No.2) Regulations, S.I. No. 221 of 1973
		Road Traffic Act, 1968 (Part V) (Amendment) Regulations, S.I. No. 240 of 1976
	30	*Road Traffic Act, 1968 (Part V) Regulations, S.I. No. 196 of 1969*
		Road Traffic Act, 1968 (Part V) (Amendment) Regulations, S.I. No. 138 of 1973
		Road Traffic Act, 1968 (Part V) (Amendment) (No.2) Regulations, S.I. No. 221 of 1973
	33	*Road Traffic Act, 1968 (Part V) Regulations, S.I. No. 196 of 1969*
		Road Traffic Act, 1968 (Part V) (Amendment) Regulations, S.I. No. 138 of 1973
		Road Traffic Act, 1968 (Part V) (Amendment) (No.2) Regulations, S.I. No. 221 of 1973
	36	*Road Traffic Act, 1968 (Part V) Regulations, S.I. No. 196 of 1969*
	37	**Medical Bureau of Road Safety (Establishment) Order, S.I. No. 241 of 1968**
		Medical Bureau of Road Safety (Establishment) Order, 1968 (Amendment) Order, S.I. No. 364 of 1983
	39	**Medical Bureau of Road Safety (Establishment) Order, S.I. No. 241 of 1968**
		Medical Bureau of Road Safety (Establishment) Order, 1968 (Amendment) Order, S.I. No. 364 of 1983
	40	**Medical Bureau of Road Safety (Establishment) Order, S.I. No. 241 of 1968**
		Medical Bureau of Road Safety (Establishment) Order, 1968 (Amendment) Order, S.I. No. 364 of 1983
	43	*Road Traffic Act, 1968 (Part V) Regulations, S.I. No. 196 of 1969*
		Road Traffic Act, 1968 (Part V) (Amendment) Regulations, S.I. No. 138 of 1973
		Road Traffic Act, 1968 (Part V) (Amendment) (No.2) Regulations, S.I. No. 221 of 1973
		Road Traffic Act, 1968 (Part V) (Amendment) Regulations, S.I. No. 336 of 1974
		Road Traffic Act, 1968 (Part V) (Amendment) Regulations, S.I. No. 240 of 1976

Statutory Authority	Section	Statutory Instrument
Road Traffic Act, No. 25 of 1968 (*Cont.*)	45	*Road Traffic Act, 1968 (Commencement) Order, S.I. No. 139 of 1969*
		Road Traffic Act, 1968 (Part V) Regulations, S.I. No. 196 of 1969
		Road Traffic (Speed Limits) (County of Louth) (Amendment) Regulations, S.I. No. 83 of 1971
		Road Traffic Act, 1968 (Part V) (Amendment) Regulations, S.I. No. 138 of 1973
		Road Traffic (Speed Limits) (County of Donegal) Regulations, S.I. No. 267 of 1977
	46	*Road Traffic Act, 1968 (Part V) Regulations, S.I. No. 196 of 1969*
		Road Traffic (Speed Limits) (County of Louth) (Amendment) Regulations, S.I. No. 83 of 1971
		Road Traffic Act, 1968 (Part V) (Amendment) (No.2) Regulations, S.I. No. 221 of 1973
		Road Traffic (Speed Limits) (County of Donegal) Regulations, S.I. No. 267 of 1977
	47	*Road Traffic Act, 1968 (Part V) Regulations, S.I. No. 196 of 1969*
		Road Traffic Act, 1968 (Part V) (Amendment) Regulations, S.I. No. 138 of 1973
		Road Traffic Act, 1968 (Part V) (Amendment) (No.2) Regulations, S.I. No. 221 of 1973
		Road Traffic Act, 1968 (Part V) (Amendment) Regulations, S.I. No. 336 of 1974
		Road Traffic Act, 1968 (Part V) (Amendment) Regulations, S.I. No. 240 of 1976
	60	**Road Traffic General Bye-laws (Amendment) Regulations, S.I. No. 281 of 1975**
		Road Traffic General Bye-laws (Amendment) Regulations, S.I. No. 275 of 1983
Road Traffic (Amendment) Act, No. 19 of 1978	4	*Road Traffic (Amendment) Act, 1978 (Commencement) Order, S.I. No. 192 of 1978*
	26	**Road Traffic (Amendment) Act, 1978 (Part III) Regulations, S.I. No. 193 of 1978**
		Road Traffic (Amendment) Act, 1978 (Part III) Regulations, S.I. No. 363 of 1983
Road Transport Act, No. 2 of 1932	3	*Road Transport Order [Vol. XIX p. 1089] S.R.& O. No. 23 of 1932*
	4	**Road Transport Regulations [Vol. XIX p. 1093] S.R.& O. No. 26 of 1932**
		Road Transport (Road Transport Act, 1932) Regulations [Vol. XIX p. 1107] S.R.& O. No. 135 of 1933
		Road Transport (Road Transport Act, 1932) Regulations [Vol. XXXVIII p. 395] S.R.& O. No. 201 of 1946
		Road Transport (Road Transport Act, 1932) Regulations [Vol. XXXVIII p. 401] S.R.& O. No. 82 of 1947

Statutory Authority	Section	Statutory Instrument
Road Transport Act, No. 2 of 1932 (*Cont.*)		*Road Transport Act, 1932 Regulations, S.I. No. 64 of 1949*
		Road Transport Act, 1932 Regulations, S.I. No. 68 of 1955
	23	**Road Transport Act, 1932 Regulations, S.I. No. 256 of 1951**
		Road Transport Act, 1932 Regulations, S.I. No. 242 of 1952
		Road Transport Act, 1932 Regulations, S.I. No. 64 of 1953
		Road Transport Act, 1932 Regulations, S.I. No. 118 of 1956
		Road Transport Act, 1932 Regulations, S.I. No. 147 of 1960
		Road Transport Act, 1932 Regulations, S.I. No. 272 of 1961
		Road Transport Act, 1932 Regulations, S.I. No. 203 of 1962
		Road Transport Act, 1932 Regulations, S.I. No. 57 of 1964
Road Transport Act, No. 8 of 1933		**Railway Tribunal (Additional) Rules [Vol. XIX p. 295] S.R.& O. No. 659 of 1935**
	5(1)	*Road Transport Act, 1933 (Appointed Day) Order, S.R.& O. No. 126 of 1933*
		Road Transport Act, 1933 (Appointed Day) Order, S.R.& O. No. 140 of 1934
	6	**Road Transport Act, 1933 (Part II) Regulations Order, S.R.& O. No. 120 of 1933**
		Road Transport Act, 1933 (Part V) Regulations, S.R.& O. No. 119 of 1933
		Road Transport Act, 1933 (Section 29) Regulations, S.R.& O. No. 173 of 1934
		Road Transport Act, 1933 (Part II) Regulations (Amendment) Order, S.R.& O. No. 316 of 1937
		Road Transport Act, 1933 (Part II) Regulations, S.I. No. 8 of 1952
		Road Transport Act, 1933 Regulations, S.I. No. 69 of 1955
		Road Transport Act, 1971 (Fees) Regulations, S.I. No. 183 of 1971
		Road Transport Acts (Fees) Regulations, S.I. No. 256 of 1977
		Road Transport Acts (Fees) Regulations, S.I. No. 277 of 1982
		Road Transport Act, 1986 (Merchandise Licence Application Form) Regulations, S.I. No. 302 of 1986
		Road Transport Acts (Fees) Regulations, S.I. No. 312 of 1986
		Road Transport Act, 1933 (Part II) (Amendment) Regulations, S.I. No. 315 of 1986
	10	*Road Transport (Vehicle Plate Issuing Stations) Order [Vol. XIX p. 1199] S.R.& O. No. 125 of 1933*

Statutory Authority	Section	Statutory Instrument
Road Transport Act, No. 8 of 1933 *(Cont.)*		*Road Transport (Vehicle Plate Issuing Stations) (Amendment) Order [Vol. XIX p. 1203] S.R.& O. No. 180 of 1933*
		Road Transport (Vehicle Plate Issuing Stations) Order, S.I. No. 106 of 1986
	30(7)	**Road Transport Act, 1933 (Part II) (Amendment) Regulations, S.I. No. 315 of 1986**
	34(1)	**Road Transport Act, 1933 (Part II) (Amendment) Regulations, S.I. No. 315 of 1986**
	47(2)	**Railway Tribunal (Road Transport) Fees Order [Vol. XIX p. 1209] S.R.& O. No. 265 of 1935**
Road Transport Act, No. 8 of 1971	6	**Road Transport Act, 1971 (Fees) Regulations, S.I. No. 183 of 1971**
		Road Transport Acts (Fees) Regulations, S.I. No. 256 of 1977
		Road Transport Acts (Fees) Regulations, S.I. No. 277 of 1982
		Road Transport Acts (Fees) Regulations, S.I. No. 312 of 1986
	8(2)	**Road Transport (International Road Haulage) Order, S.I. No. 25 of 1974**
		Road Transport (International Carriage of Goods by Road) Order, S.I. No. 48 of 1976
		Road Transport (International Carriage of Goods by Road) Order, S.I. No. 106 of 1977
		Road Transport (International Carriage of Goods by Road) (No.2) Order, S.I. No. 258 of 1977
		Road Transport (International Carriage of Goods by Road) Order, S.I. No. 159 of 1980
		Road Transport (International Carriage of Goods by Road) Order, S.I. No. 153 of 1981
		Road Transport (International Carriage of Goods by Road) (No.2) Order, S.I. No. 216 of 1981
		Road Transport (International Carriage of Goods by Road) (No.3) Order, S.I. No. 325 of 1981
		Road Transport (International Carriage of Goods by Road) (No.4) Order, S.I. No. 326 of 1981
		Road Transport (International Carriage of Goods by Road) Order, S.I. No. 42 of 1982
		Road Transport (International Carriage of Goods by Road) (No.2) Order, S.I. No. 270 of 1982
	11	*Road Transport Act, 1971 (Commencement) Order, S.I. No. 166 of 1971*
Road Transport Act, No. 8 of 1978	5	**Road Transport Act, 1978 (Section 5) Order, S.I. No. 160 of 1980**
		Road Transport Act, 1978 (Section 5) Order, S.I. No. 152 of 1981
		Road Transport Act, 1978 (Section 5) (No.2) Order, S.I. No. 323 of 1981
		Road Transport Act, 1978 (Section 5) (No.3) Order, S.I. No. 324 of 1981
		Road Transport Act, 1978 (Section 5) Order, S.I. No. 41 of 1982

Statutory Authority	Section	Statutory Instrument
Road Transport Act, No. 8 of 1978 (*Cont.*)		**Road Transport Act, 1978 (Section 5) (No.2) Order, S.I. No. 267 of 1982**
		Road Transport Act, 1978 (Section 5) (No.3) Order, S.I. No. 268 of 1982
		Road Transport Act, 1978 (Section 5) (No.4) Order, S.I. No. 269 of 1982
		Road Transport Act, 1978 (Section 5) Order, S.I. No. 331 of 1983
		Road Transport Act, 1978 (Section 5) (No.2) Order, S.I. No. 332 of 1983
Road Transport Act, No. 16 of 1986	10	**Road Transport Acts (Fees) Regulations, S.I. No. 312 of 1986**
	21	*Road Transport Act, 1986 (Commencement) Order, S.I. No. 240 of 1986*
		Road Transport Act, 1986 (Commencement) (No.2) Order, S.I. No. 313 of 1986
		Road Transport Act, 1986 (Commencement) (No.3) Order, S.I. No. 454 of 1986
Roads Act, No. 72 of 1920		*Road Vehicles (Additional Index Mark) Order, S.I. No. 282 of 1948*
		Road Vehicles (Additional Index Mark) Order, S.I. No. 42 of 1949
		Road Vehicles (Additional Index Mark) Order, S.I. No. 121 of 1950
		Road Vehicles (Additional Index Mark) Order, S.I. No. 229 of 1951
		Road Vehicles (Additional Index Mark) (No.2) Order, S.I. No. 370 of 1951
		Road Vehicles (Additional Index Mark) Order, S.I. No. 171 of 1953
		Road Vehicles (Additional Index Mark) (No.2) Order, S.I. No. 411 of 1953
		Road Vehicles (Additional Index Marks) Order, S.I. No. 95 of 1954
		Road Vehicles (Additional Index Marks) (No.2) Order, S.I. No. 178 of 1954
	1	**Road Vehicles (Registration and Licensing) Order, S.I. No. 15 of 1958**
	3(1)	*Road Fund Accounts Order [Vol. XIX p. 567] S.R.& O. No. 12 of 1924*
	5	**Road Vehicles (Registration and Licensing) Regulations, S.I. No. 13 of 1958**
		Road Vehicles (Registration and Licensing) (Amendment) Regulations, S.I. No. 217 of 1959
		Road Vehicles (Registration and Licensing) (Amendment) (No.3) Regulations, S.I. No. 371 of 1977
		Road Vehicles (Registration and Licensing) Regulations, S.I. No. 311 of 1982
		Road Vehicles (Registration and Licensing) (Amendment) Regulations, S.I. No. 293 of 1985
		Road Vehicles (Registration and Licensing) (Amendment) Regulations, S.I. No. 441 of 1986

Statutory Authority	Section	Statutory Instrument
Roads Act, No. 72 of 1920 (*Cont.*)	6	*Road Vehicles (Additional Index Marks) Order, S.I. No. 154 of 1955*
		Road Vehicles (Additional Index Marks) (No.2) Order, S.I. No. 249 of 1955
		Road Vehicles (Registration and Licensing) Regulations, S.I. No. 13 of 1958
		Road Vehicles (Registration and Licensing) (Amendment) Regulations, S.I. No. 340 of 1974
		Road Vehicles (Registration and Licensing) (Amendment) Regulations, S.I. No. 38 of 1976
		Road Vehicles (Registration and Licensing) (Amendment) Regulations, S.I. No. 122 of 1977
		Road Vehicles (Registration and Licensing) (Amendment) (No.2) Regulations, S.I. No. 185 of 1977
		Road Vehicles (Registration and Licensing) (Amendment) (No.3) Regulations, S.I. No. 371 of 1977
		Road Vehicles (Registration and Licensing) Regulations, S.I. No. 311 of 1982
		Road Vehicles (Registration and Licensing) (Amendment) Regulations, S.I. No. 293 of 1985
		Road Vehicles (Registration and Licensing) (Amendment) Regulations, S.I. No. 441 of 1986
	9	**Road Vehicles (Registration and Licensing) Regulations, S.I. No. 13 of 1958**
	12	**Road Vehicles (Seating Capacity) Regulations [Vol. XIX p. 569] S.R.& O. No. 56 of 1929**
		Road Vehicles (International Circulation) Regulations [Vol. XII p. 203] S.R.& O. No. 50 of 1932
		Road Vehicles (Seating Capacity) Regulations [Vol. XIX p. 575] S.R.& O. No. 98 of 1932
		Road Vehicles (International Circulation) Regulations [Vol. XII p. 233] S.R.& O. No. 119 of 1934
		Road Vehicles (International Circulation) (Amendment) Regulations [Vol. XII p. 265] S.R.& O. No. 98 of 1937
		Road Vehicles (Registration and Licensing) Regulations [Vol. XIX p. 581] S.R.& O. No. 64 of 1938
		Road Vehicles (International Circulation) (Amendment) Regulations [Vol. XII p. 269] S.R.& O. No. 190 of 1938
		Road Vehicles (Seating Capacity) Regulations, 1932 (Revocation) Order, S.I. No. 356 of 1952
		Road Vehicles (Registration and Licensing) (Amendment) Regulations, S.I. No. 358 of 1952
		Road Vehicles (Additional Index Marks) Order, S.I. No. 154 of 1955

Roads Act, No. 72 of 1920 (*Cont.*)

Road Vehicles (Additional Index Marks) (No.2) Order, S.I. No. 249 of 1955

Road Vehicles (Additional Index Marks) Regulations, S.I. No. 254 of 1956

Road Vehicles (Additional Index Marks) (No.2) Regulations, S.I. No. 265 of 1956

Road Vehicles (Additional Index Marks) Regulations, S.I. No. 165 of 1957

Road Vehicles (Registration and Licensing) Regulations, S.I. No. 13 of 1958

Road Vehicles (Index Marks) Regulations, S.I. No. 14 of 1958

Road Vehicles (Index Marks) (Amendment) Regulations, S.I. No. 132 of 1958

Road Vehicles (Registration and Licensing) (Amendment) Regulations, S.I. No. 198 of 1958

Road Vehicles (Index Marks) (Amendment) (No.2) Regulations, S.I. No. 248 of 1958

Road Vehicles (Index Marks) (Amendment) Regulations, S.I. No. 8 of 1959

Road Vehicles (Index Marks) (Amendment) (No.2) Regulations, S.I. No. 107 of 1959

Road Vehicles (Index Marks) (Amendment) (No.3) Regulations, S.I. No. 136 of 1959

Road Vehicles (Registration and Licensing) (Amendment) Regulations, S.I. No. 217 of 1959

Road Vehicles (Index Marks) (Amendment) Regulations, S.I. No. 46 of 1960

Road Vehicles (Registration and Licensing) (Amendment) Regulations, S.I. No. 84 of 1960

Road Vehicles (Registration and Licensing) (Amendment) (No.2) Regulations, S.I. No. 196 of 1960

Road Vehicles (Index Marks) (Amendment) (No.2) Regulations, S.I. No. 244 of 1960

Mechanically Propelled Vehicles (International Circulation) Order, S.I. No. 269 of 1961

Road Vehicles (Index Marks) (Amendment) Regulations, S.I. No. 283 of 1961

Mechanically Propelled Vehicles (International Circulation) (Amendment) Order, S.I. No. 12 of 1962

Road Vehicles (Registration and Licensing) (Amendment) Regulations, S.I. No. 13 of 1962

Road Vehicles (Index Marks) (Amendment) Regulations, S.I. No. 69 of 1963

Road Vehicles (Index Marks) (Amendment) Regulations, S.I. No. 8 of 1964

Road Vehicles (Index Marks) (Amendment) Regulations, S.I. No. 30 of 1965

Road Vehicles (Index Marks) (Amendment) Regulations, S.I. No. 128 of 1967

Statutory Authority	Section	Statutory Instrument
aint Laurence's Hospital Act, No. 3 f 1943 (*Cont.*)	5(4)	**Saint Laurence's Hospital (Constitution of Board of Governors) Order, S.I. No. 40 of 1950**
	22	**Saint Laurence's Hospital (Acquisition of Land) Order [Vol. XXXIII p. 619] S.R.& O. No. 167 of 1945**
aint Stephen's Green (Dublin) Act, No. 134 of 1877(Private)		**Saint Stephen's Green Bye-laws, S.I. No. 175 of 1962**
ale of Food and Drugs Act, No. 51 f 1899	4	*Sale of Milk (Ireland) Regulations, 1901 (Revocation) Regulations [Vol. XX p. 1] S.R.& O. No. 79 of 1936*
ale of Food and Drugs (Milk) Act, No. 3 of 1935	2	*Milk (Percentage of Milk-fat and Milk-solids) Regulations [Vol. XX p. 5] S.R.& O. No. 77 of 1936*
		Milk (Percentage of Milk-fat and Milk-solids) (No.2) Regulations [Vol. XX p. 11] S.R.& O. No. 321 of 1936
	2(3)	*Sale of Food and Drugs (Milk) Act, 1935 (Section 2, Appointed Day) Order [Vol. XX p. 17] S.R.& O. No. 78 of 1936*
ale of Food and Drugs (Milk) Act, No. 44 of 1936	3	**Sale of Food and Drugs (Milk Sampling) Regulations [Vol. XX p. 21] S.R.& O. No. 312 of 1936**
		Sale of Food and Drugs (Milk Sampling) (Amendment) Regulations [Vol. XXXIII p. 629] S.R.& O. No. 246 of 1941
almon Conservancy Fund Act, No. 4 of 1954		*Salmon Export Levy Order, S.I. No. 52 of 1954*
		Salmon Export Levy Regulations, S.I. No. 53 of 1954
		Salmon Export Levy (Revocation) Order, S.I. No. 289 of 1954
		Salmon Export Levy Order, S.I. No. 115 of 1957
		Salmon Export Levy Regulations, S.I. No. 116 of 1957
Savings Bank (Barrister) Act, No. 52 of 1876	2(2)	**Savings Banks (Disputes) Order, S.I. No. 19 of 1966**
Savings Banks Act, No. 12 of 1920	1	**Post Office Savings Bank (Limit of Deposits) Order, S.I. No. 90 of 1958**
		Post Office Savings Bank (Limit of Deposits) Order, S.I. No. 171 of 1961
		Post Office Savings Bank (Limit of Deposits) Order, 1961 (Revocation) Order, S.I. No. 62 of 1969
Savings Banks Act, No. 23 of 1958	5(2)	**Trustee Savings Banks Regulations, S.I. No. 275 of 1958**
Scholarship Exchange (Ireland and the United States of America) Act, No. 24 of 1957	19	*Scholarship Exchange (Ireland and the United States of America) Act, 1957 (Commencement) Order, S.I. No. 270 of 1957*
School Attendance Act, No. 17 of 1926		**School Attendance (Hours of Attendance) Order [Vol. XXXIII p. 614] S.R.& O. No. 356 of 1943**

Statutory Authority	Section	Statutory Instrument
School Attendance Act, No. 17 of 1926 *(Cont.)*	9	**School Attendance (Constitution of Areas) Order [Vol. XX p. 43] S.R.& O. No. 77 of 1926**
		School Attendance (Variation of Areas) Order, (1929) [Vol. XX p. 95] S.R.& O. No. 20 of 1930
	10	**School Attendance Committees Order [Vol. XX p. 185] S.R.& O. No. 94 of 1930**
		School Attendance (Dublin City School Attendance Committees) (No.2) Order [Vol. XXXIII p. 635] S.R.& O. No. 78 of 1943
		School Attendance (Dun Laoghaire Borough School Attendance Committees) Order, S.I. No. 50 of 1949
		School Attendance (Dublin City School Attendance Committees) Order, S.I. No. 259 of 1950
		School Attendance (Cork City School Attendance Committees) Order, S.I. No. 260 of 1950
		School Attendance (Dun Laoghaire Borough School Attendance Committees) Order, S.I. No. 261 of 1950
		School Attendance (Waterford City School Attendance Committees) Order, S.I. No. 262 of 1950
		School Attendance Committees Order, S.I. No. 196 of 1954
	10(8)	*Cork City School Attendance Committee Order [Vol. XX p. 179] S.R.& O. No. 69 of 1930*
		Dublin City School Attendance Committees Order [Vol. XX p. 195] S.R.& O. No. 97 of 1930
		Dun Laoghaire Borough School Attendance Committees Order [Vol. XX p. 203] S.R.& O. No. 98 of 1930
		Waterford City School Attendance Committees Order [Vol. XX p. 221] S.R.& O. No. 57 of 1931
	11(5)	**School Attendance Committees (Qualifications of Officers) Order, S.I. No. 329 of 1956**
		School Attendance Committees (Qualifications Officers) Order, S.I. No. 167 of 1972
	14(1)	**School Attendance (County Borough of Limerick) Order, XX-161, S.R.& O. No. 4 of 1927**
	23	*School Attendance (Hours of Attendance) Order [Vol. XX p. 115] S.R.& O. No. 79 of 1926*
		School Attendance (Statutory Forms) Order [Vol. XX p. 129] S.R.& O. No. 80 of 1926
		School Attendance (Principal Teachers' Returns) Order [Vol. XX p. 149] S.R.& O. No. 81 of 1926
		School Attendance (Registers and Records) Order [Vol. XX p. 173] S.R.& O. No. 77 of 1927
		School Attendance (Statutory Forms) Order, (1929) [Vol. XX p. 143] S.R.& O. No. 19 of 1930
		School Attendance (Hours of Attendance) Order [Vol. XX p. 123] S.R.& O. No. 68 of 1930

Statutory Authority	Section	Statutory Instrument
School Attendance Act, No. 17 of 1926 (*Cont.*)		**School Attendance Committees (Qualifications of Officers) Order [Vol. XX p. 211] S.R.& O. No. 28 of 1931**
		School Attendance Committees (Qualifications of Officers) Order [Vol. XX p. 217] S.R.& O. No. 32 of 1932
		School Attendance Committees (Qualifications of Officers) Order, S.I. No. 329 of 1956
		School Attendance Committees (Qualifications of Officers) Order, S.I. No. 167 of 1972
	24(1)	**School Attendance Act, 1926 (Extension of Application) Order, S.I. No. 105 of 1972**
	27(2)	*School Attendance Act, 1926 (Commencement) No.1 Order [Vol. XX p. 31] S.R.& O. No. 51 of 1926*
		School Attendance Act, 1926 (Commencement) No.2 Order [Vol. XX p. 35] S.R.& O. No. 78 of 1926
		School Attendance Act, 1926 (Commencement) No.3 Order [Vol. XX p. 39] S.R.& O. No. 82 of 1926
Scrap Iron (Control of Export) Act, No. 6 of 1938	2	*Scrap Iron (Prohibition of Export) Order [Vol. XXXIII p. 647] S.R.& O. No. 178 of 1939*
		Scrap Iron (Prohibition of Export) Order [Vol. XXXIII p. 651] S.R.& O. No. 216 of 1940
		Scrap Iron (Prohibition of Export) Order [Vol. XXXIII p. 655] S.R.& O. No. 338 of 1941
		Scrap Iron (Prohibition of Export) Order [Vol. XXXIII p. 659] S.R.& O. No. 16 of 1945
Sea Fisheries Act, No. 4 of 1931	2	*Sea Fisheries (Transfer of Properties) Order [Vol. XX p. 247] S.R.& O. No. 613 of 1935*
Sea Fisheries Act, No. 7 of 1952	3	*Sea Fisheries Act, 1952 (Commencement) (No.1) Order, S.I. No. 100 of 1952*
		Sea Fisheries Act, 1952 (Commencement) (No.2) Order, S.I. No. 155 of 1952
		Sea Fisheries Act, 1952 (Commencement) (No.3) Order, S.I. No. 3 of 1960
	8	**Pelagic Fish (Handling, Storage and Transport) Regulations, S.I. No. 156 of 1979**
		Shellfish (Handling, Storage and Transport) Regulations, S.I. No. 157 of 1979
	8(1)	**Demersal Fish (Handling, Storage and Transport) Regulations, S.I. No. 223 of 1967**
		Demersal Fish (Handling, Storage and Transport) Regulations, S.I. No. 27 of 1973
		Demersal Fish (Handling, Storage and Transport) Regulations, 1967 (Amendment) Regulations, S.I. No. 117 of 1983
	9	*Licensing of Sea-fishing Vessels Regulations, S.I. No. 4 of 1960*

Statutory Authority	Section	Statutory Instrument
Sea Fisheries Protection Act, No. 53 of 1933	7	**Sea-fishing Boats (Order to Stop) (Amendment) Regulations [Vol. XXXIII p. 663] S.R.& O. No. 138 of 1940**
	7(4)	**Sea-fishing Boats (Order to Stop) Regulations [Vol. XX p. 257] S.R.& O. No. 39 of 1934**
Sea Fisheries (Protection of Immature Fish) Act, No. 33 of 1937	2	**Undersized Sea-fish Order [Vol. XX p. 263] S.R.& O. No. 67 of 1938**
		Undersized Sea-fish Order, S.I. No. 44 of 1951
		Undersized Sea-fish (Crabs and Lobsters) Order, S.I. No. 359 of 1951
		Undersized Sea-fish (Escallops) Order, S.I. No. 40 of 1959
	3	*Fishing Nets (Regulation of Mesh) Order, S.I. No. 44 of 1954*
		Fishing Nets (Regulation of Mesh) Order, 1954 (Amendment) Order, S.I. No. 145 of 1956
		Fishing Nets (Regulation of Mesh) Order, 1954 (Amendment) Order, S.I. No. 88 of 1958
	11	*Undersized Sea-fish Order, S.I. No. 44 of 1951*
		Undersized Sea-fish (Crabs and Lobsters) Order, S.I. No. 359 of 1951
Seanad Bye-elections Act, No. 1 of 1930	10(1)	*Seanad Bye-elections (Forms) Order [Vol. XX p. 269] S.R.& O. No. 51 of 1930*
Seanad Electoral (Panel Members) Act, No. 43 of 1937	4	*Seanad Electoral (University Members) (Prescribed Matters) Regulations [Vol. XX p. 353] S.R.& O. No. 18 of 1938*
	7	*Seanad Bye-elections (Prescribed Forms) (Panel) Regulations [Vol. XXXIII p. 667] S.R.& O. No. 360 of 1940*
	15	*Seanad Electoral (Charges of Returning Officers in University Constituencies) Order [Vol. XX p. 385] S.R.& O. No. 31 of 1938*
	37	*Seanad Electorate (Councils) No.2 Regulations [Vol. XX p. 305] S.R.& O. No. 32 of 1938*
Seanad Electoral (Panel Members) Act, No. 42 of 1947	5	*Seanad General Election (Panel Members) (Prescribed Forms) Regulations, S.I. No. 207 of 1948*
		Seanad Bye-Elections (Panel Members) (Prescribed Forms) Regulations, S.I. No. 148 of 1949
		Seanad (Registration of Nominating Bodies) Regulations, S.I. No. 309 of 1950
		Seanad (Registration of Nominating Bodies) Regulations, S.I. No. 371 of 1951
		Seanad Electoral (Panel Members) (Prescribed Forms) Regulations, S.I. No. 91 of 1954
		Seanad Electoral (Panel Members) (Prescribed Forms) (Amendment) Regulations, S.I. No. 202 of 1972
	9(2)(a)	**Seanad (Registration of Nominating Bodies) Regulations, S.I. No. 309 of 1950**

Statutory Authority	Section	Statutory Instrument
Seanad Electoral (Panel Members) Act, No. 42 of 1947 (*Cont.*)	10	**Seanad (Registration of Nominating Bodies) Regulations, S.I. No. 309 of 1950**
	11	**Seanad (Registration of Nominating Bodies) Regulations, S.I. No. 309 of 1950**
	13	**Seanad (Registration of Nominating Bodies) Regulations, S.I. No. 309 of 1950**
	15	**Seanad (Registration of Nominating Bodies) Regulations, S.I. No. 309 of 1950**
	16	*Seanad (Registration of Nominating Bodies) Regulations, S.I. No. 371 of 1951*
	24	*Seanad (Panel Members) General Election Order, S.I. No. 208 of 1948*
Seanad Electoral (Panel Members) Act, No. 1 of 1954	1	*Seanad Electoral (Panel Members) Act, 1954 (Date of Commencement) Order, S.I. No. 70 of 1954*
Seanad Electoral (University Members) Act, No. 30 of 1937	4	**Seanad Electoral (University Members) (Prescribed Matters) (Amendment) Regulations, S.I. No. 201 of 1972**
	12	*Seanad (University Members) General Election Order, S.I. No. 209 of 1948*
	15	*Seanad Electoral (Charges of Returning Officers in University Constituencies) Order, S.I. No. 200 of 1951*
		Seanad Electoral (Charges of Returning Officers in University Constituencies) Order, S.I. No. 211 of 1961
		Seanad Electoral (Charges of Returning Officers in University Constituencies) (No.2) Order, S.I. No. 277 of 1961
		Seanad Electoral (Charges of Returning Officers in University Constituencies) Order, S.I. No. 145 of 1965
		Seanad Electoral (Charges of Returning Officers in University Constituencies) Order, S.I. No. 129 of 1969
		Seanad Electoral (Charges of Returning Officers in University Constituencies) Order, S.I. No. 77 of 1973
		Seanad Electoral (Charges of Returning Officers in University Constituencies) Order, S.I. No. 205 of 1977
		Seanad Electoral (Charges of Returning Officers in University Constituencies) Order, S.I. No. 384 of 1979
		Seanad Electoral (Charges of Returning Officers in University Constituencies) Order, S.I. No. 236 of 1981
		Seanad Electoral (Charges of Returning Officers in University Constituencies) Order, S.I. No. 23 of 1983

Statutory Authority	Section	Statutory Instrument
Seanad Electoral (University Members) Act, No. 30 of 1937 (*Cont.*)	25	**Seanad Elections (University Members) Free Postage Regulations, S.I. No. 194 of 1961**
		Seanad Elections (University Members) Free Postage (Amendment) Scheme, S.I. No. 289 of 1984
Seed Production Act, No. 14 of 1955	16	**Seed Production (Sugar Beet) Area and Plant Prohibition Order, S.I. No. 203 of 1955**
Shannon Act, No. 41 of 1885	6	*Kilrush Pier, County Clare Order [Vol. XX p. 391] S.R.& O. No. 161 of 1933*
	Sch. I	*Kilrush Pier, County Clare Order [Vol. XX p. 391] S.R.& O. No. 161 of 1933*
Shannon Electricity Act, No. 26 of 1925		**Shannon Electricity (Assessment of Compensation) Rules [Vol. XX p. 397] S.R.& O. No. 83 of 1926**
Shannon Fisheries Act, No. 4 of 1935	6(1)	**Shannon Fisheries (Transfer by Minister for Industry and Commerce) No.1 Order [Vol. XX p. 411] S.R.& O. No. 264 of 1936**
	19(1)	*Shannon Fisheries (Closing of Free Gap) (No.9) Order [Vol. XXXVIII p. 409] S.R.& O. No. 4 of 1947*
		Shannon Fisheries (Closing of Free Gap) (No.10) Order [Vol. XXXVIII p. 415] S.R.& O. No. 387 of 1947
		Shannon Fisheries (Closing of Free Gap) (No.11) Order, S.I. No. 364 of 1948
		Shannon Fisheries (Closing of Free Gap) (No.12) Order, S.I. No. 336 of 1949
		Shannon Fisheries (Closing of Free Gap) (No.13) Order, S.I. No. 37 of 1951
		Shannon Fisheries (Closing of Free Gap) (No.14) Order, S.I. No. 383 of 1951
		Shannon Fisheries (Closing of Free Gap) (No.15) Order, S.I. No. 41 of 1953
		Shannon Fisheries (Closing of Free Gap) (No.16) Order, S.I. No. 408 of 1953
		Shannon Fisheries (Closing of Free Gap) (No.17) Order, S.I. No. 249 of 1954
		Shannon Fisheries (Closing of Free Gap) (No.18) Order, S.I. No. 262 of 1955
	22(2)	*Shannon Fisheries (Weekly Close Season) (Variation) Order [Vol. XXXIII p. 689] S.R.& O. No. 3 of 1940*
	23	**Shannon Tidal Waters (Issue of Fishing Licences) Regulations [Vol. XX p. 401] S.R.& O. No. 664 of 1935**

Statutory Authority	Section	Statutory Instrument
Shannon Fisheries Act, No. 7 of 1938	4(1)	*Shannon Fisheries Act, 1938 (Appointed Day) Order [Vol. XX p. 121] S.R.& O. No. 91 of 1938*
Shannon Free Airport Development Company Limited (Amendment) Act, No. 9 of 1970	12	*Shannon Free Airport Development Company Limited (Amendment) Act, 1970 (Commencement) Order, S.I. No. 179 of 1970*
Shannon Navigation Act, No. 61 of 1839	48	**Saleen Pier (Quayage and Wharfage Rates) Order, S.I. No. 156 of 1962**
Sheepskin (Control of Export) Act, No. 13 of 1934	2(1)	*Sheepskin (Control of Export) Act (Prohibition of Export) Order, S.R.& O. No. 374 of 1934*
		Sheepskin (Control of Export) Act (Prohibition of Export) Order [Vol. XX p. 429] S.R.& O. No. 72 of 1935
		Sheepskin (Control of Export) Act (Prohibition of Export) Order [Vol. XX p. 433] S.R.& O. No. 69 of 1936
		Sheepskin (Control of Export) Act (Prohibition of Export) Order [Vol. XX p. 437] S.R.& O. No. 21 of 1937
		Sheepskin (Control of Export) Act (Prohibition of Export) Order [Vol. XX p. 441] S.R.& O. No. 70 of 1938
		Sheepskin (Prohibition of Export) Order [Vol. XXXIII p. 693] S.R.& O. No. 73 of 1939
		Sheepskin (Prohibition of Export) Order [Vol. XXXIII p. 697] S.R.& O. No. 97 of 1940
		Sheepskin (Prohibition of Export) Order [Vol. XXXIII p. 701] S.R.& O. No. 153 of 1941
		Sheepskin (Prohibition of Export) Order [Vol. XXXIII p. 705] S.R.& O. No. 134 of 1942
		Sheepskin (Prohibition of Export) Order [Vol. XXXIII p. 709] S.R.& O. No. 107 of 1943
		Sheepskin (Prohibition of Export) Order [Vol. XXXIII p. 713] S.R.& O. No. 95 of 1944
		Sheepskin (Prohibition of Export) Order [Vol. XXXIII p. 717] S.R.& O. No. 67 of 1945
		Sheepskin (Prohibition of Export) Order [Vol. XXXVIII p. 459] S.R.& O. No. 108 of 1946
		Sheepskin (Prohibition of Export) Order [Vol. XXXVIII p. 463] S.R.& O. No. 170 of 1947
		Sheepskin (Prohibition of Export) Order, S.I. No. 119 of 1948
		Sheepskin (Prohibition of Export) Order, S.I. No. 94 of 1949
		Sheepskin (Prohibition of Export) Order, S.I. No. 87 of 1950
		Sheepskin (Prohibition of Export) Order, S.I. No. 85 of 1951
		Sheepskin (Prohibition of Export) Order, S.I. No. 58 of 1952

Statutory Authority	Section	Statutory Instrument
Sheepskin (Control of Export) Act, No. 13 of 1934 (*Cont.*)		*Sheepskin (Prohibition of Export) Order, S.I. No. 112 of 1953*
		Sheepskin (Prohibition of Export) Order, S.I. No. 58 of 1954
		Sheepskin (Prohibition of Export) Order, S.I. No. 51 of 1955
Shipping Investment Grants Act, No. 11 of 1969	12	*Shipping Investments Grants Act, 1969 (Commencement) Order, S.I. No. 111 of 1969*
Shops (Conditions of Employment) Act, No. 4 of 1938	1(2)	*Shops (Conditions of Employment) Act, 1938 (Commencement) Order [Vol. XX p. 445] S.R.& O. No. 80 of 1938*
	12	**Shops (Conditions of Employment) Act, 1938 Regulations [Vol. XX p. 449] S.R.& O. No. 96 of 1938**
	20(9)	*Hotels (Working Hours) Order [Vol. XX p. 471] S.R.& O. No. 189 of 1938*
	21(2)	**Shops (Conditions of Employment) Act, 1938 (Section 21) (Amendment) Order [Vol. XXXIII p. 72] S.R.& O. No. 248 of 1943**
	31(5)	*Shops (Conditions of Employment) Act, 1938 (Form of Application to the District Court under Section 31 (4)) Regulations [Vol. XX p. 463] S.R.& O. No. 170 of 1938*
Shops (Hours of Trading) Act, No. 3 of 1938		**Hairdressing Shops (Hours of Trading on Weekdays) (Borough of Dun Laoghaire) Order, S.I. No. 7 of 1948**
	1(2)	*Shops (Hours of Trading) Act, 1938 (Commencement) Order [Vol. XX p. 477] S.R.& O. No. 81 of 1938*
	10	*Shops (Form of Half-holiday Notice) Regulations [Vol. XX p. 481] S.R.& O. No. 95 of 1938*
		Shops (Form of Half-holiday Notice) (No.2) Regulations [Vol. XX p. 487] S.R.& O. No. 187 of 1938
	16	**Shops (Hours of Trading) Act, 1938 (Part II) (Exempted Businesses) Order [Vol. XX p. 497] S.R.& O. No. 264 of 1938**
	16(3)	**Shops (Hours of Trading) Act, 1938 (Part II) (Exempted Businesses) Order [Vol. XXXIII p. 747] S.R.& O. No. 304 of 1940**
	22(2)	**Shops (Hours of Trading) Act, 1938 (Part III) (Exempted Business) (Exclusion) Order [Vol. XXXVIII p. 451] S.R.& O. No. 363 of 1947**
	22(3)	**Shops (Hours of Trading) Act, 1938 (Part III) (Exempted Businesses) Order [Vol. XXXIII p. 753] S.R.& O. No. 305 of 1940**
		Shops (Hours of Trading) Act, 1938 (Exempted Business for Purposes of Part III) Order [Vol. XXXVIII p. 455] S.R.& O. No. 365 of 1947
		Shops (Hours of Trading) Act, 1938 (Part III) (Exempted Business) Order, S.I. No. 137 of 1948

Shop (Hours of Trading) Act, No. 3 of 1938 (*Cont.*)	25	*Victuallers' Shops (Hours of Trading on Weekdays) (Dublin City) Order [Vol. XX p. 503] S.R.& O. No. 303 of 1938*

Boot-repairing Shops (Hours of Trading on Weekdays) (Dublin City, Dun Laoghaire and Bray) Order [Vol. XXXIII p. 729] S.R.& O. No. 19 of 1939

Drapery and Boot Shops (Hours of Trading on Weekdays) (Wexford Borough) Order [Vol. XXXIII p. 741] S.R.& O. No. 275 of 1944

Barbers' Shops (Hours of Trading on Weekdays) (Dublin City) Order [Vol. XXXIII p. 725] S.R.& O. No. 276 of 1944

Drapery and Boot Shops (Hours of Trading on Weekdays) (Westport) Order [Vol. XXXIII p. 735] S.R.& O. No. 334 of 1945

Drapery and Boot Shops (Hours of Trading on Weekdays) (Longford Urban District) Order [Vol. XXXVIII p. 431] S.R.& O. No. 147 of 1946

Barbers' Shops (Hours of Trading on Weekdays) (Athlone Urban District) Order [Vol. XXXVIII p. 421] S.R.& O. No. 295 of 1946

Hardware, Drapery and Boot Shops (Hours of Trading on Weekdays) (Drogheda and Dundalk) Order [Vol. XXXVIII p. 435] S.R.& O. No. 245 of 1947

Shops (Hours of Trading on Weekdays) Order [Vol. XXXVIII p. 441] S.R.& O. No. 362 of 1947

Drapery, Footwear and Hardware Shops (Hours of Trading on Weekdays) (Athlone Urban District) Order [Vol. XXXVIII p. 427] S.R.& O. No. 399 of 1947

Hairdressing Shops (Hours of Trading on Weekdays) (Urban District of Dundalk) Order, S.I. No. 6 of 1948

Hairdressing Shops (Hours of Trading on Weekdays) (County Borough of Limerick) Order, S.I. No. 36 of 1948

Victuallers' Shops (Hours of Trading on Weekdays) (Dublin, Dun Laoghaire and Bray) Order, S.I. No. 175 of 1948

Hairdressing Shops (Hours of Trading on Weekdays) (County Borough of Waterford) Order, S.I. No. 176 of 1948

General Drapery and Footwear Shops (Hours of Trading on Weekdays) (Castlerea) Order, S.I. No. 309 of 1948

Hairdressing Shops (Hours of Trading) (County Borough of Cork) Order, S.I. No. 338 of 1948

Hairdressing Shops (Hours of Trading on Weekdays) (County Borough of Dublin) Order, S.I. No. 240 of 1949

Shops (Hours of Trading on Weekdays) Order, 1947 (Revocation) Order, S.I. No. 355 of 1952

Statutory Authority	Section	Statutory Instrument
Shop (Hours of Trading) Act, No. 3 of 1938 (*Cont.*)	25(3)	**General Drapery and Footwear Shops (Hours of Trading on Weekdays) (Castlerea) Order, 1948 (Amendment) Order, S.I. No. 221 of 1949**
	27(1)	**Shops (Hours of Trading on Weekdays) Order, 1947 (Suspensory) Order, S.I. No. 197 of 1951**
		Shops (Hours of Trading on Weekdays) Order, 1947 (Suspensory) (No.2) Order, S.I. No. 243 of 1951
		Shops (Hours of Trading on Weekdays) Order, 1947 (Suspensory) Order, S.I. No. 176 of 1952
		Shops (Hours of Trading on Weekdays) Order, 1947 (Suspensory) (No.2) Order, S.I. No. 287 of 1952
		Drapery and Footwear Shops (Hours of Trading on Weekdays) (Urban District of Ballinasloe) Order, 1955 (Suspensory) O, S.I. No. 262 of 1957
	31(3)	**Shops (Hours of Trading) Act, 1938 (Part IV) (Exempted Businesses) Order [Vol. XXXIII p. 757] S.R.& O. No. 306 of 1940**
	33(1)	**Shops (Hours of Trading) Act, 1938 (Part IV) (Exempted Area) Order [Vol. XX p. 493] S.R.& O. No. 188 of 1938**
	34	**Hairdressing Shops (Sunday Trading) (Dublin City) Order, S.I. No. 37 of 1953**
Slaughter of Animals Act, No. 45 of 1935	1(2)	*Slaughter of Animals Act, 1935 (Dublin County Borough and Dun Laoghaire Borough) (Date of Commencement) Order [Vol. XX p. 531] S.R.& O. No. 370 of 1936*
		Slaughter of Animals Act, 1935 (Date of Commencement) (No.2) Order [Vol. XX p. 535] S.R. & O. No. 153 of 1937
	15(5)	**Slaughter of Animals (Approved Instruments) (Pigs) Order, S.I. No. 227 of 1973**
	16(1)	**Slaughter of Animals (Approved Instruments) Order [Vol. XX p. 525] S.R.& O. No. 323 of 1936**
		Slaughter of Animals (Approved Instruments) (Pigs) Order, S.I. No. 227 of 1973
	16(3)	**Slaughter of Animals (Approved Instruments) Order [Vol. XX p. 525] S.R.& O. No. 323 of 1936**
	Part III	**Slaughter of Animals (Slaughter Licence) Regulations [Vol. XX p. 509] S.R.& O. No. 303 of 1936**
Slaughter of Cattle and Sheep Act, No. 42 of 1934	2(1)	*Slaughter of Cattle and Sheep Act, 1934 (Part VIII) (Commencement) Order [Vol. XX p. 543] S.R.& O. No. 284 of 1934*
		Slaughter of Cattle and Sheep Act, 1934 (Parts I, II, III, V, VII and IX) (Commencement) Order [Vol. XX p. 539] S.R.& O. No. 285 of 1934
	4	*Cattle and Sheep (Export Licence) Regulations [Vol. XXXVIII p. 471] S.R.& O. No. 82 of 1946*
		Cattle and Sheep (Export Licence) Regulations, 1946 (Revocation) Regulations, S.I. No. 230 of 1953

Statutory Authority	Section	Statutory Instrument
Slaughter of Cattle and Sheep Act, No. 42 of 1934 (*Cont.*)	4(1)	**Slaughter of Cattle and Sheep (Registration and Levy) Regulations [Vol. XX p. 547] S.R.& O. No. 324 of 1934**
		Beef Supply (Returns) Regulations [Vol. XX p. 781] S.R.& O. No. 373 of 1934
		Slaughter of Sheep and Lambs (Rates of Levy) Regulations [Vol. XX p. 585] S.R.& O. No. 181 of 1935
		Cattle and Sheep (Return by Unregistered Slaughterer) Order [Vol. XX p. 819] S.R.& O. No. 537 of 1935
		Slaughter of Cattle and Sheep (Prohibitory Notice and Withdrawal Notice) Order [Vol. XX p. 577] S.R.& O. No. 538 of 1935
		Slaughter of Cattle and Sheep (Levy) (Amendment) Regulations [Vol. XX p. 563] S.R.& O. No. 114 of 1936
		Slaughter of Cattle and Sheep (Application for Manufacturing Licences) Regulations [Vol. XX p. 569] S.R.& O. No. 144 of 1937
	25(1)	*Cattle (Minimum Price and Calculation of Price) Regulations [Vol. XX p. 807] S.R.& O. No. 359 of 1934*
	29	*Cattle (Export Prohibition) Order [Vol. XXXVIII p. 467] S.R.& O. No. 83 of 1946*
		Cattle and Sheep (Export Prohibition) Order, S.I. No. 118 of 1952
		Cattle and Sheep (Export Prohibition) (Amendment) Order, S.I. No. 120 of 1952
		Cattle and Sheep (Export Prohibition) Orders (Revocation) Order, S.I. No. 149 of 1952
		Cattle (Export Prohibition) Order, 1946 (Revocation) Order, S.I. No. 231 of 1953
	45(1)	*Beef Supply (Appointed Area No.1) Order [Vol. XX p. 589] S.R.& O. No. 367 of 1934*
		Beef Supply (Appointed Area No.2) Order [Vol. XX p. 597] S.R.& O. No. 368 of 1934
		Beef Supply (Appointed Area No.3) Order [Vol. XX p. 631] S.R.& O. No. 369 of 1934
		Beef Supply (Appointed Area No.4) Order [Vol. XX p. 653] S.R.& O. No. 370 of 1934
		Beef Supply (Appointed Area No.1) Order [Vol. XX p. 677] S.R.& O. No. 586 of 1935
		Beef Supply (Appointed Area No.2) Order [Vol. XX p. 689] S.R.& O. No. 587 of 1935
		Beef Supply (Appointed Area No.3) Order [Vol. XX p. 725] S.R.& O. No. 588 of 1935
		Beef Supply (Appointed Area No.4) Order [Vol. XX p. 749] S.R.& O. No. 589 of 1935
	45(4)	*Beef Supply (Appointed Areas) (Amendment) Order [Vol. XX p. 671] S.R.& O. No. 92 of 1935*
		Beef Supply (Appointed Areas) (Revocation) Order [Vol. XX p. 769] S.R.& O. No. 599 of 1935

Statutory Authority	Section	Statutory Instrument
Slaughter of Cattle and Sheep Act, No. 42 of 1934 (*Cont.*)	46	*Beef Voucher (Amendment) Regulations [Vol. XX p. 793] S.R.& O. No. 93 of 1935*
		Cattle (Minimum Price and Calculation of Price) (Amendment) Regulations [Vol. XX p. 813] S.R.& O. No. 95 of 1935
		Cattle (Minimum Price and Calculation of Price) (Revocation) Regulations [Vol. XX p. 815] S.R.& O. No. 564 of 1935
		Beef Voucher (Amendment) (No.2) Regulations [Vol. XX p. 797] S.R.& O. No. 603 of 1935
	46(1)	*Beef Voucher Regulations [Vol. XX p. 785] S.R.& O. No. 351 of 1934*
Slaughter of Cattle and Sheep (Amendment) Act, No. 37 of 1935	3	*Beef Supply (Price to Recipients) Regulations [Vol. XX p. 775] S.R.& O. No. 602 of 1935*
		Beef Supply (Price to Recipients) (Amendment) Regulations [Vol. XX p. 825] S.R.& O. No. 113 of 1936
	19	*Beef Supply (Price to Recipients) (Amendment) Regulations [Vol. XX p. 825] S.R.& O. No. 113 of 1936*
	19(1)	*Slaughter of Cattle and Sheep (Amendment) Act, 1935 (Section 19, Appointed Day) Order [Vol. XX p. 839] S.R.& O. No. 601 of 1935*
	21(1)	*Canned Beef Supply Order [Vol. XX p. 829] S.R.& O. No. 600 of 1935*
	21(4)	*Canned Beef Supply (Amendment) Order [Vol. XX p. 835] S.R.& O. No. 127 of 1936*
Slaughter of Cattle and Sheep (Amendment) Act, No. 33 of 1936	4	**Slaughter of Cattle and Sheep Acts, 1934 and 1935 (Cesser) Order [Vol. XX p. 843] S.R.& O. No. 211 of 1936**
		Slaughter of Cattle and Sheep Acts, 1934 and 1935 (Cesser) (No.2) Order [Vol. XX p. 847] S.R.& O. No. 340 of 1936
Slaughtered and Detained Animals (Compensation) Act, No. 22 of 1938	3	*Detained Animals (Compensation for Depreciation) Regulations [Vol. XX p. 851] S.R.& O. No. 227 of 1938*
Small Dwellings Acquisition Act, No. 11 of 1957	2	**Small Dwellings Acquisition (Submissions to Commissioner of Valuation) (Fees) Regulations, S.I. No. 173 of 1957**
Social Welfare Act, No. 17 of 1948	22	**National Health Insurance (Rules for Insured Persons) Order, S.I. No. 201 of 1950**
		National Health Insurance (Rules for Insured Persons (Amendment) Order, S.I. No. 295 of 1952
	25(2)	*Social Welfare Act, 1948 (Section 23 (1) Commencement) Order, S.I. No. 301 of 1948*

Statutory Authority	Section	Statutory Instrument
Social Welfare Act, No. 14 of 1950	4(1)	*Social Welfare (Dissolution of Cumann an Arachais Naisiunta ar Shlainte) Order, S.I. No. 182 of 1950*
	5	**National Health Insurance (Rules for Insured Persons) Order, S.I. No. 201 of 1950**
		National Health Insurance (Rules for Insured Persons (Amendment) Order, S.I. No. 295 of 1952
	14	**Irish National Health Insurance Fund (Investment of Surplus Sums) Regulations, S.I. No. 241 of 1951**
	20(2)	**National Health Insurance (Administration of Benefits) Order, S.I. No. 190 of 1950**
		National Health Insurance (Rules for Insured Persons) Order, S.I. No. 201 of 1950
		National Health Insurance (Rules for Insured Persons (Amendment) Order, S.I. No. 295 of 1952
	20(3)	**National Health Insurance (Decisions and Appeals) Order, S.I. No. 189 of 1950**
Social Welfare Act, No. 16 of 1951	4(3)	*Social Welfare Act, 1951 (Sections 4 and 5) (Appointed Day) Order, S.I. No. 250 of 1951*
Social Welfare Act, No. 11 of 1952		**Insurance (Intermittent Unemployment) (Insurance Year) Regulations, S.I. No. 274 of 1952**
		Insurance (Intermittent Unemployment) (Contributions) Amendment Regulations, S.I. No. 1 of 1953
		Insurance (Intermittent Unemployment) (Supplementary Benefit) (Amendment) Regulations, S.I. No. 15 of 1953
		Insurance (Intermittent Unemployment) Act, 1942 (Amendment of Rates of Weekly Contributions) Regulations, S.I. No. 134 of 1953
		Social Welfare (Unemployment Benefit and Miscellaneous Provisions) (Transitional) (Amendment) Regulations, S.I. No. 124 of 1954
		Social Welfare (Unemployment Benefit and Miscellaneous Provisions) (Transitional) (Amendment) (No.2) Regulations, S.I. No. 265 of 1954
		Insurance (Intermittent Unemployment) Act, 1942 (Amendment of Rates of Supplementary Benefit) Regulations, S.I. No. 290 of 1954
	2	**Social Welfare (Occupational Injuries) Regulations, S.I. No. 77 of 1967**
		Social Welfare (Occupational Injuries) (Amendment) Regulations, S.I. No. 183 of 1969
		Social Welfare (Occupational Injuries) (Amendment) Regulations, S.I. No. 206 of 1970
		Social Welfare (Occupational Injuries) (Amendment) Regulations, S.I. No. 232 of 1971

Social Welfare Act, No. 11 of 1952 (*Cont.*)		**Social Welfare (Collection of Employment Contributions by the Collector-General) Regulations, S.I. No. 77 of 1979**
		Social Welfare (Collection of Employment Contributions for Special Contributors) Regulations, S.I. No. 120 of 1979
	2(1)	**Social Welfare (Disability, Unemployment and Marriage Benefit) Regulations, S.I. No. 7 of 1953**
		Social Welfare (General Benefit) Regulations, S.I. No. 16 of 1953
	2(4)	*Social Welfare (Persons Treated as Employers) Regulations, S.I. No. 21 of 1953*
		Social Welfare (Persons Treated as Employers) Regulations, S.I. No. 79 of 1967
		Social Welfare (Persons Treated as Employers) (No.2) Regulations, S.I. No. 192 of 1967
		Social Welfare (Persons Treated as Employers) Regulations, S.I. No. 76 of 1975
	2(6)	*Social Welfare (Normal Residence) Regulations, S.I. No. 211 of 1974*
		Social Welfare (Normal Residence) (Amendment) Regulations, S.I. No. 45 of 1978
	3	**Social Welfare (Overlapping Payments) Regulations, S.I. No. 212 of 1952**
		Social Welfare (Insurance Inclusions and Exclusions) Regulations, S.I. No. 373 of 1952
		Social Welfare (Claims and Payments) Regulations, S.I. No. 374 of 1952
		Social Welfare (Maternity Allowance) Regulations, S.I. No. 375 of 1952
		Social Welfare (Insurance Appeals) Regulations, S.I. No. 376 of 1952
		Social Welfare (Medical Certification Agreements) Regulations, S.I. No. 378 of 1952
		Social Welfare (Treatment Benefit) (Temporary Financial Provisions) Regulations, S.I. No. 379 of 1952
		Social Welfare (Collection of Contributions) Regulations, S.I. No. 381 of 1952
		Social Welfare (Unemployment Benefit and Miscellaneous Provisions) (Transitional) Regulations, S.I. No. 2 of 1953
		Social Welfare (Disability Benefit, Marriage Benefit and Maternity Benefit) (Voluntary Contributors) (Transitional) Regulations, S.I. No. 4 of 1953
		Social Welfare (Contributions) Regulations, S.I. No. 5 of 1953
		Social Welfare (Disability Benefit, Marriage Benefit, Maternity Benefit and Miscellaneous Provisions) (Transitional) Regulations, S.I. No. 6 of 1953
		Social Welfare (Disability, Unemployment and Marriage Benefit) Regulations, S.I. No. 7 of 1953

Statutory Authority	Section	Statutory Instrument
Social Welfare Act, No. 11 of 1952 *(Cont.)*		**Social Welfare (Unemployment Benefit and Miscellaneous Provisions) (Transitional) (Amendment) Regulations, S.I. No. 92 of 1955**
		Social Welfare (Overlapping Benefits) (Amendment) Regulations, S.I. No. 142 of 1955
		Social Welfare (Overlapping Benefits) (Amendment) (No.2) Regulations, S.I. No. 145 of 1955
		Social Welfare (Contributions) (Amendment) Regulations, S.I. No. 215 of 1955
		Social Welfare (Unemployment Benefit) (Additional Condition) Regulations, S.I. No. 241 of 1955
		Social Welfare (Unemployment Benefit and Miscellaneous Provisions) (Transitional) (Amendment) (No.2) Regulations, S.I. No. 242 of 1955
		Social Welfare (Claims and Payments) (Amendment) Regulations, S.I. No. 85 of 1956
		Social Welfare (Unemployment Benefit and Miscellaneous Provisions) (Transitional) (Amendment) Regulations, S.I. No. 136 of 1956
		Social Welfare (Modification of Contribution Conditions for Benefit) Regulations, S.I. No. 156 of 1956
		Social Welfare (Disability, Unemployment and Marriage Benefit) (Amendment) Regulations, S.I. No. 157 of 1956
		Social Welfare (Overlapping Benefits) (Amendment) Regulations, S.I. No. 225 of 1956
		Social Welfare (Disability, Unemployment and Marriage Benefit) (Amendment) (No.2) Regulations, S.I. No. 226 of 1956
		Social Welfare (Modifications of Insurance) Regulations, S.I. No. 236 of 1956
		Social Welfare (Unemployment Benefit) (Additional Condition) Regulations, S.I. No. 291 of 1956
		Social Welfare (Contributions) (Amendment) Regulations, S.I. No. 15 of 1957
		Social Welfare (Overlapping Benefits) (Amendment) Regulations, S.I. No. 142 of 1957
		Social Welfare (Unemployment Benefit) (Additional Condition) Regulations, S.I. No. 239 of 1957
		Social Welfare (Unemployment Benefit) (Additional Condition) Regulations, S.I. No. 233 of 1958
		Social Welfare (Modifications of Insurance) (Amendment) Regulations, S.I. No. 9 of 1959
		Social Welfare (Overlapping Benefits) (Amendment) Regulations, S.I. No. 131 of 1959
		Social Welfare (Unemployment Benefit) (Additional Condition) Regulations, S.I. No. 200 of 1959
		Social Welfare (Treatment Benefit) (Amendment) Regulations, S.I. No. 43 of 1960
		Social Welfare (Treatment Benefit) (Amendment) (No.2) Regulations, S.I. No. 126 of 1960
		Social Welfare (Contributions) (Amendment) Regulations, S.I. No. 132 of 1960

Statutory Authority	Section	Statutory Instrument

Social Welfare Act, No. 11 of 1952
(Cont.)

Social Welfare (Overlapping Benefits) (Amendment) Regulations, S.I. No. 163 of 1960

Social Welfare (Modifications of Insurance) (Amendment) Regulations, S.I. No. 170 of 1960

Social Welfare (Treatment Benefit) (Amendment) (No.3) Regulations, S.I. No. 193 of 1960

Social Welfare (General Benefit) (Amendment) Regulations, S.I. No. 221 of 1960

Social Welfare (Absence from the State) (Amendment) Regulations, S.I. No. 222 of 1960

Social Welfare (Disability, Unemployment and Marriage Benefit) (Amendment) Regulations, S.I. No. 249 of 1960

Social Welfare (Old Age (Contributory) Pension) (Transitional) Regulations, S.I. No. 255 of 1960

Social Welfare (Claims and Payments) (Amendment) Regulations, S.I. No. 259 of 1960

Social Welfare (Modifications of Insurance) (Amendment) (No.2) Regulations, S.I. No. 272 of 1960

Social Welfare (Old Age (Contributory) Pension) Regulations, S.I. No. 274 of 1960

Social Welfare (Voluntary Contributors) (Amendment) Regulations, S.I. No. 277 of 1960

Social Welfare (Overlapping Benefits) (Amendment) (No.2) Regulations, S.I. No. 278 of 1960

Social Welfare (Old Age (Contributory) Pension) (Transitional) (Amendment) Regulations, S.I. No. 138 of 1961

Social Welfare (Contributions) (Amendment) Regulations, S.I. No. 139 of 1961

Social Welfare (Overlapping Benefits) (Amendment) Regulations, S.I. No. 160 of 1961

Social Welfare (Voluntary Contributors) Regulations, S.I. No. 170 of 1961

Social Welfare (Overlapping Benefits) (Amendment) (No.2) Regulations, S.I. No. 270 of 1961

Social Welfare (Disability, Unemployment and Marriage Benefit) (Amendment) Regulations, S.I. No. 135 of 1962

Social Welfare (Old Age (Contributory) Pension) (Amendment) Regulations, S.I. No. 136 of 1962

Social Welfare (Overlapping Benefits) (Amendment) Regulations, S.I. No. 138 of 1962

Social Welfare (Contributions) (Amendment) Regulations, S.I. No. 210 of 1962

Social Welfare (Disability, Unemployment and Marriage Benefit) (Amendment) (No.2) Regulations, S.I. No. 227 of 1962

Social Welfare (Overlapping Benefits) (Amendment) (No.2) Regulations, S.I. No. 236 of 1962

Social Welfare (General Benefit) (Amendment) Regulations, S.I. No. 126 of 1963

Social Welfare Act, No. 11 of 1952
(*Cont.*)

Social Welfare (Assistance Decisions and Appeals) Regulations, S.I. No. 127 of 1963

Social Welfare (Modifications of Insurance) (Amendment) Regulations, S.I. No. 168 of 1963

Social Welfare (Overlapping Benefits) (Amendment) Regulations, S.I. No. 217 of 1963

Social Welfare (Old Age (Contributory) Pension) (Transitional) (Amendment) Regulations, S.I. No. 229 of 1963

Social Welfare (Old Age (Contributory) Pension) (Amendment) Regulations, S.I. No. 247 of 1963

Social Welfare (Disability, Unemployment and Marriage Benefit) (Amendment) Regulations, S.I. No. 258 of 1963

Social Welfare (Contributions) (Amendment) Regulations, S.I. No. 263 of 1963

Social Welfare (Claims and Payments) (Amendment) Regulations, S.I. No. 118 of 1964

Social Welfare (Overlapping Benefits) (Amendment) Regulations, S.I. No. 183 of 1964

Social Welfare (Modifications of Insurance) (Amendment) Regulations, S.I. No. 202 of 1964

Social Welfare (Share Fishermen) Regulations, S.I. No. 244 of 1964

Social Welfare (Disability, Unemployment and Marriage Benefit) (Amendment) Regulations, S.I. No. 18 of 1965

Social Welfare (Disability, Unemployment and Marriage Benefit) (Amendment) (No.2) Regulations, S.I. No. 52 of 1965

Social Welfare (Overlapping Benefits) (Amendment) Regulations, S.I. No. 61 of 1965

Social Welfare (Absence from the State) Regulations, S.I. No. 64 of 1965

Social Welfare (Old Age (Contributory) Pension) (Amendment) Regulations, S.I. No. 173 of 1965

Social Welfare (Overlapping Benefits) (Amendment) (No.2) Regulations, S.I. No. 178 of 1965

Social Welfare (Disability, Unemployment and Marriage Benefit) (Amendment) (No.3) Regulations, S.I. No. 229 of 1965

Social Welfare (Contributions) (Amendment) Regulations, S.I. No. 258 of 1965

Social Welfare (Widows' and Orphans' (Contributory) Pensions) (Transitional) (Amendment) Regulations, S.I. No. 234 of 1966

Social Welfare (Widows' and Orphans' (Contributory) Pensions) Regulations, S.I. No. 235 of 1966

Social Welfare (Unemployment Benefit) (Contributions and Additional Condition) Regulations, S.I. No. 241 of 1966

Social Welfare (Overlapping Benefits) (Amendment) Regulations, S.I. No. 247 of 1966

Social Welfare Act, No. 11 of 1952
(*Cont.*)

Social Welfare (Claims and Payments) (Amendment) Regulations, S.I. No. 289 of 1966

Social Welfare (Occupational Injuries) Regulations, S.I. No. 77 of 1967

Social Welfare (Occupational Injuries) (Prescribed Diseases) Regulations, S.I. No. 78 of 1967

Social Welfare (Persons Treated as Employers) Regulations, S.I. No. 79 of 1967

Social Welfare (Insurable (Occupational Injuries) Employment) Regulations, S.I. No. 80 of 1967

*Social Welfare (Modifications of Insurance) (Amend-
ment) Regulations, S.I. No. 81 of 1967*

Social Welfare (Claims and Payments) (Amendment) Regulations, S.I. No. 85 of 1967

Social Welfare (Contributions) (Amendment) Regulations, S.I. No. 89 of 1967

Social Welfare (Collection of Contributions) Regulations, S.I. No. 90 of 1967

Social Welfare (Overlapping Benefits) (Amendment) Regulations, S.I. No. 91 of 1967

Social Welfare (Absence from the State) Regulations, S.I. No. 97 of 1967

Social Welfare (Overlapping Benefits) (Amendment) (No.2) Regulations, S.I. No. 190 of 1967

Social Welfare (Persons Treated as Employers) (No.2) Regulations, S.I. No. 192 of 1967

Social Welfare (Modifications of Insurance) (Amendment) (No.2) Regulations, S.I. No. 193 of 1967

Social Welfare (Absence from the State) (Amendment) Regulations, S.I. No. 229 of 1967

Social Welfare (Disability, Unemployment and Marriage Benefit) (Amendment) Regulations, S.I. No. 231 of 1967

Social Welfare (Old Age (Contributory) Pension) (Amendment) Regulations, S.I. No. 248 of 1967

Social Welfare (Contributions) (Amendment) (No.2) Regulations, S.I. No. 278 of 1967

Social Welfare (Widows' and Orphans' (Contributory) Pensions) (Transitional) (Amendment) Regulations, S.I. No. 288 of 1967

Social Welfare (Widows' and Orphans' (Contributory) Pension) (Amendment) Regulations, S.I. No. 299 of 1967

Social Welfare (Contributions) (Amendment) Regulations, S.I. No. 1 of 1968

Social Welfare (Insurance Inclusions and Exclusions) Regulations, S.I. No. 51 of 1968

Social Welfare (Modifications of Insurance) (Amendment) Regulations, S.I. No. 164 of 1968

Social Welfare (Contributions) (Amendment) (No.2) Regulations, S.I. No. 226 of 1968

Statutory Authority	Section	Statutory Instrument

Social Welfare Act, No. 11 of 1952
(*Cont.*)

Social Welfare (Prescribed Female Relative) Regulations, S.I. No. 227 of 1968

Social Welfare (Insurable (Occupational Injuries) Employment) (Amendment) Regulations, S.I. No. 229 of 1968

Social Welfare (Old Age (Contributory) Pension) (Amendment) Regulations, S.I. No. 233 of 1968

Social Welfare (Widows' and Orphans' (Contributory) Pensions) (Amendment) Regulations, S.I. No. 235 of 1968

Social Welfare (Disability, Unemployment and Marriage Benefit) (Amendment) Regulations, S.I. No. 270 of 1968

Social Welfare (Modifications of Insurance) (Amendment) (No.2) Regulations, S.I. No. 281 of 1968

Social Welfare (Subsidiary Employments) (Amendment) Regulations, S.I. No. 17 of 1969

Social Welfare (Prescribed Female Relative) (Transitional) Regulations, S.I. No. 55 of 1969

Social Welfare (Treatment Benefit) (Amendment) Regulations, S.I. No. 141 of 1969

Social Welfare (Occupational Injuries) (Amendment) Regulations, S.I. No. 183 of 1969

Social Welfare (Contributions) (Amendment) Regulations, S.I. No. 192 of 1969

Social Welfare (Contributions) (Amendment) (No.2) Regulations, S.I. No. 221 of 1969

Social Welfare (Widows' and Orphans' (Contributory) Pension) (Amendment) Regulations, S.I. No. 237 of 1969

Social Welfare (Old Age (Contributory) Pension) (Amendment) Regulations, S.I. No. 238 of 1969

Social Welfare (Modifications of Insurance) (Amendment) Regulations, S.I. No. 240 of 1969

Social Welfare (Disability, Unemployment and Marriage Benefit) (Amendment) Regulations, S.I. No. 257 of 1969

Social Welfare (Overlapping Benefits) (Amendment) Regulations, S.I. No. 262 of 1969

Social Welfare (Prescribed Female Relative) Regulations, S.I. No. 268 of 1969

Social Welfare (Subsidiary Employments) Regulations, S.I. No. 26 of 1970

Social Welfare (Prescribed Female Relative) (Amendment) Regulations, S.I. No. 186 of 1970

Social Welfare (Occupational Injuries) (Amendment) Regulations, S.I. No. 206 of 1970

Social Welfare (Invalidity Pension) Regulations, S.I. No. 218 of 1970

Social Welfare (General Benefit) (Amendment) Regulations, S.I. No. 219 of 1970

Social Welfare (Absence from the State) (Amendment) Regulations, S.I. No. 220 of 1970

Statutory Authority	Section	Statutory Instrument

Social Welfare Act, No. 11 of 1952
(*Cont.*)

Social Welfare (Overlapping Benefits) (Amendment) Regulations, S.I. No. 221 of 1970

Social Welfare (Contributions) (Amendment) Regulations, S.I. No. 222 of 1970

Social Welfare (Retirement Pension and Invalidity Pension) (Transitional) Regulations, S.I. No. 224 of 1970

Social Welfare (Retirement Pension) Regulations, S.I. No. 225 of 1970

Social Welfare (Old Age (Care) Allowance) Regulations, S.I. No. 226 of 1970

Social Welfare (Deserted Wife's Allowance) Regulations, S.I. No. 227 of 1970

Social Welfare (Claims and Payments) (Amendment) Regulations, S.I. No. 228 of 1970

Social Welfare (Old Age (Contributory) Pension) (Amendment) Regulations, S.I. No. 229 of 1970

Social Welfare (Disability, Unemployment and Marriage Benefit) (Amendment) Regulations, S.I. No. 232 of 1970

Social Welfare (Widows' and Orphans' (Contributory) Pensions) (Amendment) Regulations, S.I. No. 233 of 1970

Social Welfare (Modifications of Insurance) (Amendment) Regulations, S.I. No. 243 of 1970

Social Welfare (Maternity Allowance) (Amendment) Regulations, S.I. No. 44 of 1971

Social Welfare (Modifications of Insurance) (Amendment) Regulations, S.I. No. 55 of 1971

Social Welfare (Contributions) (Amendment) Regulations, S.I. No. 85 of 1971

Social Welfare (Overlapping Benefits) (Amendment) Regulations, S.I. No. 87 of 1971

Social Welfare (Death Grant) Regulations, S.I. No. 98 of 1971

Social Welfare (Death Grant) (Transitional) Regulations, S.I. No. 99 of 1971

Social Welfare (Occupational Injuries) (Amendment) Regulations, S.I. No. 232 of 1971

Social Welfare (Claims and Payments) (Amendment) Regulations, S.I. No. 233 of 1971

Social Welfare (Contributions) (Amendment) (No.2) Regulations, S.I. No. 247 of 1971

Social Welfare (Disability, Unemployment and Marriage Benefit) (Amendment) Regulations, S.I. No. 249 of 1971

Social Welfare (Old Age and Widows' and Orphans' (Contributory) Pensions and Retirement Pension) (Amendment) Regulations, S.I. No. 267 of 1971

Social Welfare (Contributions) (Amendment) (No.3) Regulations, S.I. No. 293 of 1971

Social Welfare (Insurance Inclusions and Exclusions) Regulations, S.I. No. 315 of 1971

Social Welfare Act, No. 11 of 1952
(*Cont.*)

Social Welfare (Deserted Wife's Allowance) (Amendment) Regulations, S.I. No. 74 of 1972

Social Welfare (Contributions) (Amendment) Regulations, S.I. No. 76 of 1972

Social Welfare (Subsidiary Employments) Regulations, S.I. No. 77 of 1972

Social Welfare (Invalidity Pension) (Amendment) Regulations, S.I. No. 143 of 1972

Social Welfare (Overlapping Benefits) (Amendment) Regulations, S.I. No. 213 of 1972

Social Welfare (Death Grant) (Amendment) Regulations, S.I. No. 218 of 1972

Social Welfare (Occupational Injuries) (Amendment) Regulations, S.I. No. 219 of 1972

Social Welfare (Contributions) (Amendment) (No.2) Regulations, S.I. No. 222 of 1972

Social Welfare (Old Age and Widows' and Orphans' (Contributory) Pensions and Retirement Pension) (Amendment) Regulations, S.I. No. 238 of 1972

Social Welfare (Disability, Unemployment and Marriage Benefit) (Amendment) Regulations, S.I. No. 244 of 1972

Social Welfare (Modifications of Insurance) (Amendment) Regulations, S.I. No. 245 of 1972

Social Welfare (Prescribed Relative) Regulations, S.I. No. 248 of 1972

Social Welfare (Old Age (Care) Allowance) (Amendment) Regulations, S.I. No. 252 of 1972

Social Welfare (Claims and Payments) (Amendment) Regulations, S.I. No. 277 of 1972

Social Welfare (Contributions) (Amendment) (No.3) Regulations, S.I. No. 344 of 1972

Social Welfare (Payments to Appointed Persons) Regulations, S.I. No. 143 of 1973

Social Welfare (Unemployment Benefit) (Contributions and Additional Condition) (Revocation) Regulations, S.I. No. 150 of 1973

Social Welfare (Occupational Injuries) (Amendment) Regulations, S.I. No. 182 of 1973

Social Welfare (Disability, Unemployment and Marriage Benefit) (Amendment) Regulations, S.I. No. 183 of 1973

Social Welfare (Old Age and Widows' and Orphans' (Contributory) Pensions and Retirement Pension) (Amendment) Regulations, S.I. No. 189 of 1973

Social Welfare (Social Assistance Allowance) Regulations, S.I. No. 190 of 1973

Social Welfare (Claims and Payments) (Amendment) Regulations, S.I. No. 191 of 1973

Social Welfare (Deserted Wife's Benefit) Regulations, S.I. No. 202 of 1973

Social Welfare (Prescribed Relative) (Amendment) Regulations, S.I. No. 206 of 1973

Statutory Authority	Section	Statutory Instrument

Social Welfare Act, No. 11 of 1952
(*Cont.*)

Social Welfare (General Benefit) (Amendment) Regulations, S.I. No. 207 of 1973

Social Welfare (Payments to Appointed Persons) (No.2) Regulations, S.I. No. 219 of 1973

Social Welfare (Contributions) (Amendment) Regulations, S.I. No. 231 of 1973

Social Welfare (Modifications of Insurance) (Amendment) Regulations, S.I. No. 232 of 1973

Social Welfare (Overlapping Benefits) (Amendment) Regulations, S.I. No. 237 of 1973

Social Welfare (Pay-related Contributions) Regulations, S.I. No. 354 of 1973

Social Welfare (Occupational Injuries) (Prescribed Diseases) (Amendment) Regulations, S.I. No. 357 of 1973

Social Welfare (Pay-related Benefit) Regulations, S.I. No. 16 of 1974

Social Welfare (Prescribed Relative) (Amendment) Regulations, S.I. No. 26 of 1974

Social Welfare (Alteration of Rates of Contributions) Regulations, S.I. No. 37 of 1974

Social Welfare (Agricultural Employees) Regulations, S.I. No. 38 of 1974

Social Welfare (Scale of Pay-related Contributions) Regulations, S.I. No. 74 of 1974

Social Welfare (Special Contributors for Pay-related Benefit) Regulations, S.I. No. 77 of 1974

Social Welfare (Administration of Pay-related Benefit) Regulations, S.I. No. 78 of 1974

Social Welfare (Pay-related Contributions) Regulations, S.I. No. 79 of 1974

Social Welfare (Alteration of Rates of Contributions) (No.2) Order, S.I. No. 93 of 1974

Social Welfare (Members of the Defence Forces) Regulations, S.I. No. 94 of 1974

Social Welfare (Deserted Wife's Allowance) (Amendment) Regulations, S.I. No. 178 of 1974

Social Welfare (Disability and Unemployment Benefit) Regulations, S.I. No. 182 of 1974

Social Welfare (Disability and Unemployment Benefit) (No.2) Regulations, S.I. No. 201 of 1974

Social Welfare (Deserted Wife's Benefit) (Transitional) Regulations, S.I. No. 202 of 1974

Social Welfare (Payment of Benefit After Death) Regulations, S.I. No. 208 of 1974

Social Welfare (Single Women's Allowance) Regulations, S.I. No. 209 of 1974

Social Welfare (Occupational Injuries) (Amendment) Regulations, S.I. No. 210 of 1974

Social Welfare (Normal Residence) Regulations, S.I. No. 211 of 1974

Statutory Authority	Section	Statutory Instrument
Social Welfare Act, No. 11 of 1952 (*Cont.*)		**Social Welfare (Old Age and Widows' and Orphans' (Contributory) Pensions, Retirement Pension and Deserted Wife's Benefit) (Amendment) Regulations, S.I. No. 219 of 1974**
		Social Welfare (Prisoner's Wife's Allowance) Regulations, S.I. No. 220 of 1974
		Social Welfare (Prescribed Relative) (Amendment) (No.2) Regulations, S.I. No. 221 of 1974
		Social Welfare (Overlapping Benefits) (Amendment) Regulations, S.I. No. 224 of 1974
		Social Welfare (Occupational Injuries) (Amendment) (No.2) Regulations, S.I. No. 243 of 1974
		Social Welfare (Contributions) (Amendment) Regulations, S.I. No. 300 of 1974
		Social Welfare (Modifications of Insurance) (Amendment) Regulations, S.I. No. 365 of 1974
		Social Welfare (Subsidiary Employments) Regulations, S.I. No. 370 of 1974
		Social Welfare (Old Age and Widows' and Orphans' (Contributory) Pensions, Retirement Pension and Deserted Wife's Benefit) (Amendment) Regulations, S.I. No. 67 of 1975
		Social Welfare (Disability and Unemployment Benefit) (Amendment) Regulations, S.I. No. 68 of 1975
		Social Welfare (Occupational Injuries) (Amendment) Regulations, S.I. No. 69 of 1975
		Social Welfare (Persons Treated as Employers) Regulations, S.I. No. 76 of 1975
		Social Welfare (Contributions) (Amendment) Regulations, S.I. No. 84 of 1975
		Social Welfare (Payments to Appointed Persons) (Amendment) Regulations, S.I. No. 117 of 1975
		Social Welfare (Modifications of Insurance) (Amendment) Regulations, S.I. No. 182 of 1975
		Social Welfare (Variation of Rates of Payments) Regulations, S.I. No. 215 of 1975
		Social Welfare (Occupational Injuries) (Amendment) (No.2) Regulations, S.I. No. 231 of 1975
		Social Welfare (Old Age and Widows' and Orphans' (Contributory) Pensions, Retirement Pension and Deserted Wife's Benefit) (Amendment) (No.2) Regulations, S.I. No. 232 of 1975
		Social Welfare (Disability and Unemployment Benefit) (Amendment) (No.2) Regulations, S.I. No. 233 of 1975
		Social Welfare (Old Age and Widows' and Orphans' (Contributory) Pensions, Retirement Pension and Deserted Wife's Benefit) (Amendment) Regulations, S.I. No. 72 of 1976

Social Welfare Act, No. 11 of 1952
(*Cont.*)

Social Welfare (Disability and Unemployment Benefit) (Amendment) Regulations, S.I. No. 75 of 1976

Social Welfare (Occupational Injuries) (Amendment) Regulations, S.I. No. 76 of 1976

Social Welfare (Modifications of Insurance) (Amendment) Regulations, S.I. No. 77 of 1976

Social Welfare (Contributions) (Amendment) Regulations, S.I. No. 101 of 1976

Social Welfare (Deserted Wife's Allowance) (Amendment) Regulations, S.I. No. 122 of 1976

Social Welfare (Pay-Related Benefit) Regulations, S.I. No. 124 of 1976

Social Welfare (Pay-Related Contributions) (Amendment) Regulations, S.I. No. 145 of 1976

Social Welfare (Collection of Contributions) (Amendment) Regulations, S.I. No. 222 of 1976

Social Welfare (Variation of Rates of Payments) Regulations, S.I. No. 259 of 1976

Social Welfare (Old Age and Widows' and Orphans' (Contributory) Pensions, Retirement Pension and Deserted Wife's Benefit) (Amendment) (No.2) Regulations, S.I. No. 264 of 1976

Social Welfare (Occupational Injuries) (Amendment) Regulations, S.I. No. 96 of 1977

Social Welfare (Old Age and Widows' and Orphans' (Contributory) Pensions, Retirement Pension and Deserted Wife's Benefit) (Amendment) Regulations, S.I. No. 98 of 1977

Social Welfare (Disability and Unemployment Benefit) (Amendment) Regulations, S.I. No. 99 of 1977

Social Welfare (Overlapping Benefits) (Amendment) Regulations, S.I. No. 100 of 1977

Social Welfare (Contributions) (Amendment) Regulations, S.I. No. 126 of 1977

Social Welfare (Overlapping Benefits) (Amendment) (No.2) Regulations, S.I. No. 182 of 1977

Social Welfare (Occupational Injuries) (Prescribed Diseases) (Amendment) Regulations, S.I. No. 211 of 1977

Social Welfare (Subsidiary Employments) Regulations, S.I. No. 235 of 1977

Social Welfare (Variation of Rates of Payments) Regulations, S.I. No. 313 of 1977

Social Welfare (Occupational Injuries) (Amendment) (No.2) Regulations, S.I. No. 316 of 1977

Social Welfare (Disability and Unemployment Benefit) (Amendment) (No.2) Regulations, S.I. No. 317 of 1977

Social Welfare (Old Age and Widows' and Orphans' (Contributory) Pensions, Retirement Pension and Deserted Wife's Benefit) (Amendment) (No.2) Regulations, S.I. No. 319 of 1977

Statutory Authority	Section	Statutory Instrument

Social Welfare Act, No. 11 of 1952
(*Cont.*)

Social Welfare (Alteration of Rates of Contributions) Regulations, S.I. No. 374 of 1977

Social Welfare (Normal Residence) (Amendment) Regulations, S.I. No. 45 of 1978

Social Welfare (Occupational Injuries) (Amendment) Regulations, S.I. No. 89 of 1978

Social Welfare (Single Women's Allowance) (Amendment) Regulations, S.I. No. 90 of 1978

Social Welfare (Social Assistance Allowance) (Amendment) Regulations, S.I. No. 91 of 1978

Social Welfare (Deserted Wife's Allowance) (Amendment) Regulations, S.I. No. 92 of 1978

Social Welfare (Prisoner's Wife's Allowance) (Amendment) Regulations, S.I. No. 93 of 1978

Social Welfare (Deserted Wife's Benefit) (Amendment) Regulations, S.I. No. 94 of 1978

Social Welfare (Subsidiary Employments) Regulations, S.I. No. 100 of 1978

Social Welfare (Death Grant) (Amendment) Regulations, S.I. No. 103 of 1978

Social Welfare (Disability and Unemployment Benefit) (Amendment) Regulations, S.I. No. 104 of 1978

Social Welfare (Old Age and Widows' and Orphans' (Contributory) Pensions, Retirement Pension and Deserted Wife's Benefit) (Amendment) Regulations, S.I. No. 105 of 1978

Social Welfare (Modifications of Insurance) (Amendment) Regulations, S.I. No. 106 of 1978

Social Welfare (Contributions) (Amendment) Regulations, S.I. No. 113 of 1978

Social Welfare (Rates of Contribution and Yearly Reckonable Earnings) (Confirmation and Variation) Regulations, S.I. No. 65 of 1979

Social Welfare (Collection of Employment Contributions by the Collector-General) Regulations, S.I. No. 77 of 1979

Social Welfare (Contributions) (Transitional) Regulations, S.I. No. 86 of 1979

Social Welfare (Modifications of Insurance) Regulations, S.I. No. 87 of 1979

Social Welfare (Occupational Injuries) (Amendment) Regulations, S.I. No. 99 of 1979

Social Welfare (Disability and Unemployment Benefit) (Amendment) Regulations, S.I. No. 100 of 1979

Social Welfare (Claims and Payments) (Amendment) Regulations, S.I. No. 101 of 1979

Social Welfare (Pay-related Benefit) (Amendment) Regulations, S.I. No. 102 of 1979

Social Welfare (Old Age and Widows' and Orphans' (Contributory) Pensions, Retirement Pension and Deserted Wife's Benefit) (Amendment) Regulations, S.I. No. 117 of 1979

Social Welfare Act, No. 11 of 1952
(*Cont.*)

Social Welfare (Overlapping Benefits) (Amendment) Regulations, S.I. No. 118 of 1979

Social Welfare (Voluntary Contributors) Regulations, S.I. No. 119 of 1979

Social Welfare (Collection of Employment Contributions for Special Contributors) Regulations, S.I. No. 120 of 1979

Social Welfare (Subsidiary Employments) Regulations, S.I. No. 127 of 1979

Social Welfare (Treatment Benefit) (Amendment) Regulations, S.I. No. 130 of 1979

Social Welfare (Contributions) (Amendment) Regulations, S.I. No. 135 of 1979

Social Welfare (Employment of Inconsiderable Extent) Regulations, S.I. No. 136 of 1979

Social Welfare (Pay-related Benefit) Regulations, S.I. No. 141 of 1979

Social Welfare (Assistance) Regulations, S.I. No. 236 of 1979

Social Welfare (Variation of Rates of Payments) Regulations, S.I. No. 320 of 1979

Social Welfare (Occupational Injuries) (Amendment) (No.2) Regulations, S.I. No. 326 of 1979

Social Welfare (Old Age and Widows' and Orphans' (Contributory) Pensions, Retirement Pension and Deserted Wife's Benefit) (Amendment) (No.2) Regulations, S.I. No. 330 of 1979

Social Welfare (Disability and Unemployment Benefit) (Amendment) (No.2) Regulations, S.I. No. 332 of 1979

Social Welfare (Occupational Injuries) (Amendment) Regulations, S.I. No. 83 of 1980

Social Welfare (Pay-Related Benefit) (Amendment) Regulations, S.I. No. 98 of 1980

Social Welfare (Old Age and Widows' and Orphans' (Contributory) Pensions, Retirement Pension and Deserted Wife's Benefit) (Amendment) Regulations, S.I. No. 99 of 1980

Social Welfare (Death Grant) (Amendment) Regulations, S.I. No. 103 of 1980

Social Welfare (Disability and Unemployment Benefit) (Amendment) Regulations, S.I. No. 104 of 1980

Social Welfare (Modifications of Insurance) (Amendment) Regulations, S.I. No. 106 of 1980

Social Welfare (Contributions) (Amendment) Regulations, S.I. No. 107 of 1980

Social Welfare (Treatment Benefit) (Amendment) Regulations, S.I. No. 108 of 1980

Social Welfare (Contributions) (Amendment) Regulations, S.I. No. 162 of 1980

Social Welfare (Contributions) (Transitional) (Amendment) Regulations, S.I. No. 163 of 1980

Social Welfare (Disability and Unemployment Benefit) (Amendment) (No.2) Regulations, S.I. No. 287 of 1980

Social Welfare (Modification of Contribution Conditions for Benefit) Regulations, S.I. No. 383 of 1980

Social Welfare (Contributions) (Transitional) (Amendment) Regulations, S.I. No. 7 of 1981

4   *Social Welfare (Voluntary Contributors) Regulations, S.I. No. 13 of 1953*

Social Welfare (Voluntary Contributors) (Amendment) Regulations, S.I. No. 277 of 1960

Social Welfare (Voluntary Contributors) Regulations, S.I. No. 170 of 1961

4(2)   **Social Welfare (Voluntary Contributors) Regulations, S.I. No. 119 of 1979**

4(4)   **Social Welfare (Insurance Inclusions and Exclusions) Regulations, S.I. No. 373 of 1952**

Social Welfare (Insurance Inclusions and Exclusions) Regulations, S.I. No. 315 of 1971

4(5)   **Social Welfare (Insurance Inclusions and Exclusions) Regulations, S.I. No. 373 of 1952**

Social Welfare (Insurance Inclusions and Exclusions) Regulations, S.I. No. 51 of 1968

Social Welfare (Insurance Inclusions and Exclusions) Regulations, S.I. No. 315 of 1971

6   *Social Welfare (Collection of Contributions) Regulations, S.I. No. 381 of 1952*

Social Welfare (Collection of Contributions) Regulations, S.I. No. 90 of 1967

Social Welfare (Pay-Related Contributions) Regulations, S.I. No. 354 of 1973

Social Welfare (Collection of Employment Contributions by the Collector-General) Regulations, S.I. No. 77 of 1979

Social Welfare (Collection of Employment Contributions for Special Contributors) Regulations, S.I. No. 120 of 1979

6(2)   **Social Welfare (Voluntary Contributors) Regulations, S.I. No. 119 of 1979**

6(9)   **Social Welfare (Alteration of Rates of Contributions) Regulations, S.I. No. 37 of 1974**

Social Welfare (Alteration of Rates of Contributions) (No.2) Order, S.I. No. 93 of 1974

Social Welfare (Alteration of Rates of Contributions) Regulations, S.I. No. 374 of 1977

7   **Social Welfare (Contributions) Regulations, S.I. No. 5 of 1953**

Social Welfare (Contributions) (Amendment) Regulations, S.I. No. 215 of 1955

Social Welfare (Contributions) (Amendment) Regulations, S.I. No. 132 of 1960

Social Welfare Act, No. 11 of 1952
(*Cont.*)

Social Welfare (Contributions) (Amendment) Regulations, S.I. No. 139 of 1961

Social Welfare (Unemployment Benefit) (Contributions and Additional Condition) Regulations, S.I. No. 241 of 1966

Social Welfare (Contributions) (Amendment) Regulations, S.I. No. 89 of 1967

Social Welfare (Contributions) (Amendment) Regulations, S.I. No. 1 of 1968

Social Welfare (Contributions) (Amendment) Regulations, S.I. No. 192 of 1969

Social Welfare (Contributions) (Amendment) Regulations, S.I. No. 222 of 1970

Social Welfare (Contributions) (Amendment) Regulations, S.I. No. 85 of 1971

Social Welfare (Crediting of Contributions) Regulations, S.I. No. 180 of 1971

Social Welfare (Contributions) (Amendment) (No.3) Regulations, S.I. No. 293 of 1971

Social Welfare (Contributions) (Amendment) Regulations, S.I. No. 76 of 1972

Social Welfare (Contributions) (Amendment) (No.3) Regulations, S.I. No. 344 of 1972

Social Welfare (Contributions) (Amendment) Regulations, S.I. No. 231 of 1973

Social Welfare (Crediting of Contributions) Regulations, S.I. No. 17 of 1974

Social Welfare (Contributions) (Amendment) Regulations, S.I. No. 84 of 1975

Social Welfare (Contributions) (Amendment) Regulations, S.I. No. 101 of 1976

Social Welfare (Contributions) (Amendment) Regulations, S.I. No. 126 of 1977

Social Welfare (Contributions) (Amendment) Regulations, S.I. No. 113 of 1978

Social Welfare (Contributions) (Transitional) Regulations, S.I. No. 86 of 1979

Social Welfare (Contributions) (Amendment) Regulations, S.I. No. 135 of 1979

Social Welfare (Contributions) (Amendment) Regulations, S.I. No. 107 of 1980

Social Welfare (Contributions) (Amendment) Regulations, S.I. No. 162 of 1980

8   *Social Welfare (Collection of Contributions) Regulations, S.I. No. 381 of 1952*

Social Welfare (Contributions) Regulations, S.I. No. 5 of 1953

Social Welfare (Contributions) (Amendment) Regulations, S.I. No. 15 of 1957

Social Welfare (Collection of Contributions) Regulations, S.I. No. 90 of 1967

Social Welfare (Contributions) (Amendment) Regulations, S.I. No. 222 of 1970

906

Social Welfare (Modifications of Insurance (Amendment) Regulations, S.I. No. 243 of 1970

Social Welfare (Modifications of Insurance (Amendment) Regulations, S.I. No. 55 of 1971

Social Welfare (Modifications of Insurance (Amendment) Regulations, S.I. No. 245 of 1972

Social Welfare (Modifications of Insurance (Amendment) Regulations, S.I. No. 232 of 1973

Social Welfare (Modifications of Insurance (Amendment) Regulations, S.I. No. 182 of 1975

Social Welfare (Modifications of Insurance (Amendment) Regulations, S.I. No. 77 of 1976

Social Welfare (Modifications of Insurance (Amendment) Regulations, S.I. No. 106 of 1978

Social Welfare (Collection of Employment Contributions by the Collector-General) Regulations, S.I. No. 77 of 1979

Social Welfare (Modifications of Insurance) Regulations, S.I. No. 87 of 1979

Social Welfare (Collection of Employment Contributions for Special Contributors) Regulations, S.I. No. 120 of 1979

Social Welfare (Modifications of Insurance) (Amendment) Regulations, S.I. No. 106 of 1980

13   **Social Welfare (Contributions) (Amendment) Regulations, S.I. No. 139 of 1961**

Social Welfare (Absence from the State) Regulations, S.I. No. 64 of 1965

Social Welfare (Modifications of Insurance) (Amendment) Regulations, S.I. No. 81 of 1967

Social Welfare (Absence from the State) Regulations, S.I. No. 97 of 1967

Social Welfare (Absence from the State) (Amendment) Regulations, S.I. No. 229 of 1967

Social Welfare (Absence from the State) (Amendment) Regulations, S.I. No. 220 of 1970

Social Welfare (Administration of Pay-related Benefit) Regulations, S.I. No. 78 of 1974

Social Welfare (Modifications of Insurance) Regulations, S.I. No. 87 of 1979

14   **Social Welfare (Modification of Contribution Conditions for Benefit) Regulations, S.I. No. 156 of 1956**

Social Welfare (Modification of Contribution Conditions for Benefit) Regulations, S.I. No. 383 of 1980

15   **Social Welfare (Disability, Unemployment and Marriage Benefit) Regulations, S.I. No. 7 of 1953**

Social Welfare (Disability, Unemployment and Marriage Benefit) (Amendment) Regulations, S.I. No. 135 of 1962

Social Welfare (Disability, Unemployment and Marriage Benefit) (Amendment) Regulations, S.I. No. 18 of 1965

Statutory Authority	Section	Statutory Instrument
ocial Welfare Act, No. 11 of 1952 (*Cont.*)		Social Welfare (Disability, Unemployment and Marriage Benefit) (Amendment) (No.2) Regulations, S.I. No. 52 of 1965
		Social Welfare (Disability and Unemployment Benefit) Regulations, S.I. No. 182 of 1974
		Social Welfare (Disability and Unemployment Benefit) (Amendment) (No.2) Regulations, S.I. No. 287 of 1980
	16	Social Welfare (Disability, Unemployment and Marriage Benefit) Regulations, S.I. No. 7 of 1953
	17	Social Welfare (Disability and Unemployment Benefit) Regulations, S.I. No. 182 of 1974
		Social Welfare (Disability and Unemployment Benefit) (Amendment) (No.2) Regulations, S.I. No. 287 of 1980
	17(1)	Social Welfare (Disability, Unemployment and Marriage Benefit) Regulations, S.I. No. 7 of 1953
		Social Welfare (Disability, Unemployment and Marriage Benefit) (Amendment) Regulations, S.I. No. 135 of 1962
		Social Welfare (Disability, Unemployment and Marriage Benefit) (Amendment) Regulations, S.I. No. 18 of 1965
	17(5)	*Social Welfare (Unemployment Benefit) (Additional Condition) Regulations, S.I. No. 375 of 1953*
		Social Welfare (Unemployment Benefit) (Additional Condition) Regulations, S.I. No. 264 of 1954
		Social Welfare (Unemployment Benefit) (Additional Condition) Regulations, S.I. No. 241 of 1955
		Social Welfare (Unemployment Benefit) (Additional Condition) Regulations, S.I. No. 291 of 1956
		Social Welfare (Unemployment Benefit) (Additional Condition) Regulations, S.I. No. 239 of 1957
		Social Welfare (Unemployment Benefit) (Additional Condition) Regulations, S.I. No. 233 of 1958
		Social Welfare (Unemployment Benefit) (Additional Condition) Regulations, S.I. No. 200 of 1959
		Social Welfare (Share Fishermen) Regulations, S.I. No. 244 of 1964
		Social Welfare (Unemployment Benefit) (Contributions and Additional Condition) Regulations, S.I. No. 241 of 1966
	20	Social Welfare (Maternity Allowance) Regulations, S.I. No. 375 of 1952
		Social Welfare (Maternity Allowance) (Amendment) Regulations, S.I. No. 44 of 1971
	25(1)	*Social Welfare (Treatment Benefit) Regulations, S.I. No. 23 of 1953*
		Social Welfare (Treatment Benefit) Regulations, S.I. No. 156 of 1954
		Social Welfare (Treatment Benefit) (Amendment) (No.2) Regulations, S.I. No. 126 of 1960

Statutory Authority	Section	Statutory Instrument
Social Welfare Act, No. 11 of 1952 (*Cont.*)		Social Welfare (Treatment Benefit) (Amendment (No.3) Regulations, S.I. No. 193 of 1960
		Social Welfare (Treatment Benefit) (Amendment Regulations, S.I. No. 141 of 1969
		Social Welfare (Treatment Benefit) (Amendment Regulations, S.I. No. 130 of 1979
		Social Welfare (Treatment Benefit) (Amendment Regulations, S.I. No. 108 of 1980
	25(1)(2)	Social Welfare (Treatment Benefit) (Amendment Regulations, S.I. No. 43 of 1960
	25(2)	*Social Welfare (Treatment Benefit) Regulations, S.I. No. 23 of 1953*
		Social Welfare (Treatment Benefit) Regulations, S.I No. 156 of 1954
		Social Welfare (Treatment Benefit) (Amendment (No.2) Regulations, S.I. No. 126 of 1960
		Social Welfare (Treatment Benefit) (Amendment (No.3) Regulations, S.I. No. 193 of 1960
		Social Welfare (Treatment Benefit) (Amendment Regulations, S.I. No. 141 of 1969
	25C	Social Welfare (Invalidity Pension) Regulations, S.I. No. 218 of 1970
		Social Welfare (Invalidity Pension) (Amendment Regulations, S.I. No. 143 of 1972
	25D	Social Welfare (Retirement Pension) Regulations, S.I. No. 225 of 1970
	26(4)	*Social Welfare (Prescribed Female Relative) Regulations, S.I. No. 227 of 1968*
		Social Welfare (Prescribed Female Relative) Regulations, S.I. No. 268 of 1969
		Social Welfare (Prescribed Female Relative) (Amendment) Regulations, S.I. No. 186 of 1970
		Social Welfare (Prescribed Relative) Regulations, S.I. No. 248 of 1972
		Social Welfare (Prescribed Relative) (Amendment) Regulations, S.I. No. 206 of 1973
		Social Welfare (Prescribed Relative) (Amendment) Regulations, S.I. No. 26 of 1974
		Social Welfare (Prescribed Relative) (Amendment) (No.2) Regulations, S.I. No. 221 of 1974
	28	Social Welfare (Disability, Unemployment and Marriage Benefit) Regulations, S.I. No. 7 of 1953
		Social Welfare (Disability, Unemployment and Marriage Benefit) (Amendment) Regulations, S.I. No. 157 of 1956
		Social Welfare (Disability, Unemployment and Marriage Benefit) (Amendment) (No.2) Regulations, S.I. No. 226 of 1956
		Social Welfare (Disability, Unemployment and Marriage Benefit) (Amendment) Regulations, S.I. No. 249 of 1960

Social Welfare Act, No. 11 of 1952
(*Cont.*)

Social Welfare (Disability, Unemployment and Marriage Benefit) (Amendment) (No.2) Regulations, S.I. No. 227 of 1962

Social Welfare (Disability, Unemployment and Marriage Benefit) (Amendment) Regulations, S.I. No. 258 of 1963

Social Welfare (Disability, Unemployment and Marriage Benefit) (Amendment) (No.3) Regulations, S.I. No. 229 of 1965

Social Welfare (Disability, Unemployment and Marriage Benefit) (Amendment) Regulations, S.I. No. 231 of 1967

Social Welfare (Disability, Unemployment and Marriage Benefit) (Amendment) Regulations, S.I. No. 270 of 1968

Social Welfare (Disability, Unemployment and Marriage Benefit) (Amendment) Regulations, S.I. No. 257 of 1969

Social Welfare (Disability, Unemployment and Marriage Benefit) (Amendment) Regulations, S.I. No. 232 of 1970

Social Welfare (Disability, Unemployment and Marriage Benefit) (Amendment) Regulations, S.I. No. 249 of 1971

Social Welfare (Disability, Unemployment and Marriage Benefit) (Amendment) Regulations, S.I. No. 244 of 1972

Social Welfare (Disability, Unemployment and Marriage Benefit) (Amendment) Regulations, S.I. No. 183 of 1973

Social Welfare (Disability and Unemployment Benefit) (No.2) Regulations, S.I. No. 201 of 1974

Social Welfare (Disability and Unemployment Benefit) (Amendment) Regulations, S.I. No. 68 of 1975

Social Welfare (Disability and Unemployment Benefit) (Amendment) (No.2) Regulations, S.I. No. 233 of 1975

Social Welfare (Disability and Unemployment Benefit) (Amendment) Regulations, S.I. No. 75 of 1976

Social Welfare (Disability and Unemployment Benefit) (Amendment) Regulations, S.I. No. 99 of 1977

Social Welfare (Disability and Unemployment Benefit) (Amendment) (No.2) Regulations, S.I. No. 317 of 1977

Social Welfare (Disability and Unemployment Benefit) (Amendment) Regulations, S.I. No. 104 of 1978

Social Welfare (Disability and Unemployment Benefit) (Amendment) Regulations, S.I. No. 100 of 1979

Social Welfare (Disability and Unemployment Benefit) (Amendment) (No.2) Regulations, S.I. No. 332 of 1979

Social Welfare Act, No. 11 of 1952
(*Cont.*)

      Social Welfare (Disability and Unemployment Benefit) (Amendment) Regulations, S.I. No. 104 of 1980

28A   **Social Welfare (Old Age (Contributory) Pension) Regulations, S.I. No. 274 of 1960**

Social Welfare (Old Age (Contributory) Pension) (Amendment) Regulations, S.I. No. 136 of 1962

Social Welfare (Old Age (Contributory) Pension) (Amendment) Regulations, S.I. No. 247 of 1963

Social Welfare (Old Age (Contributory) Pension) (Amendment) Regulations, S.I. No. 173 of 1965

Social Welfare (Widows' and Orphans' (Contributory) Pensions) Regulations, S.I. No. 235 of 1966

Social Welfare (Old Age (Contributory) Pension) (Amendment) Regulations, S.I. No. 248 of 1967

Social Welfare (Widows' and Orphans' (Contributory) Pension) (Amendment) Regulations, S.I. No. 299 of 1967

Social Welfare (Old Age (Contributory) Pension) (Amendment) Regulations, S.I. No. 233 of 1968

Social Welfare (Widows' and Orphans' (Contributory) Pensions) (Amendment) Regulations, S.I. No. 235 of 1968

Social Welfare (Widows' and Orphans' (Contributory) Pension) (Amendment) Regulations, S.I. No. 237 of 1969

Social Welfare (Old Age (Contributory) Pension) (Amendment) Regulations, S.I. No. 238 of 1969

Social Welfare (Old Age (Contributory) Pension) (Amendment) Regulations, S.I. No. 229 of 1970

Social Welfare (Widows' and Orphans' (Contributory) Pensions) (Amendment) Regulations, S.I. No. 233 of 1970

Social Welfare (Old Age and Widows' and Orphans' (Contributory) Pensions and Retirement Pension) (Amendment) Regulations, S.I. No. 267 of 1971

Social Welfare (Old Age and Widows' and Orphans' (Contributory) Pensions and Retirement Pension) (Amendment) Regulations, S.I. No. 238 of 1972

Social Welfare (Old Age and Widows' and Orphans' (Contributory) Pensions and Retirement Pension) (Amendment) Regulations, S.I. No. 189 of 1973

Social Welfare (Old Age and Widows' and Orphans' (Contributory) Pensions, Retirement Pension and Deserted Wife's Benefit) (Amendment) Regulations, S.I. No. 219 of 1974

Social Welfare (Old Age and Widows' and Orphans' (Contributory) Pensions, Retirement Pension and Deserted Wife's Benefit) (Amendment) Regulations, S.I. No. 67 of 1975

Social Welfare (Old Age and Widows' and Orphans' (Contributory) Pensions, Retirement Pension and Deserted Wife's Benefit) (Amendment) (No.2) Regulations, S.I. No. 232 of 1975

Statutory Authority	Section	Statutory Instrument

Social Welfare Act, No. 11 of 1952
(*Cont.*)

Social Welfare (Old Age and Widows' and Orphans' (Contributory) Pensions, Retirement Pension and Deserted Wife's Benefit) (Amendment) Regulations, S.I. No. 72 of 1976

Social Welfare (Old Age and Widows' and Orphans' (Contributory) Pensions, Retirement Pension and Deserted Wife's Benefit) (Amendment) (No.2) Regulations, S.I. No. 264 of 1976

Social Welfare (Old Age and Widows' and Orphans' (Contributory) Pensions, Retirement Pension and Deserted Wife's Benefit) (Amendment) Regulations, S.I. No. 98 of 1977

Social Welfare (Old Age and Widows' and Orphans' (Contributory) Pensions, Retirement Pension and Deserted Wife's Benefit) (Amendment) (No.2) Regulations, S.I. No. 319 of 1977

Social Welfare (Old Age and Widows' and Orphans' (Contributory) Pensions, Retirement Pension and Deserted Wife's Benefit) (Amendment) Regulations, S.I. No. 105 of 1978

Social Welfare (Old Age and Widows' and Orphans' (Contributory) Pensions, Retirement Pension and Deserted Wife's Benefit) (Amendment) Regulations, S.I. No. 117 of 1979

Social Welfare (Old Age and Widows' and Orphans' (Contributory) Pensions, Retirement Pension and Deserted Wife's Benefit) (Amendment) (No.2) Regulations, S.I. No. 330 of 1979

Social Welfare (Old Age and Widows' and Orphans' (Contributory) Pensions, Retirement Pension and Deserted Wife's Benefit) (Amendment) Regulations, S.I. No. 99 of 1980

28B **Social Welfare (Retirement Pension) Regulations, S.I. No. 225 of 1970**

Social Welfare (Death Grant) Regulations, S.I. No. 98 of 1971

Social Welfare (Old Age and Widows' and Orphans' (Contributory) Pensions and Retirement Pension) (Amendment) Regulations, S.I. No. 267 of 1971

Social Welfare (Death Grant) (Amendment) Regulations, S.I. No. 218 of 1972

Social Welfare (Old Age and Widows' and Orphans' (Contributory) Pensions and Retirement Pension) (Amendment) Regulations, S.I. No. 238 of 1972

Social Welfare (Old Age and Widows' and Orphans' (Contributory) Pensions and Retirement Pension) (Amendment) Regulations, S.I. No. 189 of 1973

Social Welfare (Old Age and Widows' and Orphans' (Contributory) Pensions, Retirement Pension and Deserted Wife's Benefit) (Amendment) Regulations, S.I. No. 219 of 1974

Social Welfare (Old Age and Widows' and Orphans' (Contributory) Pensions, Retirement Pension and Deserted Wife's Benefit) (Amendment) (No.2) Regulations, S.I. No. 232 of 1975

Social Welfare Act, No. 11 of 1952
(*Cont.*)

Social Welfare (Old Age and Widows' and Orphans' (Contributory) Pensions, Retirement Pension and Deserted Wife's Benefit) (Amendment) Regulations, S.I. No. 72 of 1976

Social Welfare (Old Age and Widows' and Orphans' (Contributory) Pensions, Retirement Pension and Deserted Wife's Benefit) (Amendment) (No.2) Regulations, S.I. No. 264 of 1976

Social Welfare (Old Age and Widows' and Orphans' (Contributory) Pensions, Retirement Pension and Deserted Wife's Benefit) (Amendment) Regulations, S.I. No. 98 of 1977

Social Welfare (Old Age and Widows' and Orphans' (Contributory) Pensions, Retirement Pension and Deserted Wife's Benefit) (Amendment) (No.2) Regulations, S.I. No. 319 of 1977

Social Welfare (Death Grant) (Amendment) Regulations, S.I. No. 103 of 1978

Social Welfare (Old Age and Widows' and Orphans' (Contributory) Pensions, Retirement Pension and Deserted Wife's Benefit) (Amendment) Regulations, S.I. No. 105 of 1978

Social Welfare (Old Age and Widows' and Orphans' (Contributory) Pensions, Retirement Pension and Deserted Wife's Benefit) (Amendment) Regulations, S.I. No. 117 of 1979

Social Welfare (Old Age and Widows' and Orphans' (Contributory) Pensions, Retirement Pension and Deserted Wife's Benefit) (Amendment) (No.2) Regulations, S.I. No. 330 of 1979

Social Welfare (Old Age and Widows' and Orphans' (Contributory) Pensions, Retirement Pension and Deserted Wife's Benefit) (Amendment) Regulations, S.I. No. 99 of 1980

Social Welfare (Death Grant) (Amendment) Regulations, S.I. No. 103 of 1980

28C   Social Welfare (Old Age and Widows' and Orphans' (Contributory) Pensions and Retirement Pension) (Amendment) Regulations, S.I. No. 189 of 1973

Social Welfare (Deserted Wife's Benefit) Regulations, S.I. No. 202 of 1973

Social Welfare (Old Age and Widows' and Orphans' (Contributory) Pensions, Retirement Pension and Deserted Wife's Benefit) (Amendment) Regulations, S.I. No. 219 of 1974

Social Welfare (Old Age and Widows' and Orphans' (Contributory) Pensions, Retirement Pension and Deserted Wife's Benefit) (Amendment) Regulations, S.I. No. 67 of 1975

Social Welfare (Old Age and Widows' and Orphans' (Contributory) Pensions, Retirement Pension and Deserted Wife's Benefit) (Amendment) (No.2) Regulations, S.I. No. 232 of 1975

Social Welfare Act, No. 11 of 1952
(*Cont.*)

Social Welfare (Old Age and Widows' and Orphans' (Contributory) Pensions, Retirement Pension and Deserted Wife's Benefit) (Amendment) Regulations, S.I. No. 72 of 1976

Social Welfare (Old Age and Widows' and Orphans' (Contributory) Pensions, Retirement Pension and Deserted Wife's Benefit) (Amendment) (No.2) Regulations, S.I. No. 264 of 1976

Social Welfare (Old Age and Widows' and Orphans' (Contributory) Pensions, Retirement Pension and Deserted Wife's Benefit) (Amendment) Regulations, S.I. No. 98 of 1977

Social Welfare (Old Age and Widows' and Orphans' (Contributory) Pensions, Retirement Pension and Deserted Wife's Benefit) (Amendment) (No.2) Regulations, S.I. No. 319 of 1977

Social Welfare (Deserted Wife's Benefit) (Amendment) Regulations, S.I. No. 94 of 1978

Social Welfare (Old Age and Widows' and Orphans' (Contributory) Pensions, Retirement Pension and Deserted Wife's Benefit) (Amendment) Regulations, S.I. No. 105 of 1978

Social Welfare (Old Age and Widows' and Orphans' (Contributory) Pensions, Retirement Pension and Deserted Wife's Benefit) (Amendment) Regulations, S.I. No. 117 of 1979

Social Welfare (Old Age and Widows' and Orphans' (Contributory) Pensions, Retirement Pension and Deserted Wife's Benefit) (Amendment) (No.2) Regulations, S.I. No. 330 of 1979

Social Welfare (Old Age and Widows' and Orphans' (Contributory) Pensions, Retirement Pension and Deserted Wife's Benefit) (Amendment) Regulations, S.I. No. 99 of 1980

29   Social Welfare (Claims and Payments) Regulations, S.I. No. 374 of 1952

Social Welfare (Claims and Payments) (Amendment) Regulations, S.I. No. 85 of 1956

Social Welfare (Claims and Payments) (Amendment) Regulations, S.I. No. 259 of 1960

Social Welfare (Claims and Payments) (Amendment) Regulations, S.I. No. 118 of 1964

Social Welfare (Claims and Payments) (Amendment) Regulations, S.I. No. 289 of 1966

Social Welfare (Claims and Payments) (Amendment) Regulations, S.I. No. 85 of 1967

Social Welfare (Occupational Injuries) (Medical Care) Regulations, S.I. No. 92 of 1967

Social Welfare (Claims and Payments) (Amendment) Regulations, S.I. No. 228 of 1970

Social Welfare (Claims and Payments) (Amendment) Regulations, S.I. No. 191 of 1973

Social Welfare (Administration of Pay-related Benefit) Regulations, S.I. No. 78 of 1974

Social Welfare Act, No. 11 of 1952
(*Cont.*)

Social Welfare (Claims and Payments) (Amendment) Regulations, S.I. No. 101 of 1979

Social Welfare (Assistance) Regulations, S.I. No. 236 of 1979

31   *Social Welfare (Modifications of Insurance) Regulations, S.I. No. 10 of 1953*

Social Welfare (General Benefit) Regulations, S.I. No. 16 of 1953

Social Welfare (Absence from the State) Regulations, S.I. No. 17 of 1953

Social Welfare (Modifications of Insurance) Regulations, S.I. No. 236 of 1956

Social Welfare (General Benefit) (Amendment) Regulations, S.I. No. 221 of 1960

Social Welfare (Absence from the State) (Amendment) Regulations, S.I. No. 222 of 1960

Social Welfare (Absence from the State) Regulations, S.I. No. 64 of 1965

Social Welfare (Occupational Injuries) Regulations, S.I. No. 77 of 1967

Social Welfare (Modifications of Insurance) (Amendment) Regulations, S.I. No. 81 of 1967

Social Welfare (Absence from the State) Regulations, S.I. No. 97 of 1967

Social Welfare (Absence from the State) (Amendment) Regulations, S.I. No. 229 of 1967

Social Welfare (General Benefit) (Amendment) Regulations, S.I. No. 219 of 1970

Social Welfare (Absence from the State) (Amendment) Regulations, S.I. No. 220 of 1970

Social Welfare (General Benefit) (Amendment) Regulations, S.I. No. 207 of 1973

Social Welfare (Administration of Pay-related Benefit) Regulations, S.I. No. 78 of 1974

Social Welfare (Modifications of Insurance) Regulations, S.I. No. 87 of 1979

32   **Social Welfare (Overlapping Benefits) Regulations, S.I. No. 14 of 1953**

Social Welfare (Overlapping Benefits) (Amendment) Regulations, S.I. No. 155 of 1954

Social Welfare (Overlapping Benefits) (Amendment) Regulations, S.I. No. 142 of 1955

Social Welfare (Overlapping Benefits) (Amendment) (No.2) Regulations, S.I. No. 145 of 1955

Social Welfare (Overlapping Benefits) (Amendment) Regulations, S.I. No. 225 of 1956

Social Welfare (Overlapping Benefits) (Amendment) Regulations, S.I. No. 142 of 1957

Social Welfare (Overlapping Benefits) (Amendment) Regulations, S.I. No. 131 of 1959

Social Welfare (Overlapping Benefits) (Amendment) Regulations, S.I. No. 163 of 1960

Statutory Authority	Section	Statutory Instrument
Social Welfare Act, No. 11 of 1952 (*Cont.*)		**Social Welfare (Overlapping Benefits) (Amendment) (No.2) Regulations, S.I. No. 278 of 1960**
		Social Welfare (Overlapping Benefits) (Amendment) Regulations, S.I. No. 160 of 1961
		Social Welfare (Overlapping Benefits) (Amendment) Regulations, S.I. No. 138 of 1962
		Social Welfare (Overlapping Benefits) (Amendment) (No.2) Regulations, S.I. No. 236 of 1962
		Social Welfare (Overlapping Benefits) (Amendment) Regulations, S.I. No. 217 of 1963
		Social Welfare (Overlapping Benefits) (Amendment) Regulations, S.I. No. 183 of 1964
		Social Welfare (Overlapping Benefits) (Amendment) Regulations, S.I. No. 61 of 1965
		Social Welfare (Overlapping Benefits) (Amendment) (No.2) Regulations, S.I. No. 178 of 1965
		Social Welfare (Overlapping Benefits) (Amendment) Regulations, S.I. No. 247 of 1966
		Social Welfare (Overlapping Benefits) (Amendment) Regulations, S.I. No. 91 of 1967
		Social Welfare (Overlapping Benefits) (Amendment) (No.2) Regulations, S.I. No. 190 of 1967
		Social Welfare (Overlapping Benefits) (Amendment) Regulations, S.I. No. 262 of 1969
		Social Welfare (Overlapping Benefits) (Amendment) Regulations, S.I. No. 221 of 1970
		Social Welfare (Overlapping Benefits) (Amendment) Regulations, S.I. No. 87 of 1971
		Social Welfare (Overlapping Benefits) (Amendment) Regulations, S.I. No. 213 of 1972
		Social Welfare (Overlapping Benefits) (Amendment) Regulations, S.I. No. 237 of 1973
		Social Welfare (Administration of Pay-related Benefit) Regulations, S.I. No. 78 of 1974
		Social Welfare (Overlapping Benefits) (Amendment) Regulations, S.I. No. 224 of 1974
		Social Welfare (Overlapping Benefits) (Amendment) Regulations, S.I. No. 100 of 1977
		Social Welfare (Overlapping Benefits) (Amendment) (No.2) Regulations, S.I. No. 182 of 1977
		Social Welfare (Overlapping Benefits) (Amendment) Regulations, S.I. No. 118 of 1979
	32(4)	**Social Welfare (Overlapping Benefits) (Amendment) (No.2) Regulations, S.I. No. 270 of 1961**
	37	*Social Welfare (Voluntary Contributors) Regulations, S.I. No. 13 of 1953*
	37(2)	**Social Welfare (Voluntary Contributors) Regulations, S.I. No. 119 of 1979**
	42	**Social Welfare (Collection of Employment Contributions for Special Contributors) Regulations, S.I. No. 120 of 1979**

Statutory Authority	Section	Statutory Instrument
Social Welfare Act, No. 11 of 1952 (*Cont.*)	44	**Social Welfare (Insurance Appeals) Regulations, S.I. No. 376 of 1952**
	47	**Social Welfare (Claims and Payments) Regulations, S.I. No. 374 of 1952**
		Social Welfare (Claims and Payments) (Amendment) Regulations, S.I. No. 259 of 1960
		Social Welfare (Claims and Payments) (Amendment) Regulations, S.I. No. 289 of 1966
		Social Welfare (Claims and Payments) (Amendment) Regulations, S.I. No. 85 of 1967
		Social Welfare (Occupational Injuries) (Medical Care) Regulations, S.I. No. 92 of 1967
		Social Welfare (Claims and Payments) (Amendment) Regulations, S.I. No. 228 of 1970
		Social Welfare (Claims and Payments) (Amendment) Regulations, S.I. No. 277 of 1972
		Social Welfare (Payments to Appointed Persons) Regulations, S.I. No. 143 of 1973
		Social Welfare (Claims and Payments) (Amendment) Regulations, S.I. No. 191 of 1973
		Social Welfare (Payments to Appointed Persons) (No.2) Regulations, S.I. No. 219 of 1973
		Social Welfare (Administration of Pay-related Benefit) Regulations, S.I. No. 78 of 1974
		Social Welfare (Payments to Appointed Persons) (Amendment) Regulations, S.I. No. 117 of 1975
		Social Welfare (Claims and Payments) (Amendment) Regulations, S.I. No. 101 of 1979
		Social Welfare (Assistance) Regulations, S.I. No. 236 of 1979
	47(2)	*Social Welfare (Absence from the State) Regulations, S.I. No. 17 of 1953*
		Social Welfare (Absence from the State) Regulations, S.I. No. 97 of 1967
	47(2)(a)	*Social Welfare (Modifications of Insurance) Regulations, S.I. No. 10 of 1953*
		Social Welfare (Modifications of Insurance) Regulations, S.I. No. 236 of 1956
		Social Welfare (Modifications of Insurance) (Amendment) Regulations, S.I. No. 81 of 1967
		Social Welfare (Modifications of Insurance) Regulations, S.I. No. 87 of 1979
	48	**Social Welfare (General Benefit) Regulations, S.I. No. 16 of 1953**
		Social Welfare (General Benefit) (Amendment) Regulations, S.I. No. 126 of 1963
		Social Welfare (Occupational Injuries) Regulations, S.I. No. 77 of 1967
		Social Welfare (General Benefit) (Amendment) Regulations, S.I. No. 219 of 1970

Social Welfare Act, No. 11 of 1952
(*Cont.*)

Social Welfare (General Benefit) (Amendment) Regulations, S.I. No. 207 of 1973

Social Welfare (Administration of Pay-related Benefit) Regulations, S.I. No. 78 of 1974

50   **Social Welfare (Certificates of Births, Marriages and Deaths) Regulations, S.I. No. 384 of 1952**

52   *Social Welfare (Collection of Contributions) Regulations, S.I. No. 381 of 1952*

Social Welfare (Collection of Contributions) Regulations, S.I. No. 90 of 1967

Social Welfare (Collection of Employment Contributions by the Collector-General) Regulations, S.I. No. 77 of 1979

Social Welfare (Contributions) (Transitional) Regulations, S.I. No. 86 of 1979

Social Welfare (Collection of Employment Contributions for Special Contributors) Regulations, S.I. No. 120 of 1979

52(3)   *Social Welfare (Collection of Contributions) (Amendment) Regulations, S.I. No. 222 of 1976*

52(4)   **Social Welfare (Claims and Payments) Regulations, S.I. No. 374 of 1952**

Social Welfare (Claims and Payments) (Amendment) Regulations, S.I. No. 85 of 1967

64   *Social Welfare (Northern Ireland Reciprocal Arrangements) Order, S.I. No. 56 of 1953*

Social Welfare (Great Britain Reciprocal Arrangements) Order, S.I. No. 73 of 1953

Social Welfare (Isle of Man Reciprocal Arrangements) Order, S.I. No. 203 of 1954

Social Welfare (Great Britain Reciprocal Arrangements) Order, S.I. No. 96 of 1960

Social Welfare (Northern Ireland Reciprocal Arrangements) Order, S.I. No. 213 of 1964

Social Welfare (United Kingdom Reciprocal Arrangements) Order, S.I. No. 67 of 1966

66   *Social Welfare (Treatment Benefit) (Temporary Financial Provisions) Regulations, S.I. No. 379 of 1952*

Social Welfare (Unemployment Benefit and Miscellaneous Provisions) (Transitional) Regulations, S.I. No. 2 of 1953

Social Welfare (Disability Benefit, Marriage Benefit and Maternity Benefit) (Voluntary Contributors) (Transitional) Regulations, S.I. No. 4 of 1953

Social Welfare (Disability Benefit, Marriage Benefit, Maternity Benefit and Miscellaneous Provisions) (Transitional) Regulations, S.I. No. 6 of 1953

Social Welfare (Widows' and Orphans' (Contributory) Pensions) (Transitional) Regulations, S.I. No. 12 of 1953

Statutory Authority	Section	Statutory Instrument
Social Welfare Act, No. 11 of 1952 (*Cont.*)		**Social Welfare (Treatment Benefit) (Transitional) Regulations, S.I. No. 22 of 1953**
		Social Welfare (Disability Benefit, Marriage Benefit and Maternity Benefit) (Voluntary Contributors) (Transitional) (Amendment) Regulations, S.I. No. 273 of 1954
		Social Welfare (Treatment Benefit) (Transitional) (Amendment) Regulations, S.I. No. 274 of 1954
		Social Welfare (Unemployment Benefit and Miscellaneous Provisions) (Transitional) (Amendment) Regulations, S.I. No. 92 of 1955
		Social Welfare (Unemployment Benefit and Miscellaneous Provisions) (Transitional) (Amendment) (No.2) Regulations, S.I. No. 242 of 1955
		Social Welfare (Unemployment Benefit and Miscellaneous Provisions) (Transitional) (Amendment) Regulations, S.I. No. 136 of 1956
		Social Welfare (Widows' and Orphans' (Contributory) Pensions) (Transitional) (Amendment) Regulations, S.I. No. 234 of 1966
		Social Welfare (Widows' and Orphans' (Contributory) Pensions) (Transitional) (Amendment) Regulations, S.I. No. 288 of 1967
		Social Welfare (Prescribed Female Relative) (Transitional) Regulations, S.I. No. 55 of 1969
		Social Welfare (Deserted Wife's Benefit) (Transitional) Regulations, S.I. No. 202 of 1974
	66A	**Social Welfare (Old Age (Contributory) Pension) (Transitional) Regulations, S.I. No. 255 of 1960**
		Social Welfare (Old Age (Contributory) Pension) (Transitional) (Amendment) Regulations, S.I. No. 138 of 1961
		Social Welfare (Old Age (Contributory) Pension) (Transitional) (Amendment) Regulations, S.I. No. 229 of 1963
	66B	**Social Welfare (Retirement Pension and Invalidity Pension) (Transitional) Regulations, S.I. No. 224 of 1970**
		Social Welfare (Death Grant) (Transitional) Regulations, S.I. No. 99 of 1971
	69	**Social Welfare (Medical Certification Agreements) Regulations, S.I. No. 378 of 1952**
		Social Welfare (Unemployment Benefit and Miscellaneous Provisions) (Transitional) Regulations, S.I. No. 2 of 1953
		Social Welfare (Disability Benefit, Marriage Benefit, Maternity Benefit and Miscellaneous Provisions) (Transitional) Regulations, S.I. No. 6 of 1953
		Social Welfare (Widows' and Orphans' (Contributory) Pensions) (Transitional) Regulations, S.I. No. 12 of 1953
		Social Welfare (Widows' and Orphans' (Contributory) Pensions) (Transitional) (Amendment) Regulations, S.I. No. 234 of 1966

Statutory Authority	Section	Statutory Instrument
Social Welfare Act, No. 11 of 1952 (*Cont.*)		**Social Welfare (Widows' and Orphans' (Contributory) Pensions) (Transitional) (Amendment) Regulations, S.I. No. 288 of 1967**
		Social Welfare (Deserted Wife's Benefit) (Transitional) Regulations, S.I. No. 202 of 1974
	70	*Social Welfare (Voluntary Contributors) Regulations, S.I. No. 13 of 1953*
	71	**Social Welfare Act, 1952 (Section 71) Order, S.I. No. 168 of 1952**
		Social Welfare Act, 1952 (Section 71) (No.2) Order, S.I. No. 386 of 1952
		Social Welfare (Determination of Expenditure on Pensions) Order, S.I. No. 310 of 1953
		Social Welfare Act, 1952 (Section 71) Order, S.I. No. 407 of 1953
	72	*Social Welfare (Appointed Day) Order, S.I. No. 372 of 1952*
	75	**Social Welfare (Overlapping Benefits) Regulations, S.I. No. 14 of 1953**
		Social Welfare (Overlapping Benefits) (Amendment) Regulations, S.I. No. 155 of 1954
		Social Welfare (Overlapping Benefits) (Amendment) Regulations, S.I. No. 142 of 1955
		Social Welfare (Overlapping Benefits) (Amendment) (No.2) Regulations, S.I. No. 278 of 1960
		Social Welfare (Overlapping Benefits) (Amendment) Regulations, S.I. No. 61 of 1965
		Social Welfare (Overlapping Benefits) (Amendment) Regulations, S.I. No. 247 of 1966
		Social Welfare (Overlapping Benefits) (Amendment) Regulations, S.I. No. 221 of 1970
		Social Welfare (Overlapping Benefits) (Amendment) Regulations, S.I. No. 87 of 1971
		Social Welfare (Overlapping Benefits) (Amendment) Regulations, S.I. No. 237 of 1973
		Social Welfare (Administration of Pay-related Benefit) Regulations, S.I. No. 78 of 1974
		Social Welfare (Overlapping Benefits) (Amendment) Regulations, S.I. No. 224 of 1974
		Social Welfare (Overlapping Benefits) (Amendment) Regulations, S.I. No. 100 of 1977
		Social Welfare (Overlapping Benefits) (Amendment) (No.2) Regulations, S.I. No. 182 of 1977
		Social Welfare (Overlapping Benefits) (Amendment) Regulations, S.I. No. 118 of 1979
	75(1)	**Social Welfare (Overlapping Payments) Regulations, S.I. No. 212 of 1952**
	77(3)	*Social Welfare (Prescribed Female Relative) Regulations, S.I. No. 227 of 1968*
	77(5)	*Social Welfare (Prescribed Female Relative) Regulations, S.I. No. 268 of 1969*

Statutory Authority	Section	Statutory Instrument
Social Welfare Act, No. 11 of 1952 (*Cont.*)	Sch. I Part I par. 5	*Social Welfare (Subsidiary Employments) Regulations, S.I. No. 370 of 1974*
	Sch. I Part II par. 4	**Social Welfare (Employment by a Prescribed Relative) Regulations, S.I. No. 19 of 1953**
	Sch. I Part II par. 5	*Social Welfare (Subsidiary Employments) Regulations, S.I. No. 18 of 1953*
		Social Welfare (Subsidiary Employments) (No.2) Regulations, S.I. No. 321 of 1953
		Social Welfare (Subsidiary Employments) (Amendment) Regulations, S.I. No. 17 of 1969
		Social Welfare (Subsidiary Employments) Regulations, S.I. No. 26 of 1970
		Social Welfare (Subsidiary Employments) Regulations, S.I. No. 77 of 1972
		Social Welfare (Subsidiary Employments) Regulations, S.I. No. 235 of 1977
		Social Welfare (Subsidiary Employments) Regulations, S.I. No. 100 of 1978
		Social Welfare (Subsidiary Employments) Regulations, S.I. No. 127 of 1979
	Sch. I Part II par. 6	*Social Welfare (Employment of Inconsiderable Extent) Regulations, S.I. No. 20 of 1953*
		Social Welfare (Employment of Inconsiderable Extent) (No.2) Regulations, S.I. No. 290 of 1953
		Social Welfare (Employment of Inconsiderable Extent) Regulations, S.I. No. 136 of 1979
Social Welfare Act, No. 12 of 1970	21	**Social Welfare (Old Age (Care) Allowance) Regulations, S.I. No. 226 of 1970**
		Social Welfare (Deserted Wife's Allowance) Regulations, S.I. No. 227 of 1970
		Social Welfare (Deserted Wife's Allowance) (Amendment) Regulations, S.I. No. 74 of 1972
		Social Welfare (Old Age (Care) Allowance) (Amendment) Regulations, S.I. No. 252 of 1972
		Social Welfare (Payments to Appointed Persons) Regulations, S.I. No. 143 of 1973
		Social Welfare (Overlapping Benefits) (Amendment) Regulations, S.I. No. 237 of 1973
		Social Welfare (Deserted Wife's Allowance) (Amendment) Regulations, S.I. No. 178 of 1974
		Social Welfare (Deserted Wife's Allowance) (Amendment) Regulations, S.I. No. 122 of 1976
		Social Welfare (Deserted Wife's Allowance) (Amendment) Regulations, S.I. No. 92 of 1978
	22	**Social Welfare (Deserted Wife's Allowance) Regulations, S.I. No. 227 of 1970**
		Social Welfare (Deserted Wife's Allowance) (Amendment) Regulations, S.I. No. 74 of 1972

Statutory Authority	Section	Statutory Instrument
Social Welfare Act, No. 12 of 1970 (*Cont.*)		**Social Welfare (Payments to Appointed Persons) Regulations, S.I. No. 143 of 1973**
		Social Welfare (Overlapping Benefits) (Amendment) Regulations, S.I. No. 237 of 1973
		Social Welfare (Deserted Wife's Allowance) (Amendment) Regulations, S.I. No. 178 of 1974
		Social Welfare (Deserted Wife's Allowance) (Amendment) Regulations, S.I. No. 122 of 1976
		Social Welfare (Overlapping Benefits) (Amendment) (No.2) Regulations, S.I. No. 182 of 1977
		Social Welfare (Deserted Wife's Allowance) (Amendment) Regulations, S.I. No. 92 of 1978
		Social Welfare (Overlapping Benefits) (Amendment) Regulations, S.I. No. 118 of 1979
		Social Welfare (Assistance) Regulations, S.I. No. 236 of 1979
Social Welfare Act, No. 15 of 1972	15(3)	*Social Welfare Act, 1972 (Appointed Day) Order, S.I. No. 237 of 1972*
Social Welfare Act, No. 10 of 1973	8	**Social Welfare (Social Assistance Allowance) Regulations, S.I. No. 190 of 1973**
		Social Welfare (Payments to Appointed Persons) (No.2) Regulations, S.I. No. 219 of 1973
		Social Welfare (Overlapping Benefits) (Amendment) Regulations, S.I. No. 237 of 1973
		Social Welfare (Overlapping Benefits) (Amendment) (No.2) Regulations, S.I. No. 182 of 1977
		Social Welfare (Social Assistance Allowance) (Amendment) Regulations, S.I. No. 91 of 1978
		Social Welfare (Overlapping Benefits) (Amendment) Regulations, S.I. No. 118 of 1979
		Social Welfare (Assistance) Regulations, S.I. No. 236 of 1979
	12(2)	*Social Welfare Act, 1973 (Commencement of Section 12) Order, S.I. No. 4 of 1974*
Social Welfare Act, No. 12 of 1974	2	*Social Welfare Act, 1974 (Commencement) Order, S.I. No. 196 of 1974*
Social Welfare Act, No. 1 of 1975	16	**Social Welfare (Variation of Rates of Payments) Regulations, S.I. No. 215 of 1975**
		Social Welfare (Variation of Rates of Payments) Regulations, S.I. No. 259 of 1976
		Social Welfare (Variation of Rates of Payments) Regulations, S.I. No. 313 of 1977
		Social Welfare (Variation of Rates of Payments) Regulations, S.I. No. 320 of 1979
Social Welfare Act, No. 5 of 1984	17	*Social Welfare Act, 1984 (Part III) (Commencement) Order, S.I. No. 277 of 1984*
	30	*Social Welfare Act, 1984 (Part IV) (Commencement) Order, S.I. No. 158 of 1984*

Statutory Authority	Section	Statutory Instrument
Social Welfare (Amendment) Act, No. 36 of 1958	4(3)	*Social Welfare (Amendment) Act, 1958 (Commencement) Order, S.I. No. 271 of 1958*
Social Welfare (Amendment) Act, No. 25 of 1960	24	*Social Welfare (Amendment) Act, 1960 (Commencement) Order, S.I. No. 208 of 1960*
Social Welfare (Amendment) Act, No. 25 of 1978	3	*Social Welfare (Amendment) Act, 1978 (Commencement) Order, S.I. No. 62 of 1979*
		Social Welfare (Amendment) Act, 1978 (Commencement) Order, S.I. No. 316 of 1980
	5(4)	**Social Welfare (Rates of Contribution and Yearly Reckonable Earnings) (Confirmation and Variation) Regulations, S.I. No. 65 of 1979**
	11	**Social Welfare (Collection of Employment Contributions by the Collector-General) Regulations, S.I. No. 77 of 1979**
		Social Welfare (Collection of Employment Contributions for Special Contributors) Regulations, S.I. No. 120 of 1979
	12	**Social Welfare (Collection of Employment Contributions by the Collector-General) Regulations, S.I. No. 77 of 1979**
		Social Welfare (Collection of Employment Contributions for Special Contributors) Regulations, S.I. No. 120 of 1979
	16(2)	**Social Welfare (Rates of Contribution and Yearly Reckonable Earnings) (Confirmation and Variation) Regulations, S.I. No. 65 of 1979**
	20	*Social Welfare (Contributions) (Transitional) Regulations, S.I. No. 86 of 1979*
		Social Welfare (Voluntary Contributors) Regulations, S.I. No. 119 of 1979
		Social Welfare (Pay-related Benefit) Regulations, S.I. No. 141 of 1979
		Social Welfare (Contributions) (Transitional) (Amendment) Regulations, S.I. No. 163 of 1980
		Social Welfare (Contributions) (Transitional) (Amendment) Regulations, S.I. No. 7 of 1981
Social Welfare (Children's Allowances) Act, No. 12 of 1952	2	*Social Welfare (Children's Allowances) Act, 1952 (Section 2) Order, S.I. No. 203 of 1952*
	5(k)	**Social Welfare (Assistance Decisions and Appeals) Regulations, S.I. No. 9 of 1953**
		Social Welfare (Assistance Decisions and Appeals) (No.2) Regulations, S.I. No. 305 of 1953
		Social Welfare (Assistance Decisions and Appeals) Regulations, S.I. No. 127 of 1963
Social Welfare (Consolidation) Act, No. 1 of 1981	2	**Social Welfare (Adult Dependent) Regulations, S.I. No. 369 of 1986**
	2(4)	*Social Welfare (Special Provisions for Volunteer Workers) Regulations, S.I. No. 161 of 1985*

Statutory Authority	Section	Statutory Instrument
Social Welfare (Consolidation) Act, No. 1 of 1981 (*Cont.*)	2(6)	**Social Welfare (Normal Residence) Regulations, S.I. No. 367 of 1986**
	3	**Social Welfare (Old Age and Widows' and Orphans' (Contributory) Pensions, Retirement Pension and Deserted Wife's Benefit) (Amendment) Regulations, S.I. No. 110 of 1981**
		Social Welfare (Modifications of Insurance) (Amendment) Regulations, S.I. No. 123 of 1981
		Social Welfare (Disability Benefit and Unemployment Benefit) (Amendment) Regulations, S.I. No. 131 of 1981
		Social Welfare (Pay-related Benefit) (Amendment) Regulations, S.I. No. 135 of 1981
		Social Welfare (Occupational Injuries) Regulations, S.I. No. 136 of 1981
		Social Welfare (Maternity Allowance) (Additional Benefit) Regulations, S.I. No. 138 of 1981
		Social Welfare (Maternity Allowance) (Amendment) Regulations, S.I. No. 139 of 1981
		Social Welfare (Variation of Rates of Payments) Regulations, S.I. No. 312 of 1981
		Social Welfare (Occupational Injuries) (Amendment) Regulations, S.I. No. 340 of 1981
		Social Welfare (Old Age and Widows' and Orphans' (Contributory) Pensions, Retirement Pension and Deserted Wife's Benefit) (Amendment) (No.2) Regulations, S.I. No. 346 of 1981
		Social Welfare (Disability Benefit and Unemployment Benefit) (Amendment) (No.2) Regulations, S.I. No. 347 of 1981
		Social Welfare (Contributions) (Amendment) Regulations, S.I. No. 377 of 1981
		Social Welfare (Occupational Injuries) (Amendment) Regulations, S.I. No. 78 of 1982
		Social Welfare (Maternity Allowance) (Additional Benefit) (Amendment) Regulations, S.I. No. 80 of 1982
		Social Welfare (Modifications of Insurance) (Amendment) Regulations, S.I. No. 82 of 1982
		Social Welfare (Death Grant) (Amendment) Regulations, S.I. No. 91 of 1982
		Social Welfare (Disability Benefit and Unemployment Benefit) (Amendment) Regulations, S.I. No. 92 of 1982
		Social Welfare (Old Age and Widows' and Orphans' (Contributory) Pensions, Retirement Pension and Deserted Wife's Benefit) S.I. No. 93 of 1982
		Social Welfare (Collection of Employment Contributions by the Collector-General) (Amendment) Regulations, S.I. No. 94 of 1982
		Social Welfare (Pay-related Benefit) (Amendment) Regulations, S.I. No. 95 of 1982
		Social Welfare (Subsidiary Employments) Regulations, S.I. No. 172 of 1982

Social Welfare (Consolidation) Act,
No. 1 of 1981 (*Cont.*)

Social Welfare (Contributions) (Amendment) Regulations, S.I. No. 242 of 1982

Social Welfare (Temporary Provisions) Regulations, S.I. No. 281 of 1982

Social Welfare (Social Welfare Tribunal) Regulations, S.I. No. 309 of 1982

Social Welfare (Temporary Provisions) (No.2) Regulations, S.I. No. 325 of 1982

Social Welfare (Pay-related Benefit) (Amendment) Regulations, S.I. No. 92 of 1983

Social Welfare (Maternity Allowance) (Additional Benefit) (Amendment) Regulations, S.I. No. 95 of 1983

Social Welfare (Collection of Employment Contributions by the Collector-General) (Amendment) Regulations, S.I. No. 96 of 1983

Social Welfare (Disability Benefit and Unemployment Benefit) (Amendment) Regulations, S.I. No. 156 of 1983

Social Welfare (Occupational Injuries) (Amendment) Regulations, S.I. No. 157 of 1983

Social Welfare (Contributions) Regulations, S.I. No. 179 of 1983

Social Welfare (Old Age and Widows' and Orphans' (Contributory) Pensions, Retirement Pension and Deserted Wife's Benefit) (Amendment) Regulations, S.I. No. 182 of 1983

Social Welfare (Overlapping Benefits) (Amendment) Regulations, S.I. No. 253 of 1983

Social Welfare (Variation of Rates of Unemployment Assistance) Regulations, S.I. No. 268 of 1983

Social Welfare (Temporary Provisions) Regulations, S.I. No. 354 of 1983

Social Welfare (Occupational Injuries) (No.2) Regulations, S.I. No. 391 of 1983

Social Welfare (Occupational Injuries) (Prescribed Diseases) Regulations, S.I. No. 392 of 1983

Social Welfare (Supplementary Welfare Allowances) Regulations, S.I. No. 413 of 1983

Social Welfare (Amendment of Miscellaneous Social Insurance Provisions) Regulations, S.I. No. 90 of 1984

Social Welfare (Voluntary Contributors) (Amendment) Regulations, S.I. No. 91 of 1984

Social Welfare (Old Age and Blind Pensions) Regulations, S.I. No. 159 of 1984

Social Welfare (Pay-related Benefit) (Enterprise Allowance) Regulations, S.I. No. 214 of 1984

Social Welfare (Contributions) Regulations, S.I. No. 224 of 1984

Social Welfare (Family Income Supplement) Regulations, S.I. No. 278 of 1984

Social Welfare (Overlapping Benefits) (Amendment) Regulations, S.I. No. 279 of 1984

Statutory Authority	Section	Statutory Instrument
Social Welfare (Consolidation) Act, No. 1 of 1981 (*Cont.*)		*Social Welfare (Temporary Provisions) Regulations, S.I. No. 317 of 1984*
		Social Welfare (Supplementary Welfare Allowances) Regulations, S.I. No. 373 of 1984
		Social Welfare (Amendment of Miscellaneous Social Insurance Provisions) Regulations, S.I. No. 101 of 1985
		Social Welfare (Occupational Injuries) (Prescribed Diseases) (Amendment) Regulations, S.I. No. 102 of 1985
		Social Welfare (Special Provisions for Volunteer Workers) Regulations, S.I. No. 161 of 1985
		Social Welfare (Amendment of Miscellaneous Social Insurance Provisions) (No.2) Regulations, S.I. No. 229 of 1985
		Social Welfare (Family Income Supplement) (Amendment) Regulations, S.I. No. 337 of 1985
		Social Welfare (Temporary Provisions) Regulations, S.I. No. 393 of 1985
		Social Welfare (Insurance Inclusions and Exclusions) Regulations, 1985, S.I. No. 437 of 1985
		Social Welfare (Supplementary Welfare Allowances) Regulations, S.I. No. 443 of 1985
		Social Welfare (Amendment of Miscellaneous Social Insurance Provisions Regulations, S.I. No. 81 of 1986
		Social Welfare (Amendment of Miscellaneous Social Insurance Provisions) (No.2) Regulations, S.I. No. 237 of 1986
		Social Welfare (Amendment of Miscellaneous Social Insurance Provisions) (No.3) Regulations, S.I. No. 255 of 1986
		Social Welfare (Preservation of Rights) Regulations, S.I. No. 366 of 1986
		Social Welfare (Normal Residence) Regulations, S.I. No. 367 of 1986
		Social Welfare (Overlapping Benefits) (Amendment) Regulations, S.I. No. 368 of 1986
		Social Welfare (Adult Dependent) Regulations, S.I. No. 369 of 1986
		Social Welfare (Temporary Provisions) Regulations, S.I. No. 387 of 1986
		Social Welfare (Preservation of Rights) (No.2) Order, S.I. No. 422 of 1986
		Social Welfare (Family Income Supplement) (Amendment) Regulations, S.I. No. 446 of 1986
	3(2)	**Social Welfare (Rent Allowance) Regulations, S.I. No. 220 of 1982**
		Social Welfare (Rent Allowance) Regulations, S.I. No. 186 of 1983
		Social Welfare (Rent Allowance) (Amendment) Regulations, S.I. No. 352 of 1983

Statutory Authority	Section	Statutory Instrument
Social Welfare (Consolidation) Act, No. 1 of 1981 (*Cont.*)		Social Welfare (Rent Allowance) (Amendment) Regulations, S.I. No. 171 of 1984
		Social Welfare (Rent Allowance) (Amendment) Regulations, S.I. No. 236 of 1985
		Social Welfare (Rent Allowance) (Amendment) Regulations, S.I. No. 218 of 1986
	3(3)	Social Welfare (Rent Allowance) Regulations, S.I. No. 220 of 1982
		Social Welfare (Rent Allowance) Regulations, S.I. No. 186 of 1983
		Social Welfare (Rent Allowance) (Amendment) Regulations, S.I. No. 352 of 1983
		Social Welfare (Rent Allowance) (Amendment) Regulations, S.I. No. 171 of 1984
		Social Welfare (Rent Allowance) (Amendment) Regulations, S.I. No. 236 of 1985
		Social Welfare (Rent Allowance) (Amendment) Regulations, S.I. No. 218 of 1986
	5(4)	Social Welfare (Insurance Inclusions and Exclusions) Regulations, 1985, S.I. No. 437 of 1985
	5(5)	Social Welfare (Insurance Inclusions and Exclusions) Regulations, 1985, S.I. No. 437 of 1985
	7	Social Welfare (Modifications of Insurance) (Amendment) Regulations, S.I. No. 123 of 1981
		Social Welfare (Modifications of Insurance) (Amendment) Regulations, S.I. No. 82 of 1982
		Social Welfare (Amendment of Miscellaneous Social Insurance Provisions) Regulations, S.I. No. 90 of 1984
	7(1)(a)	Social Welfare (Amendment of Miscellaneous Social Insurance Provisions Regulations, S.I. No. 81 of 1986
	8	Social Welfare (Maternity Allowance) Regulations, S.I. No. 83 of 1986
	11(1)(a)	*Social Welfare (Voluntary Contributors) (Amendment) Regulations, S.I. No. 91 of 1984*
		Social Welfare (Amendment of Miscellaneous Social Insurance Provisions) Regulations, S.I. No. 101 of 1985
		Social Welfare (Amendment of Miscellaneous Social Insurance Provisions Regulations, S.I. No. 81 of 1986
	14	Social Welfare (Contributions) Regulations, S.I. No. 179 of 1983
		Social Welfare (Contributions) Regulations, S.I. No. 224 of 1984
		Social Welfare (Amendment of Miscellaneous Social Insurance Provisions) Regulations, S.I. No. 101 of 1985

Social Welfare (Consolidation) Act,
No. 1 of 1981 (*Cont.*)

Social Welfare (Disability Benefit and Unemployment Benefit) (Amendment) Regulations, S.I. No. 156 of 1983

Social Welfare (Amendment of Miscellaneous Social Insurance Provisions) Regulations, S.I. No. 90 of 1984

Social Welfare (Amendment of Miscellaneous Social Insurance Provisions) (No.2) Regulations, S.I. No. 229 of 1985

Social Welfare (Amendment of Miscellaneous Social Insurance Provisions) (No.3) Regulations, S.I. No. 255 of 1986

38(10) Social Welfare (Amendment of Miscellaneous Social Insurance Provisions Regulations, S.I. No. 81 of 1986

41 *Social Welfare (Special Provisions for Volunteer Workers) Regulations, S.I. No. 161 of 1985*

42 Social Welfare (Occupational Injuries) Regulations, S.I. No. 136 of 1981

Social Welfare (Occupational Injuries) (Amendment) Regulations, S.I. No. 340 of 1981

Social Welfare (Occupational Injuries) (Amendment) Regulations, S.I. No. 78 of 1982

Social Welfare (Occupational Injuries) (Amendment) Regulations, S.I. No. 157 of 1983

Social Welfare (Amendment of Miscellaneous Social Insurance Provisions) Regulations, S.I. No. 90 of 1984

Social Welfare (Amendment of Miscellaneous Social Insurance Provisions) (No.2) Regulations, S.I. No. 229 of 1985

Social Welfare (Amendment of Miscellaneous Social Insurance Provisions Regulations, S.I. No. 81 of 1986

Social Welfare (Amendment of Miscellaneous Social Insurance Provisions) (No.3) Regulations, S.I. No. 255 of 1986

43 Social Welfare (Occupational Injuries) Regulations, S.I. No. 136 of 1981

Social Welfare (Occupational Injuries) (Amendment) Regulations, S.I. No. 340 of 1981

Social Welfare (Occupational Injuries) (Amendment) Regulations, S.I. No. 78 of 1982

Social Welfare (Occupational Injuries) (Amendment) Regulations, S.I. No. 157 of 1983

Social Welfare (Amendment of Miscellaneous Social Insurance Provisions) Regulations, S.I. No. 90 of 1984

Social Welfare (Amendment of Miscellaneous Social Insurance Provisions) (No.2) Regulations, S.I. No. 229 of 1985

Social Welfare (Amendment of Miscellaneous Social Insurance Provisions) (No.3) Regulations, S.I. No. 255 of 1986

Statutory Authority	Section	Statutory Instrument
Social Welfare (Consolidation) Act, No. 1 of 1981 (*Cont.*)	43(4)	**Social Welfare (Occupational Injuries) (No.2) Regulations, S.I. No. 391 of 1983**
	45	**Social Welfare (Occupational Injuries) Regulations, S.I. No. 136 of 1981**
		Social Welfare (Amendment of Miscellaneous Social Insurance Provisions) (No.2) Regulations, S.I. No. 237 of 1986
	46	**Social Welfare (Occupational Injuries) Regulations, S.I. No. 136 of 1981**
		Social Welfare (Occupational Injuries) (Amendment) Regulations, S.I. No. 340 of 1981
		Social Welfare (Occupational Injuries) (Amendment) Regulations, S.I. No. 78 of 1982
		Social Welfare (Occupational Injuries) (Amendment) Regulations, S.I. No. 157 of 1983
		Social Welfare (Amendment of Miscellaneous Social Insurance Provisions) Regulations, S.I. No. 90 of 1984
		Social Welfare (Amendment of Miscellaneous Social Insurance Provisions) (No.2) Regulations, S.I. No. 229 of 1985
		Social Welfare (Amendment of Miscellaneous Social Insurance Provisions) (No.3) Regulations, S.I. No. 255 of 1986
	48	**Social Welfare (Amendment of Miscellaneous Social Insurance Provisions Regulations, S.I. No. 81 of 1986**
	54	**Social Welfare (Occupational Injuries) (Prescribed Diseases) Regulations, S.I. No. 392 of 1983**
		Social Welfare (Occupational Injuries) (Prescribed Diseases) (Amendment) Regulations, S.I. No. 102 of 1985
	56	*Social Welfare (Special Provisions for Volunteer Workers) Regulations, S.I. No. 161 of 1985*
	61	**Social Welfare (Occupational Injuries) Regulations, S.I. No. 136 of 1981**
		Social Welfare (Amendment of Miscellaneous Social Insurance Provisions Regulations, S.I. No. 81 of 1986
		Social Welfare (Amendment of Miscellaneous Social Insurance Provisions) (No.2) Regulations, S.I. No. 237 of 1986
	73	**Social Welfare (Pay-related Benefit) (Amendment) Regulations, S.I. No. 135 of 1981**
		Social Welfare (Pay-related Benefit) (Amendment) Regulations, S.I. No. 95 of 1982
		Social Welfare (Temporary Provisions) Regulations, S.I. No. 281 of 1982
		Social Welfare (Temporary Provisions) (No.2) Regulations, S.I. No. 325 of 1982
		Social Welfare (Pay-related Benefit) (Amendment) Regulations, S.I. No. 92 of 1983

933

Social Welfare (Consolidation) Act,
No. 1 of 1981 (*Cont.*)

Social Welfare (Old Age and Widows' and Orphans' (Contributory) Pensions, Retirement Pension and Deserted Wife's Benefit) (Amendment) Regulations, S.I. No. 182 of 1983

Social Welfare (Amendment of Miscellaneous Social Insurance Provisions) Regulations, S.I. No. 90 of 1984

Social Welfare (Amendment of Miscellaneous Social Insurance Provisions) (No.2) Regulations, S.I. No. 229 of 1985

Social Welfare (Amendment of Miscellaneous Social Insurance Provisions) (No.3) Regulations, S.I. No. 255 of 1986

93

Social Welfare (Old Age and Widows' and Orphans' (Contributory) Pensions, Retirement Pension and Deserted Wife's Benefit) (Amendment) Regulations, S.I. No. 110 of 1981

Social Welfare (Old Age and Widows' and Orphans' (Contributory) Pensions, Retirement Pension and Deserted Wife's Benefit) (Amendment) (No.2) Regulations, S.I. No. 346 of 1981

Social Welfare (Old Age and Widows' and Orphans' (Contributory) Pensions, Retirement Pension and Deserted Wife's Benefit) S.I. No. 93 of 1982

Social Welfare (Old Age and Widows' and Orphans' (Contributory) Pensions, Retirement Pension and Deserted Wife's Benefit) (Amendment) Regulations, S.I. No. 182 of 1983

Social Welfare (Amendment of Miscellaneous Social Insurance Provisions) Regulations, S.I. No. 90 of 1984

Social Welfare (Amendment of Miscellaneous Social Insurance Provisions) (No.2) Regulations, S.I. No. 229 of 1985

Social Welfare (Amendment of Miscellaneous Social Insurance Provisions) (No.3) Regulations, S.I. No. 255 of 1986

101

Social Welfare (Old Age and Widows' and Orphans' (Contributory) Pensions, Retirement Pension and Deserted Wife's Benefit) (Amendment) Regulations, S.I. No. 110 of 1981

Social Welfare (Old Age and Widows' and Orphans' (Contributory) Pensions, Retirement Pension and Deserted Wife's Benefit) (Amendment) (No.2) Regulations, S.I. No. 346 of 1981

Social Welfare (Old Age and Widows' and Orphans' (Contributory) Pensions, Retirement Pension and Deserted Wife's Benefit) S.I. No. 93 of 1982

Social Welfare (Old Age and Widows' and Orphans' (Contributory) Pensions, Retirement Pension and Deserted Wife's Benefit) (Amendment) Regulations, S.I. No. 182 of 1983

Social Welfare (Amendment of Miscellaneous Social Insurance Provisions) Regulations, S.I. No. 90 of 1984

Statutory Authority	Section	Statutory Instrument
Social Welfare (Consolidation) Act, No. 1 of 1981 (*Cont.*)		**Social Welfare (Amendment of Miscellaneous Social Insurance Provisions) (No.2) Regulations, S.I. No. 229 of 1985**
		Social Welfare (Amendment of Miscellaneous Social Insurance Provisions) (No.3) Regulations, S.I. No. 255 of 1986
	108	**Social Welfare (Death Grant) (Amendment) Regulations, S.I. No. 91 of 1982**
	110	**Social Welfare (Amendment of Miscellaneous Social Insurance Provisions) Regulations, S.I. No. 101 of 1985**
		Social Welfare (Special Provisions for Volunteer Workers) Regulations, S.I. No. 161 of 1985
	112	**Social Welfare (Pay-related Benefit) (Enterprise Allowance) Regulations, S.I. No. 214 of 1984**
		Social Welfare (Amendment of Miscellaneous Social Insurance Provisions Regulations, S.I. No. 81 of 1986
	115	**Social Welfare (Family Income Supplement) Regulations, S.I. No. 278 of 1984**
		Social Welfare (Family Income Supplement) (Amendment) Regulations, S.I. No. 337 of 1985
	115(3)	**Social Welfare (Amendment of Miscellaneous Social Insurance Provisions) Regulations, S.I. No. 101 of 1985**
	129	**Social Welfare (Amendment of Miscellaneous Social Insurance Provisions Regulations, S.I. No. 81 of 1986**
	130	**Social Welfare (Amendment of Miscellaneous Social Insurance Provisions Regulations, S.I. No. 81 of 1986**
		Social Welfare (Overlapping Benefits) (Amendment) Regulations, S.I. No. 368 of 1986
	130(4)	**Social Welfare (Overlapping Benefits) (Amendment) Regulations, S.I. No. 279 of 1984**
	170	**Social Welfare (Old Age and Blind Pensions) Regulations, S.I. No. 159 of 1984**
	209	*Social Welfare (Supplementary Welfare Allowances) (Amendment) Regulations, S.I. No. 49 of 1985*
		Social Welfare (Supplementary Welfare Allowances) (Amendment) (No.2) S.I. No. 334 of 1985
	218(8)	*Social Welfare (Supplementary Welfare Allowances) Regulations, S.I. No. 413 of 1983*
	218(9)	*Social Welfare (Supplementary Welfare Allowances) Regulations, S.I. No. 373 of 1984*
		Social Welfare (Supplementary Welfare Allowances) Regulations, S.I. No. 443 of 1985
	219	**Social Welfare (Overlapping Benefits) (Amendment) Regulations, S.I. No. 253 of 1983**
		Social Welfare (Overlapping Benefits) (Amendment) Regulations, S.I. No. 368 of 1986

Statutory Authority	Section	Statutory Instrument
Social Welfare (Consolidation) Act, No. 1 of 1981 (*Cont.*)	232D	**Social Welfare (Family Income Supplement) Regulations, S.I. No. 278 of 1984**
	232F	**Social Welfare (Family Income Supplement) Regulations, S.I. No. 278 of 1984**
		Social Welfare (Family Income Supplement) (Amendment) Regulations, S.I. No. 337 of 1985
		Social Welfare (Family Income Supplement) (Amendment) Regulations, S.I. No. 446 of 1986
	301B	**Social Welfare (Social Welfare Tribunal) Regulations, S.I. No. 309 of 1982**
	303	**Registration of Births, Deaths and Marriages (Reduced Fees) Regulations, S.I. No. 46 of 1982**
		Registration of Births, Deaths and Marriages (Reduced Fees) (Amendment) Regulations, S.I. No. 148 of 1983
		Registration of Births, Deaths and Marriages (Reduced Fees) (Amendment) Regulations, S.I. No. 359 of 1984
	308	**Social Welfare (Variation of Rates of Payments) Regulations, S.I. No. 312 of 1981**
		Social Welfare (Temporary Provisions) Regulations, S.I. No. 281 of 1982
		Social Welfare (Temporary Provisions) (No.2) Regulations, S.I. No. 325 of 1982
		Social Welfare (Variation of Rates of Unemployment Assistance) Regulations, S.I. No. 268 of 1983
		Social Welfare (Temporary Provisions) Regulations, S.I. No. 354 of 1983
		Social Welfare (Temporary Provisions) Regulations, S.I. No. 317 of 1984
		Social Welfare (Temporary Provisions) Regulations, S.I. No. 393 of 1985
		Social Welfare (Temporary Provisions) Regulations, S.I. No. 387 of 1986
	310	*Social Welfare (Consolidation) Act, 1981 (Commencement) Order, S.I. No. 63 of 1981*
	Sch. I Part II par. 4	**Social Welfare (Subsidiary Employments) Regulations, S.I. No. 172 of 1982**
Social Welfare (Miscellaneous Provisions) Act, No. 21 of 1957	7	*Social Welfare (Miscellaneous Provisions) Act, 1957 (Date of Commencement) Order, S.I. No. 269 of 1957*
Social Welfare (Miscellaneous Provisions) Act, No. 26 of 1963	13	**Social Welfare (Claims and Payments) (Amendment) Regulations, S.I. No. 289 of 1966**
Social Welfare (Miscellaneous Provisions) Act, No. 28 of 1964	5(4)	*Social Welfare (Miscellaneous Provisions) Act, 1964 (Appointed Day) Order, S.I. No. 238 of 1964*
	8(2)	*Social Welfare (Miscellaneous Provisions) Act, 1964 (Appointed Day) Order, S.I. No. 238 of 1964*

Statutory Authority	Section	Statutory Instrument
Social Welfare (Miscellaneous Provisions) Act, No. 20 of 1965	6(2)	**Social Welfare (Remuneration Limit for Insured Persons) Order, S.I. No. 163 of 1971**
	6(3)	*Social Welfare (Miscellaneous Provisions) Act, 1965 (Appointed Day) Order, S.I. No. 172 of 1965*
	7	**Social Welfare (Crediting of Contributions) Regulations, S.I. No. 193 of 1965**
	8(3)	**Unemployment Assistance (Specified Areas) Order, S.I. No. 236 of 1965**
Social Welfare (Miscellaneous Provisions) Act, No. 24 of 1966	5(2)	*Social Welfare (Miscellaneous Provisions) Act, 1966 (Appointed Day) Order, S.I. No. 225 of 1966*
	15	**Social Welfare (United Kingdom Reciprocal Arrangements) Order, S.I. No. 218 of 1968**
		Social Welfare (United Kingdom Reciprocal Arrangements) Order, S.I. No. 270 of 1971
Social Welfare (No.2) Act, No. 14 of 1974	3	**Social Welfare (Single Women's Allowance) (Amendment) Regulations, S.I. No. 90 of 1978**
	8	**Social Welfare (Single Women's Allowance) Regulations, S.I. No. 209 of 1974**
		Social Welfare (Overlapping Benefits) (Amendment) Regulations, S.I. No. 224 of 1974
		Social Welfare (Overlapping Benefits) (Amendment) (No.2) Regulations, S.I. No. 182 of 1977
		Social Welfare (Assistance) Regulations, S.I. No. 236 of 1979
	9	**Social Welfare (Prisoner's Wife's Allowance) Regulations, S.I. No. 220 of 1974**
		Social Welfare (Overlapping Benefits) (Amendment) Regulations, S.I. No. 224 of 1974
		Social Welfare (Overlapping Benefits) (Amendment) (No.2) Regulations, S.I. No. 182 of 1977
		Social Welfare (Prisoner's Wife's Allowance) (Amendment) Regulations, S.I. No. 93 of 1978
		Social Welfare (Overlapping Benefits) (Amendment) Regulations, S.I. No. 118 of 1979
		Social Welfare (Assistance) Regulations, S.I. No. 236 of 1979
	10	**Social Welfare (Payment of Benefit After Death) Regulations, S.I. No. 208 of 1974**
Social Welfare (No.2) Act, No. 23 of 1982	2	*Social Welfare (No.2) Act, 1982 (Commencement) Order, S.I. No. 308 of 1982*
Social Welfare (No.2) Ac , No. 14 of 1985	20	*Social Welfare (Preservation of Rights) Regulations, S.I. No. 366 of 1986*
		Social Welfare (Preservation of Rights) (No.2) Order, S.I. No. 422 of 1986
	24	*Social Welfare (No.2) Act, 1985 (Section 6) (Commencement) Order, S.I. No. 173 of 1986*
		Social Welfare (No.2) Act, 1985 (Commencement) Order, S.I. No. 365 of 1986

Statutory Authority	Section	Statutory Instrument
Social Welfare (Occupational Injuries) Act, No. 16 of 1966	1	**Social Welfare (Occupational Injuries) Regulations, S.I. No. 77 of 1967**
		Social Welfare (Occupational Injuries) (Amendment) Regulations, S.I. No. 206 of 1970
		Social Welfare (Occupational Injuries) (Amendment) Regulations, S.I. No. 232 of 1971
		Social Welfare (Occupational Injuries) (Amendment) Regulations, S.I. No. 219 of 1972
		Social Welfare (Administration of Pay-Related Benefit) Regulations, S.I. No. 78 of 1974
		Social Welfare (Occupational Injuries) (Amendment) Regulations, S.I. No. 210 of 1974
		Social Welfare (Occupational Injuries) (Amendment) (No.2) Regulations, S.I. No. 243 of 1974
		Social Welfare (Occupational Injuries) (Amendment) Regulations, S.I. No. 69 of 1975
		Social Welfare (Occupational Injuries) (Amendment) (No.2) Regulations, S.I. No. 231 of 1975
		Social Welfare (Occupational Injuries) (Amendment) Regulations, S.I. No. 76 of 1976
		Social Welfare (Occupational Injuries) (Amendment) Regulations, S.I. No. 96 of 1977
		Social Welfare (Occupational Injuries) (Amendment) (No.2) Regulations, S.I. No. 316 of 1977
		Social Welfare (Occupational Injuries) (Amendment) Regulations, S.I. No. 89 of 1978
		Social Welfare (Occupational Injuries) (Amendment) (No.2) Regulations, S.I. No. 326 of 1979
		Social Welfare (Occupational Injuries) (Amendment) Regulations, S.I. No. 83 of 1980
	1(4)	*Social Welfare (Occupational Injuries) Act, 1966 (Appointed Day) Order, S.I. No. 35 of 1967*
	1(7)	*Social Welfare (Modifications of Insurance) (Amendment) Regulations, S.I. No. 81 of 1967*
		Social Welfare (Modifications of Insurance) Regulations, S.I. No. 87 of 1979
		Social Welfare (Occupational Injuries) (Amendment) Regulations, S.I. No. 99 of 1979
	3	**Social Welfare (Insurable (Occupational Injuries) Employment) Regulations, S.I. No. 80 of 1967**
	3(9)	**Social Welfare (Insurable (Occupational Injuries) Employment) (Amendment) Regulations, S.I. No. 229 of 1968**
	3(10)	*Social Welfare (Modifications of Insurance) (Amendment) Regulations, S.I. No. 81 of 1967*
		Social Welfare (Modifications of Insurance) Regulations, S.I. No. 87 of 1979
	6	*Social Welfare (Modifications of Insurance) (Amendment) Regulations, S.I. No. 81 of 1967*
		Social Welfare (Modifications of Insurance) (Amendment) Regulations, S.I. No. 164 of 1968

Social Welfare (Occupational Injuries) Act, No. 16 of 1966 (*Cont.*)		Social Welfare (Modifications of Insurance) Regulations, S.I. No. 87 of 1979
	8	Social Welfare (Occupational Injuries) Regulations, S.I. No. 77 of 1967
		Social Welfare (Occupational Injuries) (Amendment) Regulations, S.I. No. 206 of 1970
		Social Welfare (Occupational Injuries) (Amendment) Regulations, S.I. No. 232 of 1971
		Social Welfare (Occupational Injuries) (Amendment) (No.2) Regulations, S.I. No. 326 of 1979
		Social Welfare (Occupational Injuries) (Amendment) Regulations, S.I. No. 83 of 1980
	9	Social Welfare (Occupational Injuries) Regulations, S.I. No. 77 of 1967
		Social Welfare (Occupational Injuries) (Amendment) Regulations, S.I. No. 206 of 1970
		Social Welfare (Occupational Injuries) (Amendment) Regulations, S.I. No. 232 of 1971
		Social Welfare (Occupational Injuries) (Amendment) (No.2) Regulations, S.I. No. 326 of 1979
		Social Welfare (Occupational Injuries) (Amendment) Regulations, S.I. No. 83 of 1980
	13	Social Welfare (Occupational Injuries) Regulations, S.I. No. 77 of 1967
		Social Welfare (Occupational Injuries) (Amendment) (No.2) Regulations, S.I. No. 326 of 1979
		Social Welfare (Occupational Injuries) (Amendment) Regulations, S.I. No. 83 of 1980
	14	Social Welfare (Occupational Injuries) Regulations, S.I. No. 77 of 1967
		Social Welfare (Occupational Injuries) (Amendment) Regulations, S.I. No. 183 of 1969
		Social Welfare (Occupational Injuries) (Amendment) Regulations, S.I. No. 206 of 1970
		Social Welfare (Occupational Injuries) (Amendment) Regulations, S.I. No. 232 of 1971
	15	Social Welfare (Occupational Injuries) Regulations, S.I. No. 77 of 1967
		Social Welfare (Occupational Injuries) (Amendment) Regulations, S.I. No. 183 of 1969
		Social Welfare (Occupational Injuries) (Amendment) Regulations, S.I. No. 206 of 1970
		Social Welfare (Occupational Injuries) (Amendment) Regulations, S.I. No. 232 of 1971
	18	Social Welfare (Occupational Injuries) (Amendment) Regulations, S.I. No. 183 of 1969
	19	Social Welfare (Occupational Injuries) (Amendment) Regulations, S.I. No. 183 of 1969
	22	Social Welfare (Claims and Payments) (Amendment) Regulations, S.I. No. 85 of 1967

Statutory Authority	Section	Statutory Instrument
Social Welfare (Occupational Injuries) Act, No. 16 of 1966 (*Cont.*)		**Social Welfare (Claims and Payments) (Amendment) Regulations, S.I. No. 233 of 1971**
	23	**Social Welfare (Occupational Injuries) Regulations, S.I. No. 77 of 1967**
		Social Welfare (Occupational Injuries) (Prescribed Diseases) Regulations, S.I. No. 78 of 1967
		Social Welfare (Occupational Injuries) (Prescribed Diseases) (Amendment) Regulations, S.I. No. 357 of 1973
		Social Welfare (Occupational Injuries) (Prescribed Diseases) (Amendment) Regulations, S.I. No. 211 of 1977
	24	**Social Welfare (Occupational Injuries) Regulations, S.I. No. 77 of 1967**
		Social Welfare (Claims and Payments) (Amendment) Regulations, S.I. No. 85 of 1967
	26	**Social Welfare (Occupational Injuries) Regulations, S.I. No. 77 of 1967**
		Social Welfare (Occupational Injuries) (Medical Care) (Amendment) Regulations, S.I. No. 234 of 1967
	27	**Social Welfare (Claims and Payments) (Amendment) Regulations, S.I. No. 85 of 1967**
		Social Welfare (Modifications of Insurance) Regulations, S.I. No. 87 of 1979
	28	**Social Welfare (Claims and Payments) (Amendment) Regulations, S.I. No. 85 of 1967**
		Social Welfare (Modifications of Insurance) Regulations, S.I. No. 87 of 1979
	30	**Social Welfare (Claims and Payments) (Amendment) Regulations, S.I. No. 85 of 1967**
	31	**Social Welfare (Occupational Injuries) Regulations, S.I. No. 77 of 1967**
		Social Welfare (Occupational Injuries) (Amendment) (No.2) Regulations, S.I. No. 243 of 1974
	32	**Social Welfare (Occupational Injuries) Regulations, S.I. No. 77 of 1967**
	33	**Social Welfare (Occupational Injuries) Regulations, S.I. No. 77 of 1967**
Social Welfare (Pay-related Benefit) Act, No. 2 of 1973	1	*Social Welfare (Pay-related Benefit) Regulations, S.I. No. 16 of 1974*
		Social Welfare (Pay-related Benefit) Regulations, S.I. No. 124 of 1976
		Social Welfare (Pay-related Benefit) Regulations, S.I. No. 141 of 1979
	4	*Social Welfare (Pay-related Benefit) Regulations, S.I. No. 16 of 1974*
		Social Welfare (Pay-related Benefit) Regulations, S.I. No. 124 of 1976

Statutory Authority	Section	Statutory Instrument
Social Welfare (Pay-related Benefit) Act, No. 2 of 1973 (*Cont.*)		*Social Welfare (Pay-related Benefit) (Amendment) Regulations, S.I. No. 102 of 1979* **Social Welfare (Pay-related Benefit) Regulations, S.I. No. 141 of 1979** **Social Welfare (Pay-related Benefit) (Amendment) Regulations, S.I. No. 98 of 1980**
	5	*Social Welfare (Pay-related Contributions) Regulations, S.I. No. 354 of 1973* *Social Welfare (Special Contributors for Pay-related Benefit) Regulations, S.I. No. 77 of 1974* *Social Welfare (Pay-related Contributions) Regulations, S.I. No. 79 of 1974*
	6	*Social Welfare (Pay-related Contributions) Regulations, S.I. No. 354 of 1973*
	7	*Social Welfare (Pay-related Contributions) Regulations, S.I. No. 354 of 1973* *Social Welfare (Special Contributors for Pay-related Benefit) Regulations, S.I. No. 77 of 1974* **Social Welfare (Pay-related Contributions) (Amendment) Regulations, S.I. No. 145 of 1976** **Social Welfare (Collection of Employment Contributions by the Collector-General) Regulations, S.I. No. 77 of 1979** **Social Welfare (Collection of Employment Contributions for Special Contributors) Regulations, S.I. No. 120 of 1979**
	8	*Social Welfare (Pay-related Contributions) Regulations, S.I. No. 354 of 1973* *Social Welfare (Pay-related Benefit) Regulations, S.I. No. 16 of 1974* *Social Welfare (Special Contributors for Pay-related Benefit) Regulations, S.I. No. 77 of 1974* **Social Welfare (Administration of Pay-related Benefit) Regulations, S.I. No. 78 of 1974** *Social Welfare (Pay-related Benefit) Regulations, S.I. No. 124 of 1976* **Social Welfare (Collection of Employment Contributions by the Collector-General) Regulations, S.I. No. 77 of 1979** **Social Welfare (Collection of Employment Contributions for Special Contributors) Regulations, S.I. No. 120 of 1979** **Social Welfare (Pay-related Benefit) Regulations, S.I. No. 141 of 1979**
	9	*Social Welfare (Pay-related Contributions) Regulations, S.I. No. 354 of 1973* *Social Welfare (Pay-related Benefit) Regulations, S.I. No. 16 of 1974* *Social Welfare (Scale of Pay-related Contributions) Regulations, S.I. No. 74 of 1974* **Social Welfare (Collection of Employment Contributions by the Collector-General) Regulations, S.I. No. 77 of 1979**

Statutory Authority	Section	Statutory Instrument
Social Welfare (Pay-related Benefit) Act, No. 2 of 1973 (*Cont.*)	18	*Social Welfare (Pay-related Benefit) Act, 1973 (Commencement) Order, S.I. No. 355 of 1973*
Social Welfare (Pay-related Benefit) Act, No. 8 of 1975	5	*Social Welfare (Extension of Duration of Pay-related Benefit) Order, S.I. No. 206 of 1975*
	6	*Social Welfare (Pay-related Benefit) Act, 1975 (Commencement) Order, S.I. No. 114 of 1975*
Social Welfare (Reciprocal Arrangements) Act, No. 10 of 1948	3	**Social Welfare (Great Britain Reciprocal Arrangements) Order, S.I. No. 310 of 1948**
		Social Welfare (Great Britain Reciprocal Arrangements) Order, S.I. No. 52 of 1949
		Social Welfare (Great Britain Reciprocal Arrangements) (No.2) Order, S.I. No. 73 of 1949
		Social Welfare (Northern Ireland Reciprocal Arrangements) Order, S.I. No. 97 of 1949
		Social Welfare (Great Britain Reciprocal Arrangements) Order, S.I. No. 22 of 1952
		Social Welfare (Great Britain Reciprocal Arrangements) (No.2) Order, S.I. No. 77 of 1952
		Social Welfare (Isle of Man Reciprocal Arrangements) Order, S.I. No. 309 of 1952
	3(1)	**Workmen's Compensation (Modifications Pursuant to Reciprocal Arrangements) (Great Britain) Order, S.I. No. 97 of 1960**
		Workmen's Compensation (Modifications Pursuant to Reciprocal Arrangements) (Northern Ireland) Order, S.I. No. 214 of 1964
Social Welfare (Supplementary Welfare Allowances) Act, No. 28 of 1975	4	**Social Welfare (Supplementary Welfare Allowances) Regulations, S.I. No. 168 of 1977**
	8	**Social Welfare (Supplementary Welfare Allowances) Regulations, S.I. No. 168 of 1977**
	10(3)	**Social Welfare (Variation of Rates of Supplementary Welfare Allowance) Regulations, S.I. No. 169 of 1977**
		Social Welfare (Variation of Rates of Supplementary Welfare Allowance) (No.2) Regulations, S.I. No. 318 of 1977
		Social Welfare (Variation of Weekly Amounts of Supplementary Welfare Allowance) Regulations, S.I. No. 323 of 1979
	11	**Social Welfare (Supplementary Welfare Allowances) Regulations, S.I. No. 168 of 1977**
	20	**Social Welfare (Supplementary Welfare Allowances) Regulations, S.I. No. 168 of 1977**
	21	**Social Welfare (Supplementary Welfare Allowances) Regulations, S.I. No. 168 of 1977**
		Social Welfare (Variation of Rates of Supplementary Welfare Allowance) Regulations, S.I. No. 169 of 1977

Statutory Authority	Section	Statutory Instrument
Social Welfare (Supplementary Welfare Allowances) Act, No. 28 of 1975 (*Cont.*)		**Social Welfare (Overlapping Benefits) (Amendment) (No.2) Regulations, S.I. No. 182 of 1977**
		Social Welfare (Variation of Rates of Supplementary Welfare Allowance) (No.2) Regulations, S.I. No. 318 of 1977
		Social Welfare (Variation of Weekly Amounts of Supplementary Welfare Allowance) Regulations, S.I. No. 323 of 1979
	25	**Social Welfare (Supplementary Welfare Allowances) Regulations, S.I. No. 168 of 1977**
	28	*Social Welfare (Supplementary Welfare Allowances) Act, 1975 (Commencement) Order, S.I. No. 156 of 1977*
Social Welfare (Treatment Benefit) Regulations, S.I. No. 23 of 1953	2	*Social Welfare (Commencement of Dental Benefit) Order, S.I. No. 195 of 1953*
Solicitors Act, No. 36 of 1954	4	*Solicitors Act, 1954 (Fees) Regulations, S.I. No. 299 of 1954*
		Solicitors Act, 1954 (Apprentices' Fees) Regulations, S.I. No. 300 of 1954
		Solicitors (Disciplinary Committee) Rules, S.I. No. 33 of 1955
		Solicitors Act, 1954 (Practising Certificates and Restrictions on Solicitors) Regulations, S.I. No. 60 of 1955
		Solicitors Act, 1954 (Apprenticeship and Education) Regulations, S.I. No. 90 of 1955
		Solicitors Act, 1954 (Professional Practice, Conduct and Discipline) Regulations, S.I. No. 151 of 1955
		Solicitors Act, 1954 (Apprenticeship and Education) Regulations, S.I. No. 217 of 1955
		Solicitors' Accounts Regulations, S.I. No. 218 of 1955
		Solicitors (Compensation Fund) Regulations, S.I. No. 234 of 1955
		Solicitors Act, 1954 (Apprentices' Fees) Regulations, S.I. No. 140 of 1956
		Solicitors Act, 1954 (Apprenticeship and Education) (Amendment) Regulations, S.I. No. 307 of 1956
		Solicitors' Accounts Regulations, S.I. No. 308 of 1956
		Solicitors' Accounts Regulations, S.I. No. 252 of 1957
		Solicitors' Accounts (Amendment) Regulations, S.I. No. 193 of 1958
		Solicitors Act, 1954 (Apprenticeship and Education) (Amendment) Regulations, S.I. No. 94 of 1960
		Solicitors Act, 1954 (Apprentices' Fees) Regulations, S.I. No. 131 of 1960
		Solicitors' Accounts (Amendment) Regulations, S.I. No. 51 of 1961

Social Welfare (Supplementary
Welfare Allowances) Act, No. 28 of
1975 (*Cont.*)

Solicitors Act, 1954 (Apprentices' Fees) Regulations,
S.I. No. 131 of 1962

Solicitors (Compensation Fund) Regulations, S.I.
No. 115 of 1963

Solicitors' Accounts (Amendment) Regulations, S.I.
No. 163 of 1965

Solicitors Act, 1954 (Apprenticeship and Education)
(Amendment) Regulations, S.I. No. 201 of 1965

Solicitors' Accounts (Amendment) Regulations, S.I.
No. 75 of 1966

Solicitors' Accounts (Amendment No.2) Regula-
tions, S.I. No. 193 of 1966

Solicitors Act, 1954 (Apprenticeship and Education)
(Amendment) Regulations, S.I. No. 230 of 1966

Solicitors' Accounts Regulations, S.I. No. 44 of 1967

Solicitors Act, 1954 (Apprenticeship and Education)
(Amendment) Regulations, S.I. No. 17 of 1968

Solicitors Act, 1954 (Fees) Regulations, S.I. No. 240
of 1968

Solicitors Act, 1954 (Apprenticeship and Education)
(Amendment) Regulations, S.I. No. 110 of 1969

Solicitors' Accounts (Amendment) Regulations, S.I.
No. 94 of 1970

Solicitors' Accounts (Amendment) (No.2) Regula-
tions, S.I. No. 107 of 1970

Solicitors Act, 1954 (Apprenticeship and Education)
(Amendment) Regulations, S.I. No. 108 of 1970

Solicitors' Accounts (Amendment No.3) Regula-
tions, S.I. No. 231 of 1970

Solicitors Act, 1954 (Fees) (Amendment) Regula-
tions, S.I. No. 245 of 1970

Solicitors' Accounts (Amendment) Regulations, S.I.
No. 196 of 1971

Solicitors Act, 1954 (Apprenticeship and Education)
(Amendment) Regulations, S.I. No. 218 of 1971

Solicitors Practising Certificate Fees Regulations,
S.I. No. 341 of 1971

Solicitors (Professional Practice, Conduct and
Discipline) (Amendment) Regulations, S.I. No.
344 of 1971

Solicitors Act, 1954 (Apprenticeship and Education)
(Amendment) Regulations, S.I. No. 49 of 1972

Solicitors Act, 1954 (Apprenticeship and Education)
(Amendment) Regulations, S.I. No. 47 of 1973

Solicitors Act, 1954 (Fees) Regulations, S.I. No. 315
of 1973

Solicitors Act, 1954 (Apprenticeship and Education)
(Amendment No.2) Regulations, S.I. No. 333 of
1973

Solicitors Act, 1954 (Apprenticeship and Education)
(Amendment No.1) Regulations, S.I. No. 138 of
1974

Social Welfare (Supplementary
Welfare Allowances) Act, No. 28 of
1975 (*Cont.*)

Solicitors Acts, 1954 and 1960 (Apprenticeship and Education) Regulations, S.I. No. 66 of 1975

Solicitors Acts, 1954 and 1960 (Fees) Regulations, S.I. No. 288 of 1975

Solicitors' Accounts (Amendment) Regulations, S.I. No. 125 of 1976

Solicitors Acts, 1954 and 1960 (Fees) Regulations, S.I. No. 302 of 1976

Solicitors' Accounts (Amendment) Regulations, S.I. No. 242 of 1977

Solicitors Acts, 1954 and 1960 (Fees) Regulations, S.I. No. 363 of 1978

Solicitors Acts, 1954 and 1960 (Fees) Regulations, S.I. No. 401 of 1979

Solicitors Acts, 1954 and 1960 (Apprenticeship and Education Regulations, S.I. No. 226 of 1981

Solicitors Acts, 1954 and 1960 (Fees) Regulations, S.I. No. 365 of 1982

Solicitors Acts, 1954 and 1960 (Fees) Regulations, S.I. No. 380 of 1983

Solicitors' Accounts Regulations, S.I. No. 204 of 1984

Solicitors' Accounts Regulations (No.2) S.I. No. 304 of 1984

Solicitors Acts, 1954 and 1960 (Fees) Regulations, S.I. No. 341 of 1984

Solicitors Acts, 1954 and 1960 (Fees) Regulations, S.I. No. 424 of 1985

5   *Solicitors Act, 1954 (Fees) Regulations, S.I. No. 299 of 1954*

Solicitors Act, 1954 (Apprentices' Fees) Regulations, S.I. No. 300 of 1954

Solicitors (Disciplinary Committee) Rules, S.I. No. 33 of 1955

Solicitors Act, 1954 (Practising Certificates and Restrictions on Solicitors) Regulations, S.I. No. 60 of 1955

Solicitors Act, 1954 (Apprenticeship and Education) Regulations, S.I. No. 90 of 1955

Solicitors Act, 1954 (Professional Practice, Conduct and Discipline) Regulations, S.I. No. 151 of 1955

Solicitors Act, 1954 (Apprenticeship and Education) Regulations, S.I. No. 217 of 1955

Solicitors' Accounts Regulations, S.I. No. 218 of 1955

Solicitors (Compensation Fund) Regulations, S.I. No. 234 of 1955

Solicitors Act, 1954 (Apprentices' Fees) Regulations, S.I. No. 140 of 1956

Solicitors Act, 1954 (Apprenticeship and Education) (Amendment) Regulations, S.I. No. 307 of 1956

Solicitors Act, No. 36 of 1954 (*Cont.*)		*Solicitors' Accounts Regulations, S.I. No. 308 of 1956*
		Solicitors' Accounts Regulations, S.I. No. 252 of 1957
		Solicitors' Accounts (Amendment) Regulations, S.I. No. 193 of 1958
		Solicitors Act, 1954 (Apprenticeship and Education) (Amendment) Regulations, S.I. No. 94 of 1960
		Solicitors Act, 1954 (Apprentices' Fees) Regulations, S.I. No. 131 of 1960
		Solicitors' Accounts (Amendment) Regulations, S.I. No. 51 of 1961
		Solicitors Act, 1954 (Apprentices' Fees) Regulations, S.I. No. 131 of 1962
		Solicitors (Compensation Fund) Regulations, S.I. No. 115 of 1963
		Solicitors' Accounts (Amendment) Regulations, S.I. No. 163 of 1965
		Solicitors Act, 1954 (Apprenticeship and Education) (Amendment) Regulations, S.I. No. 201 of 1965
		Solicitors' Accounts (Amendment) Regulations, S.I. No. 75 of 1966
		Solicitors' Accounts (Amendment No.2) Regulations, S.I. No. 193 of 1966
		Solicitors Act, 1954 (Apprenticeship and Education) (Amendment) Regulations, S.I. No. 230 of 1966
		Solicitors' Accounts Regulations, S.I. No. 44 of 1967
		Solicitors Act, 1954 (Apprenticeship and Education) (Amendment) Regulations, S.I. No. 17 of 1968
		Solicitors Act, 1954 (Fees) Regulations, S.I. No. 240 of 1968
		Solicitors Act, 1954 (Apprenticeship and Education) (Amendment) Regulations, S.I. No. 110 of 1969
		Solicitors' Accounts (Amendment) Regulations, S.I. No. 94 of 1970
		Solicitors' Accounts (Amendment) (No.2) Regulations, S.I. No. 107 of 1970
		Solicitors Act, 1954 (Apprenticeship and Education) (Amendment) Regulations, S.I. No. 108 of 1970
		Solicitors' Accounts (Amendment No.3) Regulations, S.I. No. 231 of 1970
		Solicitors Act, 1954 (Fees) (Amendment) Regulations, S.I. No. 245 of 1970
		Solicitors' Accounts (Amendment) Regulations, S.I. No. 196 of 1971
		Solicitors Act, 1954 (Apprenticeship and Education) (Amendment) Regulations, S.I. No. 218 of 1971
		Solicitors Practising Certificate Fees Regulations, S.I. No. 341 of 1971
		Solicitors (Professional Practice, Conduct and Discipline) (Amendment) Regulations, S.I. No. 344 of 1971

Statutory Authority	Section	Statutory Instrument
Social Welfare (Supplementary Welfare Allowances) Act, No. 28 of 1975 (*Cont.*)		*Solicitors Act, 1954 (Apprenticeship and Education) (Amendment) Regulations, S.I. No. 49 of 1972*
		Solicitors Act, 1954 (Apprenticeship and Education) (Amendment) Regulations, S.I. No. 47 of 1973
		Solicitors Act, 1954 (Fees) Regulations, S.I. No. 315 of 1973
		Solicitors Act, 1954 (Apprenticeship and Education) (Amendment No.2) Regulations, S.I. No. 333 of 1973
		Solicitors Act, 1954 (Apprenticeship and Education) (Amendment No.1) Regulations, S.I. No. 138 of 1974
		Solicitors Acts, 1954 and 1960 (Apprenticeship and Education) Regulations, S.I. No. 66 of 1975
		Solicitors Acts, 1954 and 1960 (Fees) Regulations, S.I. No. 288 of 1975
		Solicitors' Accounts (Amendment) Regulations, S.I. No. 125 of 1976
		Solicitors Acts, 1954 and 1960 (Fees) Regulations, S.I. No. 302 of 1976
		Solicitors' Accounts (Amendment) Regulations, S.I. No. 242 of 1977
		Solicitors Acts, 1954 and 1960 (Apprentices' Fees) Regulations, S.I. No. 273 of 1978
		Solicitors Acts, 1954 and 1960 (Fees) Regulations, S.I. No. 363 of 1978
		Solicitors Acts, 1954 and 1960 (Fees) Regulations, S.I. No. 401 of 1979
		Solicitors Acts, 1954 and 1960 (Apprentices' Fees) (No.2) Regulations, S.I. No. 204 of 1981
		Solicitors Acts, 1954 and 1960 (Apprenticeship and Education Regulations, S.I. No. 226 of 1981
		Solicitors Acts, 1954 and 1960 (Fees) Regulations, S.I. No. 365 of 1982
		Solicitors Acts, 1954 and 1960 (Apprentices' Fees) Regulations, S.I. No. 40 of 1983
		Solicitors Acts, 1954 and 1960 (Fees) Regulations, S.I. No. 380 of 1983
		Solicitors Acts, 1954 and 1960 (Apprentices' Fees) Regulations, S.I. No. 48 of 1984
		Solicitors' Accounts Regulations, S.I. No. 204 of 1984
		Solicitors' Accounts Regulations (No.2) S.I. No. 304 of 1984
		Solicitors Acts, 1954 and 1960 (Fees) Regulations, S.I. No. 341 of 1984
		Solicitors Acts, 1954 and 1960 (Apprentices' Fees) Regulations, S.I. No. 421 of 1985
		Solicitors Acts, 1954 and 1960 (Fees) Regulations, S.I. No. 424 of 1985
		Solicitors Acts, 1954 and 1968 (Apprentices' Fees) Regulations, S.I. No. 30 of 1986
		Solicitors (Professional Practice, Conduct and Discipline) Regulations, S.I. No. 405 of 1986
	20	*Solicitors (Disciplinary Committee) Rules, S.I. No. 33 of 1955*

Statutory Authority	Section	Statutory Instrument
Social Welfare (Supplementary Welfare Allowances) Act, No. 28 of 1975 (*Cont.*)	25	*Solicitors Act, 1954 (Apprenticeship and Education) (Amendment No.1) Regulations, S.I. No. 138 of 1974*
		Solicitors Acts, 1954 and 1960 (Apprenticeship and Education) Regulations, S.I. No. 66 of 1975
		Solicitors Acts, 1954 and 1960 (Apprenticeship and Education Regulations, S.I. No. 226 of 1981
	40	**Solicitors Act, 1954 (Practising Certificates and Restrictions on Solicitors) Regulations, S.I. No. 60 of 1955**
		Solicitors Act, 1954 (Apprenticeship and Education) Regulations, S.I. No. 90 of 1955
		Solicitors Act, 1954 (Apprenticeship and Education) Regulations, S.I. No. 217 of 1955
		Solicitors Act, 1954 (Apprenticeship and Education) (Amendment) Regulations, S.I. No. 307 of 1956
		Solicitors Act, 1954 (Apprenticeship and Education) (Amendment) Regulations, S.I. No. 94 of 1960
		Solicitors Act, 1954 (Apprenticeship and Education) (Amendment) Regulations, S.I. No. 201 of 1965
		Solicitors Act, 1954 (Apprenticeship and Education) (Amendment) Regulations, S.I. No. 230 of 1966
		Solicitors Act, 1954 (Apprenticeship and Education) (Amendment) Regulations, S.I. No. 17 of 1968
		Solicitors Act, 1954 (Apprenticeship and Education) (Amendment) Regulations, S.I. No. 110 of 1969
		Solicitors Act, 1954 (Apprenticeship and Education) (Amendment) Regulations, S.I. No. 108 of 1970
		Solicitors Act, 1954 (Apprenticeship and Education) (Amendment) Regulations, S.I. No. 218 of 1971
		Solicitors Act, 1954 (Apprenticeship and Education) (Amendment) Regulations, S.I. No. 49 of 1972
		Solicitors Act, 1954 (Apprenticeship and Education) (Amendment) Regulations, S.I. No. 47 of 1973
		Solicitors Act, 1954 (Apprenticeship and Education) (Amendment No.2) Regulations, S.I. No. 333 of 1973
		Solicitors Act, 1954 (Apprenticeship and Education) (Amendment No.1) Regulations, S.I. No. 138 of 1974
		Solicitors Acts, 1954 and 1960 (Apprenticeship and Education) Regulations, S.I. No. 66 of 1975
		Solicitors Acts, 1954 and 1960 (Apprenticeship and Education Regulations, S.I. No. 226 of 1981
	66	*Solicitors' Accounts Regulations, S.I. No. 218 of 1955*
		Solicitors' Accounts Regulations, S.I. No. 308 of 1956
		Solicitors' Accounts Regulations, S.I. No. 252 of 1957
		Solicitors' Accounts (Amendment) Regulations, S.I. No. 193 of 1958

Statutory Authority	Section	Statutory Instrument
Solicitors Act, No. 36 of 1954 (*Cont.*)		*Solicitors' Accounts (Amendment) Regulations, S.I. No. 51 of 1961*
		Solicitors' Accounts (Amendment) Regulations, S.I. No. 163 of 1965
		Solicitors' Accounts (Amendment) Regulations, S.I. No. 75 of 1966
		Solicitors' Accounts (Amendment No.2) Regulations, S.I. No. 193 of 1966
		Solicitors' Accounts Regulations, S.I. No. 44 of 1967
		Solicitors' Accounts (Amendment) Regulations, S.I. No. 94 of 1970
		Solicitors' Accounts (Amendment) (No.2) Regulations, S.I. No. 107 of 1970
		Solicitors' Accounts (Amendment No.3) Regulations, S.I. No. 231 of 1970
		Solicitors' Accounts (Amendment) Regulations, S.I. No. 196 of 1971
		Solicitors' Accounts (Amendment) Regulations, S.I. No. 125 of 1976
		Solicitors' Accounts (Amendment) Regulations, S.I. No. 242 of 1977
		Solicitors' Accounts Regulations, S.I. No. 204 of 1984
		Solicitors' Accounts Regulations (No.2) S.I. No. 304 of 1984
	71	**Solicitors Act, 1954 (Professional Practice, Conduct and Discipline) Regulations, S.I. No. 151 of 1955**
		Solicitors' Accounts Regulations, S.I. No. 218 of 1955
		Solicitors' Accounts Regulations, S.I. No. 308 of 1956
		Solicitors' Accounts Regulations, S.I. No. 252 of 1957
		Solicitors' Accounts (Amendment) Regulations, S.I. No. 193 of 1958
		Solicitors' Accounts (Amendment) Regulations, S.I. No. 51 of 1961
		Solicitors' Accounts (Amendment) Regulations, S.I. No. 163 of 1965
		Solicitors' Accounts (Amendment) Regulations, S.I. No. 75 of 1966
		Solicitors' Accounts (Amendment No.2) Regulations, S.I. No. 193 of 1966
		Solicitors' Accounts Regulations, S.I. No. 44 of 1967
		Solicitors' Accounts (Amendment) Regulations, S.I. No. 94 of 1970
		Solicitors' Accounts (Amendment) (No.2) Regulations, S.I. No. 107 of 1970
		Solicitors' Accounts (Amendment No.3) Regulations, S.I. No. 231 of 1970
		Solicitors' Accounts (Amendment) Regulations, S.I. No. 196 of 1971

Social Welfare (Supplementary Welfare Allowances) Act, No. 28 of 1975 (*Cont.*)

Solicitors (Professional Practice, Conduct and Discipline) (Amendment) Regulations, S.I. No. 344 of 1971

Solicitors' Accounts (Amendment) Regulations, S.I. No. 125 of 1976

Solicitors' Accounts (Amendment) Regulations, S.I. No. 242 of 1977

Solicitors' Accounts Regulations, S.I. No. 204 of 1984

Solicitors' Accounts Regulations (No.2) S.I. No. 304 of 1984

Solicitors (Professional Practice, Conduct and Discipline) Regulations, S.I. No. 405 of 1986

79   *Solicitors Act, 1954 (Fees) Regulations, S.I. No. 299 of 1954*

Solicitors Acts, 1954 (Apprentice's Fees) Regulations, S.I. No. 300 of 1954

Solicitors Act, 1954 (Apprentices' Fees) Regulations, S.I. No. 140 of 1956

Solicitors Act, 1954 (Fees) Regulations, S.I. No. 240 of 1968

Solicitors Act, 1954 (Fees) (Amendment) Regulations, S.I. No. 245 of 1970

Solicitors Practising Certificate Fees Regulations, S.I. No. 341 of 1971

Solicitors Act, 1954 (Fees) Regulations, S.I. No. 315 of 1973

Solicitors Acts, 1954 and 1960 (Fees) Regulations, S.I. No. 288 of 1975

Solicitors Acts, 1954 and 1960 (Fees) Regulations, S.I. No. 302 of 1976

Solicitors Acts, 1954 and 1960 (Fees) Regulations, S.I. No. 363 of 1978

Solicitors Acts, 1954 and 1960 (Fees) Regulations, S.I. No. 401 of 1979

Solicitors Acts, 1954 and 1960 (Fees) Regulations, S.I. No. 365 of 1982

Solicitors Acts, 1954 and 1960 (Fees) Regulations, S.I. No. 380 of 1983

Solicitors Acts, 1954 and 1960 (Fees) Regulations, S.I. No. 341 of 1984

Solicitors Acts, 1954 and 1960 (Fees) Regulations, S.I. No. 424 of 1985

82   *Solicitors Act, 1954 (Fees) Regulations, S.I. No. 299 of 1954*

Solicitors Acts, 1954 (Apprentice's Fees) Regulations, S.I. No. 300 of 1954

Solicitors Act, 1954 (Apprentices' Fees) Regulations, S.I. No. 140 of 1956

Solicitors Act, 1954 (Apprentices' Fees) Regulations, S.I. No. 131 of 1960

Solicitors Act, 1954 (Apprentices' Fees) Regulations, S.I. No. 131 of 1962

Solicitors Act, 1954 (Fees) Regulations, S.I. No. 240 of 1968

Statutory Authority	Section	Statutory Instrument
Social Welfare (Supplementary Welfare Allowances) Act, No. 28 of 1975 (*Cont.*)		*Solicitors Act, 1954 (Fees) (Amendment) Regulations, S.I. No. 245 of 1970*
		Solicitors Practising Certificate Fees Regulations, S.I. No. 341 of 1971
		Solicitors Act, 1954 (Fees) Regulations, S.I. No. 315 of 1973
		Solicitors Acts, 1954 and 1960 (Fees) Regulations, S.I. No. 288 of 1975
		Solicitors Acts, 1954 and 1960 (Fees) Regulations, S.I. No. 302 of 1976
		Solicitors Acts, 1954 and 1960 (Apprentices' Fees) Regulations, S.I. No. 273 of 1978
		Solicitors Acts, 1954 and 1960 (Fees) Regulations, S.I. No. 363 of 1978
		Solicitors Acts, 1954 and 1960 (Fees) Regulations, S.I. No. 401 of 1979
		Solicitors Acts, 1954 and 1960 (Apprentices' Fees) (No.2) Regulations, S.I. No. 204 of 1981
		Solicitors Acts, 1954 and 1960 (Fees) Regulations, S.I. No. 365 of 1982
		Solicitors Acts, 1954 and 1960 (Apprentices' Fees) Regulations, S.I. No. 40 of 1983
		Solicitors Acts, 1954 and 1960 (Fees) Regulations, S.I. No. 380 of 1983
		Solicitors Acts, 1954 and 1960 (Apprentices' Fees) Regulations, S.I. No. 48 of 1984
		Solicitors Acts, 1954 and 1960 (Fees) Regulations, S.I. No. 341 of 1984
		Solicitors Acts, 1954 and 1960 (Apprentices' Fees) Regulations, S.I. No. 421 of 1985
		Solicitors Acts, 1954 and 1960 (Fees) Regulations, S.I. No. 424 of 1985
		Solicitors Acts, 1954 and 1968 (Apprentices' Fees) Regulations, S.I. No. 30 of 1986
	Sch. V par. 19	*Solicitors (Compensation Fund) Regulations, S.I. No. 234 of 1955*
Solicitors Acts, 1954 and 1960,		*Solicitors Acts, 1954 and 1960 (Apprentices' Fees) Regulations, S.I. No. 308 of 1975*
		Solicitors Acts, 1954 and 1960 (Apprentices' Fees) Regulations, S.I. No. 330 of 1977
		Solicitors Acts, 1954 and 1960 (Apprentices' Fees) Regulations, S.I. No. 203 of 1981
Solicitors (Amendment) Act, No. 37 of 1960	16	**Solicitors (Disciplinary Committee) Rules, S.I. No. 30 of 1961**
	24	**Solicitors (Compensation Fund) Regulations, S.I. No. 115 of 1963**
Solicitors' Remuneration Act, No. 44 of 1881		*Solicitors' Remuneration General Order, S.I. No. 199 of 1957*
		Solicitors' Remuneration General Order, S.I. No. 165 of 1960

Statutory Authority	Section	Statutory Instrument
Solicitors' Remuneration Act, No. 44 of 1881 (*Cont.*)		Solicitors' Remuneration General Order, S.I. No. 128 of 1964
		Solicitors' Remuneration General Order, S.I. No. 286 of 1970
		Solicitors' Remuneration General Order, S.I. No. 227 of 1972
		Solicitors' Remuneration General Order, S.I. No. 329 of 1978
		Solicitors' Remuneration General Order, S.I. No. 361 of 1982
		Solicitors' Remuneration General Order, S.I. No. 155 of 1984
	3	Solicitors' Remuneration General Order, S.I. No. 379 of 1986
	6	Solicitors' Remuneration General Order, 1957 (Disallowance) Order, S.I. No. 232 of 1957
		Solicitors' Remuneration General Order, 1971 (Disallowance) Order, S.I. No. 61 of 1972
Spanish Civil War (Non-intervention) Act, No. 1 of 1937	2(1)	*Spanish Civil War (Non-intervention) Act, 1937 (Commencement) Order [Vol. XX p. 857] S.R.& O. No. 34 of 1937*
	2(2)	*Spanish Civil War (Non-intervention) Act, 1937 (Continuation) Order [Vol. XX p. 875] S.R.& O. No. 193 of 1937*
	7(1)	*Spanish Civil War (Non-intervention) Act, 1937 (Appointed Countries) Order [Vol. XX p. 861] S.R.& O. No. 35 of 1937*
	10(1)	*Spanish Civil War (Export of War Material) Order [Vol. XX p. 867] S.R.& O. No. 36 of 1937*
Spirits Act, No. 24 of 1880	159	Spirits and Wine (Amendment) Regulations, S.I. No. 419 of 1979
Standard Time (Amendment) Act, No. 17 of 1971	1	*Winter Time Order, S.I. No. 67 of 1981*
		Winter Time Order, S.I. No. 212 of 1982
		Winter Time Order, S.I. No. 45 of 1986
State Financial Transactions (Special Provisions) Act, No. 23 of 1984	2(1)(a)	*State Financial Transactions (Special Provisions) Act, 1984 (Section 2) (Commencement) Order, S.I. No. 350 of 1984*
	2(1)(b)	State Financial Transactions (Special Provisions) Act, 1984 (Section 2 (3)) (Cesser) Order, S.I. No. 32 of 1985
		State Financial Transactions (Special Provisions) Act, 1984 (Section 2 (2)) (Cesser) Order, S.I. No. 332 of 1986
	2(3)	*State Financial Transactions (Special Provisions) Act, 1984 (Section 2 (3)) Order, S.I. No. 351 of 1984*
		State Financial Transactions (Special Provisions) Act, 1984 (Section 2 (3)) (No.2) Order, S.I. No. 370 of 1984

Statutory Authority	Section	Statutory Instrument
State Financial Transactions (Special Provisions) Act, No. 23 of 1984 (*Cont.*)		*State Financial Transactions (Special Provisions) Act, 1984 (Section 2 (3)) Order, S.I. No. 6 of 1985*
		State Financial Transactions (Special Provisions) Act, 1984 (Section 2 (3)) (No.2) Order, S.I. No. 19 of 1985
		State Financial Transactions (Special Provisions) Act, 1984 (Section 2 (3)) (No.3) Order, S.I. No. 31 of 1985
	3	*State Financial Transactions (Special Provisions) Act, 1984 (Section 3) Order, S.I. No. 33 of 1985*
		State Financial Transactions (Special Provisions) Act, 1984 (Section 3) (No.2) Order, S.I. No. 55 of 1985
State Guarantees Act, No. 9 of 1954	9	**State Guarantees Act, 1954 (Amendment of Schedule) Order, S.I. No. 256 of 1957**
		State Guarantees Act, 1954 (Amendment of Schedule) Order, S.I. No. 74 of 1958
		State Guarantees Act, 1954 (Amendment of Schedule) Order, S.I. No. 49 of 1959
		State Guarantees Act, 1954 (Amendment of Schedule) (No.2) Order, S.I. No. 236 of 1959
		State Guarantees Act, 1954 (Amendment of Schedule) Order, S.I. No. 74 of 1961
		State Guarantees Act, 1954 (Amendment of Schedule) (No.2) Order, S.I. No. 88 of 1961
		State Guarantees Act, 1954 (Amendment of Schedule) Order, S.I. No. 23 of 1964
		State Guarantees Act, 1954 (Amendment of Schedule) (No.2) Order, S.I. No. 185 of 1964
		State Guarantees Act, 1954 (Amendment of Schedule) Order, S.I. No. 251 of 1965
		State Guarantees Act, 1954 (Amendment of Schedule) (No.2) Order, S.I. No. 257 of 1965
		State Guarantees Act, 1954 (Amendment of Schedule) Order, S.I. No. 246 of 1966
		State Guarantees Act, 1954 (Amendment of Schedule) Order, S.I. No. 203 of 1978
		State Guarantees Act, 1954 (Amendment of Schedule) Order, S.I. No. 331 of 1980
		State Guarantees Act, 1954 (Amendment of Schedule) Order, S.I. No. 348 of 1981
		State Guarantees Act, 1954 (Amendment of Schedule) Order, S.I. No. 266 of 1983
		State Guarantees Act, 1954 (Amendment of Schedule) Order, S.I. No. 243 of 1984
		State Guarantees Act, 1954 (Amendment of Schedule) Order, (1985) S.I. No. 63 of 1986
	11(2)	*State Guarantees Act, 1954 (Commencement) Order, S.I. No. 209 of 1954*
State Lands (Workhouses) Act, No. 8 of 1962	4(2)	*State Lands (Workhouses) Act, 1962 (Commencement) Order, S.I. No. 115 of 1962*

Statutory Authority	Section	Statutory Instrument
Statistics Act, No. 12 of 1926		*Statistics (Road Motor Passenger Services) Order, 1927, Cessation of Collection of Statistics Order [Vol. XX p. 1081] S.R.& O. No. 63 of 1932*
		Statistics (Road Motor Passenger Services: Particulars as to Staff) Order, 1928, Cessation of Collection of Statistics Order [Vol. XX p. 1091] S.R.& O. No. 64 of 1932
	3(1)	**Statistics (Sea and Inland Fisheries) Transfer Order [Vol. XX p. 887] S.R.& O. No. 25 of 1927**
	11	*Statistics (Census of Population) Order, S.I. No. 93 of 1971*
		Statistics (Census of Population) Order, S.I. No. 55 of 1979
		Statistics (Census of Population) Order, S.I. No. 60 of 1981
		Statistics (Census of Population) Order, S.I. No. 61 of 1986
	16	*Statistics (Census of Population) Order, S.I. No. 93 of 1971*
		Statistics (Census of Population) Order, S.I. No. 55 of 1979
		Statistics (Census of Population) Order, S.I. No. 60 of 1981
		Statistics (Census of Population) Order, S.I. No. 61 of 1986
	16(1)	*Statistics (Census of Production) Order [Vol. XX p. 947] S.R.& O. No. 46 of 1926*
		Statistics (Census of Population) Order [Vol. XX p. 897] S.R.& O. No. 76 of 1926
		Statistics (Salmon, Sea-trout and Eels) Order [Vol. XX p. 1093] S.R.& O. No. 45 of 1927
		Statistics (Census of Production) (Forms) Order [Vol. XX p. 1027] S.R.& O. No. 63 of 1927
		Statistics (Slaughter of Animals for Food) Order, (1926) [Vol. XX p. 1153] S.R.& O. No. 65 of 1927
		Statistics (Road Motor Passenger Services) Order [Vol. XX p. 1077] S.R.& O. No. 90 of 1927
		Statistics (Census of Population Publication) Order [Vol. XX p. 939] S.R.& O. No. 20 of 1928
		Statistics (Salmon, Sea-trout and Eels) Order [Vol. XX p. 1103] S.R.& O. No. 32 of 1928
		Statistics (Road Motor Passenger Services: Particulars as to Staff) Order [Vol. XX p. 1083] S.R.& O. No. 52 of 1928
		Statistics (Census of Production) Order [Vol. XX p. 967] S.R.& O. No. 38 of 1929
		Statistics (Road Motor Passenger Services: Particulars as to Staff) Order [Vol. XX p. 1080] S.R.& O. No. 42 of 1929
		Statistics (Census of Production) (Forms) Order [Vol. XX p. 1031] S.R.& O. No. 3 of 1930

Statutory Authority	Section	Statutory Instrument
Statistics Act, No. 12 of 1926 *(Cont.)*		*Statistics (Salmon, Sea-trout and Eels) Order [Vol. XX p. 1113] S.R.& O. No. 43 of 1930*
		Statistics (Census of Production) Order [Vol. XX p. 975] S.R.& O. No. 27 of 1931
		Statistics (Slaughter of Animals for Food) Order [Vol. XX p. 1159] S.R.& O. No. 53 of 1931
		Statistics (Census of Production) (Forms) Order [Vol. XX p. 1035] S.R.& O. No. 4 of 1932
		Statistics (Census of Production) Order [Vol. XX p. 893] S.R.& O. No. 58 of 1932
		Statistics (Salmon, Sea-trout and Eels) Order [Vol. XX p. 1123] S.R.& O. No. 83 of 1932
		Statistics (Census of Production) (Forms) Order [Vol. XX p. 1039] S.R.& O. No. 7 of 1933
		Statistics (Census of Distribution) Order [Vol. XX p. 891] S.R.& O. No. 103 of 1933
		Statistics (Census of Production) (Forms) Order [Vol. XX p. 1045] S.R.& O. No. 3 of 1934
		Statistics (Salmon, Sea-trout and Eels) Order [Vol. XX p. 1133] S.R.& O. No. 383 of 1934
		Statistics (Census of Production) Order [Vol. XX p. 987] S.R.& O. No. 15 of 1935
		Statistics (Census of Production) (Forms) Order [Vol. XX p. 1051] S.R.& O. No. 30 of 1935
		Statistics (Census of Production) (Forms) Order [Vol. XX p. 1057] S.R.& O. No. 49 of 1936
		Statistics (Census of Population) Order [Vol. XX p. 911] S.R.& O. No. 96 of 1936
		Statistics (Salmon, Sea-trout and Eels) Order [Vol. XX p. 1143] S.R.& O. No. 366 of 1936
		Statistics (Census of Production) Order [Vol. XX p. 991] S.R.& O. No. 392 of 1936
		Statistics (Census of Production) (Forms) Order [Vol. XX p. 1063] S.R.& O. No. 46 of 1937
		Statistics (Census of Production) Order [Vol. XX p. 1003] S.R.& O. No. 296 of 1937
		Statistics (Census of Production) (Forms) Order [Vol. XX p. 1071] S.R.& O. No. 16 of 1938
		Statistics (Census of Population Publication) Order [Vol. XX p. 941] S.R.& O. No. 75 of 1938
		Statistics (Census of Production) Order [Vol. XX p. 1015] S.R.& O. No. 319 of 1938
		Statistics (Salmon, Sea-trout and Eels) Order [Vol. XXXIII p. 891] S.R.& O. No. 3 of 1939
		Statistics (Census of Production) (Forms) Order [Vol. XXXIII p. 849] S.R.& O. No. 15 of 1939
		Statistics (Census of Population) Order [Vol. XXXIII p. 779] S.R.& O. No. 391 of 1939
		Statistics (Census of Production) (Forms) Order [Vol. XXXIII p. 855] S.R.& O. No. 48 of 1940
		Statistics (Salmon, Sea-trout and Eels) Order [Vol. XXXIII p. 901] S.R.& O. No. 314 of 1940

Statutory Authority	Section	Statutory Instrument

Statistics Act, No. 12 of 1926
(Cont.)

Statistics (Census of Population) Order [Vol. XXXIII p. 791] S.R.& O. No. 359 of 1940

Statistics (Census of Production) (Forms) Order [Vol. XXXIII p. 861] S.R.& O. No. 42 of 1941

Statistics (Census of Population) Order [Vol. XXXIII p. 803] S.R.& O. No. 556 of 1941

Statistics (Census of Production) (Forms) Order [Vol. XXXIII p. 867] S.R.& O. No. 52 of 1942

Statistics (Salmon, Sea-trout and Eels) Order [Vol. XXXIII p. 911] S.R.& O. No. 463 of 1942

Statistics (Census of Population) Order [Vol. XXXIII p. 815] S.R.& O. No. 518 of 1942

Statistics (Census of Production) (Forms) Order [Vol. XXXIII p. 873] S.R.& O. No. 41 of 1943

Statistics (Agricultural Returns) Order [Vol. XXXIII p. 761] S.R.& O. No. 179 of 1943

Statistics (Census of Population) Order [Vol. XXXIII p. 827] S.R.& O. No. 422 of 1943

Statistics (Census of Production) (Forms) Order [Vol. XXXIII p. 879] S.R.& O. No. 68 of 1944

Statistics (Agricultural Returns) Order [Vol. XXXIII p. 767] S.R.& O. No. 163 of 1944

Statistics (Census of Population) Order [Vol. XXXIII p. 839] S.R.& O. No. 350 of 1944

Statistics (Salmon, Sea-trout and Eels) Order [Vol. XXXIII p. 921] S.R.& O. No. 1 of 1945

Statistics (Census of Production) (Forms) Order [Vol. XXXIII p. 885] S.R.& O. No. 30 of 1945

Statistics (Agricultural Returns) Order [Vol. XXXIII p. 773] S.R.& O. No. 118 of 1945

Statistics (Salmon, Sea-trout and Eels) (No.2) Order [Vol. XXXIII p. 929] S.R.& O. No. 354 of 1945

Statistics (Census of Production) Order [Vol. XXX-VIII p. 503] S.R.& O. No. 60 of 1946

Statistics (Census of Production) (Forms) Order [Vol. XXXVIII p. 533] S.R.& O. No. 92 of 1946

Statistics (Census of Population) Order [Vol. XXX-VIII p. 479] S.R.& O. No. 97 of 1946

Statistics (Census of Production) Order [Vol. XXX-VIII p. 517] S.R.& O. No. 34 of 1947

Statistics (Census of Production) (Forms) Order [Vol. XXXVIII p. 539] S.R.& O. No. 133 of 1947

Statistics (Census of Production) Order, S.I. No. 49 of 1948

Statistics (Census of Production) (Forms) Order, S.I. No. 127 of 1948

Statistics (Census of Production) Order, S.I. No. 90 of 1949

Statistics (Census of Production) (Forms) Order, S.I. No. 122 of 1949

Statistics (Census of Population) (Publication) Order, S.I. No. 245 of 1949

Statutory Authority	Section	Statutory Instrument
Statistics Act, No. 12 of 1926 (*Cont.*)		*Statistics (Census of Production) Order, S.I. No. 25 of 1950*
		Statistics (Census of Population) (Forms) Order, S.I. No. 57 of 1950
		Statistics (Census of Production) Order, S.I. No. 17 of 1951
		Statistics (Census of Production) (Forms) Order, S.I. No. 58 of 1951
		Statistics (Census of Population) Order, S.I. No. 73 of 1951
		Statistics (Census of Distribution) Order, S.I. No. 20 of 1952
		Statistics (Census of Production) (Forms) Order, S.I. No. 25 of 1952
		Statistics (Census of Distribution) Order, S.I. No. 44 of 1953
		Statistics (Census of Production) Order, S.I. No. 72 of 1953
		Statistics (Census of Production) (Forms) Order, S.I. No. 106 of 1953
		Statistics (Census of Production) Order, S.I. No. 26 of 1954
		Statistics (Census of Distribution) Order, S.I. No. 48 of 1954
		Statistics (Census of Production) (Forms) Order, S.I. No. 51 of 1954
		Statistics (Census of Distribution) Order, S.I. No. 15 of 1955
		Statistics (Census of Production) Order, S.I. No. 80 of 1955
		Statistics (Census of Distribution) Order, S.I. No. 6 of 1956
		Statistics (Census of Population) Order, S.I. No. 71 of 1956
		Statistics (Census of Production) Order, S.I. No. 104 of 1956
		Statistics (Census of Distribution) Order, S.I. No. 39 of 1957
		Statistics (Census of Production) Order, S.I. No. 85 of 1957
		Statistics (Census of Distribution) Order, S.I. No. 62 of 1958
		Statistics (Census of Production) Order, S.I. No. 106 of 1958
		Statistics (Census of Distribution) Order, S.I. No. 43 of 1959
		Statistics (Census of Production) Order, S.I. No. 77 of 1959
		Statistics (Census of Distribution) Order, S.I. No. 5 of 1960
		Statistics (Census of Distribution) Order, S.I. No. 3 of 1961

Statutory Authority	Section	Statutory Instrument
Statistics Act, No. 12 of 1926 *(Cont.)*		*Statistics (Census of Population) Order, S.I. No. 64 of 1961*
		Statistics (Census of Production) Order, S.I. No. 87 of 1961
		Statistics (Census of Production) Order, S.I. No. 79 of 1962
		Statistics (Census of Production) Order, S.I. No. 71 of 1963
		Statistics (Census of Production) Order, S.I. No. 105 of 1964
		Statistics (Census of Production) Order, S.I. No. 107 of 1965
		Statistics (Census of Population) Order, S.I. No. 40 of 1966
		Statistics (Census of Production) Order, S.I. No. 129 of 1966
		Statistics (Census of Production) Order, S.I. No. 278 of 1966
		Statistics (Census of Distribution and Services) Order, S.I. No. 67 of 1967
		Statistics (Census of Production) Order, S.I. No. 129 of 1967
		Statistics (Census of Building and Construction) Order, S.I. No. 186 of 1967
		Statistics (Census of Production) Order, S.I. No. 97 of 1968
		Statistics (Census of Building and Construction) Order, S.I. No. 98 of 1968
		Statistics (Census of Building and Construction) Order, S.I. No. 48 of 1969
		Statistics (Census of Production) Order, S.I. No. 101 of 1969
		Statistics (Census of Building and Construction) Order, S.I. No. 45 of 1970
		Statistics (Trade Statistics) (Shannon Free Airport) Order, S.I. No. 68 of 1970
		Statistics (Census of Production) Order, S.I. No. 195 of 1970
		Statistics (Census of Building and Construction) Order, S.I. No. 84 of 1971
		Statistics (Census of Production) Order, S.I. No. 116 of 1971
		Statistics (Census of Building and Construction) Order, S.I. No. 34 of 1972
		Statistics (Census of Distribution and Services) Order, S.I. No. 56 of 1972
		Statistics (Census of Production) Order, S.I. No. 141 of 1972
		Statistics (Census of Building and Construction) Order, S.I. No. 111 of 1973
		Statistics (Census of Production) Order, S.I. No. 233 of 1973
		Statistics (Census of Building and Construction) Order, S.I. No. 120 of 1974

Statutory Authority	Section	Statutory Instrument
Statistics Act, No. 12 of 1926 *(Cont.)*		*Statistics (Census of Production) Order, S.I. No. 194 of 1974*
		Statistics (Census of Production) Order, S.I. No. 124 of 1975
		Statistics (Census of Building and Construction) Order, S.I. No. 148 of 1975
		Statistics (Census of Production) Order, S.I. No. 177 of 1976
		Statistics (Census of Building and Construction) Order, S.I. No. 247 of 1976
		Statistics (Census of Building and Construction) Order, S.I. No. 116 of 1977
		Statistics (Census of Production) Order, S.I. No. 322 of 1977
		Statistics (Census of Production) (No.2) Order, S.I. No. 391 of 1977
		Statistics (Census of Distribution) Order, S.I. No. 101 of 1978
		Statistics (Census of Production) Order, S.I. No. 147 of 1978
		Statistics (Census of Building and Construction) Order, S.I. No. 180 of 1978
		Statistics (Census of Production) (No.2) Order, S.I. No. 234 of 1978
		Statistics (Census of Building and Construction) Order, S.I. No. 185 of 1979
		Statistics (Census of Production) Order, S.I. No. 219 of 1979
		Statistics (Census of Production) Order, S.I. No. 214 of 1980
		Statistics (Census of Building and Construction) Order, S.I. No. 336 of 1980
		Statistics (Census of Production) Order, S.I. No. 291 of 1981
		Statistics (Census of Building and Construction) Order, S.I. No. 439 of 1981
		Statistics (Census of Production) Order, S.I. No. 219 of 1982
		Statistics (Census of Building and Construction) Order, S.I. No. 360 of 1982
		Statistics (Census of Production) Order, S.I. No. 258 of 1983
		Statistics (Census of Building and Construction) Order, S.I. No. 353 of 1983
		Statistics (Census of Building and Construction) Order, S.I. No. 161 of 1984
		Statistics (Census of Production) (No.1) Order, S.I. No. 24 of 1985
		Statistics (Census of Building and Construction) Order, S.I. No. 219 of 1985
		Statistics (Census of Production) (No.2) Order, S.I. No. 423 of 1985

Statutory Authority	Section	Statutory Instrument

Statistics Act, No. 12 of 1926 *(Cont.)*

Statistics (Census of Production) Order, S.I. No. 295 of 1986

Statistics (Census of Building and Construction) Order, S.I. No. 381 of 1986

Statutory Undertakings (Continuance of Charges) (No. 2) Act, No. 16 of 1923

Grand Canal Company (Revision of Charges) Order [Vol. XX p. 1165] S.R.& O. No. 36 of 1927

Statutory Undertakings (Temporary Increase of Charges) Act, No. 34 of 1918

Gas Charges: Revocation of Temporary Increase of Charges, Cork [Vol. XX p. 1169] S.R.& O. No. 1 of 1923

Gas Charges: Revocation of Temporary Increase of Charges, Dundalk [Vol. XX p. 1171] S.R.& O. No. 2 of 1923

Gas Charges: Revocation of Temporary Increase of Charges, Thurles [Vol. XX p. 1173] S.R.& O. No. 3 of 1923

Gas Charges: Revocation of Temporary Increase of Charges, Tipperary [Vol. XX p. 1175] S.R.& O. No. 4 of 1923

Gas Charges: Revocation of Temporary Increase of Charges, Waterford [Vol. XX p. 1177] S.R.& O. No. 5 of 1923

Stock Transfer Act, No. 34 of 1963 — Section 1

Stock Transfer (Recognition of Stock Exchanges) Regulations, S.I. No. 5 of 1964

Stock Transfer (Recognition of Stock Exchanges) (Amendment) Regulations, S.I. No. 22 of 1964

Stock Transfer (Recognition of Stock Exchanges) Regulations, S.I. No. 191 of 1965

Stock Transfer (Recognition of Stock Exchanges) Regulations, S.I. No. 251 of 1966

Stock Transfer (Recognition of Stock Exchanges) Regulations, S.I. No. 100 of 1973

Section 5

Stock Transfer Act, 1963 (Amendment of Forms) Regulations, S.I. No. 92 of 1975

Stock Transfer (Forms) Regulations, S.I. No. 139 of 1980

Section 7(2)

Stock Transfer Act, 1963 (Commencement) Order, S.I. No. 4 of 1964

Street and House to House Collections Act, No. 13 of 1962 — Section 2

House to House Collections Order, S.I. No. 75 of 1972

Section 28

Street and House to House Collections (Prescribed Forms) Regulations, S.I. No. 134 of 1962

Street Trading Act, No. 15 of 1926 — Section 13

Street Trading (City of Dublin) Regulations [Vol. XX p. 1179] S.R.& O. No. 63 of 1926

Street Trading (City of Dublin) Regulations Amendment Order [Vol. XX p. 1193] S.R.& O. No. 18 of 1929

Street Trading (City of Dublin) Regulations Amendment Order [Vol. XX p. 1197] S.R.& O. No. 90 of 1930

Statutory Authority	Section	Statutory Instrument

Street Trading Act, No. 15 of 1926
(*Cont.*)

Street Trading (Wexford Urban District) Regulations, (1930) [Vol. XX p. 1213] S.R.& O. No. 3 of 1931

Street Trading (City of Dublin) Regulations Amendment Order [Vol. XX p. 1201] S.R.& O. No. 110 of 1932

Street Trading (Bray Urban District) Regulations [Vol. XX p. 1231] S.R.& O. No. 408 of 1935

Street Trading (City of Dublin) Regulations Amendment Order [Vol. XX p. 1207] S.R.& O. No. 309 of 1938

Street Trading (County Borough of Cork) Order [Vol. XXXIII p. 937] S.R.& O. No. 43 of 1941

Borough of Sligo Street Trading Regulations [Vol. XXXVIII p. 545] S.R.& O. No. 43 of 1946

Street Trading (City of Dublin) Regulations, 1926 (Amendment) Regulations, S.I. No. 315 of 1948

Street Trading (Henry Street, Dublin, December, 1949) Regulations, S.I. No. 319 of 1949

Street Trading (Urban District of Castleblayney) Regulations, S.I. No. 54 of 1950

Street Trading (Henry Street, Dublin, December, 1950) Regulations, S.I. No. 285 of 1950

Street Trading (Henry Street, Dublin, December, 1951) Regulations, S.I. No. 329 of 1951

Street Trading (Henry Street, Dublin, December, 1952) Regulations, S.I. No. 326 of 1952

Street Trading (Henry Street, Dublin, December, 1953) Regulations, S.I. No. 350 of 1953

Street Trading (Henry Street, Dublin, December, 1954 Regulations, S.I. No. 238 of 1954

Street Trading (Borough of Galway) Regulations, S.I. No. 219 of 1955

Street Trading (Urban District of Naas) Regulations, S.I. No. 220 of 1955

Street Trading (Henry Street, Dublin, December, 1955) Regulations, S.I. No. 222 of 1955

Street Trading (Henry Street, Dublin, December, 1956) Regulations, S.I. No. 278 of 1956

Street Trading (City of Dublin) Regulations, 1926 (Amendment) Regulations, S.I. No. 240 of 1957

Street Trading (Borough of Galway) Regulations, S.I. No. 157 of 1960

Street Trading (County Borough of Limerick) Regulations, S.I. No. 226 of 1961

Street Trading (Urban District of Youghal) Regulations, S.I. No. 161 of 1962

Street Trading (Borough of Clonmel) Regulations, S.I. No. 284 of 1966

Street Trading (Urban District of Listowel) Regulations, S.I. No. 288 of 1966

Street Trading (Urban District of Tralee) Regulations, S.I. No. 325 of 1975

Statutory Authority	Section	Statutory Instrument

Street Trading Act, No. 15 of 1926 *(Cont.)* — **Street Trading (Urban District of Midleton) Regulations, S.I. No. 71 of 1977**

Succession Act, No. 27 of 1965

	2	*Succession Act, 1965 (Commencement) Order, S.I. No. 168 of 1966*
	34(3)	*Succession Act, 1965 (Forms of Administration Bond) Rules, S.I. No. 1 of 1967*
		Succession Act, 1965 (Form of Administration Bond) (No.2) Rules, S.I. No. 18 of 1967
	129	**District Probate Registries (Places and Districts) Order, S.I. No. 274 of 1966**

Sugar (Control of Import) Act, No. 16 of 1936

	2	*Sugar (Prohibition of Import) Order [Vol. XXXIII p. 961] S.R.& O. No. 167 of 1942*
		Sugar (Prohibition of Import) Order [Vol. XXXIII p. 967] S.R.& O. No. 149 of 1943
		Sugar (Prohibition of Import) Order [Vol. XXXIII p. 971] S.R.& O. No. 126 of 1944
		Sugar (Prohibition of Import) Order [Vol. XXXIII p. 975] S.R.& O. No. 92 of 1945
		Sugar (Prohibition of Import) Order [Vol. XXXVIII p. 561] S.R.& O. No. 136 of 1946
		Sugar (Prohibition of Import) Order [Vol. XXXVIII p. 565] S.R.& O. No. 219 of 1947
		Sugar (Prohibition of Import) Order, S.I. No. 202 of 1948
		Sugar (Prohibition of Import) Order, S.I. No. 125 of 1949
		Sugar (Prohibition of Import) Order, S.I. No. 102 of 1950
		Sugar (Prohibition of Import) Order, S.I. No. 106 of 1951
		Sugar (Prohibition of Import) Order, S.I. No. 93 of 1952
		Sugar (Prohibition of Import) Order, S.I. No. 142 of 1953
		Sugar (Prohibition of Import) Order, S.I. No. 69 of 1954
		Sugar (Prohibition of Import) Order, S.I. No. 64 of 1955
		Sugar (Prohibition of Import) Order, 1955 (Amendment) Order, S.I. No. 262 of 1956
		Sugar (Prohibition of Import) Order, S.I. No. 319 of 1956
		Sugar (Prohibition of Import) Order, 1956 (Amendment) Order, S.I. No. 112 of 1957
		Sugar (Prohibition of Import) Order, S.I. No. 267 of 1957
		Sugar (Prohibition of Import) Order, S.I. No. 255 of 1958
		Sugar (Prohibition of Import) Order, S.I. No. 220 of 1959
		Sugar (Prohibition of Import) Order, S.I. No. 251 of 1960

Statutory Authority	Section	Statutory Instrument
Street Trading Act, No. 15 of 1926 (*Cont.*)		*Sugar (Prohibition of Import) Order, S.I. No. 296 of 1961*
	2(1)	*Sugar (Prohibition of Import) Order [Vol. XX p. 1247] S.R.& O. No. 105 of 1936*
		Sugar (Prohibition of Import) Order [Vol. XX p. 1251] S.R.& O. No. 61 of 1937
		Sugar (Prohibition of Import) Order [Vol. XX p. 1255] S.R.& O. No. 111 of 1938
		Sugar (Prohibition of Import) Order [Vol. XXXIII p. 949] S.R.& O. No. 110 of 1939
		Sugar (Prohibition of Import) Order [Vol. XXXIII p. 953] S.R.& O. No. 111 of 1940
		Sugar (Prohibition of Import) Order [Vol. XXXIII p. 957] S.R.& O. No. 200 of 1941
	5	*Sugar (Prohibition of Import) Order [Vol. XXXIII p. 961] S.R.& O. No. 167 of 1942*
		Sugar (Prohibition of Import) Order [Vol. XXXIII p. 967] S.R.& O. No. 149 of 1943
		Sugar (Prohibition of Import) Order [Vol. XXXIII p. 971] S.R.& O. No. 126 of 1944
		Sugar (Prohibition of Import) Order [Vol. XXXIII p. 975] S.R.& O. No. 92 of 1945
		Sugar (Prohibition of Import) Order [Vol. XXXVIII p. 561] S.R.& O. No. 136 of 1946
		Sugar (Prohibition of Import) Order [Vol. XXXVIII p. 565] S.R.& O. No. 219 of 1947
		Sugar (Prohibition of Import) Order, S.I. No. 202 of 1948
		Sugar (Prohibition of Import) Order, S.I. No. 125 of 1949
		Sugar (Prohibition of Import) Order, S.I. No. 102 of 1950
		Sugar (Prohibition of Import) Order, S.I. No. 106 of 1951
		Sugar (Prohibition of Import) Order, S.I. No. 93 of 1952
		Sugar (Prohibition of Import) Order, S.I. No. 142 of 1953
		Sugar (Prohibition of Import) Order, S.I. No. 69 of 1954
		Sugar (Prohibition of Import) Order, S.I. No. 64 of 1955
		Sugar (Prohibition of Import) Order, 1955 (Amendment) Order, S.I. No. 262 of 1956
		Sugar (Prohibition of Import) Order, S.I. No. 319 of 1956
		Sugar (Prohibition of Import) Order, 1956 (Amendment) Order, S.I. No. 112 of 1957
		Sugar (Prohibition of Import) Order, S.I. No. 267 of 1957
		Sugar (Prohibition of Import) Order, S.I. No. 255 of 1958
		Sugar (Prohibition of Import) Order, S.I. No. 220 of 1959

Statutory Authority	Section	Statutory Instrument
Sugar (Control of Import) Act, No. 16 of 1936 *(Cont.)*		*Sugar (Prohibition of Import) Order, S.I. No. 251 of 1960*
		Sugar (Prohibition of Import) Order, S.I. No. 296 of 1961
Sugar Manufacture Act, No. 31 of 1933	15	**Erin Foods Limited (Balance Sheet and Profit and Loss Account) Regulations, S.I. No. 195 of 1965**
	15(6)	**Comhlucht Siuicre Eireann Teoranta (Balance Sheet) Regulations [Vol. XX p. 1259] S.R.& O. No. 270 of 1934**
Summer Time Act, No. 8 of 1925	3(1)	*Summer Time Order [Vol. XXXVIII p. 569] S.R.& O. No. 71 of 1947*
		Summer Time Order, S.I. No. 128 of 1948
		Summer Time Order, S.I. No. 23 of 1949
		Summer Time Order, S.I. No. 41 of 1950
		Summer Time Order, S.I. No. 27 of 1951
		Summer Time Order, S.I. No. 73 of 1952
		Summer Time Order, S.I. No. 11 of 1961
		Summer Time (No.2) Order, S.I. No. 232 of 1961
		Summer Time Order, S.I. No. 182 of 1962
		Summer Time Order, S.I. No. 167 of 1963
		Summer Time Order, S.I. No. 257 of 1964
		Summer Time Order, S.I. No. 198 of 1967
Superannuation Act, No. 67 of 1887	1	**Superannuation Act, 1887 (Section 1) Warrant [Vol. XXXIII p. 979] S.R.& O. No. 91 of 1945**
		Superannuation Act, 1887 (Section 1) Warrant [Vol. XXXVIII p. 573] S.R.& O. No. 236 of 1946
		Superannuation Act, 1887 (Section 1) Warrant, S.I. No. 110 of 1974
		Superannuation Act, 1887 (Section 1) Warrant, S.I. No. 153 of 1975
		Superannuation Act, 1887 (Section 1) Warrant, S.I. No. 297 of 1978
	8	**Superannuation Act, 1887 (Section 8) Regulations, S.I. No. 205 of 1956**
Superannuation Act, No. 10 of 1909	5	**Superannuation Act, 1887 (Section 1) Warrant [Vol. XXXIII p. 979] S.R.& O. No. 91 of 1945**
		Superannuation Act, 1887 (Section 1) Warrant [Vol. XXXVIII p. 573] S.R.& O. No. 236 of 1946
		Superannuation Act, 1887 (Section 1) Warrant, S.I. No. 110 of 1974
		Superannuation Act, 1887 (Section 1) Warrant, S.I. No. 153 of 1975
		Superannuation Act, 1887 (Section 1) Warrant, S.I. No. 297 of 1978
Superannuation Act, No. 39 of 1936	21	**Superannuation (Reckoning of Teaching Service) Regulations, S.I. No. 327 of 1951**
		Superannuation (Reckoning of Teaching Service) Regulations, S.I. No. 218 of 1956

Statutory Authority	Section	Statutory Instrument
Superannuation Act, No. 39 of 1936 (*Cont.*)		**Superannuation (Reckoning of Teaching Service) Regulations, S.I. No. 321 of 1971**
Superannuation Act, No. 14 of 1954	2	**Superannuation (Female Civil Servants) Regulations, S.I. No. 76 of 1954**
		Superannuation (Female Civil Servants) Regulations, S.I. No. 55 of 1981
Superannuation Act, No. 38 of 1956	2	*Superannuation Act, 1956 (Appointed Day) Order, S.I. No. 21 of 1957*
	3	**Superannuation (Allocation of Pension) Regulations, S.I. No. 20 of 1957**
Superannuation and Pensions Act, No. 34 of 1923		**Royal Irish Constabulary (Resigned and Dismissed) Pensions Order [Vol. XX p. 1279] S.R.& O. No. 57 of 1929**
	5	**Royal Irish Constabulary (Resigned and Dismissed) Pensions Order [Vol. XX p. 1285] S.R.& O. No. 52 of 1936**
	5(1)	**Royal Irish Constabulary (Resigned and Dismissed) Pensions Order [Vol. XX p. 1273] S.R.& O. No. 9 of 1924**
	7	**Congested Districts Board Funds – Determination as a Public Fund [Vol. XX p. 1289] S.R.& O. No. 36 of 1924**
Superannuation and Pensions Act, No. 11 of 1929		**Royal Irish Constabulary (Resigned and Dismissed) Pensions Order [Vol. XX p. 1279] S.R.& O. No. 57 of 1929**
Superannuation and Pensions Act, No. 24 of 1963	4(1)	**Superannuation (Designation of Approved Organisations) Regulations, S.I. No. 111 of 1964**
		Superannuation (Designation of Approved Organisations) Regulations, S.I. No. 231 of 1966
		Superannuation (Designation of Approved Organisations) Regulations, S.I. No. 268 of 1967
		Superannuation (Designation of Approved Organisations) Regulations, S.I. No. 191 of 1968
		Superannuation (Designation of Approved Organisations) Regulations, S.I. No. 182 of 1969
		Superannuation (Designation of Approved Organisations) Regulations, S.I. No. 28 of 1970
		Superannuation (Designation of Approved Organisations) (No.2) Regulations, S.I. No. 64 of 1970
		Superannuation (Designation of Approved Organisations) (No.3) Regulations, S.I. No. 163 of 1970
		Superannuation (Designation of Approved Organisations) (No.4) Regulations, S.I. No. 261 of 1970
		Superannuation (Designation of Approved Organisations) Regulations, S.I. No. 86 of 1971

Superannuation and Pensions Act,
No. 24 of 1963 (*Cont.*)

Superannuation (Designation of Approved Organisations) (No.2) Regulations, S.I. No. 295 of 1971

Superannuation (Designation of Approved Organisations) Regulations, S.I. No. 338 of 1972

Superannuation (Designation of Approved Organisations) Regulations, S.I. No. 298 of 1974

Superannuation (Designation of Approved Organisations) Regulations, S.I. No. 98 of 1976

Superannuation (Designation of Approved Organisations) Regulations, S.I. No. 181 of 1978

Superannuation (Designation of Approved Organisations) Regulations, S.I. No. 379 of 1979

Superannuation (Designation of Approved Organisations) Regulations, S.I. No. 437 of 1981

Superannuation (Designation of Approved Organisations) Regulations, S.I. No. 271 of 1983

Superannuation (Designation of Approved Organisations) Regulations, S.I. No. 10 of 1984

Superannuation (Designation of Approved Organisations) (No.2) Regulations, S.I. No. 239 of 1984

Superannuation (Designation of Approved Organisations) Regulations, S.I. No. 266 of 1985

Superannuation (Designation of Approved Organisations) (No.2) Regulations, S.I. No. 412 of 1985

Superannuation (Designation of Approved Organisations) Regulations, S.I. No. 283 of 1986

Superannuation (Designation of Approved Organisations) (No.2) Regulations, S.I. No. 413 of 1986

Superannuation and Pensions Act,
No. 22 of 1976

2

Civil Service Widows' and Children's Contributory Pension Scheme, S.I. No. 132 of 1977

Civil Service Widows' and Children's Ex-gratia Pension Scheme, S.I. No. 133 of 1977

Widows' and Children's (Miscellaneous Offices) Ex-gratia Pension Scheme, S.I. No. 4 of 1978

Widows' and Children's (Miscellaneous Offices) Contributory Pension Scheme, S.I. No. 5 of 1978

Civil Service Widows' and Children's Ex-gratia Pension (Amendment) Scheme, S.I. No. 175 of 1979

Civil Service Widows' and Children's Contributory Pension (Amendment) Scheme, S.I. No. 177 of 1979

Widows' and Children's (Miscellaneous Officers) Contributory Pension (Amendment) Scheme, S.I. No. 178 of 1979

Widows' and Children's (Miscellaneous Officers) Ex-gratia Pension (Amendment) Scheme, S.I. No. 179 of 1979

Statutory Authority	Section	Statutory Instrument
Superannuation and Pensions Act, No. 22 of 1976 (*Cont.*)		**Land Commissioners' Pension Scheme, S.I. No. 217 of 1979**
		National Gallery of Ireland (Director) Pension Scheme, S.I. No. 341 of 1979
		Civil Service Widows' and Children's Contributory Pension (Amendment) Scheme, S.I. No. 56 of 1981
	3	**Civil Service Superannuation Regulations, S.I. No. 188 of 1980**
		Civil Service Superannuation (No.2) Regulations, S.I. No. 362 of 1980
		Civil Service Superannuation (Amendment) Regulations, S.I. No. 215 of 1982
		Civil Service Superannuation Regulations, S.I. No. 335 of 1982
		Civil Service Superannuation Regulations, S.I. No. 169 of 1983
		Civil Service Superannuation (No.2) Regulations, S.I. No. 343 of 1983
Superannuation and Pensions Acts, 1923 and 1929,		**Royal Irish Constabulary (Resigned and Dismissed) Pensions Order, S.I. No. 285 of 1949**
Supplies and Services (Temporary Provisions) Act, No. 22 of 1946		*Carriage of Wheat Order [Vol. XXXIX p. 59] S.R.& O. No. 291 of 1946*
		Tillage Order [Vol. XXXIX p. 1069] S.R.& O. No. 343 of 1946
		Glucose and Saccharin (Suspension of Customs Duties) Order [Vol. XXXIX p. 637] S.R.& O. No. 367 of 1946
		Personal Clothing and Wearing Apparel (Suspension of Customs Duty) Order [Vol. XXXIX p. 831] S.R.& O. No. 369 of 1946
		Boots and Shoes (Suspension of Customs Duty) Order [Vol. XXXIX p. 39] S.R.& O. No. 370 of 1946
		Fur Clothing (Reduction of Customs Duty) Order [Vol. XXXIX p. 629] S.R.& O. No. 401 of 1946
		Jams, Marmalades and Fruit Jellies (Suspension of Customs Duties) Order [Vol. XXXIX p. 707] S.R.& O. No. 29 of 1947
		Transport of Wood Fuel Order [Vol. XXXIX p. 1195] S.R.& O. No. 48 of 1947
		Social Welfare Schemes (Cash Supplements) Order [Vol. XXXIX p. 969] S.R.& O. No. 76 of 1947
		Fur Clothing (Reduction of Customs Duty) Order [Vol. XXXIX p. 633] S.R.& O. No. 104 of 1947
		Customs Duties (Miscellaneous Suspensions) Order [Vol. XXXIX p. 357] S.R.& O. No. 105 of 1947
		Coal (Suspension of Customs Duty) Order [Vol. XXXIX p. 315] S.R.& O. No. 106 of 1947
		Transport of Wood Fuel Order, 1947 (Revocation) Order [Vol. XXXIX p. 1199] S.R.& O. No. 217 of 1947
		Threshing (Maximum Charges) Order [Vol. XXXIX p. 1065] S.R.& O. No. 257 of 1947

Statutory Authority	Section	Statutory Instrument

Supplies and Services (Temporary Provisions) Act, No. 22 of 1946 (*Cont.*)

Electric Filament Lamps (Suspension of Customs Duties) Order [Vol. XXXIX p. 399] S.R.& O. No. 260 of 1947

Carriage of Wheat Order [Vol. XXXIX p. 63] S.R.& O. No. 283 of 1947

Register of Population Order [Vol. XXXIX p. 937] S.R.& O. No. 295 of 1947

Social Welfare Schemes (Cash Supplements) Order, 1947 (First Amendment) Order [Vol. XXXIX p. 993] S.R.& O. No. 307 of 1947

Customs Duties (Miscellaneous Suspensions) (No.2) Order [Vol. XXXIX p. 363] S.R.& O. No. 360 of 1947

Social Welfare Schemes (Cash Supplements) Order (Second Amendment) Order [Vol. XXXIX p. 997] S.R.& O. No. 366 of 1947

Coal (Suspension of Customs Duty) (No.2) Order [Vol. XXXIX p. 319] S.R.& O. No. 374 of 1947

Personal Clothing and Wearing Apparel (Suspension of Customs Duty) Order [Vol. XXXIX p. 835] S.R.& O. No. 375 of 1947

Tillage Order [Vol. XXXIX p. 1105] S.R.& O. No. 384 of 1947

Exchange Control Order [Vol. XXXIX p. 409] S.R.& O. No. 394 of 1947

Binder Twine (Suspension of Customs Duty) Order [Vol. XXXIX p. 29] S.R.& O. No. 441 of 1947

Personal Clothing and Wearing Apparel (Customs Duty) Order, S.I. No. 14 of 1948

Customs Duties (Miscellaneous Suspensions) Order, 1947 (Amendment) Order, S.I. No. 15 of 1948

Emergency Powers (No.320) Order, 1944 (Amendment) (No.1) Order, S.I. No. 16 of 1948

Emergency Powers (No.315) Order, 1944 (Revocation) Order, S.I. No. 22 of 1948

Emergency Powers (Sacks) (Revocation) Order, S.I. No. 24 of 1948

Emergency Powers (No.2) Order, 1939 (Revocation) Order, S.I. No. 40 of 1948

Emergency Powers (No.114) Order, 1941 (Revocation) Order, S.I. No. 41 of 1948

Social Welfare (Substitutive Allowances) (Amendment) Order, S.I. No. 75 of 1948

Coal (Suspension of Customs Duty) Order, S.I. No. 88 of 1948

Customs Duties (Miscellaneous Suspensions) Order, S.I. No. 89 of 1948

Emergency Powers (No.46) Order, 1940 (Revocation) Order, S.I. No. 126 of 1948

Minimum Fares on Omnibuses Order, 1947 (Revocation) Order, S.I. No. 142 of 1948

Emergency Powers (Control of Timber) Orders (Revocation) Order, S.I. No. 204 of 1948

Statutory Authority	Section	Statutory Instrument

Supplies and Services (Temporary Provisions) Act, No. 22 of 1946 *(Cont.)*

Onions (Regulation of Import) Order, S.I. No. 276 of 1948

Carriage of Wheat Order, S.I. No. 283 of 1948

Emergency Powers (No.320) Order, 1944 (Amendment) (No.2) Order, S.I. No. 290 of 1948

Customs Duties (Miscellaneous Suspensions) (No.2) Order, S.I. No. 318 of 1948

Coal (Suspension of Customs Duty) (No.2) Order, S.I. No. 319 of 1948

Emergency Powers (No.157) Order, 1942 (Seventh Amendment) Order, S.I. No. 357 of 1948

Customs Duties (Miscellaneous Suspensions) (No.3) Order, S.I. No. 403 of 1948

Foot Appliances (Suspension of Customs Duty) Order, S.I. No. 435 of 1948

Customs Duties (Miscellaneous Suspensions) (No.2) Order, 1948 (Amendment) Order, S.I. No. 4 of 1949

Emergency Powers (No.323) Order, 1944 (Revocation) Order, S.I. No. 6 of 1949

Emergency Powers (No.358) Order, 1945 (Amendment) Order, S.I. No. 16 of 1949

Emergency Powers (No.165) Order, 1942 (Revocation) Order, S.I. No. 33 of 1949

Customs Duties (Miscellaneous Suspensions) Order, S.I. No. 75 of 1949

Manuscript Books (Reduction of Customs Duty) Order, S.I. No. 76 of 1949

Coal (Suspension of Customs Duty) Order, S.I. No. 77 of 1949

Emergency Powers (Coras Iompair Eireann) Directions, 1944 (Revocation) Directions, S.I. No. 123 of 1949

Tobacco Order, S.I. No. 134 of 1949

Emergency Powers Order, 1939 (Partial Revocation) Order, S.I. No. 184 of 1949

Emergency Powers (No.178) Order, 1942 (Revocation) Order, (1942) S.I. No. 185 of 1949

Emergency Powers (No.123) Order, 1941 (Amendment) Order, S.I. No. 196 of 1949

Emergency Powers (No.282) Order, 1943 (Amendment) Order, S.I. No. 197 of 1949

Carriage of Milk Order, S.I. No. 198 of 1949

Carriage of Wheat Order, S.I. No. 244 of 1949

Coal (Suspension of Customs Duty) (No.2) Order, S.I. No. 258 of 1949

Customs Duties (Miscellaneous Suspensions) (No.2) Order, S.I. No. 259 of 1949

Carriage of Milk (No.2) Order, S.I. No. 260 of 1949

Personal Clothing and Wearing Apparel (Customs Duty) Order, 1948 (Partial Revocation) Order, S.I. No. 295 of 1949

Statutory Authority	Section	Statutory Instrument

Supplies and Services (Temporary Provisions) Act, No. 22 of 1946 *(Cont.)*

Electric Filament Lamps (Screw Cap) (Suspension of Customs Duties) Order, S.I. No. 297 of 1949

Emergency Powers (No.258) Order, 1943 (Amendment) Order, S.I. No. 326 of 1949

Emergency Powers (No.282) Order, 1943 (Amendment) (No.2) Order, S.I. No. 327 of 1949

Emergency Powers (No.317) Order, 1944 (Revocation) Order, S.I. No. 335 of 1949

Emergency Powers (No.206) Order, 1942 (Revocation) Order, S.I. No. 42 of 1950

Mats (Suspension of Customs Duty) Order, S.I. No. 70 of 1950

Emergency Powers (No.375) Order, 1946 (Revocation) Order, S.I. No. 71 of 1950

Emergency Powers (No.320) Order, 1944 (Amendment) Order, S.I. No. 73 of 1950

Customs Duties (Miscellaneous Suspensions) Order, S.I. No. 77 of 1950

Coal (Suspension of Customs Duty) Order, S.I. No. 78 of 1950

Emergency Powers (No.312) Order, 1944 (Revocation) Order, S.I. No. 95 of 1950

Aluminium Knitting Pins (Suspension of Customs Duty) Order, S.I. No. 96 of 1950

Emergency Powers (No.286) Order, 1943 (Revocation) Order, S.I. No. 108 of 1950

Tobacco Order, 1949 (Revocation) Order, S.I. No. 185 of 1950

Emergency Powers (Nos.90 and 316) Orders (Revocation) Order, S.I. No. 186 of 1950

Emergency Powers (No.287) Order, 1943 (Revocation) Order, S.I. No. 194 of 1950

Emergency Powers (No.282) Order, 1943 (Amendment) Order, S.I. No. 224 of 1950

Carriage of Wheat Order, S.I. No. 225 of 1950

Emergency Powers (No.320) Order, 1944 (Second Amendment) Order, S.I. No. 233 of 1950

Carriage of Milk Order, S.I. No. 235 of 1950

Emergency Powers (No.358) Order, 1945 (Amendment) Order, S.I. No. 247 of 1950

Coal (Suspension of Customs Duty) (No.2) Order, S.I. No. 248 of 1950

Customs Duties (Miscellaneous Suspensions) (No.2) Order, S.I. No. 250 of 1950

Emergency Powers (No.320) Order, 1944 (Third Amendment) Order, S.I. No. 257 of 1950

Emergency Powers (No.228) Order, 1942 (Revocation) Order, S.I. No. 265 of 1950

Emergency Powers (No.352) Order, 1945 (Revocation) Order, S.I. No. 272 of 1950

Social Welfare Schemes (Cash Supplements, Supplementary Allowances and Substitutive Allowances) Orders (Revocation) Order, S.I. No. 288 of 1950

Statutory Authority	Section	Statutory Instrument
Supplies and Services (Temporary Provisions) Act, No. 22 of 1946 (*Cont.*)		*Carriage of Sugar Beet Order, S.I. No. 310 of 1950*
		Banks (Closing) Order, S.I. No. 312 of 1950
		Carriage of Sugar Beet Order, 1950 (Revocation) Order, S.I. No. 34 of 1951
		Banks (Closing) (No.6) Order, S.I. No. 35 of 1951
		Turbary Rights Order, S.I. No. 40 of 1951
		Coal (Suspension of Customs Duty) Order, S.I. No. 71 of 1951
		Customs Duties (Miscellaneous Suspensions) Order, S.I. No. 74 of 1951
		Emergency Powers (No.157) Order, 1942 (Eighth Amendment) Order, S.I. No. 107 of 1951
		Carriage of Wheat Order, S.I. No. 245 of 1951
		Carriage of Milk Order, S.I. No. 259 of 1951
		Emergency Powers (No.258) Order, 1943 (Second Amendment) Order, S.I. No. 267 of 1951
		Customs Duties (Knitted Fabric) Order, S.I. No. 302 of 1951
		Emergency Powers (No.282) Order, 1943 (Amendment) Order, S.I. No. 303 of 1951
		Emergency Powers (No.123) Orders (Revocation) Order, S.I. No. 312 of 1951
		Emergency Powers (No.157) Order, 1942 (Ninth Amendment) Order, S.I. No. 339 of 1951
		Emergency Powers (No.320) Order, 1944 (Cycle Components) (Amendment) Order, S.I. No. 341 of 1951
		Emergency Powers (No.157) Order, 1942 (Tenth Amendment) Order, S.I. No. 355 of 1951
		Emergency Powers (No.320) Order, 1944 (Cotton Thread and Ply Yarn Amendment) Order, S.I. No. 26 of 1952
		Emergency Powers (No.276) Order, 1943 (Revocation) Order, S.I. No. 34 of 1952
		Emergency Powers (No.358) Orders (Revocation) Order, S.I. No. 41 of 1952
		Coal (Suspension of Customs Duty) Order, S.I. No. 59 of 1952
		Customs Duties (Miscellaneous Suspensions) Order, S.I. No. 72 of 1952
		Emergency Powers (No.282) Order, 1943 (Rope Cord and Twine Amendment) Order, S.I. No. 95 of 1952
		Binder Twine (Suspension of Customs Duty) Order, 1947 (Revocation) Order, S.I. No. 96 of 1952
		Emergency Powers (No.282) Order, 1943 (Cardboard Boxes Amendment) Order, S.I. No. 140 of 1952
		Emergency Powers (No.18) Order, 1939 (Revocation) Order, S.I. No. 141 of 1952
		Emergency Powers (No.320) Order, 1944 (Jute Yarns and Jute Goods) (Amendment) Order, S.I. No. 164 of 1952

Statutory Authority	Section	Statutory Instrument

Supplies and Services (Temporary
Provisions) Act, No. 22 of 1946
(*Cont.*)

*Customs Duties (Textile Floor Coverings) Order,
S.I. No. 216 of 1952*

*Customs Duties (Miscellaneous Suspensions) Order,
1947 (Boots and Shoes Components) (Amendment) Order, S.I. No. 231 of 1952*

*Emergency Powers (No.320) Order, 1944 (Wire
Netting) (Amendment) Order, S.I. No. 236 of
1952*

Carriage of Wheat Order, S.I. No. 248 of 1952

*Customs Duties (Miscellaneous Suspensions) Order,
1952 (Galvanised Bins and Troughs Amendment)
Order, S.I. No. 252 of 1952*

*Emergency Powers (Nos.247 and 342) Orders
(Revocation) Order, S.I. No. 271 of 1952*

*Emergency Powers (Nos.282 and 320) Orders (Termination of Suspension of certain Package Duties)
Order, S.I. No. 282 of 1952*

Carriage of Milk Order, S.I. No. 283 of 1952

*Emergency Powers (No.320) Order, 1944 (Iron and
Steel Fencing Material Amendment) Order, S.I.
No. 296 of 1952*

Emergency Powers (No.101) Order, 1941 (Revocation) Order, S.I. No. 312 of 1952

*Turbary Rights Order, 1951 (Revocation) Order,
S.I. No. 329 of 1952*

*Coal (Suspension of Customs Duty) Order, S.I.
No. 95 of 1953*

*Emergency Powers (Nos.192 and 320) Orders (Termination of Suspension of Customs Duties on
Motor Car Tyres) Order, S.I. No. 107 of 1953*

*Customs Duties (Miscellaneous Suspensions) Order,
S.I. No. 120 of 1953*

*Emergency Powers (No.282) Order, 1943 (Imitation
Parchment Paper) (Amendment) Order, S.I.
No. 124 of 1953*

*Emergency Powers (No.320) Order, 1944 (Scythes,
Sickles, etc.) (Amendment) Order, S.I. No. 126 of
1953*

Wheat Milling Order, S.I. No. 129 of 1953

Emergency Powers Order, 1939 (Partial Revocation) Order, S.I. No. 194 of 1953

*Emergency Powers (No.282) Order, 1943 (Termination of Suspension of Duty on Roofing Felt, etc)
Order, S.I. No. 209 of 1953*

Emergency Powers (No.117) Order, 1941 (Revocation) Order, S.I. No. 218 of 1953

Emergency Powers (No.329) Order, 1944 (Revocation) Order, S.I. No. 219 of 1953

*Asbestos Articles (Termination of Suspension of
Customs Duty) Order, S.I. No. 276 of 1953*

Carriage of Wheat Order, S.I. No. 278 of 1953

Carriage of Milk Order, S.I. No. 301 of 1953

Statutory Authority	Section	Statutory Instrument
Supplies and Services (Temporary Provisions) Act, No. 22 of 1946 (*Cont.*)		*Emergency Powers (No.282) Order, 1943 (Toilet Paper) (Amendment) Order, S.I. No. 311 of 1953*
		Emergency Powers (No.251) Order, 1943 (Revocation) Order, S.I. No. 412 of 1953
		Emergency Powers (No.277) Order, 1943 (Revocation) Order, S.I. No. 419 of 1953
		Emergency Powers (Orders Relating to Pigs, Pork and Bacon) (Revocation) Order, S.I. No. 5 of 1954
		Emergency Powers (No.258) Order, 1943 (Silk and Artificial Silk) (Amendment) Order, S.I. No. 11 of 1954
		Emergency Powers (No.282) Order, 1943 (Milk Cans Amendment) Order, S.I. No. 31 of 1954
		Customs Duties (Miscellaneous Suspensions) Order, S.I. No. 57 of 1954
		Carriage of Wheat Order, S.I. No. 190 of 1954
		Carriage of Milk Order, S.I. No. 205 of 1954
		Emergency Powers (No.157) Orders (Revocation) Order, S.I. No. 210 of 1954
		Emergency Powers (No.282) Order, 1943 (Quilts and Quilt Covers) (Amendment) Order, S.I. No. 214 of 1954
		Emergency Powers (No.320) Order, 1944 (Rubber Solution Amendment) Order, S.I. No. 236 of 1954
		Wheat Milling Order, S.I. No. 74 of 1955
		Wheat Milling (Amendment) Order, S.I. No. 160 of 1955
		Carriage of Wheat Order, S.I. No. 168 of 1955
		Carriage of Milk Order, S.I. No. 174 of 1955
		Emergency Powers (No.254) Order, 1943 (Revocation) Order, S.I. No. 199 of 1955
		Emergency Powers (No.282) Order, 1943 (Varnish) (Amendment) Order, S.I. No. 264 of 1955
		Emergency Powers (No.320) Order, 1944 (Single Yarns) (Amendment) Order, S.I. No. 41 of 1956
		Emergency Powers (No.293) Order, 1943 (Amendment) Order, S.I. No. 91 of 1956
		Emergency Powers (Nos.270 and 283) Orders (Revocation) Order, S.I. No. 32 of 1957
		Emergency Powers (Coras Iompair Eireann) (Reduction of Railway Services) Order, 1944 (Revocation) Order, S.I. No. 60 of 1957
		Emergency Powers (No.282) Order, 1943 (Brass Couplings) (Amendment) Order, S.I. No. 127 of 1957
		Emergency Powers (No.145) Order, 1942 (Revocation) Order, S.I. No. 129 of 1957
		Emergency Powers (No.95) Order, 1941 (Revocation) Order, S.I. No. 211 of 1957
	2	*Minimum Fares on Omnibuses Order [Vol. XXXIX p. 763] S.R.& O. No. 316 of 1947*

Statutory Authority	Section	Statutory Instrument
Supplies and Services (Temporary Provisions) Act, No. 22 of 1946 (*Cont.*)		*Banks (Closing) (No.1) Order [Vol. XXXIX p. 13] S.R.& O. No. 321 of 1947*
		Banks (Closing) (No.2) Order [Vol. XXXIX p. 17] S.R.& O. No. 322 of 1947
		Banks (Closing) (No.3) Order [Vol. XXXIX p. 21] S.R.& O. No. 325 of 1947
		Social Welfare (Substitutive Allowances) Order, S.I. No. 8 of 1948
		Banks (Closing) Order, S.I. No. 1 of 1951
		Banks (Closing) (No.2) Order, S.I. No. 5 of 1951
		Banks (Closing) (No.3) Order, S.I. No. 10 of 1951
		Banks (Closing) (No.4) Order, S.I. No. 13 of 1951
		Banks (Closing) (No.5) Order, S.I. No. 20 of 1951
		Banks (Closing) (No.7) Order, S.I. No. 38 of 1951
		Banks (Closing) Order, S.I. No. 292 of 1954
		Customs Duties (Miscellaneous Suspensions) Order, S.I. No. 54 of 1955
		Customs Duties (Miscellaneous Suspensions) Order, S.I. No. 61 of 1956
		Superphosphates (Suspension of Customs Duty) Order, S.I. No. 283 of 1956
	4	*Customs Duties (Miscellaneous Suspensions) Order, S.I. No. 54 of 1955*
		Customs Duties (Knitted Fabric) Order, 1951 (Revocation) Order, S.I. No. 33 of 1956
		Customs Duties (Miscellaneous Suspensions) Order, S.I. No. 61 of 1956
		Emergency Powers (No.39) Order, 1940 (Revocation) Order, S.I. No. 107 of 1956
		Manuscript Books (Reduction of Customs Duty) Order, 1949 (Revocation) Order, S.I. No. 108 of 1956
		Wheat Milling Orders (Revocation) Order, S.I. No. 237 of 1956
		Customs Duties (Miscellaneous Suspensions) Order, S.I. No. 63 of 1957
		Emergency Powers (No.301) Order, 1943 (Revocation) Order, S.I. No. 79 of 1957
Supplies and Services (Temporary Provisions) Act,1946 (Continuance and Amendment) Act, No. 34 of 1950	3	*Prices Advisory Body Order, S.I. No. 2 of 1951*
Tariff Commission Act, No. 40 of 1926	3	*Tariff Commission (Proceedings) Regulations [Vol. XXI p. 1] S.R.& O. No. 24 of 1927*
		Tariff Commission (Proceedings) Regulations [Vol. XXI p. 9] S.R.& O. No. 55 of 1933
Teachers' Superannuation Act, No. 32 of 1928		**National School Teachers' Superannuation (Amendment) (No.2) Scheme [Vol. XXXIV p. 1] S.R.& O. No. 272 of 1940**

Statutory Authority	Section	Statutory Instrument
Teacher's Superannuation Act, No. 32 of 1928 (*Cont.*)		**Secondary Teachers' Superannuation (Amendment) Scheme [Vol. XXXIV p. 33] S.R.& O. No. 141 of 1942**
		National School Teachers' Superannuation (Amendment) Scheme [Vol. XXXIV p. 15] S.R.& O. No. 400 of 1942
		National School Teachers' Superannuation (Amendment) Scheme [Vol. XXXIV p. 25] S.R.& O. No. 134 of 1943
		National School Teachers' Superannuation (Amendment) Scheme [Vol. XXXVIII p. 585] S.R.& O. No. 330 of 1947
		Secondary Teachers' Superannuation (Amendment) Scheme [Vol. XXXVIII p. 599] S.R.& O. No. 358 of 1947
		National School Teachers' Superannuation (Amendment) Scheme, S.I. No. 423 of 1948
		Secondary Teachers' Superannuation (Amendment) Scheme, S.I. No. 322 of 1949
		National School Teachers' Superannuation (Amendment) Scheme, S.I. No. 180 of 1950
		Secondary Teachers' Superannuation (Amendment) Scheme, S.I. No. 48 of 1951
		Secondary Teachers' Superannuation (Amendment) Scheme, S.I. No. 56 of 1952
		National School Teachers' Superannuation (Amendment) Scheme, S.I. No. 255 of 1953
		National School Teachers' Superannuation (Amendment) Scheme, S.I. No. 72 of 1954
		Secondary Teachers' Superannuation (Amendment) Scheme, S.I. No. 234 of 1954
		Secondary Teachers' Superannuation (Amendment) Scheme, S.I. No. 153 of 1956
		Secondary Teachers' Superannuation (Amendment) Scheme, S.I. No. 112 of 1963
		Secondary Teachers' Superannuation (Amendment) (No.2) Scheme, S.I. No. 244 of 1963
		Secondary Teachers' Superannuation (Amendment) Scheme, S.I. No. 125 of 1966
		Secondary Teachers' Superannuation (Amendment) Scheme, S.I. No. 35 of 1968
	2	**Secondary Teachers' Superannuation Scheme [Vol. XXI p. 23] S.R.& O. No. 19 of 1929**
		Secondary Teachers' Superannuation (Amendment) Scheme [Vol. XXI p. 41] S.R.& O. No. 54 of 1932
		Secondary Teachers' Superannuation (Amendment) Scheme [Vol. XXI p. 55] S.R.& O. No. 107 of 1933
		National School Teachers' Superannuation Scheme [Vol. XXI p. 89] S.R.& O. No. 23 of 1934
		Secondary Teachers' Superannuation (Amendment) Scheme [Vol. XXI p. 73] S.R.& O. No. 48 of 1935

Statutory Authority	Section	Statutory Instrument
Teacher's Superannuation Act, No. 32 of 1928 (*Cont.*)		**Secondary Teachers' Superannuation (Amendment) Scheme, S.I. No. 35 of 1972**
		Secondary Teachers' Superannuation (Amendment) (No.2) Scheme, S.I. No. 171 of 1972
	3	**Secondary Teachers' Superannuation (Amendment) Scheme, S.I. No. 35 of 1972**
		Secondary Teachers' Superannuation (Amendment) (No.2) Scheme, S.I. No. 171 of 1972
	6	**National School Teachers' Superannuation (Amendment) Scheme, S.I. No. 247 of 1958**
		National School Teachers' Superannuation (Amendment) Scheme, S.I. No. 156 of 1964
		National School Teachers' Superannuation (Amendment) Scheme, S.I. No. 45 of 1967
		Secondary Teachers' Superannuation (Amendment) Scheme, S.I. No. 46 of 1967
		Secondary Teachers' Superannuation (Amendment) Scheme, S.I. No. 35 of 1972
		Secondary Teachers' Superannuation (Amendment) (No.2) Scheme, S.I. No. 171 of 1972
		National School Teachers' Superannuation (Amendment) Scheme, S.I. No. 173 of 1972
Tearmai Dlithiula Gaeilge (Acht) No. 18 of 1945	3	**Tearmai Dlithiula Gaeilge (Uimh.1) (An tOrdu) [Vol. XXXVII p. 819] S.R.& O. No. 249 of 1947**
		Tearmai Dlithiula Gaeilge (Uimh.2) (An tOrdu) S.I. No. 42 of 1948
		Tearmai Dlithiula Gaeilge (Uimh.3) (An tOrdu) S.I. No. 47 of 1948
		Tearmai Dlithiula Gaeilge (Uimh.5) (An tOrdu) S.I. No. 2 of 1950
		Tearmai Dlithiula Gaeilge (Uimh.6) (An tOrdu) S.I. No. 3 of 1950
		Tearmai Dlithiula Gaeilge (Uimh.7) (An tOrdu) S.I. No. 289 of 1950
		Tearmai Dlithiula Gaeilge (Uimh.8) (An tOrdu) S.I. No. 290 of 1950
		Tearmai Dlithiula Gaeilge (Uimh.9) (An tOrdu) S.I. No. 291 of 1950
		Tearmai Dlithiula Gaeilge (Uimh.10) (An tOrdu) S.I. No. 51 of 1956
	3(1)	**Tearmai Dlithiula Gaeilge (Uimh.4) (An tOrdu) S.I. No. 68 of 1949**
Telegraph Act, No. 58 of 1885	2	*Telephone Regulations [Vol. XXXIV p. 49] S.R.& O. No. 62 of 1942*
		Telephone (Amendment) (No.1) Regulations, S.I. No. 276 of 1951
		Telephone Regulations, S.I. No. 227 of 1953
		Telegraph (Inland Written Telegram) Amendment (No.6) Warrant, S.I. No. 144 of 1955
		Telex Regulations, S.I. No. 229 of 1955

Statutory Authority	Section	Statutory Instrument
Telegraph Act, No. 582 of 1885 (*Cont.*)		*Telephone (Amendment) (No.1) Regulations, S.I. No. 117 of 1956*
		Telephone (Amendment) Regulations, S.I. No. 179 of 1958
		Telephone Regulations, S.I. No. 118 of 1959
		Telegraph (Inland Written Telegram) Amendment (No.7) Warrant, S.I. No. 51 of 1960
		Telegraph (Inland Written Telegram) Amendment (No.8) Warrant, S.I. No. 179 of 1963
		Telegraph (Inland Written Telegram) Amendment (No.9) Warrant, S.I. No. 115 of 1964
		Telephone (Amendment) Regulations, S.I. No. 153 of 1964
		Telex (Amendment) Regulations, S.I. No. 229 of 1964
		Telephone (Amendment) Regulations, S.I. No. 33 of 1965
		Telephone (Amendment) Regulations, S.I. No. 274 of 1968
		Telegraph (Inland Written Telegram) Amendment (No.10) Warrant, S.I. No. 277 of 1968
		Telephone (Amendment) Regulations, S.I. No. 185 of 1969
		Telegraph (Inland Written Telegram) Amendment (No.11) Warrant, S.I. No. 212 of 1970
		Telephone (Amendment) Regulations, S.I. No. 213 of 1970
		Telex (Amendment) Regulations, S.I. No. 4 of 1971
		Telegraph (Inland Written Telegram) Amendment (No.12) Warrant, S.I. No. 62 of 1971
		Telephone (Amendment) Regulations, S.I. No. 63 of 1971
		Telephone (Amendment) (No.2) Regulations, S.I. No. 269 of 1971
		Telephone (Amendment) Regulations, S.I. No. 193 of 1973
		Telegraph (Inland Written Telegram) Amendment (No.13) Warrant, S.I. No. 282 of 1974
		Telex (Amendment) Regulations, S.I. No. 309 of 1974
		Telex (Amendment) (No.2) Regulations, S.I. No. 355 of 1974
		Telephone (Amendment) Regulations, S.I. No. 363 of 1974
		Telegraph (Inland Written Telegram) Amendment (No.14) Warrant, S.I. No. 364 of 1974
		Telex (Amendment) Regulations, S.I. No. 311 of 1975
		Telegraph (Inland Written Telegram) Amendment (No.15) Warrant, S.I. No. 312 of 1975
		Telephone (Amendment) Regulations, S.I. No. 313 of 1975

Statutory Authority	Section	Statutory Instrument

Telegraph Act, No. 582 of 1885
(*Cont.*)

Telegraph (Inland Written Telegram) Amendment (No.16) Warrant, S.I. No. 72 of 1977

Telex (Amendment) Regulations, S.I. No. 73 of 1977

Telephone (Amendment) Regulations, S.I. No. 74 of 1977

Telephone (Amendment) Regulations, S.I. No. 315 of 1979

Telegraph (Inland Written Telegram) Amendment (No.17) Warrant, S.I. No. 316 of 1979

Telex (Amendment) Regulations, S.I. No. 317 of 1979

Telephone Regulations, S.I. No. 195 of 1980

Telegraph (Inland Written Telegram) Regulations, S.I. No. 196 of 1980

Telex Regulations, S.I. No. 197 of 1980

Telephone (Amendment) Regulations, S.I. No. 332 of 1980

Telephone (Amendment) Regulations, S.I. No. 106 of 1981

Telex (Amendment) Regulations, S.I. No. 107 of 1981

Telegraph (Foreign Written Telegram) (Amendment) Regulations, S.I. No. 108 of 1981

Telegraph (Inland Written Telegram) (Amendment) Regulations, S.I. No. 109 of 1981

Telephone (Amendment) (No.2) Regulations, S.I. No. 294 of 1981

Telex (Amendment) (No.2) Regulations, S.I. No. 295 of 1981

Telegraph (Inland Written Telegram) Amendment (No.2) Regulations, S.I. No. 296 of 1981

Telegraph (Foreign Written Telegram) (Amendment) (No.2) Regulations, S.I. No. 297 of 1981

Telephone (Amendment) (No.3) Regulations, S.I. No. 402 of 1981

Telex (Amendment) (No.3) Regulations, S.I. No. 403 of 1981

Telephone (Amendment) Regulations, S.I. No. 39 of 1982

Telex (Amendment) Regulations, S.I. No. 40 of 1982

Telephone (Amendment) (No.2) Regulations, S.I. No. 64 of 1982

Telex (Amendment) (No.2) Regulations, S.I. No. 65 of 1982

Telegraph (Inland Written Telegram) (Amendment) Regulations, S.I. No. 66 of 1982

Telegraph (Foreign Written Telegram) (Amendment) Regulations, S.I. No. 67 of 1982

Telephone (Amendment) Regulations, S.I. No. 73 of 1983

Telex (Amendment) Regulations, S.I. No. 74 of 1983

Telegraph Act, No. 582 of 1885
(*Cont.*)

Telegraph (Inland Written Telegram) (Amendment) Regulations, S.I. No. 75 of 1983

Telegraph (Foreign Written Telegram) (Amendment) Regulations, S.I. No. 76 of 1983

Telegraph Acts, 1863 to 1904,

Telegraph (Foreign Written Telegram) Regulations, S.I. No. 198 of 1980

Telegraph Acts, 1863 to 1921,

Telephone Amendment (No.1) Warrant [Vol. XXI p. 123] S.R.& O. No. 74 of 1926

Telegraph Acts, 1863 to 1928,

Telegraph (Inland Written Telegram) Amendment (No.1) Warrant [Vol. XXI p. 127] S.R.& O. No. 45 of 1928

Telegraph (Inland Written Telegram) Amendment (No.2) Warrant, (1933) [Vol. XXI p. 135] S.R.& O. No. 15 of 1934

Telegraph (Inland Written Telegram) Amendment (No.3) Warrant [Vol. XXI p. 139] S.R.& O. No. 204 of 1936

Telegraph (Inland Written Telegram) Amendment (No.4) Warrant [Vol. XXI p. 143] S.R.& O. No. 133 of 1937

Telegraph (Inland Written Telegram) Amendment (No.5) Warrant [Vol. XXI p. 149] S.R.& O. No. 327 of 1938

Telegraph (Foreign Written Telegram) (Amendment) (No.2) Regulations [Vol. XXXIV p. 45] S.R.& O. No. 51 of 1940

Telephone Regulations [Vol. XXXIV p. 49] S.R.& O. No. 62 of 1942

Telephone Regulations, S.I. No. 227 of 1953

Therapeutic Substances Act, No. 25 of 1932

Therapeutic Substances (Saorstat Eireann) Amendment (No.2) Regulations [Vol. XXI p. 263] S.R.& O. No. 46 of 1936

Therapeutic Substances (Saorstat Eireann) Amendment Regulations [Vol. XXI p. 257] S.R.& O. No. 71 of 1936

Therapeutic Substances (Saorstat Eireann) Amendment Regulations [Vol. XXI p. 295] S.R.& O. No. 284 of 1937

Therapeutic Substances (Saorstat Eireann) Amendment Regulations [Vol. XXI p. 301] S.R.& O. No. 21 of 1938

Therapeutic Substances (Amendment) Regulations [Vol. XXXIV p. 75] S.R.& O. No. 253 of 1939

Therapeutic Substances (Amendment) Regulations [Vol. XXXIV p. 83] S.R.& O. No. 14 of 1941

Therapeutic Substances (Emergency Amendment) Order [Vol. XXXIV p. 107] S.R.& O. No. 555 of 1942

Therapeutic Substances (Amendment) Regulations [Vol. XXXIV p. 93] S.R.& O. No. 121 of 1945

Statutory Authority	Section	Statutory Instrument
Therapeutic Substances Act, No. 25 of 1932 (*Cont.*)		*Therapeutic Substances (Amendment) (No.2) Regulations [Vol. XXXIV p. 103] S.R.& O. No. 353 of 1945*
		Therapeutic Substances (Amendment) Regulations [Vol. XXXVIII p. 609] S.R.& O. No. 241 of 1946
		Therapeutic Substances (Amendment) Regulations [Vol. XXXVIII p. 613] S.R.& O. No. 345 of 1947
		Therapeutic Substances (Amendment) Regulations, S.I. No. 263 of 1948
		Therapeutic Substances (Amendment) Regulations, S.I. No. 143 of 1953
		Therapeutic Substances (Amendment) Regulations, S.I. No. 198 of 1954
	2(4)	**Therapeutic Substances (Advisory Committee) Rules [Vol. XXI p. 153] S.R.& O. No. 106 of 1933**
		Therapeutic Substances (Saorstat Eireann) Regulations [Vol. XXI p. 161] S.R.& O. No. 365 of 1934
		Therapeutic Substances (Saorstat Eireann) Amendment Regulations [Vol. XXI p. 245] S.R.& O. No. 563 of 1935
	5	**Therapeutic Substances (Amendment) Regulations, S.I. No. 149 of 1955**
	14	**Therapeutic Substances (Fees) Regulations, S.I. No. 183 of 1954**
Therapeutic Substances (Amendment) Regulations [Vol. XXXVIII p. 609] S.R.& O. No. 241 of 1946	2	**Therapeutic Substances (Penicillin) Order [Vol. XXXVIII p. 623] S.R.& O. No. 242 of 1946**
Thionscail na Gaeltachta (Acht um) No. 29 of 1957	2	*Thionscail na Gaeltachta, 1957 (An La Bunuithe) (An tOrdu fan Acht um) S.I. No. 89 of 1958*
Thomond College of Education, Limerick Act, No. 34 of 1980	17(2)	*Thomond College of Education, Limerick, Act, 1980 (Commencement) Order, S.I. No. 214 of 1981*
Tobacco Act, No. 37 of 1934		*Tobacco (Growers' Arrangements) Regulations [Vol. XXI p. 337] S.R.& O. No. 316 of 1934*
		Tobacco (Growers' Arrangements) Regulations [Vol. XXI p. 345] S.R.& O. No. 163 of 1935
	8	**Tobacco Growing Regulations [Vol. XXI p. 325] S.R.& O. No. 352 of 1934**
	9(1)	**Tobacco Rehandlers' Regulations [Vol. XXI p. 381] S.R.& O. No. 384 of 1934**
	9(2)	**Tobacco Act (Manufacturers' Returns Regulations) Order [Vol. XXI p. 357] S.R.& O. No. 340 of 1934**
	11(1)	*Tobacco (Areas for 1935) Order [Vol. XXI p. 305] S.R.& O. No. 68 of 1935*
		Tobacco (Areas for 1936) Order [Vol. XXI p. 309] S.R.& O. No. 4 of 1936

Statutory Authority	Section	Statutory Instrument
Tobacco Act, No. 37 of 1934 (*Cont.*)		*Tobacco (Areas for 1937) Order [Vol. XXI p. 313]* S.R. & O. No. 2 of 1937
		Tobacco (Areas for 1938) Order [Vol. XXI p. 317] S.R. & O. No. 6 of 1938
		Tobacco (Areas for 1939) Order [Vol. XXI p. 321] S.R. & O. No. 335 of 1938
		Tobacco (Areas for 1940) Order [Vol. XXXIV p. 115] S.R. & O. No. 20 of 1940
		Tobacco (Areas for 1941) Order [Vol. XXXIV p. 119] S.R. & O. No. 365 of 1940
		Tobacco (Areas for 1942) Order [Vol. XXXIV p. 123] S.R. & O. No. 12 of 1942
		Tobacco (Areas for 1943) Order [Vol. XXXIV p. 127] S.R. & O. No. 553 of 1942
		Tobacco (Areas for 1944) Order [Vol. XXXIV p. 131] S.R. & O. No. 73 of 1944
		Tobacco (Areas for 1945) Order [Vol. XXXIV p. 135] S.R. & O. No. 309 of 1944
		Tobacco (Areas for 1946) Order [Vol. XXXIV p. 139] S.R. & O. No. 293 of 1945
		Tobacco (Areas for 1947) Order [Vol. XXXVIII p. 627] S.R. & O. No. 338 of 1946
		Tobacco (Areas for 1948) Order [Vol. XXXVIII p. 633] S.R. & O. No. 440 of 1947
		Tobacco (Areas for 1949) Order, S.I. No. 55 of 1949
		Tobacco (Areas for 1950) Order, S.I. No. 21 of 1950
		Tobacco (Areas for 1951) Order, S.I. No. 326 of 1950
		Tobacco (Areas for 1952) Order, S.I. No. 360 of 1951
		Tobacco (Areas for 1953) Order, S.I. No. 344 of 1952
		Tobacco (Areas for 1954) Order, S.I. No. 382 of 1953
		Tobacco (Areas for 1955) Order, S.I. No. 240 of 1954
		Tobacco (Areas for 1956) Order, S.I. No. 129 of 1956
		Tobacco (Areas for 1957) Order, S.I. No. 43 of 1957
		Tobacco (Areas for 1958) Order, S.I. No. 5 of 1958
		Tobacco (Areas for 1959) Order, S.I. No. 256 of 1958
		Tobacco (Areas for 1960) Order, S.I. No. 223 of 1959
		Tobacco (Areas for 1961) Order, S.I. No. 256 of 1960
		Tobacco (Areas for 1962) Order, S.I. No. 297 of 1961
		Tobacco (Areas for 1963) Order, S.I. No. 207 of 1962
		Tobacco (Areas for 1964) Order, S.I. No. 250 of 1963

Statutory Authority	Section	Statutory Instrument
Tobacco Act, No. 37 of 1934 (*Cont.*)		*Tobacco (Areas for 1965) Order, S.I. No. 284 of 1964*
		Tobacco (Areas for 1966) Order, S.I. No. 248 of 1965
		Tobacco (Areas for 1967) Order, S.I. No. 267 of 1966
		Tobacco (Areas for 1968) Order, S.I. No. 281 of 1967
		Tobacco (Areas for 1969) Order, S.I. No. 261 of 1968
		Tobacco (Areas for 1970) Order, S.I. No. 242 of 1969
		Tobacco (Areas for 1971) Order, S.I. No. 294 of 1970
		Tobacco (Areas for 1972) Order, S.I. No. 324 of 1971
	12	**Tobacco Growing Regulations [Vol. XXI p. 325] S.R.& O. No. 352 of 1934**
	28(1)	**Tobacco Rehandlers' Regulations [Vol. XXI p. 381] S.R.& O. No. 384 of 1934**
		Tobacco (Growers' Returns) Regulations [Vol. XXI p. 351] S.R.& O. No. 164 of 1935
	35(1)	**Tobacco Rehandlers' Regulations [Vol. XXI p. 381] S.R.& O. No. 384 of 1934**
	35(2)	**Tobacco Rehandlers' Regulations [Vol. XXI p. 381] S.R.& O. No. 384 of 1934**
	42	*Tobacco Rehandlers' (Charges) Regulations [Vol. XXI p. 361] S.R.& O. No. 283 of 1934*
		Tobacco Rehandlers' (Charges) Regulations [Vol. XXI p. 365] S.R.& O. No. 627 of 1935
		Tobacco Rehandlers' (Charges) Regulations [Vol. XXI p. 369] S.R.& O. No. 348 of 1936
		Tobacco Rehandlers' (Charges) Regulations [Vol. XXI p. 373] S.R.& O. No. 268 of 1937
		Tobacco Rehandlers' (Charges) Regulations [Vol. XXI p. 377] S.R.& O. No. 298 of 1938
		Tobacco Rehandlers' (Charges) Regulations [Vol. XXXIV p. 145] S.R.& O. No. 406 of 1939
		Tobacco Rehandlers' (Charges) Regulations [Vol. XXXIV p. 149] S.R.& O. No. 364 of 1940
		Tobacco Rehandlers' (Charges) Regulations [Vol. XXXIV p. 153] S.R.& O. No. 515 of 1941
		Tobacco Rehandlers' (Charges) Regulations [Vol. XXXIV p. 157] S.R.& O. No. 554 of 1942
		Tobacco Rehandlers' (Charges) Regulations, (1943) [Vol. XXXIV p. 161] S.R.& O. No. 44 of 1944
		Tobacco Rehandlers' (Charges) Regulations [Vol. XXXIV p. 165] S.R.& O. No. 310 of 1944
		Tobacco Rehandlers' (Charges) Regulations [Vol. XXXIV p. 169] S.R.& O. No. 292 of 1945
		Tobacco Rehandlers' (Charges) Regulations [Vol. XXXVIII p. 639] S.R.& O. No. 339 of 1946

Statutory Authority	Section	Statutory Instrument
Tobacco Act, No. 37 of 1934 (*Cont.*)		*Tobacco Rehandlers' (Charges) Regulations [Vol. XXXVIII p. 643] S.R.& O. No. 439 of 1947*
		Tobacco Rehandlers' (Charges) Regulations, S.I. No. 432 of 1948
		Tobacco Rehandlers' (Charges) Regulations, S.I. No. 339 of 1949
		Tobacco Rehandlers' (Charges) Regulations, S.I. No. 325 of 1950
		Tobacco Rehandlers' (Charges) Regulations, S.I. No. 323 of 1951
		Tobacco Rehandlers' (Charges) Regulations, S.I. No. 229 of 1952
		Tobacco Rehandlers' (Charges) Regulations, S.I. No. 196 of 1953
		Tobacco Rehandlers' (Charges) Regulations, S.I. No. 117 of 1954
	43(1)	**Tobacco Rehandlers' Regulations [Vol. XXI p. 381] S.R.& O. No. 384 of 1934**
Tobacco Products (Control of Advertising, Sponsorship and Sales Promotion) Act, No. 27 of 1978	2	*Tobacco Products (Control of Advertising, Sponsorship and Sales Promotion) Regulations, S.I. No. 350 of 1979*
		Tobacco Products (Control of Advertising, Sponsorship and Sales Promotion) Regulations, S.I. No. 7 of 1986
		Tobacco (Control of Advertising, Sponsorship and Sales Promotion) (No.2) Regulations, S.I. No. 107 of 1986
Toghchain Udaras na Gaeltachta (Na Rialachain um) S.I. No. 355 of 1979	6	*Udaras na Gaeltachta (An La Votaiochta) (An tOrdu um) S.I. No. 356 of 1979*
		Udaras na Gaeltachta (An La Votaiochta) (An tOrdu um) S.I. No. 202 of 1984
Totalisator Act, No. 22 of 1929	6(1)	**Totalisator (Double Event) Regulations, (1935) [Vol. XXI p. 437] S.R.& O. No. 26 of 1936**
		Totalisator (Amendment) Regulations [Vol. XXI p. 427] S.R.& O. No. 134 of 1938
		Totalisator Regulations [Vol. XXXIV p. 173] S.R.& O. No. 195 of 1944
		Totalisator (Amendment) Regulations, S.I. No. 146 of 1956
		Greyhound Race Track (Totalisator) Regulations, S.I. No. 23 of 1960
		Totalisator (Multiple Event) Regulations, S.I. No. 7 of 1966
		Totalisator (Multiple Event) (Amendment) Regulations, S.I. No. 151 of 1966
		Totalisator (Amendment) Regulations, S.I. No. 58 of 1967
		Totalisator (Amendment) Regulations, S.I. No. 142 of 1968
		Greyhound Race Track (Totalisator) Regulations, S.I. No. 102 of 1969

Statutory Authority	Section	Statutory Instrument
Totalisator Act, No. 22 of 1929 (*Cont.*)		**Totalisator (Horse Racing) Regulations, S.I. No. 57 of 1971**
		Totalisator (Greyhound Race Track) Regulations, S.I. No. 58 of 1971
		Totalisator (Horse Racing) (Amendment) Regulations, S.I. No. 274 of 1971
		Totalisator (Horse Racing) (Amendment) Regulations, S.I. No. 160 of 1981
		Totalisator (Horse Racing) (Extended Forecast) Regulations, S.I. No. 275 of 1984
Tourist Traffic Act, No. 24 of 1939		*Tourist Traffic Act, 1939 (Commencement of Sections 33, 34, 35, 36 and 37) Order [Vol. XXXIV p. 177] S.R.& O. No. 52 of 1944*
	37B	*Tourist Traffic Act, 1939 (Commencement) Order, S.I. No. 61 of 1969*
Tourist Traffic Act, No. 5 of 1955	2	*Tourist Traffic Act, 1955 (Commencement) Order, S.I. No. 113 of 1955*
Town and Regional Planning Act, No. 22 of 1934		*Town and Regional Planning Regulations [Vol. XXI p. 451] S.R.& O. No. 334 of 1934*
		Town and Regional Planning Regulations [Vol. XXXIV p. 181] S.R.& O. No. 180 of 1939
	1(2)	*Town and Regional Planning Act, 1934 (Date of Commencement) Order [Vol. XXI p. 447] S.R.& O. No. 335 of 1934*
	21	*Cork County Borough (Extension of Planning District) Order, S.I. No. 7 of 1950*
		Cork County Borough (Extension of Planning District) Order, S.I. No. 328 of 1953
		County Cork Borough (Extension of Planning District) Order, S.I. No. 250 of 1960
		Borough of Wexford (Extension of Planning District) Order, S.I. No. 66 of 1961
	21(5)	*Cork County Borough (Extension of Planning District) Order, 1960 (Revocation) Order, S.I. No. 86 of 1961*
	24	*Town and Regional Planning Regulations, S.I. No. 321 of 1956*
Town and Regional Planning (Amendment) Act, No. 11 of 1939		*Town and Regional Planning Regulations [Vol. XXXIV p. 181] S.R.& O. No. 180 of 1939*
Towns Improvement (Ireland) Act, No. 103 of 1854		**Towns Improvement (Ireland) Act, 1854 (Tramore) Order, S.I. No. 121 of 1948**
	15	**Towns Improvement (Ireland) Act, 1854 (Shannon) Order, S.I. No. 399 of 1981**
		Towns Improvement (Ireland) Act, 1854 (Greystones) Order, S.I. No. 162 of 1983

Statutory Authority	Section	Statutory Instrument
Trade Boards Act, No. 22 of 1909	11	Paper Box Trade Board Regulations [Vol. XXI p. 571] S.R.& O. No. 10 of 1923
		Tailoring Trade Board (Irish Free State) Regulations [Vol. XXI p. 601] S.R.& O. No. 26 of 1926
		Women's Clothing and Millinery Trade Board Regulations [Vol. XXI p. 621] S.R.& O. No. 27 of 1926
		Shirtmaking Trade Board (Irish Free State) Regulations [Vol. XXI p. 587] S.R.& O. No. 21 of 1931
		Aerated Waters Trade Board Regulations [Vol. XXI p. 493] S.R.& O. No. 45 of 1933
		Boot and Shoe Repairing Trade Board Regulations [Vol. XXI p. 501] S.R.& O. No. 46 of 1933
		Brush and Broom Trade Board Regulations [Vol. XXI p. 509] S.R.& O. No. 47 of 1933
		Linen and Cotton Embroidery Trade Board Regulations [Vol. XXI p. 551] S.R.& O. No. 48 of 1933
		Sugar Confectionery and Food Preserving Trade Board Regulations [Vol. XXI p. 591] S.R.& O. No. 50 of 1933
		Tobacco Trade Board Regulations [Vol. XXI p. 611] S.R.& O. No. 51 of 1933
		General Waste Materials Reclamation Trade Board [Vol. XXI p. 529] S.R.& O. No. 52 of 1933
		Packing Trade Board Regulations [Vol. XXI p. 561] S.R.& O. No. 232 of 1934
		Rope, Twine and Net Trade Board Regulations [Vol. XXI p. 575] S.R.& O. No. 319 of 1934
		Button-making Trade Board Regulations [Vol. XXI p. 519] S.R.& O. No. 658 of 1935
		Women's Clothing and Millinery Trade Board (Amendment) Regulations [Vol. XXI p. 627] S.R.& O. No. 684 of 1935
		Handkerchief and Household Piece Goods Trade Board Regulations [Vol. XXI p. 541] S.R.& O. No. 9 of 1936
		Tailoring Trade Board (Amendment) Regulations [Vol. XXI p. 605] S.R.& O. No. 34 of 1938
		Women's Clothing and Millinery Trade Board (Amendment) Regulations [Vol. XXI p. 633] S.R.& O. No. 337 of 1938
		Trade Boards (Hand Embroidery Trade) Regulations [Vol. XXXIV p. 191] S.R.& O. No. 397 of 1939
		Trade Boards (Tailoring Trade) (Amendment) Regulations [Vol. XXXIV p. 201] S.R.& O. No. 269 of 1944
		Trade Boards (Women's Clothing and Millinery Trade) (Amendment) Regulations [Vol. XXXIV p. 205] S.R.& O. No. 271 of 1944
		Trade Boards (Sugar Confectionery and Food Preserving Trade) (Amendment) Regulations [Vol. XXXIV p. 197] S.R.& O. No. 157 of 1945

Statutory Authority	Section	Statutory Instrument
Trade Boards Act, No. 22 of 1909 (*Cont.*)	18	*Trade Boards Acts 1909 to 1918 (Amendment) Regulations [Vol. XXI p. 485] S.R.& O. No. 21 of 1923*
Trade Boards Act, No. 32 of 1918	1	*Trade Boards (Hand Embroidery Trade) Special Order [Vol. XXXIV p. 209] S.R.& O. No. 375 of 1939*
	1(2)	*Trade Boards (Packing) Order, (1924) [Vol. XXI p. 649] S.R.& O. No. 20 of 1934*
		Trade Boards (Handkerchief and Household Piece Goods) Order [Vol. XXI p. 655] S.R.& O. No. 50 of 1935
	1(5)	*Trade Boards (Sugar Confectionery and Food Preserving Trade) Special Order [Vol. XXXIV p. 213] S.R.& O. No. 156 of 1945*
	2(1)	*Trade Boards (Women's Clothing and Millinery) Order [Vol. XXI p. 641] S.R.& O. No. 8 of 1926*
		Trade Boards (Tailoring) Order [Vol. XXI p. 645] S.R.& O. No. 9 of 1926
		Trade Boards (Tailoring) Order, 1926 (Variation) Order [Vol. XXXIV p. 219] S.R.& O. No. 268 of 1944
		Trade Boards (Women's Clothing and Millinery) Order, 1926 (Variation) Order [Vol. XXXIV p. 223] S.R.& O. No. 270 of 1944
	Sch. I par. 9	*Trade Boards Draft Special Orders Inquiry Procedure Regulations [Vol. XXI p. 637] S.R.& O. No. 44 of 1925*
Trade Boards Acts, 1909 to 1918,		*Trade Boards (District Trade Committees) Regulations [Vol. XXI p. 189] S.R.& O. No. 53 of 1928*
Trade Loans (Guarantee) Act, No. 5 of 1939	12	**Trade Loans Regulations, S.I. No. 352 of 1953**
Trade Marks Act, No. 9 of 1963	1	*Trade Marks Act, 1963 (Commencement) Order, S.I. No. 34 of 1964*
	3	**Trade Marks Rules, S.I. No. 268 of 1963**
		Trade Marks Rules, 1963 (Amendment) Rules, S.I. No. 76 of 1964
		Trade Marks Rules, 1963 (Amendment) Rules, S.I. No. 187 of 1980
		Trade Marks Rules, 1963 (Amendment) Rules, S.I. No. 199 of 1983
		Trade Marks Rules, 1963 (Amendment) Rules, S.I. No. 46 of 1985
		Trade Marks Rules, 1963 (Amendment) Rules, S.I. No. 77 of 1986
	4	**Trade Marks Rules, 1963 (Amendment) Rules, S.I. No. 64 of 1968**
		Trade Marks Rules, 1963 (Amendment) Rules, S.I. No. 19 of 1974

Statutory Authority	Section	Statutory Instrument
Trade Marks Act, No. 9 of 1963 (*Cont.*)		**Trade Marks Rules, 1963 (Amendment) Rules, S.I. No. 265 of 1977**
		Trade Marks Rules, 1963 (Amendment) Rules, S.I. No. 187 of 1980
		Trade Marks Rules, 1963 (Amendment) Rules, S.I. No. 199 of 1983
		Trade Marks Rules, 1963 (Amendment) Rules, S.I. No. 46 of 1985
		Trade Marks Rules, 1963 (Amendment) Rules, S.I. No. 77 of 1986
	69	**Register of Trade Mark Agents Rules, S.I. No. 35 of 1964**
		Register of Trade Marks Agents (Amendment) Rules, 1985, S.I. No. 371 of 1985
	70(5)	**Patents, Designs and Trade Marks (International Arrangements) (Amendment) Order, S.I. No. 32 of 1968**
Trade Union Act, No. 31 of 1871	13	*Trade Union (Fees) Regulations, S.I. No. 86 of 1978*
		Trade Union (Fees) Regulations, S.I. No. 292 of 1983
Trade Union Act, No. 22 of 1941		**Trade Union Act, 1941 (Trade Union Tribunal and Appeal Board) Regulations [Vol. XXXIV p. 249] S.R.& O. No. 129 of 1943**
	3	**Trade Union Act, 1941 (Application for Negotiation Licence) Regulations [Vol. XXXIV p. 233] S.R.& O. No. 106 of 1942**
		Trade Union (Inspection of Register of Members) Regulations [Vol. XXXIV p. 227] S.R.& O. No. 156 of 1942
		Trade Union Act, 1971 (Notice of Intention to Apply for Negotiation Licence) Regulations, S.I. No. 158 of 1972
	6	*Trade Union Act, 1941 (Commencement of Section 6) Order [Vol. XXXIV p. 245] S.R.& O. No. 590 of 1941*
	6(6)	**Trade Union Act, 1941 (Exclusion from Section 6) Order, S.I. No. 221 of 1957**
		Trade Union Act, 1941 (Exclusion from Section 6) Order, S.I. No. 17 of 1960
		Trade Union Act, 1941 (Exclusion from Section 6) (No.2) Order, S.I. No. 233 of 1960
		Trade Union Act, 1941 (Exclusion from Section 6) Order, S.I. No. 58 of 1963
		Trade Union Act, 1941 (Exclusion from Section 6) (No.2) Order, S.I. No. 63 of 1963
		Trade Union Act, 1941 (Exclusion from Section 6) (No.1) Order, S.I. No. 54 of 1965
		Trade Union Act, 1941 (Exclusion from Section 6) (No.2) Order, S.I. No. 55 of 1965
		Trade Union Act, 1941 (Exclusion from Section 6) (No.3) Order, S.I. No. 56 of 1965

Statutory Authority	Section	Statutory Instrument
Trade Union Act, No. 22 of 1941 (*Cont.*)		**Trade Union Act, 1941 (Revocation of Negotiation Licence) (No.1) Order, S.I. No. 114 of 1986**
		Trade Union Act, 1941 (Revocation of Negotiation Licence) (No.2) Order, S.I. No. 115 of 1986
		Trade Union Act, 1941 (Revocation of Negotiation Licence) (No.3) Order, S.I. No. 116 of 1986
		Trade Union Act, 1941 (Revocation of Negotiation Licence) (No.4) Order, S.I. No. 117 of 1986
		Trade Union Act, 1941 (Revocation of Negotiation Licence) (No.5) Order, S.I. No. 118 of 1986
		Trade Union Act, 1941 (Revocation of Negotiation Licence) (No.6) Order, S.I. No. 119 of 1986
		Trade Union Act, 1941 (Revocation of Negotiation Licence) (No.7) Order, S.I. No. 120 of 1986
		Trade Union Act, 1941 (Revocation of Negotiation Licence) (No.8) Order, S.I. No. 121 of 1986
		Trade Union Act, 1941 (Revocation of Negotiation Licence) (No.9) Order, S.I. No. 122 of 1986
		Trade Union Act, 1941 (Revocation of Negotiation Licence) (No.10) Order, S.I. No. 123 of 1986
		Trade Union Act, 1941 (Revocation of Negotiation Licence) (No.11) Order, S.I. No. 124 of 1986
		Trade Union Act, 1941 (Revocation of Negotiation Licence) (No.12) Order, S.I. No. 125 of 1986
		Trade Union Act, 1941 (Revocation of Negotiation Licence) (No.13) Order, S.I. No. 126 of 1986
		Trade Union Act, 1941 (Revocation of Negotiation Licence) (No.14) Order, S.I. No. 127 of 1986
		Trade Union Act, 1941 (Revocation of Negotiation Licence) (No.15) Order, S.I. No. 128 of 1986
		Trade Union Act, 1941 (Revocation of Negotiation Licence) (No.16) Order, S.I. No. 129 of 1986
		Trade Union Act, 1941 (Revocation of Negotiation Licence) (No.17) Order, S.I. No. 130 of 1986
		Trade Union Act, 1941 (Revocation of Negotiation Licence) (No.18) Order, S.I. No. 131 of 1986
		Trade Union Act, 1941 (Revocation of Negotiation Licence) (No.19) Order, S.I. No. 132 of 1986
		Trade Union Act, 1941 (Revocation of Negotiation Licence) (No.20) Order, S.I. No. 133 of 1986
		Trade Union Act, 1941 (Revocation of Negotiation Licence) (No.21) Order, S.I. No. 134 of 1986
		Trade Union Act, 1941 (Revocation of Negotiation Licence) (No.22) Order, S.I. No. 135 of 1986
		Trade Union Act, 1941 (Revocation of Negotiation Licence) (No.23) Order, S.I. No. 136 of 1986
		Trade Union Act, 1941 (Revocation of Negotiation Licence) (No.24) Order, S.I. No. 137 of 1986
		Trade Union Act, 1941 (Revocation of Negotiation Licence) (No.25) Order, S.I. No. 138 of 1986
		Trade Union Act, 1941 (Revocation of Negotiation Licence) (No.26) Order, S.I. No. 139 of 1986

Statutory Authority	Section	Statutory Instrument
Trade Union Act, No. 22 of 1941 (*Cont.*)		**Trade Union Act, 1941 (Revocation of Negotiation Licence) (No.27) Order, S.I. No. 140 of 1986**
		Trade Union Act, 1941 (Revocation of Negotiation Licence) (No.28) Order, S.I. No. 141 of 1986
		Trade Union Act, 1941 (Revocation of Negotiation Licence) (No.29) Order, S.I. No. 142 of 1986
		Trade Union Act, 1941 (Revocation of Negotiation Licence) (No.30) Order, S.I. No. 143 of 1986
		Trade Union Act, 1941 (Revocation of Negotiation Licence) (No.31) Order, S.I. No. 144 of 1986
		Trade Union Act, 1941 (Revocation of Negotiation Licence) (No.32) Order, S.I. No. 145 of 1986
		Trade Union Act, 1941 (Revocation of Negotiation Licence) (No.33) Order, S.I. No. 146 of 1986
		Trade Union Act, 1941 (Revocation of Negotiation Licence) (No.34) Order, S.I. No. 147 of 1986
		Trade Union Act, 1941 (Revocation of Negotiation Licence) (No.35) Order, S.I. No. 148 of 1986
		Trade Union Act, 1941 (Revocation of Negotiation Licence) (No.36) Order, S.I. No. 149 of 1986
		Trade Union Act, 1941 (Revocation of Negotiation Licence) (No.37) Order, S.I. No. 150 of 1986
		Trade Union Act, 1941 (Revocation of Negotiation Licence) (No.38) Order, S.I. No. 151 of 1986
		Trade Union Act, 1941 (Revocation of Negotiation Licence) (No.39) Order, S.I. No. 152 of 1986
		Trade Union Act, 1941 (Revocation of Negotiation Licence) (No.40) Order, S.I. No. 153 of 1986
		Trade Union Act, 1941 (Revocation of Negotiation Licence) (No.41) Order, S.I. No. 154 of 1986
		Trade Union Act, 1941 (Revocation of Negotiation Licence) (No.42) Order, S.I. No. 155 of 1986
		Trade Union Act, 1941 (Revocation of Negotiation Licence) (No.43) Order, S.I. No. 156 of 1986
		Trade Union Act, 1941 (Revocation of Negotiation Licence) (No.44) Order, S.I. No. 157 of 1986
		Trade Union Act, 1941 (Revocation of Negotiation Licence) (No.45) Order, S.I. No. 158 of 1986
		Trade Union Act, 1941 (Revocation of Negotiation Licence) (No.46) Order, S.I. No. 159 of 1986
		Trade Union Act, 1941 (Revocation of Negotiation Licence) (No.47) Order, S.I. No. 160 of 1986
		Trade Union Act, 1941 (Revocation of Negotiation Licence) (No.48) Order, S.I. No. 161 of 1986
		Trade Union Act, 1941 (Revocation of Negotiation Licence) (No.49) Order, S.I. No. 162 of 1986
		Trade Union Act, 1941 (Revocation of Negotiation Licence) (No.50) Order, S.I. No. 163 of 1986
		Trade Union Act, 1941 (Revocation of Negotiation Licence) (No.51) Order, S.I. No. 164 of 1986
		Trade Union Act, 1941 (Revocation of Negotiation Licence) (No.52) Order, S.I. No. 165 of 1986

Statutory Authority	Section	Statutory Instrument
Trade Union Act, No. 22 of 1941 (*Cont.*)		**Trade Union Act, 1941 (Revocation of Negotiation Licence) (No.53) Order, S.I. No. 166 of 1986**
		Trade Union Act, 1941 (Revocation of Negotiation Licence) (No.54) Order, S.I. No. 167 of 1986
		Trade Union Act, 1941 (Revocation of Negotiation Licence) (No.55) Order, S.I. No. 168 of 1986
		Trade Union Act, 1941 (Revocation of Negotiation Licence) (No.56) Order, S.I. No. 169 of 1986
		Trade Union Act, 1941 (Revocation of Negotiation Licence) (No.57) Order, S.I. No. 170 of 1986
		Trade Union Act, 1941 (Revocation of Negotiation Licence) (No.58) Order, S.I. No. 171 of 1986
	18	*Trade Union Act, 1941 (Commencement of Part III) Order [Vol. XXXIV p. 241] S.R.& O. No. 84 of 1943*
Trade Union Act, No. 17 of 1947	2	**Trade Union Act, 1947 (Section 2) (No.1) Order, S.I. No. 279 of 1948**
		Trade Union Act, 1949 (Section 2) (No.1) Order, S.I. No. 6 of 1950
		Trade Union Act, 1949 (Section 2) (No.2) Order, S.I. No. 136 of 1950
		Trade Union Act, 1950 (Section 2) (No.2) Order, S.I. No. 220 of 1950
		Trade Union Act, 1951 (Section 2) (No.1) Order, S.I. No. 23 of 1952
		Trade Union Act, 1951 (Section 2) (No.2) Order, S.I. No. 52 of 1952
		Trade Union Act, 1951 (Section 2) (No.3) Order, S.I. No. 117 of 1952
		Trade Union Act, 1952 (Section 3) Order, S.I. No. 199 of 1954
		Trade Union Act, 1952 (Section 3) Order, S.I. No. 87 of 1955
		Trade Union Act, 1952 (Section 3) (No.2) Order, S.I. No. 190 of 1955
		Trade Union Act, 1952 (Section 3) Order, S.I. No. 119 of 1956
		Trade Union Act, 1952 (Section 3) (No.2) Order, S.I. No. 150 of 1956
		Trade Union Act, 1952 (Section 3) (No.3) Order, S.I. No. 213 of 1956
		Trade Union Act, 1952 (Section 3) (No.1) Order, S.I. No. 117 of 1957
		Trade Union Act, 1952 (Section 3) (No.2) Order, S.I. No. 235 of 1957
		Trade Union Act, 1952 (Section 3) (No.1) Order, S.I. No. 175 of 1959
		Trade Union Act, 1952 (Section 3) Order, S.I. No. 11 of 1960
		Trade Union Act, 1952 (Section 3) Order, S.I. No. 4 of 1961

Statutory Authority	Section	Statutory Instrument
Trade Union Act, No. 17 of 1947 *(Cont.)*		**Trade Union Act, 1952 (Section 3) (No.2) Order, S.I. No. 32 of 1961**
Trade Union Act, No. 4 of 1975	13	**Trade Union Amalgamation Regulations, S.I. No. 53 of 1976**
		Trade Union (Fees) Regulations, S.I. No. 86 of 1978
		Trade Union (Fees) Regulations, S.I. No. 292 of 1983
	17(3)	*Trade Union Act, 1975 (Section 17) (Commencement) Order, S.I. No. 177 of 1983*
Tramways (Ireland) Act, No. 152 of 1860	27	**Coras Iompair Eireann (Bantry Pier Railway) Abandonment Order, S.I. No. 48 of 1950**
Tramways (Ireland) Acts, 1860 to 1900,		**Dublin and Blessington Steam Tramway (Committee of Management) Order [Vol. X p. 847] S.R.& O. No. 109 of 1927**
Transport Act, No. 21 of 1944	4	**Transport Act, 1944 Regulations [Vol. XXXIV p. 269] S.R.& O. No. 45 of 1945**
	44(2)	**Coras Iompair Eireann Superannuation Scheme for Regular Wages Staff (Confirmation) Order [Vol. XXXIV p. 259] S.R.& O. No. 242 of 1945**
		Coras Iompair Eireann Amending Superannuation Scheme for Regular Wages Staff (Confirmation) Order, S.I. No. 115 of 1949
	44(3)	**Coras Iompair Eireann Amending Superannuation Scheme for Regular Wages Staff (Confirmation) Order, S.I. No. 115 of 1949**
	45(3)	**Transport Act, 1944 (Section 45) Order [Vol. XXXIV p. 315] S.R.& O. No. 55 of 1945**
	74	**Transport Act, 1944 (Alteration of Maximum Railway Charges) Order [Vol. XXXVIII p. 647] S.R.& O. No. 107 of 1947**
	89	*Transport Act, 1944 (Alteration of Maximum Railway Charges of the Great Northern Railway Company (Ireland)) Order [Vol. XXXVIII p. 667] S.R.& O. No. 284 of 1947*
		Transport Act, 1944 (Alteration of Maximum Charges of the County Donegal Railways Joint Committee and the Strabane and Letterkenny Railway Company) Order [Vol. XXXVIII p. 691] S.R.& O. No. 401 of 1947
		Transport Act, 1944 (Alteration of Maximum Railway Charges of the Londonderry and Lough Swilly Railway Company) Order, S.I. No. 130 of 1948
		Transport Act, 1944 (Alteration of Maximum Railway Charges of the Great Northern Railway Company (Ireland) Order) S.I. No. 110 of 1949
		Transport Act, 1944 (Alteration of Maximum Railway Charges of the Londonderry and Lough Swilly Railway Company) Order, S.I. No. 113 of 1949

Transport Act, No. 21 of 1944
(*Cont.*)

Transport Act, 1944 (Alteration of Maximum Railway Charges of the Dundalk, Newry and Greenore Railway Company) Order, S.I. No. 129 of 1949

Transport Act, 1944 (Alteration of Maximum Railway Charges of the Great Northern Railway Company (Ireland)) Order, S.I. No. 255 of 1951

Transport Act, 1944 (Alteration of Maximum Railway Charges of the Londonderry and Lough Swilly Railway Company) Order, S.I. No. 271 of 1951

Transport Act, 1944 (Alteration of Maximum Railway Charges of the County Donegal Railways Joint Committee and the Strabane and Letterkenny Railway Company) Order, S.I. No. 277 of 1951

Transport Act, 1944 (Alteration of Maximum Railway Charges of the Sligo, Leitrim and Northern Counties Railway Company) Order, S.I. No. 287 of 1951

Transport Act, 1944 (Alteration of Maximum Railway Charges of the Great Northern Railway Company (Ireland)) Order, 1951 (Amendment) Order, S.I. No. 243 of 1952

Transport Act, 1944 (Alteration of Maximum Railway Charges of the Sligo, Leitrim and Northern Counties Railway Company) Order, S.I. No. 280 of 1952

Transport Act, 1944 (Alteration of Maximum Railway Charges of the Great Northern Railway Company (Ireland)) Order, S.I. No. 105 of 1953

Transport Act, 1944 (Alteration of Maximum Railway Charges of the Sligo, Leitrim and Northern Counties Railway Company) Order, S.I. No. 122 of 1953

Transport Act, 1944 (Alteration of Maximum Railway Charges of the County Donegal Railways Joint Committee and the Strabane and Letterkenny Railway Company) Order, S.I. No. 315 of 1953

Transport Act, 1944 (Alteration of Maximum Railway Charges of the Sligo, Leitrim and Northern Counties Railway Company) Order, S.I. No. 77 of 1956

Transport Act, 1944 (Alteration of Maximum Railway Charges of the County Donegal Railways Joint Committee and the Strabane and Letterkenny Railway Company) Order, S.I. No. 88 of 1956

Transport Act, 1944 (Alteration of Maximum Railway Charges of the County Donegal Railways Joint Committee and the Strabane and Letterkenny Railway Company) Order, S.I. No. 147 of 1958

99   **River Shannon Navigation (Maximum Charges) Order, S.I. No. 161 of 1953**

Transport Act, No. 12 of 1950
(*Cont.*)

Great Southern Railways Company Amending Superannuation Scheme for Regular Wages Staff (Confirmation) Order, S.I. No. 75 of 1980

Coras Iompair Eireann Superannuation Scheme for Regular Wages Staff (Amendment) Scheme (Confirmation) Order, S.I. No. 181 of 1982

Great Southern Railways Company Pension Scheme for Regular Wages Staff (Amendment) Scheme (Confirmation) Order, S.I. No. 182 of 1982

Coras Iompair Eireann Superannuation Scheme, 1951 (Amendment) Scheme, 1982 (Confirmation) Order, S.I. No. 245 of 1982

Coras Iompair Eireann Salaried Officers' and Clerks' (G. S. R.) Superannuation Scheme (Amendment) Scheme, 1982 (Confirmation) Order, S.I. No. 246 of 1982

Coras Iompair Eireann Superannuation Scheme, 1951 (Amendment) Scheme, 1982 (Confirmation) (No.2) Order, S.I. No. 345 of 1982

Coras Iompair Eireann Salaried Officers' and Clerks' (G. S. R.) Superannuation Scheme (Amendment) Scheme, 1982 (Confirmation) (No.2) Order, S.I. No. 346 of 1982

Coras Iompair Eireann Salaried Officers' and Clerks' (G. N. R., C. D. R. and I. R. C. H.) Superannuation Scheme, 1977 (Amendment) Scheme, 1982 (Confirmation) (No.2) Order, S.I. No. 347 of 1982

Coras Iompair Eireann Pension Scheme for Regular Wages Staff (Amendment) Scheme (Confirmation) Order, S.I. No. 132 of 1985

Coras Iompair Eireann Salaried Officers' and Clerks' (G. S. R.) Superannuation Scheme (Amendment) Scheme (Confirmation) Order, S.I. No. 286 of 1985

Coras Iompair Eireann Superannuation Scheme, 1951 (Amendment) Scheme (Confirmation) Order, S.I. No. 287 of 1985

Coras Iompair Eireann Pension Scheme for Regular Wages Staff (Amendment) Scheme (Confirmation) (No.2) Order, S.I. No. 288 of 1985

Great Southern Railways Company Pension Scheme for Regular Wages Staff (Amendment) Scheme (Confirmation) Order, S.I. No. 289 of 1985

Great Northern Railway Company (Ireland) Pension Fund for Wages Staff (Amendment) Scheme (Confirmation) Order, S.I. No. 290 of 1985

Coras Iompair Eireann Pension Scheme for Regular Wages Staff (Amendment) Scheme (Confirmation) (No.3) Order, S.I. No. 319 of 1985

Great Southern Railways Company Pension Scheme for Regular Wages Staff (Amendment) Scheme (Confirmation) (No.2) Order, S.I. No. 320 of 1985

Great Northern Railway Company (Ireland) Pension Fund for Wages Staff (Amendment) Scheme (Confirmation) (No.2) Order, S.I. No. 321 of 1985

Transport Act, No. 12 of 1950
(*Cont.*)

Coras Iompair Eireann Superannuation Scheme, 1951 (Amendment) Scheme (Confirmation) Order, S.I. No. 339 of 1986

44(4) **Coras Iompair Eireann Superannuation Scheme, 1951 (Confirmation) Order, S.I. No. 353 of 1951**

Coras Iompair Eireann Amending Superannuation Scheme for Regular Wages Staff (Confirmation) Order, S.I. No. 34 of 1955

Coras Iompair Eireann Amending Superannuation Scheme for Regular Wages Staff (Confirmation) Order, S.I. No. 226 of 1957

Coras Iompair Eireann Amending Superannuation Scheme for Regular Wages Staff (Confirmation) Order, S.I. No. 56 of 1961

Great Southern Railways Company Amending Superannuation Scheme for Regular Wages Staff (Confirmation) Order, S.I. No. 57 of 1961

Coras Iompair Eireann Superannuation Scheme, 1951 (Amendment) Scheme, 1962 (Confirmation) Order, S.I. No. 221 of 1963

Female Clerks' Provident Fund (Amendment) Scheme (Confirmation) Order, S.I. No. 17 of 1964

Dundalk Foremen's Annuity Fund (Amendment) Scheme (Confirmation) Order, S.I. No. 62 of 1964

Coras Iompair Eireann Amending Superannuation Scheme for Regular Wages Staff (Confirmation) Order, S.I. No. 48 of 1965

Great Southern Railways Company Pension (Amendment) Scheme for Regular Wages Staff (Confirmation) Order, S.I. No. 49 of 1965

Coras Iompair Eireann Amending Superannuation Scheme for Regular Wages Staff (Confirmation) Order, S.I. No. 7 of 1967

Great Southern Railways Company Amending Superannuation Scheme for Regular Wages Staff (Confirmation) Order, S.I. No. 8 of 1967

Coras Iompair Eireann Amending Superannuation Scheme for Regular Wages Staff (Confirmation) Order, S.I. No. 58 of 1969

Great Southern Railways Company Amending Superannuation Scheme for Regular Wages Staff (Confirmation) Order, S.I. No. 59 of 1969

Coras Iompair Eireann Amending Superannuation Scheme for Regular Wages Staff (Confirmation) Order, S.I. No. 77 of 1971

Great Southern Railways Company Amending Superannuation Scheme for Regular Wages Staff (Confirmation) Order, S.I. No. 78 of 1971

Coras Iompair Eireann Superannuation Scheme, 1951 (Amendment) Scheme, 1968 (Confirmation) Order, S.I. No. 80 of 1971

Great Southern Railways Company Amending Superannuation Scheme for Regular Wages Staff (Confirmation) Order, S.I. No. 250 of 1974

Statutory Authority	Section	Statutory Instrument

Transport Act, No. 12 of 1950
(*Cont.*)

Coras Iompair Eireann Amending Superannuation Scheme for Regular Wages Staff (Confirmation) Order, S.I. No. 252 of 1974

Coras Iompair Eireann Superannuation Scheme, 1951 (Amendment) Scheme, 1973 (Confirmation) Order, S.I. No. 254 of 1974

Coras Iompair Eireann Superannuation Scheme, 1951 (Amendment) Scheme, 1976 (Confirmation) Order, S.I. No. 47 of 1977

Coras Iompair Eireann Superannuation Scheme, 1951 (Amendment) Scheme, 1981 (Confirmation) Order, S.I. No. 126 of 1981

44(5) Coras Iompair Eireann Amending Superannuation Scheme for Regular Wages Staff (Confirmation) Order, S.I. No. 34 of 1955

Coras Iompair Eireann Amending Superannuation Scheme for Regular Wages Staff (Confirmation) Order, S.I. No. 226 of 1957

Coras Iompair Eireann Amending Superannuation Scheme for Regular Wages Staff (Confirmation) Order, S.I. No. 56 of 1961

Great Southern Railways Company Amending Superannuation Scheme for Regular Wages Staff (Confirmation) Order, S.I. No. 57 of 1961

Coras Iompair Eireann Superannuation Scheme, 1951 (Amendment) Scheme, 1962 (Confirmation) Order, S.I. No. 221 of 1963

Coras Iompair Eireann Amending Superannuation Scheme for Regular Wages Staff (Confirmation) Order, S.I. No. 48 of 1965

Great Southern Railways Company Pension (Amendment) Scheme for Regular Wages Staff (Confirmation) Order, S.I. No. 49 of 1965

Coras Iompair Eireann Amending Superannuation Scheme for Regular Wages Staff (Confirmation) Order, S.I. No. 7 of 1967

Great Southern Railways Company Amending Superannuation Scheme for Regular Wages Staff (Confirmation) Order, S.I. No. 8 of 1967

Coras Iompair Eireann Amending Superannuation Scheme for Regular Wages Staff (Confirmation) Order, S.I. No. 58 of 1969

Great Southern Railways Company Amending Superannuation Scheme for Regular Wages Staff (Confirmation) Order, S.I. No. 59 of 1969

Coras Iompair Eireann Amending Superannuation Scheme for Regular Wages Staff (Confirmation) Order, S.I. No. 77 of 1971

Great Southern Railways Company Amending Superannuation Scheme for Regular Wages Staff (Confirmation) Order, S.I. No. 78 of 1971

Coras Iompair Eireann Superannuation Scheme, 1951 (Amendment) Scheme, 1968 (Confirmation) Order, S.I. No. 80 of 1971

Statutory Authority	Section	Statutory Instrument

Transport Act, No. 12 of 1950
(*Cont.*)

Great Southern Railways Company Amending Superannuation Scheme for Regular Wages Staff (Confirmation) Order, S.I. No. 250 of 1974

Coras Iompair Eireann Amending Superannuation Scheme for Regular Wages Staff (Confirmation) Order, S.I. No. 252 of 1974

Coras Iompair Eireann Superannuation Scheme, 1951 (Amendment) Scheme, 1973 (Confirmation) Order, S.I. No. 254 of 1974

Coras Iompair Eireann Superannuation Scheme, 1951 (Amendment) Scheme, 1976 (Confirmation) Order, S.I. No. 47 of 1977

Coras Iompair Eireann Superannuation Scheme, 1951 (Amendment) Scheme, 1981 (Confirmation) Order, S.I. No. 126 of 1981

44(6) **Great Northern Railway Company (Ireland) Pension Fund for Wages Staff (Amendment) Scheme (Confirmation) Order, S.I. No. 291 of 1977**

Great Northern Railway Company (Ireland) Pension Fund for Wages Staff (Amendment) Scheme (Confirmation) Order, S.I. No. 76 of 1980

Great Northern Railway Company (Ireland) Pension Fund for Wages Staff (Amendment) Scheme (Confirmation) Order, S.I. No. 183 of 1982

45 *Coras Iompair Eireann Salaried Officers' and Clerks' (G. S. R.) Superannuation Scheme (Amendment) Scheme, 1976 (Confirmation) Order, S.I. No. 46 of 1977*

55 *Coras Iompair Eireann (Woodenbridge-Shillelagh Railway Line) Exemption Order, S.I. No. 128 of 1953*

Coras Iompair Eireann (Schull-Skibbereen Railway Line) Exemption Order, S.I. No. 156 of 1953

Coras Iompair Eireann (Birdhill-Killaloe Railway Line) Exemption Order, S.I. No. 157 of 1953

Coras Iompair Eireann (Tralee-Dingle Railway Line) Exemption Order, S.I. No. 205 of 1953

Coras Iompair Eireann (Fermoy-Mitchelstown Railway Line) Exemption Order, S.I. No. 354 of 1953

Coras Iompair Eireann (Cork-Macroom Railway Line) Exemption Order, S.I. No. 355 of 1953

Coras Iompair Eireann (Goold's Cross-Cashel Railway Line) Exemption Order, S.I. No. 387 of 1953

Coras Iompair Eireann (Kilmessan-Athboy Railway Line) Exemption Order, S.I. No. 6 of 1954

Coras Iompair Eireann (Banteer-Newmarket Railway Line) Exemption Order, S.I. No. 5 of 1955

Coras Iompair Eireann (Crossdoney-Killeshandra Railway Line) Exemption Order, S.I. No. 6 of 1955

Statutory Authority	Section	Statutory Instrument
Transport Act, No. 12 of 1950 *(Cont.)*	56	*Coras Iompair Eireann (Naas-Corbally Canal) Order, S.I. No. 69 of 1953*
		Coras Iompair Eireann (Broadstone Branch of the Royal Canal) O, S.I. No. 241 of 1957
Transport Act, No. 19 of 1958	9	*Coras Iompair Eireann (Dundrum-Limerick Junction) (Grange Level Crossing) Order, S.I. No. 157 of 1962*
		Coras Iompair Eireann (Castlebellingham-Dundalk) (Commons Level Crossing) Order, S.I. No. 161 of 1963
		Coras Iompair Eireann (Limerick Junction-Knocklong) (Emly Level Crossing) Order, S.I. No. 147 of 1964
		Coras Iompair Eireann (Castlebellingham-Dundalk) (Dromiskin Level Crossing) Order, S.I. No. 220 of 1964
		Coras Iompair Eireann (Bennettsbridge-Kilkenny) (Ballyredding Level Crossing) Order, S.I. No. 47 of 1968
		Coras Iompair Eireann (Killarney-Tralee) (Farranfore Level Crossing) Order, S.I. No. 261 of 1971
		Coras Iompair Eireann (Athlone-Roscommon) (Ballymurray Level Crossing) Order, S.I. No. 291 of 1975
		Coras Iompair Eireann (Killonan-Birdhill) (Richill Level Crossing) Order, S.I. No. 89 of 1976
		Coras Iompair Eireann (Mallow-Banteer) (Newbury West Level Crossing) Order, S.I. No. 92 of 1976
		Coras Iompair Eireann (Killarney-Tralee) (Farranfore Level Crossing) (Amendment) Order, S.I. No. 377 of 1980
		Coras Iompair Eireann (Bennetsbridge-Kilkenny) (Ballyredding Level Crossing) (Amendment) Order, S.I. No. 64 of 1981
		Coras Iompair Eireann (Sydney Parade-Booterstown) (Merrion Level Crossing) Order, S.I. No. 62 of 1984
		Coras Iompair Eireann (Bayside-Howth) (Sutton Level Crossing) Order, S.I. No. 80 of 1984
		Coras Iompair Eireann (Howth Junction-Howth) (Kilbarrack Level Crossing Order, S.I. No. 81 of 1984
		Coras Iompair Eireann (Lansdowne Road-Sydney Parade) (Sandymount Avenue Level Crossing) Order, S.I. No. 99 of 1984
		Coras Iompair Eireann (Pearse Station-Lansdowne Road) (Lansdowne Road Level Crossing) Order, S.I. No. 130 of 1984
		Coras Iompair Eireann (Lansdowne Road-Sydney Parade) (Serpentine Avenue Level Crossing) Order, S.I. No. 143 of 1984
		Coras Iompair Eireann (Lansdowne Road-Sydney Parade) (Sydney Parade Avenue Level Crossing) O, S.I. No. 144 of 1984

Statutory Authority	Section	Statutory Instrument
Transport Act, No. 19 of 1958 (*Cont.*)		**Coras Iompair Eireann (Navan-Kingscourt) (Moathill Level Crossing) Order, S.I. No. 61 of 1985**
		Coras Iompair Eireann (Dunleer-Dundalk) (Dromiskin Level Crossing) Order, S.I. No. 62 of 1985
		Coras Iompair Eireann (Limerick Junction-Thurles) (Grange Level Crossing) Order, S.I. No. 349 of 1986
		Coras Iompair Eireann (Limerick Junction-Rathluirc) (Emily Level Crossing) Order, S.I. No. 350 of 1986
	11	*3% Transport Stock 1955–60 (Conversion) Regulations, S.I. No. 119 of 1960*
	14(6)	*Transport Act, 1958 (Section 14 (6)) Order, S.I. No. 249 of 1958*
		Transport Act, 1958 (Section 14 (6)) Order, S.I. No. 135 of 1959
		Transport Act, 1958 (Section 14 (6)) (No.2) Order, S.I. No. 166 of 1959
		Transport Act, 1958 (Section 14 (6)) (No.3) Order, S.I. No. 167 of 1959
		Transport Act, 1958 (Extension of Section 14 to Certain Employees of Coras Iompair Eireann) Order, S.I. No. 37 of 1960
		Transport Act, 1958 (Extension of Section 14 to Certain Employees of Coras Iompair Eireann) (No.2) Order, S.I. No. 123 of 1960
		Transport Act, 1958 (Section 14 (6)) Order, S.I. No. 274 of 1961
		Transport Act, 1958 (Section 14 (6)) Order, S.I. No. 36 of 1963
		Transport Act, 1958 (Section 14 (6)) (No.2) Order, S.I. No. 103 of 1963
		Transport Act, 1958 (Section 14 (6)) (No.3) Order, S.I. No. 125 of 1963
	21	**Sligo, Leitrim and Northern Counties Railway (Abandonment) Order, S.I. No. 181 of 1958**
	27(2)	**Transport Act, 1958 (Markets and Fairs) Order, S.I. No. 173 of 1958**
Transport Act, No. 31 of 1959	2	**Coras Iompair Eireann (Members) Superannuation Scheme, S.I. No. 139 of 1960**
		Coras Iompair Eireann (Members) Superannuation Scheme, 1960 (Amendment) Scheme, S.I. No. 103 of 1964
		Coras Iompair Eireann (Members) Superannuation Scheme, 1960 (Amendment) Scheme, S.I. No. 286 of 1966
Transport Act, No. 17 of 1963	6	**Transport Act, 1963 (Railway Works) Order, S.I. No. 84 of 1966**
		Transport Act, 1963 (Railway Works) Order, S.I. No. 202 of 1967

Statutory Authority	Section	Statutory Instrument
Transport Act, No. 17 of 1963 (*Cont.*)		*Transport Act, 1963 (Railway Works) Order, S.I. No. 252 of 1968*
		Transport Act, 1963 (Railway Works) Order, S.I. No. 162 of 1979
Transport Act, No. 30 of 1964	6(2)	*Transport Act, 1964 (Section 6) Order, S.I. No. 267 of 1969*
Transport (Miscellaneous Provisions) Act, No. 21 of 1955	2(3)	*Carriage of Wheat Order, S.I. No. 84 of 1956*
		Carriage of Wheat (No.2) Order, S.I. No. 234 of 1956
		Carriage of Wheat Order, S.I. No. 160 of 1957
		Carriage of Wheat Order, S.I. No. 180 of 1958
		Carriage of Wheat Order, S.I. No. 149 of 1959
		Carriage of Wheat Order, S.I. No. 172 of 1960
		Carriage of Wheat Order, S.I. No. 162 of 1961
		Carriage of Wheat Order, S.I. No. 140 of 1962
		Carriage of Wheat Order, S.I. No. 154 of 1963
		Carriage of Wheat Order, S.I. No. 201 of 1964
		Carriage of Wheat Order, S.I. No. 164 of 1965
		Carriage of Wheat Order, S.I. No. 184 of 1966
		Carriage of Wheat Order, S.I. No. 187 of 1967
		Carriage of Wheat Order, S.I. No. 174 of 1968
		Carriage of Wheat Order, S.I. No. 163 of 1969
		Carriage of Wheat Order, S.I. No. 188 of 1970
		Carriage of Wheat Order, S.I. No. 222 of 1971
		Carriage of Wheat Order, S.I. No. 204 of 1972
	3	*Carriage of Commodities Order, S.I. No. 132 of 1965*
		Carriage of Commodities Order, 1965 (Revocation) Order, S.I. No. 135 of 1965
Transport (Miscellaneous Provisions) Act, No. 14 of 1971	6	*Transport (Miscellaneous Provisions) Act, 1971 (Transfer Date – Part II) Order, S.I. No. 212 of 1971*
	12	*County Donegal Railways Joint Committee (Dissolution) Order, S.I. No. 16 of 1981*
	22	**Coras Iompair Eireann (Kilcock-Enfield) (Ferns Lock Level Crossing) Order, S.I. No. 290 of 1975**
		Coras Iompair Eireann (Athenry-Galway) (Healy's Level Crossing) Order, S.I. No. 174 of 1977
		Coras Iompair Eireann (Athenry-Galway) (French-port Level Crossing) Order, S.I. No. 175 of 1977
		Coras Iompair Eireann (Sutton-Howth) (Cosh Level Crossing) Order, S.I. No. 24 of 1983
		Coras Iompair Eireann (Howth-Sutton) (Claremont Level Crossing) Order, S.I. No. 116 of 1984
		Coras Iompair Eireann (Dalkey-Bray) (Bray Level Crossing) Order, S.I. No. 169 of 1984
		Coras Iompair Eireann (Athenry-Galway) (Garraun Level Crossing) Order, S.I. No. 47 of 1985

Statutory Authority	Section	Statutory Instrument
Transport (Miscellaneous Provisions) Act, No. 14 of 1971 (*Cont.*)		Coras Iompair Eireann (Athlone-Roscommon) (Wood O'Berries Level Crossing) Order, S.I. No. 222 of 1986
Transport (Tour Operators and Travel Agents) Act, No. 3 of 1982	1	*Transport (Tour Operators and Travel Agents) Act, 1983 (Commencement) Order, S.I. No. 99 of 1983*
	7	Tour Operators (Licensing) Regulations, S.I. No. 100 of 1983
		Travel Agents (Licensing) Regulations, S.I. No. 101 of 1983
		Tour Operators (Licensing) (Amendment) Regulations, S.I. No. 165 of 1985
		Travel Agents (Licensing) (Amendment) Regulations, S.I. No. 166 of 1985
		Tour Operators (Licensing) (Amendment) Regulations, S.I. No. 215 of 1986
		Travel Agents (Licensing) (Amendment) Regulations, S.I. No. 216 of 1986
		Tour Operators (Licensing) (Amendment) (No.2) Regulations, S.I. No. 435 of 1986
	12	Tour Operators (Licensing) Regulations, S.I. No. 100 of 1983
		Travel Agents (Licensing) Regulations, S.I. No. 101 of 1983
		Tour Operators (Licensing) (Amendment) Regulations, S.I. No. 165 of 1985
		Travel Agents (Licensing) (Amendment) Regulations, S.I. No. 166 of 1985
		Tour Operators (Licensing) (Amendment) Regulations, S.I. No. 215 of 1986
		Travel Agents (Licensing) (Amendment) Regulations, S.I. No. 216 of 1986
	14	Tour Operators and Travel Agents (Bonding) Regulations, S.I. No. 102 of 1983
	16	*Traveller's Protection Fund Regulations, S.I. No. 103 of 1983*
		Traveller's Protection Fund Regulations, S.I. No. 139 of 1984
		Traveller's Protection Fund (Amendment) Regulations, S.I. No. 434 of 1986
	18	Transport (Tour Operators and Travel Agents) Act, 1982 (Claims by Customers) Regulations, S.I. No. 104 of 1983
	25	Tour Operators (Licensing) Regulations, S.I. No. 100 of 1983
		Travel Agents (Licensing) Regulations, S.I. No. 101 of 1983
		Tour Operators and Travel Agents (Bonding) Regulations, S.I. No. 102 of 1983
		Traveller's Protection Fund Regulations, S.I. No. 103 of 1983

Statutory Authority	Section	Statutory Instrument
Transport (Tour Operators and Travel Agents) Act, No. 3 of 1982 (*Cont.*)		**Transport (Tour Operators and Travel Agents) Act, 1982 (Claims by Customers) Regulations, S.I. No. 104 of 1983**
		Traveller's Protection Fund Regulations, S.I. No. 139 of 1984
		Tour Operators (Licensing) (Amendment) Regulations, S.I. No. 165 of 1985
		Travel Agents (Licensing) (Amendment) Regulations, S.I. No. 166 of 1985
		Tour Operators (Licensing) (Amendment) Regulations, S.I. No. 215 of 1986
		Travel Agents (Licensing) (Amendment) Regulations, S.I. No. 216 of 1986
		Traveller's Protection Fund (Amendment) Regulations, S.I. No. 434 of 1986
		Tour Operators (Licensing) (Amendment) (No.2) Regulations, S.I. No. 435 of 1986
Treaties of Peace (Austria and Bulgaria) Act, No. 6 of 1920	1	**Treaty of Peace (Austria) (Collection of Debts) Order [Vol. XXI p. 673] S.R.& O. No. 21 of 1927**
Treaty of Peace Act, No. 33 of 1919	1	**Treaty of Peace (Germany) (Collection of Debts) Order [Vol. XXI p. 663] S.R.& O. No. 20 of 1927**
Trustee (Authorised Investments) Act, No. 8 of 1958	2(1)	**Trustee (Authorised Investments) Order, S.I. No. 285 of 1967**
		Trustee (Authorised Investments) Order, S.I. No. 241 of 1969
		Trustee (Authorised Investments) Order, S.I. No. 377 of 1974
		Trustee (Authorised Investments) Order, S.I. No. 41 of 1977
		Trustee (Authorised Investments) (No.2) Order, S.I. No. 344 of 1977
		Trustee (Authorised Investments) Order, S.I. No. 407 of 1979
		Trustee (Authorised Investments) Order, S.I. No. 58 of 1983
		Trustee (Authorised Investments) (No.2) Order, S.I. No. 366 of 1983
		Trustee (Authorised Investments) Order, S.I. No. 224 of 1985
		Trustee (Authorised Investments) Order, S.I. No. 372 of 1986
Trustee Savings Banks Act, No. 11 of 1965	2(c)	*Trustee Savings Banks Regulations, S.I. No. 109 of 1968*
		Trustee Savings Banks (No.2) Regulations, S.I. No. 256 of 1968
Turf Development Act, No. 10 of 1946	3	*Turf Development Act, 1946 (Appointment of Establishment Date) Order [Vol. XXXVIII p. 721] S.R.& O. No. 212 of 1946*

Statutory Authority	Section	Statutory Instrument
Turf Development Act, No. 10 of 1946 *(Cont.)*	4	Turf Development Act, 1946 (Section 31) Regulations [Vol. XXXVIII p. 725] S.R.& O. No. 309 of 1946
		Turf Development Act, 1946 (Section 31) Regulations [Vol. XXXVIII p. 733] S.R.& O. No. 331 of 1946
		Turf Development Act, 1946 (Section 31) Regulations [Vol. XXXVIII p. 739] S.R.& O. No. 332 of 1946
		Turf Development Act, 1946 (Section 31) (No.1) Regulations [Vol. XXXVIII p. 745] S.R.& O. No. 31 of 1947
		Turf Development Act, 1946 (Section 31) (No.2) Regulations [Vol. XXXVIII p. 751] S.R.& O. No. 32 of 1947
		Turf Development Act, 1946 (Section 31) (No.3) Regulations [Vol. XXXVIII p. 757] S.R.& O. No. 33 of 1947
		Turf Development Act, 1946 (Section 31) (No.4) Regulations [Vol. XXXVIII p. 763] S.R.& O. No. 152 of 1947
		Turf Development Act, 1946 (Section 31) (No.5) Regulations [Vol. XXXVIII p. 769] S.R.& O. No. 181 of 1947
		Turf Development Act, 1946 (Section 31) (No.6) Regulations [Vol. XXXVIII p. 775] S.R.& O. No. 291 of 1947
		Turf Development Act, 1946 (Section 31) Regulations, S.I. No. 13 of 1948
	31	Turf Development Act, 1946 (Section 31) Regulations [Vol. XXXVIII p. 725] S.R.& O. No. 309 of 1946
		Turf Development Act, 1946 (Section 31) Regulations [Vol. XXXVIII p. 733] S.R.& O. No. 331 of 1946
		Turf Development Act, 1946 (Section 31) Regulations [Vol. XXXVIII p. 739] S.R.& O. No. 332 of 1946
		Turf Development Act, 1946 (Section 31) (No.1) Regulations [Vol. XXXVIII p. 745] S.R.& O. No. 31 of 1947
		Turf Development Act, 1946 (Section 31) (No.2) Regulations [Vol. XXXVIII p. 751] S.R.& O. No. 32 of 1947
		Turf Development Act, 1946 (Section 31) (No.3) Regulations [Vol. XXXVIII p. 757] S.R.& O. No. 33 of 1947
		Turf Development Act, 1946 (Section 31) (No.4) Regulations [Vol. XXXVIII p. 763] S.R.& O. No. 152 of 1947
		Turf Development Act, 1946 (Section 31) (No.5) Regulations [Vol. XXXVIII p. 769] S.R.& O. No. 181 of 1947
		Turf Development Act, 1946 (Section 31) (No.6) Regulations [Vol. XXXVIII p. 775] S.R.& O. No. 291 of 1947

Statutory Authority	Section	Statutory Instrument
Turf Development Act, No. 10 of 1946 (*Cont.*)		**Turf Development Act, 1946 (Section 31) Regulations, S.I. No. 13 of 1948**
	43	**Turf Development Act, 1946 (Transport Works) (No.1) Order, S.I. No. 202 of 1950**
		Turf Development Act, 1946 (Transport Works) (No.2) Order, S.I. No. 203 of 1950
		Turf Development Act, 1946 (Transport Works) Order, S.I. No. 373 of 1951
		Turf Development Act, 1946 (Transport Works) Order, S.I. No. 112 of 1952
		Turf Development Act, 1946 (Transport Works) (No.2) Order, S.I. No. 327 of 1952
		Turf Development Act, 1946 (Transport Works) (No.1) Order, S.I. No. 299 of 1953
		Turf Development Act, 1946 (Transport Works) (No.1) Order, S.I. No. 92 of 1954
		Turf Development Act, 1946 (Transport Works) (No.1) Order, S.I. No. 37 of 1956
		Turf Development Act, 1946 (Transport Works) (No.2) Order, S.I. No. 123 of 1956
		Turf Development Act, 1946 (Transport Works) Order, S.I. No. 115 of 1958
		Turf Development Act, 1946 (Transport Works) (No.2) Order, S.I. No. 214 of 1958
		Turf Development Act, 1946 (Transport Works) Order, S.I. No. 194 of 1960
		Turf Development Act, 1946 (Transport Works) Order, S.I. No. 224 of 1961
		Turf Development Act, 1946 (Transport Works) Order, S.I. No. 186 of 1964
		Turf Development Act, 1946 (Transport Works) (No.2) Order, S.I. No. 187 of 1964
		Turf Development Act, 1946 (Transport Works) (No.3) Order, S.I. No. 188 of 1964
		Turf Development Act, 1946 (Transport Works) Order, S.I. No. 93 of 1966
		Turf Development Act, 1946 (Transport Works) (No.1) Order, S.I. No. 169 of 1967
		Turf Development Act, 1946 (Transport Works) (No.2) Order, S.I. No. 249 of 1967
	57	*Bord na Mona (Payment of Interest) Order, S.I. No. 249 of 1952*
		Bord na Mona (Payment of Interest) Order, S.I. No. 250 of 1955
	71(1)	**Turf (Suspension of Section 9 (1) of the Road Transport Act, 1933) Order [Vol. XXXVIII p. 781] S.R.& O. No. 267 of 1946**
Turf Development Act, No. 19 of 1953	6	**Turf Development Act, 1953 (Regular Works Employees) Superannuation Scheme, S.I. No. 10 of 1963**

Statutory Authority	Section	Statutory Instrument
Turf Development Act, No. 19 of 1953 *(Cont.)*		**Turf Development Act, 1953 (Regular Works Employees) Superannuation (Amendment) Scheme, S.I. No. 116 of 1967**
	7	**Turf Development Act, 1953 (Regular Works Employees) Superannuation Scheme, S.I. No. 10 of 1963**
Turf Development Act, No. 28 of 1968	2	*Bord na Mona (Waiver of Interest and Deferment of Repayment of Advances) Order, S.I. No. 283 of 1968*
		Bord na Mona (Waiver of Interest and Deferment of Repayment of Advances) Order, S.I. No. 83 of 1969
		Bord na Mona (Waiver of Interest and Deferment of Repayment of Advances) (No.2) Order, S.I. No. 208 of 1969
		Bord na Mona (Waiver of Interest) Order, S.I. No. 53 of 1970
		Bord na Mona (Waiver of Interest) (No.2) Order, S.I. No. 242 of 1970
	3	*Bord na Mona (Waiver of Interest and Deferment of Repayment of Advances) Order, S.I. No. 283 of 1968*
		Bord na Mona (Waiver of Interest and Deferment of Repayment of Advances) Order, S.I. No. 83 of 1969
		Bord na Mona (Waiver of Interest and Deferment of Repayment of Advances) (No.2) Order, S.I. No. 208 of 1969
		Bord na Mona (Deferment of Repayment of Advances) Order, S.I. No. 266 of 1969
Udaras na Gaeltachta (Acht um) No. 5 of 1979	2(1)	*Udaras na Gaeltachta (An La Ceaptha) (An tOrdu um) S.I. No. 425 of 1979*
	3	*Udaras na Gaeltachta, 1979 (Tosach Feidhme Chuid IV) (An tOrdu fan Acht um) S.I. No. 354 of 1979*
		Udaras na Gaeltachta, 1979 (Tosach Feidhme Codanna I go III) (An tOrdu fan Acht um) S.I. No. 424 of 1979
	33	**Toghchain Udaras na Gaeltachta (Na Rialachain um) S.I. No. 355 of 1979**
Undeveloped Areas Act, No. 1 of 1952	3(1)	*Undeveloped Areas Act, 1952 (Section 3) Order, S.I. No. 284 of 1953*
		Undeveloped Areas Act, 1952 (Section 3) Order, S.I. No. 229 of 1958
		Undeveloped Areas Act, 1952 (Section 3) Order, S.I. No. 70 of 1959

Statutory Authority	Section	Statutory Instrument
Undeveloped Areas Act, No. 1 of 1952 (*Cont.*)		*Undeveloped Areas Act, 1952 (Extension of Area of Application) Order, S.I. No. 158 of 1959*
		Undeveloped Areas Act, 1952 (Extension of Area of Application) Order, S.I. No. 21 of 1961
		Undeveloped Areas Act, 1952 (Extension of Area of Application) (No.3) Order, S.I. No. 209 of 1961
		Undeveloped Areas Act, 1952 (Extension of Area of Application) (No.2) Order, S.I. No. 235 of 1961
		Undeveloped Areas Act, 1952 (Extension of Area of Application) (No.4) Order, S.I. No. 237 of 1961
		Undeveloped Areas Act, 1952 (Extension of Area of Application) (No.5) Order, S.I. No. 238 of 1961
		Undeveloped Areas Act, 1952 (Section 3) Order, S.I. No. 56 of 1963
		Undeveloped Areas Act, 1952 (Area of Application) (Extension of) Order, S.I. No. 184 of 1967
Unemployment Assistance Act, No. 46 of 1933	3	*Unemployment Assistance (Qualification Certificate) (Date of Operation) Order [Vol. XXI p. 767] S.R.& O. No. 32 of 1934*
		Unemployment Assistance (Applications for Unemployment Assistance) (Date of Operation) Order [Vol. XXI p. 685] S.R.& O. No. 110 of 1934
	4(3)	*Unemployment Assistance (Employment Period) Order [Vol. XXI p. 839] S.R.& O. No. 84 of 1935*
		Unemployment Assistance (Second Employment Period) Order, 1935 [Vol. XXI p. 845] S.R.& O. No. 252 of 1935
		Unemployment Assistance (Employment Period) Order [Vol. XXI p. 851] S.R.& O. No. 66 of 1936
		Unemployment Assistance (Second Employment Period) Order [Vol. XXI p. 857] S.R.& O. No. 157 of 1936
		Unemployment Assistance (Employment Period) Order [Vol. XXI p. 863] S.R.& O. No. 30 of 1937
		Unemployment Assistance (Second Employment Period) Order, 1937 [Vol. XXI p. 869] S.R.& O. No. 102 of 1937
		Unemployment Assistance (Employment Period) Order [Vol. XXI p. 875] S.R.& O. No. 38 of 1938
		Unemployment Assistance (Second Employment Period) Order [Vol. XXI p. 881] S.R.& O. No. 117 of 1938
		Unemployment Assistance (Employment Period) Order [Vol. XXXIV p. 325] S.R.& O. No. 40 of 1939
		Unemployment Assistance (Second Employment Period) Order [Vol. XXXIV p. 367] S.R.& O. No. 130 of 1939

Statutory Authority	Section	Statutory Instrument
Unemployment Assistance Act, No. 46 of 1933 (*Cont.*)		*Unemployment Assistance (Third Employment Period) Order [Vol. XXXIV p. 417] S.R.& O. No. 306 of 1939*
		Unemployment Assistance (Employment Period) Order [Vol. XXXIV p. 331] S.R.& O. No. 86 of 1940
		Unemployment Assistance (Second Employment Period) Order [Vol. XXXIV p. 373] S.R.& O. No. 87 of 1940
		Unemployment Assistance (Third Employment Period) Order [Vol. XXXIV p. 423] S.R.& O. No. 172 of 1940
		Unemployment Assistance (Employment Period) Order [Vol. XXXIV p. 337] S.R.& O. No. 64 of 1941
		Unemployment Assistance (Employment Period) Order [Vol. XXXIV p. 343] S.R.& O. No. 80 of 1942
		Unemployment Assistance (Second Employment Period) Order [Vol. XXXIV p. 379] S.R.& O. No. 232 of 1942
		Unemployment Assistance (Employment Period) Order [Vol. XXXIV p. 349] S.R.& O. No. 72 of 1943
		Unemployment Assistance (Second Employment Period) Order [Vol. XXXIV p. 393] S.R.& O. No. 213 of 1943
		Unemployment Assistance (Employment Period) Order [Vol. XXXIV p. 355] S.R.& O. No. 70 of 1944
		Unemployment Assistance (Second Employment Period) Order [Vol. XXXIV p. 401] S.R.& O. No. 176 of 1944
		Unemployment Assistance (Employment Period) Order [Vol. XXXIV p. 361] S.R.& O. No. 35 of 1945
		Unemployment Assistance (Second Employment Period) Order [Vol. XXXIV p. 409] S.R.& O. No. 126 of 1945
		Unemployment Assistance (Employment Period) Order [Vol. XXXVIII p. 785] S.R.& O. No. 50 of 1946
		Unemployment Assistance (Second Employment Period) Order [Vol. XXXVIII p. 789] S.R.& O. No. 169 of 1946
		Unemployment Assistance (Employment Period) Order [Vol. XXXVIII p. 795] S.R.& O. No. 67 of 1947
		Unemployment Assistance (Second Employment Period) Order [Vol. XXXVIII p. 799] S.R.& O. No. 186 of 1947
		Unemployment Assistance (Employment Period) Order, S.I. No. 85 of 1948
		Unemployment Assistance (Second Employment Period) Order, S.I. No. 193 of 1948

Statutory Authority	Section	Statutory Instrument
Unemployment Assistance Act, No. 46 of 1933 (*Cont.*)		*Unemployment Assistance (Employment Period) Order, S.I. No. 51 of 1949*
		Unemployment Assistance (Second Employment Period) Order, S.I. No. 179 of 1949
		Unemployment Assistance (Employment Period) Order, S.I. No. 53 of 1950
		Unemployment Assistance (Second Employment Period) Order, S.I. No. 152 of 1950
		Unemployment Assistance (Employment Period) Order, S.I. No. 53 of 1951
		Unemployment Assistance (Second Employment Period) Order, S.I. No. 157 of 1951
		Unemployment Assistance (Employment Period) Order, S.I. No. 46 of 1952
		Unemployment Assistance (Second Employment Period) Order, S.I. No. 144 of 1952
		Unemployment Assistance (Employment Period) Order, S.I. No. 94 of 1953
		Unemployment Assistance (Second Employment Period) Order, S.I. No. 191 of 1953
		Unemployment Assistance (Employment Period) Order, S.I. No. 45 of 1954
		Unemployment Assistance (Second Employment Period) Order, S.I. No. 122 of 1954
		Unemployment Assistance (Employment Period) Order, S.I. No. 32 of 1955
		Unemployment Assistance (Second Employment Period) Order, S.I. No. 109 of 1955
		Unemployment Assistance (Employment Period) Order, S.I. No. 29 of 1956
		Unemployment Assistance (Second Employment Period) Order, S.I. No. 135 of 1956
		Unemployment Assistance (Employment Period) Order, S.I. No. 45 of 1957
		Unemployment Assistance (Second Employment Period) Order, S.I. No. 121 of 1957
		Unemployment Assistance (Employment Period) Order, S.I. No. 63 of 1958
		Unemployment Assistance (Second Employment Period) Order, S.I. No. 125 of 1958
		Unemployment Assistance (Employment Period) Order, S.I. No. 38 of 1959
		Unemployment Assistance (Second Employment Period) Order, S.I. No. 93 of 1959
		Unemployment Assistance (Employment Period) Order, S.I. No. 42 of 1960
		Unemployment Assistance (Second Employment Period) Order, S.I. No. 110 of 1960
		Unemployment Assistance (Employment Period) Order, S.I. No. 45 of 1961
		Unemployment Assistance (Second Employment Period) Order, S.I. No. 107 of 1961

Statutory Authority	Section	Statutory Instrument
Unemployment Assistance Act, No. 46 of 1933 (*Cont.*)		*Unemployment Assistance (Employment Period) Order, S.I. No. 38 of 1962*
		Unemployment Assistance (Second Employment Period) Order, S.I. No. 83 of 1962
		Unemployment Assistance (Employment Period) Order, S.I. No. 39 of 1963
		Unemployment Assistance (Second Unemployment Period) Order, S.I. No. 91 of 1963
		Unemployment Assistance (Employment Period) Order, S.I. No. 53 of 1964
		Unemployment Assistance (Second Employment Period) Order, S.I. No. 114 of 1964
		Unemployment Assistance (Employment Period) Order, S.I. No. 43 of 1965
		Unemployment Assistance (Second Employment Period) Order, S.I. No. 114 of 1965
		Unemployment Assistance (Employment Period) Order, S.I. No. 49 of 1966
		Unemployment Assistance (Second Employment Period) Order, S.I. No. 118 of 1966
		Unemployment Assistance (Employment Period) Order, S.I. No. 57 of 1967
		Unemployment Assistance (Employment Period) (Revocation) Order, S.I. No. 72 of 1967
		Unemployment Assistance (Employment Period) Order, S.I. No. 128 of 1971
		Unemployment Assistance (Employment Period) (No.2) Order, S.I. No. 142 of 1971
		Unemployment Assistance (Employment Period) (Amendment) Order, S.I. No. 154 of 1971
	7	**Unemployment Assistance (Unemployment Appeals Committee Regulations) Order [Vol. XXI p. 809] S.R.& O. No. 35 of 1934**
	7(1)	**Unemployment Assistance (Qualification Certificate Regulations) Order [Vol. XXI p. 771] S.R.& O. No. 33 of 1934**
		Unemployment Assistance (Calculation of Means Regulations) Order [Vol. XXI p. 761] S.R.& O. No. 34 of 1934
		Unemployment Assistance (Birth, Marriage or Death Certificates Regulations) Order [Vol. XXI p. 751] S.R.& O. No. 36 of 1934
		Unemployment Assistance (References and Reports to the Unemployment Appeals Committee Regulations) Order [Vol. XXI p. 817] S.R.& O. No. 37 of 1934
		Unemployment Assistance (Umpire Regulations) Order [Vol. XXI p. 833] S.R.& O. No. 123 of 1934
		Unemployment Assistance (Reference and Reports to Courts of Referees Regulations) Order [Vol. XXI p. 825] S.R.& O. No. 124 of 1934

Statutory Authority	Section	Statutory Instrument
Unemployment Assistance Act, No. 46 of 1933 (*Cont.*)		**Unemployment Assistance (Application for Assistance Regulations) Order [Vol. XXI p. 689] S.R.& O. No. 126 of 1934**
		Unemployment Assistance (Employment Period) Order [Vol. XXI p. 839] S.R.& O. No. 84 of 1935
		Unemployment Assistance (Application for Assistance Regulations) Order [Vol. XXI p. 711] S.R.& O. No. 85 of 1935
		Unemployment Assistance (Second Employment Period) Order, 1935 [Vol. XXI p. 845] S.R.& O. No. 252 of 1935
		Unemployment Assistance (Application for Assistance Regulations) (No.2) Order [Vol. XXI p. 719] S.R.& O. No. 253 of 1935
		Unemployment Assistance (Qualification Certificate Regulations) Amendment Order [Vol. XXI p. 791] S.R.& O. No. 574 of 1935
		Unemployment Assistance (Application for Assistance Regulations) (Amendment) Order [Vol. XXI p. 727] S.R.& O. No. 575 of 1935
		Unemployment Assistance (Employment Period) Order [Vol. XXI p. 851] S.R.& O. No. 66 of 1936
		Unemployment Assistance (Application for Assistance Regulations) Order [Vol. XXI p. 743] S.R.& O. No. 67 of 1936
		Unemployment Assistance (Second Employment Period) Order [Vol. XXI p. 857] S.R.& O. No. 157 of 1936
		Unemployment Assistance (Employment Period) Order [Vol. XXI p. 863] S.R.& O. No. 30 of 1937
		Unemployment Assistance (Second Employment Period) Order, 1937 [Vol. XXI p. 869] S.R.& O. No. 102 of 1937
		Unemployment Assistance (Employment Period) Order [Vol. XXI p. 875] S.R.& O. No. 38 of 1938
		Unemployment Assistance (Second Employment Period) Order [Vol. XXI p. 881] S.R.& O. No. 117 of 1938
		Unemployment Assistance (Qualification Certificate Regulations) Amendment Order [Vol. XXI p. 799] S.R.& O. No. 194 of 1938
		Unemployment Assistance (Qualification Certificate Regulations) (Amendment) (No.2) Order [Vol. XXI p. 805] S.R.& O. No. 229 of 1938
		Unemployment Assistance (Employment Period) Order [Vol. XXXIV p. 325] S.R.& O. No. 40 of 1939
		Unemployment Assistance (Second Employment Period) Order [Vol. XXXIV p. 367] S.R.& O. No. 130 of 1939

Unemployment Assistance Act,
No. 46 of 1933 (*Cont.*)

Unemployment Assistance (Third Employment Period) Order [Vol. XXXIV p. 417] S.R.& O. No. 306 of 1939

Unemployment Assistance (Employment Period) Order [Vol. XXXIV p. 331] S.R.& O. No. 86 of 1940

Unemployment Assistance (Second Employment Period) Order [Vol. XXXIV p. 373] S.R.& O. No. 87 of 1940

Unemployment Assistance (Third Employment Period) Order [Vol. XXXIV p. 423] S.R.& O. No. 172 of 1940

Unemployment Assistance (Employment Period) Order [Vol. XXXIV p. 337] S.R.& O. No. 64 of 1941

Unemployment Assistance (Employment Period) Order [Vol. XXXIV p. 343] S.R.& O. No. 80 of 1942

Unemployment Assistance (Second Employment Period) Order [Vol. XXXIV p. 379] S.R.& O. No. 232 of 1942

Unemployment Assistance (Employment Period) Order [Vol. XXXIV p. 349] S.R.& O. No. 72 of 1943

Unemployment Assistance (Second Employment Period) Order [Vol. XXXIV p. 393] S.R.& O. No. 213 of 1943

Unemployment Assistance (Employment Period) Order [Vol. XXXIV p. 355] S.R.& O. No. 70 of 1944

Unemployment Assistance (Second Employment Period) Order [Vol. XXXIV p. 401] S.R.& O. No. 176 of 1944

Unemployment Assistance (Employment Period) Order [Vol. XXXIV p. 361] S.R.& O. No. 35 of 1945

Unemployment Assistance (Second Employment Period) Order [Vol. XXXIV p. 409] S.R.& O. No. 126 of 1945

Unemployment Assistance (Employment Period) Order [Vol. XXXVIII p. 785] S.R.& O. No. 50 of 1946

Unemployment Assistance (Second Employment Period) Order [Vol. XXXVIII p. 789] S.R.& O. No. 169 of 1946

Unemployment Assistance (Employment Period) Order [Vol. XXXVIII p. 795] S.R.& O. No. 67 of 1947

Unemployment Assistance (Second Employment Period) Order [Vol. XXXVIII p. 799] S.R.& O. No. 186 of 1947

Unemployment Assistance (Employment Period) Order, S.I. No. 85 of 1948

Unemployment Assistance (Second Employment Period) Order, S.I. No. 193 of 1948

Statutory Authority	Section	Statutory Instrument
Unemployment Assistance Act, No. 46 of 1933 (*Cont.*)		**Unemployment Assistance (Application for Assistance Regulations) (Amendment) Order, S.I. No. 411 of 1948**
		Unemployment Assistance (Employment Period) Order, S.I. No. 51 of 1949
		Unemployment Assistance (Second Employment Period) Order, S.I. No. 179 of 1949
		Unemployment Assistance (Employment Period) Order, S.I. No. 53 of 1950
		Unemployment Assistance (Second Employment Period) Order, S.I. No. 152 of 1950
		Unemployment Assistance (Employment Period) Order, S.I. No. 53 of 1951
		Unemployment Assistance (Second Employment Period) Order, S.I. No. 157 of 1951
		Unemployment Assistance (Employment Period) Order, S.I. No. 46 of 1952
		Unemployment Assistance (Second Employment Period) Order, S.I. No. 144 of 1952
		Unemployment Assistance (Qualification Certificate Regulations) (Amendment) Order, S.I. No. 167 of 1952
		Unemployment Assistance (Application for Assistance Regulations) (Amendment) Order, S.I. No. 169 of 1952
		Unemployment Assistance (Application for Assistance Regulations) (Amendment) (No.2) Order, S.I. No. 387 of 1952
		Unemployment Assistance (Qualification Certificate Regulations) (Amendment) Order, S.I. No. 3 of 1953
		Unemployment Assistance (Employment Period) Order, S.I. No. 94 of 1953
		Unemployment Assistance (Second Employment Period) Order, S.I. No. 191 of 1953
		Unemployment Assistance (Employment Period) Order, S.I. No. 45 of 1954
		Unemployment Assistance (Second Employment Period) Order, S.I. No. 122 of 1954
		Unemployment Assistance (Employment Period) Order, S.I. No. 32 of 1955
		Unemployment Assistance (Second Employment Period) Order, S.I. No. 109 of 1955
		Unemployment Assistance (Employment Period) Order, S.I. No. 29 of 1956
		Unemployment Assistance (Second Employment Period) Order, S.I. No. 135 of 1956
		Unemployment Assistance (Employment Period) Order, S.I. No. 45 of 1957
		Unemployment Assistance (Second Employment Period) Order, S.I. No. 121 of 1957
		Unemployment Assistance (Employment Period) Order, S.I. No. 63 of 1958

Statutory Authority	Section	Statutory Instrument
Unemployment Assistance Act, No. 46 of 1933 (*Cont.*)		*Unemployment Assistance (Second Employment Period) Order, S.I. No. 125 of 1958*
		Unemployment Assistance (Employment Period) Order, S.I. No. 38 of 1959
		Unemployment Assistance (Second Employment Period) Order, S.I. No. 93 of 1959
		Unemployment Assistance (Employment Period) Order, S.I. No. 42 of 1960
		Unemployment Assistance (Second Employment Period) Order, S.I. No. 110 of 1960
		Unemployment Assistance (Application for Assistance Regulations) (Amendment) Order, S.I. No. 155 of 1960
		Unemployment Assistance (Employment Period) Order, S.I. No. 45 of 1961
		Unemployment Assistance (Second Employment Period) Order, S.I. No. 107 of 1961
		Unemployment Assistance (Qualification Certificate Regulations) (Amendment) Order, S.I. No. 161 of 1961
		Unemployment Assistance (Employment Period) Order, S.I. No. 38 of 1962
		Unemployment Assistance (Second Employment Period) Order, S.I. No. 83 of 1962
		Unemployment Assistance (Qualification Certificate Regulations) (Amendment) Order, S.I. No. 137 of 1962
		Unemployment Assistance (Employment Period) Order, S.I. No. 39 of 1963
		Unemployment Assistance (Second Unemployment Period) Order, S.I. No. 91 of 1963
		Unemployment Assistance (Employment Period) Order, S.I. No. 53 of 1964
		Unemployment Assistance (Second Employment Period) Order, S.I. No. 114 of 1964
		Unemployment Assistance (Employment Period) Order, S.I. No. 43 of 1965
		Unemployment Assistance (Second Employment Period) Order, S.I. No. 114 of 1965
		Unemployment Assistance (Employment Period) Order, S.I. No. 49 of 1966
		Unemployment Assistance (Second Employment Period) Order, S.I. No. 118 of 1966
		Unemployment Assistance (Employment Period) Order, S.I. No. 57 of 1967
		Unemployment Assistance (Employment Period) (Revocation) Order, S.I. No. 72 of 1967
		Unemployment Assistance (Employment Period) Order, S.I. No. 128 of 1971
		Unemployment Assistance (Employment Period) (No.2) Order, S.I. No. 142 of 1971
		Unemployment Assistance (Employment Period) (Amendment) Order, S.I. No. 154 of 1971

Statutory Authority	Section	Statutory Instrument
Unemployment Assistance Acts, 1933 to 1940,		**Unemployment Assistance (Night Work) Regulations [Vol. XXXIV p. 439] S.R.& O. No. 231 of 1940**
Unemployment Assistance (Amendment) Act, No. 38 of 1935	4	**Unemployment Assistance (Dependants) (Specified Day) Order, S.I. No. 388 of 1952**
	4(3)	*Unemployment Assistance (Amendment) Act, 1935 (Date of Operation of Section 4) Order [Vol. XXI p. 887] S.R.& O. No. 578 of 1935*
	8(6)	*Unemployment Assistance (Amendment) Act, 1935 (Date of Operation of Section 8) Order [Vol. XXI p. 891] S.R.& O. No. 579 of 1935*
	11(2)	*Unemployment Assistance (Amendment) Act, 1935 (Date of Operation of Section 11) Order [Vol. XXI p. 895] S.R.& O. No. 580 of 1935*
	17	**Unemployment Assistance (Deceased or Insane Persons) (Appointment of Representatives Regulations) Order (1935) [Vol. p. XX] S.R.& O. No. 33 of 1936**
	19(1)	**Unemployment Assistance (Deceased or Insane Persons) (Appointment of Representatives Regulations) Order (1935) [Vol. p. XX] S.R.& O. No. 33 of 1936**
Unemployment Assistance (Amendment) Act, No. 2 of 1938	2	*Unemployment Assistance (Date of Publication of Census) Order [Vol. XXI p. 915] S.R.& O. No. 214 of 1938*
	2(1)	*Unemployment Assistance (Date of Publication of Census) Order, S.I. No. 45 of 1951*
		Unemployment Assistance (Date of Publication of Census) Order, S.I. No. 76 of 1953
		Unemployment Assistance (Date of Publication of Census) Order, S.I. No. 257 of 1957
		Unemployment Assistance (Date of Publication of Census) Order, S.I. No. 104 of 1963
		Unemployment Assistance (Date of Publication of Census) Order, S.I. No. 183 of 1967
		Unemployment Assistance (Date of Publication of Census) Order, S.I. No. 270 of 1980
	3(1)	**Unemployment Assistance (Declaration of Urban Area) Order, S.I. No. 332 of 1975**
	4(4)	*Unemployment Assistance (Amendment) Act, 1938 (Section 4) (Commencement) Order [Vol. XXI p. 907] S.R.& O. No. 24 of 1938*
	5(2)	*Unemployment Assistance (Amendment) Act, 1938 (Section 5) (Appointed Day) Order [Vol. XXI p. 911] S.R.& O. No. 25 of 1938*
Unemployment Insurance Act, No. 30 of 1920		*Unemployment Insurance (Collection of Contributions) (Amendment) Regulations [Vol. XXI p. 925] S.R.& O. No. 356 of 1936*
	1	*Unemployment Insurance (Inclusion) Order, S.I. No. 209 of 1950*

Statutory Authority	Section	Statutory Instrument
Unemployment Insurance Act, No. 30 of 1920 (*Cont.*)	4	*Unemployment Insurance (Inclusion) Order, (1944) [Vol. XXXIV p. 443] S.R.& O. No. 81 of 1945*
	18	*Unemployment Insurance (Insurance Industry Special Scheme) Amendment Order, (1930) [Vol. XXI p. 945] S.R.& O. No. 2 of 1931*
		Unemployment Insurance (Insurance Industry Special Scheme) Amendment Order, (1931) [Vol. XXI p. 949] S.R.& O. No. 22 of 1932
	28	*Unemployment Insurance (Repayment and Return of Contributions) (Amendment) Regulations [Vol. XXI p. 965] S.R.& O. No. 15 of 1924*
	33	*Unemployment Insurance (Stamps) Regulations [Vol. XXI p. 971] S.R.& O. No. 45 of 1931*
	35	*Unemployment Insurance (Repayment and Return of Contributions) (Amendment) Regulations [Vol. XXI p. 965] S.R.& O. No. 15 of 1924*
		Unemployment Insurance (Night Work) Regulations, (1926) [Vol. XII p. 959] S.R.& O. No. 34 of 1927
		Unemployment Insurance (Deceased or Insane Persons) (Appointment of Representatives) Regulations, (1926) [Vol. XXI p. 929] S.R.& O. No. 35 of 1927
		Unemployment Insurance (Insurance Year) (Amendment) Regulations [Vol. XXI p. 955] S.R.& O. No. 98 of 1927
	Sch. I Part II par. (j)	*Unemployment Insurance (Subsidiary Employments) Special Order, (1944) [Vol. XXXIV p. 449] S.R.& O. No. 80 of 1945*
		Unemployment Insurance (Subsidiary Employments) Special Order, S.I. No. 359 of 1949
Unemployment Insurance Act, No. 17 of 1923	6(4)	*Unemployment Insurance (Computation of Periods) Regulations [Vol. XXI p. 1007] S.R.& O. No. 13 of 1923*
Unemployment Insurance Act, No. 26 of 1924	8(2)	*Unemployment Insurance (Insurance Industry Special Scheme) Amendment Order (No.2), (1924) [Vol. XXI p. 941] S.R.& O. No. 23 of 1925*
Unemployment Insurance Act, No. 21 of 1926		*Unemployment Insurance (Compensation for Refund) Regulations, (1926) [Vol. XXI p. 1009] S.R.& O. No. 29 of 1927*
	5	*Unemployment Insurance (Insurance Year) (Amendment) Regulations [Vol. XXI p. 955] S.R.& O. No. 98 of 1927*
Unemployment Insurance Act, No. 33 of 1930	5(2)	*Unemployment Insurance Act, 1930 (Date of Operation) Order, (1930) [Vol. XXI p. 1021] S.R.& O. No. 5 of 1931*
Unemployment Insurance Act, No. 37 of 1946	3(2)	*Unemployment Insurance Act, 1946 (Commencement of Part II) Order [Vol. XXXVIII p. 805] S.R.& O. No. 100 of 1947*

Statutory Authority	Section	Statutory Instrument
Unemployment Insurance Act, No. 37 of 1946 (*Cont.*)	12	*Unemployment Insurance Act, 1946 (Amendment of Part II) Regulations, S.I. No. 227 of 1948*
	13	*Unemployment Insurance (Special Benefit) Regulations [Vol. XXXVIII p. 809] S.R.& O. No. 185 of 1947*
Unemployment Insurance Acts, 1920 to 1924,		*Unemployment Insurance (Mercantile Marine) (Collection of Contributions) (Amendment) Regulations [Vol. XXI p. 1003] S.R.& O. No. 39 of 1926*
Unemployment Insurance Acts, 1920 to 1926,		*Unemployment Insurance (Benefit) (Amendment) Regulations, (1928) [Vol. XXI p. 919] S.R.& O. No. 20 of 1929*
Unemployment Insurance Acts, 1920 to 1952,		*Unemployment Insurance (Collection of Contributions) (Amendment) Regulations, S.I. No. 290 of 1952*
Unemployment (Relief Works) Act, No. 34 of 1940	1	**Unemployment (Relief Works) (Acquisition of Lands) Regulations [Vol. XXXIV p. 461] S.R.& O. No. 338 of 1940**
	12(1)	**Unemployment (Relief Works) (Acquisition of Lands) Regulations [Vol. XXXIV p. 461] S.R.& O. No. 338 of 1940**
	21	**Unemployment (Relief Works) (Acquisition of Lands) Regulations [Vol. XXXIV p. 461] S.R.& O. No. 338 of 1940**
Unfair Dismissals Act, No. 10 of 1977	17	**Unfair Dismissals (Claims and Appeals) Regulations, S.I. No. 286 of 1977**
		Unfair Dismissals (Calculation of Weekly Remuneration) Regulations, S.I. No. 287 of 1977
	22(2)	*Unfair Dismissals Act, 1977 (Commencement) Order, S.I. No. 138 of 1977*
Unit Trusts Act, No. 17 of 1972	10(3)	**Unit Trusts Act, 1972 (Section 10 (3)) Order, S.I. No. 294 of 1974**
	25(2)	*Unit Trusts Act, 1972 (Commencement) Order, S.I. No. 144 of 1973*
University College, Galway Act, No. 35 of 1929	2(2)	**University College, Galway (Increase of Grant) Order [Vol. XXI p. 1025] S.R.& O. No. 3 of 1932**
		University College, Galway (Increase of Grant) Order [Vol. XXI p. 1031] S.R.& O. No. 5 of 1938
University Colleges Act, No. 30 of 1940	2	*University College, Dublin (Extension of Term of Office of Governing Body) Order [Vol. XXXIV p. 485] S.R.& O. No. 356 of 1940*
		University College, Cork (Extension of Term of Office of Governing Body) Order [Vol. XXXIV p. 469] S.R.& O. No. 357 of 1940
		University College, Galway (Extension of Term of Office of Governing Body) Order [Vol. XXXIV p. 501] S.R.& O. No. 358 of 1940

Statutory Authority	Section	Statutory Instrument
University Colleges Act, No. 30 of 1940 (*Cont.*)		*University College, Dublin (Extension of Term of Office of Governing Body) Order [Vol. XXXIV p. 489] S.R.& O. No. 506 of 1941*
		University College, Cork (Extension of Term of Office of Governing Body) Order [Vol. XXXIV p. 473] S.R.& O. No. 507 of 1941
		University College, Galway (Extension of Term of Office of Governing Body) Order [Vol. XXXIV p. 505] S.R.& O. No. 508 of 1941
		University College, Dublin (Extension of Term of Office of Governing Body) Order [Vol. XXXIV p. 495] S.R.& O. No. 335 of 1942
		University College, Cork (Extension of Term of Office of Governing Body) Order [Vol. XXXIV p. 479] S.R.& O. No. 336 of 1942
		University College, Galway (Extension of Term of Office of Governing Body) Order [Vol. XXXIV p. 511] S.R.& O. No. 337 of 1942
Urban Renewal Act, No. 19 of 1986	6	**Urban Renewal Act, 1986 (Designated Areas) Order, S.I. No. 238 of 1986**
	7	**Urban Renewal Act, 1986 (Remission of Rates) Scheme, S.I. No. 276 of 1986**
		Urban Renewal Act, 1986 (Remission of Rates) (Custom House Docks Area) Scheme, S.I. No. 341 of 1986
	8	*Urban Renewal Act, 1986 (Establishment of Custom House Docks Development Authority) Order, S.I. No. 330 of 1986*
Vaccination Amendment (Ireland) Act, No. 87 of 1868		**Vaccination Regulations [Vol. XXXIV p. 517] S.R.& O. No. 127 of 1942**
Vaccination Amendment (Ireland) Act, No. 70 of 1879		**Vaccination Regulations [Vol. XXXIV p. 517] S.R.& O. No. 127 of 1942**
Vaccination (Ireland) Act, No. 64 of 1858		*Dispensary (Boards of Health) (Amendment) Order [Vol. XXII p. 1] S.R.& O. No. 67 of 1925*
		Vaccination Regulations [Vol. XXXIV p. 517] S.R.& O. No. 127 of 1942
Vaccination (Ireland) Act, No. 52 of 1863		**Vaccination Regulations [Vol. XXXIV p. 517] S.R.& O. No. 127 of 1942**
Vaccination (Ireland) Acts, 1858 to 1879,		**Dispensary and Vaccination (Rules and Regulations) Order [Vol. XVIII p. 561] S.R.& O. No. 38 of 1934**
Value-added Tax Act, No. 22 of 1972	1(1)	*Value-added Tax (Specified Day) Order, S.I. No. 180 of 1972*
	5	**Value-added Tax (Place of Supply of Certain Services) Regulations, S.I. No. 343 of 1985**
	6(2)	**Value-added Tax (Exempted Activities) (No.1) Order, S.I. No. 430 of 1985**

Statutory Authority	Section	Statutory Instrument
Value-added Tax Act, No. 22 of 1972 (*Cont.*)	9(4)	*Value-added Tax (Appointed Day) Order, S.I. No. 192 of 1972*
	10	**Value-added Tax (Imported Goods) Regulations, S.I. No. 279 of 1982**
	11(8)	**Value-added Tax (Reduction of Rate) (No.1) Order, S.I. No. 268 of 1972**
		Value-added Tax (Reduction of Rate) (No.2) Order, S.I. No. 326 of 1972
		Value-added Tax (Reduction of Rate) (No.3) Order, S.I. No. 69 of 1973
		Value-added Tax (Reduction of Rate) (No.4) Order, S.I. No. 146 of 1978
		Value-added Tax (Reduction of Rate) (No.5) Order, S.I. No. 53 of 1981
	13	**Value-added Tax (Exported Goods) Regulations, S.I. No. 230 of 1984**
		Value-added Tax (Goods exported in Baggage) Regulations, S.I. No. 231 of 1984
	15	**Value-added Tax (Imported Goods) Regulations, S.I. No. 129 of 1983**
		Value-added Tax (Remission and Repayment on Certain Importations) Regulations, S.I. No. 344 of 1985
	20(3)	**Value-added Tax (Refund of Tax) (No.1) Order, S.I. No. 267 of 1972**
		Value-added Tax (Refund of Tax) (No.2) Order, S.I. No. 269 of 1972
		Value-added Tax (Refund of Tax) (No.3) Order, S.I. No. 327 of 1972
		Value-added Tax (Refund of Tax) (No.4) Order, S.I. No. 328 of 1972
		Value-added Tax (Refund of Tax) (No.5) Order, S.I. No. 70 of 1973
		Value-added Tax (Refund of Tax) (No.6) Order, S.I. No. 238 of 1973
		Value-added Tax (Refund of Tax) (No.7) Order, S.I. No. 290 of 1974
		Value-added Tax (Refund of Tax) (No.8) Order, S.I. No. 145 of 1978
		Value-added Tax (Refund of Tax) (No.9) Order, S.I. No. 59 of 1979
		Value-added Tax (Refund of Tax) (Revocation) Order, S.I. No. 232 of 1979
		Value-added Tax (Refund of Tax) (No.10) Order, S.I. No. 275 of 1979
		Value-added Tax (Refund of Tax) (No.11) Order, S.I. No. 239 of 1980
		Value-added Tax (Refund of Tax) (No.12) Order, S.I. No. 262 of 1980
		Value-added Tax (Refund of Tax) (No.13) Order, S.I. No. 263 of 1980

Statutory Authority	Section	Statutory Instrument
Veterinary Surgeons Act, No. 36 of 1931	27	**Veterinary Surgeons (Registration Fees and Annual Fees) Order, S.I. No. 74 of 1973**
		Veterinary Surgeons (Registration Fees and Annual Fees) Order, S.I. No. 33 of 1977
		Veterinary Surgeons (Registration Fees and Annual Fees) Order, S.I. No. 24 of 1982
	28	**Veterinary Surgeons (Annual Fee in Respect of Registration) Order, S.I. No. 64 of 1964**
		Veterinary Surgeons (Registration Fees and Annual Fees) Order, S.I. No. 74 of 1973
		Veterinary Surgeons (Registration Fees and Annual Fees) Order, S.I. No. 33 of 1977
		Veterinary Surgeons (Registration Fees and Annual Fees) Order, S.I. No. 24 of 1982
		Veterinary Surgeons (Registration Fees and Annual Fees) Order, S.I. No. 40 of 1985
Veterinary Surgeons Act, No. 18 of 1952	2	**Veterinary Surgeons (Qualifying Degrees) Order, S.I. No. 85 of 1954**
	4	**Veterinary Surgeons Order, S.I. No. 68 of 1954**
		Veterinary Surgeons (Confirmation of Agreement) Order, S.I. No. 319 of 1972
	5	**Veterinary Surgeons Order, S.I. No. 68 of 1954**
		Veterinary Surgeons Order, S.I. No. 15 of 1972
Vital Statistics and Births, Deaths and Marriages Registration Act, No. 8 of 1952	2	**Vital Statistics Regulations, S.I. No. 280 of 1954**
		Vital Statistics (Foetal Deaths) Regulations, S.I. No. 302 of 1956
		Vital Statistics (Amendment) Regulations, S.I. No. 261 of 1957
	4	*Oifig an Ard-Chlaraitheora (Hours of Business) Regulations, S.I. No. 60 of 1953*
		Oifig an Ard-Chlaraitheora (Hours of Business) Regulations, S.I. No. 227 of 1965
		Oifig an Ard-Chlaraitheora (Hours of Business) Regulations, S.I. No. 114 of 1967
		Oifig an Ard-Chlaraitheora (Hours of Business) (Temporary) Regulations, S.I. No. 302 of 1970
		Oifig an Ard-Chlaraitheora (Hours of Business) Regulations, S.I. No. 339 of 1971
		Oifig an Ard-Chlaraitheora (Hours of Business) Regulations, S.I. No. 112 of 1974
		Oifig an Ard-Chlaraitheora (Hours of Business) (Temporary) Regulations, S.I. No. 287 of 1976
		Oifig an Ard-Chlaraitheora (Hours of Business) (Temporary) Regulations, S.I. No. 70 of 1979
		Oifig an Ard-Chlaraitheora (Hours of Business) (Temporary) Regulations, S.I. No. 421 of 1981
		Oifig an Ard-Chlaraitheora (Hours of Business) (Temporary) Regulations, S.I. No. 370 of 1982
		Oifig an Ard-Chlaraitheora (Hours of Business) (Temporary) Regulations, S.I. No. 89 of 1983

Statutory Authority	Section	Statutory Instrument
Vital Statistics and Births, Deaths and Marriages Registration Act, No. 8 of 1952 *(Cont.)*		**Registration of Births, Deaths and Marriages (Fees** *and Allowances) Regulations, S.I. No. 149 of 1983*
		Registration of Births, Deaths and Marriages (Fees and Allowances) Regulations, S.I. No. 347 of 1984
		Registration of Births, Deaths and Marriages (Reduced Fees) (Amendment) Regulations, S.I. No. 359 of 1984
	9(3)	**Births, Deaths and Marriages (Fees for Certificates) Regulations, S.I. No. 61 of 1953**
	14	*Vital Statistics and Births, Deaths and Marriages Registration Act, 1952 (Commencement) Order, S.I. No. 59 of 1953*
Vocational Education Act, No. 29 of 1930		**Vocational Education Act, 1930 (Requisitions for Birth Certificates) Regulations [Vol. XXII p. 237] S.R.& O. No. 86 of 1930**
		Vocational Education Act, 1930 (Requisitions for Birth Certificates) (Amendment) Regulations, S.I. No. 318 of 1953
	4(2)	**Vocational Education Act, 1930 (Extension of Technical Education) Order, S.I. No. 74 of 1949**
	4(3)	**Vocational Education ("Technical Education") Order [Vol. XXII p. 183] S.R.& O. No. 366 of 1934**
	28(1)	**Vocational Education (Acquisition of Land) Regulations [Vol. XXII p. 121] S.R.& O. No. 78 of 1931**
	50(2)	**Vocational Education (Borrowing) Regulations [Vol. XXII p. 61] S.R.& O. No. 35 of 1931**
		Vocational Education (Borrowing) (Amendment) Regulations, S.I. No. 209 of 1965
	53	**Vocational Education (Grants) Regulations [Vol. XXII p. 73] S.R.& O. No. 55 of 1931**
		Vocational Education (Grants) Amending Regulations, (1931) [Vol. XXII p. 77] S.R.& O. No. 69 of 1932
		Vocational Education (Special Additional Grants) Regulations [Vol. XXII p. 81] S.R.& O. No. 104 of 1933
		Vocational Education (Special Additional Grants) Regulations [Vol. XXII p. 87] S.R.& O. No. 200 of 1934
		Vocational Education (Special Additional Grants) Regulations [Vol. XXII p. 93] S.R.& O. No. 655 of 1935
		Vocational Education (Special Additional Grants) Regulations [Vol. XXII p. 99] S.R.& O. No. 295 of 1936
		Vocational Education (Special Additional Grants) Regulations [Vol. XXII p. 105] S.R.& O. No. 271 of 1937
		Vocational Education (Additional Grants) Regulations [Vol. XXII p. 111] S.R.& O. No. 265 of 1938

Vocational Education Act, No. 29 of
1930 (*Cont.*)

Vocational Education (Additional Grants) Regulations [Vol. XXXIV p. 545] S.R.& O. No. 171 of 1939

Vocational Education Act, 1930 (Grants under Section 53) Regulations [Vol. XXXIV p. 555] S.R.& O. No. 105 of 1940

Vocational Education Act, 1930 (Grants under Section 53) Regulations [Vol. XXXIV p. 561] S.R.& O. No. 341 of 1941

Vocational Education Act, 1930 (Grants under Section 53) Regulations [Vol. XXXIV p. 567] S.R.& O. No. 270 of 1942

Vocational Education Act, 1930 (Grants under Section 53) Regulations [Vol. XXXIV p. 575] S.R.& O. No. 256 of 1943

Vocational Education Act, 1930 (Grants under Section 53) Regulations [Vol. XXXIV p. 583] S.R.& O. No. 173 of 1944

Vocational Education Act, 1930 (Grants under Section 53) Regulations [Vol. XXXIV p. 591] S.R.& O. No. 152 of 1945

Vocational Education Act, 1930 (Grants under Section 53) Regulations [Vol. XXXVIII p. 821] S.R.& O. No. 113 of 1946

Vocational Education Act, 1930 (Grants under Section 53) Regulations [Vol. XXXVIII p. 829] S.R.& O. No. 121 of 1947

Vocational Education Act, 1930 (Grants under Section 53) Regulations, S.I. No. 156 of 1948

Vocational Education Act, 1930 (Grants under Section 53) Regulations, S.I. No. 95 of 1949

Vocational Education Act, 1930 (Grants under Section 53) Regulations, S.I. No. 117 of 1950

Vocational Education Act, 1930 (Grants under Section 53) Regulations, S.I. No. 155 of 1951

Vocational Education Act, 1930 (Grants under Section 53) Regulations, S.I. No. 240 of 1952

Vocational Education Act, 1930 (Grants under Section 53) Regulations, S.I. No. 207 of 1953

Vocational Education Act, 1930 (Grants under Section 53) Regulations, S.I. No. 139 of 1954

Vocational Education Act, 1930 (Grants under Section 53) Regulations, S.I. No. 210 of 1955

Vocational Education Act, 1930 (Grants under Section 53) Regulations, S.I. No. 159 of 1956

Vocational Education Act, 1930 (Grants under Section 53) Regulations, S.I. No. 227 of 1957

Vocational Education Act, 1930 (Grants under Section 53) Regulations, S.I. No. 199 of 1958

Vocational Education (Grants for Annual Schemes of Committees) Regulations, S.I. No. 218 of 1959

Vocational Education (Grants for Annual Schemes of Committees) Regulations, S.I. No. 211 of 1960

Vocational Education (Grants for Annual Schemes of Committees) Regulations, S.I. No. 189 of 1961

Vocational Education Act, No. 29 of
1930 (*Cont.*)

Vocational Education (Grants for Annual Schemes of Committees) Regulations, S.I. No. 170 of 1962

Vocational Education (Grants for Annual Schemes of Committees) Regulations, S.I. No. 219 of 1963

Vocational Education (Grants for Annual Schemes of Committees) Regulations, S.I. No. 228 of 1964

Vocational Education (Grants for Annual Schemes of Committees) Regulations, (1965) S.I. No. 5 of 1966

Vocational Education (Grants for Annual Schemes of Committees) Regulations, S.I. No. 66 of 1966

Vocational Education (Grants for Annual Schemes of Committees) Regulations, S.I. No. 55 of 1967

Vocational Education (Grants for Annual Schemes of Committees) Regulations, S.I. No. 53 of 1968

Vocational Education (Grants for Annual Schemes of Committees) Regulations, S.I. No. 43 of 1969

Vocational Education (Grants for Annual Schemes of Committees) Regulations, S.I. No. 58 of 1970

Vocational Education (Grants for Annual Schemes of Committees) Regulations, S.I. No. 120 of 1971

Vocational Education (Grants for Annual Schemes of Committees) Regulations, S.I. No. 89 of 1972

Vocational Education (Grants for Annual Schemes of Committees) Regulations, S.I. No. 90 of 1973

Vocational Education (Grants for Annual Schemes of Committees) Regulations, S.I. No. 87 of 1974

Vocational Education (Grants for Annual Schemes of Committees) (No.2) Regulations, S.I. No. 375 of 1974

Vocational Education (Grants for Annual Schemes of Communities) Regulations, S.I. No. 328 of 1975

Vocational Education (Grants for Annual Schemes of Committees) Regulations, S.I. No. 313 of 1976

Vocational Education (Grants for Annual Schemes of Committees) Regulations, S.I. No. 392 of 1977

Vocational Education (Grants for Annual Schemes of Committees) Regulations, S.I. No. 380 of 1978

Vocational Education (Grants for Annual Schemes of Committees) Regulations, S.I. No. 412 of 1979

Vocational Education (Grants for Annual Schemes of Committees) Regulations, S.I. No. 403 of 1980

Vocational Education (Grants for Annual Schemes of Committees) Regulations, S.I. No. 434 of 1981

Vocational Education (Grants for Annual Schemes of Committees) Regulations, S.I. No. 372 of 1982

Vocational Education (Grants for Annual Schemes of Committees) Regulations, S.I. No. 397 of 1983

Vocational Education (Grants for Annual Schemes of Committees) Regulations, S.I. No. 364 of 1984

Vocational Education (Grants for Annual Schemes of Committees) Regulations, S.I. No. 431 of 1985

Statutory Authority	Section	Statutory Instrument
Vocational Education Act, No. 29 of 1930 *(Cont.)*		**Vocational Education (Grants for Annual Schemes of Committees) Regulations, S.I. No. 453 of 1986**
	54	**Vocational Education (Expenses of Attending Conferences) Regulations [Vol. XXII p. 69] S.R.& O. No. 37 of 1931**
		Vocational Education (Expenses of Attending Conferences) Regulations, 1931 (Amendment) Regulations, S.I. No. 104 of 1948
	60	*Vocational Education Act, 1930 (Miscellaneous Orders and Regulations) (Revocation) Order, S.I. No. 23 of 1973*
	60(1)	*Vocational Education Act, 1930 (Application to Part V to Cork City) Order [Vol. XXII p. 187] S.R.& O. No. 12 of 1938*
		Vocational Education Act, 1930 (Application of Part V to Limerick City) Order [Vol. XXXIV p. 551] S.R.& O. No. 363 of 1942
		Vocational Education Act, 1930 (Application of Part V to Waterford City) Order [Vol. XXXVIII p. 817] S.R.& O. No. 360 of 1946
	103	**County Kerry Vocational Education Committee (Special Provision) (Gaeltacht) Order, S.I. No. 372 of 1953**
	103(1)	**County Donegal Vocational Education Committee (Special Provision) (Gaeltacht) Order [Vol. XXII p. 141] S.R.& O. No. 252 of 1934**
		County Clare Vocational Education Committee (Special Provision) (Gaeltacht) Order [Vol. XXII p. 149] S.R.& O. No. 253 of 1934
		County Mayo Vocational Education Committee (Special Provision) (Gaeltacht) Order [Vol. XXII p. 155] S.R.& O. No. 320 of 1934
		County Galway Vocational Education Committee (Special Provision) (Gaeltacht) Order [Vol. XXII p. 161] S.R.& O. No. 675 of 1935
		Town of Galway Vocational Education Committee (Special Provision) (Gaeltacht) Order [Vol. XXII p. 167] S.R.& O. No. 250 of 1937
		County Cork Vocational Education Committee (Special Provision) (Gaeltacht) Order [Vol. XXII p. 175] S.R.& O. No. 173 of 1938
	103(4)	**Vocational Education (Gaeltacht) Order [Vol. XXII p. 125] S.R.& O. No. 85 of 1933**
	108	*Vocational Education Committees (City of Limerick Vocational Education Committee) Regulations, S.I. No. 214 of 1970*
	109	**Vocational Education Act, 1930 (Grants under Section 109) Regulations [Vol. XXXIV p. 599] S.R.& O. No. 386 of 1939**
		Vocational Education Act, 1930 (Grants under Section 109) Regulations, 1939 (Amendment) Regulations, S.I. No. 135 of 1948

Vocational Education Act, No. 29 of
1930 (*Cont.*)

**Vocational Education Act, 1930 (Grants under
Section 109) Regulations, 1939 (Amendment)
Regulations, S.I. No. 8 of 1955**

*Vocational Education Act, 1930 (Grants under
Section 109) Regulations, 1939 (Amendment)
Regulations, S.I. No. 203 of 1958*

**Vocational Education Act, 1930 (Grants under
Section 109) Regulations, 1939 (Amendment)
Regulations, S.I. No. 69 of 1960**

**Vocational Education Act, 1930 (Grants Under
Section 109) Regulations, 1939 (Amendment)
Regulations, S.I. No. 275 of 1961**

*Vocational Education Act, 1930 (Grants Under
Section 109) Regulations, 1939 (Amendment)
Regulations, S.I. No. 44 of 1963*

*Vocational Education Act, 1930 (Grants under
Section 109) Regulations, 1939 (Amendment)
Regulations, S.I. No. 39 of 1965*

**Vocational Education Act, 1930 (Grants under
Section 109) Regulations, 1939 (Amendment)
Regulations, S.I. No. 287 of 1966**

*Vocational Education Act, 1930 (Grants under
Section 109) Regulations, 1939 (Amendment)
Regulations, S.I. No. 46 of 1968*

*Vocational Education Act, 1930 (Grants under
Section 109) Regulations, 1939 (Amendment)
Regulations, S.I. No. 73 of 1973*

*Vocational Education Act, 1930 (Grants under
Section 109) Regulations, 1939 (Amendment)
(No.2) Regulations, S.I. No. 342 of 1973*

125   *Vocational Education Act, 1930 (Miscellaneous
Orders and Regulations) (Revocation) Order, S.I.
No. 23 of 1973*

125(1) *Vocational Education Regulations (No.1) [Vol.
XXII p. 5] S.R.& O. No. 86 of 1930*

**Vocational Education (Accounts, Audit and
Procedure) Regulations [Vol. XXII p. 19] S.R.&
O. No. 20 of 1931**

**Vocational Education (Contracts) Regulations [Vol.
XXII p. 67] S.R.& O. No. 36 of 1931**

**Vocational Education (Form of Summons) Regu-
lations [Vol. XXII p. 117] S.R.& O. No. 58 of
1931**

*Vocational Education Act, 1930 (Part V) (Principal
Teachers' Returns) Regulations [Vol. XXII
p. 191] S.R.& O. No. 28 of 1938*

*Vocational Education Act, 1930 (Part V) (Registers
and Records) Regulations [Vol. XXII p. 203]
S.R.& O. No. 29 of 1938*

*Vocational Education Act, 1930 (Part V) (Statutory
Forms) Regulations [Vol. XXII p. 213] S.R.& O.
No. 33 of 1938*

**Vocational Education Act, (1930) S.R.& O. No. 118
of 1938**

Statutory Authority	Section	Statutory Instrument
Vocational Education Act, No. 29 of 1930 (*Cont.*)		**Vocational Education (Contracts) (Amendment) Regulations, S.I. No. 234 of 1964**
		Vocational Education (Contracts) (Amendment) Regulations, S.I. No. 20 of 1978
		Vocational Education (Contracts) (Amendment) Regulations, S.I. No. 69 of 1982
Vocational Education Acts, 1930 to 1944,		**Vocational Education Act, 1930 (Sections 44 and 46) Regulations [Vol. XXXIV p. 625] S.R.& O. No. 153 of 1945**
Vocational Education (Amendment) Act, No. 9 of 1944	6	**Vocational Education Committees (Age Limit for Officers) Declaration, S.I. No. 56 of 1958**
	6(1)	*Vocational Education Committees (Age Limit for Officers) Order [Vol. XXXVIII p. 837] S.R.& O. No. 37 of 1947*
	11	**Vocational Education Committees (Age Limit for Officers) Declaration, S.I. No. 56 of 1958**
Vocational Education (Amendment) Act, No. 1 of 1947	6(4)	*Vocational Education Committees (Allowances to Members) Rules [Vol. XXXVIII p. 841] S.R.& O. No. 293 of 1947*
		Vocational Education Committees (Allowances to Members) Rules, S.I. No. 114 of 1963
		Vocational Education Committees (Allowances to Members) (Amendment) Rules, S.I. No. 226 of 1964
		Vocational Education Committees (Allowances to Members) (Amendment) Rules, S.I. No. 3 of 1969
		Vocational Education Committees (Allowances to Members) (Amendment) Rules, S.I. No. 313 of 1972
		Vocational Education Committees (Allowances to Members) (Amendment) Rules, S.I. No. 151 of 1975
		Vocational Education Committees (Allowances to Members) (Amendment) Rules, S.I. No. 284 of 1976
		Vocational Education Committees (Allowances to Members) (Amendment) Rules, S.I. No. 23 of 1978
		Vocational Education Committees (Allowances to Members) (Amendment) Rules, S.I. No. 114 of 1980
		Vocational Education Committees (Allowances to Members) (Amendment) Rules, S.I. No. 133 of 1981
		Vocational Education Committees (Allowances to Members) (Amendment) Rules, S.I. No. 68 of 1982
		Vocational Education Committees (Allowances to Members) (Amendment) Rules, S.I. No. 60 of 1984
Voluntary Health Insurance Act, No. 1 of 1957	2	*Voluntary Health Insurance Act, 1957 (Establishment Day) Order, S.I. No. 24 of 1957*

Statutory Authority	Section	Statutory Instrument
Voluntary Health Insurance Act, No. 1 of 1957 (*Cont.*)	23(4)	*Voluntary Health Insurance Act, 1957 (Commencement of Sections 23 and 24) Order, S.I. No. 46 of 1957*
Water Supplies Act, No. 1 of 1942	8	**Water Supplies (Application for Provisional Order) Regulations [Vol. XXXIV p. 651] S.R.& O. No. 265 of 1945**
	25	**Water Supplies (Application for Provisional Order) Regulations [Vol. XXXIV p. 651] S.R.& O. No. 265 of 1945**
Waterford City Management Act, No. 25 of 1939	6	**Waterford County Borough Electoral Areas Order, S.I. No. 12 of 1967**
		Waterford County Borough (Electoral Areas) (Amendment) Order, S.I. No. 113 of 1985
	11(2)	**Waterford City Management (Reserved Functions) Order, S.I. No. 422 of 1985**
Weights and Measures Act, No. 49 of 1878	39	**Weights and Measures Fees Order [Vol. XXII p. 243] S.R.& O. No. 13 of 1924**
Weights and Measures Act, No. 21 of 1889	8	**Weights and Measures Fees Order [Vol. XXII p. 243] S.R.& O. No. 13 of 1924**
		Weights and Measures (Departmental Fees) Order [Vol. XXII p. 333] S.R.& O. No. 78 of 1928
	15	**Weights and Measures (Departmental Fees) Order [Vol. XXII p. 333] S.R.& O. No. 78 of 1928**
Weights and Measures Act, No. 28 of 1904		**Weights and Measures (Alteration of Fees) Order [Vol. XXII p. 345] S.R.& O. No. 19 of 1926**
	5	*Weights and Measures (Standard Bottles) Regulations [Vol. XXII p. 341] S.R.& O. No. 5 of 1926*
		Weights and Measures (Amending) Regulations [Vol. XXII p. 351] S.R.& O. No. 108 of 1927
		Weights and Measures (Amending) Regulations [Vol. XXII p. 355] S.R.& O. No. 19 of 1928
		Weights and Measures (Amendment) Regulations, S.I. No. 271 of 1957
		Weights and Measures (Taximeter: Section 136 of the Road Traffic Act, 1933) (Amendment) Regulations, S.I. No. 139 of 1958
	6	**Weights and Measures Fees Order [Vol. XXII p. 243] S.R.& O. No. 13 of 1924**
		Weights and Measures (Departmental Fees) Order [Vol. XXII p. 333] S.R.& O. No. 78 of 1928
	8	**Weights and Measures Fees Order [Vol. XXII p. 243] S.R.& O. No. 13 of 1924**
		Weights and Measures (Departmental Fees) Order [Vol. XXII p. 333] S.R.& O. No. 78 of 1928
	9	*Weights and Measures (Verification and Stamping Fees) Order [Vol. XXII p. 357] S.R.& O. No. 23 of 1929*

Statutory Authority	Section	Statutory Instrument
Weights and Measures Act, No. 28 of 1904 (*Cont.*)		*Weights and Measures (Additional Fees) Order [Vol. XXII p. 365] S.R.& O. No. 20 of 1932*
		Weights and Measures (Verification and Stamping Fees) Order [Vol. XXXIV p. 657] S.R.& O. No. 168 of 1945
		Weights and Measures (Verification and Stamping Fees) Order, S.I. No. 137 of 1978
		Weights and Measures (Verification and Stamping Fees) Order, S.I. No. 351 of 1981
		Weights and Measures (Verification and Stamping Fees) Order, S.I. No. 351 of 1983
Weights and Measures Act, No. 3 of 1928	7	*Weights and Measures (Bottle Factory) Regulations [Vol. XXII p. 375] S.R.& O. No. 73 of 1928*
	8	*Weights and Measures (Verification and Stamping of Bottles) (Fees) Regulations [Vol. XXXIV p. 663] S.R.& O. No. 82 of 1942*
		Weights and Measures (Verification and Stamping of Bottles) (Fees) Regulations [Vol. XXXVIII p. 845] S.R.& O. No. 308 of 1946
	8(1)	*Weights and Measures (Stamping of Bottles Fees) Regulations [Vol. XXII p. 379] S.R.& O. No. 16 of 1929*
		Weights and Measures (Stamping of Bottles Fees) Amending Regulations [Vol. XXII p. 383] S.R.& O. No. 54 of 1931
	13	*Weights and Measures (Stamps) Regulations [Vol. XXII p. 371] S.R.& O. No. 72 of 1928*
		Weights and Measures (Stamps) Regulations, S.I. No. 137 of 1958
	15	**Weights and Measures (Departmental Fees) Order [Vol. XXII p. 333] S.R.& O. No. 78 of 1928**
Weights and Measures Acts, 1878 to 1928,		**Weights and Measures (General) Regulations [Vol. XXII p. 249] S.R.& O. No. 71 of 1928**
		Weights and Measures (General) (Amendment) Regulations [Vol. XXII p. 317] S.R.& O. No. 80 of 1928
		Weights and Measures (Temporary Amending) Regulations [Vol. XXII p. 319] S.R.& O. No. 10 of 1931
		Weights and Measures (Glass Measures) Regulations [Vol. XXII p. 325] S.R.& O. No. 14 of 1931
		Weights and Measures (Amending) Regulations [Vol. XXII p. 323] S.R.& O. No. 100 of 1932
		Weights and Measures (Amendment) Regulations [Vol. XXII p. 329] S.R.& O. No. 13 of 1938
Weights and Measures Acts, 1878 to 1936,		**Weights and Measures (Amendment) Regulations [Vol. XXXIV p. 671] S.R.& O. No. 313 of 1940**
		Weights and Measures (Amendment) Regulations, S.I. No. 87 of 1948
		Weights and Measures (Amendment) Regulations, S.I. No. 385 of 1952

Statutory Authority	Section	Statutory Instrument
Weights and Measures (General) Regulations [Vol. XXII p. 249] S.R.& O. No. 71 of 1928	40	**Standard Bottles (Continuation of Use in Trade) Order [Vol. XXII p. 327] S.R.& O. No. 2 of 1929**
Weights and Measures (General) (Amendment) Regulations [Vol. XXII p. 317] S.R.& O. No. 80 of 1928	6	**Standard Bottles (Continuation of Use in Trade) Order [Vol. XXII p. 327] S.R.& O. No. 2 of 1929**
Weights and Measures (Metric System) Act, No. 46 of 1897	2	**Weights and Measures (Metric Equivalents) Order, S.I. No. 91 of 1976**
Whale Fisheries Act, No. 4 of 1937	2(2)	**Whale Fisheries Act, 1937 (Extension to Sperm Whales) Order [Vol. XXII p. 395] S.R.& O. No. 158 of 1937**
		Whale Fisheries Act, 1937 (Extension to Mammals of the Order Cetacea) Order, S.I. No. 240 of 1982
	4(2)	*Whale Measurement Regulations [Vol. XXII p. 387] S.R.& O. No. 157 of 1937*
		Whale Measurement (No.2) Regulations [Vol. XXII p. 391] S.R.& O. No. 240 of 1937
	31	*Whale Measurement Regulations [Vol. XXII p. 387] S.R.& O. No. 157 of 1937*
		Whale Measurement (No.2) Regulations [Vol. XXII p. 391] S.R.& O. No. 240 of 1937
Wheat Milling Order, S.I. No. 74 of 1955	3	*Wheat Milling (General Quota Variation) Order, S.I. No. 88 of 1955*
		Wheat Milling (General Quota Variation) Order, 1955 (Revocation) Order, S.I. No. 96 of 1956
Wicklow County (Extension of Boundary) Provisional Order, 1957	2	*Wicklow County (Extension of Boundary) Provisional Order, 1957 (Commencement) Order, S.I. No. 214 of 1957*
Widows' and Orphans' Pensions Act, No. 29 of 1935	2	**Widows' and Orphans' Pensions (Appointed Days) Order [Vol. XXII p. 575] S.R.& O. No. 123 of 1937**
		Widows' and Orphans' Pensions (Full-time Instruction) Regulations [Vol. XXII p. 569] S.R.& O. No. 291 of 1937
		Widows' and Orphans' Pensions (Full-time Instruction) (Amendment) Regulations [Vol. XXXIV p. 693] S.R.& O. No. 220 of 1939
	4(3)	**Widows' and Orphans' Pensions (Excepted Employments) (No.2) Order [Vol. XXII p. 563] S.R.& O. No. 163 of 1937**
		Widows' and Orphans' Pensions (Excepted Employments) Order [Vol. XXXVIII p. 867] S.R.& O. No. 248 of 1947
	5(2)	*Widows' and Orphans' Pensions (Excepted Persons) Regulations [Vol. XXII p. 429] S.R.& O. No. 665 of 1935*
		Widows' and Orphans' Pensions (Excepted Persons) (Amendment) Regulations [Vol. XXXIV p. 689] S.R.& O. No. 352 of 1942

Statutory Authority	Section	Statutory Instrument

Widows' and Orphans' Pensions
Act, No. 29 of 1935 (*Cont.*)

Widows' and Orphans' Pensions (Apportionment of Sums Received on Account of Contributions) Regulations [Vol. XXXVIII p. 851] S.R.& O. No. 221 of 1946

65(1)(g) **Widows' and Orphans' Pensions (Payments on Death) Regulations [Vol. XXII p. 521] S.R.& O. No. 133 of 1936**

65(1)(h) **Widows' and Orphans' Pensions (Payments on Death) Regulations [Vol. XXII p. 521] S.R.& O. No. 133 of 1936**

65(1)(i) *Widows' and Orphans' Pensions (Calculation of Means Regulations) Order [Vol. XXII p. 405] S.R.& O. No. 590 of 1935*

Widows' and Orphans' Pensions (Birth, Marriage or Death Certificates) Regulations [Vol. XXII p. 411] S.R.& O. No. 609 of 1935

Widows' and Orphans' Pensions (Excepted Persons) Regulations [Vol. XXII p. 429] S.R.& O. No. 665 of 1935

Widows' and Orphans' Pensions (Collection of Contributions for Excepted Persons) Regulations [Vol. XXII p. 487] S.R.& O. No. 48 of 1936

Widows' and Orphans' Pensions (Voluntary Contributors) Regulations [Vol. XXII p. 529] S.R.& O. No. 341 of 1936

Widows' and Orphans' Pensions (Unified Society's Returns) Regulations [Vol. XXII p. 557] S.R.& O. No. 96 of 1937

Widows' and Orphans' Pensions (Voluntary Contributors) Regulations [Vol. XXII p. 541] S.R.& O. No. 253 of 1938

Widows' and Orphans' Pensions (Calculation of Means) Regulations [Vol. XXXIV p. 683] S.R.& O. No. 9 of 1940

Widows' and Orphans' Pensions (Excepted Persons) (Amendment) Regulations [Vol. XXXIV p. 689] S.R.& O. No. 352 of 1942

Widows' and Orphans' Pensions (Excepted Persons) Regulations [Vol. XXXVIII p. 861] S.R.& O. No. 217 of 1946

Widows' and Orphans' Pensions (Collection of Contributions for Excepted Persons) (Amendment) Regulations [Vol. XXXVIII p. 855] S.R.& O. No. 225 of 1946

Widows' and Orphans' Pensions (Voluntary Contributors) (Amendment) Regulations [Vol. XXXVIII p. 871] S.R.& O. No. 227 of 1946

65(e) **Widows' and Orphans' Pensions (Calculation of Contributions) Regulations [Vol. XXII p. 511] S.R.& O. No. 132 of 1936**

70(1) *Widows' and Orphans' Pensions (Voluntary Contributors) Regulations [Vol. XXII p. 529] S.R.& O. No. 341 of 1936*

Statutory Authority	Section	Statutory Instrument
Widows' and Orphans' Pensions Act, No. 29 of 1935 (*Cont.*)		**Widows' and Orphans' Pensions (Voluntary Contributors) Regulations [Vol. XXII p. 541] S.R.& O. No. 253 of 1938**
		Widows' and Orphans' Pensions (Voluntary Contributors) (Amendment) Regulations [Vol. XXXVIII p. 871] S.R.& O. No. 227 of 1946
	71(1)	*Widows' and Orphans' Pensions (Voluntary Contributors) Regulations [Vol. XXII p. 529] S.R.& O. No. 341 of 1936*
		Widows' and Orphans' Pensions (Voluntary Contributors) Regulations [Vol. XXII p. 541] S.R.& O. No. 253 of 1938
		Widows' and Orphans' Pensions (Voluntary Contributors) (Amendment) Regulations [Vol. XXXVIII p. 871] S.R.& O. No. 227 of 1946
	71(2)	*Widows' and Orphans' Pensions (Voluntary Contributors) Regulations [Vol. XXII p. 529] S.R.& O. No. 341 of 1936*
		Widows' and Orphans' Pensions (Voluntary Contributors) Regulations [Vol. XXII p. 541] S.R.& O. No. 253 of 1938
		Widows' and Orphans' Pensions (Voluntary Contributors) (Amendment) Regulations [Vol. XXXVIII p. 871] S.R.& O. No. 227 of 1946
	72	*Widows' and Orphans' Pensions (Voluntary Contributors) Regulations [Vol. XXII p. 529] S.R.& O. No. 341 of 1936*
		Widows' and Orphans' Pensions (Voluntary Contributors) Regulations [Vol. XXII p. 541] S.R.& O. No. 253 of 1938
		Widows' and Orphans' Pensions (Voluntary Contributors) (Amendment) Regulations [Vol. XXXVIII p. 871] S.R.& O. No. 227 of 1946
	73	**Widows' and Orphans' Pensions (Unified Society's Returns) Regulations [Vol. XXII p. 557] S.R.& O. No. 96 of 1937**
	Sch. I par. 1(1)(a)	**Widows' and Orphans' Pensions (Calculation of Means) Regulations [Vol. XXXIV p. 683] S.R.& O. No. 9 of 1940**
	Sch. I par. 1(1)(d)	**Widows' and Orphans' Pensions (Calculation of Means) Regulations [Vol. XXXIV p. 683] S.R.& O. No. 9 of 1940**
	Sch. I par. 1(1)(e)	**Widows' and Orphans' Pensions (Calculation of Means) Regulations [Vol. XXXIV p. 683] S.R.& O. No. 9 of 1940**
Widows' and Orphans' Pensions Act, No. 11 of 1937	7(1)	*Widows' and Orphans' Pensions (Date of Publication of Census) Order [Vol. XXII p. 579] S.R.& O. No. 251 of 1938*
Widows' and Orphans' Pensions Acts, 1935 to 1948		**Widows' and Orphans' Pensions (Apportionment of Sums Received on Account of Contributions) Regulations, S.I. No. 325 of 1949**
Wild Birds Protection Act, No. 16 of 1930	2	*Wild Birds (County Clare) Order, S.I. No. 167 of 1954*

Statutory Authority	Section	Statutory Instrument
Wild Birds Protection Act, No. 16 of 1930 (*Cont.*)	2(2)	*Wild Birds (County Longford) Order [Vol. XXII p. 595] S.R.& O. No. 13 of 1931*
		Wild Birds (County Longford) Order [Vol. XXII p. 599] S.R.& O. No. 119 of 1932
		Wild Birds (County Waterford) Order [Vol. XXII p. 689] S.R.& O. No. 233 of 1938
		Wild Birds (County Cork) Order [Vol. XXXIV p. 697] S.R.& O. No. 157 of 1940
		Wild Birds (County Donegal) Order [Vol. XXXIV p. 703] S.R.& O. No. 294 of 1944
	2(3)	*Wild Birds (North Bull Island) Order [Vol. XXII p. 615] S.R.& O. No. 46 of 1931*
		Wild Birds (County Dublin) Order [Vol. XXII p. 623] S.R.& O. No. 356 of 1935
		Wild Birds (Lough Rusheen, Barna) Order [Vol. XXXIV p. 757] S.R.& O. No. 120 of 1945
		Wild Birds (County Roscommon) Order [Vol. XXXIV p. 735] S.R.& O. No. 138 of 1945
		Wild Birds (County Monaghan) Order [Vol. XXXIV p. 731] S.R.& O. No. 344 of 1945
		Wild Birds (North Bull Island Area) Order, S.I. No. 149 of 1950
		Wild Birds (The Lough, Cork City, Area) Order, S.I. No. 124 of 1963
	3	*Wild Birds (City of Dublin) Order [Vol. XXII p. 633] S.R.& O. No. 129 of 1934*
	7	*Wild Birds (County Wexford) Order [Vol. XXII p. 583] S.R.& O. No. 12 of 1931*
		Wild Birds (County Galway) Order [Vol. XXII p. 603] S.R.& O. No. 29 of 1931
		Wild Birds (County Westmeath) Order [Vol. XXII p. 607] S.R.& O. No. 30 of 1931
		Wild Birds (County Roscommon) Order [Vol. XXII p. 611] S.R.& O. No. 33 of 1931
		Wild Birds (County Dublin) Order [Vol. XXII p. 619] S.R.& O. No. 60 of 1931
		Wild Birds (County Donegal) Order [Vol. XXII p. 639] S.R.& O. No. 19 of 1933
		Wild Birds (County Kerry) Order [Vol. XXII p. 655] S.R.& O. No. 20 of 1933
		Wild Birds (County Mayo) Order [Vol. XXII p. 665] S.R.& O. No. 21 of 1933
		Wild Birds (County Waterford) Order [Vol. XXII p. 677] S.R.& O. No. 22 of 1933
		Wild Birds (County Wexford) Order [Vol. XXII p. 587] S.R.& O. No. 23 of 1933
		Wild Birds (County Cavan) Order [Vol. XXII p. 693] S.R.& O. No. 124 of 1933
		Wild Birds (County Tipperary, South Riding) Order [Vol. XXII p. 697] S.R.& O. No. 107 of 1934
		Wild Birds (City of Dublin) Order [Vol. XXII p. 633] S.R.& O. No. 129 of 1934

Statutory Authority	Section	Statutory Instrument
Wild Birds Protection Act, No. 16 of 1930 (*Cont.*)		*Wild Birds (County Tipperary, North Riding) Order [Vol. XXII p. 703] S.R.& O. No. 131 of 1934*
		Wild Birds (County Cork) Order [Vol. XXII p. 707] S.R.& O. No. 149 of 1934
		Wild Birds (County Louth) Order [Vol. XXII p. 711] S.R.& O. No. 318 of 1934
		Wild Birds (County Dublin) No.2 Order [Vol. XXII p. 629] S.R.& O. No. 679 of 1935
		Wild Birds (County Wexford) Order [Vol. XXII p. 591] S.R.& O. No. 306 of 1936
		Wild Birds (County Donegal) Order [Vol. XXII p. 643] S.R.& O. No. 307 of 1936
		Wild Birds (County Mayo) Order [Vol. XXII p. 671] S.R.& O. No. 344 of 1936
		Wild Birds (County Waterford) Order [Vol. XXII p. 683] S.R.& O. No. 186 of 1937
		Wild Birds (County Kerry) Order [Vol. XXII p. 659] S.R.& O. No. 227 of 1937
		Wild Birds (County Donegal) Order [Vol. XXII p. 649] S.R.& O. No. 310 of 1938
		Wild Birds (County Dublin) Order [Vol. XXXIV p. 709] S.R.& O. No. 114 of 1939
		Wild Birds (County Wexford) Order [Vol. XXXIV p. 739] S.R.& O. No. 112 of 1940
		Wild Birds (County Mayo) Order [Vol. XXXIV p. 721] S.R.& O. No. 280 of 1940
		Wild Birds (County Wicklow) Order [Vol. XXXIV p. 751] S.R.& O. No. 431 of 1941
		Wild Birds (County Waterford) Order [Vol. XXXIV p. 743] S.R.& O. No. 208 of 1942
		Wild Birds (County Kerry) Order [Vol. XXXIV p. 717] S.R.& O. No. 210 of 1942
		Wild Birds (County Dublin) Order [Vol. XXXIV p. 713] S.R.& O. No. 311 of 1943
		Wild Birds (County Wexford) Order [Vol. XXXIV p. 747] S.R.& O. No. 224 of 1944
		Wild Birds (County Mayo) Order [Vol. XXXIV p. 727] S.R.& O. No. 289 of 1944
		Wild Birds (County Wicklow) Order [Vol. XXX-VIII p. 883] S.R.& O. No. 301 of 1946
		Wild Birds (County Dublin) Order [Vol. XXXVIII p. 875] S.R.& O. No. 302 of 1946
		Wild Birds (County Kerry) Order [Vol. XXXVIII p. 879] S.R.& O. No. 396 of 1947
		Wild Birds (County Tipperary, South Riding) Order, S.I. No. 25 of 1948
		Wild Birds (County Louth) Order, S.I. No. 26 of 1948
		Wild Birds (County Wexford) Order, S.I. No. 27 of 1948
		Wild Birds (County Galway) Order, S.I. No. 28 of 1948

Statutory Authority	Section	Statutory Instrument
Wild Birds Protection Act, No. 16 of 1930 (*Cont.*)		*Wild Birds (County Mayo) Order, S.I. No. 29 of 1948*
		Wild Birds (County Donegal) Order, S.I. No. 30 of 1948
		Wild Birds (County Cork) Order, S.I. No. 308 of 1948
		Wild Birds (County Wicklow) Order, S.I. No. 144 of 1949
		Wild Birds (County Kerry) Order, S.I. No. 146 of 1949
		Wild Birds (County Mayo) Order, S.I. No. 182 of 1949
		Wild Birds (County Cavan) Order, S.I. No. 183 of 1949
		Wild Birds (County Dublin) Order, S.I. No. 208 of 1949
		Wild Birds (County Galway) Order, S.I. No. 216 of 1949
		Wild Birds (County Roscommon) Order, S.I. No. 235 of 1949
		Wild Birds (County Wexford) Order, S.I. No. 253 of 1950
		Wild Birds (County Mayo) Order, S.I. No. 43 of 1951
		Wild Birds (County Monaghan) Order, S.I. No. 121 of 1952
		Wild Birds (County Kerry) Order, S.I. No. 351 of 1953
		Wild Birds (County Dublin) Order, S.I. No. 126 of 1954
		Wild Birds (County Dublin) (No.2) Order, S.I. No. 298 of 1954
	7(1)	*Wild Birds (The Lough, Cork City, Area) Order, S.I. No. 124 of 1963*
Wildlife Act, No. 39 of 1976	1(2)	*Wildlife Act, 1976 (Commencement) Order, S.I. No. 154 of 1977*
	8	**Wildlife (Wild Birds) (Open Seasons) (Amendment) Order, S.I. No. 229 of 1980**
		Wildlife (Wild Birds) (Open Seasons) (Amendment) Order, S.I. No. 266 of 1982
		Wildlife Act, 1976 (Birds of Prey) Regulations, S.I. No. 8 of 1984
		Wildlife (Wild Birds) (Open Seasons) (Amendment) Order, S.I. No. 283 of 1984
		Wildlife Act, 1976 (Section 27) (No.2) Order, S.I. No. 12 of 1985
		Wildlife (Wild Birds) (Open Seasons) (Amendment) Order, S.I. No. 346 of 1985
		Wildlife (Wild Birds) (Open Seasons) (Amendment) Order, S.I. No. 307 of 1986
	8(2)	**Wildlife (Wild Mammals) (Open Seasons) (Amendment) Order, S.I. No. 306 of 1986**

Statutory Authority	Section	Statutory Instrument
Wildlife Act, No. 39 of 1976 (*Cont.*)	13	**Wildlife Advisory Council Order, S.I. No. 79 of 1978**
	15	**Nature Reserve (Derry Clare) Establishment Order, S.I. No. 177 of 1980**
		Nature Reserve (Glen of the Downs) Establishment Order, S.I. No. 178 of 1980
		Nature Reserve (Ballykeefe) Establishment Order, S.I. No. 386 of 1980
		Nature Reserve (Caher (Murphy)) Establishment Order, S.I. No. 387 of 1980
		Nature Reserve (Kyleadohir) Establishment Order, S.I. No. 388 of 1980
		Nature Reserve (Garryrickin) Establishment Order, S.I. No. 389 of 1980
		Nature Reserve (Wexford Wildfowl Reserve) Establishment Order, S.I. No. 205 of 1981
		Nature Reserve (Lough Hyne) Establishment Order, S.I. No. 206 of 1981
		Nature Reserve (Grantstown Wood and Granston Lough) Establishment Order, S.I. No. 378 of 1982
		Nature Reserve (Coolacurragh Wood) Establishment Order, S.I. No. 379 of 1982
		Nature Reserve (Uragh Wood) Establishment Order, S.I. No. 380 of 1982
		Nature Reserve (Deputy's Pass) Establishment Order, S.I. No. 381 of 1982
		Nature Reserve (The Raven) Establishment Order, S.I. No. 200 of 1983
		Nature Reserve (Vale of Clara) Establishment Order, S.I. No. 374 of 1983
		Nature Reserve (Rosturra Wood) Establishment Order, S.I. No. 375 of 1983
		Nature Reserve (Derrycrag Wood) Establishment Order, S.I. No. 376 of 1983
		Nature Reserve (Pollnaknockaun Wood) Establishment Order, S.I. No. 377 of 1983
		Nature Reserve (Ballynastaig Wood) Establishment Order, S.I. No. 378 of 1983
		Nature Reserve (Coole-Garryland) Establishment Order, S.I. No. 379 of 1983
		Nature Reserve (Oldhead Wood) Establishment Order, S.I. No. 333 of 1984
		Nature Reserve (Pettigo Plateau) Establishment Order, S.I. No. 334 of 1984
		Nature Reserve (Dromore) Establishment Order, S.I. No. 379 of 1985
		Nature Reserve (Richmond Esker) Establishment Order, S.I. No. 380 of 1985
		Nature Reserve (Capel Island and Knockadoon Head) Establishment Order, S.I. No. 381 of 1985
		Nature Reserve (Slieve Bloom Mountains) Establishment Order, S.I. No. 382 of 1985

Statutory Authority	Section	Statutory Instrument
Wildlife Act, No. 39 of 1976 (*Cont.*)		**Nature Reserve (Timahoe Esker) Establishment Order, S.I. No. 383 of 1985**
		Nature Reserve (Rathmullan Wood) Establishment Order, S.I. No. 343 of 1986
		Nature Reserve (Duntally Wood) Establishment Order, S.I. No. 344 of 1986
		Nature Reserve (Ballyarr Wood) Establishment Order, S.I. No. 345 of 1986
		Nature Reserve (Keelhilla Slievecannan) Establishment Order, S.I. No. 346 of 1986
		Nature Reserve (Pollardstown Fen) Establishment Order, S.I. No. 414 of 1986
		Nature Reserve (Knockmoyle/Sheakin) Establishment Order, S.I. No. 415 of 1986
		Nature Reserve (Owenboy) Establishment Order, S.I. No. 416 of 1986
		Nature Reserve (Ballygilgan/Lissadell) Establishment Order, S.I. No. 417 of 1986
		Nature Reserve (Ballyteige) Establishment Order, S.I. No. 418 of 1986
		Nature Reserve (Eirk Bog) Establishment Order, S.I. No. 419 of 1986
		Nature Reserve (Mount Brandon) Establishment Order, S.I. No. 420 of 1986
	16	**Nature Reserve (Knockadoon Head and Capel Island) Recognition Order, S.I. No. 384 of 1985**
	21	**Flora (Protection) Order, S.I. No. 338 of 1980**
	22	**Wildlife Act, 1976 (Protection of Bullfinches) Regulations, S.I. No. 283 of 1980**
	23	**Wildlife Act, 1976 (Protection of Wild Animals) Regulations, S.I. No. 282 of 1980**
	24	*Wild Birds (Open Seasons) Order, S.I. No. 243 of 1977*
		Wild Birds (Open Seasons) Order, S.I. No. 201 of 1978
		Wildlife (Wild Birds) (Open Seasons) Order, S.I. No. 192 of 1979
		Wildlife (Wild Birds) (Open Seasons) (Amendment) Order, S.I. No. 229 of 1980
		Wildlife (Wild Birds) (Open Seasons) (Amendment) Order, S.I. No. 266 of 1982
		Wildlife (Wild Birds) (Open Seasons) (Amendment) Order, S.I. No. 283 of 1984
		Wildlife (Wild Birds) (Open Seasons) (Amendment) Order, S.I. No. 346 of 1985
		Wildlife (Wild Birds) (Open Seasons) (Amendment) (No.2) Order, S.I. No. 347 of 1985
		Wildlife (Wild Birds) (Open Seasons) (Amendment) Order, S.I. No. 307 of 1986
	25	*Wildlife (Wild Mammals) (Open Seasons) Order, S.I. No. 240 of 1977*

Statutory Authority	Section	Statutory Instrument
Wildlife Act, No. 39 of 1976 (*Cont.*)		*Wildlife (Wild Mammals) (Open Seasons) Order, S.I. No. 202 of 1978*
		Wildlife (Wild Mammals) (Open Seasons) Order, S.I. No. 193 of 1979
		Wildlife (Wild Mammals) (Open Seasons) (Amendment) Order, S.I. No. 306 of 1986
	27	*Wildlife Act, 1976 (Section 27) Order, S.I. No. 3 of 1982*
		Wildlife Act, 1976 (Section 27) (No.2) Order, S.I. No. 15 of 1982
		Wildlife Act, 1976 (Section 27) Order, S.I. No. 11 of 1985
	33(4)	**Wildlife Act, 1976 (Firearms and Ammunition) Regulations, S.I. No. 239 of 1977**
	34(4)	**Wildlife Act, 1976 (Approved Traps, Snares and Nets) Regulations, S.I. No. 307 of 1977**
	41	**Wildlife Act, 1976 (Birds of Prey) Regulations, S.I. No. 8 of 1984**
	44	**Wildlife Act, 1976 (Section 44) (Recognised Bodies) Regulations, S.I. No. 335 of 1977**
		Wildlife Act, 1976 (Section 44) (Recognised Bodies) Regulations, S.I. No. 233 of 1980
	46	**Wildlife Act, 1976 (Wildlife Dealing) Regulations, S.I. No. 253 of 1977**
	53	**Wildlife Act, 1976 (Control of Export of Fauna) Regulations, S.I. No. 235 of 1979**
	59	**Nature Reserve (Lough Hyne) Regulations, S.I. No. 207 of 1981**
	78(7)	**Wildlife Act, 1976 (Certificate of Peace Commissioner) Regulations, S.I. No. 210 of 1977**
Wireless Telegraphy Act, No. 45 of 1926	3(6)	**Wireless Telegraphy Act, 1926 (Section 3) (Exemption of Sound Broadcasting Receivers) Order, S.I. No. 211 of 1972**
		Wireless Telegraphy Act, 1926 (Section 3) (Exemption of Certain Wired Broadcast Relay Stations) Order, S.I. No. 200 of 1976
	6	*Wireless Receiving Licences Regulations [Vol. XXII p. 715] S.R.& O. No. 1 of 1927*
		Wireless Receiving Licences (No.2) Regulations [Vol. XXII p. 723] S.R.& O. No. 54 of 1927
		Wireless Telegraphy (Experimenter's Licence) Regulations [Vol. XXII p. 753] S.R.& O. No. 330 of 1937
	6(1)	*Wireless Receiving Licences (Amendment) Regulations [Vol. XXII p. 727] S.R.& O. No. 249 of 1934*
		Wireless (Receiving Licences) Regulations [Vol. XXII p. 737] S.R.& O. No. 261 of 1937
		Wireless (Receiving Licences) (Amendment) (No.1) Regulations [Vol. XXXIV p. 763] S.R.& O. No. 117 of 1940

Statutory Authority	Section	Statutory Instrument
Wireless Telegraphy Act, No. 45 of 1926 (*Cont.*)		*Wireless (Receiving Licences) (Amendment) (No.2) Regulations, S.I. No. 282 of 1949*
		Wireless Telegraphy (Business Radio Licence) Regulations, S.I. No. 320 of 1949
		Wireless Telegraphy (Experimenter's Licence) (Amendment) (No.1) Regulations, S.I. No. 232 of 1951
		Wireless (Receiving Licences) (Amendment) (No.3) Regulations, S.I. No. 55 of 1953
		Wireless Telegraphy (Business Radio Licence) Regulations, S.I. No. 2 of 1956
		Wireless Telegraphy (Business Radio Licence) Regulations, S.I. No. 181 of 1957
		Wireless (Receiving Licences) (Amendment) Regulations, S.I. No. 174 of 1961
		Broadcasting (Receiving Licences) Regulations, S.I. No. 279 of 1961
		Broadcasting (Receiving Licences) (Amendment) Regulations, S.I. No. 199 of 1963
		Broadcasting (Receiving Licences) (Amendment) Regulations, S.I. No. 141 of 1970
		Broadcasting (Receiving Licences) (Amendment) Regulations, S.I. No. 241 of 1971
		Broadcasting (Receiving Licences) (Amendment) Regulations, S.I. No. 210 of 1972
		Broadcasting (Receiving Licences) (Amendment) Regulations, S.I. No. 274 of 1973
		Wireless Telegraphy (Wired Broadcast Relay Licence) Regulations, S.I. No. 67 of 1974
		Broadcasting (Receiving Licences) (Amendment) Regulations, S.I. No. 270 of 1974
		Broadcasting (Receiving Licences) (Amendment) Regulations, S.I. No. 4 of 1976
		Broadcasting (Receiving Licences) (Amendment) Regulations, S.I. No. 76 of 1977
		Broadcasting (Receiving Licences) (Amendment) Regulations, S.I. No. 319 of 1978
		Wireless Telegraphy (Business Radio Licence) (Amendment) Regulations, S.I. No. 193 of 1980
		Wireless Telegraphy (Experimenter's Licence) (Amendment) Regulations, S.I. No. 194 of 1980
		Broadcasting (Receiving Licences) (Amendment) Regulations, S.I. No. 359 of 1980
		Wireless Telegraphy (Business Radio Licence) (Amendment) Regulations, S.I. No. 114 of 1981
		Wireless Telegraphy (Experimenter's Licence) (Amendment) Regulations, S.I. No. 115 of 1981
		Wireless Telegraphy (Personal Radio Licence) Regulations, S.I. No. 8 of 1982
		Wireless Telegraphy (Business Radio Licence) (Amendment) Regulations, S.I. No. 73 of 1982
		Wireless Telegraphy (Experimenter's Licence) (Amendment) Regulations, S.I. No. 74 of 1982

Statutory Authority	Section	Statutory Instrument
Wireless Telegraphy Act, No. 45 of 1926 (*Cont.*)		**Broadcasting (Receiving Licences) (Amendment) Regulations, S.I. No. 83 of 1983**
		Wireless Telegraphy (Experimenter's Licence) (Amendment) Regulations, S.I. No. 87 of 1983
		Wireless Telegraphy (Business Radio Licence) (Amendment) Regulations, S.I. No. 88 of 1983
		Broadcasting (Receiving Licences) (Amendment) Regulations, S.I. No. 248 of 1984
		Wireless Telegraphy (Business Radio Licence) (Amendment) Regulations, S.I. No. 84 of 1985
		Wireless Telegraphy (Experimenter's Licence) (Amendment) Regulations, S.I. No. 85 of 1985
		Broadcasting (Receiving Licences) (Amendment) Regulations, S.I. No. 37 of 1986
		Wireless Telegraphy (Experimenter's Licence) (Amendment) Regulations, S.I. No. 74 of 1986
		Wireless Telegraphy (Business Radio Licence) (Amendment) Regulations, S.I. No. 75 of 1986
	12A	**Broadcasting Authority (Control of Interference) Order, S.I. No. 113 of 1960**
		Wireless Telegraphy (Control of Interference from Electric Motors) Regulations, S.I. No. 108 of 1963
		Wireless Telegraphy (Control of Interference from Ignition Apparatus) Regulations, S.I. No. 223 of 1963
	19	**Broadcasting (Advisory Committee) Order [Vol. XXII p. 733] S.R.& O. No. 31 of 1927**
Wireless Telegraphy Act, No. 5 of 1972	2(4)	*Wireless Telegraphy Act, 1972 (Appointed Day) Order, S.I. No. 35 of 1973*
	4(1)	**Wireless Telegraphy Act, 1972 (Period for the Purpose of Section 4) Order, S.I. No. 34 of 1973**
	7	**Wireless Telegraphy (Control of Sale, Letting On Hire or Manufacture, and Importation of Radio Transceivers) Order, S.I. No. 400 of 1981**
	15	**Wireless Telegraphy Act, 1972 (Form of Notice for the Purpose of Section 2) Regulations, S.I. No. 36 of 1973**
Wool Marketing Act, No. 26 of 1968	2	*Wool Marketing Act, 1968 (Establishment Day) Order, S.I. No. 77 of 1969*
	4(3)	*Wool Marketing Act, 1968 (Commencement) (Section 4) Order, S.I. No. 214 of 1974*
	5(4)	*Register of Buyers of Wool Order, S.I. No. 144 of 1971*
	8	**Wool Marketing (Registration Fee and Standards for Premises, Plant and Machinery) Regulations, S.I. No. 85 of 1970**
	8(1)	**Wool Marketing (Wool Exporter's Licence) (Fee) Regulations, S.I. No. 213 of 1974**

Statutory Authority	Section	Statutory Instrument
Wool Marketing Act, No. 26 of 1968 (*Cont.*)	11	**Wool Marketing (Registration Fee and Standards for Premises, Plant and Machinery) Regulations, S.I. No. 85 of 1970**
		Wool Marketing Regulations, S.I. No. 86 of 1970
		Wool Marketing Regulations, S.I. No. 143 of 1971
		Wool Marketing (Amendment) Regulations, S.I. No. 85 of 1980
	12(3)	*Wool Marketing (An Comhairle Olla) Order, S.I. No. 30 of 1978*
	21	**Wool Marketing Regulations, S.I. No. 143 of 1971**
Wool Marketing Act, No. 11 of 1984	2(1)	*Wool Marketing Act, 1984 (Section 3 (1)) (Commencement) Order, S.I. No. 308 of 1984*
Worker Participation (State Enterprises) Act, No. 6 of 1977	3(1)	*Worker Participation (State Enterprises) Act, 1977 (Appointed Day) (British and Irish Steam Packet Company Ltd.) Order, S.I. No. 227 of 1978*
		Worker Participation (State Enterprises) Act, 1977 (Appointed Day) (Electricity Supply Board) Order, S.I. No. 229 of 1978
		Worker Participation (State Enterprises) Act, 1977 (Appointed Day) (Nitrigin Eireann Teoranta) Order, S.I. No. 237 of 1978
		Worker Participation (State Enterprises) Act, 1977 (Appointed Day) (Bord na Mona) Order, S.I. No. 239 of 1978
		Worker Participation (State Enterprises) Act, 1977 (Appointed Day) (Comhlucht Siuicre Eireann Teoranta) Order, S.I. No. 2 of 1979
		Worker Participation (State Enterprises) Act, 1977 (Appointed Day) (Coras Iompair Eireann) Order, S.I. No. 184 of 1980
		Worker Participation (State Enterprises) Act, 1977 (Appointed Day) (Aer Lingus Teoranta/Aer Linte Eireann Teoranta) Order, S.I. No. 3 of 1981
	6(2)	*Worker Participation (British and Irish Steam Packet Company Ltd.) (Nomination Day) Regulations, S.I. No. 228 of 1978*
		Worker Participation (Electricity Supply Board) (Nomination Day) Regulations, S.I. No. 230 of 1978
		Worker Participation (Nitrigin Eireann Teoranta) (Nomination Day) Regulations, S.I. No. 238 of 1978
		Worker Participation (Bord na Mona) (Nomination Day) Regulations, S.I. No. 240 of 1978
		Worker Participation (Comhlucht Siuicre Eireann Teoranta) (Nomination Day) Regulations, S.I. No. 1 of 1979
		Worker Participation (Coras Iompair Eireann) (Nomination Day) Regulations, S.I. No. 185 of 1980
		Worker Participation (Aer Lingus Teoranta/Aer Linte Eireann Teoranta) (Nomination Day) Regulations, S.I. No. 4 of 1981

Worker Participation (State
Enterprises) Act, No. 6 of 1977
(Cont.)

Worker Participation (Electricity Supply Board) (Nomination Day) Regulations, S.I. No. 264 of 1981

Worker Participation (Bord na Mona) (Nomination Day) Regulations, S.I. No. 265 of 1981

Worker Participation (British and Irish Steam Packet Company Limited) (Nomination Day) Regulations, S.I. No. 266 of 1981

Worker Participation (Nitrigin Eireann Teoranta) (Nomination Day) Regulations, S.I. No. 322 of 1981

Worker Participation (Comhlucht Siuicre Eireann Teoranta) (Nomination Day) Regulations, S.I. No. 2 of 1982

Worker Participation (Coras Iompair Eireann) (Nomination Day) Regulations, S.I. No. 152 of 1983

Worker Participation (Aer Lingus Teoranta and Aerlinte Eireann Teoranta) (Nomination Day) Regulations, S.I. No. 2 of 1984

Worker Participation (Nitrigin Eireann Teoranta) (Nomination Day) Regulations, S.I. No. 197 of 1984

Worker Participation (Electricity Supply Board) (Nomination Day) Regulations, S.I. No. 198 of 1984

Worker Participation (British and Irish Steam Packet Company Limited) (Nomination Day) Regulations, S.I. No. 199 of 1984

Worker Participation (Bord Na Mona) (Nomination Day) Regulations, S.I. No. 219 of 1984

Worker Participation (Comhlucht Siuicre Eireann Teoranta) (Nomination Day) Regulations, S.I. No. 7 of 1985

Worker Participation (Coras Iompair Eireann) (Nomination Day) Regulations, S.I. No. 174 of 1986

9   **Worker Participation (State Enterprises) (Preliminary Poll) Regulations, S.I. No. 46 of 1978**

Worker Participation (State Enterprises) (General) Regulations, S.I. No. 47 of 1978

Worker Participation (State Enterprises) (Postal Voting) Regulations, S.I. No. 48 of 1978

23   **Worker Participation (State Enterprises) Order, S.I. No. 186 of 1978**

Worker Participation (State Enterprises) Order, S.I. No. 100 of 1980

25   **Worker Participation (British and Irish Steam Packet Company Ltd) Order, S.I. No. 196 of 1979**

27   **Worker Participation (State Enterprises) (General) Regulations, S.I. No. 47 of 1978**

28   **Worker Participation (State Enterprises) Order, S.I. No. 100 of 1980**

Statutory Authority	Section	Statutory Instrument
Workmen's Compensation Act, No. 9 of 1934 (*Cont.*)	76	**Workmen's Compensation Act, 1934 (Industrial Diseases) Order [Vol. XXII p. 833] S.R.& O. No. 190 of 1934**
		Workmen's Compensation Act, 1934 (Industrial Diseases) Order, 1934 (Amendment) Order [Vol. XXXIV p. 785] S.R.& O. No. 26 of 1945
		Workmen's Compensation Act, 1934 (Industrial Disease) Order, S.I. No. 60 of 1956
	76(1)(vi)	**Workmen's Compensation Act, 1934 (Certifying Surgeons and Medical Referees) Order [Vol. XXII p. 817] S.R.& O. No. 188 of 1934**
	77(4)	**Workmen's Compensation Act, 1934 (Certifying Surgeons and Medical Referees) Order [Vol. XXII p. 817] S.R.& O. No. 188 of 1934**
		Workmen's Compensation Act, 1934 (Certifying Surgeons and Medical Referees) Order, 1934 (Amendment) Order, S.I. No. 13 of 1950
		Workmen's Compensation Act, 1934 (Certifying Surgeons and Medical Referees) Order, 1934 (Amendment) Order, S.I. No. 269 of 1965
Workmen's Compensation (Amendment) Act, No. 23 of 1948	2	*Workmen's Compensation (Amendment) Act, 1948 (Appointed Day) Order, S.I. No. 429 of 1948*
Workmen's Compensation (Amendment) Act, No. 25 of 1953	2	*Workmen's Compensation (Amendment) Act, 1953 (Appointed Day) Order, S.I. No. 285 of 1953*
	10(3)	**Workmen's Compensation (Amendment) Act, 1953 (Prescribed Declarations) Regulations, S.I. No. 286 of 1953**
	11	**Workmen's Compensation (Certificate of Births and Marriages) Regulations, S.I. No. 316 of 1953**
Workmen's Compensation (Amendment) Act, No. 16 of 1955	2	*Workmen's Compensation (Amendment) Act, 1955 (Appointed Day) Order, S.I. No. 146 of 1955*
Youth Employment Agency Act, No. 32 of 1981	1	**Youth Employment Levy Regulations, S.I. No. 84 of 1982**
		Youth Employment Levy (Amendment) Regulations, S.I. No. 52 of 1983
	20	**Youth Employment Levy Regulations, S.I. No. 84 of 1982**
		Youth Employment Levy (Amendment) Regulations, S.I. No. 52 of 1983
		Youth Employment Levy (Amendment) Regulations, S.I. No. 75 of 1984
	31	*Youth Employment Agency Act, 1981 (Commencement) Order, S.I. No. 16 of 1982*